The Wisdom of Niccolò Machiavelli

by Niccolò Machiavelli

The Wisdom of Niccolò Machiavelli

By Niccolò Machiavelli

Start Publishing PD LLC

Cover art: Shutterstock/Taisiya Kozorez

Cover design: Jennifer Do

10 9 8 7 6 5 4 3 2 1

ISBN 979-8-8809-2287-1

The Prince

Niccolò Machiavelli,

To the Magnificent Laurence sonne to *Peter of Medicis* health.

They that desire to ingratiate themselves with a Prince, commonly use to offer themselves to his view, with things of that nature as such persons take most pleasure and delight in: whereupon we see they are many times presented with Horses and Armes, cloth of gold, pretious stones, and such like ornaments, worthy of their greatness. Having then a mind to offer up my self to your Magnificence, with some testimony of my service to you, I found nothing in my whole inventory, that I think better of, or more esteeme, than the knowlege of great mens actions, which I have learned by a long experience of modern affairs, and a continual reading of those of the ancients. Which, now that I have with great diligence long workt it out, and throughly sifted, I commend to your Magnificence. And, however I may well think this work unworthy of your view; yet such is your humanity, that I doubt not but it shall find acceptance, considering, that for my part I am not able to tender a greater gift, than to present you with the means, whereby in a very short time you may be able to understand all that, which I, in the space of many years, and with many sufferances and dangers, have made proof and gaind the knowledge of. And this work I have not set forth either with elegancy of discourse or stile, nor with any other ornament whereby to captivate the reader, as others use, because I would not have it gain its esteem from elsewhere than from the truth of the matter, and the gravity of the subject. Nor can this be thought presumption, if a man of humble and low condition venture to dilate and discourse upon the governments of Princes; for even as they that with their pensils designe out countreys, get themselves into the plains below to consider the nature of the mountains, and other high places above; and again to consider the plains below, they get up to the tops of the mountains; in like manner to understand the nature of the people, it is fit to be a Prince; and to know well the dispositions of Princes, sutes best with the understanding of a subject. Your Magnificence then may be pleased, to receive this small present, with the same mind that I send it; which if you shall throughly peruse and consider, you shall perceive therein that I exceedingly wish, that you may attain to that greatness, which your own fortune, and your excellent endowments promise you: and if your Magnificence from the very point of your Highness shall sometime cast your eyes upon these inferior places, you shall see how undeservedly I undergoe an extream and continual despight of Fortune.

Chapter. I

How many sorts of Principalities there are, and how many wayes they are attained to.

All States, all Dominions that have had, or now have rule over men, have been and are, either Republiques or Principalities. Principalities are either hereditary, whereof they of the blood of the Lord thereof have long time been Princes; or else they are new; and those that are new, are either all new, as was the Dutchy of Millan to Francis Sforce; or are as members adjoyned to the hereditary State of the Prince that gains it; as the Kingdom of Naples is to the King of Spain. These Dominions so gotten, are accustomed either to live under a Prince, or to enjoy their liberty; and are made conquest of, either with others forces, or ones own, either by fortune, or by valor.

Chapter II: Of Hereditary Principalities.

I will not here discourse of Republiques, because I have other where treated of them at large: I will apply my self only to a Principality, and proceed, while I weave this web, by arguing thereupon, how these Principallities can be governed and maintained. I say then that in States of inheritance, and accustomed to the blood of their Princes, there are far fewer difficulties to keep them, than in the new: for it suffices only not to transgress the course his Ancestors took, and so afterward to temporise with those accidents that can happen; that if such a Prince be but of ordinary industry, he shall allwaies be able to maintain himself in his State, unless by some extraordinary or excessive power he be deprived thereof; and when he had lost it, upon the least sinister chance that befalls the usurper, he recovers it again. We have in Italy the Duke of Ferrara for example hereof, who was of ability to resist the Venetians, in the year 84, and to withstand Pope Julius in the tenth for no other reason, than because he had of old continued in that rule; for the natural Prince hath fewer occasions, and less heed to give offence, whereupon of necessity he must be more beloved; and unless it be that some extravagant vices of his bring him into hatred, it is agreeable to reason, that naturally he should be well beloved by his own subjects: and in the antiquity and continuation of the Dominion, the remembrances and occasions of innovations are quite extinguished: for evermore one change leaves a kind of breach or dent, to fasten the building of another.

Chapter III: Of mixt Principalities.

But the difficulties consist in the new Principality; and first, if it be not all new, but as a member, so that it may be termed altogether as mixt; and the variations thereof proceed in the first place from a natural difficulty, which we commonly finde in all new Principalities; for men do willingly change their Lord, beleeving to better their condition; and this beliefe causes them to take armes against him that rules over them, whereby they deceive themselves, because they find after by experience, they have made it worse: which depends upon another natural and ordinary necessity, forcing him alwaies to offend those, whose Prince he newly becomes, as well by his soldiers he is put to entertain upon them as by many other injuries, which a new conquest draws along with it; in such manner as thou findest all those thine enemies, whom thou hast endammaged in the seizing of that Principality, and afterwards canst not keep them thy friends that have seated thee in it, for not being able to satisfie them according to their expectations, nor put in practice strong remedies against them, being obliged to them. For however one be very well provided with strong armies, yet hath he alwaies need of the favor of the inhabitants in the Countrey, to enter thereinto. For these reasons, Lewis the twelfth, King of France, suddenly took Milan, and as soon lost it; and the first time Lodwick his own forces served well enough to wrest it out of his hands; for those people that had opened him the gates, finding themselves deceived of their opinion, and of that future good which they had promised themselves, could not endure the distastes the new Prince gave them. True it is, that Countreys that have rebelled again the second time, being recovered, are harder lost; for their Lord, taking occasion from their rebellion, is less respective of persons, but cares only to secure himself, by punishing the delinquents, to clear all suspicions, and to provide for himself where he thinks he is weakest: so that if to make France lose Milan the first time, it was enough for Duke Lodwick to make some small stir only upon the confines; yet afterwards, before they could make him lose it the second time, they had need of the whole world together against him, and that all his armies should be wasted and driven out of Italy; which proceeded from the forenamed causes: however though both the first and second time it was taken from him. The generall causes of the first we have treated of; it remains now that we see those of the second; and set down the remedies that he had, or any one else can have that should chance to be in those termes he was, whereby he might be able to maintain himself better in his conquest than the King of France did. I say therefore, that these States which by Conquest are annexed to the ancient states of their conqueror, are either of the same province and the same language, or otherwise; and when they are, it is very easy to hold them, especially when they are not used to live free; and to enjoy them securely, it is enough to have extinguished the Princes line who ruled over them: For in other matters, allowing them their ancient conditions, and there being not much difference of manners betwixt them, men ordinarily live quiet enough; as we have seen that Burgundy did, Britany, Gascony, and Normandy, which so long time continued with France: for however there be some difference of language between them, yet can they easily comport one with another; and whosoever makes the conquest of them, meaning to hold them, must have two regards; the first, that the race of their former Prince be quite extinguished; the other, that he change nothing, neither in their lawes nor taxes, so that in a very short time they become one entire body with their ancient Principality. But when any States are gaind in a Province disagreeing in language, manners, and orders, here are the difficulties, and here is there need of good fortune, and great industry to maintain them; and it would be one of the best and livelyest remedies, for the Conqueror to goe in person and dwell there; this would make the possession hereof more secure and durable; as the Turk hath done in Greece, who among all the other courses taken by him for to hold that State, had he not gone thither himself in person to dwell, it had never been possible for him to have kept it: for abiding there, he sees the disorders growing in their beginnings, and forthwith can remedy them; whereas being not there present, they are heard of when they are grown to some height, and then is there no help for them. Moreover, the Province is not pillaged by the officers thou sendest thither: the subjects are much satisfied of having recourse to the Prince near at hand, whereupon have they more reason to love him, if they mean to be good; and intending to do otherwise, to fear him: and forrein Princes will be well aware how they invade that State; insomuch, that making his abode there, he can very hardly lose it. Another remedy, which is also a better, is to send Colonies into one or two places, which may be as it were the keys of that State; for it is necessary either to do this, or to maintain there many horse and foot. In these colonies the Prince makes no great expence, and either without his charge, or at a very small rate, he may both send and maintain them; and gives offence only to them from whom he takes their fields and houses, to bestow them on those new inhabitants who are but a very small part of that State; and those that he offends, remaining dispersed and poore, can never hurt him: and all the rest on one part, have no offence given them, and therefore a small matter keeps them in quiet: on the other side, they are wary not to erre, for fear it befalls not them, as it did those that were dispoild. I conclude then, that those colonies that are not chargeable, are the more trusty, give the less offence; and they that are offended, being but poor and scattered, can do but little harme, as I have said; for it is to be noted, that men must either be dallyed and flattered withall, or else be quite crusht; for they revenge themselves of small dammages; but of great ones they are not able; so that when wrong is done to any man, it ought so to be done, that it need fear no return of revenge again. But in lieu of Colonies, by maintaining soldiers there, the expence is great; for the whole revenues of that State are to be spent in the keeping of it; so the conquest proves but a loss to him that hath got it, and endammages him rather; for it hurts that whole State to remove the army from place to place, of which annoyance every one hath a feeling, and so becomes enemie to thee; as they are enemies, I wis, who are outraged by thee in their own houses, whensoever they are able to do thee mischief. Every way then is this guard unprofitable. Besides, he that is in a different Province, (as it is said) should make himself Head and defender of his less powerfull neighbors, and devise alwaies to weaken those that are more mighty therein, and take care that upon no chance there enter not any foreiner as mighty as himself; for it will alwaies come to pass, that they shall be brought in by those that are discontented, either upon ambition, or fear; as the Etolians brought the Romans into Greece; and they were brought into every countrey they came, by the Natives; and the course of the matter is, that so soon as a powerfull Stranger enters a countrey, all those that are the less powerfull there, cleave to him, provoked by an envy they beare him that is more mighty than they; so that for these of the weaker sort, he may easily gain them without any pains: for presently all of them together very willingly make one lump with that he hath gotten: He hath only to beware that these increase not their strengths, nor their authorities, and so he shall easily be able by his own forces, and their assistances, to take down those that are mighty, and remain himself absolute arbitre of that Countrey. And he that playes not well this part, shall quickly lose what he hath gotten; and while he holds it, shall find therein a great many troubles and vexations. The Romans in the Provinces they seiz'd on, observed well these points, sent colonies thither, entertained the weaker sort, without augmenting any thing their power, abated the forces of those that were mighty, and permitted not any powerfull forreiner to gain too much reputation there. And I will content my self only with the countrey of Greece for example hereof. The Achayans and Etolians were entertained by them, the Macedons kingdome was brought low, Antiochus was driven thence, nor ever did the Achayans or Etolians deserts prevail so far for them, that they would ever promise to enlarge their State, nor the perswasions of Philip induce them ever to be his friends, without bringing him lower; nor yet could Antiochus his power make them ever consent that he should hold any State in that countrey: for the Romans did in these cases that which all judicious Princes ought to do, who are not only to have regard unto all present mischiefs, but also to the future, and to provide for those with all industry; for by taking order for those when they are afarre off, it is easie to prevent them; but by delaying till they come near hand to thee, the remedy comes too late; for this malignity is grown incurable: and it befalls this, as the physicians say of the hectick feaver, that in the beginning it is easily cur'd, but hardly known; but in the course of time, not having been known in the beginning, nor cured, it becomes easie to know, but hard to cure. Even so falls it out in matters of State; for by knowing it aloof off (which is given only to a wise man to do) the mischiefs that then spring up, are quickly helped; but when, for not having been perceived, they are suffered to increase, so that every one sees them, there is then no cure for them: therefore the Romans, seeing these inconvenients afar off, alwaies prevented them, and never sufferd them to follow; for to escape a war, because they knew that a war is not undertaken, but deferred for anothers advantage; therefore would they rather make a war with Philip and Antiochus in Greece, to the end it should not afterwards be made with them in Italy, though for that time they were able to avoid both the one and the other, which they thought not good to do: nor did they approve of that saying that is ordinarily in the mouthes of the Sages of our dayes, *to enjoy the benefits of the present time*; but that rather, to take the benefit of their valor and wisdome; for time drives forward everything, and may bring with it as well good as evil, and evil as good. But let us return to France, and examine if any of the things prescribed have been done by them: and we will speak of Lewis, and not of Charles, as of whom by reason of the long possession he held in Italy we better knew the wayes he went: and you shall see he did the clean contrary to what should have been done by him that would maintain a State of different Language and conditions. King Lewis was brought into Italy by the Venetians ambition, who would have gotten for their shares half the State of Lombardy: I will not blame his comming, or the course he took, because he had a mind to begin to set a foot in Italy; but having not any friends in the country, all gates being barred against him, by reason of King Charles his carriage there, he was constrained to joyn friendship with those he could; and this consideration well taken, would have proved lucky to him, when in the rest of his courses he had not committed any error. The King then having conquered Lombardy, recovered presently all that reputation that Charles had lost him; Genua yeelded to him, the Florentines became friends with him; the Marquess of Mantua, the Duke of Ferrara, the Bentivolti, the Lady of Furli, the Lord of Faenza, Pesaro Rimino, Camerino, and Piombino, the Lucheses, Pisans and Sienses, every one came and offered him friendship: then might the Venetians consider the rashness of the course they had taken, who, only to get into their hands two Townes in Lombardy, made the King Lord of two thirds in Italy. Let any man now consider with how small difficulty could the King have maintained his reputation in Italy, if he had followed these aforenamed rules, and secured and defended those his friends, who because their number was great, and they weak and fearful, some of the Church, and others of the Venetians were alwaies forced to hold with him, and by their means he might easily have been able to secure himself against those that were mightiest: but he was no sooner got into Milan, than he took a quite wrong course, by giving ayd to Pope Alexander, to seize upon Romania, and perceiv'd not that by this resolution he weakned himself, ruining his own friends, and those had cast themselves into his bosom, making the Church puissant, by adding to their Spiritual power, they gaind their authority, and so much temporal estate. And having once got out of the way, he was constrained to go on forward; insomuch as to stop Alexanders ambition, and that he should not become Lord of all Tuscany, of force he was to come into Italy: and this sufficed him not, to have made the Church mighty, and taken away his own friends; but for the desire he had to get the Kingdome of Naples, he divided it with the King of Spain: and where before he was the sole arbitre of Italy, he brought in a competitor, to the end that all the ambitious persons of that country, and all that were ill affected to him, might have otherwhere to make their recourse: and whereas he might have left in that Kingdome some Vice-King of his own, he took him from thence, to place another there, that might afterward chace him thence. It is a thing indeed very natural and ordinary, to desire to be of the getting hand: and alwaies when men undertake it, if they can effect it, they shall be prais'd for it, or at least not blam'd: but when they are not able, and yet will undertake it, here lies the blame, here is the error committed. If France then was able with her own power to assail the Kingdome of Naples, she might well have done it; but not being able, she should not have divided it: and if the division she made of Lombardy with the Venetians, deserv'd some excuse, thereby to set one foot in Italy; yet this merits blame, for not being excused by that necessity. Lewis then committed these five faults; extinguisht the feebler ones, augmented the State of another that was already powerful in Italy, brought thereinto a very puissant forreiner, came not thither himself to dwell there, nor planted any colonies there: which faults while he liv'd, he could not but be the worse for; yet all could not have gone so ill, had he not committed the sixt, to take from the Venetians their State; for if he had not enlarg'd the Churches territories nor brought the Spaniard into Italy, it had bin necessary to take them lower; but having first taken those other courses, he should never have given way to their destruction; for while they had been strong, they would alwaies have kept the others off from venturing on the conquest of Lombardy. For the Venetians would never have given their consents thereto, unless they should have been made Lords of it themselves; and the others would never have taken it from France, to give it them: and then they would never have dar'd to go and set upon them both together. And if any one should say, that King Lewis yeelded Romania to Alexander, and the Kingdome of Naples to Spain, to avoid a war; I answer with the reasons above alledged, that one should never suffer any disorder to follow, for avoiding of a war; for that war is not sav'd, but put off to thy disadvantage. And if any others argue, that the King had given his word to the Pope, to do that exploit for him, for dissolving of his marriage, and for giving the Cardinals Cap to him of Roan; I answer with that which hereafter I shall say touching Princes words, how they ought to be kept. King Lewis then lost Lombardy, for not having observ'd some of those termes which others us'd, who have possessed themselves of countries, and desir'd to keep them. Nor is this any strange thing, but very ordinary and reasonable: and to this purpose I spake at Nantes with that French Cardinal, when Valentine (for so ordinarily was Cæsar Borgia Pope Alexanders son call'd) made himself master of Romania; for when the Cardinal said to me, that the Italians understood not the feats of war; I answered, the Frenchmen understood not matters of State: for had they been well vers'd therein, they would never have suffer'd the Church to have grown to that greatness. And by experience we have seen it, that the power hereof in Italy, and that of Spain also, was caused by France, and their own ruine proceeded from themselves. From whence a general rule may be taken, which never, or very seldom fails, *That he that gives the means to another to become powerful, ruines himself*; for that power is caus'd by him either with his industry, or with his force; and as well the one as the other of these two is suspected by him that is grown puissant.

Chapter IV: Wherefore Darius his Kingdome taken by Alexander, rebelled not against Alexanders Successors after his death.

The difficulties being consider'd, which a man hath in the maintaining of a State new gotten, some might marvaile how it came to pass, that Alexander the great subdued all Asia in a few years; and having hardly possessed himself of it, died; whereupon it seemed probable that all that State should have rebelled; nevertheless his Successors kept the possession of it, nor found they other difficulty in holding it, than what arose among themselves through their own ambition. I answer, that all the Principalities whereof we have memory left us, have been governed in two several manners; either by a Prince, and all the rest Vassals, who as ministers by his favor and allowance, do help to govern that Kingdom; or by a Prince and by Barons, who not by their Princes favor, but by the antiquity of blood hold that degree. And these kinds of Barons have both states of their own, and Vassals who acknowledge them for their Lords; and bare them a true natural affection. Those States that are govern'd by a Prince and by Vassals, have their Prince ruling over them with more authority; for in all his countrey, there is none acknowledged for superior, but himself: and if they yeeld obedience to any one else, it is but as to his minister and officer, nor beare they him any particular good will. The examples of these two different Governments now in our dayes, are, the Turk, and the King of France. The Turks whole Monarchy is govern'd by one Lord, and the rest are all his Vassals; and dividing his whole Kingdom into divers Sangiacques or Governments, he sends several thither, and those he chops and changes, as he pleases. But the King of France is seated in the midst of a multitude of Lords, who of old have been acknowledg'd for such by their subjects, and being belov'd by them, enjoy their preheminencies; nor can the King take their States from them without danger. He then that considers the one and the other of these two States, shall find difficulty in the conquest of the Turks State; but when once it is subdu'd, great facility to hold it. The reasons of these difficulties in taking of the Turks Kingdom from him, are, because the Invader cannot be called in by the Princes of that Kingdom, nor hope by the rebellion of those which he hath about him, to be able to facilitate his enterprize: which proceeds from the reasons aforesaid; for they being all his slaves, and oblig'd to him, can more hardly be corrupted; and put case they were corrupted, little profit could he get by it, they not being able to draw after them any people, for the reasons we have shewed: whereupon he that assails the Turk, must think to find him united; and must rather relie upon his own forces, than in the others disorders: but when once he is overcome and broken in the field, so that he cannot repair his armies, there is nothing else to be doubted than the Royal blood, which being once quite out, there is none else left to be feard, none of the others having any credit with the people. And as the conqueror before the victory could not hope in them; so after it, ought he not to fear them. The contrary falls out in Kingdoms governed as is that of France: for it is easie to be enterd by the gaining of any Baron in the Kingdom; for there are alwaies some malecontents to be found, and those that are glad of innovation. Those for the reasons alledg'd are able to open thee a way into that State, and to further thy victory, which afterwards to make good to thee, draws with it exceeding many difficulties, as well with those that have ayded thee, as those thou hast supprest. Nor is it enough for thee to root out the Princes race: for there remaine still those Lords who quickly will be the ring-leaders of new changes; and in case thou art not able to content these, nor extinguish them, thou losest that State, whensoever the occasion is offerd. Now if thou shalt consider what sort of government that of Darius was, thou shalt find it like to the Turks dominion, and therefore Alexander was necessitated first to defeat him utterly, and drive him out of the field; after which victory Darius being dead, that State was left secure to Alexander, for the reasons we treated of before: and his successors, had they continued in amity, might have enjoy'd it at ease: nor ever arose there in that Kingdome other tumults, than those they themselves stir'd up. But of the States that are order'd and grounded as that of France, it is impossible to become master at such ease: and from hence grew the frequent rebellions of Spain, France, and Greece against the Romans, by reason of the many Principalities those States had: whereof while the memory lasted, the Romans were alwayes doubtfull of the possession of them; but the memory of them being quite wip't out, by the power and continuance of the Empire, at length they enjoy'd it securely; and they also were able afterwards fighting one with another, each of one them to draw after them the greater part of those provinces, according as their authority had gain'd them credit therein: and that because the blood of their ancient Lords was quite spent, they acknowledg'd no other but the Romans. By the consideration then of these things, no man will marvaile that Alexander had so little trouble to keep together the State of Asia; and that others have had such great difficulties to maintain their conquest, as Pyrrhus, and many others; which proceeds not from the small or great valour of the conquerour, but from the difference of the subject.

Chapter V: In what manner Cities and Principalities are to be govern'd, which, before they were conquer'd, liv'd under their own Laws.

When those States that are conquered, as it is said, have been accustomed to live under their own Laws, and in liberty, there are three wayes for a man to hold them. The first is to demolish all their strong places; the other, personally to goe and dwell there; the third, to suffer them to live under their own Laws, drawing from them some tribute, and creating therein an Oligarchy, that may continue it in thy service: for that State being created by that Prince, knowes it cannot consist without his aid and force, who is like to doe all he can to maintain it; and with more facility is a City kept by meanes of her own Citizens, which hath been us'd before to live free, than by any other way of keeping. We have for example the Spartans and the Romans; the Spartans held Athens and Thebes, creating there an Oligarchy: yet they lost it. The Romans to be sure of Capua, Carthage, and Numantia, dismantell'd them quite, and so lost them not: they would have kept Greece as the Spartans had held them, leaving them free, and letting them enjoy their own Laws; and it prospered not with them: so that they were forc'd to deface many Cities of that province to hold it. For in truth there is not a surer way to keep them under, than by demolishments; and whoever becomes master of a City us'd to live free, and dismantells it not, let him look himselfe to bee ruin'd by it; for it alwayes in time of rebellion takes the name of liberty for refuge, and the ancient orders it had; which neither by length of time, nor for any favours afforded them, are ever forgotten; and for any thing that can be done, or order'd, unlesse the inhabitants be disunited and dispers'd, that name is never forgotten, nor those customes: but presently in every chance recourse is thither made: as Pisa did after so many yeeres that she had been subdu'd by the Florentines. But when the Cities or the Provinces are accustomed to live under a Prince, and that whole race is quite extirpated: on one part being us'd to obey; on the other, not having their old Prince; they agree not to make one from among themselves: they know not how to live in liberty, in such manner that they are much slower to take armes; and with more facility may a Prince gaine them, and secure himselfe of them. But in Republiques there is more life in them, more violent hatred, more earnest desire of revenge; nor does the remembrance of the ancient liberty ever leave them, or suffer them to rest; so that the safest way, is, either to ruine them, or dwell among them.

Chapter VI: Of new Principalities, that are conquer'd by ones own armes and valour.

Let no man marvaile, if in the discourse I shall make of new Principalities, both touching a Prince, and touching a State, I shall alledge very famous examples: for seeing men almost alwayes walk in the pathes beaten by others, and proceed in their actions by imitation; and being that others wayes cannot bee exactly follow'd, nor their vertues, whose patterne thou set'st before thee, attain'd unto; a wise man ought alwayes to tread the footsteps of the worthiest persons, and imitate those that have been the most excellent: to the end that if his vertue arrive not thereto, at least it may yeeld some favour thereof, and doe as good Archers use, who thinking the place they intend to hit, too farre distant, and knowing how farr the strength of their bow will carry, they lay their ayme a great deale higher than the mark; not for to hit so high with their arrow, but to bee able with the help of so high an aime to reach the place they shoot at. I say, that in Principalities wholly new, where there is a new Prince, there is more and lesse difficulty in maintaining them, as the vertue of their Conquerour is greater or lesser. And because this successe, to become a Prince of a private man, presupposes either vertue, or fortune; mee thinks the one and other of these two things in part should mitigate many difficulties; however he that hath lesse stood upon fortune, hath maintain'd himselfe the better. Moreover it somewhat facilitates the matter in that the Prince is constrain'd, because he hath not other dominions, in person to come and dwell there. But to come to these who by their own vertues, and not by fortune, attain'd to be Princes; the excellentest of these are Moses, Cyrus, Romulus, Theseus, and such like; and though of Moses we are not to reason, he onely executing the things that were commanded him by God; yet merits he well to be admir'd, were it only for that grace that made him worthy to converse with God. But considering Cyrus, and the others, who either got or founded Kingdomes, we shall find them all admirable; and if there particular actions and Lawes be throughly weigh'd, they will not appeare much differing from those of Moyses, which he receiv'd from so Sovraigne an instructer. And examining their lives and actions, it will not appeare, that they had other help of fortune, than the occasion, which presented them with the matter wherein they might introduce what forme they then pleas'd; and without that occasion, the vertue of their mind had been extinguish'd; and without that vertue, the occasion had been offer'd in vaine. It was then necessary for Moses to find the people of Israel slaves in Ægypt, and oppress'd by the Ægyptians, to the end that they to get out of their thraldome, should bee willing to follow him. It was fit that Romulus should not be kept in Albia, but expos'd presently after his birth, that he might become King of Rome, and founder of that City. There was need that Cyrus should find the Persians discontented with the Medes government, and the Medes delicate and effeminate through their long peace. Theseus could not make proof his vertue, had not he found the Athenians dispers'd. These occasions therefore made these men happy, and their excellent vertue made the occasion be taken notice of, whereby their countrey became enobled, and exceeding fortunate. They, who by vertuous waies, like unto these, become Princes, attain the Principality with difficulty, but hold it with much ease; and the difficulties they find in gaining the Principality, arise partly from the new orders and courses they are forc'd to bring in, to lay the foundation of their State, and work their own security. And it is to be consider'd, how there is not any thing harder to take in hand, nor doubtfuller to succeed, nor more dangerous to mannage, than to be the chief in bringing in new orders; for this Chief finds all those his enemies, that thrive upon the old orders; and hath but luke warme defenders of all those that would do well upon the new orders, which luke-warme temper proceeds partly from fear of the opposers who have the laws to their advantage; partly from the incredulity of the men who truly beleeve not a new thing, unless there be some certain proof given them thereof. Whereupon it arises, that whensoever they that are adversaries, take the occasion to assayle, they do it factiously; and these others defend but cooly, so that their whole party altogether runs a hazzard. Therefore it is necessary, being we intend throughly to discourse this part, to examine if these innovators stand of themselves, or if they depend upon others; that is, if to bring their work to effect, it be necessary they should intreat, or be able to constrain; in the first case they allwayes succeed ill, and bring nothing to pass; but when they depend of themselves, and are able to force, then seldom it is that they hazzard. Hence came it that all the prophets that were arm'd, prevail'd; but those that were unarm'd, were too weak: for besides what we have alledg'd, the nature of the people is changeable, and easie to be perswaded to a matter; but it is hard also to settle them in that perswasion. And therefore it behoves a man to be so provided, that when they beleeve no longer, he may be able to compel them thereto by force. Moses, Cyrus, Theseus, and Romulus would never have been able to cause their Laws to be obey'd, had they been disarm'd; as in our times it befel Fryer Jerome Savanarola, who perished in his new constitutions, when the multitude began not to beleeve him; neither had he the means to keep them firme, that had beleev'd; not to force beleefe in them that had not beleev'd him. Wherefore such men as these, in their proceedings find great difficulty, and all their dangers are in the way, and these they must surmount by their vertue; but having once master'd them, and beginning to be honored by all, when they have rooted those out that envi'd their dignities, they remain powerful, secure, honorable, and happy. To these choice examples, I will add one of less remark; but it shall hold some proportion with them, and this shall suffice me for all others of this kind, which is Hiero the Siracusan. He of a private man, became Prince of Siracusa, nor knew he any other ayd of fortune than the occasion: for the Siracusans being oppress'd, made choyce of him for their Captain, whereupon he deserv'd to be made their Prince: and he was of such vertue even in his private fortune, that he who writes of him, sayes, he wanted nothing of reigning, but a Kingdom; this man extinguish'd all the old soldiery, ordaind the new; left the old allyances, entertained new; and as he had friendship, and soldiers that were his own, upon that ground he was able to build any edifice; so that he indured much trouble in gaining, and suffered but little in maintaining.

Chapter VII: Of new Principalities, gotten by fortune, and other mens forces.

They who by fortune only become Princes of private men, with small pains attain to it, but have much ado to maintain themselves in it; and find no difficulty at all in the way, because they are carried thither with wings: but all the difficulties arise there, after they are plac'd in them. And of such sort are those who have an estate given them for money, by the favor of some one that grants it them: as it befell many in Greece, in the cities of Jonia, and Hellespont; where divers Princes were made by Darius, as well for his own safety as his glory; as also them that were made Emperors; who from private men by corrupting the soldiers, attaind to the Empire. These subsist meerly upon the will, and fortune of those that have advanced them; which are two voluble and unsteady things; and they neither know how, nor are able to continue in that dignity: they know not how, because unless it be a man of great understanding and vertue, it is not probable that he who hath always liv'd a private life, can know how to command: neither are they able, because they have not any forces that can be friendly or faithful to them. Moreover those States that suddenly fall into a mans hands, as all other things in nature that spring and grow quickly, cannot well have taken root, nor have made their correspondencies so firm, but that the first storm that takes them, ruines them; in case these, who (as it is said) are thus on a sudden clambred up to be Princes, are not of that worth and vertue as to know how to prepare themselves to maintain that which chance hath cast into their bosoms, and can afterwards lay those foundations, which others have cast before they were Princes. For the one and the other of these wayes about the attaining to be a Prince, by Vertue, or by Fortune, I will alledge you two examples which have been in the dayes of our memory. These were Francis Sforza, and Cæsar Borgia; Francis by just means and with a great deal of vertue, of a private man got to be Duke of Millan; and that which with much pains he had gaind, he kept with small ado. On the other side Cæesar Borgia (commonly termed Duke Valentine) got his state by his Fathers fortune, and with the same lost it; however that for his own part no pains was spar'd, nor any thing omitted, which by a discreet and valorus man ought to have been done, to fasten his roots in those Estates, which others armes or fortune had bestowed on him; for (as it was formerly said) he that lays not the foundations first, yet might be able by means of his extraordinary vertues to lay them afterwards, however it be with the great trouble of the architect, and danger of the edifice. If therefore we consider all the Dukes progresses, we may perceive how great foundations he had cast for his future power, which I judge a matter not superfluous to run over; because I should not well know, what better rules I might give to a new Prince, than the pattern of his actions; and however the courses he took, availd him not, yet was it not his fault, but it proceeded from an extraordinary and extream malignity of fortune. Pope Alexander the sixt, desiring to make the Duke his son a great man, had a great many difficulties, present and future: first he saw no way there was whereby he might be able to make him Lord of any State, that was not the Churches; and if he turnd to take that from the Church, he knew that the Duke of Milan, and the Venetians would never agree to it; for Faenza and Riminum were under the Venetians protection. Moreover, he saw that the armes of Italy, and those whereof in particular he might have been able to make some use, were in their hands, who ought to fear the Popes greatness; and therefore could not any wayes rely upon them: being all in the Orsins and Colonies hands, and those of their faction. It was necessary then, that those matters thus appointed by them should be disturbed, and the States of Italy disordered, to be able safely to master part of them, which he then found easie to do, seeing the Venetians upon three considerations had us'd the means to bring the French men back again into Italy: which he not only did not withstand, but furthered, with a resolution of King Lewis his ancient marriage. The King then past into Italy with the Venetians ayd, and Alexanders consent; nor was he sooner arrived in Milan, than the Pope had soldiers from him for the service of Romania, which was quickly yeelded up to him upon the reputation of the Kings forces. The Duke then having made himself master of Romania, and beaten the Colonies, desiring to hold it,

and proceed forward, two things hindered him: the one, his own soldiers, which he thought were not true to him; the other, the French mens good wills; that is to say, he feared that the Princes soldiers, whereof he had served himself, would fail him, and not only hinder his conquest, but take from him what he had gotten; and that the King also would serve him the same turn. He had experience of the Orsini upon an occasion, when after the taking of Faenza he assaulted Bolonia, to which assault he saw them go very cold. And touching the King, he discovered his mind, when having taken the Dutchy of Urbin, he invaded Tuscany; from which action the King made him retire; whereupon the Duke resolved to depend no more upon fortune, and other mens armes. And the first thing he did, was, to weaken the Orsini, and Colonnies factions in Rome: for he gain'd all their adherents that were gentlemen, giving them large allowances, and honoring them according to their qualities with charges and governments; so that in a few months the good will they bare to the parties was quite extinguisht, and wholly bent to the Duke. After this, he waited an occasion to root out the Orsini, having before dispersed those of the family of Colonnia, which fell out well to his hand; and he us'd it better. For the Orsini being too late aware, that the Dukes and the Churches greatness was their destruction, held a Council together in a dwelling house of theirs in the country adjoyning to Perusia. From thence grew the rebellion of Urbin, and the troubles of Romania, and many other dangers befell the Duke, which he overcame all with the help of the French: and having regained his reputation, trusting neither France, nor any forrein forces, to the end he might not be put to make trial of them again, he betook himself to his sleghts; and he knew so well to disguise his intention, that the Orsins, by the mediation of Paul Orsine, were reconciled to him, to whom the Duke was no way wanting in all manner of courtesies whereby to bring them into security, giving them rich garments, money, and horses, til their own simplicities led them all to Sinigallia, into his hands. These heads being then pluck'd off, and their partisans made his friends; the Duke had laid very good foundations, to build his own greatness on, having in his power all Romania with the Dutchy of Urbin, and gained the hearts of those people, by beginning to give them some relish of their well being. And because this part is worthy to be taken notice of, and to be imitated by others, I will not let it escape. The Duke, when he had taken Romania, finding it had been under the hands of poor Lords who had rather pillag'd their subjects, than chastis'd or amended them, giving them more cause of discord, than of peace and union, so that the whole countrey was fraught with robberies, quarrels, and other sorts of insolencies; thought the best way to reduce them to termes of pacification, and obedience to a Princely power, was, to give them some good government: and therefore he set over them one Remiro D'Orco, a cruel hasty man, to whom he gave an absolute power. This man in a very short time setled peace and union amongst them with very great reputation. Afterwards the Duke thought such excessive authority serv'd not so well to his purpose, and doubting it would grow odious, he erected a civil Judicature in the midst of the countrey, where one excellent Judge did Preside, and thither every City sent their Advocate: and because he knew the rigors past had bred some hatred against him, to purge the minds of those people, and to gain them wholly to himself, he purpos'd to shew, that if there was any cruelty used, it proceeded not from any order of his, but from the harsh disposition of his Officers. Whereupon laying hold on him, at this occasion, he caus'd his head to be struck off one morning early in the market place at Cesena, where he was left upon a gibbet, with a bloody sword by his side; the cruelty of which spectacle for a while satisfied and amaz'd those people. But to return from whence we have digressd: I say, that the Duke finding himself very strong, and in part out of doubt of the present dangers, because he was arm'd after his own manner, and had in some good measure suppress'd those forces, which, because of their vicinity, were able to annoy him, he wanted nothing else to go on with his Conquest, but the consideration of France: for he knew, that the King, who now, though late, was advis'd of his error, would never suffer him: and hereupon he began to seek after new allyances, and to waver with France, when the French came towards Naples against the Spaniards, who then besieged Gagetta; and his design was only to be out of their danger, which had been effected for him, had Pope Alexander lived. And thus were his businesses carried touching his present estate. As for the future, he had reason to doubt lest the new successor to the Papacy would not be his friend, and would endeavor to take that from him that Alexander had bestowed on him; and he thought to provide for this foure waies: First by rooting out the races of all those Lords he had dispoyled, whereby to take those occasions from the Pope. Secondly, by gaining all the gentlemen of Rome, whereby he might be able with those to keep the Pope in some awe. Thirdly, to make the Colledge of Cardinals as much at his devotion as possibly might be. Fourthly, by making of so large Conquests, before the Popes death, as that he might be able of himself to withstand the first fury of his enemies. Three of these fowre at Pope Alexanders death he had effected, and the fourth he had neare brought to a point. For of those Lords he had stript, he put to death as many as he could come at, and very few escap'd him: he gaind him the Roman Gentlemen: and in the Colledge he had made a great faction. And touching his new Conquest, he had a designe to become Lord of Tuscany. And he had possessed himself already of Perusia, and Pombin, and taken protection of Pisa: and so soon as he should have cast off his respect to France (which now he meant to hold no longer) being the French were now driven out of the Kingdome of Naples by the Spaniards, so that each of them was forc'd to buy his friendship at any termes; he was then to leap into Pisa. After this Lucca and Siena were presently to fall to him, partly for envy to the Florentines, and partly for fear. The Florentines had no way to escape him: all which, had it succeeded with him, as without question it had, the very same year that Alexander dy'd, he had made himself master of so great forces, and such reputation, that he would have been able to have stood upon his own bottom, without any dependance of fortune, or resting upon others helps, but only upon his own strength and valor. But Alexander dy'd five years after that he had begun to draw forth his sword: and left him setled only in the State of Romania, with all his other designes in the ayre, sick unto death, between two very strong armies of his enemies; and yet was there in this Duke such a spirit and courage; and he understood so well, how men are to be gaind, and how to be lost, and so firm were the grounds he had laid in a short time, that, had he not had those armies upon his back, or had been in health, he would have carried through his purpose in spight of all opposition; and that the foundations he grounded upon were good, it appeard in that Romania held for him above a moneth, and he remained secure in Rome, though even at deaths doore: and however the Baglioni, Vitelli, and Orsini came into Rome; yet found they none would take their parts against him. And this he was able to have effected, that if he could not have made him Pope whom be would, he could have hindred him that he would not should be Pope. But had he been in health when Alexander dy'd, every thing had gone easily with him; and he told me on that day that Julius the second was created Pope, that he had fore-thought on all that which could happen, in case his father chanc'd to dye, and for every thing provided its remedy, this onely excepted, that he foresaw not that he should at the same time be brought unto deaths dore also. Having then collected all the Dukes actions, me thinks I could not well blame him, but rather (as I have here done) set him as a pattern to be followed by all those who by fortune and others armes have been exalted to an Empire. For he being of great courage, and having lofty designes, could not carry himself otherwise; and the only obstacle of his purposes was the brevity of Alexanders life, and his own sickness. Whoever therefore deemes it necessary in his entrance into a new Principality, to secure himself of his enemies, and gain him friends, to overcome either by force or by cunning, to make himself beloved, or feared of his people, be followed and reverenced by his soldiers, to root out those that can, or owe thee any hurt, to change the ancient orders with new wayes, to be severe, and yet acceptable, magnanimous, and liberall; to extinguish the unfaithfull soldiery, and create new; to maintain to himself the armities of Kings and Princes, so that they shall either with favor benefit thee, or be wary how to offend thee; cannot find more fresh and lively examples than the actions of this man. He deserves to be found fault withall for the creation of Julius the second, wherein an evil choice was made for him: for, as it is said, not being able to make a Pope to his mind, he could have withheld any one from being Pope; and should never have consented that any one of those Cardinals should have got the Papacy, whom he had ever done harme to; or who having attaind the Pontificate were likely to be afraid of him: because men ordinarily do hurt either for fear, or hatred. Those whom he had offended, were among others, he who had the title of St. Peter ad Vincula, Colonna, St. George, and Ascanius; all the others that were in possibility of the Popedome, were such as might have feard him rather, except the Cardinal of Roan, and the Spaniards; these by reason of their allyance and obligation with him, the other because of the power they had, having the Kingdome of France on their party; wherefore the Duke above all things should have created a Spanyard Pope, and in case he could not have done that, he should have agreed that Roan should have been, and not St. Peter ad Vincula. And whoever beleeves, that with great personages new benefits blot on the remembrance of old injuries, is much deceiv'd. The Duke therefore in this election, was the cause of his own ruine at last.

Till wee come to this seaventh Chapter, I find not any thing much blame-worthy, unlesse it be on ground he layes in the second Chapter; whereupon hee builds most of this Fabrick, viz. That Subjects must either be dallyed or flatterd withall, or quite crusht. Whereby our Author advises his Prince to support his authority with two Cardinall Vertues, Dissimulation, and Cruelty. He considers not herein that the head is but a member of the body, though the principall; and the end of the parts is the good of the whole. And here he goes against himselfe in the twenty sixt Chapter of his Rep. 1. 1. where hee blames Philip of Macedon for such courses, terming them very cruell, and against all Christian manner of living; and that every man should refuse to be a King, and desire rather to live a private life, than to reigne so much to the ruine of mankind. The life of Cæsar Borgia, which is here given as a paterne to new Princes, we shall find to have been nothing else but a cunning carriage of things so, that he might thereby first deceive and inveigle, and then suppresse all those that could oppose or hinder his ambition. For if you runne over his life, you shall see the Father Pope Alexander the sixt and him, both imbarqued for his advancement, wherein they engag'd the Papall authority, and reputation of Religion; for faith and conscience these men never knew, though they exacted it of others: there was never promise made, but it was only so farre kept as servd for advantage; Liberality was made use of: Clemency and Cruelty, all alike, as they might serve to worke with their purposes. All was sacrific'd to ambition; no friendship could tye these men, nor any religion: and no marvell: for ambition made them forget both God and man. But see the end of all this cunning: though this Cæsar Borgia contrived all his businesse so warily, that our Author much commends him, and hee had attaind neere the pitch of his hopes, and had provided for each misadventure could befall him its remedy; Policy shewd it selefe short-sighted; for hee foresaw not at the time of his Fathers death, he himself should bee brought unto deaths doore also. And me thinks this Example might have given occasion to our Author to confesse, that surely there is a God that ruleth the earth. And many times God cutts off those cunning and mighty men in the hight of their purposes, when they think they have neare surmounted all dangers and difficulties. 'To the intent that the living may know, that the most high ruleth in the Kingdome of men, and giveth it to whomsoever he will, and setteth up over it the basest of men.' Daniel. 4. 17.

Chapter VIII: Concerning those who by wicked meanes have attaind to a Principality.

But because a man becomes a Prince of a private man two wayes, which cannot wholly be attributed either to Fortune or Vertue, I think not fit to let them passe me: howbeit the one of them may be more largely discoursed upon, where the Republicks are treated of. These are, when by some wicked and unlawfull meanes a man rises to the Principality; or when a private person by the favour of his fellow Citizens becomes Prince of his countrey. And speaking of the first manner, it shall be made evident by two Examples, the one ancient, the other moderne, without entring otherwise into the justice or merit of this part; for I take it that these are sufficient for any body that is forc'd to follow them. Agathocles the Sicilian, not of a private man onely, but from a base and abject fortune, got to be King of Siracusa. This man borne but of a Potter, continued alwayes a wicked life throughout all the degrees of this fortune: neverthelesse he accompanied his lewdnesse with such a courage and resolution, that applying himselfe to military affaires, by the degrees thereof he attained to bee Prætour of Siracusa, and being setled in that degree, and having determined that he would become Prince, and hold that by violence and without obligation to any other, which by consent had been granted him: and to this purpose haveing had some private intelligence touching his designe with Amilcar the Carthaginian, who was imployd with his army in Sicily, one morining gatherd the people together and the Senate of Syracusa, as if he had some what to advise with them of matters belonging to the Commonwealth, and upon a signe given, caus'd his souldiers to kill his Senatours, and the richest of the people; who being slaine, he usurp'd the Principality of that City without any civill strife: and however he was twice broken by the Carthaginians, and at last besieged, was able not onely to defend his own City, but leaving part of his own army at the defence thereof, with the other invaded Affrique, and in a short time freed Siracusa from the siege, and brought the Carthaginians into extreme necessity, who were constraind to accord with him, be contented with the possession of Affrique, and quitt Sicily to Agathocles. He then that should consider the actions and valour of this man, would not see any, or very few things to be attributed unto Fortune; seeing that as is formerly sayd, not by any ones favour, but by the degrees of service in warre with many sufferings and dangers, to which he had risen, he came to the Principality; and that hee maintained afterwards with so many resolute and hazardous undertakings. Yet cannot this be term'd vertue or valour to slay his own Citizens, betray his friends, to be without faith, without pitty, without religion, which wayes are of force to gaine dominion, but not glory: for if Agathocles his valour bee well weighd, in his enturing upon, and comming off from dangers, and the greatnesse of his courage, in supporting and mastering of adversities, no man can see why he should be thought any way inferiour even to the ablest Captaines. Notwithstanding his beastly cruelty and inhumanity with innumerable wickednesses, allow not that he should be celebrated among the most excellent men. That cannot then be attributed to Fortune or Vertue, which without the one or the other was attaind to by him. In our dayes, while Alexander the sixth held the sea, Oliverotte of Fermo, who some few yeeres before had been left young by his parents, was brought up under the care of an uncle of his on the mothers side, called John Foliani, and in the beginning of his youth given, by him to serve in the warres under Paulo Vitelli: to the end that being well instructed in that discipline, he might rise to some worthy degree in the warrs. Afterwards when Paulo was dead, he served under Vitellozzo his brother, and in very short time, being ingenious, of a good personage, and brave courage, he became one of the prime men among the troops he served in: but thinking it but servile to depend upon another, he plotted by the ayd of some Citizens of Fermo (who lik'd rather the thraldome of their City than the liberty of it) and by the favour of the Vitelli, to make himselfe master of Fermo; and writ to John Foliani, that having been many yeeres from home, he had a mind to come and see him and the City, and in some part take notice of his own patrimony; and because he had not imployd himselfe but to purchase honour, to the end his Citizens might perceive, that he had not vainely spent his time, he had a desire to come in good equipage and accompanied with a hundred horse of his friends and servants; and he intreated him that he would be pleasd so to take order, that he might be honourably received by the inhabitants of Fermo, which turnd as well to his honor that was his uncle, as his that was the nephew. In this, John faild not in any office of courtesie due to his nephew: and caused him to be well receivd by them of Fermo, and lodged him in his own house: where having passed some dayes, and stayd to put in order somewhat that was necessary for his intended villany, he made a very solemne feast, whether he invited John Foliani, and all the prime men of Fermo: and when all their chear was ended, and all their other entertainments, as in such feasts it is customary, Oliverotto of purpose mov'd some grave discourses; speaking of the greatnesse of Pope Alexander, and Cæsar his son, and their undertakings; where unto John and the others making answer, he of a sudden stood up, saying, that those were things to be spoken of in a more secret place, and so retir'd into a chamber, whether John and all the other Citizens followd him; nor were they sooner set downe there, than from some secret place therein camp forth diverse souldiers, who slew John and all the others: after which homicide Oliverotto got a horsebacke and ravaged the whole towne, and besieged the supreme Magistrate in the palace, so that for feare they were all constraind to obey him, and to settle a government, whereof hee made himselfe Prince; and they being all dead who, had they been discontented with him, could have hurt him; he strengthned himselfe with new civill and military orders, so that in the space of a yeer that he held the Principality, he was not only secure in the City of Fermo, but became fearefull to all his neighbours; and the conquest of him would have prov'd difficult, as that of Agathocles, had he not let himselfe been deceivd by Cæsar Borgia, when at Sinigallia, as before was said, he took the Orsini and Vitelli: where he also being taken a yeere after he had committed the parricide, was strangled together with Vitellozzo (whome he had had for master both of his vertues and vices.) Some man might doubt from whence it should proceed, that Agathocles, and such like, after many treacheries and cruelties, could possibly live long secure in his own countrey, and defend himselfe from his forrein enemies, and that never any of his own Citizens conspir'd against him, seeing that by means of cruelty, many others have never been able even in peaceable times to maintaine their States, much lesse in the doubtfull times of warre. I beleeve that this proceeds from the well, or ill using of those cruelties: they may bee termd well us'd (if it bee lawfull to say well of evill) that are put in practice only once of necessity for securities sake, not insisting therein afterwards; but there is use made of them for the subjects profit, as much as may be. But those that are ill us'd, are such as though they bee but few in the beginning, yet they multiply rather in time, than diminish. They that take that first way, may with the help of God, and mens care, find some remedy for their State, as Agathocles did: for the others, it is impossible they should continue. Whereupon it is to be noted, that in the laying hold of a State, the usurper thereof ought to runne over and execute all his cruelties at once, that he be not forced often to returne to them, and that he may be able, by not renewing of them, to give men some security, and gaine their affections by doing them some courtesies. Hee that carries it otherwise, either for fearefullnesse, or upon evill advice, is alwayes constraind to hold his sword drawne in his hand; nor ever can hee rely upon his subjects, there being no possibility for them, because of his daily and continuall injuries, to live in any safety: for his injuries should bee done altogether, that being seldomer tasted, they might lesse offend; his favours should bee bestowd by little, and little to the end they might keep their taste the better; and above all things a Prince must live with his subjects in such sort, that no accident either of good or evill can make him vary: for necessity comming upon him by reason of adversities, thou hast not time given thee to make advantage of thy cruelties; and the favours which then thou bestowest, will little help thee, being taken as if they came from thee perforce, and so yeeld no returne of thanks.

Chapter IX: Of the Civill Principality.

But comming to the other part, when a principall Citizen, not by villany, or any other insufferable violence, but by the favour of his fellow-citizens becomes Prince of his native countrey: which we may terme a Civill Principality; nor to attaine hereunto is Vertue wholly or Fortune wholly necessary, but rather a fortunate cunning: I say, this Principality is climb'd up to, either by the peoples help, or the great mens. For, in every City we finde these two humours differ; and they spring from this, that the people desire not to be commanded nor oppressed by the great ones, and the great ones are desirous to command and oppresse the people: and from these two several appetites, arise in the City one of these three effects, either a Principality, or Liberty, or Tumultuary licentiousnesse. The Principality is caused either by the people, or the great ones, according as the one or other of these factions have the occasion offerd; for the great ones seeing themselves not able to resist the people, begin to turne the whole reputation to one among them, and make him Prince, whereby they may under his shadow vent their spleenes. The people also, not being able to support the great mens insolencies, converting the whole reputation to one man, create him their Prince, to be protected by his authority. He that comes to the Principality by the assistance of the great ones, subsists with more difficulty, than he that attaines to it by the peoples favour; for he being made Prince, hath many about him, who account themselves his equalls, and therefore cannot dispose nor command them at his pleasure. But he that gaines the Principality by the peoples favor, finds himselfe alone in his throne, and hath none or very few neare him that are not very supple to bend: besides this, the great ones cannot upon easie termes be satisfied, or without doing of wrong to others, where as a small matter contents the people: for the end which the people propound to themselves, is more honest than that of the great men, these desiring to oppresse, they only not to be oppressed. To this may be added also, that the Prince which is the peoples enemy, can never well secure himselfe of them, because of their multitude; well may hee bee sure of the Nobles, they being but a few. The worst that a Prince can look for of the people become his enemy, is to be abandoned by them: but when the great ones once grow his enemies, he is not only to feare their abandoning of him, but their making of a party against him also: for there being in them more forecast and craft, they alwayes take time by the forelocks whereby to save themselves, and seeke credit with him who they hope shall get the mastery. The Prince likewise is necessitated alwayes to live with the same people, but can doe well enough without the same great men; he being able to create new ones, and destroy them again every day, and to take from them, and give them credit as he pleases: and to cleare this part, I say, that great men ought to be considerd two wayes principally, that is, if they take thy proceedings so much to heart, as to engage their fortunes wholly in thine, in case they lye not alwayes catching at spoyle, they ought to be well honourd and esteem'd: those that bind themselves not to thy fortune, are to be considerd also two wayes; either they doe it for lack of courage, and naturall want of spirit, and then shouldst thou serve thy selfe of them, and of them especially that are men of good advice; for if thy affaires prosper, thou dost thy selfe honour thereby; if crost, thou needst not feare them: but when they oblige not themselves to thee of purpose, and upon occasion of ambition, it is a signe they think more of themselves than of thee: and of these the Prince ought to beware, and account of them as his discoverd enemyes: for alwayes in thy adversity they will give a hand too to ruine thee. Therefore ought hee that comes to be Prince by the peoples favour, keepe them his friends: which he may easily doe, they desiring only to live free from oppression: but he that becomes Prince by the great mens favour, against the will of the people, ought above all things to gaine the people to him, which he may easily effect, when he takes upon him their protection: And because men when they find good, where they look for evill, are thereby more endered to their benefactour, therefore growes the people so pliant in their subjection to him, as if by their favours he had attaind his dignity. And the Prince is able to gaine them to his side by many wayes, which because they vary according to the subject, no certaine rule can be given thereupon; wherefore we shall let them passe I will only conclude, that it is necessary for a Prince to have the people his friend; otherwise in his adversities he hath no helpe. Nabis Prince of the Spartans supported the siege of all Greece, and an exceeding victorious army of the Romans, and against those defended his native countrey and State, and this suffic'd him alone, that as the danger came upon him, he secur'd himself of a fewer; whereas if the people had been his enemy, this had nothing availd him. And let no man think to overthrow this my opinion with that common proverb, that He who relyes upon the people, layes his foundation in the dirt; for that is true where a private Citizen grounds upon them, making his account that the people shall free him, when either his enemyes or the Magistrates oppresse him: In this case he should find himself often deceiv'd, as it befell the Gracchyes in Rome, and in Florence George Scali: but he being a Prince that grounds thereupon, who can command, and is a man of courage, who hath his wits about him in his adversityes, and wants not other preparations, and holds together the whole multitude animated with his valour and orders, shall not prove deceiv'd by them, and shall find he hath layd good foundations. These Principalityes are wont to be upon the point of falling when they goe about to skip from the civil order to the absolute: for these Princes either command of themselves, or by the Magistrate; in this last case their State is more weak and dangerous, because they stand wholly at the will and pleasure of these Citizens, who then are set over the Magistrates, who especially in adverse times are able with facility to take their State from them either by rising up against them, or by not obeying them; and then the Prince is not at hand in those dangers to take the absolute authority upon him: for the Citizens and subjects that are accustomed to receive the commands from the Magistrates, are not like in those fractions to obey his: and in doubtfull times he shall alwayes have greatest penury of whom he may trust; for such a Prince cannot ground upon that which he sees in peaceable times, when the Citizens have need of the State; for then every one runs, and every one promises, and every one will venture his life for him, where there is no danger neare; but in times of hazzard, when the State hath need of Citizens, there are but few of them then, and so much the more is this experience dangerous, in that it can be but once made. Therefore a prudent Prince ought to devise a way whereby his Citizens alwayes and in any case and quality of time may have need of his government, and they shall alwaies after prove faithfull to him.

Chapter X: In what manner the Forces of all Principalities ought to be measured.

It is requisite in examining the quality of those Principalities, to have another consideration of them, that is, if a Prince have such dominions, that he is able in case of necessity to subsist of himself, or else whether he hath alwaies need of another to defend him. And to cleer this point the better, I judge them able to stand of themselves, who are of power either for their multitudes of men, or quantity of money, to bring into the field a compleat armie, and joyn battel with whoever comes to assail them: and so I think those alwaies to stand in need of others help, who are not able to appear in the field against the enemy, but are forc'd to retire within their walls and guard them. Touching the first case, we have treated already, and shall adde somwhat thereto as occasion shall require. In the second case, we cannot say other, save only to encourage such Princes to fortifie and guard their own Capital city, and of the countrey about, not to hold much account; and whoever shall have well fortified that town, and touching other matters of governments shall have behaved himself towards his subjects, as hath been formerly said, and hereafter shall be, shall never be assaild but with great regard; for men willingly undertake not enterprises, where they see difficulty to work them through; nor can much facility be there found, where one assails him, who hath his town strong and wel guarded, and is not hated of his people. The cities of Germany are very free; they have but very little of the countrey about them belonging to them; and they obey the Emperor, when they please, and they stand not in fear, neither of him nor any other Potentate about them: for they are in such a manner fortified, that every one thinks the siege of any of them would prove hard and tedious: for all of them have ditches, and rampires, and good store of Artillery, and alwaies have their publick cellars well provided with meat and drink and firing for a yeer: besides this, whereby to feed the common people, and without any loss to the publick, they have alwaies in common whereby they are able for a year to imploy them in the labor of those trades that are the sinews and the life of that city, and of that industry whereby the commons ordinarily supported themselves: they hold up also the military exercises in repute, and hereupon have they many orders to maintain them. A Prince then that is master of a good strong city, and causeth not himself to be hated, cannot be assaulted; and in case he were, he that should assail him, would be fain to quit him with shame: for the affairs of the world are so various, that it is almost impossible that an army can lie incampt before a town for the space of a whole yeer: and if any should reply, that the people having their possessions abroad, in case they should see them a fire, would not have patience, and the tedious siege and their love to themselves would make them forget their Prince: I answer that a Prince puissant and couragious, will easily master those difficulties, now giving his subjects hope, that the mischief will not be of durance; sometimes affright them with the cruelty of their enemies, and other whiles cunningly securing himself of those whom he thinks too forward to run to the enemy. Besides this by ordinary reason the enemy should burne and waste their countrey, upon his arrival, and at those times while mens minds are yet warme, and resolute in their defence: and therefore so much the less ought a Prince doubt: for after some few dayes, that their courages grow coole, the dammages are all done, and mischiefs received, and there is no help for it, and then have they more occasion to cleave faster to their Prince, thinking he is now more bound to them, their houses having for his defence been fired, and their possessions wasted; and mens nature is as well to hold themselves oblig'd for the kindnesses they do, as for those they receive; whereupon if all be well weigh'd, a wise Prince shall not find much difficulty to keep sure and true to him his Citizens hearts at the beginning and latter end of the siege, when he hath no want of provision for food and ammunition.

Chapter XI: Concerning Ecclesiastical Principalities.

There remains now only that we treat of the Ecclesiastical Principalities, about which all the difficulties are before they are gotten: for they are attained to either by vertue, or Fortune; and without the one or the other they are held: for they are maintaind by orders inveterated in the religion, all which are so powerfull and of such nature, that they maintain their Princes in their dominions in what manner soever they proceed and live. These only have an Estate and defend it not; have subjects and govern them not; and yet their States because undefended, are not taken from them; nor their subjects, though not govern'd, care not, think not, neither are able to aliene themselves from them. These Principalities then are only happy and secure: but they being sustained by superior causes, whereunto humane understanding reaches not, I will not meddle with them: for being set up and maintained by God, it would be the part of a presumptuous and rash man to enter into discourse of them. Yet if any man should ask me whence it proceeds, that the Church in temporal power hath attaind to such greatness, seeing that till the time of Alexander the sixt, the Italian Potentates, and not only they who are entituled the potentates, but every Baron and Lord though of the meanest condition in regard of the temporality, made but small account of it; and now a King of France trembles at the power thereof; and it hath been able to drive him out of Italy, and ruine the Venetians; and however this be well known, me thinks it is not superstitious in some part to recall it to memory. Before that Charles King of France past into Italy, this countrey was under the rule of the Pope, Venetians, the King of Naples, the Duke of Milan, and the Florentines. These Potentates took two things principally to their care; the one, that no forreiner should invade Italy; the other that no one of them should inlarge their State. They, against whom this care was most taken, were the Pope and the Venetians; and to restrain the Venetians, there needed the union of all the rest, as it was in the defence of Ferrara; and to keep the Pope low, they served themselves of the Barons of Rome, who being divided into two factions, the Orsini and Colonnesi, there was alwaies occasion of offence between them, who standing ready with their armes in hand in the view of the Pope, held the Popedome weak and feeble: and however sometimes there arose a couragious Pope, as was Sextus; yet either his fortune, or his wisdome was not able to free him of these incommodities, and the brevity of their lives was the cause thereof; for in ten years, which time, one with another, Popes ordinarily liv'd, with much ado could they bring low one of the factions. And if, as we may say, one had near put out the Colonnesi, there arose another enemy to the Orsini, who made them grow again, so that there was never time quite to root them out. This then was the cause, why the Popes temporal power was of small esteem in Italy; there arose afterwards Pope Alexander the sixt, who of all the Popes that ever were, shewed what a Pope was able to do with money and forces: and he effected, by means of his instrument, Duke Valentine, and by the ocasion of the French mens passage, all those things which I have formerly discoursed upon in the Dukes actions: and however his purpose was nothing at all to inlarge the Church dominions, but to make the Duke great; yet what he did, turnd to the Churches advantage, which after his death when the Duke was taken away, was the heir of all his pains. Afterwards succeeded Pope Julius, and found the Church great, having all Romania, and all the Barons of Rome being quite rooted out, and by Alexanders persecutions, all their factions worne down; he found also the way open for the heaping up of moneys, never practised before Alexanders time; which things Julius not only follow'd, but augmented; and thought to make himself master of Bolonia, and extinguish the Venetians, and chase the French men out of Italy: and these designes of his prov'd all lucky to him, and so much the more to his praise in that he did all for the good of the Church, and in no private regard: he kept also the factions of the Orsins and Colonnesi, in the same State he found them: and though there were among them some head whereby to cause an alteration; yet two things have held them quiet; the one the power of the Church, which somewhat affrights them; the other because they have no Cardinals of their factions, who are the primary causes of all the troubles amongst them: nor shall these parties ever be at rest, while they have Cardinals; because they nourish the factions both in Rome, and abroad; and the Barons then are forced to undertake the defence of them: and thus from the Prelates ambitions arise the discords and tumults among the Barons. And now hath Pope Leo his Holiness found the Popedome exceeding puissant, of whom it is hoped, that if they amplified it by armes, he by his goodness, and infinite other vertues, will much more advantage and dignifie it.

Chapter XII: How many sorts of Military discipline there are and touching Mercenary soldiers.

Having treated particularly of the qualities of those Principalities, which in the beginning I propounded to discourse upon, and considered in some part the reasons of their well and ill being, and shewd the waies whereby many have sought to gain, and hold them, it remains now that I speak in general of the offences and defences, that may chance in each of the forenamed. We have formerly said that it is necessary for a Prince to have good foundations laid; otherwise it must needs be that he go to wrack. The Principal foundations that all States have, as well new, as old, or mixt, are good laws, and good armes; and because there cannot be good laws, where there are not good armes; and where there are good armes, there must needs be good laws, I will omit to discourse of the laws, and speak of armes. I say then that the armes, wherewithall a Prince defends his State, either are his own, or mercenary, or auxiliary, or mixt. Those that are mercenary and auxiliar, are unprofitable, and dangerous, and if any one holds his State founded upon mercenary armes, he shall never be quiet, nor secure, because they are never well united, ambitious, and without discipline, treacherous, among their friends stour, among their enemies cowardly; they have no fear of God, nor keep any faith with men; and so long only defer they the doing of mischief, till the enemy comes to assul thee; and in time of peace thou art despoyled by them, in war by thy enemies: the reason hereof is, because they have no other love, nor other cause to keep them in the field, but only a small stipend, which is not of force to make them willing to hazard their lives for thee: they are willing indeed to be thy soldiers, till thou goest to fight; but then they fly, or run away; which thing would cost me but small pains to perswade; for the ruine of Italy hath not had any other cause now a dayes, than for that it hath these many years rely'd upon mercenary armes; which a good while since perhaps may have done some man some service, and among themselves they may have been thought valiant: but so soon as any forrein enemy appeared, they quickly shewed what they were. Whereupon Charles the King of France, without opposition, made himself master of all Italy: and he that said, that the causes thereof were our faults, said true; but these were not those they beleeved, but what I have told; and because they were the Princes faults, they also have suffered the punishment. I will fuller shew the infelicity of these armes. The mercenary Captains are either very able men, or not: if they be, thou canst not repose any trust in them: for they will alwaies aspire unto their own proper advancements, either by suppressing of thee that art their Lord, or by suppressing of some one else quite out of thy purpose: but if the Captain be not valorous, he ordinarily ruines thee: and in case it be answered, that whoever shall have his armes in his hands, whether mercenary or not, will do so: I would reply, that armes are to be imployed either by a Prince, or Common-wealth. The Prince ought to go in person, and performe the office of a commander: the Republick is to send forth her Citizens: and when she sends forth one that proves not of abilities, she ought to change him then; and when he does prove valorous, to bridle him so by the laws, that he exceed not his commission. And by experience we see, that Princes and Republiques of themselves alone, make very great conquests; but that mercenary armes never do other than harme; and more hardly falls a Republick armed with her own armes under the obedience of one of her own Citizens, than one that is armed by forrein armes. Rome and Sparta subsisted many ages armed and free. The Swissers are exceedingly well armed, and yet very free. Touching mercenary armes that were of old, we have an example of the Carthagians, who near upon were oppress'd by their own mercenary soldiers, when the first war with the Romans was finished; however the Carthagians had their own Citizens for their Captains. Philip of Macedon was made by the Thebans after Epaminondas his death, General of their Armies; and after the victory, he took from them liberty. The Milaneses when Duke Philip was dead, entertaind Francis Sforza into their pay against the Venetians, who having vanquisht their enemie at Caravaggio, afterwards joyned with them, where by to usurp upon the Milaneses his Masters. Sforza his father, being in Joan the Queen of Naples pay, left her on a sudden disarmed; whereupon she, to save her Kingdom, was constraind to cast her self into the King of Arrragon's bosome. And in case the Venetians and the Florentines have formerly augmented their State with these kind of armes, and their own Captains, and yet none of them have ever made themselves their Princes, but rather defended them: I answer, that the Florentines in this case have had fortune much their friend: for of valorous Captains, which they might any way fear, some have not been victors, some have had opposition, and others have laid the aim of their ambitions another way. He who overcame not, was John Aouto, of whose faith there could no proof be made, being he vanquisht not; but every one will acknowledge, that, had he vanquisht, the Florentines were at his discretion. Sforza had alwaies the Bracceschi for his adversaries, so that they were as a guard one upon another. Francis converted all his ambition against Lombardy. Braccio against the Church, and the Kingdome of Naples. But let us come to that which followed a while agoe. The Florentines made Paul Vitelli their General, a throughly advis'd man, and who from a private fortune had rose to very great reputation: had he taken Pisa, no man will deny but that the Florentines must have held fast with him; for had he been entertained in their enemies pay, they had no remedy; and they themselves holding of him, of force were to obey him. The Venetians, if we consider their proceedings, we shall see wrought both warily and gloriously, while themselves made war, which was before their undertakings by land, where the gentlemen with their own Commons in armes behav'd themselves bravely: but when they began to fight by land, they lost their valor, and follow'd the customes of Italy; and in the beginning of their enlargement by land, because they had not much territory, and yet were of great reputation, they had not much cause to fear their Captains; but as they began to extend their bounds, which was under their Commander Carminiola, they had a taste of this error: for perceiving he was exceeding valorous, having under his conduct beaten the Duke of Milan; and knowing on the other side, how he was cold in the war, they judg'd that they could not make any great conquest with him; and because they neither would, nor could cashier him, that they might not lose what they had gotten, they were forced for their own safeties to put him to death. Since they have had for their General Bartholomew of Berganio, Robert of St. Severin, the Count of Petilian, and such like: whereby they were to fear their losses, as well as to hope for gain: as it fell out afterwards at Vayla, where in one day they lost that, which with so much pains they had gotten in eight hundred years: for from these kind of armes grow slack and slow and weak gains; but sudden and wonderfull losses: And because I am now come with these examples into Italy, which now these many years, have been governd by mercenary armes, I will search deeper into them, to the end that their course and progress being better discoverd, they may be the better amended. You have to understand, that so soon as in these later times the yoak of the Italian Empire began to be shaken off, and the Pope had gotten reputation in the temporality, Italy was divided into several States: for many of the great cities took armes against their Nobility; who under the Emperors protection had held them in oppression; and the Pope favored these, whereby he might get himself reputation, in the temporality; of many others, their Citizens became Princes, so that hereupon Italy being come into the Churches hands as it were, and some few Republicks, those Priests and Citizens not accustomed to the use of armes, began to take strangers to their pay. The first that gave reputation to these soldiers was Alberick of Como in Romania. From his discipline among others descended Brachio and Sforza, who in their time were the arbitres of Italy; after these followed all others, who even till our dayes have commanded the armes of Italy; and the success of their valor hath been, that it was overrun by Charles, pillaged by Lewis, forc'd by Ferdinand, and disgrac'd by the Swissers. The order which they have held, hath been, first whereby to give reputation to their own armes to take away the credit of the Infantry. This they did, because they having no State of their own, but living upon their industry, their few foot gave them no reputation, and many they were not able to maintain; whereupon they reduc'd themselves to cavalery, and so with a supportable number they were entertained and honored: and matters were brought to such termes, that in an army of twenty thousand soldiers you should not find two thousand foot. They had moreover us'd all industry to free themselves and their soldiers of all pains and fear, in their skirmishes, not killing, but taking one another prisoners, and without ransome for their freedom; they repaired not all to their tents by night, nor made palizado or trench thereabout, nor lay in the field in the summer: and all these things were thus contrived and agreed of among them in their military orders, whereby (as is said) to avoid pains and dangers, insomuch as they have brought Italy into slavery and disgrace.

Chapter XIII: Of Auxiliary Soldiers, mixt, and native.

The Auxiliary forces, being the other kind of unprofitable armes, are, when any puissant one is called in, who with his forces comes to assist and defend thee; such as in these later times did Pope Julius use, who having seen the evil proof of his mercenary soldiers in the enterprize of Ferrara, applied himself to the Auxiliaries, and agreed with Ferdinand King of Spain, that with his Forces he should aid him. These armes may be profitable and advantagious for themselves; but for him that calls them in, hurtfull; because in losing, thou art left defeated; and conquering, thou becomest their prisoner. And however that of these examples the ancient stories are full fraught; yet will I not part from this of Pope Julius the second, which is as yet fresh: whose course could not have been more inconsiderate, for the desire he had to get Ferrara, putting himself wholly into strangers hands: but his good fortune caused another cause to arise, that hindred him from receiving the fruit of his evil choice; for his Auxiliaries being broken at Ravenna, and the Swissers thereupon arriving, who put the Conquerors to flight beyond all opinion, even their own and others, he chanced not to remain his enemies prisoner, they being put to flight, nor prisoner to his Auxiliaries, having vanquished by other forces than theirs. The Florentines being wholly disarmed, brought ten thousand French to Pisa for to take it: by which course they ran more hazzard, than in any time of their troubles. The Emperor of Constantinople, to oppress his neighbors, brought into Greece ten thousand Turks, who when the war was ended, could not be got out thence, which was the beginning of Greeces servitude under the Infidels. He then that will in no case be able to overcome, let him serve himself of these armes; for they are much more dangerous than the mercenaries; for by those thy ruine is more suddenly executed; for they are all united, and all bent to the obedience of another. But for the mercenaries to hurt thee, when they have vanquished, there is no more need of time, and greater occasion, they not being all united in a body, and being found out and paid by thee, wherein a third that thou mak'st their head, cannot suddenly gaine so great authority, that he can endammage thee. In summe, in the mercenaries their sloth and lazinesse to fight is more dangerous: in the auxiliaries their valour. Wherefore a wise Prince hath alwayes avoyded these kind of armes, and betaken himselfe to his owne, and desired rather to loss with his owne, than conquer with anothers, accounting that not a true victorie which was gotten with others armes. I will not doubt to alleadge Cæsar Borgia, and his actions. This Duke entred into Romania with auxiliarie armes, bringing with him all French souldiers: but afterwards not accounting those armes secure, bent himselfe to mercenaries, judging lesse danger to be in those, and tooke in pay the Orsini and the Vitelli, which afterwards in the proof of them, finding wavering, unfaithful, and dangerous, he extinguishd, and betook himselfe to his owne; and it may easily be perceiv'd what difference there is between the one and the other of these armes, considering the difference that was between the Dukes reputation, when he had the French men alone, and when he had the Orsini and Vitelli; but when he remaind with his own, and stood of himselfe, we shall find it was much augmented: nor ever was it of grate esteeme, but when every one saw, that he wholly possessed his owne armes. I thought not to have parted from the Italian examples of late memory; but that I must not let passe that of Hiero the Siracusan, being one of those I formerly nam'd. This man (as I said before) being made general of the Siracusans forces, knew presently that mercenary souldiery was nothing for their profit in that they were hirelings, as our Italians are; and finding no way either to hold, or cashier them made them all bee cut to peeces, and afterwards waged warre with his owne men, and none others. I will also call to memory a figure of the old Testament serving just to this purpose. When David presented himselfe before Saul to goe to fight with Goliah the Philistins Champion, Saul to encourage him, clad him with his owne armes, which David when he had them upon back, refused, saying, he was not able to make any proofe of himself therein, and therefore would goe meet the enemy with his own sling and sword. In summe, others armes either fall from thy shoulders, or cumber or streighten thee. Charls the seventh, Father of Lewis the eleventh, having by his good fortune and valour set France at liberty from the English, knew well this necessity of being arm'd with his owne armes, and settled in his Kingdome the ordinances of men at armes, and infantry. Afterwards King Lewis his sonne abolisht those of the infantry, and began to take the Swissers to pay; which errour follow'd by the others, is (as now indeed it appeares) the cause of that Kingdomes dangers. For having given reputation to the Swissers,

they have renderd all their own armes contemptible; for this hath wholly ruind their foot, and oblig'd their men at armes to forrein armes: for being accustomed to serve with the Swissers, they think they are not able to overcome without them. From whence it comes that the French are not of force against the Swissers, and without them also against others they use not to adventure. Therefore are the French armies mixt, part mercenaries, and part natives, which armes are farre better than the simple mercenaries or simple auxiliaries, and much inferiour to the natives; and let the said example suffice for that: for the Kingdome of France would have been unconquerable, if Charles his order had been augmented and maintaind: but men in their small wisdome begin a thing, which then because it hath some favour of good, discovers not the poyson that lurkes thereunder, as I before said of the hectick feavers. Wherefore that Prince which perceives not mischiefes, but as they grow up, is not truely wise; and this is given but to few: and if we consider the first ruine of the Romane Empire, we shall find it was from taking the Goths first into their pay; for from that beginning the forces of the Romane Empire began to grow weak, and all the valour that was taken hence was given to them. I conclude then that without having armes of their owne, no Principality can be secure, or rather is wholly oblig'd to fortune, not having valour to shelter it in adversity. And it was alwayes the opinion and saying of wise men, that nothing is so weak and unsetled, as is the reputation of power not founded upon ones owne proper forces: which are those that are composed of thy subjects, or Citizens, or servants; all the rest are mercenary or auxiliary; and the manner how to order those well, is easie to find out, if those orders above nam'd by me, shall be but run over, and if it shall be but consider'd, how Philip Alexander the Great his Father, and in what manner many Republicks and Princes have armd and appointed themselves, to which appointments I referre my selfe wholly.

Chapter XIV: What belongs to the Prince touching military Discipline.

A prince then ought to have no other ayme, nor other thought, nor take any thing else for his proper art, but warr, and the orders and discipline thereof: for that is the sole arte which belongs to him that commands, and is of so great excellency, that not only those that are borne Princes, it maintains so; but many times raises men from a private fortune to that dignity. And it is seene by the contrary, that when Princes have given themselves more to their delights, than to the warres, they have lost their States; and the first cause that makes thee lose it, is the neglect of that arte; and the cause that makes thee gaine it, is that thou art experienc'd and approvd in that arte. Francis Sforza by being a man at armes, of a private man became Duke of Milan; and his sons by excusing themselves of the troubles and paines belonging to those imployments of Princes, became private men. For among other mischiefes thy neglect of armes brings upon thee, it causes thee to be contemnd, which is one of those disgraces, from which a Prince ought to keepe himselfe, as hereafter shall be sayd: for from one that is disarmd to one that is armd there is no proportion; and reason will not, that he who is in armes, should willingly yeeld obedience to him that is unfurnishd of them, and that he that is disarmd should be in security among his armed vassalls; for there being disdaine in the one, and suspicion in the other, it is impossible these should ever well cooperate. And therefore a Prince who is quite unexperienced in matter of warre, besides the other infelicities belonging to him, as is said, cannot be had in any esteeme among his souldiers, nor yet trust in them. Wherefore he ought never to neglect the practice of the arte of warre, and in time of peace should he exercise it more than in the warre; which he may be able to doe two wayes; the one practically, and in his labours and recreations of his body, the other theoretically. And touching the practick part, he ought besides the keeping of his own subjects well traind up in the discipline and exercise of armes, give himselfe much to the chase, whereby to accustome his body to paines, and partly to understand the manner of situations, and to know how the mountaines arise, which way the vallyes open themselves, and how the plaines are distended flat abroad, and to conceive well the nature of the rivers, and marrish ground, and herein to bestow very much care, which knowledge is profitable in two kinds: first he learnes thereby to know his own countrey, and is the better enabled to understand the defence thereof, and afterwards by meanes of this knowledge and experience in these situations, easily comprehends any other situation, which a new he hath need to view, for the little hillocks, vallies, plaines, rivers, and marrish places. For example, they in Tuscany are like unto those of other countries: so that from the knowledge of the site of one country, it is easie to attain to know that of others. And that Prince that wants this skill, failes of the principall part a Commander should be furnisht with; for this shows the way how to discover the enemy, to pitch the camp, to lead their armies, to order their battells, and also to besiege a town at thy best advantage, Philopomenes Prince of the Achayans, among other praises Writers give him, they say, that in time of peace, he thought not upon any thing so much as the practise of warre; and whensoever he was abroad in the field to disport himselfe with his friends, would often stand still, and discourse with them, in case the enemies were upon the top of that hill, and we here with our army, whether of us two should have the advantage, and how might we safely goe to find them, keeping still our orders; and if we would retire our selves, what course should we take if they retir'd, how should we follow them? and thus on the way, propounded them all such accidents could befall in any army; would heare their opinions, and tell his owne, and confirme it by argument; so that by his continuall thought hereupon, when ever he led any army no chance could happen, for which he had not a remedy. But touching the exercise of the mind, a Prince ought to read Histories, and in them consider the actions of the worthiest men, marke how they have behav'd themselves in the warrs, examine the occasions of their victories, and their losses; wherby they may be able to avoyd these, and obtaine those; and above all, doe as formerly some excellent man hath done, who hath taken upon him to imitate, if any one that hath gone before him hath left his memory glorious; the course he took, and kept alwaies near unto him the remembrances of his actions and worthy deeds: as it is said, that Alexander the great imitated Achilles; Cæsar Alexander, and Scipio Cyrus. And whoever reads the life of Cyrus, written by Xenophon, may easily perceive afterwards in Scipio's life how much glory his imitation gaind him, and how much Scipio did conforme himselfe in his chastity, affability, humanity, and liberality with those things, that are written by Xenophon of Cyrus. Such like wayes ought a wise Prince to take, nor ever be idle in quiet times, but by his paines then, as it were provide himself of store, whereof he may make some use in his adversity, the end that when the times change, he may be able to resist the stormes of his hard fortune.

Chapter XV: Of those things, in respect whereof, men, and especially Princes, are praised, or dispraised.

It now remaines that we consider what the conditions of a Prince ought to be, and his termes of government over his subjects, and towards his friends. And because I know that many have written hereupon; I doubt, lest I venturing also to treat thereof, may be branded with presumption, especially seeing I am like enough to deliver an opinion different from others. But my intent being to write for the advantage of him that understands me, I thought it fitter to follow the effectuall truth of the matter, than the imagination thereof; And many Principalities and Republiques, have been in imagination, which neither have been seen nor knowne to be indeed: for there is such a distance between how men doe live, and how men ought to live; that he who leaves that which is done, for that which ought to be done, learnes sooner his ruine than his preservation; for that man who will professe honesty in all his actions, must needs goe to ruine among so many that are dishonest. Whereupon it is necessary for a Prince, desiring to preserve himselfe, to be able to make use of that honestie, and to lay it aside againe, as need shall require. Passing by then things that are only in imagination belonging to a Prince, to discourse upon those that are really true; I say that all men, whensoever mention is made of them, and especially Princes, because they are placed aloft in the view of all, are taken notice of for some of these qualities, which procure them either commendations or blame: and this is that some one is held liberal, some miserable, (miserable I say, nor covetous; for the covetous desire to have, though it were by rapine; but a miserable man is he, that too much for bears to make use of his owne) some free givers, others extortioners; some cruell, others pitious; the one a Leaguebreaker, another faithfull; the one effeminate and of small courage, the other fierce and couragious; the one courteous, the other proud; the one lascivious, the other chaste; the one of faire dealing, the other wily and crafty; the one hard, the other easie; the one grave, the other light; the one religious, the other incredulous, and such like. I know that every one will confesse, it were exceedingly praise worthy for a Prince to be adorned with all these above nam'd qualities that are good: but because this is not possible, nor doe humane conditions admit such perfection in vertues, it is necessary for him to be so discret, that he know how to avoid the infamie of those vices which would thrust him out of his State; and if it be possible, beware of those also which are not able to remove him thence; but where it cannot be, let them passe with lesse regard. And yet, let him not stand much upon it, though he incurre the infamie of those vices, without which he can very hardly save his State: for if all be throughly considerd, some thing we shall find which will have the colour and very face of Vertue, and following them, they will lead the to thy destruction; whereas some others that shall as much seeme vice, if we take the course they lead us, shall discover unto us the way to our safety and well-being.

The second blemish in this our Authours book, I find in his fifteenth Chapter: where he instructs his Prince to use such an ambidexterity as that he may serve himselfe either of vertue, or vice, according to his advantage, which in true pollicy is neither good in attaining the Principality nor in securing it when it is attaind. For Politicks, presuppose Ethiques, which will never allow this rule: as that a man might make this small difference between vertue, and vice, that he may indifferently lay aside, or take up the one or the other, and put it in practise as best conduceth to the end he propounds himselfe. I doubt our Authour would have blamd Davids regard to Saul when 1 Sam. 24. in the cave he cut off the lap of Sauls garment, and spared his head; and afterwards in the 26. when he forbad Abishai to strike him as he lay sleeping. Worthy of a Princes consideration is that saying of Abigal to David 1 Sam. 25. 30.

'It shall come to passe when the Lord shall have done to my Lord according to all that he hath spoken concerning thee, and shall have appointed thee Ruler over Israel, that this shall be no grief to thee, nor offence of heart unto my Lord, that thou hast forborne to shed blood, etc.'

For surely the conscience of this evill ground whereupon they have either built, or underpropped their tyranny, causes men, as well met us *as spes in longum projicere,* which sets them a work on further mischiefe.

Chapter XVI: Of Liberality, and Miserablenesse.

Beginning then at the first of the above mentioned qualities, I say that it would be very well to be accounted liberall: neverthelesse, liberality used in such a manner, as to make thee be accounted so, wrongs thee: for in case it be used vertuously, and as it ought to be, it shall never come to be taken notice of, so as to free thee from the infamie of its contrary. And therefore for one to hold the name of liberal among men, it were needfull not to omit any sumptuous quality, insomuch that a Prince alwayes so dispos'd, shall waste all his revenues, and at the end shall be forc'd, if he will still maintaine that reputation of liberality, heavily to burthen his subjects, and become a great exactour; and put in practise all those things that can be done to get mony: Which begins to make him hatefull to his subjects, and fall into every ones contempt, growing necessitous: so that having with this liberality wrong'd many, and imparted of his bounty but to a few; he feels every first mischance, and runs a hazard of every first danger: Which he knowing, and desiring to withdraw himself from, incurs presently the disgrace of being termed miserable. A Prince therefore not being able to use this vertue of liberality, without his own damage, in such a sort, that it may be taken notice of, ought, if he be wise, not to regard the name of Miserable; for in time he shall alwaies be esteemed the more liberal, seeing that by his parsimony his own revenues are sufficient for him; as also he can defend himself against whoever makes war against him, and can do some exploits without grieving his subjects: so that he comes to use his liberality to all those, from whom he takes nothing, who are infinite in number; and his miserableness towards those to whom he gives nothing, who are but a few. In our dayes we have not seen any, but those who have been held miserable, do any great matters; but the others all quite ruin'd. Pope Julius the second, however he serv'd himself of the name of Liberal, to get the Papacy, yet never intended he to continue it, to the end he might be able to make war against the King of France: and he made so many wars without imposing any extraordinary tax, because his long thrift supplyed his large expences. This present King of Spain could never have undertaken, nor gone through with so many exploits, had he been accounted liberal. Wherefore a Prince ought little to regard (that he may not be driven to pillage his subjects, that he may be able to defend himself, that he may not fall into poverty and contempt, that he be not forced to become an extortioner) though he incurre the name of miserable; for this is one of those vices, which does not pluck him from his throne. And if any one should say, Cæsar by his liberality obtained the Empire, and many others (because they both were, and were esteemd liberal) attaind to exceeding great dignities. I answer, either thou art already come to be a Prince, or thou art in the way to it; in the first case, this liberality is hurtful; in the second, it is necessary to be accounted so; and Cæsar was one of those that aspired to the Principality of Rome. But if after he had gotten it, he had survived, and not forborne those expences, he would quite have ruined that Empire. And if any one should reply; many have been Princes, and with their armies have done great exploits, who have been held very liberal. I answer, either the Prince spends of his own and his subjects, or that which belongs to others: in the first, he ought to be sparing; in the second, he should not omit any part of liberality. And that Prince that goes abroad with his army, and feeds upon prey, and spoyle, and tributes, and hath the disposing of that which belongs to others, necessarily should use this liberality; otherwise would his soldiers never follow him; and of that which is neither thine, nor thy subjects, thou mayest well be a free giver, as were Cyrus, Cæsar and Alexander; for the spending of that which is anothers, takes not away thy reputation, but rather adds to it, only the wasting of that which is thine own hurts thee; nor is there any thing consumes itself so much as liberality, which whilest thou usest, thou losest the means to make use of it, and becomest poore and abject; or to avoid this poverty, an extortioner and hatefull person. And among all those things which a Prince ought to beware of is, to be dispised, and odious; to one and the other of which, liberality brings thee. Wherefore there is more discretion to hold the stile of Miserable, which begets an infamy without hatred, than to desire that of Liberal, whereby to incurre the necessity of being thought an extortioner, which procures an infamy with hatred.

Chapter XVII: Of Cruelty, and Clemency, and whether it is better to be belov'd, or feard.

Descending afterwards unto the other fore-alledged qualities, I say, that every Prince should desire to be held pitiful, and not cruel. Nevertheless ought he beware that he ill uses not this pitty. Cæsar Borgia was accounted cruel, yet had his cruelty redrest the disorders in Romania, setled it in union, and restored it to peace, and fidelity: which, if it be well weighed, we shall see was an act of more pitty, than that of the people of Florence, who to avoyd the terme of cruelty, suffered Pistoya to fall to destruction. Wherefore a Prince ought not to regard the infamy of cruelty, for to hold his subjects united and faithfull: for by giving a very few proofes of himself the other way, he shall be held more pittiful than they, who through their too much pitty, suffer disorders to follow, from whence arise murthers and rapines: for these are wont to hurt an intire universality, whereas the executions practised by a Prince, hurt only some particular. And among all sorts of Princes, it is impossible for a new Prince to avoyd the name of cruel, because all new States are full of dangers: whereupon Virgil by the mouth of Dido excuses the inhumanity of her Kingdom, saying,

Res dura et Regni novitas me talia cogunt Moliri et latè fines custode tenere.

My hard plight and new State force me to guard My confines all about with watch and ward.

Nevertheless ought he to be judicious in his giving belief to any thing, or moving himself thereat, nor make his people extreamly afraid of him; but proceed in a moderate way with wisdome, and humanity, that his too much confidence make him not unwary, and his too much distrust intolerable; from hence arises a dispute, whether it is better to be belov'd or feard: I answer, a man would wish he might be the one and the other: but because hardly can they subsist both together, it is much safer to be feard, than be loved; being that one of the two must needs fail; for touching men, we may say this in general, they are unthankful, unconstant, dissemblers, they avoyd dangers, and are covetous of gain; and whilest thou doest them good, they are wholly thine; their blood, their fortunes, lives and children are at thy service, as is said before, when the danger is remote; but when it approaches, they revolt. And that Prince who wholly relies upon their words, unfurnished of all other preparations, goes to wrack: for the friendships that are gotten with rewards, and not by the magnificence and worth of the mind, are dearly bought indeed; but they will neither keep long, nor serve well in time of need: and men do less regard to offend one that is supported by love, than by fear. For love is held by a certainty of obligation, which because men are mischievous, is broken upon any occasion of their own profit. But fear restrains with a dread of punishment which never forsakes a man. Yet ought a Prince cause himself to be belov'd in such a manner, that if he gains not love, he may avoid hatred: for it may well stand together, that a man may be feard and not hated; which shall never fail, if he abstain from his subjects goods, and their wives; and whensoever he should be forc'd to proceed against any of their lives, do it when it is to be done upon a just cause, and apparent conviction; but above all things forbeare to lay his hands on other mens goods; for men forget sooner the death of their father, than the loss of their patrimony. Moreover the occasions of taking from men their goods, do never fail: and alwaies he that begins to live by rapine, finds occasion to lay hold upon other mens goods: but against mens lives, they are seldome found, and sooner fail. But where a Prince is abroad in the field with his army, and hath a multitude of soldiers under his government, then is it necessary that he stands not much upon it, though he be termed cruel: for unless he be so, he shall never have his soldiers live in accord one with another, nor ever well disposed to any brave piece of service. Among Hannibals actions of mervail, this is reckoned for one, that having a very huge army, gathered out of several nations, and all led to serve in a strange countrey, there was never any dissention neither amongst themselves, nor against their General, as well in their bad fortune as their good. Which could not proceed from any thing else than from that barbarous cruelty of his, which together with his exceeding many vertues, rendred him to his soldiers both venerable and terrible; without which, to that effect his other vertues had served him to little purpose: and some writers though not of the best advised, on one side admire these his worthy actions, and on the otherside, condemn the principal causes thereof. And that it is true, that his other vertues would not have suffic'd him, we may consider in Scipio, the rarest man not only in the dayes he liv'd, but even in the memory of man; from whom his army rebel'd in Spain: which grew only upon his too much clemency, which had given way to his soldiers to become more licentious, than was well tollerable by military discipline: for which he was reprov'd by Fabius Maximus in the Senate, who termed him the corrupter of the Roman soldiery. The Locrensians having been destroyed by a Lieutenant of Scipio's, were never reveng'd by him, nor the insolence of that Lieutenant punisht; all this arising from his easie nature: so that one desiring to excuse him in the Senate, said, that there were many men knew better how to keep themselves from faults, than to correct the faults of other men: which disposition of his in time would have wrong'd Scipio's reputation and glory, had he therewith continu'd in his commands: but living under the government of the Senate, this quality of his that would have disgrac'd him not only was conceal'd, but prov'd to the advancement of his glory. I conclude then, returning to the purpose of being feard, and belov'd; insomuch as men love at their own pleasure, and to serve their own turne, and their fear depends upon the Princes pleasure, every wise Prince ought to ground upon that which is of himself, and not upon that which is of another: only this, he ought to use his best wits to avoid hatred, as was said.

Chapter XVIII: In what manner Princes ought to keep their words.

How commendable in a Prince it is to keep his word, and live with integrity, not making use of cunning and subtlety, every one knows well: yet we see by experience in these our dayes, that those Princes have effected great matters, who have made small reckoning of keeping their words, and have known by their craft to turne and wind men about, and in the end, have overcome those who have grounded upon the truth. You must then know, there are two kinds of combating or fighting; the one by right of the laws, the other meerly by force. That first way is proper to men, the other is also common to beasts: but because the first many times suffices not, there is a necessity to make recourse to the second; wherefore it behooves a Prince to know how to make good use of that part which belongs to a beast, as well as that which is proper to a man. This part hath been covertly shew'd to Princes by ancient writers; who say that Achilles and many others of those ancient Princes were intrusted to Chiron the Senator, to be brought up under his discipline: the moral of this, having for their teacher one that was half a beast and half a man, was nothing else, but that it was needful for a Prince to understand how to make his advantage of the one and the other nature, because neither could subsist without the other. A Prince then being necessitated to know how to make use of that part belonging to a beast, ought to serve himself of the conditions of the Fox and the Lion; for the Lion cannot keep himself from snares, nor the Fox defend himself against the Wolves. He had need then be a Fox, that he may beware of the snares, and a Lion that he may scare the wolves. Those that stand wholly upon the Lion, understand not well themselves. And therefore a wise Prince cannot, nor ought not keep his faith given when the observance thereof turnes to disadvantage, and the occasions that made him promise, are past. For if men were all good, this rule would not be allowable; but being they are full of mischief, and would not make it good to thee, neither art thou tyed to keep it with them: nor shall a Prince ever want lawfull occasions to give colour to this breach. Very many modern examples hereof might be alledg'd, wherein might be shewed how many peaces concluded, and how many promises made, have been violated and broken by the infidelity of Princes; and ordinarily things have best succeeded with him that hath been nearest the Fox in condition. But it is necessary to understand how to set a good colour upon this disposition, and to be able to fain and dissemble throughly; and men are so simple, and yeeld so much to the present necessities, that he who hath a mind to deceive, shall alwaies find another that will be deceivd. I will not conceal any one of the examples that have been of late. Alexander the sixth, never did any thing else than deceive men, and never meant otherwise, and alwaies found whom to work upon; yet never was there man would protest more effectually, nor aver any thing with more solemn oaths, and observe them less than he; nevertheless, his cousenages all thriv'd well with him; for he knew how to play this part cunningly. Therefore is there no necessity for a Prince to be endued with all above written qualities, but it behooveth well that he seem to be so; or rather I will boldly say this, that having these qualities, and alwaies regulating himself by them, they are hurtfull; but seeming to have them, they are advantageous; as to seem pittiful, faithful, mild, religious, and of integrity, and indeed to be so; provided withall thou beest of such a composition, that if need require to use the contrary, thou canst, and knowest how to apply thy self thereto. And it suffices to conceive this, that a Prince, and especially a new Prince, cannot observe all those things, for which men are held good; he being often forc'd, for the maintenance of his State, to do contrary to his faith, charity, humanity, and religion: and therefore it behooves him to have a mind so disposd, as to turne and take the advantage of all winds and fortunes; and as formerly I said, not forsake the good, while he can; but to know how to make use of the evil upon necessity. A Prince then ought to have a special care, that he never let fall any words, but what are all season'd with the five above written qualities, and let him seem to him that sees and hears him, all pitty, all faith, all integrity, all humanity, all religion; nor is there any thing more necessary for him to seem to have, than this last quality: for all men in general judge thereof, rather by the sight, than by the touch; for every man may come to the sight of him, few come to the touch and feeling of him; yvery man may come to see what thou seemest, few come to perceive and understand what thou art; and those few dare not oppose the opinion of many, who have the majesty of State to protect them: And in all mens actions, especially those of Princes wherein there is no judgement to appeale unto men, forbeare to give their censures, till the events and ends of things. Let a Prince therefore take the surest courses he can to maintain his life and State: the means shall alwaies be thought honorable, and commended by every one; for the vulgar is over-taken with the appearance and event of a thing: and for the most part of people, they are but the vulgar: the others that are but few, take place where the vulgar have no subsisteance. A Prince there is in these dayes, whom I shall not do well to name, that preaches nothing else but peace and faith; but had he kept the one and the other, several times had they taken from him his state and reputation.

In the sixteenth, seventeenth, and eighteenth Chap, our Author descends to particulars, perswading his Prince in his sixteenth to such a suppleness of disposition, as that upon occasion he can make use either of liberality or miserableness, as need shall require. But that of liberality is to last no longer than while he is in the way to some designe: which if he well weigh, is not really a reward of vertue, how ere it seems; but a bait and lure to bring birds to the net. In the seventeenth Chap, he treats of clemency and cruelty, neither of which are to be exercis'd by him as acts of mercy or justice; but as they may serve to advantage his further purposes. And lest the Prince should incline too much to clemency, our Author allows rather the restraint by fear, than by love. The contrary to which all stories shew us. I will say this only, cruelty may cut of the power of some, but causes the hatred of all, and gives a will to most to take the first occasion offerd for revenge. In the eighteenth Chap, our Author discourses how Princes ought to govern themselves in keeping their promises made: whereof he sayes they ought to make such small reckoning, as that rather they should know by their craft how to turne and wind men about, whereby to take advantage of all winds and fortunes. To this I would oppose that in the fifteenth Psal. v. 5. He that sweareth to his neighbor, and disappointeth him not, though it were to his own hindrance. It was a King that writ it, and me thinks the rule he gave, should well befit both King and Subject: and surely this perswades against all taking of advantages. A man may reduce all the causes of faith-breaking to three heads. One may be, because he that promised, had no intention to keep his word; and this is a wicked and malitious way of dealing. A second may bee, because hee that promisd, repents of his promise made; and that is grounded on unconstancy, and lightness in that he would not be well resolved before he entred into covenant. The third may be, when it so falls out, that it lyes not in his power that made the promise to performe it. In which case a man ought to imitate the good debter, who having not wherewithall to pay, hides not himself, but presents his person to his creditor, willingly suffering imprisonment. The first and second are very vitious and unworthy of a Prince: in the third, men might well be directed by the examples of those two famous Romans, Regulus and Posthumius. I shall close this with the answer of Charles the fifth, when he was pressed to break his word with Luther for his safe return from Wormes; *Fides rerum promissarum etsi toto mundo exulet, tamen apud imperatorem cam consistere oportet*. Though truth be banisht out of the whole world, yet should it alwaies find harbour in an Emperors breast.

Gulielmus Xenocarus in vit. Car. Quinti.

Chapter XIX: That Princes should take a care, not to incurre contempt or hatred.

But because among the qualities, whereof formerly mention is made, I have spoken of those of most importance, I will treat of the others more briefly under these qualityes that a Prince is to beware, as in part is above-said, and that he fly those things which cause him to be odious or vile: and when ever he shall avoid this, he shall fully have plaid his part, and in the other disgraces he shall find no danger at all. There is nothing makes him so odious, as I said, as his extortion of his subjects goods, and abuse of their women, from which he ought to forbear; and so long as he wrongs not his whole people, neither in their goods, nor honors, they live content, and he hath only to strive with the Ambition of some few: which many waies and easily too, is restrain'd. To be held various, light, effeminate, faint-hearted, unresolv'd, these make him be contemnd and thought base, which a Prince should shun like rocks, and take a care that in all his actions there appear magnanimity, courage, gravity, and valor; and that in all the private affairs of his subjects, he orders it so, that his word stand irrevocable: and maintain himself in such repute, that no man may think either to deceive or wind and turn him about: that Prince that gives such an opinion of himself, is much esteemed, and against him who is so well esteemed, hardly are any conspiracies made by his subjects, or by forreiners any invasion, when once notice is taken of his worth, and how much he is reverenced by his subjects: For a Prince ought to have two fears, the one from within, in regard of his subjects; the other from abroad, in regard of his mighty neighbors; from these he defends himself by good armes and good friends; and alwayes he shall have good friends, if he have good armes; and all things shall alwaies stand sure at home, when those abroad are firme, in case some conspiracy have not disturbed them; and however the forrein matters stand but ticklishly; yet if he have taken such courses at home, and liv'd as we have prescribed, he shall never be able (in case he forsake not himself) to resist all possibility, force and violence, as I said Nabis the Spartan did: but touching his subjects, even when his affairs abroad are setled, it is to be fear'd they may conspire privily; from which a Prince sufficiently secure himself by shunning to be hated or contemned, and keeping himself in his peoples good opinion, which it is necessary for him to compass, as formerly we treated at large. And one of the powerfullest remedies a Prince can have against conspiracies, is, not to be hated nor dispised by the universality; for alwaies he that conspires, beleeves the Princes death is acceptable to the subject: but when he thinks it displeases them, he hath not the heart to venture on such a matter; for the difficulties that are on the conspirators side, are infinite. By experience it is plain, that many times plots have been laid, but few of them have succeeded luckily; for he that conspires, cannot be alone, nor can he take the company of any, but of those, who he beleeves are malecontents; and so soon as thou hast discover'd thy self to a malecontent, thou givest him means to work his own content: for by revealing thy treason, he may well hope for all manner of favour: so that seeing his gain certain of one side; and on the other, finding only doubt and danger, either he had need be a rare friend, or that he be an exceeding obstinate enemy to the Prince, if he keeps his word with thee. And to reduce this matter into short termes: I say, there is nothing but jealousie, fear, and suspect of punishment on the conspirators part to affright him; but on the Princes part, there is the majesty of the principality, the laws, the defences of his friends and the State, which do so guard him, that to all these things the peoples good wills being added, it is unpossible any one should be so head-strong as to conspire; for ordinarily where a traytor is to feare before the execution of his mischiefe, in this case he is also to feare afterwards, having the people for his enemy when the fact is commited, and therefore for this cause, not being able to hope for any refuge. Touching this matter, many examples might be brought; but I will content my selfe to name one which fell out in the memory of our Fathers. Annibal Bentivolii, grand Father of this Annibal who now lives, that was Prince in Bolonia, being slaine by the Canneschi that conspir'd against him, none of his race being left, but this John, who was then in swadling clouts; presently the people rose upon this murder, and slew all the Canneschi which proceeded from the popular affection, which the family of the Bentivolii held then in Bolonia: which was so great, that being there remain'd not any, now Anniball was dead, that was able to manage the State; and having notice that in Florence there was one borne of the Bentivolii, who till then was taken for a Smiths sonne: the citizens of Bolonia went to Florence for him, and gave the government of their City to him, which was rul'd by him, untill John was of fit yeares to governe. I conclude then, that a Prince ought to make small account of treasons, whiles he hath the people to friend: but if they be his enemies and hate him, he may well feare every thing, and every one. And well ordered States, and discreet Princes have taken care withall diligence, not to cause their great men to fall into desperation, and to content the people, and so to maintaine them: for this is one of the most important businesses belonging to a Prince. Among the Kingdomes that are well orderd and governd in our dayes, is that of France, and therein are found exceeding many good orders, whereupon the Kings liberty and security depends: of which the chiefe is the Parliament, and the authority thereof: for he that founded that Kingdome, knowing the great mens ambition and insolence; and judgeing it necessary there should be a bridle to curbe them; and on the other side knowing the hatred of the Commonalty against the great ones, grounded upon feare, intending to secure them, would not lay this care wholly upon the King, but take this trouble from him, which he might have with the great men, in case he favourd the Commonalty; or with the Commonalty, in case he favourd the great men; and thereupon set up a third judge, which was that, to the end it should keep under the great ones, and favour the meaner sort, without any imputation to the King. It was not possible to take a better, nor wiser course then this; nor a surer way to secure the King, and the Kingdome. From whence we may draw another conclusion worthie of note, that Princes ought to cause others to take upon them the matters of blame and imputation; and upon themselves to take only those of grace and favour. Here againe I conclude, that a Prince ought to make good esteeme of his Nobility; but not thereby to incur the Commons hatred: It would seeme perhaps to many, considering the life and death of many Romane Emperours, that they were examples contrary to my opinion, finding that some have liv'd worthily, and shewd many rare vertues of the minde, and yet have lost the Empire, and been put to death by their owne subjects, conspiring against them. Intending then to answer these objections, I shall discourse upon the qualities of some Emperours, declaring the occasions of their ruine, not disagreeing from that which I have alledgd; and part thereof I will bestow on the consideration of these things, which are worthy to be noted by him that reads the actions of those times: and it shall suffice me to take all those Emperours that succeeded in the Empire from Marcus the Philosopher to Maximinus, who were Mercus and Commodus his sonne, Pertinax, Julian, Severus, Antonius, Caracalla his sonne, Macrinus, Heliogabalus, Alexander, and Maximin. And first it is to be noted, that where in the other Principalities, they are to contend only with the ambition of the Nobles, and the insolence of the people; the Romane Emperours had a third difficulty, having to support the cruelty and covetousnesse of the souldiers, which was so hard a thing, that it caused the ruine of many, being hard to satisfy the souldiers, and the people; for the people love their quiet, and therefore affect modest Princes; and the souldiers love a Prince of a warlike courage, that is insolent, cruell, and plucking from every one: which things they would have them exercise upon the people, whereby they might be able to double their stipends, and satisfie their avarice and cruelty: whence it proceeds, that those Emperours who either by Nature or by Art, had not such a reputation, as therewith they could curbe the one and the other, were alwayes ruind: and the most of them, specially those who as new men came to the principality, finding the difficulty of those two different humours, applyed themselves to content the souldiers, making small account of wronging the people, which was a course then necessary; for the Princes not being able to escape the hatred of every one, ought first endeavour that they incurre not the hatred of any whole universality; and when they cannot attaine thereunto, they are to provide with all industry, to avoyd the hatred of those universalities that are the most mighty. And therefore those Emperors, who because they were but newly call'd to the Empire, had need of extraordinary favours, more willingly stuck to the soldiers, than to the people; which neverthelesse turnd to their advantage, or otherwise, according as that Prince knew how to maintaine his repute with them. From these causes aforesayd proceeded it, that Marcus Pertinax, and Alexander, though all living modestly, being lovers of justice, and enemies of cruelty, courteous and bountifull, had all from Marcus on ward, miserable ends; Marcus only liv'd and dy'd exceedingly honoured: for he came to the Empire by inheritance, and was not to acknowledge it either from the soldiers, nor from the people: afterwards being accompanyed with many vertues, which made him venerable, he held alwayes whilst he liv'd the one and the other order within their limits, and was never either hated, or contemnd. But Pertinax was created Emperour against the soldiers wills, who being accustomed to live licentiously under Commodus, could not endure that honest course that Pertinax sought to reduce them to: Whereupon having gotten himself hatred, and to this hatred added contempt, in that he was old, was ruind in the very beginning of his government. Whence it ought to be observed, that hatred is gaind as well by good deeds as bad; and therefore as I formerly said, when a Prince would maintaine the State, he is often forced not to be good: for when that generality, whether it be the people, or soldiers, or Nobility, whereof thou thinkst thou standst in need to maintain thee, is corrupted, it behoves thee to follow their humour, and content them, and then all good deeds are thy adversaries. But let us come to Alexander who was of that goodnesse, that among the prayses given him, had this for one, that in fourteen yeers wherein he held the Empire, he never put any man to death, but by course of justice; neverthelesse being held effeminate, and a man that suffered himselfe to be ruled by his mother, and thereupon fallen into contempt, the army conspird against him. Now on the contrary discoursing upon the qualities of Commodus, Severus, Antonius, Caracalla, and Maximinus, you shall find them exceeding cruell, and ravinous, who to satisfie their soldiers, forbeare no kinde of injury that could be done upon the people; and all of them, except Severus, came to evill ends: for in Severus, there was such extraordinary valour, that while he held the soldiers his freinds, however the people were much burthend by him, he might alwayes reigne happily: for his valour rendred him so admirable in the souldiers and peoples sights; that these in a manner stood amazd and astonishd, and those others reverencing and honoring him. And because the actions of this man were exceeding great, being in a new Prince, I will briefly shew how well he knew to act the Foxes and the Lions parts; the conditions of which two, I say, as before, are very necessary for a Prince to imitate. Severus having had experience of Julian the Emperours sloth, perswaded his army (whereof he was commander in Sclavonia) that they should doe well to goe to Rome to revenge Pertinax his death, who was put to death by the Imperiall guard; and under this pretence, not making any shew that he aspird unto the Empire, set his army in march directly towards Rome, and was sooner come into Italy, than it was knowne he had mov'd from his station. Being ariv'd at Rome, he was by the Senate chosen Emperour for feare, and Julian slaine. After this beginning, two difficulties yet remaind to Severus, before he could make himselfe Lord of the whole State; the one in Asia, where Niger the Generall of those armies had gotten the title of Emperour, the other in the West with Albinus, who also aspird to the Empire: and because he thought there might be some danger to discover himselfe enemy to them both, he purposed to set upon Niger, and cozen Albinus, to whom he writ, that being elected Emperour by the Senate, he would willingly communicate it with him; and thereupon sent him the title of Cæsar, and by resolution of the Senate, tooke him to him for his Colleague; which things were taken by Albinus in true meaning. But afterwards when Severus had overcome and slaine Niger, and pacified the affaires and in the East, being returned to Rome, he complaind in the Senate of Albinus, how little weighing the benefits received from him, he had sought to slay him by treason, and therefore was he forc'd to goe punish his ingratitude: afterwards he went into France, where he bereft him both of his State and life, whoever then shall in particular examine his actions, shall finde he was a very cruell Lion, and as crafty a Fox: and shall see that he was alwayes feard and reverenc'd by every one, and by the armies not hated; and shall nothing marvell that he being a new man, was able to hold together such a great Empire: for his extraordinary reputation defended him alwayes from that hatred, which the people for his extortions might have conceiv'd against him. But Antonius his sonne, was also an exceeding brave man, and endued with most excellent qualities, which causd him to be admird by the people, and acceptable to the souldiers, because he was a warlike man, enduring all kind of travell and paines, despising all delicate food, and all kinde of effeminacy, which gaind him the love of all the armies: neverthelesse his fiercenesse and cruelty were such, and so hideous, having upon many particular occasions put to death a great part of the people of Rome, and all those of Alexandria, that he grew odious to the world, and began to be feard by those also that were neare about him; so that he was slaine by a Centurion in the very midst of his army. Where it is to be noted, that these kinde of deaths, which follow upon the deliberation of a resolv'd and obstinate minde, cannot by a Prince be avoyded: for every one that feares not to dye, is able to doe it; but a Prince ought to be lesse afraid of it because it very seldome falls out. Only should he beware not to doe any extreame injury to any of those of whom he serves himself, or that he hath near about him in any imployment of his Principality, as Antonius did: who had reproachfully slaine a brother of that Centurion; also threatned him every day, and neverthelesse entertaind him still as one of the guards of his body, which was a rash course taken, and the way to destruction, as befell him. But let us come to Commodus for whom it was very easie to hold the Empire, by reason it descended upon him by inheritance, being Marcus his sonne, and it had been enough for him to follow his fathers footsteps, and then had he contented both the people and the soldiers: but being of a cruell and savage disposition, whereby to exercise his actions upon the people, he gave himselfe to entertaine armies, and those in all licentiousnesse. On the other part not maintaining his dignity, but often descending upon the stages to combate with fencers, and doing such other like base things, little worthy of the Imperiall majesty, he became contemptible in the soldiers sight; and being hated of one part, and despisd of the other, he was conspird against, and slaine. It remaines now, that we declare Maximinus his conditions, who was a very warlike man; and the armies loathing Alexanders effeminacy, whereof I spake before, when they had slain him, chose this man Emperour, who not long continued so, because two things there were that brought him into hatred and contempt; the one because he was very base, having kept cattell in Thrace, which was well knowne to every one, and made them to scorne him; the other, because in the beginning of his Principality having delayd to goe to Rome, and enter into possession of the Imperiall throne, he had gaind the infamy of being thought exceeding cruell, having by his Prefects in Rome, and in every place of the Empire, exercisd many cruelties, insomuch that the whole world being provok'd against him to contempt for the basenesse of his blood; on the other side upon the hatred conceiv'd against him for feare of his crulty; first Affrica, afterwards the Senate, with all the people of Rome and all Italy, conspired against him, with whom his own army took part; which incamping before Aquileya, and finding some difficulty to take the town, being weary of his cruelties, and because they saw he had so many enemies, fearing him the lesse, slew him. I purpose not to say any thing either of Heliogabalus, Macrinus, or Julian, who because they were throughly base, were sudenly extinguished: but I will come to the conclusion of this discourse; and I say, that the Princes of our times have lesse of this difficulty to satisfie the Soldiers extraordinarily in their government; for notwithstanding that there be some considerations to be had of them, yet presently are those armies dissolved, because none of these Princes do use to maintaine any armies together, which are annex'd and inveterated with the governments of the provinces, as were the armies of the Romane Empire. And therefore if then it was necessary rather to content the soldiers than the people, it was because the soldiers were more powerfull than the people: now is it more necessary for all Princes, (except the Turk and the Souldan) to satisfie their people than their soldiers, because the people are more mighty than they; wherein I except the Turk, he alwayes maintaining about his person 12000 foot, and 15000 horse, upon which depends the safety and strength of his Kingdome; and it is necessary that laying aside all other regard of his people, he maintaine these his friends. The Souldans Kingdome is like hereunto, which being wholy in the souldiers power, he must also without respect of his people keep them his friends. And you are to consider, that this State of the Souldans differs much from all the other Principalities: For it is very like the Papacy, which cannot be termd an hereditary Principality: nor a new Principality: for the sons of the deceasd Prince are not heires and Lords thereof, but he that is chosen receives that dignity from those who have the authority in them. And this order being of antiquity, cannot be termd a new Principality, because therein are none of those difficulties that are in new ones: for though the Prince be new, yet are the orders of that state ancient, and ordaind to receive him, as if he were their hereditary Prince. But let us returne to our matter; whosoever shall consider our discourse before, shall perceive that either hatred, or contempt have caus'd the ruine of the afore-named Emperors; and shall know also, from it came that part of them proceeding one way, and part a contrary; yet in any of them the one had a happy success, and the others unhappy: for it was of no availe, but rather hurtful for Pertinax and Alexander, because they were new Princes, to desire to imitate Marcus, who by inheritance came to the Principality: and in like manner it was a wrong to Caracalla, Commodus, and Maximus, to imitate Severus, because none of them were endued with so great valor as to follow his steps therein. Wherefore a new Prince in his Principality cannot well imitate Marcus his actions; nor yet is it necessary to follow those of Severus: but he ought make choyce of those parts in Severus which are necessary for the founding of a State; and to take from Marcus those that are fit and glorious to preserve a State which is already established and setled.

Chapter XX: Whether the Citadels and many other things which Princes often make use of, are profitable or dammageable.

Some Princes, whereby they might safely keep their State, have disarmed their subjects; some others have held the towns under their dominion, divided into factions; others have maintain'd enmities against themselves; others have appli'd themselves to gain them, where they have suspected at their entrance into the government; others have built Fortresses; and others again have ruined and demolished them: and however that upon all these things, a man cannot well pass a determinate sentence, unless one comes to the particulars of these States, where some such like determinations were to be taken; yet I shall speak of them in so large a manner, as the matter of it self will bear. It was never then that a new Prince would disarme his own subjects; but rather when he hath found them disarmed, he hath alwaies arm'd them. For being belov'd, those armes become thine; those become faithful, which thou hadst in suspicion; and those which were faithful, are maintaind so; and thy subjects are made thy partisans; and because all thy subjects cannot be put in armes, when thou bestowest favors on those thou armest, with the others thou canst deal more for thy safety; and that difference of proceeding which they know among them, obliges them to thee; those others excuse thee, judgeing it necessary that they have deservd more, who have undergone more danger, and so have greater obligation: but when thou disarmst them, thou beginst to offend them, that thou distrustest them, either for cowardise, or small faith; and the one or the other of those two opinions provokes their hatred against thee; and because thou canst not stand disarmed, thou must then turn thy self to mercenary Soldiery, whereof we have formerly spoken what it is, and when it is good; it can never be so much as to defend thee from powerful enemies, and suspected subjects; therefore as I have said, a new Prince in a new Principality hath alwaies ordaind them armes. Of examples to this purpose, Histories are full. But when a Prince gains a new State, which as a member he adds to his ancient dominions, then it is necessary to disarme that State, unless it be those whom thou hast discoverd to have assisted thee in the conquest thereof; and these also in time and upon occasions, it is necessary to render delicate and effeminate, and so order them, that all the arms of thy State be in the hands of thy own Soldiers, who live in thy ancient State near unto thee. Our ancestors and they that were accounted Sages, were wont to say that it was necessary to hold Pistoya in factions, and Pisa with Fortresses; and for this cause maintaind some towns subject to them in differences, whereby to hold it more easily. This, at what time Italy was ballanc'd in a certain manner, might be well done; but mee thinks it cannot now a dayes be well given for a precept; for I do not beleeve, that divisions made can do any good; rather it must needs be, that when the enemy approaches them, Cities divided are presently lost; for alwaies the weaker part will cleave to the forrein power, and the other not be able to subsist. The Venetians (as I think) mov'd by the aforesaid reasons, maintaind the factions of the Guelfes and Gibellins, in their townes; and however they never suffered them to spill one anothers blood, yet they nourish'd these differences among them, to the end that the citizens imployd in these quarrels, should not plot any thing against them: which as it proved, never serv'd them to any great purpose: for being defeated at Vayla, presently one of those two factions took courage and seizd upon their whole State. Therefore such like waies argue the Princes weakness; for in a strong principality they never will suffer such divisions; for they shew them some kind of profit in time of peace, being they are able by means thereof more easily to mannage their subjects: but war comming, such like orders discover their fallacy. Without doubt, Princes become great, when they overcome the difficulties and oppositions that are made against them; and therefore Fortune especially when she hath to make any new Prince great, who hath more need to gain reputation than an hereditary Prince, causes enemies to rise against him, and him to undertake against them: to the end he may have occasion to master them, and know that ladder, which his enemies have set him upon, whereby to rise yet higher. And therefore many think, that a wise Prince when he hath the occasion, ought cunningly to nourish some enmity, that by the suppressing thereof, his greatness may grow thereupon. Princes, especially those that are new, have found more faith and profit in those men, who in the beginning of their State, have been held suspected, than in those who at their entrance have been their confidents. Pandulphus Petrucci, Prince of Siena, governd his State, more with them that had been suspected by him, than with the others. But of this matter we cannot speak at large, because it varies according to the subject; I will only say this, that those men, who in the beginning of a Principality were once enemies, if they be of quality so that to maintain themselves they have need of support, the Prince might alwaies with the greatest facility gain for his; and they are the rather forced to serve him faithfully, insomuch as they know it is more necessary for them by their deeds to cancel that sinister opinion, which was once held of them; and so the Prince ever draws from these more advantage, than from those, who serving him too supinely, neglect his affairs. And seing the matter requires it, I will not omit to put a Prince in mind, who hath anew made himself master of a State, by means of the inward helps he had from thence that he consider well the cause that mov'd them that favor'd him to favor him, if it be not a natural affection towards him;

for if it be only because they were not content with their former government, with much pains and difficulties shall he be able to keep them long his friends, because it will be impossible for him to content them. By these examples then which are drawn out of ancient and modern affaires, searching into the cause hereof, we shall find it much more easie to gain those men for friends, who formerly were contented with the State, and therefore were his enemies: than those, who because they were not contented therewith, became his fiends, and favor'd him in getting the mastery of it. It hath been the custome of Princes, whereby to hold their States more securely, to build Citadels, which might be bridles and curbs to those that should purpose any thing against them, and so to have a secure retreat from the first violences. I commend this course, because it hath been used of old; notwithstanding Nicholas Vitelli in our dayes hath been known to demolish two Citadels in the town of Castello, the better to keep the State; Guidubaldo Duke of Urbin being to return into his State, out of which he was driven by Cæsar Borgia, raz'd all the Fortresses of that Countrey, and thought he should hardlyer lose that State again without them. The Bentivolii returning into Bolonia, used the like courses. Citadels then are profitable, or not, according to the times; and if they advantage thee in one part, they do thee harme in another; and this part may be argued thus. That Prince who stands more in fear of his own people than of strangers, ought to build Fortresses: but he that is more afraid of strangers than of his people, should let them alone. Against the house of Sforza, the Castle of Milan, which Francis Sforza built, hath and will make more war, than any other disorder in that State: and therefore the best Citadel that may be, is not to incurre the peoples hatred; for however thou holdest a Fortress, and the people hate thee, thou canst hardly scape them; for people, when once they have taken armes, never want the help of strangers at their need to take ther parts. In our dayes we never saw that they ever profited any Prince, unless it were the Countess of Furli, when Count Hieronymo of Furli her husband was slain; for by means thereof she escap'd the peoples rage, and attended aid from Milan, and so recover'd her State: and then such were the times that the stranger could not assist the people: but afterwards they serv'd her to little purpose, when Cæsar Borgia assaild her, and that the people which was her enemy, sided with the stranger. Therefore both then, and at first, it would have been more for her safety, not to have been odious to the people, than to have held the Fortresses. These things being well weigh'd then, I will commend those that shall build up Fortresses, and him also that shall not; and I will blame him, howsoever he be, that relying upon those, shall make small account of being hated by his people.

Chapter XXI: How a Prince ought to behave himself to gain reputation.

There is nothing gains a Prince such repute as great exploits, and rare tryals of himself in Heroick actions. We have now in our dayes Ferdinand King of Arragon the present King of Spain: he in a manner may be termed a new Prince; for from a very weak King, he is now become for fame and glory, the first King of Christendome, and if you shall wel consider his actions, you shall find them all illustrious, and every one of them extraordinary. He in the beginning of his reign assaild Granada, and that exploit was the ground of his State. At first he made that war in security, and without suspicion he should be any waies hindred, and therein held the Barons of Castiglias minds busied, who thinking upon that war, never minded any innovation; in this while he gaind credit and authority with them, they not being aware of it; was able to maintain with the Church and the peoples money all his soldiers, and to lay a foundation for his military ordinances with that long war, which afterwards gaind him exceeding much honor. Besides this, to the end he might be able hereamong to undertake greater matters, serving himself alwaies of the colour of religion, he gave himself to a kind of religious cruelty, chasing and dispoyling those Jewes out of the Kingdome; nor can this example be more admirable and rare: under the same cloke he invaded Affrick and went through with his exploit in Italy: and last of all hath he assaild France, and so alwaies proceeded on forwards contriving of great matters, which alwaies have held his subjects minds in peace and admiration, and busied in attending the event, what it should be: and these his actions have thus grown, one upon another, that they have never given leisure to men so to rest, as they might ever plot any thing against them. Moreover it much avails a Prince to give extraordinary proofes of himself touching the government within, such as those we have heard of Bernard of Milan, whensoever occasion is given by any one, that may effectuate some great thing either of good or evil, in the civil government; and to find out some way either to reward or punish it, whereof in the world much notice may be taken. And above all things a Prince ought to endeavor in all his actions to spread abroad a fame of his magnificence and worthiness. A Prince also is well esteemed, when he is a true friend, or a true enemy; when without any regard he discovers himself in favor of one against another; which course shall be alwaies more profit, than to stand neuter: for if two mighty ones that are thy neighbors, come to fall out, or are of such quality, that one of them vanquishing, thou art like to be in fear of the vanquisher, or not; in either of these two cases, it will ever prove more for thy profit, to discover thy self, and make a good war of it: for in the first case, if thou discoverest not thy selfe, thou shalt alwaies be a prey to him that overcomes, to the contentment and satisfaction of the vanquisht; neither shalt thou have reason on thy side, nor any thing else to defend or receive thee. For he that overcomes, will not have any suspected friends that give him no assistance in his necessity: and he that loses, receives thee not, because thou wouldest not with thy armes in hand run the hazzard of his fortune. Antiochus passed into Greece, thereunto induc'd by the Etolians, to chace the Romans thence: and sent his Ambassadors to the Achayans, who were the Romans friends, to perswade them to stand neuters; on the other side the Romans moved them to joyne armes with theirs: this matter came to be deliberated on in the council of the Achayans, where Antiochus his Ambassador encouraged them to stand neuters, whereunto the Romans Ambassador answerd; Touching the course, that is commended to you, as best and profitablest for your State, to wit, not to intermeddle in the war between us, nothing can be more against you: because, not taking either part, you shall remain without thanks, and without reputation a prey to the conqueror. And it will alwaies come to pass that he who is not thy friend, will requite thy neutrality; and he that is thy friend, will urge thee to discover thy self by taking arms for him: and evil advised Princes; to avoyd the present dangers, folow often times that way of neutrality, and most commonly go to ruine: but when a Prince discovers himself strongly in favor of a party; if he to whom thou cleavest, overcomes; however that he be puissant, and thou remainest at his disposing, he is oblig'd to thee, and there is a contract of friendship made; and men are never so openly dishonest, as with such a notorious example of dishonesty to oppress thee. Besides victories are never so prosperous, that the conqueror is like neglect all respects, and especially of justice. But if he to whom thou stickst, loses, thou art received by him; and, while he is able, he aydes thee, and so thou becomest partner of a fortune that may arise again; the second case, when they that enter into the lists together, are of such quality, that thou needest not fear him that vanquisheth, so much the more is it discretion in thee to stick to him; for thou goest to ruine one with his assistance, who ought to do the best he could to save him, if he were well advised; and he overcomming, is left at thy discretion; and it is unpossible but with thy ayd he must overcome. And here it is to be noted, that a Prince should be well aware never to joyn with any one more powerfull than himself, to offend another, unless upon necessity, as formerly is said. For when he overcomes, thou art left at his discretion, and Princes ought avoid as much as they are able, to stand at anothers discretion. The Venetians took part with France against the Duke of Milan, and yet could have avoided that partaking, from which proceeded their ruine. But when it cannot be avoyded, as it befel the Florentines when the Pope and the King of Spain went both with their armies to

Lombardy, there the Prince ought to side with them for the reasons aforesaid. Nor let any State think they are able to make such sure parties, but rather that they are all doubtfull; for in the order of things we find it alwaies, that whensoever a man seeks to avoid one inconvenient, he incurs another. But the principal point of judgement, is in discerning between the qualities of inconvenients, and not taking the bad for the good. Moreover a Prince ought to shew himself a lover of vertue, and that he honors those that excel in every Art. Afterwards ought he encourage his Citizens, whereby they may be enabled quickly to exercise their faculties as well in merchandise, and husbandry, as in any other kind of traffick, to the end that no man forbear to adorne and cultivate his possessions for fear that he be despoyled of them; or any other to open the commerce upon the danger of heavy impositions: but rather to provide rewards for those that shall set these matters afoot, or for any one else that shall any way amplifie his City or State. Besides he ought in the fit times of the year entertain the people with Feasts and Maskes; and because every City is devided into Companies, and arts, and Tribes, he ought to take special notice of those bodies, and some times afford them a meeting, and give them some proof of his humanity, and magnificence; yet withall holding firme the majestie of his State; for this must never fail in any case.

Chapter XXII: Touching Princes Secretaries.

It is no small importance to a Prince, the choyce he makes, of servants being ordinarily good or bad, as his wisdome is. And the first conjecture one gives of a great man, and of his understanding, is, upon the sight of his followers and servants he hath about him, when they prove able and faithful, and then may he alwaies be reputed wise because he hath known how to discern those that are able, and to keep them true to him. But when they are otherwise, there can be no good conjecture made of him; for the first error he commits, is in this choyce. There was no man that had any knowledge of Antonio of Vanafro, the servant of Pandulfus Petrucci Prince of Sicily, who did not esteem Pandulfus for a very discreet man, having him for his servant. And because there are three kinds of understandings; the one that is advised by it self; the other that understands when it is informed by another; the third that neither is advised by it self nor by the demonstration of another; the first is best, the second is good, and the last quite unprofitable. Therefore it was of necessity, that if Pandulfus attaind not the first degree, yet he got to the second; for whenever any one hath the judgement to discerne between the good and the evil, that he does and sayes, however that he hath not his distinction from himself, yet still comes he to take notice of the good or evil actions of that servant; and those he cherishes, and these he suppresses; insomuch that the servant finding no means to deceive his master, keeps himself upright and honest. But how a Prince may throughly understand his servant, here is the way that never fails. When thou seest the servant study more for his own advantage than thine, and that in all his actions, he searches most after his own profit; this man thus qualified, shall never prove good servant, nor canst thou ever relie upon him: for he that holds the Sterne of the State in hand, ought never call home his cares to his own particular, but give himself wholly over to his Princes service, nor ever put him in minde of any thing not appertaining to him. And on the other side the Prince to keep him good to him, ought to take a care for his servant, honoring him, enriching, and obliging him to him, giving him part both of dignities and offices, to the end that the many honors and much wealth bestowed on him, may restrain his desires from other honors, and other wealth, and that those many charges cause him to fear changes that may fall, knowing he is not able to stand without his master. And when both the Princes and the servants are thus disposed, they may rely the one upon the other: when otherwise, the end will ever prove hurtfull for the one as well as for the other.

Chapter XXIII: That Flatterers are to be avoyded.

I will not omit one principle of great inportance, being an errour from which Princes with much difficulty defend themselves, unlesse they be very discreet, and make a very good choice; and this is concerning flatterers; whereof all writings are full: and that because men please themselves so much in their own things, and therein cozen themselves, that very hardly can they escape this pestilence; and desiring to escape it, there is danger of falling into contempt; for there is no other way to be secure from flattery, but to let men know, that they displease thee not in telling thee truth: but when every one hath this leave, thou losest thy reverence. Therefore ought a wise Prince take a third course, making choyce of some understanding men in his State, and give only to them a free liberty of speaking to him the truth; and touching those things only which he inquires of, and nothing else; but he ought to be inquisitive of every thing, and hear their opinions, and then afterwards advise himself after his own manner; and in these deliberations, and with every one of them so carrie himself, that they all know, that the more freely they shall speak, the better they shall be liked of: and besides those, not give eare to any one; and thus pursue the thing resolved on, and thence continue obstinate in the resolution taken. He who does otherwise, either falls upon flatterers, or often changes upon the varying of opinions, from whence proceeds it that men conceive but slightly of him. To this purpose I will alledge you a moderne example. Peter Lucas a servant of Maximilians the present Emperor, speaking of his Majesty, said that he never advised with any body, nor never did any thing after his own way: which was because he took a contrary course to what we have now said: for the Emperor is a close man, who communicates his secrets to none, nor takes counsel of any one; but as they come to be put in practise, they begin to be discovered and known, and so contradicted by those that are near about him; and he as being an easy man, is quickly wrought from them. Whence it comes that what he does to day, he undoes on the morrow; and that he never understands himself what he would, nor what he purposes, and that there is no grounding upon any of his resolutions. A Prince therefore ought alwayes to take counsell, but at his owne pleasure, and not at other mens; or rather should take away any mans courage to advise him of any thing, but what he askes: but he ought well to aske at large, and then touching the things inquird of, be a patient hearer of the truth; and perceiving that for some respect the truth were conceald from him, be displeased thereat. And because some men have thought that a Prince that gaines the opinion to bee wise, may bee held so, not by his owne naturall indowments, but by the good counsells he hath about him; without question they are deceivd; for this is a generall rule and never failes, that a Prince who of himselfe is not wise, can never be well advised, unlesse he should light upon one alone, wholly to direct and govern him, who himself were a very wise man. In this case it is possible he may be well governd: but this would last but little: for that governor in a short time would deprive him of his State; but a Prince not having any parts of nature, being advised of more then one, shall never be able to unite these counsels: of himself shall he never know how to unite them; and each one of the Counsellers, probably will follow that which is most properly his owne; and he shall never find the meanes to amend or discerne these things; nor can they fall out otherwise, because men alwayes prove mischievous, unlesse upon some necessity they be forc'd to become good: we conclude therefore, that counsells from whencesoever they proceed, must needs take their beginning from the Princes wisdome, and not the wisdome of the Prince from good counsells.

In this Chapter our Authour prescribes some rules how to avoyd flattery, and not to fall into contempt. The extent of these two extreames is so large on both sides, that there is left but a very narrow path for the right temper to walke between them both: and happy were that Prince, who could light on so good a Pilote as to bring him to Port between those rocks and those quicksands. Where Majesty becomes familiar, unlesse endued with a super-eminent vertue, it loses all awfull regards: as the light of the Sunne, because so ordinary, because so common, we should little value, were it not that all Creatures feele themselves quickned by the rayes thereof. On the other side, *Omnis insipiens arrogantiâ et plausibus capitur*, Every foole is taken with his owne pride and others flatteryes: and this foole keeps company so much with all great wise men, that hardly with a candle and lantern can they be discernd betwixt. The greatest men are more subject to grosse and palpable flatteries; and especially the greatest of men, who are Kings and Princes: for many seek the Rulers favour. *Prov.* 28. 26. For there are divers meanes whereby private men are instructed; Princes have not that good hap: but they whose instruction is of most importance, so soone as they have taken the government upon them, no longer suffer any reproovers: for but few have accesse unto them, and they who familiary converse with them, doe and say all for favour. Isocrat, to Nicocles, All are afraid to give him occasion of displeasure, though by telling him truth. To this purpose therefore sayes one; a Prince excells in learning to ride the great horse, rather than in any other exercise, because his horse being no flatterer, will shew him he makes no difference between him and another man, and unlesse he keepe his seate well, will lay him on the ground. This is plaine dealing. Men are more subtile, more double-hearted, they have a heart and a heart neither is their tongue their hearts true interpreter. Counsell in the heart of man is like deepe waters; but a man of understanding will draw it out. *Prov.* 20. 5. This understanding is most requisite in a Prince, inasmuch as the whole Globe is in his hand, and the inferiour Orbes are swayed by the motion of the highest. And therefore surely it is the honour of a King to search out such a secret: *Prov.* 25. 2. His counsellours are his eyes and eares; as they ought to be dear to him, so they ought to be true to him, and make him the true report of things without disguise. If they prove false eyes, let him pluck them out; he may as they use glasse eyes, take them forth without paine, and see never a whit the worse for it. The wisdome of a Princes Counsellours is a great argument of the Princes wisdome. And being the choyce of them imports the Princes credit and safety, our Authour will make him amends for his other errours by his good advice in his 22 Chap. whether I referre him.

Chapter XXIV: Wherefore the Princes of Italy have lost their States.

When these things above said are well observ'd, they make a new Prince seeme as if he had been of old, and presently render him more secure and firme in the State, than if he had already grown ancient therein: for a new Prince is much more observd in his action, than a Prince by inheritance; and when they are known to bee vertuous, men are much more gaind and oblig'd to them thereby, than by the antiquity of their blood: for men are much more taken by things present, than by things past, and when in the present they find good, they content themselves therein, and seeke no further; or rather they undertake the defence of him to their utmost, when the Prince is not wanting in other matters to himself; and so shall he gaine double glory to have given a beginning to a new Principality, adornd, and strengthnd it with good lawes, good arms, good friends, and good examples; as he shall have double shame, that is born a Prince, and by reason of his small discretion hath lost it. And if we shall consider those Lords, that in Italy have lost their States in our dayes, as the King of Naples, the Duke of Milan, and others; first we shall find in them a common defect, touching their armes, for the reasons which have been above discoursd at length. Afterwards we shall see some of them, that either shall have had the people for their enemies; or be it they had the people to friend, could never know how to assure themselves of the great ones: for without such defects as these, States are not lost, which have so many nerves, that they are able to maintaine an army in the feld. Philip of Macedon, not the father of Alexander the Great, but he that was vanquished by Titus Quintius, had not much State in regard of the greatnesse of the Romanes and of Greece that assail'd him; neverthelesse in that he was a warlike man and knew how to entertaine the people, and assure himself of the Nobles, for many yeares he made the warre good against them: and though at last some town perhaps were taken from him, yet the Kingdome remaind in his hands still. Wherefore these our Princes who for many yeares had continued in their Principalities, for having afterwards lost them, let them not blame Fortune, but their own sloth; because they never having thought during the time of quiet, that they could suffer a change (which is the common fault of men, while faire weather lasts, not to provide for the tempest) when afterwards mischiefes came upon them, thought rather upon flying from them, than upon their defence, and hop'd that the people, weary of the vanquishers insolence, would recall them: which course when the others faile, is good: but very ill is it to leave the other remedies for that: for a man wou'd never go to fall, beleeving another would come to take him up: which may either not come to passe, or if it does, it is not for thy security, because that defence of his is vile, and depends not upon thee; but those defences only are good, certaine, and durable, which depend upon thy owne selfe, and thy owne vertues.

Chapter XXV: How great power Fortune hath in humane affaires, and what meanes there is to resist it.

It is not unknown unto me, how that many have held opinion, and still hold it, that the affaires of the world are so governd by fortune, and by God, that men by their wisdome cannot amend or alter them; or rather that there is no remedy for them: and hereupon they would think that it were of no availe to take much paines in any thing, but leave all to be governd by chance. This opinion hath gain'd the more credit in our dayes, by reason of the great alteration of things, which we have of late seen, and do every day see, beyond all humane conjecture: upon which, I sometimes thinking, am in some parte inclind to their opinion: neverthelesse not to extinguish quite our owne free will, I think it may be true, that Fortune is the mistrisse of one halfe of our actions; but yet that she lets us have rule of the other half, or little lesse. And I liken her to a precipitous torrent, which when it rages, over-flows the plaines, overthrowes the trees, and buildings, removes the earth from one side, and laies it on another, every one flyes before it, every one yeelds to the fury thereof, as unable to withstand it; and yet however it be thus, when the times are calmer, men are able to make provision against these excesses, with banks and fences so, that afterwards when it swels again, it shall all passe smoothly along, within its channell, or else the violence thereof shall not prove so licentious and hurtfull. In like manner befals it us with fortune, which there shewes her power where vertue is not ordeind to resist her, and thither turnes she all her forces, where she perceives that no provisions nor resistances are made to uphold her. And if you shall consider Italy, which is the seat of these changes, and that which hath given them their motions, you shall see it to be a plaine field, without any trench or bank; which had it been fenc'd with convenient vertue as was Germany, Spain or France; this inundation would never have causd these great alterations it hath, or else would it not have reach'd to us: and this shall suffice to have said, touching the opposing of fortune in generall. But restraining my selfe more to particulars, I say that to day we see a Prince prosper and flourish and to morrow utterly go to ruine; not seeing that he hath altered any condition or quality; which I beleeve arises first from the causes which we have long since run over, that is because that Prince that relies wholly upon fortune, runnes as her wheele turnes. I beleeve also, that he proves the fortunate man, whose manner of proceeding meets with the quality of the time; and so likewise he unfortunate from whose course of proceeding the times differ: for we see that men, in the things that induce them to the end, (which every one propounds to himselfe, as glory and riches) proceed therein diversly; some with respects, others more bold, and rashly; one with violence, and th'other with cunning; the one with patience, th'other with its contrary; and every one of severall wayes may attaine thereto; we see also two very respective and wary men, the one come to his purpose, and th'other not; and in like maner two equally prosper, taking divers course; the one being wary the other head-strong; which proceeds from nothing else, but from the quality of the times, which agree, or not, with their proceedings. From hence arises that which I said, that two working diversly, produce the same effect: and two equaly working, the one attains his end, the other not. Hereupon depends the alteration of the good; for if to one that behaves himself with warinesse and patience, times and affaires turne so favourably, that the carriage of his businesse prove well, he prospers; but if the times and affaires chance, he is ruind, because he changes not his manner of proceeding: nor is there any man so wise, that can frame himselfe hereunto; as well because he cannot go out of the way, from that whereunto Nature inclines him: as also, for that one having alwayes prosperd, walking such a way, cannot be perswaded to leave it; and therefore the respective and wary man, when it is fit time for him to use violence and force, knows not how to put it in practice, whereupon he is ruind: but if he could change his disposition with the times and the affaires, he should not change his fortune. Pope Julius the second proceeded in all his actions with very great violence, and found the times and things so conformable to that his manner of proceeding that in all of them he had happy successe. Consider the first exploit he did at Bolonia, even while John Bentivolio lived: the Venetians were not well contented therewith; the King of Spaine likewise with the French, had treated of that enterprise; and notwithstanding al this, he stirrd up by his own rage and fiercenesse, personally undertook that expedition: which action of his put in suspence and stopt Spaine and the Venetians; those for feare, and the others for desire to recover the Kingdome of Naples; and on the other part drew after him the King of France; for that King seeing him already in motion, and desiring to hold him his friend, whereby to humble the Venetians, thought he could no way deny him his souldiers, without doing him an open injury. Julius then effected that with his violent and heady motion, which no other Pope with all humane wisdome could ever have done; for if he had expected to part from Rome with his conclusions settled, and all his affaires ordered before hand, as any other Pope would have done, he had never brought it to passe: For the King of France would have devised a thousand excuses, and others would have put him in as many feares. I will let passe his other actions, for all of them were alike, and all of them prov'd lucky to him; and the brevity of his life never sufferd him to feele the contrary: for had he litt upon such times afterwards, that it had been necessary for him to proceed with respects, there had been his utter ruine; for he would never have left those wayes, to which he had been naturally inclind. I conclude then, fortune varying, and men continuing still obstinate to their own wayes, prove happy, while these accord together: and as they disagree, prove unhappy: and I think it true, that it is better to be heady than wary; because Fortune is a mistresse; and it is necessary, to keep her in obedience to ruffle and force her: and we see, that she suffers her self rather to be masterd by those, than by others that proceed coldly. And therefore, as a mistresse, shee is a friend to young men, because they are lesse respective, more rough, and command her with more boldnesse.

I have considered the 25 Chapter, as representing me a full view of humane policy and cunning: yet me thinks it cannot satisfie a Christian in the causes of the good and bad successe of things. The life of man is like a game at Tables; skill availes much I grant, but that's not all: play thy game well, but that will not winne: the chance thou throwest must accord with thy play. Examine this; play never so surely, play never so probably, unlesse the chance thou castest, lead thee forward to advantage, all hazards are losses, and thy sure play leaves thee in the lurch. The sum of this is set down in Ecclesiastes chap. 9. v. 11. The race is not to the swift, nor the battell to the strong: neither yet bread to the wise, nor yet riches to men of understanding, nor yet favour to men of skill; but time and chance hapeneth to them all. Our cunning Author for all his exact rules he delivere in his books, could not fence against the despight of Fortune, as he complaines in his Epistle to this booke. Nor that great example of policy, Duke Valentine, whome our Author commends to Princes for his crafts-master, could so ruffle or force his mistresse Fortune, that he could keep her in obedience. Man can contribute no more to his actions than vertue and wisdome: but the successe depends upon a power above. Surely there is the finger of god; or as Prov. 16. v. 33. 'The lot is cast into the lap, but the whole disposing thereof is of the Lord.' It was not Josephs wisdome made all things thrive under his hand; but because the Lord was with him; and that which he did, the Lord made it to prosper, Gen. 39. Surely this is a blessing proceeding from the divine providence, which beyond humane capacity so cooperateth with the causes, as that their effects prove answerable, and sometimes (that we may know there is something above the ordinary causes) the success returns with such a supereminency of worth, that it far exceeds the vertue of the ordinary causes.

Chapter XXV: An Exhortation to free Italy from the Barbarians.

Having then weighed all things above discours'd, and devising with my self, whether at this present in Italy the time might serve to honor a new Prince, and whether there were matter that might minister occasion to a wise and valorous Prince, to introduce such a forme, that might do honor to him, and good to the whole generality of the people in the countrey: me thinks so many things concurre in favor of a new Prince, that I know not whether there were ever any time more proper for this purpose. And if as I said, it was necessary, desiring to see Moses his vertue, that the children of Israel should be inthrald in Ægypt; and to have experience of the magnanimity of Cyrus his mind, that the Persians should be oppress'd by the Medes; and to set forth the excellency of Theseus, that the Athenians should be dispersed; so at this present now we are desirous to know the valor of an Italian spirit, it were necessary Italy should be reduc'd to the same termes it is now in, and were in more slavery than the Hebrews were; more subject than the Persians, more scatterd than the Athenians; without head, without order, battered, pillaged, rent asunder, overrun, and had undergone all kind of destruction. And however even in these later dayes, we have had some kind of shew of hope in some one, whereby we might have conjectur'd, that he had been ordained for the deliverance hereof, yet it prov'd afterwards, that in the very height of all his actions he was curb'd by fortune, insomuch that this poore countrey remaining as it were without life, attends still for him that shall heal her wounds, give an end to all those pillagings and sackings of Lombardy, to those robberies and taxations of the Kingdome, and of Tuscany, and heal them of their soars, now this long time gangren'd. We see how she makes her prayers to God, that he send some one to redeem her from these Barbarous cruelties and insolencies. We see her also wholly ready and disposed to follow any colours, provided there be any one take them up. Nor do we see at this present, that she can look for other, than your Illustrious Family, to become Cheiftain of this deliverance, which hath now by its own vertue and Fortune been so much exalted, and favored by God and the Church, whereof it now holds the Principality: and this shall not be very hard for you to do, if you shall call to mind the former actions, and lives of those that are above named. And though those men were very rare and admirable, yet were they men, and every one of them began upon less occasion than this; for neither was their enterprize more just than this, nor more easie; nor was God more their friend, than yours. Here is very great justice: for that war is just, that is necessary; and those armes are religious, when there is no hope left otherwhere, but in them. Here is an exceeding good disposition thereto: nor can there be, where there is a good disposition, a giant difficulty, provided that use be made of those orders, which I propounded for aim and direction to you. Besides this, here we see extraordinary things without example effected by God; the sea was opened, a cloud guided the way, devotion poured forth the waters, and it rain'd down Manna; all these things have concurred in your greatness, the rest is left for you to do. God will not do every thing himself, that he may not take from us our free will, and of that glory that belongs to us. Neither is it a marvel, if any of the aforenamed Italians have not been able to compass that, which we may hope your illustrious family shall: though in so many revolutions of Italy, and so many feats of war, it may seem that the whole military vertue therein be quite extinguisht; for this arises from that the ancient orders thereof were not good; and there hath since been none that hath known how to invent new ones. Nothing can so much honor a man rising anew, as new laws and new ordinances devised by him: these things when they have a good foundation given them, and contain in them their due greatness, gain him reverence and admiration; and in Italy their wants not the matter wherein to introduce any forme. Here is great vertue in the members, were it not wanting in the heads. Consider in the single fights that have been, and duels, how much the Italians have excel'd in their strength, activity and address; but when they come to armies, they appear not, and all proceeds from the weakness of the Chieftaines; for they that understand the managing of these matters, are not obeyed; and every one presumes to understand; hitherto there having not been any one so highly raised either by fortune or vertue, as that others would submit unto him. From hence proceeds it, that in so long time, and in so many battels fought for these last past 20 years, when there hath been an army wholly Italian, it alwaies hath had evil success; whereof the river Tarus first was witness, afterwards Alexandria, Capua, Genua, Vayla, Bolonia, Mestri. Your Illustrious family then being desirous to tread the footsteps of these Worthyes who redeem'd their countreys, must above all things as the very foundation of the whole fabrick, be furnished with soldiers of your own natives: because you cannot have more faithful, true, nor better soldiers; and though every one of them be good, all together they will become better when they shall find themselves entertained, commanded, and honored by their own Prince. Wherefore it is necessary to provide for those armes, whereby to be able with the Italian valor to make a defence against forreiners. And however the Swisse infantry and Spanish be accounted terrible; yet is there defect in both of them, by which a third order might not only oppose them, but may be confident to vanquish them: for the Spaniards are not able to indure the Horse, and the Swisse are to feare the foot, when they incounter with them, as resolute in the fight as they; whereupon it hath been seen, and upon experience shall be certain, that the Spaniards are not able to beare up against the French Cavalery, and the Swisses have been routed by the Spanish Foot. And though touching this last, there hath not been any entire experience had, yet was there some proof thereof given in the battel of Ravenna, when the Spanish Foot affronted the Dutch battalions, which keep the same rank the Swisses do, where the Spaniards with their nimbleness of body, and the help of their targets entred in under their Pikes, and there stood safe to offend them, the Dutch men having no remedy: and had it not been for the Cavalery that rusht in upon them, they had quite defeated them. There may then (the defect of the one and other of these two infantries being discoverd) another kind of them be anew ordained, which may be able to make resistance against the Horse, and not fear the Foot, which shall not be a new sort of armes, but change of orders. And these are some of those things which ordained a new, gain reputation and greatness to a new Prince. Therefore this occasion should not be let pass, to the end that Italy after so long a time may see some one redeemer of hers appear. Nor can I express with what dearness of affection he would be received in all those countreys which have suffered by those forrein scums, with what thirst of revenge, with what resolution of fidelity, with what piety, with what tears. Would any gates be shut again him? Any people deny him obedience? Any envy oppose him? Would not every Italian fully consent with him? This government of the Barbarians stinks in every ones nostrils. Let your Illustrious Family then undertake this worthy exployt with that courage and those hopes wherewith such just actions are to be attempted; to the end that under your colours, this countrey may be enabled, and under the protection of your fortune that saying of Petrarch be verifyed.

Virtù contr' al fuore Prendera l'arme, e fia il combatter corto: Che l'antico valore Ne gli Italici cor non è morto.

Vertue against fury shall advance the fight, And it i' th' combate soon shall put to flight: For th' old Roman valor is not dead, Nor in th' Italians brests extinguished.

The Art of War

Translator: Peter Whitehorne and Edward Dacres

The Proheme of Nicholas Machiavell,

Citezein and Secretarie of Florence, upon his booke of the Arte of Warre, unto Laurence Philippe Strozze, one of the nobilitie of Florence.

There have Laurence, many helde, and do holde this opinion, that there is no maner of thing, whiche lesse agreeth the one with the other, nor that is so much unlike, as the civil life to the Souldiours. Wherby it is often seen, that if any determin in thexercise of that kinde of service to prevaile, that incontinent he doeth not only chaunge in apparel, but also in custome and maner, in voice, and from the facion of all civil use, he doeth alter: For that he thinketh not meete to clothe with civell apparell him, who wil be redie, and promt to all kinde of violence, nor the civell customes, and usages maie that man have, the whiche judgeth bothe those customes to be effeminate, and those usages not to be agreable to his profession: Nor it semes not convenient for him to use the civill gesture and ordinarie wordes, who with fasing and blasphemies, will make afraied other menne: the whiche causeth in this time, suche opinion to be moste true. But if thei should consider thauncient orders, there should nothing be founde more united, more confirmable, and that of necessitie ought to love so much the one the other, as these: for as muche as all the artes that are ordeined in a common weale, in regarde or respecte of common profite of menne, all the orders made in the same, to live with feare of the Lawe, and of God should be vaine, if by force of armes their defence wer not prepared, which, well ordeined, doe maintain those also whiche be not well ordeined. And likewise to the contrarie the good orders, without the souldiours help, no lesse or otherwise doe disorder, then the habitacion of a sumptuous and roiall palais, although it wer decte with gold and precious stones, when without being covered, should not have wherewith to defende it from the raine. And if in what so ever other orders of Cities and Kyngdomes, there hath been used al diligence for to maintain men faithfull, peaceable, and full of the feare of God, in the service of warre, it was doubled: if for in what man ought the countrie to seke greater faith, then in him, who must promise to die for the same? In whom ought there to bee more love of peace, then in him, whiche onely by the warre maie be hurte? In whome ought there to bee more feare of *God*, then in him, which every daie committyng himself to infinite perilles, hath moste neede of his helpe? This necessitie considered wel, bothe of them that gave the lawes to Empires, and of those that to the exercise of service wer apoincted, made that the life of Souldiours, of other menne was praised, and with all studie folowed and imitated. But the orders of service of war, beyng altogether corrupted, and a greate waie from the auncient maners altered, there hath growen these sinisterous opinions, which maketh men to hate the warlike service, and to flie the conversacion of those that dooe exercise it. Albeit I judgeing by the same, that I have seen and redde, that it is not a thyng impossible, to bryng it again to the auncient maners, and to give it some facion of the vertue passed, I have determined to the entente not to passe this my idell time, without doyng some thyng, to write that whiche I doe understande, to the satisfaction of those, who of aunciente actes, are lovers of the science of warre. And although it be a bold thing to intreate of the same matter, wher of otherwise I have made no profession, notwithstanding I beleve it is no errour, to occupie with wordes a degree, the whiche many with greater presumpcion with their deedes have occupied: for as muche as the errours that I maie happen to make by writing, may be without harme to any man corrected: but those the whiche of them be made in doyng cannot be knowen without the ruine of Empires. Therefore Laurence you ought to consider the qualitie of this my laboure, and with your judgement to give it that blame, or that praise, as shall seeme unto you it hath deserved. The whiche I sende unto you, as well to shewe my selfe gratefull, although my habilitie reche not to the benefites, which I have received of you, as also for that beyng the custome to honour with like workes them who for nobilitie, riches, wisedome, and liberalitie doe shine: I knowe you for riches, and nobilitie, not to have many peeres, for wisedome fewe, and for liberalitie none.

The First Booke

Forasmuch as I beleve that after death, al men maie be praised without charge, al occasion and suspecte of flatterie beyng taken awaie, I shal not doubte to praise our Cosimo Ruchellay, whose name was never remembred of me without teares, havyng knowen in him those condicions, the whiche in a good frende or in a citezien, might of his freendes, or of his countrie, be desired: for that I doe not knowe what thyng was so muche his, not excepting any thing (saving his soule) which for his frendes willingly of him should not have been spent: I knowe not what enterprise should have made him afraide, where the same should have ben knowen to have been for the benefite of his countrie. And I doe painly confesse, not to have mette emongest so many men, as I have knowen, and practised withal, a man, whose minde was more inflamed then his, unto great and magnificent thynges. Nor he lamented not with his frendes of any thyng at his death, but because he was borne to die a yong manne within his owne house, before he had gotten honour, and accordynge to his desire, holpen any manne: for that he knewe, that of him coulde not be spoken other, savyng that there should be dead a good freende. Yet it resteth not for this, that we, and what so ever other that as we did know him, are not able to testifie (seeyng his woorkes doe not appere) of his lawdable qualities. True it is, that fortune was not for al this, so muche his enemie, that it left not some brief record of the readinesse of his witte, as doeth declare certaine of his writinges, and settyng foorthe of amorous verses, wherin (although he were not in love) yet for that he would not consume time in vain, til unto profounder studies fortune should have brought him, in his youthfull age he exercised himselfe. Whereby moste plainly maie be comprehended, with how moche felicitie he did describe his conceiptes, and how moche for Poetrie he should have ben estemed, if the same for the ende therof, had of him ben exercised. Fortune having therfore deprived us from the use of so great a frende, me thinketh there can bee founde no other remedie, then as muche as is possible, to seke to enjoye the memorie of the same, and to repeate suche thynges as hath been of him either wittely saied, or wisely disputed. And for as much as there is nothyng of him more freshe, then the reasonyng, the whiche in his last daies Signior Fabricio Collonna, in his orchard had with him, where largely of the same gentilman were disputed matters of warre, bothe wittely and prudently, for the moste parte of Cosimo demaunded, I thought good, for that I was present there with certain other of our frendes, to bring it to memorie, so that reading the same, the frendes of Cosimo, whiche thether came, might renewe in their mindes, the remembraunce of his vertue: and the other part beyng sorie for their absence, might partly learne hereby many thynges profitable, not onely to the life of Souldiours, but also to civil mennes lives, which gravely of a moste wise man was disputed. Therfore I saie, that Fabricio Collonna retournyng out of Lombardie, where longe time greatly to his glorie, he had served in the warres the catholike kyng, he determined, passyng by Florence, to rest himself certain daies in the same citee, to visite the Dukes excellencie, and to see certaine gentilmen, whiche in times paste he had been acquainted withal. For whiche cause, unto Cosimo it was thought beste to bid him into his orchard, not so muche to use his liberalitee, as to have occasion to talke with him at leasure, and of him to understande and to learne divers thinges, accordyng as of suche a man maie bee hoped for, semyng to have accasion to spende a daie in reasonyng of suche matters, which to his minde should best satisfie him. Then Fabricio came, accordyng to his desire, and was received of Cosimo together, with certain of his trustie frendes, emongest whome wer Zanoby Buondelmonti, Baptiste Palla, and Luigi Allamanni, all young men loved of him and of the very same studies moste ardente, whose good qualities, for as muche as every daie, and at every houre thei dooe praise themselves, we will omit. Fabricio was then accordyng to the time and place honoured, of all those honours, that thei could possible devise: But the bankettyng pleasures beyng passed, and the tabel taken up, and al preparacion of feastinges consumed, the which are sone at an ende in sight of greate men, who to honorable studies have their mindes set, the daie beyng longe, and the heate muche, Cosimo judged for to content better his desire, that it wer well doen, takyng occasion to avoide the heate, to bring him into the moste secret, and shadowest place of his garden. Where thei beyng come, and caused to sit, some upon herbes, some in the coldest places, other upon litle seates which there was ordeined, under the shadow of moste high trees, Fabricio praiseth the place, to be delectable, and particularly consideryng the trees, and not knowyng some of them, he did stande musinge in his minde, whereof Cosimo beeyng a ware saied, you have not peradventure ben acquainted with some of these sortes of trees: But doe not marvell at it, for as muche as there bee some, that were more estemed of the antiquitie, then thei are commonly now a daies: and he tolde him the names of them, and how Barnardo his graundfather did travaile in suche kinde of plantyng: Fabricio replied, I thought it shuld be the same you saie, and this place, and this studie, made me to remember certaine Princes of the Kyngdome of Naples, whiche of these anncient tillage and shadow doe delight. And staiyng upon this talke, and somewhat standyng in a studdie, saied moreover, if I thought I should not offende, I woud tell my opinion, but I beleeve I shall not, commonyng with friendes, and to dispute of thynges, and not to condemne them. How much better thei should have doen (be it spoken without displeasure to any man) to have sought to been like the antiquitie in thinges strong, and sharpe, not in the delicate and softe: and in those that thei did in the Sunne, not in the shadowe: and to take the true and perfecte maners of the antiquitie: not those that are false and corrupted: for that when these studies pleased my Romaines, my countrie fell into ruin. Unto which Cosimo answered. But to avoide the tediousnesse to repeate so many times he saied, and the other answered, there shall be onely noted the names of those that speakes, without rehersing other.

Then Cosimo saied, you have opened the waie of a reasoning, which I have desired, and I praie you that you will speake withoute respecte, for that that I without respecte will aske you, and if I demaundyng, or repliyng shall excuse, or accuse any, it shal not be to excuse, or accuse, but to understande of you the truth.

Fabricio. And I shall be very well contented to tell you that, whiche I understand of al the same that you shall aske me, the whiche if it shall be true, or no, I wil report me to your judgemente: and I will be glad that you aske me, for that I am to learne, as well of you in askyng me, as you of me in aunsweryng you: for as muche as many times a wise demaunder, maketh one to consider many thynges, and to knowe many other, whiche without havyng been demaunded, he should never have knowen.

Cosimo. I will retourne to thesame, that you said first, that my graundfather and those your Princes, should have doen more wisely, to have resembled the antiquitie in hard thinges, then in the delicate, and I will excuse my parte, for that, the other I shall leave to excuse for you. I doe not beleve that in his tyme was any manne, that so moche detested the livyng in ease, as he did, and that so moche was a lover of the same hardenesse of life, whiche you praise: notwithstandyng he knewe not how to bee able in persone, nor in those of his sonnes to use it, beeyng borne in so corrupte a worlde, where one that would digresse from the common use, should bee infamed and disdained of every man: consideryng that if one in the hottest day of Summer being naked, should wallowe hymself upon the Sande, or in Winter in the moste coldest monethes upon the snowe, as Diogenes did, he should be taken as a foole. If one, (as the Spartans were wonte to doe) should nourishe his children in a village, makyng them to slepe in the open aire, to go with hedde and feete naked, to washe them selves in the colde water for to harden them, to be able to abide moche paine, and for to make theim to love lesse life, and to feare lesse death, he should be scorned, and soner taken as a wilde beast, then as a manne. If there wer seen also one, to nourishe himself with peason and beanes, and to despise gold, as Fabricio doeth, he should bee praised of fewe, and followed of none: so that he being afraied of this present maner of livyng, he left thauncient facions, and thesame, that he could with lest admiracion imitate in the antiquitie, he did.

Fabricio. You have excused it in this parte mooste strongly: and surely you saie the truthe: but I did not speake so moche of this harde maner of livyng, as of other maners more humaine, and whiche have with the life now a daies greater conformitie. The whiche I doe not beleve, that it hath been difficulte to bryng to passe unto one, who is nombred emongest Princes of a citee: for the provyng whereof, I will never seke other, then thexample of the Romaines. Whose lives, if thei wer well considred, and thorders of thesame common weale, there should therin be seen many things, not impossible to induce into a cominaltie, so that it had in her any good thing.

Cosimo. What thynges are those, that you would induce like unto the antiquitie.

Fabricio. To honour, and to reward vertue, not to despise povertie, to esteme the maners and orders of warfare, to constrain the citezeins to love one an other, to live without sectes, to esteme lesse the private, than the publike, and other like thinges, that easily might bee with this time accompanied: the which maners ar not difficult to bring to passe, when a man should wel consider them, and entre therin by due meanes: for asmoche as in thesame, the truth so moche appereth, that every common wit, maie easely perceive it: which thing, who that ordeineth, doth plant trees, under the shadowe wherof, thei abide more happie, and more pleasantly, then under these shadowes of this goodly gardeine.

Cosimo. I will not speake any thyng againste thesame that you have saied, but I will leave it to bee judged of these, whom easely can judge, and I will tourne my communicacion to you, that is an accusar of theim, the whiche in grave, and greate doynges, are not followers of the antiquitie, thinkyng by this waie more easely to be in my entent satisfied. Therfore, I would knowe of you whereof it groweth, that of the one side you condempne those, that in their doynges resemble not the antiquitie? Of the other, in the warre, whiche is your art, wherin you are judged excellent, it is not seen, that you have indevoured your self, to bryng the same to any soche ende, or any thyng at all resembled therein the auncient maners.

Fabricio. You are happened upon the poincte, where I loked: for that my talke deserved no other question: nor I desired other: and albeit that I could save my self with an easie excuse, not withstandyng for my more contentacion, and yours, seyng that the season beareth it, I will enter in moche longer reasoning. Those men, whiche will enterprise any thyng, ought firste with all diligence to prepare theim selves, to be ready and apte when occasion serveth, to accomplish that, which thei have determined to worke: and for that when the preparacions are made craftely, thei are not knowen, there cannot be accused any man of any negligence, if firste it be not disclosed by thoccasion: in the which working not, is after seen, either that there is not prepared so moche as suffiseth, or that there hath not been of any part therof thought upon. And for as moche as to me there is not come any occasion to be able, to shewe the preparacions made of me, to reduce the servise of warre into his auncient orders, if I have not reduced it, I cannot be of you, nor of other blamed: I beleve this excuse shuld suffise for answere to your accusement.

Cosimo. It should suffice, when I wer certain, that thoccasion were not come.

Fabricio. But for that I know, that you maie doubt whether this occasion hath been cum, or no, I will largely (when you with pacience will heare me) discourse what preparacions are necessary first to make, what occasion muste growe, what difficultie doeth let, that the preparacions help not, and why thoccasion cannot come, and how these things at ones, which some contrary endes, is most difficill, and most easie to do.

Cosimo. You cannot do bothe to me, and unto these other, a thing more thankfull then this. And if to you it shall not be tedious to speake, unto us it shal never be grevous to heare: but for asmoch as this reasonyng ought to be long, I will with your license take helpe of these my frendes: and thei, and I praie you of one thyng, that is, that you will not bee greved, if some tyme with some question of importaunce, we interrupte you.

Why a good man ought never to use the exercise of armes, as his art.

Fabricio. I am moste well contented, that you **Cosimo** with these other younge men here, doe aske me: for that I beleve, that youthfulnes, will make you lovers of warlike thinges, and more easie to beleve thesame, that of me shalbe saied. These other, by reason of havyng nowe their hedde white, and for havyng upon their backes their bloude congeled, parte of theim are wonte to bee enemies of warre, parte uncorrectable, as those, whom beleve, that tymes, and not the naughtie maners, constraine men to live thus: so that safely aske you all of me, and without respecte: the whiche I desire, as well, for that it maie be unto me a little ease, as also for that I shall have pleasure, not to leave in your mynde any doubt. I will begin at your woordes, where you saied unto me, that in the warre, that is my arte, I had not indevoured to bryng it to any aunciente ende: whereupon I saie, as this beyng an arte, whereby men of no maner of age can live honestly, it cannot bee used for an arte, but of a common weale: or of a kyngdome: and the one and the other of these, when thei bee well ordeined, will never consente to any their Citezeins, or Subjectes, to use it for any arte, nor never any good manne doeth exercise it for his particulare arte: for as moche as good he shall never bee judged, whom maketh an excersise thereof, where purposing alwaies to gaine thereby, it is requisite for hym to be ravenyng, deceiptfull, violente, and to have many qualities, the whiche of necessitie maketh hym not good: nor those menne cannot, whiche use it for an arte, as well the greate as the leaste, bee made otherwise: for that this arte doeth not nourishe them in peace. Wherfore thei ar constrained either to thinke that there is no peace, or so moche to prevaile in the tyme of warre, that in peace thei maie bee able to kepe them selves: and neither of these two thoughtes happeneth in a good man: for that in mindyng to bee able to finde himself at all tymes, dooe growe robberies, violence, slaughters, whiche soche souldiours make as well to the frendes, as to the enemies: and in mindyng not to have peace, there groweth deceiptes, whiche the capitaines use to those, whiche hire them, to the entent the warre maie continue, and yet though the peace come often, it happeneth that the capitaines beyng deprived of their stipendes, and of their licencious livyng, thei erecte an ansigne of adventures, and without any pitie thei put to sacke a province. Have not you in memorie of your affaires, how that beyng many Souldiours in Italie without wages, bicause the warre was ended, thei assembled together many companies, and went taxyng the tounes, and sackyng the countrie, without beyng able to make any remedie? Have you not red, that the Carthagenes souldiours, the first warre beyng ended which thei had with the Romaines, under Matho, and Spendio, twoo capitaines, rebelliously constituted of theim, made more perillous warre to the Carthaginens, then thesame whiche thei had ended with the Romaines? In the time of our fathers, Frances Sforza, to the entente to bee able to live honourably in the time of peace, not only beguiled the Millenars, whose souldiour he was, but he toke from them their libertie and became their Prince. Like unto him hath been all the other souldiours of Italie whiche have used warfare, for their particulare arte, and albeeit thei have not through their malignitie becomen Dukes of Milein, so moche the more thei deserve to bee blamed: for that although thei have not gotten so moch as he, thei have all (if their lives wer seen) sought to bring the like thynges to passe. Sforza father of Fraunces, constrained Quene Jone, to caste her self into the armes of the king of Aragon, havyng in a sodain forsaken her, and in the middest of her enemies, lefte her disarmed, onely to satisfie his ambicion, either in taxyng her, or in takyng from her the Kyngdome. Braccio with the verie same industrie, sought to possesse the kyngdome of Naples, and if he had not been overthrowen and slaine at Aquila, he had brought it to passe. Like disorders growe not of other, then of soche men as hath been, that use the exercise of warfare, for their proper arte. Have not you a Proverbe, whiche fortefieth my reasons, whiche saieth, that warre maketh Theves, and peace hangeth theim up? For as moche as those, whiche knowe not how to live of other exercise, and in the same finding not enie man to sustayne theym, and havyng not so moche power, to knowe how to reduce theim selves together, to make an open rebellion, they are constrayned of necessetie to Robbe in the highe waies, and Justice is enforced to extinguishe theim.

Cosimo. You have made me to esteme this arte of warfare almoste as nothyng, and I have supposed it the moste excellentes, and moste honourableste that hath been used: so that if you declare me it not better, I cannot remaine satisfied: For that when it is thesame, that you saie, I knowe not, whereof groweth the glorie of Cesar, of Pompei, of Scipio, of Marcello, and of so many Romaine Capitaines, whiche by fame are celebrated as Goddes.

Fabricio. I have not yet made an ende of disputyng al thesame, that I purposed to propounde: whiche were twoo thynges, the one, that a good manne could not use this exercise for his arte: the other, that a common weale or a kingdome well governed, did never permitte, that their Subjectes or Citezeins should use it for an arte. Aboute the firste, I have spoken as moche as hath comen into my mynde: there remaineth in me to speake of the seconde where I woll come to aunswere to this your laste question, and I saie that Pompey and Cesar, and almoste all those Capitaines, whiche were at Rome, after the laste Carthagenens warre, gotte fame as valiaunt men, not as good, and those whiche lived before them, gotte glorie as valiaunte and good menne: the whiche grewe, for that these tooke not the exercise of warre for their arte: and those whiche I named firste, as their arte did use it. And so longe as the common weale lived unspotted, never any noble Citezein would presume, by the meane of soche exercise, to availe thereby in peace, breakyng the lawes, spoilyng the Provinces, usurpyng, and plaiyng the Tyraunte in the countrie, and in every maner prevailyng: nor any of how lowe degree so ever thei were, would goe aboute to violate the Religion, confederatyng theim selves with private men, not to feare the Senate, or to followe any tirannicall insolence, for to bee able to live with the arte of warre in all tymes. But those whiche were Capitaines, contented with triumphe, with desire did tourne to their private life, and those whiche were membres, would be more willyng to laie awaie their weapons, then to take them, and every manne tourned to his science, whereby thei gotte their livyng: Nor there was never any, that would hope with praie, and with this arte, to be able to finde theim selves. Of this there maie be made concernyng Citezeins, moste evidente conjecture, by the ensample of Regolo Attillio, who beyng Capitain of the Romaine armies in Affrica, and havyng as it wer overcome the Carthegenens, he required of the Senate, licence to retourne home, to kepe his possessions, and told them, that thei were marde of his housbandmen. Whereby it is more clere then the Sunne, that if thesame manne had used the warre as his arte, and by meanes thereof, had purposed to have made it profitable unto him, havyng in praie so many Provinces, he would not have asked license, to returne to kepe his feldes: for as moche as every daie he might otherwise, have gotten moche more, then the value of al those possessions: but bicause these good men and soche as use not the warre for their arte, will not take of thesame any thing then labour, perilles, and gloris, when thei are sufficiently glorious, thei desire to returne home, and to live of their owne science. Concernyng menne of lowe degree, and common souldiours, to prove that thei kepte the verie same order, it doeth appeare that every one willingly absented theim selves from soche exercise, and when thei served not in the warre, thei would have desired to serve, and when thei did serve, thei would have desired leave not to have served: whiche is wel knowen through many insamples, and inespecially seeyng how emonge the firste privileges, whiche the Romaine people gave to their Citezeins was, that thei should not be constrained against their willes, to serve in the warres. Therefore Rome so long as it was well governed, whiche was untill the commyng of Graccus, it had not any Souldiour that would take this exercise for an arte, and therefore it had fewe naughtie, and those few wer severely punished. Then a citee well governed, ought to desire, that this studie of warre, be used in tyme of peace for exercise, and in the time of warre, for necessitie and for glorie: and to suffer onely the common weale to use it for an arte, as Rome did, and what so ever Citezein, that hath in soche exercise other ende, is not good, and what so ever citee is governed otherwise, is not well ordeined.

Cosimo. I remain contented enough and satisfied of thesame, whiche hetherto you have told, and this conclusion pleaseth me verie wel whiche you have made, and as muche as is loked for touching a common welth, I beleve that it is true, but concerning Kinges, I can not tell nowe, for that I woulde beleve that a Kinge would have about him, whome particularly should take suche exercise for his arte.

Fabricio. A kingdome well ordred ought moste of all to avoide the like kinde of men, for only thei, are the destruction of their king, and all together ministers of tiranny, and alledge me not to the contrarie anie presente kingdome, for that I woll denie you all those to be kingdomes well ordered, bicause the kingdomes whiche have good orders, give not their absolute Empire unto their king, saving in the armies, for as much as in this place only, a quicke deliberation is necessarie, and for this cause a principall power ought to be made. In the other affaires, he ought not to doe any thing without councell, and those are to be feared, which councell him, leaste he have some aboute him which in time of peace desireth to have warre bicause they are not able without the same to live, but in this, I wilbe a little more large: neither to seke a kingdome altogether good, but like unto those whiche be nowe a daies where also of a king those ought to be feared, whiche take the warre for theire art, for that the strength of armies without any doubte are the foote menne: so that if a king take not order in suche wise, that his men in time of peace may be content to returne home, and to live of their owne trades, it will follow of necessitie, that he ruinate: for that there is not found more perilous men, then those, whiche make the warre as their arte: bicause in such case, a king is inforsed either alwaies to make warre, or to paie them alwaies, or else to bee in perill, that they take not from him his kingdome. To make warre alwaies, it is not possible: to paie them alwaies it can not be: see that of necessitie, he runneth in peril to lese the state. The Romaines (as I have saide) so long as they were wise and good, would never permitte, that their Citizeins should take this exercise for their arte, although they were able to nurrishe them therin alwaies, for that that alwaies they made warre: but to avoide thesame hurte, whiche this continuall exercise might doe them, seyng the time did not varie, they changed the men, and from time to time toke such order with their legions, that in xv. yeres alwaies, they renewed them: and so thei had their men in the floure of their age, that is from xviij. to xxxiij. yeres, in which time the legges, the handes, and the yes answere the one the other, nor thei tarried not till there strengthe should decaie, and there naghtines increase, as it did after in the corrupted times. For as muche as Octavian first, and after Tiberius, minding more their own proper power, then the publicke profite, began to unarme the Romaine people, to be able easely to commaunde them, and to kepe continually those same armies on the frontries of the Empire: and bicause also they judged those, not sufficient to kepe brideled the people and Romaine Senate, they ordeined an armie called Pretoriano, which laie harde by the walles of Rome, and was as a rocke on the backe of the same Citie. And for as much as then thei began frely to permitte, that suche men as were apoincted in suche exercises, should use the service of warre for their arte, streight waie the insolence of theim grewe, that they became fearful unto the Senate, and hurtefull to the Emperour, whereby ensued suche harme, that manie were slaine thorough there insolensie: for that they gave, and toke awaie the Empire, to whome they thought good. And some while it hapned, that in one self time there were manie Emperours, created of divers armies, of whiche thinges proceded first the devision of the Empire, and at laste the ruine of the same. Therefore kinges ought, if thei wil live safely, to have there souldiours made of men, who when it is time to make warre, willingly for his love will go to the same, and when the peace cometh after, more willingly will returne home. Whiche alwaies wilbe, when thei shalbe men that know how to live of other arte then this: and so they ought to desire, peace beyng come, that there Prince doo tourne to governe their people, the gentilmen to the tending of there possessions, and the common souldiours to their particular arte, and everie one of these, to make warre to have peace, and not to seke to trouble the peace, to have warre.

Cosimo. Truely this reasonyng of yours, I thinke to bee well considered, notwithstanding beyng almost contrarie to that, whiche till nowe I have thought, my minde as yet doeth not reste purged of all doubte, for as muche as I see manie Lordes and gentelmen, to finde them selves in time of peace, thorough the studies of warre, as your matches bee, who have provision of there princes, and of the cominaltie. I see also, almost al the gentelmen of armes, remaine with neir provision, I see manie souldiours lie in garison of Cities and fortresses, so that my thinkes, that there is place in time of peace, for everie one.

Fabricio. I doe not beleve that you beleve this, that in time of peace everie man may have place, bicause, put case that there coulde not be brought other reason, the small number, that all they make, whiche remaine in the places alledged of you, would answer you. What proporcion have the souldiours, whiche are requiset to bee in the warre with those, whiche in the peace are occupied? For as much as the fortreses, and the cities that be warded in time of peace, in the warre are warded muche more, unto whome are joyned the souldiours, whiche kepe in the fielde, whiche are a great number, all whiche in the peace be putte awaie. And concerning the garde of states, whiche are a small number, Pope July, and you have shewed to everie man, how muche are to be feared those, who will not learne to exercise any other art, then the warre, and you have for there insolence, deprived them from your garde, and have placed therin Swisers, as men borne and brought up under lawes, and chosen of the cominaltie, according to the true election: so that saie no more,

that in peace is place for everie man. Concerning men at armes, thei al remaining in peace with their wages, maketh this resolution to seme more difficulte: notwithstandyng who considereth well all, shall finde the answere easie, bicause this manner of keping men of armes, is a corrupted manner and not good, the occasion is, for that they be men, who make thereof an arte, and of them their should grow every daie a thousande inconveniencies in the states, where thei should be, if thei were accompanied of sufficient company: but beyng fewe, and not able by them selves to make an armie, they cannot often doe suche grevous hurtes, neverthelesse they have done oftentimes: as I have said of Frances, and of Sforza his father, and of Braccio of Perugia: so that this use of keping men of armes, I doe not alowe, for it is a corrupte maner, and it may make great inconveniencies.

Cosimo. Woulde you live without them? or keping them, how would you kepe them?

A kinge that hath about him any that are to much lovers of warre, or to much lovers of peace shal cause him to erre.

Fabricio. By waie of ordinaunce, not like to those of the king of Fraunce: for as muche as they be perilous, and insolent like unto ours, but I would kepe them like unto those of the auncient Romaines, whom created their chivalry of their own subjectes, and in peace time, thei sente them home unto their houses, to live of their owne trades, as more largely before this reasoning ende, I shal dispute. So that if now this part of an armie, can live in such exercise, as wel when it is peace, it groweth of the corrupt order. Concerning the provisions, which are reserved to me, and to other capitaines, I saie unto you, that this likewise is an order moste corrupted: for as much as a wise common weale, ought not to give such stipendes to any, but rather thei ought to use for Capitaines in the warre, their Citezeins, and in time of peace to will, that thei returne to their occupations. Likewise also, a wise king either ought not to give to suche, or giving any, the occasion ought to be either for rewarde of some worthy dede, or else for the desire to kepe suche a kinde of man, as well in peace as in warre. And bicause you alledged me, I will make ensample upon my self, and saie that I never used the warre as an arte, for as muche as my arte, is to governe my subjectes, and to defende them, and to be able to defende them, to love peace, and to know how to make warre, and my kinge not so muche to rewarde and esteeme me, for my knowledge in the warre, as for the knowledge that I have to councel him in peace. Then a king ought not to desire to have about him, any that is not of this condicion if he be wise, and prudently minde to governe: for that, that if he shal have about him either to muche lovers of peace, or to much lovers of warre, they shall make him to erre. I cannot in this my firste reasoning, and according to my purpose saie more, and when this suffiseth you not, it is mete, you seke of them that may satisfie you better. You maie now verie well understand, how difficulte it is to bringe in use the auncient maners in the presente warres, and what preparations are mete for a wise man to make, and what occasions ought to be loked for, to be able to execute it. But by and by, you shall know these things better, if this reasoning make you not werie, conferring what so ever partes of the auncient orders hath ben, to the maners nowe presente.

Cosimo. If we desired at the first to here your reason of these thinges, truly thesame whiche hetherto you have spoken, hath doubled our desire: wherefore we thanke you for that we have hard, and the rest, we crave of you to here.

Fabricio. Seyng that it is so your pleasure, I will begin to intreate of this matter from the beginning, to the intent it maye be better understode, being able by thesame meane, more largely to declare it. The ende of him that wil make warre, is to be able to fight with every enemy in the fielde and to be able to overcum an armie. To purpose to doe this, it is convenient to ordeine an hoost. To ordein an hoost, their must be found menne, armed, ordered, and as well in the small, as in the great orders exercised, to knowe howe to kepe araie, and to incampe, so that after bringing them unto the enemie, either standing or marching, they maie know how to behave themselves valiantly. In this thing consisteth all the industrie of the warre on the lande, whiche is the most necessarie, and the most honorablest, for he that can wel order a fielde against the enemie, the other faultes that he should make in the affaires of warre, wilbe borne with: but he that lacketh this knowledge, although that in other particulars he be verie good, he shal never bring a warre to honor: for as muche as a fielde that thou winnest, lesing? img 94 doeth cancell all other thy evill actes: so like wise lesing it, all thinges well done of thee before, remaine vaine. Therfore, beyng necessarie first to finde the menne, it is requiset to come to the choise of them. They whiche unto the warre have given rule, will that the menne be chosen out of temperate countries, to the intente they may have hardines, and prudence, for as muche as the hote countrey, bredes prudente men and not hardy, the colde, hardy, and not prudente. This rule is good to be geven, to one that were prince of all the world, bicause it is lawfull for him to choose men out of those places, whiche he shall thinke beste. But minding to give a rule, that every one may use, it is mete to declare, that everie common weale, and every kingdome, ought to choose their souldiours out of their owne countrie, whether it be hote, colde, or temperate: for that it is scene by olde ensamples, how that in every countrie with exercise, their is made good souldiours: bicause where nature lacketh, the industry supplieth, the which in this case is worthe more, then nature, and taking them in other places, you shal not have of the choise, for choise is as much to saie, as the best of a province, and to have power to chuse those that will not, as well as those that wil serve. Wherfore, you muste take your choise in those places, that are subjecte unto you, for that you cannot take whome you liste, in the countries that are not yours, but you muste take suche as will goe with you.

Cosimo. Yet there maie bee of those, that will come, taken and lefte, and therefore, thei maie be called chosen.

Oute of what countrie is best to chuse souldiours to make a good election.

Fabuicio. You saie the truthe in a certaine maner, but consider the faultes, whiche soche a chosen manne hath in himselfe, for that also many times it hapneth, that he is not a chosen manne. For those that are not thy subjectes, and whiche willyngly doe serve, are not of the beste, but rather of the worste of a Province, for as moche as if any be sclanderous, idell, unruly, without Religion, fugetive from the rule of their fathers, blasphemours, Dise plaiers, in every condicion evill brought up, bee those, whiche will serve, whose customes cannot be more contrarie, to a true and good servise: Albeit, when there bee offered unto you, so many of soche men, as come to above the nomber, that you have appoincted, you maie chuse them: but the matter beyng naught, the choise is not possible to be good: also, many times it chaunceth, that thei be not so many, as will make up the nomber, whereof you have nede, so that beyng constrained to take them al, it commeth to passe, that thei cannot then bee called chosen men, but hired Souldiours. With this disorder the armies of Italie, are made now a daies, and in other places, except in Almaine, bicause there thei doe not hire any by commaundemente of the Prince, but accordyng to the will of them, that are disposed to serve. Then consider now, what maners of those aunciente armies, maie bee brought into an armie of men, put together by like waies.

Cosimo. What waie ought to bee used then?

Fabricio. The same waie that I saied, to chuse them of their owne subjectes, and with the auethoritie of the Prince.

Cosmo. In the chosen, shall there bee likewise brought in any auncient facion?

Fabricio. You know well enough that ye: when he that should commaunde theim, were their Prince, or ordinarie lorde, whether he were made chief, or as a Citezein, and for the same tyme Capitaine, beyng a common weale, otherwise it is harde to make any thyng good.

Cosimo. Why?

Fabricio. I will tell you a nane: For this time I will that this suffise you, that it cannot be wrought well by other waie.

Whether it Be Better to Take Menne Oute of Townes or out of the Countrie to Serve.

Cosimo. Having then to make this choyse of men in their owne countries, whether judge you that it be better to take them oute of the citie, or out of the countrie?

Fabricio. Those that have written of such matters, doe all agree, that it is best to chuse them out of the countrie, being men accustomed to no ease, nurished in labours, used to stonde in the sunne, to flie the shadow, knowing how to occupy the spade, to make a diche, to carrie a burden, and to bee without any deceite, and without malisiousnes. But in this parte my opinion should be, that beyng two sortes of souldiours, on foote, and on horsebacke, that those on foote, should be chosen out of the countrie, and those on horseback, oute of the Cities.

Of what age souldiours ought to bee chosen.

Cosimo. Of what age would you choose them?

Fabricio. I would take them, when I had to make a newe armie, from xvii. to xl. yeres: when it were made alredy, and I had to restore them, of xvii. alwaies.

Cosimo. I doe not understonde well this distinction.

Fabricio. I shall tell you: when I should ordaine an hooste to make warre, where were no hooste alredy, it should be necessarie to chuse all those men, which were most fitte and apte for the warre, so that they were of servisable age, that I might bee able to instructe theim, as by me shalbe declared: but when I would make my choise of menne in places, where a powre were alredy prepared, for suppliyng of thesame, I would take them of xvii. yeres: for as much as the other of more age be alredy chosen and apoincted.

Cosimo. Then woulde you prepare a power like to those whiche is in our countrie?

Fabricio. Ye truly, it is so that I would arme them, Captaine them, exercise and order them in a maner, whiche I cannot tell, if you have ordred them so.

Cosimo. Then do you praise the keping of order?

Fabricio. Wherefore would you that I should dispraise it?

Cosimo. Bicause many wise menne have alwaies blamed it.

Fabricio. You speake against all reason, to saie that a wise man blameth order, he maie bee well thought wise, and be nothyng so.

Cosimo. The naughtie profe, which it hath alwaies, maketh us to have soche opinion thereof.

Fabricio. Take hede it be not your fault, and not the kepyng of order, the whiche you shall knowe, before this reasonyng be ended.

Cosimo. You shall doe a thyng moste thankfull, yet I will saie concernyng thesame, that thei accuse it, to the entente you maie the better justifie it. Thei saie thus, either it is unprofitable, and we trustyng on the same, shall make us to lese our state, or it shall be verteous, and by thesame meane, he that governeth may easely deprive us thereof. Thei alledge the Romaines, who by meane of their owne powers, loste their libertie. Thei alledge the Venicians, and the Frenche king, whiche Venicians, bicause thei will not be constrained, to obeie one of their owne Citezeins, use the power of straungers: and the Frenche kyng hath disarmed his people, to be able more easely to commaunde them, but thei whiche like not the ordinaunces, feare moche more the unprofitablenesse, that thei suppose maie insue thereby, then any thyng els: the one cause whiche thei allege is, bicause thei are unexperte: The other, for that thei have to serve par force: for asmoche as thei saie, that the aged bee not so dissiplinable, nor apte to learne the feate of armes, and that by force, is doen never any thyng good.

By what meanes souldiours bee made bolde and experte.

Fabricio. All these reasons that you have rehearsed, be of men, whiche knoweth the thyng full little, as I shall plainly declare. And firste, concernyng the unprofitablenesse, I tell you, that there is no service used in any countrie more profitable, then the service by the Subjectes of thesame nor thesame service cannot bee prepared, but in this maner: and for that this nedeth not to be disputed of, I will not lese moche tyme: bicause al thensamples of auncient histores, make for my purpose, and for that thei alledge the lacke of experience, and to use constraint: I saie how it is true, that the lacke of experience, causeth lacke of courage, and constrainte, maketh evill contentacion: but courage, and experience thei are made to gette, with the maner of armyng theim, exercisyng, and orderyng theim, as in proceadyng of this reasonyng, you shall heare. But concernyng constrainte, you ought to understande, that the menne, whiche are conducted to warfare, by commaundement of their Prince, thei ought to come, neither altogether forced, nor altogether willyngly, for as moche as to moche willyngnesse, would make thinconveniencies, where I told afore, that he should not be a chosen manne, and those would be fewe that would go: and so to moche constraint, will bring forth naughtie effectes. Therefore, a meane ought to be taken, where is not all constrainte, nor all willingnesse: but beyng drawen of a respecte, that thei have towardes their Prince, where thei feare more the displeasure of thesame, then the presente paine: and alwaies it shall happen to be a constrainte, in maner mingled with willingnesse, that there cannot growe soche evil contentacion, that it make evill effectes. Yet I saie not for all this, that it cannot bee overcome, for that full many tymes, were overcome the Romaine armies, and the armie of Aniball was overcome, so that it is seen, that an armie cannot be ordained so sure, that it cannot be overthrowen. Therefore, these your wise men, ought not to measure this unprofitablenesse, for havyng loste ones, but to beleve, that like as thei lese, so thei maie winne, and remeadie the occasion of the losse: and when thei shall seke this thei shall finde, that it hath not been through faulte of the waie, but of the order, whiche had not his perfeccion and as I have saied, thei ought to provide, not with blamyng the order, but with redressing it, the whiche how it ought to be doen, you shall understande, from poinct to poinct. Concernyng the doubte, leste soche ordinaunces, take not from thee thy state, by meane of one, whiche is made hedde therof, I answere, that the armure on the backes of citezeins, or subjectes, given by the disposicion of order and lawe, did never harme, but rather alwaies it doeth good, and mainteineth the citee, moche lenger in suretie, through helpe of this armure, then without. Rome continued free CCCC. yeres, and was armed. Sparta viii.C. Many other citees have been disarmed, and have remained free, lesse then xl. For as moche as citees have nede of defence, and when thei have no defence of their owne, thei hire straungers, and the straunges defence, shall hurte moche soner the common weale, then their owne: bicause thei be moche easier to be corrupted, and a citezein that becommeth mightie, maie moche soner usurpe, and more easely bryng his purpose to passe, where the people bee disarmed, that he seketh to oppresse: besides this, a citee ought to feare a greate deale more, twoo enemies then one. Thesame citee that useth straungers power, feareth at one instant the straunger, whiche it hireth, and the Citezein: and whether this feare ought to be, remember thesame, whiche I rehearsed a little a fore of Frances Sforza. That citee, whiche useth her own proper power, feareth no man, other then onely her owne Citezein. But for all the reasons that maie bee saied, this shall serve me, that never any ordeined any common weale, or Kyngdome, that would not thinke, that thei theim selves, that inhabite thesame, should with their sweardes defende it.

And if the Venicians had been so wise in this, as in all their other orders, thei should have made a new Monarchie in the world, whom so moche the more deserve blame, havyng been armed of their first giver of lawes: for havyng no dominion on the lande, thei wer armed on the sea, where thei made their warre vertuously, and with weapons in their handes, increased their countrie. But when thei were driven to make warre on the lande, to defende Vicenza, where thei ought to have sent one of their citezens, to have fought on the lande, thei hired for their capitain, the Marques of Mantua: this was thesame foolishe acte, whiche cut of their legges, from climyng into heaven, and from enlargyng their dominion: and if thei did it, bicause thei beleved that as thei knewe, how to make warre on the Sea, so thei mistrusted theim selves, to make it on the lande, it was a mistruste not wise: for as moche as more easely, a capitain of the sea, whiche is used to fight with the windes, with the water, and with men, shall become a Capitaine of the lande, where he shall fight with men onely, then a capitaine of the lande, to become a capitain of the sea. The Romanies knowyng how to fight on the lande, and on the sea, commyng to warre, with the Carthaginens, whiche were mightie on the sea, hired not Grekes, or Spaniardes, accustomed to the sea, but thei committed thesame care, to their Citezeins, whiche thei sent on the land, and thei overcame. If thei did it, for that one of their citezeins should not become a tiraunt, it was a feare smally considered: for that besides thesame reasons, whiche to this purpose, a little afore I have rehearsed, if a Citezein with the powers on the sea, was never made a tiraunt in a citee standyng in the sea, so moche the lesse he should have been able to accomplishe this with the powers of the lande: whereby thei ought to se that the weapons in the handes of their

Citezeins, could not make tirantes: but the naughtie orders of the governement, whiche maketh tirannie in a citee, and thei havyng good governement, thei nede not to feare their owne weapons: thei toke therefore an unwise waie, the whiche hath been occasion, to take from them moche glorie, and moche felicitie. Concernyng the erroure, whiche the kyng of Fraunce committeth not kepyng instructed his people in the warre, the whiche those your wise men alledge for ensample, there is no man, (his particulare passions laied a side) that doeth not judge this fault, to be in thesame kyngdome, and this negligence onely to make hym weake. But I have made to greate a digression, and peradventure am come out of my purpose, albeit I have doen it to aunswere you, and to shewe you, that in no countrie, there can bee made sure foundacion, for defence in other powers but of their owne subjectes: and their own power, cannot be prepared otherwise, then by waie of an ordinaunce, nor by other waie, to induce the facion of an armie in any place, nor by other meane to ordein an instruction of warfare. If you have red the orders, whiche those first kynges made in Rome, and inespecially Servio Tullo, you shall finde that the orders of the Classi is no other, then an ordinaunce, to bee able at a sodaine, to bryng together an armie, for defence of thesame citee. But let us retourne to our choise, I saie againe, that havyng to renewe an olde order, I would take them of xvii. havyng to make a newe armie, I would take them of all ages, betwene xvii. and xl. to be able to warre straight waie.

Of what science soldiours ought to bee chosen.

Cosimo. Would you make any difference, of what science you would chuse them?

Fabricio. The aucthours, which have written of the arte of warre, make difference, for that thei will not, that there bee taken Foulers, Fishers, Cookes, baudes, nor none that use any science of voluptuousnesse. But thei will, that there bee taken Plowmen, Ferrars, Smithes, Carpenters, Buchars, Hunters, and soche like: but I would make little difference, through conjecture of the science, concernyng the goodnesse of the man, notwithstandyng, in as moche as to be able with more profite to use theim, I would make difference, and for this cause, the countrie men, which are used to till the grounde, are more profitable then any other. Next to whom be Smithes, Carpentars, Ferrars, Masons, wherof it is profitable to have enough: for that their occupacions, serve well in many thynges: beyng a thyng verie good to have a souldiour, of whom maie be had double servise.

Howe to chose a souldiour.

Cosimo. Wherby doe thei knowe those, that be, or are not sufficient to serve.

Fabricio. I will speake of the maner of chusing a new ordinaunce, to make an armie after, for that parte of this matter, doeth come also to be reasoned of, in the election, which should be made for the replenishing, or restoring of an old ordinaunce. I saie therfore, that the goodnesse of one, whiche thou muste chuse for a Souldiour, is knowen either by experience, thorough meane of some of his worthy doynges, or by conjecture. The proofe of vertue, cannot be founde in men whiche are chosen of newe, and whiche never afore have ben chosen, and of these are

founde either fewe or none, in the ordinaunce that of newe is ordeined. It is necessarie therefore, lackyng this experience, to runne to the conjecture, whiche is taken by the yeres, by the occupacion, and by the personage: of those two first, hath been reasoned, there remaineth to speake of the thirde. And therefore, I saie how some have willed, that the souldiour bee greate, emongest whom was Pirrus. Some other have chosen theim onely, by the lustinesse of the body, as Cesar did: whiche lustinesse of bodie and mynde, is conjectured by the composicion of the members, and of the grace of the countenaunce: and therefore, these that write saie, that thei would have the iyes lively and cherefull, the necke full of sinowes, the breaste large, the armes full of muscullės, the fingers long, little beallie, the flankes rounde, the legges and feete drie: whiche partes are wont alwayes to make a manne nimble and strong, whiche are twoo thynges, that in a souldiour are sought above al other. Regarde ought to bee had above all thynges, to his customes, and that in hym bee honestie, and shame: otherwise, there shall bee chosen an instrumente of mischief, and a beginnyng of corrupcion: for that lette no manne beleve that in the dishoneste educacion, and filthy minde, there maie take any vertue, whiche is in any parte laudable. And I thinke it not superfluous, but rather I beleve it to bee necessarie, to the entente you maie the better understande, the importaunce of this chosen, to tell you the maner that the Romaine Consuls, in the beginnyng of their rule, observed in the chosing of their Romain legions: in the whiche choise of men, bicause thesame legions were mingled with old souldiours and newe, consideryng the continuall warre thei kepte, thei might in their choise procede, with the experince of the old, and with the conjecture of the newe: and this ought to be noted, that these men be chosen, either to serve incontinently, or to exercise theim incontinently, and after to serve when nede should require. But my intencion is to shew you, how an armie maie be prepared in the countrie, where there is no warlike discipline: in which countrie, chosen men cannot be had, to use them straight waie, but there, where the custome is to levie armies, and by meane of the Prince, thei maie then well bee had, as the Romaines observed, and as is observed at this daie emong the Suisers: bicause in these chosen, though there be many newe menne, there be also so many of the other olde Souldiours, accustomed to serve in the warlike orders, where the newe mingled together with the olde, make a bodie united and good, notwithstanding, that themperours after, beginning the staciones of ordinarie Souldiours, had appoincted over the newe souldiours, whiche were called tironi, a maister to exercise theim, as appeareth in the life of Massimo the Emperour. The whiche thyng, while Rome was free, not onely in the armies, but in the citee was ordeined: and the exercises of warre, beyng accustomed in thesame, where the yong men did exercise, there grewe, that beyng chosen after to goe into warre, thei were so used in the fained exercise of warfare, that thei could easely worke in the true: but those Emperours havyng after put doune these exercises, thei wer constrained to use the waies, that I have shewed you. Therefore, comyng to the maner of the chosen Romain, I saie that after the Romain Consulles (to whom was appoincted the charge of the warre) had taken the rule, myndyng to ordeine their armies, for that it was the custome, that either of them should have twoo Legions of Romaine menne, whiche was the strength of their armies, thei created xxiiii. Tribunes of warre, and thei appoincted sixe for every Legion, whom did thesame office, whiche those doe now a daies, that we call Conestables: thei made after to come together, all the Romain men apte to beare weapons and thei put the Tribunes of every Legion, seperate the one from the other. Afterwarde, by lot thei drewe the Tribes, of whiche thei had firste to make the chosen, and of thesame Tribe thei chose fower of the best, of whiche was chosen one of the Tribunes, of the first Legion, and of the other three was chosen, one of the Tribunes of the second Legion, of the other two there was chosen one of the Tribunes of the third, and the same last fell to the fowerth Legion. After these iiij, thei chose other fower, of which, first one was chosen of the Tribunes of the seconde Legion, the seconde of those of the thirde, the thirde of those of the fowerth, the fowerth remained to the first. After, thei chose other fower, the first chose the thirde, the second the fowerth, the thirde the fiveth, the fowerth remained to the seconde: and thus thei varied successively, this maner of chosyng, so that the election came to be equall, and the Legions wer gathered together: and as afore we saied, this choise might bee made to use straighte waie, for that thei made them of men, of whom a good parte were experiensed in the verie warfare in deede, and all in the fained exercised, and thei might make this choise by conjecture, and by experience. But where a power must be ordeined of newe, and for this to chuse them out of hande, this chosen cannot be made, saving by conjecture, whiche is taken by consideryng their ages and their likelinesse.

Cosimo. I beleve all to be true, as moche as of you hath been spoken: but before that you procede to other reasonyng, I woll aske of you one thing, which you have made me to remember: saiyng that the chosen, that is to be made where men were not used to warre, ought to be made by conjecture: for asmoche as I have heard some men, in many places dispraise our ordinaunce, and in especially concernyng the nomber, for that many saie, that there ought to bee taken lesse nomber, whereof is gotten this profite, that thei shall be better and better chosen, and men shal not be so moche diseased, so that there maie bee given them some rewarde, whereby thei maie bee more contented, and better bee commaunded, whereof I would understande in this parte your opinion, and whether you love better the greate nomber, than the little, and what waie you would take to chuse theim in the one, and in the other nomber.

Fabricio. Without doubte it is better, and more necessary, the great nomber, then the little: but to speake more plainly, where there cannot be ordeined a great nomber of men, there cannot be ordeined a perfect ordinaunce: and I will easely confute all the reasons of them propounded. I saie therefore firste, that the lesse nomber where is many people, as is for ensample Tuscane, maketh not that you have better, nor that the chosen be more excellent, for that myndyng in chosing the menne, to judge them by experience, there shall be founde in thesame countrie moste fewe, whom experience should make provable, bothe for that fewe hath been in warre, as also for that of those, mooste fewe have made triall, whereby thei might deserve to bee chosen before the other: so that he whiche ought in like places to chuse, it is mete he leave a parte the experience, and take them by conjecture. Then being brought likewise into soche necessitie, I would understande, if there come before me twentie young men of good stature, with what rule I ought to take, or to leave any: where without doubte, I beleve that every man will confesse, how it is lesse errour to take them al, to arme theim and exercise theim, beyng not able to knowe, whiche of theim is beste, and to reserve to make after more certaine chosen, when in practisyng theim with exercise, there shall be knowen those of moste spirite, and of moste life: which considered, the chusing in this case a fewe, to have them better, is altogether naught.

Concernyng diseasing lesse the countrie, and men, I saie that the ordinaunce, either evill or little that it bee, causeth not any disease, for that this order doeth not take menne from any of their businesse, it bindeth them not, that thei cannot go to doe any of their affaires: for that it bindeth them onely in the idell daies, to assemble together, to exercise them, the whiche thyng doeth not hurt, neither to the countrie, nor to the men, but rather to yong men it shall bryng delite: For that where vilie on the holy daies thei stande idell in tipplyng houses, thei will go for pleasure to those exercises, for that the handlyng of weapons, as it is a goodly spectacle, so unto yong men it is pleasaunt. Concernyng to bee able to paie the lesse nomber, and for this to kepe theim more obediente, and more contented, I answere, how there cannot be made an ordinaunce of so fewe, whiche maie be in maner continually paied, where thesame paiment of theirs maie satisfie them. As for ensample, if there were ordeined a power of v. thousande men, for to paie them after soche sorte, that it might be thought sufficient, to content them, it shal bee convenient to give theim at least, ten thousaunde crounes the moneth: first, this nomber of men are not able to make an armie, this paie is intolerable to a state, and of the other side, it is not sufficiente to kepe men contented, and bounde to be able to serve at al times: so that in doyng this, there shall be spent moche, and a small power kept, whiche shall not be sufficient to defend thee, or to doe any enterprise of thine. If thou shouldest give theim more, or shouldest take more, so moche more impossibilitie it should be, for thee to paie theim: if thou shouldest give them lesse, or should take lesse, so moche the lesse contentacion should be in them, or so moche the lesse profite thei shal bring thee. Therfore, those that reason of makyng an ordinaunce, and whilest thei tary at home to paie them, thei reason of a thing either impossible, or unprofitable, but it is necessarie to paie them, when thei are taken up to be led to the warre: albeit, though soche order should somewhat disease those, in time of peace, that are appoincted in thesame, which I se not how, there is for recompence all those benefites, whiche a power brynges, that is ordeined in a countrie: for that without thesame, there is nothyng sure. I conclude, that he that will have the little nomber, to be able to paie them, or for any of the other causes alledged of you, doeth not understande, for that also it maketh for my opinion, that every nomber shall deminishe in thy handes, through infinite impedimentes, whiche men have: so that the little nomber shall tourne to nothing: again havyng thordinaunce greate, thou maiest at thy pleasure use fewe of many, besides this, it must serve thee in deede, and in reputacion and alwaies the great nomber shall give thee moste reputacion. More over, makyng the ordinaunce to kepe menne exercised, if thou appoincte a fewe nomber of men in many countries, the handes of men bee so farre a sonder, the one from the other, that thou canst not without their moste grevous losse, gather them together to exercise them, and without this exercise, the ordinaunce is unprofitable, as hereafter shall be declared.

Cosimo. It suffiseth upon this my demaunde, that whiche you have saied: but I desire now, that you declare me an other doubt. Thei saie, that soche a multitude of armed men, will make confusion, discension and disorder in the countrie where thei are.

How to provid againste soche inconveniences as souldiours maie cause.

Fabricio. This is an other vaine opinion, the cause wherof, I shall tell you: soche as are ordeined to serve in the warres, maie cause disorder in twoo maners, either betwene them selves, or against other, whiche thinges moste easely maie be withstode, where the order of it self, should not withstande it: for that concernyng the discorde emong theim selves, this order taketh it waie, and doeth not nourishe it, for that in orderyng them, you give them armour and capitaines. If the countrie where you ordein them, bee so unapte for the warre, that there are not armours emong the men of thesame, and that thei bee so united, that thei have no heddes, this order maketh theim moche fearser against the straunger, but it maketh them not any thyng the more disunited, for that men well ordered, feare the lawe beyng armed, as well as unarmed, nor thei can never alter, if the capitaines, which you give them, cause not the alteracion, and the waie to make this, shall be tolde now: but if the countrie where you ordein them, be warlike and disunited, this order onely shal be occasion to unite them: bicause this order giveth them armours profitable for the warre, and heddes, extinguishers of discencion: where their owne armours bee unprofitable for the warres, and their heddes nourishers of discorde. For that so sone as any in thesame countrie is offended, he resorteth by and by to his capitain to make complaint, who for to maintain his reputacion, comforteth hym to revengement not to peace. To the contrary doeth the publike hed, so that by this meanes, thoccasion of discorde is taken awaie, and the occasion of union is prepared, and the provinces united and effeminated, gette utilitie, and maintain union: the disunited and discencious, doe agree, and thesame their fearsnesse, which is wont disordinately to worke, is tourned into publike utilitie. To minde to have them, to doe no hurt against other, it ought to bee considered, that thei cannot dooe this, except by meane of the heddes, whiche governe them. To will that the heddes make no disorder, it is necessarie to have care, that thei get not over them to much auctoritie. And you must consider that this auctoritie, is gotten either by nature, or by accidente: and as to nature, it behoveth to provide, that he which is boren in one place, be not apoincted to the men billed in the same, but be made hedde of those places, where he hath not any naturall aquaintance: and as to the accident, the thing ought to be ordeined in suche maner, that every yere the heddes maie be changed from governement to goverment: for as muche as the continuall auctoritie over one sorte of menne, breedeth among them so muche union, that it maie turne easely to the prejudice of the Prince: whiche permutations howe profitable they be to those who have used theim, and hurtefull to them that have not observed theim, it is well knowen by the kingdome of the Assirians, and by the Empire of the Romaines: where is seene, that the same kingdome indured a M. yeres without tumulte, and without any Civill warre: whiche preceded not of other, then of the permutations, whiche from place to place everie yere thesame Capitaines made, unto whome were apoincted the charge of the Armies. Nor for any other occasion in the Romaine Empire, after the bloud of Cesar was extinguished, there grewe so many civill warres, betwene the Capitaines of the hostes, and so many conspiracies of the forsaied capitaines against the Emperours, not onely kepyng continually still those capitaines alwayes in one governement. And if in some of those firste Emperoures, of those after, whom helde the Empire with reputacion, as Adriane, Marcus, Severus, and soche like, there had been so moche foresight, that thei had brought this custome of chaungyng the capitaines in thesame Empire, without doubte it should have made theim more quiete, and more durable: For that the Capitaines should have had lesse occasion to make tumultes, the Emperours lesse cause to feare, and the senate in the lackes of the successions, should have had in the election of the Emperour, more aucthoritie, and by consequence should have been better: but the naughtie custome, either for ignoraunce, or through the little diligence of menne, neither for the wicked, nor good ensamples, can be taken awaie.

Cosimo. I cannot tell, if with my questionyng, I have as it were led you out of your order, bicause from the chusyng of men, we be entred into an other matter, and if I had not been a little before excused, I should thinke to deserve some reprehension.

The nomber of horsemen, that the romanies chose for a legion, and for a consailes armie.

Fabricio. Let not this disquiete you, for that all this reasonyng was necessary, myndyng to reason of the ordinaunce, the which beyng blamed of many, it was requsite to excuse it, willyng to have this first parte of chusyng men to be alowed. But now before I discend to the other partes, I will reason of the choise of men on horsebacke. Of the antiquitie, these were made of the moste richeste, havyng regard bothe to the yeres, and to the qualitie of the man, and thei chose CCC. for a Legion, so that the Romain horse, in every Consulles armie, passed not the nomber of vi. C.

Cosimo. Would you make an ordinaunce of hors, to exercise them at home, and to use their service when nede requires?

The choosing and ordering of horsemen, that is to be observed at this present.

Fabricio. It is most necessary, and it cannot be doen otherwise, minding to have the power, that it be the owne proper, and not to purpose to take of those, which make thereof an art.

Cosimo. How would you choose them?

Fabricio. I would imitate the Romans, I would take of the richest, I would give them heads or chief Captains, in the same manner, as nowadays to other is given, and I would arm them and exercise them.

Cosimo. To these should it be well to give some provision?

Fabricio. Yea marie, but so much only as is necessary to keep the horse, for as much as bringing to thy subjects expenses, they might justly complain of thee, therefore it should be necessary, to pay them their charges of their horse.

Cosimo. What number would you make? and how would you arme them?

Fabricio. You pass into another matter. I will tell you in convenient place, which shall be when I have told you, how footmen ought to be armed, and how a power of men is prepared, for a day of battle.

The Second Booke

Howe the Romaines armed their souldiers and what weapons thei used.

I beleeve that it is necessarye, men being founde, to arme them, and minding to doo this, I suppose that it is a needefull thing to examine, what armoure the antiquitie used, and of the same to chose the best. The Romanes devided their foote men in heavie and lighte armed: Those that were light armed, they called by the name of Veliti: Under this name were understoode all those that threwe with Slinges, shot with Crossebowes, cast Dartes, and they used the most parte of them for their defence, to weare on their heade a Murion, with a Targaet on their arme: they fought out of the orders, and farre of from the heavie armed, which did weare a head peece, that came downe to their shoulders, a Corselet, which with the tases came downe to the knees, and they had the legges and armes, covered with greaves, and vambraces, with a targaet on the left arme, a yarde and a halfe long, and three quarters of a yarde brode, whiche had a hoope of Iron upon it, to bee able to sustaine a blowe, and an other under, to the intente, that it being driven to the earth, it should not breake: for to offende, they had girte on their left flanke a swoorde, the length of a yearde and a naile, on their righte side, a Dagger: they had a darte in every one of their handes, the which they called Pilo, and in the beginning of the fight, they threwe those at the enemie. This was the ordering, and importaunce of the armours of the Romanes, by the which they possessed all the world. And although some of these ancient writers gave them, besides the foresayde weapons, a staffe in their hande like unto a Partasen, I cannot tell howe a heavy staff, may of him that holdeth a Targaet be occupied: for that to handle it with both hands, the Targaet should bee an impediment, and to occupye the same with one hande, there can be done no good therewith, by reason of the weightynesse thereof: besides this, to faight in the strong, and in the orders with such long kinde of weapon, it is unprofitable, except in the first front, where they have space enough, to thrust out all the staffe, which in the orders within, cannot be done, for that the nature of the battaile (as in the order of the same, I shall tell you) is continually to throng together, which although it be an inconvenience, yet in so doing they fear lesse, then to stande wide, where the perill is most evident, so that all the weapons, which passe in length a yarde and a halfe, in the throng, be unprofitable: for that, if a man have the Partasen, and will occupye it with both handes, put case that the Targaet let him not, he can not hurte with the same an enemy, whom is upon him, if he take it with one hande, to the intent to occupy also the Targaet, being not able to take it, but in the middest, there remayneth so much of the staff behind, that those which are behinde him, shall let him to welde it. And whether it were true, either that the Romans had not this Partasen, or that having it, did little good withal, read all the battailes, in the historye thereof, celebrated of Titus Livius, and you shall see in the same, most seldom times made mencion of Partasens, but rather alwaies he saieth, that the Dartes being thrown, they laid their hands on their sweardes. Therefore I will leave this staffe, and observe, concerning the Romanes, the swoorde for to hurte, and for defense the Targaet, with the other armours aforesaide.

A brave and a terrible thing to the enemies

The Greekes did not arme them selves so heavyly, for their defense, as the Romans dyd: but for to offend the enemies, they grounded more on their staves, then on their swoordes, and in especiallye the Fallangye of Macedonia, which used staves, that they called Sarisse, seven yardes and a halfe long, with the which they opened the rankes of their enemies, and they keept the orders in their Fallangy. And although some writers saie, that they had also the Targaet, I can not tell (by the reasons aforesayde) howe the Sarisse and they coulde stande together. Besides this, in the battaile that Paulus Emilius made, with Persa king of Macedonia, I do not remember, that there is made any mention of Targaettes, but only of the Sarisse, and of the difficultie that the Romane armie had, to overcome them: so that I conjecture, that a Macedonicall Fallange, was no other wise, then is now a dayes a battaile of Suizzers, the whiche in their Pikes have all their force, and all their power. The Romanes did garnish (besides the armours) the footemen with feathers; the whiche thinges makes the fight of an armie to the friendes goodly, to the enemies terrible. The armour of the horsemen, in the same first Romane antiquitie, was a rounde Targaet, and they had their head armed, and the rest unarmed: They had a swoorde and a staffe, with an Iron head onely before, long and small: whereby it happened, that they were not able to staye the Targaet, and the staffe in the incountring broke, and they through being unarmed, were subjecte to hurtes: after, in processe of time, they armed them as the footemen, albeit they used the Targaette muche shorter, square, and the staffe more stiffe, and with twoo heades, to the entente, that breaking one of the heades, they mighte prevaile with the other. With these armours as well on foote, as on horsebacke, the Romanes conquered all the worlde, and it is to be beleeved, by the fruiet thereof, whiche is seene, that they were the beste appointed armies, that ever were: and Titus Livius in his history, doeth testifie verye often, where comming to comparison with the enemies armies, he saieth: But the Romanes, by vertue, by the kinde of their armours, and piactise in the service of warre, were superiours: and therfore I have more particularly reasoned of the armours of conquerours, then of the conquered. But nowe mee thikes good, to reason onelye of the manner of arming men at this presente. Footemen have for their defence, a breast plate, and for to offende, a launce, sixe yardes and three quarters long, which is called a pike, with a swoorde on their side, rather rounde at the poinct, then sharpe. This is the ordinarie arming of footemen nowe a dayes, for that fewe there be, which have their legges armed, and their armes, the heade none, and those fewe, beare insteede of a Pike, a Halberde, the staffe whereof as you know, is twoo yardes and a quarter long, and it hath the Iron made like an axe. Betweene them, they have Harkebutters, the which with the violence of the fire, do the same office, which in olde time the slingers did, and the Crosseboweshoters. This maner of arming, was found out by the Dutchemen, inespeciallye of Suizzers, whom being poore, and desirous to live free, they were, and be constrayned to fight, with the ambition of the Princes of Almaine, who being riche, were able to keepe horse, the which the same people could not do for povertye. Wherby it grewe, that being on foote, minding to defende them selves from the enemies, that were on horsebacke, it behooveth them to seeke of the aunciente orders, and to finde weapons, whiche from the furie of horses, should defende them: This necessitie hath made either to be maintayned, or to bee founde of them the aunciente orders, without whiche, as everye prudente man affirmeth, the footemen is altogether unprofitable. Therefore, they tooke for their weapon the Pike, a moste profitable weapon, not only to withstande horses, but to overcome them: and the Dutchemen have by vertue of these weapons, and of these orders, taken such boldnesse, that XV. or XX. thousande of them, will assault the greatest nomber of horse that maye be: and of this, there hath beene experience enough within this XXV. yeres. And the insamples of their vertue hath bene so mightie, grounded upon these weapons, and these orders, that sence King Charles passed into Italie, everye nation hath imitated them: so that the Spanish armies, are become into most great reputation.

Cosimo. Which maner of arming, do you praise moste, either these Dutchemens, or the auncient Romanes?

Whether the Romanes maner in arming of men, be better then the arming of men, that is used nowe a daies

Fabricio. The Romane without doubte, and I will tell the commoditie, and the discommoditie of the one, and the other. The Dutche footemen, are able to withstande, and overcome the horses: they bee moste speedie to marche, and to be set in araye, being not laden with armours: of the other part, they be subjecte to all blowes, both farre of, and at hande: because they be unarmed, they bee unprofitable unto the battaile on the lande, and to everye fighte, where is strong resistaunce. But the Romanes withstoode, and overcame the horses, as well as the Dutchemen, they were safe from blowes at hande, and farre of, being covered with armours: they were also better able to charge, and better able to sustaine charges, having Targaettes: they might more aptly in the preace fight with the swoorde, then these with the Pike, and though the Dutchemen have likewise swoordes, yet being without Targaets, they become in suche case unprofitable: The Romanes might safelye assault townes, having their bodies cleane covered with armour, and being better able to cover themselves with their Targaettes. So that they had no other incommoditie, then the waightynesse of their armours, and the pain to cary them: the whiche thinges thei overcame, with accustomyng the body to diseases, and with hardenyng it, to bee able to indure labour. And you knowe, how that in thinges accustomed, men suffer no grief. And you have to understand this, that the footemen maie be constrained, to faight with footemen, and with horse, and alwaies those be unprofitable, whiche cannot either sustain the horses, or beyng able to sustain them, have notwithstandyng neede to feare the footemen, whiche be better armed, and better ordeined then thei. Now if you consider the Duchemen, and the Romaines, you shall finde in the Duchemen activitie (as we have said) to overcome the horses, but greate dissavauntage, when thei faighte with menne, ordeined as thei them selves are, and armed as the Romaines were: so that there shall be this advauntage more of the one, then of thother, that the Romaines could overcome the men, and the horses, the Duchemen onely the horses.

Cosimo. I would desire, that you would come to some more particulare insample, whereby wee maie better understande.

An ensample whiche proveth that horsemen with staves, cannot prevaile against footemen with pikes, and what great advauntage the armed have, againste the unarmed. The victory of carminvola against the duchemen.

Fabricio. I saie thus, that you shall finde in many places of our histories, the Romain footemen to have overcome innumerable horses, and you shall never finde, that thei have been overcome of men on foote, for default that thei have had in their armour, or thorowe the vantage that the enemie hath had in the armours: For that if the maner of their armyng, should have had defaulte, it had been necessarie, that there should folowe, the one of these twoo thynges, either that findyng soche, as should arme theim better then thei, thei should not have gone still forwardes, with their conquestes, or that thei should have taken the straungers maners, and should have left their owne, and for that it folowed not in the one thing, nor in the other, there groweth that ther maie be easely conjectured, that the maner of their armyng, was better then thesame of any other. It is not yet thus happened to the Duchemen, for that naughtie profe, hath ben seen made them, when soever thei have chaunsed to faight with men on foote prepared, and as obstinate as thei, the whiche is growen of the vauntage, whiche thesame have incountred in thenemies armours. Philip Vicecounte of Milaine, being assaulted of xviii. thousande Suizzers, sent against theim the Counte Carminvola, whiche then was his capitaine. He with sixe thousande horse, and a fewe footemen, went to mete with them, and incounteryng theim, he was repulsed with his moste greate losse: wherby Carminvola as a prudente man, knewe straight waie the puisaunce of the enemies weapons, and how moche against the horses thei prevailed, and the debilitie of the horses, againste those on foote so appoincted: and gatheryng his men together again, he went to finde the Suizzers, and so sone as he was nere them, he made his men of armes, to a light from their horse, and in thesame mane, faightyng with them he slue theim all, excepte three thousande: the whiche seyng them selves to consume, without havyng reamedy, castyng their weapons to the grounde, yelded.

Cosimo. Whereof cometh so moche disavauntage?

The Battailes When Thei Are a Faightyng, Doe Throng Together.

Fabricio. I have a little afore tolde you, but seyng that you have not understoode it, I will rehearse it againe. The Duchemen (as a little before I saied unto you) as it were unarmed, to defende themselves, have to offende, the Pike and the swearde: thei come with these weapons, and with their orders to finde the enemies, whom if thei bee well armed, to defende theim selves, as were the menne of armes of Carminvola, whiche made theim a lighte on foote, thei come with the sweard, and in their orders to find them, and have no other difficultie, then to come nere to the Suizzers, so that thei maie reche them with the sweard, for that so sone as thei have gotten unto them, thei faight safely: for asmoche as the Duch man cannot strike thenemie with the Pike, whom is upon him, for the length of the staffe, wherefore it is conveniente for hym, to put the hande to the sweard, the whiche to hym is unprofitable, he beyng unarmed, and havyng against hym an enemie, that is all armed. Whereby he that considereth the vantage, and the disavantage of the one, and of the other, shall see, how the unarmed, shall have no maner of remeady, and the overcommyng of the firste faight, and to passe the firste poinctes of the Pikes, is not moche difficulte, he that faighteth beyng well armed: for that the battailes go (as you shall better understande, when I have shewed you, how thei are set together) and incounteryng the one the other, of necessitie thei thrust together, after soche sorte, that thei take the one thother by the bosome, and though by the Pikes some bee slaine, or overthrowen, those that remain on their feete, be so many, that thei suffice to obtaine the victorie. Hereof it grewe, that Carminvola overcame them, with so greate slaughter of the Suizzers, and with little losse of his.

Cosimo. Consider that those of Carminvola, were men of armes, whom although thei wer on foote, thei were covered all with stele, and therefore thei wer able to make the profe thei did: so that me thinkes, that a power ought to be armed as thei, mindyng to make the verie same profe.

Fabricio. If you should remember, how I tolde you the Romaines were armed, you would not thynke so: for as moche as a manne, that hath the hedde covered with Iron, the breaste defended of a Corselet, and of a Targaet, the armes and the legges armed, is moche more apt to defende hymself from the Pike, and to enter emong them, then a man of armes on foote. I wil give you a little of a late ensample. There wer come out of Cicelie, into the kyngdome of Naples, a power of Spaniardes, for to go to finde Consalvo, who was besieged in Barlet, of the Frenchemen: there made against theim Mounsier de Vhigni, with his menne of armes, and with aboute fower thousande Duchemen on foote: The Duchemen incountered with their Pikes lowe, and thei opened the power of the Spaniardes: but those beyng holp, by meane of their bucklers and of the agiletie of their bodies, mingled togethers with the Duchemen, so that thei might reche them with the swearde, whereby happened the death, almoste of all theim, and the victorie to the Spaniardes. Every man knoweth, how many Duchemen were slaine in the battaile of Ravenna, the whiche happened by the verie same occasion: for that the Spanishe souldiours, got them within a swerdes length of the Duche souldiours, and thei had destroied them all, if of the Frenche horsemen, the Duchemen on foote, had not been succored: notwithstandyng, the Spaniardes close together, brought themselves into a safe place. I conclude therefore, that a good power ought not onely to be able, to withstande the horses, but also not to have fear of menne on foote, the which (as I have many tymes saied) procedeth of the armours, and of the order.

How to arme men, and what weapons to appoincte theim, after the romaine maner, and duche facion.

Cosimo. Tell therefore, how you would arme them?

Fabricio. I would take of the Romaine armours, and of the Duchemennes weapons, and I would that the one haulfe, should bee appoincted like the Romaines, and the other haulfe like the Duchemen: for that if in sixe thousande footemen (as I shall tell you a little hereafter) I should have thre thousande men with Targaettes, after the Romain maner, and two thousande Pikes, and a thousand Harkebutters, after the Duche facion, thei should sufice me: for that I would place the Pikes, either in the fronte of the battaile, or where I should feare moste the horses, and those with the Targaetes and sweardes, shall serve me to make a backe to the Pikes, and to winne the battaile, as I shall shewe you: so that I beleeve, that a power thus ordayned, should overcome at this daye, any other power.

Cosimo. This which hath beene saide, sufficeth concerning footemen, but concerning horsemen, wee desire to understand which you thinke more stronger armed, either ours, or the antiquitie.

The victorie of lucullo, against tiarane king of armenia; for what pupose horsemen be most requisite.

Fabricio. I beleeve that in these daies, having respect to the Saddelles bolstered, and to the stiroppes not used of the antiquitie, they stande more stronglye on horsebacke, then in the olde time: I thinke also they arme them more sure: so that at this daye, a bande of men of armes, paysing very muche, commeth to be with more difficultie withstoode, then were the horsemen of old time: notwithstanding for all this, I judge, that there ought not to be made more accompt of horses, then in olde time was made, for that (as afore is sayde) manye times in our dayes, they have with the footemen receyved shame and shall receyve alwayes, where they incounter, with a power of footemen armed, and ordered, as above hath bene declared. Tigrane king of Armenia, had againste the armie of the Romanes, wherof was Capitayne Lucullo, CL. thousande horsemen, amongest the whiche, were many armed, like unto our men of armes, which they called Catafratti, and of the other parte, the Romanes were about sixe thousande, with xxv. thousand footemen: so that Tigrane seeing the armie of the enemies, saide: these be horses enough for an imbassage: notwithstanding, incountering together, he was overthrowen: and he that writeth of the same fighte, disprayseth those Catafratti, declaring them to be unprofitable; for that hee sayeth, because they had their faces covered, they had muche a doe to see, and to offende the enemie, and they falling, being laden with armour coulde not rise up again, nor welde themselves in any maner to prevaile. I say therefore, that those people or kingdomes, whiche shall esteeme more the power of horses, then the power of footemen be alwaies weake, and subjecte to all ruine, as by Italie hath been seene in our time, the whiche hath beene taken, ruinated, and over run with straungers, through not other fault, then for having taken litle care, of the service on foote, and being brought the souldiours therof, all on horsebacke. Yet there ought to bee had horses, but for seconde, and not for firste foundaion of an armie: for that to make a discovery, to over run and to destroy the enemies countrie, and to keepe troubled and disquieted, the armie of the same, and in their armours alwayes, to let them of their victuals, they are necessary, and most profitable: but concerning for the daye of battaile, and for the fighte in the fielde, whiche is the importaunce of the warre, and the ende, for which the armies are ordeined, they are more meeter to follow the enemie being discomfited then to do any other thing which in the same is to be done, and they bee in comparison, to the footemen much inferiour.

Cosimo. There is happened unto mee twoo doubtes, the one, where I knowe, that the Parthians dyd not use in the warre, other then horses, and yet they devided the worlde with the Romanes: the other is, that I woulde that you should shewe, howe the horsemen can be withstoode of footemen, and wherof groweth the strength of these, and the debilitie of those?

The reason why footmen are able to overcome horsemen; how footmen maie save them selves from horsemen; the exercise of souldiours, ought to be devided into thre partes; what exercises the auncient common weales used to exercise their youth in, and what commoditie insued thereby; how the antiquitie, learned their yong soldiours, to handell their weapons; what thantiquitie estemed moste happie in a common weale; mouster maisters; for thexercisyng of yong men unexperte.

Fabricio. Either I have tolde you, or I minded to tell you, howe that my reasoning of the affaires of warre, ought not to passe the boundes of Europe: when thus it is, I am not bounde unto you, to make accompte of the same, which is used in Asia, yet I muste saye unto you thus, that the warring of the Parthians, was altogether contrarye, to the same of the Romanes: for as muche as the Parthians, warred all on horsebacke, and in the fight, they proceeded confusedlye, and scattered, and it was a maner of fighte unstable, and full of uncertaintie. The Romanes were (it maye be sayde) almoste al on foote, and thei fought close together and sure, and thei overcame diversly, the one the other, according to the largenesse, or straightnesse of the situation: for that in this the Romaines were superiours, in thesame the Parthians, whom might make greate proofe, with thesame maner of warryng, consideryng the region, which thei had to defende, the which was moste large: for as moche as it hath the sea coaste, distant a thousande miles, the rivers thone from thother, twoo or three daies journey, the tounes in like maner and the inhabitauntes few: so that a Romaine armie heavie and slowe, by meanes of their armoures, and their orders, could not over run it, without their grevous hurt (those that defended it, being on horsebacke mooste expedite) so that thei were to daie in one place, and to morowe distaunt fiftie miles. Hereof it grewe, that the Parthians might prevaile with their chivalrie onely, bothe to the ruine of the armie of Crassus, and to the perill of thesame, of Marcus Antonius: but I (as I have told you) doe not intende in this my reasonyng, to speake of the warfare out of Europe, therfore I will stand upon thesame, whiche in times past, the Romaines ordained, and the Grekes, and as the Duchemen doe now adaies. But let us se to the other question of yours, where you desire to understande, what order, or what naturall vertue makes, that the footemen overcome the horsmen. And I saie unto you first that the horses cannot go, as the footmen in every place: Thei are slower then the footemen to obeie, when it is requisite to alter the order: for as moche, as if it be nedefull, either goyng forward, to turne backwarde, or tournyng backwarde, to go forwarde, or to move themselves standing stil, or goyng to stand still, without doubt, the horsemen cannot dooe it so redilie as the footemen: the horsemen cannot, being of some violence, disordained, returne in their orders, but with difficultie, although thesame violence cease, the whiche the footemen dooe moste easely and quickly. Besides this, it happeneth many tymes, that a hardie manne shall be upon a vile horse, and a coward upon a good, whereby it foloweth, that this evill matchyng of stomackes, makes disorder. Nor no man doeth marvell, that a bande of footemenne, susteineth all violence of horse for that a horse is a beaste, that hath sence, and knoweth the perilles, and with an ill will, will enter in them: and if you consider, what force maketh theim go forwarde, and what holdeth them backwarde, you shall se without doubt thesame to be greater, whiche kepeth them backe, then that whiche maketh them go forwardes: For that the spurre maketh theim go forwarde, and of the other side, either the swearde, or the Pike, kepeth theim backe: so that it hath been seen by the olde, and by the late experience, a bande of footemen to bee moste safe, ye, invinsible for horses. And if you should argue to this, that the heate, with whiche thei come, maketh theim more furious to incounter who that would withstande them, and lesse to regard the Pike, then the spurre: I saie, that if the horse so disposed, begin to see, that he must run upon the poincte of the Pike, either of himself, he wil refrain the course so that so sone as he shall feele himself pricked, he will stande still atones, or beeyng come to theim, he will tourne on the right, or on the lefte hande. Whereof if you wil make experience, prove to run a horse against a walle: you shall finde fewe, with what so ever furie he come withall, will strike against it. Cesar havyng in Fraunce, to faighte with the Suizzers, a lighted, and made every manne a light on foote, and to avoide from the araies, the horses, as a thyng more meete to flie, then to faight. But notwithstandyng these naturall impedimentes, whiche horses have, thesame Capitaine, whiche leadeth the footemen, ought to chuse waies, whiche have for horse, the moste impedimentes that maie bee, and seldome tymes it happeneth, but that a manne maie save hymself, by the qualitie of the countrie: for that if thou marche on the hilles, the situacion doeth save thee from thesame furie, whereof you doubt, that thei go withail in the plain, fewe plaines be, whiche through the tillage or by meanes of the woddes, doe not assure thee: for that every hillocke, every bancke, although it be but small, taketh awaie thesame heate, and every culture where bee Vines, and other trees, lettes the horses: and if thou come to battaile, the very same lettes happeneth, that chaunceth in marchyng: for as moche as every little impedemente, that the horse hath, abateth his furie. One thyng notwithstandyng, I will not forgette to tell you, how the Romaines estemed so moche their orders, and trusted so moche to their weapons, that if thei shuld have had, to chuse either so rough a place to save theim selves from horses, where thei should not have been able, to raunge their orders, or a place where thei should have nede, to feare more of horses, but ben able to deffende their battaile, alwaies thei toke this, and left that: but bicause it is tyme, to passe to the armie, having armed these souldiours, accordyng to the auncient and newe use, let us see what exercises the Romaines caused theim make, before the menne were brought to the battaile. Although thei be well chosen, and better armed, thei ought with moste greate studie be exercised, for that without this exercise, there was never any souldiour good: these exercises ought to be devided into three partes, the one, for to harden the bodie, and to make it apte to take paines, and to bee more swifter and more readier, the other, to teach them, how to handell their weapons, the third, for to learne them to kepe the orders in the armie, as well in marchyng, as in faightyng, and in the incampyng: The whiche be three principall actes, that an armie doeth: for asmoche, as if an armie marche, incampe, and faight with order, and expertly, the Capitaine leseth not his honoure, although the battaile should have no good ende. Therfore, all thauncient common weales, provided these exercises in maner, by custome, and by lawe, that there should not be left behinde any part thereof. Thei exercised then their youth, for to make them swift, in runnyng, to make theim readie, in leapyng, for to make them strong, in throwyng the barre, or in wrestlyng: and these three qualities, be as it were necessarie in souldiours. For that swiftnesse, maketh theim apte to possesse places, before the enemie, and to come to them unloked for, and at unwares to pursue them, when thei are discomfaicted: the readinesse, maketh theim apte to avoide a blowe, to leape over a diche, to winne a banke: strength, maketh them the better able to beare their armours, to incounter the enemie, to withstande a violence. And above all, to make the bodie the more apte to take paines, thei used to beare greate burthens, the whiche custome is necessarie: for that in difficulte expedicions it is requisite many tymes, that the souldiour beside his armours, beare vitualles for many daies, and if he were not accustomed to this labour, he could not dooe it: and without this, there can neither bee avoided a perill, nor a victorie gotten with fame. Concernyng to learne how to handell the weapons, thei exercised theim, in this maner: thei would have the yong menne, to put on armour, whiche should waie twise as moche, as their field armour, and in stede of a swearde, thei gave them a cudgell leaded, whiche in comparison of a verie swearde in deede, was moste heavie; thei made for every one of them, a poste to be set up in the ground, which should be in height twoo yardes and a quarter, and in soche maner, and so strong, that the blowes should not slur nor hurle it doune, against the whiche poste, the yong man with a targaet, and with the cudgell, as against an enemie did exercise, and some whiles he stroke, as though he would hurte the hedde, or the face, somewhile he retired backe, an other while he made forewarde: and thei had in this exercise, this advertisment, to make theim apt to cover theim selves, and to hurte the enemie: and havyng the counterfaight armours moste heavy, their ordinarie armours semed after unto them more lighter. The Romanies, would that their souldiours should hurte with the pricke, and not with the cutte, as well bicause the pricke is more mortalle, and hath lesse defence, as also to thentent that he that should hurt, might lye the lesse open, and be more apt to redouble it, then with cuttes. Dooe not marvaile that these auncient men, should thinke on these small thynges, for that where the incounteryng of men is reasoned of, you shall perceive, that every little vauntage, is of greate importaunce: and I remember you the same, whiche the writers of this declare, rather then I to teache you. The antiquitie estemed nothing move happie, in a common weale, then to be in thesame, many men exercised in armes: bicause not the shining of precious stones and of golde, maketh that the enemies submit themselves unto thee, but onely the fear of the weapons: afterwarde the errours whiche are made in other thynges, maie sometymes be corrected, but those whiche are dooen in the warre, the paine straight waie commyng on, cannot be amended. Besides that, the knowlege to faight, maketh men more bold, bicause no man feareth to doe that thing, which he thinketh to have learned to dooe. The antiquitie would therefore, that their Citezeins should exercise themselves, in all marcial feates, and thei made them to throwe against thesame poste, dartes moche hevier then the ordinarie: the whiche exercise, besides the makyng men expert in throwyng, maketh also the arme more nimble, and moche stronger. Thei taught them also to shote in the long bowe, to whorle with the sling: and to all these thynges, thei appoincted maisters, in soche maner, that after when thei were chosen for to go to the warre, thei were now with mynde and disposicion, souldiours. Nor there remained them to learn other, then to go in the orders, and to maintain them selves in those, either marchyng, or faightyng: The whiche moste easely thei learned, mingeling themselves with those, whiche had long tyme served, whereby thei knewe how to stande in the orders.

Cosimo. What exercises would you cause theim to make at this present?

The exercises that souldiers ought to make in these daies; the exercise of swimmyng; tiber, is a river runnyng through rome the water wher of will never corrupte; thexercise of vautyng, and the commoditie thereof; an order that is taken in certain countries, concerning exercises of warre; what knowledge a souldiour ought to have; a cohorte is a bande of men; of what nomer and of what kind of armours and weapons, a maine battaile ought to bee, and the distributing and appoinetyng of thesame; veliti are light armed men; thecapitaines that ar appointed to every band of men; twoo orders observed in an armie; how a captain muste instructe muste instructe his souldiours how thei ought to governe themselves in the battaile.

Fabricio. A good many of those, whiche have been declared, as runnyng, and wrestlyng, makyng theim to leape, makyng theim to labour in armours, moche heavier then the ordinarie, making them shoote with Crosse bowes, and longe bowes, whereunto I would joyne the harkabus, a newe instrument (as you know) verie necessarie, and to these exercises I would use, al the youth of my state, but with greater industrie, and more sollicitatenesse thesame parte, whiche I should have alreadie appoincted to serve, and alwaies in the idell daies, thei should bee exercised. I would also that thei should learne to swimme, the whiche is a thyng verie profitable: for that there be not alwaies bridges over rivers, boates be not alwaies readie: so that thy army not knowyng howe to swime, remaineth deprived of many commodities: and many occasions to woorke well, is taken awaie. The Romaines for none other cause had ordained, that the yong men should exercise them selves in Campus Martius, then onely, for that havyng Tiber at hande, thei might, beyng weried with the exercise on lande, refreshe theim selves in the water, and partly in swimmyng, to exercise them selves. I would make also, as the antiquitie, those whiche should serve on horsebacke to exercise, the whiche is moste necessarie, for that besides to know how to ride, thei muste knowe how on horsebacke thei maie prevaile of them selves. And for this thei had ordeined horses of wood, upon the which thei practised, to leape by armed, and unarmed, without any helpe, and on every hande: the whiche made, that atones, and at a beck of a capitain, the horsmen were on foote, and likewise at a token, thei mounted on horsebacke. And soche exercises, bothe on foote and on horsebacke, as thei were then easie to bee doen, so now thei should not be difficult to thesame common weale, or to thesame prince, whiche would cause them to be put in practise of their yong men. As by experience is seen, in certaine citees of the Weste countrie, where is kepte a live like maners with this order. Thei

devide all their inhabiters into divers partes: and every parte thei name of the kinde of those weapons, that thei use in the warre. And for that thei use Pikes, Halbardes, Bowes, and Harkebuses, thei call them Pike menne, Halberders, Harkebutters, and Archars: Therefore, it is mete for all the inhabiters to declare, in what orders thei will be appoincted in. And for that all men, either for age, or for other impedimentes, be not fitte for the warre, every order maketh a choise of men, and thei call them the sworen, whom in idell daies, be bounde to exercise themselves in those weapons, wherof thei be named: and every manne hath his place appoincted hym of the cominaltie, where soche exercise ought to be made: and those whiche be of thesame order, but not of the sworen, are contributaries with their money, to thesame expenses, whiche in soche exercises be necessarie: therfore thesame that thei doe, we maie doe. But our smal prudence dooeth not suffre us, to take any good waie. Of these exercises there grewe, that the antiquitie had good souldiours, and that now those of the Weste, bee better men then ours: for as moche as the antiquitie exercised them, either at home (as those common weales doe) or in the armies, as those Emperours did, for thoccasions aforesaied: but we, at home will not exercise theim, in Campe we cannot, bicause thei are not our subjectes, and for that we are not able to binde them to other exercises then thei them selves liste to doe: the whiche occacion hath made, that firste the armies bee neclected, and after, the orders, and that the kyngdomes, and the common weales, in especially Italians, live in soche debilitie. But let us tourne to our order, and folowyng this matter of exercises, I saie, how it suffiseth not to make good armies, for havyng hardened the men, made them strong, swift, and handsome, it is nedefull also, that thei learne to stande in the orders, to obeie to signes, to soundes, and to the voice of the capitain: to knowe, standyng, to retire them selves, goyng forwardes, bothe faightyng, and marchyng to maintain those: bicause without this knowlege, withal serious diligence observed, and practised, there was never armie good: and without doubt, the fierce and disordered menne, bee moche more weaker, then the fearfull that are ordered, for that thorder driveth awaie from men feare, the disorder abateth fiercenesse. And to the entente you maie the better perceive that, whiche here folowyng shalbe declared, you have to understande, how every nation, in the orderyng of their men to the warre, have made in their hoste, or in their armie, a principall member, the whiche though thei have varied with the name, thei have little varied with the nomber of the menne: for that thei all have made it, betwene sixe and viii. M. men. This nomber of men was called of the Romaines, a Legion, of Grekes a Fallange, of Frenchemen Caterva: this verie same in our tyme of the Suizzers, whom onely of the auncient warfare, kepe some shadowe, is called in their tongue that, whiche in ours signifieththe maine battaile. True it is, that every one of them, hath after devided it, accordyng to their purposes. Therefore me thinkes beste, that wee grounde our talke, upon this name moste knowen, and after, according to the aunciente, and to the orders now adaies, the beste that is possible to ordaine it; and bicause the Romaines devided their Legion, whiche was made betwene five and sixe thousande men, in ten Cohortes, I will that wee devide our main battaile, into ten battailes, and that we make it of sixe thousande menne on foote, and we will give to every battaile, CCCCL. men, of whiche shall be, CCCC. armed with heavie armour, and L. with light armour: the heavie armed, shall be CCC. Targettes with sweardes, and shalbe called Target men: and C. with Pikes, whiche shalbe called ordinarie Pikes: the light armed shalbe, L. men armed with Harkabuses, Crosse bowes, and Partisans, and smal Targaettes, and these by an aunciente name, were called ordinarie Veliti: all of the ten battailes therefore, comes to have three thousande Targaet men, a thousande ordinarie Pikes, CCCC. ordinarie Veliti, all whiche make the nomber of fower thousande and five hundred men. And we saied, that we would make the maine battaile of six thousande; therefore there must be added an other thousande, five hundred men, of whiche I will appoinet a thousande with Pikes, whom I will call extraordinarie Veliti, and thus my menne should come (as a little before I have saied) to bee made halfe of Targaetes, and halfe of Pikes and other weapons. I would appoinete to everie battaile, or bande of men, a Conestable, fower Centurions and fouretic peticapitaines, and moreover a hedde to the ordinarie Veliti. with five peticapitaines; I would give to the thousande extraordinarie Pikes, three Conestabelles, ten Centurions, and a hundred peticapitaines; to the extraodrinarie Veliti, two Conestabelles, v. Centurions, and l. peticapitaines: I would then apoinet a generall hed, over all the main battaile: I would that every Conestable should have an Ansigne, and a Drum. Thus there should be made a manne battaile of ten battailes, of three thousande Targaet men, of a thousande ordinarie Pikes, of a thousande extraordinarie of five hundred ordinarie Veliti, of five hundred extraordinarie, so there should come to bee sixe thousande men, emongeste the whiche there should bee M.D. peticapitaines, and moreover, xv. Conestables, with xv. Drummes, and xv. Ansignes, lv. Centurions, x. heddes of the ordinarie Veliti, and a Capitaine over all the maine battaile with his Asigne and Drume, and I have of purpose repeated this order the oftener, to the intent, that after when I shall shewe you, the maners of orderyng the battailes, and tharmies, you should not be confounded: I saie therefore, how that, that king, or that common weale, whiche intendeth to ordeine their subjectes to armes, ought to appoincte theim with these armoures and weapons, and with these partes, and to make in their countrie so many maine battailes, as it were able: and when thei should have ordained them, according to the forsaid distribucion, minding to exercise them in the orders, it should suffice to exercise every battaile by it self: and although the nomber of the men, of every one of them, cannot by it self, make the facion of a juste armie, notwithstandyng, every man maie learne to dooe thesame, whiche particularly appertaineth unto hym: for that in the armies, twoo orders is observed, the one, thesame that the men ought to doe in every battaile, and the other that, whiche the battaile ought to doe after, when it is with the other in an armie. And those men, whiche doe wel the first, mooste easely maie observe the seconde: But without knowyng thesame, thei can never come to the knowlege of the seconde. Then (as I have saied) every one of these battailes, maie by them selves, learne to kepe the orders of the araies, in every qualitie of movyng, and of place, and after learne to put them selves togethers, to understande the soundes, by meanes wherof in the faight thei are commaunded, to learne to know by that, as the Gallics by the whissell, what ought to be doen, either to stande still, or to tourne forward, or to tourne backwarde or whiche waie to tourne the weapons, and the face: so that knowyng how to kepe well the araie, after soche sorte, that neither place nor movyng maie disorder them, understandyng well the commaundementes of their heddes, by meanes of the sounde, and knowyng quickly, how to retourne into their place, these battailes maie after easly (as I have said) beyng brought many together, learne to do that, whiche all the body together, with the other battailes in a juste armie, is bounde to dooe. And bicause soche universall practise, is also not to bee estemed a little, ones or twise a yere, when there is peace, all the main battaile maie be brought together, to give it the facion of an whole armie, some daies exercisyng theim, as though thei should faight a fielde, settyng the fronte, and the sides with their succours in their places. And bicause a capitaine ordeineth his hoste to the fielde, either for coumpte of the enemie he seeth, or for that, of whiche without seyng he doubteth, he ought to exercise his armie in the one maner, and in the other, and to instructe theim in soche sorte, that thei maie knowe how to marche, and to faight, when nede should require, the wyng to his souldiours, how thei should governe theim selves, when thei should happen to be assaulted of this, or of that side: and where he ought to instructe theim how to faight againste the enemie, whom thei should see: he must shewe them also, how the faight is begun, and where thei ought to retire: being overthrowen, who hath to succeade in their places, to what signes, to what soundes, to what voices, thei ought to obeie, and to practise them in soche wise in the battaile, and with fained assaultes, that thei may desire the verie thyng in deede. For that an armie is not made coragious, bicause in thesame be hardie menne, but by reason the orders thereof bee well appoineted: For as moche as if I be one of the first faighters, and do knowe, beyng overcome, where I maie retire, and who hath to succeade in my place, I shall alwaies faight with boldnes, seing my succour at hand. If I shall be one of the seconde faighters, the first being driven backe, and overthrowen, I shall not bee afraied, for that I shall have presuposed that I maie bee, and I shall have desire to be thesame, whiche maie give the victory to my maister, and not to bee any of the other. These exercises bee moste necessarie, where an armie is made of newe, and where the old armie is, thei bee also necessarie: for that it is also seen, how the Romaines knew from their infancie, thorder of their armies, notwithstandyng, those capitaines before thei should come to thenemie, continually did exercise them in those. And Josephus in his historie saieth, that the continuall exercises of the Romaine armies, made that all thesame multitude, whiche folowe the campe for gain, was in the daie of battaile profitable: bicause thei all knewe, how to stande in the orders, and to faight kepyng the same: but in the armies of newe men, whether thou have putte theim together, to faight straight waie, or that thou make a power to faight, when neede requires, without these exercises, as well of the battailes severally by themselves, as of all the armie, is made nothing: wherefore the orders beying necessarie, it is conveniente with double industrie and laboure, to shewe them unto soche as knoweth them not, and for to teache it, many excellent capitaines have travailed, without any respecte.

Cosimo. My thinkes that this reasoning, hath sumwhat transported you: for asmoche, as havyng not yet declared the waies, with the whiche the battailes bee exercised, you have reasoned of the whole armie, and of the daie of battaile.

The chief importance in the exercisyng of bandes of men; three principall for thorderyng of menne into battaile raie; the manner how to bryng a bande of men into battaile raie after a square facion; the better waie for the ordring of a band of men in battaile raie, after the first facion; how to exercise men, and to take soche order, whereby a band of men that were by whatsoever chance disordred maye straighte wai be brought into order againe; what advertisement ought to bee used in tourning about a whole bande of menne, after soche sorte, as though it were but one bodie; how to order a band of menne after soche sort that thei maie make their front againste thenemie of whiche flanke thei list; how a band of man oughte to be ordered, when in marchyng thei should bee constrained to faighton their backes.

Fabricio. You saie truth, but surely thoccasion hath been the affection, whiche I beare to these orders, and the grief that I feele, seyng thei be not put in use: notwithstanding, doubt not but that I will tourne to the purpose: as I have saied, the chief importaunce that is in thexercise of the battailes, is to knowe how to kepe well the armies: and bicause I tolde you that one of these battailes, ought to bee made of fower hundred men heavie armed, I wil staie my self upon this nomber. Thei ought then to be brought into lxxx. rankes, and five to a ranke: afterward goyng fast, or softly, to knit them together, and to lose them: the whiche how it is dooen, maie bee shewed better with deedes, then with wordes. Which nedeth not gretly to be taught, for that every manne, whom is practised in servise of warre, knoweth how this order procedeth, whiche is good for no other, then to use the souldiours to keepe the raie: but let us come to putte together one of these battailes, I saie, that there is given them three facions principally, the firste, and the moste profitablest is, to make al massive, and to give it the facion of two squares, the second is, to make it square with the front horned, the thirde is, to make it with a voide space in the middest: the maner to put men together in the first facion, maie be of twoo sortes, tho together in the first facion, maie be of twoo sortes, thone is to double the rankes, that is, to make the seconde ranke enter into the first, the iiii. into the third, the sixt into the fift, and so foorth, so that where there was lxxx. rankes, five to a ranke, thei maie become xl. rankes, x. to a ranke. Afterward cause theim to double ones more in thesame maner, settyng the one ranke into an other, and so there shall remain twentie rankes, twentie men to a ranke: this maketh twoo squares aboute, for as moche as albeit that there bee as many men the one waie, as in the other, notwithstandyng to wardes the hedde, thei joine together, that the one side toucheth the other: but by the other waie, thei be distant the one from the other, at least a yarde and a haulfe, after soche sorte, that the square is moche longer, from the backe to the fronte, then from the one side to thother: and bicause we have at this presente, to speake often of the partes afore, of behinde, and of the sides of these battailes, and of all the armie together, knowe you, that when I saie either hedde or fronte, I meane the parte afore, when I shall saie backe, the part behind, when I shall saie flankes, the partes on the sides. The fiftie ordinarie veliti of the battaile, muste not mingle with the other rankes, but so sone as the battaile is facioned, thei shalbe set a long by the flankes therof. The other waie to set together the battaile is this, and bicause it is better then the firste, I will set it before your ives juste, how it ought to bee ordeined. I beleve that you remember of what nomber of menne, of what heddes it is made, and of what armours thei are armed, then the facion, that this battaile ought to have, is (as I have saied) of twentie rankes, twentie men to a ranke, five rankes of Pikes in the front, and fiftene rankes of Targaettes on the backe, twoo Centurions standying in the fronte, twoo behinde on the backe, who shall execute the office of those, whiche the antiquitie called Tergiductori. The Conestable with the Ansigne, and with the Drumme, shall stande in thesame space, that is betwene the five rankes of the Pikes, and the fiftene of the Targeaettes. Of the Peticapitaines, there shall stande one upon every side of the ranckes, so that every one, maie have on his side his men, those peticapitaines, whiche shalbe on the left hande, to have their men on the right hand, those Peticapitaines, whiche shall be on the right hand, to have their menne on the left hande: The fiftie Veliti, muste stande a long the flankes, and on the backe of the battaile. To mynde now, that this battaile maie be set together in this facion, the men goyng ordinarily, it is convenient to order them thus. Make the men to be brought into lxxx. rankes, five to a ranke, as a little afore we have said, leavyng the Veliti either at the hedde, or at the taile, so that thei stande out of this order: and it ought to be ordeined, that every Centurion have behinde his back twentie rankes, and to bee nexte behinde every Centurion, five rankes of Pikes, and the reste Targaettes. The Conestable shall stande with the Drum, and the Ansigne, in thesame space, whiche is betwene the Pikes, and the Targaettes of the seconde Centurion, and to occupie the places of three Targaette men. Of the Peticapitaines, twentie shall stand on the sides of the rankes, of the first Centurion, on the lefte hande, and twentie shall stande on the sides of the rankes, of the last Centurion on the right hande. And you muste understande, that the Peticapitaine, whiche hath to leade the Pikes, ought to have a Pike, and those that leade the Targaettes, ought to have like weapons. Then the rankes beyng brought into this order, and mindyng in marchyng, to bryng them into battaile, for to make the hedde, the first Centurion must be caused to stande still, with the firste twentie rankes, and the seconde to proceade marchyng, and tournyng on the right hand, he must go a long the sides of the twentie rankes that stande still, till he come to bee even with the other Centurion, where he must also stande still, and the thirde Centurion to procede marchyng, likewise tournyng on the right hand, and a long the sides of the rankes that stande still, must go so farre, that he be even with the other twoo Centurions, and he also standyng still, the other Centurion must folowe with his rankes, likewise tournyng on the right hande, a longe the sides of the rankes that stande still, so farre that he come to the hed of the other, and then to stand still, and straight waie twoo Centurions onely, shall depart from the front, and go to the backe of the battaile, the whiche cometh to bee made in thesame maner, and with thesame order juste, as a little afore I have shewed you. The Veliti muste stande a long, by the flankes of thesame, accordyng as is disposed in the first waie, whiche waie is called redoublyng by right line, this is called redoublyng by flanke: the first waie is more easie, this is with better order, and commeth better to passe, and you maie better correcte it, after your owne maner, for that in redoublyng by righte line, you muste bee ruled by the nomber, bicause five maketh ten, ten twentie, twentie fourtie, so that with redoublyng by right line, you cannot make a hedde of fiftene, nor of five and twentie, nor of thirtie, nor of five and thirtie, but you must go where thesame nomber will leade you. And yet it happeneth every daie in particulare affaires, that it is convenient to make the forwarde with sixe hundred, or eight hundred men, so that to redouble by right line, should disorder you: therefore this liketh me better: that difficultie that is, ought moste with practise, and with exercise to bee made easie. Therefore I saie unto you, how it importeth more then any thyng, to have the souldiours to know how to set themselves in araie quickly, and it is necessarie to keepe theim in this battaile, to exercise theim therin, and to make them to go apace, either forward or backward, to passe through difficulte places, without troublyng thorder: for asmoche as the souldiours, whiche can doe this well, be expert souldiours, and although thei have never seen enemies in the face, thei maie be called old souldiours, and contrariwise, those whiche cannot keepe these orders, though thei have been in a thousande warres, thei ought alwaies to be reputed new souldiours. This is, concernyng setting them together, when thei are marching in small rankes: but beyng set, and after beyng broken by some accident or chaunce, whiche groweth either of the situacion, or of the enemie, to make that in a sodaine, thei maie come into order againe, this is the importaunce and the difficultie, and where is nedefull moche exercise, and moche practise, and wherin the antiquitie bestowed moche studie. Therefore it is necessarie to doe twoo thynges, firste to have this battaile full of countersignes, the other, to keepe alwaies this order, that those same men maie stand alwaies in the ranke, which thei were firste placed in: as for insample, if one have begon to stande in the seconde, that he stande after alwaie in that, and not onely in that self same rancke, but in that self same place: for the observyng whereof (as I have saied) bee necessarie many countersignes. In especially it is requisite, that the Ansigne bee after soche sorte countersigned, that companyng with the other battailes, it maie be knowen from theim, accordyng as the Conestable, and the Centurions have plumes of fethers in their heddes differente, and easie to be knowen, and that whiche importeth moste, is to ordaine that the peticapitaines bee knowen. Whereunto the antiquitie had so moche care, that thei would have nothing els written in their hedde peces, but the nomber that thei were named by, callyng them firste, seconde, thirde, and fourthe xc. And yet thei were not contented with this, but made every souldiour to have written in his Targaet, the nomber of the ranke, and the nomber of the place, in whiche ranke he was appoineted. Then the menne being countersigned thus, and used to stande betwene these limites, it is an easie thyng, thei beyng disordered, to sett theim all againe quickly into order: considering, that the Ansigne standyng still, the Centurions, and the Peticapitaines maie gesse their places by the iye, and beyng brought the left of the left, the right of the right, with their accustomed distance, the souldiours led by their rule, and by the differences of the cognisances, maie be quickly in their proper places, no otherwise, then as if the boordes of a tunne should bee taken a sunder, whiche beyng first marked, moste easely maie bee set together again, where thesame beyng not countersigned, were impossible to bryng into order any more. These thynges, with diligence and with exercise, are quickely taught, and quickly learned, and beyng learned, with difficultie are forgotten: for that the newe menne, be led of the olde, and with tyme, a Province with these exercises, may become throughly practised in the war. It is also necessarie to teache theim, to tourne theim selves all at ones, and when neede requires, to make of the flankes, and of the backe, the fronte, and of the front, flankes, or backe, whiche is moste easie: bicause it suffiseth that every manne doe tourne his bodie, towardes thesame parte that he is commaunded, and where thei tourne their faces, there the fronte commeth to bee. True it is, that when thei tourne to any of the flanckes, the orders tourne out of their proporcion: for that from the breast to the backe, there is little difference, and from the one flancke to the other, there is verie moche distance, the whiche is al contrarie to the ordinarie order of the battaile: therefore it is convenient, that practise, and discrecion, doe place them as thei ought to be: but this is small disorder, for that moste easely by themselves, thei maie remedie it. But that whiche importeth more, and where is requisite more practise, is when a battaile would tourne all at ones, as though it were a whole bodie, here is meete to have greate practise, and greate discrecion: bicause mindyng to tourne, as for insample on the left hande, the left corner must stande still, and those that be next to hym that standeth still, muste marche so softly, that thei that bee in the right corner, nede not to runne: otherwise all thing should be confounded. But bicause it happeneth alwaies, when an armie marcheth from place to place, that the battailes, whiche are not placed in the front, shall be driven to faight not by hedde, but either by flancke, or by backe, so that a battaile muste in a sodaine make of flancke, or of backe, hedde: and mindyng that like battailes in soche cace, maie have their proporcion, as above is declared, it is necessarie, that thei have the Pikes on thesame flancke, that ought to be hedde, and the Peticapitaines, Centurions, and Conestables, to resorte accordyngly to their places. Therefore to mynde to dooe this, in plasyng them together, you must ordeine the fower skore rankes, of five in a ranke, thus: Set all the Pikes in the first twentie rankes, and place the Peticapitaines thereof, five in the first places, and five in the last: the other three score rankes, whiche come after, bee all of Targaettes, whiche come to bee three Centuries. Therefore, the first and the laste ranke of every Centurion, would be Peticapitaines, the Conestable with the Ansigne, and with the Drumme, muste stande in the middest of the first Centurie of Targaettes, and the Centurions in the hed of every Centurie. The bande thus ordained, when you would have the Pikes to come on the left flancke, you must redouble Centurie by Centurie, on the right flancke: if you would have them to come on the right flancke, you must redouble theim on the lefte. And so this battaile tourneth with the Pikes upon a flancke, and the Conestable in the middeste: the whiche facion it hath marchyng: but the enemie commyng, and the tyme that it would make of flancke hedde, it nedeth not but to make every man to tourne his face, towardes thesame flancke, where the Pikes be, and then the battaile tourneth with the rankes, and with the heddes in thesame maner, as is aforesaied: for that every man is in his place, excepte the Centurions, and the Centurions straight waie, and without difficultie, place themselves: But when thei in marchyng, should bee driven to faight on the backe, it is convenient to ordein the rankes after soch sorte, that settyng theim in battaile, the Pikes maie come behinde, and to doe this, there is to bee kepte no other order, then where in orderyng the battaile, by the ordinarie, every Centurie hath five rankes of Pikes before, to cause that thei maie have them behind, and in all the other partes to observe thorder, whiche I declared firste.

Cosimo. You have tolde (if I dooe well remember me) that this maner of exercise, is to bee able to bryng these battailes together into an armie, and that this practise, serveth to be able to order theim selves in the same: But if it should happen, that these CCCCL. men, should have to doe an acte seperate, how would you order them?

How a battaile is made with twoo hornes; the orderyng of a battaile with a voide space in the middeste.

Fabricio. He that leadeth them, ought then to judge, where he will place the Pikes, and there to put them, the whiche doeth not repugne in any part to the order above written: for that also, though thesame bee the maner, that is observed to faighte a fielde, together with thother battailes, notwithstandyng it is a rule, whiche serveth to all those waies, wherein a band of menne should happen to have to doe: but in shewyng you the other twoo waies of me propounded, of ordering the battailes, I shal also satisfie you more to your question: for that either thei are never used, or thei are used when a battaile is a lone, and not in companie of other, and to come to the waie of ordering them, with twoo hornes, I saie, that thou oughteste to order the lxxx. rankes, five to a ranke, in this maner. Place in the middest, one Centurion, and after hym xxv. rankes, whiche muste bee with twoo Pikes on the lefte hande, and with three Targaettes on the right, and after the first five, there must be put in the twentie folowyng, twentie Peticapitaines, all betwene the pikes, and the Targaettes, excepte those whiche beare the Pike, whom maie stand with the Pikes: after these xxv. rankes thus ordered, there is to be placed an other Centurion, and behinde hym fiftene rankes of Targaettes: after these, the Conestable betwene the Drum and the Ansigne, who also must have after him, other fiftene rankes of Targaettes: after this, the thirde Centurion must be placed, and behinde hym, xxv. rankes, in every one of whiche, ought to bee three Targaettes on the lefte flancke, and twoo Pikes on the right, and after the five first rankes, there must be xx. Peticapitaines placed betwene the Pikes, and the Targaettes: after these rankes, the fowerth Centurion must folowe. Intendying therefore, of these rankes thus ordered, to make a battaile with twoo hornes, the first Centurion must stand still, with the xxv. rankes, whiche be behinde him, after the second Centurion muste move, with the fiftene rankes of Targaettes, that bee behinde hym, and to tourne on the right hande, and up by the right flancke of the xxv. rankes, to go so farre, that he arrive to the xv. ranke, and there to stande still: after, the Conestable muste move, with the fiftene rankes of Targaettes, whiche be behinde hym, and tournyng likewise on the right hande, up by the right flancke of the fiftene rankes, that wer firste moved, muste marche so farre, that he come to their heddes, and there to stand stil: after, the thirde Centurion muste move with the xxv. rankes, and with the fowerth Centurion, whiche was behinde, and turnyng up straight, must go a long by the right flanck of the fiftene last rankes of the Targaettes, and not to stande still when he is at the heddes of them, but to followe marchyng so farre, that the laste ranke of the xxv. maie come to be even with the rankes behinde. And this dooen, the Centurion, whiche was hedde of the firste fiftene rankes of Targaettes, must go awaie from thens where he stoode, and go to the backe in the lefte corner: and thus a battaile shall be made of xxv. rankes, after twentie men to a rank, with two hornes, upon every side of the front, one horn, and every one, shall have ten rankes, five to a ranke, and there shall remain a space betwene the twoo hornes, as moche as containeth ten men, whiche tourne their sides, the one to thother. Betwene the two hornes, the capitain shall stande, and on every poinct of a horne, a Centurion: There shall bee also behinde, on every corner, a Centurion: there shal be twoo rankes of Pikes, and xx. Peticapitaines on every flancke. These twoo hornes, serve to kepe betwene theim the artillerie, when this battaile should have any withit, and the cariages: The Veliti muste stande a long the flankes, under the Pikes. But mindyng to bring this horned battaile, with a voide space in the middeste, there ought no other to bee doen, then of fiftene rankes, of twentie to a ranke, to take eight rankes, and to place them on the poinctes of the twoo hornes, whiche then of hornes, become backe of the voide space, in this place, the cariages are kept, the capitain standeth, and the Ansigne, but never the Artillerie, the whiche is placed either in the front, or a long the flankes. These be the waies, that a battaile maie use when it is constrained to passe alone through suspected places: notwithstandyng, the massive battaile without hornes, and without any soche voide place is better, yet purposyng to assure the disarmed, the same horned battaile is necessarie. The Suizzers make also many facions of battailes, emong which, thei make one like unto a crosse: bicause in the spaces that is betwen the armes therof, thei kepe safe their Harkebuters from the daunger of the enemies: but bicause soche battailes be good to faight by theim selves, and my intente is to shew, how many battailes united, do faight with thenemie, I wil not labour further in describing them.

Cosimo. My thinkes I have verie well comprehended the waie, that ought to be kept to exercise the men in these battailes: But (if I remember me well) you have saied, how that besides the tenne battailes, you joyne to the maine battaile, a thousande extraordinarie Pikes, and five hundred extraordinarie Veliti: will you not appoincte these to be exercised?

To what purpose the pikes and velite extraordinarie must serve.

Fabricio. I would have theim to bee exercised, and that with moste great diligence: and the Pikes I would exercise, at leaste Ansigne after Ansigne, in the orders of the battailes, as the other: For as moche as these should doe me more servise, then the ordinarie battailes, in all particulare affaires: as to make guides, to get booties, and to doe like thynges: but the Veliti, I would exercise at home, without bringing them together, for that their office being to faight a sonder, it is not mete, that thei should companie with other, in the common exercises: for that it shall suffice, to exercise them well in the particular exercises. Thei ought then (as I firste tolde you, nor now me thynkes no labour to rehearse it againe) to cause their men to exercise them selves in these battailes, whereby thei maie knowe how to kepe the raie, to knowe their places, to tourne quickly, when either enemie, or situacion troubleth them: for that, when thei knowe how to do this, the place is after easely learned, which a battaile hath to kepe, and what is the office thereof in the armie: and when a Prince, or a common weale, will take the paine, and will use their diligence in these orders, and in these exercisyng, it shall alwaies happen, that in their countrie, there shall bee good souldiours, and thei to be superiours to their neighbours, and shalbe those, whiche shall give, and not receive the lawes of other men: but (as I have saied) the disorder wherein thei live, maketh that thei neclecte, and doe not esteme these thynges, and therefore our armies be not good: and yet though there were either hed, or member naturally vertuous, thei cannot shewe it.

Cosimo. What carriages would you, that every one of these battailes should have?

Neither centurion nor peticapitaine, ought not to ride; what carriages the capitaines ought to have, and the nomber of carrages requisite to every bande of menne.

Fabricio. Firste, I would that neither Centurion, nor Peticapitain, should be suffered to ride: and if the Conestable would nedes ride, I would that he should have a Mule, and not a horse: I would allowe hym twoo carriages, and one to every Centurion, and twoo to every three Peticapitaines, for that so many wee lodge in a lodgyng, as in the place therof we shall tell you: So that every battaile will come to have xxxvi. carriages, the whiche I would should carrie of necessitie the tentes, the vesselles to seeth meate, axes, barres of Iron, sufficient to make the lodgynges, and then if thei can carry any other thyng, thei maie dooe it at their pleasure.

Cosimo. I beleve that the heddes of you, ordeined in every one of these battailes, be necessarie: albeit, I would doubt, lest that so many commaunders, should confounde all.

Without many capitaines, an armie cannot be governed; to what purpose ansignes ought to serve; for what purpose drummes oughte to bee used; the propertie that soundes of instrumentes have in mens myndes.

Fabricio. That should bee, when it were not referred to one man, but referryng it, thei cause order, ye and without theim, it is impossible to governe an armie: for that a wall, whiche on every parte enclineth, requireth rather to have many proppes, and thicke, although not so strong, then fewe, though thei were strong: bicause the vertue of one a lone, doeth not remedie the ruine a farre of. And therefore in tharmies, and emong every ten men, it is convenient that there bee one, of more life, of more harte, or at leaste wise of more aucthoritie, who with stomacke, with wordes, and with example, maie kepe them constante, and disposed to faight, and these thynges of me declared, bee necessarie in an armie, as the Heddes, the Ansignes, and the Drummes, is seen that wee have theim all in our armies, but none doeth his office. First to mynde that the Peticapitaines doe thesame, for whiche thei are ordeined, it is necessarie (as I have said) that there bee a difference, betwene every one of them and their men, and that thei lodge together, doyng their duties, standyng in thorder with them: for that thei placed in their places, bee a rule and a temperaunce, to maintaine the raies straight and steddie, and it is impossible that thei disorder, or disorderyng, dooe not reduce themselves quickly into their places. But we now adaies, doe not use them to other purpose, then to give theim more wages, then to other menne, and to cause that thei dooe some particulare feate: The very same happeneth of the Ansigne bearers, for that thei are kept rather to make a faire muster, then for any other warlike use: but the antiquitie used theim for guides, and to bryng theim selves againe into order: for that every man, so sone as the Ansigne stoode still, knewe the place, that he kept nere to his Ansigne, wherunto he retourned alwaies: thei knewe also, how that the same movyng, or standyng, thei should staie, or move: therfore it is necessarie in an armie, that there be many bodies, and every bande of menne to have his Ansigne, and his guide: wherfore havyng this, it is mete that thei have stomackes inough, and by consequence life enough. Then the menne ought to marche, accordyng to the Ansigne: and the Ansigne to move, accordyng to the Drumme, the whiche Drumme well ordered, commaundeth to the armie, the whiche goyng with paces, that answereth the tyme of thesame, will come to kepe easilie thorders: for whiche cause the antiquitie had Shalmes, Flutes, and soundes perfectly tymed: For as moche as like as he that daunseth, proceadeth with the tyme of the Musick, and goyng with thesame doeth not erre, even so an armie obeiyng, in movyng it self to thesame sounde, doeth not disorder: and therefore, thei varied the sounde, accordyng as thei would varie the mocion, and accordyng as thei would inflame, or quiete, or staie the mindes of men: and like as the soundes were divers, so diversly thei named them: the sounde Dorico, ingendered constancie, the sounde Frigio, furie: whereby thei saie, that Alexander beyng at the Table, and one soundyng the sounde Frigio, it kendled so moche his minde, that he laied hande on his weapons. All these maners should be necessarie to finde again: and when this should bee difficulte, at least there would not be left behind those that teache the Souldiour to obeie, the whiche every man maie varie, and ordeine after his owne facion, so that with practise, he accustome the eares of his souldiours to knowe it: But now adaies of this sounde, there is no other fruicte taken for the moste part, then to make a rumour.

Cosimo. I would desire to understande of you, if ever with your self you have discourced, whereof groweth so moche vilenesse, and so moche disorder, and so moche necligence in these daies of this exercise?

A notable discourse of the aucthour, declaryng whereof groweth so moche vilenes disorder and necligence in these daies, concernyng the exercises of warre.

Fabricio. With a good will I will tell you thesame, that I thinke. You knowe how that of the excellente men of warre, there hath been named many in Europe, fewe in Affric, and lesse in Asia: this grewe, for that these twoo laste partes of the worlde, have had not paste one kyngdome, or twoo, and fewe common weales, but Europe onely, hath had many kyngdomes, and infinite common weales, where menne became excellent, and did shewe their vertue, accordyng as thei were sette a woorke, and brought before their Prince, or common weale, or king that he be: it followeth therefore, that where be many dominions, there rise many valiaunt menne, and where be fewe, fewe. In Asia is founde Ninus, Cirus, Artasercses, Mithridates: and verie fewe other, that to these maie be compared. In Africk, is named (lettyng stande thesame auncient Egipt) Massinissa, Jugurta, and those Capitaines, whiche of the Carthaginens common weale were nourished, whom also in respecte to those of Europe, are moste fewe: bicause in Europe, be excellente men without nomber, and so many more should be, if together with those should bee named the other, that be through the malignitie of time extincte: for that the worlde hath been moste vertuous, where hath been moste states, whiche have favoured vertue of necessitie, or for other humaine passion. There rose therfore in Asia, fewe excellente menne: bicause thesame Province, was all under one kyngdome, in the whiche for the greatnesse thereof, thesame standing for the moste parte of tyme idell, there could not growe men in doynges excellent. To Africke there happened the verie same, yet there were nourished more then in Asia, by reason of the Carthaginens common weale: for that in common weales, there growe more excellent men, then in kingdomes, bicause in common weales for the most part, vertue is honoured, in Kyngdomes it is helde backe: wherby groweth, that in thone, vertuous men are nourished, in the other thei are extincte. Therefore he that shall consider the partes of Europe, shall finde it to have been full of common weales, and of princedomes, the whiche for feare, that the one had of the other, thei wer constrained to kepe lively the warlike orders, and to honor them, whiche in those moste prevailed: for that in Grece, besides the kyngdome of the Macedonians, there were many common weales, and in every one of theim, were bred moste excellente men. In Italie, were the Romaines, the Sannites, the Toscanes, the Gallie Cisalpini. Fraunce, and Almainie, wer ful of common weales and princedomes. Spaine likewise: and although in comparison of the Romaines, there are named fewe other, it groweth through the malignitie of the writers, whom folowe fortune, and to theim for the moste parte it suffised, to honour the conquerours: but it standeth not with reason, that betwene the Sannites, and the Toscanes, whom fought CL. yeres with the Romaine people, before thei wer overcome, there should not growe exceadyng many excellente menne. And so likewise in Fraunce, and in Spaine: but that vertue, whiche the writers did not celebrate in particuler menne, thei celebrated generally in the people, where thei exalte to the starres, the obstinatenesse that was in them, to defende their libertie. Beyng then true, that where bee moste dominions, there riseth moste valiaunt menne, it foloweth of necessitie, that extinguishyng those, vertue is extincte straighte waie, the occasion decaiyng, whiche maketh menne vertuous. Therefore, the Romaine Empire beyng after increased, and havyng extinguished all the common weales, and Princedomes of Europe, and of Afrike, and for the moste part those of Asia, it lefte not any waie to vertue, excepte Rome: whereby grewe, that vertuous menne began to be as fewe in Europe, as in Asia: the whiche vertue, came after to the laste caste: For as moche, as all the vertue beyng reduced to Roome, so sone as thesame was corrupted, almoste all the worlde came to bee corrupted: and the Scithian people, were able to come to spoile thesame Empire, the whiche had extinguished the vertue of other, and knewe not howe to maintaine their owne: and after, although through the inundacion of those barberous nacions, thesame Empire was devided into many partes, this vertue is not renued:

The causes why the aunciente orders are neclected.

The one cause is, for that it greveth theim moche, to take againe the orders when thei are marde, the other, bicause the maner of livyng now adaies, having respect to the Christian religion, commaundeth not thesame necessitie to menne, to defende themselves, whiche in olde tyme was: for that then, the menne overcome in warre, either were killed, or remained perpetuall slaves, where thei led their lives moste miserably: The tounes overcome, either were rased, or the inhabiters thereof driven out, their goodes taken awaie, sent dispersed through the worlde: so that the vanquished in warre, suffered all extreme miserie: of this feare, men beyng made afraied, thei wer driven to kepe lively the warlike exercises, and thei honoured soche as were excellente in theim: But nowe adaies, this feare for the moste part is not regarded: of those that are overcom, fewe bee killed, none is kepte longe in prison: for that with facelitie, thei are sette at libertie: the citees also, whiche a thousande tymes have rebelled, are not destroied, the men wherof, are let a lone with their goodes, so that the greateste hurte that is feared, is but a taske: in so moche, that men will not submit them selves to the orders of warre, and to abide alwaies under those, to avoide the perilles whereof thei are little afraied: again these Provinces of Europe, be under a verie fewe heddes, in respecte as it hath been in times past: for that al Fraunce, obeieth one kyng, al Spain, an other: Italie is in fewe partes, so that the weake citees, are defended with leanyng to hym that overcometh, and the strong states, for the causes aforesaied, feare no soche extreme ruine.

Cosimo. Yet ther hath ben seen many tounes that have ben sacked within this xxv. yeres, and lost their dominions, whose insample, ought to teache other how to live, and to take again some of those old orders.

Fabricio. You saie true: but if you note what tounes have gone to sacke, you shall not finde that thei have been the heddes of states, but of the members; as was seen sacked Tortona, and not Milaine: Capua, and not Napelles, Brescia, and not Venice, Ravenna, and not Roome: the whiche insamples maketh those that governe, not to chaunge their purposes, but rather maketh them to stande more in their opinion, to be able to redeme again all thynges with taskes, and for this, thei will not submit theim selves to the troubles of thexercises of warre, semyng unto them partly not necessarie, partly, an intrinsicate matter, whiche thei understande not: Those other, whiche bee subjectes to them, whom soche insamples ought to make afraied, have no power to remedie it: and those Princes, that have ones loste their estates, are no more able, and those which as yet kept them, know not, nor wil not. Bicause thei will without any disease rain by fortune, and not by their vertue: for that in the worlde beyng but little vertue, thei see fortune governeth all thynges. And thei will have it to rule theim, not thei to rule it. And to prove this that I have discoursed to bee true, consider Almaine, in the whiche, bicause there is many Princedomes, and common weales, there is moche vertue, and all thesame, whiche in the present service of warre is good, dependeth of the insamples of those people: who beyng all gellious of their states, fearing servitude, the which in other places is not feared, thei all maintaine theim selves Lordes, and honourable: this that I have saied, shall suffice to shewe the occacions of the presente utilitie, accordyng to my opinion: I cannot tell, whether it seeme thesame unto you, or whether there be growen in you any doubtyng.

Cosimo. None, but rather I understande all verie well: onely I desire, tournyng to our principall matter, to understande of you, how you would ordein the horses with these battailes, and how many, and how thei should be governed, and how armed.

The Armyng of Horsemen; the Weapons That Light Horsmenne Should Have; the Nombre of Horsmen Requisite for a Maine Bataille of Six Thousand Men; the Nombre of Carrages That Men of Armes and Light Horsmen Ought to Have.

Fabricio. You thinke peraventure, that I have left it behinde: whereat doe not marvell, for that I purpose for twoo causes, to speake therof little, the one is, for that the strengthe, and the importaunce of an armie, is the footemen, the other is, bicause this part of service of warre, is lesse corrupted, then thesame of footemen. For that though it be not stronger then the old, yet it maie compare with thesame, nevertheles ther hath been spoken a little afore, of the maner of exercisyng them. And concernyng tharmyng them, I would arme them as thei doe at this present, as wel the light horsemen, as the menne of armes: but the light horsemen, I would that thei should be all Crossebowe shuters, with some Harkebutters emong them: the whiche though in the other affaires of warre, thei bee little profitable, thei be for this most profitable, to make afraied the countrie menne, and to drive them from a passage, that were kept of them: bicause a Harkebutter, shall feare them more, then twentie other armed. But commyng to the nomber, I saie, that having taken in hand, to imitate the service of warre of the Romaines, I would not ordein more then three hundred horse, profitable for every maine battaile, of whiche I would that there were CL. men of armes, and CL. light horsmen, and I would give to every one of these partes, a hedde, making after emong them fiftene peticapitaines for a bande, givyng to every one of them a Trompet, and a standarde: I would that every ten menne of armes, should have five carriages, and every ten light horsemen twoo, the whiche as those of the footemen, should carrie the tentes, the vesselles, and the axes, and the stakes, and the rest of their other harneis. Nor beleve not but that it is disorder, where the menne of armes have to their service fower horse, bicause soche a thyng is a corrupt use: for that the men of armes in Almaine, are seen to bee with their horse alone, every twentie of theim, havyng onely a carte, that carrieth after them their necessary thynges. The Romaine horsemen, were likewise a lone: true it is, that the Triary lodged nere them, whiche wer bound to minister helpe unto theim, in the kepyng of their horses the whiche maie easely be imitated of us, as in the distributyng of the lodgynges, I shall shewe you. Thesame then that the Romaines did, and that whiche the Duchmen doe now a daies, we maie doe also, ye, not doyng it, we erre. These horses ordained and appoincted together with a main battaile, maie sometymes be put together, when the battailes bee assembled, and to cause that betwene theim bee made some sight of assault, the whiche should be more to make them acquainted together, then for any other necessitie. But now of this part, there hath been spoke sufficiently, wherefore let us facion the armie, to be able to come into the field against the enemie, and hope to winne it: whiche thyng is the ende, for whiche the exercise of warre is ordeined, and so moche studie therein bestowed.

The Thirde Booke

Cosimo. Seeing that we chaunge reasonyng, I will that the demaunder be chaunged: bicause I would not be thought presumptuous, the which I have alwaies blamed in other: therfore, I resigne the Dictatorship, and give this aucthoritie to hym that will have it, of these my other frendes.

Zanobi. We would be moste glad, that you should procede, but seyng that you will not, yet tell at leaste, whiche of us shall succede in your place.

Cosimo. I will give this charge to signor Fabricio.

Fabricio. I am content to take it, and I will that we folowe the Venecian custome, that is, that the youngeste speake firste: bicause this beyng an exercise for yong men, I perswade my self, that yong menne, bee moste apt to reason thereof, as thei be moste readie to execute it.

Cosimo. Then it falleth to you Luigi: and as I have pleasure of soche a successour, so you shal satisfie your self of soche a demaunder: therefore I praie you, let us tourne to the matter, and let us lese no more tyme.

The greateste disorder that is used now a daies in pitching of a fielde; the order how a romain legion was appoincted to faight; the maner that the grekes used in their falangi, when thei fought against their enemies; the order that the suizzers use in their main battailes when thei faight; howe to appoincte a main battaile with armour and weapons, and to order thesame after the Greke and Romain maner.

Fabricio. I am certain, that to mynde to shewe wel, how an armie is prepared, to faight a fielde, it should be necessarie to declare, how the Grekes, and the Romaines ordeined the bandes of their armies: Notwithstandyng, you your selves, beeyng able to rede, and to consider these tnynges, by meanes of the auncient writers. I will passe over many particulars: and I will onely bryng in those thynges, whiche I thinke necessarie to imitate, mindyng at this tyme, to give to our exercise of warre, some parte of perfection: The whiche shall make, that in one instant, I shall shewe you, how an armie is prepared to the field, and how it doeth incounter in the verie faight, and how it maie be exercised in the fained. The greatest disorder, that thei make, whiche ordeine an armie to the fielde, is in giving them onely one fronte, and to binde them to one brunt, and to one fortune: the whiche groweth, of havyng loste the waie, that the antiquitie used to receive one bande within an other: bicause without this waie, thei can neither succour the formoste, nor defende them, nor succede in the faight in their steede: the whiche of the Romaines, was moste excellently well observed. Therefore, purposyng to shewe this waie, I saie, how that the Romaines devided into iii. partes every Legion, in Hastati, Prencipi, and Triarii, of which, the Hastati wer placed in the first front, or forward of the armie, with thorders thicke and sure, behinde whom wer the Prencipi, but placed with their orders more thinne: after these, thei set the Triarii, and with so moche thinnes of orders, that thei might, if nede wer, receive betwene them the Prencipi, and the Hastati. Thei had besides these, the Slingers, and Crosbowshoters, and the other lighte armed, the whiche stoode not in these orders, but thei placed them in the bed of tharmie, betwene the horses and the other bandes of footemen: therefore these light armed, began the faight, if thei overcame (whiche happened seldom times) thei folowed the victorie: if thei were repulced, thei retired by the flanckes of the armie, or by the spaces ordained for soche purposes, and thei brought them selves emong the unarmed: after the departure of whom, the Hastati incountered with the enemie, the whiche if thei saw themselves to be overcome, thei retired by a little and little, by the rarenesse of thorders betwene the Prencipi, and together with those, thei renued the faight if these also wer repulced, thei retired al in the rarenesse of the orders of the Triarii, and al together on a heape, began againe the faight: and then, if thei were overcome, there was no more remeady, bicause there remained no more waies to renue them again. The horses stoode on the corners of the armie, to the likenes of twoo winges to a bodie, and somewhiles thei fought with the enemies horses, an other while, thei rescued the fotmen, according as nede required. This waie of renuyng theim selves three tymes, is almoste impossible to overcome: for that, fortune muste three tymes forsake thee, and the enemie to have so moche strengthe, that three tymes he maie overcome thee. The Grekes, had not in their Falangi, this maner of renuyng them selves, and although in those wer many heddes, and many orders, notwithstandyng, thei made one bodie, or els one hedde: the maner that thei kepte in rescuyng the one the other was, not to retire the one order within the other, as the Romaines, but to enter the one manne into the place of the other: the which thei did in this maner. Their Falange brought into rankes, and admit, that thei put in a ranke fiftie menne, commyng after with their hedde againste the enemie, of all the rankes the foremoste sixe, mighte faight: Bicause their Launces, the whiche thei called Sarisse, were so long, that the sixt ranke, passed with the hedde of their Launces, out of the first ranke: then in faightyng, if any of the first, either through death, or through woundes fell, straight waie there entered into his place, thesame man, that was behinde in the second ranke, and in the place that remained voide of the seconde, thesame man entred, whiche was behind hym in the thirde, and thus successively, in a sodaine the rankes behinde, restored the faultes of those afore, so that the rankes alwaies remained whole, and no place of the faighters was voide, except the laste rankes, the whiche came to consume, havyng not menne behinde their backes, whom might restore theim: So that the hurte that the first rankes suffered, consumed the laste, and the firste remained alwaies whole: and thus these Falangi by their order, might soner be consumed, then broken, for that the grosse bodie, made it more immovable. The Romaines used at the beginnyng the Falangi, and did set in order their Legions like unto them: after, this order pleased them not, and thei devided the Legions into many bodies, that is, in bandes and companies: Bicause thei judged (as a little afore I saied) that thesame bodie, should have neede of many capitaines, and that it should be made of sunderie partes, so that every one by it self, might be governed. The maine battailes of the Suizzers, use at this present, all the maners of the Falangi, as well in ordryng it grosse, and whole, as in rescuyng the one the other: and in pitchyng the field, thei set the main battailes, thone to the sides of the other: and though thei set them the one behinde the other, thei have no waie, that the firste retiryng it self, maie bee received of the seconde, but thei use this order, to the entent to bee able to succour the one thother, where thei put a maine battaile before, and an other behinde thesame on the right hande: so that if the first have nede of helpe, that then the other maie make forewarde, and succour it: the third main battaile, thei put behind these, but distant from them, a Harkebus shot: this thei doe, for that thesaid two main battailes being repulced, this maie make forwarde, and have space for theim selves, and for the repulced, and thesame that marcheth forward, to avoide the justling of the one the other: for asmoche as a grosse multitude, cannot bee received as a little bodie: and therefore, the little bodies beyng destincte, whiche were in a Romaine Legion, might be placed in soche wise, that thei might receive betwene theim, and rescue the one the other. And to prove this order of the Suizzers not to be so good, as the auncient Romaines, many insamples of the Romain Legions doe declare, when thei fought with the Grekes Falangi, where alwaies thei were consumed of theim: for that the kinde of their weapons (as I have said afore) and this waie of renuyng themselves, could do more, then the massivenesse of the Falangi. Havyng therefore, with these insamples to ordaine an armie, I have thought good, partly to retaine the maner of armyng and the orders of the Grekes Falangi, and partely of the Romain Legions: and therfore I have saied, that I would have in a main battaile, twoo thousande pikes, whiche be the weapons of the Macedonicall Falangi, and three thousande Targaettes with sweardes, whiche be the Romain weapons: I have devided the main battaile, into x. battailes, as the Romaines their Legion into ten Cohortes: I have ordeined the Veliti, that is the light armed, to begin the faight, as the Romaines used: and like as the weapons beyng mingled, doe participate of thone and of the other nacion, so the orders also doe participate: I have ordained, that every battaile shall have v. rankes of Pikes in the fronte, and the rest of Targaettes, to bee able with the front, to withstande the horses, and to enter easely into the battaile of the enemies on foot, having in the firste fronte, or vawarde, Pikes, as well as the enemie, the whiche shall suffice me to withstande them, the Targaettes after to overcome theim. And if you note the vertue of this order, you shal se al these weapons, to doe fully their office, for that the Pikes, bee profitable against the horses, and when thei come against the footemenne, thei dooe their office well, before the faight throng together, bicause so sone as thei presse together, thei become unprofitable: wherefore, the Suizzers to avoide this inconvenience, put after everye three rankes of Pikes, a ranke of Halberdes, the whiche they do to make roome to the Pikes, which is not yet so much as suffiseth. Then putting our Pikes afore, and the Targaettes behinde, they come to withstande the horses, and in the beginning of the fight, they open the rayes, and molest the footemen: But when the fight is thrust together, and that they become unprofitable, the Targaettes and swoords succeede, which may in every narowe place be handled.

Luigi. Wee looke nowe with desire to understande, howe you would ordeyne the armie to fighte the fielde, with these weapons, and with these order.

The nomber of men that was in a counsulles armie; how the Romaines placed their legions in the field; how to order an armie in the fielde to fighte a battaile, according to the minde of the authour; how the extraordinary pikes bee placed in the set battaile; the place where thextraordinarie archars and harkebutters, and the men of armes and lighte horsmen ought to stande when the field is pitched, and goeth to faighte the battaile; the ordinarie archars and harkebutters are placed aboute their owne battailes; the place where the generall hedde of a maine battaile muste stande, when thesame power of men is appoincted to faight; what menne a general capitain of a maine battaile oughte to have aboute hym; the place wher a general capitain of all thearmie must stand when the battaile is ready to be fought and what nomber of chosen men oughte to be aboute hym; how many canons is requisite for an armie, and of what sise they ought to bee; where the artillerie ought to be placed when thearmie is reedie to fight; an armie that were ordered as above is declared, maie in fighting, use the Grekes maner, and the roman fashion; to what purpose the spaces that be betwene every bande of men do serve.

Fabricio. And I will not nowe shewe you other, then this: you have to understande, how that in an ordinarye Romane armie, which they call a Consull armie, there were no more, then twoo Legions of Romane Citezens which were sixe hundred horse, and about aleven thousande footemen: they had besides as many more footemen and horsemen, whiche were sente them from their friends and confiderates, whome they divided into twoo partes, and called the one, the right horne and the other the left horne: nor they never permitted, that these aiding footemen, should passe the nomber of the footemen of their Legions, they were well contented, that the nomber of those horse shoulde be more then theirs: with this armie, which was of xxii. thousand footemen, and about twoo thousande good horse, a Consul executed all affaires, and went to all enterprises: yet when it was needefull to set against a greater force, twoo Consulles joyned together with twoo armies. You ought also to note in especially, that in all the three principall actes, which an armie doth that is, to march, to incampe, and to fight, the Romanes used to put their Legions in the middeste, for that they woulde, that the same power, wherein they most trusted, shoulde bee moste united, as in the reasoning of these three actes, shall be shewed you: those aiding footemen, through the practise they had with the Legion Souldiours, were as profitable as they, because they were instructed, according as the souldiours of the Legions were, and therefore, in like maner in pitching the field, they pitched. Then he that knoweth how the Romaines disposed a Legion in their armie, to fight a field, knoweth how they disposed all: therefor, having tolde you how they devided a Legion into three bandes, and how the one bande received the other, I have then told you, how al tharmie in a fielde, was ordained. Wherefore, I minding to ordain a field like unto the Romaines, as they had twoo Legions, I will take ii. main batailes, and these being disposed, the disposicion of all an armie shalbe understode therby: bycause in joyning more men, there is no other to be doen, then to ingrosse the orders: I thinke I neede not to rehearse how many men a maine battaile hath, and howe it hath ten battailes, and what heades bee in a battaile and what weapons they have, and which be the ordinarie Pikes and Veliti, and which the extraordinarie for that a litle a fore I told you it destinctly, and I willed you to kepe it in memorie as a necessarie thing to purpose, to understande all the other orders: and therfore I will come to the demonstracion of the order without repeating it any more: Me thinkes good, that the ten battailes of one main battaile be set on the left flanke, and the tenne other, of the other main battaile, on the right: these that are placed on the left flanke, be ordeined in this maner, there is put five battailes the one to the side of the other in the fronte, after suche sorte, that betweene the one and the other, there remaine a space of three yardes, whiche come to occupie for largenesse Cvi. yardes, of ground, and for length thirtie: behinde these five battailes, I would put three other distante by right line from the firste thirtie yardes: twoo of the whiche, should come behinde by right line, to the uttermoste of the five, and the other should kepe the space in the middeste, and so these three, shall come to occupie for bredth and length, as moche space, as the five doeth. But where the five have betwene the one, and the other, a distaunce of three yardes, these shall have a distance of xxv. yardes. After these, I would place the twoo last battailes, in like maner behinde the three by right line, and distaunte from those three, thirtie yardes, and I would place eche of theim, behinde the uttermoste part of the three, so that the space, whiche should remain betwen the one and the other, should be lxviii. yardes: then al these battailes thus ordered, will take in bredth Cvi. yardes, and in length CL. Thextraordinarie Pikes, I would deffende a long the flanckes of these battailes, on the left side, distante from them fiftene yardes, makyng Cxliij. rankes, seven to a ranke, after soche sorte, that thei maie impale with their length, all the left sixe of the tenne battailes in thesame wise, declared of me to be ordained: and there shall remain fourtie rankes to keepe the carriages, and the unarmed, whiche ought to remaine in the taile of the armie, distributyng the Peticapitaines, and the Centurions, in their places: and of the three Conestables, I would place one in the hedde, the other in the middeste, the third in the laste ranke, the whiche should execute the office of a Tergiductore, whom the antiquitie so called hym, that was appoincted to the backe of the armie. But retournyng to the hedde of the armie, I saie how that I would place nere to the extraordinarie pikes, the Veliti extraordinarie, whiche you knowe to be five hundred, and I would give them a space of xxx. yardes: on the side of these likewise on the left hande, I would place the menne of armes, and I would thei should have a space of a Cxii. yardes: after these, the light horsemen, to whom I would appoinct as moche ground to stande in, as the menne of armes have: the ordinarie veliti, I would leave about their owne battailes, who should stand in those spaces, whiche I appoincte betwene thone battaile and thother: whom should be as their ministers, if sometyme I thought not good to place them under the extraordinarie Pikes: in dooyng or not doyng whereof, I would proceade, accordyng as should tourne best to my purpose. The generall hedde of all the maine battaile, I would place in thesame space, that were betwene the first and the seconde order of the battailes, or els in the hedde, and in thesame space, that is betwene the laste battaile of the firste five, and the extraordinarie Pikes, accordyng as beste should serve my purpose, with thirtie or fourtie chosen men about hym, that knewe by prudence, how to execute a commission, and by force, to withstande a violence, and thei to be also betwen the Drumme and the Ansigne: this is thorder, with the whiche I would dispose a maine battaile, whiche should bee the disposyng of halfe the armie, and it should take in breadth three hundred fourscore and twoo yardes, and in length as moche as above is saied, not accomptyng the space, that thesame parte of the extraordinarie Pikes will take, whiche muste make a defence for the unarmed, whiche will bee aboute lxxv. yardes: the other maine battaile, I would dispose on the righte side, after the same maner juste, as I have disposed that on the lefte, leavyng betwene the one main battaile, and thother, a space of xxii. yardes: in the hedde of whiche space, I would set some little carriages of artillerie, behynde the whiche, should stande the generall capitaine of all the armie, and should have about hym with the Trumpet, and with the Capitaine standerde, twoo hundred menne at least, chosen to be on foote the moste parte, emongest whiche there should be tenne or more, mete to execute all commaundementes, and should bee in soche wise a horsebacke, and armed, that thei mighte bee on horsebacke, and on foote, accordyng as neede should require. The artillerie of the armie, suffiseth ten Cannons, for the winning of Townes, whose shotte shoulde not passe fiftie pounde: the whiche in the fielde should serve mee more for defence of the campe, then for to fight the battaile: The other artillerie, should bee rather of ten, then of fifteene pounde the shotte: this I would place afore on the front of all the armie, if sometime the countrie should not stande in such wise, that I mighte place it by the flancke in a sure place, where it mighte not of the enemie be in daunger: this fashion of an armie thus ordered, may in fighting, use the order of the Falangi, and the order of the Romane Legions: for that in the fronte, bee Pikes, all the men bee set in the rankes, after such sorte, that incountering with the enemie, and withstanding him, maye after the use of the Falangi, restore the firste ranckes, with those behinde: on the other parte, if they be charged so sore, that they be constrayned to breake the orders, and to retire themselves, they maye enter into the voide places of the seconde battailes, which they have behinde them, and unite their selves with them, and making a new force, withstande the enemie, and overcome him: and when this sufficeth not, they may in the verie same maner, retire them selves the seconde time, and the third fight: so that in this order, concerning to fight, there is to renue them selves, both according to the Greeke maner, and according to the Romane: concerning the strength of the armie, there cannot be ordayned a more stronger: for as much, as the one and the other borne therof, is exceedingly well replenished, both with heades, and weapons, nor there remayneth weake, other then the part behinde of the unarmed, and the same also, hath the flanckes impaled with the extraordinarie Pikes: nor the enemie can not of anye parte assaulte it, where he shall not finde it well appointed, and the hinder parte can not be assaulted: Because there can not bee an enemie, that hath so much puissaunce, whome equallye maye assault thee on everye side: for that hee having so great a power, thou oughtest not then to matche thy selfe in the fielde with him: but when he were three times more then thou, and as well appointed as thou, hee doth weaken him selfe in assaulting thee in divers places, one part that thou breakest, will cause all the reste go to naughte: concerning horses, although he chaunce to have more then thine, thou needest not feare: for that the orders of the Pikes, which impale thee, defende thee from all violence of them, although thy horses were repulced. The heades besides this, be disposed in such place, that they may easyly commaunde, and obeye: the spaces that bee between the one battaile, and the other, and betweene the one order, and the other, not onely serve to be able to receyve the one the other, but also to give place to the messengers, whiche should go and come by order of the Capitayne. And as I tolde you firste, howe the Romanes had for an armie, aboute foure and twentie thousande men, even so this oughte to bee: and as the other souldiours tooke ensample of the Legions, for the maner of fighting, and the fashion of the armie, so those souldiours, whiche you shoulde joyne to oure twoo mayne battailes, oughte to take the forme and order of them: whereof having put you an ensample, it is an easye matter to imitate it, for that increasing, either twoo other mayne battailes unto the armie, or as many other souldiours, as they bee, there is no other to bee done, then to double the orders, and where was put tenne battailes on the lefte parte, to put twentie, either ingrossing, or distending the orders, according as the place, or the enemie shoulde compell thee.

Luigi. Surelye sir I imagine in suche wise of this armie, that mee thinkes I nowe see it, and I burne with a desire to see it incounter, and I woulde for nothing in the worlde, that you shoulde become Fabius Maximus intendyng to kepe the enemie at a baie, and to deferre the daie of battaile: bicause I would saie worse of you, then the Romain people saied of hym.

The descripcion of a battaile that is a faightyng.

Fabricio. Doubt not: Doe you not heare the artillerie? Ours have alredie shotte, but little hurte the enemie: and thextraordinarie Veliti, issuyng out of their places together with the light horsemen, moste speadely, and with moste merveilous furie, and greateste crie that maie be, thei assaulte the enemie: whose artillerie hath discharged ones, and hath passed over the heddes of our footemen, without doyng them any hurt, and bicause it cannot shoote the seconde tyme, the Veliti, and our horsemen, have nowe gotten it, and the enemies for to defende it, are come fore warde, so that neither our ordinaunce, nor thenemies, can any more doe their office. Se with how moche vertue, strengthe and agilitie our men faighteth, and with how moche knowledge through the exercise, whiche hath made them to abide, and by the confidence, that thei have in the armie, the whiche, see, how with the pace therof, and with the men of armes on the sides, it marcheth in good order, to give the charge on the adversarie: See our artillerie, whiche to give theim place, and to leave them the space free, is retired by thesame space, from whens the Veliti issued: See how the capitaine incourageth them, sheweth them the victorie certain: See how the Veliti and light horsemen bee inlarged, and retourned on the flanckes of tharmie, to seke and view, if thei maie by the flanck, doe any injurie to the adversaries: behold how the armies be affronted. Se with how moche valiauntnesse thei have withstode the violence of thenemies, and with how moche silence, and how the capitain commaundeth the menne of armes, that thei sustain, and not charge, and that thei breake not from the order of the footemen: see how our light horsemen be gone, to give the charge on a band of the enemies Harkebutters, whiche would have hurt our men by flancke, and how the enemies horse have succoured them, so that tourned betwene the one and the other horse, thei cannot shoote, but are faine to retire behinde their owne battaile: see with what furie our Pikes doe also affront, and how the footemen be now so nere together the one to the other, that the Pikes can no more be occupied: so that according to the knowlege learned of us, our pikes do retire a little and a little betwen the targaettes. Se how in this while a great bande of men of armes of the enemies, have charged our men of armes on the lefte side, and how ours, accordyng to knowlege, bee retired under the extraordinarie Pikes, and with the help of those, giving again a freshe charge, have repulced the adversaries, and slain a good part of them: in so moche, that thordinarie pikes of the first battailes, be hidden betwene the raies of the Targaettes, thei havyng lefte the faight to the Targaet men: whom you maie see, with how moche vertue, securitie, and leasure, thei kill the enemie: see you not how moche by faightyng, the orders be thrust together? That thei can scarse welde their sweardes? Behold with how moche furie the enemies move: bicause beyng armed with the pike, and with the swerd unprofitable (the one for beyng to long, the other for findyng thenemie to well armed) in part thei fall hurt or dedde, in parte thei flie. See, thei flie on the righte corner, thei flie also on the lefte: behold, the victorie is ours. Have not we wonne a field moste happely? But with more happinesse it should bee wonne, if it were graunted me to put it in acte. And see, how there neded not the helpe of the seconde, nor of the third order, for our first fronte hath sufficed to overcome theim: in this part, I have no other to saie unto you, then to resolve if any doubt be growen you.

Questions concerning the shotyng of ordinaunce.

Luigi. You have with so moche furie wonne this fielde that I so moche mervaile and am so astonied, that I beleve that I am not able to expresse, if any doubt remain in my mynde: yet trustyng in your prudence, I will be so bolde to tell thesame that I understande. Tell me firste, why made you not your ordinaunce to shoote more then ones? And why straighte waie you made them to retire into tharmie, nor after made no mension of them? Me thought also, that you leveled the artillerie of the enemie high, and appoincted it after your own devise: the whiche might very well bee, yet when it should happen, as I beleve it chaunseth often, that thei strike the rankes, what reamedie have you? And seyng that I have begun of the artillerie, I will finishe all this question, to the intente I nede not to reason therof any more. I have heard many dispraise the armours, and the orders of the aunciente armies, arguyng, how now a daies, thei can doe little, but rather should bee altogether unprofitable, havyng respecte to the furie of the artillerie: bicause, this breaketh the orders, and passeth the armours in soche wise, that it semeth unto them a foolishenesse to make an order, whiche cannot bee kepte, and to take pain to beare a harneis, that cannot defende a man.

An aunswere to the questions that were demaunded, concernyng the shoting of ordinaunce; the best remedie to avoide the hurte that the enemie in the fielde maie doe with his ordinaunce; a policie against bowes and dartes; nothyng causeth greater confusion in an armie, than to hinder mennes fightes; nothing more blindeth the sight of men in an armie, then the smoke of ordinaunce; a policie to trouble the enemies sight; the shotte of greate ordinaunce in the fielde, is not moche to bee feared of fotemenne; bicause menne of armes stand closer together then light horsmen, thei ought to remaine behinde the armie till the enemies ordinaunce have done shootyng; the artillerie is no let, why the auncient orders of warfar ought not to be used in these daies.

Fabricio. This question of yours (bicause it hath many heddes) hath neede of a long aunswere. It is true, that I made not thartillery to shoote more than ones, and also of thesame ones, I stoode in doubte: the occasion was, for asmoche as it importeth more, for one to take hede not to be striken, then it importeth to strike the enemie. You have to understande, that to purpose that a pece of ordinaunce hurte you not, it is necessarie either to stande where it cannot reche you, or to get behinde a wall, or behinde a banke: other thing there is not that can witholde it: and it is nedefull also, that the one and the other be moste strong. Those capitaines whiche come to faight a field, cannot stand behind a wal, or behind bankes, nor where thei maie not be reached: therfore it is mete for them, seyng thei cannot finde a waie to defende them, to finde some mean, by the whiche thei maie be least hurte: nor thei cannot finde any other waie, then to prevente it quickly: the waie to prevent it, is to go to finde it out of hande, and hastely, not at leasure and in a heape: for that through spede, the blowe is not suffered to bee redoubled, and by the thinnesse, lesse nomber of menne maie be hurt. This, a bande of menne ordered, cannot dooe; bicause if thesame marche hastely, it goweth out of order: if it go scattered, the enemie shall have no paine to breake it, for that it breaketh by it self: and therfore, I ordered the armie after soche sorte, that it might dooe the one thyng and the other: for as moche as havyng set in the corners thereof, a thousande Veliti, I appoincted that after that our ordinaunce had shotte, thei should issue out together with the light horsemen, to get the enemies artillerie: and therfore, I made not my ordinance to shoote again, to the intente, to give no tyme to the enemie to shoote: Bicause space could not be given to me, and taken from other men, and for thesame occasion, where I made my ordinaunce not to shoote the seconde tyme, was for that I would not have suffered the enemie to have shot at al, if I had could: seyng that to mynde that the enemies artillerie be unprofitable, there is no other remedie, but to assaulte it spedely: for as moche as if the enemies forsake it, thou takeste it, if thei will defende it, it is requisite that thei leave it behind, so that being possessed of enemies, and of frendes, it cannot shoote. I would beleve, that with out insamples these reasons should suffice you, yet beyng able to shewe olde ensamples, to prove my saiynges true, I will. Ventidio commyng to faight a field with the Parthians, whose strength for the moste part, consisted in bowes and arrowes, he suffered theim almoste to come harde to his campe, before he drewe out his armie, the whiche onely he did, to be able quickly to prevent them: and not to give them space to shoote. Cesar when he was in Fraunce, maketh mencion, that in faighting a battaile with the enemies, he was with so moche furie assaulted of them, that his menne had no time to whorle their Dartes, accordyng to the custome of the Romaines: wherfore it is seen, that to intende, that a thyng that shooteth farre of, beyng in the field, doe not hurte thee, there is no other remedy, then with as moche celeritie as maie bee, to prevente it. An other cause moved me to procede, without shotyng the ordinaunce, whereat peradventure you will laugh: yet I judge not that it is to be dispraised. Ther is nothyng that causeth greater confusion in an armie, then to hinder mennes fightes: whereby many moste puisaunte armies have been broken, by meanes their fighte hath been letted, either with duste, or with the Sunne: yet there is nothyng, that more letteth the sight then the smoke that the artillerie maketh in shotyng: therfore, I would thinke that it wer more wisedome, to suffer the enemie to blinde hymself, then to purpose (thou being blind) to go to finde hym: for this cause, either I would not shote, or (for that this should not be proved, considering the reputacion that the artillerie hath) I would place it on the corners of the armie, so that shootyng, it should not with the smoke thereof, blinde the front of thesame, whiche is the importaunce of my men. And to prove that it is a profitable thyng, to let the sight of the enemie, there maie be brought for insample Epaminondas, whom to blind the enemies armie, whiche came to faight with hym, he caused his light horsemen, to run before the fronte of the enemies, to raise up the duste, and to lette their sight, whereby he gotte the victorie. And where it semeth unto you, that I have guided the shot of the artillerie, after my owne devise, making it to passe over the heddes of my men, I answer you, that most often tymes, and without comparison, the greate ordinaunce misse the footemen, moche soner than hitte theim: for that the footemen are so lowe, and those so difficult to shoote; that every little that thou raisest theim, thei passe over the heddes of men: and if thei be leveled never so little to lowe, thei strike in the yearth, and the blowe cometh not to theim: also the unevenesse of the grounde saveth them, for that every little hillocke, or high place that is, betwene the men and thordinance, letteth the shot therof. And concernyng horsmen, and in especially men of armes, bicause thei ought to stand more close together, then the light horsemen, and for that thei are moche higher, maie the better be stroken, thei maie, untill the artillerie have shotte, be kepte in the taile of the armie. True it is, that the Harkebutters doe moche more hurt, and the field peces, then the greate ordinance, for the whiche, the greatest remedy is, to come to hande strokes quickly: and if in the firste assaulte, there be slaine some, alwaies there shall bee slaine: but a good capitaine, and a good armie, ought not to make a coumpte of a hurte, that is particulare, but of a generall, and to imitate the Suizzers, whom never eschue to faight, beyng made afraied of the artillerie: but rather punishe with death those, whiche for feare thereof, either should go out of the ranke, or should make with his body any signe of feare. I made them (so sone as thei had shotte) to bee retired into the armie, that thei might leave the waie free for the battaile: I made no more mencion of theim, as of a thyng unprofitable, the faight beyng begun. You have also saied, that consideryng the violence of this instrument, many judge the armours, and the auncient orders to be to no purpose, and it semeth by this your talke, that men now a daies, have founde orders and armours, whiche are able to defend them against the artillerie: if you knowe this, I would bee glad that you would teache it me: for that hetherto, I never sawe any, nor I beleve that there can any be founde: so that I would understande of soche men, for what cause the souldiours on foote in these daies, weare the breastplate, or the corselet of steele, and thei on horsebacke go all armed: bicause seyng that thei blame the aunciente armyng of men as unprofitable, considryng the artillery, thei ought to despise also this? I would understande moreover, for what occasion the Suizzers, like unto the auncient orders, make a battaile close together of sixe, or eight thousande menne, and for what occasion all other have imitated theim, this order bearyng the verie same perill, concernyng the artillerie, that those other should beare, whiche should imitate the antiquitie. I beleve thei should not knowe what to answere: but if you should aske soche Souldiours, as had some judgement, thei would aunswere first, that thei go armed, for that though thesame armoure defende theim not from the artillerie: it defendeth them from crossebowes, from Pikes, from sweardes, from stones, and from all other hurt, that commeth from the enemies, thei would answere also, that thei went close together, like the Suizzers, to be able more easely to overthrow the footemen, to be able to withstand better the horse and to give more difficultie to the enemie to breake them: so that it is seen, that the souldiours have to fear, many other thynges besides the ordinance: from which thynges, with the armours, and with the orders, thei are defended: whereof foloweth, that the better that an armie is armed, and the closer that it hath the orders, and stronger, so moche the surer it is: so that he that is of thesame opinion, that you saie, it behoveth either that he bee of smalle wisedome, or that in this thyng, he hath studied verie little: for as moche as if we see, that so little a parte of the aunciente maner of armyng, whiche is used now a daies, that is the pike, and so little a parte of those orders, as are the maine battailes of the Suizzers, dooe us so moche good, and cause our armies to bee so strong, why ought not we to beleve, that the other armours, and thother orders whiche are lefte, be profitable? Seyng that if we have no regard to the artillerie, in puttyng our selves close together, as the Suizzers, what other orders maie make us more to feare thesame? For as moche as no order can cause us so moche to feare thesame, as those, whiche bryng men together. Besides this, if the artillerie of the enemies should not make me afraied, in besiegyng a Toune, where it hurteth me with more safegarde, beyng defended of a wall, I beyng not able to prevente it, but onely with tyme, with my artillerie to lette it, after soche sorte that it maie double the blowe as it liste, why should I feare thesame in the field, where I maie quickly prevent it? So that I conclude thus, that the artillerie, according to my opinion, doeth not let, that the aunciente maners cannot be used, and to shewe the auncient vertue: and if I had not talked alreadie with you of this instrument, I would of thesame, declare unto you more at length: but I will remit my self to that, whiche then I saied.

Luigi. Wee maie now understande verie well, how moche you have aboute the artillerie discoursed: and in conclusion, my thinkes you have shewed, that the preventyng it quickly, is the greatest remedie, that maie be had for thesame, beyng in the fielde, and havyng an armie againste you. Upon the whiche there groweth in me a doubte: bicause me thinkes, that the enemie might place his ordinaunce in soche wise, in his armie, that it should hurt you, and should be after soche sort garded of the footemen, that it could not be prevented. You have (if you remember your self well) in the orderyng of your armie to faight, made distaunces of three yardes, betwene the one battaile and the other, makyng those distaunces fiftene, whiche is from the battailes, to thextraordinarie pikes: if thenemie, shuld order his armie like unto yours, and should putte the artillerie a good waie within those spaces, I beleve that from thens, it should hurte you with their moste greate safegard: bicause menne can not enter into the force of their enemies to prevent it.

A generall rule againste soche thynges as cannot bee withstoode.

Fabricio. You doubt moste prudently, and I will devise with my self, either to resolve you the doubte, or shewe you the remedie: I have tolde you, that continually these battailes, either through goyng, or thorowe faightyng, are movyng, and alwaies naturally, thei come to drawe harde together, so that if you make the distaunces of a small breadth, where you set the artillerie, in a little tyme thei be shootte up, after soche sort, that the artillerie cannot any more shoote: if you make theim large, to avoide this perill, you incurre into a greater, where you through those distances, not onely give commoditie to the enemie, to take from you the artillerie, but to breake you: but you have to understande, that it is impossible to keepe the artillerie betwene the bandes, and in especially those whiche go on carriages: For that the artillerie goeth one waie, and shooteth an other waie: So that havyng to go and to shoote, it is necessary, before thei shote, that thei tourne, and for to tourne theim, thei will have so moche space, that fiftie cartes of artillerie, would disorder any armie: therfore, it is mete to kepe them out of the bandes, where thei may be overcome in the maner, as a little afore we have shewed: but admit thei might be kept, and that there might be found a waie betwen bothe, and of soche condicion, that the presyng together of men should not hinder the artillerie, and were not so open that it should give waie to the enemie, I saie, that it is remedied moste easely, with makyng distances in thy armie against it, whiche maie give free passage to the shot of those, and so the violence thereof shall come to be vain, the which maie be doen moste easely: for asmoche, as the enemie mindyng to have his artillerie stand safe, it
behoveth that he put them behinde, in the furthest part of the distances, so that the shot of the same, he purposyng that thei hurt not his owne men, ought to passe by right line, and by that very same alwaies: and therefore with givyng theim place, easely thei maie bee avoided: for that this is a generall rule, that to those thynges, whiche cannot be withstode, there must bee given waie, as the antiquitie made to the Eliphantes, and to the carres full of hookes. I beleve, ye, I am more then certaine, that it semeth unto you, that I have ordered and wonne a battaile after my own maner: notwithstanding, I answeer unto you this, when so moche as I have saied hetherto, should not suffice, that it should be impossible, that an armie thus ordered, and armed, should not overcome at the first incounter, any other armie that should bee ordained, as thei order the armies now adaies, whom most often tymes, make not but one front, havyng no targaettes, and are in soche wise unarmed, that thei cannot defende themselves from the enemie at hand, and thei order theim after soche sorte, that if thei set their battailes by flanck, the one to the other, thei make the armie thinne: if thei put the one behind the other, havyng no waie to receive the one the other, thei doe it confusedly, and apt to be easly troubled: and although thei give three names to their armies, and devide them into thre companies, vaward, battaile, and rereward, notwithstandyng it serveth to no other purpose, then to marche, and to distinguis the lodgynges: but in the daie of battaile, thei binde them all to the first brunte, and to the first fortune.

Luigi. I have noted also in the faightyng of your fielde, how your horsemen were repulced of the enemies horsemen: for whiche cause thei retired to the extraordinaire Pikes: whereby grewe, that with the aide of theim, thei withstode, and drave the enemies backe? I beleve that the Pikes maie withstande the horses, as you saie, but in a grosse and thicke maine battaile, as the Suizzers make: but you in your army, have for the hedde five rankes of Pikes, and for the flancke seven, so that I cannot tell how thei maie bee able to withstande them.

A battaile how greate so ever it bee, cannot atones occupy above v. rankes of pikes.

Fabricio. Yet I have told you, how sixe rankes of pikes wer occupied at ones, in the Macedonicall Falangi, albeit you ought to understande, that a maine battaile of Suizzers, if it were made of a thousande rankes, it cannot occupie more then fower, or at the most five: bicause the Pikes be sixe yardes and three quarters longe, one yarde and halfe a quarter, is occupied of the handes, wherefore to the firste ranke, there remaineth free five yardes and a half, and a halfe quarter of Pike: the seconde ranke besides that whiche is occupied with the hande, consumeth a yarde and half a quarter in the space, whiche remaineth betwene the one ranke and thother: so that there is not left of pike profitable, more then fower yardes and a halfe: to the thirde ranke, by this verie same reason, there remaineth three yardes and a quarter and a halfe: to the fowerth, twoo yardes and a quarter: to the fift one yard and halfe a quarter: the other rankes, for to hurte, be unprofitable, but thei serve to restore these firste rankes, as we have declared, and to bee a fortificacion to those v. Then if five of their rankes can withstande the horse, why cannot five of ours withstande theim? to the whiche also there lacketh not rankes behinde, that doeth sustain and make them the very same staie, although thei have no pikes as the other. And when the rankes of thextraordinarie pikes, which are placed on the flanckes, should seme unto you thinne, thei maie bee brought into a quadrante, and put on the flancke nere the twoo battailes, whiche I set in the laste companie of the armie: From the whiche place, thei maie easely altogether succour the fronte, and the backe of the armie, and minister helpe to the horses, accordyng as nede shall require.

Luigi. Would you alwaies use this forme of order, when you would pitche a fielde.

An advertiement concernyng the pitchying of a field.

Fabricio. No in no wise: for that you ought to varie the facion of the armie, according to the qualitie of the situacion, and the condicion and quantitie of the enemie, as before this reasonyng dooe ende, shall bee shewed certaine insamples: but this forme is given unto you, not so moche as moste strongeste of all, where in deede it is verie strong, as to the intente that thereby you maie take a rule, and an order to learne to knowe the waies to ordeine the other: for as moche, as every science hath his generalitie, upon the whiche a good part of it is grounded. One thing onely I advise you, that you never order an armie, after soche sorte, that those that faight afore, cannot bee sucoured of theim, whiche be set behind: bicause he that committeth this errour, maketh the greateste parte of his armie to bee unprofitable, and if it incounter any strength, it cannot overcome.

Luigi. There is growen in me, upon this parte a doubte. I have seen that in the placyng of the battailes, you make the fronte of five on a side, the middeste of three, and the last partes of twoo, and I beleve, that it were better to ordain them contrariwise: for that I thinke, that an armie should with more difficultie bee broken, when he that should charge upon it, the more that he should entre into the-same, so moche the stronger he should finde it: and the order devised of you, me thinkes maketh, that the more it is entered into, so moche the weaker it is founde.

How the front of the armie ought to bee made; how the middell part of the armie ought to be ordered.

Fabricio. If you should remember how to the Triarii, whom were the thirde order of the Romain Legions, there were not assigned more then sixe hundred men, you would doubt lesse, havyng understode how thei were placed in the laste companie: For that you should see, how I moved of this insample, have placed in the last companie twoo battailes, whiche are nine hundred men, so that I come rather (folowyng the insample of the Romaine people) to erre, for havyng taken to many, then to fewe: and although this insample should suffice, I will tell you the reason, the which is this. The first fronte of the armie, is made perfectly whole and thicke, bicause it must withstande the brunt of the enemies, and it hath not to receive in it any of their felowes: and for this, it is fitte that it bee full of menne: bicause a fewe menne, should make it weake, either thinnesse, or for lacke of sufficiente nomber: but the seconde companie, for as moche as it must first receive their frendes, to sustain the enemie, it is mete that it have greate spaces, and for this it behoveth, that it be of lesse nomber then the first: for that if it wer of greater nomber, or equall, it should bee conveniente, either not to leave the distaunces, the whiche should be disorder, or leavyng theim, to passe the boundes of thoseafore, the whiche should make the facion of the armie unperfecte: and it is not true that you saie, that the enemie, the more that he entereth into the maine battaile, so moche the weaker he findeth it: for that the enemie, can never faight with the seconde order, except the first be joined with thesame: so that he cometh to finde the middest of the maine battaile more stronger, and not more weaker, havyng to faight with the first, and with the seconde order altogether: the verie same happeneth, when the enemie should come to the thirde companie: for that there, not with twoo battailes, whiche is founde freshe, but with all the maine battaile he must faight: and for that this last part hath to receive moste men, the spaces therof is requisite to be greatest, and that whiche receiveth them, to be the leste nomber.

The orderyng of the hinder part of tharmy.

Luigi. It pleaseth me thesame that you have told: but answere me also this: if the five first battailes doe retire betwene the three seconde battailes, and after the eight betwene the twoo thirde, it semeth not possible, that the eight beyng brought together, and then the tenne together, maie bee received when thei bee eight, or when thei be tenne in the verie same space, whiche received the five.

The retire of the pikes, to place the targaet men.

Fabricio. The first thyng that I aunswere is, that it is not the verie same space: For that the five have fower spaces in the middeste, whiche retiryng betwene the thre, or betwene the twoo, thei occupie: then there remaineth thesame space, that is betwene the one maine battaile and other and thesame that is, betwene the battailes, and the extraordinarie Pikes, al the whiche spaces makes largenesse: besides this, it is to bee considered, that the battailes kepe other maner of spaces, when thei bee in the orders without beyng altered, then when thei be altered: for that in the alteracion: either thei throng together, or thei inlarge the orders: thei inlarge theim, when thei feare so moche, that thei fall to fliyng, thei thrust them together, when thei feare in soche wise, that thei seke to save them selves, not with runnyng a waie, but with defence: So that in this case, thei should come to be destingueshed, and not to be inlarged. Moreover, the five rankes of the Pikes, that are before, so sone as thei have begun the faighte, thei ought betwene their battailes to retire, into the taile of the armie, for to give place to the Targaet men, that thei maie faighte: and thei goyng into the taile of the armie, maie dooe soche service as the capitain should judge, were good to occupie theim aboute, where in the forward, the faight beyng mingled, thei should otherwise bee altogether unprofitable. And for this the spaces ordained, come to bee for the remnaunte of the menne, wide inough to receive them: yet when these spaces should not suffice, the flankes on the sides be men, and not walles, whom givyng place, and inlargyng them selves, maie make the space to containe so moche, that it maie bee sufficient to receive theim.

How the pikes that are placed on the flankes of the armie ought to governe them selves when the rest of the armie is driven to retire.

Luigi. The rankes of the extraordinarie Pikes, whiche you place on the flanckes of the armie, when the first battailes retire into the second, will you have them to stande still, and remain with twoo homes to the armie? Or will you that thei also retire together, with the battailes? The whiche when thei should do, I see not how thei can, havyng no battailes behinde with distaunces that maie receive them.

Thexercise of the army in generall; the nomber that is mete to be written in the ansigne of every band of men; the degrees of honours in an armie, whiche soche a man ought to rise by, as should bee made a generall capitain.

Fabricio. If the enemie overcome theim not, when he inforceth the battailes to retire, thei maie stande still in their order, and hurte the enemie on the flanck, after that the firste battailes retired: but if he should also overcome theim, as semeth reason, beyng so puisaunte, that he is able to repulce the other, thei also ought to retire: whiche thei maie dooe excellently well, although thei have not behinde, any to receive them: bicause from the middest thei maie redouble by right line, entring the one ranke into the other, in the maner whereof wee reasoned, when it was spoken of the order of redoublyng: True it is, that to mynde redoublyng to retire backe, it behoveth to take an other waie, then thesame that I shewed you: for that I told you, that the second ranke, ought to enter into the first, the fowerth into the thirde, and so foorth: in this case, thei ought not to begin before, but behinde, so that redoublyng the rankes, thei maie come to retire backewarde not to tourne forward: but to aunswere to all thesame, that upon this foughten field by me shewed, might of you bee replied. I saie unto you again, that I have ordained you this armie, and shewed this foughten field for two causes, thone, for to declare unto you how it is ordered, the other to shewe you how it is exercised: thorder, I beleve you understande moste well: and concernyng the exersice, I saie unto you, that thei ought to be put together in this forme, as often times as maie be: for as moche as the heddes learne therby, to kepe their battailes in these orders: for that to particulare souldiours, it appertaineth to keepe well the orders of every battaile, to the heddes of the battailes, it appertaineth to keepe theim well in every order of the armie, and that thei knowe how to obeie, at the commaundement of the generall capitain: therefore, it is conveniente that thei knowe, how to joyne the one battaile with thother, that thei maie knowe how to take their place atones: and for this cause it is mete that thansigne of every battaile, have written in some evident part, the nomber therof: as well for to be able to commaunde them, as also for that the capitain, and the souldiours by thesame nomber, maie more easely knowe theim againe: also the maine battailes, ought to be nombred, and to have the nomber in their principal Ansigne: Therefore it is requisite, to knowe of what nomber the maine battaile shall be, that is placed on the left, or on the right horne of what nombers the battailes bee, that are set in the fronte, and in the middeste, and so foorthe of the other. The antiquitie would also, that these nombers should bee steppes to degrees, of honors of the armies: as for insample, the first degree, is the Peticapitain, the seconde, the hedde of fiftie ordinarie Veliti, the thirde, the Centurion, the fowerth, the hedde of the first battaile, the fifte, of the second, the sixt, of the thirde, and so forthe, even to the tenth battaile, the whiche must be honoured in the seconde place, nexte the generall capitaine of a maine battaile: nor any ought to come to thesame hedde, if first, he have not risen up by all these degrees. And bicause besides these heddes, there be the three Conestables of the extraordinarie Pikes, and twoo of the extraordinarie Veliti, I would that thei should be in the same degree of the Conestable of the first battaile: nor I would not care, that there were sixe men of like degree, to thintent, that every one of them might strive, who should doe beste, for to be promised to be hedde of the seconde battaile. Then every one of these heddes, knowyng in what place his battaile ought to be sette in, of necessitie it must folowe, that at a sounde of the Trompette, so sone as the hedde standarde shall bee erected, all the armie shall be in their places: and this is the first exercise, whereunto an armie ought to bee accustomed, that is to set theim quickly together: and to doe this, it is requisite every daie, and divers times in one daie, to set them in order, and to disorder them.

Luigi. What armes would you that thansignes of all the armie, shoul'd have beside the nomber?

The armes that oughte to bee in the standarde, and in the ansignes of an armie; the second and thirde exercise of an armie; the fowerth exercise of an armie; the soundes of the instrumentes of musicke, that the antiquitie used in their armies; what is signified by the sounde of the trompet.

Fabricio. The standarde of the generall Capitaine oughte to have the armes of the Prince of the armie, all the other, maie have the verie same armes, and to varie with the fieldes, or to varie with the armes, as should seme beste to the Lorde of the armie: Bicause this importeth little, so that the effect growe, that thei be knowen the one from the other. But let us passe to the other exercise: the which is to make them to move, and with a convenient pace to marche, and to se, that marehyng thei kepe the orders. The third exercise is, that thei learne to handle themselves in thesame maner, whiche thei ought after to handle theimselves in the daie of battaile, to cause the artillerie to shoote, and to bee drawen out of the waie, to make the extraordinarie Veliti to issue out, after a likenes of an assault, to retire theim: To make that the firste battailes, as though thei wer sore charged, retire into the spaces of the second: and after, all into the thirde, and from thens every one to retourne to his place: and in soche wise to use theim in this exercise, that to every manne, all thyng maie be knowen, and familiar: the which with practise, and with familiaritie, is brought to passe moste quickly. The fowerth exercise is, that thei learne to knowe by meane of the sounde, and of the Ansigne, the commaundemente of their capitaine: for as moche as that, whiche shall be to them pronounced by voice, thei without other commaundemente, maie understande: and bicause the importaunce of this commaundement, ought to growe of the sounde, I shall tell you what soundes the antiquitie used. Of the Lacedemonians, accordyng as Tucidido affirmeth, in their armies were used Flutes: for that thei judged, that this armonie, was moste mete to make their armie to procede with gravetie, and with furie: the Carthaginens beyng moved by this verie same reason, in the first assaulte, used the violone. Aliatte kyng of the Lidians, used in the warre the violone, and the Flutes: but Alexander Magnus, and the Romaines, used hornes, and Trumpettes, as thei, that thought by vertue of soche instrumentes, to bee able to incourage more the myndes of Souldiours, and make theim to faight the more lustely: but as we have in armyng the armie, taken of the Greke maner, and of the Romaine, so in distrihutyng the soundes, we will keepe the customes of the one, and of the other nacion: therefore, nere the generall capitain, I would make the Trompettes to stand, as a sounde not onely apt to inflame the armie, but apte to bee heard in all the whole tumoult more, then any other sounde: all the other soundes, whiche should bee aboute the Conestables, and the heddes of maine battailes I would, that thei should bee smalle Drummes, and Flutes, sounded not as thei sounde theim now but as thei use to sounde theim at feastes. The capitaine then with the Trompet, should shewe when thei must stande still, and go forward, or tourne backward, when the artillerie must shoote, when the extraordinarie Veliti must move, and with the varietie or distinccion of soche soundes, to shewe unto the armie all those mocions, whiche generally maie bee shewed, the whiche Trompettes, should bee after followed of the Drummes, and in this exercise, bicause it importeth moche, it behoveth moche to exercise the armie. Concernyng the horsemen, there would be used likewise Trompettes, but of a lesse sounde, and of a divers voice from those of the Capitaine. This is as moche as is come into my remembraunce, aboute the order of the armie, and of the exercise of thesame.

Luigi. I praie you let it not be grevous unto you to declare unto me an other thyng, that is, for what cause you made the light horsmen, and the extraordinarie Veliti, to goe with cries, rumours, and furie, when thei gave the charge? And after in the incountering of the rest of tharmie, you shewed, that the thing folowed with a moste greate scilence? And for that I understande not the occasion of this varietie, I would desire that you would declare it unto me.

The cries, and rumours, wher with the firste charge is given unto the enemies, and the silence that ought to bee used after, when the faight is ones begunne.

Fabricio. The opinion of auncient capitaines, hath been divers about the commyng to handes, whether thei ought with rumour to go a pace, or with scilence to go faire and softely: this laste waie, serveth to kepe the order more sure, and to understande better the commaundementes of the Capitaine: the firste, serveth to incourage more the mindes of men: and for that I beleve, that respecte ought to bee had to the one, and to the other of these twoo thynges, I made the one goe with rumour, and thother with scilence: nor me thinkes not in any wise, that the continuall rumours bee to purpose: bicause thei lette the commaundementes, the whiche is a thyng moste pernicious: nor it standeth not with reason, that the Romaines used, except at the firste assaulte to make rumour: for that in their histories, is seen many tymes to have happened, that through the wordes, and comfortinges of the capitain the souldiours that ranne awaie, were made to stande to it, and in sundrie wise by his commaundemente, to have varied the orders, the whiche should not have followed, if the rumoures had been louder then his voyce.

The Fowerth Booke

Luigi. Seng that under my governement, a field hath been wonne so honourably, I suppose that it is good, that I tempt not fortune any more, knowyng how variable, and unstable she is: and therefore, I desire to give up my governement, and that Zanobi do execute now this office of demaundyng, mindyng to followe the order, whiche concerneth the youngeste: and I knowe he will not refuse this honoure, or as we would saie, this labour, as well for to doe me pleasure, as also for beyng naturally of more stomach than I: nor it shall not make hym afraied, to have to enter into these travailes, where he maie bee as well overcome, as able to conquere.

Zanobi. I am readie to do what soever shall please you to appoinete me, although that I desire more willingly to heare: for as moche as hetherto, your questions have satisfied me more, then those should have pleased me, whiche in harkenyng to your reasonyng, hath chaunced to come into my remembraunce. But sir, I beleve that it is good, that you lese no tyme, and that you have pacience, if with these our Ceremonies we trouble you.

Fabricio. You doe me rather pleasure, for that this variacion of demaunders, maketh me to knowe the sundrie wittes and sunderie appetites of yours: But remaineth there any thyng, whiche seemeth unto you good, to bee joyned to the matter, that alreadie hath been reasoned of?

Zanobi. Twoo thinges I desire, before you passe to an other parte: the one is, to have you to shewe, if in orderyng armies, there needeth to bee used any other facion: the other, what respectes a capitaine ought to have, before he conducte his men to the faight, and in thesame an accidente risyng or growyng, what reamedie maie be had.

To deffende moche the fronte of an armie, is most perillous; what is beste for a capitaine to dooe, where his power is, moche lesse then thenemies power; a general rule; the higher grounde ought to be chosen; an advertisement not to place an armie wher the enemie maie se what the same doeth; respectes for the sonne and winde; the variyng of order and place maie cause the conquered to become victorius; a policie in the ordering of men and pitchyng of a fielde; how to compasse about the enemies power; how a capitaine maie faight and bee as it were sure, not to be overcome; how to trouble the orders of the enemie; what a capitaine oughte to dooe when he hath not so many horsmen as the enemie; a greate aide for horsemen; the policies used betwene aniball and scipio.

Fabricio. I will inforce my self to satisfie you, I will not answere now distinctly to your questions: for that whileste I shall aunswere to one, many tymes it will come to passe, that I muste aunswere to an other. I have tolde you, how I have shewed you a facion of an armie, to the intent, that accordyng to thesame, there maie bee given all those facions, that the enemie, and the situacion requireth: For as moche as in this case, bothe accordyng to the power thereof, and accordyng to the enemie, it proceadeth: but note this, that there is not a more perillous facion, then to deffende moche the front of tharmie, if then thou have not a most puisant, and moste great hoste: otherwise, thou oughtest to make it rather grosse, and of small largenesse, then of moche largenes and thin: for when thou hast fewe men in comparison to thenemie, thou oughtest to seke other remedies, as is to ordain thine army in soche a place, wher thou maiest be fortefied, either through rivers, or by meanes of fennes, after soch sort, that thou canst not bee compassed aboute, or to inclose thy self on the flanckes with diches, as Cesar did in Fraunce. You have to take in this cace, this generall rule, to inlarge your self, or to draw in your self with the front, according to your nomber, and thesame of the enemie. For thenemies being of lesse nomber, thou oughtest to seke large places, havyng in especially thy men well instructed: to the intent thou maiest, not onely compasse aboute the enemie, but to deffende thy orders: for that in places rough and difficulte, beyng not able to prevaile of thy orders, thou commeste not to have any advauntage, hereby grewe, that the Romaines almoste alwaies, sought the open fieldes, and advoided the straightes. To the contrarie, as I have said, thou oughtest to doe, if thou hast fewe menne, or ill instructed: for that then thou oughteste to seeke places, either where the little nomber maye be saved, and where the small experience dooe not hurte thee: Thou oughtest also to chuse the higher grounde, to be able more easily to infest them: notwithstandyng, this advertisment ought to be had, not to ordaine thy armie, where the enemie maie spie what thou doest and in place nere to the rootes of the same, where the enemies armie maie come: For that in this case, havyng respecte unto the artillerie, the higher place shall gette thee disadvauntage: Bicause that alwaies and commodiously, thou mightest of the enemies artillerie bee hurte, without beyng able to make any remedy, and thou couldest not commodiously hurte thesame, beyng hindered by thine owne men. Also, he that prepareth an armie to faight a battaile, ought to have respecte, bothe to the Sunne, and to the Winde, that the one and the other, doe not hurte the fronte, for that the one and the other, will let thee the sight, the one with the beames, and the other with the duste: and moreover, the Winde hindereth the weapons, whiche are stroken at the enemie, and maketh their blowes more feable: and concerning the Sunne, it sufficeth not to have care, that at the firste it shine not in the face, but it is requisite to consider, that increasyng the daie, it hurte thee not: and for this, it should bee requsite in orderyng the men, to have it all on the backe, to the entente it should have to passe moche tyme, to come to lye on the fronte. This waie was observed of Aniball at Canne, and of Mario against the Cimbrians. If thou happen to be moche inferiour of horses, ordaine thine armie emongeste Vines, and trees, and like impedimentes, as in our time the Spaniardes did, when thei overthrewe the Frenchmenne at Cirignuola. And it hath been seen many times, with all one Souldiours, variyng onely the order, and the place, that thei have become of losers victorers: as it happened to the Carthageners, whom havyng been overcome of Marcus Regolus divers tymes, were after by the counsaill of Santippo a Lacedemonian, victorious: whom

made them to go doune into the plaine, where by vertue of the horses, and of Eliphantes, thei were able to overcome the Romaines. It semes unto me, accordyng to the auncient insamples that almoste all the excellente Capitaines, when thei have knowen, that the enemie hath made strong one side of his battaile, thei have not set against it, the moste strongest parte, but the moste weakest, and thother moste strongest thei have set against the most weakest: after in the beginning the faighte, thei have commaunded to their strongest parte, that onely thei sustaine the enemie, and not to preace upon hym, and to the weaker, that thei suffer them selves to be overcome, and to retire into the hindermoste bandes of the armie. This breadeth twoo greate disorders to the enemie: the firste, that he findeth his strongest parte compassed about, the second is, that semyng unto him to have the victorie, seldome tymes it happeneth, that thei disorder not theim selves, whereof groweth his sodain losse. Cornelius Scipio beyng in Spain, againste Asdruball of Carthage, and understanding how to Asdruball it was knowen, that he in the orderyng the armie, placed his Legions in the middest, the whiche was the strongest parte of his armie, and for this how Asdruball with like order ought to procede: after when he came to faighte the battaile, he chaunged order, and put his Legions on the hornes of the armie, and in the middest, placed all his weakeste men: then commyng to the handes, in a sodain those men placed in the middeste, he made to marche softly, and the hornes of the armie, with celeritie to make forwarde, so that onely the hornes of bothe the armies fought, and the bandes in the middest, through beyng distaunt the one from the other, joyned not together, and thus the strongest parte of Scipio, came to faight with the weakest of Asdruball, and overcame hym. The whiche waie was then profitable, but now havyng respect to the artillerie, it cannot be used: bicause the same space, whiche should remain in the middest, betwene the one armie and the other, should give tyme to thesame to shoote: The whiche is moste pernicious, as above is saied: Therefore it is requisite to laie this waie aside, and to use, as a little afore we saied, makyng all the armie to incounter, and the weakest parte to give place. When a capitaine perceiveth, that he hath a greater armie then his enemie, mindyng to compasse hym aboute, before he be aware let hym ordaine his fronte equall, to thesame of his adversaries, after, so sone as the faight is begun, let hym make the fronte by a little and little to retire, and the flanckes to deffende, and alwaies it shall happen, that the enemie shal find hymself, before he be aware compassed about. When a capitain will faight, as it wer sure not to be broken, let hym ordaine his armie in place, where he hath refuge nere, and safe, either betwene Fennes, or betwene hilles, or by some strong citee: for that in this case, he cannot bee followed of the enemie, where the enemie maie be pursued of him: this poincte was used of Aniball, when fortune began to become his adversarie, and that he doubted of the valiauntnesse of Marcus Marcello. Some to trouble the orders of the enemie, have commaunded those that were light armed, to begin the faight, and that beyng begunne, to retire betwene the orders: and when the armies were after buckled together, and that the fronte of either of them were occupied in faightyng, thei have made theim to issue out by the flanckes of the battaile, and thesame have troubled and broken. If any perceive hymself to bee inferiour of horse, he maie besides the waies that are alredie shewed, place behinde his horsemen a battaile of Pikes, and in faightyng take order, that thei give waie to the Pikes, and he shall remain alwaies superiour. Many have accustomed to use certain fotemenne lighte armed, to faighte emong horsemen, the whiche hath been to the chivalrie moste greate helpe. Of all those, which have prepared armies to the field, be moste praised Aniball and Scipio, when thei fought in Africk: and for that Aniball had his armie made of Carthaginers, and of straungers of divers nacions, he placed in the first fronte thereof lxxx. Elephantes, after he placed the straungers, behinde whom he sette his Carthaginers, in the hindermoste place, he putte the Italians, in whom he trusted little: the whiche thing he ordained so, for that the straungers havyng before theim the enemie, and behinde beyng inclosed of his men, could not flie: so that being constrained to faight thei should overcome, or wearie the Romaines, supposyng after with his freshe and valiaunte men, to be then able easely to overcome the Romaines, beeyng wearied. Against this order, Scipio set the Astati, the Prencipi, and the Triarii, in the accustomed maner, to bee able to receive the one the other, and to rescue the one the other: he made the fronte of the armie, full of voide spaces, and bicause it should not be perceived but rather should seme united, he filled them ful of veliti, to whom he commaunded, that so sone as the Eliphantes came, thei should avoide, and by the ordinarie spaces, should enter betwene the Legins, and leave open the waie to the Eliphauntes, and so it came to passe, that it made vaine the violence of theim, so that commyng to handes, he was superiour.

Zanobi. You have made me to remember, in alledging me this battaile, how Scipio in faighting, made not the Astati to retire into thorders of the Prencipi, but he devided theim, and made theim to retire in the hornes of the armie, to thintent thei might give place to the Prencipi, when he would force forwarde: therfore I would you should tell me, what occasion moved hym, not to observe the accustomed order.

Cartes full of hookes made to destroie the enemies; the remedy that was used against cartes full of hookes; the straunge maner that Silla used in orderyng his army against Archelaus; how to trouble in the faighte the armie of the enemies; a policie of Caius Sulpitius, to make his enemies afraied; a policie of Marius againste the Duchmenne; a policie of greate importaunce, while a battaile is a faightyng; how horsemen maie bee disordered; how the Turke gave the Sophie an overthrowe; how the Spaniardes overcame the armie of Amilcare; how to traine the enemie, to his destruccion; a policie of Tullo Hostilio and Lucius Silla in dessemlyng of a mischaunce; sertorius slue a man for telling him of the death of one of his capitaines; howe certaine captaines have staied their men that hath been running awaie; Attillius constrained his men that ran awaie to tourne again and to faight; how Philip King of Macedonia made his men afraied to run awaie; victorie ought with all celeritie to bee folowed; what a capitaine ought to dooe, when he should chaunce to receive an overthrowe; how Martius overcame the armie of the Carthaginers; a policie of Titus Dimius to hide a losse, whiche he had received in a faight; a general rule; aniball; scipio; asdruball; a capitaine ought not to faight without advantage, excepte he be constrained; how advauntage maie bee taken of the enemies; furie withstode, converteth into vilenesse; what maner of men a capitaine ought to have about him continually, to consult withall; the condicions of the capitain of the enemies, and of those that are about hym is moste requisite to bee knowen; a timerous army is not to be conducted to faight; how to avoide the faightyng of a fielde.

Fabricio. I will tell you. Aniball had putte all the strengthe of his armie, in the seconde bande: wherefore Scipio for to set againste thesame like strengthe, gathered the Prencipi and the Triarii together: So that the distaunces of the Prencipi, beyng occupied of the Triarii, there was no place to bee able to receive the Astati: and therefore he made the Astati to devide, and to go in the hornes of the armie, and he drewe them not betwene the Prencipi. But note, that this waie of openyng the first bande, for to give place to the seconde, cannot bee used, but when a man is superiour to his enemie: for that then there is commoditie to bee able to dooe it, as Scipio was able: but beyng under, and repulced, it cannot be doen, but with thy manifest ruine: and therefore it is convenient to have behinde, orders that maie receive thee, but let us tourne to our reasonyng. The auncient Asiaticans, emongest other thynges devised of them to hurt the enemies, used carres. The whiche had on the sides certaine hookes, so that not onely thei served to open with their violence the bandes, but also to kill with the hookes the adversaries: against the violence of those, in thre maners thei provided, either thei sustained theim with the thickenesse of the raies, or thei received theim betwene the bandes, as the Eliphantes were received, or els thei made with arte some strong resistence: As Silla a Romaine made againste Archelaus, whom had many of these cartes, whiche thei called hooked, who for to sustaine theim, drave many stakes into the grounde, behinde his first bandes of men, whereby the cartes beyng stopped, lost their violence. And the newe maner that Silla used against hym in orderyng the armie, is to bee noted: for that he put the Veliti, and the horse, behinde, and all the heavie armed afore, leavyng many distaunces to be able to sende before those behinde, when necessite required: whereby the fight beyng begun, with the helpe of the horsemen, to the whiche he gave the waie, he got the victorie. To intende to trouble in the faight the enemies armie, it is conveniente to make some thyng to growe, that maie make theim afraied, either with showyng of newe helpe that commeth, or with showyng thynges, whiche maie represente a terrour unto theim: after soche sorte, that the enemies begiled of that sight, maie be afraied, and being made afraied, thei maie easely bee overcome: the whiche waies Minutio Rufo used, and Accilio Glabrione Consulls of Rome. Caius Sulpitius also set a greate many of sackes upon Mules, and other beastes unprofitable for the warre, but in soche wise ordained, that thei semed men of armes, and he commaunded, that thei should appere upon a hill, while he were a faightyng with the Frenchemen, whereby grewe his victorie. The verie same did Marius, when he foughte against the Duchemen. Then the fained assaultes availyng moche, whilest the faight continueth, it is conveniente, that the very assaultes in deede, dooe helpe moche: inespecially if at unwares in the middest of the faight, the enemie might bee assaulted behinde, or on the side: the whiche hardely maie be doen, if the countrie helpe thee not: for that when it is open, parte of thy men cannot bee hid, as is mete to bee doen in like enterprises: but in woddie or hille places, and for this apt for ambusshes parte of thy men maie be well hidden, to be able in a sodain, and contrary to thenemies opinion to assaut him, whiche thyng alwaies shall be occasion to give thee the victorie. It hath been sometyme of greate importaunce, whilest the faighte continueth, to sowe voices, whiche doe pronounce the capitaine of thenemies to be dedde, or to have overcome on the other side of the armie: the whiche many times to them that have used it, hath given the victorie. The chivalrie of the enemies maie bee easely troubled, either with sightes, or with rumours, not used: as Creso did, whom put Camelles againste the horses of the adversaries, and Pirrus sette againste the Romaine horsemen Eliphantes, the sighte of whiche troubled and disordered them. In our time, the Turke discomfited the Sophi in Persia, and the Soldane in Surria with no other, then with the noise of Harkabuses, the whiche in soche wise, with their straunge rumours, disturbed the horses of those, that the Turke mighte easely overcome them: The Spaniardes to overcome the armie of Amilcare, put in the firste fronte Cartes full of towe drawen of oxen, and comming to handes, thei kindeled fire to thesame, wherfore the oxen to flie from the fire, thrust into the armie of Amilcar, and opened it. Thei are wonte (as we have saied) to begile the enemie in the faight, drawyng him into their ambusshes, where the Countrie is commodious for the same purpose, but where it were open and large, many have used to make diches, and after have covered them lightly with bowes and yearth, and lefte certain spaces whole, to be able betnene those to retire: after, so sone as the faight hath been begunne, retiryng by those, and the enemie folowing them, hath fallen in the pittes. If in the faight there happen thee, any accident that maie feare thy souldiours, it is a moste prudente thyng, to knowe how to desemble it, and to pervert it to good, as Tullo Hostilio did, and Lucius Silla: whom seyng while thei fought, how a parte of his men wer gone to the enemies side, and how thesame thing had verie moche made afraied his men, he made straighte waie throughout all the armie to be understoode, how all thing proceded, accordyng to his order: the whiche not onely did not trouble the armie, but it increased in them so moche stomack, that he remained victorious. It happened also to Silla, that havyng sente certaine souldiours to doe some businesse, and thei beyng slain he saied, to the intent his armie should not be made afraied thereby, that he had with crafte sent theim into the handes of the enemies, for that he had found them nothyng faithfull. Sertorius faightyng a battaile in Spaine, slue one, whom signified unto hym the death of one of his capitaines, for feare that tellyng the very same to other, he should make theim afraied. It is a moste difficult thyng, an armie beyng now moved to flie, to staie it, and make it to faight. And you have to make this distinccion: either that it is all moved, and then to be impossible to tourne it, or there is moved a parte thereof, and then there is some remedie. Many Romain capitaines, with making afore those whiche fled, have caused them to staie, making them ashamed of running awaie, as Lucius Silla did, where alredy parte of his Legions beyng tourned to flight, driven awaie by the men of Mithridates, he made afore them with a swearde in his hande criyng: if any aske you, where you left your capitaine, saie, we have left hym in Boecia, where he faighteth. Attillius a consull set againste that ran awaie, them that ranne not awaie, and made them to understande, that if thei would not tourne, thei should be slaine of their frendes, and of their enemies. Philip of Macedonia understanding how his men feared the Scithian Souldiours, placed behinde his armie, certaine of his moste trustie horsemen, and gave commission to theim, that thei should kill whom so ever fledde: wherfore, his men mindyng rather to die faightyng, then fliyng, overcame. Many Romaines, not so moche to staie a flight, as for to give occasion to their men, to make greater force, have whileste thei have foughte, taken an Ansigne out of their owne mennes handes, and throwen it emongeste the enemies, and appoincted rewardes to hym that could get it again. I doe not beleve that it is out of purpose, to joyne to this reasonyng those thynges, whiche chaunce after the faight, in especially beyng brief thinges, and not to be left behinde, and to this reasonyng conformable inough. Therefore I saie, how the fielde is loste, or els wonne: when it is wonne, the victorie ought with all celeritie to be folowed, and in this case to imitate Cesar, and not Aniball, whom staiyng after that he had discomfited the Romaines at Canne, loste the Empire of Rome: The other never rested after the victorie, but folowed the enemie beyng broken, with greater violence and furie, then when he assalted hym whole: but when a capitaine dooeth

loese, he ought to see, if of the losse there maie growe any utilite unto hym, inespecially if there remain any residue of tharmie. The commoditie maie growe of the small advertisment of the enemie, whom moste often times after the victorie, becometh negligent, and giveth thee occasion to oppresse hym, as Marcius a Romaine oppressed the armie of the Carthaginers, whom having slain the twoo Scipions, and broken their armie, not estemyng thesame remnaunt of menne, whiche with Marcius remained a live, were of hym assaulted and overthrowen: for that it is seen, that there is no thing so moche to bee brought to passe, as thesame, whiche the enemie thinketh, that thou canst not attempte: bicause for the moste parte, men bee hurte moste, where thei doubt leaste: therefore a capitain ought when he cannot doe this, to devise at least with diligence, that the losse bee lesse hurtfull, to dooe this, it is necessarie for thee to use meanes, that the enemie maie not easely folowe thee, or to give him occasion to make delaie: in the first case, some after thei have been sure to lese, have taken order with their heddes, that in divers partes, and by divers waies thei should flie, havyng appoincted wher thei should after assemble together: the which made, that thenemie (fearing to devide the armie) was faine to let go safe either all, or the greatest part of them. In the seconde case, many have cast before the enemie, their dearest thinges, to the entent that he tariyng about the spoile, might give them more laisure to flie. Titus Dimius used no small policie to hide the losse, whiche he had received in the faight, for asmoche as havyng fought untill night, with great losse of his menne, he made in the night to be buried, the greatest part of them, wherefore in the mornyng, the enemies seyng so many slaine of theirs, and so fewe of the Romaines, belevyng that thei had the disavauntage, ran awaie. I trust I have thus confusedly, as I saied, satisfied in good part your demaunde: in dede about the facions of the armies, there resteth me to tell you, how some tyme, by some Capitaines, it hath been used to make theim with the fronte, like unto a wedge, judgyng to bee able by soche meane, more easely to open the enemies armie. Against this facion, thei have used to make a facion like unto a paire of sheres, to be able betwene thesame voide place, to receive that wedge, and to compasse it about, and to faight with it on every side: whereupon I will that you take this generall rule, that the greatest remedie that is used againste a devise of the enemie, is to dooe willingly thesame, whiche he hath devised that thou shalt dooe perforce: bicause that doyng it willingly, thou doest it with order, and with thy advauntage, and his disadvauntage, if thou shouldest doe it beyng inforced, it should be thy undoyng: For the provyng whereof, I care not to reherse unto you, certain thynges alredy tolde. The adversary maketh the wedge to open thy bandes: if thou gowest with them open, thou disorderest hym, and he disordereth not thee. Aniball set the Elephantes in the fronte of his armie, to open with theim the armie of Scipio. Scipio went with it open, and it was the occasion of his victorie, and of the ruine of hym. Asdruball placed his strongest men in the middest of the fronte of his armie, to overthrowe Scipios menne: Scipio commaunded, that by them selves thei should retire and he broke theim: So that like devises when thei are foreseen, bee the causes of the victorie of him, against whom thei be prepared. There remaineth me also, if I remember my self well, to tell you what respectes a Capitaine ought to have, before he leade his men to faight: upon whiche I have to tell you firste, how a capitaine ought never to faight a battaile, except he have advauntage, or be constrained. The vantage groweth of the situacion, of the order, of havyng more, or better menne: the necessitie groweth when thou seest how that not faightyng, thou muste in any wise lose, as should bee for lackyng of money, and for this, thy armie to bee ready all maner of waies to resolve, where famishemente is ready to assaulte thee, where the enemie looketh to bee ingrosed with newe men: in these cases, thou oughtest alwaies to faight, although with thy disadvauntage: for that it is moche better to attempte fortune, where she maie favour thee, then not attemptyng, to see thy certaine ruine: and it is as grevous a faulte in this case, in a capitain not to faight, as to have had occasion to overcome, and not to have either knowen it through ignoraunce, or lefte it through vilenesse. The advauntages some tymes the enemie giveth thee, and some tymes thy prudence: Many in passyng Rivers have been broken of their enemie, that hath been aware thereof, whom hath taried, till the one halfe hath been of the one side, and the other halfe on the other, and then hath assaulted them: as Cesar did to the Suizzers, where he destroied the fowerth parte of theim, through beyng halfe over a river. Some tyme thy enemie is founde wearie, for havyng folowed thee to undescritely, so that findyng thy self freshe and lustie, thou oughtest not to let passe soche an occasion: besides this, if the enemie offer unto thee in the mornyng betymes to faight, thou maiest a good while deferre to issue out of thy lodgyng, and when he hath stoode long in armour, and that he hath loste that same firste heate, with the whiche he came, thou maiest then faight with him. This waie Scipio and Metellus used in Spaine: the one against Asdruball, the other against Sertorius. If the enemie be deminished of power, either for havyng devided the armie, as the Scipions in Spain, or for some other occasion, thou oughteste to prove chaunce. The greateste parte of prudent capitaines, rather receive the violence of the enemies, then go with violence to assalte them: for that the furie is easely withstoode of sure and steddie menne, and the furie beyng sustained, converteth lightly into vilenesse: Thus Fabius did againste the Sannites, and against the Galles, and was victorious and his felowe Decius remained slain. Some fearing the power of their enemies, have begun the faight a little before night, to the intent that their men chaunsyng to bee overcome, might then by the helpe of the darkenesse thereof, save theim selves. Some havyng knowen, how the enemies armie beyng taken of certaine supersticion, not to faight in soche a tyme, have chosen thesame tyme to faighte, and overcome: The whiche Cesar observed in Fraunce, againste Arionistus, and Vespasian in Surrie, againste the Jewes. The greatest and moste importaunte advertismente, that a capitaine ought to have, is to have aboute hym faithfull menne, that are wise and moste expert in the warre, with whom he must continually consulte and reason of his men, and of those of the enemies, whiche is the greater nomber, whiche is beste armed, or beste on horsebacke, or best exercised, whiche be moste apte to suffer necessitie, in whom he trusteth moste, either in the footemen, or in the horsemen: after thei ought to consider the place where thei be, and whether it be more to the purpose for thenemie, then for him: which of theim hath victualles moste commodious: whether it be good to deferre the battaile, or to faight it: what good might bee given hym, or taken awaie by tyme: for that many tymes, souldiours seyng the warre to be delaied, are greved, and beyng wearie, in the pain and in the tediousnesse therof, wil forsake thee. It importeth above all thyng, to knowe the capitain of the enemies, and whom he hath aboute hym, whether he be rashe, or politike, whether he be fearfull, or hardie: to see how thou maiest truste upon the aidyng souldiours. And above all thyng thou oughtest to take hede, not to conducte the armie to faight when it feareth, or when in any wise it mistrusteth of the victorie: for that the greatest signe to lose, is thei beleve not to be able to winne: and therfore in this case, thou oughtest to avoide the faightyng of the fielde, either with doyng as Fabius Maximus, whom incampyng in strong places, gave no courage to Aniball, to goe to finde hym, or when thou shouldest thinke, that the enemie also in strong places, would come to finde thee, to departe out of the fielde, and to devide the menne into thy tounes to thentent that tediousnesse of winnyng them, maie wearie hym.

Zanobi. Cannot the faightyng of the battaile be otherwise avoided, then in devidyng the armie in sunderie partes and placyng the men in tounes?

Fabius Maximus.

Fabricio. I beleve that ones alreadie, with some of you I have reasoned, how that he, that is in the field, cannot avoide to faight the battaile, when he hath an enemie, which will faight with hym in any wise, and he hath not, but one remedie, and that is, to place him self with his armie distant fiftie miles at leaste, from his adversarie, to be able betymes to avoide him, when he should go to finde hym. For Fabius Maximus never avoided to faight the battaile with Aniball, but he would have it with his advauntage: and Aniball did not presume to bee able to overcome hym, goyng to finde hym in the places where he incamped: where if he had presupposed, to have been able to have overcome, it had been conveniente for Fabius, to have fought the battaile with hym, or to have avoided.

Philip king of Macedonia, overcome by the Romaines; How Cingentorige avoided the faightyng of the fielde with Cesar; The ignorance of the Venecians; What is to be doen wher soldiours desire to faight, contrary to their capitaines minde; How to incourage souldiers; An advertisment to make the soldiour most obstinately to faight.

Philip Kyng of Macedonia, thesame that was father to Perse, commyng to warre with the Romaines, pitched his campe upon a verie high hill, to the entent not to faight with theim: but the Romaines wente to find hym on thesame hill, and discomfaited hym. Cingentorige capitain of the Frenche menne, for that he would not faight the field with Cesar, whom contrarie to his opinion, had passed a river, got awaie many miles with his men. The Venecians in our tyme, if thei would not have come to have fought with the Frenche kyng, thei ought not to have taried till the Frenche armie, had passed the River Addus, but to have gotten from them as Cingentorige, where thei havyng taried knewe not how to take in the passyng of the men, the occasion to faight the battaile, nor to avoide it: For that the Frenche men beyng nere unto them, as the Venecians went out of their Campe, assaulted theim, and discomfited theim: so it is, that the battaile cannot bee avoided, when the enemie in any wise will faight, nor let no man alledge Fabius, for that so moche in thesame case, he did flie the daie of battaile, as Aniball. It happeneth many tymes, that thy souldiours be willyng to faight, and thou knoweste by the nomber, and by the situacion, or for some other occasion to have disadvauntage, and desirest to make them chaunge from this desire: it happeneth also, that necessitie, or occasion, constraineth thee to faight, and that thy souldiours are evill to be trusted, and smally disposed to faight: where it is necessarie in thone case, to make theim afraied, and in the other to incourage theim: In the firste case, when perswacions suffiseth not, there is no better waie, then to give in praie, a part of them unto thenemie, to thintent those that have, and those that have not fought, maie beleve thee: and it may very wel be doen with art, thesame which to Fabius Maximus hapned by chaunce. Tharmie of Fabius (as you knowe) desired to faight with Aniballs armie: the very same desire had the master of his horses: to Fabius it semed not good, to attempte the faight: so that through soche contrary opinions, he was fain to devide the armie: Fabius kept his men in the campe, the other fought, and commyng into great perill, had been overthrowen, if Fabius had not rescued him: by the whiche insample the maister of the horse, together with all the armie, knewe how it was a wise waie to obeie Fabius. Concernyng to incourage theim to faight, it should be well doen, to make them to disdain the enemies, shewyng how thei speake slaunderous woordes of them, to declare to have intelligence with them, and to have corrupted part of them, to incampe in place, where thei maie see the enemies, and make some light skirmishe with them, for that the thyng that is dailie seen, with more facilitie is despised: to shewe theim to bee unworthie, and with an oracion for the purpose, to reprehende them of their cowardnesse, and for to make them ashamed, to tell theim that you will faight alone, when thei will not beare you companie. And you ought above all thyng to have this advertismente, mindyng to make the Souldiour obstinate to faight, not to permitte, that thei maie send home any of their substaunce, or to leave it in any place, till the warre bee ended, that thei maie understande, that although fliyng save their life, yet it saveth not theim their goodes, the love whereof, is wonte no lesse then thesame, to make men obstinate in defence.

Zanobi. You have tolde, how the souldiours maie be tourned to faight, with speakyng to theim: doe you meane by this, that all the armie must bee spoken unto, or to the heddes thereof?

It is requisite for excellent Capitaines to bee good orators; Alexander Magnus used openly to perswade his armie; The effecteousnes of speking; Souldiours ought to be accustomed to heare their Capitaine speake; How in olde time souldiers were threatened for their faltes; Enterprises maie the easelier be brought to passe by meanes of religion; Sertorius; A policie of Silla; A policie of Charles the seventh king of Fraunce against the Englishmen; How souldiers maiebee made to esteme little their enemies; The surest wai to make souldiours moste obstinat to faight; By what meanes obstinatenesse to faighte is increased.

Fabricio. To perswade, or to diswade a thyng unto fewe, is verie easie, for that if woordes suffise not, you maie then use aucthoritie and force: but the difficultie is, to remove from a multitude an evill opinion, and that whiche is contrary either to the common profite, or to thy opinion, where cannot be used but woordes, the whiche is meete that thei be heard of every man, mindyng to perswade them all. Wherfore, it was requisite that the excellente Capitaines were oratours: for that without knowyng how to speake to al the army, with difficultie maie be wrought any good thing: the whiche altogether in this our tyme is laied aside. Rede the life of Alexander Magnus, and you shall see how many tymes it was necessarie for hym to perswade, and to speake publikly to his armie: otherwise he should never have brought theim, beyng become riche, and full of spoile, through the desertes of Arabia, and into India with so moche his disease, and trouble: for that infinite tymes there growe thynges, wherby an armie ruinateth, when the capitain either knoweth not, or useth not to speake unto thesame, for that this speakyng taketh awaie feare, in courageth the mindes, increaseth the obstinatenes to faight, discovereth the deceiptes, promiseth rewardes, sheweth the perilles, and the waie to avoide theim, reprehendeth, praieth, threatened, filleth full of hope, praise, shame, and doeth all those thynges, by the whiche the humaine passions are extincte or kendled: wherefore, that prince, or common weale, whiche should appoincte to make a newe power, and cause reputacion to their armie, ought to accustome the Souldiours thereof, to heare the capitain to speake, and the capitain to know how to speake unto them. In kepyng desposed the souldiours in old tyme, to faight for their countrie, the religion availed moche, and the othes whiche thei gave them, when thei led theim to warfare: for as moche as in al their faultes, thei threatned them not onely with those punishementes, whiche might be feared of men but with those whiche of God might be looked for: the whiche thyng mingled with the other Religious maners, made many tymes easie to the auncient capitaines all enterprises, and will doe alwaies, where religion shall be feared, and observed. Sertorius prevailed, by declaryng that he spake with a Stagge, the whiche in Goddes parte, promised hym the victorie. Silla saied, he spoke with an Image, whiche he had taken out of the Temple of Apollo. Many have tolde how God hath appered unto them in their slepe, whom hath admonished them to faight. In our fathers time, Charles the seventh kyng of Fraunce, in the warre whiche he made againste the Englishemen, saied, he counsailed with a maide, sent from God, who was called every where the Damosell of Fraunce, the which was occacion of his victorie. There maie be also used meanes, that maie make thy men to esteme little the enemie, as Agesilao a Spartaine used, whom shewed to his souldiours, certain Persians naked, to the intent that seyng their delicate members, thei should not have cause to feare them. Some have constrained their men to faight through necessitie, takyng awaie from them all hope of savyng theim selves, savyng in overcommyng. The whiche is the strongest, and the beste provision that is made, to purpose to make the souldiour obstinate to faight: whiche obstinatenesse is increased by the confidence, and love of the Capitaine, or of the countrie. Confidence is caused through the armour, the order the late victorie, and the opinion of the Capitaine. The love of the countrie, is caused of nature: that of the Capitain, through vertue, more then by any other benefite: the necessities maie be many, but that is strongest, whiche constraineth thee; either to overcome, or to dye.

The Fiveth Booke

How the Romaines marched with their armies; How the Romaines ordered their armie when it happened to be assaulted on the waie; How the main battailes ought to marche; The orderyng of an armie after soche sorte, that it maie marche safelie through the enemies countrie and be alwaies in a redines to faight; The place in the armie wher the bowmen and Harkabutters are appoincted; The place in the armie wher thextraordinarie Pikes are appoincted. The place in the armie wherthe generall capitain must be; Where the artillerie must be placed. The light horsmenne must be sente before to discover the countrie and the menne of armes to come behind tharmy; A generall rule concernyng horse; Wher the carriages and the unarmed are placed; The waie must be made plaine wher the armie shall marche in order; How many miles a day an armie maie marche in battaile raie, to bee able to incampe before sunne set; The orderyng of the armie, when it is assaulted on the vawarde; The orderyng of tharmie when thenemie commes to assaulte it behinde; How the armie is ordered when it is assaulted of any of the sides; doen when the army is assaulted on twoo sides.

Fabricio. I have shewed you, how an armi, is ordained to faight a fielde with an other armie, which is seen pitched against it, and have declared unto you, howe the same is overcome, and after many circumstaunces, I have likewise shewed you, what divers chaunces, maie happen about thesame, so that me thinkes tyme to shewe you now, how an armie is ordered, againste thesame enemie, whiche otherwise is not seen, but continually feared, that he assaulte thee: this happeneth when an armie marcheth through the enemies countrie, or through suspected places. Firste, you must understande, how a Romaine armie, sent alwaies ordinarely afore, certaine bandes of horsemen, as spies of the waie: after followed the right horne, after this, came all the carriages, whiche to thesame apperteined, after this, came a Legion, after it, the carriages therof, after that, an other legion, and next to it, their carriages, after whiche, came the left horne, with the carriages thereof at their backe, and in the laste part, folowed the remnaunte of the chivalrie: this was in effecte the maner, with whiche ordinarily thei marched: and if it happened that the armie were assaulted in the waie on the fronte, or on the backe, thei made straight waie all the carriages to bee drawen, either on the right, or on the lefte side, accordyng as chaunsed, or as thei could beste, havyng respecte to the situacion: and all the men together free from their impedimentes, made hedde on that parte, where the enemie came. If thei were assaulted on the flancke, thei drue the carriages towardes thesame parte that was safe, and of the other, thei made hedde. This waie beyng well and prudently governed, I have thought meete to imitate, sending afore the light horsemen, as exploratours of the Countrie: Then havyng fower maine battailes I would make them to marche in araie, and every one with their carriages folowyng theim. And for that there be twoo sortes of carriages, that is partainyng to particulare souldiours, and partainyng to the publike use of all the Campe, I would devide the publike Carriages into fower partes, and to every maine battaile, I would appoinct his parte, deviding also the artillerie into fower partes, and all the unarmed, so that every nomber of armed menne, should equally have their impedimentes. But bicause it happeneth some times, that thei marche through the countrie, not onely suspected, but so daungerous, that thou fearest every hower to be assaulted, thou art constrained for to go more sure, to chaunge the forme of marchyng, and to goe in soche wise prepared, that neither the countrie menne, nor any armie, maie hurte thee, findyng thee in any parte unprovided. In soche case, the aunciente capitaines were wont, to marche with the armie quadrante, whiche so thei called this forme, not for that it was altogether quadrante, but for that it was apte to faight of fower partes, and thei saied, that thei wente prepared, bothe for the waie, and for the faight: from whiche waie, I will not digresse, and I will ordaine my twoo maine battailes, whiche I have taken for to make an armie of, to this effect. Mindyng therefore, to marche safely through the enemies Countrie, and to bee able to aunswere hym on every side, when at unwares the armie might chaunce to be assaulted, and intendyng therefore, accordyng to the antiquitie, to bryng thesame into a square, I would devise to make a quadrant, that the rome therof should be of space on every part Clix. yardes, in this maner. First I would put the flanckes, distant the one flanck from the other, Clix. yardes, and I would place five battailes for a flancke, in a raie in length, and distant the one from the other, twoo yardes and a quarter: the whiche shall occupie with their spaces, every battaile occupiyng thirtie yardes, Clix. yardes. Then betwen the hedde and the taile of these two flanckes, I would place the other tenne battailes, in every parte five, orderyng them after soche sorte, that fower should joyne to the hedde of the right flanck, and fower to the taile of the lefte flancke, leaving betwene every one of them, a distance of thre yardes: one should after joyne to the hedde of the lefte flancke, and one to the taile of the right flancke: and for that the space that is betwene the one flancke and the other, is Clix. yardes, and these battailes whiche are set the one to the side of the other by breadth, and not by length, will come to occupie with the distaunces one hundred yardes and a halfe yarde, there shall come betwene theim fower battailes, placed in the fronte on the right flancke, and the one placed in thesame on the lefte, to remaine a space of fiftie and eighte yardes and a halfe, and the verie same space will come to remaine in the battailes, placed in the hinder parte: nor there shall bee no difference, saving that the one space shall come on the parte behind towardes the right horne, and thother shall come on the parte afore, towardes the lefte home. In the space of the lviii. yardes and a halfe before, I would place all the ordinarie Veliti, in thesame behinde, the extraordinarie, which wil come to be a thousande for a space, and mindyng to have the space that ought to be within the armie, to be every waie Clix. yardes, it is mete that the five battailes, whiche are placed in the hedde, and those whiche are placed in the taile, occupie not any parte of the space, whiche the flanckes keepe: and therefore it shall be convenient, that the five battailes behinde, doe touche with the fronte, the taile of their flanckes, and those afore, with the taile to touche he hedde, after soche sorte, that upon every corner of the ame armie, there maie remaine a space, to receive an other battaile: and for that there bee fower spaces, I would take fower bandes of the extraordinarie Pikes, and in every corner I would place one, and the twoo Ansignes of the foresaied Pikes, whiche shall remain overplus, I would sette in the middest of the rome of this armie, in a square battaile, on the hedde whereof, should stande the generall capitaine, with his menne about him. And for that these battailes ordeined thus, marche all one waie, but faight not all one waie, in puttyng them together, those sides ought to be ordained to faight, whiche are not defended of thother battailes. And therfore it ought to be considered, that the five battailes that be in the front, have all their other partes defended, excepte the fronte: and therfore these ought to bee put together in good order, and with the Pikes afore. The five battailes whiche are behinde, have all their sides defended, except the parte behinde, and therefore those ought to bee put together in soche wise, that the Pikes come behind, as in the place therof we shall shewe. The five battailes that bee in the right flancke, have all their sides defended, except the right flancke. The five that be on the left flanck, have all their partes defended, excepte the lefte flancke: and therefore in orderyng the battailes, thei ought to bee made, that the Pikes maie tourne on the same flanck, that lieth open: and the Peticapitaines to stand on the hedde, and on the taile, so that nedyng to faight, all the armour and weapons maie be in their due places, the waie to doe this, is declared where we reasoned of the maner of orderyng the battailes. The artillerie I would devide, and one parte I would place without, on the lefte flancke, and the other on the right. The light horsemen, I would sende afore to discover the countrie. Of the menne of armes, I would place part behinde, on the right home, and parte on the lefte, distante about thirtie yardes from the battailes: and concerning horse, you have to take this for a general rule in every condicion, where you ordaine an armie, that alwaies thei ought to be put, either behinde, or on the flanckes of thesame: he that putteth them afore, over against the armie, it behoveth hym to doe one of these twoo thinges, either that he put them so moche afore, that beyng repulced, thei maie have so moche space, that maie give them tyme, to be able to go a side from thy footemen, and not to runne upon them, or to order them in soche wise, with so many spaces, that the horses by those maie enter betwene them, without disorderyng them. Nor let no man esteme little this remembraunce, for as moche as many capitaines, whom havyng taken no hede thereof, have been ruinated, and by themselves have been disordered, and broken. The carriages and the unarmed menne are placed, in the rome that remaineth within the armie, and in soche sorte equally devided, that thei maie give the waie easely, to whom so ever would go, either from the one corner to the other, or from the one hedde, to the other of the armie. These battailes without the artillerie and the horse, occupie every waie from the utter side, twoo hundred and eleven yardes and a halfe of space: and bicause this quadrante is made of twoo main battailes, it is convenient to distinguishe, what part thone maine battaile maketh, and what the other: and for that the main battailes are called by the nomber, and every of theim hath (as you knowe) tenne battailes, and a generall hed, I would cause that the first main battaile, should set the first v. battailes therof in the front, the other five, in the left flanck, and the capitain of the same should stande in the left corner of the front. The seconde maine battaile, should then put the firste five battailes therof, in the right flanck, and the other five in the taile, and the hedde capitain of thesame, should stande in the right corner, whom should come to dooe the office of the Tergiductor. The armie ordained in this maner, ought to be made to move, and in the marchyng, to observe all this order, and without doubte, it is sure from all the tumultes of the countrie men. Nor the capitain ought not to make other provision, to the tumultuarie assaultes, then to give sometyme Commission to some horse, or Ansigne of Veliti, that thei set themselves in order: nor it shall never happen that these tumultuous people, will come to finde thee at the drawyng of the swerd, or pikes poincte: for that men out of order, have feare of those that be in araie: and alwaies it shall bee seen, that with cries and rumours, thei will make a greate assaulte, without otherwise commyng nere unto thee, like unto barking curres aboute a Mastie. Aniball when he came to the hurte of the Romaines into Italie, he passed through all Fraunce, and alwaies of the Frenche tumultes, he took small regarde. Mindyng to marche, it is conveniente to have plainers and labourers afore, whom maie make thee the waie plaine, whiche shall bee garded of those horsemen, that are sent afore to viewe the countrie: an armie in this order maie marche tenne mile the daie, and shall have tyme inough to incampe, and suppe before Sunne goyng doune, for that ordinarely, an armie maie marche twentie mile: if it happen that thou be assaulted, of an armie set in order, this assaulte cannot growe sodainly: for that an armie in order, commeth with his pace, so that thou maiest have tyme inough, to set thy self in order to faight the field, and reduce thy menne quickly into thesame facion, or like to thesame facion of an armie, which afore is shewed thee. For that if thou be assaulted, on the parte afore, thou needeste not but to cause, that the artillerie that be on the flanckes, and the horse that be behinde, to come before, and place theimselves in those places, and with those distaunces, as afore is declared. The thousande Veliti that bee before, must go out of their place, and be devided into CCCCC. for a parte, and go into their place, betwene the horse and the hornes of tharmy: then in the voide place that thei shal leave, the twoo Ansignes of the extraordinarie Pikes muste entre, whiche I did set in the middest of the quadrante of the armie. The thousande Veliti, whiche I placed behinde, must departe from thesame place, and devide them selves in the flanckes of the battailes, to the fortificacion of those: and by the open place that thei shal leave, all the carriages and unarmed menne must go out, and place themselves on the backe of the battaile. Then the rome in the middeste beyng voided, and every man gone to his place: the five battailes, whiche I placed behinde on the armie, must make forward in the voide place, that is betwene the one and the other flanck, and marche towardes the battailes, that stand in the hedde, and three of theim, muste stande within thirtie yardes of those, with equall distances, betwene the one and the other, and the other twoo shal remain behinde, distaunte other thirtie yardes: the whiche facion maie bee ordained in a sodaine, and commeth almoste to bee like, unto the firste disposicion, whiche of tharmy afore we shewed. And though it come straighter in the fronte, it commeth grosser in the flanckes, whiche giveth it no lesse strength: but bicause the five battailes, that be in the taile, have the Pikes on the hinder parte, for the occasion that before we have declared, it is necessarie to make theim to come on the parte afore, mindyng to have theim to make a backe to the front of tharmie: and therfore it behoveth either to make them to tourne battaile after battaile, as a whole body, or to make them quickly to enter betwen thorders of targettes, and conduct them afore, the whiche waie is more spedy, and of lesse disorder, then to make them to turn al together: and so thou oughtest to doe of all those, whiche remain behind in every condicion of assault, as I shal shewe you. If it appere that thenemie come on the part behinde, the first thyng that ought to bee dooen, is to cause that every man tourne his face where his backe stode, and straight waie tharmie cometh to have made of taile, hed, and of hed taile: then al those waies ought to be kept, in orderyng thesame fronte, as I tolde afore. If the enemie come to incounter the right flancke, the face of thy armie ought to bee made to tourne towardes thesame side: after, make all those thynges in fortificacion of thesame hedde, whiche above is saied, so that the horsemen, the Veliti, and the artillerie, maie be in places conformable to the hed thereof: onely you have this difference, that in variyng the hed of those, which are transposed, some have to go more, and some lesse. In deede makyng hedde of the right flancke, the Veliti ought to enter in the spaces, that bee betwene the horne of the armie, and those horse, whiche were nerest to the lefte flancke, in whose place ought to enter, the twoo Ansignes of the extraordinarie Pikes, placed in the middest: But firste the carriages and the unarmed, shall goe out by the open place, avoidyng the rome in the middest, and retiryng themselves behinde the lefte flancke, whiche shall come to bee then the taile of the armie: the other Veliti that were placed in the taile, accordyng to the principall orderyng of the armie, in this case, shall not move: Bicause the same place should not remaine open, whiche of taile shall come to be flancke: all other thyng ought to bee dooen, as in orderyng of the firste hedde is saied: this that is told about the makyng hed of the right flanck, must be understode to be told, havyng nede to make it of the left flanck: for that the very same order ought to bee observed. If the enemie should come grose, and in order to assaulte thee on twoo sides, those twoo sides, whiche he commeth to assaulte thee on, ought to bee made stronge with the other twoo sides, that are not assaulted, doublyng the orders in eche of theim, and devidyng for bothe partes the artillerie, the Veliti, and the horse. If he come on three or on fower sides, it is necessarie that either thou or he lacke prudence: for that if thou shalt bee wise, thou wilte never putte thy self in place, that the enemie on three or fower sides, with a greate nomber of men, and in order, maie assault thee: for that mindyng, safely to hurte thee, it is requisit, that he be so great, that on every side, he maie assault thee, with as many men, as thou haste almoste in al thy army: and if thou be so unwise, that thou put thy self in the daunger and force of an enemie, whom hath three tymes more menne ordained then thou, if thou catche hurte, thou canste blame no man but thy self: if it happen not through thy faulte, but throughe some mischaunce, the hurt shall be without the shame, and it shal chaunce unto thee, as unto the Scipions in Spaine, and to Asdruball in Italie but if the enemie have not many more men then thou, and intende for to disorder thee, to assaulte thee on divers sides, it shal be his foolishnesse, and thy good fortune: for as moche as to doe so, it is convenient, that he become so thinne in soche wise, that then easely thou maiste overthrow one bande, and withstande an other, and in short time ruinate him: this maner of ordering an armie against an enemie, whiche is not seen, but whiche is feared, is a necessarie and a profitable thing, to accustome thy souldiours, to put themselves together, and to march with soche order, and in marchyng, to order theimselves to faight, accordyng to the first hedde, and after to retourne in the forme, that thei marched in, then to make hedde of the taile, after, of the flanckes, from these, to retourne into the first facion: the whiche exercises and uses bee necessarie, mindyng to have an armie, throughly instructed and practised: in whiche thyng the Princes and the capitaines, ought to take paine. Nor the discipline of warre is no other, then to knowe how to commaunde, and to execute these thynges. Nor an instructed armie is no other, then an armie that is wel practised in these orders: nor it cannot be possible, that who so ever in this time, should use like disciplin shall ever bee broken. And if this quadrante forme whiche I have shewed you, is somewhat difficulte, soche difficultnesse is necessarie, takyng it for an exercise: for as moche as knowyng well, how to set theim selves in order, and to maintaine theim selves in the same, thei shall knowe after more easely, how to stand in those, whiche should not have so moche difficultie.

Zanobi. I beleve as you saie, that these orders bee verie necessarie, and I for my parte, knowe not what to adde or take from it: true it is, that I desire to know of you twoo thynges, the one, if when you will make of the taile, or of the flancke hedde, and would make them to tourne, whether this be commaunded by the voice, or with the sounde: thother, whether those that you sende afore, to make plain the waie, for the armie to marche, ought to be of the verie same souldiours of your battailes, or other vile menne appoincted, to like exercise.

Commaundementes of Capitaines being not wel understoode, maie be the destruction of an armie; Respect that is to be had in commaundementes made with the sounde of the Trompet; In commaundmentes made with the voice, what respect is to be had; Of Pianars.

Fabricio. Your firste question imported moche: for that many tymes the commaundementes of Capitaines, beyng not well understoode, or evill interpreted, have disordered their armie: therfore the voices, with the whiche thei commaunde in perilles, ought to bee cleare, and nete. And if thou commaunde with the sounde, it is convenient to make, that betwene the one waie and the other, there be so moche difference, that the one cannot be chaunged for the other: and if thou commaundest with the voice, thou oughteste to take heede, that thou flie the general voices, and to use the particulares, and of the particulars, to flie those, whiche maie be interpreted sinisterly. Many tymes the saiyng backe, backe, hath made to ruinate an armie; therfore this voice ought not to be used, but in steede therof to use, retire you. If you will make theim to tourne, for to chaunge the hedde, either to flanck, or to backe, use never to saie tourne you, but saie to the lefte, to the right, to the backe, to the front: thus all the other voices ought to be simple, and nete, as thrust on, march, stande stronge, forwarde, retourne you: and all those thynges, whiche maie bee dooen with the voice, thei doe, the other is dooen with the sounde. Concernyng those menne, that must make the waies plaine for the armie to marche, whiche is your seconde question, I would cause my owne souldiours to dooe this office, as well bicause in the aunciente warfare thei did so, as also for that there should be in the armie, lesser nomber of unarmed men, and lesse impedimentes: and I would choose out of every battaile, thesame nomber that should nede, and I would make theim to take the instrumentes, meete to plaine the grounde withall, and their weapons to leave with those rankes, that should bee nereste them, who should carrie them, and the enemie commyng, thei shall have no other to doe, then to take them again, and to retourne into their araie.

Zanobi. Who shall carrie thinstrumentes to make the waie plaine withall?

Fabricio. The Cartes that are appoincted to carrie the like instrumentes.

Zanobi. I doubte whether you should ever brynge these our souldiours, to labour with Shovell or Mattocke, after soche sorte.

The victualles that thantiquitie made provision of, for their armies.

Fabricio. All these thynges shall bee reasoned in the place thereof, but now I will let alone this parte, and reason of the maner of the victualing of the armie: for that me thinketh, havyng so moche traivailed theim, it is tyme to refreshe them, and to comfort them with meate. You have to understande, that a Prince ought to ordaine his armie, as expedite as is possible, and take from thesame all those thynges, whiche maie cause any trouble or burthen unto it, and make unto hym any enterprise difficulte. Emongest those thynges that causeth moste difficultie, is to be constrained to keepe the armie provided of wine, and baked bread. The antiquitie cared not for Wine, for that lackyng it, thei dranke water, mingeled with a little vinegre, to give it a taste: For whiche cause, emong the municions of victualles for the hoste, vineger was one, and not wine. Thei baked not the breade in Ovens, as thei use for Citees, but thei provided the Meale, and of thesame, every Souldiour after his owne maner, satisfied hym self, havyng for condimente Larde and Baken, the whiche made the breade saverie, that thei made, and maintained theim strong, so that the provision of victualles for the armie, was Meale, Vineger, Larde, and Bacon, and for the horses Barley. Thei had ordinarely heardes of greate beastes and small, whiche folowed the armie, the whiche havyng no nede to bee carried, caused not moche impedimente. Of this order there grewe, that an armie in old time, marched somtymes many daies through solitarie places, and difficulte, without sufferyng disease of victualles: for that thei lived of thyngs, whiche easely thei might convey after them. To the contrarie it happeneth in the armies, that are now a daies, whiche mindyng not to lacke wine, and to eate baked breade in thesame maner, as when thei are at home, whereof beyng not able to make provision long, thei remaine often tymes famished, or though thei be provided, it is dooen with disease, and with moste greate coste: therfore I would reduce my armie to this maner of living: and I would not that thei should eate other bread, then that, which by themselves thei should bake. Concernyng wine, I would not prohibite the drinkyng thereof, nor yet the commyng of it into the armie, but I would not use indevour, nor any labour for to have it, and in the other provisions, I would governe my self altogether, like unto the antiquitie: the whiche thing, if you consider well, you shall see how moche difficultie is taken awaie, and how moche trouble and disease, an armie and a capitaine is avoided of, and how moche commoditie shall bee given, to what so ever enterprise is to bee dooen.

Zanobi. We have overcome thenemie in the field, marched afterward upon his countrie, reason would, that spoiles be made, tounes sacked, prisoners taken, therefore I would knowe how the antiquitie in these thynges, governed them selves.

The occasions why the warres made nowe adaies, doe impoverishe the conquerors as well as the conquered; The order that the Romaines toke, concerning the spoile and the booties that their souldiours gotte; An order that the antiquitie tooke, concernyng their soldiours wages.

Fabricio. Beholde, I will satisfie you. I beleve you have considered, for that once alredie with some of you I have reasoned, howe these present warres, impoverishe as well those lordes that overcome, as those that leese: for that if the one leese his estate, the other leeseth his money, and his movables: the whiche in olde time was not, for that the conquerour of the warre, waxed ritche. This groweth of keepyng no compte in these daies of the spoiles, as in olde tyme thei did, but thei leave it to the discreacion of the souldiours. This manner maketh twoo moste great disorders: the one, that whiche I have tolde: the other that the souldiour becometh more covetous to spoyle, and lesse observeth the orders: and manie times it hath been seen, howe the covetousnesse of the praye, hath made those to leese, whome were victorious. Therefore the Romaines whiche were princes of armies, provided to the one and to the other of these inconvenienses, ordainyng that all the spoyle should apertaine to the publicke, and that the publicke after should bestowe it, as shoulde be thought good: and therfore thei had in tharmie the questours, whom were as we would say, the chamberlaines, to whose charge all the spoyle and booties were committed: whereof the consull was served to geve the ordinarie pay to the souldiours, to succour the wounded, and the sicke, and for the other businesse of the armie. The consull might well, and he used it often, to graunte a spoyle to soldiours: but this grauntyng, made no disorder: for that the armie beyng broken all the pray was put in the middest, and distributed by hedde, accordyng to the qualitee of everie man: the which maner thei constituted, to thintente, that the soldiours should attend to overcome, and not to robbe: and the Romaine Legions overcame the enemies, and folowed them not, for that thei never departed from their orders: onely there folowed them, the horsemenne with those that were light armed, and if there were any other souldiours then those of the legions, they likewyse pursued the chase. Where if the spoyle shoulde have ben his that gotte it, it had not ben possible nor reasonable, to have kepte the legions steddie, and to withstonde manie perils; hereby grewe therefore, that the common weale inritched, and every Consull carried with his triumphe into the treasurie, muche treasure, whiche all was of booties and spoiles. An other thing the antiquetie did upon good consideration, that of the wages, whiche they gave to every souldiour, the thirde parte they woulde shoulde be laied up nexte to him, whome carried the ansigne of their bande, whiche never gave it them againe, before the warre was ended: this thei did, beyng moved of twoo reasons, the first was to thintente, that the souldiour should thrive by his wages, because the greatest parte of them beyng yonge men, and carelesse, the more thei have, so muche the more without neede thei spende, the other cause was, for that knowyng, that their movabelles were nexte to the ansigne, thei should be constrained to have more care thereof, and with more obstinatenesse to defende it: and this made them stronge and to holde together: all which thynges is necessarie to observe, purposinge to reduce the exercise of armes unto the intier perfection therof.

Zanobi. I beleeve that it is not possible, that to an armie that marcheth from place to place, there fal not perrilous accidentes, where the industerie of the capitaine is needefull, and the worthinesse of the souldiours, mindyng to avoyde them. Therefore I woulde be glad, that you remembring any, would shew them.

Captaines mai incurre the daunger of ambusshes twoo maner of wayes; How to avoide the perill of ambusshes; Howe ambusshes have ben perceived; Howe the Capitaine of the enemies ought to be esteemed; Where men be in greatest perill; The description of the countrey where an army muste marche, is most requiset for a Capitaine to have; A most profitable thyng it is for a capitayne to be secrete in all his affaires; An advertisment concernyng the marchyng of an armie; The marching of an armie ought to be ruled by the stroke of the Drumme; The condicion of the enemie ought to be considered.

Fabricio. I shall contente you with a good will, beyng inespetially necessarie, intendyng to make of this exercise a perfecte science. The Capitaines ought above all other thynges, whileste thei marche with an armie, to take heede of ambusshes, wherein they incurre daunger twoo waies, either marchynge thou entrest into them, or thoroughe crafte of the enemie thou arte trained in before thou arte aware. In the first case, mindyng to avoide suche perill, it is necessarie to sende afore double warde, whome may discover the countrey, and so muche the more dilligence ought to be used, the more that the countrey is apte for ambusshes, as be the woddie or hilly countries, for that alwaies thei be layd either in a wodde, or behind a hille: and as the ambusshe not forseene, doeth ruin thee, so forseyng the same, it cannot hurte thee. Manie tymes birdes or muche duste have discovered the enemie: for that alwayes where the enemie cometh to finde thee, he shall make great duste, whiche shall signifie unto thee his comyng: so often tymes a Capitaine seyng in the places where he ought to passe, Doves to rise, or other of those birdes that flie in flockes, and to tourne aboute and not to light, hath knowen by the same the ambusshe of the enemies to be there, and sendynge before his men, and sertainely understandyng it, hath saved him selfe and hurte his enemie. Concernyng the seconde case, to be trained in, (which these our men cal to be drawen to the shot) thou ought to take heede, not straight way to beleve those thinges, which are nothyng reasonable, that thei be as they seeme: as shoulde be, if the enemie should set afore thee a praie, thou oughtest to beleeve that in the same is the hooke, and that therin is hid the deceipte. If many enemies be driven away by a fewe of thine, if a fewe enemies assaulte manie of thine, if the enemies make a sodeine flight, and not standynge with reason, alwaies thou oughtest in suche cases to feare deceipte, and oughtest never to beleeve that the enemie knoweth not how to doe his businesse, but rather intendyng that he may begile thee the lesse, and mindyng to stand in lesse peril, the weaker that he is, and the lesse craftier that the enemie is, so muche the more thou oughtest to esteeme him: and thou muste in this case use twoo sundrie poinctes, for that thou oughtest to feare him in thy minde and with the order, but with wordes, and with other outewarde demonstracion, to seeme to dispyse him: because this laste way, maketh that the souldiours hope the more to have the victorie: the other maketh thee more warie, and lesse apte to be begyled. And thou hast to understand, that when men marche thoroughe the enemies countrey, they ar in muche more, and greater perils, then in fayghtyng the fielde: and therefore the Capitaine in marchyng, ought to use double diligence: and the first thyng that he ought to doo, is to get described, and payncted oute all the countrie, thorough the which he must marche, so that he maye know the places, the number, the distances, the waies, the hilles, the rivers, the fennes, and all the quallites of them: and to cause this to bee knowen, it is convenient to have with him diversly, and in sundrie maners such men, as know the places, and to aske them with diligence, and to se whether their talke agree, and accordyng to the agreyng therof, to note: he oughte also to sende afore the horsemen, and with them prudente heddes, not so muche to discover the enemie, as to viewe the countrey, to se whether it agree with the description, and with the knowledge that they have of the same. Also the guydes that are sente, ought to be kepte with hope of rewarde, and feare of paine. And above all thynges it ought to be provided, that the armie knowe not to what businesse he leadeth them: for that there is nothyng in the warre more profitable, then to keepe secret the thynges that is to be dooen: and to thintente a suddeine assaulte dooe not trouble thy soldiours, thou oughteste to see them to stande reddie with their weapons, because the thynges that ar provided for, offend lesse. Manie for to avoyde the confusion of marchyng, have placed under the standerde, the carriages, and the unarmed, and have commaunded them to folow the same, to the intente that in marchyng needyng to staye, or to retire, they might dooe it more easely, which thyng as profitable, I alowe very muche. Also in marchyng, advertismente ought to be had, that the one parte of the armie goe not a sunder from the other, or that thoroughe some goyng fast, and some softe, the armie become not slender: the whiche thynges, be occation of dissorder: therfore the heddes muste be placed in suche wise, that they may maintaine the pace even, causing to goe softe those that goe to fast, and to haste forward the other that goe to sloe, the whiche pace can not bee better ruled, then by the stroke of the drumme. The waies ought to be caused to be inlarged, so that alwaies at least a bande of iiii. hundred men may marche in order of battaile. The custome and the qualitie of the enemie ought to be considered, and whether that he wil assaulte thee either in the mornyng, or at none or in the evenynge, and whether he be more puisante with fotemen or horsemen, and accordyng as thou understandest, to ordeine and to provide for thy self. But let us come to some particular accidente. It hapneth sometime, that thou gettyng from the enemie, because thou judgest thy selfe inferiour, and therfore mindynge not to faight with him, and he comyng at thy backe, thou arivest at the banke of a river, passyng over the which, asketh time, so that the enemie is redie to overtake thee and to fayght with thee. Some, which chaunsing to bee in suche perill, have inclosed their armie on the hinder parte with a diche, and fillyng the same full of towe, and firyng it, have then passed with the armie without beyng able to be letted of the enemie, he beyng by the same fire that was betwene them held backe.

Annone of Carthage.

Zanobi. I am harde of beliefe, that this fyre coulde stay theim, in especially because I remember that I have harde, howe Annone of Carthage, beyng besieged of enemies, inclosed him selfe on the same parte, with wodde, which he did set on fire where he purposed to make eruption. Wherfore the enemies beyng not intentive on the same parte to looke to him, he made his armie to passe over the same flame, causing every man to holde his Target before his face for to defend them from the fire, and smoke.

Nabide a spartayne; Quintus Luttatius pollecie to passe over a river; How to passe a ryver without a bridge; A polecie of Cesar to passe a river, where his enemie beyng on the other side therof sought to lette hym.

Fabricio. You saye well: but consider you howe I have saied, and howe Annone did: for as muche as I saied that they made a diche, and filled it with towe, so that he, that woulde passe over the same, should be constrained to contende with the diche and with fire: Annone made the fire, without the diche, and because he intended to passe over it, he made it not great, for that otherwise without the diche, it shoulde have letted him. Dooe you not knowe, that Nabide a Spartan beyng besieged in Sparta of the Romaines, set fire on parte of his towne to let the way to the Romaines, who alredie wer entred in? And by meane of the same flame not onely hindered their way, but drave them oute: but let us turne to our matter. Quintus Luttatius a Romaine, havyng at his backe the Cimbri, and commyng to a river, to thentente the enemie should give him time to passe over, semed to geve time to them to faight with him: and therfore he fained that he would lodge there, and caused trenches to be made, and certaine pavilions to be erected, and sent certayne horsemen into the countrie for forredge: so that the Cimbrise beleevyng, that he incamped, they also incamped, and devided them selves into sundrie partes, to provide for victuals, wherof Luttatius being aware, passed the river they beyng not able to let him. Some for to passe a river havynge no bridge, have devided it, and one parte they have turned behynde their backes, and the other then becomynge shalower, with ease they have passed it: when the rivers be swift, purposyng to have their footemen to passe safely, they place their strongest horses on the higher side, that thei may sustain the water, and an other parte be lowe that may succour the men, if any of the river in passyng should be overcome with the water: They passe also rivers, that be verie deepe, with bridges, with botes, and with barrelles: and therfore it is good to have in a redinesse in an armie wherewith to be able to make all these thynges. It fortuneth sometime that in passyng a river, the enemie standynge agaynst thee on the other banke, doeth let thee: to minde to overcome this difficultie, I know not a better insample to folow, then the same of Cesar, whome havynge his armie on the banke of a river in Fraunce, and his passage beynge letted of Vergintorige a Frenche man, the whiche on the other side of the river had his men, marched many daies a longe the river, and the like did the enemie: wherfore Cesar incamping in a woddie place, apte to hide men, he tooke out of every legion three cohortes, and made them to tarie in the same place, commaundynge theim that so soone as he was departed, they shoulde caste over a bridge, and should fortefie it, and he with his other menne folowed on the waye: wherfore Vergintorige seyng the number of the legions, thinkyng that there was not left anie parte of theim behinde, folowed also his way: but Cesar when he supposed that the bridge was made, tourned backewarde, and findynge all thinges in order, passed the river without difficultee.

Zanobi. Have ye any rule to know the foordes?

How to know the Foordes of a river.

Fabricio. Yea, we have: alwaies the river, in that parte, whiche is betwene the water, that is stilleste, and the water that runneth fastest, there is least depth and it is a place more meete to be looked on, then any other where. For that alwaies in thesame place, the river is moste shallowest. The whiche thyng, bicause it hath been proved many tymes, is moste true.

Zanobi. If it chaunce that the River hath marde the Foorde, so that the horses sincke, what reamedy have you?

Howe to escape oute of a straight where the same is besette with enemies; Howe Lutius Minutius escaped out of a strayght wherin he was inclosed of his enemies; Howe some Capitaynes have suffered them selves to be compassed aboute of their enemies; A polecie of Marcus Antonius; A defence for the shotte of arrowes.

Fabricio. The remedie is to make hardels of roddes whiche must be placed in the bottome of the river, and so to passe upon those: but let us folowe our reasonyng. If it happen that a capitain be led with his armie, betwen two hilles, and that he have not but twoo waies to save hymself, either that before, or that behinde, and those beyng beset of thenemies, he hath for remidie to doe the same, which some have doen heretofore: that which have made on their hinder parte a greate trenche, difficult to passe over, and semed to the enemie, to mynde to kepe him of, for to be able with al his power, without neding to feare behinde, to make force that waie, whiche before remaineth open. The whiche the enemies belevyng, have made theim selves stronge, towardes the open parte, and have forsaken the inclosed and he then castyng a bridge of woode over the Trenche, for soche an effect prepared, bothe on thesame parte, with out any impedimente hath passed, and also delivered hymself out of the handes of the enemie. Lucius Minutus a Consul of Rome, was in Liguria with an armie, and was of the enemies inclosed, betwene certaine hilles, whereby he could not go out: therefore he sente certaine souldiours of Numidia on horsebacke, whiche he had in his armie (whom were evill armed, and upon little leane horses) towardes the places that were kepte of the enemies, whom at the first sight made the enemies, to order theim selves together, to defende the passage: but after that thei sawe those men ill apoincted, and accordyng to their facion evill horsed, regardyng theim little, enlarged the orders of their warde, wherof so sone as the Numidians wer a ware, givyng the spurres to their horses, and runnyng violently upon theim, passed before thei could provide any remedy, whom beyng passed, destroied and spoiled the countrie after soche sorte, that thei constrained the enemies, to leave the passage free to the armie of Lucius. Some capitaine, whiche hath perceived hymself to be assaulted of a greate multitude of enemies, hath drawen together his men, and hath given to the enemie commoditie, to compasse hym all about, and then on thesame part, whiche he hath perceived to be moste weake, hath made force, and by thesame waie, hath caused to make waie, and saved hymself.

Marcus Antonius retiryng before the armie of the Parthians, perceived how the enemies every daie before Sunne risyng, when he removed, assaulted him, and all the waie troubled hym: in so moch, that he determined not to departe the nexte daie, before None: so that the Parthians beleving, that he would not remove that daie, retourned to their tentes. Whereby Marcus Antonius might then all the reste of the daie, marche without any disquietnesse. This self same man for to avoide the arrowes of the Parthians, commaunded his men, that when the Parthians came towardes them, thei should knele, and that the second ranke of the battailes, should cover with their Targaettes, the heddes of the firste, the thirde, the seconde, the fowerth the third, and so successively, that all the armie came, to be as it were under a pentehouse, and defended from the shotte of the enemies. This is as moche as is come into my remembraunce, to tell you, which maie happen unto an armie marchyng: therefore, if you remember not any thyng els, I will passe to an other parte.

The Sixthe Booke

Zanobi. I beleve that it is good, seyng the reasonyng must be chaunged, that Baptiste take his office, and I to resigne myne, and wee shall come in this case, to imitate the good Capitaines (accordyng as I have nowe here understoode of the gentilman) who place the beste souldiours, before and behinde the armie, semyng unto theim necessarie to have before, soche as maie lustely beginne the faight, and soche as behinde maie lustely sustaine it. Now seyng Cosimus began this reasonyng prudently, Baptiste prudently shall ende it. As for Luigi and I, have in this middeste intertained it, and as every one of us hath taken his part willingly, so I beleve not, that Baptiste wil refuse it.

Baptiste. I have let my self been governed hetherto, so I minde to doe still. Therfore be contente sir, to folowe your reasonyng, and if we interrupte you with this practise of ours, have us excused.

How the Grekes incamped; Howe the Romaines incamped; The maner of the incamping of an armie; The lodging for the generall capitaine.

Fabricio. You dooe me, as all readie I have saied, a moste greate pleasure; for this your interrupting me, taketh not awaie my fantasie, but rather refresheth me. But mindyng to followe our matter I saie, how that it is now tyme, that we lodge this our armie, for that you knowe every thyng desireth reste and saftie, bicause to reste, and not to reste safely, is no perfecte reste: I doubte moche, whether it hath not been desired of you, that I should firste have lodged them, after made theim to marche, and laste of all to faight, and we have doen the contrary: whereunto necessitie hath brought us, for that intendyng to shewe, how an armie in going, is reduced from the forme of marching, to thesame maner of faightyng, it was necessarie to have firste shewed, how thei ordered it to faight. But tournyng to our matter, I saie, that minding to have the Campe sure, it is requisite that it be strong, and in good order: the industrie of the Capitaine, maketh it in order, the situacion, or the arte, maketh it stronge. The Grekes sought strong situacions, nor thei would never place theim selves, where had not been either cave, or bancke of a river, or multitude of trees, or other naturall fortificacion, that might defende theim: but the Romaines not so moche incamped safe through the situacion, as through arte, nor thei would never incampe in place, where thei should not have been able to have raunged all their bandes of menne, accordyng to their discipline. Hereby grewe, that the Romaines might kepe alwaies one forme of incamping, for that thei would, that the situacion should bee ruled by them, not thei by the situacion: the which the Grekes could not observe, for that beyng ruled by the situacion, and variyng the situacion and forme, it was conveniente, that also thei should varie the maner of incampyng, and the facion of their lodgynges. Therefore the Romaines, where the situacion lacked strength thei supplied thesame with arte, and with industrie. And for that I in this my declaracion, have willed to imitate the Romaines, I will not departe from the maner of their incamping, yet not observyng altogether their order, but takyng thesame parte, whiche semeth unto me, to be mete for this present tyme. I have told you many tymes, how the Romaines had in their consull armies, twoo Legions of Romaine men, whiche were aboute a leven thousande footemen, and sixe hundred horsemen, and moreover thei had an other leven thousande footemen, sente from their frendes in their aide: nor in their armie thei had never more souldiers that were straungers, then Romaines, excepte horsemenne, whom thei cared not, though thei were more in nomber then theirs: and in all their doynges, thei did place their Legions in the middeste, and the aiders, on the sides: the whiche maner, thei observed also in incampyng, as by your self you maie rede, in those aucthoures, that write of their actes: and therefore I purpose not to shewe you distinctly how thei incamped, but to tell you onely with what order, I at this presente would incampe my armie, whereby you shall then knowe, what parte I have taken out of the Romaine maners. You knowe, that in stede of twoo Romaine Legions, I have taken twoo maine battailes of footemen, of sixe thousande footemen, and three hundred horsemen, profitable for a maine battaile, and into what battailes, into what weapons, into what names I have devided theim: you knowe howe in orderyng tharmie to marche, and to faight, I have not made mencion of other men, but onely have shewed, how that doublyng the men, thei neded not but to double the orders: but mindyng at this presente, to shew you the maner of incampyng, me thinketh good not to stande onely with twoo maine battailes, but to bryng together a juste armie, made like unto the Romaines, of twoo maine battailes, and of as many more aidyng men: the whiche I make, to the intent that the forme of the incampyng, maie be the more perfect, by lodgyng a perfecte armie: whiche thyng in the other demonstracions, hath not semed unto me so necessarie. Purposing then, to incampe a juste armie, of xxiiii. thousande footemen, and of twoo thousande good horsemenne, beeyng devided into fower maine battailes, twoo of our owne menne, and twoo of straungers, I would take this waie. The situacion beyng founde, where I would incampe, I would erecte the hed standarde, and aboute it, I would marke out a quadrant, whiche should have every side distante from it xxxvii. yardes and a half, of whiche every one of them should lye, towardes one of the fower regions of heaven, as Easte, Weste, Southe, and Northe: betwene the whiche space, I would that the capitaines lodgyng should be appoincted. And bicause I beleve that it is wisedom, to devide the armed from the unarmed, seyng that so, for the moste parte the Romaines did, I would therefore seperate the menne, that were cumbered with any thing, from the uncombered. I would lodge all, or the greatest parte of the armed, on the side towardes the Easte, and the unarmed, and the cumbred, on the Weste side, makyng Easte the hedde, and Weste the backe of the Campe, and Southe, and Northe should be the flanckes: and for to distinguishe the lodgynges of the armed, I would take this waie. I would drawe a line from the hedde standarde, and lead it towardes the Easte, the space of CCCCC.x. yardes and a half: I would after, make two other lines, that should place in the middeste the same, and should bee as longe as that, but distante eche of theim from it a leven yardes and a quarter: in the ende whereof, I would have the Easte gate, and the space that is betwene the twoo uttermoste lines, should make a waie, that should go from the gate, to the capitaines lodging, whiche shall come to be xxii. yardes and a halfe broad, and CCCClxxii. yardes and a halfe longe, for the xxxvii. yardes and a halfe, the lodgyng of the Capitaine will take up: and this shall bee called the Capitaine waie. Then there shall be made an other waie, from the Southe gate, to the Northe gate, and shall passe by the hedde of the capitaine waie, and leave the Capitaines lodgyng towardes theaste, whiche waie shalbe ix.C.xxxvii. yardes and a halfe long (for the length therof wilbe as moche as the breadth of all the lodgynges) and shall likewise be xxii. yardes and a half broad, and shalbe called the crosse waie. Then so sone as the Capitaines lodgyng, were appoincted out, and these twoo waies, there shall bee begun to be appoincted out, the lodginges of our own two main battailes, one of the whiche, I would lodge on the right hand of the capitaines waie, and the other, on the lefte: and therefore passing over the space, that the breadth of the crosse waie taketh, I would place xxxii. lodgynges, on the lefte side of the capitain waie, and xxxii. on the right side, leavyng betwene the xvi. and the xvii. lodgyng, a space of xxii. yardes and a halfe, the whiche should serve for a waie overthwart, whiche should runne overthwarte, throughout all the lodgynges of the maine battailes as in the distributyng of them shall bee seen.

The lodgings for the men of armes, and their Capitaine; Note, which is breadth and whiche length in the square campe; The lodgings for the lighte horsemen, and their capitain; The lodgings for the footemen of twoo ordinary main battailes; The lodgings for the conestables; The nomber of footemen appoincted to every lodging; The lodynges for the chiefe Capitaines of the maine battayles and for the treasurers, marshals and straungers; Lodginges for the horsemen, of the extraordinarie mayne battailes; The lodgynges for the extraordinarie Pykes and Veliti; How the Artillerie must be placed in the Campe; Lodgynges for the unarmed men, and the places that are apoineted for the impedimentes of the campe.

Of these twoo orders of lodgynges in the beginnyng of the head, whiche shall come to joygne to the crosse waye, I would lodge the Capitaine of the men of armes, in the xv. lodgynges, which on everie side foloweth next, their men of armes, where eche main battaile, havyng a CL. men of armes, it will come to ten men of armes for a lodgyng. The spaces of the Capitaines lodgynges, should be in bredth xxx. and in length vii. yardes and a halfe. And note that when so ever I sai bredeth, it signifieth the space of the middest from Southe to Northe, and saiyng length, that whiche is from weste to Easte. Those of the men of armes, shoulde be xi. yardes and a quarter in length, and xxii. yardes and a halfe in bredeth. In the other xv. lodgynges, that on everie syde should folowe, the whiche should have their beginnyng on the other side of the overthwarte way, and whiche shall have the very same space, that those of the men of armes had, I woulde lodge the light horsemen: wherof beynge a hundred and fiftie, it will come to x. horsemen for a lodgyng, and in the xvi. that remaineth, I woulde lodge their Capitaine, gevynge him the verie same space, that is geven to the Capitain of the men of armes: and thus the lodginges of the horsemen of two maine battailes, will come to place in the middest the Capitaine way, and geve rule to the lodginges of the footemen, as I shall declare. You have noted how I have lodged the CCC. horsemen of everie main battaile with their Capitaines, in xxxii. lodgynges placed on the Captaine waie, havynge begun from the crosse waie, and how from the xvi. to the xvii. there remaineth a space of xxii. yardes and a halfe, to make awaie overthwarte. Mindyng therefore to lodge the xx. battailes, which the twoo ordinarie maine battailes have, I woulde place the lodgyng of everie twoo battailes, behinde the lodgynges of the horsemen, everie one of whiche, should have in length xi. yardes and a quarter, and in bredeth xxii. yardes and a half as those of the horsemens, and shoulde bee joigned on the hinder parte, that thei shoulde touche the one the other. And in every first lodgyng on everie side which cometh to lie on the crosse waie, I woulde lodge the Counstable of a battaile, whiche should come to stand even with the lodgyng of the Capitayne of the men of armes, and this lodgyng shall have onely of space for bredeth xv. yardes, and for length vii. yardes and a halfe. In the other xv. lodgynges, that on everie side followeth after these, even unto the overthwarte way, I would lodge on everie part a battaile of foote men, whiche beyng iiii. hundred and fiftie, there will come to a lodgyng xxx. The other xv. lodgynges, I woulde place continually on every side on those of the light horse men, with the verie same spaces, where I woulde lodge on everie part, an other battaile of fote men, and in the laste lodgyng, I would place on every parte the Conestable of the battaile, whiche will come to joigne with the same of the Capitaine of the lighte horsemen, with the space of vii. yardes and a halfe for length, and xv. for bredeth: and so these two firste orders of lodgynges, shal be halfe of horsemen, and halfe of footemen. And for that I woulde (as in the place therof I have tolde you) these horse menne shoulde be all profitable, and for this havynge no servauntes whiche in kepyng the horses, or in other necessarie thynges might helpe them, I woulde that these footemen, who lodge behynde the horse, should bee bounde to helpe to provide, and to keepe theim for their maisters: and for this to bee exempted from the other doynges of the Campe. The whiche maner, was observed of the Romanies. Then leavyng after these lodgynges on everie parte, a space of xxii. yardes and a halfe, whiche shoulde make awaye, that shoulde be called the one, the firste waye on the righte hande, and the other the firste waie on the lefte hand, I woulde pitche on everie side an other order of xxxii. double lodgynges, whiche should tourne their hinder partes the one againste the other with the verie same spaces, as those that I have tolde you of, and devided after the sixtenth in the verie same maner for to make the overthwarte waie, where I would lodge on every side iiii. battailes of footemen, with their constables in bothe endes. Then leavyng on every side an other space of xxii. yardes and a halfe, that shoulde make a waie, whiche shoulde be called of the one side, the seconde waie on the right hande, and on the other syde, the seconde way on the lefte hande, I would place an other order on everie side of xxxii. double lodgynges, with the verie same distance and devisions, where I would lodge on everie side, other iiii. battailes with their Constables: and thus the horesemenne and the bandes of the twoo ordinarie maine battailes, should come to be lodged in three orders of lodgynges, on the one side of the capitaine waie, and in three other orders of lodgynges on the other side of the Capitaine waie. The twoo aidyng maine battels (for that I cause them to be made of the verie same nation) I woulde lodge them on everie parte of these twoo ordinarie maine battailes, with the very same orders of double lodgynges, pitchyng first one order of lodgynges, where should lodge halfe the horsemen, and half the foote men, distance xxii. yardes and a halfe from the other, for to make a way whiche should be called the one, the thirde waie on the right hande, and the other the thirde waie on the lefte hande. And after, I woulde make on everie side, twoo other orders of lodgynges, in the verie same maner destinguesshed and ordeined, as those were of the ordinarie maine battelles, which shall make twoo other wayes, and they all should be called of the numbre, and of the hande, where thei should be placed: in suche wyse, that all this side of the armie, shoulde come to be lodged in xii. orders of double lodgynges, and in xiii. waies, reckenynge captaine waie, and crosse waie: I would there should remayne a space from the lodgynges to the Trenche of lxxv. yardes rounde aboute: and if you recken al these spaces, you shall see that from the middest of the Capitaines lodgyng to the easte gate, there is Dx. yardes. Now there remaineth twoo spaces, whereof one is from the Capitaines lodgyng to the Southe gate, the other is from thense to the Northe gate: whiche come to be (either of them measurynge them from the poincte in the middest) CCCC.lxxvi. yardes. Then takyng out of everie one of these spaces xxxvii. yardes and a halfe, whiche the Capitaynes lodgynge occupieth, and xxxiiii. yardes everie waie for a market place, and xxii. yardes and a halfe for way that devides everie one of the saied spaces in the middest, and lxxv. yardes, that is lefte on everie part betweene the lodgynges and the Trenche, there remaineth on every side a space for lodginges of CCC. yardes broade, and lxxv. yardes longe, measurynge the length with the space that the Captaines lodgynge taketh up. Devidynge then in the middest the saied lengthe, there woulde be made on every hande of the Capitaine xl. lodgynges xxxvii. yardes and a halfe longe, and xv. broade, whiche will come to be in all lxxx. lodgynges, wherin shall be lodged the heddes of the maine battailes, the Treasurers, the Marshalles of the fielde, and all those that shoulde have office in the armie, leavyng some voide for straungers that shoulde happen to come, and for those that shall serve for good will of the Capitaine. On the parte behinde the Capitaines lodgynge, I would have a way from Southe to Northe xxiii. yardes large, and shoulde be called the bed way, whiche shall come to be placed a longe by the lxxx. lodgynges aforesayd: for that this waie, and the crosseway, shall come to place in the middest betweene them bothe the Capitaines lodgynge, and the lxxx. lodgynges that be on the sides therof. From this bed waie, and from over agaynst the captaines lodgyng, I would make an other waie, which shoulde goe from thens to the weste gate, lykewyse broade xxii. yardes and a halfe, and should aunswer in situation and in length to the Captaine way, and should be called the market waie. These twoo waies beynge made, I woulde ordeine the market place, where the market shall bee kepte, whiche I woulde place on the head of the market way over against the capitaines lodgynge, and joigned to the head way, and I woulde have it to be quadrante, and woulde assigne lxxxx. yardes and three quarters to a square: and on the right hande and lefte hande, of the saied market place, I would make two orders of lodginges, where everie order shal have eight double lodginges, which shall take up in length, ix. yardes, and in bredeth xxii. yardes and a halfe, so that there shall come to be on every hande of the market place, xvi. lodgynges that shall place the same in the middest which shall be in al xxxii. wherin I woulde lodge those horsemen, which shoulde remaine to the aidyng mayne battailes: and when these should not suffise, I woulde assigne theim some of those lodginges that placeth between them the Capitaines lodgynge, and in especially those, that lie towardes the Trenche. There resteth now to lodge the Pikes, and extraordinarie Veliti, that everie main battaile hath, which you know accordynge to our order, how everie one hath besides the x. battailes M. extraordinarie Pikes, and five hundreth Veliti: so that the twoo cheefe maine battailes, have two thousande extraordinarie Pikes, and a thousande extraordinarie Veliti, and the ayders as many as those, so that yet there remaineth to be lodged, vi. M. menne, whome I woulde lodge all on the weste side, and a longe the Trenche. Then from the ende of the hed waye, towardes Northe, leavyng the space of lxxv. yardes from them to the trenche, I woulde place an order of v. double lodgynges, whiche in all shoulde take up lvi. yardes in lengthe, and xxx. in bredeth: so that the bredeth devided, there will come to everie lodgyng xi. yardes and a quarter for lengthe, and for bredeth twoo and twentie yardes and a half. And because there shall be x. lodgynges, I will lodge three hundred men, apoinctyng to every lodging xxx. men: leavyng then a space of three and twentie yardes and a quarter, I woulde place in like wise, and with like spaces an other order of five double lodgynges, and againe an other, till there were five orders of five double lodgynges: which wil come to be fiftie lodgynges placed by right line on the Northe side, every one of them distante from the Trenche lxxv. yardes, which will lodge fifteene hundred men. Tournyng after on the lefte hande towardes the weste gate, I woulde pitche in all the same tracte, whiche were from them to the saied gate, five other orders of double lodgynges, with the verie same spaces, and with the verie same maner: true it is, that from the one order to the other, there shall not be more then a xi. yardes and a quarter of space: wherin shall be lodged also fifteene hundred men: and thus from the Northe gate to the weste, as the Trenche turneth, in a hundred lodginges devided in x. rewes of five double lodgynges in a rowe, there will be lodged all the Pikes and extraordinarie Veliti of the cheefe maine battayles. And so from the west gate to the Southe, as the Trenche tourneth even in the verie same maner, in other ten rewes of ten lodgynges in a rewe, there shall be lodged the pikes, and extraordinarie Veliti of the aidyng mayne battailes. Their headdes or their counstables may take those lodgynges, that shal seeme unto them moste commodious, on the parte towardes the trenche. The Artillerie, I woulde dispose throughoute all the Campe, a longe the banke of the Trenche: and in all the other space that shoulde remaine towardes weste, I woulde lodge all the unarmed, and place all the impedimentes of the Campe.

And it is to be understoode, that under this name of impedimentes (as you know) the antiquitee mente all the same trayne, and all those thynges, which are necessarie for an armie, besides the souldiours: as are Carpenters, Smithes, Masons, Ingeners, Bombardiers, althoughe that those might be counted in the numbre of the armed, herdemen with their herdes of motons and beeves whiche for victuallyng of the armie, are requiset: and moreover maisters of all sciences, together with publicke carriages of the publicke munition, whiche pertaine as well to victuallyng, as to armynge. Nor I would not distinguishe these lodginges perticularly, only I would marke out the waies which should not be occupied of them: then the other spaces, that betweene the waies shall remaine, whiche shall be fower, I woulde appoincte theim generally for all the saied impedimentes, that is one for the herdemen, the other for artificers and craftes men, the thirde for publicke carriages of victuals, the fowerth for the municion of armour and weapons. The waies whiche I woulde shoulde be lefte without ocupiyng them, shal be the market waie, the head waye, and more over a waie that shoulde be called the midde waye, whiche should goe from Northe to Southe, and should passe thoroughe the middest of the market waie, whiche from the weste parte, shoulde serve for the same purpose that the overthwarte way doeth on the east parte. And besides this, a waye whiche shall goe aboute on the hinder parte, alonge the lodgynges of the Pikes and extraordinarie Veliti, and all these wayes shall be twoo and tweentie yardes and a halfe broade. And the Artilerie, I woulde place a longe the Trenche of the Campe, rounde aboute the same.

Baptiste. I confesse that I understand not, nor I beleeve that also to saye so, is any shame unto me, this beyng not my exercise: notwithstandyng, this order pleaseth me muche: onely I woulde that you shoulde declare me these doubtes: The one, whie you make the waie, and the spaces aboute so large. The other, that troubleth me more, is these spaces, whiche you apoincte oute for the lodgynges, howe they ought to be used.

The Campe ought to be all waies of one facion.

Fabricio. You must note, that I make all the waies, xxii. yardes and a halfe broade, to the intente that thorowe them, maie go a battaile of men in araie, where if you remember wel, I tolde you how every bande of menne, taketh in breadth betwene xviii. and xxii. yardes of space to marche or stande in. Nowe where the space that is betwene the trenche, and the lodgynges, is lxxv. yardes broade, thesame is moste necessarie, to the intent thei maie there order the battailes, and the artillerie, bothe to conducte by thesame the praies, and to have space to retire theim selves with newe trenches, and newe fortificacion if neede were: The lodginges also, stande better so farre from the diches, beyng the more out of daunger of fires, and other thynges, whiche the enemie, might throwe to hurte them. Concernyng the seconde demaunde, my intent is not that every space, of me marked out, bee covered with a pavilion onely, but to be used, as tourneth commodious to soch as lodge there, either with more or with lesse Tentes, so that thei go not out of the boundes of thesame. And for to marke out these lodginges, there ought to bee moste cunnyng menne, and moste excellente Architectours, whom, so sone as the Capitaine hath chosen the place, maie knowe how to give it the facion, and to distribute it, distinguishyng the waies, devidyng the lodgynges with Coardes and staves, in soche practised wise, that straight waie, thei maie bee ordained, and devided: and to minde that there growe no confusion, it is conveniente to tourne the Campe, alwaies one waie, to the intente that every manne maie knowe in what waie, in what space he hath to finde his lodgyng: and this ought to be observed in every tyme, in every place, and after soche maner, that it seme a movyng Citee, the whiche where so ever it goweth, carrieth with it the verie same waies, the verie same habitacions, and the verie same aspectes, that it had at the firste: The whiche thing thei cannot observe, whom sekyng strong situacions, must chaunge forme, accordyng to the variacion of the grounde: but the Romaines in the plaine, made stronge the place where thei incamped with trenches, and with Rampires, bicause thei made a space about the campe, and before thesame a ditche, ordinary broad fower yardes and a halfe, and depe aboute twoo yardes and a quarter, the which spaces, thei increased, according as thei intended to tarie in a place, and accordyng as thei feared the enemie. I for my parte at this presente, would not make the listes, if I intende not to Winter in a place: yet I would make the Trenche and the bancke no lesse, then the foresaied, but greater, accordyng to necessitie. Also, consideryng the artellerie, I would intrench upon every corner of the Campe, a halfe circle of ground, from whens the artillerie might flancke, whom so ever should seke to come over the Trenche. In this practise in knowyng how to ordain a campe, the souldiours ought also to be exercised, and to make with them the officers expert, that are appoincted to marke it out, and the Souldiours readie to knowe their places: nor nothyng therein is difficulte, as in the place thereof shall bee declared: wherefore, I will goe forewarde at this tyme to the warde of the campe, bicause without distribucion of the watche, all the other pain that hath been taken, should be vain.

Baptiste. Before you passe to the watche, I desire that you would declare unto me, when one would pitche his campe nere the enemie, what waie is used: for that I knowe not, how a man maie have tyme, to be able to ordaine it without perill.

Fabricio. You shall understande this, that no Capitaine will lye nere the enemie, except he, that is desposed to faight the fielde, when so ever his adversarie will: and when a capitaine is so disposed, there is no perill, but ordinarie: for that the twoo partes of the armie, stande alwaies in a redinesse, to faight the battaile, and thother maketh the lodginges. The Romaines in this case, gave this order of fortifiyng the Campe, unto the Triarii: and the Prencipi, and the Astati, stoode in armes. This thei did, for as moche as the Triarii, beyng the last to faight, might have time inough, if the enemie came, to leave the woorke, and to take their weapons, and to get them into their places. Therfore, accordyng unto the Romaines maner, you ought to cause the Campe to be made of those battailes, whiche you will set in the hinder parte of the armie, in the place of the Triarii. But let us tourne to reason of the watche.

Theantiquitie used no Scoutes; The watche and warde of the Campe.

I thinke I have not founde, emongest the antiquitie, that for to warde the campe in the night, thei have kepte watche without the Trenche, distaunte as thei use now a daies, whom thei call Scoutes: the whiche I beleve thei did, thinkyng that the armie might easely bee deceived, through the difficultie, that is in seeyng them againe, for that thei might bee either corrupted, or oppressed of the enemie: So that to truste either in parte, or altogether on them, thei judged it perillous. And therefore, all the strength of the watche, was with in the trenche, whiche thei did withall diligence kepe, and with moste greate order, punished with death, whom so ever observed not thesame order: the whiche how it was of them ordained, I will tell you no other wise, leaste I should bee tedious unto you, beyng able by your self to see it, if as yet you have not seen it: I shall onely briefly tell that, whiche shall make for my purpose, I wold cause to stand ordinarely every night, the thirde parte of the armie armed, and of thesame, the fowerth parte alwaies on foote, whom I would make to bee destributed, throughout all the banckes, and throughout all the places of the armie, with double warde, placed in every quadrante of thesame: Of whiche, parte should stande still, parte continually should go from the one corner of the Campe, to the other: and this order, I would observe also in the daie, when I should have the enemie nere.

Dilligence ought to be used, to knowe who lieth oute of the Campe, and who they be that cometh of newe; Claudius Nero; The justice that ought to be in a campe. The fauts that the antiquitie punisshed with Death; Where greate punishementes be, there oughte likewise to bee great rewardes; It was no marvel that the Romaines became mightie Princes; A meane to punishe and execute Justice, without raising tumultes; Manlius Capitolinus; Souldiours sworen to kepe the discipline of warre.

Concernyng the givyng of the watche worde, and renuyng thesame every evening, and to doe the other thynges, whiche in like watches is used, bicause thei are thynges well inough knowen, I will speake no further of them: onely I shall remember one thyng, for that it is of greate importaunce, and whiche causeth great saulfgarde observyng it, and not observyng it, moche harme: The whiche is, that there be observed greate diligence, to knowe at night, who lodgeth not in the Campe, and who commeth a newe: and this is an easie thing to see who lodgeth, with thesame order that wee have appoincted: for as moche as every lodgyng havyng the determined nomber of menne, it is an easie matter to see, if thei lacke, or if there be more menne: and when thei come to be absente without lisence, to punishe them as Fugetives, and if there bee more, to understande what thei be, what they make there, and of their other condicions. This diligence maketh that the enemie cannot but with difficultie, practise with thy capitaines, and have knowlege of thy counsailes: which thing if of the Romaines, had not been diligently observed, Claudius Nero could not, havyng Aniball nere hym, depart from his Campe, whiche he had in Lucania, and to go and to retourne from Marca, without Aniball should have firste heard thereof some thyng. But it suffiseth not to make these orders good, excepte thei bee caused to bee observed, with a greate severtie: for that there is nothyng that would have more observacion, then is requisite in an armie: therefore the lawes for the maintenaunce of thesame, ought to be sharpe and harde, and the executour therof moste harde. The Romaines punished with death him that lacked in the watch, he that forsoke the place that was given hym to faight in, he that caried any thynge, hidde out of the Campe, if any manne should saie, that he had doen some worthy thing in the faight, and had not doen it, if any had fought without the commaundemente of the Capitaine, if any had for feare, caste awaie his weapons: and when it happened, that a Cohorte, or a whole Legion, had committed like fault, bicause thei would not put to death all, thei yet tooke al their names, and did put them in a bagge, and then by lotte, thei drue oute the tenthe parte, and so those were put to death: the whiche punishemente, was in soche wise made, that though every man did not feele it every man notwithstandyng feared it: and bicause where be greate punishementes, there ought to be also rewardes, mindyng to have menne at one instant, to feare and to hope, thei had appoincted rewardes to every worthie acte: as he that faighting, saved the life of one of his Citezeins, to hym that firste leapte upon the walle of the enemies Toune, to hym that entered firste into the Campe of the enemies, to hym that had in faightyng hurte, or slaine the enemie, he that had stroken him from his horse: and so every vertuous act, was of the Consulles knowen and rewarded, and openly of every manne praised: and soche as obtained giftes, for any of these thynges, besides the glorie and fame, whiche thei got emongest the souldiours, after when thei returned into their countrie, with solemne pompe, and with greate demonstracion emong their frendes and kinsfolkes, thei shewed them. Therefore it was no marveile, though thesame people gotte so moche dominion, having so moche observacion in punishemente, and rewarde towardes theim, whom either for their well doyng, or for their ill doyng, should deserve either praise or blame: Of whiche thynges it were convenient, to observe the greater parte. Nor I thinke not good to kepe secrete, one maner of punishmente of theim observed, whiche was, that so sone as the offendour, was before the Tribune, or Consulle convicted, he was of the same lightely stroken with a rodde: after the whiche strikyng, it was lawfull for the offendour to flie, and to all the Souldiours to kill hym: so that straight waie, every man threwe at hym either stones, or dartes, or with other weapons, stroke hym in soche wise, that he went but little waie a live, and moste fewe escaped, and to those that so escaped, it was not lawfull for them to retourne home, but with so many incommodities, and soche greate shame and ignomie, that it should have ben moche better for him to have died. This maner is seen to be almoste observed of the Suizzers, who make the condempned to be put to death openly, of thother souldiours, the whiche is well considered, and excellently dooen: for that intendyng, that one be not a defendour of an evill doer, the greateste reamedie that is founde, is to make hym punisher of thesame: bicause otherwise, with other respecte he favoureth hym: where when he hymself is made execucioner, with other desire, he desireth his punishemente, then when the execucion commeth to an other. Therefore mindyng, not to have one favored in his faulte of the people, a greate remedie it is, to make that the people, maie have hym to judge. For the greater proofe of this, thinsample of Manlius Capitolinus might be brought, who being accused of the Scenate, was defended of the people, so longe as thei were not Judge, but becommyng arbitratours in his cause, thei condempned hym to death. This is then a waie to punishe, without raisyng tumultes, and to make justise to be kepte: and for as moche as to bridell armed menne, neither the feare of the Lawes, nor of menne suffise not, the antiquitie joined thereunto the aucthoritie of God: and therefore with moste greate Ceremonies, thei made their souldiours to sweare, to kepe the discipline of warre, so that doyng contrariewise, thei should not onely have to feare the Lawes, and menne, but God: and thei used all diligence, to fill them with Religion.

Women and idell games, were not suffered by the antiquitie, to bee in their armies.

Baptiste. Did the Romaines permitte, that women might bee in their armies, or that there might be used these idell plaies, whiche thei use now a daies.

Fabricio. Thei prohibited the one and thother, and this prohibicion was not moche difficulte: For that there were so many exercises, in the whiche thei kept every daie the souldiours, some whiles particularely, somewhiles generally occupied that thei had no time to thinke, either on Venus, or on plaies, nor on any other thyng, whiche sedicious and unproffitable souldiours doe.

Baptiste. I am herein satisfied, but tell me, when the armie had to remove, what order kepte thei?

Ordre in the removing the armie by the soundes of a Trumpet.

Fabricio. The chief Trumpet sounded three tymes, at the firste sound, thei toke up the Tentes, and made the packes, at the seconde, thei laded the carriage, at the thirde, thei removed in thesame maner aforsaied, with the impedimentes after every parte of armed men, placyng the Legions in the middeste: and therefore you ought to cause after thesame sorte, an extraordinarie maine battaile to remove: and after that, the particulare impedimentes therof, and with those, the fowerth part of the publike impedimentes, which should bee all those, that were lodged in one of those partes, whiche a little afore we declared: and therfore it is conveniente, to have every one of them, appointed to a maine battaile, to the entente that the armie removyng, every one might knowe his place in marchyng: and thus every maine battaile ought to goe awaie, with their owne impedimentes, and with the fowerth parte of the publike impedimentes, followyng after in soche maner, as wee shewed that the Romaines marched.

Baptiste. In pitchyng the Campe, had thei other respectes, then those you have tolde?

Respectes to be had for incampyng; How to choose a place to incampe; How to avoide diseases from the armie; The wonderfull commoditie of exercise; The provision of victualles that ought alwaies to bee in a readinesse in an armie.

Fabricio. I tell you again, that the Romaines when thei encamped, would be able to kepe the accustomed fashion of their maner, the whiche to observe, thei had no other respecte: but concernyng for other consideracions, thei had twoo principall, the one, to incampe theim selves in a wholesome place, the other, to place themselves, where thenemie could not besiege theim, nor take from them the waie to the water, or victualles. Then for to avoide infirmitie, thei did flie from places Fennie, or subjecte to hurtfull windes: whiche thei knewe not so well, by the qualitie of the situacion, as by the face of the inhabitours: for when thei sawe theim evill coloured, or swollen, or full of other infeccion, thei would not lodge there: concernyng thother respecte to provide not to be besieged, it is requisite to consider the nature of the place, where the friendes lye, and thenemies, and of this to make a conjecture, if thou maiest be besieged or no: and therefore it is meete, that the Capitaine be moste experte, in the knowlege of situacions of countries, and have aboute him divers men, that have the verie same expertenes. Thei avoide also diseases, and famishment, with causyng the armie to kepe no misrule, for that to purpose to maintain it in health, it is nedefull to provide, that the souldiours maie slepe under tentes, that thei maie lodge where bee Trees, that make shadowe, where woodde is for to dresse their meate, that thei go not in the heate, and therefore thei muste bee drawen out of the campe, before daie in Summer, and in Winter, to take hede that thei marche not in the Snowe, and in the Froste, without havyng comoditie to make fire, and not to lack necessarie aparel, nor to drink naughtie water: those that fall sicke by chaunce, make them to bee cured of Phisicions: bicause a capitain hath no reamedie, when he hath to faight with sicknesse, and with an enemie: but nothing is so profitable, to maintaine the armie in health, as is the exercise: and therfore the antiquitie every daie, made them to exercise: wherby is seen how muche exercise availeth: for that in the Campe, it kepeth thee in health, and in the faight victorious. Concernyng famishemente, it is necessarie to see, that the enemie hinder thee not of thy victualles, but to provide where thou maieste have it, and to see that thesame whiche thou haste, bee not loste: and therefore it is requisite, that thou have alwaies in provision with the armie, sufficiente victuall for a monethe, and then removyng into some strong place, thou muste take order with thy nexte frendes, that daily thei maie provide for thee, and above al thinges bestowe the victual with diligence, givyng every daie to every manne, a reasonable measure, and observe after soche sorte this poincte, that it disorder thee not: bicause all other thyng in the warre, maie with tyme be overcome, this onely with tyme overcometh thee: nor there shall never any enemie of thyne, who maie overcome thee with famishemente, that will seeke to overcome thee with iron. For that though the victory be not so honourable, yet it is more sure and more certaine: Then, thesame armie cannot avoide famishemente, that is not an observer of justice, whiche licenciously consumeth what it liste: bicause the one disorder, maketh that the victualls commeth not unto you, the other, that soche victuall as commeth, is unprofitably consumed: therefore thantiquitie ordained, that thei should spende thesame, whiche thei gave, and in thesame tyme when thei appoincted: for that no souldiour did eate, but when the Capitaine did eate: The whiche how moche it is observed of the armies nowe adaies, every manne knoweth, and worthely thei can not bee called menne of good order and sober, as the antiquitie, but lasivious and drunkardes.

Baptiste. You saied in the beginnyng of orderynge the Campe, that you woulde not stande onely uppon twoo maine battailes, but woulde take fower, for to shewe how a juste armie incamped: therfore I would you shoulde tell me twoo thynges, the one, when I shoulde have more or lesse men, howe I ought to incampe them, the other, what numbre of souldiours should suffice you to faight against what so ever enemie that were.

Howe to lodge in the Campe more or lesse menne, then the ordinarie; The nombre of men that an army ought to be made of, to bee able to faighte with the puisantest enemie that is; Howe to cause men to do soche a thing as shold bee profitable for thee, and hurtfull to them selves; Howe to overcome menne at unwares; How to tourne to commoditie the doynges of soche, as use to advertise thy enemie of thy proceadynges; How to order the campe, that the enemie shal not perceive whether the same bee deminished, or increased; A saiyng of Metellus; Marcus Crassus; How to understand the secretes of thy enemie; A policie of Marius, to understande howe he might truste the Frenchmen; What some Capitaines have doen when their countrie have been invaded of enemies; To make the enemie necligente in his doynges; Silla Asdruball; The policie of Aniball, where by he escaped out of the danger of Fabius Maximus; A Capitayne muste devise how to devide the force of his enemies; How to cause the enemie to have in suspect his most trusty men; Aniball Coriolanus; Metellus against Jugurte; A practis of the Romayne oratours, to bryng Aniball out of Credit with Antiochus; Howe to cause the enemie to devide his power; Howe Titus Didius staied his enemies that wer going to incounter a legion of men that were commyng in his ayde; Howe some have caused the enemie to devide his force; A policie to winne the enemies countrie before he be aware; Howe to reforme sedicion and discorde; The benefitte that the reputacion of the Capitaine causeth, which is only gotten by vertue; The chiefe thyng that a capitayne ought to doe; When paie wanteth, punishment is not to be executed; The inconvenience of not punisshynge; Cesar chaunsynge to fall, made the same to be supposed to signifi good lucke; Religion taketh away fantasticall opinions; In what cases a Capitaine ought not to faight with his enemie if he may otherwyse choose; A policie of Fulvius wherby he got and spoyled his enemies Campe; A policie to disorder the enemie; A policie to overcome the enemie; A policie; How to beguile the enemie; Howe Mennonus trained his enemies oute of stronge places to bee the better able to overcom them.

Fabricio. To the first question I answer you, that if the armie be more or lesse, then fower or sixe thousande souldiours, the orders of lodgynges, may bee taken awaie or joined, so many as suffiseth: and with this way a man may goe in more, and in lesse, into infinite: Notwithstandynge the Romaines, when thei joigned together twoo consull armies, thei made twoo campes, and thei tourned the partes of the unarmed, thone against thother. Concernyng the second question, I say unto you, that the Romaines ordinary armie, was about xxiiii. M. souldiours: but when thei were driven to faight against the greatest power that might be, the moste that thei put together, wer L. M. With this number, thei did set against two hundred thousand Frenchemen, whome assaulted them after the first warre, that thei had with the Carthageners. With this verie same numbre, thei fought againste Anniball. And you muste note, that the Romaines, and the Grekes, have made warre with fewe, fortefiyng themselves thorough order, and thorough arte: the west, and the easte, have made it with multitude: But the one of these nacions, doeth serve with naturall furie: as doe the men of the west partes, the other through the great obedience whiche those men have to their kyng. But in Grece, and in Italy, beyng no naturall furie, nor the naturall reverence towardes their king, it hath been necessary for them to learne the discipline of warre, the whiche is of so muche force, that it hath made that a fewe, hath been able to overcome the furie, and the naturall obstinatenesse of manie. Therefore I saie, that mindyng to imitate the Romaines, and the Grekes, the number of L. M. souldiers ought not to bee passed, but rather to take lesse: because manie make confucion, nor suffer not the discipline to be observed, and the orders learned, and Pirrus used to saie, that with xv. thousande men he woulde assaile the worlde: but let us pas to an other parte. We have made this our armie to winne a field and shewed the travailes, that in the same fight may happen: we have made it to marche, and declared of what impedimentes in marchyng it may be disturbed: and finally we have lodged it: where not only it ought to take a littell reste of the labours passed, but also to thinke howe the warre ought to be ended: for that in the lodgynges, is handeled many thynges, inespecially thy enemies as yet remainyng in the fielde, and in suspected townes, of whome it is good to be assured, and those that be enemies to overcome them: therfore it is necessarie to come to this demonstracion, and to passe this difficultie with the same glorie, as hitherto we have warred. Therfore comynge to particular matters, I saie that if it shoulde happen, that thou wouldest have manie men, or many people to dooe a thyng, whiche were to thee profittable, and to theim greate hurte, as should be to breake downe the wall of their citie, or to sende into exile many of them, it is necessarie for thee, either to beguile them in such wise that everie one beleeve not that it toucheth him: so that succouryng not the one the other, thei may finde them selves al to be oppressed without remedie, or els unto all to commaunde the same, whiche they ought to dooe in one selfe daie, to the intente that every man belevyng to be alone, to whome the commaundement is made, maie thinke to obey and not to remedie it: and so withoute tumulte thy commaundement to be of everie man executed. If thou shouldest suspecte the fidelitie of anie people, and woulde assure thee, and overcome them at unawares, for to colour thy intente more easelie, thou canst not doe better, then to counsel with them of some purpose of thine, desiryng their aide, and to seeme to intende to make an other enterprise, and to have thy minde farre from thinkyng on them: the whiche will make, that thei shall not think on their owne defence, beleevyng not that thou purposest to hurte them, and thei shal geve thee commoditie, to be able easely to satisfie thy desire. When thou shouldest perceive, that there were in thine armie some, that used to advertise thy enemie of thy devises, thou canst not doe better, myndynge to take commoditie by their traiterous mindes, then to commen with them of those thynges, that thou wilte not doe, and those that thou wilt doe, to kepe secret, and to say to doubte of thynges, that thou doubtest not, and those of whiche thou doubtest, to hide: the which shall make thenemie to take some enterprise in hand, beleving to know thy devises, where by easly thou maiest beguile and opresse hym. If thou shouldest intende (as Claudius Nero did) to deminishe thy armie, sendynge helpe to some freende, and that the enemie shoulde not bee aware therof, it is necessarie not to deminishe the lodgynges, but to maintayne the signes, and the orders whole, makyng the verie same fires, and the verye same wardes throughout all the campe, as wer wont to be afore. Lykewise if with thy armie there should joigne new men, and wouldest that the enemie shoulde not know that thou werte ingrosed, it is necessarie not to increase the lodgynges: Because keepyng secrete doynges and devises, hath alwaies been moste profitable. Wherfore Metellus beyng with an armie in Hispayne, to one, who asked him what he would doe the nexte daie, answered, that if his sherte knew therof, he would bourne it. Marcus Craussus, unto one, whome asked him, when the armie shoulde remove, saied beleevest thou to be alone not to here the trumpet? If thou shouldest desire to understande the secretes of thy enemie, and to know his orders, some have used to sende embassadours, and with theim in servauntes aparel, moste expertest men in warre: whom havynge taken occasion to se the enemies armie, and to consider his strengthe and weakenesse, it hath geven them oportunitie to overcome him. Some have sente into exile one of their familiars, and by meanes of the same, hath knowen the devises of his adversarie. Also like secrettes are understoode of the enemies when for this effecte there were taken any prisoners. Marius whiche in the warre that he made with the Cimbrie, for to know the faieth of those Frenchmen, who then inhabited Lombardie, and were in leage with the Romaine people, sent them letters open, and sealed: and in the open he wrote, that they shoulde not open the sealed, but at a certaine time, and before the same time demaundyng them againe, and finding them opened, knew thereby that their faithe was not to be trusted. Some Capitaines, being invaded, have not desired to goe to meete the enemie, but have gone to assaulte his countrey, and constrained him to retorne to defende his owne home: The whiche manie times hath come wel to passe, for that those soldiours beginnyng to fil them selves with booties, and confidence to overcome, shall sone make the enemies souldiours to wexe afraide, when they supposynge theim selves conquerours, shal understand to become losers: So that to him that hath made this diversion, manie times it hath proved well. But onely it may be doen by him, whiche hath his countrey stronger then that of the enemies, because when it were otherwise, he should goe to leese. It hath been often a profitable thyng to a capitaine, that hath been besieged in his lodgynges by the enemie, to move an intreatie of agreemente, and to make truse with him for certaine daies: the which is wonte to make the enemies more necligente in all doynges: so that avaylynge thee of their necligence, thou maiest easely have occacion to get thee oute of handes. By this way Silla delivered him selfe twise from the enemies: and with this verie same deceipte, Asdruball in Hispayne got oute of the force of Claudious Nero, whome had besieged him. It helpeth also to deliver a man out of the daunger of the enemie, to do some thyng beside the forsaied, that may keepe him at a baye: this is dooen in two maners, either to assaulte him with parte of thy power, so that he beyng attentive to the same faight, may geve commoditie to the reste of thy men to bee able to save theim selves, or to cause to rise some newe accidente, which for the strayngenesse of the thynge, maie make him to marvell, and for this occasion to stande doubtefull, and still: as you knowe howe Anniball dyd, who beynge inclosed of Fabius Maximus, tied in the nighte small Bavens kindeled beetweene the hornes of manie Oxen, so that Fabius astonied at the strangenesse of the same sight, thought not to lette him at all the passage. A Capitayne oughte amonge all other of his affaires, with al subtiltie to devise to devide the force of the enemie, either with makyng him to suspecte his owne menne, in whome he trusteth, or to give him occasion, that he maye seperate his menne, and therby to be come more weake. The fyrste way is dooen with keepyng saulfe the thynges of some of those whiche he hath aboute him, as to save in the warre their menne and their possessions, renderynge theim their children, or other their necessaries withoute raunsome. You know that Anniball havynge burned all the fieldes aboute Rome, he made onely to bee reserved saulfe those of Fabius Maximus. You know how Coriolanus comyng with an armie to Rome, preserved the possessions of the nobilitie, and those of the comminaltie he bourned, and sacked. Metellus havinge an armie againste Jugurte, all the oratours, whiche of Jugurte were sente him, were required of him, that they woulde geve him Jugurte prisoner, and after to the verie same men writyng letters of the verie same matter, wrought in suche wise, that in shorte tyme Jugurte havyng in suspecte all his counsellours, in diverse maners put them to death. Anniball beynge fled to Antiochus, the Romaine oratours practised with him so familiarly, that Antiochus beyng in suspecte of him, trusted not anie more after to his counselles. Concernyng to devide the enemies men, there is no more certainer waie, then to cause their countrie to be assaulted to the intente that being constrained to goe to defende the same, they maie forsake the warre. This way Fabius used havynge agaynst his armie the power of the Frenchemen, of the Tuscans, Umbries and Sannites. Titus Didius havyng a few men in respecte to those of the enemies, and lookynge for a legion from Rome, and the enemies purposinge to goe to incounter it, to the intente that they should not goe caused to bee noised through all his armie, that he intended the nexte daie to faighte the field with the enemies: after he used means, that certaine of the prisoners, that he had taken afore, had occasion to runne awaie. Who declaryng the order that the Consull had taken to faighte the nexte daie, by reason wherof the enemies beyng afraide to deminishe their owne strength, went not to incounter the same legion, and by this way thei wer conducted safe. The which means serveth not to devide the force of the enemies, but to augmente a mans owne. Some have used to devide the enemies force, by lettyng him to enter into their countrie, and in profe have let him take manie townes, to the intente that puttynge in the same garrisons, he might thereby deminishe his power, and by this waie havynge made him weake, have assaulted and overcomen him. Some other mindyng to goe into one province, have made as though they woulde have invaded an other, and used so much diligence, that sodenly entryng into the same, where it was not doubted that they woulde enter, they have first wonne it, before the ennemie coulde have time to succour it: for that thy enemie beynge not sure, whether thou purposest to tourne backe, to the place fyrste of thee threatned, is constrained not to forsake the one place, to succour the other, and so many times he defendeth neither the one nor the other. It importeth besides the sayde thynges to a Capitaine, if there growe sedicion or discorde amonge the souldiours, to knowe with arte howe to extynguishe it: The beste waie is to chastise the headdes of the faultes, but it muste be doen in such wise, that thou maiest first have oppressed them, before they be able to be aware: The way is if they be distante from thee, not onely to call the offenders, but together with theim all the other, to the entente that not beleevynge, that it is for any cause to punishe them, they become not contumelius, but geve commoditie to the execution of the punishemente: when thei be present, thou oughtest to make thy selfe stronge with those that be not in faulte, and by meane of their helpe to punishe the other. When there hapneth discorde amonge them, the beste waye is, to bryng them to the perill, the feare whereof is wonte alwaies to make them agree. But that, which above all other thynge kepeth the armie in unitee, is the reputacion of the Capitaine, the whiche onely groweth of his vertue: because neither bloud, nor authoritie gave it ever without vertue. And the chiefe thyng, whiche of a Capitain is looked for to be doen, is, to keepe his souldiours punisshed, and paied: for that when so ever the paie lacketh, it is conveniente that the punisshement lacke: because thou canst not correcte a souldiour, that robbeth, if thou doest not paie him, nor the same mindynge to live, cannot abstaine from robbynge: but if thou paiest him and punisshest him not, he beecometh in everie condicion insolente: For that thou becomest of small estimacion, where thou chaunsest not to bee able to maintaine the dignitie of thy degree, and not mainetainyng it, there foloweth of necessitee tumulte, and discorde, whiche is the ruine of an armie. Olde Capitaines had a troubell, of the which the presente be almoste free, whiche was to interprete to their purpose the sinister auguries: because if there fell a thunderbolte in an armie, if the sunne were darkened or the Moone, if there came an erthequake, if the Capitaine either in gettyng up, or in lightynge of his horse fell, it was of the souldiours interpreted sinisterously: And it ingendred in them so moche feare, that comynge to faight the fielde, easely they should have lost it: and therefore the aunciente Capitaines so sone as a lyke accidente grewe, either they shewed the cause of the same, and redused it to a naturall cause, or they interpreted it to their purpose. Cesar fallyng in Africa, in comyng of the sea saied, Africa I have taken thee. Moreover manie have declared the cause of the obscuryng of the Moone, and of earthquakes: which thing in our time cannot happen, as well because our men be not so supersticious, as also for that our religion taketh away altogether such opinions: al be it when they should chaunse, the orders of the antiquitie ought to be imitated. When either famishement, or other naturall necessitie, or humaine passion, hath broughte thy enemie to an utter desperation, and he driven of the same, cometh to faight with thee, thou oughtest to stande within thy campe, and as muche as lieth in thy power, to flie the faight. So the Lacedemonians did against the Masonians, so Cesar did against Afranio, and Petreio. Fulvius beyng Consul, against the Cimbrians, made his horsemen manie daies continually to assaulte the enemies, and considered how thei issued out of their campe for to folow them: wherfore he sette an ambusshe behinde the Campe of the Cimbrians, and made them to be assaulted of his horsmen, and the Cimbrians issuyng oute of their campe for to follow them. Fulvio gotte it, and sacked it. It hath ben of great utilitie to a Capitaine, havyng his armie nere to the enemies armie, to sende his menne with the enemies ansignes to robbe, and to burne his owne countrey, whereby the enemies beleevynge those to bee menne, whiche are come in their aide, have also runne to helpe to make them the pray: and for this disorderyng them selves, hathe therby given oportunitie to the adversary to overcome them. This waie Alexander of Epirus used againste the Illirans and Leptenus of Siracusa against the Carthaginers and bothe to the one and to the other, the devise came to passe most happely. Manie have overcome the enemie, gevyng him occasion to eate and to drinke oute of measure, fayning to have feared, and leaving their Campes full of wyne and herdes of cattell, wherof the enemie beyng filled above all naturall use, have then assaulted him, and with his destruction overthrowen him. So Tamirus did against Cirus, and Tiberius Graccus agaynst the Spaniardes. Some have poysoned the wine, and other thynges to feede on, for to be able more easely to overcome them. I saied a littel afore how I founde not, that the antiquetie kepte in the night Scoutes abroade, and supposed that they did it for to avoide the hurte, whiche might growe therby: because it is founde, that through no other meane then throughe the watche man, whiche was set in the daie to watche the enemie, hath been cause of the ruin of him, that set him there: for that manie times it hath hapned, that he beyng taken, hath been made perforce to tell theim the token, whereby they might call his felowes, who commyng to the token, have been slaine or taken. It helpeth to beguile the enemie sometime to varie a custome of thine, whereupon he having grounded him self, remaineth ruinated: as a Capitaine did once, whome usinge to cause to be made signes to his men for comynge of the enemies in the night with fire, and in the daie with smoke, commaunded that withoute anie intermission, they shoulde make smoke and fire, and after commynge upon them the enemie, they should reste, whome beleevyng to come without beynge seen, perceivyng no signe to be made of beyng discovered, caused (through goeyng disordered) more easie the victorie to his adversarie. Mennonus a Rodian mindynge to drawe from stronge places the enemies armie, sente one under colour of a fugitive, the whiche affirmed, howe his armie was in discorde, and that the greater parte of them wente awaie: and for to make the thynge to be credited, he caused to make in sporte, certaine tumultes amonge the lodgynges: whereby the enemie thvnkyng thereby to be able to discomfaighte them, assaultynge theim, were overthrowen.

The enemie ought not to be brought into extreme desperacion; How Lucullus constrained certaine men that ran awaie from him to his enemies, to fayght whether they wold or not.

Besides thesaied thynges, regarde ought to be had not to brynge the enemie into extreme desperacion: whereunto Cesar had regarde, faightyng with the Duchemen, who opened them the waie, seyng, howe thei beyng not able to flie, necessitie made them strong, and would rather take paine to followe theim, when thei fled, then the perill to overcome them, when thei defended them selves. Lucullus seyng, how certaine Macedonian horsemenne, whiche were with hym, went to the enemies parte, straight waie made to sounde to battaile, and commaunded, that the other men should folowe hym: whereby the enemies beleving, that Lucullus would begin the faight, went to incounter the same Macedonians, with soche violence, that thei were constrained to defende themselves: and so thei became against their willes, of fugetives, faighters. It importeth also to knowe, how to be assured of a toune, when thou doubteste of the fidelitie thereof, so sone as thou haste wonne the fielde, or before, the whiche certain old insamples maie teache thee.

A policie wher by Pompey got a towne; How Publius Valerius assured him self of a towne; A policie that Alexander Magnus used to be assured of all Tracia, which Philip kynge of Spaine did practise to be asured of England when he wente to sainct Quintens; Examples for Capitaines to winne the hartes of the people.

Pompei doubtyng of the Catinensians, praied them that thei would bee contente, to receive certaine sicke menne, that he had in his armie, and sendyng under the habite of sicke persones, most lustie menne, gotte the toune. Publius Valerius, fearyng the fidelitie of the Epidannians, caused to come, as who saieth, a Pardon to a churche without the toune, and when al the people wer gone for Pardon, he shutte the gates, receivyng after none in, but those whom he trusted. Alexander Magnus, mindyng to goe into Asia, and to assure himself of Thracia, toke with him all the principall of thesame Province, givyng theim provision, and he set over the common people of Thracia, men of lowe degree, and so he made the Princes contented with paiyng theim, and the people quiete, havyng no heddes that should disquiete them: But emong all the thynges, with the whiche the Capitaines, winne the hartes of the people, be the insamples of chastitie and justice, as was thesame of Scipio in Spaine, when he rendered that yong woman, moste faire of personage to her father, and to her housebande: the whiche made him more, then with force of armes to winne Spain.

Cesar having caused that woodde to bee paied for, whiche he had occupied for to make the Listes, about his armie in Fraunce, got so moche a name of justice, that he made easier the conquest of thesame province. I cannot tell what remaineth me, to speake more upon these accidentes, for that concerning this matter, there is not lefte any parte, that hath not been of us disputed. Onely there lacketh to tell, of the maner of winnyng, and defendyng a toune: the whiche I am readie to doe willingly, if you be not now wearie.

Baptiste. Your humanitie is so moche, that it maketh us to followe our desires, without beyng afraied to be reputed presumptuous, seyng that you liberally offer thesame, whiche we should have been ashamed, to have asked you: Therefore, we saie unto you onely this, that to us you cannot dooe a greater, nor a more gratefuller benefite, then to finishe this reasonyng. But before that you passe to that other matter, declare us a doubte, whether it bee better to continewe the warre, as well in the Winter, as thei use now adaies, or to make it onely in the Sommer, and to goe home in the Winter, as the antiquitie did.

Warre ought not to be made in winter; Rough situacions, colde and watrie times, are enemies to the oder of warre; An overthrowe caused by winter.

Fabricio. See, that if the prudence of the demaunder were not, there had remained behinde a speciall part, that deserveth consideracion. I answere you againe, that the antiquitie did all thynges better, and with more prudence then wee: and if wee in other things commit some erroure, in the affaires of warre, wee commit all errour. There is nothing more undiscrete, or more perrillous to a Capitayne, then to make warre in the Winter, and muche more perrill beareth he, that maketh it, then he that abideth it: the reason is this. All the industrie that is used in the discipline of warre, is used for to bee prepared to fighte a fielde with thy enemie, because this is the ende, whereunto a Capitayne oughte to goo or endevour him selfe: For that the foughten field, geveth thee the warre wonne or loste: then he that knoweth best how to order it, and he that hath his army beste instructed, hath moste advauntage in this, and maye beste hope to overcome. On the other side, there is nothing more enemie to the orders, and then the rough situacions, or the colde watery time: for that the rough situacions, suffereth thee not to deffende thy bandes, according to thee discipline: the coulde and watery times, suffereth thee not to keepe thy men together, nor thou canst not bring them in good order to the enemy: but it is convenient for thee to lodge them a sunder of necessitie, and without order, being constrayned to obeye to Castells, to Boroughes, and to the Villages, that maye receyve thee, in maner that all thy laboure of thee, used to instructe the army is vaine. Nor marvayle you not though now a daies, they warre in the Winter, because the armies being without discipline, know not the hurt that it dooth them, in lodging not together, for that it is no griefe to them not to be able to keepe those orders, and to observe that discipline, which they have not: yet they oughte to see howe much harme, the Camping in the Winter hath caused, and to remember, how the Frenchmen in the yeare of oure Lorde God, a thousande five hundred and three, were broken at Gariliano of the Winter, and not of the Spaniardes: For as much as I have saide, he that assaulteth, hath more disadvauntage then he that defendeth: because the fowle weather hurteth him not a littell, being in the dominion of others and minding to make warre. For that he is constrayned, either to stande together with his men, and to sustaine the incommoditie of water and colde, or to avoide it to devide his power: But he that defendeth, may chuse the place as he listeth, and tary him with his freshe men: and he in a sodayne may set his men in araye, and goo to find a band of the enemies men, who cannot resiste the violence of them. So the Frenchemen were discomfited, and so they shall alwayes be discomfited, which will assaulte in the Winter an enemye, whoo hath in him prudence. Then he that will that force, that orders, that discipline and vertue, in anye condition availe him not, let him make warre in the fielde in the winter: and because that the Romaines woulde that all these thinges, in which they bestowed so much diligence, should availe them, fleedde no otherwise the Winter, then the highe Alpes, and difficulte places, and whatsoever other thing shoulde let them, for being able to shewe their arte and their vertue. So this suffiseth to your demaund, wherefore we wil come to intreate of the defending and besieging of tounes, and of their situacions and edifications.

The Seventh Booke

Tounes and Fortresses maie be strong twoo waies; The place that now a daies is moste sought to fortifie in; How a Toune walle ought to bee made; The walle of a toune ought to bee high, and the diche within, and not without; The thickenes that a Toune walle ought to bee of, and the distaunces betwene everie flancker, and of what breadth and deapth the dich ought to bee; How the ordinaunce is planted, for the defence of a toune; The nature of the batterie.

You oughte to knowe, how that tounes and fortresses, maie bee strong either by nature, or by industrie; by nature, those bee strong, whiche bee compassed aboute with rivers, or with Fennes, as Mantua is and Ferrara, or whiche bee builded upon a Rocke, or upon a stepe hille, as Monaco, and Sanleo: For that those that stande upon hilles, that be not moche difficulct to goe up, be now a daies, consideryng the artillerie and the Caves, moste weake. And therfore moste often times in building, thei seke now a daies a plain, for to make it stronge with industrie. The firste industrie is, to make the walles crooked, and full of tournynges, and of receiptes: the whiche thyng maketh, that thenemie cannot come nere to it, bicause he maie be hurte, not onely on the front, but by flancke. If the walles be made high, thei bee to moche subjecte to the blowes of the artillerie: if thei be made lowe, thei bee moste easie to scale. If thou makeste the diches on the out side thereof, for to give difficultie to the Ladders, if it happen that the enemie fill them up (whiche a great armie maie easely dooe) the wall remaineth taken of thenemie. Therefore purposyng to provide to the one and thother foresaid inconveniences, I beleve (savyng alwaies better judgement) that the walle ought to be made highe, and the Diche within, and not without. This is the moste strongeste waie of edificacion, that is made, for that it defendeth thee from the artillerie, and from Ladders, and it giveth not facilitie to the enemie, to fill up the diche: Then the walle ought to be high, of that heighth as shall bee thought beste, and no lesse thick, then two yardes and a quarter, for to make it more difficult to ruinate. Moreover it ought to have the toures placed, with distances of CL. yardes betwen thone and thother: the diche within, ought to be at leaste twoo and twentie yardes and a halfe broad, and nine depe, and al the yearth that is digged out, for to make the diche, muste be throwen towardes the Citee, and kepte up of a walle, that muste be raised from the bottome of the diche, and goe so high over the toune, that a man maie bee covered behinde thesame, the whiche thing shal make the depth of the diche the greater. In the bottome of the diche, within every hundred and l. yardes, there would be a slaughter house, which with the ordinaunce, maie hurte whom so ever should goe doune into thesame: the greate artillerie that defende the citee, are planted behinde the walle, that shutteth the diche, bicause for to defende the utter walle, being high, there cannot bee occupied commodiously, other then smalle or meane peeses. If the enemie come to scale, the heigth of the firste walle moste easely defendeth thee: if he come with ordinaunce, it is convenient for hym to batter the utter walle: but it beyng battered, for that the nature of the batterie is, to make the walle to fall, towardes the parte battered, the ruine of the walle commeth, finding no diche that receiveth and hideth it, to redouble the profunditie of thesame diche: after soche sorte, that to passe any further, it is not possible, findyng a ruine that with holdeth thee, a diche that letteth thee, and the enemies ordinaunce, that from the walle of the diche, moste safely killeth thee. Onely there is this remedie, to fill the diche: the whiche is moste difficulte to dooe, as well bicause the capacitie thereof is greate, as also for the difficultie, that is in commyng nere it, the walle beeyng strong and concaved, betwene the whiche, by the reasons aforesaied, with difficultie maie be entered, havyng after to goe up a breache through a ruin, whiche giveth thee moste greate difficultie, so that I suppose a citee thus builded, to be altogether invinsible.

Baptiste. When there should bee made besides the diche within, a diche also without, should it not bee stronger?

Fabricio. It should be without doubt, but mindyng to make one diche onely, myne opinion is, that it standeth better within then without.

Baptiste. Would you, that water should bee in the diches, or would you have them drie?

A drie diche is moste sureste.

Fabricio. The opinion of men herein bee divers, bicause the diches full of water, saveth thee from mines under grounde, the Diches without water, maketh more difficulte the fillyng of them: but I havyng considered all, would make them without water, for that thei bee more sure: For diches with water, have been seen in the Winter to bee frosen, and to make easie the winnyng of a citee, as it happened to Mirandola, when Pope Julie besieged it: and for to save me from mines, I would make it so deepe, that he that would digge lower, should finde water.

An advertisemente for the buildyng and defending of a Toune or Fortresse; Small fortresses cannot bee defended; A toune of war or Fortresse, ought not to have in them any retiring places; Cesar Borgia; The causes of the losse of the Fortresse of Furlie, that was thought invincible; Howe the houses that are in a toune of war or Fortresse ought to be builded.

The Fortresses also, I would builde concernyng the diches and the walles in like maner, to the intent thei should have the like difficultie to be wonne. One thyng I will earnestly advise hym, that defendeth a Citee: and that is, that he make no Bulwarkes without distaunte from the walle of thesame: and an other to hym that buildeth the Fortresse, and this is, that he make not any refuge place in them, in whiche he that is within, the firste walle beyng loste, maie retire: That whiche maketh me to give the firste counsaile is, that no manne ought to make any thyng, by meane wherof, he maie be driven without remedie to lese his firste reputacion, the whiche losyng, causeth to be estemed lesse his other doinges, and maketh afraied them, whom have taken upon theim his defence, and alwaies it shall chaunce him this, whiche I saie, when there are made Bulwarkes out of the Toune, that is to bee defended, bicause alwaies he shall leese theim, little thynges now a daies, beyng not able to bee defended, when thei be subject to the furie of ordinance, in soche wise that lesyng them, thei be beginning and cause of his ruine. When Genua rebelled againste king Leus of Fraunce, it made certaine Bulwarkes alofte on those hilles, whiche bee about it, the whiche so sone as thei were loste, whiche was sodainly, made also the citee to be loste. Concernyng the second counsaile, I affirme nothyng to be to a Fortresse more perilous, then to be in thesame refuge places, to be able to retire: Bicause the hope that menne have thereby, maketh that thei leese the utter warde, when it is assaulted: and that loste, maketh to bee loste after, all the Fortresse. For insample there is freshe in remembraunce, the losse of the Fortresse of Furly, when Catherin the Countesse defended it againste Cesar Borgia, sonne to Pope Alexander the vi. who had conducted thether the armie of the king of Fraunce: thesame Fortresse, was al full of places, to retire out of one into an other: for that there was firste the kepe, from the same to the Fortresse, was a diche after soche sorte, that thei passed over it by a draw bridge: the fortresse was devided into three partes, and every parte was devided from the other with diches, and with water, and by Bridges, thei passed from the one place to the other: wherefore the Duke battered with his artillerie, one of the partes of the fortresse, and opened part of the walle: For whiche cause Maister Jhon Casale, whiche was appoincted to that Warde, thought not good to defende that breache, but abandoned it for to retire hymself into the other places: so that the Dukes men having entered into that parte without incounter, in a sodaine thei gotte it all: For that the Dukes menne became lordes of the bridges, whiche went from one place to an other. Thei loste then this Fortresse, whiche was thought invinsible, through two defaultes, the one for havyng so many retiryng places, the other, bicause every retiryng place, was not Lorde of the bridge thereof. Therefore, the naughtie builded Fortresse, and the little wisedome of them that defended it, caused shame to the noble enterprise of the countesse, whoe had thought to have abidden an armie, whiche neither the kyng of Naples, nor the Duke of Milaine would have abidden: and although his inforcementes had no good ende, yet notwithstandyng he gotte that honoure, whiche his valiauntnesse had deserved: The whiche was testified of many Epigrammes, made in those daies in his praise. Therefore, if I should have to builde a Fortresse, I would make the walles strong, and the diches in the maner as we have reasoned, nor I would not make therein other, then houses to inhabite, and those I would make weake and lowe, after soche sorte that thei should not let him that should stande in the middest of the Market place, the sight of all the walle, to the intente that the Capitain might see with the iye, where he maie succour: and that every manne should understande, that the walle and the diche beyng lost, the fortresse were lost. And yet when I should make any retiryng places, I would make the bridges devided in soche wise, that every parte should be Lorde of the bridges of his side, ordainyng, that thei should fall upon postes, in the middest of the diche.

Baptiste. You have saied that littel thynges now a daies can not bee defended, and it seemed unto me to have understoode the contrarie, that the lesser that a thyng wer, the better it might be defended.

The fortifiyng of the entrance of a Toune.

Fabricio. You have not understoode well, because that place cannot be now a daies called stronge, wher he that defendeth it, hath not space to retire with new diches, and with new fortificacions, for that the force of the ordinance is so much, that he that trusteth uppon the warde of one wall and of one fortification only, is deceived: and because the Bulwarkes (mindyng that they passe not their ordinarie measure, for that then they shoulde be townes and Castels) be not made, in suche wise that men maie have space within them to retire, thei are loste straight waie. Therefore it is wisdom to let alone those Bulwarkes without, and to fortifie thenterance of the toune, and to kever the gates of the same with turnyngs after suche sort, that men cannot goe in nor oute of the gate by right line: and from the tournynges to the gate, to make a diche with a bridge. Also they fortifie the gate, with a Percullis, for to bee abell to put therin their menne, when they be issued out to faight, and hapnyng that the enemies pursue them, to avoide, that in the mingelynge together, they enter not in with them: and therfore these be used, the which the antiquitie called Cattarratte, the whiche beyng let fall, exclude thenemies, and save the freendes, for that in suche a case, men can do no good neither by bridges nor by a gate, the one and the other beynge ocupied with prease of menne.

Baptiste. I have seene these Perculleses that you speake of, made in Almayne of littell quarters of woodde after the facion of a grate of Iron, and these percullises of ouers, be made of plankes all massive: I woulde desire to understande whereof groweth this difference, and which be the strongest.

Battelments ought to be large and thicke and the flanckers large within.

Fabricio. I tell you agayne, that the manners and orders of the warre, throughe oute all the worlde, in respecte to those of the antiquitie, be extinguesshed, and in Italye they bee altogether loste, for if there bee a thing somewhat stronger then the ordinarye, it groweth of the insample of other countries. You mighte have understoode and these other may remember, with howe muche debilitie before, that king Charles of Fraunce in the yere of our salvation a thousande CCCC. xciiii. had passed into Italie, they made the batelmentes not halfe a yarde thicke, the loopes, and the flanckers were made with a litle opening without, and muche within, and with manye other faultes whiche not to be tedious I will let passe: for that easely from thinne battelments the defence is taken awaye, the flanckers builded in the same maner, moste easylye are opened: Nowe of the Frenchemen is learned to make the battelment large and thicke, and the flanckers to bee large on the parte within, and to drawe together in the middeste of the wall, and then agayn to waxe wider unto the uttermost parte without: this maketh that the ordinaunce hardlye can take away the defence. Therfore the Frenchmen have, manye other devises like these, the whiche because they have not beene seene of our men, they have not beene considered. Among whiche, is this kinde of perculles made like unto a grate, the which is a greate deale better then oures: for that if you have for defence of a gate a massive parculles as oures, letting it fall, you shutte in your menne, and you can not though the same hurte the enemie, so that hee with axes, and with fire, maye breake it downe safely: but if it bee made like a grate, you maye, it being let downe, through those holes and through those open places, defende it with Pikes, with crosbowes, and with all other kinde of weapons.

Baptiste. I have seene in Italye an other use after the outelandishe fashion, and this is, to make the carriage of the artillery with the spokes of the wheele crooked towardes the Axeltree. I woulde knowe why they make them so: seeming unto mee that they bee stronger when they are made straighte as those of oure wheeles.

Neither the ditche, wall tillage, nor any kinde of edificacion, ought to be within a mile of a toune of warre.

Fabricio. Never beleeve that the thinges that differ from the ordinarie wayes, be made by chaunce: and if you shoulde beleeve that they make them so, to shewe fayrer, you are deceaved: because where strength is necessarie, there is made no counte of fayrenesse: but all groweth, for that they be muche surer and muche stronger then ours. The reason is this: the carte when it is laden, either goeth even, or leaning upon the righte, or upon the lefte side: when it goeth even, the wheeles equally sustayne the wayght, the which being equallye devided betweene them, doth not burden much, but leaning, it commeth to have all the paise of the cariage on the backe of that wheele upon the which it leaneth. If the spokes of the same be straight they wil soone breake: for that the wheele leaning, the spokes come also to leane, and not to sustaine the paise by the straightnesse of them, and so when the carte goeth even, and when they are least burdened, they come to bee strongest: when the Carte goeth awrye, and that they come to have moste paise, they bee weakest. Even the contrarie happeneth to the crooked spokes of the Frenche Cartes, for that when the carte leaning upon one side poincteth uppon them, because they bee ordinary crooked, they come then to bee straight, and to be able to sustayne strongly al the payse, where when the carte goeth even, and that they bee crooked, they sustayne it halfe: but let us tourne to our citie and Fortresse. The Frenchemen use also for more safegarde of the gates of their townes, and for to bee able in sieges more easylye to convey and set oute men of them, besides the sayde thinges, an other devise, of which I have not seene yet in Italye anye insample: and this is, where they rayse on the oute side from the ende of the drawe bridge twoo postes, and upon either of them they joigne a beame, in suche wise that the one halfe of them comes over the bridge, the other halfe with oute: then all the same parte that commeth withoute, they joygne together with small quarters of woodde, the whiche they set thicke from one beame to an other like unto a grate, and on the parte within, they fasten to the ende of either of the beames a chaine: then when they will shutte the bridge on the oute side, they slacke the chaines, and let downe all the same parte like unto a grate, the whiche comming downe, shuttethe the bridge, and when they will open it, they drawe the chaines, and the same commeth to rise up, and they maye raise it up so much that a man may passe under it, and not a horse, and so much that there maye passe horse and man, and shutte it againe at ones, for that it falleth and riseth as a window of a battelment. This devise is more sure than the Parculles, because hardely it maye be of the enemye lette in such wise, that it fall not downe, falling not by a righte line as the Parculles, which easely may be underpropped. Therfore they which will make a citie oughte to cause to be ordained all the saide things: and moreover aboute the walle, there woulde not bee suffered any grounde to be tilled, within a myle thereof, nor any wall made, but shoulde be all champaine, where should be neither ditch nor banck, neither tree nor house, which might let the fighte, and make defence for the enemie that incampeth.

The provision that is meete to be made for the defence of a toune.

And noote, that a Towne, whiche hathe the ditches withoute, with the banckes higher then the grounde, is moste weake: for as muche as they make defence to the enemye which assaulteth thee, and letteth him not hurte thee, because easely they may be opened, and geve place to his artillerye: but let us passe into the Towne. I will not loose so muche time in shewing you howe that besides the foresayde thinges, it is requisite to have provision of victualles, and wherewith to fight, for that they be thinges that everye man underdeth, and without them, all other provision is vaine: and generally twoo thinges oughte to be done, to provide and to take the commoditie from the enemie that he availe not by the things of thy countrey: therfore the straw, the beastes, the graine, whiche thou canste not receive into house, ought to be destroied. Also he that defendeth a Towne, oughte to provide that nothing bee done tumultuouslye and disordinatelye, and to take suche order, that in all accidentes everye man maye knowe what he hath to doo.

What incoragethe the enemy most that besiegeth a toune; What he that besiegeth and he that defendeth oughte to doo; Advertisementes for a besieged towne; Howe the Romaines vitaled Casalino besieged of Aniball; A policie for the besieged.

The order that oughte to be taken is thus, that the women, the olde folkes, the children, and the impotent, be made to keepe within doores, that the Towne maye be left free, to yong and lustie men, whom being armed, must be destributed for the defence of the same, appointing part of them to the wall, parte to the gates, parte to the principall places of the Citie, for to remedie those inconveniences, that might growe within: an other parte must not be bound to any place, but be ready to succour all, neede requiring: and the thing beeing ordained thus, with difficultie tumulte can growe, whiche maye disorder thee. Also I will that you note this, in the besieging and defending of a Citie, that nothing geveth so muche hoope to the adversarye to be able to winne a towne, as when he knoweth that the same is not accustomed to see the enemie: for that many times for feare onely without other experience of force, cities have bene loste: Therefore a man oughte, when he assaulteth a like Citie, to make all his ostentacions terrible. On the other parte he that is assaulted, oughte to appoincte to the same parte, whiche the enemie fighteth againste, strong men and suche as opinion makethe not afraide, but weapons onely: for that if the first proofe turne vaine, it increaseth boldenesse to the besieged, and then the enemie is constrained to overcome them within, with vertue and reputacion. The instrumentes wherwith the antiquitie defended townes, where manie: as balistes, onagris, scorpions, Arcubalistes, Fustibals, Slinges: and also those were manie with which thei gave assaultes. As Arrieti, Towers, Musculi Plutei, Viney, Falci, testudeni, in steede of which thynges be now a daies the ordinance, the whiche serve him that bessegeth, and him that defendeth: and therfore I will speake no forther of theim: But let us retourne to our reasonyng and let us come to particular offences. They ought to have care not to be taken by famine, and not to be overcome through assaultes: concernyng famin, it hath ben tolde, that it is requiset before the siege come, to be well provided of vitualles. But when a towne throughe longe siege, lacketh victuals, some times hath ben seen used certaine extraordinarie waies to be provided of their friendes, whome woulde save them: inespeciall if through the middest of the besieged Citie there runne a river, as the Romaines vittelled their castell called Casalino besieged of Anibal, whom being not able by the river to sende them other victual then Nuttes, wherof castyng in the same great quantitie, the which carried of the river, without beyng abel to be letted, fedde longe time the Casalinians. Some besieged, for to shew unto the enemie, that they have graine more then inough and for to make him to dispaire, that he cannot, by famin overcome theim, have caste breade oute of the gates, or geven a Bullocke graine to eate, and after have suffered the same to be taken, to the intent that kilde and founde full of graine, might shewe that aboundance, whiche they had not. On the other parte excellent Capitaines have used sundrie waies to werie the enemie.

A policie of Fabius in besieging of a toune; A policie of Dionisius in besiegynge of a toune.

Fabius suffered them whome he besieged, to sowe their fieldes, to the entente that thei should lacke the same corne, whiche they sowed.

Dionisius beynge in Campe at Regio, fained to minde to make an agreement with them, and duryng the practise therof he caused him selfe to be provided of their victuales, and then when he had by this mean got from them their graine, he kepte them straight and famished them.

Howe Alexander wanne Leucadia.

Alexander Magnus mindyng to winne Leucadia overcame all the Castels aboute it, and by that means drivyng into the same citie a great multitude of their owne countrie men, famished them.

The besieged ought to take heed of the first brunte; The remedie that townes men have, when the enemies ar entred into the towne; How to make the townes men yeelde.

Concernynge the assaultes, there hath been tolde that chiefely thei ought to beware of the firste bronte, with whiche the Romaines gotte often times manie townes, assaultyng them sodainly, and on every side: and thei called it *Aggredi urbem corona.* As Scipio did, when he wanne newe Carthage in Hispayne: the which brunte if of a towne it be withstoode, with difficultie after will bee overcome: and yet thoughe it should happen that the enemie were entred into the citie, by overcomynge the wall, yet the townes men have some remedie, so thei forsake it not: for as much as manie armies through entring into a toune, have ben repulced or slaine: the remedie is, that the townes men doe keepe them selves in highe places, and from the houses, and from the towers to faight with them: the whiche thynge, they that have entered into the citie, have devised to overcome in twoo manners: the one with openyng the gates of the citie, and to make the waie for the townes men, that thei might safely flie: the other with sendynge foorthe a proclamacion, that signifieth, that none shall be hurte but the armed, and to them that caste their weapons on the grounde, pardon shall be graunted: the whiche thynge hath made easie the victorie of manie cities.

How townes or cities are easelie wonne; How duke Valentine got the citie of Urbine; The besieged ought to take heede of the deciptes and policies of the enemie; How Domitio Calvino wan a towne.

Besides this, the Citees are easie to bee wonne, if thou come upon them unawares: whiche is dooen beyng with thy armie farre of, after soche sort, that it be not beleved, either that thou wilte assaulte theim, or that thou canst dooe it, without commyng openly, bicause of the distance of the place: wherefore, if thou secretely and spedely assaulte theim, almoste alwaies it shall followe, that thou shalte gette the victorie. I reason unwillingly of the thynges succeded in our tyme, for that to me and to mine, it should be a burthen, and to reason of other, I cannot tel what to saie: notwithstanding, I cannot to this purpose but declare, the insample of Cesar Borgia, called duke Valentine, who beyng at Nocera with his menne, under colour of goyng to besiege Camerino, tourned towardes the state of Urbin, and gotte a state in a daie, and without any paine, the whiche an other with moche time and cost, should scante have gotten. It is conveniente also to those, that be besieged, to take heede of the deceiptes, and of the policies of the enemie, and therefore the besieged ought not to truste to any thyng, whiche thei see the enemie dooe continually, but let theim beleve alwaies, that it is under deceipte, and that he can to their hurte varie it. Domitio Calvino besiegyng a toune, used for a custome to compasse aboute every daie, with a good parte of his menne, the wall of the same: whereby the Tounes menne, belevyng that he did it for exercise, slacked the Ward: whereof Domicius beyng aware, assaulted and overcame them.

A policie to get a towne.

Certaine Capitaines understandyng, that there should come aide to the besieged, have apareled their Souldiours, under the Ansigne of those, that should come, and beyng let in, have gotte the Toune.

How Simon of Athens wan a towne; A policie to get a towne; How Scipio gotte certaine castels in Afrike.

Simon of Athens set fire in a night on a Temple, whiche was out of the toune, wherefore, the tounes menne goyng to succour it, lefte the toune in praie to the enemie. Some have slaine those, whiche from the besieged Castle, have gone a foragyng, and have appareled their souldiours, with the apparell of the forragers, whom after have gotte the toune. The aunciente Capitaines, have also used divers waies, to destroie the Garison of the Toune, whiche thei have sought to take. Scipio beyng in Africa, and desiring to gette certaine Castles, in whiche were putte the Garrisons of Carthage, he made many tymes, as though he would assaulte theim, albeit, he fained after, not onely to abstaine, but to goe awaie from them for feare: the whiche Aniball belevyng to bee true, for to pursue hym with greater force, and for to bee able more easely to oppresse him, drewe out all the garrisons of theim: The whiche Scipio knowyng, sente Massinissa his Capitaine to overcome them.

Howe Pirrus wan the chiefe Citie of Sclavonie; A policie to get a towne; How the beseiged are made to yelde; Howe to get a towne by treason; A policie of Aniball for the betraiyng of a Castell; How the besieged maie be begiled; How Formion overcame the Calcidensians; What the besieged muste take heede of; Liberalitie maketh enemies frendes; The diligence that the besieged ought to use in their watche and ward.

Pirrus makyng warre in Sclavonie, to the chiefe citee of the same countrie, where were brought many menne in Garrison, fained to dispaire to bee able to winne it, and tourning to other places, made that the same for to succour them, emptied it self of the warde, and became easie to bee wonne. Many have corrupted the water, and have tourned the rivers an other waie to take Tounes. Also the besieged, are easely made to yelde them selves, makyng theim afraied, with signifiyng unto them a victorie gotten, or with new aides, whiche come in their disfavour. The old Capitaines have sought to gette Tounes by treason, corruptyng some within, but thei have used divers meanes. Sum have sente a manne of theirs, whiche under the name of a fugetive, might take aucthoritie and truste with the enemies, who after have used it to their profite. Some by this meanes, have understode the maner of the watche, and by meanes of the same knowledge, have taken the Toune. Some with a Carte, or with Beames under some colour, have letted the gate, that it could not bee shutte, and with this waie, made the entrie easie to the enemie. Aniball perswaded one, to give him a castle of the Romaines, and that he should fain to go a huntyng in the night, makyng as though he could not goe by daie, for feare of the enemies, and tournyng after with the Venison, should put in with hym certaine of his menne, and so killyng the watchmen, should give hym the gate. Also the besieged are beguiled, with drawyng them out of the Toune, and goyng awaie from them, faining to flie when thei assault thee. And many (emong whom was Anibal) have for no other intente, let their Campe to be taken, but to have occasion to get betwene theim and home, and to take their Toune. Also, thei are beguiled with fainyng to departe from them, as Formion of Athens did, who havyng spoiled the countrie of the Calcidensians, received after their ambassadours, fillyng their Citee with faire promises, and hope of safetie, under the which as simple menne, thei were a little after of Formione oppressed. The besieged ought to beware of the men, whiche thei have in suspecte emong them: but some times thei are wont, as well to assure them selves with deserte, as with punishemente. Marcellus knoweyng how Lucius Bancius a Nolane, was tourned to favour Aniball so moche humanitie and liberalitie, he used towardes him, that of an enemie, he made him moste frendely. The besieged ought to use more diligence in the warde, when the enemie is gone from theim, then when he is at hande. And thei ought to warde those places, whiche thei thinke, that maie bee hurt least: for that many tounes have been loste, when thenemie assaulteth it on thesame part, where thei beleve not possible to be assaulted. And this deceipt groweth of twoo causes, either for the place being strong, and to beleve, that it is invinsible, or through craft beyng used of the enemie, in assaltyng theim on one side with fained alaroms, and on the other without noise, and with verie assaltes in deede: and therefore the besieged, ought to have greate advertisment, and above all thynges at all times, and in especially in the night to make good watche to bee kepte on the walles, and not onely to appoincte menne, but Dogges, and soche fiearse Mastives, and lively, the whiche by their sente maie descrie the enemie, and with barkyng discover him: and not Dogges onely, but Geese have ben seen to have saved a citee, as it happened to Roome, when the Frenchemen besieged the Capitoll.

An order of Alcibiades for the dew keping of watch and warde.

Alcibiades for to see, whether the warde watched, Athense beeyng besieged of the Spartaines, ordained that when in the night, he should lifte up a light, all the ward should lift up likewise, constitutyng punishmente to hym that observed it not.

The secrete conveighyng of Letters; The defence against a breach; How the antiquitie got tounes by muining under grounde.

Isicrates of Athens killed a watchman, which slept, saiyng that he lefte him as he found him. Those that have been besieged, have used divers meanes, to sende advise to their frendes: and mindyng not to send their message by mouth, thei have written letters in Cifers, and hidden them in sundrie wise: the Cifers be according, as pleaseth him that ordaineth them, the maner of hidyng them is divers. Some have written within the scaberde of a sweard: Other have put the Letters in an unbaked lofe, and after have baked the same, and given it for meate to hym that caried theim. Certaine have hidden them, in the secreteste place of their bodies: other have hidden them in the collor of a Dogge, that is familiare with hym, whiche carrieth theim: Some have written in a letter ordinarie thinges, and after betwene thone line and thother, have also written with water, that wetyng it or warming it after, the letters should appere. This waie hath been moste politikely observed in our time: where some myndyng to signifie to their freendes inhabityng within a towne, thinges to be kept secret, and mindynge not to truste any person, have sente common matters written, accordyng to the common use and enterlined it, as I have saied above, and the same have made to be hanged on the gates of the Temples, the whiche by countersignes beyng knowen of those, unto whome they have been sente, were taken of and redde: the whiche way is moste politique, bicause he that carrieth them maie bee beguiled, and there shall happen hym no perill. There be moste infinite other waies, whiche every manne maie by himself rede and finde: but with more facilitie, the besieged maie bee written unto, then the besieged to their frendes without, for that soche letters cannot be sent, but by one, under colour of a fugetive, that commeth out of a toune: the whiche is a daungerous and perilous thing, when thenemie is any whit craftie: But those that sende in, he that is sente, maie under many colours, goe into the Campe that besiegeth, and from thens takyng conveniente occasion, maie leape into the toune: but lette us come to speake of the present winnyng of tounes. I saie that if it happen, that thou bee besieged in thy citee, whiche is not ordained with diches within, as a little before we shewed, to mynde that thenemie shall not enter through the breach of the walle, whiche the artillerie maketh: bicause there is no remedie to lette thesame from makyng of a breache, it is therefore necessarie for thee, whileste the ordinance battereth, to caste a diche within the wall which is battered, and that it be in bredth at leaste twoo and twentie yardes and a halfe, and to throwe all thesame that is digged towardes the toun, whiche maie make banke, and the diche more deper: and it is convenient for thee, to sollicitate this worke in soche wise, that when the walle falleth, the Diche maie be digged at least, fower or five yardes in depth: the whiche diche is necessarie, while it is a digging, to shutte it on every side with a slaughter house: and when the wall is so strong, that it giveth thee time to make the diche, and the slaughter houses, that battered parte, commeth to be moche stronger, then the rest of the citee: for that soche fortificacion, cometh to have the forme, of the diches which we devised within: but when the walle is weake, and that it giveth thee not tyme, to make like fortificacions, then strengthe and valiauntnesse muste bee shewed, settyng againste the enemies armed menne, with all thy force. This maner of fortificacion was observed of the Pisans, when you besieged theim, and thei might doe it, bicause thei had strong walles, whiche gave them time, the yearth beyng softe and moste meete to raise up banckes, and to make fortificacions: where if thei had lacked this commoditie, thei should have loste the toune. Therefore it shall bee alwaies prudently doen, to provide afore hand, makyng diches within the citee, and through out all the circuite thereof, as a little before wee devised: for that in this case, the enemie maie safely be taried for at laisure, the fortificacions beyng redy made. The antiquitie many tymes gotte tounes, with muinyng under ground in twoo maners, either thei made a waie under grounde secretely, whiche risse in the toune, and by thesame entered, in whiche maner the Romaines toke the citee of Veienti, or with the muinyng, thei overthrewe a walle, and made it ruinate: this laste waie is now a daies moste stronge, and maketh, that the citees placed high, be most weake, bicause thei maie better bee under muined: and puttyng after in a Cave of this Gunne pouder, whiche in a momente kindelyng, not onely ruinateth a wall, but it openeth the hilles, and utterly dissolveth the strength of them.

The reamedie against Caves or undermuinynges; What care the besieged ought to have; What maketh a citee or campe difficulte to bee defended; By what meanes thei that besiege ar made afraied; Honour got by constancie.

The remedie for this, is to builde in the plain, and to make the diche that compasseth thy citee, so deepe, that the enemie maie not digge lower then thesame, where he shall not finde water, whiche onely is enemie to the caves: for if thou be in a toune, which thou defendest on a high ground, thou canst not remedie it otherwise, then to make within thy walles many deepe Welles, the whiche be as drouners to thesame Caves, that the enemie is able to ordain against thee. An other remedie there is, to make a cave againste it, when thou shouldeste bee aware where he muineth, the whiche waie easely hindereth hym, but difficultly it is foreseen, beyng besieged of a craftie enemie. He that is besieged, ought above al thinges to have care, not to bee oppressed in the tyme of reste: as is after a battaile fought, after the watche made, whiche is in the Mornyng at breake of daie, and in the Evenyng betwen daie and night, and above al, at meale times: in whiche tyme many tounes have been wonne, and armies have been of them within ruinated: therefore it is requisite with diligence on all partes, to stande alwaies garded, and in a good part armed. I will not lacke to tell you, how that, whiche maketh a citee or a campe difficult to be defended, is to be driven to kepe sundred all the force, that thou haste in theim, for that the enemie beyng able to assaulte thee at his pleasure altogether, it is conveniente for thee on every side, to garde every place, and so he assaulteth thee with all his force, and thou with parte of thine defendest thee. Also, the besieged maie bee overcome altogether, he without cannot bee, but repulced: wherefore many, whom have been besieged, either in a Campe, or in a Toune, although thei have been inferiour of power, have issued out with their men at a sodaine, and have overcome the enemie. This Marcellus of Nola did: this did Cesar in Fraunce, where his Campe beeyng assaulted of a moste great nomber of Frenchmen, and seeyng hymself not able to defende it, beyng constrained to devide his force into many partes, and not to bee able standyng within the Listes, with violence to repulce thenemie: he opened the campe on thone side, and turning towardes thesame parte with all his power, made so moche violence against them, and with moche valiantnes, that he vanquisshed and overcame them. The constancie also of the besieged, causeth many tymes displeasure, and maketh afraied them that doe besiege. Pompei beyng against Cesar, and Cesars armie beeyng in greate distresse through famine, there was brought of his bredde to Pompei, whom seyng it made of grasse, commaunded, that it should not bee shewed unto his armie, least it shoulde make them afraide, seyng what enemies they had against theim. Nothyng caused so muche honour to the Romaines in the warre of Aniball, as their constancie: for as muche as in what so ever envious, and adverse fortune thei were troubled, they never demaunded peace, thei never made anie signe of feare, but rather when Aniball was aboute Rome, thei solde those fieldes, where he had pitched his campe, dearer then ordinarie in other times shoulde have been solde: and they stoode in so much obstinacie in their enterprises, that for to defende Rome, thei would not raise their campe from Capua, the whiche in the verie same time that Roome was besieged, the Romaines did besiege.

I knowe that I have tolde you of manie thynges, the whiche by your selfe you might have understoode, and considered, notwithstandyng I have doen it (as to daie also I have tolde you) for to be abell to shewe you better by meane therof, the qualitie of this armie, and also for to satisfie those, if there be anie, whome have not had the same commoditie to understand them as you. Nor me thinkes that there resteth other to tell you, then certaine generall rules, the whiche you shal have moste familiar, which be these.

Generall rules of warre.

The same that helpeth the enemie, hurteth thee: and the same that helpeth thee, hurteth the enemie.

He that shall be in the warre moste vigilant to observe the devises of the enemie, and shall take moste payne to exercise his armie, shall incurre least perilles and maie hope moste of the victorie.

Never conducte thy men to faight the field, if first them hast not confirmed their mindes and knowest them to be without feare, and to be in good order: for thou oughteste never to enterprise any dangerous thyng with thy souldiours, but when thou seest, that they hope to overcome.

It is better to conquere the enemie with faminne, then with yron: in the victorie of which, fortune maie doe much more then valiantnesse.

No purpose is better then that, whiche is hidde from the enemie untill thou have executed it.

To know in the warre how to understande occasion, and to take it, helpeth more then anie other thynge.

Nature breedeth few stronge menne, the industrie and the exercise maketh manie.

Discipline maie doe more in warre, then furie.

When anie departe from the enemies side for to come to serve thee, when thei be faithfull, thei shalbe unto thee alwaies great gaines: for that the power of thadversaries are more deminisshed with the losse of them, that runne awaie, then of those that be slaine, although that the name of a fugetive be to new frendes suspected, to olde odius.

Better it is in pitchyng the fielde, to reserve behynde the first front aide inoughe, then to make the fronte bigger to disperse the souldiours.

He is difficultely overcome, whiche can know his owne power and the same of the enemie.

The valiantenesse of the souldiours availeth more then the multitude.

Some times the situacion helpeth more then the valiantenesse.

New and sudden thynges, make armies afrayde.

Slowe and accustomed thinges, be littell regarded of them. Therfore make thy armie to practise and to know with small faightes a new enemie, before thou come to faight the fielde with him.

He that with disorder foloweth the enemie after that he is broken, will doe no other, then to become of a conquerour a loser.

He that prepareth not necessarie victualles to live upon, is overcome without yron.

He that trusteth more in horsemen then in footemen, more in footemen then in horsemen, must accommodate him selfe with the situacion.

When thou wilte see if in the daie there be comen anie spie into the Campe, cause everie man to goe to his lodgynge.

Chaunge purpose, when thou perceivest that the enemie hath forseene it.

How to consulte.

Consulte with many of those thinges, which thou oughtest to dooe: the same that thou wilt after dooe, conferre with fewe.

Souldiours when thei abide at home, are mainteined with feare and punishemente, after when thei ar led to the warre with hope and with rewarde.

Good Capitaines come never to faight the fielde, excepte necessitie constraine theim, and occasion call them.

Cause that thenemies know not, how thou wilte order thy armie to faight, and in what so ever maner that thou ordainest it, make that the firste bande may be received of the seconde and of the thirde.

In the faight never occupie a battell to any other thyng, then to the same, for whiche thou haste apoineted it, if thou wilt make no disorder.

The sodene accidentes, with difficultie are reamedied: those that are thought upon, with facilitie.

What thynges are the strength of the warre.

Men, yron, money, and bread, be the strengthe of the warre, but of these fower, the first twoo be moste necessarie: because men and yron, finde money and breade: but breade and money fynde not men and yron.

The unarmed riche man, is a bootie to the poore souldiour.

Accustome thy souldiours to dispise delicate livyng and lacivius aparell.

This is as muche as hapneth me generally to remember you, and I know that there might have ben saied manie other thynges in all this my reasonynge: as should be, howe and in howe manie kinde of waies the antiquitie ordered their bandes, how thei appareled them, and how in manie other thynges they exercised them, and to have joygned hereunto manie other particulars, the whiche I have not judged necessarie to shew, as wel for that you your self may se them, as also for that my intente hath not been to shew juste how the olde servis of warre was apoincted, but howe in these daies a servis of warre might be ordained, whiche should have more vertue then the same that is used. Wherfore I have not thought good of the auncient thynges to reason other, then that, which I have judged to suche introduction necessarie. I know also that I might have delated more upon the service on horsebacke, and after have reasoned of the warre on the Sea: for as muche as he that destinguissheth the servis of warre, saieth, how there is an armie on the sea, and of the lande, on foote, and on horsebacke. Of that on the sea, I will not presume to speake, for that I have no knowledge therof: but I will let the Genoues, and the Venecians speake therof, whome with like studies have heretofore doen great thinges.

Also of horses, I wil speake no other, then as afore I have saied, this parte beynge (as I have declared) least corrupted. Besides this, the footemen being wel ordained, which is the puissance of the armie, good horses of necessitie will come to be made.

Provisions that maie bee made to fill a Realme full of good horse; The knowledge that a capitaine oughte to have.

Onely I counsel him that would ordayne the exercise of armes in his owne countrey, and desireth to fill the same with good horses, that he make two provisions: the one is, that he destribute Mares of a good race throughe his dominion, and accustome his menne to make choise of coltes, as you in this countrie make of Calves and Mules: the other is, that to thentente the excepted might finde a byer, I woulde prohibet that no man should kepe a Mule excepte he woulde keepe a horse: so that he that woulde kepe but one beaste to ride on, shoulde be constrained to keepe a horse: and moreover that no man should weare fine cloathe except he which doeth keepe a horse: this order I under stande hath beene devised of certaine princes in our time, whome in short space have therby, brought into their countrey an excellente numbre of good horses. Aboute the other thynges, as much as might be looked for concernynge horse, I remit to as much as I have saied to daie, and to that whiche they use. Peradventure also you woulde desire to understand what condicions a Capitaine ought to have: wherof I shal satisfie you moste breeflie: for that I cannot tell how to chose anie other man then the same, who shoulde know howe to doe all those thynges whiche this daie hath ben reasoned of by us: the which also should not suffise, when he should not knowe howe to devise of him selfe: for that no man without invencion, was ever excellent in anie science: and if invencion causeth honour in other thynges, in this above all, it maketh a man honorable: for everie invention is seen, although it were but simple, to be of writers celebrated: as it is seen, where Alexander Magnus is praised, who for to remove his Campe moste secretely, gave not warnyng with the Trumpette, but with a hatte upon a Launce. And was praised also for havyng taken order that his souldiours in buckelynge with the enemies, shoulde kneele with the lefte legge, to bee able more strongly to withstande their violence: the whiche havyng geven him the victorie, it got him also so muche praise, that all the Images, whiche were erected in his honour, stoode after the same facion. But because it is tyme to finishe this reasonyng, I wil turne againe to my first purpose, and partly I shall avoide the same reproche, wherin they use to condempne in this towne, such as knoweth not when to make an ende.

The auctor retorneth to his first purpose and maketh a littel discorse to make an ende of his reasonyng.

If you remembre Cosimus you tolde me, that I beyng of one side an exalter of the antiquitie, and a dispraiser of those, which in waightie matters imitated them not, and of the other side, I havynge not in the affaires of war, wherin I have taken paine, imitated them, you coulde not perceive the occasion: wherunto I answered, how that men which wil doo any thing, muste firste prepare to knowe how to doe it, for to be able, after to use it, when occasion permitteth: whether I doe know how to bryng the servis of warre to the auncient manners or no, I will be judged by you, whiche have hearde me upon this matter longe dispute wherby you may know, how much time I have consumed in these studies: and also I beleeve that you maie imagen, how much desire is in me to brynge it to effecte: the whiche whether I have been able to have doen, or that ever occasion hath been geven me, most easely you maie conjecture: yet for to make you more certaine and for my better justificacion, I will also aledge the occasions: and as much as I have promised, I will partely performe, to shew you the difficultie and the facelitie, whiche bee at this presente in suche imitacions.

A prince may easelie brynge to intiere perfection the servis of warre; Two sortes of Capitaines worthie to bee praysed.

Therfore I saie, how that no deede that is doen now a daies emong men, is more easie to be reduced unto the aunciente maners, then the service of Warre: but by them onely that be Princes of so moche state, who can at least gather together of their owne subjectes, xv. or twentie thousande yong menne: otherwise, no thyng is more difficulte, then this, to them whiche have not soche commoditie: and for that you maie the better understande this parte, you have to knowe, howe that there bee of twoo condicions, Capitaines to bee praised: The one are those, that with an armie ordained through the naturalle discipline thereof, have dooen greate thynges: as were the greater parte of the Romaine Citezeins, and suche as have ledde armies, the which have had no other paine, then to maintaine them good, and to se them guided safely: the other are they, whiche not onely have had to overcome the enemie, but before they come to the same, have been constrained to make good and well ordered their armie: who without doubte deserve muche more praise, then those have deserved, which with olde armies, and good, have valiantely wrought. Of these, such wer Pelopida, and Epaminonda, Tullus Hostillius, Phillip of Macedony father of Alexander, Cirus kyng of the Percians, Graccus a Romaine: they all were driven first to make their armies good, and after to faighte with them: they all coulde doe it, as well throughe their prudence, as also for havynge subjectes whome thei might in like exercises instruct: nor it shuld never have ben otherwise possible, that anie of theim, though they had ben never so good and ful of al excellencie, should have been able in a straunge countrey, full of men corrupted, not used to anie honest obedience, to have brought to passe anie laudable worke. It suffiseth not then in Italie, to know how to governe an army made, but first it is necessarie to know how to make it and after to know how to commaunde it: and to do these things it is requisit they bee those princes, whome havyng much dominion, and subjectes inoughe, maie have commoditie to doe it: of whiche I can not bee, who never commaunded, nor cannot commaunde, but to armies of straungers, and to men bounde to other, and not to me: in whiche if it be possible, or no, to introduce anie of those thynges that this daie of me hath ben reasoned, I will leave it to your judgement.

Albeit when coulde I make one of these souldiours which now a daies practise, to weare more armur then the ordinarie, and besides the armur, to beare their owne meate for two or three daies, with a mattocke: When coulde I make theim to digge, or keepe theim every daie manie howers armed, in fained exercises, for to bee able after in the verie thyng in deede to prevaile? When woulde thei abstaine from plaie, from laciviousnesse, from swearynge, from the insolence, whiche everie daie they committe? when would they be reduced into so muche dissepline, into so much obedience and reverence, that a tree full of appels in the middest of their Campe, shoulde be founde there and lefte untouched? As is redde, that in the auncient armies manie times hapned. What thynge maye I promis them, by meane wherof thei may have me in reverence to love, or to feare, when the warre beyng ended, they have not anie more to doe with me? wher of maie I make them ashamed, whiche be borne and brought up without shame? whie shoulde thei be ruled by me who knowe me not? By what God or by what sainctes may I make them to sweare? By those that thei worship, or by those that they blaspheme? Who they worship I knowe not anie: but I knowe well they blaspheme all. How shoulde I beleeve that thei will keepe their promise to them, whome everie hower they dispise? How can they, that dispise God, reverence men? Then what good fashion shoulde that be, whiche might be impressed in this matter? And if you should aledge unto me that Suyzzers and Spaniardes bee good souldiours, I woulde confesse unto you, how they be farre better then the Italians: but if you note my reasonynge, and the maner of procedyng of bothe, you shall see, howe they lacke many thynges to joygne to the perfection of the antiquetie. And how the Suyzzers be made good of one of their naturall uses caused of that, whiche to daie I tolde you: those other are made good by mean of a necessitie: for that servyng in a straunge countrie, and seemyng unto them to be constrained either to die, or to overcome, thei perceivynge to have no place to flie, doe become good: but it is a goodnesse in manie partes fawtie: for that in the same there is no other good, but that they bee accustomed to tarie the enemie at the Pike and sweardes poincte: nor that, which thei lacke, no man should be meete to teache them, and so much the lesse, he that coulde not speake their language.

The Auctor excuseth the people of Italie to the great reproche of their pryncces for their ignorance in the affaires of warre.

But let us turne to the Italians, who for havynge not had wise Princes, have not taken anie good order: and for havyng not had the same necessitie, whiche the Spaniardes have hadde, they have not taken it of theim selves, so that they remaine the shame of the worlde: and the people be not to blame, but onely their princes, who have ben chastised, and for their ignorance have ben justely punisshed, leesinge moste shamefully their states, without shewing anie vertuous ensample. And if you will see whether this that I say be trew: consider how manie warres have ben in Italie since the departure of kyng Charles to this day, where the war beyng wonte to make men warlyke and of reputacion, these the greater and fierser that they have been, so muche the more they have made the reputacion of the members and of the headdes therof to bee loste. This proveth that it groweth, that the accustomed orders were not nor bee not good, and of the newe orders, there is not anie whiche have knowen how to take them. Nor never beleeve that reputacion will be gotten, by the Italians weapons, but by the same waie that I have shewed, and by means of theim, that have great states in Italie: for that this forme maie be impressed in simple rude men, of their owne, and not in malicious, ill brought up, and straungers. Nor there shall never bee founde anie good mason, whiche will beleeve to be able to make a faire image of a peece of Marbell ill hewed, but verye well of a rude peece.

A discription of the folishenesse of the Italian princes; Cesar and Alexander, were the formoste in battell; The Venecians and the duke of Ferare began to have reduced the warfare to the Aunciente maners; He that despiseth the servis of warre, despiseth his own welthe.

Our Italian Princes beleved, before thei tasted the blowes of the outlandishe warre, that it should suffice a Prince to knowe by writynges, how to make a subtell answere, to write a goodly letter, to shewe in saiynges, and in woordes, witte and promptenesse, to knowe how to canvas a fraude, to decke theim selves with precious stones and gold, to slepe and to eate with greater glorie then other: To keepe many lascivious persones aboute them, to governe theim selves with their subjectes, covetuously and proudely: To rotte in idlenesse, to give the degrees of the exercise of warre, for good will, to despise if any should have shewed them any laudable waie, minding that their wordes should bee aunswers of oracles: nor the sely wretches were not aware, that thei prepared theim selves to bee a praie, to whom so ever should assaulte theim. Hereby grewe then in the thousande fower hundred nintie and fower yere, the greate feares, the sodain flightes, and the marveilous losses: and so three most mightie states which were in Italie, have been divers times sacked and destroied. But that which is worse, is where those that remaine, continue in the verie same erroure, and live in the verie same disorder, and consider not, that those, who in old time would kepe their states, caused to be dooen these thynges, which of me hath been reasoned, and that their studies wer, to prepare the body to diseases, and the minde not to feare perilles. Whereby grewe that Cesar, Alexander, and all those menne and excellente Princes in old tyme, were the formoste emongest the faighters, goyng armed on foote: and if thei loste their state, thei would loose their life, so that thei lived and died vertuously. And if in theim, or in parte of theim, there might bee condempned to muche ambicion to reason of: yet there shall never bee founde, that in theim is condempned any tendernesse or any thynge that maketh menne delicate and feable: the whiche thyng, if of these Princes were redde and beleved, it should be impossible, that thei should not change their forme of living, and their provinces not to chaunge fortune. And for that you in the beginnyng of this our reasonyng, lamented your ordinaunces, I saie unto you, that if you had ordained it, as I afore have reasoned, and it had given of it self no good experience, you might with reason have been greved therewith: but if it bee not so ordained, and exercised, as I have saied, it maie be greeved with you, who have made a counterfaite thereof, and no perfecte figure. The Venecians also, and the Duke of Ferare, beganne it, and followed it not, the whiche hath been through their faulte, not through their menne. And therfore I assure you, that who so ever of those, whiche at this daie have states in Italie, shall enter firste into this waie, shall be firste, before any other, Lorde of this Province, and it shall happen to his state, as to the kyngdome of the Macedonians, the which commyng under Philip, who had learned the maner of settyng armies in order of Epaminondas a Thebane, became with this order, and with these exercises (whileste the reste of Grece stoode in idlenesse, and attended to risite comedes) so puisant, that he was able in few yeres to possesse it all, and to leave soche foundacion to his sonne, that he was able to make hymself, prince of all the world. He then that despiseth these studies, if he be a Prince, despiseth his Princedome: if he bee a Citezein, his Citee. Wherefore, I lamente me of nature, the whiche either ought not to have made me a knower of this, or it ought to have given me power, to have been able to have executed it: For now beyng olde, I cannot hope to have any occasion, to bee able so to dooe: In consideracion whereof, I have been liberall with you, who beeyng grave yong menne, maie (when the thynges saied of me shall please you) at due tymes in favour of your Princes, helpe theim and counsaile them, wherein I would have you not to bee afraied, or mistrustfull, bicause this Province seemes to bee altogether given, to raise up againe the thynges dedde, as is seen by the perfeccion that poesie, paintyng, and writing, is now brought unto: Albeit, as moche as is looked for of me, beyng strooken in yeres, I do mistruste. Where surely, if Fortune had heretofore graunted me so moche state, as suffiseth for a like enterprise, I would not have doubted, but in moste shorte tyme, to have shewed to the worlde, how moche the aunciente orders availe: and without peradventure, either I would have increased it with glory, or loste it without shame.

The ende of the seventh and laste booke of the arte of warre, of Nicholas Machiavell, Citezein and Secretarie of Florence, translated out of Italian into Englishe: By Peter Whitehorne, felow of Graise Inne.

Discourses on the First Decade of Titus Livius

by Niccolò Machiavelli Citizen and Secretary of Florence
Translated from the Italian by Ninian Hill Thomson, M.A.

Niccolò Machiavelli to Zanobi Buondelmonti and Cosimo Rucellai
Health.

I send you a gift, which if it answers ill the obligations I owe you, is at any rate the greatest which Niccolò Machiavelli has it in his power to offer. For in it I have expressed whatever I have learned, or have observed for myself during a long experience and constant study of human affairs. And since neither you nor any other can expect more at my hands, you cannot complain if I have not given you more.

You may indeed lament the poverty of my wit, since what I have to say is but poorly said; and tax the weakness of my judgment, which on many points may have erred in its conclusions. But granting all this, I know not which of us is less beholden to the other: I to you, who have forced me to write what of myself I never should have written; or you to me, who have written what can give you no content.

Take this, however, in the spirit in which all that comes from a friend should be taken, in respect whereof we always look more to the intention of the giver than to the quality of the gift. And, believe me, that in one thing only I find satisfaction, namely, in knowing that while in many matters I may have made mistakes, at least I have not been mistaken in choosing you before all others as the persons to whom I dedicate these Discourses; both because I seem to myself, in doing so, to have shown a little gratitude for kindness received, and at the same time to have departed from the hackneyed custom which leads many authors to inscribe their works to some Prince, and blinded by hopes of favour or reward, to praise him as possessed of every virtue; whereas with more reason they might reproach him as contaminated with every shameful vice.

To avoid which error I have chosen, not those who are but those who from their infinite merits deserve to be Princes; not such persons as have it in their power to load me with honours, wealth, and preferment, but such as though they lack the power, have all the will to do so. For men, if they would judge justly, should esteem those who are, and not those whose means enable them to be generous; and in like manner those who know how to govern kingdoms, rather than those who possess the government without such knowledge. For Historians award higher praise to Hiero of Syracuse when in a private station than to Perseus the Macedonian when a King affirming that while the former lacked nothing that a Prince should have save the name, the latter had nothing of the King but the kingdom.

Make the most, therefore, of this good or this evil, as you may esteem it, which you have brought upon yourselves; and should you persist in the mistake of thinking my opinions worthy your attention, I shall not fail to proceed with the rest of the History in the manner promised in my Preface. *Farewell.*

Book I: Preface.

Albeit the jealous temper of mankind, ever more disposed to censure than to praise the work of others, has constantly made the pursuit of new methods and systems no less perilous than the search after unknown lands and seas; nevertheless, prompted by that desire which nature has implanted in me, fearlessly to undertake whatsoever I think offers a common benefit to all, I enter on a path which, being hitherto untrodden by any, though it involve me in trouble and fatigue, may yet win me thanks from those who judge my efforts in a friendly spirit. And although my feeble discernment, my slender experience of current affairs, and imperfect knowledge of ancient events, render these efforts of mine defective and of no great utility, they may at least open the way to some other, who, with better parts and sounder reasoning and judgment, shall carry out my design; whereby, if I gain no credit, at all events I ought to incur no blame.

When I see antiquity held in such reverence, that to omit other instances, the mere fragment of some ancient statue is often bought at a great price, in order that the purchaser may keep it by him to adorn his house, or to have it copied by those who take delight in this art; and how these, again, strive with all their skill to imitate it in their various works; and when, on the other hand, I find those noble labours which history shows to have been wrought on behalf of the monarchies and republics of old times, by kings, captains, citizens, lawgivers, and others who have toiled for the good of their country, rather admired than followed, nay, so absolutely renounced by every one that not a trace of that antique worth is now left among us, I cannot but at once marvel and grieve; at this inconsistency; and all the more because I perceive that, in civil disputes between citizens, and in the bodily disorders into which men fall, recourse is always had to the decisions and remedies, pronounced or prescribed by the ancients.

For the civil law is no more than the opinions delivered by the ancient jurisconsults, which, being reduced to a system, teach the jurisconsults of our own times how to determine; while the healing art is simply the recorded experience of the old physicians, on which our modern physicians found their practice. And yet, in giving laws to a commonwealth, in maintaining States and governing kingdoms, in organizing armies and conducting wars, in dealing with subject nations, and in extending a State's dominions, we find no prince, no republic, no captain, and no citizen who resorts to the example of the ancients.

This I persuade myself is due, not so much to the feebleness to which the present methods of education have brought the world, or to the injury which a pervading apathy has wrought in many provinces and cities of Christendom, as to the want of a right intelligence of History, which renders men incapable in reading it to extract its true meaning or to relish its flavour. Whence it happens that by far the greater number of those who read History, take pleasure in following the variety of incidents which it presents, without a thought to imitate them; judging such imitation to be not only difficult but impossible; as though the heavens, the sun, the elements, and man himself were no longer the same as they formerly were as regards motion, order, and power.

Desiring to rescue men from this error, I have thought fit to note down with respect to all those books of Titus Livius which have escaped the malignity of Time, whatever seems to me essential to a right understanding of ancient and modern affairs; so that any who shall read these remarks of mine, may reap from them that profit for the sake of which a knowledge of History is to be sought. And although the task be arduous, still, with the help of those at whose instance I assumed the burthen, I hope to carry it forward so far, that another shall have no long way to go to bring it to its destination.

Chapter I.—*Of the Beginnings of Cities in general, and in particular of that of Rome.*

No one who reads how the city of Rome had its beginning, who were its founders, and what its ordinances and laws, will marvel that so much excellence was maintained in it through many ages, or that it grew afterwards to be so great an Empire.

And, first, as touching its origin, I say, that all cities have been founded either by the people of the country in which they stand, or by strangers. Cities have their origins in the former of these two ways when the inhabitants of a country find that they cannot live securely if they live dispersed in many and small societies, each of them unable, whether from its situation or its slender numbers, to stand alone against the attacks of its enemies; on whose approach there is no time left to unite for defence without abandoning many strongholds, and thus becoming an easy prey to the invader. To escape which dangers, whether of their own motion or at the instance of some of greater authority among them, they restrict themselves to dwell together in certain places, which they think will be more convenient to live in and easier to defend.

Among many cities taking their origin in this way were Athens and Venice; the former of which, for reasons like those just now mentioned, was built by a scattered population under the direction of Theseus. To escape the wars which, on the decay of the Roman Empire daily renewed in Italy by the arrival of fresh hordes of Barbarians, numerous refugees, sheltering in certain little islands in a corner of the Adriatic Sea, gave beginning to Venice; where, without any recognized leader to direct them, they agreed to live together under such laws as they thought best suited to maintain them. And by reason of the prolonged tranquility which their position secured, they being protected by the narrow sea and by the circumstance that the tribes who then harassed Italy had no ships wherewith to molest them, they were able from very small beginnings to attain to that greatness they now enjoy.

In the second case, namely of a city being founded by strangers, the settlers are either wholly independent, or they are controlled by others, as where colonies are sent forth either by a prince or by a republic, to relieve their countries of an excessive population, or to defend newly acquired territories which it is sought to secure at small cost. Of this sort many cities were settled by the Romans, and in all parts of their dominions. It may also happen that such cities are founded by a prince merely to add to his renown, without any intention on his part to dwell there, as Alexandria was built by Alexander the Great. Cities like these, not having had their beginning in freedom, seldom make such progress as to rank among the chief towns of kingdoms.

The city of Florence belongs to that class of towns which has not been independent from the first; for whether we ascribe its origin to the soldiers of Sylla, or, as some have conjectured, to the mountaineers of Fiesole (who, emboldened by the long peace which prevailed throughout the world during the reign of Octavianus, came down to occupy the plain on the banks of the Arno), in either case, it was founded under the auspices of Rome nor could, at first, make other progress than was permitted by the grace of the sovereign State.

The origin of cities may be said to be independent when a people, either by themselves or under some prince, are constrained by famine, pestilence, or war to leave their native land and seek a new habitation. Settlers of this sort either establish themselves in cities which they find ready to their hand in the countries of which they take possession, as did Moses; or they build new ones, as did Æneas. It is in this last case that the merits of a founder and the good fortune of the city founded are best seen; and this good fortune will be more or less remarkable according to the greater or less capacity of him who gives the city its beginning.

The capacity of a founder is known in two ways: by his choice of a site, or by the laws which he frames. And since men act either of necessity or from choice, and merit may seem greater where choice is more restricted, we have to consider whether it may not be well to choose a sterile district as the site of a new city, in order that the inhabitants, being constrained to industry, and less corrupted by ease, may live in closer union, finding less cause for division in the poverty of their land; as was the case in Ragusa, and in many other cities built in similar situations. Such a choice were certainly the wisest and the most advantageous, could men be content to enjoy what is their own without seeking to lord it over others. But since to be safe they must be strong, they are compelled avoid these barren districts, and to plant themselves in more fertile regions; where, the fruitfulness of the soil enabling them to increase and multiply, they may defend themselves against any who attack them, and overthrow any who would withstand their power.

And as for that languor which the situation might breed, care must be had that hardships which the site does not enforce, shall be enforced by the laws; and that the example of those wise nations be imitated, who, inhabiting most fruitful and delightful countries, and such as were likely to rear a listless and effeminate race, unfit for all manly exercises, in order to obviate the mischief wrought by the amenity and relaxing influence of the soil and climate, subjected all who were to serve as soldiers to the severest training; whence it came that better soldiers were raised in these countries than in others by nature rugged and barren. Such, of old, was the kingdom of the Egyptians, which, though of all lands the most bountiful, yet, by the severe training which its laws enforced, produced most valiant soldiers, who, had their names not been lost in antiquity, might be thought to deserve more praise than Alexander the Great and many besides, whose memory is still fresh in men's minds. And even in recent times, any one contemplating the kingdom of the Soldan, and the military order of the Mamelukes before they were destroyed by Selim the Grand Turk, must have seen how carefully they trained their soldiers in every kind of warlike exercise; showing thereby how much they dreaded that indolence to which their genial soil and climate might have disposed them, unless neutralized by strenuous laws. I say, then, that it is a prudent choice to found your city in a fertile region when the effects of that fertility are duly balanced by the restraint of the laws.

When Alexander the Great thought to add to his renown by founding a city, Dinocrates the architect came and showed him how he might build it on Mount Athos, which not only offered a strong position, but could be handled that the city built there might present a semblance of the human form, which would be a thing strange and striking, and worthy of so great a monarch. But on Alexander asking how the inhabitants were to live, Dinocrates answered that he had not thought of that. Whereupon, Alexander laughed, and leaving Mount Athos as it stood, built Alexandria; where, the fruitfulness of the soil, and the vicinity of the Nile and the sea, might attract many to take up their abode.

To him, therefore, who inquires into the origin of Rome, if he assign its beginning to Æneas, it will seem to be of those cities which were founded by strangers if to Romulus, then of those founded by the natives of the country. But in whichever class we place it, it will be seen to have had its beginning in freedom, and not in subjection to another State. It will be seen, too, as hereafter shall be noted, how strict was the discipline which the laws instituted by Romulus, Numa, and its other founders made compulsory upon it; so that neither its fertility, the proximity of the sea, the number of its victories, nor the extent of its dominion, could for many centuries corrupt it, but, on the contrary, maintained it replete with such virtues as were never matched in any other commonwealth.

And because the things done by Rome, and which Titus Livius has celebrated, were effected at home or abroad by public or by private wisdom, I shall begin by treating, and noting the consequences of those things done at home in accordance with the public voice, which seem most to merit attention; and to this object the whole of this first Book or first Part of my Discourses, shall be directed.

Chapter II.—*Of the various kinds of Government; and to which of them the Roman Commonwealth belonged.*

I forego all discussion concerning those cities which at the outset have been dependent upon others, and shall speak only of those which from their earliest beginnings have stood entirely clear of all foreign control, being governed from the first as pleased themselves, whether as republics or as princedoms.

These as they have had different origins, so likewise have had different laws and institutions. For to some at their very first commencement, or not long after, laws have been given by a single legislator, and all at one time; like those given by Lycurgus to the Spartans; while to others they have been given at different times, as need rose or accident determined; as in the case of Rome. That republic, indeed, may be called happy, whose lot has been to have a founder so prudent as to provide for it laws under which it can continue to live securely, without need to amend them; as we find Sparta preserving hers for eight hundred years, without deterioration and without any dangerous disturbance. On the other hand, some measure of unhappiness attaches to the State which, not having yielded itself once for all into the hands of a single wise legislator, is obliged to recast its institutions for itself; and of such States, by far the most unhappy is that which is furthest removed from a sound system of government, by which I mean that its institutions lie wholly outside the path which might lead it to a true and perfect end. For it is scarcely possible that a State in this position can ever, by any chance, set itself to rights, whereas another whose institutions are imperfect, if it have made a good beginning and such as admits of its amendment, may in the course of events arrive at perfection. It is certain, however, that such States can never be reformed without great risk; for, as a rule, men will accept no new law altering the institutions of their State, unless the necessity for such a change be demonstrated; and since this necessity cannot arise without danger, the State may easily be overthrown before the new order of things is established. In proof whereof we may instance the republic of Florence, which was reformed in the year 1502, in consequence of the affair of Arezzo, but was ruined in 1512, in consequence of the affair of Prato.

Desiring, therefore, to discuss the nature of the government of Rome, and to ascertain the accidental circumstances which brought it to its perfection, I say, as has been said before by many who have written of Governments, that of these there are three forms, known by the names Monarchy, Aristocracy, and Democracy, and that those who give its institutions to a State have recourse to one or other of these three, according as it suits their purpose. Other, and, as many have thought, wiser teachers, will have it, that there are altogether six forms of government, three of them utterly bad, the other three good in themselves, but so readily corrupted that they too are apt to become hurtful. The good are the three above named; the bad, three others dependent upon these, and each so like that to which it is related, that it is easy to pass imperceptibly from the one to the other. For a Monarchy readily becomes a Tyranny, an Aristocracy an Oligarchy, while a Democracy tends to degenerate into Anarchy. So that if the founder of a State should establish any one of these three forms of Government, he establishes it for a short time only, since no precaution he may take can prevent it from sliding into its contrary, by reason of the close resemblance which, in this case, the virtue bears to the vice.

These diversities in the form of Government spring up among men by chance. For in the beginning of the world, its inhabitants, being few in number, for a time lived scattered after the fashion of beasts; but afterwards, as they increased and multiplied, gathered themselves into societies, and, the better to protect themselves, began to seek who among them was the strongest and of the highest courage, to whom, making him their head, they tendered obedience. Next arose the knowledge of such things as are honourable and good, as opposed to those which are bad and shameful. For observing that when a man wronged his benefactor, hatred was universally felt for the one and sympathy for the other, and that the ungrateful were blamed, while those who showed gratitude were honoured, and reflecting that the wrongs they saw done to others might be done to themselves, to escape these they resorted to making laws and fixing punishments against any who should transgress them; and in this way grew the recognition of Justice. Whence it came that afterwards, in choosing their rulers, men no longer looked about for the strongest, but for him who was the most prudent and the most just.

But, presently, when sovereignty grew to be hereditary and no longer elective, hereditary sovereigns began to degenerate from their ancestors, and, quitting worthy courses, took up the notion that princes had nothing to do but to surpass the rest of the world in sumptuous display and wantonness, and whatever else ministers to pleasure so that the prince coming to be hated, and therefore to feel fear, and passing from fear to infliction of injuries, a tyranny soon sprang up. Forthwith there began movements to overthrow the prince, and plots and conspiracies against him undertaken not by those who were weak, or afraid for themselves, but by such as being conspicuous for their birth, courage, wealth, and station, could not tolerate the shameful life of the tyrant. The multitude, following the lead of these powerful men, took up arms against the prince and, he being got rid of, obeyed these others as their liberators; who, on their part, holding in hatred the name of sole ruler, formed themselves into a government and at first, while the recollection of past tyranny was still fresh, observed the laws they themselves made, and postponing personal advantage to the common welfare, administered affairs both publicly and privately with the utmost diligence and zeal. But this government passing, afterwards, to their descendants who, never having been taught in the school of Adversity, knew nothing of the vicissitudes of Fortune, these not choosing to rest content with mere civil equality, but abandoning themselves to avarice, ambition, and lust, converted, without respect to civil rights what had been a government of the best into a government of the few; and so very soon met with the same fate as the tyrant.

For the multitude loathing its rulers, lent itself to any who ventured, in whatever way, to attack them; when some one man speedily arose who with the aid of the people overthrew them. But the recollection of the tyrant and of the wrongs suffered at his hands being still fresh in the minds of the people, who therefore felt no desire to restore the monarchy, they had recourse to a popular government, which they established on such a footing that neither king nor nobles had any place in it. And because all governments inspire respect at the first, this government also lasted for a while, but not for long, and seldom after the generation which brought it into existence had died out. For, suddenly, liberty passed into license, wherein neither private worth nor public authority was respected, but, every one living as he liked, a thousand wrongs were done daily. Whereupon, whether driven by necessity, or on the suggestion of some wiser man among them and to escape anarchy, the people reverted to a monarchy, from which, step by step, in the manner and for the causes already assigned, they came round once more to license. For this is the circle revolving within which all States are and have been governed; although in the same State the same forms of Government rarely repeat themselves, because hardly any State can have such vitality as to pass through such a cycle more than once, and still together. For it may be expected that in some sea of disaster, when a State must always be wanting prudent counsels and in strength, it will become subject to some neighbouring and better-governed State; though assuming this not to happen, it might well pass for an indefinite period from one of these forms of government to another.

I say, then, that all these six forms of government are pernicious—the three good kinds, from their brief duration the three bad, from their inherent badness. Wise legislators therefore, knowing these defects, and avoiding each of these forms in its simplicity, have made choice of a form which shares in the qualities of all the first three, and which they judge to be more stable and lasting than any of these separately. For where we have a monarchy, an aristocracy, and a democracy existing together in the same city, each of the three serves as a check upon the other.

Among those who have earned special praise by devising a constitution of this nature, was Lycurgus, who so framed the laws of Sparta as to assign their proper functions to kings, nobles, and commons; and in this way established a government, which, to his great glory and to the peace and tranquility of his country, lasted for more than eight hundred years. The contrary, however, happened in the case of Solon; who by the turn he gave to the institutions of Athens, created there a purely democratic government, of such brief duration, that I himself lived to witness the beginning of the despotism of Pisistratus. And although, forty years later, the heirs of Pisistratus were driven out, and Athens recovered her freedom, nevertheless because she reverted to the same form government as had been established by Solon, she could maintain it for only a hundred years more; for though to preserve it, many ordinances were passed for repressing the ambition of the great and the turbulence of the people, against which Solon had not provided, still, since neither the monarchic nor the aristocratic element was given a place in her constitution, Athens, as compared with Sparta, had but a short life.

But let us now turn to Rome, which city, although she had no Lycurgus to give her from the first such a constitution as would preserve her long in freedom, through a series of accidents, caused by the contests between the commons and the senate, obtained by chance what the foresight of her founders failed to provide. So that Fortune, if she bestowed not her first favours on Rome, bestowed her second; because, although the original institutions of this city were defective, still they lay not outside the true path which could bring them to perfection. For Romulus and the other kings made many and good laws, and such as were not incompatible with freedom; but because they sought to found a kingdom and not a commonwealth, when the city became free many things were found wanting which in the interest of liberty it was necessary to supply, since these kings had not supplied them. And although the kings of Rome lost their sovereignty, in the manner and for the causes mentioned above, nevertheless those who drove them out, by at once creating two consuls to take their place, preserved in Rome the regal authority while banishing from it the regal throne, so that as both senate and consuls were included in that republic, it in fact possessed two of the elements above enumerated, to wit, the monarchic and the aristocratic.

It then only remained to assign its place to the popular element, and the Roman nobles growing insolent from causes which shall be noticed hereafter, the commons against them, when, not to lose the whole of their power, they were forced to concede a share to the people; while with the share which remained, the senate and consuls retained so much authority that they still held their own place in the republic. In this way the tribunes of the people came to be created, after whose creation the stability of the State was much augmented, since each the three forms of government had now its due influence allowed it. And such was the good fortune of Rome that although her government passed from the kings to the nobles, and from these to the people, by the steps and for the reasons noticed above, still the entire authority of the kingly element was not sacrificed to strengthen the authority of the nobles, nor were the nobles divested of their authority to bestow it on the commons; but three, blending together, made up a perfect State; which perfection, as shall be fully shown in the next two Chapters, was reached through the dissensions of the commons and the senate.

Chapter III.—*Of the Accidents which led in Rome to the creation of Tribunes of the People; whereby the Republic was made more perfect.*

They who lay the foundations of a State and furnish it with laws must, as is shown by all who have treated of civil government, and by examples of which history is full, assume that 'all men are bad, and will always, when they have free field, give loose to their evil inclinations; and that if these for a while remain hidden, it is owing to some secret cause, which, from our having no contrary experience, we do not recognize at once, but which is afterwards revealed by Time, of whom we speak as the father of all truth.

In Rome, after the expulsion of the Tarquins, it seemed as though the closest union prevailed between the senate and the commons, and that the nobles, laying aside their natural arrogance, had learned so to sympathize with the people as to have become supportable by all, even of the humblest rank. This dissimulation remained undetected, and its causes concealed, while the Tarquins lived; for the nobles dreading the Tarquins, and fearing that the people, if they used them ill, might take part against them, treated them with kindness. But no sooner were the Tarquins got rid of, and the nobles thus relieved of their fears, when they began to spit forth against the commons all the venom which before they had kept in their breasts, offending and insulting them in every way they could; confirming what I have observed already, that men never behave well unless compelled, and that whenever they are free to act as they please, and are under no restraint everything falls at once into confusion and disorder. Wherefore it has been said that as poverty and hunger are needed to make men industrious, so laws are needed to make them good. When we do well without laws, laws are not needed; but when good customs are absent, laws are at once required.

On the extinction of the Tarquins, therefore, the dread of whom had kept the nobles in check, some new safeguard had to be contrived, which should effect the same result as had been effected by the Tarquins while they lived. Accordingly, after much uproar and confusion, and much danger of violence ensuing between the commons and the nobles, to insure the safety of the former, tribunes were created, and were invested with such station and authority as always afterwards enabled them to stand between the people and the senate, and to resist the insolence of the nobles.

Chapter IV.—*That the Dissensions between the Senate and Commons of Rome, made Rome free and powerful.*

Touching those tumults which prevailed in Rome from the extinction of the Tarquins to the creation of the tribunes the discussion of which I have no wish to avoid, and as to certain other matters of a like nature, I desire to say something in opposition to the opinion of many who assert that Rome was a turbulent city, and had fallen into utter disorder, that had not her good fortune and military prowess made amends for other defects, she would have been inferior to every other republic.

I cannot indeed deny that the good fortune and the armies of Rome were the causes of her empire; yet it certainly seems to me that those holding this opinion fail to perceive, that in a State where there are good soldiers there must be good order, and, generally speaking, good fortune. And looking to the other circumstances of this city, I affirm that those who condemn these dissensions between the nobles and the commons, condemn what was the prime cause of Rome becoming free; and give more heed to the tumult and uproar wherewith these dissensions were attended, than to the good results which followed from them; not reflecting that while in every republic there are two conflicting factions, that of the people and that of the nobles, it is in this conflict that all laws favourable to freedom have their origin, as may readily be seen to have been the case in Rome. For from the time of the Tarquins to that of the Gracchi, a period of over three hundred years, the tumults in Rome seldom gave occasion to punishment by exile, and very seldom to bloodshed. So that we cannot truly declare those tumults to have been disastrous, or that republic to have been disorderly, which during all that time, on account of her internal broils, banished no more than eight or ten of her citizens, put very few to death, and rarely inflicted money penalties. Nor can we reasonably pronounce that city ill-governed wherein we find so many instances of virtue; for virtuous actions have their origin in right training, right training in wise laws, and wise laws in these very tumults which many would thoughtlessly condemn. For he who looks well to the results of these tumults will find that they did not lead to banishments, nor to violence hurtful to the common good, but to laws and ordinances beneficial to the public liberty. And should any object that the behaviour of the Romans was extravagant and outrageous; that for the assembled people to be heard shouting against the senate, the senate against the people; for the whole commons to be seen rushing wildly through the streets, closing their shops, and quitting the town, were things which might well affright him even who only reads of them; it may be answered, that the inhabitants of all cities, more especially of cities which seek to make use of the people in matters of importance, have their own ways of giving expression to their wishes; among which the city of Rome had the custom, that when its people sought to have a law passed they followed one or another of those courses mentioned above, or else refused to be enrolled as soldiers when, to pacify them, something of their demands had to be conceded. But the demands of a free people are hurtful to freedom, since they originate either in being oppressed, or in the fear that they are about to be so. When this fear is groundless, it finds its remedy in public meetings, wherein some worthy person may come forward and show the people by argument that they are deceiving themselves. For though they be ignorant, the people are not therefore, as Cicero says, incapable of being taught the truth, but are readily convinced when it is told them by one in whose honesty they can trust.

We should, therefore, be careful how we censure the government of Rome, and should reflect that all the great results effected by that republic, could not have come about without good cause. And if the popular tumults led the creation of the tribunes, they merit all praise; since these magistrates not only gave its due influence to the popular voice in the government, but also acted as the guardians of Roman freedom, as shall be clearly shown in the following Chapter.

Chapter V.—*Whether the Guardianship of public Freedom is safer in the hands of the Commons or of the Nobles; and whether those who seek to acquire Power or they who seek to maintain it are the greater cause of Commotions.*

Of the provisions made by wise founders of republics, one of the most necessary is for the creation of a guardianship of liberty; for according as this is placed in good or bad hands, the freedom of the State will be more or less lasting. And because in every republic we find the two parties of nobles and commons, the question arises, to which of these two this guardianship can most safely be entrusted. Among the Lacedæmonians of old, as now with the Venetians, it was placed in the hands of the nobles, but with the Romans it was vested in the commons. We have, therefore, to determine which of these States made the wiser choice. If we look to reasons, something is to be said on both sides of the question; though were we to look to results, we should have to pronounce in favour of the nobles, inasmuch as the liberty of Sparta and Venice has had a longer life than that of Rome.

As touching reasons, it may be pleaded for the Roman method, that they are most fit to have charge of a thing, who least desire to pervert it to their own ends. And, doubtless, if we examine the aims which the nobles and the commons respectively set before them, we shall find in the former a great desire to dominate, in the latter merely a desire not to be dominated over, and hence a greater attachment to freedom, since they have less to gain than the others by destroying it. Wherefore, when the commons are put forward as the defenders of liberty, they may be expected to take better care of it, and, as they have no desire to tamper with it themselves, to be less apt to suffer others to do so.

On the other hand, he who defends the method followed by the Spartans and Venetians, may urge, that by confiding this guardianship to the nobles, two desirable ends are served: first, that from being allowed to retain in their own hands a weapon which makes them the stronger party in the State, the ambition of this class is more fully satisfied; and, second, that an authority is withdrawn from the unstable multitude which as used by them is likely to lead to endless disputes and tumults, and to drive the nobles into dangerous and desperate courses. In instance whereof might be cited the case of Rome itself, wherein the tribunes of the people being vested with this authority, not content to have one consul a plebeian, insisted on having both; and afterwards laid claim to the censorship, the prætorship and all the other magistracies in the city. Nor was this enough for them, but, carried away by the same factious spirit, they began after a time to pay court to such men as they thought able to attack the nobility, and so gave occasion to the rise of Marius and the overthrow of Rome.

Wherefore one who weighs both sides of the question well, might hesitate which party he should choose as the guardian of public liberty, being uncertain which class is more mischievous in a commonwealth, that which would acquire what it has not, or that which would keep the authority which it has already. But, on the whole, on a careful balance of arguments we may sum up thus:—Either we have to deal with a republic eager like Rome to extend its power, or with one content merely to maintain itself; in the former case it is necessary to do in all things as Rome did; in the latter, for the reasons and in the manner to be shown in the following Chapter, we may imitate Venice and Sparta.

But reverting to the question which class of citizens is more mischievous in a republic, those who seek to acquire or those who fear to lose what they have acquired already, I note that when Marcus Menenius and Marcus Fulvius, both of them men of plebeian birth, were made the one dictator, the other master of the knights, that they might inquire into certain plots against Rome contrived in Capua, they had at the same time authority given them by the people to investigate whether, in Rome itself, irregular and corrupt practices had been used to obtain the consulship and other honours of the city. The nobles suspecting that the powers thus conferred were to be turned against them, everywhere gave out that if honours had been sought by any by irregular and unworthy means, it was not by them, but by the plebeians, who, with neither birth nor merit to recommend them, had need to resort to corruption. And more particularly they accused the dictator himself. And so telling was the effect of these charges, that Menenius, after haranguing the people and complaining to them of the calumnies circulated against him, laid down his dictatorship, and submitted himself to whatever judgment might be passed upon him. When his cause came to be tried he was acquitted; but at the hearing it was much debated, whether he who would retain power or he who would acquire it, is the more dangerous citizen; the desires of both being likely to lead to the greatest disorders.

Nevertheless, I believe that, as a rule, disorders are more commonly occasioned by those seeking to preserve power, because in them the fear of loss breeds the same passions as are felt by those seeking to acquire; since men never think they hold what they have securely, unless when they are gaining something new from others. It is also to be said that their position enables them to operate changes with less effort and greater efficacy. Further, it may be added, that their corrupt and insolent behaviour inflames the minds of those who have nothing, with the desire to have; either for the sake of punishing their adversaries by despoiling them, or to obtain for themselves a share of those riches and honours which they see the others abuse.

Chapter VI.- Whether it was possible in Rome to contrive such a Government as would have composed the Differences between the Commons and the Senate.

I have spoken above of the effects produced in Rome by the controversies between the commons and the senate. Now, as these lasted down to the time of the Gracchi, when they brought about the overthrow of freedom, some may think it matter for regret that Rome should not have achieved the great things she did, without being torn by such disputes. Wherefore, it seems to me worth while to consider whether the government of Rome could ever have been constituted in such a way as to prevent like controversies.

In making this inquiry we must first look to those republics which have enjoyed freedom for a great while, undisturbed by any violent contentions or tumults, and see what their government was, and whether it would have been possible to introduce it into Rome. Of such republics we have an example in ancient times in Sparta, in modern times in Venice, of both which States I have already made mention. Sparta created for herself a government consisting of a king and a limited senate. Venice has made no distinction in the titles of her rulers, all qualified to take part in her government being classed under the one designation of "Gentlemen," an arrangement due rather to chance than to the foresight of those who gave this State its constitution. For many persons, from causes already noticed, seeking shelter on these rocks on which Venice now stands, after they had so multiplied that if they were to continue to live together it became necessary for them to frame laws, established a form of government; and assembling often in their councils to consult for the interests of their city, when it seemed to them that their numbers were sufficient for political existence, they closed the entrance to civil rights against all who came afterwards to live there, not allowing them to take any part in the management of affairs. And when in course of time there came to be many citizens excluded from the government, to add to the importance of the governing body, they named these "Gentlemen" (*gentiluomini*), the others "Plebeians" (*popolani*). And this distinction could grow up and maintain itself without causing disturbance; for as at the time of its origin, whosoever then lived in Venice was made one of the governing body, none had reason to complain; while those who came to live there afterwards, finding the government in a completed form, had neither ground nor opportunity to object. No ground, because nothing was taken from them; and no opportunity, because those in authority kept them under control, and never employed them in affairs in which they could acquire importance. Besides which, they who came later to dwell in Venice were not so numerous as to destroy all proportion between the governors and the governed; the number of the "Gentlemen" being as great as, or greater than that of the "Plebeians." For these reasons, therefore, it was possible for Venice to make her constitution what it is, and to maintain it without divisions.

Sparta, again, being governed, as I have said, by a king and a limited senate, was able to maintain herself for the long period she did, because, from the country being thinly inhabited and further influx of population forbidden, and from the laws of Lycurgus (the observance whereof removed all ground of disturbance) being held in high esteem, the citizens were able to continue long in unity. For Lycurgus having by his laws established in Sparta great equality as to property, but less equality as to rank, there prevailed there an equal poverty; and the commons were less ambitious, because the offices of the State, which were held to their exclusion, were confined to a few; and because the nobles never by harsh treatment aroused in them any desire to usurp these offices. And this was due to the Spartan kings, who, being appointed to that dignity for life, and placed in the midst of this nobility, had no stronger support to their authority than in defending the people against injustice. Whence it resulted that as the people neither feared nor coveted the power which they did not possess, the conflicts which might have arisen between them and the nobles were escaped, together with the causes which would have led to them; and in this way they were able to live long united. But of this unity in Sparta there were two chief causes: one, the fewness of its inhabitants, which allowed of their being governed by a few; the other, that by denying foreigners admission into their country, the people had less occasion to become corrupted, and never so increased in numbers as to prove troublesome to their few rulers.

Weighing all which circumstances, we see that to have kept Rome in the same tranquility wherein these republics were kept, one of two courses must have been followed by her legislators; for either, like the Venetians, they must have refrained from employing the commons in war, or else, like the Spartans, they must have closed their country to foreigners. Whereas, in both particulars, they did the opposite, arming the commons and increasing their number, and thus affording endless occasions for disorder. And had the Roman commonwealth grown to be more tranquil, this inconvenience would have resulted, that it must at the same time have grown weaker, since the road would have been closed to that greatness to which it came, for in removing the causes of her tumults, Rome must have interfered with the causes of her growth.

And he who looks carefully into the matter will find, that in all human affairs, we cannot rid ourselves of one inconvenience without running into another. So that if you would have your people numerous and warlike, to the

Chapter VI.—*Whether it was possible in Rome to contrive such a Government as would have composed the Differences between the Commons and the Senate.*

I have spoken above of the effects produced in Rome by the controversies between the commons and the senate. Now, as these lasted down to the time of the Gracchi, when they brought about the overthrow of freedom, some may think it matter for regret that Rome should not have achieved the great things she did, without being torn by such disputes. Wherefore, it seems to me worth while to consider whether the government of Rome could ever have been constituted in such a way as to prevent like controversies.

In making this inquiry we must first look to those republics which have enjoyed freedom for a great while, undisturbed by any violent contentions or tumults, and see what their government was, and whether it would have been possible to introduce it into Rome. Of such republics we have an example in ancient times in Sparta, in modern times in Venice, of both which States I have already made mention. Sparta created for herself a government consisting of a king and a limited senate. Venice has made no distinction in the titles of her rulers, all qualified to take part in her government being classed under the one designation of "Gentlemen," an arrangement due rather to chance than to the foresight of those who gave this State its constitution. For many persons, from causes already noticed, seeking shelter on these rocks on which Venice now stands, after they had so multiplied that if they were to continue to live together it became necessary for them to frame laws, established a form of government; and assembling often in their councils to consult for the interests of their city, when it seemed to them that their numbers were sufficient for political existence, they closed the entrance to civil rights against all who came afterwards to live there, not allowing them to take any part in the management of affairs. And when in course of time there came to be many citizens excluded from the government, to add to the importance of the governing body, they named these "Gentlemen" (*gentiluomini*), the others "Plebeians" (*popolani*). And this distinction could grow up and maintain itself without causing disturbance; for as at the time of its origin, whosoever then lived in Venice was made one of the governing body, none had reason to complain; while those who came to live there afterwards, finding the government in a completed form, had neither ground nor opportunity to object. No ground, because nothing was taken from them; and no opportunity, because those in authority kept them under control, and never employed them in affairs in which they could acquire importance. Besides which, they who came later to dwell in Venice were not so numerous as to destroy all proportion between the governors and the governed; the number of the "Gentlemen" being as great as, or greater than that of the "Plebeians." For these reasons, therefore, it was possible for Venice to make her constitution what it is, and to maintain it without divisions.

Sparta, again, being governed, as I have said, by a king and a limited senate, was able to maintain herself for the long period she did, because, from the country being thinly inhabited and further influx of population forbidden, and from the laws of Lycurgus (the observance whereof removed all ground of disturbance) being held in high esteem, the citizens were able to continue long in unity. For Lycurgus having by his laws established in Sparta great equality as to property, but less equality as to rank, there prevailed there an equal poverty; and the commons were less ambitious, because the offices of the State, which were held to their exclusion, were confined to a few; and because the nobles never by harsh treatment aroused in them any desire to usurp these offices. And this was due to the Spartan kings, who, being appointed to that dignity for life, and placed in the midst of this nobility, had no stronger support to their authority than in defending the people against injustice. Whence it resulted that as the people neither feared nor coveted the power which they did not possess, the conflicts which might have arisen between them and the nobles were escaped, together with the causes which would have led to them; and in this way they were able to live long united. But of this unity in Sparta there were two chief causes: one, the fewness of its inhabitants, which allowed of their being governed by a few; the other, that by denying foreigners admission into their country, the people had less occasion to become corrupted, and never so increased in numbers as to prove troublesome to their few rulers.

Weighing all which circumstances, we see that to have kept Rome in the same tranquility wherein these republics were kept, one of two courses must have been followed by her legislators; for either, like the Venetians, they must have refrained from employing the commons in war, or else, like the Spartans, they must have closed their country to foreigners. Whereas, in both particulars, they did the opposite, arming the commons and increasing their number, and thus affording endless occasions for disorder. And had the Roman commonwealth grown to be more tranquil, this inconvenience would have resulted, that it must at the same time have grown weaker, since the road would have been closed to that greatness to which it came, for in removing the causes of her tumults, Rome must have interfered with the causes of her growth.

And he who looks carefully into the matter will find, that in all human affairs, we cannot rid ourselves of one inconvenience without running into another. So that if you would have your people numerous and warlike, to the end that with their aid you may establish a great empire, you will have them of such a sort as you cannot afterwards control at your pleasure; while should you keep them few and unwarlike, to the end that you may govern them easily, you will be unable, should you extend your dominions, to preserve them, and will become so contemptible as to be the prey of any who attack you. For which reason in all our deliberations we ought to consider where we are likely to encounter least inconvenience, and accept that as the course to be preferred, since we shall never find any line of action entirely free from disadvantage.

Rome might, therefore, following the example of Sparta, have created a king for life and a senate of limited numbers, but desiring to become a great empire, she could not, like Sparta, have restricted the number of her citizens. So that to have created a king for life and a limited senate had been of little service to her.

Were any one, therefore, about to found a wholly new republic, he would have to consider whether he desired it to increase as Rome did in territory and dominion, or to continue within narrow limits. In the former case he would have to shape its constitution as nearly as possible on the pattern of the Roman, leaving room for dissensions and popular tumults, for without a great and warlike population no republic can ever increase, or increasing maintain itself. In the second case he might give his republic a constitution like that of Venice or Sparta; but since extension is the ruin of such republics, the legislator would have to provide in every possible way against the State which he had founded making any additions to its territories. For these, when superimposed upon a feeble republic, are sure to be fatal to it: as we see to have been the case with Sparta and Venice, the former of which, after subjugating nearly all Greece, on sustaining a trifling reverse, betrayed the insufficiency of her foundations, for when, after the revolt of Thebes under Pelopidas, other cities also rebelled, the Spartan kingdom was utterly overthrown. Venice in like manner, after gaining possession of a great portion of Italy (most of it not by her arms but by her wealth and subtlety), when her strength was put to the proof, lost all in one pitched battle.

I can well believe, then, that to found a republic which shall long endure, the best plan may be to give it internal institutions like those of Sparta or Venice; placing it in a naturally strong situation, and so fortifying it that none can expect to get the better of it easily, yet, at the same time, not making it so great as to be formidable to its neighbours; since by taking these precautions, it might long enjoy its independence. For there are two causes which lead to wars being made against a republic; one, your desire to be its master, the other the fear lest it should master you; both of which dangers the precaution indicated will go far to remove. For if, as we are to assume, this republic be well prepared for defence, and consequently difficult of attack, it will seldom or never happen that any one will form the design to attack it, and while it keeps within its own boundaries, and is seen from experience not to be influenced by ambition, no one will be led, out of fear for himself, to make war upon it, more particularly when its laws and constitution forbid its extension. And were it possible to maintain things in this equilibrium, I veritably believe that herein would be found the true form of political life, and the true tranquility of a republic. But all human affairs being in movement, and incapable of remaining as they are, they must either rise or fall; and to many conclusions to which we are not led by reason, we are brought by necessity. So that when we have given institutions to a State on the footing that it is to maintain itself without enlargement, should necessity require its enlargement, its foundations will be cut from below it, and its downfall quickly ensue. On the other hand, were a republic so favoured by Heaven as to lie under no necessity of making war, the result of this ease would be to make it effeminate and divided which two evils together, and each by itself, would insure its ruin. And since it is impossible, as I believe, to bring about an equilibrium, or to adhere strictly to the mean path, we must, in arranging our republic, consider what is the more honourable course for it to take, and so contrive that even if necessity compel its enlargement, it may be able to keep what it gains.

But returning to the point first raised, I believe it necessary for us to follow the method of the Romans and not that of the other republics, for I know of no middle way. We must, consequently, put up with those dissensions which arise between commons and senate, looking on them as evils which cannot be escaped if we would arrive at the greatness of Rome.

In connection with the arguments here used to prove that the authority of the tribunes was essential in Rome to the guardianship of freedom, we may naturally go on to show what advantages result to a republic from the power of impeachment; which, together with others, was conferred upon the tribunes; a subject to be noticed in the following Chapter.

Chapter VII.—*That to preserve Liberty in a State there must exist the Right to accuse.*

To those set forward in a commonwealth as guardians of public freedom, no more useful or necessary authority can be given than the power to accuse, either before the people, or before some council or tribunal, those citizens who in any way have offended against the liberty of their country.

A law of this kind has two effects most beneficial to a State: *first*, that the citizens from fear of being accused, do not engage in attempts hurtful to the State, or doing so, are put down at once and without respect of persons: and *next*, that a vent is given for the escape of all those evil humours which, from whatever cause, gather in cities against particular citizens; for unless an outlet be duly provided for these by the laws, they flow into irregular channels and overwhelm the State. There is nothing, therefore, which contributes so much to the stability and permanence of a State, as to take care that the fermentation of these disturbing humours be supplied by operation of law with a recognized outlet. This might be shown by many examples, but by none so clearly as by that of Coriolanus related by Livius, where he tells us, that at a time when the Roman nobles were angry with the plebeians (thinking that the appointment of tribunes for their protection had made them too powerful), it happened that Rome was visited by a grievous famine, to meet which the senate sent to Sicily for corn. But Coriolanus, hating the commons, sought to persuade the senate that now was the time to punish them, and to deprive them of the authority which they had usurped to the prejudice of the nobles, by withholding the distribution of corn, and so suffering them to perish of hunger. Which advice of his coming to the ears of the people, kindled them to such fury against him, that they would have slain him as he left the Senate House, had not the tribunes cited him to appear and answer before them to a formal charge.

In respect of this incident I repeat what I have just now said, how useful and necessary it is for republics to provide by their laws a channel by which the displeasure of the multitude against a single citizen may find a vent. For when none such is regularly provided, recourse will be had to irregular channels, and these will assuredly lead to much worse results. For when a citizen is borne down by the operation or the ordinary laws, even though he be wronged, little or no disturbance is occasioned to the state: the injury he suffers not being wrought by private violence, nor by foreign force, which are the causes of the overthrow of free institutions, but by public authority and in accordance with public ordinances, which, having definite limits set them, are not likely to pass beyond these so as to endanger the commonwealth. For proof of which I am content to rest on this old example of Coriolanus, since all may see what a disaster it would have been for Rome had he been violently put to death by the people. For, as between citizen and citizen, a wrong would have been done affording ground for fear, fear would have sought defence, defence have led to faction, faction to divisions in the State, and these to its ruin. But the matter being taken up by those whose office it was to deal with it, all the evils which must have followed had it been left in private hands were escaped.

In Florence, on the other hand, and in our own days, we have seen what violent commotions follow when the people cannot show their displeasure against particular citizens in a form recognized by the laws, in the instance of Francesco Valori, at one time looked upon as the foremost citizen of our republic. But many thinking him ambitious, and likely from his high spirit and daring to overstep the limits of civil freedom, and there being no way to oppose him save by setting up an adverse faction, the result was, that, apprehending irregular attacks, he sought to gain partisans for his support; while his opponents, on their side, having no course open to them of which the laws approved, resorted to courses of which the laws did not approve, and, at last, to open violence. And as his influence had to be attacked by unlawful methods, these were attended by injury not to him only, but to many other noble citizens; whereas, could he have been met by constitutional restraints, his power might have been broken without injury to any save himself. I might also cite from our Florentine history the fall of Piero Soderini, which had no other cause than there not being in our republic any law under which powerful and ambitious citizens can be impeached. For to form a tribunal by which a powerful citizen is to be tried, eight judges only are not enough; the judges must be numerous, because a few will always do the will of a few. But had there been proper methods for obtaining redress, either the people would have impeached Piero if he was guilty, and thus have given vent to their displeasure without calling in the Spanish army; or if he was innocent, would not have ventured, through fear of being accused themselves, to have taken proceedings against him. So that in either case the bitter spirit which was the cause of all the disorder would have had an end. Wherefore, when we find one of the parties in a State calling in a foreign power, we may safely conclude that it is because the defective laws of that State provide no escape for those malignant humours which are natural to men; which can best be done by arranging for an impeachment before a sufficient number of judges, and by giving countenance to this procedure. This was so well contrived in Rome that in spite of the perpetual struggle maintained between the commons and the senate, neither the senate nor the commons, nor any single citizen, ever sought redress at the hands of a foreign power; for having a remedy at home, there was no need to seek one abroad.

Although the examples above cited be proof sufficient of what I affirm, I desire to adduce one other, recorded by Titus Livius in his history, where he relates that a sister of Aruns having been violated by a Lucumo of Clusium, the chief of the Etruscan towns, Aruns being unable, from the interest of her ravisher, to avenge her, betook himself to the Gauls who ruled in the province we now name Lombardy, and besought them to come with an armed force to Clusium; showing them how with advantage to themselves they might avenge his wrongs. Now, had Aruns seen that he could have had redress through the laws of his country, he never would have resorted to these Barbarians for help.

But as the right to accuse is beneficial in a republic, so calumny, on the other hand, is useless and hurtful, as in the following Chapter I shall proceed to show.

Chapter VIII.—*That Calumny is as hurtful in a Commonwealth as the power to accuse is useful.*

Such were the services rendered to Rome by Furius Camillus in rescuing her from the oppression of the Gauls, that no Roman, however high his degree or station, held it derogatory to yield place to him, save only Manlius Capitolinus, who could not brook such glory and distinction being given to another. For he thought that in saving the Capitol, he had himself done as much as Camillus to preserve Rome, and that in respect of his other warlike achievements he was no whit behind him. So that, bursting with jealousy, and unable to remain at rest by reason of the other's renown, and seeing no way to sow discord among the Fathers, he set himself to spread abroad sinister reports among the commons; throwing out, among other charges, that the treasure collected to be given to the Gauls, but which, afterwards, was withheld, had been embezzled by certain citizens, and if recovered might be turned to public uses in relieving the people from taxes or from private debts. These assertions so prevailed with the commons that they began to hold meetings and to raise what tumults they liked throughout the city. But this displeasing the senate, and the matter appearing to them grave and dangerous, they appointed a dictator to inquire into it, and to restrain the attacks of Manlius. The dictator, forthwith, caused Manlius to be cited before him; and these two were thus brought face to face in the presence of the whole city, the dictator surrounded by the nobles, and Manlius by the commons. The latter, being desired to say with whom the treasure of which he had spoken was to be found, since the senate were as anxious to know this as the commons, made no direct reply, but answered evasively that it was needless to tell them what they already knew. Whereupon the dictator ordered him to prison.

In this passage we are taught how hateful a thing is calumny in all free States, as, indeed, in every society, and how we must neglect no means which may serve to check it. And there can be no more effectual means for checking calumny than by affording ample facilities for impeachment, which is as useful in a commonwealth as the other is pernicious. And between them there is this difference, that calumny needs neither witness, nor circumstantial proof to establish it, so that any man may be calumniated by any other; but not impeached; since impeachment demands that there be substantive charges made, and trustworthy evidence to support them. Again, it is before the magistrates, the people, or the courts of justice that men are impeached; but in the streets and market places that they are calumniated. Calumny, therefore, is most rife in that State wherein impeachment is least practised, and the laws least favour it. For which reasons the legislator should so shape the laws of his State that it shall be possible therein to impeach any of its citizens without fear or favour; and, after duly providing for this, should visit calumniators with the sharpest punishments. Those punished will have no cause to complain, since it was in their power to have impeached openly where they have secretly calumniated. Where this is not seen to, grave disorders will always ensue. For calumnies sting without disabling; and those who are stung being more moved by hatred of their detractors than by fear of the things they say against them, seek revenge.

This matter, as we have said, was well arranged for in Rome, but has always been badly regulated in our city of Florence. And as the Roman ordinances with regard to it were productive of much good, so the want of them in Florence has bred much mischief. For any one reading the history of our city may perceive, how many calumnies have at all times been aimed against those of its citizens who have taken a leading part in its affairs. Thus, of one it would be said that he had plundered the public treasury, of another, that he had failed in some enterprise because he had been bribed; of a third, that this or the other disaster had originated in his ambition. Hence hatred sprung up on every side, and hatred growing to division, these led to factions, and these again to ruin. But had there existed in Florence some procedure whereby citizens might have been impeached, and calumniators punished, numberless disorders which have taken there would have been prevented. For citizens who were impeached, whether condemned or acquitted, would have had no power to injure the State; and they would have been impeached far seldomer than they have been calumniated; for calumny, as I have said already, is an easier matter than impeachment.

Some, indeed, have made use of calumny as a means for raising themselves to power, and have found their advantage in traducing eminent citizens who withstood their designs; for by taking the part of the people, and confirming them in their ill-opinion of these great men, they made them their friends. Of this, though I could give many instances, I shall content myself with one. At the siege of Lucca the Florentine army was commanded by Messer Giovanni Guicciardini, as its commissary, through whose bad generalship or ill-fortune the town was not taken. But whatever the cause of this failure, Messer Giovanni had the blame; and the rumour ran that he had been bribed by the people of Lucca. Which calumny being fostered by his enemies, brought Messer Giovanni to very verge of despair; and though to clear himself he would willingly have given himself up to the Captain of Justice he found he could not, there being no provision in the laws of the republic which allowed of his doing so. Hence arose the bitterest hostility between the friends of Messer Giovanni, who were mostly of the old nobility (*grandi*), and those who sought to reform the government of Florence; and from this and the like causes, the affair grew to such dimensions as to bring about the downfall of our republic.

Manlius Capitolinus, then, was a calumniator, not an accuser; and in their treatment of him the Romans showed how calumniators should be dealt with; by which I mean, that they should be forced to become accusers; and if their accusation be proved true, should be rewarded, or at least not punished, but if proved false should be punished as Manlius was.

Chapter IX.—*That to give new Institutions to a Commonwealth, or to reconstruct old Institutions on an entirely new basis, must be the work of one Man.*

It may perhaps be thought that I should not have got so far into the history of Rome, without some mention of those who gave that city its institutions, and saying something of these institutions themselves, so far as they relate to religion and war. As I have no wish to keep those who would know my views on these matters in suspense, I say at once, that to many it might seem of evil omen that the founder of a civil government like Romulus, should first have slain his brother, and afterwards have consented to the death of Titus Tatius the Sabine, whom he had chosen to be his colleague in the kingship; since his countrymen, if moved by ambition and lust of power to inflict like injuries on any who opposed their designs, might plead the example of their prince. This view would be a reasonable one were we to disregard the object which led Romulus to put those men to death. But we must take it as a rule to which there are very few if any exceptions, that no commonwealth or kingdom ever has salutary institutions given it from the first or has its institutions recast in an entirely new mould, unless by a single person. On the contrary, it must be from one man that it receives its institutions at first, and upon one man that all similar reconstruction must depend. For this reason the wise founder of a commonwealth who seeks to benefit not himself only, or the line of his descendants, but his State and country, must endeavour to acquire an absolute and undivided authority. And none who is wise will ever blame any action, however extraordinary and irregular, which serves to lay the foundation of a kingdom or to establish a republic. For although the act condemn the doer, the end may justify him; and when, as in the case of Romulus, the end is good, it will always excuse the means; since it is he who does violence with intent to injure, not he who does it with the design to secure tranquility, who merits blame. Such a person ought however to be so prudent and moderate as to avoid transmitting the absolute authority he acquires, as an inheritance to another; for as men are, by nature, more prone to evil than to good, a successor may turn to ambitious ends the power which his predecessor has used to promote worthy ends. Moreover, though it be one man that must give a State its institutions, once given they are not so likely to last long resting for support on the shoulders of one man only, as when entrusted to the care of many, and when it is the business of many to maintain them. For though the multitude be unfit to set a State in order, since they cannot, by reason of the divisions which prevail among them, agree wherein the true well-being of the State lies, yet when they have once been taught the truth, they never will consent to abandon it. And that Romulus, though he put his brother to death, is yet of those who are to be pardoned, since what he did was done for the common good and not from personal ambition, is shown by his at once creating a senate, with whom he took counsel, and in accordance with whose voice he determined. And whosoever shall well examine the authority which Romulus reserved to himself, will find that he reserved nothing beyond the command of the army when war was resolved on, and the right to assemble the senate. This is seen later, on Rome becoming free by the expulsion of the Tarquins, when the Romans altered none of their ancient institutions save in appointing two consuls for a year instead of a king for life; for this proves that all the original institutions of that city were more in conformity with a free and constitutional government, than with an absolute and despotic one.

In support of what has been said above, I might cite innumerable instances, as of Moses, Lycurgus, Solon, and other founders of kingdoms and commonwealths, who, from the full powers given them, were enabled to shape their laws to the public advantage; but passing over these examples, as of common notoriety, I take one, not indeed so famous, but which merits the attention of all who desire to frame wise laws. Agis, King of Sparta, desiring to bring back his countrymen to those limits within which the laws of Lycurgus had held them, because he thought that, from having somewhat deviated from them, his city had lost much of its ancient virtue and, consequently much of its strength and power, was, at the very outset of his attempts, slain by the Spartan Ephori, as one who sought to make himself a tyrant. But Cleomenes coming after him in the kingdom, and, on reading the notes and writings which he found of Agis wherein his designs and intentions were explained, being stirred by the same desire, perceived that he could not confer this benefit on his country unless he obtained sole power. For he saw that the ambition of others made it impossible for him to do what was useful for many against the will of a few. Wherefore, finding fit occasion, he caused the Ephori and all others likely to throw obstacles in his way, to be put to death; after which, he completely renewed the laws of Lycurgus. And the result of his measures would have been to give fresh life to Sparta, and to gain for himself a renown not inferior to that of Lycurgus, had it not been for the power of the Macedonians and the weakness of the other Greek States. For while engaged with these reforms, he was attacked by the Macedonians, and being by himself no match for them, and having none to whom he could turn for help, he was overpowered; and his plans, though wise and praiseworthy, were never brought to perfection.

All which circumstances considered, I conclude that he who gives new institutions to a State must stand alone; and that for the deaths of Remus and Tatius, Romulus is to be excused rather than blamed.

Chapter X. — That in proportion as the Founder of a Kingdom or Commonwealth merits Praise, he who founds a Tyranny deserves Blame.

Of all who are praised they are praised the most, who are the authors and founders of religions. After whom come the founders of kingdoms and commonwealths. Next to these, they have the greatest name who as commanders of armies have added to their own dominions or those of their country. After these, again, are ranked men of letters, who being of various shades of merit are celebrated each in his degree. To all others, whose number is infinite, is ascribed that measure of praise to which his profession or occupation entitles him. And, conversely, all who contribute to the overthrow of religion, or to the ruin of kingdoms and commonwealths, all who are foes to letters and to the arts which confer honour and benefit on the human race (among whom I reckon the impious, the cruel, the ignorant, the indolent, the base and the worthless), are held in infamy and detestation.

No one, whether he be wise or foolish, bad or good, if asked to choose between these two kinds of men, will ever be found to withhold praise from what deserves praise, or blame from what is to be blamed. And yet almost all, deceived by a false good and a false glory, allow themselves either ignorantly or wilfully to follow in the footsteps such as deserve blame rather than praise; and, have it in their power to establish, to their lasting renown, a commonwealth or kingdom, turn aside to create a tyranny without a thought how much they thereby lose in name, fame, security, tranquillity, and peace of mind; and in name how much infamy, scorn, danger, and disquiet they incur. But were they to read history, and turn to profit the lessons of the past, it seems impossible that those living in a republic as private citizens, should not prefer their native city, to play the part of Scipio rather of Caesar; or that those, who by good fortune or merit have risen to be rulers, should not seek rather to resemble Agesilaus, Timoleon, and Dion, than to Nabis, Phalaris and Dionysius; since they would see how the latter are loaded with infamy, while the former have been extolled beyond bounds. They would see, too, how Timoleon and others like him, had as great authority in their country as Dionysius or Phalaris in theirs, while enjoying far greater security.

Nor let any one finding Caesar celebrated by a crowd of writers, be misled by his glory. For those who praise him have been corrupted by good fortune, and overawed by the greatness of that empire which, being governed in his name, would not suffer any to speak their minds openly concerning him. But let him who desires to know how historians would have written of Caesar had they been free to declare their thoughts mark what they say of Catiline, than whom Caesar is more hateful, in proportion as he who does is more to be condemned than he who only desires to do evil. Let him see also what praises they lavish upon Brutus, because being unable, out of respect for his power, to reproach Caesar, they magnify his enemy. And if he who has become prince in any State will but reflect, how, after Rome was made an empire, far greater praise was earned by those emperors who lived within the laws, and worthily, than by those who lived in the contrary way, he will see that Titus, Nerva, Trajan, Hadrian, Antoninus and Marcus had no need of praetorian cohorts, or of countless legions to guard them, but were defended by their own good lives, the good-will of their subjects, and the attachment of the senate. In like manner he will perceive in the case of Caligula, Nero, Vitellius, and every many more of those evil emperors, that all the armies of the east and of the west were of no avail to protect them from the enemies whom their bad and depraved lives raised up against them. And were the history of these emperors rightly studied, it would be a sufficient lesson to any prince how to distinguish the paths which lead to honour and safety from those which end in shame and insecurity. For of the twenty-six emperors from Caesar to Maximinus, sixteen came to a violent, ten only to a natural death; and though one or two of those who died by violence may have been good princes, as Galba or Pertinax, they met their fate in consequence of that corruption which their predecessors had left behind in the army. And if among those who died a natural death, there be found some bad emperors, like Severus, it is to be ascribed to their signal good fortune and to their great abilities, advantages seldom found united in the same man. From the study of this history we may also learn how a good government is to be established; for while all the emperors who succeeded to the throne by birth, except Titus, were bad, all were good who succeeded by adoption, as in the case of the five from Nerva to Marcus. But so soon as the empire fell once more to the heirs by birth, its ruin recommenced.

Let a prince therefore look to that period which extends from Nerva to Marcus, and contrast it with that which went before and that which came after, and then let him say in which of them he would wish to have been born or to have reigned. For during these times in which good men governed, he will see the prince secure in the midst of happy subjects, and the whole world filled with peace and justice. He will find the senate maintaining its authority, the magistrates enjoying their honours, rich men their wealth, rank and merit held in respect, ease and content everywhere prevailing, rancour, licence, corruption and ambition everywhere quenched, and that golden age restored in which every one might hold and support what opinions he pleased. He will see, in short, the world triumphing, the sovereign honoured and revered, the people animated with love, and rejoicing in their security. But should he turn to examine the times of the other emperors, he will find them wasted by battle, torn

Chapter X.—*That in proportion as the Founder of a Kingdom or Commonwealth merits Praise, he who founds a Tyranny deserves Blame.*

Of all who are praised they are praised the most, who are the authors and founders of religions. After whom come the founders of kingdoms and commonwealths. Next to these, they have the greatest name who as commanders of armies have added to their own dominions or those of their country. After these, again, are ranked men of letters, who being of various shades of merit are celebrated each in his degree. To all others, whose number is infinite, is ascribed that measure of praise to which his profession or occupation entitles him. And, conversely, all who contribute to the overthrow of religion, or to the ruin of kingdoms and commonwealths, all who are foes to letters and to the arts which confer honour and benefit on the human race (among whom I reckon the impious, the cruel, the ignorant, the indolent, the base and the worthless), are held in infamy and detestation.

No one, whether he be wise or foolish, bad or good, if asked to choose between these two kinds of men, will ever be found to withhold praise from what deserves praise, or blame from what is to be blamed. And yet almost all, deceived by a false good and a false glory, allow themselves either ignorantly or wilfully to follow in the footsteps such as deserve blame rather than praise; and, have it in their power to establish, to their lasting renown, a commonwealth or kingdom, turn aside to create a tyranny without a thought how much they thereby lose in name, fame, security, tranquility, and peace of mind; and in name how much infamy, scorn, danger, and disquiet they are? But were they to read history, and turn to profit the lessons of the past, it seems impossible that those living in a republic as private citizens, should not prefer their native city, to play the part of Scipio rather of Cæsar; or that those who by good fortune or merit have risen to be rulers, should not seek rather to resemble Agesilaus, Timoleon, and Dion, than to Nabis, Phalaris and Dionysius; since they would see how the latter are loaded with infamy, while the former have been extolled beyond bounds. They would see, too, how Timoleon and others like him, had as great authority in their country as Dionysius or Phalaris in theirs, while enjoying far greater security. Nor let any one finding Cæsar celebrated by a crowd of writers, be misled by his glory; for those who praise him have been corrupted by good fortune, and overawed by the greatness of that empire which, being governed in his name, would not suffer any to speak their minds openly concerning him. But let him who desires to know how historians would have written of Cæsar had they been free to declare their thoughts mark what they say of Catiline, than whom Cæsar is more hateful, in proportion as he who does is more to be condemned than he who only desires to do evil. Let him see also what praises they lavish upon Brutus, because being unable, out of respect for his power, to reproach Cæsar, they magnify his enemy. And if he who has become prince in any State will but reflect, how, after Rome was made an empire, far greater praise was earned those emperors who lived within the laws, and worthily, than by those who lived in the contrary way, he will see that Titus, Nerva, Trajan, Hadrian, Antoninus and Marcus had no need of prætorian cohorts, or of countless legions to guard them, but were defended by their own good lives, the good-will of their subjects, and the attachment of the senate. In like manner he will perceive in the case of Caligula, Nero, Vitellius, and ever so many more of those evil emperors, that all the armies of the east and of the west were of no avail to protect them from the enemies whom their bad and depraved lives raised up against them. And were the history of these emperors rightly studied, it would be a sufficient lesson to any prince how to distinguish the paths which lead to honour and safety from those which end in shame and insecurity. For of the twenty-six emperors from Cæsar to Maximinus, sixteen came to a violent, ten only to a natural death; and though one or two of those who died by violence may have been good princes, as Galba or Pertinax, they met their fate in consequence of that corruption which their predecessors had left behind in the army. And if among those who died a natural death, there be found some bad emperors, like Severus, it is to be ascribed to their signal good fortune and to their great abilities, advantages seldom found united in the same man. From the study this history we may also learn how a good government is to be established; for while all the emperors who succeeded to the throne by birth, except Titus, were bad, all were good who succeeded by adoption; as in the case of the five from Nerva to Marcus. But so soon as the empire fell once more to the heirs by birth, its ruin recommenced.

Let a prince therefore look to that period which extends from Nerva to Marcus, and contrast it with that which went before and that which came after, and then let him say in which of them he would wish to have been born or to have reigned. For during these times in which good men governed, he will see the prince secure in the midst of happy subjects, and the whole world filled with peace and justice. He will find the senate maintaining its authority, the magistrates enjoying their honours, rich citizens their wealth, rank and merit held in respect, ease and content everywhere prevailing, rancour, licence corruption and ambition everywhere quenched, and that golden age restored in which every one might hold and support what opinions he pleased. He will see, in short, the world triumphing, the sovereign honoured and revered, the people animated with love, and rejoicing in their security. But should he turn to examine the times of the other emperors, he will find them wasted by battles, torn by seditions, cruel alike in war and peace; many princes perishing by the sword; many wars foreign and domestic; Italy overwhelmed with unheard-of disasters; her towns destroyed and plundered; Rome burned; the Capitol razed to the ground by Roman citizens; the ancient temples desolated; the ceremonies of religion corrupted; the cities rank with adultery; the seas covered with exiles and the islands polluted with blood. He will see outrage follow outrage; rank, riches, honours, and, above all, virtue imputed as mortal crimes; informers rewarded; slaves bribed to betray their masters, freedmen their patrons, and those who were without enemies brought to destruction by their friends; and then he will know the true nature of the debt which Rome, Italy, and the world owe to Cæsar; and if he possess a spark of human feeling, will turn from the example of those evil times, and kindle with a consuming passion to imitate those which were good.

And in truth the prince who seeks for worldly glory should desire to be the ruler of a corrupt city; not that, like Cæsar, he may destroy it, but that, like Romulus, he may restore it; since man cannot hope for, nor Heaven offer any better opportunity of fame. Were it indeed necessary in giving a constitution to a State to forfeit its sovereignty, the prince who, to retain his station, should withhold a constitution, might plead excuse; but for him who in giving a constitution can still retain his sovereignty, no excuse is to be made.

Let those therefore to whom Heaven has afforded this opportunity, remember that two courses lie open to them; one which will render them secure while they live and glorious when they die; another which exposes them to continual difficulties in life, and condemns them to eternal infamy after death.

Chapter XI.—*Of the Religion of the Romans.*

Though Rome had Romulus for her first founder, and as a daughter owed him her being and nurture, nevertheless, when the institutions of Romulus were seen by Heaven to be insufficient for so great a State, the Roman senate were moved to choose Numa Pompilius as his successor, that he might look to all matters which Romulus had neglected. He finding the people fierce and turbulent, and desiring with the help of the peaceful arts to bring them to order and obedience, called in the aid of religion as essential to the maintenance of civil society, and gave it such a form, that for many ages God was nowhere so much feared as in that republic. The effect of this was to render easy any enterprise in which the senate or great men of Rome thought fit to engage. And whosoever pays heed to an infinity of actions performed, sometimes by the Roman people collectively, often by single citizens, will see, that esteeming the power of God beyond that of man, they dreaded far more to violate their oath than to transgress the laws; as is clearly shown by the examples of Scipio and of Manlius Torquatus. For after the defeat of the Romans by Hannibal at Cannæ, many citizens meeting together, resolved, in their terror and dismay, to abandon Italy and seek refuge in Sicily. But Scipio, getting word of this, went among them, and menacing them with his naked sword, made them swear never to abandon their country. Again, when Lucius Manlius was accused by the tribune Marcus Pomponius, before the day fixed for trial, Titus Manlius, afterwards named Torquatus, son to Lucius, went to seek this Marcus, and threatening him with death if he did not withdraw the charge against his father, compelled him to swear compliance; and he, through fear, having sworn, kept his oath. In the first of these two instances, therefore, citizens whom love of their country and its laws could not have retained in Italy, were kept there by the oath forced upon them; and in the second, the tribune Marcus, to keep his oath, laid aside the hatred he bore the father, and overlooked the injury done him by the son, and his own dishonour. And this from no other cause than the religion which Numa had impressed upon this city.

And it will be plain to any one who carefully studies Roman History, how much religion helped in disciplining the army, in uniting the people, in keeping good men good, and putting bad men to shame; so that had it to be decided to which prince, Romulus or Numa, Rome owed the greater debt, I think the balance must turn in favour of Numa; for when religion is once established you may readily bring in arms; but where you have arms without religion it is not easy afterwards to bring in religion. We see, too, that while Romulus in order to create a senate, and to establish his other ordinances civil and military, needed no support from Divine authority, this was very necessary to Numa, who feigned to have intercourse with a Nymph by whose advice he was guided in counselling the people. And this, because desiring to introduce in Rome new and untried institutions, he feared that his own authority might not effect his end. Nor, indeed, has any attempt ever been made to introduce unusual laws among a people, without resorting to Divine authority, since without such sanction they never would have been accepted. For the wise recognize many things to be good which do not bear such reasons on the face of them as command their acceptance by others; wherefore, wise men who would obviate these difficulties, have recourse to Divine aid. Thus did Lycurgus, thus Solon, and thus have done many besides who have had the same end in view.

The Romans, accordingly, admiring the prudence and virtues of Numa, assented to all the measures which he recommended. This, however, is to be said, that the circumstance of these times being deeply tinctured with religious feeling, and of the men with whom he had to deal being rude and ignorant, gave Numa better facility to carry out his plans, as enabling him to mould his subjects readily to any new impression. And, doubtless, he who should seek at the present day to form a new commonwealth, would find the task easier among a race of simple mountaineers, than among the dwellers in cities where society is corrupt; as the sculptor can more easily carve a fair statue from a rough block, than from the block which has been badly shaped out by another. But taking all this into account, I maintain that the religion introduced by Numa was one of the chief causes of the prosperity of Rome, since it gave rise to good ordinances, which in turn brought with them good fortune, and with good fortune, happy issues to whatsoever was undertaken.

And as the observance of the ordinances of religion is the cause of the greatness of a State, so their neglect is the occasion of its decline; since a kingdom without the fear of God must either fall to pieces, or must be maintained by the fear of some prince who supplies that influence not supplied by religion. But since the lives of princes are short, the life of this prince, also, and with it his influence, must soon come to an end; whence it happens that a kingdom which rests wholly on the qualities of its prince, lasts for a brief time only; because these qualities, terminating with his life, are rarely renewed in his successor. For as Dante wisely says:—

"Seldom through the boughs doth human worth renew itself; for such the will of Him who gives it, that to Him we may ascribe it."[1]

It follows, therefore, that the safety of a commonwealth or kingdom lies, not in its having a ruler who governs it prudently while he lives, but in having one who so orders things, that when he dies, the State may still maintain itself. And though it be easier to impose new institutions or a new faith on rude and simple men, it is not therefore impossible to persuade their adoption by men who are civilized, and who do not think themselves rude. The people of Florence do not esteem themselves rude or ignorant, and yet were persuaded by the Friar Girolamo Savonarola that he spoke with God. Whether in this he said truth or no, I take not on me to pronounce, since of so great a man we must speak with reverence; but this I do say, that very many believed him without having witnessed anything extraordinary to warrant their belief; his life, his doctrines, the matter whereof he treated, being sufficient to enlist their faith.

Let no man, therefore, lose heart from thinking that he cannot do what others have done before him; for, as I said in my Preface, men are born, and live, and die, always in accordance with the same rules.

[Footnote 1:

L'umana probitate: e questo vuole Quei che la dà, perchè da lui si chiami. *Purg*. vii. 121-123.]

Chapter XII.—*That it is of much moment to make account of Religion; and that Italy, through the Roman Church, being wanting therein, has been ruined.*

Princes and commonwealths that would save themselves from growing corrupted, should before all things keep uncorrupted the rites and ceremonies of religion, and always hold them in reverence; since we can have no surer sign of the decay of a province than to see Divine worship held therein in contempt. This is easily understood when it is seen on what foundation that religion rests in which a man is born. For every religion has its root in certain fundamental ordinances peculiar to itself.

The religion of the Gentiles had its beginning in the responses of the oracles and in the prognostics of the augurs and soothsayers. All their other ceremonies and observances depended upon these; because men naturally believed that the God who could forecast their future weal or woe, could also bring them to pass. Wherefore the temples, the prayers, the sacrifices, and all the other rites of their worship, had their origin in this, that the oracles of Delos, of Dodona, and others celebrated in antiquity, held the world admiring and devout. But, afterwards, when these oracles began to shape their answers to suit the interests of powerful men, and their impostures to be seen through by the multitude, men grew incredulous and ready to overturn every sacred institution. For which reason, the rulers of kingdoms and commonwealths should maintain the foundations of the faith which they hold; since thus it will be easy for them to keep their country religious, and, consequently, virtuous and united. To which end they should countenance and further whatsoever tells in favour of religion, even should they think it untrue; and the wiser they are, and the better they are acquainted with natural causes, the more ought they to do so. It is from this course having been followed by the wise, that the miracles celebrated even in false religions, have come to be held in repute; for from whatever source they spring, discreet men will extol them, whose authority afterwards gives them currency everywhere.

These miracles were common enough in Rome, and among others this was believed, that when the Roman soldiers were sacking the city of Veii, certain of them entered the temple of Juno and spoke to the statue of the goddess, saying, "*Wilt thou come with us to Rome?*" when to some it seemed that she inclined her head in assent, and to others that they heard her answer, "*Yea.*" For these men being filled with religious awe (which Titus Livius shows us by the circumstance that, in entering the temple, they entered devoutly, reverently, and without tumult), persuaded themselves they heard that answer to their question, which, perhaps, they had formed beforehand in their minds. But their faith and belief were wholly approved of and confirmed by Camillus and by the other chief men of the city.

Had religion been maintained among the princes of Christendom on the footing on which it was established by its Founder, the Christian States and republics had been far more united and far more prosperous than they now are; nor can we have surer proof of its decay than in witnessing how those countries which are the nearest neighbours of the Roman Church, the head of our faith, have less devoutness than any others; so that any one who considers its earliest beginnings and observes how widely different is its present practice, might well believe its ruin or its chastisement to be close at hand.

But since some are of opinion that the welfare of Italy depends upon the Church of Rome, I desire to put forward certain arguments which occur to me against that view, and shall adduce two very strong ones, which, to my mind, admit of no answer. The first is, that, through the ill example of the Roman Court, the country has lost all religious feeling and devoutness, a loss which draws after it infinite mischiefs and disorders; for as the presence of religion implies every excellence, so the contrary is involved in its absence. To the Church, therefore, and to the priests, we Italians owe this first debt, that through them we have become wicked and irreligious. And a still greater debt we owe them for what is the immediate cause of our ruin, namely, that by the Church our country is kept divided. For no country was ever united or prosperous which did not yield obedience to some one prince or commonwealth, as has been the case with France and Spain. And the Church is the sole cause why Italy stands on a different footing, and is subject to no one king or commonwealth. For though she holds here her seat, and exerts her temporal authority, she has never yet gained strength and courage to seize upon the entire country, or make herself supreme; yet never has been so weak that when in fear of losing her temporal dominion, she could not call in some foreign potentate to aid her against any Italian State by which she was overmatched. Of which we find many instances, both in early times, as when by the intervention of Charles the Great she drove the Lombards, who had made themselves masters of nearly the whole country, out of Italy; and also in recent times, as when, with the help of France, she first stripped the Venetians of their territories, and then, with the help of the Swiss, expelled the French.

The Church, therefore, never being powerful enough herself to take possession of the entire country, while, at the same time, preventing any one else from doing so, has made it impossible to bring Italy under one head; and has been the cause of her always living subject to many princes or rulers, by whom she has been brought to such division and weakness as to have become a prey, not to Barbarian kings only, but to any who have thought fit to attack her. For this, I say, we Italians have none to thank but the Church. And were any man powerful enough to transplant the Court of Rome, with all the authority it now wields over the rest of Italy, into the territories of the Swiss (the only people who at this day, both as regards religion and military discipline, live like the ancients,) he would have clear proof of the truth of what I affirm, and would find that the corrupt manners of that Court had, in a little while, wrought greater mischief in these territories than any other disaster which could ever befall them.

Chapter XIII.—*Of the use the Romans made of Religion in giving Institutions to their City, in carrying out their Enterprises, and in quelling Tumults.*

Here it seems to me not out of place to cite instances of the Romans seeking assistance from religion in reforming their institutions and in carrying out their warlike designs. And although many such are related by Titus Livius, I content myself with mentioning the following only: The Romans having appointed tribunes with consular powers, all of them, save one, plebeians, it so chanced that in that very year they were visited by plague and famine, accompanied by many strange portents. Taking occasion from this, the nobles, at the next creation of tribunes, gave out that the gods were angry with Rome for lowering the majesty

of her government, nor could be appeased but by the choice of tribunes being restored to a fair footing. Whereupon the people, smitten with religious awe, chose all the tribunes from the nobles. Again, at the siege of Veii, we find the Roman commanders making use of religion to keep the minds of their men well disposed towards that enterprise. For when, in the last year of the siege, the soldiers, disgusted with their protracted service, began to clamour to be led back to Rome, on the Alban lake suddenly rising to an uncommon height, it was found that the oracles at Delphi and elsewhere had foretold that Veii should fall that year in which the Alban lake overflowed. The hope of near victory thus excited in the minds of the soldiers, led them to put up with the weariness of the war, and to continue in arms; until, on Camillus being named dictator, Veii was taken after a ten years' siege. In these cases, therefore, we see religion, wisely used, assist in the reduction of this city, and in restoring the tribuneship to the nobles; neither of which ends could well have been effected without it.

One other example bearing on the same subject I must not omit. Constant disturbances were occasioned in Rome by the tribune Terentillus, who, for reasons to be noticed in their place, sought to pass a certain law. The nobles, in their efforts to baffle him, had recourse to religion, which they sought to turn to account in two ways. For first they caused the Sibylline books to be searched, and a feigned answer returned, that in that year the city ran great risk of losing its freedom through civil discord; which fraud, although exposed by the tribunes, nevertheless aroused such alarm in the minds of the commons that they slackened in their support of their leaders. Their other contrivance was as follows: A certain Appius Herdonius, at the head of a band of slaves and outlaws, to the lumber of four thousand, having seized the Capitol by night, an alarm was spread that were the Equians and Volscians, those perpetual enemies of the Roman name, then to attack the city, they might succeed in taking it. And when, in spite of this, the tribunes stubbornly persisted in their efforts to pass the law, declaring the act of Herdonius to be a device of the nobles and no real danger. Publius Rubetius, a citizen of weight and authority, came forth from the Senate House, and in words partly friendly and partly menacing, showed them the peril in which the city stood, and that their demands were unseasonable; and spoke to such effect that the commons bound themselves by oath to stand by the consul; in fulfilment of which engagement they aided the consul, Publius Valerius, to carry the Capitol by assault. But Valerius being slain in the attack, Titus Quintius was at once appointed in his place, who, to leave the people no breathing time, nor suffer their thoughts to revert to the Terentillian law, ordered them to quit Rome and march against the Volscians; declaring them bound to follow him by virtue of the oath they had sworn not to desert the consul. And though the tribunes withstood him, contending that the oath had been sworn to the dead consul and not to Quintius, yet the people under the influence of religious awe, chose rather to obey the consul than believe the tribunes. And Titus Livius commends their behaviour when he says: "*That neglect of the gods which now prevails, had not then made its way nor was it then the practice for every man to interpret his oath, or the laws, to suit his private ends.*" The tribunes accordingly, fearing to lose their entire ascendency, consented to obey the consul, and to refrain for a year from moving in the matter of the Terentillian law; while the consuls, on their part, undertook that for a year the commons should not be called forth to war. And thus, with the help of religion, the senate were able to overcome a difficulty which they never could have overcome without it.

Chapter XIV.—*That the Romans interpreted the Auspices to meet the occasion; and made a prudent show of observing the Rites of Religion even when forced to disregard them; and any who rashly slighted Religion they punished.*

Auguries were not only, as we have shown above, a main foundation of the old religion of the Gentiles, but were also the cause of the prosperity of the Roman commonwealth. Accordingly, the Romans gave more heed to these than to any other of their observances; resorting to them in their consular comitia; in undertaking new enterprises; in calling out their armies; in going into battle; and, in short, in every business of importance, whether civil or military. Nor would they ever set forth on any warlike expedition, until they had satisfied their soldiers that the gods had promised them victory.

Among other means of declaring the auguries, they had in their armies a class of soothsayers, named by them *pullarii*, whom, when they desired to give battle, they would ask to take the auspices, which they did by observing the behaviour of fowls. If the fowls pecked, the engagement was begun with a favourable omen. If they refused, battle was declined. Nevertheless, when it was plain on the face of it that a certain course had to be taken, they take it at all hazards, even though the auspices were adverse; contriving, however, to manage matters so adroitly as not to appear to throw any slight on religion; as was done by the consul Papirius in the great battle he fought with the Samnites wherein that nation was finally broken and overthrown. For Papirius being encamped over against the Samnites, and perceiving that he fought, victory was certain, and consequently being eager to engage, desired the omens to be taken. The fowls refused to peck; but the chief soothsayer observing the eagerness of the soldiers to fight and the confidence felt both by them and by their captain, not to deprive the army of such an opportunity of glory, reported to the consul that the auspices were favourable. Whereupon Papirius began to array his army for battle. But some among the soothsayers having divulged to certain of the soldiers that the fowls had not pecked, this was told to Spurius Papirius, the nephew of the consul, who reporting it to his uncle, the latter straightway bade him mind his own business, for that so far as he himself and the army were concerned, the auspices were fair; and if the soothsayer had lied, the consequences were on his head. And that the event might accord with the prognostics, he commanded his officers to place the soothsayers in front of the battle. It so chanced that as they advanced against the enemy, the chief soothsayer was killed by a spear thrown by a Roman soldier; which, the consul hearing of, said, "*All goes well, and as the Gods would have it, for by the death of this liar the army is purged of blame and absolved from whatever displeasure these may have conceived against it.*" And contriving, in this way to make his designs tally with the auspices, he joined battle, without the army knowing that the ordinances of religion had in any degree been disregarded.

But an opposite course was taken by Appius Pulcher, in Sicily, in the first Carthaginian war. For desiring to join battle, he bade the soothsayers take the auspices, and on their announcing that the fowls refused to feed, he answered, "*Let us see, then, whether they will drink,*" and, so saying, caused them to be thrown into the sea. After which he fought and was defeated. For this he was condemned at Rome, while Papirius was honoured; not so much because the one had gained while the other had lost a battle, as because in their treatment of the auspices the one had behaved discreetly, the other with rashness. And, in truth, the sole object of this system of taking the auspices was to insure the army joining battle with that confidence of success which constantly leads to victory; a device followed not by the Romans only, but by foreign nations as well; of which I shall give an example in the following Chapter.

Chapter XV.—*How the Samnites, as a last resource in their broken Fortunes, had recourse to Religion.*

The Samnites, who before had met with many defeats at the hands of the Romans, were at last decisively routed by them in Etruria, where their armies were cut to pieces and their commanders slain. And because their allies also, such as the Etruscans, the Umbrians, and the Gauls, were likewise vanquished, they "*could now no longer*" as Livius tells us, "*either trust to their own strength or to foreign aid; yet, for all that, would not cease from hostilities, nor resign themselves to forfeit the liberty which they had unsuccessfully defended, preferring new defeats to an inglorious submission.*" They resolved, therefore, to make a final effort; and as they knew that victory was only to be secured by inspiring their soldiers with a stubborn courage, to which end nothing could help so much as religion, at the instance of their high priest, Ovius Paccius, they revived an ancient sacrificial rite performed by them in the manner following. After offering solemn sacrifice they caused all the captains of their armies, standing between the slain victims and the smoking altars, to swear never to abandon the war. They then summoned the common soldiers, one by one, and before the same altars, and surrounded by a ring of many centurions with drawn swords, first bound them by oath never to reveal what they might see or hear; and then, after imprecating the Divine wrath, and reciting the most terrible incantations, made them vow and swear to the gods, as they would not have a curse light on their race and offspring, to follow wherever their captains led, never to turn back from battle, and to put any they saw turn back to death. Some who in their terror declined to swear, were forthwith slain by the centurions. The rest, warned by their cruel fate, complied. Assembling thereafter to the number of forty thousand, one-half of whom, to render their appearance of unusual splendour were clad in white, with plumes and crests over their helmets, they took up their ground in the neighbourhood of Aquilonia. But Papirius, being sent against them, bade his soldiers be of good cheer, telling them "*that feathers made no wounds, and that a Roman spear would pierce a painted shield;*" and to lessen the effect which the oath taken by the Samnites had upon the minds of the Romans, he said that such an oath must rather distract than strengthen those bound by it, since they had to fear, at once, their enemies, their comrades, and their Gods. In the battle which ensued, the Samnites were routed, any firmness lent them by religion or by the oath they had sworn, being balanced by the Roman valour, and the terror inspired by past defeats. Still we see that, in their own judgment, they had no other refuge to which to turn, nor other remedy for restoring their broken hopes; and this is strong testimony to the spirit which religion rightly used can arouse.

Some of the incidents which I have now been considering may be thought to relate rather to the foreign than to the domestic affairs of Rome, which last alone form the proper subject of this Book; nevertheless since the matter connects itself with one of the most important institutions of the Roman republic, I have thought it convenient to notice it here, so as not to divide the subject and be obliged to return to it hereafter.

Chapter XVI.—*That a People accustomed to live under a Prince, if by any accident it become free, can hardly preserve that Freedom.*

Should a people accustomed to live under a prince by any accident become free, as did the Romans on the expulsion of the Tarquins, we know from numberless instances recorded in ancient history, how hard it will be for it to maintain that freedom. And this is no more than we might expect. For a people in such circumstances may be likened to the wild animal which, though destined by nature to roam at large in the woods, has been reared in the cage and in constant confinement and which, should it chance to be set free in the open country, being unused to find its own food, and unfamiliar with the coverts where it might lie concealed, falls a prey to the first who seeks to recapture it. Even thus it fares with the people which has been accustomed to be governed by others; since ignorant how to act by itself either for attack or defence, and neither knowing foreign princes nor being known of them, it is speedily brought back under the yoke, and often under a heavier yoke than that from which it has just freed its neck. These difficulties will be met with, even where the great body of the citizens has not become wholly corrupted; but where the corruption is complete, freedom, as shall presently be shown, is not merely fleeting but impossible. Wherefore my remarks are to be taken as applying to those States only wherein corruption has as yet made no great progress, and in which there is more that is sound than unsound.

To the difficulties above noticed, another has to be added, which is, that a State in becoming free makes for itself bitter enemies but not warm friends. All become its bitter enemies who, drawing their support from the wealth of the tyrant, flourished under his government. For these men, when the causes which made them powerful are withdrawn, can no longer live contented, but are one and all impelled to attempt the restoration of the tyranny in hopes of regaining their former importance. On the other hand, as I have said, the State which becomes free does not gain for itself warm friends. For a free government bestows its honours and rewards in accordance with certain fixed rules, and on considerations of merit, without which none is honoured or rewarded. But when a man obtains only those honours or rewards which he seems to himself to deserve, he will never admit that he is under any obligation to those who bestow them. Moreover the common benefits that all derive from a free government, which consist in the power to enjoy what is our own, openly and undisturbed, in having to feel no anxiety for the honour of wife or child, nor any fear for personal safety, are hardly recognized by men while they still possess them, since none will ever confess obligation to him who merely refrains from injury. For these reasons, I repeat, a State which has recently become free, is likely to have bitter enemies and no warm friends.

Now, to meet these difficulties and their attendant disorders, there is no more potent, effectual, wholesome, and necessary remedy than *to slay the sons of Brutus*. They, as the historian tells us, were along with other young Romans led to conspire against their country, simply because the unusual privileges which they had enjoyed under the kings, were withheld under the consuls; so that to them it seemed as though the freedom of the people implied their servitude. Any one, therefore, who undertakes to control a people, either as their prince or as the head of a commonwealth, and does not make sure work with all who are hostile to his new institutions, founds a government which cannot last long. Undoubtedly those princes are to be reckoned unhappy, who, to secure their position, are forced to advance by unusual and irregular paths, and with the people for their enemies. For while he who has to deal with a few adversaries only, can easily and without much or serious difficulty secure himself, he who has an entire people against him can never feel safe and the greater the severity he uses the weaker his authority becomes; so that his best course is to strive to make the people his friends.

But since these views may seem to conflict with what I have said above, treating there of a republic and here of a prince, that I may not have to return to the subject again, I will in this place discuss it briefly. Speaking, then of those princes who have become the tyrants of their country, I say that the prince who seeks to gain over an unfriendly people should first of all examine what it is the people really desire, and he will always find that they desire two things: first, to be revenged upon those who are the cause of their servitude; and second, to regain their freedom. The first of these desires the prince can gratify wholly, the second in part. As regards the former, we have an instance exactly in point. Clearchus, tyrant of Heraclea, being in exile, it so happened that on a feud arising between the commons and the nobles of that city, the latter, perceiving they were weaker than their adversaries, began to look with favour on Clearchus, and conspiring with him, in opposition to the popular voice recalled him to Heraclea and deprived the people of their freedom. Clearchus finding himself thus placed between the arrogance of the nobles, whom he could in no way either satisfy or correct, and the fury of the people, who could not put up with the loss of their freedom, resolved to rid himself at a stroke from the harassment of the nobles and recommend himself to the people. Wherefore, watching his opportunity, he caused all the nobles to be put to death, and thus, to the extreme delight of the people, satisfied one of those desires by which they are possessed, namely, the desire for vengeance.

As for the other desire of the people, namely, to recover their freedom, the prince, since he never can content them in this, should examine what the causes are which make them long to be free; and he will find a very few of them desiring freedom that they may obtain power, but all the rest, whose number is countless, only desiring it that they may live securely. For in all republics, whatever the form of their government, barely forty or fifty citizens have any place in the direction of affairs; who, from their number being so small, can easily be reckoned with, either by making away with them, or by allowing them such a share of honours as, looking to their position, may reasonably content them. All those others whose sole aim it is to live safely, are well contented where the prince enacts such laws and ordinances as provide for the general security, while they establish his own authority; and when he does this, and the people see that nothing induces him to violate these laws, they soon begin to live happily and without anxiety. Of this we have an example in the kingdom of France, which enjoys perfect security from this cause alone, that its kings are bound to compliance with an infinity of laws upon which the well-being of the whole people depends. And he who gave this State its constitution allowed its kings to do as they pleased as regards arms and money; but provided that as regards everything else they should not interfere save as the laws might direct. Those rulers, therefore, who omit to provide sufficiently for the safety of their government at the outset, must, like the Romans, do so on the first occasion which offers; and whoever lets the occasion slip, will repent too late of not having acted as he should. The Romans, however, being still uncorrupted at the time when they recovered their freedom, were able, after slaying the sons of Brutus and getting rid of the Tarquins, to maintain it with all those safeguards and remedies which we have elsewhere considered. But had they already become corrupted, no remedy could have been found, either in Rome or out of it, by which their freedom could have been secured; as I shall show in the following Chapter.

Chapter XVII.—*That a corrupt People obtaining Freedom can hardly preserve it.*

I believe that if her kings had not been expelled, Rome must very soon have become a weak and inconsiderable State. For seeing to what a pitch of corruption these kings had come, we may conjecture that if two or three more like reigns had followed, and the taint spread from the head to the members, so soon as the latter became infected, cure would have been hopeless. But from the head being removed while the trunk was still sound, it was not difficult for the Romans to return to a free and constitutional government.

It may be assumed, however, as most certain, that a corrupted city living under a prince can never recover its freedom, even were the prince and all his line to be exterminated. For in such a city it must necessarily happen that one prince will be replaced by another, and that things will never settle down until a new lord be established; unless, indeed, the combined goodness and valour of some one citizen should maintain freedom, which, even then, will endure only for his lifetime; as happened twice in Syracuse, first under the rule of Dion, and again under that of Timoleon, whose virtues while they lived kept their city free, but on whose death it fell once more under a tyranny.

But the strongest example that can be given is that of Rome, which on the expulsion of the Tarquins was able at once to seize on liberty and to maintain it; yet, on the deaths of Cæsar, Caligula, and Nero, and on the extinction of the Julian line, was not only unable to establish her freedom, but did not even venture a step in that direction. Results so opposite arising in one and the same city can only be accounted for by this, that in the time of the Tarquins the Roman people were not yet corrupted, but in these later times had become utterly corrupt. For on the first occasion, nothing more was needed to prepare and determine them to shake off their kings, than that they should be bound by oath to suffer no king ever again to reign in Rome; whereas, afterwards, the authority and austere virtue of Brutus, backed by all the legions of the East, could not rouse them to maintain their hold of that freedom, which he, following in the footsteps of the first Brutus, had won for them; and this because of the corruption wherewith the people had been infected by the Marian faction, whereof Cæsar becoming head, was able so to blind the multitude that it saw not the yoke under which it was about to lay its neck.

Though this example of Rome be more complete than any other, I desire to instance likewise, to the same effect, certain peoples well known in our own days; and I maintain that no change, however grave or violent, could ever restore freedom to Naples or Milan, because in these States the entire body of the people has grown corrupted. And so we find that Milan, although desirous to return to a free form of government, on the death of Filippo Visconti, had neither the force nor the skill needed to preserve it.

Most fortunate, therefore, was it for Rome that her kings grew corrupt soon, so as to be driven out before the taint of their corruption had reached the vitals of the city. For it was because these were sound that the endless commotions which took place in Rome, so far from being hurtful, were, from their object being good, beneficial to the commonwealth. From which we may draw this inference, that where the body of the people is still sound, tumults and other like disorders do little hurt, but that where it has become corrupted, laws, however well devised, are of no advantage, unless imposed by some one whose paramount authority causes them to be observed until the community be once more restored to a sound and healthy condition.

Whether this has ever happened I know not, nor whether it ever can happen. For we see, as I have said a little way back, that a city which owing to its pervading corruption has once begun to decline, if it is to recover at all, must be saved not by the excellence of the people collectively, but of some one man then living among them, on whose death it at once relapses into its former plight; as happened with Thebes, in which the virtue of Epaminondas made it possible while he lived to preserve the form of a free Government, but which fell again on his death into its old disorders; the reason being that hardly any ruler lives so long as to have time to accustom to right methods a city which has long been accustomed to wrong. Wherefore, unless things be put on a sound footing by some one ruler who lives to a very advanced age, or by two virtuous rulers succeeding one another, the city upon their death at once falls back into ruin; or, if it be preserved, must be so by incurring great risks, and at the cost of much blood. For the corruption I speak of, is wholly incompatible with a free government, because it results from an inequality which pervades the State and can only be removed by employing unusual and very violent remedies, such as few are willing or know how to employ, as in another place I shall more fully explain.

Chapter XVIII.—*How a Free Government existing in a corrupt City may be preserved, or not existing may be created.*

I think it neither out of place, nor inconsistent with what has been said above, to consider whether a free government existing in a corrupt city can be maintained, or, not existing, can be introduced. And on this head I say that it is very difficult to bring about either of these results, and next to impossible to lay down rules as to how it may be done; because the measures to be taken must vary with the degree of corruption which prevails.

Nevertheless, since it is well to reason things out, I will not pass this matter by, but will assume, in the first place, the case of a very corrupt city, and then take the case of one in which corruption has reached a still greater height; but where corruption is universal, no laws or institutions will ever have force to restrain it. Because as good customs stand in need of good laws for their support, so laws, that they may be respected, stand in need of good customs. Moreover, the laws and institutions established in a republic at its beginning, when men were good, are no longer suitable when they have become bad; but while the laws of a city are altered to suit its circumstances, its institutions rarely or never change; whence it results that the introduction of new laws is of no avail, because the institutions, remaining unchanged, corrupt them.

And to make this plainer, I say that in Rome it was first of all the institutions of the State, and next the laws as enforced by the magistrates, which kept the citizens under control. The institutions of the State consisted in the authority of the people, the senate, the tribunes, and the consuls; in the methods of choosing and appointing magistrates; and in the arrangements for passing laws. These institutions changed little, if at all, with circumstances. But the laws by which the people were controlled, as for instance the law relating to adultery, the sumptuary laws, the law as to canvassing at elections, and many others, were altered as the citizens grew more and more corrupted. Hence, the institutions of the State remaining the same although from the corruption of the people no longer suitable, amendments in the laws could not keep men good, though they might have proved very useful if at the time when they were made the institutions had likewise been reformed.

That its original institutions are no longer adapted to a city that has become corrupted, is plainly seen in two matters of great moment, I mean in the appointment of magistrates and in the passing of laws. For the Roman people conferred the consulship and other great offices of their State on none save those who sought them; which was a good institution at first, because then none sought these offices save those who thought themselves worthy of them, and to be rejected was held disgraceful; so that, to be deemed worthy, all were on their best behaviour. But in a corrupted city this institution grew to be most mischievous. For it was no longer those of greatest worth, but those who had most influence, who sought the magistracies; while all who were without influence, however deserving, refrained through fear. This untoward result was not reached all at once, but like other similar results, by gradual steps. For after subduing Africa and Asia, and reducing nearly the whole of Greece to submission, the Romans became perfectly assured of their freedom, and seemed to themselves no longer to have any enemy whom they had cause to fear. But this security and the weakness of their adversaries led them in conferring the consulship, no longer to look to merit, but only to favour, selecting for the office those who knew best how to pay court to them, not those who knew best how to vanquish their enemies. And afterwards, instead of selecting those who were best liked, they came to select those who had most influence; and in this way, from the imperfection of their institutions, good men came to be wholly excluded.

Again, as to making laws, any of the tribunes and certain others of the magistrates were entitled to submit laws to the people; but before these were passed it was open to every citizen to speak either for or against them. This was a good system so long as the citizens were good, since it is always well that every man should be able to propose what he thinks may be of use to his country, and that all should be allowed to express their views with regard to his proposal; so that the people, having heard all, may resolve on what is best. But when the people grew depraved, this became a very mischievous institution; for then it was only the powerful who proposed laws, and these not in the interest of public freedom but of their own authority; and because, through fear, none durst speak against the laws they proposed, the people were either deceived or forced into voting their own destruction.

In order, therefore, that Rome after she had become corrupted might still preserve her freedom, it was necessary that, as in the course of events she had made new laws, so likewise she should frame new institutions, since different institutions and ordinances are needed in a corrupt State from those which suit a State which is not corrupted; for where the matter is wholly dissimilar, the form cannot be similar.

But since old institutions must either be reformed all at once, as soon as they are seen to be no longer expedient, or else gradually, as the imperfection of each is recognized, I say that each of these two courses is all but impossible. For to effect a gradual reform requires a sagacious man who can discern mischief while it is still remote and in the germ. But it may well happen that no such person is found in a city; or that, if found, he is unable to persuade others of what he is himself persuaded. For men used to live in one way are loath to leave it for another, especially when they are not brought face to face with the evil against which they should guard, and only have it indicated to them by conjecture. And as for a sudden reform of institutions which are seen by all to be no longer good, I say that defects which are easily discerned are not easily corrected, because for their correction it is not enough to use ordinary means, these being in themselves insufficient; but recourse must be had to extraordinary means, such as violence and arms; and, as a preliminary, you must become prince of the city, and be able to deal with it at your pleasure. But since the restoration of a State to new political life presupposes a good man, and to become prince of a city by violence presupposes a bad man, it can, consequently, very seldom happen that, although the end be good, a good man will be found ready to become a prince by evil ways, or that a bad man having become a prince will be disposed to act virtuously, or think of turning to good account his ill-acquired authority.

From all these causes comes the difficulty, or rather the impossibility, which a corrupted city finds in maintaining an existing free government, or in establishing a new one. So that had we to establish or maintain a government in that city, it would be necessary to give it a monarchical, rather than a popular form, in order that men too arrogant to be restrained by the laws, might in some measure be kept in check by a power almost absolute; since to attempt to make them good otherwise would be a very cruel or a wholly futile endeavour. This, as I have said, was the method followed by Cleomenes; and if he, that he might stand alone, put to death the Ephori; and if Romulus, with a like object, put to death his brother and Titus Tatius the Sabine, and if both afterwards made good use of the authority they thus acquired, it is nevertheless to be remembered that it was because neither Cleomenes nor Romulus had to deal with so corrupt a people as that of which I am now speaking, that they were able to effect their ends and to give a fair colour to their acts.

Chapter XIX.—*After a strong Prince a weak Prince may maintain himself: but after one weak Prince no Kingdom can stand a second.*

When we contemplate the excellent qualities of Romulus, Numa, and Tullus, the first three kings of Rome, and note the methods which they followed, we recognize the extreme good fortune of that city in having her first king fierce and warlike, her second peaceful and religious, and her third, like the first, of a high spirit and more disposed to war than to peace. For it was essential for Rome that almost at the outset of her career, a ruler should be found to lay the foundations of her civil life; but, after that had been done, it was necessary that her rulers should return to the virtues of Romulus, since otherwise the city must have grown feeble, and become a prey to her neighbours.

And here we may note that a prince who succeeds to another of superior valour, may reign on by virtue of his predecessor's merits, and reap the fruits of his labours; but if he live to a great age, or if he be followed by another who is wanting in the qualities of the first, that then the kingdom must necessarily dwindle. Conversely, when two consecutive princes are of rare excellence, we commonly find them achieving results which win for them enduring renown. David, for example, not only surpassed in learning and judgment, but was so valiant in arms that, after conquering and subduing all his neighbours, he left to his young son Solomon a tranquil State, which the latter, though unskilled in the arts of war, could maintain by the arts of peace, and thus happily enjoy the inheritance of his father's valour. But Solomon could not transmit this inheritance to his son Rehoboam, who neither resembling his grandfather in valour, nor his father in good fortune, with difficulty made good his right to a sixth part of the kingdom. In like manner Bajazet, sultan of the Turks, though a man of peace rather than of war, was able to enjoy the labours of Mahomet his father, who, like David, having subdued his neighbours, left his son a kingdom so safely established that it could easily be retained by him by peaceful arts. But had Selim, son to Bajazet, been like his father, and not like his grandfather, the Turkish monarchy must have been overthrown; as it is, he seems likely to outdo the fame of his grandsire.

I affirm it to be proved by these examples, that after a valiant prince a feeble prince may maintain himself; but that no kingdom can stand when two feeble princes follow in succession, unless, as in the case of France, it be supported by its ancient ordinances. By feeble princes, I mean such as are not valiant in war. And, to put the matter shortly, it may be said, that the great valour of Romulus left Numa a period of many years within which to govern Rome by peaceful arts; that after Numa came Tullus, who renewed by his courage the fame of Romulus; and that he in turn was succeeded by Ancus, a prince so gifted by nature that he could equally avail himself of the methods of peace or war; who setting himself at first to pursue the former, when he found that his neighbours judged him to be effeminate, and therefore held him in slight esteem, understood that to preserve Rome he must resort to arms and resemble Romulus rather than Numa. From whose example every ruler of a State may learn that a prince like Numa will hold or lose his power according as fortune and circumstances befriend him; but that the prince who resembles Romulus, and like him is fortified with foresight and arms, will hold his State whatever befall, unless deprived of it by some stubborn and irresistible force. For we may reckon with certainty that if Rome had not had for her third king one who knew how to restore her credit by deeds of valour, she could not, or at any rate not without great difficulty, have afterwards held her ground, nor could ever have achieved the great exploits she did.

And for these reasons Rome, while she lived under her kings, was in constant danger of destruction through a king who might be weak or bad.

Chapter XX.—*That the consecutive Reigns of two valiant Princes produce great results: and that well-ordered Commonwealths are assured of a Succession of valiant Rulers by whom their Power and Growth are rapidly extended.*

When Rome had driven out her kings, she was freed from those dangers to which, as I have said, she was exposed by the possible succession of a weak or wicked prince. For the chief share in the government then devolved upon the consuls, who took their authority not by inheritance, nor yet by craft or by ambitious violence, but by the free suffrages of their fellow-citizens, and were always men of signal worth; by whose valour and good fortune Rome being constantly aided, was able to reach the height of her greatness in the same number of years as she had lived under her kings. And since we find that two successive reigns of valiant princes, as of Philip of Macedon and his son Alexander, suffice to conquer the world, this ought to be still easier for a commonwealth, which has it in its power to choose, not two excellent rulers only, but an endless number in succession. And in every well ordered commonwealth provision will be made for a succession of this sort.

Chapter XXI.—*That it is a great reproach to a Prince or to a Commonwealth to be without a national Army.*

Those princes and republics of the present day who lack forces of their own, whether for attack or defence, should take shame to themselves, and should be convinced by the example of Tullus, that their deficiency does not arise from want of men fit for warlike enterprises, but from their own fault in not knowing how to make their subjects good soldiers. For after Rome had been at peace for forty years, Tullus, succeeding to the kingdom, found not a single Roman who had ever been in battle. Nevertheless when he made up his mind to enter on a war, it never occurred to him to have recourse to the Samnites, or the Etruscans, or to any other of the neighbouring nations accustomed to arms, but he resolved, like the prudent prince he was, to rely on his own countrymen. And such was his ability that, under his rule, the people very soon became admirable soldiers. For nothing is more true than that where a country, having men, lacks soldiers, it results from some fault in its ruler, and not from any defect in the situation or climate. Of this we have a very recent instance. Every one knows, how, only the other day, the King of England invaded the realm of France with an army raised wholly from among his own people, although from his country having been at peace for thirty years, he had neither men nor officers who had ever looked an enemy in the face. Nevertheless, he did not hesitate with such troops as he had, to attack a kingdom well provided with officers and excellent soldiers who had been constantly under arms in the Italian wars. And this was possible through the prudence of the English king and the wise ordinances of his kingdom, which never in time of peace relaxes its warlike discipline. So too, in old times, Pelopidas and Epaminondas the Thebans, after they had freed Thebes from her tyrants, and rescued her from thraldom to Sparta, finding themselves in a city used to servitude and surrounded by an effeminate people, scrupled not, so great was their courage, to furnish these with arms, and go forth with them to meet and to conquer the Spartan forces on the field. And he who relates this, observes, that these two captains very soon showed that warriors are not bred in Lacedæmon alone, but in every country where men are found, if only some one arise among them who knows how to direct them to arms; as we see Tullus knew how to direct the Romans. Nor could Virgil better express this opinion, or show by fitter words that he was convinced of its truth than, when he says:—

"To arms shall Tullus rouse His sluggish warriors."[1]

[Footnote 1: Residesque movebit Tullus in arma viros. *Virg. Aen.* vi. 814.]

Chapter XXII.—*What is to be noted in the combat of the three Roman Horatii and the three Alban Curiatii.*

It was agreed between Tullus king of Rome, and Metius king of Alba, that the nation whose champions were victorious in combat should rule over the other. The three Alban Curiatii were slain; one of the Roman Horatii survived. Whereupon the Alban king with all his people became subject to the Romans. The surviving Horatius returning victorious to Rome, and meeting his sister, wife to one of the dead Curiatii, bewailing the death of her husband, slew her; and being tried for this crime, was, after much contention, liberated, rather on the entreaties of his father than for his own deserts.

Herein three points are to be noted. *First*, that we should never peril our whole fortunes on the success of only a part of our forces. *Second*, that in a well-governed State, merit should never be allowed to balance crime. And *third*, that those are never wise covenants which we cannot or should not expect to be observed. Now, for a State to be enslaved is so terrible a calamity that it ought never to have been supposed possible that either of these kings or nations would rest content under a slavery resulting from the defeat of three only of their number. And so it appeared to Metius; for although on the victory of the Roman champions, he at once confessed himself vanquished, and promised obedience; nevertheless, in the very first expedition which he and Tullus undertook jointly against the people of Veii, we find him seeking to circumvent the Roman, as though perceiving too late the rash part he had played.

This is enough to say of the third point which I noted as deserving attention. Of the other two I shall speak in the next two Chapters.

Chapter XXIII.—*That we should never hazard our whole Fortunes where we put not forth our entire Strength; for which reason to guard a Defile is often hurtful.*

It was never judged a prudent course to peril your whole fortunes where you put not forth your whole strength; as may happen in more ways than one. One of these ways was that taken by Tullus and Metius, when each staked the existence of his country and the credit of his army on the valour and good fortune of three only of his soldiers, that being an utterly insignificant fraction of the force at his disposal. For neither of these kings reflected that all the labours of their predecessors in framing such institutions for their States, as might, with the aid of the citizens themselves, maintain them long in freedom, were rendered futile, when the power to ruin all was left in the hands of so small a number. No rasher step, therefore, could have been taken, than was taken by these kings.

A like risk is almost always incurred by those who, on the approach of an enemy, resolve to defend some place of strength, or to guard the defiles by which their country is entered. For unless room be found in this place of strength for almost all your army, the attempt to hold it will almost always prove hurtful. If you can find room, it will be right to defend your strong places; but if these be difficult of access, and you cannot there keep your entire force together, the effort to defend is mischievous. I come to this conclusion from observing the example of those who, although their territories be enclosed by mountains and precipices, have not, on being attacked by powerful enemies, attempted to fight on the mountains or in the defiles, but have advanced beyond them to meet their foes; or, if unwilling to advance, have awaited attack behind their mountains, on level and not on broken ground. The reason of which is, as I have above explained, that many men cannot be assembled in these strong places for their defence; partly because a large number of men cannot long subsist there, and partly because such places being narrow and confined, afford room for a few only; so that no enemy can there be withstood, who comes in force to the attack; which he can easily do, his design being to pass on and not to make a stay; whereas he who stands on the defensive cannot do so in force, because, from not knowing when the enemy may enter the confined and sterile tracts of which I speak, he may have to lodge himself there for a long time. But should you lose some pass which you had reckoned on holding, and on the defence of which your country and army have relied, there commonly follows such panic among your people and among the troops which remain to you, that you are vanquished without opportunity given for any display of valour, and lose everything without bringing all your resources into play.

Every one has heard with what difficulty Hannibal crossed the Alps which divide France from Lombardy, and afterwards those which separate Lombardy from Tuscany. Nevertheless the Romans awaited him, in the first instance on the banks of the Ticino, in the second on the plain of Arezzo, preferring to be defeated on ground which at least gave them a chance of victory, to leading their army into mountain fastnesses where it was likely to be destroyed by the mere difficulties of the ground. And any who read history with attention will find, that very few capable commanders have attempted to hold passes of this nature, as well for the reasons already given, as because to close them all were impossible. For mountains, like plains, are traversed not only by well-known and frequented roads, but also by many by-ways, which, though unknown to strangers, are familiar to the people of the country, under whose guidance you may always, and in spite of any opposition, be easily conducted to whatever point you please. Of this we have a recent instance in the events of the year 1515. For when Francis I. of France resolved on invading Italy in order to recover the province of Lombardy, those hostile to his attempt looked mainly to the Swiss, who it was hoped would stop him in passing through their mountains. But this hope was disappointed by the event. For leaving on one side two or three defiles which were guarded by the Swiss, the king advanced by another unknown pass, and was in Italy and upon his enemies before they knew. Whereupon they fled terror-stricken into Milan; while the whole population of Lombardy, finding themselves deceived in their expectation that the French would be detained in the mountains, went over to their side.

Chapter XXIV.—*That well-ordered States always provide Rewards and Punishments for their Citizens; and never set off Deserts against Misdeeds.*

The valour of Horatius in vanquishing the Curiatii deserved the highest reward. But in slaying his sister he had been guilty of a heinous crime. And so displeasing to the Romans was an outrage of this nature, that although his services were so great and so recent, they brought him to trial for his life. To one looking at it carelessly, this might seem an instance of popular ingratitude, but he who considers the matter more closely, and examines with sounder judgment what the ordinances of a State should be, will rather blame the Roman people for acquitting Horatius than for putting him on his trial. And this because no well-ordered State ever strikes a balance between the services of its citizens and their misdeeds; but appointing rewards for good actions and punishment for bad, when it has rewarded a man for acting well, will afterwards, should he act ill, chastise him, without regard to his former deserts. When these ordinances are duly observed, a city will live long in freedom, but when they are neglected, it must soon come to ruin. For when a citizen has rendered some splendid service to his country, if to the distinction which his action in itself confers, were added an over-weening confidence that any crime he might thenceforth commit would pass unpunished, he would soon become so arrogant that no civil bonds could restrain him.

Still, while we would have punishment terrible to wrongdoers, it is essential that good actions should be rewarded, as we see to have been the case in Rome. For even where a republic is poor, and has but little to give, it ought not to withhold that little; since a gift, however small, bestowed as a reward for services however great, will always be esteemed most honourable and precious by him who receives it. The story of Horatius Cocles and that of Mutius Scævola are well known: how the one withstood the enemy on the bridge while it was being cut down, and the other thrust his hand into the fire in punishment of the mistake made when he sought the life of Porsenna the Etruscan king. To each of these two, in requital of their splendid deeds, two ploughgates only of the public land were given. Another famous story is that of Manlius Capitolinus, to whom, for having saved the Capitol from the besieging Gauls, a small measure of meal was given by each of those who were shut up with him during the siege. Which recompense, in proportion to the wealth of the citizens of Rome at that time, was thought ample; so that afterwards, when Manlius, moved by jealousy and malice, sought to arouse sedition in Rome, and to gain over the people to his cause, they without regard to his past services threw him headlong from that Capitol in saving which he had formerly gained so great a renown.

Chapter XXV.—*That he who would reform the Institutions of a free State, must retain at least the semblance of old Ways.*

Whoever takes upon him to reform the government of a city, must, if his measures are to be well received and carried out with general approval, preserve at least the semblance of existing methods, so as not to appear to the people to have made any change in the old order of things; although, in truth, the new ordinances differ altogether from those which they replace. For when this is attended to, the mass of mankind accept what seems as what is; nay, are often touched more nearly by appearances than by realities.

This tendency being recognized by the Romans at the very outset of their civil freedom, when they appointed two consuls in place of a single king, they would not permit the consuls to have more than twelve lictors, in order that the old number of the king's attendants might not be exceeded. Again, there being solemnized every year in Rome a sacrificial rite which could only be performed by the king in person, that the people might not be led by the absence of the king to remark the want of any ancient observance, a priest was appointed for the due celebration of this rite, to whom was given the name of *Rex sacrificulus,* and who was placed under the orders of the chief priest. In this way the people were contented, and had no occasion from any defect in the solemnities to desire the return of their kings. Like precautions should be used by all who would put an end to the old government of a city and substitute new and free institutions. For since novelty disturbs men's minds, we should seek in the changes we make to preserve as far as possible what is ancient, so that if the new magistrates differ from the old in number, in authority, or in the duration of their office, they shall at least retain the old names.

This, I say, should be seen to by him who would establish a constitutional government, whether in the form of a commonwealth or of a kingdom. But he who would create an absolute government of the kind which political writers term a tyranny, must renew everything, as shall be explained in the following Chapter.

Chapter XXVI.—*A new Prince in a City or Province of which he has taken Possession, ought to make Everything new.*

Whosoever becomes prince of a city or State, more especially if his position be so insecure that he cannot resort to constitutional government either in the form of a republic or a monarchy, will find that the best way to preserve his princedom is to renew the whole institutions of that State; that is to say, to create new magistracies with new names, confer new powers, and employ new men, and like David when he became king, exalt the humble and depress the great, "*filling the hungry with good things, and sending the rich empty away.*" Moreover, he must pull down existing towns and rebuild them, removing their inhabitants from one place to another; and, in short, leave nothing in the country as he found it; so that there shall be neither rank, nor condition, nor honour, nor wealth which its possessor can refer to any but to him. And he must take example from Philip of Macedon, the father of Alexander, who by means such as these, from being a petty prince became monarch of all Greece; and of whom it was written that he shifted men from province to province as a shepherd moves his flocks from one pasture to another.

These indeed are most cruel expedients, contrary not merely to every Christian, but to every civilized rule of conduct, and such as every man should shun, choosing rather to lead a private life than to be a king on terms so hurtful to mankind. But he who will not keep to the fair path of virtue, must to maintain himself enter this path of evil. Men, however, not knowing how to be wholly good or wholly bad, choose for themselves certain middle ways, which of all others are the most pernicious, as shall be shown by an instance in the following Chapter.

Chapter XXVII.—*That Men seldom know how to be wholly good or wholly bad.*

When in the year 1505, Pope Julius II. went to Bologna to expel from that city the family of the Bentivogli, who had been princes there for over a hundred years, it was also in his mind, as a part of the general design he had planned against all those lords who had usurped Church lands, to remove Giovanpagolo Baglioni, tyrant of Perugia. And coming to Perugia with this intention and resolve, of which all men knew, he would not wait to enter the town with a force sufficient for his protection, but entered it unattended by troops, although Giovanpagolo was there with a great company of soldiers whom he had assembled for his defence. And thus, urged on by that impetuosity which stamped all his actions, accompanied only by his body-guard, he committed himself into the hands of his enemy, whom he forthwith carried away with him, leaving a governor behind to hold the town for the Church. All prudent men who were with the Pope remarked on his temerity, and on the pusillanimity of Giovanpagolo; nor could they conjecture why the latter had not, to his eternal glory, availed himself of this opportunity for crushing his enemy, and at the same time enriching himself with plunder, the Pope being attended by the whole College of Cardinals with all their luxurious equipage. For it could not be supposed that he was withheld by any promptings of goodness or scruples of conscience; because in the breast of a profligate living in incest with his sister, and who to obtain the princedom had put his nephews and kinsmen to death, no virtuous impulse could prevail. So that the only inference to be drawn was, that men know not how to be splendidly wicked or wholly good, and shrink in consequence from such crimes as are stamped with an inherent greatness or disclose a nobility of nature. For which reason Giovanpagolo, who thought nothing of incurring the guilt of incest, or of murdering his kinsmen, could not, or more truly durst not, avail himself of a fair occasion to do a deed which all would have admired; which would have won for him a deathless fame as the first to teach the prelates how little those who live and reign as they do are to be esteemed; and which would have displayed a greatness far transcending any infamy or danger that could attach to it.

Chapter XXVIII.—*Whence it came that the Romans were less ungrateful to their Citizens than were the Athenians.*

In the histories of all republics we meet with instances of some sort of ingratitude to their great citizens, but fewer in the history of Rome than of Athens, or indeed of any other republic. Searching for the cause of this, I am persuaded that, so far as regards Rome and Athens, it was due to the Romans having had less occasion than the Athenians to look upon their fellow-citizens with suspicion For, from the expulsion of her kings down to the times of Sylla and Marius, the liberty of Rome was never subverted by any one of her citizens; so that there never was in that city grave cause for distrusting any man, and in consequence making him the victim of inconsiderate injustice. The reverse was notoriously the case with Athens; for that city, having, at a time when she was most flourishing, been deprived of her freedom by Pisistratus under a false show of good-will, remembering, after she regained her liberty, her former bondage and all the wrongs she had endured, became the relentless chastiser, not of offences only on the part of her citizens, but even of the shadow of an offence. Hence the banishment and death of so many excellent men, and hence the law of ostracism, and all those other violent measures which from time to time during the history of that city were directed against her foremost citizens. For this is most true which is asserted by the writers on civil government, that a people which has recovered its freedom, bites more fiercely than one which has always preserved it.

And any who shall weigh well what has been said, will not condemn Athens in this matter, nor commend Rome, but refer all to the necessity arising out of the different conditions prevailing in the two States. For careful reflection will show that had Rome been deprived of her freedom as Athens was, she would not have been a whit more tender to her citizens. This we may reasonably infer from remarking what, after the expulsion of the kings, befell Collatinus and Publius Valerius; the former of whom, though he had taken part in the liberation of Rome, was sent into exile for no other reason than that he bore the name of Tarquin; while the sole ground of suspicion against the latter, and what almost led to his banishment, was his having built a house upon the Cælian hill. Seeing how harsh and suspicious Rome was in these two instances, we may surmise that she would have shown the same ingratitude as Athens, had she, like Athens, been wronged by her citizens at an early stage of her growth, and before she had attained to the fulness of her strength.

That I may not have to return to this question of ingratitude, I shall say all that remains to be said about it in my next Chapter.

Chapter XXIX.—*Whether a People or a Prince is the more ungrateful.*

In connection with what has been said above, it seems proper to consider whether more notable instances of ingratitude are supplied by princes or peoples. And, to go to the root of the matter, I affirm that this vice of ingratitude has its source either in avarice or in suspicion. For a prince or people when they have sent forth a captain on some important enterprise, by succeeding in which he earns a great name, are bound in return to reward him; and if moved by avarice and covetousness they fail to do so, or if, instead of rewarding, they wrong and disgrace him, they commit an error which is not only without excuse, but brings with it undying infamy. And, in fact, we find many princes who have sinned in this way, for the cause given by Cornelius Tacitus when he says, that "*men are readier to pay back injuries than benefits, since to requite a benefit is felt to be a burthen, to return an injury a gain.*"[1]

When, however, reward is withheld, or, to speak more correctly, where offence is given, not from avarice but from suspicion, the prince or people may deserve some excuse; and we read of many instances of ingratitude proceeding from this cause. For the captain who by his valour has won new dominions for his prince, since while overcoming his enemies, he at the same time covers himself with glory and enriches his soldiers, must needs acquire such credit with his own followers, and with the enemy, and also with the subjects of his prince, as cannot be wholly agreeable to the master who sent him forth. And since men are by nature ambitious as well as jealous, and none loves to set a limit to his fortunes, the suspicion which at once lays hold of the prince when he sees his captain victorious, is sure to be inflamed by some arrogant act or word of the captain himself. So that the prince will be unable to think of anything but how to secure himself; and to this end will contrive how he may put his captain to death, or at any rate deprive him of the credit he has gained with the army and among the people; doing all he can to show that the victory was not won by his valour, but by good fortune, or by the cowardice of the enemy, or by the skill and prudence of those commanders who were with him at this or the other battle.

After Vespasian, who was then in Judæa, had been proclaimed emperor by his army, Antonius Primus, who commanded another army in Illyria, adopted his cause, and marching into Italy against Vitellius who had been proclaimed emperor in Rome, courageously defeated two armies under that prince, and occupied Rome; so that Mutianus, who was sent thither by Vespasian, found everything done to his hand, and all difficulties surmounted by the valour of Antonius. But all the reward which Antonius had for his pains, was, that Mutianus forthwith deprived him of his command of the army, and by degrees diminished his authority in Rome till none was left him. Thereupon Antonius went to join Vespasian, who was still in Asia; by whom he was so coldly received and so little considered, that in despair he put himself to death. And of cases like this, history is full. Every man living at the present hour knows with what zeal and courage Gonsalvo of Cordova, while conducting the war in Naples against the French, conquered and subdued that kingdom for his master Ferdinand of Aragon; and how his services were requited by Ferdinand coming from Aragon to Naples, and first of all depriving him of the command of the army, afterwards of the fortresses, and finally carrying him back with him to Spain, where soon after he died in disgrace.

This jealousy, then, is so natural to princes, that they cannot guard themselves against it, nor show gratitude to those who serving under their standard have gained great victories and made great conquests on their behalf. And if it be impossible for princes to free their minds from such suspicions, there is nothing strange or surprising that a people should be unable to do so. For as a city living under free institutions has two ends always before it, namely to acquire liberty and to preserve it, it must of necessity be led by its excessive passion for liberty to make mistakes in the pursuit of both these objects. Of the mistakes it commits in the effort to acquire liberty, I shall speak, hereafter, in the proper place. Of mistakes committed in the endeavour to preserve liberty are to be noted, the injuring those citizens who ought to be rewarded, and the suspecting those who should be trusted. Now, although in a State which has grown corrupt these errors occasion great evils, and commonly lead to a tyranny, as happened in Rome when Cæsar took by force what ingratitude had denied him, they are nevertheless the cause of much good in the republic which has not been corrupted, since they prolong the duration of its free institutions, and make men, through fear of punishment, better and less ambitious. Of all peoples possessed of great power, the Romans, for the reasons I have given, have undoubtedly been the least ungrateful, since we have no other instance of their ingratitude to cite, save that of Scipio. For both Coriolanus and Camillus were banished on account of the wrongs which they inflicted on the commons; and though the former was not forgiven because he constantly retained ill will against the people, the latter was not only recalled, but for the rest of his life honoured as a prince. But the ingratitude shown towards Scipio arose from the suspicion wherewith the citizens came to regard him, which they had not felt in the case of the others, and which was occasioned by the greatness of the enemy whom he had overthrown, the fame he had won by prevailing in so dangerous and protracted a war, the suddenness of his victories, and, finally, the favour which his youth, together with his prudence and his other memorable qualities had gained for him. These qualities were, in truth, so remarkable that the very magistrates, not to speak of others, stood in awe of his authority, a circumstance displeasing to prudent citizens, as before unheard of in Rome. In short, his whole bearing and character were so much out of the common, that even the elder Cato, so celebrated for his austere virtue, was the first to declare against him, saying that no city could be deemed free which contained a citizen who was feared by the magistrates. And since, in this instance, the Romans followed the opinion of Cato, they merit that excuse which, as I have said already, should be extended to the prince or people who are ungrateful through suspicion.

In conclusion it is to be said that while this vice of ingratitude has its origin either in avarice or in suspicion, commonwealths are rarely led into it by avarice, and far seldomer than princes by suspicion, having, as shall presently be shown, far less reason than princes for suspecting.

[Footnote 1: Proclivius est injuriæ quam beneficio vicem exsolvere, quia gratia oneri, ultio in quastu habetur. *Tacit. Hist.* iv. 2.]

Chapter XXX.—*How Princes and Commonwealths may avoid the vice of Ingratitude; and how a Captain or Citizen may escape being undone by it.*

That he may not be tormented by suspicion, nor show ungrateful, a prince should go himself on his wars as the Roman emperors did at first, as the Turk does now, and, in short, as all valiant princes have done and do. For when it is the prince himself who conquers, the glory and the gain are all his own; but when he is absent, since the glory is another's, it will seem to the prince that he profits nothing by the gain, unless that glory be quenched which he knew not how to win for himself; and when he thus becomes ungrateful and unjust, doubtless his loss is greater than his gain. To the prince, therefore, who, either through indolence or from want of foresight, sends forth a captain to conduct his wars while he himself remains inactive at home, I have no advice to offer which he does not already know. But I would counsel the captain whom he sends, since I am sure that he can never escape the attacks of ingratitude, to follow one or other of two courses, and either quit his command at once after a victory, and place himself in the hands of his prince, while carefully abstaining from every vainglorious or ambitious act, so that the prince, being relieved from all suspicion, may be disposed to reward, or at any rate not to injure him; or else, should he think it inexpedient for him to act in this way, to take boldly the contrary course, and fearlessly to follow out all such measures as he thinks will secure for himself, and not for his prince, whatever he has gained; conciliating the good-will of his soldiers and fellow-citizens, forming new friendships with neighbouring potentates, placing his own adherents in fortified towns, corrupting the chief officers of his army and getting rid of those whom he fails to corrupt, and by all similar means endeavouring to punish his master for the ingratitude which he looks for at his hands. These are the only two courses open; but since, as I said before, men know not how to be wholly good or wholly bad, it will never happen that after a victory a captain will quit his army and conduct himself modestly, nor yet that he will venture to use those hardy methods which have in them some strain of greatness; and so, remaining undecided, he will be crushed while he still wavers and doubts.

A commonwealth desiring to avoid the vice of ingratitude is, as compared with a prince, at this disadvantage, that while a prince can go himself on his expeditions, the commonwealth must send some one of its citizens. As a remedy, I would recommend that course being adopted which was followed by the Roman republic in order to be less ungrateful than others, having its origin in the nature of the Roman government. For the whole city, nobles and commons alike, taking part in her wars, there were always found in Rome at every stage of her history, so many valiant and successful soldiers, that by reason of their number, and from one acting as a check upon another, the nation had never ground to be jealous of any one man among them; while they, on their part, lived uprightly, and were careful to betray no sign of ambition, nor give the people the least cause to distrust them as ambitious; so that he obtained most glory from his dictatorship who was first to lay it down. Which conduct, as it excited no suspicion, could occasion no ingratitude.

We see, then, that the commonwealth which would have no cause to be ungrateful, must act as Rome did; and that the citizen who would escape ingratitude, must observe those precautions which were observed by Roman citizens.

Chapter XXXI.—*That the Roman Captains were never punished with extreme severity for Misconduct; and where loss resulted to the Republic merely through their Ignorance or Want of Judgment, were not punished at all.*

The Romans were not only, as has been said above, less ungrateful than other republics, but were also more lenient and more considerate than others in punishing the captains of their armies. For if these erred of set purpose, they chastised them with gentleness; while if they erred through ignorance, so far from punishing, they even honoured and rewarded them. And this conduct was well considered. For as they judged it of the utmost moment, that those in command of their armies should, in all they had to do, have their minds undisturbed and free from external anxieties, they would not add further difficulty and danger to a task in itself both dangerous and difficult, lest none should ever be found to act with valour. For supposing them to be sending forth an army against Philip of Macedon in Greece or against Hannibal in Italy, or against any other enemy at whose hands they had already sustained reverses, the captain in command of that expedition would be weighted with all the grave and important cares which attend such enterprises. But if to all these cares, had been added the example of Roman generals crucified or otherwise put to death for having lost battles, it would have been impossible for a commander surrounded by so many causes for anxiety to have acted with vigour and decision. For which reason, and because they thought that to such persons the mere ignominy of defeat was in itself punishment enough, they would not dishearten their generals by inflicting on them any heavier penalty.

Of errors committed not through ignorance, the following is an instance. Sergius and Virginius were engaged in the siege of Veii, each being in command of a division of the army, and while Sergius was set to guard against the approach of the Etruscans, it fell to Virginius to watch the town. But Sergius being attacked by the Faliscans and other tribes, chose rather to be defeated and routed than ask aid from Virginius, who, on his part, awaiting the humiliation of his rival, was willing to see his country dishonoured and an army destroyed, sooner than go unasked to his relief. This was notable misconduct, and likely, unless both offenders were punished, to bring discredit on the Roman name. But whereas another republic would have punished these men with death, the Romans were content to inflict only a money fine: not because the offence did not in itself deserve severe handling, but because they were unwilling, for the reasons already given, to depart in this instance from their ancient practice.

Of errors committed through ignorance we have no better example than in the case of Varro, through whose rashness the Romans were defeated by Hannibal at Cannæ, where the republic well-nigh lost its liberty. But because he had acted through ignorance and with no evil design, they not only refrained from punishing him, but even treated him with distinction; the whole senate going forth to meet him on his return to Rome, and as they could not thank him for having fought, thanking him for having come back, and for not having despaired of the fortunes his country.

Again, when Papirius Cursor would have had Fabius put to death, because, contrary to his orders, he had fought with the Samnites, among the reasons pleaded by the father of Fabius against the persistency of the dictator, he urged that never on the occasion of the defeat of any of their captains had the Romans done what Papirius desired them to do on the occasion of a victory.

Chapter XXXII.—*That a Prince or Commonwealth should not delay conferring Benefits until they are themselves in difficulties.*

The Romans found it for their advantage to be generous to the commons at a season of danger, when Porsenna came to attack Rome and restore the Tarquins. For the senate, apprehending that the people might choose rather to take back their kings than to support a war, secured their adherence by relieving them of the duty on salt and of all their other burthens; saying that "*the poor did enough for the common welfare in rearing their offspring.*" In return for which indulgence the commons were content to undergo war, siege, and famine. Let no one however, relying on this example, delay conciliating the people till danger has actually come; or, if he do, let him not hope to have the same good fortune as the Romans. For the mass of the people will consider that they have to thank not him, but his enemies, and that there is ground to fear that when the danger has passed away, he will take back what he gave under compulsion, and, therefore, that to him they lie under no obligation. And the reason why the course followed by the Romans succeeded, was that the State was still new and unsettled. Besides which, the people knew that laws had already been passed in their favour, as, for instance, the law allowing an appeal to the tribunes, and could therefore persuade themselves that the benefits granted them proceeded from the good-will entertained towards them by the senate, and were not due merely to the approach of an enemy. Moreover, the memory of their kings, by whom they had in many ways been wronged and ill-treated, was still fresh in their minds. But since like conditions seldom recur, it can only rarely happen that like remedies are useful. Wherefore, all, whether princes or republics, who hold the reins of government, ought to think beforehand of the adverse times which may await them, and of what help they may then stand in need; and ought so to live with their people as they would think right were they suffering under any calamity. And, whosoever, whether prince or republic, but prince more especially, behaves otherwise, and believes that after the event and when danger is upon him he will be able to win men over by benefits, deceives himself, and will not merely fail to maintain his place, but will even precipitate his downfall.

Chapter XXXIII.—*When a Mischief has grown up in, or against a State, it is safer to temporize with than to meet it with Violence.*

As Rome grew in fame, power, and dominion, her neighbours, who at first had taken no heed to the injury which this new republic might do them, began too late to see their mistake, and desiring to remedy what should have been remedied before, combined against her to the number of forty nations. Whereupon the Romans, resorting to a method usual with them in seasons of peril, appointed a dictator; that is, gave power to one man to decide without advice, and carry out his resolves without appeal. Which expedient, as it then enabled them to overcome the dangers by which they were threatened, so always afterwards proved most serviceable, when, at any time during the growth of their power, difficulties arose to embarrass their republic.

In connection with this league against Rome we have first to note, that when a mischief which springs up either in or against a republic, and whether occasioned by internal or external causes, has grown to such proportions that it begins to fill the whole community with alarm, it is a far safer course to temporize with it than to attempt to quell it by violence. For commonly those who make this attempt only add fuel to the flame, and hasten the impending ruin. Such disorders arise in a republic more often from internal causes than external, either through some citizen being suffered to acquire undue influence, or from the corruption of some institution of that republic, which had once been the life and sinew of its freedom; and from this corruption being allowed to gain such head that the attempt to check it is more dangerous than to let it be. And it is all the harder to recognize these disorders in their beginning, because it seems natural to men to look with favour on the beginnings of things. Favour of this sort, more than by anything else, is attracted by those actions which seem to have in them a quality of greatness, or which are performed by the young. For when in a republic some young man is seen to come forward endowed with rare excellence, the eyes of all the citizens are at once turned upon him, and all, without distinction, concur to do him honour; so that if he have one spark of ambition, the advantages which he has from nature, together with those he takes from this favourable disposition of men's minds, raise him to such a pitch of power, that when the citizens at last see their mistake it is almost impossible for them to correct it; and when they do what they can to oppose his influence the only result is to extend it. Of this I might cite numerous examples, but shall content myself with one relating to our own city.

Cosimo de' Medici, to whom the house of the Medici in Florence owes the origin of its fortunes, acquired so great a name from the favour wherewith his own prudence and the blindness of others invested him, that coming to be held in awe by the government, his fellow-citizens deemed it dangerous to offend him, but still more dangerous to let him alone. Nicolò da Uzzano, his cotemporary, who was accounted well versed in all civil affairs, but who had made a first mistake in not discerning the dangers which might grow from the rising influence of **Cosimo**, would never while he lived, permit a second mistake to be made in attempting to crush him; judging that such an attempt would be the ruin of the State, as in truth it proved after his death. For some who survived him, disregarding his counsels, combined against **Cosimo** and banished him from Florence. And so it came about that the partisans of **Cosimo**, angry at the wrong done him, soon afterwards recalled him and made him prince of the republic, a dignity he never would have reached but for this open opposition. The very same thing happened in Rome in the case of Cæsar. For his services having gained him the good-will of Pompey and other citizens, their favour was presently turned to fear, as Cicero testifies where he says that "it was late that Pompey began to fear Cæsar." This fear led men to think of remedies, and the remedies to which they resorted accelerated the destruction of the republic.

I say, then, that since it is difficult to recognize these disorders in their beginning, because of the false impressions which things produce at the first, it is a wiser course when they become known, to temporize with them than to oppose them; for when you temporize, either they die out of themselves, or at any rate the injury they do is deferred. And the prince who would suppress such disorders or oppose himself to their force and onset, must always be on his guard, lest he help where he would hinder, retard when he would advance, and drown the plant he thinks to water. He must therefore study well the symptoms of the disease; and, if he believe himself equal to the cure, grapple with it fearlessly; if not, he must let it be, and not attempt to treat it in any way. For, otherwise, it will fare with him as it fared with those neighbours of Rome, for whom it would have been safer, after that city had grown to be so great, to have sought to soothe and restrain her by peaceful arts, than to provoke her by open war to contrive new means of attack and new methods of defence. For this league had no other effect than to make the Romans more united and resolute than before, and to bethink themselves of new expedients whereby their power was still more rapidly advanced; among which was the creation of a dictator; for this innovation not only enabled them to surmount the dangers which then threatened them, but was afterwards the means of escaping infinite calamities into which, without it, the republic must have fallen.

Chapter XXXIV.—*That the authority of the Dictator did good and not harm to the Roman Republic: and that it is not those Powers which are given by the free suffrages of the People, but those which ambitious Citizens usurp for themselves, that are pernicious to a State.*

Those citizens who first devised a dictatorship for Rome have been blamed by certain writers, as though this had been the cause of the tyranny afterwards established there. For these authors allege that the first tyrant of Rome governed it with the title of Dictator, and that, but for the existence of the office, Cæsar could never have cloaked his usurpation under a constitutional name. He who first took up this opinion had not well considered the matter, and his conclusion has been accepted without good ground. For it was not the name nor office of Dictator which brought Rome to servitude, but the influence which certain of her citizens were able to assume from the prolongation of their term of power; so that even had the name of Dictator been wanting in Rome, some other had been found to serve their ends, since power may readily give titles, but not titles power. We find, accordingly, that while the dictatorship was conferred in conformity with public ordinances, and not through personal influence, it was constantly beneficial to the city. For it is the magistracies created and the powers usurped in unconstitutional ways that hurt a republic, not those which conform to ordinary rule; so that in Rome, through the whole period of her history, we never find a dictator who acted otherwise than well for the republic. For which there were the plainest reasons. In the first place, to enable a citizen to work harm and to acquire undue authority, many circumstances must be present which never can be present in a State which is not corrupted. For such a citizen must be exceedingly rich, and must have many retainers and partisans, whom he cannot have where the laws are strictly observed, and who, if he had them, would occasion so much alarm, that the free suffrage of the people would seldom be in his favour. In the second place, the dictator was not created for life, but for a fixed term, and only to meet the emergency for which he was appointed. Power was indeed given him to determine by himself what measures the exigency demanded; to do what he had to do without consultation; and to punish without appeal. But he had no authority to do anything to the prejudice of the State, as it would have been to deprive the senate or the people of their privileges, to subvert the ancient institutions of the city, or introduce new. So that taking into account the brief time for which his office lasted, its limited authority, and the circumstance that the Roman people were still uncorrupted, it was impossible for him to overstep the just limits of his power so as to injure the city; and in fact we find that he was always useful to it.

And, in truth, among the institutions of Rome, this of the dictatorship deserves our special admiration, and to be linked with the chief causes of her greatness; for without some such safeguard a city can hardly pass unharmed through extraordinary dangers. Because as the ordinary institutions of a commonwealth work but slowly, no council and no magistrate having authority to act in everything alone, but in most matters one standing in need of the other, and time being required to reconcile their differences, the remedies which they provide are most dangerous when they have to be applied in cases which do not brook delay. For which reason, every republic ought to have some resource of this nature provided by its constitution; as we find that the Republic of Venice, one of the best of those now existing, has in cases of urgent danger reserved authority to a few of her citizens, if agreed among themselves, to determine without further consultation what course is to be followed. When a republic is not provided with some safeguard such as this, either it must be ruined by observing constitutional forms, or else, to save it, these must be broken through. But in a republic nothing should be left to be effected by irregular methods, because, although for the time the irregularity may be useful, the example will nevertheless be pernicious, as giving rise to a practice of violating the laws for good ends, under colour of which they may afterwards be violated for ends which are not good. For which reason, that can never become a perfect republic wherein every contingency has not been foreseen and provided for by the laws, and the method of dealing with it defined. To sum up, therefore, I say that those republics which cannot in sudden emergencies resort either to a dictator or to some similar authority, will, when the danger is serious, always be undone.

We may note, moreover, how prudently the Romans, in introducing this new office, contrived the conditions under which it was to be exercised. For perceiving that the appointment of a dictator involved something of humiliation for the consuls, who, from being the heads of the State, were reduced to render obedience like every one else, and anticipating that this might give offence, they determined that the power to appoint should rest with the consuls, thinking that when the occasion came when Rome should have need of this regal authority, they would have the consuls acting willingly and feeling the less aggrieved from the appointment being in their own hands. For those wounds or other injuries which a man inflicts upon himself by choice, and of his own free will, pain him far less than those inflicted by another. Nevertheless, in the later days of the republic the Romans were wont to entrust this power to a consul instead of to a dictator, using the formula, *Videat consul ne quid respublica detrimenti capiat.*

But to return to the matter in hand, I say briefly, that when the neighbours of Rome sought to crush her, they led her to take measures not merely for her readier defence, but such as enabled her to attack them with a stronger force, with better skill, and with an undivided command.

Chapter XXXV—*Why the Creation of the Decemvirate in Rome, although brought about by the free and open Suffrage of the Citizens, was hurtful to the Liberties of that Republic*

The fact of those ten citizens who were chosen by the Roman people to make laws for Rome, in time becoming her tyrants and depriving her of her freedom, may seem contrary to what I have said above, namely that it is the authority which is violently usurped, and not that conferred by the free suffrages of the people which is injurious to a republic. Here, however, we have to take into account both the mode in which, and the term for which authority is given. Where authority is unrestricted and is conferred for a long term, meaning by that for a year or more, it is always attended with danger, and its results will be good or bad according as the men are good or bad to whom it is committed. Now when we compare the authority of the Ten with that possessed by the dictator, we see that the power placed in the hands of the former was out of all proportion greater than that entrusted to the latter. For when a dictator was appointed there still remained the tribunes, the consuls, and the senate, all of them invested with authority of which the dictator could not deprive them. For even if he could have taken his consulship from one man, or his status as a senator from another, he could not abolish the senatorial rank nor pass new laws. So that the senate, the consuls, and the tribunes continuing to exist with undiminished authority were a check upon him and kept him in the right road. But on the creation of the Ten, the opposite of all this took place. For on their appointment, consuls and tribunes were swept away, and express powers were given to the new magistrates to make laws and do whatever else they thought fit, with the entire authority of the whole Roman people. So that finding themselves alone without consuls or tribunes to control them, and with no appeal against them to the people, and thus there being none to keep a watch upon them, and further being stimulated by the ambition of Appius, in the second year of their office they began to wax insolent.

Let it be noted, therefore, that when it is said that authority given by the public vote is never hurtful to any commonwealth, it is assumed that the people will never be led to confer that authority without due limitations, or for other than a reasonable term. Should they, however either from being deceived or otherwise blinded, be induced to bestow authority imprudently, as the Romans bestowed it on the Ten, it will always fare with them as with the Romans. And this may readily be understood on reflecting what causes operated to keep the dictator good, what to make the Ten bad, and by observing how those republics which have been accounted well governed, have acted when conferring authority for an extended period, as the Spartans on their kings and the Venetians on their doges; for it will be seen that in both these instances the authority was controlled by checks which made it impossible for it to be abused. But where an uncontrolled authority is given, no security is afforded by the circumstance that the body of the people is not corrupted; for in the briefest possible time absolute authority will make a people corrupt, and obtain for itself friends and partisans. Nor will it be any hindrance to him in whom such authority is vested, that he is poor and without connections, for wealth and every other advantage will quickly follow, as shall be shown more fully when we discuss the appointment of the Ten.

Chapter XXXVI.—*That Citizens who have held the higher Offices of a Commonwealth should not disdain the lower*.

Under the consuls M. Fabius and Cn. Manlius, the Romans had a memorable victory in a battle fought with the Veientines and the Etruscans, in which Q. Fabius, brother of the consul, who had himself been consul the year before, was slain. This event may lead us to remark how well the methods followed by the city of Rome were suited to increase her power, and how great a mistake is made by other republics in departing from them. For, eager as the Romans were in the pursuit of glory, they never esteemed it a dishonour to obey one whom before they had commanded, or to find themselves serving in the ranks of an army which once they had led. This usage, however, is opposed to the ideas, the rules, and the practice which prevail at the present day, as, for instance, in Venice, where the notion still obtains that a citizen who has filled a great office should be ashamed to accept a less; and where the State itself permits him to decline it. This course, assuming it to lend lustre to individual citizens, is plainly to the disadvantage of the community, which has reason to hope more from, and to trust more to, the citizen who descends from a high office to fill a lower, than him who rises from a low office to fill a high one; for in the latter no confidence can reasonably be placed, unless he be seen to have others about him of such credit and worth that it may be hoped their wise counsels and influence will correct his inexperience. But had the usage which prevails in Venice and in other modern commonwealths and kingdoms, prevailed in Rome whereby he who had once been consul was never afterwards to go with the army except as consul, numberless results must have followed detrimental to the free institutions of that city; as well from the mistakes which the inexperience of new men would have occasioned, as because from their ambition having a freer course, and from their having none near them in whose presence they might fear to do amiss, they would have grown less scrupulous; and in this way the public service must have suffered grave harm.

Chapter XXXVII.—*Of the Mischief bred in Rome by the Agrarian Law: and how it is a great source of disorder in a Commonwealth to pass a Law opposed to ancient Usage and with stringent retrospective Effect.*

It has been said by ancient writers that to be pinched by adversity or pampered by prosperity is the common lot of men, and that in whichever way they are acted upon the result is the same. For when no longer urged to war on one another by necessity, they are urged by ambition, which has such dominion in their hearts that it never leaves them to whatsoever heights they climb. For nature has so ordered it that while they desire everything, it is impossible for them to have everything, and thus their desires being always in excess of their capacity to gratify them, they remain constantly dissatisfied and discontented. And hence the vicissitudes in human affairs. For some seeking to enlarge their possessions, and some to keep what they have got, wars and enmities ensue, from which result the ruin of one country and the growth of another.

I am led to these reflections from observing that the commons of Rome were not content to secure themselves against the nobles by the creation of tribunes, a measure to which they were driven by necessity, but after effecting this, forthwith entered upon an ambitious contest with the nobles, seeking to share with them what all men most esteem, namely, their honours and their wealth. Hence was bred that disorder from which sprang the feuds relating to the Agrarian Laws, and which led in the end to the downfall of the Roman republic. And although it should be the object of every well-governed commonwealth to make the State rich and keep individual citizens poor it must be allowed that in the matter of this law the city of Rome was to blame; whether for having passed it at first in such a shape as to require it to be continually recast; or for having postponed it so long that its retrospective effect was the occasion of tumult; or else, because, although rightly framed at first, it had come in its operation to be perverted. But in whatever way it happened, so it was, that this law was never spoken of in Rome without the whole city being convulsed.

The law itself embraced two principal provisions. By one it was enacted that no citizen should possess more than a fixed number of acres of land; by the other that all lands taken from the enemy should be distributed among the whole people. A twofold blow was thus aimed at the nobles; since all who possessed more land than the law allowed, as most of the nobles did, fell to be deprived of it; while by dividing the lands of the enemy among the whole people, the road to wealth was closed. These two grounds of offence being given to a powerful class, to whom it appeared that by resisting the law they did a service to the State, the whole city, as I have said, was thrown into an uproar on the mere mention of its name. The nobles indeed sought to temporize, and to prevail by patience and address; sometimes calling out the army, sometimes opposing another tribune to the one who was promoting the law, and sometimes coming to a compromise by sending a colony into the lands which were to be divided; as was done in the case of the territory of Antium, whither, on a dispute concerning the law having arisen, settlers were sent from Rome, and the land made over to them. In speaking of which colony Titus Livius makes the notable remark, that hardly any one in Rome could be got to take part in it, so much readier were the commons to indulge in covetous schemes at home, than to realize them by leaving it.

The ill humour engendered by this contest continued to prevail until the Romans began to carry their arms into the remoter parts of Italy and to countries beyond its shores; after which it seemed for a time to slumber—and this, because the lands held by the enemies of Rome, out of sight of her citizens and too remote to be conveniently cultivated, came to be less desired. Whereupon the Romans grew less eager to punish their enemies by dividing their lands, and were content, when they deprived any city of its territory, to send colonists to occupy it. For causes such as these, the measure remained in abeyance down to the time of the Gracchi; but being by them revived, finally overthrew the liberty of Rome. For as it found the power of its adversaries doubled, such a flame of hatred was kindled between commons and senate, that, regardless of all civil restraints, they resorted to arms and bloodshed. And as the public magistrates were powerless to provide a remedy, each of the two factions having no longer any hopes from them, resolved to do what it could for itself, and to set up a chief for its own protection. On reaching this stage of tumult and disorder, the commons lent their influence to Marius, making him four times consul; whose authority, lasting thus long, and with very brief intervals, became so firmly rooted that he was able to make himself consul other three times. Against this scourge, the nobles, lacking other defence, set themselves to favour Sylla, and placing him at the head of their faction, entered on the civil wars; wherein, after much blood had been spilt, and after many changes of fortune, they got the better of their adversaries. But afterwards, in the time of Cæsar and Pompey, the distemper broke out afresh; for Cæsar heading the Marian party, and Pompey, that of Sylla, and war ensuing, the victory remained with Cæsar, who was the first tyrant in Rome; after whose time that city was never again free. Such, therefore, was the beginning and such the end of the Agrarian Law.

But since it has elsewhere been said that the struggle between the commons and senate of Rome preserved her liberties, as giving rise to laws favourable to freedom, it might seem that the consequences of the Agrarian Law are opposed to that view. I am not, however, led to alter my opinion on this account; for I maintain that the ambition of the great is so pernicious that unless controlled and counteracted in a variety of ways, it will always reduce a city to speedy ruin. So that if the controversy over the Agrarian Laws took three hundred years to bring Rome to slavery, she would in all likelihood have been brought to slavery in a far shorter time, had not the commons, by means of this law, and by other demands, constantly restrained the ambition of the nobles.

We may also learn from this contest how much more men value wealth than honours; for in the matter of honours, the Roman nobles always gave way to the commons without any extraordinary resistance; but when it came to be a question of property, so stubborn were they in its defence, that the commons to effect their ends had to resort to those irregular methods which have been described above. Of which irregularities the prime movers were the Gracchi, whose motives are more to be commended than their measures; since to pass a law with stringent retrospective effect, in order to remove an abuse of long standing in a republic, is an unwise step, and one which, as I have already shown at length, can have no other result than to accelerate the mischief to which the abuse leads; whereas, if you temporize, either the abuse develops more slowly, or else, in course of time, and before it comes to a head, dies out of itself.

Chapter XXXVIII.—*That weak Republics are irresolute and undecided; and that the course they may take depends more on Necessity than Choice.*

A terrible pestilence breaking out in Rome seemed to the Equians and Volscians to offer a fit opportunity for crushing her. The two nations, therefore, assembling a great army, attacked the Latins and Hernicians and laid waste their country. Whereupon the Latins and Hernicians were forced to make their case known to the Romans, and to ask to be defended by them. The Romans, who were sorely afflicted by the pestilence, answered that they must look to their own defence, and with their own forces, since Rome was in no position to succour them.

Here we recognize the prudence and magnanimity of the Roman senate, and how at all times, and in all changes of fortune, they assumed the responsibility of determining the course their country should take; and were not ashamed, when necessary, to decide on a course contrary to that which was usual with them, or which they had decided to follow on some other occasion. I say this because on other occasions this same senate had forbidden these nations to defend themselves; and a less prudent assembly might have thought it lowered their credit to withdraw that prohibition. But the Roman senate always took a sound view of things, and always accepted the least hurtful course as the best. So that, although it was distasteful to them not to be able to defend their subjects, and equally distasteful—both for the reasons given, and for others which may be understood—that their subjects should take up arms in their absence, nevertheless knowing that these must have recourse to arms in any case, since the enemy was upon them, they took an honourable course in deciding that what had to be done should be done with their leave, lest men driven to disobey by necessity should come afterwards to disobey from choice. And although this may seem the course which every republic ought reasonably to follow, nevertheless weak and badly-advised republics cannot make up their minds to follow it, not knowing how to do themselves honour in like extremities.

After Duke Valentino had taken Faenza and forced Bologna to yield to his terms, desiring to return to Rome through Tuscany, he sent one of his people to Florence to ask leave for himself and his army to pass. A council was held in Florence to consider how this request should be dealt with, but no one was favourable to the leave asked for being granted. Wherein the Roman method was not followed. For as the Duke had a very strong force with him, while the Florentines were so bare of troops that they could not have prevented his passage, it would have been far more for their credit that he should seem to pass with their consent, than that he should pass in spite of them; because, while discredit had to be incurred either way, they would have incurred less by acceding to his demand.

But of all courses the worst for a weak State is to be irresolute; for then whatever it does will seem to be done under compulsion, so that if by chance it should do anything well, this will be set down to necessity and not to prudence. Of this I shall cite two other instances happening in our own times, and in our own country. In the year 1500, King Louis of France, after recovering Milan, being desirous to restore Pisa to the Florentines, so as to obtain payment from them of the fifty thousand ducats which they had promised him on the restitution being completed, sent troops to Pisa under M. Beaumont, in whom, though a Frenchman, the Florentines put much trust. Beaumont accordingly took up his position with his forces between Cascina and Pisa, to be in readiness to attack the town. After he had been there for some days making arrangements for the assault, envoys came to him from Pisa offering to surrender their city to the French if a promise were given in the king's name, not to hand it over to the Florentines until four months had run. This condition was absolutely rejected by the Florentines, and the siege being proceeded with, they were forced to retire with disgrace. Now the proposal of the Pisans was rejected by the Florentines for no other reason than that they distrusted the good faith of the King, into whose hands their weakness obliged them to commit themselves, and did not reflect how much more it was for their interest that, by obtaining entrance into Pisa, he should have it in his power to restore the town to them, or, failing to restore it, should at once disclose his designs, than that remaining outside he should put them off with promises for which they had to pay. It would therefore have been a far better course for the Florentines to have agreed to Beaumont taking possession on whatever terms.

This was seen afterwards by experience in the year 1502, when, on the revolt of Arezzo, M. Imbalt was sent by the King of France with French troops to assist the Florentines. For when he got near Arezzo, and began to negotiate with the Aretines, who, like the Pisans, were willing to surrender their town on terms, the acceptance of these terms was strongly disapproved in Florence; which Imbalt learning, and thinking that the Florentines were acting with little sense, he took the entire settlement of conditions into his own hands, and, without consulting the Florentine commissioners, concluded an arrangement to his own satisfaction, in execution of which he entered Arezzo with his army. And he let the Florentines know that he thought them fools and ignorant of the ways of the world; since if they desired to have Arezzo, they could signify their wishes to the King, who would be much better able to give it them when he had his soldiers inside, than when he had them outside the town.

Nevertheless, in Florence they never ceased to blame and abuse M. Imbalt, until at last they came to see that if Beaumont had acted in the same way, they would have got possession Of Pisa as well as of Arezzo.

Applying what has been said to the matter in hand, we find that irresolute republics, unless upon compulsion, never follow wise courses; for wherever there is room for doubt, their weakness will not suffer them to come to any resolve; so that unless their doubts be overcome by some superior force which impels them forward, they remain always in suspense.

Chapter XXXIX.—*That often the same Accidents are seen to befall different Nations.*

Any one comparing the present with the past will soon perceive that in all cities and in all nations there prevail the same desires and passions as always have prevailed; for which reason it should be an easy matter for him who carefully examines past events, to foresee those which are about to happen in any republic, and to apply such remedies as the ancients have used in like cases; or finding none which have been used by them, to strike out new ones, such as they might have used in similar circumstances. But these lessons being neglected or not understood by readers, or, if understood by them, being unknown to rulers, it follows that the same disorders are common to all times.

In the year 1494 the Republic of Florence, having lost a portion of its territories, including Pisa and other towns, was forced to make war against those who had taken possession of them, who being powerful, it followed that great sums were spent on these wars to little purpose. This large expenditure had to be met by heavy taxes which gave occasion to numberless complaints on the part of the people; and inasmuch as the war was conducted by a council of ten citizens, who were styled "the Ten of the War," the multitude began to regard these with displeasure, as though they were the cause of the war and of the consequent expenditure; and at last persuaded themselves that if they got rid of this magistracy there would be an end to the war. Wherefore when the magistracy of "the Ten" should have been renewed, the people did not renew it, but, suffering it to lapse, entrusted their affairs to the "Signory." This course was most pernicious, since not only did it fail to put an end to the war, as the people expected it would, but by setting aside men who had conducted it with prudence, led to such mishaps that not Pisa only, but Arezzo also, and many other towns besides were lost to Florence. Whereupon, the people recognizing their mistake, and that the evil was in the disease and not in the physician, reinstated the magistracy of the Ten.

Similar dissatisfaction grew up in Rome against the consular authority. For the people seeing one war follow another, and that they were never allowed to rest, when they should have ascribed this to the ambition of neighbouring nations who desired their overthrow, ascribed it to the ambition of the nobles, who, as they believed, being unable to wreak their hatred against them within the city, where they were protected by the power of the tribunes, sought to lead them outside the city, where they were under the authority of the consuls, that they might crush them where they were without help. In which belief they thought it necessary either to get rid of the consuls altogether, or so to restrict their powers as to leave them no authority over the people, either in the city or out of it.

The first who attempted to pass a law to this effect was the tribune Terentillus, who proposed that a committee of five should be named to consider and regulate the power of the consuls. This roused the anger of the nobles, to whom it seemed that the greatness of their authority was about to set for ever, and that no part would be left them in the administration of the republic. Such, however, was the obstinacy of the tribunes, that they succeeded in abolishing the consular title, nor were satisfied until, after other changes, it was resolved that, in room of consuls, tribunes should be appointed with consular powers; so much greater was their hatred of the name than of the thing. For a long time matters remained on this footing; till eventually, the commons, discovering their mistake, resumed the appointment of consuls in the same way as the Florentines reverted to "the Ten of the War."

Chapter XL.—*Of the creation of the Decemvirate in Rome, and what therein is to be noted. Wherein among other Matters is shown how the same Causes may lead to the Safety or to the Ruin of a Commonwealth.*

It being my desire to treat fully of those disorders which arose in Rome on the creation of the decemvirate, I think it not amiss first of all to relate what took place at the time of that creation, and then to discuss those circumstances attending it which seem most to deserve notice. These are numerous, and should be well considered, both by those who would maintain the liberties of a commonwealth and by those who would subvert them. For in the course of our inquiry it will be seen that many mistakes prejudicial to freedom were made by the senate and people, and that many were likewise made by Appius, the chief decemvir, prejudicial to that tyranny which it was his aim to establish in Rome.

After much controversy and wrangling between the commons and the nobles as to the framing of new laws by which the freedom of Rome might be better secured, Spurius Posthumius and two other citizens were, by general consent, despatched to Athens to procure copies of the laws which Solon had drawn up for the Athenians, to the end that these might serve as a groundwork for the laws of Rome. On their return, the next step was to depute certain persons to examine these laws and to draft the new code. For which purpose a commission consisting of ten members, among whom was Appius Claudius, a crafty and ambitious citizen, was appointed for a year; and that the commissioners in framing their laws might act without fear or favour, all the other magistracies, and in particular the consulate and tribuneship, were suspended, and the appeal to the people discontinued; so that the decemvirs came to be absolute in Rome. Very soon the whole authority of the commissioners came to be centred in Appius, owing to the favour in which he was held by the commons. For although before he had been regarded as the cruel persecutor of the people, he now showed himself so conciliatory in his bearing that men wondered at the sudden change in his character and disposition.

This set of commissioners, then, behaved discreetly, being attended by no more than twelve lictors, walking in front of that decemvir whom the rest put forward as their chief; and though vested with absolute authority, yet when a Roman citizen had to be tried for murder, they cited him before the people and caused him to be judged by them. Their laws they wrote upon ten tables, but before signing them they exposed them publicly, that every one might read and consider them, and if any defect were discovered in them, it might be corrected before they were finally passed. At this juncture Appius caused it to be notified throughout the city that were two other tables added to these ten, the laws would be complete; hoping that under this belief the people would consent to continue the decemvirate for another year. This consent the people willingly gave, partly to prevent the consuls being reinstated, and partly because they thought they could hold their ground without the aid of the tribunes, who, as has already been said, were the judges in criminal cases.

On it being resolved to reappoint the decemvirate, all the nobles set to canvass for the office, Appius among the foremost; and such cordiality did he display towards the commons while seeking their votes, that the other candidates, "*unable to persuade themselves that so much affability on the part of so proud a man was wholly disinterested,*" began to suspect him; but fearing to oppose him openly, sought to circumvent him, by putting him forward, though the youngest of them all, to declare to the people the names of the proposed decemvirs; thinking that he would not venture to name himself, that being an unusual course in Rome, and held discreditable. "*But what they meant as a hindrance, he turned to account,*" by proposing, to the surprise and displeasure of the whole nobility, his own name first, and then nominating nine others on whose support he thought he could depend.

The new appointments, which were to last for a year, having been made, Appius soon let both commons and nobles know the mistake they had committed, for throwing off the mask, he allowed his innate arrogance to appear, and speedily infected his colleagues with the same spirit; who, to overawe the people and the senate, instead of twelve lictors, appointed one hundred and twenty. For a time their measures were directed against high and low alike; but presently they began to intrigue with the senate, and to attack the commons; and if any of the latter, on being harshly used by one decemvir, ventured to appeal to another, he was worse handled on the appeal than in the first instance. The commons, on discovering their error, began in their despair to turn their eyes towards the nobles, "*and to look for a breeze of freedom from that very quarter whence fearing slavery they had brought the republic to its present straits.*" To the nobles the sufferings of the commons were not displeasing, from the hope "*that disgusted with the existing state of affairs, they too might come to desire the restoration of the consuls.*"

When the year for which the decemvirs were appointed at last came to an end, the two additional tables of the law were ready, but had not yet been published. This was made a pretext by them for prolonging their magistracy, which they took measures to retain by force, gathering round them for this purpose a retinue of young noblemen, whom they enriched with the goods of those citizens whom they had condemned. "*Corrupted by which gifts, these youths came to prefer selfish licence to public freedom.*"

It happened that at this time the Sabines and Volscians began to stir up a war against Rome, and it was during the alarm thereby occasioned that the decemvirs were first made aware how weak was their position. For without the senate they could take no warlike measures, while by assembling the senate they seemed to put an end to their own authority. Nevertheless, being driven to it by necessity, they took this latter course. When the senate met, many of the senators, but particularly Valerius and Horatius, inveighed against the insolence of the decemvirs, whose power would forthwith have been cut short, had not the senate through jealousy of the commons declined to exercise their authority. For they thought that were the decemvirs to lay down office of their own free will, tribunes might not be reappointed. Wherefore they decided for war, and sent forth the armies under command of certain of the decemvirs. But Appius remaining behind to govern the city, it so fell out that he became enamoured of Virginia, and that when he sought to lay violent hands upon her, Virginius, her father, to save her from dishonour, slew her. Thereupon followed tumults in Rome, and mutiny among the soldiers, who, making common cause with the rest of the plebeians, betook themselves to the Sacred Hill, and there remained until the decemvirs laid down their office; when tribunes and consuls being once more appointed, Rome was restored to her ancient freedom.

In these events we note, first of all, that the pernicious step of creating this tyranny in Rome was due to the same causes which commonly give rise to tyrannies in cities; namely, the excessive love of the people for liberty, and the passionate eagerness of the nobles to govern. For when they cannot agree to pass some measure favourable to freedom, one faction or the other sets itself to support some one man, and a tyranny at once springs up. Both parties in Rome consented to the creation of the decemvirs, and to their exercising unrestricted powers, from the desire which the one had to put an end to the consular name, and the other to abolish the authority of the tribunes. When, on the appointment of the decemvirate, it seemed to the commons that Appius had become favourable to their cause, and was ready to attack the nobles, they inclined to support him. But when a people is led to commit this error of lending its support to some one man, in order that he may attack those whom it holds in hatred, if he only be prudent he will inevitably become the tyrant of that city. For he will wait until, with the support of the people, he can deal a fatal blow to the nobles, and will never set himself to oppress the people until the nobles have been rooted out. But when that time comes, the people, although they recognize their servitude, will have none to whom they can turn for help.

Had this method, which has been followed by all who have successfully established tyrannies in republics, been followed by Appius, his power would have been more stable and lasting; whereas, taking the directly opposite course, he could not have acted more unwisely than he did. For in his eagerness to grasp the tyranny, he made himself obnoxious to those who were in fact conferring it, and who could have maintained him in it; and he destroyed those who were his friends, while he sought friendship from those from whom he could not have it. For although it be the desire of the nobles to tyrannize, that section of them which finds itself outside the tyranny is always hostile to the tyrant, who can never succeed in gaining over the entire body of the nobles by reason of their greed and ambition; for no tyrant can ever have honours or wealth enough to satisfy them all.

In abandoning the people, therefore, and siding with the nobles, Appius committed a manifest mistake, as well for the reasons above given, as because to hold a thing by force, he who uses force must needs be stronger than he against whom it is used. Whence it happens that those tyrants who have the mass of the people for their friends and the nobles for their enemies, are more secure than those who have the people for their enemies and the nobles for their friends; because in the former case their authority has the stronger support. For with such support a ruler can maintain himself by the internal strength of his State, as did Nabis, tyrant of Sparta, when attacked by the Romans and by the whole of Greece; for making sure work with the nobles, who were few in number, and having the people on his side, he was able with their assistance to defend himself; which he could not have done had they been against him. But in the case of a city, wherein the tyrant has few friends, its internal strength will not avail him for its defence, and he will have to seek aid from without in one of three shapes. For either he must hire foreign guards to defend his person; or he must arm the peasantry, so that they may play the part which ought to be played by the citizens; or he must league with powerful neighbours for his defence. He who follows these methods and observes them well, may contrive to save himself, though he has the people for his enemy. But Appius could not follow the plan of gaining over the peasantry, since in Rome they and the people were one. And what he might have done he knew not how to do, and so was ruined at the very outset.

In creating the decemvirate, therefore, both the senate and the people made grave mistakes. For although, as already explained, when speaking of the dictatorship, it is those magistrates who make themselves, and not those made by the votes of the people, that are hurtful to freedom; nevertheless the people, in creating magistrates ought to take such precautions as will make it difficult for these to become bad. But the Romans when they ought to have set a check on the decemvirs in order to keep them good, dispensed with it, making them the sole magistrates of Rome, and setting aside all others; and this from the excessive desire of the senate to get rid of the tribunes, and of the commons to get rid of the consuls; by which objects both were so blinded as to fall into all the disorders which ensued. For, as King Ferrando was wont to say, men often behave like certain of the smaller birds, which are so intent on the prey to which nature incites them, that they discern not the eagle hovering overhead for their destruction.

In this Discourse then the mistakes made by the Roman people in their efforts to preserve their freedom and the mistakes made by Appius in his endeavour to obtain the tyranny, have, as I proposed at the outset, been plainly shown.

Chapter XLI.—*That it is unwise to pass at a bound from leniency to severity, or to a haughty bearing from a humble.*

Among the crafty devices used by Appius to aid him in maintaining his authority, this, of suddenly passing from one character to the other extreme, was of no small prejudice to him. For his fraud in pretending to the commons to be well disposed towards them, was happily contrived; as were also the means he took to bring about the reappointment of the decemvirate. Most skilful, too, was his audacity in nominating himself contrary to the expectation of the nobles, and in proposing colleagues on whom he could depend to carry out his ends. But, as I have said already, it was not happily contrived that, after doing all this, he should suddenly turn round, and from being the friend, reveal himself the enemy of the people; haughty instead of humane; cruel instead of kindly; and make this change so rapidly as to leave himself no shadow of excuse, but compel all to recognize the doubleness of his nature. For he who has once seemed good, should he afterwards choose, for his own ends, to become bad, ought to change by slow degrees, and as opportunity serves; so that before his altered nature strip him of old favour, he may have gained for himself an equal share of new, and thus his influence suffer no diminution. For otherwise, being at once unmasked and friendless, he is undone:

Chapter XLII.—*How easily Men become corrupted.*

In this matter of the decemvirate we may likewise note the ease wherewith men become corrupted, and how completely, although born good and well brought up, they change their nature. For we see how favourably disposed the youths whom Appius gathered round him became towards his tyranny, in return for the trifling benefits which they drew from it; and how Quintus Fabius, one of the second decemvirate and a most worthy man, blinded by a little ambition, and misled by the evil counsels of Appius, abandoning his fair fame, betook himself to most unworthy courses, and grew like his master.

Careful consideration of this should make those who frame laws for commonwealths and kingdoms more alive to the necessity of placing restraints on men's evil appetites, and depriving them of all hope of doing wrong with impunity.

Chapter XLIII.—*That Men fighting in their own Cause make good and resolute Soldiers.*

From what has been touched upon above, we are also led to remark how wide is the difference between an army which, having no ground for discontent, fights in its own cause, and one which, being discontented, fights to satisfy the ambition of others. For whereas the Romans were always victorious under the consuls, under the decemvirs they were always defeated. This helps us to understand why it is that mercenary troops are worthless; namely, that they have no incitement to keep them true to you beyond the pittance which you pay them, which neither is nor can be a sufficient motive for such fidelity and devotion as would make them willing to die in your behalf. But in those armies in which there exists not such an attachment towards him for whom they fight as makes them devoted to his cause, there never will be valour enough to withstand an enemy if only he be a little brave. And since such attachment and devotion cannot be looked for from any save your own subjects, you must, if you would preserve your dominions, or maintain your commonwealth or kingdom, arm the natives of your country; as we see to have been done by all those who have achieved great things in war.

Under the decemvirs the ancient valour of the Roman soldiers had in no degree abated; yet, because they were no longer animated by the same good will, they did not exert themselves as they were wont. But so soon as the decemvirate came to an end, and the soldiers began once more to fight as free men, the old spirit was reawakened, and, as a consequence, their enterprises, according to former usage, were brought to a successful close.

Chapter XLIV.—*That the Multitude is helpless without a Head: and that we should not with the same breath threaten and ask leave.*

When Virginia died by her father's hand, the commons of Rome withdrew under arms to the Sacred Hill. Whereupon the senate sent messengers to demand by what sanction they had deserted their commanders and assembled there in arms. And in such reverence was the authority of the senate held, that the commons, lacking leaders, durst make no reply. "Not," says Titus Livius, "that they were at a loss what to answer, but because they had none to answer for them;" words which clearly show how helpless a thing is the multitude when without a head.

This defect was perceived by Virginius, at whose instance twenty military tribunes were appointed by the commons to be their spokesmen with the senate, and to negotiate terms; who, having asked that Valerius and Horatius might be sent to them, to whom their wishes would be made known, these declined to go until the decemvirs had laid down their office. When this was done, and Valerius and Horatius came to the hill where the commons were assembled, the latter demanded that tribunes of the people should be appointed; that in future there should be an appeal to the people from the magistrates of whatever degree; and that all the decemvirs should be given up to them to be burned alive. Valerius and Horatius approved the first two demands, but rejected the last as inhuman; telling the commons that "they were rushing into that very cruelty which they themselves had condemned in others;" and counselling them to say nothing about the decemvirs, but to be satisfied to regain their own power and authority; since thus the way would be open to them for obtaining every redress.

Here we see plainly how foolish and unwise it is to ask a thing and with the same breath to say, "I desire this that I may inflict an injury." For we should never declare our intention beforehand, but watch for every opportunity to carry it out. So that it is enough to ask another for his weapons, without adding, "With these I purpose to destroy you;" for when once you have secured his weapons, you can use them afterwards as you please.

Chapter XLV.—*That it is of evil example, especially in the Maker of a Law, not to observe the Law when made: and that daily to renew acts of injustice in a City is most hurtful to the Governor.*

Terms having been adjusted, and the old order of things restored in Rome, Virginius cited Appius to defend himself before the people; and on his appearing attended by many of the nobles, ordered him to be led to prison. Whereupon Appius began to cry out and appeal to the people. But Virginius told him that he was unworthy to be allowed that appeal which he had himself done away with, or to have that people whom he had wronged for his protectors. Appius rejoined, that the people should not set at nought that right of appeal which they themselves had insisted on with so much zeal. Nevertheless, he was dragged to prison, and before the day of trial slew himself. Now, though the wicked life of Appius merited every punishment, still it was impolitic to violate the laws, more particularly a law which had only just been passed; for nothing, I think, is of worse example in a republic, than to make a law and not to keep it; and most of all, when he who breaks is he that made it.

After the year 1494, the city of Florence reformed its government with the help of the Friar Girolamo Savonarola, whose writings declare his learning, his wisdom, and the excellence of his heart. Among other ordinances for the safety of the citizens, he caused a law to be passed, allowing an appeal to the people from the sentences pronounced by "the Eight" and by the "Signory" in trials for State offences; a law he had long contended for, and carried at last with great difficulty. It so happened that a very short time after it was passed, five citizens were condemned to death by the "Signory" for State offences, and that when they sought to appeal to the people they were not permitted to do so, and the law was violated. This, more than any other mischance, helped to lessen the credit of the Friar; since if his law of appeal was salutary, he should have caused it to be observed; if useless, he ought not to have promoted it. And his inconsistency was the more remarked, because in all the sermons which he preached after the law was broken, he never either blamed or excused the person who had broken it, as though unwilling to condemn, while unable to justify what suited his purposes. This, as betraying the ambitious and partial turn of his mind, took from his reputation and exposed him to much obloquy.

Another thing which greatly hurts a government is to keep alive bitter feelings in men's minds by often renewed attacks on individuals, as was done in Rome after the decemvirate was put an end to. For each of the decemvirs, and other citizens besides, were at different times accused and condemned, so that the greatest alarm was spread through the whole body of the nobles, who came to believe that these prosecutions would never cease until their entire order was exterminated. And this must have led to grave mischief had not Marcus Duilius the tribune provided against it, by an edict which forbade every one, for the period of a year, citing or accusing any Roman citizen, an ordinance which had the effect of reassuring the whole nobility. Here we see how hurtful it is for a prince or commonwealth to keep the minds of their subjects in constant alarm and suspense by continually renewed punishments and violence. And, in truth, no course can be more pernicious. For men who are in fear for their safety will seize on every opportunity for securing themselves against the dangers which surround them, and will grow at once more daring, and less scrupulous in resorting to new courses. For these reasons we should either altogether avoid inflicting injury, or should inflict every injury at a stroke, and then seek to reassure men's minds and suffer them to settle down and rest.

Chapter XLVI.—*That Men climb from one step of Ambition to another, seeking at first to escape Injury and then to injure others.*

As the commons of Rome on recovering their freedom were restored to their former position—nay, to one still stronger since many new laws had been passed which confirmed and extended their authority,—it might reasonably have been hoped that Rome would for a time remain at rest. The event, however, showed the contrary, for from day to day there arose in that city new tumults and fresh dissensions. And since the causes which brought this about have been most judiciously set forth by Titus Livius, it seems to me much to the purpose to cite his own words when he says, that "whenever either the commons or the nobles were humble, the others grew haughty; so that if the commons kept within due bounds, the young nobles began to inflict injuries upon them, against which the tribunes, who were themselves made the objects of outrage, were little able to give redress; while the nobles on their part, although they could not close their eyes to the ill behaviour of their young men, were yet well pleased that if excesses were to be committed, they should be committed by their own faction, and not by the commons. Thus the desire to secure its own liberty prompted each faction to make itself strong enough to oppress the other. For this is the common course of things, that in seeking to escape cause for fear, men come to give others cause to be afraid by inflicting on them those wrongs from which they strive to relieve themselves; as though the choice lay between injuring and being injured."

Herein, among other things, we perceive in what ways commonwealths are overthrown, and how men climb from one ambition to another; and recognize the truth of those words which Sallust puts in the mouth of Cæsar, that "*all ill actions have their origin in fair beginnings.*" [1] For, as I have said already, the ambitious citizen in a commonwealth seeks at the outset to secure himself against injury, not only at the hands of private persons, but also of the magistrates; to effect which he endeavours to gain himself friends. These he obtains by means honourable in appearance, either by supplying them with money or protecting them against the powerful. And because such conduct seems praiseworthy, every one is readily deceived by it, and consequently no remedy is applied. Pursuing these methods without hindrance, this man presently comes to be so powerful that private citizens begin to fear him, and the magistrates to treat him with respect. But when he has advanced thus far on the road to power without encountering opposition, he has reached a point at which it is most dangerous to cope with him; it being dangerous, as I have before explained, to contend with a disorder which has already made progress in a city. Nevertheless, when he has brought things to this pass, you must either endeavour to crush him, at the risk of immediate ruin, or else, unless death or some like accident interpose, you incur inevitable slavery by letting him alone. For when, as I have said, it has come to this that the citizens and even the magistrates fear to offend him and his friends, little further effort will afterwards be needed to enable him to proscribe and ruin whom he pleases.

A republic ought, therefore, to provide by its ordinances that none of its citizens shall, under colour of doing good, have it in their power to do evil, but shall be suffered to acquire such influence only as may aid and not injure freedom. How this may be done, shall presently be explained.

[Footnote 1: Quod omnia mala exempla ex bonis initiis orta sunt. (Sall. Cat. 51.)]

Chapter XLVII.—*That though Men deceive themselves in Generalities, in Particulars they judge truly.*

The commons of Rome having, as I have said, grown disgusted with the consular name, and desiring either that men of plebeian birth should be admitted to the office or its authority be restricted, the nobles, to prevent its degradation in either of these two ways, proposed a middle course, whereby four tribunes, who might either be plebeians or nobles, were to be created with consular authority. This compromise satisfied the commons, who thought they would thus get rid of the consulship, and secure the highest offices of the State for their own order. But here a circumstance happened worth noting. When the four tribunes came to be chosen, the people, who had it in their power to choose all from the commons, chose all from the nobles. With respect to which election Titus Livius observes, that "*the result showed that the people when declaring their honest judgment after controversy was over, were governed by a different spirit from that which had inspired them while contending for their liberties and for a share in public honours.*" The reason for this I believe to be, that men deceive themselves more readily in generals than in particulars. To the commons of Rome it seemed, in the abstract, that they had every right to be admitted to the consulship, since their party in the city was the more numerous, since they bore the greater share of danger in their wars, and since it was they who by their valour kept Rome free and made her powerful. And because it appeared to them, as I have said, that their desire was a reasonable one, they were resolved to satisfy it at all hazards. But when they had to form a particular judgment on the men of their own party, they recognized their defects, and decided that individually no one of them was deserving of what, collectively, they seemed entitled to; and being ashamed of them, turned to bestow their honours on those who deserved them. Of which decision Titus Livius, speaking with due admiration, says, "*Where shall we now find in any one man, that modesty, moderation, and magnanimity which were then common to the entire people?*"

As confirming what I have said, I shall cite another noteworthy incident, which occurred in Capua after the rout of the Romans by Hannibal at Cannæ. For all Italy being convulsed by that defeat, Capua too was threatened with civil tumult, through the hatred which prevailed between her people and senate. But Pacuvius Calavius, who at this time filled the office of chief magistrate, perceiving the danger, took upon himself to reconcile the contending factions. With this object he assembled the Senate and pointed out to them the hatred in which they were held by the people, and the risk they ran of being put to death by them, and of the city, now that the Romans were in distress, being given up to Hannibal. But he added that, were they to consent to leave the matter with him, he thought he could contrive to reconcile them; in the meanwhile, however, he must shut them up in the palace, that, by putting it in the power of the people to punish them, he might secure their safety.

The senate consenting to this proposal, he shut them up in the palace, and summoning the people to a public meeting, told them the time had at last come for them to trample on the insolence of the nobles, and requite the wrongs suffered at their hands; for he had them all safe under bolt and bar; but, as he supposed they did not wish the city to remain without rulers, it was fit, before putting the old senators to death, they should appoint others in their room. Wherefore he had thrown the names of all the old senators into a bag, and would now proceed to draw them out one by one, and as they were drawn would cause them to be put to death, so soon as a successor was found for each. When the first name he drew was declared, there arose a great uproar among the people, all crying out against the cruelty, pride, and arrogance of that senator whose name it was. But on Pacuvius desiring them to propose a substitute, the meeting was quieted, and after a brief pause one of the commons was nominated. No sooner, however, was his name mentioned than one began to whistle, another to laugh, some jeering at him in one way and some in another. And the same thing happening in every case, each and all of those nominated were judged unworthy of senatorial rank. Whereupon Pacuvius, profiting by the opportunity, said, "Since you are agreed that the city would be badly off without a senate, but are not agreed whom to appoint in the room of the old senators, it will, perhaps, be well for you to be reconciled to them; for the fear into which they have been thrown must have so subdued them, that you are sure to find in them that affability which hitherto you have looked for in vain." This proposal being agreed to, a reconciliation followed between the two orders; the commons having seen their error so soon as they were obliged to come to particulars.

A people therefore is apt to err in judging of things and their accidents in the abstract, but on becoming acquainted with particulars, speedily discovers its mistakes. In the year 1494, when her greatest citizens were banished from Florence, and no regular government any longer existed there, but a spirit of licence prevailed, and matters went continually from bad to worse, many Florentines perceiving the decay of their city, and discerning no other cause for it, blamed the ambition of this or the other powerful citizen, who, they thought, was fomenting these disorders with a view to establish a government to his own liking, and to rob them of their liberties. Those who thought thus, would hang about the arcades and public squares, maligning many citizens, and giving it to be understood that if ever they found themselves in the Signory, they would expose the designs of these citizens and have them punished. From time to time it happened that one or another of those who used this language rose to be of the chief magistracy, and so soon as he obtained this advancement, and saw things nearer, became aware whence the disorders I have spoken of really came, the dangers attending them, and the difficulty in dealing with them; and recognizing that they were the growth of the times, and not occasioned by particular men, suddenly altered his views and conduct; a nearer knowledge of facts freeing him from the false impressions he had been led into on a general view of affairs. But those who had heard him speak as a private citizen, when they saw him remain inactive after he was made a magistrate, believed that this arose not from his having obtained any better knowledge of things, but from his having been cajoled or corrupted by the great. And this happening with many men and often, it came to be a proverb among the people, that "*men had one mind in the market-place, another in the palace.*"

Reflecting on what has been said, we see how quickly men's eyes may be opened, if knowing that they deceive themselves in generalities, we can find a way to make them pass to particulars; as Pacuvius did in the case of the Capuans, and the senate in the case of Rome. Nor do I believe that any prudent man need shrink from the judgment of the people in questions relating to particulars, as, for instance, in the distribution of honours and dignities. For in such matters only, the people are either never mistaken, or at any rate far seldomer than a small number of persons would be, were the distribution entrusted to them.

It seems to me, however, not out of place to notice in the following Chapter, a method employed by the Roman senate to enlighten the people in making this distribution.

Chapter XLVIII.—*He who would not have an Office bestowed on some worthless or wicked Person, should contrive that it be solicited by one who is utterly worthless and wicked, or else by one who is in the highest degree noble and good.*

Whenever the senate saw a likelihood of the tribunes with consular powers being chosen exclusively from the commons, it took one or other of two ways,—either by causing the office to be solicited by the most distinguished among the citizens; or else, to confess the truth, by bribing some base and ignoble fellow to fasten himself on to those other plebeians of better quality who were seeking the office, and become a candidate conjointly with them. The latter device made the people ashamed to give, the former ashamed to refuse.

This confirms what I said in my last Chapter, as to the people deceiving themselves in generalities but not in particulars.

Chapter XLIX.—*That if Cities which, like Rome, had their beginning in Freedom, have had difficulty in framing such Laws as would preserve their Freedom, Cities which at the first have been in Subjection will find this almost impossible.*

How hard it is in founding a commonwealth to provide it with all the laws needed to maintain its freedom, is well seen from the history of the Roman Republic. For although ordinances were given it first by Romulus, then by Numa, afterwards by Tullus Hostilius and Servius, and lastly by the Ten created for the express purpose, nevertheless, in the actual government of Rome new needs were continually developed, to meet which, new ordinances had constantly to be devised; as in the creation of the censors, who were one of the chief means by which Rome was kept free during the whole period of her constitutional government. For as the censors became the arbiters of morals in Rome, it was very much owing to them that the progress of the Romans towards corruption was retarded. And though, at the first creation of the office, a mistake was doubtless made in fixing its term at five years, this was corrected not long after by the wisdom of the dictator Mamercus, who passed a law reducing it to eighteen months; a change which the censors then in office took in such ill part, that they deprived Mamercus of his rank as a senator. This step was much blamed both by the commons and the Fathers; still, as our History does not record that Mamercus obtained any redress, we must infer either that the Historian has omitted something, or that on this head the laws of Rome were defective; since it is never well that the laws of a commonwealth should suffer a citizen to incur irremediable wrong because he promotes a measure favourable to freedom.

But returning to the matter under consideration, we have, in connection with the creation of this new office, to note, that if those cities which, as was the case with Rome, have had their beginning in freedom, and have by themselves maintained that freedom, have experienced great difficulty in framing good laws for the preservation of their liberties, it is little to be wondered at that cities which at the first were dependent, should find it not difficult merely but impossible so to shape their ordinances as to enable them to live free and undisturbed. This difficulty we see to have arisen in the case of Florence, which, being subject at first to the power of Rome and subsequently to that of other rulers, remained long in servitude, taking no thought for herself; and even afterwards, when she could breathe more freely and began to frame her own laws, these, since they were blended with ancient ordinances which were bad, could not themselves be good; and thus for the two hundred years of which we have trustworthy record, our city has gone on patching her institutions, without ever possessing a government in respect of which she could truly be termed a commonwealth.

The difficulties which have been felt in Florence are the same as have been felt in all cities which have had a like origin; and although, repeatedly, by the free and public votes of her citizens, ample authority has been given to a few of their number to reform her constitution, no alteration of general utility has ever been introduced, but only such as forwarded the interests of the party to which those commissioned to make changes belonged. This, instead of order, has occasioned the greatest disorder in our city.

But to come to particulars, I say, that among other matters which have to be considered by the founder of a commonwealth, is the question into whose hands should be committed the power of life and death over its citizens' This was well seen to in Rome, where, as a rule, there was a right of appeal to the people, but where, on any urgent case arising in which it might have been dangerous to delay the execution of a judicial sentence, recourse could be had to a dictator with powers to execute justice at once; a remedy, however, never resorted to save in cases of extremity. But Florence, and other cities having a like origin, committed this power into the hands of a foreigner, whom they styled Captain, and as he was open to be corrupted by powerful citizens this was a pernicious course. Altering this arrangement afterwards in consequence of changes in their government, they appointed eight citizens to discharge the office of Captain. But this, for a reason already mentioned, namely that a few will always be governed by the will of a few and these the most powerful, was a change from bad to worse.

The city of Venice has guarded herself against a like danger. For in Venice ten citizens are appointed with power to punish any man without appeal; and because, although possessing the requisite authority, this number might not be sufficient to insure the punishment of the powerful, in addition to their council of Ten, they have also constituted a council of Forty, and have further provided that the council of the "*Pregai*," which is their supreme council, shall have authority to chastise powerful offenders. So that, unless an accuser be wanting, a tribunal is never wanting in Venice to keep powerful citizens in check.

But when we see how in Rome, with ordinances of her own imposing, and with so many and so wise legislators, fresh occasion arose from day to day for framing new laws favourable to freedom, it is not to be wondered at that, in other cities less happy in their beginnings, difficulties should have sprung up which no ordinances could remedy.

Chapter L.—*That neither any Council nor any Magistrate should have power to bring the Government of a City to a stay.*

T.Q. Cincinnatus and Cn. Julius Mento being consuls of Rome, and being at variance with one another, brought the whole business of the city to a stay; which the senate perceiving, were moved to create a dictator to do what, by reason of their differences, the consuls would not. But though opposed to one another in everything else, the consuls were of one mind in resisting the appointment of a dictator; so that the senate had no remedy left them but to seek the help of the tribunes, who, supported by their authority, forced the consuls to yield.

Here we have to note, first, the usefulness of the tribunes' authority in checking the ambitious designs, not only of the nobles against the commons, but also of one section of the nobles against another; and next, that in no city ought things ever to be so ordered that it rests with a few to decide on matters, which, if the ordinary business of the State is to proceed at all, must be carried out. Wherefore, if you grant authority to a council to distribute honours and offices, or to a magistrate to administer any branch of public business, you must either impose an obligation that the duty confided shall be performed, or ordain that, on failure to perform, another may and shall do what has to be done. Otherwise such an arrangement will be found defective and dangerous; as would have been the case in Rome, had it not been possible to oppose the authority of the tribunes to the obstinacy of the consuls.

In the Venetian Republic, the great council distributes honours and offices. But more than once it has happened that the council, whether from ill-humour or from being badly advised, has declined to appoint successors either to the magistrates of the city or to those administering the government abroad. This gave rise to the greatest confusion and disorder; for, on a sudden, both the city itself and the subject provinces found themselves deprived of their lawful governors; nor could any redress be had until the majority of the council were pacified or undeceived. And this disorder must have brought the city to a bad end, had not provision been made against its recurrence by certain of the wiser citizens, who, finding a fit opportunity, passed a law that no magistracy, whether within or without the city, should ever be deemed to have been vacated until it was filled up by the appointment of a successor. In this way the council was deprived of its facilities for stopping public business to the danger of the State.

Chapter LI.—*What a Prince or Republic does of Necessity, should seem to be done by Choice.*

In all their actions, even in those which are matters of necessity rather than choice, prudent men will endeavour so to conduct themselves as to conciliate good-will. This species of prudence was well exercised by the Roman senate when they resolved to grant pay from the public purse to soldiers on active service, who, before, had served at their own charges. For perceiving that under the old system they could maintain no war of any duration, and, consequently, could not undertake a siege or lead an army to any distance from home, and finding it necessary to be able to do both, they decided on granting the pay I have spoken of. But this, which they could not help doing, they did in such a way as to earn the thanks of the people, by whom the concession was so well received that all Rome was intoxicated with delight. For it seemed to them a boon beyond any they could have ventured to hope for, or have dreamed of demanding. And although the tribunes sought to make light of the benefit, by showing the people that their burthens would be increased rather than diminished by it, since taxes would have to be imposed out of which the soldier's stipend might be paid, they could not persuade them to regard the measure otherwise than with gratitude; which was further increased by the manner in which the senate distributed the taxes, imposing on the nobles all the heavier and greater, and those which had to be paid first.

Chapter LII.—*That to check the arrogance of a Citizen who is growing too powerful in a State, there is no safer Method, or less open to objection, than to forestall him in those Ways whereby he seeks to advance himself.*

It has been seen in the preceding chapter how much credit the nobles gained with the commons by a show of good-will towards them, not only in providing for their military pay, but also in adjusting taxation. Had the senate constantly adhered to methods like these, they would have put an end to all disturbances in Rome, and have deprived the tribunes of the credit they had with the people, and of the influence thence arising. For in truth, in a commonwealth, and especially in one which has become corrupted, there is no better, or easier, or less objectionable way of opposing the ambition of any citizen, than to anticipate him in those paths by which he is seen to be advancing to the ends he has in view. This plan, had it been followed by the enemies of **Cosimo** de' Medici, would have proved a far more useful course for them than to banish him from Florence; since if those citizens who opposed him had adopted his methods for gaining over the people, they would have succeeded, without violence or tumult, in taking his most effective weapon from his hands.

The influence acquired in Florence by Piero Soderini was entirely due to his skill in securing the affections of the people, since in this way he obtained among them a name for loving the liberties of the commonwealth. And truly, for those citizens who envied his greatness it would have been both easier and more honourable, and at the same time far less dangerous and hurtful to the State, to forestall him in those measures by which he was growing powerful, than to oppose him in such a manner that his overthrow must bring with it the ruin of the entire republic. For had they, as they might easily have done, deprived him of the weapons which made him formidable, they could then have withstood him in all the councils, and in all public deliberations, without either being suspected or feared. And should any rejoin that, if the citizens who hated Piero Soderini committed an error in not being beforehand with him in those ways whereby he came to have influence with the people, Piero himself erred in like manner, in not anticipating his enemies in those methods whereby they grew formidable to him; I answer that Piero is to be excused, both because it would have been difficult for him to have so acted, and because for him such a course would not have been honourable. For the paths wherein his danger lay were those which favoured the Medici, and it was by these that his enemies attacked him, and in the end overthrew him. But these paths Piero could not pursue without dishonour, since he could not, if he was to preserve his fair fame, have joined in destroying that liberty which he had been put forward to defend. Moreover, since favours to the Medicean party could not have been rendered secretly and once for all, they would have been most dangerous for Piero, who, had he shown himself friendly to the Medici, must have become suspected and hated by the people; in which case his enemies would have had still better opportunities than before for his destruction.

Men ought therefore to look to the risks and dangers of any course which lies before them, nor engage in it when it is plain that the dangers outweigh the advantages, even though they be advised by others that it is the most expedient way to take. Should they act otherwise, it will fare with them as with Tullius, who, in seeking to diminish the power of Marcus Antonius, added to it. For Antonius, who had been declared an enemy by the senate, having got together a strong force, mostly made up of veterans who had shared the fortunes of Cæsar, Tullius counselled the senate to invest Octavianus with full authority, and to send him against Antonius with the consuls and the army; affirming, that so soon as those veterans who had served with Cæsar saw the face of him who was Cæsar's nephew and had assumed his name, they would rally to his side and desert Antonius, who might easily be crushed when thus left bare of support.

But the reverse of all this happened. For Antonius persuaded Octavianus to take part with him, and to throw over Tullius and the senate. And this brought about the ruin of the senate, a result which might easily have been foreseen. For remembering the influence of that great captain, who, after overthrowing all opponents, had seized on sovereign power in Rome, the senate should have turned a deaf ear to the persuasions of Tullius, nor ever have believed it possible that from Cæsar's heir, or from soldiers who had followed Cæsar, they could look for anything that consisted with the name of Freedom.

Chapter LIII.—*That the People, deceived by a false show of Advantage, often desire what would be their Ruin; and that large Hopes and brave Promises easily move them.*

When Veii fell, the commons of Rome took up the notion that it would be to the advantage of their city were half their number to go and dwell there. For they argued that as Veii lay in a fertile country and was a well-built city, a moiety of the Roman people might in this way be enriched; while, by reason of its vicinity to Rome, the management of civil affairs would in no degree be affected. To the senate, however, and the wiser among the citizens, the scheme appeared so rash and mischievous that they publicly declared they would die sooner than consent to it. The controversy continuing, the commons grew so inflamed against the senate that violence and bloodshed must have ensued; had not the senate for their protection put forward certain old and esteemed citizens, respect for whom restrained the populace and put a stop to their violence.

Two points are here to be noted. First, that a people deceived by a false show of advantage will often labour for its own destruction; and, unless convinced by some one whom it trusts, that the course on which it is bent is pernicious, and that some other is to be preferred, will bring infinite danger and injury upon the State. And should it so happen, as sometimes is the case, that from having been deceived before, either by men or by events, there is none in whom the people trust, their ruin is inevitable. As to which Dante, in his treatise "De Monarchia," observes that the people will often raise the cry, *"Flourish our death and perish our life."*[1] From which distrust it arises that often in republics the right course is not followed; as when Venice, as has been related, on being attacked by many enemies, could not, until her ruin was complete, resolve to make friends with any one of them by restoring those territories she had taken from them, on account of which war had been declared and a league of princes formed against her.

In considering what courses it is easy, and what it is difficult to persuade a people to follow, this distinction may be drawn: Either what you would persuade them to, presents on the face of it a semblance of gain or loss, or it seems a spirited course or a base one. When any proposal submitted to the people holds out promise of advantage, or seems to them a spirited course to take, though loss lie hid behind, nay, though the ruin of their country be involved in it, they will always be easily led to adopt it; whereas it will always be difficult to persuade the adoption of such courses as wear the appearance of disgrace or loss, even though safety and advantage be bound up with them. The truth of what I say is confirmed by numberless examples both Roman and foreign, modern and ancient. Hence grew the ill opinion entertained in Rome of Fabius Maximus, who could never persuade the people that it behoved them to proceed warily in their conflict with Hannibal, and withstand his onset without fighting. For this the people thought a base course, not discerning the advantage resulting from it, which Fabius could by no argument make plain to them. And so blinded are men in favour of what seems a spirited course, that although the Romans had already committed the blunder of permitting Varro, master of the knights to Fabius, to join battle contrary to the latter's desire, whereby the army must have been destroyed had not Fabius by his prudence saved it, this lesson was not enough; for afterwards they appointed this Varro to be consul, for no other reason than that he gave out, in the streets and market-places, that he would make an end of Hannibal as soon as leave was given him to do so. Whence came the battle and defeat of Cannæ, and well-nigh the destruction of Rome.

Another example taken from Roman history may be cited to the same effect. After Hannibal had maintained himself for eight or ten years in Italy, during which time the whole country had been deluged with Roman blood, a certain Marcus Centenius Penula, a man of mean origin, but who had held some post in the army, came forward and proposed to the senate that were leave given him to raise a force of volunteers in any part of Italy he pleased, he would speedily deliver Hannibal into their hands, alive or dead. To the senate this man's offer seemed a rash one; but reflecting that were they to refuse it, and were the people afterwards to hear that it had been made, tumults, ill will, and resentment against them would result, they granted the permission asked; choosing rather to risk the lives of all who might follow Penula, than to excite fresh discontent on the part of the people, to whom they knew that such a proposal would be welcome, and that it would be very hard to dissuade them from it. And so this adventurer, marching forth with an undisciplined and disorderly rabble to meet Hannibal, was, with all his followers, defeated and slain in the very first encounter.

In Greece, likewise, and in the city of Athens, that most grave and prudent statesman, Nicias, could not convince the people that the proposal to go and attack Sicily was disadvantageous; and the expedition being resolved on, contrary to his advice and to the wishes of the wiser among the citizens, resulted in the overthrow of the Athenian power. Scipio, on being appointed consul, asked that the province of Africa might be awarded to him, promising that he would utterly efface Carthage; and when the senate, on the advice of Fabius, refused his request, he threatened to submit the matter to the people as very well knowing that to the people such proposals are always acceptable.

I might cite other instances to the same effect from the history of our own city, as when Messer Ercole Bentivoglio and Antonio Giacomini, being in joint command of the Florentine armies, after defeating Bartolommeo d'Alviano at San Vincenzo, proceeded to invest Pisa. For this enterprise was resolved on by the people in consequence of the brave promises of Messer Ercole; and though many wise citizens disapproved of it, they could do nothing to prevent it, being carried away by the popular will, which took its rise in the assurances of their captain.

I say, then, that there is no readier way to bring about the ruin of a republic, when the power is in the hands of the people, than to suggest daring courses for their adoption. For wherever the people have a voice, such proposals will always be well received, nor will those persons who are opposed to them be able to apply any remedy. And as this occasions the ruin of States, it likewise, and even more frequently, occasions the private ruin of those to whom the execution of these proposals is committed; because the people anticipating victory, do not when there comes defeat ascribe it to the short means or ill fortune of the commander, but to his cowardice and incapacity; and commonly either put him to death, or imprison or banish him; as was done in the case of numberless Carthaginian generals and of many Athenian, no successes they might previously have obtained availing them anything; for all past services are cancelled by a present loss. And so it happened with our Antonio Giacomini, who not succeeding as the people had expected, and as he had promised, in taking Pisa, fell into such discredit with the people, that notwithstanding his countless past services, his life was spared rather by the compassion of those in authority than through any movement of the citizens in his behalf.

[Footnote 1: "Viva la sua morte e muoia la sua vita." The quotation does *not* seem to be from the "De Monarchia."]

Chapter LIV.—*Of the boundless Authority which a great Man may use to restrain an excited Multitude.*

The next noteworthy point in the passage referred to in the foregoing Chapter is, that nothing tends so much to restrain an excited multitude as the reverence felt for some grave person, clothed with authority, who stands forward to oppose them. For not without reason has Virgil said—

"If then, by chance, some reverend chief appear, Known for his deeds and for his virtues dear, Silent they wait his words and bend a listening ear."[1]

He therefore who commands an army or governs a city wherein tumult shall have broken out, ought to assume the noblest and bravest bearing he can, and clothe himself with all the ensigns of his station, that he may make himself more revered. It is not many years since Florence was divided into two factions, the *Frateschi* and *Arrabbiati*, as they were named, and these coming to open violence, the *Frateschi*, among whom was Pagolo Antonio Soderini, a citizen of great reputation in these days, were worsted. In the course of these disturbances the people coming with arms in their hands to plunder the house of Soderini, his brother Messer Francesco, then bishop of Volterra and now cardinal, who happened to be dwelling there, so soon as he heard the uproar and saw the crowd, putting on his best apparel and over it his episcopal robes, went forth to meet the armed multitude, and by his words and mien brought them to a stay; and for many days his behaviour was commended by the whole city. The inference from all which is, that there is no surer or more necessary restraint on the violence of an unruly multitude, than the presence of some one whose character and bearing command respect.

But to return once more to the passage we are considering, we see how stubbornly the people clung to this scheme of transplanting themselves to Veii, thinking it for their advantage, and not discerning the mischief really involved in it; so that in addition to the many dissensions which it occasioned, actual violence must have followed, had not the senate with the aid of certain grave and reverend citizens repressed the popular fury.

[Footnote 1: Tum pietate gravem ac meritis si forte virum quem Conspexere, silent, arrectisque auribus adstant. *Virg. Aen.*, I. 154.]

Chapter LV.—*That Government is easily carried on in a City wherein the body of the People is not corrupted: and that a Princedom is impossible where Equality prevails, and a Republic where it does not.*

Though what we have to fear or hope from cities that have grown corrupted has already been discussed, still I think it not out of place to notice a resolution passed by the senate touching the vow which Camillus made to Apollo of a tenth of the spoil taken from the Veientines. For this spoil having fallen into the hands of the people, the senate, being unable by other means to get any account of it, passed an edict that every man should publicly offer one tenth part of what he had taken. And although this edict was not carried out, from the senate having afterwards followed a different course, whereby, to the content of the people, the claim of Apollo was otherwise satisfied, we nevertheless see from their having entertained such a proposal, how completely the senate trusted to the honesty of the people, when they assumed that no one would withhold any part of what the edict commanded him to give; on the other hand, we see that it never occurred to the people that they might evade the law by giving less than was due, their only thought being to free themselves from the law by openly manifesting their displeasure. This example, together with many others already noticed, shows how much virtue and how profound a feeling of religion prevailed among the Roman people, and how much good was to be expected from them. And, in truth, in the country where virtue like this does not exist, no good can be looked for, as we should look for it in vain in provinces which at the present day are seen to be corrupted; as Italy is beyond all others, though, in some degree, France and Spain are similarly tainted. In which last two countries, if we see not so many disorders spring up as we see daily springing up in Italy, this is not so much due to the superior virtue of their inhabitants (who, to say truth, fall far short of our countrymen), as to their being governed by a king who keeps them united, not merely by his personal qualities, but also by the laws and ordinances of the realm which are still maintained with vigour. In Germany, however, we do see signal excellence and a devout religious spirit prevail among the people, giving rise to the many free States which there maintain themselves, with such strict observance of their laws that none, either within or without their walls, dare encroach on them.

That among this last-named people a great share of the ancient excellence does in truth still flourish, I shall show by an example similar to that which I have above related of the senate and people of Rome. It is customary with the German Free States when they have to expend any large sum of money on the public account, for their magistrates or councils having authority given them in that behalf, to impose a rate of one or two in the hundred on every man's estate; which rate being fixed, every man, in conformity with the laws of the city, presents himself before the collectors of the impost, and having first made oath to pay the amount justly due, throws into a chest provided for the purpose what he conscientiously believes it fair for him to pay, of which payment none is witness save himself. From this fact it may be gathered what honesty and religion still prevail among this people. For we must assume that each pays his just share, since otherwise the impost would not yield the sum which, with reference to former imposts, it was estimated to yield; whereby the fraud would be detected, and thereupon some other method for raising money have to be resorted to.

At the present time this virtue is the more to be admired, because it seems to have survived in this province only. That it has survived there may be ascribed to two circumstances: *first*, that the natives have little communication with their neighbours, neither visiting them in their countries nor being visited by them; being content to use such commodities, and subsist on such food, and to wear garments of such materials as their own land supplies; so that all occasion for intercourse, and every cause of corruption is removed. For living after this fashion, they have not learned the manners of the French, the Italians, or the Spaniards, which three nations together are the corruption of the world. The *second* cause is, that these republics in which a free and pure government is maintained will not suffer any of their citizens either to be, or to live as gentlemen; but on the contrary, while preserving a strict equality among themselves, are bitterly hostile to all those gentlemen and lords who dwell in their neighbourhood; so that if by chance any of these fall into their hands, they put them to death, as the chief promoters of corruption and the origin of all disorders.

But to make plain what I mean when I speak of *gentlemen*, I say that those are so to be styled who live in opulence and idleness on the revenues of their estates, without concerning themselves with the cultivation of these estates, or incurring any other fatigue for their support. Such persons are very mischievous in every republic or country. But even more mischievous are they who, besides the estates I have spoken of, are lords of strongholds and castles, and have vassals and retainers who render them obedience. Of these two classes of men the kingdom of Naples, the country round Rome, Romagna, and Lombardy are full; and hence it happens that in these provinces no commonwealth or free form of government has ever existed; because men of this sort are the sworn foes to all free institutions.

And since to plant a commonwealth in provinces which are in this condition were impossible, if these are to be reformed at all, it can only be by some one man who is able there to establish a kingdom; the reason being that when the body of the people is grown so corrupted that the laws are powerless to control it, there must in addition to the laws be introduced a stronger force, to wit, the regal, which by its absolute and unrestricted authority may curb the excessive ambition and corruption of the great. This opinion may be supported by the example of Tuscany, in which within a narrow compass of territory there have long existed the three republics of Florence, Lucca, and Siena, while the other cities of that province, although to a certain extent dependent, still show by their spirit and by their institutions that they preserve, or at any rate desire to preserve, their freedom: and this because there are in Tuscany no lords possessed of strongholds, and few or no gentlemen, but so complete an equality prevails, that a prudent statesman, well acquainted with the history of the free States of antiquity, might easily introduce free institutions. Such, however, has been the unhappiness of this our country, that, up to the present hour, it has never produced any man with the power and knowledge which would have enabled him to act in this way.

From what has been said, it follows, that he who would found a commonwealth in a country wherein there are many gentlemen, cannot do so unless he first gets rid of them; and that he who would found a monarchy or princedom in a country wherein great equality prevails, will never succeed, unless he raise above the level of that equality many persons of a restless and ambitious temperament, whom he must make gentlemen not in name merely but in reality, by conferring on them castles and lands, supplying them with riches, and providing them with retainers; that with these gentlemen around him, and with their help, he may maintain his power, while they through him may gratify their ambition; all others being constrained to endure a yoke, which force and force alone imposes on them. For when in this way there comes to be a proportion between him who uses force and him against whom it is used, each stands fixed in his own station.

But to found a commonwealth in a country suited for a kingdom, or a kingdom in a country suited to be a commonwealth, requires so rare a combination of intelligence and power, that though many engage in the attempt, few are found to succeed. For the greatness of the undertaking quickly daunts them, and so obstructs their advance they break down at the very outset. The case of the Venetian Republic, wherein none save gentlemen are permitted to hold any public office, does, doubtless, seem opposed to this opinion of mine that where there are gentlemen it is impossible to found a commonwealth. But it may be answered that the case of Venice is not in truth an instance to the contrary; since the gentlemen of Venice are gentlemen rather in name than in reality, inasmuch as they draw no great revenues from lands, their wealth consisting chiefly in merchandise and chattels, and not one of them possessing a castle or enjoying any feudal authority. For in Venice this name of gentleman is a title of honour and dignity, and does not depend on any of those circumstances in respect of which the name is given in other States. But as in other States the different ranks and classes are divided under different names, so in Venice we have the division into gentlemen (*gentiluomini*) and plebeians (*popolani*), it being understood that the former hold, or have the right to hold all situations of honour, from which the latter are entirely excluded. And in Venice this occasions no disturbance, for reasons which I have already explained.

Let a commonwealth, then, be constituted in the country where a great equality is found or has been made; and, conversely, let a princedom be constituted where great inequality prevails. Otherwise what is constituted will be discordant in itself, and without stability.

Chapter LVI.—*That when great Calamities are about to befall a City or Country, Signs are seen to presage, and Seers arise who foretell them.*

Whence it happens I know not, but it is seen from examples both ancient and recent, that no grave calamity has ever befallen any city or country which has not been foretold by vision, by augury, by portent, or by some other Heaven-sent sign. And not to travel too far afield for evidence of this, every one knows that long before the invasion of Italy by Charles VIII. of France, his coming was foretold by the friar Girolamo Savonarola; and how, throughout the whole of Tuscany, the rumour ran that over Arezzo horsemen had been seen fighting in the air. And who is there who has not heard that before the death of the elder Lorenzo de' Medici, the highest pinnacle of the cathedral was rent by a thunderbolt, to the great injury of the building? Or who, again, but knows that shortly before Piero Soderini, whom the people of Florence had made gonfalonier for life, was deprived of his office and banished, the palace itself was struck by lightning?

Other instances might be cited, which, not to be tedious, I shall omit, and mention only a circumstance which Titus Livius tells us preceded the invasion of the Gauls. For he relates how a certain plebeian named Marcus Ceditius reported to the senate that as he passed by night along the Via Nova, he heard a voice louder than mortal, bidding him warn the magistrates that the Gauls were on their way to Rome.

The causes of such manifestations ought, I think, to be inquired into and explained by some one who has a knowledge, which I have not, of causes natural and supernatural. It may, however, be, as certain wise men say, that the air is filled with intelligent beings, to whom it is given to forecast future events; who, taking pity upon men, warn them beforehand by these signs to prepare for what awaits them. Be this as it may, certain it is that such warnings are given, and that always after them new and strange disasters befall nations.

Chapter LVII.—*That the People are strong collectively, but individually weak.*

After the ruin brought on their country by the invasion of the Gauls, many of the Romans went to dwell in Veii, in opposition to the edicts and commands of the senate, who, to correct this mischief, publicly ordained that within a time fixed, and under penalties stated, all should return to live in Rome. The persons against whom these proclamations were directed at first derided them; but, when the time came for them to be obeyed, all obeyed them. And Titus Livius observes that, "*although bold enough collectively, each separately, fearing to be punished, made his submission.*" And indeed the temper of the multitude in such cases, cannot be better described than in this passage. For often a people will be open-mouthed in condemning the decrees of their prince, but afterwards, when they have to look punishment in the face, putting no trust in one another, they hasten to comply. Wherefore, if you be in a position to keep the people well-disposed towards you when they already are so, or to prevent them injuring you in case they be ill-disposed, it is clearly of little moment whether the feelings with which they profess to regard you, be favourable or no. This applies to all unfriendliness on the part of a people, whencesoever it proceed, excepting only the resentment felt by them on being deprived either of liberty, or of a prince whom they love and who still survives. For the hostile temper produced by these two causes is more to be feared than any beside, and demands measures of extreme severity to correct it. The other untoward humours of the multitude, should there be no powerful chief to foster them, are easily dealt with; because, while on the one hand there is nothing more terrible than an uncontrolled and headless mob, on the other, there is nothing feebler. For though it be furnished with arms it is easily subdued, if you have some place of strength wherein to shelter from its first onset. For when its first fury has somewhat abated, and each man sees that he has to return to his own house, all begin to lose heart and to take thought how to insure their personal safety, whether by flight or by submission. For which reason a multitude stirred in this way, if it would avoid dangers such as I speak of, must at once appoint a head from among its own numbers, who may control it, keep it united, and provide for its defence; as did the commons of Rome when, after the death of Virginia, they quitted the city, and for their protection created twenty tribunes from among themselves. Unless this be done, what Titus Livius has observed in the passage cited, will always prove true, namely, that a multitude is strong while it holds together, but so soon as each of those who compose it begins to think of his own private danger, it becomes weak and contemptible.

Chapter LVIII.—*That a People is wiser and more constant than a Prince*

That "*nothing is more fickle and inconstant than the multitude*" is affirmed not by Titus Livius only, but by all other historians, in whose chronicles of human actions we often find the multitude condemning some citizen to death, and afterwards lamenting him and grieving greatly for his loss, as the Romans grieved and lamented for Manlius Capitolinus, whom they had themselves condemned to die. In relating which circumstance our author observes "*In a short time the people, having no longer cause to fear him, began to deplore his death*" And elsewhere, when speaking of what took place in Syracuse after the murder of Hieronymus, grandson of Hiero, he says, "*It is the nature of the multitude to be an abject slave, or a domineering master*"

It may be that in attempting to defend a cause, which, as I have said, all writers are agreed to condemn, I take upon me a task so hard and difficult that I shall either have to relinquish it with shame or pursue it with opprobrium. Be that as it may, I neither do, nor ever shall judge it a fault, to support opinion by arguments, where it is not sought to impose them by violence or authority I maintain, then, that this infirmity with which historians tax the multitude, may with equal reason be charged against every individual man, but most of all against princes, since all who are not controlled by the laws, will commit the very same faults as are committed by an uncontrolled multitude. Proof whereof were easy, since of all the many princes existing, or who have existed, few indeed are or have been either wise or good.

I speak of such princes as have had it in their power to break the reins by which they are controlled, among whom I do not reckon those kings who reigned in Egypt in the most remote antiquity when that country was governed in conformity with its laws; nor do I include those kings who reigned in Sparta, nor those who in our own times reign in France, which kingdom, more than any other whereof we have knowledge at the present day, is under the government of its laws. For kings who live, as these do, subject to constitutional restraint, are not to be counted when we have to consider each man's proper nature, and to see whether he resembles the multitude. For to draw a comparison with such princes as these, we must take the case of a multitude controlled as they are, and regulated by the laws, when we shall find it to possess the same virtues which we see in them, and neither conducting itself as an abject slave nor as a domineering master.

Such was the people of Rome, who, while the commonwealth continued uncorrupted, never either served abjectly nor domineered haughtily; but, on the contrary, by means of their magistrates and their ordinances, maintained their place, and when forced to put forth their strength against some powerful citizen, as in the case of Manlius, the decemvirs, and others who sought to oppress them, did so; but when it was necessary for the public welfare to yield obedience to the dictator or consuls, obeyed. And if the Roman people mourned the loss of the dead Manlius, it is no wonder; for they mourned his virtues, which had been of such a sort that their memory stirred the regret of all, and would have had power to produce the same feelings even in a prince; all writers being agreed that excellence is praised and admired even by its enemies. But if Manlius when he was so greatly mourned, could have risen once more from the dead, the Roman people would have pronounced the same sentence against him which they pronounced when they led him forth from the prison-house, and straightway condemned him to die. And in like manner we see that princes, accounted wise, have put men to death, and afterwards greatly lamented them, as Alexander mourned for Clitus and others of his friends, and Herod for Mariamne.

But what our historian says of the multitude, he says not of a multitude which like the people of Rome is controlled by the laws, but of an uncontrolled multitude like the Syracusans, who were guilty of all these crimes which infuriated and ungoverned men commit, and which were equally committed by Alexander and Herod in the cases mentioned. Wherefore the nature of a multitude is no more to be blamed than the nature of princes, since both equally err when they can do so without regard to consequences. Of which many instances, besides those already given, might be cited from the history of the Roman emperors, and of other princes and tyrants, in whose lives we find such inconstancy and fickleness, as we might look in vain for in a people.

I maintain, therefore, contrary to the common opinion which avers that a people when they have the management of affairs are changeable, fickle, and ungrateful, that these faults exist not in them otherwise than as they exist in individual princes; so that were any to accuse both princes and peoples, the charge might be true, but that to make exception in favour of princes is a mistake; for a people in command, if it be duly restrained, will have the same prudence and the same gratitude as a prince has, or even more, however wise he may be reckoned; and a prince on the other hand, if freed from the control of the laws, will be more ungrateful, fickle, and short-sighted than a people. And further, I say that any difference in their methods of acting results not from any difference in their nature, that being the same in both, or, if there be advantage on either side, the advantage resting with the people, but from their having more or less respect for the laws under which each lives. And whosoever attentively considers the history of the Roman people, may see that for four hundred years they never relaxed in their hatred of the regal name, and were constantly devoted to the glory and welfare of their country, and will find numberless proofs given by them of their consistency in both particulars. And should any allege against me the ingratitude they showed to Scipio, I reply by what has already been said at length on that head, where I proved that peoples are less ungrateful than princes. But as for prudence and stability of purpose, I affirm that a people is more prudent, more stable, and of better judgment than a prince. Nor is it without reason that the voice of the people has been likened to the voice of God; for we see that wide-spread beliefs fulfil themselves, and bring about marvellous results, so as to have the appearance of presaging by some occult quality either weal or woe. Again, as to the justice of their opinions on public affairs, seldom find that after hearing two speakers of equal ability urging them in opposite directions, they do not adopt the sounder view, or are unable to decide on the truth of what they hear. And if, as I have said, a people errs in adopting courses which appear to it bold and advantageous, princes will likewise err when their passions are touched, as is far oftener the case with them than with a people.

We see, too, that in the choice of magistrates a people will choose far more honestly than a prince; so that while you shall never persuade a people that it is advantageous to confer dignities on the infamous and profligate, a prince may readily, and in a thousand ways, be drawn to do so. Again, it may be seen that a people, when once they have come to hold a thing in abhorrence, remain for many ages of the same mind; which we do not find happen with princes. For the truth of both of which assertions the Roman people are my sufficient witness, who, in the course of so many hundred years, and in so many elections of consuls and tribunes, never made four appointments of which they had reason to repent; and, as I have said, so detested the name of king, that no obligation they might be under to any citizen who affected that name, could shield him from the appointed penalty.

Further, we find that those cities wherein the government is in the hands of the people, in a very short space of time, make marvellous progress, far exceeding that made by cities which have been always ruled by princes; as Rome grew after the expulsion of her kings, and Athens after she freed herself from Pisistratus; and this we can ascribe to no other cause than that the rule of a people is better than the rule of a prince.

Nor would I have it thought that anything our historian may have affirmed in the passage cited, or elsewhere, controverts these my opinions. For if all the glories and all the defects both of peoples and of princes be carefully weighed, it will appear that both for goodness and for glory a people is to be preferred. And if princes surpass peoples in the work of legislation, in shaping civil institutions, in moulding statutes, and framing new ordinances, so far do the latter surpass the former in maintaining what has once been established, as to merit no less praise than they.

And to state the sum of the whole matter shortly, I say that popular governments have endured for long periods in the same way as the governments of princes, and that both have need to be regulated by the laws; because the prince who can do what he pleases is a madman, and the people which can do as it pleases is never wise. If, then, we assume the case of a prince bound, and of a people chained down by the laws, greater virtue will appear in the people than in the prince; while if we assume the case of each of them freed from all control, it will be seen that the people commits fewer errors than the prince, and less serious errors, and such as admit of readier cure. For a turbulent and unruly people may be spoken to by a good man, and readily brought back to good ways; but none can speak to a wicked prince, nor any remedy be found against him but by the sword. And from this we may infer which of the two suffers from the worse disease; for if the disease of the people may be healed by words, while that of the prince must be dealt with by the sword, there is none but will judge that evil to be the greater which demands the more violent remedy.

When a people is absolutely uncontrolled, it is not so much the follies which it commits or the evil which it actually does that excites alarm, as the mischief which may thence result, since in such disorders it becomes possible for a tyrant to spring up. But with a wicked prince the contrary is the case; for we dread present ill, and place our hopes in the future, persuading ourselves that the evil life of the prince may bring about our freedom. So that there is this distinction between the two, that with the one we fear what is, with the other what is likely to be. Again, the cruelties of a people are turned against him who it fears will encroach upon the common rights, but the cruelties of the prince against those who he fears may assert those rights.

The prejudice which is entertained against the people arises from this, that any man may speak ill of them openly and fearlessly, even when the government is in their hands; whereas princes are always spoken of with a thousand reserves and a constant eye to consequences.

But since the subject suggests it, it seems to me not out of place to consider what alliances we can most trust, whether those made with commonwealths or those made with princes.

Chapter LIX.—*To what Leagues or Alliances we may most trust; whether those we make with Commonwealths or those we make with Princes.*

Since leagues and alliances are every day entered into by one prince with another, or by one commonwealth with another, and as conventions and treaties are concluded in like manner between princes and commonwealths, it seems to me proper to inquire whether the faith of a commonwealth or that of a prince is the more stable and the safer to count on. All things considered, I am disposed to believe that in most cases they are alike, though in some they differ. Of one thing, however, I am convinced, namely, that engagements made under duress will never be observed either by prince or by commonwealth; and that if menaced with the loss of their territories, both the one and the other will break faith with you and treat you with ingratitude. Demetrius, who was named the "City-taker," had conferred numberless benefits upon the Athenians; but when, afterwards, on being defeated by his enemies, he sought shelter in Athens, as being a friendly city and under obligations to him, it was refused him; a circumstance which grieved him far more than the loss of his soldiers and army had done. Pompey, in like manner, when routed by Cæsar in Thessaly, fled for refuge to Ptolemy in Egypt, who formerly had been restored by him to his kingdom; by whom he was put to death. In both these instances the same causes were at work, although the inhumanity and the wrong inflicted were less in the case of the commonwealth than of the prince. Still, wherever there is fear, the want of faith will be the same.

And even if there be found a commonwealth or prince who, in order to keep faith, will submit to be ruined, this is seen to result from a like cause. For, as to the prince, it may easily happen that he is friend to a powerful sovereign, whom, though he be at the time without means to defend him, he may presently hope to see restored to his dominions; or it may be that having linked his fortunes with another's, he despairs of finding either faith or friendship from the enemies of his ally, as was the case with those Neapolitan princes who espoused the interests of France. As to commonwealths, an instance similar to that of the princes last named, is that of Saguntum in Spain, which awaited ruin in adhering to the fortunes of Rome. A like course was also followed by Florence when, in the year 1512, she stood steadfastly by the cause of the French. And taking everything into account, I believe that in cases of urgency, we shall find a certain degree of stability sooner in commonwealths than in princes. For though commonwealths be like-minded with princes, and influenced by the same passions, the circumstance that their movements must be slower, makes it harder for them to resolve than it is for a prince, for which reason they will be less ready to break faith.

And since leagues and alliances are broken for the sake of certain advantages, in this respect also, commonwealths observe their engagements far more faithfully than princes; for abundant examples might be cited of a very slight advantage having caused a prince to break faith, and of a very great advantage having failed to induce a commonwealth to do so. Of this we have an instance in the proposal made to the Athenians by Themistocles, when he told them at a public meeting that he had certain advice to offer which would prove of great advantage to their city, but the nature of which he could not disclose to them, lest it should become generally known, when the opportunity for acting upon it would be lost. Whereupon the Athenians named Aristides to receive his communication, and to act upon it as he thought fit. To him, accordingly, Themistocles showed how the navy of united Greece, for the safety of which the Athenians stood pledged, was so situated that they might either gain it over or destroy it, and thus make themselves absolute masters of the whole country. Aristides reporting to the Athenians that the course proposed by Themistocles was extremely advantageous but extremely dishonourable, the people utterly refused to entertain it. But Philip of Macedon would not have so acted, nor any of those other princes who have sought and found more profit in breaking faith than in any other way.

As to engagements broken off on the pretext that they have not been observed by the other side, I say nothing, since that is a matter of everyday occurrence, and I am speaking here only of those engagements which are broken off on extraordinary grounds; but in this respect, likewise, I believe that commonwealths offend less than princes, and are therefore more to be trusted.

Chapter LX.—*That the Consulship and all the other Magistracies in Rome were given without respect to Age.*

It is seen in the course of the Roman history that, after the consulship was thrown open to the commons, the republic conceded this dignity to all its citizens, without distinction either of age or blood; nay, that in this matter respect for age was never made a ground for preference among the Romans, whose constant aim it was to discover excellence whether existing in old or young. To this we have the testimony of Valerius Corvinus, himself made consul in his twenty-fourth year, who, in addressing his soldiers, said of the consulship that it was *"the reward not of birth but of desert."*

Whether the course thus followed by the Romans was well judged or not, is a question on which much might be said. The concession as to blood, however, was made under necessity, and as I have observed on another occasion, the same necessity which obtained in Rome, will be found to obtain in every other city which desires to achieve the results which Rome achieved. For you cannot subject men to hardships unless you hold out rewards, nor can you without danger deprive them of those rewards whereof you have held out hopes. It was consequently necessary to extend, betimes, to the commons the hope of obtaining the consulship, on which hope they fed themselves for a while, without actually realizing it. But afterwards the hope alone was not enough, and it had to be satisfied. For while cities which do not employ men of plebeian birth in any of those undertakings wherein glory is to be gained, as we have seen was the case with Venice, may treat these men as they please, those other cities which desire to do as Rome did, cannot make this distinction. And if there is to be no distinction in respect of blood, nothing can be pleaded for a distinction in respect of age. On the contrary, that distinction must of necessity cease to be observed. For where a young man is appointed to a post which requires the prudence which are is supposed to bring, it must be, since the choice rests with the people, that he is thus advanced in consideration of some noble action which he has performed; but when a young man is of such excellence as to have made a name for himself by some signal achievement, it were much to the detriment of his city were it unable at once to make use of him, but had to wait until he had grown old, and had lost, with youth, that alacrity and vigour by which his country might have profited; as Rome profited by the services of Valerius Corvinus, of Scipio, of Pompey, and of many others who triumphed while yet very young.

Book II: Preface.

Men do always, but not always with reason, commend the past and condemn the present, and are so much the partisans of what has been, as not merely to cry up those times which are known to them only from the records left by historians, but also, when they grow old, to extol the days in which they remember their youth to have been spent. And although this preference of theirs be in most instances a mistaken one, I can see that there are many causes to account for it; chief of which I take to be that in respect of things long gone by we perceive not the whole truth, those circumstances that would detract from the credit of the past being for the most part hidden from us, while all that gives it lustre is magnified and embellished. For the generality of writers render this tribute to the good fortune of conquerors, that to make their achievements seem more splendid, they not merely exaggerate the great things they have done, but also lend such a colour to the actions of their enemies, that any one born afterwards, whether in the conquering or in the conquered country, has cause to marvel at these men and these times, and is constrained to praise and love them beyond all others.

Again, men being moved to hatred either by fear or envy, these two most powerful causes of dislike are cancelled in respect of things which are past, because what is past can neither do us hurt, nor afford occasion for envy. The contrary, however, is the case with the things we see, and in which we take part; for in these, from our complete acquaintance with them, no part of them being hidden from us, we recognize, along with much that is good, much that displeases us, and so are forced to pronounce them far inferior to the old, although in truth they deserve far greater praise and admiration. I speak not, here, of what relates to the arts, which have such distinction inherent in them, that time can give or take from them but little of the glory which they merit of themselves. I speak of the lives and manners of men, touching which the grounds for judging are not so clear.

I repeat, then, that it is true that this habit of blaming and praising obtains, but not always true that it is wrong applied. For sometimes it will happen that this judgment is just; because, as human affairs are in constant movement, it must be that they either rise or fall. Wherefore, we may see a city or province furnished with free institutions by some great and wise founder, flourish for a while through his merits, and advance steadily on the path of improvement. Any one born therein at that time would be in the wrong to praise the past more than the present, and his error would be occasioned by the causes already noticed. But any one born afterwards in that city or province when the time has come for it to fall away from its former felicity, would not be mistaken in praising the past.

When I consider how this happens, I am persuaded that the world, remaining continually the same, has in it a constant quantity of good and evil; but that this good and this evil shift about from one country to another, as we know that in ancient times empire shifted from one nation to another, according as the manners of these nations changed, the world, as a whole, continuing as before, and the only difference being that, whereas at first Assyria was made the seat of its excellence, this was afterwards placed in Media, then in Persia, until at last it was transferred to Italy and Rome. And although after the Roman Empire, none has followed which has endured, or in which the world has centred its whole excellence, we nevertheless find that excellence diffused among many valiant nations, the kingdom of the Franks, for example, that of the Turks, that of the Soldan, and the States of Germany at the present day; and shared at an earlier time by that sect of the Saracens who performed so many great achievements and gained so wide a dominion, after destroying the Roman Empire in the East.

In all these countries, therefore, after the decline of the Roman power, and among all these races, there existed, and in some part of them there yet exists, that excellence which alone is to be desired and justly to be praised. Wherefore, if any man being born in one of these countries should exalt past times over present, he might be mistaken; but any who, living at the present day in Italy or Greece, has not in Italy become an ultramontane or in Greece a Turk, has reason to complain of his own times, and to commend those others, in which there were many things which made them admirable; whereas, now, no regard being had to religion, to laws, or to arms, but all being tarnished with every sort of shame, there is nothing to redeem the age from the last extremity of wretchedness, ignominy, and disgrace. And the vices of our age are the more odious in that they are practised by those who sit on the judgment seat, govern the State, and demand public reverence.

But, returning to the matter in hand, it may be said, that if the judgment of men be at fault in pronouncing whether the present age or the past is the better in respect of things whereof, by reason of their antiquity, they cannot have the same perfect knowledge which they have of their own times, it ought not to be at fault in old men when they compare the days of their youth with those of their maturity, both of which have been alike seen and known by them. This were indeed true, if men at all periods of their lives judged of things in the same way, and were constantly influenced by the same desires; but since they alter, the times, although they alter not, cannot but seem different to those who have other desires, other pleasures, and other ways of viewing things in their old age from those they had in their youth. For since, when they grow old, men lose in bodily strength but gain in wisdom and discernment, it must needs be that those things which in their youth seemed to them tolerable and good, should in their old age appear intolerable and evil. And whereas they should ascribe this to their judgment, they lay the blame upon the times.

But, further, since the desires of men are insatiable, Nature prompting them to desire all things and Fortune permitting them to enjoy but few, there results a constant discontent in their minds, and a loathing of what they possess, prompting them to find fault with the present, praise the past, and long for the future, even though they be not moved thereto by any reasonable cause.

I know not, therefore, whether I may not deserve to be reckoned in the number of those who thus deceive themselves, if, in these Discourses of mine, I render excessive praise to the ancient times of the Romans while I censure our own. And, indeed, were not the excellence which then prevailed and the corruption which prevails now clearer than the sun, I should proceed more guardedly in what I have to say, from fear lest in accusing others I should myself fall into this self-deception. But since the thing is so plain that every one sees it, I shall be bold to speak freely all I think, both of old times and of new, in order that the minds of the young who happen to read these my writings, may be led to shun modern examples, and be prepared to follow those set by antiquity whenever chance affords the opportunity. For it is the duty of every good man to teach others those wholesome lessons which the malice of Time or of Fortune has not permitted him to put in practice; to the end, that out of many who have the knowledge, some one better loved by Heaven may be found able to carry them out.

Having spoken, then, in the foregoing Book of the various methods followed by the Romans in regulating the domestic affairs of their city, in this I shall speak of what was done by them to spread their Empire.

Chapter I.—*Whether the Empire acquired by the Romans was more due to Valour or to Fortune.*

Many authors, and among others that most grave historian Plutarch, have thought that in acquiring their empire the Romans were more beholden to their good fortune than to their valour; and besides other reasons which they give for this opinion, they affirm it to be proved by the admission of the Romans themselves, since their having erected more temples to Fortune than to any other deity, shows that it was to her that they ascribed their success. It would seem, too, that Titus Livius was of the same mind, since he very seldom puts a speech into the mouth of any Roman in which he discourses of valour, wherein he does not also make mention of Fortune. This, however, is an opinion with which I can in no way concur, and which, I take it, cannot be made good. For if no commonwealth has ever been found to grow like the Roman, it is because none was ever found so well fitted by its institutions to make that growth. For by the valour of her armies she spread her empire, while by her conduct of affairs, and by other methods peculiar to herself and devised by her first founder, she was able to keep what she acquired, as shall be fully shown in many of the following Discourses.

The writers to whom I have referred assert that it was owing to their good fortune and not to their prudence that the Romans never had two great wars on their hands at once; as, for instance, that they waged no wars with the Latins until they had not merely overcome the Samnites, but undertook in their defence the war on which they then entered; nor ever fought with the Etruscans until they had subjugated the Latins, and had almost worn out the Samnites by frequent defeats; whereas, had any two of these powers, while yet fresh and unexhausted, united together, it may easily be believed that the ruin of the Roman Republic must have followed. But to whatsoever cause we ascribe it, it never so chanced that the Romans engaged in two great wars at the same time. On the contrary, it always seemed as though on the breaking out of one war, another was extinguished; or that on the termination of one, another broke out. And this we may plainly see from the order in which their wars succeeded one another.

For, omitting those waged by them before their city was taken by the Gauls, we find that during their struggle with the Equians and the Volscians, and while these two nations continued strong, no others rose against them. On these being subdued, there broke out the war with the Samnites; and although before the close of that contest the Latin nations had begun to rebel against Rome, nevertheless, when their rebellion came to a head, the Samnites were in league with Rome, and helped her with their army to quell the presumption of the rebels; on whose defeat the war with Samnium was renewed.

When the strength of Samnium had been drained by repeated reverses, there followed the war with the Etruscans; which ended, the Samnites were once more stirred to activity by the coming of Pyrrhus into Italy. When he, too, had been defeated, and sent back to Greece, Rome entered on her first war with the Carthaginians; which was no sooner over than all the Gallic nations on both sides of the Alps combined against the Romans, by whom, in the battle fought between Populonia and Pisa, where now stands the fortress of San Vincenzo, they were at last routed with tremendous slaughter.

This war ended, for twenty years together the Romans were engaged in no contest of importance, their only adversaries being the Ligurians, and the remnant of the Gallic tribes who occupied Lombardy; and on this footing things continued down to the second Carthaginian war, which for sixteen years kept the whole of Italy in a blaze. This too being brought to a most glorious termination, there followed the Macedonian war, at the close of which succeeded the war with Antiochus and Asia. These subdued, there remained not in the whole world, king or people who either singly or together could withstand the power of Rome.

But even before this last victory, any one observing the order of these wars, and the method in which they were conducted, must have recognized not only the good fortune of the Romans, but also their extraordinary valour and prudence. And were any one to search for the causes of this good fortune, he would have little difficulty in finding them, since nothing is more certain than that when a potentate has attained so great a reputation that every neighbouring prince or people is afraid to engage him single-handed, and stands in awe of him, none will ever venture to attack him, unless driven to do so by necessity; so that it will almost rest on his will to make war as he likes on any of his neighbours, while he studiously maintains peace with the rest; who, on their part, whether through fear of his power, or deceived by the methods he takes to dull their vigilance, are easily kept quiet. Distant powers, in the mean time, who have no intercourse with either, treat the matter as too remote to concern them in any way; and abiding in this error until the conflagration approaches their own doors, on its arrival have no resource for its extinction, save in their own strength, which, as their enemy has by that time become exceedingly powerful, no longer suffices.

I forbear to relate how the Samnites stood looking on while the Romans were subjugating the Equians and the Volscians; and, to avoid being prolix, shall content myself with the single instance of the Carthaginians, who, at the time when the Romans were contending with the Samnites and Etruscans, were possessed of great power and held in high repute, being already masters of the whole of Africa together with Sicily and Sardinia, besides occupying territory in various parts of Spain. And because their empire was so great, and at such a distance from the Roman frontier, they were never led to think of attacking the Romans or of lending assistance to the Etruscans or Samnites. On the contrary, they behaved towards the Romans as men behave towards those whom they see prosper, rather taking their part and courting their friendship. Nor did they discover their mistake until the Romans, after subduing all the intervening nations, began to assail their power both in Spain and Sicily. What happened in the case of the Carthaginians, happened also in the case of the Gauls, of Philip of Macedon, and of Antiochus, each of whom, while Rome was engaged with another of them, believed that other would have the advantage, and that there would be time enough to provide for their own safety, whether by making peace or war. It seems to me, therefore, that the same good fortune which, in this respect, attended the Romans, might be shared by all princes acting as they did, and of a valour equal to theirs.

As bearing on this point, it might have been proper for me to show what methods were followed by the Romans in entering the territories of other nations, had I not already spoken of this at length in my *Treatise on Princedoms*, wherein the whole subject is discussed. Here it is enough to say briefly, that in a new province they always sought for some friend who should be to them as a ladder whereby to climb, a door through which to pass, or an instrument wherewith to keep their hold. Thus we see them effect their entrance into Samnium through the Capuans, into Etruria through the Camertines, into Sicily through the Mamertines, into Spain through the Saguntans, into Africa through Massinissa, into Greece through the Etolians, into Asia through Eumenes and other princes, into Gaul through the Massilians and Eduans; and, in like manner, never without similar assistance in their efforts whether to acquire provinces or to keep them.

The nations who carefully attend to this precaution will be seen to stand in less need of Fortune's help than others who neglect it. But that all may clearly understand how much more the Romans were aided by valour than by Fortune in acquiring their empire, I shall in the following Chapter consider the character of those nations with whom they had to contend, and show how stubborn these were in defending their freedom.

Chapter II.—*With what Nations the Romans had to contend, and how stubborn these were in defending their Freedom.*

In subduing the countries round about them, and certain of the more distant provinces, nothing gave the Romans so much trouble, as the love which in those days many nations bore to freedom, defending it with such obstinacy as could not have been overcome save by a surpassing valour. For we know by numberless instances, what perils these nations were ready to face in their efforts to maintain or recover their freedom, and what vengeance they took against those who deprived them of it. We know, too, from history, what hurt a people or city suffers from servitude. And though, at the present day, there is but one province which can be said to contain within it free cities, we find that formerly these abounded everywhere. For we learn that in the ancient times of which I speak, from the mountains which divide Tuscany from Lombardy down to the extreme point of Italy, there dwelt numerous free nations, such as the Etruscans, the Romans, and the Samnites, besides many others in other parts of the Peninsula. Nor do we ever read of there being any kings over them, except those who reigned in Rome, and Porsenna, king of Etruria. How the line of this last-named prince came to be extinguished, history does not inform us; but it is clear that at the time when the Romans went to besiege Veii, Etruria was free, and so greatly rejoiced in her freedom, and so detested the regal name, that when the Veientines, who for their defence had created a king in Veii, sought aid from the Etruscans against Rome, these, after much deliberation resolved to lend them no help while they continued to live under a king; judging it useless to defend a country given over to servitude by its inhabitants.

It is easy to understand whence this love of liberty arises among nations, for we know by experience that States have never signally increased, either as to dominion or wealth, except where they have lived under a free government. And truly it is strange to think to what a pitch of greatness Athens came during the hundred years after she had freed herself from the despotism of Pisistratus; and far stranger to contemplate the marvellous growth which Rome made after freeing herself from her kings. The cause, however, is not far to seek, since it is the well-being, not of individuals, but of the community which makes a State great; and, without question, this universal well-being is nowhere secured save in a republic. For a republic will do whatsoever makes for its interest; and though its measures prove hurtful to this man or to that, there are so many whom they benefit, that these are able to carry them out, in spite of the resistance of the few whom they injure.

But the contrary happens in the case of a prince; for, as a rule, what helps him hurts the State, and what helps the State hurts him; so that whenever a tyranny springs up in a city which has lived free, the least evil which can befall that city is to make no further progress, nor ever increase in power or wealth; but in most cases, if not in all, it will be its fate to go back. Or should there chance to arise in it some able tyrant who extends his dominions by his valour and skill in arms, the advantage which results is to himself only, and not to the State; since he can bestow no honours on those of the citizens over whom he tyrannizes who have shown themselves good and valiant, lest afterwards he should have cause to fear them. Nor can he make those cities which he acquires, subject or tributary to the city over which he rules; because to make this city powerful is not for his interest, which lies in keeping it so divided that each town and province may separately recognize him alone as its master. In this way he only, and not his country, is the gainer by his conquests. And if any one desire to have this view confirmed by numberless other proofs, let him look into Xenophon's treatise *De Tirannide*.

No wonder, then, that the nations of antiquity pursued tyrants with such relentless hatred, and so passionately loved freedom that its very name was dear to them, as was seen when Hieronymus, grandson of Hiero the Syracusan, was put to death in Syracuse. For when word of his death reached the army, which lay encamped not far off, at first it was greatly moved, and eager to take up arms against the murderers. But on hearing the cry of liberty shouted in the streets of Syracuse, quieted at once by the name, it laid aside its resentment against those who had slain the tyrant, and fell to consider how a free government might be provided for the city.

Nor is it to be wondered at that the ancient nations took terrible vengeance on those who deprived them of their freedom; of which, though there be many instances, I mean only to cite one which happened in the city of Corcyra at the time of the Peloponnesian war. For Greece being divided into two factions, one of which sided with the Athenians, the other with the Spartans, it resulted that many of its cities were divided against themselves, some of the citizens seeking the friendship of Sparta and some of Athens. In the aforesaid city of Corcyra, the nobles getting the upper hand, deprived the commons of their freedom; these, however, recovering themselves with the help of the Athenians, laid hold of the entire body of the nobles, and cast them into a prison large enough to contain them all, whence they brought them forth by eight or ten at a time, pretending that they were to be sent to different places into banishment, whereas, in fact, they put them to death with many circumstances of cruelty. Those who were left, learning what was going on, resolved to do their utmost to escape this ignominious death, and arming themselves with what weapons they could find, defended the door of their prison against all who sought to enter; till the people, hearing the tumult and rushing in haste to the prison, dragged down the roof, and smothered the prisoners in the ruins. Many other horrible and atrocious cruelties likewise perpetrated in Greece, show it to be true that a lost freedom is avenged with more ferocity than a threatened freedom is defended.

When I consider whence it happened that the nations of antiquity were so much more zealous in their love of liberty than those of the present day, I am led to believe that it arose from the same cause which makes the present generation of men less vigorous and daring than those of ancient times, namely the difference of the training of the present day from that of earlier ages; and this, again, arises from the different character of the religions then and now prevailing. For our religion, having revealed to us the truth and the true path, teaches us to make little account of worldly glory; whereas, the Gentiles, greatly esteeming it, and placing therein their highest good, displayed a greater fierceness in their actions.

This we may gather from many of their customs, beginning with their sacrificial rites, which were of much magnificence as compared with the simplicity of our worship, though that be not without a certain dignity of its own, refined rather than splendid, and far removed from any tincture of ferocity or violence. In the religious ceremonies of the ancients neither pomp nor splendour were wanting; but to these was joined the ordinance of sacrifice, giving occasion to much bloodshed and cruelty. For in its celebration many beasts were slaughtered, and this being a cruel spectacle imparted a cruel temper to the worshippers. Moreover, under the old religions none obtained divine honours save those who were loaded with worldly glory, such as captains of armies and rulers of cities; whereas our religion glorifies men of a humble and contemplative, rather than of an active life. Accordingly, while the highest good of the old religions consisted in magnanimity, bodily strength, and all those other qualities which make men brave, our religion places it in humility, lowliness, and contempt for the things of this world; or if it ever calls upon us to be brave, it is that we should be brave to suffer rather than to do.

This manner of life, therefore, seems to have made the world feebler, and to have given it over as a prey to wicked men to deal with as they please; since the mass of mankind, in the hope of being received into Paradise, think more how to bear injuries than how to avenge them. But should it seem that the world has grown effeminate and Heaven laid aside her arms, this assuredly results from the baseness of those who have interpreted our religion to accord with indolence and ease rather than with valour. For were we to remember that religion permits the exaltation and defence of our country, we would see it to be our duty to love and honour it, and would strive to be able and ready to defend it.

This training, therefore, and these most false interpretations are the causes why, in the world of the present day, we find no longer the numerous commonwealths which were found of old; and in consequence, that we see not now among the nations that love of freedom which prevailed then; though, at the same time, I am persuaded that one cause of this change has been, that the Roman Empire by its arms and power put an end to all the free States and free institutions of antiquity. For although the power of Rome fell afterwards into decay, these States could never recover their strength or resume their former mode of government, save in a very few districts of the Empire.

But, be this as it may, certain it is that in every country of the world, even the least considerable, the Romans found a league of well-armed republics, most resolute in the defence of their freedom, whom it is clear they never could have subdued had they not been endowed with the rarest and most astonishing valour. To cite a single instance, I shall take the case of the Samnites who, strange as it may now seem, were on the admission of Titus Livius himself, so powerful and so steadfast in arms, as to be able to withstand the Romans down to the consulship of Papirius Cursor, son to the first Papirius, a period of six and forty years, in spite of numerous defeats, the loss of many of their towns, and the great slaughter which overtook them everywhere throughout their country. And this is the more remarkable when we see that country, which once contained so many noble cities, and supported so great a population, now almost uninhabited; and reflect that it formerly enjoyed a government and possessed resources making its conquest impossible to less than Roman valour.

There is no difficulty, therefore, in determining whence that ancient greatness and this modern decay have arisen, since they can be traced to the free life formerly prevailing and to the servitude which prevails now. For all countries and provinces which enjoy complete freedom, make, as I have said, most rapid progress. Because, from marriage being less restricted in these countries, and more sought after, we find there a greater population; every man being disposed to beget as many children as he thinks he can rear, when he has no anxiety lest they should be deprived of their patrimony, and knows not only that they are born to freedom and not to slavery, but that they may rise by their merit to be the first men of their country. In such States, accordingly, we see wealth multiply, both that which comes from agriculture and that which comes from manufactures. For all love to gather riches and to add to their possessions when their enjoyment of them is not likely to be disturbed. And hence it happens that the citizens of such States vie with one another in whatever tends to promote public or private well-being; in both of which, consequently, there is a wonderful growth.

But the contrary of all this takes place in those countries which live in servitude, and the more oppressive their servitude, the more they fall short of the good which all desire. And the hardest of all hard servitudes is that wherein one commonwealth is subjected to another. First, because it is more lasting, and there is less hope to escape from it; and, second, because every commonwealth seeks to add to its own strength by weakening and enfeebling all beside. A prince who gets the better of you will not treat you after this fashion, unless he be a barbarian like those eastern despots who lay countries waste and destroy the labours of civilization; but if influenced by the ordinary promptings of humanity, will, as a rule, regard all his subject States with equal favour, and suffer them to pursue their usual employments, and retain almost all their ancient institutions, so that if they flourish not as free States might, they do not dwindle as States that are enslaved; by which I mean enslaved by a stranger, for of that other slavery to which they may be reduced by one of their own citizens, I have already spoken.

Whoever, therefore, shall well consider what has been said above, will not be astonished at the power possessed by the Samnites while they were still free, nor at the weakness into which they fell when they were subjugated. Of which change in their fortunes Livius often reminds us, and particularly in connection with the war with Hannibal, where he relates that the Samnites, being ill-treated by a Roman legion quartered at Nola, sent legates to Hannibal to ask his aid; who in laying their case before him told him, that with their own soldiers and captains they had fought single handed against the Romans for a hundred years, and had more than once withstood two consuls and two consular armies; but had now fallen so low, that they were scarce able to defend themselves against one poor legion.

Chapter III.—*That Rome became great by destroying the Cities which lay round about her, and by readily admitting strangers to the rights of Citizenship.*

"Crescit interea Roma Albæ ruinis"—*Meanwhile Rome grows on the ruins of Alba.* They who would have their city become a great empire, must endeavour by every means to fill it with inhabitants; for without a numerous population no city can ever succeed in growing powerful. This may be effected in two ways, by gentleness or by force. By gentleness, when you offer a safe and open path to all strangers who may wish to come and dwell in your city, so as to encourage them to come there of their own accord; by force, when after destroying neighbouring towns, you transplant their inhabitants to live in yours. Both of these methods were practised by Rome, and with such success, that in the time of her sixth king there dwelt within her walls eighty thousand citizens fit to bear arms. For the Romans loved to follow the methods of the skilful husbandman, who, to insure a plant growing big and yielding and maturing its fruit, cuts off the first shoots it sends out, that the strength remaining in the stem, it may in due season put forth new and more vigorous and more fruitful branches. And that this was a right and a necessary course for Rome to take for establishing and extending her empire, is proved by the example of Sparta and Athens, which, although exceedingly well-armed States, and regulated by excellent laws, never reached the same greatness as the Roman Republic; though the latter, to all appearance, was more turbulent and disorderly than they, and, so far as laws went, not so perfectly governed. For this we can offer no other explanation than that already given. For by augmenting the numbers of her citizens in both the ways named, Rome was soon able to place two hundred and eighty thousand men under arms; while neither Sparta nor Athens could ever muster more than twenty thousand; and this, not because the situation of these countries was less advantageous than that of Rome, but simply from the difference in the methods they followed.

For Lycurgus, the founder of the Spartan Republic, thinking nothing so likely to relax his laws as an admixture of new citizens, did all he could to prevent intercourse with strangers; with which object, besides refusing these the right to marry, the right of citizenship, and all such other social rights as induce men to become members of a community, he ordained that in this republic of his the only money current should be of leather, so that none might be tempted to repair thither to trade or to carry on any art.

Under such circumstances the number of the inhabitants of that State could never much increase. For as all our actions imitate nature, and it is neither natural nor possible that a puny stem should carry a great branch, so a small republic cannot assume control over cities or countries stronger than herself; or, doing so, will resemble the tree whose boughs being greater than its trunk, are supported with difficulty, and snapped by every gust of wind. As it proved with Sparta. For after she had spread her dominion over all the cities of Greece, no sooner did Thebes rebel than all the others rebelled likewise, and the trunk was left stripped of its boughs. But this could not have happened with Rome, whose stem was mighty enough to bear any branch with ease.

It was, therefore, by adding to her population, and by, adopting certain other methods presently to be noticed, that Rome became so great and powerful. And this is well expressed by Titus Livius, in the words, "*Crescit interea Roma Albae ruinis.*"

Chapter IV.—*That Commonwealths have followed three Methods for extending their Power.*

Any one who has read ancient history with attention, must have observed that three methods have been used by republics for extending their power. One of these, followed by the old Etruscans, is to form a confederation of many States, wherein none has precedence over the rest in authority or rank, and each allows the others to share its acquisitions; as do the States of the Swiss League in our days, and as the Achaians and Etolians did in Greece in earlier times. And because the Etruscans were opposed to the Romans in many wars, that I may give a clearer notion of this method of theirs, I shall enlarge a little in my account of the Etruscan people.

In Italy, before the Romans became supreme, the Etruscans were very powerful, both by sea and land; and although we have no separate history of their affairs, we have some slight records left us of them, and some indications of their greatness. We know, for instance, that they planted a colony, to which they gave the name of Hadria, on the coast of the upper sea; which colony became so renowned that it lent its name to the sea itself, which to this day by the Latins is called the Hadriatic. We know, too, that their arms were obeyed from the Tiber to the foot of the mountains which enclose the greater part of the Italian peninsula; although, two hundred years before Rome grew to any great strength, they had lost their supremacy in the province now known as Lombardy, of which the French had possessed themselves. For that people, whether driven by necessity, or attracted by the excellence of the fruits, and still more of the wine of Italy, came there under their chief, Bellovesus; and after defeating and expelling the inhabitants of the country, settled themselves therein, and there built many cities; calling the district Gallia, after the name they then bore: and this territory they retained until they were subdued by the Romans.

These Etruscans, therefore, living with one another on a footing of complete equality, when they sought to extend their power, followed that first method of which I have just now spoken. Their State was made up of twelve cities, among which were Chiusi, Veii, Friuli, Arezzo, Volterra, and the like, and their government was conducted in the form of a league. They could not, however, extend their conquests beyond Italy; while even within the limits of Italy, much territory remained unoccupied by them for reasons presently to be noticed.

The second method is to provide yourself with allies or companions, taking heed, however, to retain in your own hands the chief command, the seat of government, and the titular supremacy. This was the method followed by the Romans.

The third method is to hold other States in direct subjection to you, and not merely associated with you as companions; and this was the plan pursued by the Spartans and Athenians.

Of these three methods, the last is wholly useless, as was seen in the case of the two States named, which came to ruin from no other cause than that they had acquired a dominion greater than they could maintain. For to undertake to govern cities by force, especially such cities as have been used to live in freedom, is a difficult and arduous task, in which you never can succeed without an army and that a great one. But to have such an army you must needs have associates who will help to swell the numbers of your own citizens. And because Athens and Sparta neglected this precaution, whatever they did was done in vain; whereas Rome, which offers an instance of the second of the methods we are considering, by attending to this precaution reached a power that had no limit. And as she alone has lived in this way, so she alone has attained to this pitch of power. For joining with herself many States throughout Italy as her companions, who in most respects lived with her on a footing of equality, while, as has been noted, always reserving to herself the seat of empire and the titular command, it came about that these States, without being aware of it, by their own efforts, and with their own blood, wrought out their own enslavement.

For when Rome began to send armies out of Italy, for the purpose of reducing foreign kingdoms to provinces, and of subjugating nations who, being used to live under kings, were not impatient of her yoke, and who, receiving Roman governors, and having been conquered by armies bearing the Roman name, recognized no masters save the Romans, those companions of Rome who dwelt in Italy suddenly found themselves surrounded by Roman subjects, and weighed down by the greatness of the Roman power; and when at last they came to perceive the mistake in which they had been living, it was too late to remedy it, so vast was the authority which Rome had then obtained over foreign countries, and so great the resources which she possessed within herself; having by this time grown to be the mightiest and best-armed of States. So that although these her companions sought to avenge their wrongs by conspiring against her, they were soon defeated in the attempt, and remained in a worse plight than before, since they too became subjects and no longer associates. This method, then, as I have said, was followed by the Romans alone; but no other plan can be pursued by a republic which desires to extend its power; experience having shown none other so safe and certain.

The method which consists in forming leagues, of which I have spoken above as having been adopted by the Etruscans, the Achaians, and the Etolians of old, and in our own days by the Swiss, is the next best after that followed by the Romans, for as in this way there can be no great extension of power, two advantages result: first, that you do not readily involve yourself in war; and, second, that you can easily preserve any little acquisition which you may make. The reason why you cannot greatly extend your power is, that as your league is made up of separate States with distinct seats of government, it is difficult for these to consult and resolve in concert. The same causes make these States careless to enlarge their territories; because acquisitions which have to be shared among many communities are less thought of than those made by a single republic which looks to enjoy them all to itself. Again, since leagues govern through general councils, they must needs be slower in resolving than a nation dwelling within one frontier.

Moreover, we find from experience that this method has certain fixed limits beyond which there is no instance of its ever having passed; by which I mean that some twelve or fourteen communities may league themselves together, but will never seek to pass beyond that limit: for after associating themselves in such numbers as seem to them to secure their safety against all besides, they desire no further extension of their power, partly because no necessity compels them to extend, and partly because, for the reasons already given, they would find no profit in extending. For were they to seek extension they would have to follow one of two courses: either continuing to admit new members to their league, whose number must lead to confusion; or else making subjects, a course which they will avoid since they will see difficulty in making them, and no great good in having them. Wherefore, when their number has so increased that their safety seems secured, they have recourse to two expedients: either receiving other States under their protection and engaging for their defence (in which way they obtain money from various quarters which they can easily distribute among themselves); or else hiring themselves out as soldiers to foreign States, and drawing pay from this or the other prince who employs them to carry out his enterprises; as we see done by the Swiss at the present day, and as we read was done in ancient times by certain of those nations whom we have named above. To which we have a witness in Titus Livius, who relates that when Philip of Macedon came to treat with Titus Quintius Flamininus, and while terms were being discussed in the presence of a certain Etolian captain, this man coming to words with Philip, the latter taunted him with greed and bad faith; telling him that the Etolians were not ashamed to draw pay from one side, and then send their men to serve on the other; so that often the banner of Etolia might be seen displayed in two hostile camps.

We see, therefore, that the method of proceeding by leagues has always been of the same character, and has led always to the same results. We see, likewise, that the method which proceeds by reducing States to direct subjection has constantly proved a weak one, and produced insignificant gains; and that whenever these gains have passed a certain limit, ruin has ensued. And if the latter of these two methods be of little utility among armed States, among those that are unarmed, as is now the case with the republics of Italy, it is worse than useless. We may conclude, therefore, that the true method was that followed by the Romans; which is the more remarkable as we find none who adopted it before they did, and none who have followed it since. As for leagues, I know of no nations who have had recourse to them in recent times except the Swiss and the Suevians.

But to bring my remarks on this head to an end, I affirm that all the various methods followed by the Romans in conducting their affairs, whether foreign or domestic, so far from being imitated in our day, have been held of no account, some pronouncing them to be mere fables, some thinking them impracticable, others out of place and unprofitable; and so, abiding in this ignorance, we rest a prey to all who have chosen to invade our country. But should it seem difficult to tread in the footsteps of the Romans, it ought not to appear so hard, especially for us Tuscans, to imitate the Tuscans of antiquity, who if, from the causes already assigned, they failed to establish an empire like that of Rome, succeeded in acquiring in Italy that degree of power which their method of acting allowed, and which they long preserved in security, with the greatest renown in arms and government, and the highest reputation for manners and religion. This power and this glory of theirs were first impaired by the Gauls, and afterwards extinguished by the Romans, and so utterly extinguished, that of the Etruscan Empire, so splendid two thousand years ago, we have at the present day barely a record. This it is which has led me to inquire whence this oblivion of things arises, a question of which I shall treat in the following Chapter.

Chapter V.—*That changes in Sects and Tongues, and the happening of Floods and Pestilences, obliterate the Memory of the Past.*

To those philosophers who will have it that the world has existed from all eternity, it were, I think, a good answer, that if what they say be true we ought to have record of a longer period than five thousand years; did it not appear that the memory of past times is blotted out by a variety of causes, some referable to men, and some to Heaven.

Among the causes which have a human origin are the changes in sects and tongues; because when a new sect, that is to say a new religion, comes up, its first endeavour, in order to give itself reputation, is to efface the old; and should it so happen that the founders of the new religion speak another tongue, this may readily be effected. This we know from observing the methods which Christianity has followed in dealing with the religion of the Gentiles, for we find that it has abolished all the rites and ordinances of that worship, and obliterated every trace of the ancient belief. True, it has not succeeded in utterly blotting out our knowledge of things done by the famous men who held that belief; and this because the propagators of the new faith, retaining the Latin tongue, were constrained to use it in writing the new law; for could they have written this in a new tongue, we may infer, having regard to their other persecutions, that no record whatever would have survived to us of past events. For any one who reads of the methods followed by Saint Gregory and the other heads of the Christian religion, will perceive with what animosity they pursued all ancient memorials; burning the works of poets and historians; breaking images; and destroying whatsoever else afforded any trace of antiquity. So that if to this persecution a new language had been joined, it must soon have been found that everything was forgotten.

We may believe, therefore, that what Christianity has sought to effect against the sect of the Gentiles, was actually effected by that sect against the religion which preceded theirs; and that, from the repeated changes of belief which have taken place in the course of five or six thousand years, the memory of what happened at a remote date has perished, or, if any trace of it remain, has come to be regarded as a fable to which no credit is due; like the Chronicle of Diodorus Siculus, which, professing to give an account of the events of forty or fifty thousand years, is held, and I believe justly, a lying tale.

As for the causes of oblivion which we may refer to Heaven, they are those which make havoc of the human race, and reduce the population of certain parts of the world to a very small number. This happens by plague, famine, or flood, of which three the last is the most hurtful, as well because it is the most universal, as because those saved are generally rude and ignorant mountaineers, who possessing no knowledge of antiquity themselves, can impart none to those who come after them. Or if among the survivors there chance to be one possessed of such knowledge, to give himself consequence and credit, he will conceal and pervert it to suit his private ends, so that to his posterity there will remain only so much as he may have been pleased to communicate, and no more.

That these floods, plagues, and famines do in fact happen, I see no reason to doubt, both because we find all histories full of them, and recognize their effect in this oblivion of the past, and also because it is reasonable that such things should happen. For as when much superfluous matter has gathered in simple bodies, nature makes repeated efforts to remove and purge it away, thereby promoting the health of these bodies, so likewise as regards that composite body the human race, when every province of the world so teems with inhabitants that they can neither subsist where they are nor remove elsewhere, every region being equally crowded and over-peopled, and when human craft and wickedness have reached their highest pitch, it must needs come about that the world will purge herself in one or another of these three ways, to the end that men, becoming few and contrite, may amend their lives and live with more convenience.

Etruria, then, as has been said above, was at one time powerful, abounding in piety and valour, practising her own customs, and speaking her own tongue; but all this was effaced by the power of Rome, so that, as I have observed already, nothing is left of her but the memory of a name.

Chapter VI.—*Of the Methods followed by the Romans in making War.*

Having treated of the methods followed by the Romans for increasing their power, we shall now go on to consider those which they used in making war; and in all they did we shall find how wisely they turned aside from the common path in order to render their progress to supreme greatness easy.

Whosoever makes war, whether from policy or ambition, means to acquire and to hold what he acquires, and to carry on the war he has undertaken in such a manner that it shall enrich and not impoverish his native country and State. It is necessary, therefore, whether for acquiring or holding, to consider how cost may be avoided, and everything done most advantageously for the public welfare. But whoever would effect all this, must take the course and follow the methods of the Romans; which consisted, first of all, in making their wars, as the French say, *great and short*. For entering the field with strong armies, they brought to a speedy conclusion whatever wars they had with the Latins, the Samnites, or the Etruscans.

And if we take note of all the wars in which they were engaged, from the foundation of their city down to the siege of Veii, all will be seen to have been quickly ended some in twenty, some in ten, and some in no more than six days. And this was their wont: So soon as war was declared they would go forth with their armies to meet the enemy and at once deliver battle. The enemy, on being routed, to save their country from pillage, very soon came to terms, when the Romans would take from them certain portions of their territory. These they either assigned to particular persons, or made the seat of a colony, which being settled on the confines of the conquered country served as a defence to the Roman frontier, to the advantage both of the colonists who had these lands given them, and of the Roman people whose borders were thus guarded at no expense to themselves. And no other system of defence could have been at once so safe, so strong, and so effectual. For while the enemy were not actually in the field, this guard was sufficient; and when they came out in force to overwhelm the colony, the Romans also went forth in strength and gave them battle; and getting the better of them, imposed harder terms than before, and so returned home. And in this way they came gradually to establish their name abroad, and to add to their power.

These methods they continued to employ until they changed their system of warfare, which they did during the siege of Veii; when to enable them to carry on a prolonged war, they passed a law for the payment of their soldiers, whom, up to that time they had not paid, nor needed to pay, because till then their wars had been of brief duration. Nevertheless, while allowing pay to their soldiers that they might thus wage longer wars, and keep their armies longer in the field when employed on distant enterprises, they never departed from their old plan of bringing their campaigns to as speedy an end as place and circumstances allowed, nor ever ceased to plant colonies.

Their custom of terminating their wars with despatch, besides being natural to the Romans, was strengthened by the ambition of their consuls, who, being appointed for twelve months only, six of which they had to spend in the city, were eager to bring their wars to an end as rapidly as they could, that they might enjoy the honours of a triumph. The usage of planting colonies was recommended by the great advantage and convenience which resulted from it. In dealing with the spoils of warfare their practice, no doubt, in a measure changed, so that in this respect they were not afterwards so liberal as they were at first; partly, because liberality did not seem so necessary when their soldiers were in receipt of pay; and, partly, because the spoils themselves being greater than before, they thought by their help so to enrich the public treasury as to be able to carry on their wars without taxing the city; and, in fact, by pursuing this course the public revenues were soon greatly augmented. The methods thus followed by the Romans in dividing plunder and in planting colonies had, accordingly, this result, that whereas other less prudent princes and republics are impoverished by war, Rome was enriched by it; nay, so far was the system carried, that no consul could hope for a triumph unless he brought back with him for the public treasury much gold and silver and spoils of every kind.

By methods such as these, at one time bringing their wars to a rapid conclusion by invasion and actual defeat, at another wearing out an enemy by protracted hostilities, and again by concluding peace on advantageous terms, the Romans continually grew richer and more powerful.

Chapter VII.—*Of the Quantity of Land assigned by the Romans to each Colonist.*

It would, I think, be difficult to fix with certainty how much land the Romans allotted to each colonist, for my belief is that they gave more or less according to the character of the country to which they sent them. We may, however, be sure that in every instance, and to whatever country they were sent, the quantity of land assigned was not very large: first, because, these colonists being sent to guard the newly acquired country, by giving little land it became possible to send more men; and second because, as the Romans lived frugally at home, it is unreasonable to suppose that they should wish their countrymen to be too well off abroad. And Titus Livius tells us that on the capture of Veii, the Romans sent thither a colony, allotting to each colonist three jugera and seven unciae of land, which, according to our measurement would be something under two acres.

Besides the above reasons, the Romans may likely enough have thought that it was not so much the quantity of the land allotted as its careful cultivation that would make it suffice. It is very necessary, however, that every colony should have common pasturage where all may send their cattle to graze, as well as woods where they may cut fuel; for without such conveniences no colony can maintain itself.

Chapter VIII.—*Why certain Nations leave their ancestral Seats and overflow the Countries of others.*

Having spoken above of the methods followed by the Romans in making war, and related how the Etruscans were attacked by the Gauls, it seems to me not foreign to these topics to explain that of wars there are two kinds. One kind of war has its origin in the ambition of princes or republics who seek to extend their dominions. Such were the wars waged by Alexander the Great, and by the Romans, and such are those which we see every day carried on by one potentate against another. Wars of this sort have their dangers, but do not utterly extirpate the inhabitants of a country; what the conqueror seeks being merely the submission of the conquered people, whom, generally speaking, he suffers to retain their laws, and always their houses and goods.

The other species of war is when an entire people, with all the families of which it is made up, being driven out by famine or defeat, removes from its former seat, and goes in search of a new abode and a new country, not simply with the view to establish dominion over it, but to possess it as its own, and to expel or exterminate the former inhabitants. Of this most terrible and cruel species of warfare Sallust speaks at the end of his history of the war with Jugurtha, where in mentioning that after the defeat of Jugurtha the movement of the Gauls into Italy began to be noticed, he observes that "*in the wars of the Romans with other nations the struggle was for mastery; but that always in their wars with the Gauls the struggle on both sides was for life.*" For a prince or commonwealth, when attacking another State, will be content to rid themselves of those only who are at the head of affairs; but an entire people, set in motion in the manner described, must destroy all who oppose them, since their object is to subsist on that whereon those whom they invade have hitherto subsisted.

The Romans had to pass through three of these desperate wars; the first being that in which their city was actually captured by those Gauls who, as already mentioned, had previously taken Lombardy from the Etruscans and made it their seat, and for whose invasion Titus Livius has assigned two causes. First, that they were attracted, as I have said before, by the fruitful soil and by the wine of Italy which they had not in Gaul; second, that their population having multiplied so greatly that they could no longer find wherewithal to live on at home, the princes of their land decided that certain of their number should go forth to seek a new abode; and so deciding, chose as leaders of those who were to go, two Gaulish chiefs, Bellovesus and Siccovesus; the former of whom came into Italy while the latter passed into Spain. From the immigration under Bellovesus resulted the occupation of Lombardy, and, subsequently, the first war of the Gauls with Rome. At a later date, and after the close of the first war with Carthage, came the second Gallic invasion, when more than two hundred thousand Gauls perished in battle between Piombino and Pisa. The third of these wars broke out on the descent into Italy of the Todi and Cimbri, who, after defeating several Roman armies, were themselves defeated by Marius.

In these three most dangerous contests the arms of Rome prevailed; but no ordinary valour was needed for their success. For we see afterwards, when the spirit of the Romans had declined, and their armies had lost their former excellence, their supremacy was overthrown by men of the same race, that is to say by the Goths, the Vandals, and others like them, who spread themselves over the whole of the Western Empire.

Nations such as these, quit, as I have said, their native land, when forced by famine, or by defeat in domestic wars, to seek a new habitation elsewhere. When those thus driven forth are in large numbers, they violently invade the territories of other nations, slaughtering the inhabitants, seizing on their possessions, founding new kingdoms, and giving new names to provinces; as was done by Moses, and by those tribes who overran the Roman Empire. For the new names which we find in Italy and elsewhere, have no other origin than in their having been given by these new occupants; as when the countries formerly known as Gallia Cisalpina and Gallia Transalpina took the names of Lombardy and France, from the Lombards and the Franks who settled themselves there. In the same way Sclavonia was formerly known as Illyria, Hungary as Pannonia, and England as Britain; while many other provinces which it would be tedious to enumerate, have similarly changed their designations; as when the name Judæa was given by Moses to that part of Syria of which he took possession.

And since I have said above that nations such as those I have been describing, are often driven by wars from their ancestral homes, and forced to seek a new country elsewhere, I shall cite the instance of the Maurusians, a people who anciently dwelt in Syria, but hearing of the inroad of the Hebrews, and thinking themselves unable to resist them, chose rather to seek safety in flight than to perish with their country in a vain effort to defend it. For which reason, removing with their families, they went to Africa, where, after driving out the native inhabitants, they took up their abode; and although they could not defend their own country, were able to possess themselves of a country belonging to others. And Procopius, who writes the history of the war which Belisarius conducted against those Vandals who seized on Africa, relates, that on certain pillars standing in places where the Maurusians once dwelt, he had read inscriptions in these words: "*We Maurusians who fled before Joshua, the robber, the son of Nun;*"[1] giving us to know the cause of their quitting Syria. Be this as it may, nations thus driven forth by a supreme necessity, are, if they be in great number, in the highest degree dangerous, and cannot be successfully withstood except by a people who excel in arms.

When those constrained to abandon their homes are not in large numbers, they are not so dangerous as the nations of whom I have been speaking, since they cannot use the same violence, but must trust to their address to procure them a habitation; and, after procuring it, must live with their neighbours as friends and companions, as we find Æneas, Dido, the Massilians, and others like them to have lived; all of whom contrived to maintain themselves in the districts in which they settled, by securing the good will of the neighbouring nations.

Almost all the great emigrations of nations have been and continue to be from the cold and barren region of Scythia, because from the population there being excessive, and the soil ill able to support them, they are forced to quit their home, many causes operating to drive them forth and none to keep them back. And if, for the last five hundred years, it has not happened that any of these nations has actually overrun another country, there are various reasons to account for it. First, the great clearance which that region made of its inhabitants during the decline of the Roman Empire, when more than thirty nations issued from it in succession; and next, the circumstance that the countries of Germany and Hungary, whence also these nations came, are now so much improved that men can live there in comfort, and consequently are not constrained to shift their habitations. Besides which, since these countries are occupied by a very warlike race, they serve as a sort of bulwark to keep back the neighbouring Scythians, who for this reason do not venture to attack them, nor attempt to force a passage. Nevertheless, movements on a great scale have oftentimes been begun by the Tartars, and been at once withstood by the Hungarians and Poles, whose frequent boast it is, that but for them, Italy and the Church would more than once have felt the weight of the Tartar arms.

Of the nations of whom I have been speaking, I shall now say no more.

[Footnote 1: Nos Maurusii qui fugimus a facie Jesu latronis filii Navae. *Procop. Hist. Bell. Vand. II.*]

Chapter IX.—*Of the Causes which commonly give rise to Wars between States.*

The occasion which led to war between the Romans and Samnites, who for long had been in league with one another, is of common occurrence in all powerful States, being either brought about by accident, or else purposely contrived by some one who would set war a-foot. As between the Romans and the Samnites, the occasion of war was accidental. For in making war upon the Sidicinians and afterwards on the Campanians, the Samnites had no thought of involving themselves with the Romans. But the Campanians being overpowered, and, contrary to the expectation of Romans and Samnites alike, resorting to Rome for aid, the Romans, on whose protection they threw themselves, were forced to succour them as dependants, and to accept a war which, it seemed to them, they could not with honour decline. For though they might have thought it unreasonable to be called on to defend the Campanians as friends against their own friends the Samnites, it seemed to them shameful not to defend them as subjects, or as a people who had placed themselves under their protection. For they reasoned that to decline their defence would close the gate against all others who at any future time might desire to submit themselves to their power. And, accordingly, since glory and empire, and not peace, were the ends which they always had in view, it became impossible for them to refuse this protectorship.

A similar circumstance gave rise to the first war with the Carthaginians, namely the protectorate assumed by the Romans of the citizens of Messina in Sicily, and this likewise came about by chance. But the second war with Carthage was not the result of chance. For Hannibal the Carthaginian general attacked the Saguntans, who were the friends of Rome in Spain, not from any desire to injure them, but in order to set the arms of Rome in motion, and so gain an opportunity of engaging the Romans in a war, and passing on into Italy. This method of picking a quarrel is constantly resorted to by powerful States when they are bound by scruples of honour or like considerations. For if I desire to make war on a prince with whom I am under an ancient and binding treaty, I shall find some colour or pretext for attacking the friend of that prince, very well knowing that when I attack his friend, either the prince will resent it, when my scheme for engaging him in war will be realized; or that, should he not resent it, his weakness or baseness in not defending one who is under his protection will be made apparent; either of which alternatives will discredit him, and further my designs.

We are to note, therefore, in connection with this submission of the Campanians, what has just now been said as to provoking another power to war; and also the remedy open to a State which, being unequal to its own defence, is prepared to go all lengths to ruin its assailant,—that remedy being to give itself up unreservedly to some one whom it selects for its defender; as the Campanians gave themselves up to the Romans, and as the Florentines gave themselves up to King Robert of Naples, who, after refusing to defend them as his friends against Castruccio of Lucca by whom they were hard pressed, defended them as his subjects.

Chapter X.—*That contrary to the vulgar opinion, Money is not the Sinews of War.*

Since any man may begin a war at his pleasure, but cannot at his pleasure bring it to a close, a prince before he engages in any warlike enterprise ought to measure his strength and govern himself accordingly. But he must be prudent enough not to deceive himself as to his strength, which he will always do, if he measure it by money, by advantage of position, or by the good-will of his subjects, while he is unprovided with an army of his own. These are things which may swell your strength but do not constitute it, being in themselves null and of no avail without an army on which you can depend.

Without such an army no amount of money will meet your wants, the natural strength of your country will not protect you, and the fidelity and attachment of your subjects will not endure, since it is impossible that they should continue true to you when you cannot defend them. Lakes, and mountains, and the most inaccessible strongholds, where valiant defenders are wanting, become no better than the level plain; and money, so far from being a safeguard, is more likely to leave you a prey to your enemy; since nothing can be falser than the vulgar opinion which affirms it to be the sinews of war.

This opinion is put forward by Quintus Curtius, where, in speaking of the war between Antipater the Macedonian and the King of Sparta, he relates that the latter, from want of money, was constrained to give battle and was defeated; whereas, could he have put off fighting for a few days the news of Alexander's death would have reached Greece, and he might have had a victory without a battle. But lacking money, and fearing that on that account his soldiers might desert him, he was forced to hazard an engagement. It was for this reason that Quintus Curtius declared money to be the sinews of war, a maxim every day cited and acted upon by princes less wise than they should be. For building upon this, they think it enough for their defence to have laid up great treasures; not reflecting that were great treasures all that is needed for victory, Darius of old had conquered Alexander, the Greeks the Romans, and in our own times Charles of Burgundy the Swiss; while the pope and the Florentines together would have had little difficulty in defeating Francesco Maria, nephew of Pope Julius II., in the recent war of Urbino; and yet, in every one of these instances, the victory remained with him who held the sinews of war to consist, not in money, but in good soldiers.

Croesus, king of Lydia, after showing Solon the Athenian much besides, at last displayed to him the boundless riches of his treasure-house, and asked him what he thought of his power. Whereupon Solon answered that he thought him no whit more powerful in respect of these treasures, for as war is made with iron and not with gold, another coming with more iron might carry off his gold. After the death of Alexander the Great a tribe of Gauls, passing through Greece on their way into Asia, sent envoys to the King of Macedonia to treat for terms of accord; when the king, to dismay them by a display of his resources, showed them great store of gold and silver. But these barbarians, when they saw all this wealth, in their greed to possess it, though before they had looked on peace as settled, broke off negotiations; and thus the king was ruined by those very treasures he had amassed for his defence. In like manner, not many years ago, the Venetians, with a full treasury, lost their whole dominions without deriving the least advantage from their wealth.

I maintain, therefore, that it is not gold, as is vulgarly supposed, that is the sinews of war, but good soldiers; or while gold by itself will not gain you good soldiers, good soldiers may readily get you gold. Had the Romans chosen to make war with gold rather than with iron all the treasures of the earth would not have sufficed them having regard to the greatness of their enterprises and the difficulties they had to overcome in carrying them out. But making their wars with iron they never felt any want of gold; for those who stood in fear of them brought gold into their camp.

And supposing it true that the Spartan king was forced by lack of money to risk the chances of a battle, it only fared with him in respect of money as it has often fared with others from other causes; since we see that where an army is in such straits for want of victual that it must either fight or perish by famine, it will always fight, as being the more honourable course and that on which fortune may in some way smile. So, too, it has often happened that a captain, seeing his enemy about to be reinforced, has been obliged either to trust to fortune and at once deliver battle, or else, waiting till the reinforcement is complete, to fight then, whether he will or no, and at whatever disadvantage. We find also, as in the case of Hasdrubal when beset, in the March of Ancona, at once by Claudius Nero and by the other Roman consul, that a captain, when he must either fight or fly, will always fight, since it will seem to him that by this course, however hazardous, he has at least a chance of victory, while by the other his ruin is certain.

There are many circumstances, therefore, which may force a captain to give battle contrary to his intention, among which the want of money may sometimes be one. But this is no ground for pronouncing money to be the sinews of war, any more than those other things from the want of which men are reduced to the same necessity. Once more, therefore, I repeat that not gold but good soldiers constitute the sinews of war. Money, indeed, is most necessary in a secondary place; but this necessity good soldiers will always be able to supply, since it is as impossible that good soldiers should lack money, as that money by itself should secure good soldiers. And that what I say is true is shown by countless passages in history. When Pericles persuaded the Athenians to declare war against the whole Peloponnesus, assuring them that their dexterity, aided by their wealth, was sure to bring them off victorious, the Athenians, though for a while they prospered in this war, in the end were overpowered, the prudent counsels and good soldiers of Sparta proving more than a match for the dexterity and wealth of Athens. But, indeed, there can be no better witness to the truth of my contention than Titus Livius himself. For in that passage of his history wherein he discusses whether if Alexander the Great had invaded Italy, he would have succeeded in vanquishing the Romans, three things are noted by him as essential to success in war; to wit, many and good soldiers, prudent captains, and favourable fortune; and after examining whether the Romans or Alexander would have had the advantage in each of these three particulars, he arrives at his conclusion without any mention of money.

The Campanians, therefore, when asked by the Sidicinians to arm in their behalf, must have measured their strength by wealth and not by soldiers; for after declaring in their favour and suffering two defeats, to save themselves they were obliged to become tributary to Rome.

Chapter XI.—*That it were unwise to ally yourself a Prince who has Reputation rather than Strength.*

To mark the mistake made by the Sidicinians in trusting to the protection of the Campanians, and by the Campanians in supposing themselves able to protect the Sidicinians, Titus Livius could not have expressed himself in apter words than by saying, that "*the Campanians rather lent their name to the Sidicinians than furnished any substantial aid towards their defence.*"

Here we have to note that alliances with princes who from dwelling at a distance have no facility, or who from their own embarrassments, or from other causes, have no ability to render aid, afford rather reputation than protection to those who put their trust in them. As was the case in our own times with the Florentines, when, in the year 1479, they were attacked by the Pope and the King of Naples. For being friends of the French king they drew from that friendship more reputation than help. The same would be the case with that prince who should engage in any enterprise in reliance on the Emperor Maximilian, his being one of those friendships which, in the words of our historian, *nomen magis quam praesidium adferunt.*

On this occasion, therefore, the Campanians were misled by imagining themselves stronger than they really were. For often, from defect of judgment, men take upon them to defend others, when they have neither skill nor ability to defend themselves. Of which we have a further instance in the Tarentines, who, when the Roman and Samnite armies were already drawn up against one another for battle, sent messengers to the Roman consul to acquaint him that they desired peace between the two nations, and would themselves declare war against whichsoever of the two first began hostilities. The consul, laughing at their threats, in the presence of the messengers, ordered the signal for battle to sound, and bade his army advance to meet the enemy; showing the Tarentines by acts rather than words what answer he thought their message deserved.

Having spoken in the present Chapter of unwise courses followed by princes for defending others, I shall speak in the next, of the methods they follow in defending themselves.

Chapter XII.—*Whether when Invasion is imminent it is better to anticipate or to await it.*

I have often heard it disputed by men well versed in military affairs, whether, when there are two princes of nearly equal strength, and the bolder of the two proclaims war upon the other, it is better for that other to await attack within his own frontier, or to march into the enemy's country and fight him there; and I have heard reasons given in favour of each of these courses.

They who maintain that an enemy should be attacked in his own country, cite the advice given by Croesus to Cyrus, when the latter had come to the frontiers of the Massagetæ to make war on that people. For word being sent by Tomyris their queen that Cyrus might, at his pleasure, either enter her dominions, where she would await him, or else allow her to come and meet him; and the matter being debated, Croesus, contrary to the opinion of other advisers, counselled Cyrus to go forward and meet the queen, urging that were he to defeat her at a distance from her kingdom, he might not be able to take it from her, since she would have time to repair her strength; whereas, were he to defeat her within her own dominions, he could follow her up on her flight, and, without giving her time to recover herself, deprive her of her State. They cite also the advice given by Hannibal to Antiochus, when the latter was meditating a war on the Romans. For Hannibal told him that the Romans could not be vanquished except in Italy, where an invader might turn to account the arms and resources of their friends, whereas any one making war upon them out of Italy, and leaving that country in their hands, would leave them an unfailing source whence to draw whatever reinforcement they might need; and finally, he told him, that the Romans might more easily be deprived of Rome than of their empire, and of Italy more easily than of any of their other provinces. They likewise instance Agathocles, who, being unequal to support a war at home, invaded the Carthaginians, by whom he was being attacked, and reduced them to sue for peace. They also cite Scipio, who to shift the war from Italy, carried it into Africa.

Those who hold a contrary opinion contend that to have your enemy at a disadvantage you must get him away from his home, alleging the case of the Athenians, who while they carried on the war at their convenience in their own territory, retained their superiority; but when they quitted that territory, and went with their armies to Sicily, lost their freedom. They cite also the fable of the poets wherein it is figured that Antæus, king of Libya, being assailed by the Egyptian Hercules, could not be overcome while he awaited his adversary within the bounds of his own kingdom; but so soon as he was withdrawn from these by the craft of Hercules, lost his kingdom and his life. Whence the fable runs that Antæus, being son to the goddess Earth, when thrown to the ground drew fresh strength from the Earth, his mother; and that Hercules, perceiving this, held him up away from the Earth.

Recent opinions are likewise cited as favouring this view. Every one knows how Ferrando, king of Naples, was in his day accounted a most wise prince; and how two years before his death there came a rumour that Charles VIII of France was meditating an attack upon him; and how, after making great preparations for his defence, he sickened; and being on the point of death, among other counsels left his son Alfonso this advice, that nothing in the world should tempt him to pass out of his own territory, but to await the enemy within his frontier, and with his forces unimpaired; a warning disregarded by Alfonso, who sent into Romagna an army, which he lost, and with it his whole dominions, without a battle.

Other arguments on both sides of the question in addition to those already noticed, are as follows: He who attacks shows higher courage than he who stands on his defence, and this gives his army greater confidence. Moreover, by attacking your enemy you deprive him of many opportunities for using his resources, since he can receive no aid from subjects who have been stripped of their possessions; and when an enemy is at his gates, a prince must be careful how he levies money and imposes taxes; so that, as Hannibal said, the springs which enable a country to support a war come to be dried up. Again, the soldiers of an invader, finding themselves in a foreign land, are under a stronger necessity to fight, and necessity, as has often been said, is the parent of valour.

On the other hand, it may be argued that there are many advantages to be gained by awaiting the attack of your enemy. For without putting yourself much about, you may harass him by intercepting his supplies, whether of victual or of whatsoever else an army stands in need: from your better knowledge of the country you can impede his movements; and because men muster more willingly to defend their homes than to go on distant expeditions, you can meet him with more numerous forces, if defeated you can more easily repair your strength, because the bulk of your army, finding shelter at hand, will be able to save itself, and your reserves will have no distance to come. In this way you can use your whole strength without risking your entire fortunes; whereas, in leaving your country, you risk your entire fortunes, without putting forth your whole strength. Nay, we find that to weaken an adversary still further, some have suffered him to make a march of several days into their country, and then to capture certain of their towns, that by leaving garrisons in these, he might reduce the numbers of his army, and so be attacked at greater disadvantage.

But now to speak my own mind on the matter, I think we should make this distinction. Either you have your country strongly defended, as the Romans had and the Swiss have theirs, or, like the Carthaginians of old and the King of France and the Italians at the present day, you have it undefended. In the latter case you must keep the enemy at a distance from your country, for as your strength lies not in men but in money, whenever the supply of money is cut off you are undone, and nothing so soon cuts off this supply as a war of invasion. Of which we have example in the Carthaginians, who, while their country was free from invasion, were able by means of their great revenues to carry on war in Italy against the Romans, but when they were invaded could not defend themselves even against Agathocles. The Florentines, in like manner, could make no head against Castruccio, lord of Lucca, when he attacked them in their own country; and to obtain protection, were compelled to yield themselves up to King Robert of Naples. And yet, after Castruccio's death, these same Florentines were bold enough to attack the Duke of Milan in his own country, and strong enough to strip him of his dominions. Such valour did they display in distant wars, such weakness in those that were near.

But when a country is armed as Rome was and Switzerland now is, the closer you press it, the harder it is to subdue; because such States can assemble a stronger force to resist attack than for attacking others. Nor does the great authority of Hannibal move me in this instance, since resentment and his own advantage might lead him to speak as he spoke to Antiochus. For had the Romans suffered in Gaul, and within the same space of time, those three defeats at the hands of Hannibal which they suffered in Italy, it must have made an end of them; since they could not have turned the remnants of their armies to account as they did in Italy, not having the same opportunity for repairing their strength; nor could they have met their enemy with such numerous armies. For we never find them sending forth a force of more than fifty thousand men for the invasion of any province; whereas, in defending their own country against the inroad of the Gauls at the end of the first Carthaginian war, we hear of them bringing some eighteen hundred thousand men into the field; and their failure to vanquish the Gauls in Lombardy as they had vanquished those in Tuscany arose from their inability to lead a great force so far against a numerous enemy, or to encounter him with the same advantages. In Germany the Cimbrians routed a Roman army who had there no means to repair their disaster; but when they came into Italy, the Romans could collect their whole strength, and destroy them. Out of their native country, whence they can bring no more than thirty or forty thousand men, the Swiss may readily be defeated; but in their own country, where they can assemble a hundred thousand, they are well-nigh invincible.

In conclusion, therefore, I repeat that the prince who has his people armed and trained for war, should always await a great and dangerous war at home, and never go forth to meet it. But that he whose subjects are unarmed, and whose country is not habituated to war, should always carry the war to as great a distance as he can from home. For in this way each will defend himself in the best manner his means admit.

Chapter XIII.—*That Men rise from humble to high Fortunes rather by Fraud than by Force.*

I hold it as most certain that men seldom if ever rise to great place from small beginnings without using fraud or force, unless, indeed, they be given, or take by inheritance the place to which some other has already come. Force, however, will never suffice by itself to effect this end, while fraud often will, as any one may plainly see who reads the lives of Philip of Macedon, Agathocles of Sicily, and many others like them, who from the lowest or, at any rate, from very low beginnings, rose either to sovereignty or to the highest command.

This necessity for using deceit is taught by Xenophon in his life of Cyrus; for the very first expedition on which Cyrus is sent, against the King of Armenia, is seen to teem with fraud; and it is by fraud, and not by force, that he is represented as having acquired his kingdom; so that the only inference to be drawn from his conduct, as Xenophon describes it, is, that the prince who would accomplish great things must have learned how to deceive. Xenophon, moreover, represents his hero as deceiving his maternal grandsire Cyaxares, king of the Medians, in a variety of ways; giving it to be understood that without such deceit he could not have reached the greatness to which he came. Nor do I believe that any man born to humble fortunes can be shown to have attained great station, by sheer and open force, whereas this has often been effected by mere fraud, such as that used by Giovanni Galeazzo to deprive his uncle Bernabo of the State and government of Lombardy.

The same arts which princes are constrained to use at the outset of their career, must also be used by commonwealths, until they have grown powerful enough to dispense with them and trust to strength alone. And because Rome at all times, whether from chance or choice, followed all such methods as are necessary to attain greatness, in this also she was not behindhand. And, to begin with, she could have used no greater fraud than was involved in her method above noticed, of making for herself companions; since under this name she made for herself subjects, for such the Latins and the other surrounding nations, in fact, became. For availing herself at first of their arms to subdue neighbouring countries and gain herself reputation as a State, her power was so much increased by these conquests that there was none whom she could not overcome. But the Latins never knew that they were enslaved until they saw the Samnites twice routed and forced to make terms. This success, while it added greatly to the fame of the Romans among princes at a distance, who were thereby made familiar with the Roman name though not with the Roman arms, bred at the same time jealousy and distrust among those who, like the Latins, both saw and felt these arms; and such were the effects of this jealousy and distrust, that not the Latins only but all the Roman colonies in Latium, along with the Campanians whom a little while before the Romans had defended leagued themselves together against the authority of Rome. This war was set on foot by the Latins in the manner in which, as I have already explained, most wars are begun, not by directly attacking the Romans, but by defending the Sidicinians against the Samnites who were making war upon them with the permission of the Romans. And that it was from their having found out the crafty policy of the Romans that the Latins were led to take this step, is plain from the words which Titus Livius puts in the mouth of Annius Setinus the Latin prætor, who, in addressing the Latin council, is made to say, *“For if even now we can put up with slavery under the disguise of an equal alliance, etc”*

We see, therefore, that the Romans, from the time they first began to extend their power, were not unfamiliar with the art of deceiving, an art always necessary for those who would mount to great heights from low beginnings; and which is the less to be condemned when, as in the case of the Romans, it is skilfully concealed.

Chapter XIV.—*That Men often err in thinking they can subdue Pride by Humility.*

You shall often find that humility is not merely of no service to you, but is even hurtful, especially when used in dealing with insolent men, who, through envy or other like cause, have conceived hatred against you. Proof whereof is supplied by our historian where he explains the causes of this war between the Romans and the Latins. For on the Samnites complaining to the Romans that the Latins had attacked them, the Romans, desiring not to give the Latins ground of offence, would not forbid them proceeding with the war. But the endeavour to avoid giving offence to the Latins only served to increase their confidence, and led them the sooner to declare their hostility. Of which we have evidence in the language used by the same Latin Prætor, Annius Setinus, at the aforesaid council, when he said:—"*You have tried their patience by refusing them, soldiers. Who doubts but that they are offended? Still they have put up with the affront. They have heard that we are assembling an army against their allies the Samnites; and yet they have not stirred from their city. Whence this astonishing forbearance, but from their knowing our strength and their own weakness*?" Which words give us clearly to understand how much the patience of the Romans increased the arrogance of the Latins.

A prince, therefore, should never stoop from his dignity, nor should he if he would have credit for any concession make it voluntarily, unless he be able or believe himself able to withhold it. For almost always when matters have come to such a pass that you cannot give way with credit it is better that a thing be taken from you by force than yielded through fear of force. For if you yield through fear and to escape war, the chances are that you do not escape it; since he to whom, out of manifest cowardice you make this concession, will not rest content, but will endeavour to wring further concessions from you, and making less account of you, will only be the more kindled against you. At the same time you will find your friends less zealous on your behalf, since to them you will appear either weak or cowardly. But if, so soon as the designs of your enemy are disclosed, you at once prepare to resist though your strength be inferior to his, he will begin to think more of you, other neighbouring princes will think more; and many will be willing to assist you, on seeing you take up arms, who, had you relinquished hope and abandoned yourself to despair, would never have stirred a finger to save you.

The above is to be understood as applying where you have a single adversary only; but should you have several, it will always be a prudent course, even after war has been declared, to restore to some one of their number something you have of his, so as to regain his friendship and detach him from the others who have leagued themselves against you.

Chapter XV.—That weak States are always dubious in their Resolves; and that tardy Resolves are always hurtful.

Touching this very matter, and with regard to these earliest beginnings of war between the Latins and the Romans, it may be noted, that in all our deliberations it behoves us to come quickly to a definite resolve, and not to remain always in dubiety and suspense. This is plainly seen in connection with the council convened by the Latins when they thought to separate themselves from the Romans. For the Romans suspecting the hostile humour wherewith the Latins were infected, in order to learn how things really stood, and see whether they could not win back the malcontents without recourse to arms, gave them to know that they must send eight of their citizens to Rome, as they had occasion to consult with them. On receiving which message the Latins, knowing that they had done many things contrary to the wishes of the Romans, called a council to determine who of their number should be sent, and to instruct them what they were to say. But Annius, their prætor, being present in the council when these matters were being discussed, told them *"that he thought it of far greater moment for them to consider what they were to do than what they were to say; for when their resolves were formed, it would be easy to clothe them in fit words."* This, in truth, was sound advice and such as every prince and republic should lay to heart. Because, where there is doubt and uncertainty as to what we may decide on doing, we know not how to suit our words to our conduct; whereas, with our minds made up, and the course we are to follow fixed, it is an easy matter to find words to declare our resolves. I have noticed this point the more readily, because I have often found such uncertainty hinder the public business of our own republic, to its detriment and discredit. And in all matters of difficulty, wherein courage is needed for resolving, this uncertainty will always be met with, whenever those who have to deliberate and decide are weak.

Not less mischievous than doubtful resolves are those which are late and tardy, especially when they have to be made in behalf of a friend. For from their lateness they help none, and hurt ourselves. Tardy resolves are due to want of spirit or want of strength, or to the perversity of those who have to determine, who being moved by a secret desire to overthrow the government, or to carry out some selfish purpose of their own, suffer no decision to be come to, but only thwart and hinder. Whereas, good citizens, even when they see the popular mind to be bent on dangerous courses, will never oppose the adoption of a fixed plan, more particularly in matters which do not brook delay.

After Hieronymus, the Syracusan tyrant, was put to death, there being at that time a great war between the Romans and the Carthaginians, the citizens of Syracuse fell to disputing among themselves with which nation they should take part; and so fierce grew the controversy between the partisans of the two alliances, that no course could be agreed on, and they took part with neither; until Apollonides, one of the foremost of the Syracusan citizens, told them in a speech replete with wisdom, that neither those who inclined to hold by the Romans, nor those who chose rather to side with the Carthaginians, were deserving of blame; but that what was utterly to be condemned was doubt and delay in taking one side or other; for from such uncertainty he clearly foresaw the ruin of their republic; whereas, by taking a decided course, whatever it might be, some good might come. Now Titus Livius could not show more clearly than he does in this passage, the mischief which results from resting in suspense. He shows it, likewise, in the case of the Lavinians, of whom he relates, that being urged by the Latins to aid them against Rome, they were so long in making up their minds, that when the army which they at last sent to succour the Latins was issuing from their gates, word came that the Latins were defeated. Whereupon Millionius, their prætor, said, *"With the Romans this short march will cost us dear."* But had the Lavinians resolved at once either to grant aid or to refuse it, taking a latter course they would not have given offence to the Romans, taking the former, and rendering timely help, they and the Latins together might have had a victory. But by delay they stood to lose in every way, as the event showed.

This example, had it been remembered by the Florentines, might have saved them from all that loss and vexation which they underwent at the hands of the French, at the time King Louis XII. of France came into Italy against Lodovico, duke of Milan. For when Louis first proposed to pass through Tuscany he met with no objection from the Florentines, whose envoys at his court arranged with him that they should stand neutral, while the king, on his arrival in Italy, was to maintain their government and take them under his protection; a month's time being allowed the republic to ratify these terms. But certain persons, who, in their folly, favoured the cause of Lodovico, delayed this ratification until the king was already on the eve of victory; when the Florentines suddenly becoming eager to ratify, the king would not accept their ratification, perceiving their consent to be given under constraint and not of their own good-will. This cost the city of Florence dear, and went near to lose her freedom, whereof she was afterwards deprived on another like occasion. And the course taken by the Florentines was the more to be blamed in that it was of no sort of service to Duke Lodovico, who, had he been victorious, would have shown the Florentines many more signs of his displeasure than did the king.

Although the hurt which results to republics from weakness of this sort has already been discussed in another Chapter, nevertheless, since an opportunity offered for touching upon it again, I have willingly availed myself of it, because to me it seems a matter of which republics like ours should take special heed.

Chapter XVI.—*That the Soldiers of our days depart widely from the methods of ancient Warfare.*

In all their wars with other nations, the most momentous battle ever fought by the Romans, was that which they fought with the Latins when Torquatus and Decius were consuls. For it may well be believed that as by the loss of that battle the Latins became subject to the Romans, so the Romans had they not prevailed must have become subject to the Latins. And Titus Livius is of this opinion, since he represents the armies as exactly equal in every respect, in discipline and in valour, in numbers and in obstinacy, the only difference he draws being, that of the two armies the Romans had the more capable commanders. We find, however, two circumstances occurring in the conduct of this battle, the like of which never happened before, and seldom since, namely, that to give steadiness to the minds of their soldiers, and render them obedient to the word of command and resolute to fight, one of the consuls put himself, and the other his son, to death.

The equality which Titus Livius declares to have prevailed in these two armies, arose from this, that having long served together they used the same language, discipline, and arms; that in disposing their men for battle they followed the same system; and that the divisions and officers of their armies bore the same names. It was necessary, therefore, that as they were of equal strength and valour, something extraordinary should take place to render the courage of the one army more stubborn and unflinching than that of the other, it being on this stubbornness, as I have already said, that victory depends. For while this temper is maintained in the minds of the combatants they will never turn their backs on their foe. And that it might endure longer in the minds of the Romans than of the Latins, partly chance, and partly the valour of the consuls caused it to fall out that Torquatus slew his son, and Decius died by his own hand.

In pointing out this equality of strength, Titus Livius takes occasion to explain the whole system followed by the Romans in the ordering of their armies and in disposing them for battle; and as he has treated the subject at length, I need not go over the same ground, and shall touch only on what I judge in it most to deserve attention, but, being overlooked by all the captains of our times, has led to disorder in many armies and in many battles.

From this passage of Titus Livius, then, we learn that the Roman army had three principal divisions, or battalions as we might now call them, of which they named the first *hastati*, the second *principes*, and the third *triarii*, to each of which cavalry were attached. In arraying an army for battle they set the *hastati* in front. Directly behind them, in the second rank, they placed the *principes*; and in the third rank of the same column, the *triarii*. The cavalry of each of these three divisions they disposed to the right and left of the division to which it belonged; and to these companies of horse, from their form and position, they gave the name wings (*alæ*), from their appearing like the two wings of the main body of the army. The first division, the *hastati*, which was in front, they drew up in close order to enable it to withstand and repulse the enemy. The second division, the *principes*, since it was not to be engaged from the beginning, but was meant to succour the first in case that were driven in, was not formed in close order but kept in open file, so that it might receive the other into its ranks whenever it was broken and forced to retire. The third division, that, namely, of the *triarii*, had its ranks still more open than those of the second, so that, if occasion required, it might receive the first two divisions of the *hastati* and *principes*. These divisions, therefore, being drawn up in this order, the engagement began, and if the *hastati* were overpowered and driven back, they retired within the loose ranks of the *principes*, when both these divisions, being thus united into one, renewed the conflict. If these, again, were routed and forced back, they retreated within the open ranks of the *triarii*, and all three divisions, forming into one, once more renewed the fight, in which, if they were overpowered, since they had no further means of recruiting their strength, they lost the battle. And because whenever this last division, of the *triarii*, had to be employed, the army was in jeopardy, there arose the proverb, "*Res redacta est ad triarios*," equivalent to our expression of *playing a last stake*.

The captains of our day, as they have abandoned all the other customs of antiquity, and pay no heed to any part of the ancient discipline, so also have discarded this method of disposing their men, though it was one of no small utility. For to insure the defeat of a commander who so arranges his forces as to be able thrice during an engagement to renew his strength, Fortune must thrice declare against him, and he must be matched with an adversary able three times over to defeat him; whereas he whose sole chance of success lies in his surviving the first onset, as is the case with all the armies of Christendom at the present day, may easily be vanquished, since any slight mishap, and the least failure in the steadiness of his men, may deprive him of victory.

And what takes from our armies the capacity to renew their strength is, that provision is now no longer made for one division being received into the ranks of another, which happens because at present an army is arranged for battle in one or other of two imperfect methods. For either its divisions are placed side by side, so as to form a line of great width but of no depth or solidity; or if, to strengthen it, it be drawn up in columns after the fashion of the Roman armies, should the front line be broken, no provision having been made for its being received by the second, it is thrown into complete disorder, and both divisions fall to pieces. For if the front line be driven back, it jostles the second, if the second line endeavour to advance, the first stands in its way: and thus, the first driving against the second, and the second against the third, such confusion follows that often the most trifling accident will cause the ruin of an entire army.

At the battle of Ravenna, where M. de Foix, the French commander, was slain, although according to modern notions this was a well-fought field, both the French and the Spanish armies were drawn up in the first of the faulty methods above described; that is to say, each army advanced with the whole of its battalions side by side, so that each presented a single front much wider than deep; this being always the plan followed by modern armies when, as at Ravenna, the ground is open. For knowing the disorder they fall into on retreat, forming themselves in a single line, they endeavour, as I have said, as much as possible to escape confusion by extending their front. But where the ground confines them they fall at once into the disorder spoken of, without an effort to prevent it.

Troops traversing an enemy's country, whether to pillage or carry out any other operation of war, are liable to fall into the same disorder; and at S. Regolo in the Pisan territory, and at other places where the Florentines were beaten by the Pisans during the war which followed on the revolt of Pisa after the coming of Charles of France into Italy, our defeat was due to no other cause than the behaviour of our own cavalry, who being posted in front, and being repulsed by the enemy, fell back on the infantry and threw them into confusion, whereupon the whole army took to flight; and Messer Ciriaco del Borgo, the veteran leader of the Florentine foot, has often declared in my presence that he had never been routed by any cavalry save those who were fighting on his side. For which reason the Swiss, who are the greatest proficients in modern warfare, when serving with the French, make it their first care to place themselves on their flank, so that the cavalry of their friends, if repulsed, may not throw them into disorder.

But although these matters seem easy to understand and not difficult to put in practice, none has yet been found among the commanders of our times, who attempted to imitate the ancients or to correct the moderns. For although these also have a tripartite division of their armies into van-guard, main-body, and rear-guard, the only use they make of it is in giving orders when their men are in quarters; whereas on active service it rarely happens that all divisions are not equally exposed to the same onset.

And because many, to excuse their ignorance, will have it that the destructive fire of artillery forbids our employing at the present day many of the tactics used by the ancients, I will discuss this question in the following Chapter, and examine whether artillery does in fact prevent us from using the valiant methods of antiquity.

Chapter XVII.—*What importance the Armies of the present day should allow to Artillery; and whether the commonly received opinion concerning it be just.*

Looking to the number of pitched battles, or what are termed by the French *journées*, and by the Italians *fatti d'arme*, fought by the Romans at divers times, I am led further to examine the generally received opinion, that had artillery been in use in their day, the Romans would not have been allowed, or at least not with the same ease, to subjugate provinces and make other nations their tributaries, and could never have spread their power in the astonishing way they did. For it is said that by reason of these fire-arms men can no longer use or display their personal valour as they could of old; that there is greater difficulty now than there was in former times in joining battle; that the tactics followed then cannot be followed now; and that in time all warfare must resolve itself into a question of artillery.

Judging it not out of place to inquire whether these opinions are sound, and how far artillery has added to or taken from the strength of armies, and whether its use lessens or increases the opportunities for a good captain to behave valiantly, I shall at once address myself to the first of the averments noticed above, namely, that the armies of the ancient Romans could not have made the conquests they did, had artillery then been in use.

To this I answer by saying that, since war is made for purposes either of offence or defence, we have first to see in which of these two kinds of warfare artillery gives the greater advantage or inflicts the greater hurt. Now, though something might be said both ways, I nevertheless believe that artillery is beyond comparison more hurtful to him who stands on the defensive than to him who attacks. For he who defends himself must either do so in a town or in a fortified camp. If within a town, either the town will be a small one, as fortified towns commonly are, or it will be a great one. In the former case, he who is on the defensive is at once undone. For such is the shock of artillery that there is no wall so strong that in a few days it will not batter down, when, unless those within have ample room to withdraw behind covering works and trenches, they must be beaten; it being impossible for them to resist the assault of an enemy who forces an entrance through the breaches in their walls. Nor will any artillery a defender may have be of any service to him; since it is an established axiom that where men are able to advance in numbers and rapidly, artillery is powerless to check them.

For this reason, in storming towns the furious assaults of the northern nations prove irresistible, whereas the attacks of our Italian troops, who do not rush on in force, but advance to the assault in small knots of skirmishers (*scaramouches*, as they are fitly named), may easily be withstood. Those who advance in such loose order, and with so little spirit, against a breach covered by artillery, advance to certain destruction, and as against them artillery is useful. But when the assailants swarm to the breach so massed together that one pushes on another, unless they be brought to a stand by ditches and earthworks, they penetrate everywhere, and no artillery has any effect to keep them back; and though some must fall, yet not so many as to prevent a victory.

The frequent success of the northern nations in storming towns, and more particularly the recovery of Brescia by the French, is proof sufficient of the truth of what I say. For the town of Brescia rising against the French while the citadel still held out, the Venetians, to meet any attack which might be made from the citadel upon the town, ranged guns along the whole line of road which led from the one to the other, planting them in front, and in flank, and wherever else they could be brought to bear. Of all which M. de Foix making no account, dismounted with his men-at-arms from horseback, and, advancing with them on foot through the midst of the batteries, took the town; nor do we learn that he sustained any considerable loss from the enemy's fire. So that, as I have said, he who has to defend himself in a small town, when his walls are battered down and he has no room to retire behind other works, and has only his artillery to trust to, is at once undone.

But even where the town you defend is a great one, so that you have room to fall back behind new works, artillery is still, by a long way, more useful for the assailant than for the defender. For to enable your artillery to do any hurt to those without, you must raise yourself with it above the level of the ground, since, if you remain on the level, the enemy, by erecting any low mound or earth-work, can so secure himself that it will be impossible for you to touch him. But in raising yourself above the level of the ground, whether by extending yourself along the gallery of the walls, or otherwise, you are exposed to two disadvantages; for, first, you cannot there bring into position guns of the same size or range as he who is without can bring to bear against you, since it is impossible to work large guns in a confined space; and, secondly, although you should succeed in getting your guns into position, you cannot construct such strong and solid works for their protection as those can who are outside, and on level ground, and who have all the room and every other advantage which they could desire. It is consequently impossible for him who defends a town to maintain his guns in position at any considerable height, when those who are outside have much and powerful artillery; while, if he place it lower, it becomes, as has been explained, to a great extent useless. So that in the end the defence of the city has to be effected, as in ancient times, by hand to hand fighting, or else by means of the smaller kinds of fire-arms, from which if the defender derive some slight advantage, it is balanced by the injury he sustains from the great artillery of his enemy, whereby the walls of the city are battered down and almost buried in their ditches; so that when it comes once more to an encounter at close quarters, by reason of his walls being demolished and his ditches filled up, the defender is now at a far greater disadvantage than he was formerly. Wherefore I repeat that these arms are infinitely more useful for him who attacks a town than for him who defends it.

As to the remaining method, which consists in your taking up your position in an entrenched camp, where you need not fight unless you please, and unless you have the advantage, I say that this method commonly affords you no greater facility for avoiding an engagement than the ancients had; nay, that sometimes, owing to the use of artillery, you are worse off than they were. For if the enemy fall suddenly upon you, and have some slight advantage (as may readily be the case from his being on higher ground, or from your works on his arrival being still incomplete so that you are not wholly sheltered by them), forthwith, and without your being able to prevent him, he dislodges you, and you are forced to quit your defences and deliver battle: as happened to the Spaniards at the battle of Ravenna. For having posted themselves between the river Ronco and an earthwork, from their not having carried this work high enough, and from the French having a slight advantage of ground, they were forced by the fire of the latter to quit their entrenchments come to an engagement.

But assuming the ground you have chosen for your camp to be, as it always should, higher than that occupied by the enemy, and your works to be complete and sufficient, so that from your position and preparations the enemy dare not attack you, recourse will then be had to the very same methods as were resorted to in ancient times when an army was so posted that it could not be assailed; that is to say, your country will be wasted, cities friendly to you besieged or stormed, and your supplies intercepted; until you are forced, at last, of necessity to quit your camp and to fight a pitched battle, in which, as will presently appear, artillery will be of little service to you.

If we consider, therefore, for what ends the Romans made wars, and that attack and not defence was the object of almost all their campaigns, it will be clear, if what I have said be true, that they would have had still greater advantage, and might have achieved their conquests with

even greater ease, had artillery been in use in their times.

And as to the second complaint, that by reason of artillery men can no longer display their valour as they could in ancient days, I admit it to be true that when they have to expose themselves a few at a time, men run more risks now than formerly; as when they have to scale a town or perform some similar exploit, in which they are not massed together but must advance singly and one behind another. It is true, also, that Captains and commanders of armies are subjected to a greater risk of being killed now than of old, since they an be reached everywhere by the enemy's fire; and it is no protection to them to be with those of their men who are furthest from the enemy, or to be surrounded by the bravest of their guards. Still, we do not often find either of these two dangers occasioning extraordinary loss. For towns strongly fortified are not attacked by escalade, nor will the assailing army advance against them in weak numbers; but will endeavour, as in ancient times, to reduce them by regular siege. And even in the case of towns attacked by storm, the dangers are not so very much greater now than they were formerly; for in those old days also, the defenders of towns were not without warlike engines, which if less terrible in their operation, had, so far as killing goes, much the same effect. And as for the deaths of captains and leaders of companies, it may be said that during the last twenty-four years of war in Italy, we have had fewer instances of such deaths than might be found in a period of ten years of ancient warfare. For excepting the Count Lodovico della Mirandola, who fell at Ferrara, when the Venetians a few years ago attacked that city, and the Duke de Nemours, slain at Cirignuola, we have no instance of any commander being killed by artillery. For, at Ravenna, M. de Foix died by steel and not by shot. Wherefore I say that if men no longer perform deeds of individual prowess, it results not so much from the use of artillery, as from the faulty discipline and weakness of our armies, which being collectively without valour cannot display it in particular instances.

As to the third assertion, that armies can no longer be brought to engage one another, and that war will soon come to be carried on wholly with artillery, I maintain that this allegation is utterly untrue, and will always be so held by those who are willing in handling their troops to follow the usages of ancient valour. For whosoever would have a good army must train it, either by real or by mimic warfare, to approach the enemy, to come within sword-thrust, and to grapple with him; and must rely more on foot soldiers than on horse, for reasons presently to be explained. But when you trust to your foot-soldiers, and to the methods already indicated, artillery becomes powerless to harm you. For foot-soldiers, in approaching an enemy, can with more ease escape the fire of his artillery than in ancient times they could have avoided a charge of elephants or of scythed chariots, or any other of those strange contrivances which had to be encountered by the Romans, and against which they always devised some remedy. And, certainly, as against artillery, their remedy would have been easier, by as much as the time during which artillery can do hurt is shorter than the time during which elephants and chariots could. For by these you were thrown into disorder after battle joined, whereas artillery harasses you only before you engage; a danger which infantry can easily escape, either by advancing so as to be covered by the inequalities of the ground, or by lying down while the firing continues; nay, we find from experience that even these precautions may be dispensed with, especially as against great artillery, which can hardly be levelled with such precision that its fire shall not either pass over your head from the range being too high, or fall short from its being too low.

So soon, however, as the engagement is begun, it is perfectly clear that neither small nor great artillery can harm you any longer; since, if the enemy have his artillerymen in front, you take them; if in rear, they will injure him before they injure you; and if in flank, they can never fire so effectively as to prevent your closing, with the result already explained. Nor does this admit of much dispute, since we have proof of it in the case of the Swiss at Novara, in the year 1513, when, with neither guns nor cavalry, they advanced against the French army, who had fortified themselves with artillery behind entrenchments, and routed them without suffering the slightest check from their fire. In further explanation whereof it is to be noted, that to work artillery effectively it should be protected by walls, by ditches, or by earth-works; and that whenever, from being left without such protection it has to be defended by men, as happens in pitched battles and engagements in the open field, it is either taken or otherwise becomes useless. Nor can it be employed on the flank of an army, save in the manner in which the ancients made use of their warlike engines, which they moved out from their columns that they might be worked without inconvenience, but withdrew within them when driven back by cavalry or other troops. He who looks for any further advantage from artillery does not rightly understand its nature, and trusts to what is most likely to deceive him. For although the Turk, using artillery, has gained victories over the Soldan and the Sofi, the only advantage he has had from it has been the terror into which the horses of the enemy, unused to such sounds, are thrown by the roar of the guns.

And now, to bring these remarks to a conclusion, I say briefly that, employed by an army wherein there is some strain of the ancient valour, artillery is useful; but employed otherwise, against a brave adversary, is utterly useless.

Chapter XVIII.—*That the authority of the Romans and the example of ancient Warfare should make us hold Foot Soldiers of more account than Horse.*

By many arguments and instances it can be clearly established that in their military enterprises the Romans set far more store on their infantry than on their cavalry, and trusted to the former to carry out all the chief objects which their armies were meant to effect. Among many other examples of this, we may notice the great battle which they fought with the Latins near the lake Regillus, where to steady their wavering ranks they made their horsemen dismount, and renewing the combat on foot obtained a victory. Here we see plainly that the Romans had more confidence in themselves when they fought on foot than when they fought on horseback. The same expedient was resorted to by them in many of their other battles, and always in their sorest need they found it their surest stay.

Nor are we to condemn the practice in deference to the opinion of Hannibal, who, at the battle of Cannæ, on seeing the consuls make the horsemen dismount, said scoffingly, "*Better still had they delivered their knights to me in chains.*" For though this saying came from the mouth of a most excellent soldier, still, if we are to regard authority, we ought rather to follow the authority of a commonwealth like Rome, and of the many great captains who served her, than that of Hannibal alone. But, apart from authority, there are manifest reasons to bear out what I say. For a man may go on foot into many places where a horse cannot go; men can be taught to keep rank, and if thrown into disorder to recover form; whereas, it is difficult to keep horses in line, and impossible if once they be thrown into disorder to reform them. Moreover we find that with horses as with men, some have little courage and some much; and that often a spirited horse is ridden by a faint-hearted rider, or a dull horse by a courageous rider, and that in whatever way such disparity is caused, confusion and disorder result. Again, infantry, when drawn up in column, can easily break and is not easily broken by cavalry. This is vouched, not only by many ancient and many modern instances, but also by the authority of those who lay down rules for the government of States, who show that at first wars were carried on by mounted soldiers, because the methods for arraying infantry were not yet understood, but that so soon as these were discovered, the superiority of foot over horse was at once recognized. In saying this, I would not have it supposed that horsemen are not of the greatest use in armies, whether for purposes of observation, for harrying and laying waste the enemy's country, for pursuing a retreating foe or helping to repulse his cavalry. But the substance and sinew of an army, and that part of it which ought constantly to be most considered, should always be the infantry. And among sins of the Italian princes who have made their country the slave of foreigners, there is none worse than that they have held these arms in contempt, and turned their whole attention to mounted troops.

This error is due to the craft of our captains and to the ignorance of our rulers. For the control of the armies of Italy for the last five and twenty years resting in the hands of men, who, as having no lands of their own, may be looked on as mere soldiers of fortune, these fell forthwith on contriving how they might maintain their credit by being supplied with the arms which the princes of the country were without. And as they had no subjects of their own of whom they could make use, and could not obtain constant employment and pay for a large number of foot-soldiers, and as a small number would have given them no importance, they had recourse to horsemen. For a *condottiere* drawing pay for two or three hundred horsemen was maintained by them in the highest credit, and yet the cost was not too great to be met by the princes who employed him. And to effect their object with more ease, and increase their credit still further, these adventurers would allow no merit or favour to be due to foot-soldiers, but claimed all for their horsemen. And to such a length was this bad system carried, that in the very greatest army only the smallest sprinkling of infantry was to be found. This, together with many other ill practices which accompanied it, has so weakened the militia of Italy, that the country has easily been trampled upon by all the nations of the North.

That it is a mistake to make more account of cavalry than of infantry, may be still more clearly seen from another example taken from Roman history. The Romans being engaged on the siege of Sora, a troop of horse a sally from the town to attack their camp; when the Roman master of the knights advancing with his own horsemen to give them battle, it so chanced that, at the very first onset, the leaders on both sides were slain. Both parties being thus left without commanders, and the combat, nevertheless, continuing, the Romans thinking thereby to have the advantage of their adversaries, alighted from horseback, obliging the enemy's cavalry, in order to defend themselves, to do the like. The result was that the Romans had the victory. Now there could be no stronger instance than this to show the superiority of foot over horse. For while in other battles the Roman cavalry were made by their consuls to dismount in order to succour their infantry who were in distress and in need of such aid, on this occasion they dismounted, not to succour their infantry, nor to encounter an enemy contending on foot, but because they saw that though they could not prevail against the enemy fighting as horsemen against horsemen, on foot they readily might. And from this I conclude that foot-soldiers, if rightly handled, can hardly be beaten except by other soldiers fighting on foot.

With very few cavalry, but with a considerable force of infantry, the Roman commanders, Crassus and Marcus Antonius, each for many days together overran the territories of the Parthians, although opposed by the countless horsemen of that nation. Crassus, indeed, with the greater part of his army, was left there dead, and Antonius only saved himself by his valour; but even in the extremities to which the Romans were then brought, see how greatly superior foot-soldiers are to horse. For though fighting in an open country, far from the sea-coast, and cut off from his supplies, Antonius proved himself a valiant soldier in the judgment even of the Parthians themselves, the whole strength of whose cavalry never ventured to attack the columns of his army. And though Crassus perished there, any one who reads attentively the account of his expedition must see that he was rather outwitted than defeated, and that even when his condition was desperate, the Parthians durst not close with him, but effected his destruction by hanging continually on the flanks of his army, and intercepting his supplies, while cajoling him with promises which they never kept.

It might, I grant, be harder to demonstrate this great superiority of foot over horse, had we not very many modern examples affording the clearest proof of it. For instance, at the battle of Novara, of which we have already spoken, nine thousand Swiss foot were seen to attack ten thousand cavalry together with an equal number of infantry, and to defeat them; the cavalry being powerless to injure them, while of the infantry, who were mostly Gascons, and badly disciplined, they made no account. On another occasion we have seen twenty-six thousand Swiss march on Milan to attack Francis I. of France, who had with him twenty thousand men-at-arms, forty thousand foot, and a hundred pieces of artillery; and although they were not victorious as at Novara, they nevertheless fought valiantly for two days together, and, in the end, though beaten, were able to bring off half their number. With foot-soldiers only Marcus Attilius Regulus ventured to oppose himself, not to cavalry merely, but to elephants; and if the attempt failed it does not follow that he was not justified by the valour of his men in believing them equal to surmount this danger.

I repeat, therefore, that to prevail against well-disciplined infantry, you must meet them with infantry disciplined still better, and that otherwise you advance to certain destruction. In the time of Filippo Visconti, Duke of Milan, some sixteen thousand Swiss made a descent on Lombardy, whereupon the Duke, who at that time had Il Carmagnola as his captain, sent him with six thousand men-at-arms and a slender following of foot-soldiers to meet them. Not knowing their manner of fighting, Carmagnola fell upon them with his horsemen, expecting to put them at once to rout; but finding them immovable, after losing many of his men he withdrew. But, being a most wise captain, and skilful in devising new remedies to meet unwonted dangers, after reinforcing his company he again advanced to the attack; and when about to engage made all his men-at-arms dismount, and placing them in front of his foot-soldiers, fell once more upon the Swiss, who could then no longer withstand him. For his men, being on foot and well armed, easily penetrated the Swiss ranks without hurt to themselves; and getting among them, had no difficulty in cutting them down, so that of the entire army of the Swiss those only escaped who were spared by his humanity.

Of this difference in the efficiency of these two kinds of troops, many I believe are aware; but such is the unhappiness and perversity of the times in which we live, that neither ancient nor modern examples, nor even the consciousness of error, can move our present princes to amend their ways, or convince them that to restore credit to the arms of a State or province, it is necessary to revive this branch of their militia also, to keep it near them, to make much of it, and to give it life, that in return, it may give back life and reputation to them. But as they have departed from all those other methods already spoken of, so have they departed from this, and with this result, that to them the acquisition of territory is rather a loss than a gain, as presently shall be shown.

Chapter XIX.—*That Acquisitions made by ill-governed States and such as follow not the valiant methods of the Romans, tend rather to their Ruin than to their Aggrandizement.*

To these false opinions, founded on the pernicious example first set by the present corrupt age, we owe it, that no man thinks of departing from the methods which are in use. It had been impossible, for instance, some thirty years ago, to persuade an Italian that ten thousand foot-soldiers could, on plain ground, attack ten thousand cavalry together with an equal number of infantry; and not merely attack, but defeat them; as we saw done by the Swiss at that battle of Novara, to which I have already referred so often. For although history abounds in similar examples, none would have believed them, or, believing them, would have said that nowadays men are so much better armed, that a squadron of cavalry could shatter a rock, to say nothing of a column of infantry. With such false pleas would they have belied their judgment, taking no account that with a very scanty force of foot-soldiers, Lucullus routed a hundred and fifty thousand of the cavalry of Tigranes, among whom were a body of horsemen very nearly resembling our own men-at-arms. Now, however, this error is demonstrated by the example of the northern nations.

And since what history teaches as to the superiority of foot-soldiers is thus proved to be true, men ought likewise to believe that the other methods practised by the ancients are in like manner salutary and useful. And were this once accepted, both princes and commonwealths would make fewer blunders than they do, would be stronger to resist sudden attack, and would no longer place their sole hope of safety in flight; while those who take in hand to provide a State with new institutions would know better what direction to give them, whether in the way of extending or merely of preserving; and would see that to augment the numbers of their citizens, to assume other States as companions rather than reduce them to subjection, to send out colonies for the defence of acquired territories, to hold their spoils at the credit of the common stock, to overcome enemies by inroads and pitched battles rather than by sieges, to enrich the public purse, keep down private wealth, and zealously, to maintain all military exercises, are the true ways to aggrandize a State and to extend its empire. Or if these methods for adding to their power are not to their mind, let them remember that acquisitions made in any other way are the ruin of republics, and so set bounds to their ambition, wisely regulating the internal government of their country by suitable laws and ordinances, forbidding extension, and looking only to defence, and taking heed that their defences are in good order, as do those republics of Germany which live and for long have lived, in freedom.

And yet, as I have said on another occasion, when speaking of the difference between the methods suitable for acquiring and those suitable for maintaining, it is impossible for a republic to remain long in the peaceful enjoyment of freedom within a restricted frontier. For should it forbear from molesting others, others are not likely to refrain from molesting it; whence must grow at once the desire and the necessity to make acquisitions; or should no enemies be found abroad, they will be found at home, for this seems to be incidental to all great States. And if the free States of Germany are, and have long been able to maintain themselves on their present footing, this arises from certain conditions peculiar to that country, and to be found nowhere else, without which these communities could not go on living as they do.

The district of Germany of which I speak was formerly subject to the Roman Empire, in the same way as France and Spain; but on the decline of the Empire, and when its very name came to be limited to this one province, its more powerful cities taking advantage of the weakness and necessities of the Emperors, began to free themselves by buying from them their liberty, subject to the payment of a trifling yearly tribute; until, gradually, all the cities which held directly from the Emperor, and were not subject to any intermediate lord, had, in like manner, purchased their freedom. While this went on, it so happened that certain communities subject to the Duke of Austria, among which were Friburg, the people of Schweitz, and the like, rose in rebellion against him, and meeting at the outset with good success, by degrees acquired such accession of strength that so far from returning under the Austrian yoke, they are become formidable to all their neighbours These are the States which we now name Swiss.

Germany is, consequently, divided between the Swiss, the communities which take the name of Free Towns, the Princes, and the Emperor; and the reason why, amid so many conflicting interests, wars do not break out, or breaking out are of short continuance, is the reverence in which all hold this symbol of the Imperial authority. For although the Emperor be without strength of his own, he has nevertheless such credit with all these others that he alone can keep them united, and, interposing as mediator, can speedily repress by his influence any dissensions among them.

The greatest and most protracted wars which have taken place in this country have been those between the Swiss and the Duke of Austria; and although for many years past the Empire and the dukedom of Austria have been united in the same man, he has always failed to subdue the stubbornness of the Swiss, who are never to be brought to terms save by force. Nor has the rest of Germany lent the Emperor much assistance in his wars with the Swiss, the Free Towns being little disposed to attack others whose desire is to live as they themselves do, in freedom; while the Princes of the Empire either are so poor that they cannot, or from jealousy of the power of the Emperor will not, take part with him against them.

These communities, therefore, abide contented within their narrow confines, because, having regard to the Imperial authority, they have no occasion to desire greater; and are at the same time obliged to live in unity within their walls, because an enemy is always at hand, and ready to take advantage of their divisions to effect an entrance. But were the circumstances of the country other than they are these communities would be forced to make attempts to extend their dominions, and be constrained to relinquish their present peaceful mode of life. And since the same conditions are not found elsewhere, other nations cannot adopt this way of living, but are compelled to extend their power either by means of leagues, or else by the methods used by the Romans; and any one who should act otherwise would find not safety but rather death and destruction. For since in a thousand ways, and from causes innumerable, conquests are surrounded with dangers, it may well happen that in adding to our dominions, we add nothing to our strength; but whosoever increases not his strength while he adds to his dominions, must needs be ruined. He who is impoverished by his wars, even should he come off victorious, can add nothing to his strength, since he spends more than he gains, as the Venetians and Florentines have done. For Venice has been far feebler since she acquired Lombardy, and Florence since she acquired Tuscany, than when the one was content to be mistress of the seas, and the other of the lands lying within six miles from her walls. And this from their eagerness to acquire without knowing what way to take. For which ignorance these States are the more to be blamed in proportion as there is less to excuse them; since they had seen what methods were used by the Romans, and could have followed in their footsteps; whereas the Romans, without any example set them, were able by their own prudence to shape a course for themselves.

But even to well-governed States, their conquests may chance to occasion much harm; as when some city or province is acquired abounding in luxury and delights, by whose manners the conqueror becomes infected; as happened first to the Romans, and afterwards to Hannibal on taking possession of Capua. And had Capua been at such a distance from Rome that a ready remedy could not have been applied to the disorders of the soldiery, or had Rome herself been in any degree tainted with corruption, this acquisition had certainly proved her ruin. To which Titus Livius bears witness when he says, "*Most mischievous at this time to our military discipline was Capua; for ministering to all delights, she turned away the corrupted minds of our soldiers from the remembrance of their country*." And, truly, cities and provinces like this, avenge themselves on their conquerors without blood or blow; since by infecting them with their own evil customs they prepare them for defeat at the hands of any assailant. Nor could the subject have been better handled than by Juvenal, where he says in his Satires, that into the hearts of the Romans, through their conquests in foreign lands, foreign manners found their way; and in place of frugality and other admirable virtues—

"Came luxury more mortal than the sword, And settling down, avenged a vanquished world."[1]

And if their conquests were like to be fatal to the Romans at a time when they were still animated by great virtue and prudence, how must it fare with those who follow methods altogether different from theirs, and who, to crown their other errors of which we have already said enough, resort to auxiliary and mercenary arms, bringing upon themselves those dangers whereof mention shall be made in the Chapter following.

[Footnote 1:
Sævior armis Luxuria occubuit victumque ulciscitur orbem. Juv. Sat. vi. 292.]

Chapter XX.—*Of the Dangers incurred by Princes or Republics who resort to Auxiliary or Mercenary Arms.*

Had I not already, in another treatise, enlarged on the inutility of mercenary and auxiliary, and on the usefulness of national arms, I should dwell on these matters in the present Discourse more at length than it is my design to do. For having given the subject very full consideration elsewhere, here I would be brief. Still when I find Titus Livius supplying a complete example of what we have to look for from auxiliaries, by whom I mean troops sent to our assistance by some other prince or ruler, paid by him and under officers by him appointed, it is not fit that I should pass it by in silence.

It is related, then, by our historian, that the Romans, after defeating on two different occasions armies of the Samnites with forces sent by them to succour the Capuans, whom they thus relieved from the war which the Samnites Were waging against them, being desirious to return to Rome, left behind two legions to defend the Capuans, that the latter might not, from being altogether deprived of their protection, once more become a prey to the Samnites. But these two legions, rotting in idleness began to take such delight therein, that forgetful of their country and the reverence due to the senate, they resolved to seize by violence the city they had been left to guard by their valour. For to them it seemed that the citizens of Capua were unworthy to enjoy advantages which they knew not how to defend. The Romans, however, getting timely notice of this design, at once met and defeated it, in the manner to be more fully noticed when I come to treat of conspiracies.

Once more then, I repeat, that of all the various kinds of troops, auxiliaries are the most pernicious, because the prince or republic resorting to them for aid has no authority over them, the only person who possesses such authority being he who sends them. For, as I have said, auxiliary troops are those sent to your assistance by some other potentate, under his own flag, under his own officers, and in his own pay, as were the legions sent by the Romans to Capua. Such troops, if victorious, will for the most part plunder him by whom, as well as him against whom, they are hired to fight; and this they do, sometimes at the instigation of the potentate who sends them, sometimes for ambitious ends of their own. It was not the purpose of the Romans to violate the league and treaty which they had made with Capua; but to their soldiers it seemed so easy a matter to master the Capuans, that they were readily led into this plot for depriving them of their town and territories. Many other examples might be given to the same effect, but it is enough to mention besides this instance, that of the people of Regium, who were deprived of their city and of their lives by another Roman legion sent for their protection.

Princes and republics, therefore, should resort to any other expedient for the defence of their States sooner than call in hired auxiliaries, when they have to rest their entire hopes of safety on them; since any accord or terms, however hard, which you may make with your enemy, will be carefully studied and current events well considered, it will be seen that for one who has succeeded with such assistance, hundreds have been betrayed. Nor, in truth, can any better opportunity for usurping a city or province present itself to an ambitious prince or commonwealth, than to be asked to send an army for its defence. On the other hand, he who is so greedy of conquest as to summon such help, not for purposes of defence but in order to attack others, seeks to have what he can never hold and is most likely to be taken from him by the very person who helps him to gain it. Yet such is the perversity of men that, to gratify the desire of the moment, they shut their eyes to those ills which must speedily ensue and are no more moved by example in this matter than in all those others of which I have spoken; for were they moved by these examples they would see that the more disposed they are to deal generously with their neighbours, and the more averse they are to usurp authority over them, the readier will these be to throw themselves into their arms; as will at once appear from the case of the Capuans.

Chapter XXI.—*That Capua was the first City to which the Romans sent a Prætor; nor there, until four hundred years after they began to make War.*

The great difference between the methods followed by the ancient Romans in adding to their dominions, and those used for that purpose by the States of the present time, has now been sufficiently discussed. It has been seen, too how in dealing with the cities which they did not think fit to destroy, and even with those which had made their submission not as companions but as subjects, it was customary with the Romans to permit them to live on under their own laws, without imposing any outward sign of dependence, merely binding them to certain conditions, or complying with which they were maintained in their former dignity and importance. We know, further, that the same methods continued to be followed by the Romans until they passed beyond the confines of Italy, and began to reduce foreign kingdoms and States to provinces: as plainly appears in the fact that Capua was the first city to which they sent a prætor, and him from no motive of ambition, but at the request of the Capuans themselves who, living at variance with one another, thought it necessary to have a Roman citizen in their town who might restore unity and good order among them. Influenced by this example, and urged by the same need, the people of Antium were the next to ask that they too might have a prætor given them; touching which request and in connection with which new method of governing, Titus Livius observes, *"that not the arms only but also the laws of Rome now began to exert an influence;"* showing how much the course thus followed by the Romans promoted the growth of their authority.

For those cities, more especially, which have been used to freedom or to be governed by their own citizens, rest far better satisfied with a government which they do not see, even though it involve something of oppression, than with one which standing constantly before their eyes, seems every day to reproach them with the disgrace of servitude. And to the prince there is another advantage in this method of government, namely, that as the judges and magistrates who administer the laws civil and criminal within these cities, are not under his control, no decision of theirs can throw responsibility or discredit upon him; so that he thus escapes many occasions of calumny and hatred. Of the truth whereof, besides the ancient instances which might be noted, we have a recent example here in Italy. For Genoa, as every one knows, has many times been occupied by the French king, who always, until lately, sent thither a French governor to rule in his name. Recently, however, not from choice but of necessity, he has permitted the town to be self-governed under a Genoese ruler; and any one who had to decide which of these two methods of governing gives the greater security to the king's authority and the greater content to the people themselves, would assuredly have to pronounce in favour of the latter.

Men, moreover, in proportion as they see you averse to usurp authority over them, grow the readier to surrender themselves into your hands; and fear you less on the score of their freedom, when they find you acting towards them with consideration and kindness. It was the display of these qualities that moved the Capuans to ask the Romans for a prætor; for had the Romans betrayed the least eagerness to send them one, they would at once have conceived jealousy and grown estranged.

But why turn for examples to Capua and Rome, when we have them close at hand in Tuscany and Florence? Who is there but knows what a time it is since the city of Pistoja submitted of her own accord to the Florentine supremacy? Who, again, but knows the animosity which down to the present day exists between Florence and the cities of Pisa, Lucca, and Siena? This difference of feeling does not arise from the citizens of Pistoja valuing their freedom less than the citizens of these other towns or thinking themselves inferior to them, but from the Florentines having always acted towards the former as brothers, towards the latter as foes. This it was that led the Pistojans to come voluntarily under our authority while the others have done and do all in their power to escape it. For there seems no reason to doubt, that if Florence, instead of exasperating these neighbours of hers, had sought to win them over, either by entering into league with them or by lending them assistance, she would at this hour have been mistress of Tuscany. Not that I would be understood to maintain that recourse is never to be had to force and to arms, but that these are only to be used in the last resort, and when all other remedies are unavailing.

Chapter XXII.—*That in matters of moment Men often judge amiss.*

How falsely men often judge of things, they who are present at their deliberations have constant occasion to know. For in many matters, unless these deliberations be guided by men of great parts, the conclusions come to are certain to be wrong. And because in corrupt republics, and especially in quiet times, either through jealousy or from other like causes, men of great ability are often obliged to stand aloof, it follows that measures not good in themselves are by a common error judged to be good, or are promoted by those who seek public favour rather than the public advantage. Mistakes of this sort are found out afterwards in seasons of adversity, when recourse must be had to those persons who in peaceful times had been, as it were, forgotten, as shall hereafter in its proper place be more fully explained. Cases, moreover, arise in which those who have little experience of affairs are sure to be misled, from the matters with which they have to deal being attended by many deceptive appearances such as lead men to believe whatsoever they are minded to believe.

These remarks I make with reference to the false hopes which the Latins, after being defeated by the Romans, were led to form on the persuasion of their prætor Numitius, and also with reference to what was believed by many a few years ago, when Francis, king of France, came to recover Milan from the Swiss. For Francis of Angoulême, succeeding on the death of Louis XII. to the throne of France, and desiring to recover for that realm the Duchy of Milan, on which, some years before, the Swiss had seized at the instance of Pope Julius, sought for allies in Italy to second him in his attempt; and besides the Venetians, who had already been gained over by King Louis, endeavoured to secure the aid of the Florentines and Pope Leo X.; thinking that were he to succeed in getting these others to take part with him, his enterprise would be easier. For the forces of the Spanish king were then in Lombardy, and the army of the Emperor at Verona.

Pope Leo, however, did not fall in with the wishes of Francis, being, it is said, persuaded by his advisers that his best course was to stand neutral. For they urged that it was not for the advantage of the Church to have powerful strangers, whether French or Swiss, in Italy; but that to restore the country to its ancient freedom, it must be delivered from the yoke of both. And since to conquer both, whether singly or together, was impossible, it was to be desired that the one should overthrow the other, after which the Church with her friends might fall upon the victor. And it was averred that no better opportunity for carrying out this design could ever be found than then presented itself; for both the French and the Swiss were in the field; while the Pope had his troops in readiness to appear on the Lombard frontier and in the vicinity of the two armies, where, under colour of watching his own interests, he could easily keep them until the opposed hosts came to an engagement; when, as both armies were full of courage, their encounter might be expected to be a bloody one, and likely to leave the victor so weakened that it would be easy for the Pope to attack and defeat him; and so, to his own great glory, remain master of Lombardy and supreme throughout Italy.

How baseless this expectation was, was seen from the event. For the Swiss being routed after a protracted combat, the troops of the Pope and Spain, so far from venturing to attack the conqueror, prepared for flight; nor would flight have saved them, had not the humanity or indifference of the king withheld him from pursuing his victory, and disposed him to make terms with the Church.

The arguments put forward by the Pope's advisers had a certain show of reason in their favour, which looked at from a distance seemed plausible enough; but were in reality wholly contrary to truth; since it rarely happens that the captain who wins a victory loses any great number of his men, his loss being in battle only, and not in flight. For in the heat of battle, while men stand face to face, but few fall, chiefly because such combats do not last long; and even when they do last, and many of the victorious army are slain, so splendid is the reputation which attends a victory, and so great the terror it inspires, as far to outweigh any loss the victor suffers by the slaughter of his soldiers; so that an enemy who, trusting to find him weakened, should then venture to attack him, would soon be taught his mistake, unless strong enough to give him battle at any time, before his victory as well as after. For in that case he might, as fortune and valour should determine, either win or lose; though, even then, the army which had first fought and won would have an advantage. And this we know for a truth from what befell the Latins in consequence of the mistake made by Numitius their prætor, and their blindness in believing him. For when they had already suffered defeat at the hands of the Romans, Numitius caused it to be proclaimed throughout the whole country of Latium, that now was the time to fall upon the enemy, exhausted by a struggle in which they were victorious only in name, while in reality suffering all those ills which attend defeat, and who might easily be crushed by any fresh force brought against them. Whereupon the Latins believed him, and getting together a new army, were forthwith routed with such loss as always awaits those who listen to like counsels.

Chapter XXIII.—*That in chastising their Subjects when circumstances required it the Romans always avoided half-measures.*

"Such *was now the state of affairs in Latium, that peace and war seemed alike intolerable.*" No worse calamity can befall a prince or commonwealth than to be reduced to such straits that they can neither accept peace nor support war; as is the case with those whom it would ruin to conclude peace on the terms offered, while war obliges them either to yield themselves a spoil to their allies, or remain a prey to their foes. To this grievous alternative are men led by evil counsels and unwise courses, and, as already said, from not rightly measuring their strength. For the commonwealth or prince who has rightly measured his strength, can hardly be brought so low as were the Latins, who made war with the Romans when they should have made terms, and made terms when they should have made war, and so mismanaged everything that the friendship and the enmity of Rome were alike fatal. Whence it came that, in the first place, they were defeated and broken by Manlius Torquatus, and afterwards utterly subdued by Camillus; who, when he had forced them to surrender at discretion to the Roman arms, and had placed garrisons in all their towns, and taken hostages from all, returned to Rome and reported to the senate that the whole of Latium now lay at their mercy.

And because the sentence then passed by the senate is memorable, and worthy to be studied by princes that it may be imitated by them on like occasion, I shall cite the exact words which Livius puts into the mouth of Camillus, as confirming what I have already said touching the methods used by the Romans to extend their power, and as showing how in chastising their subjects they always avoided half-measures and took a decided course. For government consists in nothing else than in so controlling your subjects that it shall neither be in their power nor for their interest to harm you. And this is effected either by making such sure work with them as puts it out of their power to do you injury, or else by so loading them with benefits that it would be folly in them to seek to alter their condition. All which is implied first in the measures proposed by Camillus, and next in the resolutions passed on these proposals by the senate. The words of Camillus were as follows: "*The immortal gods have made you so entirely masters in the matter you are now considering, that it lies with you to pronounce whether Latium shall or shall not longer exist. So far as the Latins are concerned, you can secure a lasting peace either by clemency or by severity. Would you deal harshly with those whom you have conquered and who have given themselves into your hands, you can blot out the whole Latin nation. Would you, after the fashion of our ancestors, increase the strength of Rome by admitting the vanquished to the rights of citizenship, here you have opportunity to do so, and with the greatest glory to yourselves. That, assuredly, is the strongest government which they rejoice in who obey it. Now, then, is your time, while the minds of all are bent on what is about to happen, to obtain an ascendency over them, either by punishment or by benefits.*"

Upon this motion the senate resolved, in accordance with the advice given by the consul, to take the case of each city separately, and either destroy utterly or else treat with tenderness all the more important of the Latin towns. To those cities they dealt with leniently, they granted exemptions and privileges, conferring upon them the rights of citizenship, and securing their welfare in every particular. The others they razed to the ground, and planting colonies in their room, either removed the inhabitants to Rome, or so scattered and dispersed them that neither by arms nor by counsels was it ever again in their power to inflict hurt. For, as I have said already, the Romans never, in matters of moment, resorted to half-measures. And the sentence which they then pronounced should be a pattern for all rulers, and ought to have been followed by the Florentines when, in the year 1502, Arezzo and all the Val di Chiana rose in revolt. For had they followed it, they would have established their authority on a surer footing, and added much to the greatness of their city by securing for it those lands which are needed to supply it with the necessaries of life. But pursuing that half-hearted policy which is most mischievous in executing justice, some of the Aretines they outlawed, some they condemned to death, and all they deprived of their dignities and ancient importance in their town, while leaving the town itself untouched. And if in the councils then held any Florentine recommended that Arezzo should be dismantled, they who thought themselves wiser than their fellows objected, that to do so would be little to the honour of our republic, since it would look as though she lacked strength to hold it. Reasons like this are of a sort which seem sound, but are not really so; for, by the same rule, no parricide should be put to death, nor any other malefactor, however atrocious his crimes; because, forsooth, it would be discreditable to the ruler to appear unequal to the control of a single criminal. They who hold such opinions fail to see that when men individually, or entire cities collectively, offend against the State, the prince for his own safety, and as a warning to others, has no alternative but to make an end of them; and that true honour lies in being able and in knowing how to chastise such offenders, and not in incurring endless dangers in the effort to retain them. For the prince who does not chastise offenders in a way that puts it out of their power to offend again, is accounted unwise or worthless.

How necessary it was for the Romans to execute Justice against the Latins, is further seen from the course took with the men of Privernum. And here the text of Livius suggests two points for our attention: first, as already noted, that a subjugated people is either to be caressed or crushed; and second, how much it is for our advantage to maintain a manly bearing, and to speak the truth fearlessly in the presence of the wise. For the senate being met to determine the fate of the citizens of Privernum, who after rebelling had been reduced to submission by the Roman arms, certain of these citizens were sent by their countrymen to plead for pardon. When these had come into the presence of the senate, one of them was asked by a senator, "*What punishment he thought his fellow citizens deserved?*" To which he of Privernum answered, "*Such punishment as they deserve who deem themselves worthy of freedom.*" "*But,*" said the consul, "*should we remit your punishment, what sort of peace can we hope to have with you?*" To which the other replied, "*If granted on fair terms, a firm and lasting peace; if on unfair, a peace of brief duration.*" Upon this, though many of the senators were displeased, the wiser among them declared "*that they had heard the voice of freedom and manhood, and would never believe that the man or people who so spoke ought to remain longer than was needful in a position which gave them cause for shame; since that was a safe peace which was accepted willingly; whereas good faith could not be looked for where it was sought to impose servitude.*" So saying, they decided that the people of Privernum should be admitted to Roman citizenship, with all the rights and privileges thereto appertaining; declaring that "*men whose only thought was for freedom, were indeed worthy to be Romans.*" So pleasing was this true and high answer to generous minds, while any other must have seemed at once false and shameful. And they who judge otherwise of men, and of those men, especially, who have been used to be free, or so to think themselves, are mistaken; and are led through their mistake to adopt courses unprofitable for themselves and affording no content to others. Whence, the frequent rebellions and the downfall of States.

But, returning to our subject, I conclude, as well from this instance of Privernum, as from the measures followed with the Latins, that when we have to pass sentence upon powerful States accustomed to live in freedom, we must either destroy them utterly, or else treat them with much indulgence; and that any other course we may take with them will be unprofitable. But most carefully should we avoid, as of all courses the most pernicious, such half-measures as were followed by the Samnites when they had the Romans shut up in the Caudine Forks, and would not listen to the counsels of the old man who urged them either to send their captives away with every honourable attention, or else put them all to death; but adopted a middle course, and after disarming them and making them pass under the yoke, suffered them to depart at once disgraced and angered. And no long time after, they found to their sorrow that the old man's warning was true, and that the course they had themselves chosen was calamitous; as shall, hereafter, in its place be shown.

Chapter XXIV.—*That, commonly, Fortresses do much more Harm than Good*

To the wise men of our day it may seem an oversight on the part of the Romans, that, when they sought to protect themselves against the men of Latium and Privernum, it never occurred to them to build strongholds in their cities to be a curb upon them, and insure their fidelity, especially when we remember the Florentine saying which these same wise men often quote, to the effect that Pisa and other like cities must be held by fortresses Doubtless, had those old Romans been like-minded with our modern sages, they would not have neglected to build themselves fortresses, but because they far surpassed them in courage, sense, and vigour, they refrained. And while Rome retained her freedom, and adhered to her own wise ordinances and wholesome usages, she never built a single fortress with the view to hold any city or province, though, sometimes, she may have suffered those to stand which she found already built.

Looking, therefore, to the course followed by the Romans in this particular, and to that adopted by our modern rulers, it seems proper to consider whether or not it is advisable to build fortresses, and whether they are more likely to help or to hurt him who builds them In the first place, then, we are to remember that fortresses are built either as a defence against foreign foes or against subjects In the former case, I pronounce them unnecessary, in the latter mischievous. And to state the reasons why in the latter case they are mischievous, I say that when princes or republics are afraid of their subjects and in fear lest they rebel, this must proceed from knowing that their subjects hate them, which hatred in its turn results from their own ill conduct, and that again from their thinking themselves able to rule their subjects by mere force, or from their governing with little prudence. Now one of the causes which lead them to suppose that they can rule by mere force, is this very circumstance of their people having these fortresses on their backs So that the conduct which breeds hatred is itself mainly occasioned by these princes or republics being possessed of fortresses, which, if this be true, are really far more hurtful than useful First, because, as has been said already, they render a ruler bolder and more violent in his bearing towards his subjects, and, next, because they do not in reality afford him that security which he believes them to give For all those methods of violence and coercion which may be used to keep a people under, resolve themselves into two; since either like the Romans you must always have it in your power to bring a strong army into the field, or else you must dissipate, destroy, and disunite the subject people, and so divide and scatter them that they can never again combine to injure you For should you merely strip them of their wealth, *spoliatis arma supersunt*, arms still remain to them, or if you deprive them of their weapons, *furor arma ministrat*, rage will supply them, if you put their chiefs to death and continue to maltreat the rest, heads will renew themselves like those Hydra; while, if you build fortresses, these may serve in time of peace to make you bolder in outraging your subjects, but in time of war they will prove wholly useless, since they will be attacked at once by foes both foreign and domestic, whom together it will be impossible for you to resist. And if ever fortresses were useless they are so at the present day, by reason of the invention of artillery, against the fury of which, as I have shown already, a petty fortress which affords no room for retreat behind fresh works, cannot be defended.

But to go deeper into the matter, I say, either you are a prince seeking by means of these fortresses to hold the people of your city in check; or you are a prince, or it may be a republic, desirous to control some city which you have gained in war. To the prince I would say, that, for the reasons already given, nothing can be more unserviceable than a fortress as a restraint upon your subjects, since it only makes you the readier to oppress them, and less scrupulous how you do so; while it is this very oppression which moves them to destroy you, and so kindles their hatred, that the fortress, which is the cause of all the mischief, is powerless to protect you. A wise and good prince, therefore, that he may continue good, and give no occasion or encouragement to his descendants to become evil, will never build a fortress, to the end that neither he nor they may ever be led to trust to it rather than to the good-will of their subjects. And if Francesco Sforza, who was accounted a wise ruler, on becoming Duke of Milan erected a fortress in that city, I say that herein he was unwise, and that the event has shown the building of this fortress to have been hurtful and not helpful to his heirs. For thinking that by its aid they could behave as badly as they liked to their citizens and subjects, and yet be secure, they refrained from no sort of violence or oppression, until, becoming beyond measure odious, they lost their State as soon as an enemy attacked it. Nor was this fortress, which in peace had occasioned them much hurt, any defence or of any service them in war. For had they being without it, through thoughtlessness, treated their subjects inhumanely, they must soon have discovered and withdrawn from their danger; and might, thereafter, with no other help than that of attached subjects, have withstood the attacks of the French far more successfully than they could with their fortress, but with subjects whom they had estranged.

And, in truth, fortresses are unserviceable in every way, since they may be lost either by the treachery of those to whom you commit their defence, or by the overwhelming strength of an assailant, or else by famine. And where you seek to recover a State which you have lost, and in which only the fortress remains to you, if that fortress is to be of any service or assistance to you, you must have an army wherewith to attack the enemy who has driven you out. But with such an army you might succeed in recovering your State as readily without a fortress as with one; nay, perhaps, even more readily, since your subjects, had you not used them ill, from the overweening confidence your fortress gave you, might then have felt better disposed towards you. And the event shows that in times of adversity this very fortress of Milan has been of no advantage whatever, either to the Sforzas or to the French; but, on the contrary, has brought ruin on both, because, trusting to it, they did not turn their thoughts to nobler methods for preserving that State. Guido Ubaldo, duke of Urbino and son to Duke Federigo, who in his day was a warrior of much renown, but who was driven from his dominions by Cesare Borgia, son to Pope Alexander VI., when afterwards, by a sudden stroke of good fortune, he was restored to the dukedom caused all the fortresses of the country to be dismantled, judging them to be hurtful. For as he was beloved by his subjects, so far as they were concerned he had no need for fortresses; while, as against foreign enemies, he saw he could not defend them, since this would have required an army kept constantly in the field. For which reasons he made them be razed to the ground.

When Pope Julius II. had driven the Bentivogli from Bologna, after erecting a citadel in that town, he caused the people to be cruelly oppressed by his governor; whereupon, the people rebelled, and he forthwith lost the citadel; so that his citadel, and the oppressions to which it led, were of less service to him than different behaviour on his part had been. When Niccolo da Castello, the ancestor of the Vitelli, returned to his country out of exile, he straightway pulled down the two fortresses built there by Pope Sixtus IV., perceiving that it was not by fortresses, but by the good-will of the people, that he could be maintained in his government.

But the most recent, and in all respects most noteworthy instance, and that which best demonstrates the futility of building, and the advantage of destroying fortresses, is what happened only the other day in Genoa. Every one knows how, in 1507, Genoa rose in rebellion against Louis XII. of France, who came in person and with all his forces to recover it; and after recovering it built there a citadel stronger than any before known, being, both from its position and from every other circumstance, most inaccessible to attack. For standing on the extremity of a hill, named by the Genoese Codefa, which juts out into the sea, it commanded the whole harbour and the greater part of the town. But, afterwards, in the year 1512, when the French were driven out of Italy, the Genoese, in spite of this citadel, again rebelled, and Ottaviano Fregoso assuming the government, after the greatest efforts, continued over a period of sixteen months, at last succeeded in reducing the citadel by famine. By all it was believed that he would retain it as a rock of refuge in case of any reverse of fortune, and by some he was advised to do so; but he, being a truly wise ruler, and knowing well that it is by the attachment of their subjects and not by the strength of their fortifications that princes are maintained in their governments, dismantled this citadel; and founding his authority, not upon material defences, but on his own valour and prudence, kept and still keeps it. And whereas, formerly, a force of a thousand foot-soldiers could effect a change in the government of Genoa, the enemies of Ottaviano have assailed him with ten thousand, without being able to harm him.

Here, then, we see that, while to dismantle this fortress occasioned Ottaviano no loss, its construction gave the French king no sort of advantage. For when he could come into Italy with an army, he could recover Genoa, though he had no citadel there; but when he could not come with an army, it was not in his power to hold the city by means of the citadel. Moreover it was costly for the king to build, and shameful for him to lose this fortress; while for Ottaviano it was glorious to take, and advantageous to destroy it.

Let us turn now to those republics which build fortresses not within their own territories, but in towns whereof they have taken possession. And if the above example of France and Genoa suffice not to show the futility of this course, that of Florence and Pisa ought, I think, to be conclusive. For in erecting fortresses to hold Pisa, the Florentines failed to perceive that a city which had always been openly hostile to them, which had lived in freedom, and which could cloak rebellion under the name of liberty, must, if it were to be retained at all, be retained by those methods which were used by the Romans, and either be made a companion or be destroyed. Of how little service these Pisan fortresses were, was seen on the coming of Charles VIII. of France into Italy, to whom, whether through the treachery of their defenders or from fear of worse evils, they were at once delivered up; whereas, had there been no fortresses in Pisa, the Florentines would not have looked to them as the means whereby the town was to be held; the king could not by their assistance have taken the town from the Florentines; and the methods whereby it had previously been preserved might, in all likelihood, have continued sufficient to preserve it; and, at any rate, had served that end no worse than the fortresses.

These, then, are the conclusions to which I come, namely, that fortresses built to hold your own country under are hurtful, and that those built to retain acquired territories are useless; and I am content to rely on the example of the Romans, who in the towns they sought to hold by the strong hand, rather pulled down fortresses than built them. And if any, to controvert these views of mine, were to cite the case of Tarentum in ancient times, or of Brescia in recent, as towns which when they rebelled were recovered by means of their citadels; I answer, that for the recovery of Tarentum, Fabius Maximus was sent at the end of a year with an army strong enough to retake it even had there been no fortress there; and that although he availed himself of the fortress for the recovery of the town, he might, without it, have resorted to other means which would have brought about the same result. Nor do I see of what service a citadel can be said to be, when to recover the city you must employ a consular army under a Fabius Maximus. But that the Romans would, in any case, have recovered Tarentum, is plain from what happened at Capua, where there was no citadel, and which they retook, simply by the valour of their soldiers.

Again, as regards Brescia, I say that the circumstances attending the revolt of that town were such as occur but seldom, namely, that the citadel remaining in your hands after the defection of the city, you should happen to have a great army nigh at hand, as the French had theirs on this occasion. For M. de Foix being in command of the king's forces at Bologna, on hearing of the loss of Brescia, marched thither without an hour's delay, and reaching Brescia in three days, retook the town with the help of the citadel. But here, again, we see that, to be of any service, the citadel of Brescia had to be succoured by a de Foix, and by that French army which in three days' time marched to its relief. So that this instance cannot be considered conclusive as against others of a contrary tendency. For, in the course of recent wars, many fortresses have been taken and retaken, with the same variety of fortune with which open country has been acquired or lost; and this not only in Lombardy, but also in Romagna, in the kingdom of Naples, and in all parts of Italy.

And, further, touching the erection of fortresses as a defence against foreign enemies, I say that such defences are not needed by the prince or people who possess a good army; while for those who do not possess a good army, they are useless. For good armies without fortresses are in themselves a sufficient defence: whereas, fortresses without good armies avail nothing. And this we see in the case of those nations which have been thought to excel both in their government and otherwise, as, for instance, the Romans and the Spartans. For while the Romans would build no fortresses, the Spartans not merely abstained from building them, but would not even suffer their cities to be enclosed with walls; desiring to be protected by their own valour only, and by no other defence. So that when a Spartan was asked by an Athenian what he thought of the walls of Athens, he answered "that they were fine walls if meant to hold women only."

If a prince who has a good army has likewise, on the sea-front of his dominions, some fortress strong enough to keep an enemy in check for a few days, until he gets his forces together, this, though not necessary, may sometimes be for his advantage. But for a prince who is without a strong army to have fortresses erected throughout his territories, or upon his frontier, is either useless or hurtful, since they may readily be lost and then turned against him; or, supposing them so strong that the enemy is unable to take them by assault, he may leave them behind, and so render them wholly unprofitable. For a brave army, unless stoutly met, enters an enemy's country without regard to the towns or fortified places it leaves in its rear, as we read of happening in ancient times, and have seen done by Francesco Maria della Rovere, who no long while ago, when he marched against Urbino, made little of leaving ten hostile cities behind him.

The prince, therefore, who can bring together a strong army can do without building fortresses, while he who has not a strong army ought not to build them, but should carefully strengthen the city wherein he dwells, and keep it well stored with supplies, and its inhabitants well affected, so that he may resist attack till an accord be agreed on, or he be relieved by foreign aid. All other expedients are costly in time of peace, and in war useless.

Whoever carefully weighs all that has now been said will perceive, that the Romans, as they were most prudent in all their other methods, so also showed their wisdom in the measures they took with the men of Latium and Privernum, when, without ever thinking of fortresses, they sought security in bolder and more sagacious courses.

Chapter XXV.—*That he who attacks a City divided against itself, must not think to get possession of it through its Divisions.*

Violent dissensions breaking out in Rome between the commons and the nobles, it appeared to the Veientines and Etruscans that now was their time to deal a fatal blow to the Roman supremacy. Accordingly, they assembled an army and invaded the territories of Rome. The senate sent Caius Manlius and Marcus Fabius to meet them, whose forces encamping close by the Veientines, the latter ceased not to reproach and vilify the Roman name with every sort of taunt and abuse, and so incensed the Romans by their unmeasured insolence that, from being divided they became reconciled, and giving the enemy battle, broke and defeated them. Here, again, we see, what has already been noted, how prone men are to adopt wrong courses, and how often they miss their object when they think to secure it. The Veientines imagined that they could conquer the Romans by attacking them while they were at feud among themselves; but this very attack reunited the Romans and brought ruin on their assailants. For the causes of division in a commonwealth are, for the most part, ease and tranquillity, while the causes of union are fear and war. Wherefore, had the Veientines been wise, the more divided they saw Rome to be, the more should they have sought to avoid war with her, and endeavoured to gain an advantage over her by peaceful arts. And the best way to effect this in a divided city lies in gaining the confidence of both factions, and in mediating between them as arbiter so long as they do not come to blows; but when they resort to open violence, then to render some tardy aid to the weaker side, so as to plunge them deeper in hostilities, wherein both may exhaust their forces without being led by your putting forth an excess of strength to suspect you of a desire to ruin them and remain their master. Where this is well managed, it will almost always happen that you succeed in effecting the object you propose to yourself.

The city of Pistoja, as I have said already in connection with another matter, was won over to the Florentine republic by no other artifice than this. For the town being split by factions, the Florentines, by now favouring one side and now the other, without incurring the suspicions of either, brought both to such extremities that, wearied out with their harassed life, they threw themselves at last of their own accord into the arms of Florence. The city of Siena, again, has never made any change in her government which has had the support of the Florentines, save when that support has been slight and insignificant; for whenever the interference of Florence has been marked and decided, it has had the effect of uniting all parties in support of things as they stood.

One other instance I shall add to those already given. Oftener than once Filippo Visconti, duke of Milan, relying on their divisions, set wars on foot against the Florentines, and always without success; so that, in lamenting over these failures, he was wont to complain that the mad humours of the Florentines had cost him two millions of gold, without his having anything to show for it. The Veientines and Etruscans, therefore, as I have said already, were misled by false hopes, and in the end were routed by the Romans in a single pitched battle; and any who should look hereafter to prevail on like grounds and by similar means against a divided people, will always find themselves deceived.

Chapter XXVI.—*That Taunts and Abuse breed Hatred against him who uses them, without yielding him any Advantage.*

To abstain from threats and injurious language, is, methinks, one of the wisest precautions a man can use. For abuse and menace take nothing from the strength of an adversary; the latter only making him more cautious, while the former inflames his hatred against you, and leads him to consider more diligently how he may cause you hurt.

This is seen from the example of the Veientines, of whom I spoke in the last Chapter, who, to the injury of war against the Romans, added those verbal injuries from which all prudent commanders should compel their soldiers to refrain. For these are injuries which stir and kindle your enemy to vengeance, and yet, as has been said, in no way disable him from doing you hurt; so that, in truth, they are weapons which wound those who use them. Of this we find a notable instance in Asia, in connection with the siege of Amida. For Gabade, the Persian general, after besieging this town for a great while, wearied out at last by its protracted defence, determined on withdrawing his army; and had actually begun to strike his camp, when the whole inhabitants of the place, elated by their success, came out upon the walls to taunt and upbraid their enemies with their cowardice and meanness of spirit, and to load them with every kind of abuse. Stung by these insults, Gabade, changing his resolution, renewed the siege with such fury that in a few days he stormed and sacked the town. And the very same thing befell the Veientines, who, not content, as we have seen, to make war on the Romans with arms, must needs assail them with foul reproaches, advancing to the palisade of their camp to revile them, and molesting them more with their tongues than with their swords, until the Roman soldiers, who at first were most unwilling to fight, forced the consuls to lead them to the attack. Whereupon, the Veientines, like those others of whom mention has just now been made, had to pay the penalty of their insolence.

Wise captains of armies, therefore, and prudent governors of cities, should take all fit precautions to prevent such insults and reproaches from being used by their soldiers and subjects, either amongst themselves or against an enemy. For when directed against an enemy they lead to the mischiefs above noticed, while still worse consequences may follow from our not preventing them among ourselves by such measures as sensible rulers have always taken for that purpose.

The legions who were left behind for the protection of Capua having, as shall in its place be told, conspired against the Capuans, their conspiracy led to a mutiny, which was presently suppressed by Valerius Corvinus; when, as one of the conditions on which the mutineers made their submission, it was declared that whosoever should thereafter upbraid any soldier of these legions with having taken part in this mutiny, should be visited with the severest punishment. So likewise, when Tiberius Gracchus was appointed, during the war with Hannibal, to command a body of slaves, whom the Romans in their straits for soldiers had furnished with arms, one of his first acts was to pass an order making it death for any to reproach his men with their servile origin. So mischievous a thing did the Romans esteem it to use insulting words to others, or to taunt them with their shame. Whether this be done in sport or earnest, nothing vexes men more, or rouses them to fiercer indignation; "*for the biting jest which flavours too much of truth, leaves always behind it a rankling memory.*"[1]

[Footnote 1: *Nam facetiæ asperæ, quando nimium ex vero traxere, acrem sui memoriam relinquunt. Tacit. An.* xv. 68.]

Chapter XXVII.—*That prudent Princes and Republics should be content to have obtained a Victory; for, commonly, when they are not, theft-Victory turns to Defeat.*

The use of dishonouring language towards an enemy is mostly caused by an insolent humour, bred by victory or the false hope of it, whereby men are oftentimes led not only to speak, but also to act amiss. For such false hopes, when they gain an entry into men's minds, cause them to overrun their goal, and to miss opportunities for securing a certain good, on the chance of obtaining some thing better, but uncertain. And this, being a matter that deserves attention, because in deceiving themselves men often injure their country, I desire to illustrate it by particular instances, ancient and recent, since mere argument might not place it in so clear a light.

After routing the Romans at Cannæ, Hannibal sent messengers to Carthage to announce his victory, and to ask support. A debate arising in the Carthaginian senate as to what was to be done, Hanno, an aged and wise citizen, advised that they should prudently take advantage of their victory to make peace with the Romans, while as conquerors they might have it on favourable terms, and not wait to make it after a defeat; since it should be their object to show the Romans that they were strong enough to fight them, but not to peril the victory they had won in the hope of winning a greater. This advice was not followed by the Carthaginian senate, but its wisdom was well seen later, when the opportunity to act upon it was gone.

When the whole East had been overrun by Alexander of Macedon, the citizens of Tyre (then at the height of its renown, and very strong from being built, like Venice, in the sea), recognizing his greatness, sent ambassadors to him to say that they desired to be his good servants, and to yield him all obedience, yet could not consent to receive either him or his soldiers within their walls. Whereupon, Alexander, displeased that a single city should venture to close its gates against him to whom all the rest of the world had thrown theirs open, repulsed the Tyrians, and rejecting their overtures set to work to besiege their town. But as it stood on the water, and was well stored with victual and all other munitions needed for its defence, after four months had gone, Alexander, perceiving that he was wasting more time in an inglorious attempt to reduce this one city than had sufficed for most of his other conquests, resolved to offer terms to the Tyrians, and to make them those concessions which they themselves had asked. But they, puffed up by their success, not merely refused the terms offered, but put to death the envoy sent to propose them. Enraged by this, Alexander renewed the siege, and with such vigour, that he took and destroyed the city, and either slew or made slaves of its inhabitants.

In the year 1512, a Spanish army entered the Florentine territory, with the object of restoring the Medici to Florence, and of levying a subsidy from the town; having been summoned thither by certain of the citizens, who had promised them that so soon as they appeared within the Florentine confines they would arm in their behalf. But when the Spaniards had come into the plain of the Arno, and none declared in their favour, being in sore need of supplies, they offered to make terms. This offer the people of Florence in their pride rejected, and so gave occasion for the sack of Prato and the overthrow of the Florentine Republic.

A prince, therefore, who is attacked by an enemy much more powerful than himself, can make no greater mistake than to refuse to treat, especially when overtures are made to him; for however poor the terms offered may be, they are sure to contain some conditions advantageous for him who accepts them, and which he may construe as a partial success. For which reason it ought to have been enough for the citizens of Tyre that Alexander was brought to accept terms which he had at first rejected; and they should have esteemed it a sufficient triumph that, by their resistance in arms, they had forced so great a warrior to bow to their will. And, in like manner, it should have been a sufficient victory for the Florentines that the Spaniards had in part yielded to their wishes, and abated something of their own demands, the purport of which was to change the government of Florence, to sever her from her allegiance to France, and, further, to obtain money from her. For if of these three objects the Spaniards had succeeded in securing the last two, while the Florentines maintained the integrity of their government, a fair share of honour and contentment would have fallen to each. And while preserving their political existence, the Florentines should have made small account of the other two conditions; nor ought they, even with the possibility and almost certainty of greater advantages before them, to have left matters in any degree to the arbitration of Fortune, by pushing things to extremes, and incurring risks which no prudent man should incur, unless compelled by necessity.

Hannibal, when recalled by the Carthaginians from Italy, where for sixteen years he had covered himself with glory, to the defence of his native country, found on his arrival that Hasdrubal and Syphax had been defeated, the kingdom of Numidia lost, and Carthage confined within the limits of her walls, and left without other resource save in him and his army. Perceiving, therefore, that this was the last stake his country had to play, and not choosing to hazard it until he had tried every other expedient, he felt no shame to sue for peace, judging that in peace rather than in war lay the best hope of safety for his country. But, when peace was refused him, no fear of defeat deterred him from battle, being resolved either to conquer, if conquer he might, or if he must fall, to fall gloriously. Now, if a commander so valiant as Hannibal, at the head of an unconquered army, was willing to sue for peace rather than appeal to battle when he saw that by defeat his country must be enslaved, what course ought to be followed by another commander, less valiant and with less experience than he? But men labour under this infirmity, that they know not where to set bounds to their hopes, and building on these without otherwise measuring their strength, rush headlong on destruction.

Chapter XXVIII.—*That to neglect the redress of Grievances, whether public or private, is dangerous for a Prince or Commonwealth.*

Certain Gauls coming to attack Etruria, and more particularly Clusium its chief city, the citizens of Clusium sought aid from Rome; whereupon the Romans sent the three Fabii, as envoys to these Gauls, to notify to them, in the name of the Roman people, that they must refrain from making war on the Etruscans. From what befell the Romans in connection with this embassy, we see clearly how far men may be carried in resenting an affront. For these envoys arriving at the very moment when the Gauls and Etruscans were about to join battle, being readier at deeds than words, took part with the Etruscans and fought in their foremost ranks. Whence it came that the Gauls recognizing the Roman envoys, turned against the Romans all the hatred which before they had felt for the Etruscans; and grew still more incensed when on making complaint to the Roman senate, through their ambassador, of the wrong done them, and demanding that the Fabii should be given up to them in atonement for their offence, not merely were the offenders not given up or punished in any way, but, on the contrary, when the comitia met were created tribunes with consular powers. But when the Gauls found these men honoured who deserved to be chastised, they concluded that what had happened had been done by way of slight and insult to them, and, burning with fury and resentment, hastened forward to attack Rome, which they took with the exception of the Capitol.

Now this disaster overtook the Romans entirely from their disregard of justice. For their envoys, who had violated the law of nations, and had therefore deserved punishment, they had on the contrary treated with honour. And this should make us reflect, how carefully all princes and commonwealths ought to refrain from committing like wrongs, not only against communities, but also against particular men. For if a man be deeply wronged, either by a private hand or by a public officer, and be not avenged to his satisfaction, if he live in a republic, he will seek to avenge himself, though in doing so he bring ruin on his country; or if he live under a prince, and be of a resolute and haughty spirit, he will never rest until he has wreaked his resentment against the prince, though he knows it may cost him dear. Whereof we have no finer or truer example than in the death of Philip of Macedon, the father of Alexander. For Pausanias, a handsome and high-born youth belonging to Philip's court, having been most foully and cruelly dishonoured by Attalus, one of the foremost men of the royal household, repeatedly complained to Philip of the outrage; who for a while put him off with promises of vengeance, but in the end, so far from avenging him, promoted Attalus to be governor of the province of Greece. Whereupon, Pausanias, seeing his enemy honoured and not punished, turned all his resentment from him who had outraged, against him who had not avenged him, and on the morning of the day fixed for the marriage of Philip's daughter to Alexander of Epirus, while Philip walked between the two Alexanders, his son and his son-in-law, towards the temple to celebrate the nuptials, he slew him.

This instance nearly resembles that of the Roman envoys; and offers a warning to all rulers never to think so lightly of any man as to suppose, that when wrong upon wrong has been done him, he will not bethink himself of revenge, however great the danger he runs, or the punishment he thereby brings upon himself.

Chapter XXIX.—*That Fortune obscures the minds of Men when she would not have them hinder her Designs.*

If we note well the course of human affairs, we shall often find things come about and accidents befall, against which it seems to be the will of Heaven that men should not provide. And if this were the case even in Rome, so renowned for her valour, religion, and wise ordinances, we need not wonder if it be far more common in other cities and provinces wherein these safeguards are wanting.

Having here a notable opportunity to show how Heaven influences men's actions, Titus Livius turns it to account, and treats the subject at large and in pregnant words, where he says, that since it was Heaven's will, for ends of its own, that the Romans should feel its power, it first of all caused these Fabii, who were sent as envoys to the Gauls, to act amiss, and then by their misconduct stirred up the Gauls to make war on Rome; and, lastly, so ordered matters that nothing worthy of their name was done by the Romans to withstand their attack. For it was fore-ordained by Heaven that Camillus, who alone could supply the remedy to so mighty an evil, should be banished to Ardea; and again, that the citizens, who had often created a dictator to meet attacks of the Volscians and other neighbouring hostile nations, should fail to do so when the Gauls were marching upon Rome. Moreover, the army which the Romans got together was but a weak one, since they used no signal effort to make it strong; nay, were so dilatory in arming that they were barely in time to meet the enemy at the river Allia, though no more than ten miles distant from Rome. Here, again, the Roman tribunes pitched their camp without observing any of the usual precautions, attending neither to the choice of ground, nor to surround themselves with trench or Palisade, nor to avail themselves of any other aid, human or Divine. In ordering their army for battle, moreover, disposed it in weak columns, and these far apart: so that neither men nor officers accomplished anything worthy of the Roman discipline. The battle was bloodless for the Romans fled before they were attacked; most of them retreating to Veii, the rest to Rome, where, without turning aside to visit their homes, they made straight for the Capitol.

Meanwhile, the senate, so far from bethinking themselves how they might defend the city, did not even attend to closing the gates; and while some of them made their escape from Rome, others entered the Capitol along with those who sought shelter there. It was only in the defence of the Capitol that any method was observed, measures being taken to prevent it being crowded with useless numbers, and all the victual which could be got, being brought into it to enable it to stand a siege. Of the women, the children, and the men whose years unfitted them for service, the most part fled for refuge to the neighbouring towns, the rest remained in Rome a prey to the invaders; so that no one who had heard of the achievements of the Romans in past years, on being told of what took place on this occasion, could have believed that it was of the same people that things so contrary were related.

Wherefore, Titus Livius, after setting forth all these disorders, concludes with the words, "*So far does Fortune darken men's minds when she would not have her ascendency gainsaid.*" Nor could any juster observation be made. And hence it is that those who experience the extremes whether of good or of evil fortune, are, commonly, little deserving either of praise or blame; since it is apparent that it is from Heaven having afforded them, or denied them opportunities for acting worthily, that they have been brought to their greatness or to their undoing. Fortune, doubtless, when she seeks to effect great ends, will often choose as her instrument a man of such sense and worth that he can recognize the opportunities which she holds out to him; and, in like manner, when she desires to bring about great calamities, will put forward such men as will of themselves contribute to that result. And all who stand in her way, she either removes by death, or deprives of the means of effecting good. And it is well seen in the passage we are considering, how Fortune, to aggrandize Rome, and raise her to the height she reached, judged it necessary, as shall be more fully shown in the following Book, to humble her; yet would not have her utterly undone. For which reason we find her causing Camillus to be banished, but not put to death; suffering Rome to be taken, but not the Capitol; and bringing it to pass that, while the Romans took no wise precaution for the defence of their city, they neglected none in defending their citadel. That Rome might be taken, Fortune caused the mass of the army, after the rout at the Allia, to direct its flight to Veii, thus withdrawing the means wherewith the city might have been defended; but while thus disposing matters, she at the same time prepared all the needful steps for its recovery, in bringing an almost entire Roman array to Veii, and Camillus to Ardea, so that a great force might be assembled for the rescue of their country, under a captain in no way compromised by previous reverses, but, on the contrary, in the enjoyment of an untarnished renown. I might cite many modern instances to confirm these opinions, but since enough has been said to convince any fair mind, I pass them over. But once more I repeat what, from all history, may be seen to be most true, that men may aid Fortune, but not withstand her; may interweave their threads with her web, but cannot break it But, for all that, they must never lose heart, since not knowing what their end is to be, and moving towards it by cross-roads and untravelled paths, they have always room for hope, and ought never to abandon it, whatsoever befalls, and into whatsoever straits they come.

Chapter XXX.—That really powerful Princes and Commonwealths do not buy Friendships with Money, but with their Valour and the Fame of their Prowess.

When besieged in the Capitol, the Romans, although expecting succour from Veii and from Camillus, were driven by famine to enter into an agreement to buy off the Gauls with gold. But at the very moment when, in pursuance of this agreement, the gold was being weighed out, Camillus came up with his army. This, says our historian, was contrived by Fortune, "*that the Romans might not live thereafter as men ransomed for a price;*" and the matter is noteworthy, not only with reference to this particular occasion, but also as it bears on the methods generally followed by this republic. For we never find Rome seeking to acquire towns or to purchase peace with money, but always confiding in her own valour, which could not, I believe, be said of any other republic.

Now, one of the tests whereby to gauge the strength of any State, is to observe on what terms it lives with its neighbours; for when it so carries itself that, to secure its friendship, its neighbours pay it tribute, this is a sure sign of its strength, but when its neighbours, though of less reputation, receive payments from it, this is a clear proof of its weakness. In the course of the Roman history we read how the Massilians, the Eduans, the Rhodians, Hiero of Syracuse, the Kings Eumenes and Massinissa, all of them neighbours to the Roman frontiers, in order to secure the friendship of Rome, submitted to imposts and tribute whenever Rome had need of them, asking no return save her protection. But with a weak State we find the reverse of all this happening. And, to begin with our own republic of Florence, we know that in times past, when she was at the height of her renown, there was never a lordling of Romagna who had not a subsidy from her, to say nothing of what she paid to the Perugians, to the Castellans, and to all her other neighbours. But had our city been armed and strong, the direct contrary would have been the case, for, to obtain her protection, all would have poured money into her lap, not seeking to sell their friendship but to purchase hers.

Nor are the Florentines the only people who have lived on this dishonourable footing. The Venetians have done the same, nay, the King of France himself, for all his great dominions, lives a tributary to the Swiss and to the King of England; and this because the French king and the others named, with a view to escape dangers rather imaginary than real, have disarmed their subjects; seeking to reap a present gain by wringing money from them, rather than follow a course which would secure their own safety and the lasting welfare of their country. Which ill-practices of theirs, though they quiet things for a time, must in the end exhaust their resources, and give rise in seasons of danger to incurable mischief and disorder. It would be tedious to count up how often in the course of their wars, the Florentines, the Venetians, and the kingdom of France have had to ransom themselves from their enemies, and to submit to an ignominy to which, once only, the Romans were very near being subjected. It would be tedious, too, to recite how many towns have been bought by the Florentines and by the Venetians, which, afterwards, have only been a trouble to them, from their not knowing how to defend with iron what they had won with gold. While the Romans continued free they adhered to this more generous and noble method, but when they came under the emperors, and these, again, began to deteriorate, and to love the shade rather than the sunshine, they also took to purchasing peace, now from the Parthians, now from the Germans, and at other times from other neighbouring nations. And this was the beginning of the decline of their great empire.

Such are the evils that befall when you withhold arms from your subjects; and this course is attended by the still greater disadvantage, that the closer an enemy presses you the weaker he finds you. For any one who follows the evil methods of which I speak, must, in order to support troops whom he thinks can be trusted to keep off his enemies, be very exacting in his dealings with those of his subjects who dwell in the heart of his dominions; since, to widen the interval between himself and his enemies, he must subsidize those princes and peoples who adjoin his frontiers. States maintained on this footing may make a little resistance on their confines; but when these are passed by the enemy no further defence remains. Those who pursue such methods as these seem not to perceive that they are opposed to reason and common sense. For the heart and vital parts of the body, not the extremities, are those which we should keep guarded, since we may live on without the latter, but must die if the former be hurt. But the States of which I speak, leaving the heart undefended, defend only the hands and feet. The mischief which has thus been, and is at this day wrought in Florence is plain enough to see. For so soon as an enemy penetrates within her frontiers, and approaches her heart, all is over with her. And the same was witnessed a few years ago in the case of the Venetians, whose city, had it not been girdled by the sea, must then have found its end. In France, indeed, a like result has not been seen so often, she being so great a kingdom as to have few enemies mightier than herself. Nevertheless, when the English invaded France in the year 1513, the whole kingdom tottered; and the King himself, as well as every one else, had to own that a single defeat might have cost him his dominions.

Chapter XXX.—*That really powerful Princes and, Commonwealths do not buy Friendships with Money, but with their Valour and the Fame of their Prowess.*

When besieged in the Capitol, the Romans although expecting succour from Veii and from Camillus, nevertheless, being straitened by famine, entered into an agreement to buy off the Gauls with gold But at the very moment when, in pursuance of this agreement, the gold was being weighed out, Camillus came up with his army. This, says our historian, was contrived by Fortune, "*that the Romans might not live thereafter as men ransomed for a price,*" and the matter is noteworthy, not only with reference to this particular occasion, but also as it bears on the methods generally followed by this republic. For we never find Rome seeking to acquire towns, or to purchase peace with money, but always confiding in her own warlike valour, which could not, I believe, be said of any other republic.

Now, one of the tests whereby to gauge the strength of any State, is to observe on what terms it lives with its neighbours: for when it so carries itself that, to secure its friendship, its neighbours pay it tribute, this is a sure sign of its strength, but when its neighbours, though of less reputation, receive payments from it, this is a clear proof of its weakness In the course of the Roman history we read how the Massilians, the Eduans, the Rhodians, Hiero of Syracuse, the Kings Eumenes and Massinissa, all of them neighbours to the Roman frontiers, in order to secure the friendship of Rome, submitted to imposts and tribute whenever Rome had need of them, asking no return save her protection. But with a weak State we find the reverse of all this happening And, to begin with our own republic of Florence, we know that in times past, when she was at the height of her renown, there was never a lordling of Romagna who had not a subsidy from her, to say nothing of what she paid to the Perugians, to the Castellans, and to all her other neighbours But had our city been armed and strong, the direct contrary would have been the case, for, to obtain her protection, all would have poured money into her lap, not seeking to sell their friendship but to purchase hers.

Nor are the Florentines the only people who have lived on this dishonourable footing The Venetians have done the same, nay, the King of France himself, for all his great dominions, lives tributary to the Swiss and to the King of England; and this because the French king and the others named, with a view to escape dangers rather imaginary than real, have disarmed their subjects; seeking to reap a present gain by wringing money from them, rather than follow a course which would secure their own safety and the lasting welfare of their country. Which ill-practices of theirs, though they quiet things for a time, must in the end exhaust their resources, and give rise in seasons of danger to incurable mischief and disorder. It would be tedious to count up how often in the course of their wars, the Florentines, the Venetians, and the kingdom of France have had to ransom themselves from their enemies, and to submit to an ignominy to which, once only, the Romans were very near being subjected. It would be tedious, too, to recite how many towns have been bought by the Florentines and by the Venetians, which, afterwards, have only been a trouble to them, from their not knowing how to defend with iron what they had won with gold. While the Romans continued free they adhered to this more generous and noble method, but when they came under the emperors, and these, again, began to deteriorate, and to love the shade rather than the sunshine, they also took to purchasing peace, now from the Parthians, now from the Germans, and at other times from other neighbouring nations. And this was the beginning of the decline of their great empire.

Such are the evils that befall when you withhold arms from your subjects; and this course is attended by the still greater disadvantage, that the closer an enemy presses you the weaker he finds you. For any one who follows the evil methods of which I speak, must, in order to support troops whom he thinks can be trusted to keep off his enemies, be very exacting in his dealings with those of his subjects who dwell in the heart of his dominions; since, to widen the interval between himself and his enemies, he must subsidize those princes and peoples who adjoin his frontiers. States maintained on this footing may make a little resistance on their confines; but when these are passed by the enemy no further defence remains. Those who pursue such methods as these seem not to perceive that they are opposed to reason and common sense. For the heart and vital parts of the body, not the extremities, are those which we should keep guarded, since we may live on without the latter, but must die if the former be hurt. But the States of which I speak, leaving the heart undefended, defend only the hands and feet. The mischief which has thus been, and is at this day wrought in Florence is plain enough to see. For so soon as an enemy penetrates within her frontiers, and approaches her heart, all is over with her. And the same was witnessed a few years ago in the case of the Venetians, whose city, had it not been girdled by the sea, must then have found its end. In France, indeed, a like result has not been seen so often, she being so great a kingdom as to have few enemies mightier than herself. Nevertheless, when the English invaded France in the year 1513, the whole kingdom tottered; and the King himself, as well as every one else, had to own that a single defeat might have cost him his dominions.

But with the Romans the reverse of all this took place. For the nearer an enemy approached Rome, the more completely he found her armed for resistance; and accordingly we see that on the occasion of Hannibal's invasion of Italy, the Romans, after three defeats, and after the slaughter of so many of their captains and soldiers, were still able, not merely to withstand the invader, but even, in the end, to come off victorious. This we may ascribe to the heart being well guarded, while the extremities were but little heeded. For the strength of Rome rested on the Roman people themselves, on the Latin league, on the confederate towns of Italy, and on her colonies, from all of which sources she drew so numerous an army, as enabled her to subdue the whole world and to keep it in subjection.

The truth of what I say may be further seen from the question put by Hanno the Carthaginian to the messengers sent to Carthage by Hannibal after his victory at Cannæ. For when these were vaunting the achievements of Hannibal, they were asked by Hanno whether any one had come forward on behalf of the Romans to propose terms of peace, and whether any town of the Latin league or of the colonized districts had revolted from the Romans. And when to both inquiries the envoys answered, "No," Hanno observed that the war was no nearer an end than on the day it was begun.

We can understand, therefore, as well from what has now been said, as from what I have often said before, how great a difference there is between the methods followed by the republics of the present times, and those followed by the republics of antiquity; and why it is that we see every day astounding losses alternate with extraordinary gains. For where men are weak, Fortune shows herself strong; and because she changes, States and Governments change with her; and will continue to change, until some one arise, who, following reverently the example of the ancients, shall so control her, that she shall not have opportunity with every revolution of the sun to display anew the greatness of her power.

Chapter XXXI.—*Of the Danger of trusting banished Men.*

The danger of trusting those who are in exile from their own country, being one to which the rulers of States are often exposed, may, I think, be fitly considered in these Discourses; and I notice it the more willingly, because I am able to illustrate it by a memorable instance which Titus Livius, though with another purpose, relates in his history. When Alexander the Great passed with his army into Asia, his brother-in-law and uncle, Alexander of Epirus, came with another army into Italy, being invited thither by the banished Lucanians, who gave him to believe that, with their aid, he might get possession of the whole of that country. But when, confiding in the promises of these exiles, and fed by the hopes they held out to him, he came into Italy, they put him to death, their fellow-citizens having offered to restore them to their country upon this condition. It behoves us, therefore, to remember how empty are the promises, and how doubtful the faith, of men in banishment from their native land. For as to their faith, it may be assumed that whenever they can effect their return by other means than yours, notwithstanding any covenants they may have made with you, they will throw you over, and take part with their countrymen. And as for the empty promises and delusive hopes which they set before you, so extreme is their desire to return home that they naturally believe many things which are untrue, and designedly misrepresent many others; so that between their beliefs and what they say they believe, they fill you with false impressions, on which if you build, your labour is in vain, and you are led to engage in enterprises from which nothing but ruin can result.

To this instance of Alexander I shall add only one other, that, namely, of Themistocles the Athenian, who, being proclaimed a traitor, fled into Asia to Darius, to whom he made such lavish promises if he would only attack Greece, that he induced him to undertake the enterprise. But afterwards, when he could not fulfil what he had promised, either from shame, or through fear of punishment, he poisoned himself. But, if such a mistake as this was made by a man like Themistocles, we may reckon that mistakes still greater will be made by those who, being of a feebler nature, suffer themselves to be more completely swayed by their feelings and wishes Wherefore, let a prince be careful how he embarks in any enterprise on the representations of an exile; for otherwise, he is likely either to be put to shame, or to incur the gravest calamities.

Because towns are sometimes, though seldom, taken by craft, through secret practices had with their inhabitants, I think it not out of place to discuss the matter in the following Chapter, wherein I shall likewise show in how many ways the Romans were wont to make such acquisitions.

Chapter XXXII.—*In how many Ways the Romans gained Possession of Towns.*

Turning their thoughts wholly to arms, the Romans always conducted their military enterprises in the most advantageous way, both as to cost and every other circumstance of war. For which reason they avoided attempting towns by siege, judging the expense and inconvenience of this method of carrying on war greatly to outweigh any advantage to be gained by it. Accordingly, they thought it better and more for their interest to reduce towns in any other way than this; and in all those years during which they were constantly engaged in wars we find very few instances of their proceeding by siege.

For the capture of towns, therefore, they trusted either to assault or to surrender. Assaults were effected either by open force, or by force and stratagem combined. When a town was assailed by open force, the walls were stormed without being breached, and the assailants were said "*aggredi urbem corona,*" because they encircled the city with their entire strength and kept up an attack on all sides. In this way they often succeeded in carrying towns, and even great towns, at a first onset, as when Scipio took new Carthage in Spain. But when they failed to carry a town by storm, they set themselves to breach the walls with battering rams and other warlike engines; or they dug mines so as to obtain an entrance within the walls, this being the method followed in taking Veii; or else, to be on a level with the defenders, they erected towers of timber or threw up mounds of earth against the outside of the walls so as to reach the top.

Of these methods of attack, the first, wherein the city was entirely surrounded, exposed the defenders to more sudden perils and left them more doubtful remedies. For while it was necessary for them to have a sufficient force at all points, it might happen that the forces at their disposal were not numerous enough to be everywhere at once, or to relieve one another. Or if their numbers were sufficient, they might not all be equally resolute in standing their ground, and their failure at any one point involved a general defeat. Consequently, as I have said, this method of attack was often successful. But when it did not succeed at the first, it was rarely renewed, being a method dangerous to the attacking army, which having to secure itself along an extended line, was left everywhere too weak to resist a sally made from the town; nay, of itself, was apt to fall into confusion and disorder. This method of attack, therefore, could be attempted once only and by way of surprise.

Against breaches in the walls the defence was, as at the present day, to throw up new works; while mines were met by counter-mines, in which the enemy were either withstood at the point of the sword, or baffled by some other warlike contrivance; as by filling casks with feathers, which, being set on fire and placed in the mine, choked out the assailants by their smoke and stench. Where towers were employed for the attack, the defenders sought to destroy them with fire; and where mounds of earth were thrown up against the walls, they would dig holes at the base of the wall against which the mound rested, and carry off the earth which the enemy were heaping up; which, being removed from within as fast as it was thrown up from without, the mound made no progress.

None of these methods of attack can long be persisted in and the assailant, if unsuccessful, must either strike his camp and seek victory in some other direction, as Scipio did when he invaded Africa and, after failing in the attempt to storm Utica, withdrew from his attack on that town and turned his strength against the Carthaginian army in the field; or else recourse must be had to regular siege, as by the Romans at Veii, Capua, Carthage, Jerusalem, and divers other cities which they reduced in this way.

The capture of towns by stratagem combined with force is effected, as by the Romans at Palæopolis, through a secret understanding with some within the walls. Many attempts of this sort have been made, both by the Romans and by others, but few successfully, because the least hindrance disarranges the plan of action, and because such hindrances are very likely to occur. For either the plot is discovered before it can be carried out, as it readily may, whether from treachery on the part of those to whom it has been communicated, or from the difficulties which attend its inception, the preliminary arrangements having to be made with the enemy and with persons with whom it is not permitted, save under some pretext or other, to hold intercourse; or if it be not discovered while it is being contrived, a thousand difficulties will still be met with in its execution. For if you arrive either before or after the appointed time, all is ruined. The faintest sound, as of the cackling of the geese in the Capitol, the least departure from some ordinary routine, the most trifling mistake or error, mars the whole enterprise. Add to which, the darkness of night lends further terror to the perils of such undertakings; while the great majority of those engaged in them, having no knowledge of the district or places into which they are brought, are bewildered and disconcerted by the least mishap, and put to flight by every imaginary danger. In secret nocturnal enterprises of this sort, no man was ever more successful than Aratus of Sicyon, although in any encounter by day there never was a more arrant coward. This we must suppose due rather to some special and occult quality inherent in the man, than to success being naturally to be looked for in the like attempts. Such enterprises, accordingly, are often planned, but few are put into execution, and fewer still with success.

When cities are acquired by surrender, the surrender is either voluntary or under compulsion; voluntary, when the citizens appeal to you for protection against some threatened danger from without, as Capua submitted to the Romans; or where they are moved by a desire to be better governed, and are attracted by the good government which he to whom they surrender is seen exercising over others who have placed themselves in his hands; as was the case with the Rhodians, the Massilians, and others who for like causes gave themselves up to the Roman people. Compulsory surrenders take place, either as the result of a protracted siege, like those we have spoken of above; or from the country being continually wasted by incursions, forays, and similar severities, to escape which a city makes its submission.

Of the methods which have been noticed, the Romans, in preference to all others, used this last; and for four hundred and fifty years made it their aim to wear out their neighbours by invasion and by defeat in the open field, while endeavouring, as I have elsewhere said, to establish their influence over them by treaties and conventions. It was to this method of warfare therefore that they always mainly trusted, because, after trying all others, they found none so free from inconvenience and disadvantage—the procedure by siege involving expense and delay, that by assault, difficulty and danger, and that by secret practice, uncertainty and doubt. They found, likewise, that while in subduing one obstinate city by siege many years might be wasted, a kingdom might be gained in a single day by the defeat of a hostile army in the field.

Chapter XXXIII.—*That the Romans intrusted the Captains of their Armies with the fullest Powers.*

In reading this History of Titus Livius with a view to profit by it, I think that all the methods of conduct followed by the Roman people and senate merit attention. And among other things fit to be considered, it should be noted, with how ample an authority they sent forth their consuls, their dictators, and the other captains of their armies, all of whom we find clothed with the fullest powers: no other prerogative being reserved to itself by the senate save that of declaring war and making peace, while everything else was left to the discretion and determination of the consul. For so soon as the people and senate had resolved on war, for instance on a war against the Latins, they threw all further responsibility upon the consul, who might fight or decline battle as he pleased, and attack this or the other city as he thought fit.

That this was so, is seen in many instances, and especially from what happened during an expedition made against the Etruscans. For the consul Fabius having routed that people near Sutrium, and thinking to pass onward through the Ciminian forest into Etruria, so far from seeking the advice of the senate, gave them no hint whatever of his design, although for its execution the war had to be carried into a new, difficult, and dangerous country. We have further witness to the same effect, in the action taken in respect of this enterprise by the senate, who being informed of the victory obtained by Fabius, and apprehending that he might decide to pass onward through the aforesaid forest, and deeming it inexpedient that he should incur risk by attempting this invasion, sent two messengers to warn him not to enter Etruria. These messengers, however, did not come up with the consul until he had already made his way into that country and gained a second victory; when, instead of opposing his further advance, they returned to Rome to announce his good fortune and the glory which he had won.

Whoever, therefore, shall well consider the character of the authority whereof I speak, will see that it was most wisely accorded; since had it been the wish of the senate that a consul, in conducting a war, should proceed step by step as they might direct him, this must have made him at once less cautious and more dilatory; because the credit of victory would not then have seemed to be wholly his own, but shared by the senate on whose advice he acted. Besides which, the senate must have taken upon itself the task of advising on matters which it could not possibly understand; for although it might contain among its members all who were most versed in military affairs, still, since these men were not on the spot, and were ignorant of many particulars which, if they were to give sound advice, it was necessary for them to know, they must in advising have made numberless mistakes. For these reasons they desired that the consul should act on his own responsibility, and that the honours of success should be wholly his; judging that the love of fame would act on him at once as a spur and as a curb, making him do whatever he had to do well.

This matter I have the rather dwelt upon because I observe that our modern republics, such as the Venetian and the Florentine, view it in a different light; so that when their captains, commissaries, or *provedditori* have a single gun to place in position, the authorities at home must be informed and consulted; a course deserving the same approval as is due to all those other methods of theirs, which, one with another, have brought Italy to her present condition.

Book III.

Chapter I.—*For a Sect or Commonwealth to last long, it must often be brought back to its Beginnings.*

Doubtless, all the things of this world have a limit set to their duration; yet those of them the bodies whereof have not been suffered to grow disordered, but have been so cared for that either no change at all has been wrought in them, or, if any, a change for the better and not for the worse, will run that course which Heaven has in a general way appointed them. And since I am now speaking of mixed bodies, for States and Sects are so to be regarded, I say that for them these are wholesome changes which bring them back to their first beginnings.

Those States consequently stand surest and endure longest which, either by the operation of their institutions can renew themselves, or come to be renewed by accident apart from any design. Nothing, however, can be clearer than that unless thus renewed these bodies do not last. Now the way to renew them is, as I have said, to bring them back to their beginnings, since all beginnings of sects, commonwealths, or kingdoms must needs have in them a certain excellence, by virtue of which they gain their first reputation and make their first growth. But because in progress of time this excellence becomes corrupted, unless something be done to restore it to what it was at first, these bodies necessarily decay; for as the physicians tell us in speaking of the human body, *"Something or other is daily added which sooner or later will require treatment."*[1]

As regards commonwealths, this return to the point of departure is brought about either by extrinsic accident or by intrinsic foresight. As to the first, we have seen how it was necessary that Rome should be taken by the Gauls, that being thus in a manner reborn, she might recover life and vigour, and resume the observances of religion and justice which she had suffered to grow rusted by neglect. This is well seen from those passages of Livius wherein he tells us that when the Roman army was 'sent forth against the Gauls, and again when tribunes were created with consular authority, no religious rites whatever were celebrated, and wherein he further relates how the Romans not only failed to punish the three Fabii, who contrary to the law of nations had fought against the Gauls, but even clothed them with honour. For, from these instances, we may well infer that the rest of the wise ordinances instituted by Romulus, and the other prudent kings, had begun to be held of less account than they deserved, and less than was essential for the maintenance of good government.

And therefore it was that Rome was visited by this calamity from without, to the end that all her ordinances might be reformed, and the people taught that it behoved them not only to maintain religion and justice, but also to esteem their worthy citizens, and to prize their virtues beyond any advantages of which they themselves might seem to have been deprived at their instance. And this, we find, was just the effect produced. For no sooner was the city retaken, than all the ordinances of the old religion were at once restored; the Fabii, who had fought in violation of the law of nations, were punished; and the worth and excellence of Camillus so fully recognized, that the senate and the whole people, laying all jealousies aside, once more committed to him the entire charge of public affairs.

It is necessary then, as I have said already, that where men dwell together in a regulated society, they be often reminded of those ordinances in conformity with which they ought to live, either by something inherent in these, or else by some external accident. A reminder is given in the former of these two ways, either by the passing of some law whereby the members of the society are brought to an account; or else by some man of rare worth arising among them, whose virtuous life and example have the same effect as a law. In a Commonwealth, accordingly, this end is served either by the virtues of some one of its citizens, or by the operation of its institutions.

The institutions whereby the Roman Commonwealth was led back to its starting point, were the tribuneship of the people and the censorship, together with all those laws which were passed to check the insolence and ambition of its citizens. Such institutions, however, require fresh life to be infused into them by the worth of some one man who fearlessly devotes himself to give them effect in opposition to the power of those who set them at defiance.

Of the laws being thus reinforced in Rome, before its capture by the Gauls, we have notable examples in the deaths of the sons of Brutus, of the Decemvirs, and of Manlius Frumentarius; and after its capture, in the deaths of Manlius Capitolinus, and of the son of Manlius Torquatus in the prosecution of his master of the knights by Papirius Cursor, and in the impeachment of the Scipios. Such examples as these, being signal and extraordinary, had the effect, whenever they took place, of bringing men back to the true standard of right; but when they came to be of rarer occurrence, they left men more leisure to grow corrupted, and were attended by greater danger and disturbance. Wherefore, between one and another of these vindications of the laws, no more than ten years, at most, ought to intervene; because after that time men begin to change their manners and to disregard the laws; and if nothing occur to recall the idea of punishment, and unless fear resume its hold on their minds, so many offenders suddenly spring up together that it is impossible to punish them without danger. And to this purport it used to be said by those who ruled Florence from the year 1434 to 1494, that their government could hardly be maintained unless it was renewed every five years; by which they meant that it was necessary for them to arouse the same terror and alarm in men's minds, as they inspired when they first assumed the government, and when all who offended against their authority were signally chastised. For when the recollection of such chastisement has died out, men are emboldened to engage in new designs, and to speak ill of their rulers; for which the only remedy is to restore things to what they were at first.

A republic may, likewise, be brought back to its original form, without recourse to ordinances for enforcing justice, by the mere virtues of a single citizen, by reason that these virtues are of such influence and authority that good men love to imitate them, and bad men are ashamed to depart from them. Those to whom Rome owed most for services of this sort, were Horatius Cocles, Mutius Scævola, the two Decii, Atilius Regulus, and divers others, whose rare excellence and generous example wrought for their city almost the same results as might have been effected by ordinances and laws. And if to these instances of individual worth had been added, every ten years, some signal enforcement of justice, it would have been impossible for Rome ever to have grown corrupted. But when both of these incitements to virtuous behavior began to recur less frequently, corruption spread, and after the time of Atilius Regulus, no like example was again witnessed. For though the two Catos came later, so great an interval had elapsed before the elder Cato appeared, and again, so long a period intervened between him and the younger, and these two, moreover, stood so much alone, that it was impossible for them, by their influence, to work any important change; more especially for the younger, who found Rome so much corrupted that he could do nothing to improve his fellow-citizens.

This is enough to say concerning commonwealths, but as regards sects, we see from the instance of our own religion that here too a like renewal is needed. For had not this religion of ours been brought back to its original condition by Saint Francis and Saint Dominick, it must soon have been utterly extinguished. They, however, by their voluntary poverty, and by their imitation of the life of Christ, rekindled in the minds of men the dying flame of faith; and by the efficacious rules which they established averted from our Church that ruin which the ill lives of its prelates and heads must otherwise have brought upon it. For living in poverty, and gaining great authority with the people by confessing them and preaching to them, they got them to believe that it is evil to speak ill even of what is evil; and that it is good to be obedient to rulers, who, if they do amiss, may be left to the judgment of God. By which teaching these rulers are encouraged to behave as badly as they can, having no fear of punishments which they neither see nor credit. Nevertheless, it is this renewal which has maintained, and still maintains, our religion.

Kingdoms also stand in need of a like renewal, and to have their laws restored to their former force; and we see how, by attending to this, the kingdom of France has profited. For that kingdom, more than any other, lies under the control of its laws and ordinances, which are maintained by its parliaments, and more especially by the parliament of Paris, from which last they derive fresh vigour whenever they have to be enforced against any prince of the realm; for this assembly pronounces sentence even against the king himself. Heretofore this parliament has maintained its name as the fearless champion of the laws against the nobles of the land; but should it ever at any future time suffer wrongs to pass unpunished, and should offences multiply, either these will have to be corrected with great disturbance to the State, or the kingdom itself must fall to pieces.

This, then, is our conclusion—that nothing is so necessary in any society, be it a religious sect, a kingdom, or a commonwealth, as to restore to it that reputation which it had at first, and to see that it is provided either with wholesome laws, or with good men whose actions may effect the same ends, without need to resort to external force. For although this last may sometimes, as in the case of Rome, afford an efficacious remedy, it is too hazardous a remedy to make us ever wish to employ it.

And that all may understand how much the actions of particular citizens helped to make Rome great, and how many admirable results they wrought in that city, I shall now proceed to set them forth and examine them; with which survey this Third Book of mine, and last division of the First Decade of Titus Livius, shall be brought to a close. But, although great and notable actions were done by the Roman kings, nevertheless, since history has treated of these at much length, here I shall pass them over, and say no more about these princes, save as regards certain things done by them with an eye to their private interest. I shall begin, therefore, with Brutus, the father of Roman freedom.

[Footnote 1: "Quod quotidie aggregatur aliquid quod quandoque indiget curatione."]

Chapter II.—*That on occasion it is wise to feign Folly.*

Never did any man by the most splendid achievements gain for himself so great a name for wisdom and prudence as is justly due to Junius Brutus for feigning to be a fool. And although Titus Livius mentions one cause only as having led him to assume this part, namely, that he might live more securely and look after his patrimony; yet on considering his behavior we may believe that in counterfeiting folly it was also his object to escape notice, and so find better convenience to overthrow the kings, and to free his country whenever an occasion offered. That this was in his mind is seen first of all from the interpretation he gave to the oracle of Apollo, when, to render the gods favourable to his designs, he pretended to stumble, and secretly kissed his mother earth; and, again, from this, that on the death of Lucretia, though her father, her husband, and others of her kinsmen were present, he was the first to draw the dagger from her wound, and bind the bystanders by oath never more to suffer king to reign in Rome.

From his example all who are discontented with their prince are taught, first of all, to measure, and to weigh their strength, and if they find themselves strong enough to disclose their hostility and proclaim open war, then to take that course as at once the nobler and less dangerous; but, if too weak to make open war, then sedulously to court the favour of the prince, using to that end all such methods as they may judge needful, adapting themselves to his pleasures, and showing delight in whatever they see him delight in. Such an intimacy, in the first place, enables you to live securely, and permits you, without incurring any risk, to share the happy fortunes of the prince, while it affords you every facility for carrying out your plans. Some, no doubt, will tell you that you should not stand so near the prince as to be involved in his downfall; nor yet at such a distance that when he falls you shall be too far off to use the occasion for rising on his ruin. But although this mean course, could we only follow it, were certainly the best, yet, since I believe it to be impracticable, we must resort to the methods above indicated, and either keep altogether aloof, or else cleave closely to the prince. Whosoever does otherwise, if he be of great station, lives in constant peril; nor will it avail him to say, "I concern myself with nothing; I covet neither honours nor preferment; my sole wish is to live a quiet and peaceful life." For such excuses, though they be listened to, are not accepted; nor can any man of great position, however much and sincerely he desire it, elect to live this life of tranquillity since his professions will not be believed; so that although he might be contented to be let alone, others will not suffer him to be so. Wherefore, like Brutus, men must feign folly; and to play the part effectively, and so as to please their prince, must say, do, see, and praise things contrary to their inclinations.

But now, having spoken of the prudence shown by Brutus when he sought to recover the freedom of Rome, let us next speak of the severity which he used to maintain it.

Chapter III.—*That to preserve a newly acquired Freedom we must slay the Sons of Brutus.*

The severity used by Brutus in preserving for Rome the freedom he had won for her, was not less necessary than useful. The spectacle of a father sitting on the judgment, and not merely sentencing his own sons to death, but being himself present at their execution, affords an example rare in history. But those who study the records of ancient times will understand, that after a change in the form of a government, whether it be from a commonwealth to a tyranny or from a tyranny to a commonwealth, those who are hostile to the new order of things must always be visited with signal punishment. So that he who sets up as a tyrant and slays not Brutus, and he who creates a free government and slays not the sons of Brutus, can never maintain himself long. But since I have elsewhere treated of this matter at large, I shall merely refer to what has there been said concerning it, and shall cite here one instance only, happening in our own days, and memorable in the history of our country.

I speak of Piero Soderini, who thought by his patience and goodness to overcome the very same temper which prompted the sons of Brutus to revert to the old government, and who failed in the endeavour. For although his sagacity should have taught him the necessity, while chance and the ambition of those who attacked him furnished him with the opportunity of making an end of them, he never could resolve to strike the blow; and not merely believed himself able to subdue disaffection by patience and kindness, and to mitigate the enmity of particular men by the rewards he held out to them, but also persuaded himself, and often declared in the presence of his friends, that he could not confront opposition openly, nor crush his adversaries, without assuming extraordinary powers and passing laws destructive of civil equality; which measures, although not afterward used by him for tyrannical ends, would so alarm the community, that after his death they would never again consent to appoint a Gonfalonier for life, an office which he judged it essential both to maintain and strengthen. Now although these scruples of his were wise and good, we ought never out of regard for what is good, to suffer an evil to run its course, since it may well happen that the evil will prevail over the good. And Piero should have believed that as his acts and intentions were to be judged by results, he might, if he lived and if fortune befriended him, have made it clear to all, that what he did was done to preserve his country, and not from personal ambition; and he might have so contrived matters that no successor of his could ever turn to bad ends the means which he had used for good ends. But he was misled by a preconceived opinion, and failed to understand that ill-will is not to be vanquished by time nor propitiated by favours. And, so, from not knowing how to resemble Brutus, he lost power, and fame, and was driven an exile from his country.

That it is as hard a matter to preserve a princedom as it is to preserve a commonwealth, will be shown in the Chapter following.

Chapter IV.—*That an Usurper is never safe in his Princedom while those live whom he has deprived of it.*

From what befell the elder Tarquin at the hands of the sons of Ancus, and Servius Tullius at the hands of Tarquin the Proud, we see what an arduous and perilous course it is to strip a king of his kingdom and yet suffer him to live on, hoping to conciliate him by benefits. We see, too, how the elder Tarquin was ruined by his belief that he held the kingdom by a just title, since it had been given him by the people and confirmed to him by the senate, never suspecting that the sons of Ancus would be so stirred by resentment that it would be impossible to content them with what contented all the rest of Rome. Servius Tullius again, was ruined through believing that he could conciliate the sons of Ancus by loading them with favours.

By the fate of the first of these kings every prince may be warned that he can never live securely in his princedom so long as those from whom he has taken it survive; while the fate of the second should remind all rulers that old injuries are not to be healed by subsequent benefits, and least of all when the new benefit is less in degree than the injury suffered. And, truly, Servius was wanting in wisdom when he imagined that the sons of Tarquin would contentedly resign themselves to be the sons-in-law of one whom they thought should be their subject. For the desire to reign is so prevailing a passion, that it penetrates the minds not only of those who are rightful heirs, but also of those who are not; as happened with the wife of the younger Tarquin, who was daughter to Servius, but who, possessed by this madness, and setting at naught all filial duty, incited her husband to take her father's kingdom, and with it his life; so much nobler did she esteem it to be a queen than the daughter of a king. But while the elder Tarquin and Servius Tullius lost the kingdom from not knowing how to secure themselves against those whom they had deprived of it, the younger Tarquin lost it from not observing the ordinances of the old kings, as shall be shown in the following Chapter.

Chapter V.—*How an Hereditary King may come to lose his Kingdom.*

Tarquin the Proud, when he had put Servius Tullius to death, inasmuch as the latter left no heirs, took secure possession of the kingdom, having nothing to fear from any of those dangers which had stood in the way of his predecessors. And although the means whereby he made himself king were hateful and monstrous, nevertheless, had he adhered to the ancient ordinances of the earlier kings, he might have been endured, nor would he have aroused both senate and people to combine against him and deprive him of his government. It was not, therefore, because his son Sextus violated Lucretia that Tarquin was driven out, but because he himself had violated the laws of the kingdom, and governed as a tyrant, stripping the senate of all authority, and bringing everything under his own control. For all business which formerly had been transacted in public, and with the sanction of the senate, he caused to be transacted in his palace, on his own responsibility, and to the displeasure of every one else, and so very soon deprived Rome of whatever freedom she had enjoyed under her other kings.

Nor was it enough for him to have the Fathers his enemies, but he must needs also kindle the commons against him, wearing them out with mere mechanic labours, very different from the enterprises in which they had been employed by his predecessors; so that when Rome overflowed with instances of his cruelty and pride, he had already disposed the minds of all the citizens to rebel whenever they found the opportunity. Wherefore, had not occasion offered in the violence done to Lucretia, some other had soon been found to bring about the same result. But had Tarquin lived like the other kings, when Sextus his son committed that outrage, Brutus and Collatinus would have had recourse to him to punish the offender, and not to the commons of Rome. And hence let princes learn that from the hour they first violate those laws, customs, and usages under which men have lived for a great while, they begin to weaken the foundations of their authority. And should they, after they have been stripped of that authority, ever grow wise enough to see how easily princedoms are preserved by those who are content to follow prudent counsels, the sense of their loss will grieve them far more, and condemn them to a worse punishment than any they suffer at the hands of others. For it is far easier to be loved by good men than by bad, and to obey the laws than to seek to control them.

And to learn what means they must use to retain their authority, they have only to take example by the conduct of good princes, such as Timoleon of Corinth, Aratus of Sicyone, and the like, in whose lives they will find such security and content, both on the side of the ruler and the ruled, as ought to stir them with the desire to imitate them, which, for the reasons already given, it is easy for them to do. For men, when they are well governed, ask no more, nor look for further freedom; as was the case with the peoples governed by the two whom I have named, whom they constrained to continue their rulers while they lived, though both of them sought repeatedly to return to private life.

But because, in this and the two preceding Chapters, I have noticed the ill-will which arose against the kings, the plots contrived by the sons of Brutus against their country, and those directed against the elder Tarquin and Servius Tullius, it seems to me not out of place to discourse of these matters more at length in the following Chapter, as deserving the attention both of princes and private citizens.

Chapter VI.—*Of Conspiracies.*

It were an omission not to say something on the subject of conspiracies, these being a source of much danger both to princes and to private men. For we see that many more princes have lost their lives and states through these than in open warfare; power to wage open war upon a prince being conceded to few, whereas power to conspire against him is denied to none. On the other hand, since conspiracies are attended at every stage by difficulties and dangers, no more hazardous or desperate undertakings can be engaged in by any private citizen; whence it comes that while many conspiracies are planned, few effect their object. Wherefore, to put princes on their guard against these dangers, and to make subjects more cautious how they take part in them, and rather learn to live content under whatever government fortune has assigned them, I shall treat of them at length, without omitting any noteworthy circumstance which may serve for the instruction of either. Though, indeed, this is a golden sentence Of Cornelius Tacitus, wherein he says that *"the past should have our reverence, the present our obedience, and that we should wish for good princes, but put up with any."*[1] For assuredly whosoever does otherwise is likely to bring ruin both on himself and on his country.

But, to go deeper into the matter, we have first of all to examine against whom conspiracies are directed; and we shall find that men conspire either against their country or their prince; and it is of these two kinds of conspiracy that at present I desire to speak. For of conspiracies which have for their object the surrender of cities to enemies who are besieging them, and of all others contrived for like ends, I have already said enough.

First, then, I shall treat of those conspiracies which are directed against a prince, and begin by inquiring into their causes, which are manifold, but of which one is more momentous than all the rest; I mean, the being hated by the whole community. For it may reasonably be assumed, that when a prince has drawn upon himself this universal hatred, he must also have given special offence to particular men, which they will be eager to avenge. And this eagerness will be augmented by the feeling of general ill-will which the prince is seen to have incurred. A prince ought, therefore, to avoid this load of public hatred. How he is to do so I need not stop here to explain, having discussed the matter already in another place; but if he can guard against this, offence given to particular men will expose him to but few attacks. One reason being, that there are few men who think so much of an injury done them as to run great risks to revenge it; another, that assuming them to have both the disposition and the courage to avenge themselves, they are restrained by the universal favour which they see entertained towards the prince.

Injuries are either to a man's life, to his property, or to his honour. As regards the first, they who threaten injuries to life incur more danger than they who actually inflict them; or rather, while great danger is incurred in threatening, none at all is incurred from inflicting such injuries. For the dead are past thinking of revenge; and those who survive, for the most part leave such thoughts to the dead. But he whose life is threatened, finding himself forced by necessity either to do or suffer, becomes a man most dangerous to the prince, as shall be fully explained hereafter.

After menaces to life, injuries to property and honour stir men more than any others, and of these a Prince has most to beware. For he can never strip a man so bare of his possessions as not to leave him some weapon wherewith to redress his wrongs, nor ever so far dishonour him as to quell the stubborn spirit which prompts revenge. Of all dishonours those done to the women of a household are the worst; after which come such personal indignities as nerved the arm of Pausanias against Philip of Macedon, and of many another against other princes; and, in our own days, it was no other reason that moved Giulio Belanti to conspire against Pandolfo, lord of Siena, than that Pandolfo, who had given him his daughter to wife, afterwards took her from him, as presently shall be told. Chief among the causes which led the Pazzi to conspire against the Medici, was the law passed by the latter depriving them of the inheritance of Giovanni Bonromei.

Another most powerful motive to conspire against a prince is the desire men feel to free their country from a usurper. This it was which impelled Brutus and Cassius to conspire against Cæsar, and countless others against such tyrants as Phalaris, Dionysius, and the like. Against this humour no tyrant can guard, except by laying down his tyranny; which as none will do, few escape an unhappy end. Whence the verses of Juvenal:—

"Few tyrants die a peaceful death, and few The kings who visit Proserpine's dread lord, Unscathed by wounds and blood."[2]

Great, as I have said already, are the dangers which men run in conspiring; for at all times they are in peril, whether in contriving, in executing, or after execution. And since in conspiracies either many are engaged, or one only (for although it cannot properly be said of *one* man that he *conspires*, there may exist in him the fixed resolve to put the prince to death), it is only the solitary plotter who escapes the first of these three stages of danger. For he runs no risk before executing his design, since as he imparts it to none, there is none to bring it to the ear of the prince. A deliberate resolve like this may be conceived by a person in any rank of life, high or low, base or noble, and whether or no he be the familiar of his prince. For every one must, at some time or other, have leave to speak to the prince, and whoever has this leave has opportunity to accomplish his design. Pausanias, of whom we have made mention so often, slew Philip of Macedon as he walked between his son and his son-in-law to the temple, surrounded by a thousand armed guards. Pausanias indeed was noble, and known to the prince, but Ferdinand of Spain was stabbed in the neck by a poor and miserable Spaniard; and though the wound was not mortal, it sufficed to show that neither courage nor opportunity were wanting to the would-be-assassin. A Dervish, or Turkish priest, drew his scimitar on Bajazet, father of the Sultan now reigning, and if he did not wound him, it was from no lack either of daring or of opportunity. And I believe that there are many who in their minds desire the deed, no punishment or danger attending the mere wish, though there be but few who dare do it. For since few or none who venture, escape death, few are willing to go forward to certain destruction.

But to pass from these solitary attempts to those in which several are engaged, I affirm it to be shown by history that all such plots have been contrived by men of great station, or by those who have been on terms of close intimacy with the prince, since no others, not being downright madmen, would ever think of conspiring. For men of humble rank, and such as are not the intimates of their prince, are neither fed by the hopes nor possessed of the opportunities essential for such attempts. Because, in the first place, men of low degree will never find any to keep faith with them, none being moved to join in their schemes by those expectations which encourage men to run great risks; wherefore, so soon as their design has been imparted to two or three, they are betrayed and ruined. Or, assuming them fortunate enough to have no traitor of their number, they will be so hampered in the execution of their plot by the want of easy access to the prince, that they are sure to perish in the mere attempt. For if even men of great position, who have ready access to the prince, succumb to the difficulties which I shall presently notice, those difficulties must be infinitely increased in the case of men who are without these advantages. And because when life and property are at stake men are not utterly reckless, on perceiving themselves to be weak they grow cautious, and though cursing the tyrant in their hearts, are content to endure him, and to wait until some one of higher station than they, comes forward to redress their wrongs. So that should we ever find these weaklings attempting anything, we may commend their courage rather than their prudence.

We see, however, that the great majority of conspirators have been persons of position and the familiars of their prince, and that their plots have been as often the consequence of excessive indulgence as of excessive injury; as when Perennius conspired against Commodus, Plautianus against Severus, and Sejanus against Tiberius; all of whom had been raised by their masters to such wealth, honours, and dignities, that nothing seemed wanting to their authority save the imperial name. That they might not lack this also, they fell to conspiring against their prince; but in every instance their conspiracies had the end which their ingratitude deserved.

The only instance in recent times of such attempts succeeding, is the conspiracy of Jacopo IV. d'Appiano against Messer Piero Gambacorti, lord of Pisa. For Jacopo, who had been bred and brought up by Piero, and loaded by him with honours, deprived him of his State. Similar to this, in our own days, was the conspiracy of Coppola against King Ferdinand of Aragon. For Coppola had reached such a pitch of power that he seemed to himself to have everything but sovereignty; in seeking to obtain which he lost his life; though if any plot entered into by a man of great position could be expected to succeed, this certainly might, being contrived, as we may say, by another king, and by one who had the amplest opportunities for its accomplishment. But that lust of power which blinds men to dangers darkened the minds of those to whom the execution of the scheme was committed; who, had they only known how to add prudence to their villainy, could hardly have missed their aim.

The prince, therefore, who would guard himself against plots, ought more to fear those men to whom he has been too indulgent, than those to whom he has done great wrongs. For the latter lack opportunities which the former have in abundance; and the moving cause is equally strong in both, lust of power being at least as strong a passion as lust of revenge. Wherefore, a prince should entrust his friends with so much authority only as leaves a certain interval between his position and theirs; that between the two something be still left them to desire. Otherwise it will be strange if he do not fare like those princes who have been named above.

But to return from this digression, I say, that having shown it to be necessary that conspirators should be men of great station, and such as have ready access to the prince, we have next to consider what have been the results of their plots, and to trace the causes which have made them succeed or fail. Now, as I have said already, we find that conspiracies are attended by danger at three stages: before during, and after their execution; for which reason very few of them have had a happy issue; it being next to impossible to surmount all these different dangers successfully. And to begin with those which are incurred beforehand, and which are graver than all the rest, I say that he must be both very prudent and very fortunate who, when contriving a conspiracy, does not suffer his secret to be discovered.

Conspiracies are discovered either by disclosures made, or by conjecture. Disclosures are made through the treachery or folly of those to whom you communicate your design. Treachery is to be looked for, because you can impart your plans only to such persons as you believe ready to face death on your behalf, or to those who are discontented with the prince. Of men whom you can trust thus implicitly, one or two may be found; but when you have to open your designs to many, they cannot all be of this nature; and their goodwill towards you must be extreme if they are not daunted by the danger and by fear of punishment. Moreover men commonly deceive themselves in respect of the love which they imagine others bear them, nor can ever be sure of it until they have put it to the proof. But to make proof of it in a matter like this is very perilous; and even if you have proved it already, and found it true in some other dangerous trial, you cannot assume that there will be the same fidelity here, since this far transcends every other kind of danger. Again, if you gauge a man's fidelity by his discontent with the prince, you may easily deceive yourself; for so soon as you have taken this discontented man into your confidence, you have supplied him with the means whereby he may become contented; so that either his hatred of the prince must be great indeed, or your influence over him extraordinary, if it keep him faithful. Hence it comes that so many conspiracies have been discovered and crushed in their earliest stage, and that when the secret is preserved among many accomplices for any length of time, it is looked on as a miracle; as in the case of the conspiracy of Piso against Nero, and, in our own days, in that of the Pazzi against Lorenzo and Giuliano de' Medici; which last, though more than fifty persons were privy to it, was not discovered until it came to be carried out.

Conspiracies are disclosed through the imprudence of a conspirator when he talks so indiscreetly that some servant, or other person not in the plot, overhears him; as happened with the sons of Brutus, who, when treating with the envoys of Tarquin, were overheard by a slave, who became their accuser; or else through your own weakness in imparting your secret to some woman or boy whom you love, or to some other such light person; as when Dymnus, who was one of those who conspired with Philotas against Alexander the Great, revealed the plot to Nicomachus, a youth whom he loved, who at once told Cebalinus, and Cebalinus the king.

Of discoveries by conjecture we have an instance in the conspiracy of Piso against Nero; for Scaevinus, one of the conspirators, the day before he was to kill Nero, made his will, liberated all his slaves and gave them money, and bade Milichus, his freedman, sharpen his old rusty dagger, and have bandages ready for binding up wounds. From all which preparations Milichus conjecturing what work was in hand, accused Scaevinus before Nero; whereupon Scaevinus was arrested, and with him Natalis, another of the conspirators, who the day before had been seen to speak with him for a long time in private; and when the two differed in their account of what then passed between them, they were put to the torture and forced to confess the truth. In this way the conspiracy was brought to light, to the ruin of all concerned.

Against these causes of the discovery of conspiracies it is impossible so to guard as that either through treachery, want of caution, or levity, the secret shall not be found out, whenever more than three or four persons are privy to it. And whenever more than one conspirator is arrested, the plot is certain to be detected, because no two persons can perfectly agree in a false account of what has passed between them. If only one be taken, should he be a man of resolute courage, he may refuse to implicate his comrades; but they on their part must have no less courage, to stay quiet where they are, and not betray themselves by flight; for if courage be absent anywhere, whether in him who is taken or in those still at large, the conspiracy is revealed. And what is related by Titus Livius as having happened in the conspiracy against Hieronymus, tyrant of Syracuse, is most extraordinary, namely, that on the capture of one of the conspirators, named Theodorus, he, with great fortitude, withheld the names of all his accomplices, and accused friends of the tyrant; while his companions, on their part, trusted so completely in his courage, that not one of them quitted Syracuse or showed any sign of fear.

All these dangers, therefore, which attend the contrivance of a plot, must be passed through before you come to its execution; or if you would escape them, you must observe the following precautions: Your first and surest, nay, to say truth, your only safeguard, is to leave your accomplices no time to accuse you; for which reason you must impart the affair to them, only at the moment when you mean it to be carried out, and not before. Those who have followed this course have wholly escaped the preliminary dangers of conspiracies, and, generally speaking, the others also; indeed, I may say that they have all succeeded, and that it is open to every prudent man to act as they did. It will be enough to give two instances of plots effected in this way. Nelematus, unable to endure the tyranny of Aristotimus, despot of Epirus, assembling many of his friends and kinsmen in his house, exhorted them to free their country; and when some of them asked for time to consider and mature their plans, he bade his slaves close the doors, and told those assembled that unless they swore to go at once and do as he directed he would make them over to Aristotimus as prisoners. Alarmed by his threats, they bound themselves by a solemn oath, and going forth at once and without delay, successfully carried out his bidding. A certain Magus having fraudulently usurped the throne of Persia; Ortanes, a grandee of that realm, discovering the fraud, disclosed it to six others of the chief nobility, telling them that it behoved them to free the kingdom from the tyranny of this impostor. And when some among them asked for time, Darius, who was one of the six summoned by Ortanes, stood up and said, "Either we go at once to do this deed, or I go to the Magus to accuse you all." Whereupon, all rising together, without time given to any to change his mind, they went forth and succeeded in effecting their end. Not unlike these instances was the plan taken by the Etolians to rid themselves of Nabis, the Spartan tyrant, to whom, under pretence of succouring him, they sent Alasamenes, their fellow-citizen, with two hundred foot soldiers and thirty horsemen. For they imparted their real design to Alasamenes only, charging the rest, under pain of exile, to obey him in whatever he commanded. Alasamenes repaired to Sparta, and never divulged his commission till the time came for executing it; and so succeeded in putting Nabis to death.

It was, therefore, by the precautions they observed, that the persons of whom I have just now spoken escaped all those perils that attend the contrivance of conspiracies; and any following their example may expect the like good fortune. And that all may learn to do as they did I shall notice the case of Piso, of which mention has before been made. By reason of his rank, his reputation, and the intimate terms on which he lived with Nero, who trusted him without reserve, and would often come to his garden to sup with him, Piso was able to gain the friendship of many persons of spirit and courage, and well fitted in every way to take part in his plot against the emperor, which, under these circumstances, might easily have been carried out. For when Nero came to his garden, Piso could readily have communicated his design to those friends of his, and with suitable words have encouraged them to do what, in fact, they would not have had time to withdraw from, and was certain to succeed. And were we to examine all similar attempts, it would be seen that there are few which might not have been effected in the manner shown. But since most men are very ignorant of practical affairs, they commit the gravest blunders, especially in matters which lie, as this does, a little way out of the beaten track.

Wherefore, the contriver of a plot ought never, if he can help it, to communicate his design until the moment when it is to be executed; or if he must communicate it, then to some one man only, with whom he has long been intimate, and whom he knows to be moved by the same feelings as himself. To find one such person is far easier than to find several, and, at the same time, involves less risk; for though this one man play you false, you are not left altogether without resource, as you are when your accomplices are numerous. For I have heard it shrewdly said that to one man you may impart anything, since, unless you have been led to commit yourself by writing, your denial will go as far as his assertion. Shun writing, therefore, as you would a rock, for there is nothing so damning as a letter under your own hand.

Plautianus, desiring to procure the deaths of the Emperor Severus and his son Caracalla, intrusted the business to the tribune Saturninus, who, being more disposed to betray than obey Plautianus, but at the same time afraid that, if it came to laying a charge, Plautianus might be believed sooner than he, asked him for a written authority, that his commission might be credited. Blinded by ambition, Plautianus complied, and forthwith was accused by Saturninus and found guilty; whereas, but for that written warrant, together with other corroborating proofs, he must have escaped by his bold denial of the charge. Against the testimony of a single witness, you have thus some defence, unless convicted by your own handwriting, or by other circumstantial proof against which you must guard. A woman, named Epicharis, who had formerly been a mistress of Nero, was privy to Piso's conspiracy, and thinking it might be useful to have the help of a certain captain of triremes whom Nero had among his body-guards, she acquainted him with the plot, but not with the names of the plotters. This fellow, turning traitor, and accusing Epicharis to Nero, so stoutly did she deny the charge, that Nero, confounded by her effrontery, let her go.

In imparting a plot to a single person there are, therefore, two risks: one, that he may come forward of his own accord to accuse you; the other, that if arrested on suspicion, or on some proof of his guilt, he may, on being convicted, in the hope to escape punishment, betray you. But in neither of these dangers are you left without a defence; since you may meet the one by ascribing the charge to the malice of your accuser, and the other by alleging that the witness his been forced by torture to say what is untrue. The wisest course, however, is to impart your design to none, but to act like those who have been mentioned above; or if you impart it, then to one only: for although even in this course there be a certain degree of danger, it is far less than when many are admitted to your confidence.

A case nearly resembling that just now noticed, is where an emergency, so urgent as to leave you no time to provide otherwise for your safety, constrains you to do to a prince what you see him minded to do to you. A necessity of this sort leads almost always to the end desired, as two instances may suffice to show. Among the closest friends and intimates of the Emperor Commodus, were two captains of the pretorian guards, Letus and Electus, while among the most favoured of his distresses was a certain Martia. But because these three often reproved him for his manner of living, as disgraceful to himself and to his station, he resolved to rid himself of them; and so wrote their names, along with those of certain others whom he meant should be put to death the next night, in a list which he placed under the pillow of his bed. But on his going to bathe, a boy, who was a favourite of his, while playing about his room and on his bed, found the list, and coming out of the chamber with it in his hand, was met by Martia, who took it from him, and on reading it and finding what it contained, sent for Letus and Electus. And all three recognizing the danger in which they stood, resolved to be beforehand with the tyrant, and losing no time, murdered him that very night.

The Emperor Caracalla, being with his armies in Mesopotamia, had with him Macrinus, who was more of a statesman than a soldier, as his prefect. But because princes who are not themselves good are always afraid lest others treat them as they deserve, Caracalla wrote to his friend Maternianus in Rome to learn from the astrologers whether any man had ambitious designs upon the empire, and to send him word. Maternianus, accordingly, wrote back that such designs were entertained by Macrinus. But this letter, ere it reached the emperor, fell into the hands of Macrinus, who, seeing when he read it that he must either put Caracalla to death before further letters arrived from Rome, or else die himself, committed the business to a centurion, named Martialis, whom he trusted, and whose brother had been slain by Caracalla a few days before, who succeeded in killing the emperor.

We see, therefore, that an urgency which leaves no room for delay has almost the same results as the method already noticed as followed by Nelematus of Epirus. We see, too, what I remarked almost at the outset of this Discourse, that the threats of princes expose them to greater danger than the wrongs they actually inflict, and lead to more active conspiracies: and, therefore, that a prince should be careful not to threaten; since men are either to be treated kindly or else got rid of, but never brought to such a pass that they have to choose between slaying and being slain.

As to the dangers attending the execution of plots, these result either from some change made in the plan, or from a failure in courage on the part of him who is to carry it out; or else from some mistake he falls into through want of foresight, or from his not giving the affair its finishing stroke, as when some are left alive whom it was meant to put to death. Now, nothing causes so much disturbance and hindrance in human affairs, as to be forced, at a moment's notice and without time allowed for reflection, to vary your plan of action and adopt a different one from that fixed on at the first. And if such changes cause confusion anywhere, it is in matters appertaining to war, and in enterprises of the kind we are now speaking of; for in such affairs as these, there is nothing so essential as that men be prepared to do the exact thing intrusted to them. But when men have for many days together turned their whole thoughts to doing a thing in a certain way and in a certain order, and the way and order are suddenly altered, it is impossible but that they should be disconcerted and the whole scheme ruined. For which reason, it is far better to do everything in accordance with the preconcerted plan, though it be seen to be attended with some disadvantages, than, in order to escape these, to involve yourself in an infinity of dangers. And this will happen when you depart from your original design without time given to form a new one. For when time is given you may manage as you please.

The conspiracy of the Pazzi against Lorenzo and Giuliano de' Medici is well known. The scheme agreed on was to give a banquet to the Cardinal S. Giorgio, at which the brothers should be put to death. To each of the conspirators a part was assigned: to one the murder, to another the seizure of the palace, while a third was to ride through the streets and call on the people to free themselves. But it so chanced that at a time when the Pazzi, the Medici, and the Cardinal were all assembled in the cathedral church of Florence to hear High Mass, it became known that Giuliano would not be present at the banquet; whereupon the conspirators, laying their heads together, resolved to do in church what they were to have done elsewhere. This, however, deranged the whole scheme. For Giovambattista of Montesecco, would have no hand in the murder if it was to be done in a church; and the whole distribution of parts had in consequence to be changed; when, as those to whom the new parts were assigned had no time allowed them to nerve their minds to their new tasks, they managed matters so badly that they were overpowered in their attempt.

Courage fails a conspirator either from his own poorness of spirit, or from his being overcome by some feeling of reverence. For such majesty and awe attend the person of a prince, that it may well happen that he softens or dismays his executioners. When Caius Marius was taken by the people of Minturnum, the slave sent in to slay him, overawed by the bearing of the man, and by the memories which his name called up, became unnerved, and powerless to perform his office. And if this influence was exercised by one who was a prisoner, and in chains, and overwhelmed by adverse fortune, how much more must reverence be inspired by a prince who is free and uncontrolled, surrounded by his retinue and by all the pomp and splendour of his station; whose dignity confounds, and whose graciousness conciliates.

Certain persons conspiring against Sitalces, king of Thrace, fixed a day for his murder, and assembled at the place appointed, whither the king had already come. Yet none of them raised a hand to harm him, and all departed without attempting anything against him or knowing why they refrained; each blaming the others. And more than once the same folly was repeated, until the plot getting wind, they were taken and punished for what they might have done, yet durst not do.

Two brothers of Alfonso, Duke of Ferrara, conspired against him, employing as their tool a certain priest named Giennes, a singing-man in the service of the Duke. He, at their request, repeatedly brought the Duke into their company, so that they had full opportunity to make away with him. Yet neither of them ever ventured to strike the blow; till at last, their scheme being discovered, they paid the penalty of their combined cowardice and temerity. Such irresolution can only have arisen from their being overawed by the majesty of the prince, or touched by his graciousness.

In the execution of conspiracies, therefore, errors and mishaps arise from a failure of prudence or courage to which all are subject, when, losing self-control, they are led in their bewilderment to do and say what they ought not. That men are thus confounded, and thrown off their balance, could not be better shown than in the words of Titus Livius, where he describes the behaviour of Alasamenes the Etolian, at the time when he resolved on the death of Nabis the Spartan, of whom I have spoken before. For when the time to act came, and he had disclosed to his followers what they had to do, Livius represents him as "*collecting his thoughts which had grown confused by dwelling on so desperate an enterprise*." For it is impossible for any one, though of the most steadfast temper and used to the sight of death and to handle deadly weapons, not to be perturbed at such a moment. For which reason we should on such occasions choose for our tools those who have had experience in similar affairs, and trust no others though reputed of the truest courage. For in these grave undertakings, no one who is without such experience, however bold and resolute, is to be trusted.

The confusion of which I speak may either cause you to drop your weapon from your hand, or to use words which will have the same results. Quintianus being commanded by Lucilla, sister of Commodus, to slay him, lay in wait for him at the entrance of the amphitheatre, and rushing upon him with a drawn dagger, cried out, "*The senate sends you this*;" which words caused him to be seized before his blow descended. In like manner Messer Antonio of Volterra, who as we have elsewhere seen was told off to kill Lorenzo de' Medici, exclaimed as he approached him, "*Ah traitor!*" and this exclamation proved the salvation of Lorenzo and the ruin of that conspiracy.

For the reasons now given, a conspiracy against a single ruler may readily break down in its execution; but a conspiracy against two rulers is not only difficult, but so hazardous that its success is almost hopeless. For to effect like actions, at the same time, in different places, is well-nigh impossible; nor can they be effected at different times, if you would not have one counteract another. So that if conspiracy against a single ruler be imprudent and dangerous, to conspire against two, is in the last degree fool-hardy and desperate. And were it not for the respect in which I hold the historian, I could not credit as possible what Herodian relates of Plautianus, namely, that he committed to the centurion Saturninus the task of slaying single-handed both Severus and Caracalla, they dwelling in different places; for the thing is so opposed to reason that on no other authority could I be induced to accept it as true.

Certain young Athenians conspired against Diocles and Hippias, tyrants of Athens. Diocles they slew; but Hippias, making his escape, avenged him. Chion and Leonidas of Heraclea, disciples of Plato, conspired against the despots Clearchus and Satirus. Clearchus fell, but Satirus survived and avenged him. The Pazzi, of whom we have spoken so often, succeeded in murdering Giuliano only. From such conspiracies, therefore, as are directed against more heads than one, all should abstain; for no good is to be got from them, whether for ourselves, for our country, or for any one else. On the contrary, when those conspired against escape, they become harsher and more unsufferable than before, as, in the examples given, Florence, Athens, and Heraclea had cause to know. True it is that the conspiracy contrived by Pelopidas for the liberation of his country, had to encounter every conceivable hindrance, and yet had the happiest end. For Pelopidas had to deal, not with two tyrants only, but with ten; and so far from having their confidence, could not, being an outlaw, even approach them. And yet he succeeded in coming to Thebes, in putting the tyrants to death, and in freeing his country. But whatever he did was done with the aid of one of the counsellors of the tyrants, a certain Charon, through whom he had all facilities for executing his design. Let none, however, take this case as a pattern;

for that it was in truth a desperate attempt, and its success a marvel, was and is the opinion of all historians, who speak of it as a thing altogether extraordinary and unexampled.

The execution of a plot may be frustrated by some groundless alarm or unforeseen mischance occurring at the very moment when the scheme is to be carried out. On the morning on which Brutus and his confederates were to slay Cæsar, it so happened that Cæsar talked for a great while with Cneus Pompilius Lenas, one of the conspirators; which some of the others observing, were in terror that Pompilius was divulging the conspiracy to Cæsar; whose life they would therefore have attempted then and there, without waiting his arrival in the senate house, had they not been reassured by seeing that when the conference ended he showed no sign of unusual emotion. False alarms of this sort are to be taken into account and allowed for, all the more that they are easily raised. For he who has not a clear conscience is apt to assume that others are speaking of him. A word used with a wholly different purpose, may throw his mind off its balance and lead him to fancy that reference is intended to the matter he is engaged on, and cause him either to betray the conspiracy by flight, or to derange its execution by anticipating the time fixed. And the more there are privy to the conspiracy, the likelier is this to happen.

As to the mischances which may befall, since these are unforeseen, they can only be instanced by examples which may make men more cautious. Giulio Belanti of Siena, of whom I have spoken before, from the hate he bore

Pandolfo Petrucci, who had given him his daughter to wife and afterwards taken her from him, resolved to murder him, and thus chose his time. Almost every day Pandolfo went to visit a sick kinsman, passing the house of Giulio on the way, who, remarking this, took measures to have his accomplices ready in his house to kill Pandolfo as he passed. Wherefore, placing the rest armed within the doorway, one he stationed at a window to give the signal of Pandolfo's approach. It so happened however, that as he came nigh the house, and after the look-out had given the signal, Pandolfo fell in with a friend who stopped him to converse; when some of those with him, going on in advance, saw and heard the gleam and clash of weapons, and so discovered the ambuscade; whereby Pandolfo was saved, while Giulio with his companions had to fly from Siena. This plot accordingly was marred, and Giulio's schemes baulked, in consequence of a chance meeting. Against such accidents, since they are out of the common course of things, no provision can be made. Still it is very necessary to take into account all that may happen, and devise what remedies you can.

It now only remains for us to consider those dangers which follow after the execution of a plot. These in fact resolve themselves into one, namely, that some should survive who will avenge the death of the murdered prince. The part of avenger is likely to be assumed by a son, a brother, or other kinsman of the deceased, who in the ordinary course of events might have looked to succeed to the princedom. And such persons are suffered to live, either from inadvertence, or from some of the causes noted already, as when Giovann' Andrea of Lampognano, with the help of his companions, put to death the Duke of Milan. For the son and two brothers of the Duke, who survived him, were able to avenge his death. In cases like this, indeed, the conspirators may be held excused, since there is nothing they can do to help themselves. But when from carelessness and want of due caution some one is allowed to live whose death ought to have been secured, there is no excuse. Certain conspirators, after murdering the lord, Count Girolamo of Forli, made prisoners of his wife and of his children who were still very young. By thinking they could not be safe unless they got possession of the citadel, which the governor refused to surrender, they obtained a promise from Madonna Caterina, for so the Countess was named, that on their permitting her to enter the citadel she would cause it to be given up to them, her children in the mean time remaining with them as hostages. On which undertaking they suffered her to enter the citadel. But no sooner had she got inside than she fell to upbraid them from the walls with the murder of her husband, and to threaten them with every kind of vengeance; and to show them how little store she set upon her children, told them scoffingly that she knew how others could be got. In the end, the rebels having no leader to advise them, and perceiving too late the error into which they had been betrayed, had to pay the penalty of their rashness by perpetual banishment.

But of all the dangers which may follow on the execution of a plot, none is so much or so justly to be feared as that the people should be well affected to the prince whom you have put to death. For against this danger conspirators have no resource which can ensure their safety. Of this we have example in the case of Cæsar, who as he had the love of the Roman people was by them avenged; for they it was who, by driving out the conspirators from Rome, were the cause that all of them, at different times and in different places, came to violent ends.

Conspiracies against their country are less danger for those who take part in them than conspiracies against princes; since there is less risk beforehand, and though there be the same danger in their execution, there is none afterwards. Beforehand, the risks are few, because a citizen may use means for obtaining power without betraying his wishes or designs to any; and unless his course be arrested, his designs are likely enough to succeed; nay, though laws be passed to restrain him, he may strike out a new path. This is to be understood of a commonwealth which has to some degree become corrupted; for in one wherein there is no taint of corruption, there being no soil in which evil seed can grow, such designs will never suggest themselves to any citizen.

In a commonwealth, therefore, a citizen may by many means and in many ways aspire to the princedom without risking destruction, both because republics are slower than princes are to take alarm, are less suspicious and consequently less cautious, and because they look with greater reverence upon their great citizens, who are in this way rendered bolder and more reckless in attacking them. Any one who has read Sallust's account of the conspiracy of Catiline, must remember how, when that conspiracy was discovered, Catiline not only remained in Rome, but even made his appearance in the senatehouse, where he was suffered to address the senate in the most insulting terms,—so scrupulous was that city in protecting the liberty of all its citizens. Nay, even after he had left Rome and placed himself at the head of his army, Lentulus and his other accomplices would not have been imprisoned, had not letters been found upon them clearly establishing their guilt. Hanno, the foremost citizen of Carthage, aspiring to absolute power, on the occasion of the marriage of a daughter contrived a plot for administering poison to the whole senate and so making himself prince. The scheme being discovered, the senate took no steps against him beyond passing a law to limit the expense of banquets and marriage ceremonies. So great was the respect they paid to his quality.

True, the *execution* of a plot against your country is attended with greater difficulty and danger, since it seldom happens that, in conspiring against so many, your own resources are sufficient by themselves; for it is not every one who, like Cæsar, Agathocles, or Cleomenes, is at the head of an army, so as to be able at a stroke, and by open force to make himself master of his country. To such as these, doubtless, the path is safe and easy enough; but others who have not such an assembled force ready at their command, must effect their ends either by stratagem and fraud, or with the help of foreign troops. Of such stratagems and frauds we have an instance in the case of Pisistratus the Athenian, who after defeating the Megarians and thereby gaining the favour of his fellow-citizens, showed himself to them one morning covered with wounds and blood, declaring that he had been thus outraged through the jealousy of the nobles, and asking that he might have an armed guard assigned for his protection. With the authority which this lent him, he easily rose to such a pitch of power as to become tyrant of Athens. In like manner Pandolfo Petrucci, on his return with the other exiles to Siena, was appointed the command of the public guard, as a mere office of routine which others had declined. Very soon, however, this armed force gave him so much importance that he became the supreme ruler of the State. And many others have followed other plans and methods, and in the course of time, and without incurring danger, have achieved their aim.

Conspirators against their country, whether trusting to their own forces or to foreign aid, have had more or less success in proportion as they have been favoured by Fortune. Catiline, of whom we spoke just now, was overthrown. Hanno, who has also been mentioned, failing to accomplish his object by poison, armed his partisans to the number of many thousands; but both he and they came to an ill end. On the other hand, certain citizens of Thebes conspiring to become its tyrants, summoned a Spartan army to their assistance, and usurped the absolute control of the city. In short, if we examine all the conspiracies which men have engaged in against their country, we shall find that few or none have been quelled in their inception, but that all have either succeeded, or have broken down in their execution. Once executed, they entail no further risks beyond those implied in the nature of a princedom. For the man who becomes a tyrant incurs all the natural and ordinary dangers in which a tyranny involves him, and has no remedies against them save those of which I have already spoken.

This is all that occurs to me to say on the subject of conspiracies. If I have noticed those which have been carried out with the sword rather than those wherein poison has been the instrument, it is because, generally speaking, the method of proceeding is the same in both. It is true, nevertheless, that conspiracies which are to be carried out by poison are, by reason of their uncertainty, attended by greater danger. For since fewer opportunities offer for their execution, you must have an understanding with persons who can command opportunities. But it is dangerous to have to depend on others. Again, many causes may hinder a poisoned draught from proving mortal; as when the murderers of Commodus, on his vomiting the poison given him, had to strangle him.

Princes, then, have no worse enemy than conspiracy, for when a conspiracy is formed against them, it either carries them off, or discredits them: since, if it succeeds, they die; while, if it be discovered, and the conspirators be put to death themselves, it will always be believed that the whole affair has been trumped up by the prince that he might glut his greed and cruelty with the goods and blood of those whom he has made away with. Let me not, however, forget to warn the prince or commonwealth against whom a conspiracy is directed, that on getting word of it, and before taking any steps to punish it, they endeavour, as far as they can, to ascertain its character, and after carefully weighing the strength of the conspirators with their own, on finding it preponderate, never suffer their knowledge of the plot to appear until they are ready with a force sufficient to crush it. For otherwise, to disclose their knowledge will only give the signal for their destruction. They must strive therefore to seem unconscious of what is going on; for conspirators who see themselves detected are driven forward by necessity and will stick at nothing. Of this precaution we have an example in Roman history, when the officers of the two legions, who, as has already been mentioned, were left behind to defend the Capuans from the Samnites, conspired together against the Capuans. For on rumours of this conspiracy reaching Rome, Rutilius the new consul was charged to see to it; who, not to excite the suspicions of the conspirators, publicly gave out that by order of the senate the Capuan legions were continued in their station. The conspirators believing this, and thinking they would have ample time to execute their plans, made no effort to hasten matters, but remained at their ease, until they found that the consul was moving one of the two legions to a distance from the other. This arousing their suspicion, led them to disclose their designs and endeavour to carry them out.

Now, we could have no more instructive example than this in whatever way we look at it. For it shows how slow men are to move in those matters wherein time seems of little importance, and how active they become when necessity urges them. Nor can a prince or commonwealth desiring for their own ends to retard the execution of a conspiracy, use any more effectual means to do so, than by artfully holding out to the conspirators some special opportunity as likely soon to present itself; awaiting which, and believing they have time and to spare for what they have to do, they will afford that prince or commonwealth all the leisure needed to prepare for their punishment. Whosoever neglects these precautions hastens his own destruction, as happened with the Duke of Athens, and with Guglielmo de' Pazzi. For the Duke, who had made himself tyrant of Florence, on learning that he was being conspired against, without further inquiry into the matter, caused one of the conspirators to be seized; whereupon the rest at once armed themselves and deprived him of his government. Guglielmo, again, being commissary in the Val di Chiana in the year 1501, and learning that a conspiracy was being hatched in Arezzo to take the town from the Florentines and give it over to the Vitelli, repaired thither with all haste; and without providing himself with the necessary forces or giving a thought to the strength of the conspirators, on the advice of the bishop, his son, had one of them arrested. Which becoming known to the others, they forthwith rushed to arms, and taking the town from the Florentines, made Guglielmo their prisoner. Where, however, conspiracies are weak, they may and should be put down without scruple or hesitation.

Two methods, somewhat opposed to one another, which have occasionally been followed in dealing with conspiracies, are in no way to be commended. One of these was that adopted by the Duke of Athens, of whom I have just now spoken, who to have it thought that he confided in the goodwill of the Florentines, caused a certain man who gave information of a plot against him, to be put to death. The other was that followed by Dion the Syracusan, who, to sound the intentions of one whom he suspected, arranged with Calippus, whom he trusted, to pretend to get up a conspiracy against him. Neither of these tyrants reaped any advantage from the course he followed. For the one discouraged informers and gave heart to those who were disposed to conspire, the other prepared an easy road to his own death, or rather was prime mover in a conspiracy against himself. As the event showed. For Calippus having free leave to plot against Dion, plotted to such effect, that he deprived him at once of his State and life.

[Footnote 1: *Tac. Hist.* iv. 8.]

[Footnote 2: *Ad generum Cereris sine caede et vulnere pauci Descendunt reges, et sicca morte tiranni. Juv. Sat.* x. 112.]

Chapter VII.—*Why it is that changes from Freedom to Servitude, and from Servitude to Freedom, are sometimes made without Bloodshed, but at other times reek with Blood.*

Since we find from history that in the countless changes which have been made from freedom to servitude and from servitude to freedom, sometimes an infinite multitude have perished, while at others not a soul has suffered (as when Rome made her change from kings to consuls, on which occasion none was banished save Tarquin, and no harm was done to any other), it may perhaps be asked, how it happens that of these revolutions, some have been attended by bloodshed and others not.

The answer I take to be this. The government which suffers change either has or has not had its beginning in violence. And since the government which has its beginning in violence must start by inflicting injuries on many, it must needs happen that on its downfall those who were injured will desire to avenge themselves; from which desire for vengeance the slaughter and death of many will result. But when a government originates with, and derives its authority from the whole community, there is no reason why the community, if it withdraw that authority, should seek to injure any except the prince from whom it withdraws it. Now the government of Rome was of this nature, and the expulsion of the Tarquins took place in this way. Of a like character was the government of the Medici in Florence, and, accordingly, upon their overthrow in the year 1494, no injury was done to any save themselves.

In such cases, therefore, the changes I speak of do not occasïon any very great danger. But the changes wrought by men who have wrongs to revenge, are always of a most dangerous kind, and such, to say the least, as may well cause dismay in the minds of those who read of them. But since history abounds with instances of such changes I need say no more about them.

Chapter VIII.—*That he who would effect Changes in a Commonwealth, must give heed to its Character and Condition*

I have said before that a bad citizen cannot work grave mischief in a commonwealth which has not become corrupted. This opinion is not only supported by the arguments already advanced, but is further confirmed by the examples of Spurius Cassius and Manlius Capitolinus. For Spurius, being ambitious, and desiring to obtain extraordinary authority in Rome, and to win over the people by loading them with benefits (as, for instance, by selling them those lands which the Romans had taken from the Hernici,) his designs were seen through by the senate, and laid him under such suspicion, that when in haranguing the people he offered them the money realized by the sale of the grain brought from Sicily at the public expense, they would have none of it, believing that he offered it as the price of their freedom. Now, had the people been corrupted, they would not have refused this bribe, but would have opened rather than closed the way to the tyranny.

The example of Manlius is still more striking. For in his case we see what excellent gifts both of mind and body, and what splendid services to his country were afterwards cancelled by that shameful eagerness to reign which we find bred in him by his jealousy of the honours paid Camillus. For so darkened did his mind become, that without reflecting what were the institutions to which Rome was accustomed, or testing the material he had to work on, when he would have seen that it was still unfit to be moulded to evil ends, he set himself to stir up tumults against the senate and against the laws of his country.

And herein we recognize the excellence of this city of Rome, and of the materials whereof it was composed. For although the nobles were wont to stand up stoutly for one another, not one of them stirred to succour Manlius, and not one of his kinsfolk made any effort on his behalf, so that although it was customary, in the case of other accused persons, for their friends to put on black and sordid raiment, with all the other outward signs of grief, in order to excite pity for the accused, none was seen to do any of these things for Manlius. Even the tribunes of the people, though constantly ready to promote whatever courses seemed to favour the popular cause, and the more vehemently the more they seemed to make against the nobles, in this instance sided with the nobles to put down the common enemy. Nay the very people themselves, keenly alive to their own interests, and well disposed towards any attempt to damage the nobles, though they showed Manlius many proofs of their regard, nevertheless, when he was cited by the tribunes to appear before them and submit his cause for their decision, assumed the part of judges and not of defenders, and without scruple or hesitation sentenced him to die. Wherefore, I think, that there is no example in the whole Roman history which serves so well as this to demonstrate the virtues of all ranks in that republic. For not a man in the whole city bestirred himself to shield a citizen endowed with every great quality, and who, both publicly and privately, had done so much that deserved praise. But in all, the love of country outweighed every other thought, and all looked less to his past deserts than to the dangers which his present conduct threatened; from which to relieve themselves they put him to death. "*Such*," says Livius, "*was the fate of a man worthy our admiration had he not been born in a free State.*"

And here two points should be noted. The first, that glory is to be sought by different methods in a corrupt city, and in one which still preserves its freedom. The second, which hardly differs from the first, that in their actions, and especially in matters of moment, men must have regard to times and circumstances and adapt themselves thereto. For those persons who from an unwise choice, or from natural inclination, run counter to the times will for the most part live unhappily, and find all they undertake issue in failure; whereas those who accommodate themselves to the times are fortunate and successful. And from the passage cited we may plainly infer, that had Manlius lived in the days of Marius and Sylla, when the body of the State had become corrupted, so that he could have impressed it with the stamp of his ambition, he might have had the same success as they had, and as those others had who after them aspired to absolute power; and, conversely, that if Sylla and Marius had lived in the days of Manlius, they must have broken down at the very beginning of their attempts.

For one man, by mischievous arts and measures, may easily prepare the ground for the universal corruption of a city; but no one man in his lifetime can carry that corruption so far, as himself to reap the harvest; or granting that one man's life might be long enough for this purpose, it would be impossible for him, having regard to the ordinary habits of men, who grow impatient and cannot long forego the gratification of their desires, to wait until the corruption was complete. Moreover, men deceive themselves in respect of their own affairs, and most of all in respect of those on which they are most bent; so that either from impatience or from self-deception, they rush upon undertakings for which the time is not ripe, and so come to an ill end. Wherefore to obtain absolute authority in a commonwealth and to destroy its liberties, you must find the body of the State already corrupted, and corrupted by a gradual wasting continued from generation to generation; which, indeed, takes place necessarily, unless, as has been already explained, the State be often reinforced by good examples, or brought back to its first beginnings by wise laws.

Manlius, therefore, would have been a rare and renowned man had he been born in a corrupt city; and from his example we see that citizens seeking to introduce changes in the form of their government, whether in favour of liberty or despotism, ought to consider what materials they have to deal with, and then judge of the difficulty of their task. For it is no less arduous and dangerous to attempt to free a people disposed to live in servitude, than to enslave a people who desire to live free.

And because it has been said above, that in their actions men must take into account the character of the times in which they live, and guide themselves accordingly, I shall treat this point more fully in the following Chapter.

Chapter IX.—*That to enjoy constant good Fortune we must change with the Times.*

I have repeatedly noted that the good or bad fortune of men depends on whether their methods of acting accord with the character of the times. For we see that in what they do some men act impulsively, others warily and with caution. And because, from inability to preserve the just mean, they in both of these ways overstep the true limit, they commit mistakes in one direction or the other. He, however, will make fewest mistakes, and may expect to prosper most, who, while following the course to which nature inclines him, finds, as I have said, his method of acting in accordance with the times in which he lives.

All know that in his command of the Roman armies, Fabius Maximus displayed a prudence and caution very different from the audacity and hardihood natural to his countrymen; and it was his good fortune that his methods suited with the times. For Hannibal coming into Italy in all the flush of youth and recent success, having already by two defeats stripped Rome of her best soldiers and filled her with dismay, nothing could have been more fortunate for that republic than to find a general able, by his deliberateness and caution, to keep the enemy at bay. Nor, on the other hand, could Fabius have fallen upon times better suited to the methods which he used, and by which he crowned himself with glory. That he acted in accordance with his natural bent, and not from a reasoned choice, we may gather from this, that when Scipio, to bring the war to an end, proposed to pass with his army into Africa, Fabius, unable to depart from his characteristic methods and habits, strenuously opposed him; so that had it rested with him, Hannibal might never have left Italy. For he perceived not that the times had changed, and that with them it was necessary to change the methods of prosecuting the war. Had Fabius, therefore, been King of Rome, he might well have caused the war to end unhappily, not knowing how to accommodate his methods to the change in the times. As it was, he lived in a commonwealth in which there were many citizens, and many different dispositions; and which as it produced a Fabius, excellent at a time when it was necessary to protract hostilities, so also, afterwards gave birth to a Scipio, at a time suited to bring them to a successful close.

And hence it comes that a commonwealth endures longer, and has a more sustained good fortune than a princedom, because from the diversity in the characters of its citizens, it can adapt itself better than a prince can to the diversity of times. For, as I have said before, a man accustomed to follow one method, will never alter it; whence it must needs happen that when times change so as no longer to accord with his method, he will be ruined. Piero Soderini, of whom I have already spoken, was guided in all his actions by patience and gentleness, and he and his country prospered while the times were in harmony with these methods. But, afterwards, when a time came when it behoved him to have done with patience and gentleness, he knew not how to drop them, and was ruined together with his country. Pope Julius II., throughout the whole of his pontificate, was governed by impulse and passion, and because the times were in perfect accord, all his undertakings prospered. But had other times come requiring other qualities, he could not have escaped destruction, since he could not have changed his methods nor his habitual line of conduct.

As to why such changes are impossible, two reasons may be given. One is that we cannot act in opposition to the bent of our nature. The other, that when a man has been very successful while following a particular method, he can never be convinced that it is for his advantage to try some other. And hence it results that a man's fortunes vary, because times change and he does not change with them. So, too, with commonwealths, which, as we have already shown at length, are ruined from not altering their institutions to suit the times. And commonwealths are slower to change than princes are, changes costing them more effort; because occasions must be waited for which shall stir the whole community, and it is not enough that a single citizen alters his method of acting.

But since I have made mention of Fabius Maximus who wore out Hannibal by keeping him at bay, I think it opportune to consider in the following Chapter whether a general who desires to engage his enemy at all risks, can be prevented by that enemy from doing so.

Chapter X.—*That a Captain cannot escape Battle when his Enemy forces it on him at all risks.*

"Cneius Sulpitius when appointed dictator against the Gauls, being unwilling to tempt Fortune by attacking an enemy whom delay and a disadvantageous position would every day render weaker, protracted the war."

When a mistake is made of a sort that all or most men are likely to fall into, I think it not amiss to mark it again and again with disapproval. Wherefore, although I have already shown repeatedly how in affairs of moment the actions of the moderns conform not to those of antiquity, still it seems to me not superfluous, in this place, to say the same thing once more. For if in any particular the moderns have deviated from the methods of the ancients, it is especially in their methods of warfare, wherein not one of those rules formerly so much esteemed is now attended to. And this because both princes and commonwealths have devolved the charge of such matters upon others, and, to escape danger, have kept aloof from all military service; so that although one or another of the princes of our times may occasionally be seen present in person with his army, we are not therefore to expect from him any further praiseworthy behaviour. For even where such personages take part in any warlike enterprise, they do so out of ostentation and from no nobler motive; though doubtless from sometimes seeing their soldiers face to face, and from retaining to themselves the title of command, they are likely to make fewer blunders than we find made by republics, and most of all by the republics of Italy, which though altogether dependent upon others, and themselves utterly ignorant of everything relating to warfare, do yet, that they may figure as the commanders of their armies, take upon them to direct their movements, and in doing so commit countless mistakes; some of which have been considered elsewhere but one is of such importance as to deserve notice here.

When these sluggard princes or effeminate republics send forth any of their Captains, it seems to them that the wisest instruction they can give him is to charge him on no account to give battle, but, on the contrary, to do what he can to avoid fighting. Wherein they imagine themselves to imitate the prudence of Fabius Maximus, who by protracting the war with Hannibal, saved the Roman commonwealth; not perceiving that in most instances such advice to a captain is either useless or hurtful. For the truth of the matter is, that a captain who would keep the field, cannot decline battle when his adversary forces it on him at all hazards. So that the instruction to avoid battle is but tantamount to saying, "You shall engage when it pleases your enemy, and not when it suits yourself." For if you would keep the field and yet avoid battle, the only safe course is to interpose a distance of at least fifty miles between you and your enemy, and afterwards to maintain so vigilant a look-out, that should he advance you will have time to make your retreat. Another method is to shut yourself up in some town. But both of these methods are extremely disadvantageous. For by following the former, you leave your country a prey to the enemy, and a valiant prince would far sooner risk the chances of battle than prolong a war in a manner so disastrous to his subjects; while by adopting the latter method, and shutting yourself up in a town with your army, there is manifest danger of your being besieged, and presently reduced by famine and forced to surrender. Wherefore it is most mischievous to seek to avoid battle in either of these two ways.

To intrench yourself in a strong position, as Fabius was wont to do, is a good method when your army is so formidable that the enemy dare not advance to attack you in your intrenchments; yet it cannot truly be said that Fabius avoided battle, but rather that he sought to give battle where he could do so with advantage. For had Hannibal desired to fight, Fabius would have waited for him and fought him. But Hannibal never dared to engage him on his own ground. So that an engagement was avoided as much by Hannibal as by Fabius, since if either had been minded to fight at all hazards the other would have been constrained to take one of three courses, that is to say, one or other of the two just now mentioned, or else to retreat. The truth of this is confirmed by numberless examples, and more particularly by what happened in the war waged by the Romans against Philip of Macedon, the father of Perseus. For Philip being invaded by the Romans, resolved not to give them battle; and to avoid battle, sought at first to do as Fabius had done in Italy, posting himself on the summit of a hill, where he intrenched himself strongly, thinking that the Romans would not venture to attack him there. But they advancing and attacking him in his intrenchments, drove him from his position; when, unable to make further resistance, he fled with the greater part of his army, and was only saved from utter destruction by the difficulty of the ground, which made it impossible for the Romans to pursue him.

Philip, therefore, who had no mind to fight, encamping too near the Romans, was forced to fly; and learning from this experience that to escape fighting it was not enough for him to intrench himself on a hill, yet not choosing to shut himself up in a walled town, he was constrained to take the other alternative of keeping at a distance of many miles from the Roman legions. Accordingly, when the Romans entered one province, he betook himself to another, and when they left a province he entered it. But perceiving that by protracting the war in this way, his condition grew constantly worse, while his subjects suffered grievously, now from his own troops, at another time from those of the enemy, he at last resolved to hazard battle, and so came to a regular engagement with the Romans.

It is for your interest, therefore, not to fight, when you possess the same advantages as Fabius, or as Cneius Sulpitius had; in other words, when your army is so formidable in itself that the enemy dare not attack you in your intrenchments, and although he has got within your territory has yet gained no footing there, and suffers in consequence from the want of necessary supplies. In such circumstances delay is useful, for the reasons assigned by Titus Livius when speaking of Sulpitius. In no other circumstances, however, can an engagement be avoided without dishonour or danger. For to retire as Philip did, is nothing else than defeat; and the disgrace is greater in proportion as your valour has been less put to the proof. And if Philip was lucky enough to escape, another, not similarly favoured by the nature of the ground, might not have the same good fortune.

That Hannibal was not a master in the arts of warfare there is none will venture to maintain. Wherefore, when he had to encounter Scipio in Africa, it may be assumed that had he seen any advantage in prolonging the war he would have done so; and, possibly, being a skilful captain and in command of a valiant army, he might have been able to do what Fabius did in Italy. But since he took not that course, we may infer that he was moved by sufficient reasons. For the captain who has got an army together, and perceives that from want of money or friends he cannot maintain it long, must be a mere madman if he do not at once, and before his army melts away, try the fortunes of battle; since he is certain to lose by delay, while by fighting he may chance to succeed. And there is this also to be kept in view, that we must strive, even if we be defeated, to gain glory; and that more glory is to be won in being beaten by force, than in a defeat from any other cause. And this we may suppose to have weighed with Hannibal. On the other hand, supposing Hannibal to have declined battle, Scipio, even if he had lacked courage to follow him up and attack him in his intrenched camp, would not have suffered thereby; for as he had defeated Syphax, and got possession of many of the African towns, he could have rested where he was in the same security and with the same convenience as if he had been in Italy. But this was not the case with Hannibal when he had to encounter Fabius, nor with the Gauls when they were opposed to Sulpitius.

Least of all can he decline battle who invades with his army the country of another; for seeking to enter his enemy's country, he must fight whenever the enemy comes forward to meet him; and is under still greater necessity to fight, if he undertake the siege of any town. As happened in our own day with Duke Charles of Burgundy, who, when beleaguering Morat, a town of the Swiss, was by them attacked and routed; or as happened with the French army encamped against Novara, which was in like manner defeated by the Swiss.

Chapter XI.—*That one who has to contend with many, though he be weaker than they, will prevail if he can withstand their first onset.*

The power exercised in Rome by the tribunes of the people was great, and, as I have repeatedly explained, was necessary, since otherwise there would have been no check on the ambition of the nobles, and the commonwealth must have grown corrupted far sooner than it did. But because, as I have said elsewhere, there is in everything a latent evil peculiar to it, giving rise to new mischances, it becomes necessary to provide against these by new ordinances. The authority of the tribunes, therefore, being insolently asserted so as to become formidable to the nobility and to the entire city, disorders dangerous to the liberty of the State must thence have resulted, had not a method been devised by Appius Claudius for controlling the ambition of the tribunes. This was, to secure that there should always be one of their number timid, or venal, or else a lover of the general good, who could be influenced to oppose the rest whenever these sought to pass any measure contrary to the wishes of the senate. This remedy was a great restraint on the excessive authority of the tribunes, and on many occasions proved serviceable to Rome.

I am led by this circumstance to remark, that when many powerful persons are united against one, who, although no match for the others collectively, is also powerful, the chances are more in favour of this single and less I powerful person, than of the many who together are much stronger. For setting aside an infinity of accidents which can be turned to better account by one than by many, it will always happen that, by exercising a little dexterity, the one will be able to divide the many, and weaken the force which was strong while it was united. In proof whereof, I shall not refer to ancient examples, though many such might be cited, but content myself with certain modern instances taken from the events of our own times.

In the year 1484, all Italy combined against the Venetians, who finding their position desperate, and being unable to keep their army any longer in the field, bribed Signer Lodovico, who then governed Milan, and so succeeded in effecting a settlement, whereby they not only recovered the towns they had lost, but also obtained for themselves a part of the territories of Ferrara; so that those were by peace the gainers, who in war had been the losers. Not many years ago the whole world was banded together against France; but before the war came to a close, Spain breaking with the confederates and entering into a separate treaty with France, the other members of the league also, were presently forced to make terms.

Wherefore we may always assume when we see a war set on foot by many against one, that this one, if he have strength to withstand the first shock, and can temporize and wait his opportunity, is certain to prevail. But unless he can do this he runs a thousand dangers: as did the Venetians in the year 1508, who, could they have temporized with the French, and so got time to conciliate some of those who had combined against them, might have escaped the ruin which then overtook them. But not possessing such a strong army as would have enabled them to temporize with their enemies, and consequently not having the time needed for gaining any to their side, they were undone. Yet we know that the Pope, as soon as he had obtained what he wanted, made friends with them, and that Spain did the like; and that both the one and the other of these powers would gladly have saved the Lombard territory for themselves, nor would, if they could have helped it, have left it to France, so as to augment her influence in Italy.

The Venetians, therefore, should have given up a part to save the rest; and had they done so at a time when the surrender would not have seemed to be made under compulsion, and before any step had been taken in the direction of war, it would have been a most prudent course; although discreditable and probably of little avail after war had been begun. But until the war broke out, few of the Venetian citizens recognized the danger, fewer still the remedy, and none ventured to prescribe it.

But to return to the point whence we started, I say that the same safeguard for their country which the Roman senate found against the ambition of the tribunes in their number, is within the reach of the prince who is attacked by many adversaries, if he only know to use prudently those methods which promote division.

Chapter XII.—*A prudent Captain will do what he can to make it necessary for his own Soldiers to fight, and to relieve his Enemy from that necessity.*

Elsewhere I have noted how greatly men are governed in what they do by Necessity, and how much of their renown is due to her guidance, so that it has even been said by some philosophers, that the hands and tongues of men, the two noblest instruments of their fame, would never have worked to perfection, nor have brought their labours to that pitch of excellence we see them to have reached, had they not been impelled by this cause. The captains of antiquity, therefore, knowing the virtues of this necessity, and seeing the steadfast courage which it gave their soldiers in battle, spared no effort to bring their armies under its influence, while using all their address to loosen its hold upon their enemies. For which reason, they would often leave open to an adversary some way which they might have closed, and close against their own men some way they might have left open.

Whosoever, therefore, would have a city defend itself stubbornly, or an army fight resolutely in the field, must before all things endeavour to impress the minds of those whom he commands with the belief that no other course is open to them. In like manner a prudent captain who undertakes the attack of a city, will measure the ease or difficulty of his enterprise, by knowing and considering the nature of the necessity which compels the inhabitants to defend it; and where he finds that necessity to be strong, he may infer that his task will be difficult, but if otherwise, that it will be easy.

And hence it happens that cities are harder to be recovered after a revolt than to be taken for the first time. Because on a first attack, having no occasion to fear punishment, since they have given no ground of offence, they readily surrender; but when they have revolted, they know that they have given ground of offence, and, fearing punishment, are not so easily brought under. A like stubbornness grows from the natural hostility with which princes or republics who are neighbours regard one another; which again is caused by the desire to dominate over those who live near, or from jealousy of their power. This is more particularly the case with republics, as in Tuscany for example; for contention and rivalry have always made, and always will make it extremely hard for one republic to bring another into subjection. And for this reason any one who considers attentively who are the neighbours of Florence, and who of Venice, will not marvel so much as some have done, that Florence should have spent more than Venice on her wars and gained less; since this results entirely from the Venetians finding their neighbouring towns less obstinate in their resistance than the Florentines theirs. For all the towns in the neighbourhood of Venice have been used to live under princes and not in freedom; and those who are used to servitude commonly think little of changing masters, nay are often eager for the change. In this way Venice, though she has had more powerful neighbours than Florence, has been able, from finding their towns less stubborn, to subdue them more easily than the latter, surrounded exclusively by free cities, has had it in her power to do.

But, to return to the matter in hand, the captain who attacks a town should use what care he can, not to drive the defenders to extremities, lest he render them stubborn; but when they fear punishment should promise them pardon, and when they fear for their freedom should assure them that he has no designs against the common welfare, but only against a few ambitious men in their city; for such assurances have often smoothed the way to the surrender of towns. And although pretexts of this sort are easily seen through, especially by the wise, the mass of the people are often beguiled by them, because desiring present tranquillity, they shut their eyes to the snares hidden behind these specious promises. By means such as these, therefore, cities innumerable have been brought into subjection, as recently was the case with Florence. The ruin of Crassus and his army was similarly caused: for although he himself saw through the empty promises of the Parthians, as meant only to blind the Roman soldiers to the necessity of defending themselves, yet he could not keep his men steadfast, they, as we clearly gather in reading the life of this captain, being deceived by the offers of peace held out to them by their enemies.

On the other hand, when the Samnites, who, at the instance of a few ambitious men, and in violation of the terms of the truce made with them, had overrun and pillaged lands belonging to the allies of Rome, afterwards sent envoys to Rome to implore peace, offering to restore whatever they had taken, and to surrender the authors of these injuries and outrages as prisoners, and these offers were rejected by the Romans, and the envoys returned to Samnium bringing with them no hope of an adjustment, Claudius Pontius, who then commanded the army of the Samnites, showed them in a remarkable speech, that the Romans desired war at all hazards, and declared that, although for the sake of his country he wished for peace, necessity constrained him to prepare for war; telling them *"that was a just war which could not be escaped, and those arms sacred in which lay their only hopes."* And building on this necessity, he raised in the minds of his soldiers a confident expectation of success. That I may not have to revert to this matter again, it will be convenient to notice here those examples from Roman history which most merit attention. When Caius Manilius was in command of the legions encamped against Veii, a division of the Veientine army having got within the Roman intrenchments, Manilius ran forward with a company of his men to defend them, and, to prevent the escape of the Veientines, guarded all the approaches to the camp. The Veientines finding themselves thus shut in, began to fight with such fury that they slew Manilius, and would have destroyed all the rest of the Roman army, had not the prudence of one of the tribunes opened a way for the Veientines to retreat. Here we see that so long as necessity compelled, the Veientines fought most fiercely, but on finding a path opened for escape, preferred flight to combat. On another occasion when the Volscians and Equians passed with their armies across the Roman frontier, the consuls were sent out to oppose them, and an engagement ensued. It so happened that when the combat was at its height, the army of the Volscians, commanded by Vectius Mescius, suddenly found themselves shut in between their own camp, which a division of the Romans had occupied, and the body of the Roman army; when seeing that they must either perish or cut a way for themselves with their swords, Vectius said to them, "*Come on, my men, here is no wall or rampart to be scaled: we fight man with man; in valour we are their equals, and necessity, that last and mightiest weapon, gives us the advantage.*" Here, then, necessity is spoken of by Titus Livius as *the last and mightiest weapon*.

Camillus, the wisest and most prudent of all the Roman commanders, when he had got within the town of Veii with his army, to make its surrender easier and not to drive its inhabitants to desperation, called out to his men, so that the Veientines might hear, to spare all whom they found unarmed. Whereupon the defenders throwing away their weapons, the town was taken almost without bloodshed. And this device was afterwards followed by many other captains.

Chapter XIII.—*Whether we may trust more to a valiant Captain with a weak Army, or to a valiant Army with a weak Captain.*

Coriolanus being banished from Rome betook himself to the Volscians, and when he had got together an army wherewith to avenge himself on his countrymen, came back to Rome; yet, again withdrew, not constrained to retire by the might of the Roman arms, but out of reverence for his mother. From this incident, says Titus Livius, we may learn that the spread of the Roman power was due more to the valour of her captains than of her soldiers. For before this the Volscians had always been routed, and only grew successful when Coriolanus became their captain.

But though Livius be of this opinion, there are many passages in his history to show that the Roman soldiers, even when left without leaders, often performed astonishing feats of valour, nay, sometimes maintained better discipline and fought with greater spirit after their consuls were slain than they had before. For example, the army under the Scipios in Spain, after its two leaders had fallen, was able by its valour not merely to secure its own safety, but to overcome the enemy and preserve the province for the Roman Republic. So that to state the case fairly, we find many instances in which the valour of the soldiers alone gained the day, as well as many in which success was wholly due to the excellence of the captain. From which it may be inferred that the one stands in need of the other.

And here the question suggests itself: which is the more formidable, a good army badly led, or a good captain commanding an indifferent army; though, were we to adopt the opinion of Cæsar on this head, we ought lightly to esteem both. For when Cæsar went to Spain against Afranius and Petreius, who were there in command of a strong army, he made little account of them, saying, "*that he went to fight an army without a captain,*" indicating thereby the weakness of these generals. And, conversely, when he went to encounter Pompeius in Thessaly, he said, "*I go against a captain without an army.*"[1]

A further question may also be raised, whether it is easier for a good captain to make a good army, or for a good army to make a good captain. As to this it might be thought there was barely room for doubt, since it ought to be far easier for many who are good to find one who is good or teach him to become so, than for one who is good to find or make many good. Lucullus when sent against Mithridates was wholly without experience in war: but his brave army, which was provided with many excellent officers, speedily taught him to be a good captain. On the other hand, when the Romans, being badly off for soldiers, armed a number of slaves and gave them over to be drilled by Sempronius Gracchus, he in a short time made them into a serviceable army. So too, as I have already mentioned, Pelopidas and Epaminondas after rescuing Thebes, their native city, from Spartan thraldom, in a short time made such valiant soldiers of the Theban peasantry, as to be able with their aid not only to withstand, but even to defeat the Spartan armies. So that the question may seem to be equally balanced, excellence on one side generally finding excellence on the other.

A good army, however, when left without a good leader, as the Macedonian army was on the death of Alexander, or as those veterans were who had fought in the civil wars, is apt to grow restless and turbulent. Wherefore I am convinced that it is better to trust to the captain who has time allowed him to discipline his men, and means wherewith to equip them, than to a tumultuary host with a chance leader of its own choosing. But twofold is the merit and twofold the glory of those captains who not only have had to subdue their enemies, but also before encountering them to organize and discipline their forces. This, however, is a task requiring qualities so seldom combined, that were many of those captains who now enjoy a great name with the world, called on to perform it, they would be much less thought of than they are.

[Footnote 1: *Professus ante inter suos, ire se ad exercitum sine duce, et inde reversurum ad ducem sine exercitu.* (*Suet. in Vita J. Caes.*)]

Chapter XIV.—*Of the effect produced in Battle by strange and unexpected Sights or Sounds.*

That the disorder occasioned by strange and unexpected sights or sounds may have momentous consequences in combat, might be shown by many instances, but by none better than by what befell in the battle fought between the Romans and the Volscians, when Quintius, the Roman general, seeing one wing of his army begin to waver, shouted aloud to his men to stand firm, for the other wing was already victorious. Which words of his giving confidence to his own troops and striking the enemy with dismay won him the battle. But if a cry like this, produce great effect on a well disciplined army, far greater must be its effect on one which is ill disciplined and disorderly. For by such a wind the whole mass will be moved, as I shall show by a well-known instance happening in our own times.

A few years ago the city of Perugia was split into the two factions of the Baglioni and the Oddi, the former holding the government, the latter being in exile. The Oddeschi, however, with the help of friends, having got together an armed force which they lodged in villages of their own near Perugia, obtained, by the favour of some of their party, an entrance into the city by night, and moving forward without discovery, came as far as the public square. And as all the streets of Perugia are barred with chains drawn across them at their corners, the Oddeschi had in front of them a man who carried an iron hammer wherewith to break the fastenings of the chains so that horsemen might pass. When the only chain remaining unbroken was that which closed the public square, the alarm having now been given, the hammerman was so impeded by the crowd pressing behind him that he could not raise his arm to strike freely. Whereupon, to get more room for his work, he called aloud to the others to stand back; and the word back passing from rank to rank those furthest off began to run, and, presently, the others also, with such precipitancy, that they fell into utter disorder. In this way, and from this trifling circumstance, the attempt of the Oddeschi came to nothing.

Here we may note that discipline is needed in an army, not so much to enable it to fight according to a settled order, as that it may not be thrown into confusion by every insignificant accident. For a tumultuary host is useless in war, simply because every word, or cry, or sound, may throw it into a panic and cause it to fly. Wherefore it behoves a good captain to provide that certain fixed persons shall receive his orders and pass them on to the rest, and to accustom his soldiers to look to these persons, and to them only, to be informed what his orders are. For whenever this precaution is neglected the gravest mishaps are constantly seen to ensue.

As regards strange and unexpected sights, every captain should endeavour while his army is actually engaged with the enemy, to effect some such feint or diversion as will encourage his own men and dismay his adversary since this of all things that can happen is the likeliest to ensure victory. In evidence whereof we may cite the example of Cneius Sulpitius, the Roman dictator, who, when about to give battle to the Gauls, after arming his sutlers and camp followers, mounted them on mules and other beasts of burden, furnished them with spears and banners to look like cavalry, and placing them behind a hill, ordered them on a given signal, when the fight was at the hottest, to appear and show themselves to the enemy. All which being carried out as he had arranged, threw the Gauls into such alarm, that they lost the battle.

A good captain, therefore, has two things to see to: first, to contrive how by some sudden surprise he may throw his enemy into confusion; and next, to be prepared should the enemy use a like stratagem against him to discover and defeat it; as the stratagem of Semiramis was defeated by the King of India. For Semiramis seeing that this king had elephants in great numbers, to dismay him by showing that she, too, was well supplied, caused the skins of many oxen and buffaloes to be sewn together in the shape of elephants and placed upon camels and sent to the front. But the trick being detected by the king, turned out not only useless but hurtful to its contriver. In a battle which the Dictator Mamercus fought against the people of Fidenae, the latter, to strike terror into the minds of the Romans, contrived that while the combat raged a number of soldiers should issue from Fidenae bearing lances tipped with fire, thinking that the Romans, disturbed by so strange a sight, would be thrown into confusion.

We are to note, however, with regard to such contrivances, that if they are to serve any useful end, they should *be formidable as well as* seem so; for when they menace a real danger, their weak points are not so soon discerned. When they have more of pretence than reality, it will be well either to dispense with them altogether, or resorting to them, to keep them, like the muleteers of Sulpitius, in the background, so that they be not too readily found out. For any weakness inherent in them is soon discovered if they be brought near, when, as happened with the elephants of Semiramis and the fiery spears of the men of Fidenae, they do harm rather than good. For although by this last-mentioned device the Romans at the first were somewhat disconcerted, so soon as the dictator came up and began to chide them, asking if they were not ashamed to fly like bees from smoke, and calling on them to turn on their enemy, and "*with her own flames efface that Fidenae whom their benefits could not conciliate,*" they took courage; so that the device proved of no service to its contrivers, who were vanquished in the battle.

Chapter XV.—*That one and not many should head an Army: and why it is harmful to have more Leaders than one.*

The men of Fidenae rising against the colonists whom the Romans had settled among them, and putting them to the sword, the Romans to avenge the insult appointed four tribunes with consular powers: one of whom they retained to see to the defence of Rome, while the other three were sent against the Fidenati and the Veientines. But these three falling out among themselves, and being divided in their counsels, returned from their mission with discredit though not with loss. Of which discredit they were themselves the cause. That they sustained no loss was due to the valour of their soldiers But the senate perceiving the source of the mischief, to the end that one man might put to rights what three had thrown into confusion, resorted to the appointment of a dictator.

Here we see the disadvantage of having several leaders in one army or in a town which has to defend itself. And the case could not be put in clearer words than by Titus Livius, where he says, "*The three tribunes with consular authority gave proof how hurtful it is in war to have many leaders; for each forming a different opinion, and each abiding by his own, they threw opportunities in the way of their enemies.*" And though this example suffice by itself to show the disadvantage in war of divided commands, to make the matter still plainer I shall cite two further instances, one ancient and one modern.

In the year 1500, Louis XII. of France, after recovering Milan, sent troops to restore Pisa to the Florentines, Giovambattista Ridolfi and Luca d'Antonio Albizzi going with them as commissaries. Now, because Giovambattista had a great name, and was older than Luca, the latter left the whole management of everything to him; and although he did not show his jealousy of him by opposing him, he betrayed it by his silence, and by being so careless and indifferent about everything, that he gave no help in the business of the siege either by word or deed, just as though he had been a person of no account. But when, in consequence of an accident, Giovambattista had to return to Florence, all this was changed; for Luca, remaining in sole charge, behaved with the greatest courage, prudence, and zeal, all which qualities had been hidden while he held a joint command. Further to bear me out I shall again borrow the words of Titus Livius, who, in relating how when Quintius and Agrippa his colleague were sent by the Romans against the Equians, Agrippa contrived that the conduct of the war should rest with Quintius, observes, "*Most wholesome is it that in affairs of great moment, supreme authority be vested in one man.*" Very different, however, is the course followed by the republics and princes of our own days, who, thinking to be better served, are used to appoint several captains or commissioners to fill one command; a practice giving rise to so much confusion, that were we seeking for the causes of the overthrow of the French and Italian armies in recent times, we should find this to be the most active of any.

Rightly, therefore, may we conclude that in sending forth an army upon service, it is wiser to entrust it to one man of ordinary prudence, than to two of great parts but with a divided command.

Chapter XVI.—*That in Times of Difficulty true Worth is sought after; whereas in quiet Times it is not the most deserving, but those who are recommended by Wealth or Connection who are most in favour.*

It always has happened and always will, that the great and admirable men of a republic are neglected in peaceful times; because at such seasons many citizens are found, who, envying the reputation these men have justly earned, seek to be regarded not merely as their equals but as their superiors. Touching this there is a notable passage in Thucydides, the Greek historian, where he tells how the republic of Athens coming victorious out of the Peloponessian war, wherein she had bridled the pride of Sparta, and brought almost the whole of Greece under her authority, was encouraged by the greatness of her renown to propose to herself the conquest of Sicily. In Athens this scheme was much debated, Alcibiades and certain others who had the public welfare very little in their thoughts, but who hoped that the enterprise, were they placed in command, might minister to their fame, recommending that it should be undertaken. Nicias, on the other hand, one of the best esteemed of the Athenian citizens, was against it, and in addressing the people, gave it as the strongest reason for trusting his advice, that in advising them not to engage in this war, he urged what was not for his own advantage; for he knew that while Athens remained at peace numberless citizens were ready to take precedence of him: whereas, were war declared, he was certain that none would rank before him or even be looked upon as his equal.

Here we see that in tranquil times republics are subject to the infirmity of lightly esteeming their worthiest citizens. And this offends these persons for two reasons: first, because they are not given the place they deserve; and second, because they see unworthy men and of abilities inferior to their own, as much or more considered than they. Injustice such as this has caused the ruin of many republics. For citizens who find themselves undeservedly slighted, and perceive the cause to be that the times are tranquil and not troubled, will strive to change the times by stirring up wars hurtful to the public welfare. When I look for remedies for this state of things, I find two: first, to keep the citizens poor, so that wealth without worth shall corrupt neither them nor others; second, to be so prepared for war as always to be ready to make war; for then there will always be a need for worthy citizens, as was the case in Rome in early times. For as Rome constantly kept her armies in the field, there was constant opportunity for men to display their valour, nor was it possible to deprive a deserving man of his post and give it to another who was not deserving. Or if ever this were done by inadvertency, or by way of experiment, there forthwith resulted such disorder and danger, that the city at once retraced its steps and reverted to the true path. But other republics which are not regulated on the same plan, and make war only when driven to it by necessity, cannot help committing this injustice, nay, will constantly run into it, when, if the great citizen who finds himself slighted be vindictive, and have some credit and following in the city, disorder will always ensue. And though Rome escaped this danger for a time, she too, as has elsewhere been said, having no longer, after she had conquered Carthage and Antiochus, any fear of war, came to think she might commit her armies to whom she would, making less account of the valour of her captains than of those other qualities which gain favour with the people. Accordingly we find Paulus Emilius rejected oftener than once when he sought the consulship; nor, in fact, obtaining it until the Macedonian war broke out, which, being judged a formidable business, was by the voice of the whole city committed to his management. After the year 1494 our city of Florence was involved in a series of wars, in conducting which none of our citizens had any success until chance threw the command into the hands of one who showed us how an army should be led. This was Antonio Giacomini, and so long as there were dangerous wars on foot, all rivalry on the part of other citizens was suspended; and whenever a captain or commissary had to be appointed he was unopposed. But when a war came to be undertaken, as to the issue of which no misgivings were felt, and which promised both honour and preferment, so numerous were the competitors for command, that three commissaries having to be chosen to conduct the siege of Pisa, Antonio was left out; and though it cannot with certainty be shown that any harm resulted to our republic from his not having been sent on this enterprise, we may reasonably conjecture that such was indeed the case. For as the people of Pisa were then without means either for subsistence or defence, it may be believed that had Antonio been there he would have reduced them to such extremities as would have forced them to surrender at discretion to the Florentines. But Pisa being besieged by captains who knew neither how to blockade nor how to storm it, held out so long, that the Florentines, who should have reduced it by force, were obliged to buy its submission. Neglect like this might well move Antonio to resentment; and he must needs have been both very patient and very forgiving if he felt no desire to revenge himself when he could, by the ruin of the city or by injuries to individual citizens. But a republic should beware not to rouse such feelings, as I shall show in the following Chapter.

Chapter XVII.—*That we are not to offend a Man, and then send him to fill an important Office or Command.*

A republic should think twice before appointing to an important command a citizen who has sustained notable wrong at the hands of his fellow-citizens. Claudius Nero, quitting the army with which he was opposing Hannibal, went with a part of his forces into the March of Ancona, designing to join the other consul there, and after joining him to attack Hasdrubal before he came up with his brother. Now Claudius had previously commanded against Hasdrubal in Spain, and after driving him with his army into such a position that it seemed he must either fight at a disadvantage or perish by famine, had been outwitted by his adversary, who, while diverting his attention with proposals of terms, contrived to slip through his hands and rob him of the opportunity for effecting his destruction. This becoming known in Rome brought Claudius into so much discredit both with the senate and people, that to his great mortification and displeasure, he was slightingly spoken of by the whole city. But being afterwards made consul and sent to oppose Hannibal, he took the course mentioned above, which was in itself so hazardous that all Rome was filled with doubt and anxiety until tidings came of Hasdrubal's defeat. When subsequently asked why he had played so dangerous a game, wherein without urgent necessity he had staked the very existence of Rome, Claudius answered, he had done so because he knew that were he to succeed he would recover whatever credit he had lost in Spain; while if he failed, and his attempt had an untoward issue, he would be revenged on that city and On those citizens who had so ungratefully and indiscreetly wronged him.

But if resentment for an offence like this so deeply moved a Roman citizen at a time when Rome was still uncorrupted, we should consider how it may act on the citizen of a State not constituted as Rome then was. And because there is no certain remedy we can apply to such disorders when they arise in republics, it follows that it is impossible to establish a republic which shall endure always; since in a thousand unforeseen ways ruin may overtake it.

Chapter XVIII.—*That it is the highest Quality of a Captain to be able to forestall the designs of his Adversary.*

It was a saying of Epaminondas the Theban that nothing was so useful and necessary for a commander as to be able to see through the intentions and designs of his adversary. And because it is hard to come at this knowledge directly, the more credit is due to him who reaches it by conjecture. Yet sometimes it is easier to fathom an enemy's designs than to construe his actions; and not so much those actions which are done at a distance from us, as those done in our presence and under our very eyes. For instance, it has often happened that when a battle has lasted till nightfall, the winner has believed himself the loser, and the loser has believed himself the winner and that this mistake has led him who made it to follow a course hurtful to himself. It was from a mistake of this sort, that Brutus and Cassius lost the battle of Philippi. For though Brutus was victorious with his wing of the army Cassius, whose wing was beaten, believed the entire army to be defeated, and under this belief gave way to despair and slew himself. So too, in our own days, in the battle fought by Francis, king of France, with the Swiss at Santa Cecilia in Lombardy, when night fell, those of the Swiss who remained unbroken, not knowing that the rest had been routed and slain, thought they had the victory; and so believing would not retreat, but, remaining on the field, renewed the combat the following morning to their great disadvantage. Nor were they the only sufferers from their mistake, since the armies of the Pope and of Spain were also misled by it, and well-nigh brought to destruction. For on the false report of a victory they crossed the Po, and had they only advanced a little further must have been made prisoners by the victorious French.

An instance is recorded of a like mistake having been made in the camps both of the Romans and of the Equians. For the Consul Sempronius being in command against the Equians, and giving the enemy battle, the engagement lasted with varying success till nightfall, when as both armies had suffered what was almost a defeat, neither returned to their camp, but each drew off to the neighboring hills where they thought they would be safer. The Romans separated into two divisions, one of which with the consul, the other with the centurion Tempanius by whose valour the army had that day been saved from utter rout. At daybreak the consul, without waiting for further tidings of the enemy, made straight for Rome; and the Equians, in like manner, withdrew to their own country. For as each supposed the other to be victorious, neither thought much of leaving their camp to be plundered by the enemy. It so chanced, however, that Tempanius, who was himself retreating with the second division of the Roman army, fell in with certain wounded Equians, from whom he learned that their commanders had fled, abandoning their camp; on hearing which, he at once returned to the Roman camp and secured it, and then, after sacking the camp of the Equians, went back victorious to Rome. His success, as we see, turned entirely on his being the first to be informed of the enemy's condition. And here we are to note that it may often happen that both the one and the other of two opposed armies shall fall into the same disorder, and be reduced to the same straits; in which case, that which soonest detects the other's distress is sure to come off best.

I shall give an instance of this which occurred recently in our own country. In the year 1498, when the Florentines had a great army in the territory of Pisa and had closely invested the town, the Venetians, who had undertaken its protection, seeing no other way to save it, resolved to make a diversion in its favour by attacking the territories of the Florentines in another quarter. Wherefore, having assembled a strong force, they entered Tuscany by the Val di Lamona, and seizing on the village of Marradi, besieged the stronghold of Castiglione which stands on the height above it. Getting word of this, the Florentines sought to relieve Marradi, without weakening the army which lay round Pisa. They accordingly raised a new levy of foot-soldiers, and equipped a fresh squadron of horse, which they despatched to Marradi under the joint command of Jacopo IV. d'Appiano, lord of Piombino, and Count Rinuccio of Marciano. These troops taking up their position on the hill above Marradi, the Venetians withdrew from the investment of Castiglione and lodged themselves in the village. But when the two armies had confronted one another for several days, both began to suffer sorely from want of victuals and other necessaries, and neither of them daring to attack the other, or knowing to what extremities the other was reduced, both simultaneously resolved to strike their camps the following morning, and to retreat, the Venetians towards Berzighella and Faenza, the Florentines towards Casaglia and the Mugello. But at daybreak, when both armies had begun to remove their baggage, it so happened that an old woman, whose years and poverty permitted her to pass unnoticed, leaving the village of Marradi, came to the Florentine camp, where were certain of her kinsfolk whom she desired to visit. Learning from her that the Venetians were in retreat, the Florentine commanders took courage, and changing their plan, went in pursuit of the enemy as though they had dislodged them, sending word to Florence that they had repulsed the Venetians and gained a victory. But in truth this victory was wholly due to their having notice of the enemy's movements before the latter had notice of theirs. For had that notice been given to the Venetians first, it would have wrought against us the same results as it actually wrought for us.

Chapter XIX.—*Whether Indulgence or Severity be more necessary for controlling a Multitude.*

The Roman Republic was distracted by the feuds of the nobles and commons. Nevertheless, on war breaking out, Quintius and Appius Claudius were sent forth in command of Roman armies. From his harshness and severity to his soldiers, Appius was so ill obeyed by them, that after sustaining what almost amounted to a defeat, he had to resign his command. Quintius, on the contrary, by kindly and humane treatment, kept his men obedient and returned victorious to Rome. From this it might seem that to govern a large body of men, it is better to be humane than haughty, and kindly rather than severe.

And yet Cornelius Tacitus, with whom many other authors are agreed, pronounces a contrary opinion where he says, "*In governing a multitude it avails more to punish than to be compliant.*"[1] If it be asked how these opposite views can be reconciled, I answer that you exercise authority either over men used to regard you as their equal, or over men who have always been subject to you. When those over whom you exercise authority are your equals, you cannot trust wholly to punishment or to that severity of which Tacitus speaks. And since in Rome itself the commons had equal weight with the nobles, none appointed their captain for a time only, could control them by using harshness and severity. Accordingly we find that those Roman captains who gained the love of their soldiers and were considerate of them, often achieved greater results than those who made themselves feared by them in an unusual degree, unless, like Manlius Torquatus, these last were endowed with consummate valour. But he who has to govern subjects such as those of whom Tacitus speaks, to prevent their growing insolent and trampling upon him by reason of his too great easiness, must resort to punishment rather than to compliance. Still, to escape hatred, punishment should be moderate in degree, for to make himself hated is never for the interest of any prince. And to escape hatred, a prince has chiefly to guard against tampering with the property of any of his subjects; for where nothing is to be gained by it, no prince will desire to shed blood, unless, as seldom happens, constrained to do so by necessity. But where advantage is to be gained thereby, blood will always flow, and neither the desire to shed it, nor causes for shedding it will ever be wanting, as I have fully shown when discussing this subject in another treatise.

Quintius therefore was more deserving of praise than Appius. Nevertheless the opinion of Tacitus, duly restricted and not understood as applying to a case like that of Appius, merits approval. But since I have spoken of punishment and indulgence, it seems not out of place to show how a single act of humanity availed more than arms with the citizens of Falerii.

[Footnote 1: "In multitudine regenda plus poena quam obsequium valet." But compare Annals, III. 55, "Obsequium inde in principem et æmulandi amoi validioi quam poena ex legibus et metus."]

Chapter XX.—*How one humane act availed more with the men of Falerii, than all the might of the Roman Arms.*

When the besieging army of the Romans lay round Falerii, the master of a school wherein the best-born youths of the city were taught, thinking to curry favour with Camillus and the Romans, came forth from the town with these boys, on pretence of giving them exercise, and bringing them into the camp where Camillus was, presented them to him, saying, "*To ransom these that city would yield itself into your hands.*" Camillus, however, not only rejected this offer, but causing the schoolmaster to be stripped and his hands tied behind him, gave each of the boys a scourge, and bade them lead the fellow back to the town scourging him as they went. When the citizens of Falerii heard of this, so much were they pleased with the humanity and integrity of Camillus, that they resolved to surrender their town to him without further defence.

This authentic instance may lead us to believe that a humane and kindly action may sometimes touch men's minds more nearly than a harsh and cruel one; and that those cities and provinces into which the instruments and engines of war, with every other violence to which men resort, have failed to force a way, may be thrown open to a single act of tenderness, mercy, chastity, or generosity. Whereof history supplies us with many examples besides the one which I have just now noticed. For we find that when the arms of Rome were powerless to drive Pyrrhus out of Italy, he was moved to depart by the generosity of Fabritius in disclosing to him the proposal which his slave had made the Romans to poison him. Again, we read how Scipio gained less reputation in Spain by the capture of New Carthage, than by his virtue in restoring a young and beautiful wife unviolated to her husband; the fame of which action won him the love of the whole province. We see, too, how much this generous temper is esteemed by a people in its great men; and how much it is praised by historians and by those who write the lives of princes, as well as by those who lay down rules of human conduct. Among whom Xenophon has taken great pains to show what honours, and victories, and how fair a fame accrued to Cyrus from his being kindly and gracious, without taint of pride, or cruelty, or luxury, or any other of those vices which cast a stain upon men's lives.

And yet when we note that Hannibal, by methods wholly opposite to these, achieved splendid victories and a great renown, I think I am bound to say something in my next Chapter as to how this happened.

Chapter XXI.—*How it happened that Hannibal pursuing a course contrary to that taken by Scipio, wrought the same results in Italy which the other achieved in Spain.*

Some, I suspect, may marvel to find a captain, taking a contrary course, nevertheless arrive at the same ends as those who have pursued the methods above spoken of; since it must seem as though success did not depend on the causes I have named; nay, that if glory and fame are to be won in other ways, these causes neither add to our strength nor advance our fortunes. Wherefore, to make my meaning plain, and not to part company with the men of whom I have been speaking, I say, that as, on the one hand, we see Scipio enter Spain, and by his humane and generous conduct at once secure the good-will of the province, and the admiration and reverence of its inhabitants, so on the other hand, we see Hannibal enter Italy, and by methods wholly opposite, to wit, by violence and rapine, by cruelty and treachery of every kind, effect in that country the very same results. For all the States of Italy revolted in his favour, and all the Italian nations ranged themselves on his side.

When we seek to know why this was, several reasons present themselves, the first being that men so passionately love change, that, commonly speaking, those who are well off are as eager for it as those who are badly off: for as already has been said with truth, men are pampered by prosperity, soured by adversity. This love of change, therefore, makes them open the door to any one who puts himself at the head of new movements in their country, and if he be a foreigner they adopt his cause, if a fellow-countryman they gather round him and become his partisans and supporters; so that whatever methods he may there use, he will succeed in making great progress. Moreover, men being moved by two chief passions, love and fear, he who makes himself feared commands with no less authority than he who makes himself loved; nay, as a rule, is followed and obeyed more implicitly than the other. It matters little, however, which of these two ways a captain chooses to follow, provided he be of transcendent valour, and has thereby won for himself a great name For when, like Hannibal or Scipio, a man is very valiant, this quality will cloak any error he may commit in seeking either to be too much loved or too much feared. Yet from each of these two tendencies, grave mischiefs, and such as lead to the ruin of a prince, may arise. For he who would be greatly loved, if he swerve ever so little from the right road, becomes contemptible; while he who would be greatly feared, if he go a jot too far, incurs hatred. And since it is impossible, our nature not allowing it, to adhere to the exact mean, it is essential that any excess should be balanced by an exceeding valour, as it was in Hannibal and Scipio. And yet we find that even they, while they were exalted by the methods they followed, were also injured by them. How they were exalted has been shown. The injury which Scipio suffered was, that in Spain his soldiers, in concert with certain of his allies, rose against him, for no other reason than that they stood in no fear of him. For men are so restless, that if ever so small a door be opened to their ambition, they forthwith forget all the love they have borne their prince in return for his graciousness and goodness, as did these soldiers and allies of Scipio; when, to correct the mischief, he was forced to use something of a cruelty foreign to his nature.

As to Hannibal, we cannot point to any particular instance wherein his cruelty or want of faith are seen to have been directly hurtful to him; but we may well believe that Naples and other towns which remained loyal to the Roman people, did so by reason of the dread which his character inspired. This, however, is abundantly clear, that his inhumanity made him more detested by the Romans than any other enemy they ever had; so that while to Pyrrhus, in Italy with his army, they gave up the traitor who offered to poison him, Hannibal, even when disarmed and a fugitive, they never forgave, until they had compassed his death.

To Hannibal, therefore, from his being accounted impious, perfidious, and cruel, these disadvantages resulted; but, on the other hand, there accrued to him one great gain, noticed with admiration by all historians, namely, that in his army, although made up of men of every race and country, no dissensions ever broke out among the soldiers themselves, nor any mutiny against their leader. This we can only ascribe to the awe which his character inspired, which together with the great name his valour had won for him, had the effect of keeping his soldiers quiet and united. I repeat, therefore, that it is of little moment which method a captain may follow if he be endowed with such valour as will bear him out in the course which he adopts. For, as I have said, there are disadvantages incident to both methods unless corrected by extraordinary valour.

And now, since I have spoken of Scipio and Hannibal, the former of whom by praiseworthy, the latter by odious qualities, effected the same results, I must not, I think, omit to notice the characters of two Roman citizens, who by different, yet both by honourable methods, obtained a like glory.

Chapter XXII.—*That the severity of Manlius Torquatus and the gentleness of Valerius Corvinus won for both the same Glory.*

There lived in Rome, at the same time, two excellent captains, Manlius Torquatus and Valerius Corvinus, equal in their triumphs and in their renown, and in the valour which in obtaining these they had displayed against the enemy; but who in the conduct of their armies and treatment of their soldiers, followed very different methods. For Manlius, in his command, resorted to every kind of severity, never sparing his men fatigue, nor remitting punishment; while Valerius, on the contrary, treated them with all kindness and consideration, and was easy and familiar in his intercourse with them. So that while the one, to secure the obedience of his soldiers, put his own son to death, the other never dealt harshly with any man. Yet, for all this diversity in their modes of acting, each had the same success against the enemy, and each obtained the same advantages both for the republic and for himself. For no soldier of theirs ever flinched in battle, or rose in mutiny against them, or in any particular opposed their will; though the commands of Manlius were of such severity that any order of excessive rigour came to be spoken of as a *Manlian order*.

Here, then, we have to consider first of all why Manlius was obliged to use such severity; next, why Valerius could behave so humanely; thirdly, how it was that these opposite methods had the same results; and lastly, which of the two methods it is better and more useful for us to follow. Now, if we well examine the character of Manlius from the moment when Titus Livius first begins to make mention of him, we shall find him to have been endowed with a rare vigour both of mind and body, dutiful in his behaviour to his father and to his country, and most reverent to his superiors. All which we see in his slaying the Gaul, in his defence of his father against the tribune, and in the words in which, before going forth to fight the Gaul, he addressed the consul, when he said, "*Although assured of victory, never will I without thy bidding engage an enemy.*" But when such a man as this attains to command, he looks to find all others like himself; his dauntless spirit prompts him to engage in daring enterprises, and to insist on their being carried out. And this is certain, that where things hard to execute are ordered to be done, the order must be enforced with sternness, since, otherwise, it will be disobeyed.

And here be it noted that if you would be obeyed you must know how to command, and that they alone have this knowledge who have measured their power to enforce, with the willingness of others to yield obedience; and who issue their orders when they find these conditions combining, but, otherwise, abstain. Wherefore, a wise man was wont to say that to hold a republic by force, there must be a proportion between him who uses the force and him against whom it is used; and that while this proportion obtains the force will operate; but that when he who suffers is stronger than he who uses the force, we may expect to see it brought to an end at any moment.

But returning to the matter in hand, I say that to command things hard of execution, requires hardness in him who gives the command, and that a man of this temper and who issues such commands, cannot look to enforce them by gentleness. He who is not of such a temper must be careful not to impose tasks of extraordinary difficulty, but may use his natural gentleness in imposing such as are ordinary. For common punishments are not imputed to the prince, but to the laws and ordinances which he has to administer.

We must believe, therefore, that Manlius was constrained to act with severity by the unusual character of the commands which his natural disposition prompted him to issue. Such commands are useful in a republic, as restoring its ordinances to their original efficacy and excellence. And were a republic, as I have before observed, fortunate enough to come frequently under the influence of men who, by their example, reinforce its laws, and not only retard its progress towards corruption, but bring it back to its first perfection, it might endure for ever.

Manlius, therefore, was of those who by the severity of their commands maintained the military discipline of Rome; urged thereto, in the first place, by his natural temper, and next by the desire that whatever he was minded to command should be done. Valerius, on the other hand, could afford to act humanely, because for him it was enough if all were done which in a Roman army it was customary to do. And, since the customs of that army were good customs, they sufficed to gain him honour, while at the same time their maintenance cost him no effort, nor threw on him the burthen of punishing transgressors; as well because there were none who trangressed, as because had there been any, they would, as I have said, have imputed their punishment to the ordinary rules of discipline, and not to the severity of their commander. In this way Valerius had room to exercise that humane disposition which enabled him at once to gain influence over his soldiers and to content them. Hence it was that both these captains obtaining the same obedience, could, while following different methods, arrive at the same ends. Those, however, who seek to imitate them may chance to fall into the errors of which I have already spoken, in connection with Hannibal and Scipio, as breeding contempt or hatred, and which are only to be corrected by the presence of extraordinary valour, and not otherwise.

It rests now to determine which of these two methods is the more to be commended. This, I take it, is matter of dispute, since both methods have their advocates. Those writers, however, who have laid down rules for the conduct of princes, describe a character approaching more nearly to that of Valerius than to that of Manlius; and Xenophon, whom I have already cited, while giving many instances of the humanity of Cyrus, conforms closely to what Livius tells us of Valerius. For Valerius being made consul against the Samnites, on the eve of battle spoke to his men with the same kindliness with which he always treated them; and Livius, after telling us what he said, remarks of him: "*Never was there a leader more familiar with his men; cheerfully sharing with the meanest among them every hardship and fatigue. Even in the military games, wherein those of the same rank were wont to make trial of their strength or swiftness, he would good-naturedly take a part, nor disdain any adversary who offered; meeting victory or defeat with an unruffled temper and an unchanged countenance. When called on to act, his bounty and generosity never fell short. When he had to speak, he was as mindful of the feelings of others as of his own dignity. And, what more than anything else secures the popular favour, he maintained when exercising his magistracies the same bearing he had worn in seeking them.*"

Of Manlius also, Titus Livius speaks in like honourable terms, pointing out that his severity in putting his son to death brought the Roman army to that pitch of discipline which enabled it to prevail against the Latins, nay, he goes so far in his praises that after describing the whole order of the battle, comparing the strength of both armies, and showing all the dangers the Romans ran, and the difficulties they had to surmount, he winds up by saying, that it was the valour of Manlius which alone gained for them this great victory, and that whichever side had Manlius for its leader must have won the day. So that weighing all that the historians tell us of these two captains, it might be difficult to decide between them.

Nevertheless, not to leave the question entirely open, I say, that for a citizen living under a republic, I think the conduct of Manlius more deserving of praise and less dangerous in its consequences. For methods like his tend only to the public good and in no way subserve private ends. He who shows himself harsh and stern at all times and to all men alike, and is seen to care only for the common welfare, will never gain himself partisans, since this is not the way to win personal friends, to whom, as I said before, the name of partisans is given. For a republic, therefore, no line of conduct could be more useful or more to be desired than this, because in following it the public interest is not neglected, and no room is given to suspect personal ambition.

But the contrary holds as to the methods followed by Valerius. For though the public service they render be the same, misgivings must needs arise that the personal good-will which, in the course of a prolonged command, a captain obtains from his soldiers, may lead to consequences fatal to the public liberty. And if this was not found to happen in the case of Valerius, it was because the minds of the Roman people were not yet corrupted, and because they had never remained for a long time and continuously under his command.

Had we, however, like Xenophon, to consider what is most for the interest of a prince, we should have to give up Manlius and hold by Valerius; for, undoubtedly, a prince should strive to gain the love of his soldiers and subjects, as well as their obedience. The latter he can secure by discipline and by his reputation for valour. But for the former he will be indebted to his affability, kindliness, gentleness, and all those other like qualities which were possessed by Valerius, and which are described by Xenophon as existing in Cyrus. That a prince should be personally loved and have his army wholly devoted to him is consistent with the character of his government; but that this should happen to a person of private station does not consist with his position as a citizen who has to live in conformity with the laws and in subordination to the magistrates. We read in the early annals of the Venetian Republic, that once, on the return of the fleet, a dispute broke out between the sailors and the people, resulting in tumults and armed violence which neither the efforts of the public officers, the respect felt for particular citizens, nor the authority of the magistrates could quell. But on a certain gentleman, who the year before had been in command of these sailors, showing himself among them, straightway, from the love they bore him, they submitted to his authority and withdrew from the fray. Which deference on their part aroused such jealousy and suspicion in the minds of the Venetian senators that very soon after they got rid of this gentleman, either by death or exile.

The sum of the matter, therefore, is, that the methods followed by Valerius are useful in a prince, but pernicious in a private citizen, both for his country and for himself, for his country, because such methods pave the way to a tyranny; for himself, because his fellow-citizens, growing suspicious of his conduct, are constrained to protect themselves to his hurt. And conversely, I maintain, that the methods of Manlius, while hurtful in a prince are useful in a citizen, and in the highest degree for his country; and, moreover, seldom give offence, unless the hatred caused by his severity be augmented by the jealousy which the fame of his other virtues inspires: a matter now to be considered in connection with the banishment of Camillas.

Chapter XXIII.—*Why Camillus was banished from Rome.*

It has been shown above how methods like those of Valerius are hurtful to the citizen who employs them and to his country, while methods like those of Manlius are advantageous for a man's country, though sometimes they be hurtful to the man himself. This is well seen in the example of Camillus, whose bearing more nearly resembled that of Manlius than that of Valerius, so that Titus Livius, in speaking of him, says, "*His virtues were at once hated and admired by his soldiers.*" What gained him their admiration was his care for their safety, his prudence, his magnanimity, and the good order he maintained in conducting and commanding them. What made him hated was his being more stern to punish than bountiful to reward; and Livius instances the following circumstances as giving rise to this hatred. First, his having applied the money got by the sale of the goods of the Veientines to public purposes, and not divided it along with the rest of the spoils. Second, his having, on the occasion of his triumph, caused his chariot to be drawn by four white horses, seeking in his pride, men said, to make himself the equal of the sun god. And, third, his having vowed to Apollo a tenth of the Veientine plunder, which, if he was to fulfil his vow, he had to recover from his soldiers, into whose hands it had already come.

Herein we may well and readily discern what causes tend to make a prince hateful to his people; the chief whereof is the depriving them of some advantage. And this is a matter of much importance. For when a man is deprived of what is in itself useful, he never forgets it, and every trifling occasion recalls it to his mind; and because such occasions recur daily, he is every day reminded of his loss. Another error which we are here taught to guard against, is the appearing haughty and proud, than which nothing is more distasteful to a people, and most of all to a free people; for although such pride and haughtiness do them no hurt, they nevertheless hold in detestation any who display these qualities. Every show of pride, therefore, a prince should shun as he would a rock, since to invite hatred without resulting advantage were utterly rash and futile.

Chapter XXIV.—*That prolonged Commands brought Rome to Servitude.*

If we well examine the course of Roman history, we shall find two causes leading to the break-up of that republic: one, the dissensions which arose in connection with the agrarian laws; the other, the prolongation of commands. For had these matters been rightly understood from the first, and due remedies applied, the freedom of Rome had been far more lasting, and, possibly, less disturbed. And although, as touching the prolongation of commands, we never find any tumult breaking out in Rome on that account, we do in fact discern how much harm was done to the city by the ascendency which certain of its citizens thereby gained. This mischief indeed would not have arisen, if other citizens whose period of office was extended had been as good and wise as Lucius Quintius, whose virtue affords a notable example. For terms of accord having been settled between the senate and commons of Rome, the latter, thinking their tribunes well able to withstand the ambition of the nobles, prolonged their authority for a year. Whereupon, the senate, not to be outdone by the commons, proposed, out of rivalry, to extend the consulship of Quintius. He, however, refused absolutely to lend himself to their designs, and insisted on their appointing new consuls, telling them that they should seek to discredit evil examples, not add to them by setting worse. Had this prudence and virtue of his been shared by all the citizens of Rome, the practice of prolonging the terms of civil offices would not have been suffered to establish itself, nor have led to the kindred practice of extending the term of military commands, which in progress of time effected the ruin of their republic.

The first military commander whose term was extended, was Publius Philo; for when his consulship was about to expire, he being then engaged in the siege of Palæopolis, the senate, seeing he had the victory in his hands, would not displace him by a successor, but appointed him *Proconsul,* which office he was the first to hold. Now, although in thus acting the senate did what they thought best for the public good, nevertheless it was this act of theirs that in time brought Rome to slavery. For the further the Romans carried their arms, the more necessary it seemed to them to grant similar extensions of command, and the oftener they, in fact, did so. This gave rise to two disadvantages: first that a smaller number of men were trained to command; second, that by the long continuance of his command a captain gained so much influence and ascendency over his soldiers that in time they came to hold the senate of no account, and looked only to him. This it was, that enabled Sylla and Marius to find adherents ready to follow them even to the public detriment, and enabled Cæsar to overthrow the liberties of his country; whereas, had the Romans never prolonged the period of authority, whether civil or military, though they might have taken longer to build up their empire, they certainly had been later in incurring servitude.

Chapter XXV.—*Of the poverty of Cincinnatus and of many other Roman Citizens.*

Elsewhere I have shown that no ordinance is of such advantage to a commonwealth, as one which enforces poverty on its citizens. And although it does not appear what particular law it was that had this operation in Rome (especially since we know the agrarian law to have been stubbornly resisted), we find, as a fact, that four hundred years after the city was founded, great poverty still prevailed there; and may assume that nothing helped so much to produce this result as the knowledge that the path to honours and preferment was closed to none, and that merit was sought after wheresoever it was to be found; for this manner of conferring honours made riches the less courted. In proof whereof I shall cite one instance only.

When the consul Minutius was beset in his camp by the Equians, the Roman people were filled with such alarm lest their army should be destroyed, that they appointed a dictator, always their last stay in seasons of peril. Their choice fell on Lucius Quintius Cincinnatus, who at the time was living on his small farm of little more than four acres, which he tilled with his own hand. The story is nobly told by Titus Livius where he says: "*This is worth listening to by those who contemn all things human as compared with riches, and think that glory and excellence can have no place unless accompanied by lavish wealth.*" Cincinnatus, then, was ploughing in his little field, when there arrived from Rome the messengers sent by the senate to tell him he had been made dictator, and inform him of the dangers which threatened the Republic. Putting on his gown, he hastened to Rome, and getting together an army, marched to deliver Minutius. But when he had defeated and spoiled the enemy, and released Minutius, he would not suffer the army he had rescued to participate in the spoils, saying, "*I will not have you share in the plunder of those to whom you had so nearly fallen a prey.*" Minutius he deprived of his consulship, and reduced to be a subaltern, in which rank he bade him remain till he had learned how to command. And before this he had made Lucius Tarquininus, although forced by his poverty to serve on foot, his master of the knights.

Here, then, we see what honour was paid in Rome to poverty, and how four acres of land sufficed to support so good and great a man as Cincinnatus. We find the same Poverty still prevailing in the time of Marcus Regulus, who when serving with the army in Africa sought leave of senate to return home that he might look after his farm which his labourers had suffered to run to waste. Here again we learn two things worthy our attention: first, the poverty of these men and their contentment under it, and how their sole study was to gain renown from war, leaving all its advantages to the State. For had they thought of enriching themselves by war, it had given them little concern that their fields were running to waste Further, we have to remark the magnanimity of these citizens, who when placed at the head of armies surpassed all princes in the loftiness of their spirit, who cared neither for king nor for commonwealth, and whom nothing could daunt or dismay; but who, on returning to private life, became once more so humble, so frugal, so careful of their slender means, and so submissive to the magistrates and reverential to their superiors, that it might seem impossible for the human mind to undergo so violent a change.

This poverty prevailed down to the days of Paulus Emilius, almost the last happy days for this republic wherein a citizen, while enriching Rome by his triumphs, himself remained poor. And yet so greatly was poverty still esteemed at this time, that when Paulus, in conferring rewards on those who had behaved well in the war, presented his own son-in-law with a silver cup, it was the first vessel of silver ever seen in his house.

I might run on to a great length pointing out how much better are the fruits of poverty than those of riches, and how poverty has brought cities, provinces, and nations to honour, while riches have wrought their ruin, had not this subject been often treated by others.

Chapter XXVI.—*How Women are a cause of the ruin of States.*

A feud broke out in Ardea touching the marriage of an heiress, whose hand was sought at the same time by two suitors, the one of plebeian, the other of noble birth. For her father being dead, her guardian wished her to wed the plebeian, her mother the noble. And so hot grew the dispute that resort was had to arms, the whole nobility siding with their fellow-noble, and all the plebeians with the plebeian. The latter faction being worsted, left the town, and sent to the Volscians for help; whereupon, the nobles sought help from Rome. The Volscians were first in the field, and on their arrival encamped round Ardea. The Romans, coming up later, shut in the Volscians between themselves and the town, and, reducing them by famine, forced them to surrender at discretion. They then entered Ardea, and putting all the ringleaders in this dispute to the sword, composed the disorders of the city.

In connection with this affair there are several points to be noted. And in the first place we see how women have been the occasion of many divisions and calamities in States, and have wrought great harm to rulers; as when, according to our historian, the violence done to Lucretia drove the Tarquins from their kingdom, and that done to Virginia broke the power of the decemvirs. And among the chief causes which Aristotle assigns for the downfall of tyrants are the wrongs done by them to their subjects in respect of their women, whether by adultery, rape, or other like injury to their honour, as has been sufficiently noticed in the Chapter wherein we treated *"of Conspiracies"*

I say, then, that neither absolute princes nor the rulers of free States should underrate the importance of matter, but take heed to the disorders which it may breed and provide against them while remedies can still be used without discredit to themselves or to their governments And this should have been done by the rulers of Ardea who by suffering the rivalry between their citizens to come to a head, promoted their divisions, and when they sought to reunite them had to summon foreign help, than which nothing sooner leads to servitude.

But now let us turn to another subject which merits attention, namely, the means whereby divided cities may be reunited; and of this I propose to speak in the following Chapter.

Chapter XXVII. *How a divided City may be reunited, and how it is a false opinion that to hold Cities in subjection they must be kept divided.*

From the example of the Roman consuls who reconciled the citizens of Ardea, we are taught the method whereby the feuds of a divided city may be composed, namely, by putting the ringleaders of the disturbances to death; and that no other remedy should be used. Three courses, indeed, are open to you, since you may either put to death, as these consuls did, or banish, or bind the citizens to live at peace with one another, taking security for their good behaviour. Of which three ways the last is the most hurtful, the most uncertain, and the least effectual; because when much blood has been shed, or other like outrage done, it cannot be that a peace imposed on compulsion should endure between men who are every day brought face to face with one another; for since fresh cause of contention may at any moment result from their meeting, it will be impossible for them to refrain from mutual injury. Of this we could have no better instance than in the city of Pistoja.

Fifteen years ago this city was divided between the Panciatichi and Cancellieri, as indeed it still continues, the only difference being that then they were in arms, whereas, now, they have laid them aside. After much controversy and wrangling, these factions would presently proceed to bloodshed, to pulling down houses, plundering property, and all the other violent courses usual in divided cities. The Florentines, with whom it lay to compose these feuds, strove for a long time to do so by using the third of the methods mentioned; but when this only led to increased tumult and disorder, losing patience, they decided to try the second method and get rid of the ringleaders of both factions by imprisoning some and banishing others. In this way a sort of settlement was arrived at, which continues in operation up to the present hour. There can be no question, however, that the first of the methods named would have been the surest. But because extreme measures have in them an element of greatness and nobility, a weak republic, so far from knowing how to use this first method, can with difficulty be brought to employ even the second. This, as I said at the beginning, is the kind of blunder made by the princes of our times when they have to decide on matters of moment, from their not considering how those men acted who in ancient days had to determine under like conditions. For the weakness of the present race of men (the result of their enfeebling education and their ignorance of affairs), makes them regard the methods followed by the ancients as partly inhuman and partly impracticable. Accordingly, they have their own newfangled ways of looking at things, wholly at variance with the true, as when the sages of our city, some time since, pronounced that *Pistoja was to be held by feuds and Pisa by fortresses*, not perceiving how useless each of these methods is in itself.

Having spoken of fortresses already at some length, I shall not further refer to them here, but shall consider the futility of trying to hold subject cities by keeping them divided. In the first place, it is impossible for the ruling power, whether prince or republic, to be friends with both factions. For wherever there is division, it is human nature to take a side, and to favour one party more than another. But if one party in a subject city be unfriendly to you, the consequence will be that you will lose that city so soon as you are involved in war, since it is impossible for you to hold a city where you have enemies both within and without. Should the ruling power be a republic, there is nothing so likely to corrupt its citizens and sow dissension among them, as having to control a divided city. For as each faction in that city will seek support and endeavour to make friends in a variety of corrupt ways, two very serious evils will result: first, that the governed city will never be contented with its governors, since there can be no good government where you often change its form, adapting yourself to the humours now of one party and now of another; and next, that the factious spirit of the subject city is certain to infect your own republic. To which Biondo testifies, when, in speaking of the citizens of Florence and Pistoja, he says, "*In seeking to unite Pistoja the Florentines themselves fell out.*"[1] It is easy, therefore, to understand how much mischief attends on such divisions. In the year 1501, when we lost Arezzo, and when all the Val di Tevere and Val di Chiana were occupied by the Vitelli and by Duke Valentino, a certain M. de Lant was sent by the King of France to cause the whole of the lost towns to be restored to the Florentines; who finding in all these towns men who came to him claiming to be of the party of the *Marnocco*[2], greatly blamed this distinction, observing, that if in France any of the king's subjects were to say that he was of the king's party, he would be punished; since the expression would imply that there was a party hostile to the king, whereas it was his majesty's desire that all his subjects should be his friends and live united without any distinction of party. But all these mistaken methods and opinions originate in the weakness of rulers, who, seeing that they cannot hold their States by their own strength and valour, have recourse to like devices; which, if now and then in tranquil times they prove of some slight assistance to them, in times of danger are shown to be worthless.

[Footnote 1: *Flav. Blondri Hist.*, dec. ii. lib. 9. Basle ed. 1559, p. 337]

[Footnote 2: The heraldic Lion of Florence.]

Chapter XXVIII. *That a Republic must keep an eye on what its Citizens are about; since often the seeds of a Tyranny lie hidden under a semblance of generous deeds.*

The granaries of Rome not sufficing to meet a famine with which the city was visited, a certain Spurius Melius, a very wealthy citizen for these days, privately laid in a supply of corn wherewith to feed the people at his own expense; gaining thereby such general favour with the commons, that the senate, apprehending that his bounty might have dangerous consequences, in order to crush him before he grew too powerful, appointed a dictator to deal with him and caused him to be put to death.

Here we have to note that actions which seem good in themselves and unlikely to occasion harm to any one, very often become hurtful, nay, unless corrected in time, most dangerous for a republic. And to treat the matter with greater fulness, I say, that while a republic can never maintain itself long, or manage its affairs to advantage, without citizens of good reputation, on the other hand the credit enjoyed by particular citizens often leads to the establishment of a tyranny. For which reasons, and that things may take a safe course, it should be so arranged that a citizen shall have credit only for such behaviour as benefits, and not for such as injures the State and its liberties. We must therefore examine by what ways credit is acquired. These, briefly, are two, public or secret. Public, when a citizen gains a great name by advising well or by acting still better for the common advantage. To credit of this sort we should open a wide door, holding out rewards both for good counsels and for good actions, so that he who renders such services may be at once honoured and satisfied. Reputation acquired honestly and openly by such means as these can never be dangerous. But credit acquired by secret practices, which is the other method spoken of, is most perilous and prejudicial. Of such secret practices may be instanced, acts of kindness done to this or the other citizen in lending him money, in assisting him to marry his daughters, in defending him against the magistrates, and in conferring such other private favours as gain men devoted adherents, and encourage them after they have obtained such support, to corrupt the institutions of the State and to violate its laws.

A well-governed republic, therefore, ought, as I have said, to throw wide the door to all who seek public favour by open courses, and to close it against any who would ingratiate themselves by underhand means. And this we find was done in Rome. For the Roman republic, as a reward to any citizen who served it well, ordained triumphs and all the other honours which it had to bestow; while against those who sought to aggrandize themselves by secret intrigues, it ordained accusations and impeachment; and when, from the people being blinded by a false show of benevolence, these proved insufficient, it provided for a dictator, who with regal authority might bring to bounds any who had strayed beyond them, as instanced in the case of Spurius Melius. And if conduct like his be ever suffered to pass unchastised, it may well be the ruin of a republic, for men when they have such examples set them are not easily led back into the right path.

Chapter XXIX.—*That the Faults of a People are due to its Prince.*

Let no prince complain of the faults committed by a people under his control; since these must be ascribed either to his negligence, or to his being himself blemished by similar defects. And were any one to consider what peoples in our own times have been most given to robbery and other like offences, he would find that they have only copied their rulers, who have themselves been of a like nature. Romagna, before those lords who ruled it were driven out by Pope Alexander VI., was a nursery of all the worst crimes, the slightest occasion giving rise to wholesale rapine and murder. This resulted from the wickedness of these lords, and not, as they asserted, from the evil disposition of their subjects. For these princes being poor, yet choosing to live as though they were rich, were forced to resort to cruelties innumerable and practised in divers ways; and among other shameful devices contrived by them to extort money, they would pass laws prohibiting certain acts, and then be the first to give occasion for breaking them; nor would they chastise offenders until they saw many involved in the same offence; when they fell to punishing, not from any zeal for the laws which they had made, but out of greed to realize the penalty. Whence flowed many mischiefs, and more particularly this, that the people being impoverished, but not corrected, sought to make good their injuries at the expense of others weaker than themselves. And thus there sprang up all those evils spoken of above, whereof the prince is the true cause.

The truth of what I say is confirmed by Titus Livius where he relates how the Roman envoys, who were conveying the spoils of the Veientines as an offering to Apollo, were seized and brought on shore by the corsairs of the Lipari islands in Sicily; when Timasitheus, the prince of these islands, on learning the nature of the offering, its destination, and by whom sent, though himself of Lipari, behaved as a Roman might, showing his people what sacrilege it would be to intercept such a gift, and speaking to such purpose that by general consent the envoys were suffered to proceed upon their voyage, taking all their possessions with them. With reference to which incident the historian observes: "*The multitude, who always take their colour from their ruler, were filled by Timasitheus with a religious awe.*" And to like purport we find it said by Lorenzo de' Medici:—

"A prince's acts his people imitate; For on their lord the eyes of all men wait."[1]

[Footnote 1: E quel che fa il signer, fanno poi molti; Chè nel signer son tutti gli occhi volti. (*La Rappresentazione di San Giovanni e Paolo.*)]

Chapter XXX.—*That a Citizen who seeks by his personal influence to render signal service to his Country, must first stand clear of Envy. How a City should prepare for its defence on the approach of an Enemy.*

When the Roman senate learned that all Etruria was assembled in arms to march against Rome, and that the Latins and Hernicians, who before had been the friends of the Romans, had ranged themselves with the Volscians the ancient enemies of the Roman name, they foresaw that a perilous contest awaited them. But because Camillus was at that time tribune with consular authority they thought all might be managed without the appointment of a dictator, provided the other tribunes, his colleagues would agree to his assuming the sole direction of affairs. This they willingly did; "*nor*," says Titus Livius, "*did they account anything as taken from their own dignity which was added to his.*"

On receiving their promise of obedience, Camillus gave orders that three armies should be enrolled. Of the first, which was to be directed against the Etruscans, he himself assumed command. The command of the second, which he meant to remain near Rome and meet any movement of the Latins and Hernicians, he gave to Quintius Servilius. The third army, which he designed for the protection of the city, and the defence of the gates and Curia, he entrusted to Lucius Quintius. And he further directed, that Horatius, one of his colleagues, should furnish supplies of arms, and corn, and of all else needful in time of war. Finally he put forward his colleague Cornelius to preside in the senate and public council, that from day to day he might advise what should be done. For in those times these tribunes were ready either to command or obey as the welfare of their country might require.

We may gather from this passage how a brave and prudent man should act, how much good he may effect, and how serviceable he may be to his country, when by the force of his character and worth he succeeds in extinguishing envy. For this often disables men from acting to the best advantage, not permitting them to obtain that authority which it is essential they should have in matters of importance. Now, envy may be extinguished in one or other of two ways: first, by the approach of some flagrant danger, whereby seeing themselves like to be overwhelmed, all forego their own private ambition and lend a willing obedience to him who counts on his valour to rescue them. As in the case of Camillas, who from having given many proofs of surpassing ability, and from having been three times dictator and always exercised the office for the public good and not for his private advantage, had brought men to fear nothing from his advancement; while his fame and reputation made it no shame for them to recognize him as their superior. Wisely, therefore, does Titus Livius use concerning him the words which I have cited.

The other way in which envy may be extinguished, is by the death, whether by violence or in the ordinary course of nature, of those who have been your rivals in the pursuit of fame or power, and who seeing you better esteemed than themselves, could never acquiesce in your superiority or put up with it in patience. For when these men have been brought up in a corrupt city, where their training is little likely to improve them, nothing that can happen will induce them to withdraw their pretensions; nay, to have their own way and satisfy their perverse humour, they will be content to look on while their country is ruined. For envy such as this there is no cure save by the death of those of whom it has taken possession. And when fortune so befriends a great man that his rivals are removed from his path by a natural death, his glory is established without scandal or offence, since he is then able to display his great qualities unhindered. But when fortune is not thus propitious to him, he must contrive other means to rid himself of rivals, and must do so successfully before he can accomplish anything. Any one who reads with intelligence the lessons of Holy Writ, will remember how Moses, to give effect to his laws and ordinances, was constrained to put to death an endless number of those who out of mere envy withstood his designs. The necessity of this course was well understood by the Friar Girolamo Savonarola, and by the Gonfalonier Piero Soderini. But the former could not comply with it, because, as a friar, he himself lacked the needful authority; while those of his followers who might have exercised that authority, did not rightly comprehend his teaching. This, however, was no fault of his; for his sermons are full of invectives and attacks against "*the wise of this world*," that being the name he gave to envious rivals and to all who opposed his reforms. As for Piero Soderini, he was possessed by the belief that in time and with favourable fortune he could allay envy by gentleness-and by benefits conferred on particular men; for as he was still in the prime of life, and in the fresh enjoyment of that good-will which his character and opinions had gained for him, he thought to get the better of all who out of jealousy opposed him, without giving occasion for tumult, violence, or disorder; not knowing how time stays not, worth suffices not, fortune shifts, and malice will not be won over by any benefit Wherefore, because they could not or knew not how to vanquish this envy, the two whom I have named came to their downfall.

Another point to be noted in the passage we are considering, is the careful provision made by Camillus for the safety of Rome both within and without the city. And, truly, not without reason do wise historians, like our author, set forth certain events with much minuteness and detail, to the end that those who come after may learn how to protect themselves in like dangers. Further, we have to note that there is no more hazardous or less useful defence than one conducted without method or system. This is shown in Camillus causing a third army to be enrolled that it might be left in Rome for the protection of the city. Many persons, doubtless, both then and now, would esteem this precaution superfluous, thinking that as the Romans were a warlike people and constantly under arms, there could be no occasion for a special levy, and that it was time enough to arm when the need came. But Camillus, and any other equally prudent captain would be of the same mind, judged otherwise, not permitting the multitude to take up arms unless they were to be bound by the rules and discipline of military service. Let him, therefore, who is called on to defend a city, taking example by Camillus, before all things avoid placing arms in the hands of an undisciplined multitude, but first of all select and enroll those whom he proposes to arm, so that they may be wholly governed by him as to where they shall assemble and whither they shall march; and then let him direct those who are not enrolled, to abide every man in his own house for its defence. Whosoever observes this method in a city which is attacked, will be able to defend it with ease; but whosoever disregards it, and follows not the example of Camillus, shall never succeed.

Chapter XXXI.—*That strong Republics and valiant Men preserve through every change the same Spirit and Bearing.*

Among other high sayings which our historian ascribes to Camillus, as showing of what stuff a truly great man should be made, he puts in his mouth the words, "*My courage came not with my dictatorship nor went with my exile;*" for by these words we are taught that a great man is constantly the same through all vicissitudes of Fortune; so that although she change, now exalting, now depressing, he remains unchanged, and retains always a mind so unmoved, and in such complete accordance with his nature as declares to all that over him Fortune has no dominion.

Very different is the behaviour of those weak-minded mortals who, puffed up and intoxicated with their success, ascribe all their felicity to virtues which they never knew, and thus grow hateful and insupportable to all around them. Whence also the changes in their fortunes. For whenever they have to look adversity in the face, they suddenly pass to the other extreme, becoming abject and base. And thus it happens that feeble-minded princes, when they fall into difficulties, think rather of flight than of defence, because, having made bad use of their prosperity, they are wholly unprepared to defend themselves.

The same merits and defects which I say are found in individual men, are likewise found in republics, whereof we have example in the case of Rome and of Venice. For no reverse of fortune ever broke the spirit of the Roman people, nor did any success ever unduly elate them; as we see plainly after their defeat at Cannæ, and after the victory they had over Antiochus. For the defeat at Cannæ, although most momentous, being the third they had met with, no whit daunted them; so that they continued to send forth armies, refused to ransom prisoners as contrary to their custom, and despatched no envoy to Hannibal or to Carthage to sue for peace; but without ever looking back on past humiliations, thought always of war, though in such straits for soldiers that they had to arm their old men and slaves. Which facts being made known to Hanno the Carthaginian, he, as I have already related, warned the Carthaginian senate not to lay too much stress upon their victory. Here, therefore, we see that in times of adversity the Romans were neither cast down nor dismayed. On the other hand, no prosperity ever made them arrogant. Before fighting the battle wherein he was finally routed, Antiochus sent messengers to Scipio to treat for an accord; when Scipio offered peace on condition that he withdrew at once into Syria, leaving all his other dominions to be dealt with by the Romans as they thought fit. Antiochus refusing these terms, fought and was defeated, and again sent envoys to Scipio, enjoining them to accept whatever conditions the victor might be pleased to impose. But Scipio proposed no different terms from those he had offered before saying that "*the Romans, as they lost not heart on defeat, so waxed not insolent with success.*"

The contrary of all this is seen in the behaviour of the Venetians, who thinking their good fortune due to valour of which they were devoid, in their pride addressed the French king as "Son of St. Mark;" and making no account of the Church, and no longer restricting their ambition to the limits of Italy, came to dream of founding an empire like the Roman. But afterwards, when their good fortune deserted them, and they met at Vailà a half-defeat at the hands of the French king, they lost their whole dominions, not altogether from revolt, but mainly by a base and abject surrender to the Pope and the King of Spain. Nay, so low did they stoop as to send ambassadors to the Emperor offering to become his tributaries, and to write letters to the Pope, full of submission and servility, in order to move his compassion. To such abasement were they brought in four days' time by what was in reality only a half-defeat. For on their flight after the battle of Vailà only about a half of their forces were engaged, and one of their two provedditori escaped to Verona with five and twenty thousand men, horse and foot. So that had there been a spark of valour in Venice, or any soundness in her military system, she might easily have renewed her armies, and again confronting fortune have stood prepared either to conquer, or, if she must fall, to fall more gloriously; and at any rate might have obtained for herself more honourable terms. But a pusillanimous spirit, occasioned by the defects of her ordinances in so far as they relate to war, caused her to lose at once her courage and her dominions. And so will it always happen with those who behave like the Venetians. For when men grow insolent in good fortune, and abject inn evil, the fault lies in themselves and in the character of their training, which, when slight and frivolous, assimilates them to itself; but when otherwise, makes them of another temper, and giving them better acquaintance with the world, causes them to be less disheartened by misfortunes and less elated by success.

And while this is true of individual men, it holds good also of a concourse of men living together in one republic, who will arrive at that measure of perfection which the institutions of their State permit. And although I have already said on another occasion that a good militia is the foundation of all States, and where that is wanting there can neither be good laws, nor aught else that is good, it seems to me not superfluous to say the same again; because in reading this history of Titus Livius the necessity of such a foundation is made apparent in every page. It is likewise shown that no army can be good unless it be thoroughly trained and exercised, and that this can only be the case with an army raised from your own subjects. For as a State is not and cannot always be at war, you must have opportunity to train your army in times of peace; but this, having regard to the cost, you can only have in respect of your own subjects.

When Camillus, as already related, went forth to meet the Etruscans, his soldiers on seeing the great army of their enemy, were filled with fear, thinking themselves too to withstand its onset. This untoward disposition being reported to Camillus, he showed himself to his men and by visiting their tents, and conversing with this and the other among them, was able to remove their misgivings; and, finally, without other word of command, he bade them *"each do his part as he had learned and been accustomed."* Now, any one who well considers the methods followed by Camillus, and the words spoken by him to encourage his soldiers to face their enemy, will perceive that these words and methods could never have been used with an army which had not been trained and disciplined in time of peace as well as of war. For no captain can trust to untrained soldiers or look for good service at their hands; nay, though he were another Hannibal, with such troops his defeat were certain. For, as a captain cannot be present everywhere while a battle is being fought, unless he have taken all measures beforehand to render his men of the same temper as himself, and have made sure that they perfectly understand his orders and arrangements, he will inevitably be destroyed.

When a city therefore is armed and trained as Rome was, and when its citizens have daily opportunity, both singly and together, to make trial of their valour and learn what fortune can effect, it will always happen, that at all times, and whether circumstances be adverse or favourable, they will remain of unaltered courage and preserve the same noble bearing. But when its citizens are unpractised in arms, and trust not to their own valour but wholly to the arbitration of Fortune, they will change their temper as she changes, and offer always the same example of behaviour as was given by the Venetians.

Chapter XXXII.—*Of the methods which some have used to make Peace impossible.*

The towns of Cære and Velitræ, two of her own colonies, revolted from Rome in expectation of being protected by the Latins. But the Latins being routed and all hopes of help from that quarter at an end, many of the townsmen recommended that envoys should be sent to Rome to make their peace with the senate. This proposal, however, was defeated by those who had been the prime movers of the revolt, who, fearing that the whole punishment might fall on their heads, to put a stop to any talk of an adjustment, incited the multitude to take up arms and make a foray into the Roman territory.

And, in truth, when it is desired that a prince or people should banish from their minds every thought of reconciliation, there is no surer or more effectual plan than to incite them to inflict grave wrong on him with whom you would not have them be reconciled; for, then, the fear of that punishment which they will seem to themselves to have deserved, will always keep them apart. At the close of the first war waged by the Romans against Carthage, the soldiers who had served under the Carthaginians in Sardinia and Sicily, upon peace being proclaimed, returned to Africa; where, being dissatisfied with their pay, they mutinied against the Carthaginians, and choosing two of their number, Mato and Spendio, to be their leaders, seized and sacked many towns subject to Carthage. The Carthaginians, being loath to use force until they had tried all other methods for bringing them to reason, sent Hasdrubal, their fellow-citizen, to mediate with them, thinking that from formerly having commanded them he might be able to exercise some influence over them. But on his arrival, Spendio and Mato, to extinguish any hope these mutineers might have had of making peace with Carthage, and so leave them no alternative but war, persuaded them that their best course was to put Hasdrubal, with all the other Carthaginian citizens whom they had taken prisoners, to death. Whereupon, they not only put them to death, but first subjected them to an infinity of tortures; crowning their wickedness by a proclamation to the effect that every Carthaginian who might thereafter fall into their hands should meet a like fate. This advice, therefore, and its consummation had the effect of rendering these mutineers relentless and inveterate in their hostility to the Carthaginians.

Chapter XXXIII.—*That to insure victory in battle you must inspire your Men with confidence in one another and in you.*

To insure an army being victorious in battle you must inspire it with the conviction that it is certain to prevail. The causes which give it this confidence are its being well armed and disciplined, and the soldiers knowing one another. These conditions are only to be found united in soldiers born and bred in the same country.

It is likewise essential that the army should think so well of its captain as to trust implicitly to his prudence; which it will always do if it see him careful of its welfare, attentive to discipline, brave in battle, and otherwise supporting well and honourably the dignity of his position. These conditions he fulfils when, while punishing faults, he does not needlessly harass his men, keeps his word with them, shows them that the path to victory is easy, and conceals from them, or makes light of things which seen from a distance might appear to threaten danger. The observance of these precautions will give an army great confidence, and such confidence leads to victory.

This confidence the Romans were wont to inspire in the minds of their soldiers by the aid of religion; and accordingly their consuls were appointed, their armies were enrolled, their soldiers marched forth, and their battles were begun, only when the auguries and auspices were favourable; and without attending to all these observances no prudent captain would ever engage in combat; knowing that unless his soldiers were first assured that the gods were on their side, he might readily suffer defeat. But if any consul or other leader ever joined battle contrary to the auspices, the Romans would punish him, as they did Claudius Pulcher.

The truth of what I affirm is plainly seen from the whole course of the Roman history, but is more particularly established by the words which Livius puts into the mouth of Appius Claudius, who, when complaining to the people of the insolence of the tribunes, and taxing them with having caused the corruption of the auspices and other rites of religion, is made to say, "*And now they would strip even religion of its authority. For what matters it, they will tell you, that the fowls refuse to peck, or come slowly from the coop, or that a cock has crowed? These are small matters doubtless; but it was by not contemning such small matters as these, that our forefathers built up this great republic.*" And, indeed, in these small matters lies a power which keeps men united and of good courage, which is of itself the chief condition of success.

But the observances of religion must be accompanied by valour, for otherwise they can nothing avail. The men of Praneste, leading forth their army against the Romans, took up their position near the river Allia, on the very spot where the Romans had been routed by the Gauls, selecting this ground that it might inspire their own side with confidence, and dishearten their enemies with the unhappy memories which it recalled But although, for the reasons already noted, this was a course which promised success, the result nevertheless showed that true valour is not to be daunted by trifling disadvantages. And this the historian well expresses by the words he puts in the mouth of the dictator as spoken to his master of the knights "*See how these fellows, in encamping on the banks of the Allia, have chosen their ground in reliance upon fortune. Do you, therefore, relying on discipline and valour, fall upon then centre.*" For true valour, tight discipline, and the feeling of security gained by repeated victories, are not to be counteracted by things of no real moment, dismayed by empty terrors, or quelled by a solitary mishap. As was well seen when the two Manlii, being consuls in command against the Volscians, rashly allowed a part of their army to go out foraging, and both those who went out and those who stayed behind found themselves attacked at the same moment For from this danger they were saved by the courage of the soldiers, and not by the foresight of the consuls. With regard to which occurrence Titus Livius observes, "*Even without a leader the steadfast valour of the soldiers was maintained.*"

Here I must not omit to notice the device practised by Fabius to give his army confidence, when he led it for the first time into Etruria. For judging such encouragement to be especially needed by his men, since they were entering an unknown country to encounter a new foe, he addressed them before they joined battle, and, after reciting many reasons for expecting a victory, told them, that "*he could have mentioned other favourable circumstances making victory certain, had it not been dangerous to disclose them.*" And as this device was dexterously used it merits imitation.

Chapter XXXIV.—*By what reports, rumours, or surmises the Citizens of a Republic are led to favour a Fellow-citizen: and-whether the Magistracies are bestowed with better judgment by a People or by a Prince.*

I have elsewhere related how Titus Manlius, afterwards named Torquatus, rescued his father from the charge laid against him by Marcus Pomponius, tribune of the people. And though the means he took to effect this were somewhat violent and irregular, so pleasing to everyone were his filial piety and affection, that not only did he escape rebuke, but when military tribunes had to be appointed his name was second on the list of those chosen. To explain his good fortune, it will, I think, be useful to consider what are the methods followed by the citizens of a republic in estimating the character of those on whom they bestow honours, so as to see whether what I have already said on this head be true, namely, that a people is more discriminating in awarding honours than a prince.

I say, then, that in conferring honours and offices, the people, when it has no knowledge of a man from his public career, follows the estimate given of him by the general voice, and by common report; or else is guided by some prepossession or preconceived opinion which it has adopted concerning him. Such impressions are formed either from consideration of a man's descent (it being assumed, until the contrary appears, that where his ancestors have been great and distinguished citizens their descendant will resemble them), or else from regard to his manners and habits; and nothing can be more in his favour than that he frequents the company of the grave and virtuous, and such as are generally reputed wise. For as we can have no better clue to a man's character than the company he keeps, he who frequents worthy company deservedly obtains a good name, since there can hardly fail to be some similarity between himself and his associates. Sometimes, however, the popular estimate of a man is founded on some remarkable and noteworthy action, though not of public moment, in which he has acquitted himself well. And of all the three causes which create a prepossession in a man's favour, none is so effectual as this last. For the presumption that he will resemble his ancestors and kinsmen is so often misleading, that men are slow to trust and quick to discard it, unless confirmed by the personal worth of him of whom they are judging.

The criterion of character afforded by a man's manners and conversation is a safer guide than the presumption of inherited excellence, but is far inferior to that afforded by his actions; for until he has given actual proof of his worth, his credit is built on mere opinion, which may readily change. But this third mode of judging, which originates in and rests upon his actions, at once gives him a name which can only be destroyed by his afterwards doing many actions of a contrary nature. Those therefore who live in a republic should conform to this third criterion, and endeavour, as did many of the Roman youth, to make their start in life with some extraordinary achievement, either by promoting a law conducive to the general well-being, or by accusing some powerful citizen as a transgressor of the laws, or by performing some similar new and notable action which cannot fail to be much spoken of.

Actions like this are necessary not only to lay a foundation for your fame, but also to maintain and extend it. To which end, they must continually be renewed, as we find done by Titus Manlius throughout the whole course of his life. For after winning his earliest renown by his bold and singular defence of his father, when some years had passed he fought his famous duel with the Gaul, from whom, when he had slain him, he took the twisted golden collar which gave him the name of Torquatus. Nor was this the last of his remarkable actions, for at a later period, when he was of ripe years, he caused his own son to be put to death, because he had fought without leave, although successfully. Which three actions gained for him at the time a greater name, and have made him more renowned through after ages than all his triumphs and victories, though of these he had as large a share as fell to the lot of any other Roman. The explanation of which is, that while in his victories Manlius had many who resembled him, in these particular actions he stood almost or entirely alone.

So, too, with the elder Scipio, all whose victories together did not obtain for him so much reputation, as did his rescue, while he was yet young, of his father at the Ticino, and his undaunted bearing after the rout at Cannæ, when with his naked sword he constrained a number of the Roman youth to swear never to abandon their country, as some among them had before been minded to do. It was these two actions, therefore, which laid the foundation of his future fame and paved the way for his triumphs in Spain and Africa. And the fair esteem in which men held him, was still further heightened when in Spain he restored a daughter to her father, a wife to her husband.

Nor is it only the citizen who seeks reputation as leading to civil honours, who must act in this way; the prince who would maintain his credit in his princedom must do likewise; since nothing helps so much to make a prince esteemed as to give signal proofs of his worth, whether by words or by deeds which tend to promote the public good, and show him to be so magnanimous, generous, and just, that he may well pass into a proverb among his subjects. But to return to the point whence I digressed, I say that if a people, when they first confer honours on a fellow-citizen, rest their judgment on any one of the three circumstances above-mentioned, they build on a reasonable foundation; but, when many instances of noble conduct have made a man favourably known, that the foundation is still better, since then there is hardly room for mistake. I speak merely of those honours which are bestowed on a man at the outset of his career, before he has come to be known by continued proof, or is found to have passed from one kind of conduct to another and dissimilar kind, and I maintain that in such cases, so far as erroneous judgments or corrupt motives are concerned, a people will always commit fewer mistakes than a prince.

But since a people may happen to be deceived as regards the character, reputation, and actions of a man, thinking them better or greater than in truth they are, an error a prince is less likely to fall into from his being informed and warned by his advisers, in order that the people may not lack similar advice, wise founders of republics have provided, that when the highest dignities of the State, to which it would be dangerous to appoint incapable men, have to be filled up, and it appears that some incapable man is the object of the popular choice, it shall be lawful and accounted honourable for any citizen to declare in the public assemblies the defects of the favoured candidate, that the people, being made acquainted therewith, may be better able to judge of his fitness. That this was the practice in Rome we have proof in the speech made by Fabius Maximus to the people during the second Punic war, when in the appointment of consuls public favour leaned towards Titus Ottacilius. For Fabius judging him unequal to the duties of the consulship at such a crisis, spoke against him and pointed out his insufficiency, and so prevented his appointment, turning the popular favour towards another who deserved it more.

In the choice of its magistrates, therefore, a people judges of those among whom it has to choose, in accordance with the surest indications it can get; and when it can be advised as princes are, makes fewer mistakes than they. But the citizen who would make a beginning by gaining the good-will of the people, must, to obtain it, perform, like Titus Manlius, some noteworthy action.

Chapter XXXV.—*Of the Danger incurred in being the first to recommend new Measures; and that the more unusual the Measures the greater the Danger.*

How perilous a thing it is to put one's self at the head of changes whereby many are affected, how difficult to guide and bring them to perfection, and when perfected to maintain them, were too wide and arduous a subject to be treated here. Wherefore I reserve it for a fitter occasion, and shall now speak only of those dangers which are incurred by the citizens of a republic or by the counsellors of a prince in being the first to promote some grave and important measure in such manner that the whole responsibility attending it rests with them. For as men judge of things by their results, any evil which ensues from such measures will be imputed to their author. And although if good ensue he will be applauded, nevertheless in matters of this kind, what a man may gain is as nothing to what he may lose.

Selim, the present sultan, or Grand Turk as he is called, being in readiness, as some who come from his country relate, to set forth on an expedition against Egypt and Syria, was urged by one of his bashaws whom he had stationed on the confines of Persia, to make war upon the Sofi. In compliance with which advice he went on this new enterprise with a vast army. But coming to a great plain, wherein were many deserts and few streams, and encountering the same difficulties as in ancient times had proved the ruin of many Roman armies, he suffered so much from pestilence and famine, that, although victorious in battle, he lost a great part of his men. This so enraged him against the bashaw on whose advice he had acted, that he forthwith put him to death.

In like manner, we read of many citizens who having strenuously promoted various measures were banished when these turned out badly. Certain citizens of Rome, for instance, were very active in forwarding a law allowing the appointment of a plebeian to be consul. This law passing, it so happened that the first plebeian consul who went forth with the armies was routed; and had it not been that the party in whose behalf the law was made was extremely powerful, its promoters would have fared badly. It is plain therefore that the counsellors whether of a republic or of a prince stand in this dilemma, that if they do not conscientiously advise whatsoever they think advantageous for their city or prince, they fail in their duty; if they do advise it, they risk their places and their lives; all men being subject to this infirmity of judging advice by the event.

When I consider in what way this reproach or this danger may best be escaped, I find no other remedy to recommend than that in giving advice you proceed discreetly not identifying yourself in a special manner with the measure you would see carried out, but offering your opinion without heat, and supporting it temperately and modestly, so that if the prince or city follow it, they shall do so of their own good-will, and not seem to be dragged into it by your importunity. When you act thus, neither prince nor people can reasonably bear you a grudge in respect of the advice given by you, since that advice was not adopted contrary to the general opinion. For your danger lies in many having opposed you, who afterwards, should your advice prove hurtful, combine to ruin you. And although in taking this course you fall short of the glory which is earned by him who stands alone against many in urging some measure which succeeds, you have nevertheless two advantages to make up for it: first, that you escape danger; and second, that when you have temperately stated your views, and when, in consequence of opposition, your advice has not been taken, should other counsels prevail and mischief come of them, your credit will be vastly enhanced. And although credit gained at the cost of misfortune to your prince or city cannot be matter of rejoicing, still it is something to be taken into account.

On this head, then, I know of no other advice to offer. For that you should be silent and express no opinion at all, were a course hurtful for your prince or city, and which would not absolve you from danger, since you would soon grow to be suspected, when it might fare with you as with the friend of Perseus the Macedonian king. For Perseus being defeated by Paulus Emilius, and making his escape with a few companions, it happened that one of them, in reviewing the past, began to point out to the king many mistakes which he had made and which had been his ruin. Whereupon Perseus turning upon him said, "*Traitor, hast thou waited till now when there is no remedy to tell me these things*?" and so saying, slew him with his own hand. Such was the penalty incurred by one who was silent when he should have spoken, and who spoke when he should have been silent; and who found no escape from danger in having refrained from giving advice. Wherefore, I believe, that the course which I have recommended should be observed and followed.

Chapter XXXVI.—*Why it has been and still may be affirmed of the Gauls, that at the beginning of a fray they are more than Men, but afterwards less than Women.*

The bravery of the Gaul who on the banks of the Anio challenged any among the Romans to fight with him, and the combat that thereupon ensued between him and Titus Manlius, remind me of what Titus Livius oftener than once observes in his history, that "*at the beginning of a fray the Gauls are more than men, but ere it is ended show themselves less than women.*"

Touching the cause of this, many are content to believe that such is their nature, which, indeed, I take to be true; but we are not, therefore, to assume that the natural temper which makes them brave at the outset, may not be so trained and regulated as to keep them brave to the end. And, to prove this, I say, that armies are of three kinds. In one of these you have discipline with bravery and valour as its consequence. Such was the Roman army, which is shown by all historians to have maintained excellent discipline as the result of constant military training. And because in a well-disciplined army none must do anything save by rule, we find that in the Roman army, from which as it conquered the world all others should take example, none either eat, or slept, or bought, or sold, or did anything else, whether in his military or in his private capacity, without orders from the consul. Those armies which do otherwise are not true armies, and if ever they have any success, it is owing to the fury and impetuosity of their onset and not to trained and steady valour. But of this impetuosity and fury, trained valour, when occasion requires, will make use; nor will any danger daunt it or cause it to lose heart, its courage being kept alive by its discipline, and its confidence fed by the hope of victory which never fails it while that discipline is maintained.

But the contrary happens with armies of the second sort, those, namely, which have impetuosity without discipline, as was the case with the Gauls whose courage in a protracted conflict gradually wore away; so that unless they succeeded in their first attack, the impetuosity to which they trusted, having no support from disciplined valour, soon cooled; when, as they had nothing else to depend on, their efforts ceased. The Romans, on the other hand, being less disquieted in danger by reason of their perfect discipline, and never losing hope, fought steadily and stubbornly to the last, and with the same courage at the end as at the outset; nay, growing heated by the conflict, only became the fiercer the longer it was continued.

In armies of the third sort both natural spirit and trained valour are wanting; and to this class belong the Italian armies of our own times, of which it may be affirmed that they are absolutely worthless, never obtaining a victory, save when, by some accident, the enemy they encounter takes to flight. But since we have daily proofs of this absence of valour, it were needless to set forth particular instances of it.

That all, however, may know on the testimony of Titus Livius what methods a good army should take, and what are taken by a bad army, I shall cite the words he represents Papirius Cursor to have used when urging that Fabius, his master of the knights, should be punished for disobedience, and denouncing the consequences which would ensue were he absolved, saying:—"*Let neither God nor man be held in reverence; let the orders of captains and the Divine auspices be alike disregarded; let a vagrant soldiery range without leave through the country of friend or foe; reckless of their military oath, let them disband at their pleasure; let them forsake their deserted standards, and neither rally nor disperse at the word of command; let them fight when they choose, by day or by night, with or without advantage of ground, with or without the bidding of their leader, neither maintaining their ranks nor observing the order of battle; and let our armies, from being a solemn and consecrated company, grow to resemble some dark and fortuitous gathering of cut-throats.*" With this passage before us, it is easy to pronounce whether the armies of our times be "*a dark and fortuitous gathering,*" or "*a solemn and consecrated company;*" nay, how far they fall short of anything worthy to be called an army, possessing neither the impetuous but disciplined valour of the Romans, nor even the mere undisciplined impetuosity of the Gauls.

Chapter XXXVII.—*Whether a general engagement should be preceded by skirmishes; and how, avoiding these, we may get knowledge of a new Enemy.*

Besides all the other difficulties which hinder men from bringing anything to its utmost perfection, it appears, as I have already observed, that in close vicinity to every good is found also an evil, so apt to grow up along with it that it is hardly possible to have the one without accepting the other. This we see in all human affairs, and the result is, that unless fortune aid us to overcome this natural and common disadvantage, we never arrive at any excellence. I am reminded of this by the combat between Titus Manlius and the Gaul, concerning which Livius writes that it "*determined the issue of the entire war; since the Gauls, abandoning their camp, hastily withdrew to the country about Tivoli, whence they presently passed into Campania.*"

It may be said, therefore, on the one hand, that a prudent captain ought absolutely to refrain from all those operations which, while of trifling moment in themselves, may possibly produce an ill effect on his army. Now, to engage in a combat wherein you risk your whole fortunes without putting forth your entire strength, is, as I observed before, when condemning the defence of a country by guarding its defiles, an utterly foolhardy course. On the other hand, it is to be said that a prudent captain, when he has to meet a new and redoubtable adversary, ought, before coming to a general engagement, to accustom his men by skirmishes and passages of arms, to the quality of their enemy; that they may learn to know him, and how to deal with him, and so free themselves from the feeling of dread which his name and fame inspire.

This for a captain is a matter of the very greatest importance, and one which it might be almost fatal for him to neglect, since to risk a pitched battle without first giving your soldiers such opportunities to know their enemy and shake off their fear of him, is to rush on certain destruction. When Valerius Corvinus was sent by the Romans with their armies against the Samnites, these being new adversaries with whom up to that time they had not measured their strength, Titus Livius tells us that before giving battle he made his men make trial of the enemy in several unimportant skirmishes, "*lest they should be dismayed by a new foe and a new method of warfare.*" Nevertheless, there is very great danger that, if your soldiers get the worst in these encounters, their alarm and self-distrust may be increased, and a result follow contrary to that intended, namely, that you dispirit where you meant to reassure.

This, therefore, is one of those cases in which the evil lies so nigh the good, and both are so mixed up together that you may readily lay hold of the one when you think to grasp the other. And with regard to this I say, that a good captain should do what he can that nothing happen which might discourage his men, nor is there anything so likely to discourage them as to begin with a defeat. For which reason skirmishes are, as a rule, to be avoided, and only to be allowed where you fight to great advantage and with a certainty of victory. In like manner, no attempt should be made to defend the passes leading into your country unless your whole army can co-operate; nor are any towns to be defended save those whose loss necessarily involves your ruin. And as to those towns which you do defend, you must so arrange, both in respect of the garrison within and the army without, that in the event of a siege your whole forces can be employed. All other towns you must leave undefended. For, provided your army be kept together, you do not, in losing what you voluntarily abandon, forfeit your military reputation, or sacrifice your hopes of final success. But when you lose what it was your purpose, and what all know it was your purpose to hold, you suffer a real loss and injury, and, like the Gauls on the defeat of their champion, you are ruined by a mishap of no moment in itself.

Philip of Macedon, the father of Perseus, a great soldier in his day, and of a great name, on being invaded by the Romans, laid waste and relinquished much of his territory which he thought he could not defend; rightly judging it more hurtful to his reputation to lose territory after an attempt to defend it, than to abandon it to the enemy as something he cared little to retain. So, likewise, after the battle of Cannæ, when their affairs were at their worst, the Romans refused aid to many subject and protected States, charging them to defend themselves as best they could. And this is a better course than to undertake to defend and then to fail; for by refusing to defend, you lose only your friend; whereas in failing, you not only lose your friend, but weaken yourself.

But to return to the matter in hand, I affirm, that even when a captain is constrained by inexperience of his enemy to make trial of him by means of skirmishes, he ought first to see that he has so much the advantage that he runs no risk of defeat; or else, and this is his better course, he must do as Marius did when sent against the Cimbrians, a very courageous people who were laying Italy waste, and by their fierceness and numbers, and from the fact of their having already routed a Roman army, spreading terror wherever they came. For before fighting a decisive battle, Marius judged it necessary to do something to lessen the dread in which these enemies were held by his army; and being a prudent commander, he, on several occasions, posted his men at points where the Cimbrians must pass, that seeing and growing familiar with their appearance, while themselves in safety and within the shelter of their intrenched camp, and finding them to be a mere disorderly rabble, encumbered with baggage, and either without weapons, or with none that were formidable, they might at last assume courage and grow eager to engage them in battle. The part thus prudently taken by Marius, should be carefully imitated by others who would escape the dangers above spoken of and not have to betake themselves like the Gauls to a disgraceful flight, on sustaining some trifling defeat.

But since in this Discourse I have referred by name to Valerius Corvinus, in my next Chapter I shall cite his words to show what manner of man a captain ought to be.

Chapter XXXVIII.—*Of the Qualities of a Captain in whom his Soldiers can confide.*

Valerius Corvinus, as I have said already, was sent in command of an army against the Samnites, who were then new enemies to Rome. Wherefore, to reassure his soldiers and familiarize them with their adversaries, he made them engage with them in various unimportant passages of arms. But not thinking this enough, he resolved before delivering battle to address his men, and by reminding them of their valour and his own, to make it plain how little they should esteem such enemies. And from the words which Titus Livius puts in his mouth we may gather what manner of man the captain ought to be in whom an army will put its trust. For he makes him say:—"*Bear ye also this in mind under whose conduct and auspices you are about to fight, and whether he whom you are to obey be great only in exhorting, bold only in words, and all unpractised in arms; or whether he be one who himself knows how to use his spear, to march before the eagles, and play his part in the thickest of the fight. Soldiers! I would have you follow my deeds and not my words, and look to me for example rather than for commands; for with this right hand I have won for myself three consulships, and an unsurpassed renown.*" Which words rightly understood give every one to know what he must do to merit a captain's rank. And if any man obtain it by other means, he will soon discover that advancement due to chance or intrigue rather takes away than brings reputation, since it is men who give lustre to titles and not titles to men.

From what has been said it will likewise be understood that if great captains when matched against an unfamiliar foe have had to resort to unusual methods for reassuring the minds even of veteran soldiers, much more will it be necessary for them to use all their address when in command of a raw and untried army which has never before looked an enemy in the face. For if an unfamiliar adversary inspire terror even in a veteran army, how much greater must be the terror which any army will inspire in the minds of untrained men. And yet we often find all these difficulties overcome by the supreme prudence of a great captain like the Roman Gracchus or the Theban Epaminondas, of whom I have before spoken, who with untried troops defeated the most practised veterans. And the method they are said to have followed was to train their men for some months in mimic warfare, so as to accustom them to discipline and obedience, after which they employed them with complete confidence on actual service.

No man, therefore, of warlike genius, need despair of creating a good army if only he have the men; for the prince who has many subjects and yet lacks soldiers, has only to thank his own inertness and want of foresight, and must not complain of the cowardice of his people.

Chapter XXXIX.—*That a Captain should have good knowledge of Places.*

Among other qualifications essential in a good captain is a knowledge, both general and particular, of places and countries, for without such knowledge it is impossible for him to carry out any enterprise in the best way. And while practice is needed for perfection in every art, in this it is needed in the highest degree. Such practice, or particular knowledge as it may be termed, is sooner acquired in the chase than in any other exercise; and, accordingly, we find it said by ancient historians that those heroes who, in their day, ruled the world, were bred in the woods and trained to the chase; for this exercise not merely gives the knowledge I speak of, but teaches countless other lessons needful in war. And Xenophon in his life of Cyrus tells us, that Cyrus, on his expedition against the King of Armenia, when assigning to each of his followers the part he was to perform, reminded them that the enterprise on which they were engaged, differed little from one of those hunting expeditions on which they had gone so often in his company; likening those who were to lie in ambush in the mountains, to the men sent to spread the toils on the hill-tops; and those who were to overrun the plain, to the beaters whose business it is to start the game from its lair that it may be driven into the toils. Now, this is related to show how, in the opinion of Xenophon, the chase is a mimic representation of war, and therefore to be esteemed by the great as useful and honourable.

Nor can that knowledge of countries which I have spoken of as necessary in a commander, be obtained in any convenient way except by the chase. For he who joins therein gains a special acquaintance with the character of the country in which it is followed; and he who has made himself specially familiar with one district, will afterwards readily understand the character of any strange country into which he comes. For all countries, and the districts of which they are made up, have a certain resemblance to one another, so that from a knowledge of one we can pass easily to the knowledge of another. He therefore who is without such practical acquaintance with some one country, can only with difficulty, and after a long time, obtain a knowledge of another, while he who possesses it can take in at a glance how this plain spreads, how that mountain slopes, whither that valley winds, and all other like particulars in respect of which he has already acquired a certain familiarity.

The truth of what I affirm is shown by Titus Livius in the case of Publius Decius, who, being military tribune in the army which the consul Cornelius led against the Samnites, when the consul advanced into a defile where the Roman army were like to be shut in by the enemy, perceiving the great danger they ran, and noting, as Livius relates, a hill which rose by a steep ascent and overhung the enemy's camp, and which, though hard of access for heavy-armed troops, presented little difficulty to troops lightly armed, turned to the consul and said:—"*Seest thou, Aulus Cornelius, yonder height over above the enemy, which they have been blind enough to neglect? There, were we manfully to seize it, might we find the citadel of our hopes and of our safety.*" Whereupon, he was sent by the consul with three thousand men to secure the height, and so saved the Roman army. And as it was part of his plan to make his own escape and carry off his men safely under shelter of night, Livius represents him as saying to his soldiers:—"*Come with me, that, while daylight still serves, we may learn where the enemy have posted their guards, and by what exit we may issue hence.*" Accordingly, putting on the cloak of a common soldier, lest the enemy should observe that an officer was making his rounds he surveyed their camp in all directions.

Now any one who carefully studies the whole of this passage, must perceive how useful and necessary it is for a captain to know the nature of places, which knowledge had Decius not possessed he could not have decided that it would be for the advantage of the Roman army to occupy this hill; nor could he have judged from a distance whether the hill was accessible or no; and when he reached the summit and desired to return to the consul, since he was surrounded on all sides by the enemy, he never could have distinguished the path it was safe for him to take, from those guarded by the foe. For all which reasons it was absolutely essential that Decius should have that thorough knowledge which enabled him by gaining possession of this hill to save the Roman army, and to discover a path whereby, in the event of his being attacked, he and his followers might escape.

Chapter XL.—*That Fraud is fair in War*.

Although in all other affairs it be hateful to use fraud, in the operations of war it is praiseworthy and glorious; so that he who gets the better of his enemy by fraud, is as much extolled as he who prevails by force. This appears in the judgments passed by such as have written of the lives of great warriors, who praise Hannibal and those other captains who have been most noted for acting in this way. But since we may read of many instances of such frauds, I shall not cite them here. This, however, I desire to say, that I would not have it understood that any fraud is glorious which leads you to break your plighted word, or to depart from covenants to which you have agreed; for though to do so may sometimes gain you territory and power, it can never, as I have said elsewhere, gain you glory.

The fraud, then, which I here speak of is that employed against an enemy who places no trust in you, and is wholly directed to military operations, such as the stratagem of Hannibal at the Lake of Thrasymene, when he feigned flight in order to draw the Roman consul and his army into an ambuscade; or when to escape from the hands of Fabius Maximus he fastened lights to the horns of his oxen. Similar to the above was the deceit practised by Pontius the Samnite commander to inveigle the Roman army into the Caudine Forks. For after he had drawn up his forces behind the hills, he sent out a number of his soldiers, disguised as herdsmen, to drive great herds of cattle across the plain; who being captured by the Romans, and interrogated as to where the Samnite army was, all of them, as they had been taught by Pontius, agreed in saying that it had gone to besiege Nocera: which being believed by the consuls, led them to advance within the Caudine Valley, where no sooner were they come than they were beset by the Samnites. And the victory thus won by a fraud would have been most glorious for Pontius had he but taken the advice of his father Herennius, who urged that the Romans should either be set at liberty unconditionally, or all be put to death; but that a mean course "*which neither gains friends nor gets rid of foes*" should be avoided. And this was sound advice, for, as has already been shown, in affairs of moment a mean course is always hurtful.

Chapter XLI.—*That our Country is to be defended by Honour or by Dishonour; and in either way is well defended.*

The consuls together with the whole Roman army fell, as I have related, into the hands of the Samnites, who imposed on them the most ignominious terms, insisting that they should be stripped of their arms, and pass under the yoke before they were allowed to return to Rome. The consuls being astounded by the harshness of these conditions and the whole army overwhelmed with dismay, Lucius Lentulus, the Roman lieutenant, stood forward and said, that in his opinion they ought to decline no course whereby their country might be saved; and that as the very existence of Rome depended on the preservation of her army, that army must be saved at any sacrifice, for whether the means be honourable or ignominious, all is well done that is done for the defence of our country. And he said that were her army preserved, Rome, in course of time, might wipe out the disgrace; but if her army were destroyed, however gloriously it might perish, Rome and her freedom would perish with it. In the event his counsel was followed.

Now this incident deserves to be noted and pondered over by every citizen who is called on to advise his country; for when the entire safety of our country is at stake, no consideration of what is just or unjust, merciful or cruel, praiseworthy or shameful, must intervene. On the contrary, every other consideration being set aside, that course alone must be taken which preserves the existence of the country and maintains its liberty. And this course we find followed by the people of France, both in their words and in their actions, with the view of supporting the dignity of their king and the integrity of their kingdom; for there is no remark they listen to with more impatience than that this or the other course is disgraceful to the king. For their king, they say, can incur no disgrace by any resolve he may take, whether it turn out well or ill; and whether it succeed or fail, all maintain that he has acted as a king should.

Chapter XLII.—*That Promises made on Compulsion are not to be observed.*

When, after being subjected to this disgrace, the consuls returned to Rome with their disarmed legions, Spurius Posthumius, himself one of the consuls, was the first to contend in the senate that the terms made in the Caudine Valley were not to be observed. For he argued that the Roman people were not bound by them, though he himself doubtless was, together with all the others who had promised peace; wherefore, if the people desired to set themselves free from every engagement, he and all the rest who had given this promise must be made over as prisoners into the hands of the Samnites. And so steadfastly did he hold to this opinion, that the senate were content to adopt it, and sending him and the rest as prisoners back to Samnium, protested to the Samnites that the peace was not binding. And so kind was Fortune to Posthumius on this occasion, that the Samnites would not keep him as a prisoner, and that on his return to Rome, notwithstanding his defeat, he was held in higher honour by the Romans than the victorious Pontius by his countrymen.

Here two points are to be noted; first, that glory may be won by any action; for although, commonly, it follow upon victory, it may also follow on defeat, if this defeat be seen to have happened through no fault of yours, or if, directly after, you perform some valiant action which cancels it. The other point to be noted is that there is no disgrace in not observing promises wrung from you by force; for promises thus extorted when they affect the public welfare will always be broken so soon as the pressure under which they were made is withdrawn, and that, too, without shame on the part of him who breaks them; of which we read many instances in history, and find them constantly occurring at the present day. Nay, as between princes, not only are such compulsory promises broken when the force which extorted them is removed, but all other promises as well, are in like manner disregarded when the causes which led to them no longer operate.

Whether this is a thing to be commended or no, and whether such methods ought or ought not to be followed by princes, has already been considered by me in my "*Treatise of the Prince*" wherefore I say no more on that subject here.

Chapter XLIII.—*That Men born in the same Province retain through all Times nearly the same Character.*

The wise are wont to say, and not without reason or at random, that he who would forecast what is about to happen should look to what has been; since all human events, whether present or to come, have their exact counterpart in the past. And this, because these events are brought about by men, whose passions and dispositions remaining in all ages the same naturally give rise to the same effects; although, doubtless, the operation of these causes takes a higher form, now in one province, and now in another, according to the character of the training wherein the inhabitants of these provinces acquire their way of life.

Another aid towards judging of the future by the past, is to observe how the same nation long retains the same customs, remaining constantly covetous or deceitful, or similarly stamped by some one vice or virtue. Any one reading the past history of our city of Florence, and noting what has recently befallen it, will find the French and German nations overflowing with avarice, pride, cruelty, and perfidy, all of which four vices have at divers times wrought much harm to our city. As an instance of their perfidy, every one knows how often payments of money were made to Charles VIII. of France, in return for which he engaged to restore the fortresses of Pisa, yet never did restore them, manifesting thereby his bad faith and grasping avarice. Or, to pass from these very recent events, all may have heard of what happened in the war in which the Florentines were involved with the Visconti, dukes of Milan, when Florence, being left without other resource, resolved to invite the emperor into Italy, that she might be assisted by his name and power in her struggle with Lombardy. The emperor promised to come with a strong army to take part against the Visconti and to protect Florence from them, on condition that the Florentines paid him a hundred thousand ducats on his setting out, and another hundred thousand on his arrival in Italy; to which terms the Florentines agreed. But although he then received payment of the first instalment and, afterwards, on reaching Verona, of the second, he turned back from the expedition without effecting anything, alleging as his excuse that he was stopped by certain persons who had failed to fulfil their engagements. But if Florence had not been urged by passion or overcome by necessity, or had she read of and understood the ancient usages of the barbarians, she would neither on this, nor on many other occasions, have been deceived by them, seeing that these nations have always been of the same character, and have always, in all circumstances, and with all men alike, used the same methods. For in ancient times we find them behaving after the same fashion to the Etruscans, who, when overpowered by the Romans, by whom they had been repeatedly routed and put to flight, perceiving that they could not stand without help, entered into a compact with the Gauls dwelling in the parts of Italy south of the Alps, to pay them a certain sum if they would unite with them in a campaign against the Romans. But the Gauls, after taking their money, refused to arm on their behalf, alleging that they had not been paid to make war on the enemies of the Etruscans, but only to refrain from pillaging their lands. And thus the people of Etruria, through the avarice and perfidy of the Gauls, were at once defrauded of their money and disappointed of the help which they had counted on obtaining.

From which two instances of the Etruscans in ancient times and of the Florentines in recent, we may see that barbaric races have constantly followed the same methods, and may easily draw our conclusions as to how far princes should trust them.

Chapter XLIV.—*That where ordinary methods fail, Hardihood and Daring often succeed.*

When attacked by the Romans, the Samnites as they could not without help stand against them in the field, resolved to leave garrisons in the towns of Samnium, and to pass with their main army into Etruria, that country being then at truce with Rome, and thus ascertain whether their actual presence in arms might not move the Etruscans to renew hostilities against Rome, which they had refused to renew when invited through envoys. During the negotiations which, on this occasion, passed between the two nations, the Samnites in explaining the chief causes that led them to take up arms, used the memorable words—"*they had risen because peace is a heavier burthen for slaves than war for freemen*" In the end, partly by their persuasions, and partly by the presence of their army, they induced the Etruscans to join forces with them.

Here we are to note that when a prince would obtain something from another, he ought, if the occasion allow, to leave him no time to deliberate, but should so contrive that the other may see the need of resolving at once; as he will, if he perceive that refusal or delay in complying with what is asked of him, will draw upon him a sudden and dangerous resentment.

This method we have seen employed with good effect in our own times by Pope Julius II. in dealing with France, and by M. de Foix, the general of the French king, in dealing with the Marquis of Mantua. For Pope Julius desiring to expel the Bentivogli from Bologna, and thinking that for this purpose he needed the help of French troops, and to have the Venetians neutral, after sounding both and receiving from both hesitating and ambiguous answers, determined to make both fall in with his views, by giving them no time to oppose him; and so, setting forth from Rome with as strong a force as he could get together, he marched on Bologna, sending word to the Venetians that they must stand aloof, and to the King of France to send him troops. The result was that in the brief time allowed them, neither of the two powers could make up their mind to thwart him; and knowing that refusal or delay would be violently resented by the Pope, they yielded to his demands, the king sending him soldiers and the Venetians maintaining neutrality.

M. de Foix, again, being with the king's army in Bologna when word came that Brescia had risen, could not rest till he had recovered that town. But, to get there he had to choose between two routes, one long and circuitous leading through the territories of the king, the other short and direct. In taking the latter route, however, not only would he have to pass through the dominions of the Marquis of Mantua, but also to make his way into these through the lakes and marshes wherewith that country abounds, by following an embanked road, closed and guarded by the marquis with forts and other defensive works. Resolving, nevertheless, to take the shortest road at all hazards, he waited till his men were already on their march before signifying to the marquis that he desired leave to pass through his country, so that no time might be left him to deliberate. Taken aback by the unexpected demand, the marquis gave the leave sought, which he never would have given had De Foix acted with less impetuosity. For he was in league with the Venetians and with the Pope, and had a son in the hands of the latter; all which circumstances would have afforded him fair pretexts for refusal. But carried away by the suddenness and urgency of the demand, he yielded. And in like manner the Etruscans yielded to the instances of the Samnites, the presence of whose army decided them to renew hostilities which before they had declined to renew.

Chapter XLV.—*Whether in battle it is better to await and repel the Enemy's attack, or to anticipate it by an impetuous onset.*

Decius and Fabius, the Roman consuls, were each of them in command of a separate army, one directed against the Samnites, the other against the Etruscans: and as both delivered battle, we have to pronounce, in respect of the two engagements, which commander followed the better method. Decius attacked his enemy at once with the utmost fury and with his whole strength. Fabius was content, at first, merely to maintain his ground; for judging that more was to be gained by a later attack, he reserved his forces for a final effort, when the ardour of the enemy had cooled and his energy spent itself. The event showed Fabius to be more successful in his tactics than Decius, who being exhausted by his first onset, and seeing his ranks begin to waver, to secure by death the glory he could no longer hope from victory, followed the example set him by his father, and sacrificed himself to save the Roman legions. Word whereof being brought to Fabius, he, to gain, while he yet lived, as much honour as the other had earned by his death, pushed forward all the troops he had reserved for his final effort, and so obtained an unexampled victory. Whence we see that of the two methods, that of Fabius was the safer and the more deserving our imitation.

Chapter XLVI.—*How the Characteristics of Families come to be perpetuated.*

Manners and institutions differing in different cities, seem here to produce a harder and there a softer race; and a like difference may also be discerned in the character of different families in the same city. And while this holds good of all cities, we have many instances of it in reading the history of Rome. For we find the Manlii always stern and stubborn; the Valerii kindly and courteous; the Claudii haughty and ambitious; and many families besides similarly distinguished from one another by their peculiar qualities.

These qualities we cannot refer wholly to the *blood*, for that must change as a result of repeated intermarriages, but must ascribe rather to the different training and education given in different families. For much turns on whether a child of tender years hears a thing well or ill spoken of, since this must needs make an impression on him whereby his whole conduct in after life will be influenced. Were it otherwise we should not have found the whole family of the Claudii moved by the desires and stirred by the passions which Titus Livius notes in many of them, and more especially in one holding the office of censor, who, when his colleague laid down his magistracy, as the law prescribed, at the end of eighteen months, would not resign, maintaining that he was entitled to hold the office for five years in accordance with the original law by which the censorship was regulated. And although his refusal gave occasion to much controversy, and bred great tumult and disturbance, no means could be found to depose him from his office, which he persisted in retaining in opposition to the will of the entire commons and a majority of the senate. And any who shall read the speech made against him by Publius Sempronius, tribune of the people, will find therein all the Claudian insolence exposed, and will recognize the docility and good temper shown by the body of the citizens in respecting the laws and institutions of their country.

Chapter XLVII.—*That love of his Country should lead a good Citizen to forget private Wrongs.*

While commanding as consul against the Samnites, Manlius was wounded in a skirmish. His army being thereby endangered, the senate judged it expedient to send Papirius Cursor as dictator to supply his place. But as it was necessary that the dictator should be nominated by Fabius, the other consul, who was with the army in Etruria, and as a doubt was felt that he might refuse to nominate Papirius, who was his enemy, the senate sent two messengers to entreat him to lay aside private animosity, and make the nomination which the public interest required. Moved by love of his country Fabius did as he was asked, although by his silence, and by many other signs, he gave it to be known that compliance was distasteful. From his conduct at this juncture all who would be thought good citizens should take example.

Chapter XLVIII.—*That on finding an Enemy make what seems a grave blunder, we should suspect some fraud to lurk behind.*

The consul having gone to Rome to perform certain ceremonial rites, and Fulvius being left in charge of the Roman army in Etruria, the Etruscans, to see whether they could not circumvent the new commander, planting an ambush not far from the Roman camp, sent forward soldiers disguised as shepherds driving large flocks of sheep so as to pass in sight of the Roman army. These pretended shepherds coming close to the wall of his camp, Fulvius, marvelling at what appeared to him unaccountable audacity, hit upon a device whereby the artifice of the Etruscans was detected and their design defeated.

Here it seems proper to note that the captain of an army ought not to build on what seems a manifest blunder on the part of an enemy; for as men are unlikely to act with conspicuous want of caution, it will commonly be found that this blunder is cover to a fraud. And yet, so blinded are men's minds by their eagerness for victory, that they look only to what appears on the surface.

After defeating the Romans on the Allia, the Gauls, hastening on to Rome, found the gates of the city left open and unguarded. But fearing some stratagem, and being unable to believe that the Romans could be so foolish and cowardly as to abandon their city, they waited during the whole of that day and the following night outside the gates, without daring to enter. In the year 1508, when the Florentines Avere engaged in besieging Pisa, Alfonso del Mutolo, a citizen of that town, happening to be taken prisoner, was released on his promise to procure the surrender to the Florentines of one of the gates of the city. Afterwards, on pretence of arranging for the execution of this surrender, he came repeatedly to confer with those whom the Florentine commissaries had deputed to treat with him, coming not secretly but openly, and accompanied by other citizens of Pisa, whom he caused to stand aside while he conversed with the Florentines. From all which circumstances his duplicity might have been suspected, since, had he meant to do as he had engaged, it was most unlikely that he should be negotiating so openly. But the desire to recover possession of Pisa so blinded the Florentines that they allowed themselves to be conducted under his guidance to the Lucca Gate, where, through his treachery, but to their own disgrace, they lost a large number of their men and officers.

Chapter XLIX.—*That a Commonwealth to preserve its Freedom has constant need of new Ordinances. Of the services in respect of which Quintius Fabius received the surname of Maximus.*

It must happen, as I have already said, in every great city, that disorders needing the care of the physician continually spring up; and the graver these disorders are, the greater will be the skill needed for their treatment. And if ever in any city, most assuredly in Rome, we see these disorders assume strange and unexpected shapes. As when it appeared that all the Roman wives had conspired to murder their husbands, many of them being found to have actually administered poison, and many others to have drugs in readiness for the purpose.

Of like nature was the conspiracy of the Bacchanals, discovered at the time of the Macedonian war, wherein many thousands, both men and women, were implicated, and which, had it not been found out, or had the Romans not been accustomed to deal with large bodies of offenders, must have proved perilous for their city. And, indeed, if the greatness of the Roman Republic were not declared by countless other signs, as well as by the manner in which it caused its laws to be observed, it might be seen in the character of the punishments which it inflicted against wrong-doers. For in vindicating justice, it would not scruple or hesitate to put a whole legion to death, to depopulate an entire city, or send eight or ten thousand men at a time into banishment, subject to the most stringent conditions, which had to be observed, not by one of these exiles only, but by all. As in the case of those soldiers who fought unsuccessfully at Cannæ, who were banished to Sicily, subject to the condition that they should not harbour in towns, and should all eat standing.

But the most formidable of all their punishments was that whereby one man out of every ten in an entire army was chosen by lot to be put to death. For correcting a great body of men no more effectual means could be devised; because, when a multitude have offended and the ringleaders are not known, all cannot be punished, their number being too great; while to punish some only, and leave the rest unpunished, were unjust to those punished and an encouragement to those passed over to offend again. But where you put to death a tenth chosen by lot, where all equally deserve death, he who is punished will blame his unlucky fortune, while he who escapes will be afraid that another time the lot may be his, and for that reason will be careful how he repeats his offence. The poisoners and the Bacchanals, therefore, were punished as their crimes deserved.

Although disorders like these occasion mischievous results in a commonwealth, still they are not fatal, since almost always there is time to correct them. But no time is given in the case of disorders in the State itself, which unless they be treated by some wise citizen, will always bring a city to destruction. From the readiness wherewith the Romans conferred the right of citizenship on foreigners, there came to be so many new citizens in Rome, and possessed of so large a share of the suffrage, that the government itself began to alter, forsaking those courses which it was accustomed to follow, and growing estranged from the men to whom it had before looked for guidance. Which being observed by Quintius Fabius when censor, he caused all those new citizens to be classed in four *Tribes*, that being reduced within this narrow limit they might not have it in their power to corrupt the entire State. And this was a wisely contrived measure, for, without introducing any violent change, it supplied a convenient remedy, and one so acceptable to the republic as to gain for Fabius the well-deserved name of Maximus.

The History of Florence

Book I: Chapter I

Irruption of Northern people upon the Roman territories—Visigoths—Barbarians called in by Stilicho—Vandals in Africa—Franks and Burgundians give their names to France and Burgundy—The Huns—Angles give the name to England—Attila, king of the Huns, in Italy—Genseric takes Rome—The Lombards.

The people who inhabit the northern parts beyond the Rhine and the Danube, living in a healthy and prolific region, frequently increase to such vast multitudes that part of them are compelled to abandon their native soil, and seek a habitation in other countries. The method adopted, when one of these provinces had to be relieved of its superabundant population, was to divide into three parts, each containing an equal number of nobles and of people, of rich and of poor. The third upon whom the lot fell, then went in search of new abodes, leaving the remaining two-thirds in possession of their native country.

These migrating masses destroyed the Roman empire by the facilities for settlement which the country offered when the emperors abandoned Rome, the ancient seat of their dominion, and fixed their residence at Constantinople; for by this step they exposed the western empire to the rapine of both their ministers and their enemies, the remoteness of their position preventing them either from seeing or providing for its necessities. To suffer the overthrow of such an extensive empire, established by the blood of so many brave and virtuous men, showed no less folly in the princes themselves than infidelity in their ministers; for not one irruption alone, but many, contributed to its ruin; and these barbarians exhibited much ability and perseverance in accomplishing their object.

The first of these northern nations that invaded the empire after the Cimbrians, who were conquered by Caius Marius, was the Visigoths—which name in our language signifies "Western Goths." These, after some battles fought along its confines, long held their seat of dominion upon the Danube, with consent of the emperors; and although, moved by various causes, they often attacked the Roman provinces, were always kept in subjection by the imperial forces. The emperor Theodosius conquered them with great glory; and, being wholly reduced to his power, they no longer selected a sovereign of their own, but, satisfied with the terms which he granted them, lived and fought under his ensigns, and authority. On the death of Theodosius, his sons Arcadius and Honorius, succeeded to the empire, but not to the talents and fortune of their father; and the times became changed with the princes. Theodosius had appointed a governor to each of the three divisions of the empire, Ruffinus to the eastern, to the western Stilicho, and Gildo to the African. Each of these, after the death of Theodosius, determined not to be governors merely, but to assume sovereign dominion over their respective provinces. Gildo and Ruffinus were suppressed at their outset; but Stilicho, concealing his design, ingratiated himself with the new emperors, and at the same time so disturbed their government, as to facilitate his occupation of it afterward. To make the Visigoths their enemies, he advised that the accustomed stipend allowed to this people should be withheld; and as he thought these enemies would not be sufficient alone to disturb the empire, he contrived that the Burgundians, Franks, Vandals, and Alans (a northern people in search of new habitations), should assail the Roman provinces.

That they might be better able to avenge themselves for the injury they had sustained, the Visigoths, on being deprived of their subsidy, created Alaric their king; and having assailed the empire, succeeded, after many reverses, in overrunning Italy, and finally in pillaging Rome.

After this victory, Alaric died, and his successor, Astolphus, having married Placidia, sister of the emperors, agreed with them to go to the relief of Gaul and Spain, which provinces had been assailed by the Vandals, Burgundians, Alans, and Franks, from the causes before mentioned. Hence it followed, that the Vandals, who had occupied that part of Spain called Betica (now Andalusia), being pressed by the Visigoths, and unable to resist them, were invited by Boniface, who governed Africa for the empire, to occupy that province; for, being in rebellion, he was afraid his error would become known to the emperor. For these reasons the Vandals gladly undertook the enterprise, and under Genseric, their king, became lords of Africa.

At this time Theodosius, son of Arcadius, succeeded to the empire; and, bestowing little attention on the affairs of the west, caused those who had taken possession to think of securing their acquisitions. Thus the Vandals ruled Africa; the Alans and Visigoths, Spain; while the Franks and Burgundians not only took Gaul, but each gave their name to the part they occupied; hence one is called France, the other Burgundy. The good fortune of these brought fresh people to the destruction of the empire, one of which, the Huns, occupied the province of Pannonia, situated upon the nearer shore of the Danube, and which, from their name, is still called Hungary. To these disorders it must be added, that the emperor, seeing himself attacked on so many sides, to lessen the number of his enemies, began to treat first with the Vandals, then with the Franks; a course which diminished his own power, and increased that of the barbarians. Nor was the island of Britain, which is now called England, secure from them;

for the Britons, being apprehensive of those who had occupied Gaul, called the Angli, a people of Germany, to their aid; and these under Vortigern their king, first defended, and then drove them from the island, of which they took possession, and after themselves named the country England. But the inhabitants, being robbed of their home, became desperate by necessity and resolved to take possession of some other country, although they had been unable to defend their own. They therefore crossed the sea with their families, and settled in the country nearest to the beach, which from themselves is called Brittany. The Huns, who were said above to have occupied Pannonia, joining with other nations, as the Zepidi, Eurili, Turingi, and Ostro, or eastern Goths, moved in search of new countries, and not being able to enter France, which was defended by the forces of the barbarians, came into Italy under Attila their king. He, a short time previously, in order to possess the entire monarchy, had murdered his brother Bleda; and having thus become very powerful, Andaric, king of the Zepidi, and Velamir, king of the Ostrogoths, became subject to him. Attila, having entered Italy, laid siege to Aquileia, where he remained without any obstacle for two years, wasting the country round, and dispersing the inhabitants. This, as will be related in its place, caused the origin of Venice. After the taking and ruin of Aquileia, he directed his course towards Rome, from the destruction of which he abstained at the entreaty of the pontiff, his respect for whom was so great that he left Italy and retired into Austria, where he died. After the death of Attila, Velamir, king of the Ostrogoths, and the heads of the other nations, took arms against his sons Henry and Uric, slew the one and compelled the other, with his Huns, to repass the Danube and return to their country; while the Ostrogoths and the Zepidi established themselves in Pannonia, and the Eruli and the Turingi upon the farther bank of the Danube.

Attila having left Italy, Valentinian, emperor of the west, thought of restoring the country; and, that he might be more ready to defend it against the barbarians, abandoned Rome, and removed the seat of government to Ravenna. The misfortunes which befell the western empire caused the emperor, who resided at Constantinople, on many occasions to give up the possession of it to others, as a charge full of danger and expense; and sometimes, without his permission, the Romans, seeing themselves so abandoned, created an emperor for their defense, or suffered some one to usurp the dominion. This occurred at the period of which we now speak, when Maximus, a Roman, after the death of Valentinian, seized the government, and compelled Eudocia, widow of the late emperor, to take him for her husband; but she, being of imperial blood, scorned the connection of a private citizen; and being anxious to avenge herself for the insult, secretly persuaded Genseric, king of the Vandals and master of Africa to come to Italy, representing to him the advantage he would derive from the undertaking, and the facility with which it might be accomplished. Tempted by the hope of booty, he came immediately, and finding Rome abandoned, plundered the city during fourteen days. He also ravaged many other places in Italy, and then, loaded with wealth, withdrew to Africa. The Romans, having returned to their city, and Maximus being dead, elected Avitus, a Roman, as his successor. After this, several important events occurred both in Italy and in the countries beyond; and after the deaths of many emperors the empire of Constantinople devolved upon Zeno, and that of Rome upon Orestes and Augustulus his son, who obtained the sovereignty by fraud. While they were designing to hold by force what they had obtained by treachery, the Eruli and the Turingi, who, after the death of Attila, as before remarked, had established themselves upon the farther bank of the Danube, united in a league and invaded Italy under Odoacer their general. Into the districts which they left unoccupied, the Longobardi or Lombards, also a northern people, entered, led by Godogo their king. Odoacer conquered and slew Orestes near Pavia, but Augustulus escaped. After this victory, that Rome might, with her change of power, also change her title, Odoacer, instead of using the imperial name, caused himself to be declared king of Rome. He was the first of those leaders who at this period overran the world and thought of settling in Italy; for the others, either from fear that they should not be able to hold the country, knowing that it might easily be relieved by the eastern emperors, or from some unknown cause, after plundering her, sought other countries wherein to establish themselves.

Chapter II: State of the Roman empire under Zeno—Theodoric king of the Ostrogoths—Character of Theodoric—Changes in the Roman empire—New languages—New names—Theodoric dies—Belisarius in Italy—Totila takes Rome—Narses destroys the Goths—New form of Government in Italy—Narses invites the Lombards into Italy—The Lombards change the form of government

At this time the ancient Roman empire was governed by the following princes: Zeno, reigning in Constantinople, commanded the whole of the eastern empire; the Ostrogoths ruled Mesia and Pannonia; the Visigoths, Suavi, and Alans, held Gascony and Spain; the Vandals, Africa; the Franks and Burgundians, France; and the Eruli and Turingi, Italy. The kingdom of the Ostrogoths had descended to Theodoric, nephew of Velamir, who, being on terms of friendship with Zeno the eastern emperor, wrote to him that his Ostrogoths thought it an injustice that they, being superior in valor to the people thereabout, should be inferior to them in dominion, and that it was impossible for him to restrain them within the limits of Pannonia. So, seeing himself under the necessity of allowing them to take arms and go in search of new abodes, he wished first to acquaint Zeno with it, in order that he might provide for them, by granting some country in which they might establish themselves, by his good favor with greater propriety and convenience. Zeno, partly from fear and partly from a desire to drive Odoacer out of Italy, gave Theodoric permission to lead his people against him, and take possession of the country. Leaving his friends the Zepidi in Pannonia, Theodoric marched into Italy, slew Odoacer and his son, and, moved by the same reasons which had induced Valentinian to do so, established his court at Ravenna, and like Odoacer took the title of king of Italy.

Theodoric possessed great talents both for war and peace; in the former he was always conqueror, and in the latter he conferred very great benefits upon the cities and people under him. He distributed the Ostrogoths over the country, each district under its leader, that he might more conveniently command them in war, and govern them in peace. He enlarged Ravenna, restored Rome, and, with the exception of military discipline, conferred upon the Romans every honor. He kept within their proper bounds, wholly by the influence of his character, all the barbarian kings who occupied the empire; he built towns and fortresses between the point of the Adriatic and the Alps, in order, with the greater facility, to impede the passage of any new hordes of barbarians who might design to assail Italy; and if, toward the latter end of his life, so many virtues had not been sullied by acts of cruelty, caused by various jealousies of his people, such as the death of Symmachus and Boethius, men of great holiness, every point of his character would have deserved the highest praise. By his virtue and goodness, not only Rome and Italy, but every part of the western empire, freed from the continual troubles which they had suffered from the frequent influx of barbarians, acquired new vigor, and began to live in an orderly and civilized manner. For surely if any times were truly miserable for Italy and the provinces overrun by the barbarians, they were those which occurred from Arcadius and Honorius to Theodoric. If we only consider the evils which arise to a republic or a kingdom by a change of prince or of government; not by foreign interference, but by civil discord (in which we may see how even slight variations suffice to ruin the most powerful kingdoms or states), we may then easily imagine how much Italy and the other Roman provinces suffered, when they not only changed their forms of government and their princes, but also their laws, customs, modes of living, religion, language, and name. Any one of such changes, by itself, without being united with others, might, with thinking of it, to say nothing of the seeing and suffering, infuse terror into the strongest minds.

From these causes proceeded the ruin as well as the origin and extension of many cities. Among those which were ruined were Aquileia, Luni, Chiusi, Popolonia, Fiesole, and many others. The new cities were Venice, Sienna, Ferrara, Aquila, with many towns and castles which for brevity we omit. Those which became extended were Florence, Genoa, Pisa, Milan, Naples, and Bologna; to all of which may be added, the ruin and restoration of Rome, and of many other cities not previously mentioned.

From this devastation and new population arose new languages, as we see in the different dialects of France, Spain and Italy; which, partaking of the native idiom of the new people and of the old Roman, formed a new manner of discourse. Besides, not only were the names of provinces changed, but also of lakes, rivers, seas, and men; for France, Spain, and Italy are full of fresh names, wholly different from the ancient; as, omitting many others, we see that the Po, the Garda, the Archipelago, are names quite different from those which the ancients used; while instead of Caesar and Pompey we have Peter, Matthew, John, etc.

Among so many variations, that of religion was not of little importance; for, while combating the customs of the ancient faith with the miracles of the new, very serious troubles and discords were created among men. And if the Christians had been united in one faith, fewer disorders would have followed; but the contentions among themselves, of the churches of Rome, Greece, and Ravenna, joined to those of the heretic sects with the Catholics, served in many ways to render the world miserable. Africa is a proof of this; having suffered more horrors from the Arian sect, whose doctrines were believed by the Vandals, than from any avarice or natural cruelty of the people themselves. Living amid so many persecutions, the countenances of men bore witness of the terrible impressions upon their minds; for besides the evils they suffered from the disordered state of the world, they scarcely could have recourse to the help of God, in whom the unhappy hope for relief; for the greater part of them, being uncertain what divinity they ought to address, died miserably, without help and without hope.

Having been the first who put a stop to so many evils, Theodoric deserves the highest praise: for during the thirty-eight years he reigned in Italy, he brought the country to such a state of greatness that her previous sufferings were no longer recognizable. But at his death, the kingdom descending to Atalaric, son of Amalasontha, his daughter, and the malice of fortune not being yet exhausted, the old evils soon returned; for Atalaric died soon after his grandfather, and the kingdom coming into the possession of his mother, she was betrayed by Theodatus, whom she had called to assist her in the government. He put her to death and made himself king; and having thus become odious to the Ostrogoths, the emperor Justinian entertained the hope of driving him out of Italy. Justinian appointed Belisarius to the command of this expedition, as he had already conquered Africa, expelled the Vandals, and reduced the country to the imperial rule.

Belisarius took possession of Sicily, and from thence passing into Italy, occupied Naples and Rome. The Goths, seeing this, slew Theodatus their king, whom they considered the cause of their misfortune, and elected Vitiges in his stead, who, after some skirmishes, was besieged and taken by Belisarius at Ravenna; but before he had time to secure the advantages of his victory, Belisarius was recalled by Justinian, and Joannes and Vitalis were appointed in his place. Their principles and practices were so different from those of Belisarius, that the Goths took courage and created Ildovadus, governor of Verona, their king. After Ildovadus, who was slain, came Totila, who routed the imperial forces, took Tuscany and Naples, and recovered nearly the whole of what Belisarius had taken from them. On this account Justinian determined to send him into Italy again; but, coming with only a small force, he lost the reputation which his former victories had won for him, in less time than he had taken to acquire it. Totila being at Ostia with his forces, took Rome before his eyes; but being unable to hold or to leave the city, he destroyed the greater part of it, drove out the citizens, and took the senators away from him. Thinking little of Belisarius, he led his people into Calabria, to attack the forces which had been sent from Greece.

Belisarius, seeing the city abandoned, turned his mind to the performance of an honourable work. Viewing the ruins of Rome, he determined to rebuild her walls and recall her inhabitants with as little delay as possible. But fortune was opposed to this laudable enterprise; for Justinian, being at this time assailed by the Parthians, recalled him; and his duty to his sovereign compelled him to abandon Italy to Totila, who again took Rome, but did not treat her with such severity as upon the former occasion; for at the entreaty of St. Benedict, who in those days had great reputation for sanctity, he endeavored to restore her. In the meantime, Justinian having arranged matters with the Parthians, again thought of sending a force to the relief of Italy; but the Sclavi, another northern people, having crossed the Danube and attacked Illyria and Thrace, prevented him, so that Totila held almost the whole country. Having conquered the Slavonians, Justinian sent Narses, a eunuch, a man of great military talent, who, having arrived in Italy, routed and slew Totila. The Goths who escaped sought refuge in Pavia, where they created Teias their king. On the other hand, Narses after the victory took Rome, and coming to an engagement with Teias near Nocera, slew him and routed his army. By this victory, the power of the Goths in Italy was quite annihilated, after having existed for seventy years, from the coming of Theodoric to the death of Teias.

No sooner was Italy delivered from the Goths than Justinian died, and was succeeded by Justin, his son, who, at the instigation of Sophia, his wife, recalled Narses, and sent Longinus in his stead. Like those who preceded him, he made his abode at Ravenna, and besides this, gave a new form to the government of Italy; for he did not appoint governors of provinces, as the Goths had done, but in every city and town of importance placed a ruler whom he called a duke. Neither in this arrangement did he respect Rome more than the other cities; for having set aside the consuls and senate, names which up to this time had been preserved, he placed her under a duke, who was sent every year from Ravenna, and called her the duchy of Rome; while to him who remained in Ravenna, and governed the whole of Italy for the emperor, was given the name of Exarch. This division of the country greatly facilitated the ruin of Italy, and gave the Lombards an early occasion of occupying it. Narses was greatly enraged with the emperor, for having recalled him from the government of the province, which he had won with his own valor and blood; while Sophia, not content with the injury done by withdrawing him, treated him in the most offensive manner, saying she wished him to come back that he might spin with the other eunuchs. Full of indignation, Narses persuaded Alboin, king of the Lombards, who then reigned in Pannonia, to invade and take possession of Italy.

The Lombards, as was said before, occupied those places upon the Danube which had been vacated by the Eruli and Turingi, when Odoacer their king led them into Italy; where, having been established for some time, their dominions were held by Alboin, a man ferocious and bold, under whom they crossed the Danube, and coming to an engagement with Cunimund, king of the Zepidi, who held Pannonia, conquered and slew him. Alboin finding Rosamond, daughter of Cunimund, among the captives, took her to wife, and made himself sovereign of Pannonia;

and, moved by his savage nature, caused the skull of Cunimund to be formed into a cup, from which, in memory of the victory, he drank. Being invited into Italy by Narses, with whom he had been in friendship during the war with the Goths, he left Pannonia to the Huns, who after the death of Attila had returned to their country. Finding, on his arrival, the province divided into so many parts, he presently occupied Pavia, Milan, Verona, Vicenza, the whole of Tuscany, and the greater part of Flamminia, which is now called Romagna. These great and rapid acquisitions made him think the conquest of Italy already secured; he therefore gave a great feast at Verona, and having become elevated with wine, ordered the skull of Cunimund to be filled, and caused it to be presented to the queen Rosamond, who sat opposite, saying loud enough for her to hear, that upon occasion of such great joy she should drink with her father. These words were like a dagger to the lady's bosom and she resolved to have revenge. Knowing that Helmichis, a noble Lombard, was in love with one of her maids, she arranged with the young woman, that Helmichis, without being acquainted with the fact, should sleep with her instead of his mistress. Having effected her design, Rosamond discovered herself to Helmichis, and gave him the choice either of killing Alboin, and taking herself and the kingdom as his reward, or of being put to death as the ravisher of the queen. Helmichis consented to destroy Alboin; but after the murder, finding they could not occupy the kingdom, and fearful that the Lombards would put them to death for the love they bore to Alboin, they seized the royal treasure, and fled with it to Longinus, at Ravenna, who received them favorably.

During these troubles the emperor Justinus died, and was succeeded by Tiberius, who, occupied in the wars with the Parthians, could not attend to the affairs of Italy; and this seeming to Longinus to present an opportunity, by means of Rosamond and her wealth, of becoming king of the Lombards and of the whole of Italy, he communicated his design to her, persuaded her to destroy Helmichis, and so take him for her husband. To this end, having prepared poisoned wine, she with her own hand presented it to Helmichis, who complained of thirst as he came from the bath. Having drunk half of it, he suspected the truth, from the unusual sensation it occasioned and compelled her to drink the remainder; so that in a few hours both came to their end, and Longinus was deprived of the hope of becoming king.

In the meantime the Lombards, having drawn themselves together in Pavia, which was become the principal seat of their empire, made Clefis their king. He rebuilt Imola, destroyed by Narses, and occupied Remini and almost every place up to Rome; but he died in the course of his victories. Clefis was cruel to such a degree, not only toward strangers, but to his own Lombards, that these people, sickened of royal power, did not create another king, but appointed among themselves thirty dukes to govern the rest. This prevented the Lombards from occupying the whole of Italy, or of extending their dominion further than Benevento; for, of the cities of Rome, Ravenna, Cremona, Mantua, Padua, Monselice, Parma, Bologna, Faenza, Forli, and Cesena, some defended themselves for a time, and others never fell under their dominion; since, not having a king, they became less prompt for war, and when they afterward appointed one, they were, by living in freedom, become less obedient, and more apt to quarrel among themselves; which from the first prevented a fortunate issue of their military expeditions, and was the ultimate cause of their being driven out of Italy. The affairs of the Lombards being in the state just described, the Romans and Longinus came to an agreement with them, that each should lay down their arms and enjoy what they already possessed.

Chapter III: Beginning of the greatness of the pontiffs in Italy—Abuse of censures and indulgences—The pope applies to Pepin, king of France, for assistance—Donation of Pepin to the pontiff—Charlemagne—End of the kingdom of the Lombards—The title of cardinal begins to be used—The empire passes to the Germans—Berengarius, duke of Fruili, created king of Italy—Pisa becomes great—Order and division of the states of Italy—Electors of the emperor created.

In these times the popes began to acquire greater temporal authority than they had previously possessed; although the immediate successors of St. Peter were more reverenced for the holiness of their lives, and the miracles which they performed; and their example so greatly extended the Christian religion, that princes of other states embraced it, in order to obviate the confusion which prevailed at that period. The emperor having become a Christian and returned to Constantinople, it followed, as was remarked at the commencement of the book, that the Roman empire was the more easily ruined, and the church more rapidly increased her authority. Nevertheless, the whole of Italy, being subject either to the emperors or the kings till the coming of the Lombards, the popes never acquired any greater authority than what reverence for their habits and doctrine gave them. In other respects they obeyed the emperors or kings; officiated for them in their affairs, as ministers or agents, and were even sometimes put to death by them. He who caused them to become of more importance in the affairs of Italy, was Theodoric, king of the Goths, when he established the seat of his empire at Ravenna; for, Rome being without a prince, the Romans found it necessary, for their safety, to yield obedience to the pope; his authority, however, was not greatly increased thereby, the only advantage being, that the church of Rome was allowed to take precedence of that of Ravenna. But the Lombards having taken possession, and Italy being divided into many parts, the pope had an opportunity of greater exertion. Being as it were the head of Rome, both the emperor of Constantinople and the Lombards respected him; so that the Romans, by his means, entered into league with the Lombards, and with Longinus, not as subjects, but as equals. Thus the popes, at one time friends of the Greeks, and at another of the Lombards, increased their own power; but upon the ruin of the eastern empire, which occurred during the time of Heraclius, their influence was reduced; for the Sclavi, of whom we spoke before, again assailed Illyria, and having occupied the country, named it Sclavonia, after themselves; and the other parts were attacked by the Persians, then by the Saracens under Mohammed, and lastly by the Turks, who took Syria, Africa, and Egypt. These causes induced the reigning pope, in his distress, to seek new friends, and he applied to the king of France. Nearly all the wars which the northern barbarians carried on in Italy, it may be here remarked, were occasioned by the pontiffs; and the hordes, with which the country was inundated, were generally called in by them. The same mode of proceeding still continued, and kept Italy weak and unsettled. And, therefore, in relating the events which have taken place from those times to the present, the ruin of the empire will be no longer illustrated, but only the increase of the pontificate and of the other principalities which ruled Italy till the coming of Charles VIII. It will be seen how the popes, first with censures, and afterward with these and arms, mingled with indulgences, became both terrible and venerable; and how, from having abused both, they ceased to possess any influence, and were wholly dependent on the will of others for assistance in their wars.

But to return to the order of our narration. Gregory III. occupied the papacy, and the kingdom of the Lombards was held by Astolphus, who, contrary to agreement, seized Ravenna, and made war upon the pope. On this account, Gregory no longer relying upon the emperor of Constantinople, since he, for the reasons above given, was unable to assist him, and unwilling to trust the Lombards, for they had frequently broken their faith, had recourse to Pepin II., who, from being lord of Austria and Brabant, had become king of France; not so much by his own valor as by that of Charles Martel, his father, and Pepin his grandfather; for Charles Martel, being governor of the kingdom, effected the memorable defeat of the Saracens near Tours, upon the Loire, in which two hundred thousand of them are said to have been left dead upon the field of battle. Hence, Pepin, by his father's reputation and his own abilities, became afterward king of France. To him Pope Gregory, as we have said, applied for assistance against the Lombards, which Pepin promised to grant, but desired first to see him and be honored with his presence. Gregory accordingly went to France, passing uninjured through the country of his enemies, so great was the respect they had for religion, and was treated honorably by Pepin, who sent an army into Italy, and besieged the Lombards in Pavia. King Astolphus, compelled by necessity, made proposals of peace to the French, who agreed to them at the entreaty of the pope—for he did not desire the death of his enemy, but that he should be converted and live. In this treaty, Astolphus promised to give to the church all the places he had taken from her; but the king's forces having returned to France, he did not fulfill the agreement, and the pope again had recourse to Pepin, who sent another army, conquered the Lombards, took Ravenna, and, contrary to the wishes of the Greek emperor, gave it to the pope, with all the places that belonged to the exarchate, and added to them Urbino and the Marca. But Astolphus, while fulfilling the terms of his agreement, died, and Desiderius, a Lombard, who was duke of Tuscany, took up arms to occupy the kingdom, and demanded assistance of the pope, promising him his friendship. The pope acceding to his request, the other princes assented. Desiderius kept faith at first, and proceeded to resign the districts to the pope, according to the agreement made with Pepin, so that an exarch was no longer sent from Constantinople to Ravenna, but it was governed according to the will of the pope. Pepin soon after died, and was succeeded by his son Charles, the same who, on account of the magnitude and success of his enterprises, was called Charlemagne, or Charles the Great. Theodore I. now succeeded to the papacy, and discord arising between him and Desiderius, the latter besieged him in Rome. The pope requested assistance of Charles, who, having crossed the Alps, besieged Desiderius in Pavai, where he took both him and his children, and sent them prisoners to France. He then went to visit the pontiff at Rome, where he Declared, *That the Pope, Being Vicar of God, Could Not Be Judged by Men*. The pope and the people of Rome made him emperor; and thus Rome began to have an emperor of the west. And whereas the popes used to be established by the emperors, the latter now began to have need of the popes at their elections; the empire continued to lose its powers, while the church acquired them; and, by these means, she constantly extended her authority over temporal princes.

The Lombards, having now been two hundred and thirty-two years in the country, were strangers only in name, and Charles, wishing to reorganize the states of Italy, consented that they should occupy the places in which they had been brought up, and call the province after their own name, Lombardy. That they might be led to respect the Roman name, he ordered all that part of Italy adjoining to them, which had been under the exarchate of Ravenna, to be called Romagna. Besides this, he created his son Pepin, king of Italy, whose dominion extended to Benevento; all the rest being possessed by the Greek emperor, with whom Charles was in league. About this time Pascal I. occupied the pontificate, and the priests of the churches of Rome, from being near to the pope, and attending the elections of the pontiff, began to dignify their own power with a title, by calling themselves cardinals, and arrogated so great authority, that having excluded the people of Rome from the election of pontiff, the appointment of a new pope was scarcely ever made except from one of their own number: thus on the death of Pascal, the cardinal of St. Sabina was created pope by the title of Eugenius II. Italy having come into the hands of the French, a change of form and order took place, the popes acquiring greater temporal power, and the new authorities adopting the titles of count and marquis, as that of duke had been introduced by Longinus, exarch of Ravenna. After the deaths of some pontiffs, Osporco, a Roman, succeeded to the papacy; but on account of his unseemly appellation, he took the name of Sergius, and this was the origin of that change of names which the popes adopt upon their election to the pontificate.

In the meantime, the Emperor Charles died and was succeeded by Lewis (the Pious), after whose death so many disputes arose among his sons, that at the time of his grandchildren, the house of France lost the empire, which then came to the Germans; the first German emperor being called Arnolfus. Nor did the Carlovingian family lose the empire only; their discords also occasioned them the loss of Italy; for the Lombards, gathering strength, offended the pope and the Romans, and Arnolfo, not knowing where to seek relief, was compelled to create Berengarius, duke of Fruili, king of Italy. These events induced the Huns, who occupied Pannonia, to assail Italy; but, in an engagement with Berengarius, they were compelled to return to Pannonia, which had from them been named Hungary.

Romano was at this time emperor of Greece, having, while prefect of the army, dethroned Constantine; and as Puglia and Calabria, which, as before observed, were parts of the Greek empire, had revolted, he gave permission to the Saracans to occupy them; and they having taken possession of these provinces, besieged Rome. The Romans, Berengarius being then engaged in defending himself against the Huns, appointed Alberic, duke of Tuscany, their leader. By his valor Rome was saved from the Saracens, who, withdrawing from the siege, erected a fortress upon Mount Gargano, by means of which they governed Puglia and Calabria, and harassed the whole country. Thus Italy was in those times very grievously afflicted, being in constant warfare with the Huns in the direction of the Alps, and, on the Neapolitan side, suffering from the inroads of the Saracens. This state of things continued many years, occupying the reigns of three Berengarii, who succeeded each other; and during this time the pope and the church were greatly disturbed; the impotence of the eastern, and the disunion which prevailed among the western princes, leaving them without defense. The city of Genoa, with all her territory upon the rivers, having been overrun by the Saracens, an impulse was thus given to the rising greatness of Pisa, in which city multitudes took refuge who had been driven out of their own country. These events occurred in the year 931, when Otho, duke of Saxony, the son of Henry and Matilda, a man of great prudence and reputation, being made emperor, the pope Agapito, begged that he would come into Italy and relieve him from the tyranny of the Berengarii.

The States of Italy were governed in this manner: Lombardy was under Berengarius III. and Alfred his son; Tuscany and Romagna were governed by a deputy of the western emperor; Puglia and Calabria were partly under the Greek emperor, and partly under the Saracens; in Rome two consuls were annually chosen from the nobility, who governed her according to ancient custom; to these was added a prefect, who dispensed justice among the people; and there was a council of twelve, who each year appointed rectors for the places subject to them. The popes had more or less authority in Rome and the rest of Italy, in proportion as they were favorites of the emperor or of the most powerful states. The Emperor Otho came into Italy, took the kingdom from the Berengarii, in which they had reigned fifty-five years, and reinstated the pontiff in his dignity. He had a son and a nephew, each named Otho, who, one after the other, succeeded to the empire. In the reign of Otho III., Pope Gregory V. was expelled by the Romans; whereupon the emperor came into Italy and replaced him; and the pope, to revenge himself on the Romans, took from them the right to create an emperor, and gave it to three princes and three bishops of Germany; the princes of Brandenburg, Palatine, and Saxony, and the bishops of Magonza, Treveri, and Colonia. This occurred in the year 1002. After the death of Otho III. the electors created Henry, duke of Bavaria, emperor, who at the end of twelve years was crowned by Pope Stephen VIII. Henry and his wife Simeonda were persons of very holy life, as is seen by the many temples built and endowed by them, of which the church of St. Miniato, near Florence, is one. Henry died in 1024, and was succeeded by Conrad of Suabia; and the latter by Henry II., who came to Rome; and as there was a schism in the church of three popes, he set them all aside, and caused the election of Clement II., by whom he was crowned emperor.

Chapter IV: Nicholas II. commits the election of the pope to the cardinals—First example of a prince deprived of his dominions by the pope—Guelphs and Ghibellines—Establishment of the kingdom of Naples—Pope Urban II. goes to France—The first crusade—New orders of knighthood—Saladin takes from the Christians their possessions in the east—Death of the Countess Matilda—Character of Frederick Barbarossa—Schism—Frederick creates an anti-pope—Building of Alexandria in Puglia—Disgraceful conditions imposed by the pope upon Henry, king of England—Reconciliation of Frederick with the pope—The kingdom of Naples passes to the Germans—Orders of St. Dominic and St. Francis.

Italy was at this time governed partly by the people, some districts by their own princes, and others by the deputies of the emperor. The highest in authority, and to whom the others referred, was called the chancellor. Of the princes, the most powerful were Godfred and the Countess Matilda his wife, who was daughter of Beatrice, the sister of Henry II. She and her husband possessed Lucca, Parma, Reggio, Mantua, and the whole of what is now called *the Patrimony of the Church*. The ambition of the Roman people caused many wars between them and the pontiffs, whose authority had previously been used to free them from the emperors; but when they had taken the government of the city to themselves, and regulated it according to their own pleasure, they at once became at enmity with the popes, who received far more injuries from them than from any Christian potentate. And while the popes caused all the west to tremble with their censures, the people of Rome were in open rebellion against them; nor had they or the popes any other purpose, but to deprive each other of reputation and authority.

Nicholas II. now attained the papacy; and as Gregory V. had taken from the Romans the right to create an emperor, he in the same manner determined to deprive them of their share in the election of the pope; and confined the creation to the cardinals alone. Nor did this satisfy him; for, having agreed with the princes who governed Calabria and Puglia, with methods which we shall presently relate, he compelled the officers whom the Romans appointed to their different jurisdictions, to render obedience to him; and some of them he even deprived of their offices. After the death of Nicholas, there was a schism in the church; the clergy of Lombardy refused obedience to Alexander II., created at Rome, and elected Cadolo of Parma anti-pope; and Henry, who hated the power of the pontiffs, gave Alexander to understand that he must renounce the pontificate, and ordered the cardinals to go into Germany to appoint a new pope. He was the first who felt the importance of spiritual weapons; for the pope called a council at Rome, and deprived Henry of both the empire and the kingdom. Some of the people of Italy took the part of the pope, others of Henry; and hence arose the factions of the Guelphs and the Ghibellines; that Italy, relieved from the inundations of barbarians, might be distracted with intestine strife. Henry, being excommunicated, was compelled by his people to come into Italy, and fall barefooted upon his knees before the pope, and ask his pardon. This occurred in the year 1082. Nevertheless, there shortly afterward arose new discords between the pope and Henry; upon which the pope again excommunicated him, and the emperor sent his son, also named Henry, with an army to Rome, and he, with the assistance of the Romans, who hated the pope, besieged him in the fortress. Robert Guiscard them came from Puglia to his relief, but Henry had left before his arrival, and returned to Germany. The Romans stood out alone, and the city was sacked by Robert, and reduced to ruins. As from this Robert sprung the establishment of the kingdom of Naples, it seems not superfluous to relate particularly his actions and origin.

Disunion having arisen among the descendants of Charlemagne, occasion was given to another northern people, called Normans, to assail France and occupy that portion of the country which is now named Normandy. A part of these people came into Italy at the time when the province was infested with the Berengarii, the Saracens, and the Huns, and occupied some places in Romagna, where, during the wars of that period, they conducted themselves valiantly. Tancred, one of these Norman princes, had many children; among the rest were William, surnamed Ferabac, and Robert, called Guiscard. When the principality was governed by William, the troubles of Italy were in some measure abated; but the Saracens still held Sicily, and plundered the coasts of Italy daily. On this account William arranged with the princes of Capua and Salerno, and with Melorco, a Greek, who governed Puglia and Calabria for the Greek emperor, to attack Sicily; and it was agreed that, if they were victorious, each should have a fourth part of the booty and the territory. They were fortunate in their enterprise, expelled the Saracens, and took possession of the island; but, after the victory, Melorco secretly caused forces to be brought from Greece, seized Sicily in the name of the emperor, and appropriated the booty to himself and his followers. William was much dissatisfied with this, but reserved the exhibition of his displeasure for a suitable opportunity, and left Sicily with the princes of Salerno and Capua. But when they had parted from him to return to their homes, instead of proceeding to Romagna he led his people towards Puglia, and took Melfi; and from thence, in a short time, recovered from the Greek emperor almost the whole of Puglia and Calabria, over which provinces, in the time of pope Nicholas II. his brother Robert Guiscard was sovereign. Robert having had many disputes with his nephews for the inheritance of these states, requested the influence of the pope to settle them; which his holiness was very willing to afford, being anxious to make a friend of Robert, to defend himself against the emperor of Germany and the insolence of the Roman people, which indeed shortly followed, when, at the instance of Gregory, he drove Henry from Rome, and subdued the people. Robert was succeeded by his sons Roger and William, to whose dominion not only was Naples added, but all the places interjacent as far as Rome, and afterward Sicily, of which Roger became sovereign; but, upon William going to Constantinople, to marry the daughter of the emperor, his dominions were wrested from him by his brother Roger. Inflated with so great an acquisition, Roger first took the title of king of Italy, but afterward contented himself with that of king of Puglia and Sicily. He was the first who established and gave that name to this kingdom, which still retains its ancient boundaries, although its sovereigns have been of many families and countries. Upon the failure of the Normans, it came to the Germans, after these to the French, then to the Aragonese, and it is now held by the Flemish.

About this time Urban II. became pope and excited the hatred of the Romans. As he did not think himself safe even in Italy, on account of the disunion which prevailed, he directed his thoughts to a generous enterprise. With his whole clergy he went into France, and at Anvers, having drawn together a vast multitude of people, delivered an oration against the infidels, which so excited the minds of his audience, that they determined to undertake the conquest of Asia from the Saracens; which enterprise, with all those of a similar nature, were afterward called crusades, because the people who joined in them bore upon their armor and apparel the figure of a cross. The leaders were Godfrey, Eustace, and Baldwin of Bouillon, counts of Boulogne, and Peter, a hermit celebrated for his prudence and sagacity. Many kings and people joined them, and contributed money; and many private persons fought under them at their own expense; so great was the influence of religion in those days upon the minds of men, excited by the example of those who were its principal ministers. The proudest successes attended the beginning of this enterprise; for the whole of Asia Minor, Syria, and part of Egypt, fell under the power of the Christians. To commemorate these events the order of the Knights of Jerusalem was created, which still continues, and holds the island of Rhodes—the only obstacle to the power of the Mohammedans. The same events gave rise to the order of the Knights Templars, which, after a short time, on account of their shameless practices, was dissolved. Various fortunes attended the crusaders in the course of their enterprises, and many nations and individuals became celebrated accordingly. The kings of France and England joined them, and, with the Venetians, Pisans, and Genoese, acquired great reputation, till the time of Saladin, when, by whose talents, and the disagreement of the Christians among themselves, the crusaders were robbed of all that glory which they had at first acquired; and, after ninety years, were driven from those places which they had so honorably and happily recovered.

After the death of Urban, Pascal II. became pope, and the empire was under the dominion of Henry IV. who came to Rome pretending friendship for the pontiff but afterward put his holiness and all his clergy in prison; nor did he release them till it was conceded that he should dispose of the churches of Germany according to his own pleasure. About this time, the Countess Matilda died, and made the church heir to all her territories. After the deaths of Pascal and Henry IV. many popes and emperors followed, till the papacy was occupied by Alexander III. and the empire by Frederick, surnamed Barbarossa. The popes during this period had met with many difficulties from the people of Rome and the emperors; and in the time of Barbarossa they were much increased. Frederick possessed military talent, but was so full of pride that he would not submit to the pontiff. However, at his election to the empire he came to Rome to be crowned, and returned peaceably to Germany, where he did not long remain in the same mind, but came again into Italy to subdue certain places in Lombardy, which did not obey him. It happened at this time that the cardinal St. Clement, of a Roman family, separated from Alexander, and was made pope by some of the cardinals. The Emperor Frederick, being encamped at Cerma, Alexander complained to him of the anti-pope, and received for answer, that they were both to go to him, and, having heard each side, he would determine which was the true pope. This reply displeased Alexander; and, as he saw the emperor was inclined to favor the anti-pope, he excommunicated him, and then fled to Philip, king of France. Frederick, in the meantime, carrying on the war in Lombardy, destroyed Milan; which caused the union of Verona, Padua, and Vicenza against him for their common defense. About the same period the anti-pope died, and Frederick set up Guido of Cremona, in his stead.

The Romans, from the absence of the pope, and from the emperor being in Lombardy, had reacquired some authority in Rome, and proceeded to recover the obedience of those places which had been subject to them. And as the people of Tusculum refused to submit to their authority, they proceeded against them with their whole force; but these, being assisted by Frederick, routed the Roman army with such dreadful slaughter, that Rome was never after either so populous or so rich. Alexander now returned to the city, thinking he could be safe there on account of the enmity subsisting between the Romans and the emperor, and from the enemies which the latter had in Lombardy. But Frederick, setting aside every other consideration, led his forces and encamped before Rome; and Alexander fled to William, king of Puglia, who had become hair of that kingdom after the death of Roger. Frederick, however, withdrew from Rome on account of the plague which then prevailed, and returned to

Germany. The cities of Lombardy in league against him, in order to command Pavia and Tortona, which adhered to the imperial party, built a city, to be their magazine in time of war, and named in Alexandria, in honor of the pope and in contempt of Frederick.

Guido the anti-pope died, and Giovanni of Fermo was appointed in his stead, who, being favored by the imperialists, lived at Montefiascone. Pope Alexander being at Tusculum, whither he had been called by the inhabitants, that with his authority he might defend them from the Romans, ambassadors came to him from Henry, king of England, to signify that he was not blamable for the death of Thomas a Becket, archbishop of Canterbury, although public report had slandered him with it. On this the pope sent two cardinals to England, to inquire into the truth of the matter; and although they found no actual charge against the king, still, on account of the infamy of the crime, and for not having honored the archbishop so much as he deserved, the sentence against the king of England was, that having called together the barons of his empire, he should upon oath before them affirm his innocence; that he should immediately send two hundred soldiers to Jerusalem, paid for one year; that, before the end of three years, he should himself proceed thither with as large an army as he could draw together; that his subjects should have the power of appealing to Rome when they thought proper; and that he should annul whatever acts had been passed in his kingdom unfavorable to ecclesiastical rule. These terms were all accepted by Henry; and thus a great king submitted to a sentence that in our day a private person would have been ashamed of. But while the pope exercised so great authority over distant princes, he could not compel obedience from the Romans themselves, or obtain their consent that he should remain in Rome, even though he promised to intermeddle only with ecclesiastical affairs.

About this time Frederick returned to Italy, and while he was preparing to carry on new wars against the pope, his prelates and barons declared that they would abandon him unless he reconciled himself with the church; so that he was obliged to go and submit to the pope at Venus, where a pacification was effected, but in which the pope deprived the emperor of all authority over Rome, and named William, king of Sicily and Puglia, a coadjutor with him. Frederick, unable to exist without war, joined the crusaders in Asia, that he might exercise that ambition against Mohammed, which he could not gratify against the vicars of Christ. And being near the river Cydnus, tempted by the clearness of its waters, bathed therein, took cold, and died. Thus the river did a greater favor to the Mohammedans than the pope's excommunications had done to the Christians; for the latter only checked his pride, while the former finished his career. Frederick being dead, the pope had now only to suppress the contumacy of the Romans; and, after many disputes concerning the creation of consuls, it was agreed that they should elect them as they had been accustomed to do, but that these should not undertake the office, till they had first sworn to be faithful to the church. This agreement being made, Giovanni the anti-pope took refuge in Mount Albano, where he shortly afterward died. William, king of Naples, died about the same time, and the pope intended to occupy that kingdom on the ground that the king had left only a natural son named Tancred. But the barons would not consent, and wished that Tancred should be king. Celestine III., the then pope, anxious to snatch the kingdom from the hands of Tancred, contrived that Henry, son of Frederick should be elected emperor, and promised him the kingdom on the condition that he should restore to the church all the places that had belonged to her. To facilitate this affair, he caused Gostanza, a daughter of William, who had been placed in a monastery and was now old, to be brought from her seclusion and become the wife of Henry. Thus the kingdom of Naples passed from the Normans, who had been the founders of it, to the Germans. As soon as the affairs of Germany were arranged, the Emperor Henry came into Italy with Gostanza his wife, and a son about four years of age named Frederick; and, as Tancred was now dead, leaving only an infant named Roger, he took possession of the kingdom without much difficulty. After some years, Henry died in Sicily, and was succeeded in the kingdom by Frederick, and in the empire by Otho, duke of Saxony, who was elected through the influence of Innocent III. But as soon as he had taken the crown, contrary to the general expectation, he became an enemy of the pope, occupied Romagna, and prepared to attack the kingdom. On this account the pope excommunicated him; he was abandoned by every one, and the electors appointed Frederick, king of Naples, emperor in his stead. Frederick came to Rome for his coronation; but the pope, being afraid of his power, would not crown him, and endeavored to withdraw him from Italy as he had done Otho. Frederick returned to Germany in anger, and, after many battles with Otho, at length conquered him. Meanwhile, Innocent died, who, besides other excellent works, built the hospital of the Holy Ghost at Rome. He was succeeded by Honorius III., in whose time the religious orders of St. Dominic and St. Francis were founded, 1218. Honorius crowned Frederick, to whom Giovanni, descended from Baldwin, king of Jerusalem, who commanded the remainder of the Christian army in Asia and still held that title, gave a daughter in marriage; and, with her portion, conceded to him the title to that kingdom: hence it is that every king of Naples is called king of Jerusalem.

Chapter V: The state of Italy—Beginning of the greatness of the house of Este—Guelphs and Ghibellines—Death of the Emperor Frederick II.—Manfred takes possession of the kingdom of Naples—Movements of the Guelphs and Ghibellines in Lombardy—Charles of Anjou invested by the pope with the kingdom of Naples and Sicily—Restless policy of the popes—Ambitious views of pope Nicholas III.—Nephews of the popes—Sicilian vespers—The Emperor Rodolph allows many cities to purchase their independence—Institution of the jubilee—The popes at Avignon.

At this time the states of Italy were governed in the following manner: the Romans no longer elected consuls, but instead of them, and with the same powers, they appointed one senator, and sometimes more. The league which the cities of Lombardy had formed against Frederick Barbarossa still continued, and comprehended Milan, Brescia, Mantua, and the greater number of the cities of Romagna, together with Verona, Vicenza, Padua, and Trevisa. Those which took part with the emperor, were Cremona, Bergamo, Parma, Reggio, and Trento. The other cities and fortresses of Lombardy, Romagna, and the march of Trevisa, favored, according to their necessities, sometimes one party, sometimes the other.

In the time of Otho III. there had come into Italy a man called Ezelin, who, remaining in the country, had a son, and he too had a son named Ezelin. This person, being rich and powerful, took part with Frederick, who, as we have said, was at enmity with the pope; Frederick, at the instigation and with the assistance of Ezelin, took Verona and Mantua, destroyed Vicenza, occupied Padua, routed the army of the united cities, and then directed his course towards Tuscany. Ezelin, in the meantime, had subdued the whole of the Trevisian March, but could not prevail against Ferrara, which was defended by Azone da Este and the forces which the pope had in Lombardy; and, as the enemy were compelled to withdraw, the pope gave Ferrara in fee to this Azone, from whom are descended those who now govern that city. Frederick halted at Pisa, desirous of making himself lord of Tuscany; but, while endeavoring to discover what friends and foes he had in that province, he scattered so many seeds of discord as occasioned the ruin of Italy; for the factions of the Guelphs and Ghibellines multiplied,—those who supported the church taking the name of Guelphs, while the followers of the emperor were called Ghibellines, these names being first heard at Pistoia. Frederick, marching from Pisa, assailed and wasted the territories of the church in a variety of ways; so that the pope, having no other remedy, unfurled against him the banner of the cross, as his predecessor had done against the Saracens. Frederick, that he might be suddenly abandoned by his people, as Frederick Barbarossa and others had been, took into his pay a number of Saracens; and to bind them to him, and establish in Italy a firm bulwark against the church, without fear of papal maledictions, he gave them Nocera in the kingdom of Naples, that, having a refuge of their own, they might be placed in greater security. The pontificate was now occupied by Innocent IV., who, being in fear of Frederick, went to Genoa, and thence to France, where he appointed a council to be held at Lyons, where it was the intention of Frederick to attend, but he was prevented by the rebellion of Parma: and, being repulsed, he went into Tuscany, and from thence to Sicily, where he died, leaving his son Conrad in Suabia; and in Puglia, Manfred, whom he had created duke of Benevento, born of a concubine. Conrad came to take possession of the kingdom, and having arrived at Naples, died, leaving an infant son named Corradino, who was then in Germany. On this account Manfred occupied the state, first as guardian of Corradino, but afterward, causing a report to be circulated that Corradino had died, made himself king, contrary to the wishes of both the pope and the Neapolitans, who, however, were obliged to submit.

While these things were occurring in the kingdom of Naples, many movements took place in Lombardy between the Guelphs and the Ghibellines. The Guelphs were headed by a legate of the pope; and the Ghibelline party by Ezelin, who possessed nearly the whole of Lombardy beyond the Po; and, as in the course of the war Padua rebelled, he put to death twelve thousand of its citizens. But before its close he himself was slain, in the eightieth year of his age, and all the places he had held became free. Manfred, king of Naples, continued those enmities against the church which had been begun by his ancestors, and kept the pope, Urban IV., in continual alarm; so that, in order to subdue him, Urban summoned the crusaders, and went to Perugia to await their arrival. Seeing them few and slow in their approach, he found that more able assistance was necessary to conquer Manfred. He therefore sought the favor of France; created Louis of Anjou, the king's brother, sovereign of Naples and Sicily, and excited him to come into Italy to take possession of that kingdom. But before Charles came to Rome the pope died, and was succeeded by Clement IV., in whose time he arrived at Ostia, with thirty galleys, and ordered that the rest of his forces should come by land. During his abode at Rome, the citizens, in order to attach him to them, made him their senator, and the pope invested him with the kingdom, on condition that he should pay annually to the church the sum of fifty thousand ducats; and it was decreed that, from thenceforth, neither Charles nor any other person, who might be king of Naples, should be emperor also. Charles marched against Manfred, routed his army, and slew him near Benevento, and then became sovereign of Sicily and Naples. Corradino, to whom, by his father's will, the state belonged, having collected a great force in Germany, marched into Italy against Charles, with whom he came to an engagement at Tagliacozzo, was taken prisoner while endeavoring to escape, and being unknown, put to death.

Italy remained in repose until the pontificate of Adrian V. Charles, being at Rome and governing the city by virtue of his office of senator, the pope, unable to endure his power, withdrew to Viterbo, and solicited the Emperor Rodolph to come into Italy and assist him. Thus the popes, sometimes in zeal for religion, at others moved by their own ambition, were continually calling in new parties and exciting new disturbances. As soon as they had made a prince powerful, they viewed him with jealousy and sought his ruin; and never allowed another to rule the country, which, from their own imbecility, they were themselves unable to govern. Princes were in fear of them; for, fighting or running away, the popes always obtained the advantage, unless it happened they were entrapped by deceit, as occurred to Boniface VIII., and some others, who under pretense of friendship, were ensnared by the emperors. Rodolph did not come into Italy, being detained by the war in which he was engaged with the king of Bohemia. At this time Adrian died, and Nicholas III., of the Orsini family, became pontiff. He was a bold, ambitious man; and being resolved at any event to diminish the power of Charles, induced the Emperor Rodolph to complain that he had a governor in Tuscany favorable to the Guelphic faction, who after the death of Manfred had been replaced by him. Charles yielded to the emperor and withdrew his governor, and the pope sent one of his nephews, a cardinal, as governor for the emperor, who, for the honor done him, restored Romagna to the church, which had been taken from her by his predecessors, and the pope made Bertoldo Orsino duke of Romagna. As Nicholas now thought himself powerful enough to oppose Charles, he deprived him of the office of senator, and made a decree that no one of royal race should ever be a senator in Rome. It was his intention to deprive Charles of Sicily, and to this end he entered into a secret negotiation with Peter, king of Aragon, which took effect in the following papacy. He also had the design of creating two kings out of his family, the one in Lombardy, the other in Tuscany, whose power would defend the church from the Germans who might design to come into Italy, and from the French, who were in the kingdom of Naples and Sicily. But with these thoughts he died. He was the first pope who openly exhibited his own ambition; and, under pretense of making the church great, conferred honors and emolument upon his own family. Previous to his time no mention is made of the nephews or families of any pontiff, but future history is full of them; nor is there now anything left for them to attempt, except the effort to make the papacy hereditary. True it is, the princes of their creating have not long sustained their honors; for the pontiffs, being generally of very limited existence, did not get their plants properly established.

To Nicholas succeeded Martin IV., of French origin, and consequently favorable to the party of Charles, who sent him assistance against the rebellion of Romagna; and while they were encamped at Furli, Guido Bonatto, an astrologer, contrived that at an appointed moment the people should assail the forces of the king, and the plan succeeding, all the French were taken and slain. About this period was also carried into effect the plot of Pope Nicholas and Peter, king of Aragon, by which the Sicilians murdered all the French that were in that island; and Peter made himself sovereign of it, saying, that it belonged to him in the right of his wife Gostanza, daughter of Manfred. But Charles, while making warlike preparations for the recovery of Sicily, died, leaving a son, Charles II., who was made prisoner in Sicily, and to recover his liberty promised to return to his prison, if within three years he did not obtain the pope's consent that the kings of Aragon should be invested with the kingdom of Sicily.

The Emperor Rodolph, instead of coming into Italy, gave the empire the advantage of having done so, by sending an ambassador, with authority to make all those cities free which would redeem themselves with money. Many purchased their freedom, and with liberty changed their mode of living. Adolpho of Saxony succeeded to the empire; and to the papacy, Pietro del Murrone, who took the name of Celestino; but, being a hermit and full of sanctity, after six months renounced the pontificate, and Boniface VIII. was elected.

After a time the French and Germans left Italy, and the country remained wholly in the hands of the Italians; but Providence ordained that the pope, when these enemies were withdrawn, should neither establish nor enjoy his authority, and raised two very powerful families in Rome, the Colonnesi and the Orsini, who with their arms, and the proximity of their abode, kept the pontificate weak. Boniface then determined to destroy the Colonnesi, and, besides excommunicating, endeavored to direct the weapons of the church against them. This, although it did them some injury, proved more disastrous to the pope; for those arms which from attachment to the faith performed valiantly against its enemies, as soon as they were directed against Christians for private ambition, ceased to do the will of those who wished to wield them. And thus the too eager desire to gratify themselves, caused the pontiffs by degrees to lose their military power. Besides what is just related, the pope deprived two cardinals of the Colonnesi family of their office; and Sciarra, the head of the house, escaping unknown, was taken by corsairs of Catalonia and put to the oar; but being afterward recognized at Marseilles, he was sent to Philip, king of France, who had been excommunicated and deprived of the kingdom. Philip, considering that in a war against the pontiff he would either be a loser or run great hazards, had recourse to deception, and simulating a wish to come to terms, secretly sent Sciarra into Italy, who, having arrived at Anagnia, where his holiness then resided, assembled a few friends, and in the night took him prisoner. And although the people of Anagnia set him

at liberty shortly after, yet from grief at the injury he died mad. Boniface was founder of the jubilee in 1300, and fixed that it should be celebrated at each revolution of one hundred years. In those times various troubles arose between the Guelph and Ghibelline factions; and the emperors having abandoned Italy, many places became free, and many were occupied by tyrants. Pope Benedict restored the scarlet hat to the cardinals of the Colonnesi family, and reblessed Philip, king of France. He was succeeded by Clement V., who, being a Frenchman, removed the papal court to Avignon in 1305.

Chapter VI: The Emperor Henry comes into Italy—The Florentines take the part of the pope—The Visconti originate the duchy of Milan—Artifice of Maffeo Visconti against the family of de la Torre—Giovanni Galeazzo Visconti, first duke of Milan—The Emperor Louis in Italy—John, king of Bohemia, in Italy—League against the king of Bohemia and the pope's legate—Origin of Venice—Liberty of the Venetians confirmed by Pepin and the Greek emperor—Greatness of Venice—Decline of Venice—Discord between the pope and the emperor—Giovanna, queen of Naples—Rienzi—The jubilee reduced to fifty years—Succession of the duke of Milan—Cardinal Egidio the pope's legate—War between the Genoese and the Venetians.

At this time, Charles II. of Naples died, and was succeeded by his son Robert. Henry of Luxemburg had been elected to the empire, and came to Rome for his coronation, although the pope was not there. His coming occasioned great excitement in Lombardy; for he sent all the banished to their homes, whether they were Guelphs or Ghibellines; and in consequence of this, one faction endeavoring to drive out the other, the whole province was filled with war; nor could the emperor with all his endeavors abate its fury. Leaving Lombardy by way of Genoa, he came to Pisa, where he endeavored to take Tuscany from King Robert; but not being successful, he went to Rome, where he remained only a few days, being driven away by the Orsini with the consent of King Robert, and returned to Pisa; and that he might more securely make war upon Tuscany, and wrest the country from the hands of the king, he caused it to be assailed by Frederick, monarch of Sicily. But when he was in hope of occupying Tuscany and robbing the king of Naples of his dominions, he died, and was succeeded by Louis of Bavaria. About the same period, John XXII. attained the papacy, during whose time the emperor still continued to persecute the Guelphs and the church, but they were defended by Robert and the Florentines. Many wars took place in Lombardy between the Visconti and the Guelphs, and in Tuscany between Castruccio of Lucca and the Florentines. As the family of Visconti gave rise to the duchy of Milan, one of the five principalities which afterward governed Italy, I shall speak of them from a rather earlier date.

Milan, upon recovering from the ruin into which she had been thrown by Frederick Barbarossa, in revenge for her injuries, joined the league formed by the Lombard cities for their common defense; this restrained him, and for awhile preserved alive the interests of the church in Lombardy. In the course of the wars which followed, the family of La Torre became very potent in that city, and their reputation increased so long as the emperor possessed little authority in the province. But Frederick II. coming into Italy, and the Ghibelline party, by the influence of Ezelin having grown powerful, seeds of the same faction sprang up in all the cities. In Milan were the Visconti, who expelled the La Torres; these, however, did not remain out, for by agreement between the emperor and the pope they were restored to their country. For when the pope and his court removed to France, and the emperor, Henry of Luxemburg, came into Italy, with the pretext of going to Rome for his crown, he was received in Milan by Maffeo Visconti and Guido della Torre, who were then the heads of these families. But Maffeo, designing to make use of the emperor for the purpose of expelling Guido, and thinking the enterprise not difficult, on account of the La Torre being of the contrary faction to the imperial, took occasion, from the remarks which the people made of the uncivil behavior of the Germans, to go craftily about and excite the populace to arm themselves and throw off the yoke of these barbarians. When a suitable moment arrived, he caused a person in whom he confided to create a tumult, upon which the people took arms against the Germans. But no sooner was the mischief well on foot, than Maffeo, with his sons and their partisans, ran to Henry, telling him that all the disturbance had been occasioned by the La Torre family, who, not content to remain peaceably in Milan, had taken the opportunity to plunder him, that they might ingratiate themselves with the Guelphs of Italy and become princes in the city; they then bade him be of good cheer, for they, with their party, whenever he wished it, were ready to defend him with their lives. Henry, believing all that Maffeo told him, joined his forces to those of the Visconti, and attacking the La Torre, who were in various parts of the city endeavoring to quell the tumult, slew all upon whom they could lay hands, and having plundered the others of their property, sent them into exile. By this artifice, Maffeo Visconti became a prince of Milan. Of him remained Galeazzo and Azzo; and, after these, Luchino and Giovanni. Giovanni became archbishop of Milan; and of Luchino, who died before him, were left Bernabo and Galeazzo; Galeazzo, dying soon after, left a son called the Count of Virtu, who after the death of the archbishop, contrived the murder of his uncle, Bernabo, became prince of Milan, and was the first who had the title of duke. The duke left Filippo and Giovanmaria Angelo, the latter of whom being slain by the people of Milan, the state fell to Filippo; but he having no male heir, Milan passed from the family of Visconti to that of Sforza, in the manner to be related hereafter.

But to return to the point from which we deviated. The Emperor Louis, to add to the importance of his party and to receive the crown, came into Italy; and being at Milan, as an excuse for taking money of the Milanese, he pretended to make them free and to put the Visconti in prison; but shortly afterwards he released them, and, having gone to Rome, in order to disturb Italy with less difficulty, he made Piero della Corvara anti-pope, by whose influence, and the power of the Visconti, he designed to weaken the opposite faction in Tuscany and Lombardy. But Castruccio died, and his death caused the failure of the emperor's purpose; for Pisa and Lucca rebelled. The Pisans sent Piero della Corvara a prisoner to the pope in France, and the emperor, despairing of the affairs of Italy, returned to Germany. He had scarcely left, before John king of Bohemia came into the country, at the request of the Ghibellines of Brescia, and made himself lord of that city and of Bergamo. And as his entry was with the consent of the pope, although he feigned the contrary, the legate of Bologna favored him, thinking by this means to prevent the return of the emperor. This caused a change in the parties of Italy; for the Florentines and King Robert, finding the legate was favorable to the enterprises of the Ghibellines, became foes of all those to whom the legate and the king of Bohemia were friendly. Without having regard for either faction, whether Guelph or Ghibelline, many princes joined them, of whom, among others, were the Visconti, the Della Scala, Filippo Gonzao of Mantua, the Carrara, and those of Este. Upon this the pope excommunicated them all. The king, in fear of the league, went to collect forces in his own country, and having returned with a large army, still found his undertaking a difficult one; so, seeing his error, he withdrew to Bohemia, to the great displeasure of the legate, leaving only Reggio and Modena guarded, and Parma in the care of Marsilio and Piero de' Rossi, who were the most powerful men in the city. The king of Bohemia being gone, Bologna joined the league; and the leaguers divided among themselves the four cities which remained of the church faction. They agreed that Parma should pertain to the Della Scalla; Reggio to the Gonzaga; Modena to the family of Este, and Lucca to the Florentines. But in taking possession of these cities, many disputes arose which were afterward in a great measure settled by the Venetians. Some, perhaps, will think it a species of impropriety that we have so long deferred speaking of the Venetians, theirs being a republic, which, both on account of its power and internal regulations, deserves to be celebrated above any principality of Italy. But that this surprise may cease when the cause is known, I shall speak of their city from a more remote period; that everyone may understand what were their beginnings, and the causes which so long withheld them from interfering in the affairs of Italy.

When Attila, king of the Huns, besieged Aquileia, the inhabitants, after defending themselves a long time, began to despair of effecting their safety, and fled for refuge to several uninhabited rocks, situated at the point of the Adriatic Sea, now called the Gulf of Venice, carrying with them whatever movable property they possessed. The people of Padua, finding themselves in equal danger, and knowing that, having became master of Aquileia, Attila would next attack themselves, also removed with their most valuable property to a place on the same sea, called Rivo Alto, to which they brought their women, children, and aged persons, leaving the youth in Padua to assist in her defense. Besides these, the people of Monselice, with the inhabitants of the surrounding hills, driven by similar fears, fled to the same rocks. But after Attila had taken Aquileia, and destroyed Padua, Monselice, Vicenza, and Verona, the people of Padua and others who were powerful, continued to inhabit the marshes about Rivo Alto; and, in like manner, all the people of the province anciently called Venetia, driven by the same events, became collected in these marshes. Thus, under the pressure of necessity, they left an agreeable and fertile country to occupy one sterile and unwholesome. However, in consequence of a great number of people being drawn together into a comparatively small space, in a short time they made those places not only habitable, but delightful; and having established among themselves laws and useful regulations, enjoyed themselves in security amid the devastations of Italy, and soon increased both in reputation and strength. For, besides the inhabitants already mentioned, many fled to these places from the cities of Lombardy, principally to escape from the cruelties of Clefis king of the Lombards, which greatly tended to increase the numbers of the new city; and in the conventions which were made between Pepin, king of France, and the emperor of Greece, when the former, at the entreaty of the pope, came to drive the Lombards out of Italy, the duke of Benevento and the Venetians did not render obedience to either the one or the other, but alone enjoyed their liberty. As necessity had led them to dwell on sterile rocks, they were compelled to seek the means of subsistence elsewhere; and voyaging with their ships to every port of the ocean, their city became a depository for the various products of the world, and was itself filled with men of every nation.

For many years the Venetians sought no other dominion than that which tended to facilitate their commercial enterprises, and thus acquired many ports in Greece and Syria; and as the French had made frequent use of their ships in voyages to Asia, the island of Candia was assigned to them in recompense for these services. While they lived in this manner, their name spread terror over the seas, and was held in veneration throughout Italy. This was so completely the case, that they were generally chosen to arbitrate in controversies between the states, as occurred in the difference between the Colleagues, on account of the cities they had divided among themselves; which being referred to the Venetians, they awarded Brescia and Bergamo to the Visconti. But when, in the course of time, urged by their eagerness for dominion, they had made themselves masters of Padua, Vicenza, Trevisa, and afterward of Verona, Bergamo, and Brescia, with many cities in Romagna and the kingdom of Naples, other nations were impressed with such an opinion of their power, that they were a terror, not only to the princes of Italy, but to the ultramontane kings. These states entered into an alliance against them, and in one day wrested from them the provinces they had obtained with so much labor and expense; and although they have in latter times reacquired some portions, still possessing neither power nor reputation, like all the other Italian powers, they live at the mercy of others.

Benedict XII. having attained the pontificate and finding Italy lost, fearing, too, that the emperor would assume the sovereignty of the country, determined to make friends of all who had usurped the government of those cities which had been accustomed to obey the emperor; that they might have occasion to dread the latter, and unite with himself in the defense of Italy. To this end he issued a decree, confirming to all the tyrants of Lombardy the places they had seized. After making this concession the pope died, and was succeeded by Clement VI. The emperor, seeing with what a liberal hand the pontiff had bestowed the dominions of the empire, in order to be equally bountiful with the property of others, gave to all who had assumed sovereignty over the cities or territories of the church, the imperial authority to retain possession of them. By this means Galeotto Malatesti and his brothers became lords of Rimino, Pesaro, and Fano; Antonio da Montefeltro, of the Marca and Urbino; Gentile da Varano, of Camerino; Guido di Polenta, of Ravenna; Sinibaldo Ordelaffi, of Furli and Cesena; Giovanni Manfredi, of Faenza; Lodovico Alidossi, of Imola; and besides these, many others in divers places. Thus, of all the cities, towns, or fortresses of the church, few remained without a prince; for she did not recover herself till the time of Alexander VI., who, by the ruin of the descendants of these princes, restored the authority of the church.

The emperor, when he made the concession before named, being at Tarento, signified an intention of going into Italy. In consequence of this, many battles were fought in Lombardy, and the Visconti became lords of Parma. Robert king of Naples, now died, leaving only two grandchildren, the issue of his sons Charles, who had died a considerable time before him. He ordered that the elder of the two, whose name was Giovanna or Joan, should be heiress of the kingdom, and take for her husband Andrea, son of the king of Hungary, his grandson. Andrea had not lived with her long, before she caused him to be murdered, and married another cousin, Louis, prince of Tarento. But Louis, king of Hungary, and brother of Andrea, in order to avenge his death, brought forces into Italy, and drove Queen Joan and her husband out of the kingdom.

At this period a memorable circumstance took place at Rome. Niccolo di Lorenzo, often called Rienzi or Cola di Rienzi, who held the office of chancellor at Campidoglio, drove the senators from Rome and, under the title of tribune, made himself the head of the Roman republic; restoring it to its ancient form, and with so great reputation of justice and virtue, that not only the places adjacent, but the whole of Italy sent ambassadors to him. The ancient provinces, seeing Rome arise to new life, again raised their heads, and some induced by hope, others by fear, honored him as their sovereign. But Niccolo, notwithstanding his great reputation, lost all energy in the very beginning of his enterprise; and as if oppressed with the weight of so vast an undertaking, without being driven away, secretly fled to Charles, king of Bohemia, who, by the influence of the pope, and in contempt of Louis of Bavaria, had been elected emperor. Charles, to ingratiate himself with the pontiff, sent Niccolo to him, a prisoner. After some time, in imitation of Rienzi, Francesco Baroncegli seized upon the tribunate of Rome, and expelled the senators; and the pope, as the most effectual means of repressing him, drew Niccolo from his prison, sent him to Rome, and restored to him the office of tribune; so that he reoccupied the state and put Francesco to death; but the Colonnesi becoming his enemies, he too, after a short time, shared the same fate, and the senators were again restored to their office. The king of Hungary, having driven out Queen Joan, returned to his kingdom; but the pope, who chose to have the queen in the neighborhood of Rome rather than the king, effected her restoration to the sovereignty, on the condition that her husband, contenting himself with the title of prince of Tarento, should not be called king. Being the year 1350, the pope thought that the jubilee, appointed by Boniface VIII. to take place at the conclusion of each century, might be renewed at the end of each fifty years; and having issued a decree for the establishment of it, the Romans, in acknowledgment of the benefit, consented that he should send four cardinals to reform the government of the city, and appoint senators according to his own pleasure. The pope again declared Louis of Tarento, king, and in gratitude for the benefit, Queen Joan gave Avignon, her inheritance, to the church. About this time Luchino Visconti died, and his brother the archbishop, remaining lord of Milan, carried on many wars against Tuscany and his neighbors, and became very powerful. Bernabo and Galeazzo, his nephews, succeeded him; but Galeazzo soon after died, leaving Giovan Galeazzo, who shared the state with Bernabo. Charles, king of Bohemia, was then emperor, and the pontificate was occupied by Innocent VI., who sent Cardinal Egidio, a Spaniard, into Italy. He restored the reputation of the church, not only in Rome and Romagna, but throughout the whole of Italy; he recovered Bologna from the archbishop of Milan, and compelled the Romans to accept a foreign senator appointed annually by the pope. He made honorable terms with the Visconti, and routed and took prisoner, John Agut, an Englishman, who with four thousand English had fought on the side of the Ghibellines in Tuscany. Urban V., hearing of so many victories, resolved to visit Italy and Rome, whither also the emperor came; after remaining a few months, he returned to the kingdom of Bohemia, and the pope to Avignon. On the death of Urban, Gregory XI. was created pope; and, as the Cardinal Egidio was dead, Italy again recommenced her ancient discords, occasioned by the union of the other powers against the Visconti;

and the pope, having first sent a legate with six thousand Bretons, came in person and established the papal court at Rome in 1376, after an absence of seventy-one years in France. To Gregory XI., succeeded Urban VI., but shortly afterwards Clement VI. was elected at Fondi by ten cardinals, who declared the appointment of Urban irregular. At this time, the Genoese threw off the yoke of the Visconti under whom they had lived many years; and between them and the Venetians several important battles were fought for the island of Tenedos. Although the Genoese were for a time successful, and held Venice in a state of siege during many months, the Venetians were at length victorious; and by the intervention of the pope, peace was made in the year 1381. In these wars, artillery was first used, having been recently invented by the Dutch.

Chapter VII: Schism in the church—Ambitious views of Giovanni Galeazzo Visconti—The pope and the Romans come to an agreement—Boniface IX. introduces the practice of Annates—Disturbance in Lombardy—The Venetians acquire dominion on terra firma—Differences between the pope and the people of Rome—Council of Pisa—Council of Constance—Filippo Visconti recovers his dominion—Giovanna II. of Naples—Political condition of Italy.

A schism having thus arisen in the church, Queen Joan favored the schismatic pope, upon which Urban caused Charles of Durazzo, descended from the kings of Naples, to undertake the conquest of her dominions. Having succeeded in his object, she fled to France, and he assumed the sovereignty. The king of France, being exasperated, sent Louis of Anjou into Italy to recover the kingdom for the queen, to expel Urban from Rome, and establish the anti-pope. But in the midst of this enterprise Louis died, and his people being routed returned to France. In this conjuncture the pope went to Naples, where he put nine cardinals into prison for having taken the part of France and the anti-pope. He then became offended with the king, for having refused to make his nephew prince of Capua; and pretending not to care about it, requested he would grant him Nocera for his habitation, but, having fortified it, he prepared to deprive the king of his dominions. Upon this the king pitched his camp before the place, and the pope fled to Naples, where he put to death the cardinals whom he had imprisoned. From thence he proceeded to Rome, and, to acquire influence, created twenty-nine cardinals. At this time Charles, king of Naples, went to Hungary, where, having been made king, he was shortly afterward killed in battle, leaving a wife and two children at Naples. About the same time Giovanni Galeazzo Visconti murdered Bernabo his uncle and took the entire sovereignty upon himself; and, not content with being duke of Milan and sovereign of the whole of Lombardy, designed to make himself master of Tuscany; but while he was intent upon occupying the province with the ultimate view of making himself king of Italy, he died. Boniface IX. succeeded Urban VI. The anti-pope, Clement VI., also died, and Benedict XIII. was appointed his successor.

Many English, Germans, and Bretons served at this period in the armies of Italy, commanded partly by those leaders who had from time to time authority in the country, and partly by such as the pontiffs sent, when they were at Avignon. With these warriors the princes of Italy long carried on their wars, till the coming of Lodovico da Cento of Romagna, who formed a body of Italian soldiery, called the Company of St. George, whose valor and discipline soon caused the foreign troops to fall into disrepute, and gave reputation to the native forces of the country, of which the princes afterward availed themselves in their wars with each other. The pope, Boniface IX., being at enmity with the Romans, went to Scesi, where he remained till the jubilee of 1400, when the Romans, to induce him to return to the city, consented to receive another foreign senator of his appointing, and also allowed him to fortify the castle of Saint Angelo: having returned upon these conditions, in order to enrich the church, he ordained that everyone, upon vacating a benefice, should pay a year's value of it to the Apostolic Chamber.

After the death of Giovanni Galeazzo, duke of Milan, although he left two children, Giovanmaria and Filippo, the state was divided into many parts, and in the troubles which ensued Giovanmaria was slain. Filippo remained some time in the castle of Pavia, from which, through the fidelity and virtue of the castellan, he escaped. Among others who occupied cities possessed by his father, was Guglielmo della Scala, who, being banished, fell into the hands of Francesco de Carrera, lord of Padua, by whose means he recovered the state of Verona, in which he only remained a short time, for he was poisoned, by order of Francesco, and the city taken from him. These things occasioned the people of Vicenza, who had lived in security under the protection of the Visconti, to dread the greatness of the lord of Padua, and they placed themselves under the Venetians, who, engaging in arms with him, first took Verona and then Padua.

At this time Pope Boniface died, and was succeeded by Innocent VII. The people of Rome supplicated him to restore to them their fortresses and their liberty; but as he would not consent to their petition, they called to their assistance Ladislaus, king of Naples. Becoming reconciled to the people, the pope returned to Rome, and made his nephew Lodovico count of La Marca. Innocent soon after died, and Gregory XII. was created, upon the understanding to renounce the papacy whenever the anti-pope would also renounce it. By the advice of the cardinals, in order to attempt the reunion of the church, Benedict, the anti-pope, came to Porto Venere, and Gregory to Lucca, where they made many endeavors, but effected nothing. Upon this, the cardinals of both the popes abandoned them, Benedict going to Spain, and Gregory to Rimini. On the other hand, the cardinals, with the favor of Balthazar Cossa, cardinal and legate of Bologna, appointed a council at Pisa, where they created Alexander V., who immediately excommunicated King Ladislaus, and invested Louis of Anjou with the kingdom; this prince, with the Florentines, Genoese, and Venetians, attacked Ladislaus and drove him from Rome. In the head of the war Alexander died, and Balthazar Cossa succeeded him, with the title of John XXIII. Leaving Bologna, where he was elected, he went to Rome, and found there Louis of Anjou, who had brought the army from Provence, and coming to an engagement with Ladislaus, routed him. But by the mismanagement of the leaders, they were unable to prosecute the victory, so that the king in a short time gathered strength and retook Rome. Louis fled to Provence, the pope to Bologna; where, considering how he might diminish the power of Ladislaus, he caused Sigismund, king of Hungary, to be elected emperor, and advised him to come to Italy. Having a personal interview at Mantua, they agreed to call a general council, in which the church should be united; and having effected this, the pope thought he should be fully enabled to oppose the forces of his enemies.

At this time there were three popes, Gregory, Benedict, and Giovanni, which kept the church weak and in disrepute. The city of Constance, in Germany, was appointed for the holding of the council, contrary to the expectation of Pope John. And although the death of Ladislaus had removed the cause which induced the pope to call the council, still, having promised to attend, he could not refuse to go there. In a few months after his arrival at Constance he discovered his error, but it was too late; endeavoring to escape, he was taken, put into prison, and compelled to renounce the papacy. Gregory, one of the anti-popes, sent his renunciation; Benedict, the other, refusing to do the same, was condemned as a heretic; but, being abandoned by his cardinals, he complied, and the council elected Oddo, of the Colonnesi family, pope, by the title of Martin V. Thus the church was united under one head, after having been divided by many pontiffs.

Filippo Visconti was, as we have said, in the fortress of Pavia. But Fazino Cane, who in the affairs of Lombardy had become lord of Vercelli, Alessandria, Novara, and Tortona, and had amassed great riches, finding his end approach, and having no children, left his wife Beatrice heiress of his estates, and arranged with his friends that a marriage should be effected between her and Filippo. By this union Filippo became powerful, and reacquired Milan and the whole of Lombardy. By way of being grateful for these numerous favors, as princes commonly are, he accused Beatrice of adultery and caused her to be put to death. Finding himself now possessed of greater power, he began to think of warring with Tuscany and of prosecuting the designs of Giovanni Galeazzo, his father.

Ladislaus, king of Naples, at his death, left to his sister Giovanna the kingdom and a large army, under the command of the principal leaders of Italy, among the first of whom was Sforza of Cotignuola, reputed by the soldiery of that period to be a very valiant man. The queen, to shun the disgrace of having kept about her person a certain Pandolfello, whom she had brought up, took for her husband Giacopo della Marca, a Frenchman of the royal line, on the condition that he should be content to be called Prince of Tarento, and leave to her the title and government of the kingdom. But the soldiery, upon his arrival in Naples, proclaimed him king; so that between the husband and the wife wars ensued; and although they contended with varying success, the queen at length obtained the superiority, and became an enemy of the pope. Upon this, in order to reduce her to necessity, and that she might be compelled to throw herself into his lap, Sforza suddenly withdrew from her service without giving her any pervious notice of his intention to do so. She thus found herself at once unarmed, and not having any other source, sought the assistance of Alfonzo, king of Aragon and Sicily, adopted him as her son, and engaged Braccio of Montone as her captain, who was of equal reputation in arms with Sforza, and inimical to the pope, on account of his having taken possession of Perugia and some other places belonging to the church. After this, peace was made between the queen and the pontiff; but King Alfonzo, expecting she would treat him as she had her husband, endeavored secretly to make himself master of the strongholds; but, possessing acute observation, she was beforehand with him, and fortified herself in the castle of Naples. Suspicions increasing between them, they had recourse to arms, and the queen, with the assistance of Sforza, who again resumed her service, drove Alfonzo out of Naples, deprived him of his succession, and adopted Louis of Anjou in his stead. Hence arose new contests between Braccio, who took the part of Alfonzo, and Sforza, who defended the cause of the queen. In the course of the war, Sforza was drowned in endeavoring to pass the river Pescara; the queen was thus again unarmed, and would have been driven out of the kingdom, but for the assistance of Filippo Visconti, the duke of Milan, who compelled Alfonzo to return to Aragon. Braccio, undaunted at the departure of Alfonzo, continued the enterprise against the queen, and besieged L'Aquilla; but the pope, thinking the greatness of Braccio injurious to the church, received into his pay Francesco, the son of Sforza, who went in pursuit of Braccio to L'Aquilla, where he routed and slew him. Of Braccio remained Oddo, his son, from whom the pope took Perugia, and left him the state of Montone alone; but he was shortly afterward slain in Romagna, in the service of the Florentines; so that of those who had fought under Braccio, Niccolo Piccinino remained of greatest reputation.

Having continued our general narration nearly to the period which we at first proposed to reach, what remains is of little importance, except the war which the Florentines and Venetians carried on against Filippo duke of Milan, of which an account will be given when we speak particularly of Florence. I shall, therefore, continue it no further, briefly explaining the condition of Italy in respect of her princes and her arms, at the period to which we have now come. Joan II. held Naples, La Marca, the Patrimony and Romagna; some of these places obeyed the church, while others were held by vicars or tyrants, as Ferrara, Modena, and Reggio, by those of the House of Este; Faenza by the Manfredi; Imola by the Alidossi; Furli by the Ordelaffi; Rimini and Psaro by the Malatesti; and Camerino by those of Varano. Part of Lombardy was subject to the Duke Filippo, part to the Venetians; for all those who had held single states were set aside, except the House of Gonzaga, which ruled in Mantua. The greater part of Tuscany was subject to the Florentines. Lucca and Sienna alone were governed by their own laws; Lucca was under the Guinigi; Sienna was free. The Genoese, being sometimes free, at others, subject to the kings of France or the Visconti, lived unrespected, and may be enumerated among the minor powers.

None of the principal states were armed with their own proper forces. Duke Filippo kept himself shut up in his apartments, and would not allow himself to be seen; his wars were managed by commissaries. The Venetians, when they directed their attention to terra firma, threw off those arms which had made them terrible upon the seas, and falling into the customs of Italy, submitted their forces to the direction of others. The practice of arms being unsuitable to priests or women, the pope and Queen Joan of Naples were compelled by necessity to submit to the same system which others practiced from defect of judgment. The Florentines also adopted the same custom, for having, by their frequent divisions, destroyed the nobility, and their republic being wholly in the hands of men brought up to trade, they followed the usages and example of others.

Thus the arms of Italy were either in the hands of the lesser princes, or of men who possessed no state; for the minor princes did not adopt the practice of arms from any desire of glory, but for the acquisition of either property or safety. The others (those who possessed no state) being bred to arms from their infancy, were acquainted with no other art, and pursued war for emolument, or to confer honor upon themselves. The most noticed among the latter were Carmignola, Francesco Sforza, Niccolo Piccinino the pupil of Braccio, Agnolo della Pergola, Lorenzo di Micheletto Attenduli, il Tartaglia, Giacopaccio, Cecolini da Perugia, Niccolo da Tolentino, Guido Torello, Antonia dal Ponte ad Era, and many others. With these, were those lords of whom I have before spoken, to which may be added the barons of Rome, the Colonnesi and the Orsini, with other lords and gentlemen of the kingdoms of Naples and Lombardy, who, being constantly in arms, had such an understanding among themselves, and so contrived to accommodate things to their own convenience, that of those who were at war, most commonly both sides were losers; and they had made the practice of arms so totally ridiculous, that the most ordinary leader, possessed of true valor, would have covered these men with disgrace, whom, with so little prudence, Italy honored.

With these idle princes and such contemptible arms, my history must, therefore, be filled; to which, before I descend, it will be necessary, as was at first proposed, to speak of the origin of Florence, that it may be clearly understood what was the state of the city in those times, and by what means, through the labours of a thousand years, she became so imbecile.

Book II: Chapter I: The custom of ancient republics to plant colonies, and the advantage of it—Increased population tends to make countries more healthy—Origin of Florence—Aggrandizement of Florence—Origin of the name of Florence—Destruction of Florence by Totila—The Florentines take Fiesole—The first division in Florence, and the cause of it—Buondelmonti—Buondelmonti slain—Guelphs and Ghibellines in Florence—Guelphic families—Ghibelline families—The two factions come to terms.

Among the great and wonderful institutions of the republics and principalities of antiquity that have now gone into disuse, was that by means of which towns and cities were from time to time established; and there is nothing more worthy the attention of a great prince, or of a well-regulated republic, or that confers so many advantages upon a province, as the settlement of new places, where men are drawn together for mutual accommodation and defense. This may easily be done, by sending people to reside in recently acquired or uninhabited countries. Besides causing the establishment of new cities, these removals render a conquered country more secure, and keep the inhabitants of a province properly distributed. Thus, deriving the greatest attainable comfort, the inhabitants increase rapidly, are more prompt to attack others, and defend themselves with greater assurance. This custom, by the unwise practice of princes and republics, having gone into desuetude, the ruin and weakness of territories has followed; for this ordination is that by which alone empires are made secure, and countries become populated. Safety is the result of it; because the colony which a prince establishes in a newly acquired country, is like a fortress and a guard, to keep the inhabitants in fidelity and obedience. Neither can a province be wholly occupied and preserve a proper distribution of its inhabitants without this regulation; for all districts are not equally healthy, and hence some will abound to overflowing, while others are void; and if there be no method of withdrawing them from places in which they increase too rapidly, and planting them where they are too few the country would soon be wasted; for one part would become a desert, and the other a dense and wretched population. And, as nature cannot repair this disorder, it is necessary that industry should effect it, for unhealthy localities become wholesome when a numerous population is brought into them. With cultivation the earth becomes fruitful, and the air is purified with fires—remedies which nature cannot provide. The city of Venice proves the correctness of these remarks. Being placed in a marshy and unwholesome situation, it became healthy only by the number of industrious individuals who were drawn together. Pisa, too, on account of its unwholesome air, was never filled with inhabitants, till the Saracens, having destroyed Genoa and rendered her rivers unnavigable, caused the Genoese to migrate thither in vast numbers, and thus render her populous and powerful. Where the use of colonies is not adopted, conquered countries are held with great difficulty; districts once uninhabited still remain so, and those which populate quickly are not relieved. Hence it is that many places of the world, and particularly in Italy, in comparison of ancient times, have become deserts. This has wholly arisen and proceeded from the negligence of princes, who have lost all appetite for true glory, and of republics which no longer possess institutions that deserve praise. In ancient times, by means of colonies, new cities frequently arose, and those already begun were enlarged, as was the case with Florence, which had its beginning from Fiesole, and its increase from colonies.

It is exceedingly probable, as Dante and Giovanni Villani show, that the city of Fiesole, being situate upon the summit of the mountain, in order that her markets might be more frequented, and afford greater accommodation for those who brought merchandise, would appoint the place in which to told them, not upon the hill, but in the plain, between the foot of the mountain and the river Arno. I imagine these markets to have occasioned the first erections that were made in those places, and to have induced merchants to wish for commodious warehouses for the reception of their goods, and which, in time, became substantial buildings. And afterward, when the Romans, having conquered the Carthaginians, rendered Italy secure from foreign invasion, these buildings would greatly increase; for men never endure inconveniences unless some powerful necessity compels them. Thus, although the fear of war induces a willingness to occupy places strong and difficult of access, as soon as the cause of alarm is removed, men gladly resort to more convenient and easily attainable localities. Hence, the security to which the reputation of the Roman republic gave birth, caused the inhabitants, having begun in the manner described, to increase so much as to form a town, this was at first called the Villa Arnina. After this occurred the civil wars between Marius and Sylla; then those of Caesar, and Pompey; and next those of the murderers of Caesar, and the parties who undertook to avenge his death. Therefore, first by Sylla, and afterward by the three Roman citizens, who, having avenged the death of Caesar, divided the empire among themselves, colonies were sent to Fiesole, which, either in part or in whole, fixed their habitations in the plain, near to the then rising town. By this increase, the place became so filled with dwellings, that it might with propriety be enumerated among the cities of Italy.

There are various opinions concerning the derivation of the word Florentia. Some suppose it to come from Florinus, one of the principal persons of the colony; others think it was originally not Florentia, but Fluentia, and suppose the word derived from *fluente*, or flowing of the Arno; and in support of their opinion, adduce a passage from Pliny, who says, "the Fluentini are near the flowing of the Arno." This, however, may be incorrect, for Pliny speaks of the locality of the Florentini, not of the name by which they were known. And it seems as if the word Fluentini were a corruption, because Frontinus and Cornelius Tacitus, who wrote at nearly the same period as Pliny, call them Florentia and Florentini; for, in the time of Tiberius, they were governed like the other cities of Italy. Besides, Cornelius refers to the coming of ambassadors from the Florentines, to beg of the emperor that the waters of the Chiane might not be allowed to overflow their country; and it is not at all reasonable that the city should have two names at the same time. Therefore I think that, however derived, the name was always Florentia, and that whatever the origin might be, it occurred under the Roman empire, and began to be noticed by writers in the times of the first emperors.

When the Roman empire was afflicted by the barbarians, Florence was destroyed by Totila, king of the Ostrogoths; and after a period of two hundred and fifty years, rebuilt by Charlemagne; from whose time, till the year 1215, she participated in the fortune of the rest of Italy; and, during this period, first the descendants of Charles, then the Berengarii, and lastly the German emperors, governed her, as in our general treatise we have shown. Nor could the Florentines, during those ages, increase in numbers, or effect anything worthy of memory, on account of the influence of those to whom they were subject. Nevertheless, in the year 1010, upon the feast of St. Romolo, a solemn day with the Fiesolani, they took and destroyed Fiesole, which must have been performed either with the consent of the emperors, or during the interim from the death of one to the creation of his successor, when all assumed a larger share of liberty. But then the pontiffs acquired greater influence, and the authority of the German emperors was in its wane, all the places of Italy governed themselves with less respect for the prince; so that, in the time of Henry III. the mind of the country was divided between the emperor and the church. However, the Florentines kept themselves united until the year 1215, rendering obedience to the ruling power, and anxious only to preserve their own safety. But, as the diseases which attack our bodies are more dangerous and mortal in proportion as they are delayed, so Florence, though late to take part in the sects of Italy, was afterward the more afflicted by them. The cause of her first division is well known, having been recorded by Dante and many other writers; I shall, however, briefly notice it.

Among the most powerful families of Florence were the Buondelmonti and the Uberti; next to these were the Amidei and the Donati. Of the Donati family there was a rich widow who had a daughter of exquisite beauty, for whom, in her own mind, she had fixed upon Buondelmonti, a young gentleman, the head of the Buondelmonti family, as her husband; but either from negligence, or, because she thought it might be accomplished at any time, she had not made known her intention, when it happened that the cavalier betrothed himself to a maiden of the Amidei family. This grieved the Donati widow exceedingly; but she hoped, with her daughter's beauty, to disturb the arrangement before the celebration of the marriage; and from an upper apartment, seeing Buondelmonti approach her house alone, she descended, and as he was passing she said to him, "I am glad to learn you have chosen a wife, although I had reserved my daughter for you;" and, pushing the door open, presented her to his view. The cavalier, seeing the beauty of the girl, which was very uncommon, and considering the nobility of her blood, and her portion not being inferior to that of the lady whom he had chosen, became inflamed with such an ardent desire to possess her, that, not thinking of the promise given, or the injury he committed in breaking it, or of the evils which his breach of faith might bring upon himself, said, "Since you have reserved her for me, I should be very ungrateful indeed to refuse her, being yet at liberty to choose;" and without any delay married her. As soon as the fact became known, the Amidei and the Uberti, whose families were allied, were filled with rage, and having assembled with many others, connections of the parties, they concluded that the injury could not be tolerated without disgrace, and that the only vengeance proportionate to the enormity of the offence would be to put Buondelmonti to death. And although some took into consideration the evils that might ensue upon it, Mosca Lamberti said, that those who talk of many things effect nothing, using that trite and common adage, *Cosa fatta capo ha*. Thereupon, they appointed to the execution of the murder Mosca himself, Stiatti Uberti, Lambertuccio Amidei, and Oderigo Fifanti, who, on the morning of Easter day, concealed themselves in a house of the Amidei, situate between the old bridge and St. Stephen's, and as Buondelmonti was passing upon a white horse, thinking it as easy a matter to forget an injury as reject an alliance, he was attacked by them at the foot of the bridge, and slain close by a statue of Mars. This murder divided the whole city; one party espousing the cause of the Buondelmonti, the other that of the Uberti; and as these families possessed men and means of defense, they contended with each other for many years, without one being able to destroy the other.

Florence continued in these troubles till the time of Frederick II., who, being king of Naples, endeavored to strengthen himself against the church; and, to give greater stability to his power in Tuscany, favored the Uberti and their followers, who, with his assistance, expelled the Buondelmonti; thus our city, as all the rest of Italy had long time been, became divided into Guelphs and Ghibellines; and as it will not be superfluous, I shall record the names of the families which took part with each faction. Those who adopted the cause of the Guelphs were the Buondelmonti, Nerli, Rossi, Frescobaldi, Mozzi, Bardi, Pulci, Gherardini, Foraboschi, Bagnesi, Guidalotti,

Sacchetti, Manieri, Lucardesi, Chiaramontesi, Compiobbesi, Cavalcanti, Giandonati, Gianfigliazzi, Scali, Gualterotti, Importuni, Bostichi, Tornaquinci, Vecchietti, Tosinghi, Arrigucci, Agli, Sizi, Adimari, Visdomini, Donati, Passi, della Bella, Ardinghi, Tedaldi, Cerchi. Of the Ghibelline faction were the Uberti, Manelli, Ubriachi, Fifanti, Amidei, Infangati, Malespini, Scolari, Guidi, Galli, Cappiardi, Lamberti, Soldanieri, Cipriani, Toschi, Amieri, Palermini, Migliorelli, Pigli, Barucci, Cattani, Agolanti, Brunelleschi, Caponsacchi, Elisei, Abati, Tidaldini, Giuochi, and Galigai. Besides the noble families on each side above enumerated, each party was joined by many of the higher ranks of the people, so that the whole city was corrupted with this division. The Guelphs being expelled, took refuge in the Upper Val d'Arno, where part of their castles and strongholds were situated, and where they strengthened and fortified themselves against the attacks of their enemies. But, upon the death of Frederick, the most unbiased men, and those who had the greatest authority with the people, considered that it would be better to effect the reunion of the city, than, by keeping her divided, cause her ruin. They therefore induced the Guelphs to forget their injuries and return, and the Ghibellines to lay aside their jealousies and receive them with cordiality.

Chapter II: New form of government in Florence—Military establishments—The greatness of Florence—Movements of the Ghibellines—Ghibellines driven out of the city—Guelphs routed by the forces of the king of Naples—Florence in the power of the king of Naples—Project of the Ghibellines to destroy Florence opposed by Farinata degli Uberti—Adventures of the Guelphs of Florence—The pope gives his standard to the Guelphs—Fears of the Ghibellines and their preparations for the defense of their power—Establishment of trades' companies, and their authority—Count Guido Novello expelled—He goes to Prato—The Guelphs restored to the city—The Ghibellines quit Florence—The Florentines reform the government in favor of the Guelphs—The pope endeavors to restore the Ghibellines and excommunicates Florence—Pope Nicholas III. endeavors to abate the power of Charles king of Naples.

Being united, the Florentines thought the time favorable for the ordination of a free government, and that it would be desirable to provide their means of defense before the new emperor should acquire strength. They therefore divided the city into six parts, and elected twelve citizens, two for each sixth, to govern the whole. These were called Anziani, and were elected annually. To remove the cause of those enmities which had been observed to arise from judicial decisions, they provided two judges from some other state,—one called captain of the people, the other podesta, or provost,—whose duty it was to decide in cases, whether civil or criminal, which occurred among the people. And as order cannot be preserved without a sufficient force for the defense of it, they appointed twenty banners in the city, and seventy-six in the country, upon the rolls of which the names of all the youth were armed; and it was ordered that everyone should appear armed, under his banner, whenever summoned, whether by the captain of the people or the Anziani. They had ensigns according to the kind of arms they used, the bowmen being under one ensign, and the swordsmen, or those who carried a target, under another; and every year, upon the day of Pentecost, ensigns were given with great pomp to the new men, and new leaders were appointed for the whole establishment. To give importance to their armies, and to serve as a point of refuge for those who were exhausted in the fight, and from which, having become refreshed, they might again make head against the enemy, they provided a large car, drawn by two oxen, covered with red cloth, upon which was an ensign of white and red. When they intended to assemble the army, this car was brought into the New Market, and delivered with pomp to the heads of the people. To give solemnity to their enterprises, they had a bell called Martinella, which was rung during a whole month before the forces left the city, in order that the enemy might have time to provide for his defense; so great was the virtue then existing among men, and with so much generosity of mind were they governed, that as it is now considered a brave and prudent act to assail an unprovided enemy, in those days it would have been thought disgraceful, and productive only of a fallacious advantage. This bell was also taken with the army, and served to regulate the keeping and relief of guard, and other matters necessary in the practice of war.

With these ordinations, civil and military, the Florentines established their liberty. Nor is it possible to imagine the power and authority Florence in a short time acquired. She became not only the head of Tuscany, but was enumerated among the first cities of Italy, and would have attained greatness of the most exalted kind, had she not been afflicted with the continual divisions of her citizens. They remained under the this government ten years, during which time they compelled the people of Pistoria, Arezzo, and Sienna, to enter into league with them; and returning with the army from Sienna, they took Volterra, destroyed some castles, and led the inhabitants to Florence. All these enterprises were effected by the advice of the Guelphs, who were much more powerful than the Ghibellines, for the latter were hated by the people as well on account of their haughty bearing while in power, during the time of Frederick, as because the church party was in more favor than that of the emperor; for with the aid of the church they hoped to preserve their liberty, but, with the emperor, they were apprehensive of losing it.

The Ghibellines, in the meantime, finding themselves divested of authority, could not rest, but watched for an occasion of repossessing the government; and they thought the favorable moment come, when they found that Manfred, son of Frederick, had made himself sovereign of Naples, and reduced the power of the church. They, therefore, secretly communicated with him, to resume the management of the state, but could not prevent their proceedings from coming to the knowledge of the Anziani, who immediately summoned the Uberti to appear before them; but instead of obeying, they took arms and fortified themselves in their houses. The people, enraged at this, armed themselves, and with the assistance of the Guelphs, compelled them to quit the city, and, with the whole Ghibelline party, withdraw to Sienna. They then asked assistance of Manfred king of Naples, and by the able conduct of Farinata degli Uberti, the Guelphs were routed by the king's forces upon the river Arbia, with so great slaughter, that those who escaped, thinking Florence lost, did not return thither, but sought refuge at Lucca.

Manfred sent the Count Giordano, a man of considerable reputation in arms, to command his forces. He after the victory, went with the Ghibellines to Florence, and reduced the city entirely to the king's authority, annulling the magistracies and every other institution that retained any appearance of freedom. This injury, committed with little prudence, excited the ardent animosity of the people, and their enmity against the Ghibellines, whose ruin it eventually caused, was increased to the highest pitch. The necessities of the kingdom compelling the Count Giordano to return to Naples, he left at Florence as regal vicar the Count Guido Novallo, lord of Casentino, who called a council of Ghibellines at Empoli. There it was concluded, with only one dissenting voice, that in order to preserve their power in Tuscany, it would be necessary to destroy Florence, as the only means of compelling the Guelphs to withdraw their support from the party of the church. To this so cruel a sentence, given against such a noble city, there was not a citizen who offered any opposition, except Farinata degli Uberti, who openly defended her, saying he had not encountered so many dangers and difficulties, but in the hope of returning to his country; that he still wished for what he had so earnestly sought, nor would he refuse the blessing which fortune now presented, even though by using it, he were to become as much an enemy of those who thought otherwise, as he had been of the Guelphs; and that no one need be afraid the city would occasion the ruin of their country, for he hoped that the valor which had expelled the Guelphs, would be sufficient to defend her. Farinata was a man of undaunted resolution, and excelled greatly in military affairs: being the head of the Ghibelline party, and in high estimation with Manfred, his authority put a stop to the discussion, and induced the rest to think of some other means of preserving their power.

The Lucchese being threatened with the anger of the count, for affording refuge to the Guelphs after the battle of the Arbia, could allow them to remain no longer; so leaving Lucca, they went to Bologna, from whence they were called by the Guelphs of Parma against the Ghibellines of that city, where, having overcome the enemy, the possessions of the latter were assigned to them; so that having increased in honors and riches, and learning that Pope Clement had invited Charles of Anjou to take the kingdom from Manfred, they sent ambassadors to the pope to offer him their services. His holiness not only received them as friends, but gave them a standard upon which his insignia were wrought. It was ever after borne by the Guelphs in battle, and is still used at Florence. Charles having taken the kingdom from Manfred, and slain him, to which success the Guelphs of Florence had contributed, their party became more powerful, and that of the Ghibellines proportionately weaker. In consequence of this, those who with Count Novello governed the city, thought it would be advisable to attach to themselves, with some concession, the people whom they had previously aggravated with every species of injury; but these remedies which, if applied before the necessity came would have been beneficial, being offered when they were no longer considered favors, not only failed of producing any beneficial results to the donors, but hastened their ruin. Thinking, however, to win them to their interests, they restored some of the honors of which they had deprived them. They elected thirty-six citizens from the higher rank of the people, to whom, with two cavaliers, knights or gentlemen, brought from Bologna, the reformation of the government of the city was confided. As soon as they met, they classed the whole of the people according to their arts or trades, and over each art appointed a magistrate, whose duty was to distribute justice to those placed under him. They gave to each company or trade a banner, under which every man was expected to appear armed, whenever the city required it. These arts were at first twelve, seven major and five minor. The minor arts were afterward increased to fourteen, so that the whole made, as at present, twenty-one. The thirty-six reformers also effected other changes for the common good.

Count Guido proposed to lay a tax upon the citizens for the support of the soldiery; but during the discussion found so much difficulty, that he did not dare to use force to obtain it; and thinking he had now lost the government, called together the leaders of the Ghibellines, and they determined to wrest from the people those powers which they had with so little prudence conceded. When they thought they had sufficient force, the thirty-six being assembled, they caused a tumult to be raised, which so alarmed them that they retired to their houses, when suddenly the banners of the Arts were unfurled, and many armed men drawn to them. These, learning that Count Guido and his followers were at St. John's, moved toward the Holy Trinity, and chose Giovanni Soldanieri for their leader. The count, on the other hand, being informed where the people were assembled, proceeded in that direction; nor did the people shun the fight, for, meeting their enemies where now stands the residence of the Tornaquinci, they put the count to flight, with the loss of many of his followers. Terrified with this result, he was afraid his enemies would attack him in the night, and that his own party, finding themselves beaten, would murder him. This impression took such hold of his mind that, without attempting any other remedy, he sought his safety rather in flight than in combat, and, contrary to the advice of the rectors, went with all his people to Prato. But, on finding himself in a place of safety, his fears fled; perceiving his error he wished to correct it, and on the following day, as soon as light appeared, he returned with his people to Florence, to enter the city by force which he had abandoned in cowardice. But his design did not succeed; for the people, who had had difficulty in expelling him, kept him out with facility; so that with grief and shame he went to the Casentino, and the Ghibellines withdrew to their villas.

The people being victorious, by the advice of those who loved the good of the republic, determined to reunite the city, and recall all the citizens as well Guelph as Ghibelline, who yet remained without. The Guelphs returned, after having been expelled six years; the recent offences of the Ghibellines were forgiven, and themselves restored to their country. They were, however, most cordially hated, both by the people and the Guelphs, for the latter could not forget their exile, and the former but too well remembered their tyranny when they were in power; the result was, that the minds of neither party became settled.

While affairs were in this state at Florence, a report prevailed that Corradino, nephew of Manfred, was coming with a force from Germany, for the conquest of Naples; this gave the Ghibellines hope of recovering power, and the Guelphs, considering how they should provide for their security, requested assistance from Charles for their defense, in case of the passage of Corradino. The coming of the forces of Charles rendered the Guelphs insolent, and so alarmed the Ghibellines that they fled the city, without being driven out, two days before the arrival of the troops.

The Ghibellines having departed, the Florentines reorganized the government of the city, and elected twelve men who, as the supreme power, were to hold their magistracy two months, and were not called Anziani or "ancients," but Buono Uomini or "good men." They also formed a council of eighty citizens, which they called the Credenza. Besides these, from each sixth, thirty citizens were chosen, who, with the Credenza and the twelve Buono Uomini, were called the General Council. They also appointed another council of one hundred and twenty citizens, elected from the people and the nobility, to which all those things were finally referred that had undergone the consideration of the other councils, and which distributed the offices of the republic. Having formed this government, they strengthened the Guelphic party by appointing its friends to the principal offices of state, and a variety of other measures, that they might be enabled to defend themselves against the Ghibellines, whose property they divided into three parts, one of which was applied to the public use, another to the Capitani, and the third was assigned to the Guelphs, in satisfaction of the injuries they had received. The pope, too, in order to keep Tuscany in the Guelphic interest, made Charles imperial vicar over the province. While the Florentines, by virtue of the new government, preserved their influence at home by laws, and abroad with arms, the pope died, and after a dispute, which continued two years, Gregory X. was elected, being then in Syria, where he had long lived; but not having witnessed the working of parties, he did not estimate them in the manner his predecessors had done, and passing through Florence on his way to France, he thought it would be the office of a good pastor to unite the city, and so far succeeded that the Florentines consented to receive the Syndics of the Ghibellines in Florence to consider the terms of their recall. They effected an agreement, but the Ghibellines without were so terrified that they did not venture to return. The pope laid the whole blame upon the city, and being enraged excommunicated her, in which state of contumacy she remained as long as the pontiff lived; but was reblessed by his successor Innocent V.

The pontificate was afterward occupied by Nicholas III. of the Orsini family. It has to be remarked that it was invariably the custom of the popes to be jealous of those whose power in Italy had become great, even when its growth had been occasioned by the favors of the church; and as they always endeavored to destroy it, frequent troubles and changes were the result. Their fear of a powerful person caused them to increase the influence of one previously weak; his becoming great caused him also to be feared, and his being feared made them seek the means of destroying him. This mode of thinking and operation occasioned the kingdom of Naples to be taken from Manfred and given to Charles, but as soon as the latter became powerful his ruin was resolved upon. Actuated by these motives, Nicholas III. contrived that, with the influence of the emperor, the government of Tuscany should be taken from Charles, and Latino his legate was therefore sent into the province in the name of the empire.

Chapter III: Changes in Florence—The Ghibellines recalled—New form of government in Florence—The Signory created—Victory over the Aretins—The Gonfalonier of Justice created—Ubaldo Ruffoli the first Gonfalonier—Giano della Bella—New reform by his advice—Giano della Bella becomes a voluntary exile—Dissensions between the people and the nobility—The tumults composed—Reform of Government—Public buildings—The prosperous state of the city.

Florence was at this time in a very unhappy condition; for the great Guelphic families had become insolent, and set aside the authority of the magistrates; so that murders and other atrocities were daily committed, and the perpetrators escaped unpunished, under the protection of one or other of the nobility. The leaders of the people, in order to restrain this insolence, determined to recall those who had been expelled, and thus gave the legate an opportunity of uniting the city. The Ghibellines returned, and, instead of twelve governors, fourteen were appointed, seven for each party, who held their office one year, and were to be chosen by the pope. The Florentines lived under this government two years, till the pontificate of Martin, who restored to Charles all the authority which had been taken from him by Nicholas, so that parties were again active in Tuscany; for the Florentines took arms against the emperor's governor, and to deprive the Ghibellines of power, and restrain the nobility, established a new form of government. This was in the year 1282, and the companies of the Arts, since magistrates had been appointed and colors given to them, had acquired so great influence, that of their own authority they ordered that, instead of fourteen citizens, three should be appointed and called Priors, to hold the government of the republic two months, and chosen from either the people or the nobility. After the expiration of the first magistracy they were augmented to six, that one might be chosen from each sixth of the city, and this number was preserved till the year 1342, when the city was divided into quarters, and the Priors became eight, although upon some occasions during the interim they were twelve.

This government, as will be seen hereafter, occasioned the ruin of the nobility; for the people by various causes excluded them from all participation in it, and then trampled upon them without respect. The nobles at first, owing to their divisions among themselves, made no opposition; and each being anxious to rob the other of influence in the state, they lost it altogether. To this government a palace was given, in which they were to reside constantly, and all requisite officers were appointed; it having been previously the custom of councils and magistrates to assemble in churches. At first they were only called Priors, but to increase their distinction the word signori, or lords, was soon afterward adopted. The Florentines remained for some time in domestic quiet, during which they made war with the Aretins for having expelled the Guelphs, and obtained a complete victory over them at Campaldino. The city being increased in riches and population, it was found expedient to extend the walls, the circle of which was enlarged to the extent it at present remains, although its diameter was previously only the space between the old bridge and the church of St. Lorenzo.

Wars abroad and peace within the city had caused the Guelph and Ghibelline factions to become almost extinct; and the only party feeling which seemed occasionally to glow, was that which naturally exists in all cities between the higher classes and the people; for the latter, wishing to live in conformity with the laws, and the former to be themselves the rulers of the people, it was not possible for them to abide in perfect amity together. This ungenial disposition, while their fear of the Ghibellines kept them in order, did not discover itself, but no sooner were they subdued than it broke forth, and not a day passed without some of the populace being injured, while the laws were insufficient to procure redress, for every noble with his relations and friends defended himself against the forces of the Priors and the Capitano. To remedy this evil, the leaders of the Arts' companies ordered that every Signory at the time of entering upon the duties of office should appoint a Gonfalonier of Justice, chosen from the people, and place a thousand armed men at his disposal divided into twenty companies of fifty men each, and that he, with his gonfalon or banner and his forces, should be ready to enforce the execution of the laws whenever called upon, either by the Signors themselves or the Capitano. The first elected to this high office was Ubaldo Ruffoli. This man unfurled his gonfalon, and destroyed the houses of the Galletti, on account of a member of that family having slain one of the Florentine people in France. The violent animosities among the nobility enabled the companies of the Arts to establish this law with facility; and the former no sooner saw the provision which had been made against them than they felt the acrimonious spirit with which it was enforced. At first it impressed them with greater terror, but they soon after returned to their accustomed insolence, for one or more of their body always making part of the Signory, gave them opportunities of impeding the Gonfalonier, so that he could not perform the duties of his office. Besides this, the accuser always required a witness of the injury he had received, and no one dared to give evidence against the nobility. Thus in a short time Florence again fell into the same disorders as before, and the tyranny exercised against the people was as great as ever; for the decisions of justice were either prevented or delayed, and sentences were not carried into execution.

In this unhappy state, the people not knowing what to do, Giano della Bella, of a very noble family, and a lover of liberty, encouraged the heads of the Arts to reform the constitution of the city; and by his advice it was ordered that the Gonfalonier should reside with the Priors, and have four thousand men at his command. They deprived the nobility of the right to sit in the Signory. They condemned the associates of a criminal to the same penalty as himself, and ordered that public report should be taken as evidence. By these laws, which were called the ordinations of justice, the people acquired great influence, and Giano della Bella not a small share of trouble; for he was thoroughly hated by the great, as the destroyer of their power, while the opulent among the people envied him, for they thought he possessed too great authority. This became very evident upon the first occasion that presented itself.

It happened that a man from the class of the people was killed in a riot, in which several of the nobility had taken a part, and among the rest Corso Donati, to whom, as the most forward of the party, the death was attributed. He was, therefore, taken by the captain of the people, and whether he was really innocent of the crime or the Capitano was afraid of condemning him, he was acquitted. This acquittal displeased the people so much, that, seizing their arms, they ran to the house of Giano della Bella, to beg that he would compel the execution of those laws which he had himself made. Giano, who wished Corso to be punished, did not insist upon their laying down their arms, as many were of opinion he ought to have done, but advised them to go to the Signory, complain of the fact, and beg that they would take it into consideration. The people, full of wrath, thinking themselves insulted by the Capitano and abandoned by Giano della Bella, instead of going to the Signory went to the palace of the Capitano, of which they made themselves masters, and plundered it.

This outrage displeased the whole city, and those who wished the ruin of Giano laid the entire blame upon him; and as in the succeeding Signory there was an enemy of his, he was accused to the Capitano as the originator of the riot. While the case was being tried, the people took arms, and, proceeding to his house, offered to defend him against the Signory and his enemies. Giano, however, did not wish to put this burst of popular favor to the proof, or trust his life to the magistrates, for he feared the malignity of the latter and the instability of the former; so, in order to remove an occasion for his enemies to injure him, or his friends to offend the laws, he determined to withdraw, deliver his countrymen from the fear they had of him, and, leaving the city which at his own charge and peril he had delivered from the servitude of the great, become a voluntary exile.

After the departure of Giano della Bella the nobility began to entertain hopes of recovering their authority; and judging their misfortune to have arisen from their divisions, they sent two of their body to the Signory, which they thought was favorable to them, to beg they would be pleased to moderate the severity of the laws made against them. As soon as their demand became known, the minds of the people were much excited; for they were afraid the Signors would submit to them; and so, between the desire of the nobility and the jealousy of the people, arms were resorted to. The nobility were drawn together in three places: near the church of St. John, in the New Market, and in the Piazza of the Mozzi, under three leaders, Forese Adimari, Vanni de Mozzi, and Geri Spini. The people assembled in immense numbers, under their ensigns, before the palace of the Signory, which at that time was situated near St. Procolo; and, as they suspected the integrity of the Signory, they added six citizens to their number to take part in the management of affairs.

While both parties were preparing for the fight, some individuals, as well of the people as of the nobility, accompanied by a few priests of respectable character, mingled among them for the purpose of effecting a pacification, reminding the nobility that their loss of power, and the laws which were made against them, had been occasioned by their haughty conduct, and the mischievous tendency of their proceedings; that resorting to arms to recover by force what they had lost by illiberal measures and disunion, would tend to the destruction of their country and increase the difficulties of their own position; that they should bear in mind that the people, both in riches, numbers, and hatred, were far stronger than they; and that their nobility, on account of which they assumed to be above others, did not contribute to win battles, and would be found, when they came to arms, to be but an empty name, and insufficient to defend them against so many. On the other hand, they reminded the people that it is not prudent to wish always to have the last blow; that it is an injudicious step to drive men to desperation, for he who is without hope is also without fear; that they ought not to forget that in the wars the nobility had always done honor to the country, and therefore it was neither wise nor just to pursue them with so much bitterness; and that although the nobility could bear with patience the loss of the supreme magistracy, they could not endure that, by the existing laws, it should be in the power of everyone to drive them from their country; and, therefore, it would be well to qualify these laws, and, in furtherance of so good a result, be better to lay down their arms than, trusting to numbers, try the fortune of a battle; for it is often seen that the many are overcome by the few. Variety of opinion was found among the people; many wished to decide the question by arms at once, for they were assured it would have to be done some time, and that it would be better to do so then than delay till the enemy had acquired greater strength; and that if they thought a mitigation of the laws would satisfy them, that then they would be glad to comply, but that the pride of the nobility was so great they would not submit unless they were compelled. To many others, who were more peaceable and better disposed, it appeared a less evil to qualify the laws a little than to come to battle; and their opinion prevailing, it was provided that no accusation against the nobility could be received unless supported with sufficient testimony.

Although arms were laid aside, both parties remained full of suspicion, and each fortified itself with men and places of strength. The people reorganized the government, and lessened the number of its officers, to which measure they were induced by finding that the Signors appointed from the families, of which the following were the heads, had been favorable to the nobility, viz.: the Mancini, Magalotti, Altoviti, Peruzzi, and Cerretani. Having settled the government, for the greater magnificence and security of the Signory, they laid the foundation of their palace; and to make space for the piazza, removed the houses that had belonged to the Uberti; they also at the same period commenced the public prisons. These buildings were completed in a few years; nor did our city ever enjoy a greater state of prosperity than in those times: filled with men of great wealth and reputation; possessing within her walls 30,000 men capable of bearing arms, and in the country 70,000, while the whole of Tuscany, either as subjects or friends, owed obedience to Florence. And although there might be some indignation and jealousy between the nobility and the people, they did not produce any evil effect, but all lived together in unity and peace. And if this peace had not been disturbed by internal enmities there would have been no cause of apprehension whatever, for the city had nothing to fear either from the empire or from those citizens whom political reasons kept from their homes, and was in condition to meet all the states of Italy with her own forces. The evil, however, which external powers could not effect, was brought about by those within.

Chapter IV: The Cerchi and the Donati—Origin of the Bianca and Nera factions in Pistoia—They come to Florence—Open enmity of the Donati and the Cerchi—Their first conflict—The Cerchi head the Bianca faction—The Donati take part with the Nera—The pope's legate at Florence increases the confusion with an interdict—New affray between the Cerchi and the Donati—The Donati and others of the Nera faction banished by the advice of Dante Alighieri—Charles of Valois sent by the pope to Florence—The Florentines suspect him—Corso Donati and the rest of the Nera party return to Florence—Veri Cerchi flies—The pope's legate again in Florence—The city again interdicted—New disturbances—The Bianchi banished—Dante banished—Corso Donati excites fresh troubles—The pope's legate endeavors to restore the emigrants but does not succeed—Great fire in Florence.

The Cerchi and the Donati were, for riches, nobility, and the number and influence of their followers, perhaps the two most distinguished families in Florence. Being neighbors, both in the city and the country, there had arisen between them some slight displeasure, which, however, had not occasioned an open quarrel, and perhaps never would have produced any serious effect if the malignant humors had not been increased by new causes. Among the first families of Pistoia was the Cancellieri. It happened that Lore, son of Gulielmo, and Geri, son of Bertacca, both of this family, playing together, and coming to words, Geri was slightly wounded by Lore. This displeased Gulielmo; and, designing by a suitable apology to remove all cause of further animosity, he ordered his son to go to the house of the father of the youth whom he had wounded and ask pardon. Lore obeyed his father; but this act of virtue failed to soften the cruel mind of Bertacca, and having caused Lore to be seized, in order to add the greatest indignity to his brutal act, he ordered his servants to chop off the youth's hand upon a block used for cutting meat upon, and then said to him, "Go to thy father, and tell him that sword wounds are cured with iron and not with words."

The unfeeling barbarity of this act so greatly exasperated Gulielmo that he ordered his people to take arms for his revenge. Bertacca prepared for his defense, and not only that family, but the whole city of Pistoia, became divided. And as the Cancellieri were descended from a Cancelliere who had had two wives, of whom one was called Bianca (white), one party was named by those who were descended from her *Bianca*; and the other, by way of greater distinction, was called *Nera* (black). Much and long-continued strife took place between the two, attended with the death of many men and the destruction of much property; and not being able to effect a union among themselves, but weary of the evil, and anxious either to bring it to an end, or, by engaging others in their quarrel, increase it, they came to Florence, where the Neri, on account of their familiarity with the Donati, were favored by Corso, the head of that family; and on this account the Bianchi, that they might have a powerful head to defend them against the Donati, had recourse to Veri de Cerchi, a man in no respect inferior to Corso.

This quarrel, and the parties in it, brought from Pistoia, increased the old animosity between the Cerchi and the Donati, and it was already so manifest, that the Priors and all well-disposed men were in hourly apprehension of its breaking out, and causing a division of the whole city. They therefore applied to the pontiff, praying that he would interpose his authority between these turbulent parties, and provide the remedy which they found themselves unable to furnish. The pope sent for Veri, and charged him to make peace with the Donati, at which Veri exhibited great astonishment, saying that he had no enmity against them, and that as pacification presupposes war, he did not know, there being no war between them, how peacemaking could be necessary. Veri having returned from Rome without anything being effected, the rage of the parties increased to such a degree, that any trivial accident seemed sufficient to make it burst forth, as indeed presently happened.

It was in the month of May, during which, and upon holidays, it is the custom of Florence to hold festivals and public rejoicings throughout the city. Some youths of the Donati family, with their friends, upon horseback, were standing near the church of the Holy Trinity to look at a party of ladies who were dancing; thither also came some of the Cerchi, like the Donati, accompanied with many of the nobility, and, not knowing that the Donati were before them, pushed their horses and jostled them; thereupon the Donati, thinking themselves insulted, drew their swords, nor were the Cerchi at all backward to do the same, and not till after the interchange of many wounds, they separated. This disturbance was the beginning of great evils; for the whole city became divided, the people as well as the nobility, and the parties took the names of the Bianchi and the Neri. The Cerchi were at the head of the Bianchi faction, to which adhered the Adimari, the Abati, a part of the Tosinghi, of the Bardi, of the Rossi, of the Frescobaldi, of the Nerli, and of the Manelli; all the Mozzi, the Scali, Gherardini, Cavalcanti, Malespini, Bostichi, Giandonati, Vecchietti, and Arrigucci. To these were joined many families of the people, and all the Ghibellines then in Florence, so that their great numbers gave them almost the entire government of the city.

The Donati, at the head of whom was Corso, joined the Nera party, to which also adhered those members of the above-named families who did not take part with the Bianchi; and besides these, the whole of the Pazzi, the Bisdomini, Manieri, Bagnesi, Tornaquinci, Spini, Buondelmonti, Gianfigliazzi, and the Brunelleschi. Nor did the evil confine itself to the city alone, for the whole country was divided upon it, so that the Captains of the Six Parts, and whoever were attached to the Guelphic party or the well-being of the republic, were very much afraid that this new division would occasion the destruction of the city, and give new life to the Ghibelline faction. They, therefore, sent again to Pope Boniface, desiring that, unless he wished that city which had always been the shield of the church should either be ruined or become Ghibelline, he would consider some means for her relief. The pontiff thereupon sent to Florence, as his legate, Cardinal Matteo d'Acquasparta, a Portuguese, who, finding the Bianchi, as the most powerful, the least in fear, not quite submissive to him, he interdicted the city, and left it in anger, so that greater confusion now prevailed than had done previously to his coming.

The minds of men being in great excitement, it happened that at a funeral which many of the Donati and the Cerchi attended, they first came to words and then to arms, from which, however, nothing but merely tumult resulted at the moment. However, having each retired to their houses, the Cerchi determined to attack the Donati, but, by the valor of Corso, they were repulsed and great numbers of them wounded. The city was in arms. The laws and the Signory were set at nought by the rage of the nobility, and the best and wisest citizens were full of apprehension. The Donati and their followers, being the least powerful, were in the greatest fear, and to provide for their safety they called together Corso, the Captains of the Parts, and the other leaders of the Neri, and resolved to apply to the pope to appoint some personage of royal blood, that he might reform Florence; thinking by this means to overcome the Bianchi. Their meeting and determination became known to the Priors, and the adverse party represented it as a conspiracy against the liberties of the republic. Both parties being in arms, the Signory, one of whom at that time was the poet Dante, took courage, and from his advice and prudence, caused the people to rise for the preservation of order, and being joined by many from the country, they compelled the leaders of both parties to lay aside their arms, and banished Corso, with many of the Neri. And as an evidence of the impartiality of their motives, they also banished many of the Bianchi, who, however, soon afterward, under pretense of some justifiable cause, returned.

Corso and his friends, thinking the pope favorable to their party, went to Rome and laid their grievances before him, having previously forwarded a statement of them in writing. Charles of Valois, brother of the king of France, was then at the papal court, having been called into Italy by the king of Naples, to go over into Sicily. The pope, therefore, at the earnest prayers of the banished Florentines, consented to send Charles to Florence, till the season suitable for his going to Sicily should arrive. He therefore came, and although the Bianchi, who then governed, were very apprehensive, still, as the head of the Guelphs, and appointed by the pope, they did not dare to oppose him, and in order to secure his friendship, they gave him authority to dispose of the city as he thought proper.

Thus authorized, Charles armed all his friends and followers, which step gave the people so strong a suspicion that he designed to rob them of their liberty, that each took arms, and kept at his own house, in order to be ready, if Charles should make any such attempt. The Cerchi and the leaders of the Bianchi faction had acquired universal hatred by having, while at the head of the republic, conducted themselves with unbecoming pride; and this induced Corso and the banished of the Neri party to return to Florence, knowing well that Charles and the Captains of the Parts were favorable to them. And while the citizens, for fear of Charles, kept themselves in arms, Corso, with all the banished, and followed by many others, entered Florence without the least impediment. And although Veri de Cerchi was advised to oppose him, he refused to do so, saying that he wished the people of Florence, against whom he came, should punish him. However, the contrary happened, for he was welcomed, not punished by them; and it behooved Veri to save himself by flight.

Corso, having forced the Pinti Gate, assembled his party at San Pietro Maggiore, near his own house, where, having drawn together a great number of friends and people desirous of change, he set at liberty all who had been imprisoned for offenses, whether against the state or against individuals. He compelled the existing Signory to withdraw privately to their own houses, elected a new one from the people of the Neri party, and for five days plundered the leaders of the Bianchi. The Cerchi, and the other heads of their faction, finding Charles opposed to them, withdrew from the city, and retired to their strongholds. And although at first they would not listen to the advice of the pope, they were now compelled to turn to him for assistance, declaring that instead of uniting the city, Charles had caused greater disunion than before. The pope again sent Matteo d'Acquasparta, his legate, who made peace between the Cerchi and the Donati, and strengthened it with marriages and new betrothals. But wishing that the Bianchi should participate in the employments of the government, to which the Neri who were then at the head of it would not consent, he withdrew, with no more satisfaction nor less enraged than on the former occasion, and left the city interdicted for disobedience.

Both parties remained in Florence, and equally discontented; the Neri from seeing their enemies at hand, and apprehending the loss of their power, and the Bianchi from finding themselves without either honor or authority; and to these natural causes of animosity new injuries were added. Niccolo de' Cerchi, with many of his friends, went to his estates, and being arrived at the bridge of Affrico, was attacked by Simone, son of Corso Donati. The contest was obstinate, and one each side had a sorrowful conclusion; for Niccolo was slain, and Simone was so severely wounded that he died on the following night.

This event again disturbed the entire city; and although the Neri were most to blame, they were defended by those who were at the head of affairs; and before sentence was delivered, a conspiracy of the Bianchi with Piero Ferrante, one of the barons who had accompanied Charles, was discovered, by whose assistance they sought to be replaced in the government. The matter became known from letters addressed to him by the Cerchi, although some were of opinion that they were not genuine, but written and pretended to be found, by the Donati, to abate the infamy which their party had acquired by the death of Niccolo. The whole of the Cerchi were, however, banished,—with their followers of the Bianchi party, of whom was Dante the poet,—their property confiscated, and their houses pulled down. They sought refuge, with a great number of Ghibellines who had joined them, in many places, seeking fresh fortunes in new undertakings. Charles, having effected the purpose of his coming, left the city, and returned to the pope to pursue his enterprise against Sicily, in which he was neither wiser nor more fortunate than he had been at Florence; so that with disgrace and the loss of many of his followers, he withdrew to France.

After the departure of Charles, Florence remained quiet. Corso alone was restless, thinking he did not possess that sort of authority in the city which was due to his rank; for the government being in the hands of the people, he saw the offices of the republic administered by many inferior to himself. Moved by passions of this kind, he endeavored, under the pretense of an honorable design, to justify his own dishonorable purposes, and accused many citizens who had the management of the public money, of applying it to their private uses, and recommended that they should be brought to justice and punished. This opinion was adopted by many who had the same views as himself; and many in ignorance joined them, thinking Corso actuated only by pure patriotism. On the other hand, the accused citizens, enjoying the popular favor, defended themselves, and this difference arose to such a height, that, after civil means, they had recourse to arms. Of the one party were Corso and Lottieri, bishop of Florence, with many of the nobility and some of the people; on the other side were the Signory, with the greater part of the people; so that skirmishes took place in many parts of the city. The Signory, seeing their danger great, sent for aid to the Lucchese, and presently all the people of Lucca were in Florence. With their assistance the disturbances were settled for the moment, and the people retained the government and their liberty, without attempting by any other means to punish the movers of the disorder.

The pope had heard of the tumults at Florence, and sent his legate, Niccolo da Prato, to settle them, who, being in high reputation both for his quality, learning, and mode of life, presently acquired so much of the people's confidence, that authority was given him to establish such a government as he should think proper. As he was of Ghibelline origin, he determined to recall the banished; but designing first to gain the affections of the lower orders, he renewed the ancient companies of the people, which increased the popular power and reduced that of the nobility. The legate, thinking the multitude on his side, now endeavored to recall the banished, and, after attempting in many ways, none of which succeeded, he fell so completely under the suspicion of the government, that he was compelled to quit the city, and returned to the pope in great wrath, leaving Florence full of confusion and suffering under an interdict. Neither was the city disturbed with one division alone, but by many; first the enmity between the people and the nobility, then that of the Ghibellines and the Guelphs, and lastly, of the Bianchi and the Neri. All the citizens were, therefore, in arms, for many were dissatisfied with the departure of the legate, and wished for the return of the banished. The first who set this disturbance on foot were the Medici and the Guinigi, who, with the legate, had discovered themselves in favor of the rebels; and thus skirmishes took place in many parts of the city.

In addition to these evils a fire occurred, which first broke out at the garden of St. Michael, in the houses of the Abati; it thence extended to those of the Capoinsacchi, and consumed them, with those of the Macci, Amieri, Toschi, Cipriani, Lamberti, Cavalcanti, and the whole of the New Market; from thence it spread to the gate of St. Maria, and burned it to the ground; turning from the old bridge, it destroyed the houses of the Gherardini, Pulci, Amidei, and Lucardesi, and with these so many others that the number amounted to seventeen hundred. It was the opinion of many that this fire occurred by accident during the heat of the disturbances. Others affirm that it was begun willfully by Neri Abati, prior of St. Pietro Scarragio, a dissolute character, fond of mischief, who, seeing the people occupied with the combat, took the opportunity of committing a wicked act, for which the citizens, being thus employed, could offer no remedy. And to insure his success, he set fire to the house of his own brotherhood, where he had the best opportunity of doing it. This was in the year 1304, Florence being afflicted both with fire and the sword. Corso Donati alone remained unarmed in so many tumults; for he thought he would more easily become the arbitrator between the contending parties when, weary of strife, they should be inclined to accommodation. They laid down their arms, however, rather from satiety of evil than from any desire of union; and the only consequence was, that the banished were not recalled, and the party which favored them remained inferior.

Chapter V. The emigrants attempt to re-enter Florence, but are not allowed to do so—The companies of the people restored—Restless conduct of Corso Donati—The ruin of Corso Donati—Corso Donati accused and condemned—Riot at the house of Corso—Death of Corso—His character—Fruitless attempt of the Emperor Henry against the Florentines—The emigrants are restored to the city—The citizens place themselves under the king of Naples for five years—War with Uguccione della Faggiuola—The Florentines routed—Florence withdraws herself from subjection to King Robert, and expels the Count Novello—Lando d'Agobbio—His tyranny—His departure.

The legate being returned to Rome, and hearing of the new disturbance which had occurred, persuaded the pope that if he wished to unite the Florentines, it would be necessary to have twelve of the first citizens appear before him; and having thus removed the principal causes of disunion, he might easily put a stop to it. The pope took this advice, and the citizens, among whom was Corso Donati, obeyed the summons. These having left the city, the legate told the exiles that now, when the city was deprived of her leaders, was the time for them to return. They, therefore, having assembled, came to Florence, and entering by a part of the wall not yet completed, proceeded to the piazza of St. Giovanni. It is worthy of remark, that those who, a short time previously, when they came unarmed and begged to be restored to their country, had fought for their return, now, when they saw them in arms and resolved to enter by force, took arms to oppose them (so much more was the common good esteemed than private friendship), and being joined by the rest of the citizens compelled them to return to the place whence they had come. They failed in their undertaking by having left part of their force at Lastra, and by not having waited the arrival of Tolosetto Uberti, who had to come from Pistoia with three hundred horse; for they thought celerity rather than numbers would give them the victory; and it often happens, in similar enterprises, that delay robs us of the occasion, and too great anxiety to be forward prevents us of the power, or makes us act before we are properly prepared.

The banished having retired, Florence again returned to her old divisions; and in order to deprive the Cavalcanti of their authority, the people took from them the Stinche, a castle situated in the Val di Greve, and anciently belonging to the family. And as those who were taken in it were the first who were put into the new prisons, the latter were, and still continue, named after it, the Stinche. The leaders of the republic also re-established the companies of the people, and gave them the ensigns that were first used by the companies of the Arts; the heads of which were called Gonfaloniers of the companies and colleagues of the Signory; and ordered, that when any disturbance arose they should assist the Signory with arms, and in peace with counsel. To the two ancient rectors they added an executor, or sheriff, who, with the Gonfaloniers, was to aid in repressing the insolence of the nobility.

In the meantime the pope died. Corso, with the other citizens, returned from Rome; and all would have been well if his restless mind had not occasioned new troubles. It was his common practice to be of a contrary opinion to the most powerful men in the city; and whatever he saw the people inclined to do, he exercised his utmost influence to effect, in order to attach them to himself; so that he was a leader in all differences, at the head of every new scheme, and whoever wished to obtain anything extraordinary had recourse to him. This conduct caused him to be hated by many of the highest distinction; and their hatred increased to such a degree that the Neri faction to which he belonged, became completely divided; for Corso, to attain his ends, had availed himself of private force and authority, and of the enemies of the state. But so great was the influence attached to his person, that everyone feared him. Nevertheless, in order to strip him of the popular favor (which by this means may easily be done), a report was set on foot that he intended to make himself prince of the city; and to the design his conduct gave great appearance of probability, for his way of living quite exceeded all civil bounds; and the opinion gained further strength, upon his taking to wife a daughter of Uguccione della Faggiuola, head of the Ghibelline and Bianchi faction, and one of the most powerful men in Tuscany.

When this marriage became known it gave courage to his adversaries, and they took arms against him; and for the same reason the people ceased to defend him, and the greater part of them joined the ranks of his enemies, the leaders of whom were Rosso della Tosa, Pazzino dei Pazzi, Geri Spini, and Berto Brunelleschi. These, with their followers, and the greater part of the people, assembled before the palace of the Signory, by whose command a charge was made before Piero Branca, captain of the people, against Corso, of intending, with the aid of Uguccione, to usurp the government. He was then summoned, and for disobedience, declared a rebel; nor did two hours pass over between the accusation and the sentence. The judgment being given, the Signory, with the companies of the people under their ensigns, went in search of him, who, although seeing himself abandoned by many of his followers, aware of the sentence against him, the power of the Signory, and the multitude of his enemies, remained undaunted, and fortified his houses, in the hope of defending them till Uguccione, for whom he had sent, should come to his relief. Their residences, and the streets approaching them, were barricaded and taken possession of by

Chapter V: The emigrants attempt to re-enter Florence, but are not allowed to do so—The companies of the people restored—Restless conduct of Corso Donati—The ruin of Corso Donati—Corso Donati accused and condemned—Riot at the house of Corso—Death of Corso—His character—Fruitless attempt of the Emperor Henry against the Florentines—The emigrants are restored to the city—The citizens place themselves under the king of Naples for five years—War with Uguccione della Faggiuola—The Florentines routed—Florence withdraws herself from subjection to King Robert, and expels the Count Novello—Lando d'Agobbio—His tyranny—His departure.

The legate being returned to Rome, and hearing of the new disturbance which had occurred, persuaded the pope that if he wished to unite the Florentines, it would be necessary to have twelve of the first citizens appear before him, and having thus removed the principal causes of disunion, he might easily put a stop to it. The pontiff took this advice, and the citizens, among whom was Corso Donati, obeyed the summons. These having left the city, the legate told the exiles that now, when the city was deprived of her leaders, was the time for them to return. They, therefore, having assembled, came to Florence, and entering by a part of the wall not yet completed, proceeded to the piazza of St. Giovanni. It is worthy of remark, that those who, a short time previously, when they came unarmed and begged to be restored to their country, had fought for their return, now, when they saw them in arms and resolved to enter by force, took arms to oppose them (so much more was the common good esteemed than private friendship), and being joined by the rest of the citizens, compelled them to return to the places whence they had come. They failed in their undertaking by having left part of their force at Lastra, and by not having waited the arrival of Tolosetto Uberti, who had to come from Pistoia with three hundred horse; for they thought celerity rather than numbers would give them the victory; and it often happens, in similar enterprises, that delay robs us of the occasion, and too great anxiety to be forward prevents us of the power, or makes us act before we are properly prepared.

The banished having retired, Florence again returned to her old divisions; and in order to deprive the Cavalcanti of their authority, the people took from them the Stinche, a castle situated in the Val di Greve, and anciently belonging to the family. And as those who were taken in it were the first who were put into the new prisons, the latter were, and still continue, named after it,—the Stinche. The leaders of the republic also re-established the companies of the people, and gave them the ensigns that were first used by the companies of the Arts; the heads of which were called Gonfaloniers of the companies and colleagues of the Signory; and ordered, that when any disturbance arose they should assist the Signory with arms, and in peace with counsel. To the two ancient rectors they added an executor, or sheriff, who, with the Gonfaloniers, was to aid in repressing the insolence of the nobility.

In the meantime the pope died. Corso, with the other citizens, returned from Rome; and all would have been well if his restless mind had not occasioned new troubles. It was his common practice to be of a contrary opinion to the most powerful men in the city; and whatever he saw the people inclined to do, he exercised his utmost influence to effect, in order to attach them to himself; so that he was a leader in all differences, at the head of every new scheme, and whoever wished to obtain anything extraordinary had recourse to him. This conduct caused him to be hated by many of the highest distinction; and their hatred increased to such a degree that the Neri faction to which he belonged, became completely divided; for Corso, to attain his ends, had availed himself of private force and authority, and of the enemies of the state. But so great was the influence attached to his person, that everyone feared him. Nevertheless, in order to strip him of the popular favor (which by this means may easily be done), a report was set on foot that he intended to make himself prince of the city; and to the design his conduct gave great appearance of probability, for his way of living quite exceeded all civil bounds; and the opinion gained further strength, upon his taking to wife a daughter of Uguccione della Faggiuola, head of the Ghibelline and Bianchi faction, and one of the most powerful men in Tuscany.

When this marriage became known it gave courage to his adversaries, and they took arms against him; for the same reason the people ceased to defend him, and the greater part of them joined the ranks of his enemies, the leaders of whom were Rosso della Tosa, Pazino dei Pazzi, Geri Spini, and Berto Brunelleschi. These, with their followers, and the greater part of the people, assembled before the palace of the Signory, by whose command a charge was made before Piero Branca, captain of the people, against Corso, of intending, with the aid of Uguccione, to usurp the government. He was then summoned, and for disobedience, declared a rebel; nor did two hours pass over between the accusation and the sentence. The judgment being given, the Signory, with the companies of the people under their ensigns, went in search of him, who, although seeing himself abandoned by many of his followers, aware of the sentence against him, the power of the Signory, and the multitude of his enemies, remained undaunted, and fortified his houses, in the hope of defending them till Uguccione, for whom he had sent, should come to his Relief. His residences, and the streets approaching them, were barricaded and taken possession of by his partisans, who defended them so bravely that the enemy, although in great numbers, could not force them, and the battle became one of the hottest, with wounds and death on all sides. But the people, finding they could not drive them from their ground, took possession of the adjoining houses, and by unobserved passages obtained entry. Corso, thus finding himself surrounded by his foes, no longer retaining any hope of assistance from Uguccione, and without a chance of victory, thought only of effecting his personal safety, and with Gherardo Bordoni, and some of his bravest and most trusted friends, fought a passage through the thickest of their enemies, and effected their escape from the city by the Gate of the Cross. They were, however, pursued by vast numbers, and Gherardo was slain upon the bridge of Affrico by Boccaccio Cavicciulli. Corso was overtaken and made prisoner by a party of Catalan horse, in the service of the Signory, at Rovezzano. But when approaching Florence, that he might avoid being seen and torn to pieces by his victorious enemies, he allowed himself to fall from horseback, and being down, one of those who conducted him cut his throat. The body was found by the monks of San Salvi, and buried without any ceremony due to his rank. Such was the end of Corso, to whom his country and the Neri faction were indebted for much both of good and evil; and if he had possessed a cooler spirit he would have left behind him a more happy memory. Nevertheless, he deserves to be enumerated among the most distinguished men our city has produced. True it is, that his restless conduct made both his country and his party forgetful of their obligation to him. The same cause also produced his miserable end, and brought many troubles upon both his friends and his country. Uguccione, coming to the assistance of his relative, learned at Remoli that Corso had been overcome by the people, and finding that he could not render him any assistance, in order to avoid bringing evil upon himself without occasion, he returned home.

After the death of Corso, which occurred in the year 1308, the disturbances were appeased, and the people lived quietly till it was reported that the Emperor Henry was coming into Italy, and with him all the Florentine emigrants, to whom he had promised restoration to their country. The leaders of the government thought, that in order to lessen the number of their enemies, it would be well to recall, of their own will, all who had been expelled, excepting such as the law had expressly forbidden to return. Of the number not admitted, were the greater part of the Ghibellines, and some of those of the Bianchi faction, among whom were Dante Alighieri, the sons of Veri de' Cerchi and of Giano della Bella. Besides this they sent for aid to Robert, king of Naples, and not being able to obtain it of him as friends, they gave their city to him for five years, that he might defend them as his own people. The emperor entered Italy by the way of Pisa, and proceeded by the marshes to Rome, where he was crowned in the year 1312. Then, having determined to subdue the Florentines, he approached their city by the way of Perugia and Arezzo, and halted with his army at the monastery of San Salvi, about a mile from Florence, where he remained fifty days without effecting anything. Despairing of success against Florence, he returned to Pisa, where he entered into an agreement with Frederick, king of Sicily, to undertake the conquest of Naples, and proceeded with his people accordingly; but while filled with the hope of victory, and carrying dismay into the heart of King Robert, having reached Buonconvento, he died.

Shortly after this, Uguccione della Faggiuola, having by means of the Ghibelline party become lord of Pisa and of Lucca, caused, with the assistance of these cities, very serious annoyance to the neighbouring places. In order to effect their relief the Florentines requested King Robert would allow his brother Piero to take the command of their armies. On the other hand, Uguccione continued to increase his power; and either by force or fraud obtained possession of many castles in the Val d'Arno and the Val di Nievole; and having besieged Monte Cataini, the Florentines found it would be necessary to send to its relief, that they might not see him burn and destroy their whole territory. Having drawn together a large army, they entered the Val di Nievole where they came up with Uguccione, and were routed after a severe battle in which Piero the king's brother and 2,000 men were slain; but the body of the Prince was never found. Neither was the victory a joyful one to Uguccione; for one of his sons, and many of the leaders of his army, fell in the strife.

The Florentines after this defeat fortified their territory, and King Robert sent them, for commander of their forces, the Count d'Andria, usually called Count Novello, by whose deportment, or because it is natural to the Florentines to find every state tedious, the city, notwithstanding the war with Uguccione, became divided into friends and enemies of the king. Simon della Tosa, the Magalotti, and certain others of the people who had attained greater influence in the government than the rest, were leaders of the party against the king. By these means messengers were sent to France, and afterward into Germany, to solicit leaders and forces that they might drive out the count, whom the king had appointed governor; but they failed of obtaining any. Nevertheless they did not abandon their undertaking, but still desirous of one whom they might worship, after an unavailing search in France and Germany, they discovered him at Agobbio, and having expelled the Count Novello, caused Lando d'Agobbio to be brought into the city as Bargello (sheriff), and gave him the most unlimited power of the citizens. This man was cruel and rapacious; and going through the country accompanied with an armed force, he put many to death at the mere instigation of those who had endowed him with authority. His insolence rose to such a height, that he stamped base metal with the impression used upon the money of the state, and no one had sufficient courage to oppose him, so powerful had he become by the discords of Florence. Great, certainly, but unhappy city! which neither the memory of past divisions, the fear of her enemies, nor a king's authority, could unite for her own advantage; so that she found herself in a state of the utmost wretchedness, harassed without by Uguccione, and plundered within by Lando d'Agobbio.

The friends of the king and those who opposed Lando and his followers, were either of noble families or the highest of the people, and all Guelphs; but their adversaries being in power they could not discover their minds without incurring the greatest danger. Being, however, determined to deliver themselves from such disgraceful tyranny, they secretly wrote to King Robert, requesting him to appoint for his vicar in Florence Count Guido da Battifolle. The king complied; and the opposite party, although the Signory were opposed to the king, on account of the good quality of the count, did not dare to resist him. Still his authority was not great, because the Signory and Gonfaloniers of the companies were in favor of Lando and his party.

During these troubles, the daughter of King Albert of Bohemia passed through Florence, in search of her husband, Charles, the son of King Robert, and was received with the greatest respect by the friends of the king, who complained to her of the unhappy state of the city, and of the tyranny of Lando and his partisans; so that through her influence and the exertions of the king's friends, the citizens were again united, and before her departure, Lando was stripped of all authority and send back to Agobbio, laden with blood and plunder. In reforming the government, the sovereignty of the city was continued to the king for another three years, and as there were then in office seven Signors of the party of Lando, six more were appointed of the king's friends, and some magistracies were composed of thirteen Signors; but not long afterward the number was reduced to seven according to ancient custom.

Chapter VI: War with Castruccio—Castruccio marches against Prato and retires without making any attempt—The emigrants not being allowed to return, endeavor to enter the city by force, and are repulsed—Change in the mode of electing the great officers of state—The Squittini established—The Florentines under Raymond of Cardona are routed by Castruccio at Altopascio—Treacherous designs of Raymond—The Florentines give the sovereignty of the city to Charles duke of Cambria, who appoints the duke of Athens for his vicar—The duke of Calabria comes to Florence—The Emperor Louis of Bavaria visits Italy—The excitement he produces—Death of Castruccio and of Charles duke of Calabria—Reform of government.

About the same time, Uguccione lost the sovereignty of Lucca and of Pisa, and Castruccio Castracani, a citizen of Lucca, became lord of them, who, being a young man, bold and fierce, and fortunate in his enterprises, in a short time became the head of the Ghibellines in Tuscany. On this account the discords among the Florentines were laid aside for some years, at first to abate the increasing power of Castruccio, and afterward to unite their means for mutual defense against him. And in order to give increased strength and efficacy to their counsels, the Signory appointed twelve citizens whom they called Buonomini, or good men, without whose advice and consent nothing of any importance could be carried into effect. The conclusion of the sovereignty of King Robert being come, the citizens took the government into their own hands, reappointed the usual rectors and magistracies, and were kept united by the dread of Castruccio, who, after many efforts against the lords of Lunigiano, attacked Prato, to the relief of which the Florentines having resolved to go, shut up their shops and houses, and proceeded thither in a body, amounting to twenty thousand foot and one thousand five hundred horse. And in order to reduce the number of Castruccio's friends and augment their own, the Signory declared that every rebel of the Guelphic party who should come to the relief of Prato would be restored to his country; they thus increased their army with an addition of four thousand men. This great force being quickly brought to Prato, alarmed Castruccio so much, that without trying the fortune of battle, he retired toward Lucca. Upon this, disturbances arose in the Florentine camp between the nobility and the people, the latter of whom wished to pursue the foe and destroy him; the former were for returning home, saying they had done enough for Prato in hazarding the safety of Florence on its account, which they did not regret under the circumstances, but now, that necessity no longer existing, the propriety of further risk ceased also, as there was little to be gained and much to lose. Not being able to agree, the question was referred to the Signory, among whom the difference of opinion was equally great; and as the matter spread throughout the city, the people drew together, and used such threatening language against the nobility that they, being apprehensive for their safety, yielded; but the resolution being adopted too late, and by many unwillingly, gave the enemy time to withdraw in safety to Lucca.

This unfortunate circumstance made the people so indignant against the great that the Signory refused to perform the promise made to the exiles, and the latter, anticipating the fact, determined to be beforehand, and were at the gates of Florence to gain admittance into the city before the rest of the forces; but their design did not take effect, for their purpose being foreseen, they were repulsed by those who had remained at home. They then endeavored to acquire by entreaty what they had failed to obtain by force; and sent eight men as ambassadors to the Signory, to remind them of the promise given, and of the dangers they had undergone, in hope of the reward which had been held out to them. And although the nobility, who felt the obligation on account of their having particularly undertaken to fulfill the promise for which the Signory had bound themselves, used their utmost exertion in favor of the exiles, so great was the anger of the multitude on account of their only partial success against Castruccio, that they could not obtain their admission. This occasioned cost and dishonor to the city; for many of the nobility, taking offense at this proceeding, endeavored to obtain by arms that which had been refused to their prayers, and agreed with the exiles that they should come armed to the city, and that those within would arm themselves in their defense. But the affair was discovered before the appointed day arrived, so that those without found the city in arms, and prepared to resist them. So completely subdued were those within, that none dared to take arms; and thus the undertaking was abandoned, without any advantage having been obtained by the party. After the departure of the exiles it was determined to punish those who had been instrumental in bringing them to the city; but, although everyone knew who were the delinquents, none ventured to name and still less to accuse them. It was, therefore, resolved that in order to come at the truth, everyone should write the names of those he believed to be guilty, and present the writing secretly to the Capitano. By this means, Amerigo Donati, Teghiajo, Frescobaldi, and Lotteringo Gherardini were accused; but, the judges being more favorably disposed to them than, perhaps, their misdeeds deserved, each escaped by paying a fine.

The tumults which arose in Florence from the coming of the rebels to the gates, showed that one leader was insufficient for the companies of the people; they, therefore, determined that in future each should have three or four; and to every Gonfalonier two or three Pennonieri (pennon bearers) were added, so that if the whole body were not drawn out, a part might operate under one of them. And as happens in republics, after any disturbance, some old laws are annulled and others renewed, so on this occasion, as it had been previously customary to appoint the Signory for a time only, the then existing Signors and the Colleagues, feeling themselves possessed of sufficient power, assumed the authority to fix upon the Signors that would have to sit during the next forty months, by putting their names into a bag or purse, and drawing them every two months. But, before the expiration of the forty months, many citizens were jealous that their names had not been deposited among the rest, and a new embborsation was made. From this beginning arose the custom of embosing or enclosing the names of all who should take office in any of the magistracies for a long time to come, as well those whose offices employed them within the city as those abroad, though previously the councils of the retiring magistrates had elected those who were to succeed them. These embosations were afterward called Squittini, or pollings,—and it was thought they would prevent much trouble to the city, and remove the cause of those tumults which every three, or at most five, years, took place upon the creation of magistrates, from the number of candidates for office. And not being able to adopt a better expedient, they made use of this, but did not observe the defects which lay concealed under such a trivial accommodation.

In 1325, Castruccio, having taken possession of Pistoia, became so powerful that the Florentines, fearing his greatness, resolved, before he should get himself firmly seated in his new conquest, to attack him and withdraw it from his authority. Of their citizens and friends they mustered an army amounting to 20,000 foot and 3,000 horse, and with this body encamped before Altopascio, with the intention of taking the place and thus preventing it from relieving Pistoia. Being successful in the first part of their design, they marched toward Lucca, and laid the country waste in their progress; but from the little prudence and less integrity of their leader, Ramondo di Cardona, they made but small progress; for he, having observed them upon former occasions very prodigal of their liberty, placing it sometimes in the hands of a king, at others in those of a legate, or persons of even inferior quality, thought, if he could bring them into some difficulty, it might easily happen that they would make him their prince. Nor did he fail frequently to mention these matters, and required to have that authority in the city which had been given him over the army, endeavoring to show that otherwise he could not enforce the obedience requisite to a leader. As the Florentines did not consent to this, he wasted time, and allowed Castruccio to obtain the assistance which the Visconti and other tyrants of Lombardy had promised him, and thus become very strong. Ramondo, having willfully let the opportunity of victory pass away, now found himself unable to escape; for Castruccio coming up with him at Altopascio, a great battle ensued in which many citizens were slain and taken prisoners, and among the former fell Ramondo, who received from fortune that reward of bad faith and mischievous counsels which he had richly deserved from the Florentines. The injury they suffered from Castruccio, after the battle, in plunder, prisoners, destruction, and burning of property, is quite indescribable; for, without any opposition, during many months, he led his predatory forces wherever he thought proper, and it seemed sufficient to the Florentines if, after such a terrible event, they could save their city.

Still they were not so absolutely cast down as to prevent them from raising great sums of money, hiring troops, and sending to their friends for assistance; but all they could do was insufficient to restrain such a powerful enemy; so that they were obliged to offer the sovereignty to Charles duke of Calabria, son of King Robert, if they could induce him to come to their defense; for these princes, being accustomed to rule Florence, preferred her obedience to her friendship. But Charles, being engaged in the wars of Sicily, and therefore unable to undertake the sovereignty of the city, sent in his stead Walter, by birth a Frenchman, and duke of Athens. He, as viceroy, took possession of the city, and appointed the magistracies according to his own pleasure; but his mode of proceeding was quite correct, and so completely contrary to his real nature, that everyone respected him.

The affairs of Sicily being composed, Charles came to Florence with a thousand horse. He made his entry into the city in July, 1326, and his coming prevented further pillage of the Florentine territory by Castruccio. However, the influence which they acquired without the city was lost within her walls, and the evils which they did not suffer from their enemies were brought upon them by their friends; for the Signory could not do anything without the consent of the duke of Calabria, who, in the course of one year, drew from the people 400,000 florins, although by the agreement entered into with him, the sum was not to exceed 200,000; so great were the burdens with which either himself or his father constantly oppressed them.

To these troubles were added new jealousies and new enemies; for the Ghibellines of Lombardy became so alarmed upon the arrival of Charles in Tuscany, that Galeazzo Visconti and the other Lombard tyrants, by money and promises, induced Louis of Bavaria, who had lately been elected emperor contrary to the wish of the pope, to come into Italy. After passing through Lombardy he entered Tuscany, and with the assistance of Castruccio, made himself master of Pisa, from whence, having been pacified with sums of money, he directed his course towards Rome. This caused the duke of Calabria to be apprehensive for the safety of Naples; he therefore left Florence, and appointed as his viceroy Filippo da Saggineto.

After the departure of the emperor, Castruccio made himself master of Pisa, but the Florentines, by a treaty with Pistoia, withdrew her from obedience to him. Castruccio then besieged Pistoia, and persevered with so much vigor and resolution, that although the Florentines often attempted to relieve her, by attacking first his army and then his country, they were unable either by force or policy to remove him; so anxious was he to punish the Pistolesi and subdue the Florentines. At length the people of Pistoia were compelled to receive him for their sovereign; but this event, although greatly to his glory, proved but little to his advantage, for upon his return to Lucca he died. And as one event either of good or evil seldom comes alone, at Naples also died Charles duke of Calabria and lord of Florence, so that in a short time, beyond the expectation of their most sanguine hopes, the Florentines found themselves delivered from the domination of the one and the fear of the other. Being again free, they set about the reformation of the city, annulled all the old councils, and created two new ones, the one composed of 300 citizens from the class of the people, the other of 250 from the nobility and the people.

The first was called the Council of the People, the other the Council of the Commune.

Chapter VII: The Emperor at Rome—The Florentines refuse to purchase Lucca, and repent of it—Enterprises of the Florentines—Conspiracy of the Bardi and the Frescobaldi—The conspiracy discovered and checked—Maffeo da Marradi appeases the tumult—Lucca is purchased by the Florentines and taken by the Pisans—The duke of Athens at Florence—The nobility determine to make him prince of the city.

The emperor, being arrived at Rome, created an anti-pope, did many things in opposition to the church, and attempted many others, but without effect, so that at last he retired with disgrace, and went to Pisa, where, either because they were not paid, or from disaffection, about 800 German horse mutinied, and fortified themselves at Montechiaro upon the Ceruglio; and when the emperor had left Pisa to go into Lombardy, they took possession of Lucca and drove out Francesco Castracani, whom he had left there. Designing to turn their conquest to account, they offered it to the Florentines for 80,000 florins, which, by the advice of Simone della Tosa, was refused. This resolution, if they had remained in it, would have been of the greatest utility to the Florentines; but as they shortly afterward changed their minds, it became most pernicious; for although at the time they might have obtained peaceful possession of her for a small sum and would not, they afterward wished to have her and could not, even for a much larger amount; which caused many and most hurtful changes to take place in Florence. Lucca, being refused by the Florentines, was purchased by Gherardino Spinoli, a Genoese, for 30,000 florins. And as men are often less anxious to take what is in their power than desirous of that which they cannot attain, as soon as the purchase of Gherardino became known, and for how small a sum it had been bought, the people of Florence were seized with an extreme desire to have it, blaming themselves and those by whose advice they had been induced to reject the offer made to them. And in order to obtain by force what they had refused to purchase, they sent troops to plunder and overrun the country of the Lucchese.

About this time the emperor left Italy. The anti-pope, by means of the Pisans, became a prisoner in France; and the Florentines from the death of Castruccio, which occurred in 1328, remained in domestic peace till 1340, and gave their undivided attention to external affairs, while many wars were carried on in Lombardy, occasioned by the coming of John king of Bohemia, and in Tuscany, on account of Lucca. During this period Florence was ornamented with many new buildings, and by the advice of Giotto, the most distinguished painter of his time, they built the tower of Santa Reparata. Besides this, the waters of the Arno having, in 1333, risen twelve feet above their ordinary level, destroyed some of the bridges and many buildings, all which were restored with great care and expense.

In the year 1340, new sources of disagreement arose. The great had two ways of increasing or preserving their power; the one, so to restrain the emborsation of magistrates, that the lot always fell upon themselves or their friends; the other, that having the election of the rectors, they were always favorable to their party. This second mode they considered of so great importance, that the ordinary rectors not being sufficient for them, they on some occasions elected a third, and at this time they had made an extraordinary appointment, under the title of captain of the guard, of Jacopo Gabrielli of Agobbio, and endowed him with unlimited authority over the citizens. This man, under the sanction of those who governed, committed constant outrages; and among those whom he injured were Piero de' Bardi and Bardo Frescobaldi. These being of the nobility, and naturally proud, could not endure that a stranger, supported by a few powerful men, should without cause injure them with impunity, and consequently entered into a conspiracy against him and those by whom he was supported. They were joined by many noble families, and some of the people, who were offended with the tyranny of those in power. Their plan was, that each should bring into his house a number of armed men, and on the morning after the day of All Saints, when almost all would be in the temples praying for their dead, they should take arms, kill the Capitano and those who were at the head of affairs, and then, with a new Signory and new ordinances, reform the government.

But, as the more a dangerous business is considered, the less willingly it is undertaken, it commonly happens, when there is any time allowed between the determining upon a perilous enterprise and its execution, that the conspiracy by one means or another becomes known. Andrea de' Bardi was one of the conspirators, and upon reconsideration of the matter, the fear of the punishment operated more powerfully upon him than the desire of revenge, and he disclosed the affair to Jacopo Alberti, his brother-in-law. Jacopo acquainted the Priors, and they informed the government. And as the danger was near, All Saints' day being just at hand, many citizens met together in the palace; and thinking their peril increased by delay, they insisted that the Signory should order the alarm to be rung, and called the people together in arms. Taldo Valori was at this time Gonfalonier, and Francesco Salviati one of the Signory, who, being relatives of the Bardi, were unwilling to summon the people with the bell, alleging as a reason that it is by no means well to assemble them in arms upon every slight occasion, for power put into the hands of an unrestrained multitude was never beneficial; that it is an easy matter to excite them to violence, but a difficult thing to restrain them; and that, therefore, it would be taking a more prudent course if they were to inquire into the truth of the affair, and punish the delinquents by the civil authority, than to attempt, upon a simple information, to correct it by such a tumultuous means, and thus hazard the safety of the city. None would listen to these remarks; the Signory were assailed with insolent behavior and indecent expressions, and compelled to sound the alarm, upon which the people presently assembled in arms. On the other hand, the Bardi and the Frescobaldi, finding themselves discovered, that they might conquer with glory or die without shame, armed themselves, in the hope that they would be able to defend that part of the city beyond the river, where their houses were situated; and they fortified the bridge in expectation of assistance, which they expected from the nobles and their friends in the country. Their design was frustrated by the people who, in common with themselves, occupied this part of the city; for these took arms in favor of the Signory, so that, seeing themselves thus circumstanced, they abandoned the bridges, and betook themselves to the street in which the Bardi resided, as being a stronger situation than any other; and this they defended with great bravery.

Jacopo d'Agobbio, knowing the whole conspiracy was directed against himself, in fear of death, terrified and vanquished, kept himself surrounded with forces near the palace of the Signory; but the other rectors, who were much less blamable, discovered greater courage, and especially the podesta or provost, whose name was Maffeo da Marradi. He presented himself among the combatants without any fear, and passing the bridge of the Rubaconte amid the swords of the Bardi, made a sign that he wished to speak to them. Upon this, their reverence for the man, his noble demeanor, and the excellent qualities he was known to possess, caused an immediate cessation of the combat, and induced them to listen to him patiently. He very gravely, but without the use of any bitter or aggravating expressions, blamed their conspiracy, showed the danger they would incur if they still contended against the popular feeling, gave them reason to hope their complaints would be heard and mercifully considered, and promised that he himself would use his endeavors in their behalf. He then returned to the Signory, and implored them to spare the blood of the citizens, showing the impropriety of judging them unheard, and at length induced them to consent that the Bardi and the Frescobaldi, with their friends, should leave the city, and without impediment be allowed to retire to their castles. Upon their departure the people being again disarmed, the Signory proceeded against those only of the Bardi and Frescobaldi families who had taken arms. To lessen their power, they bought of the Bardi the castle of Mangona and that of Vernia; and enacted a law which provided that no citizen should be allowed to possess a castle or fortified place within twenty miles of Florence.

After a few months, Stiatta Frescobaldi was beheaded, and many of his family banished. Those who governed, not satisfied with having subdued the Bardi and the Frescobaldi, as is most commonly the case, the more authority they possessed the worse use they made of it and the more insolent they became. As they had hitherto had one captain of the guard who afflicted the city, they now appointed another for the country, with unlimited authority, to the end that those whom they suspected might abide neither within nor without. And they excited them to such excesses against the whole of the nobility, that these were driven to desperation, and ready to sell both themselves and the city to obtain revenge. The occasion at length came, and they did not fail to use it.

The troubles of Tuscany and Lombardy had brought the city of Lucca under the rule of Mastino della Scala, lord of Verona, who, though bound by contract to assign her to the Florentines, had refused to do so; for, being lord of Parma, he thought he should be able to retain her, and did not trouble himself about his breach of faith. Upon this the Florentines joined the Venetians, and with their assistance brought Mastino to the brink of ruin. They did not, however, derive any benefit from this beyond the slight satisfaction of having conquered him; for the Venetians, like all who enter into league with less powerful states than themselves, having acquired Trevigi and Vicenza, made peace with Mastino without the least regard for the Florentines. Shortly after this, the Visconti, lords of Milan, having taken Parma from Mastino, he found himself unable to retain Lucca, and therefore determined to sell it. The competitors for the purchase were the Florentines and the Pisans; and in the course of the treaty the Pisans, finding that the Florentines, being the richer people, were about to obtain it, had recourse to arms, and, with the assistance of the Visconti, marched against Lucca. The Florentines did not, on that account, withdraw from the purchase, but having agreed upon the terms with Mastino, paid part of the money, gave security for the remainder, and sent Naddo Rucellai, Giovanni di Bernadino de' Medici, and Rosso di Ricciardo de' Ricci, to take possession, who entered Lucca by force, and Mastino's people delivered the city to them. Nevertheless, the Pisans continued the siege, and the Florentines used their utmost endeavors to relieve her; but after a long war, loss of money, and accumulation of disgrace, they were compelled to retire, and the Pisans became lords of Lucca.

The loss of this city, as in like cases commonly happens, exasperated the people of Florence against the members of the government; at every street corner and public place they were openly censured, and the entire misfortune was laid to the charge of their greediness and mismanagement. At the beginning of the war, twenty citizens had been appointed to undertake the direction of it, who appointed Malatesta da Rimini to the command of the forces. He having exhibited little zeal and less prudence, they requested assistance from Robert king of Naples, and he sent them Walter duke of Athens, who, as Providence would have it, to bring about the approaching evils, arrived at Florence just at the moment when the undertaking against Lucca had entirely failed. Upon this the Twenty, seeing the anger of the people, thought to inspire them with fresh hopes by the appointment of a new leader, and thus remove, or at least abate, the causes of calumny against themselves. As there was much to be feared, and that the duke of Athens might have greater authority to defend them, they first chose him for their coadjutor, and then appointed him to the command of the army. The nobility, who were discontented from the causes above mentioned, having many of them been acquainted with Walter, when upon a former occasion he had governed Florence for the duke of Calabria, thought they had now an opportunity, though with the ruin of the city, of subduing their enemies; for there was no means of prevailing against those who had oppressed them but of submitting to the authority of a prince who, being acquainted with the worth of one party and the insolence of the other, would restrain the latter and reward the former. To this they added a hope of the benefits they might derive from him when he had acquired the principality by their means. They, therefore, took several occasions of being with him secretly, and entreated he would take the command wholly upon himself, offering him the utmost assistance in their power. To their influence and entreaty were also added those of some families of the people; these were the Peruzzi, Acciajuoli, Antellesi, and Buonaccorsi, who, being overwhelmed with debts, and without means of their own, wished for those of others to liquidate them, and, by the slavery of their country, to deliver themselves from their servitude to their creditors. These demonstrations excited the ambitious mind of the duke to greater desire of dominion, and in order to gain himself the reputation of strict equity and justice, and thus increase his favor with the plebeians, he prosecuted those who had conducted the war against Lucca, condemned many to pay fines, others to exile, and put to death Giovanni de' Medici, Naddo Rucellai, and Guglielmo Altoviti.

Chapter VIII: The Duke of Athens requires to be made prince of Florence—The Signory address the duke upon the subject—The plebeians proclaim him prince of Florence for life—Tyrannical proceedings of the duke—The city disgusted with him—Conspiracies against the duke—The duke discovers the conspiracies, and becomes terrified—The city rises against him—He is besieged in the palace—Measures adopted by the citizens for reform of the government—The duke is compelled to withdraw from the city—Miserable deaths of Guglielmo da Scesi and his son—Departure of the duke of Athens—His character.

These executions greatly terrified the middle class of citizens, but gave satisfaction to the great and to the plebeians;—to the latter, because it is their nature to delight in evil; and to the former, by thus seeing themselves avenged of the many wrongs they had suffered from the people. When the duke passed along the streets he was hailed with loud cheers, the boldness of his proceedings was praised, and both parties joined in open entreaties that he would search out the faults of the citizens, and punish them.

The office of the Twenty began to fall into disuse, while the power of the duke became great, and the influence of fear excessive; so that everyone, in order to appear friendly to him, caused his arms to be painted over their houses, and the name alone was all he needed to be absolutely prince. Thinking himself upon such a footing that he might safely attempt anything, he gave the Signory to understand that he judged it necessary for the good of the city, that the sovereignty should be freely given to him, and that as the rest of the citizens were willing that it should be so, he desired they would also consent. The Signory, notwithstanding many had foreseen the ruin of their country, were much disturbed at this demand; and although they were aware of the dangerous position in which they stood, that they might not be wanting in their duty, resolutely refused to comply. The duke had, in order to assume a greater appearance of religion and humanity, chosen for his residence the convent of the Minor Canons of St. Croce, and in order to carry his evil designs into effect, proclaimed that all the people should, on the following morning, present themselves before him in the piazza of the convent. This command alarmed the Signory much more than his discourse to them had done, and they consulted with those citizens whom they thought most attached to their country and to liberty; but they could not devise any better plan, knowing the power of which the duke was possessed, than to endeavor by entreaty to induce him either to forego his design or to make his government less intolerable. A party of them was, therefore, appointed to wait upon him, one of whom addressed him in the following manner:—

"We appear before you, my lord, induced first by the demand which you have made, and then by the orders you have given for a meeting of the people; for it appears to us very clearly, that it is your intention to effect by extraordinary means the design from which we have hitherto withheld our consent. It is not, however, our intention to oppose you with force, but only to show what a heavy charge you take upon yourself, and the dangerous course you adopt; to the end that you may remember our advice and that of those who, not by consideration of what is beneficial for you, but for the gratification of their own unreasonable wishes, have advised you differently. You are endeavoring to reduce to slavery a city that has always existed in freedom; for the authority which we have at times conceded to the kings of Naples was companionship and not servitude. Have you considered the mighty things which the name of liberty implies to such a city as this, and how delightful it is to those who hear it? It has a power which nothing can subdue, time cannot wear away, nor can any degree of merit in a prince countervail the loss of it. Consider, my lord, how great the force must be that can keep a city like this in subjection, no foreign aid would enable you to do it; neither can you confide in those at home; for they who are at present your friends, and advise you to adopt the course you now pursue, as soon as with your assistance they have overcome their enemies, will at once turn their thoughts toward effecting your destruction, and then take the government upon themselves. The plebeians, in whom you confide, will change upon any accident, however trivial; so that in a very short time you may expect to see the whole city opposed to you, which will produce both their ruin and your own. Nor will you be able to find any remedy for this; for princes who have but few enemies may make their government very secure by the death or banishment of those who are opposed to them; but when the hatred is universal, no security whatever can be found, for you cannot tell from what direction the evil may commence; and he who has to apprehend every man his enemy cannot make himself assured of anyone. And if you should attempt to secure a friend or two, you would only increase the dangers of your situation; for the hatred of the rest would be increased by your success, and they would become more resolutely disposed to vengeance.

"That time can neither destroy nor abate the desire for freedom is most certain; for it has been often observed, that those have reassumed their liberty who in their own persons had never tasted of its charms, and love it only from remembrance of what they have heard their fathers relate; and, therefore, when recovered, have preserved it with indomitable resolution and at every hazard. And even when their fathers could not remember it, the public buildings, the halls of the magistracy, and the insignia of free institutions, remind them of it; and these things cannot fail to be known and greatly desired by every class of citizens.

"What is it you imagine you can do, that would be an equivalent for the sweets of liberty, or make men lose the desire of their present conditions? No; if you were to join the whole of Tuscany to the Florentine rule, if you were to return to the city daily in triumph over her enemies, what could it avail? The glory would not be ours, but yours. We should not acquire fellow-citizens, but partakers of our bondage, who would serve to sink us still deeper in ignominy. And if your conduct were in every respect upright, your demeanor amiable, and your judgments equitable, all these would be insufficient to make you beloved. If you imagine otherwise, you deceive yourself; for, to one accustomed to the enjoyment of liberty, the slightest chains feel heavy, and every tie upon his free soul oppresses him. Besides, it is impossible to find a violent people associated with a good prince, for of necessity they must soon become alike, or their difference produce the ruin of one of them. You may, therefore, be assured, that you

will either have to hold this city by force, to effect which, guards, castles, and external aid have oft been found insufficient, or be content with the authority we have conferred; and this we would advise, reminding you that no dominion can be durable to which the governed do not consent; and we have no wish to lead you, blinded by ambition, to such a point that, unable either to stand or advance, you must, to the great injury of both, of necessity fall."

This discourse did not in the slightest degree soften the obdurate mind of the duke, who replied that it was not his intention to rob the city of her liberty, but to restore it to her; for those cities alone are in slavery that are disunited, while the united are free. As Florence, by her factions and ambition, had deprived herself of liberty, he should restore, not take it from her; and as he had been induced to take this charge upon himself, not from his own ambition, but at the entreaty of a great number of citizens, they would do well to be satisfied with that which produced contentment among the rest. With regard to the danger he might incur, he thought nothing of it; for it was not the part of a good man to avoid doing good from his apprehension of evil, and it was the part of a coward to shun a glorious undertaking because some uncertainty attended the success of the attempt; and he knew he should so conduct himself, that they would soon see they had entertained great apprehensions and been in little danger.

The Signory then agreed, finding they could not do better, that on the following morning the people should be assembled in their accustomed place of meeting, and with their consent the Signory should confer upon the duke the sovereignty of the city for one year, on the same conditions as it had been intrusted to the duke of Calabria. It was upon the 8th of November, 1342, when the duke, accompanied by Giovanni della Tosa and all his confederates, with many other citizens, came to the piazza or court of the palace, and having, with the Signory mounted upon the ringhiera, or rostrum (as the Florentines call those steps which lead to the palace), the agreement which had been entered into between the Signory and himself was read. When they had come to the passage which gave the government to him for one year, the people shouted, "FOR LIFE." Upon this, Francesco Rustichelli, one of the Signory, arose to speak, and endeavored to abate the tumult and procure a hearing; but the mob, with their hootings, prevented him from being heard by anyone; so that with the consent of the people the duke was elected, not for one year merely, but for life. He was then borne through the piazza by the crowd, shouting his name as they proceeded.

It is the custom that he who is appointed to the guard of the palace shall, in the absence of the Signory, remain locked within. This office was at that time held by Rinieri di Giotto, who, bribed by the friends of the duke, without waiting for any force, admitted him immediately. The Signory, terrified and dishonored, retired to their own houses; the palace was plundered by the followers of the duke, the Gonfalon of the people torn to pieces, and the arms of the duke placed over the palace. All this happened to the indescribable sorrow of good men, though to the satisfaction of those who, either from ignorance or malignity, were consenting parties.

The duke, having acquired the sovereignty of the city, in order to strip those of all authority who had been defenders of her liberty, forbade the Signory to assemble in the palace, and appointed a private dwelling for their use. He took their colors from the Gonfaloniers of the companies of the people; abolished the ordinances made for the restraint of the great; set at liberty those who were imprisoned; recalled the Bardi and the Frescobaldi from exile, and forbade everyone from carrying arms about his person. In order the better to defend himself against those within the city, he made friends of all he could around it, and therefore conferred great benefits upon the Aretini and other subjects of the Florentines. He made peace with the Pisans, although raised to power in order that he might carry on war against them; ceased paying interest to those merchants who, during the war against Lucca, had lent money to the republic; increased the old taxes, levied new ones, and took from the Signory all authority. His rectors were Baglione da Perugia and Guglielmo da Scesi, who, with Cerrettieri Bisdomini, were the persons with whom he consulted on public affairs. He imposed burdensome taxes upon the citizens; his decisions between contending parties were unjust; and that precision and humanity which he had at first assumed, became cruelty and pride; so that many of the greatest citizens and noblest people were, either by fines, death, or some new invention, grievously oppressed. And in completing the same bad system, both without the city and within, he appointed six rectors for the country, who beat and plundered the inhabitants. He suspected the great, although he had been benefited by them, and had restored many to their country; for he felt assured that the generous minds of the nobility would not allow them, from any motives, to submit contentedly to his authority. He also began to confer benefits and advantages upon the lowest orders, thinking that with their assistance, and the arms of foreigners, he would be able to preserve the tyranny. The month of May, during which feasts are held, being come, he caused many companies to be formed of the plebeians and very lowest of the people, and to these, dignified with splendid titles, he gave colors and money; and while one party went in bacchanalian procession through the city, others were stationed in different parts of it, to receive them as guests. As the report of the duke's authority spread abroad, many of French origin came to him, for all of whom he found offices and emoluments, as if they had been the most trustworthy of men; so that in a short time Florence became not only subject to French dominion, but adopted their dress and manners; for men and women, without regard to propriety or sense of shame, imitated them. But that which disgusted the people most completely was the violence which, without any distinction of quality or rank, he and his followers committed upon the women.

The people were filled with indignation, seeing the majesty of the state overturned, its ordinances annihilated, its laws annulled, and every decent regulation set at naught; for men unaccustomed to royal pomp could not endure to see this man surrounded with his armed satellites on foot and on horseback; and having now a closer view of their disgrace, they were compelled to honor him whom they in the highest degree hated. To this hatred, was added the terror occasioned by the continual imposition of new taxes and frequent shedding of blood, with which he impoverished and consumed the city.

The duke was not unaware of these impressions existing strongly in the people's minds, nor was he without fear of the consequences; but still pretended to think himself beloved; and when Matteo di Morozzo, either to acquire his favor or to free himself from danger, gave information that the family of the Medici and some others had entered into a conspiracy against him he not only did not inquire into the matter, but caused the informer to be put to a cruel death. This mode of proceeding restrained those who were disposed to acquaint him of his danger and gave additional courage to such as sought his ruin. Bertone Cini, having ventured to speak against the taxes with which the people were loaded, had his tongue cut out with such barbarous cruelty as to cause his death. This shocking act increased the people's rage, and their hatred of the duke; for those who were accustomed to discourse and to act upon every occasion with the greatest boldness, could not endure to live with their hands tied and forbidden to speak.

This oppression increased to such a degree, that not merely the Florentines, who though unable to preserve their liberty cannot endure slavery, but the most servile people on earth would have been roused to attempt the recovery of freedom; and consequently many citizens of all ranks resolved either to deliver themselves from this odious tyranny or die in the attempt. Three distinct conspiracies were formed; one of the great; another of the people, and the third of the working classes; each of which, besides the general causes which operated upon the whole, were

excited by some other particular grievance. The great found themselves deprived of all participation in the government; the people had lost the power they possessed, and the artificers saw themselves deficient in the usual remuneration of their labor.

Agnolo Acciajuoli was at this time archbishop of Florence, and by his discourses had formerly greatly favored the duke, and procured him many followers among the higher class of the people. But when he found him lord of the city, and became acquainted with his tyrannical mode of proceeding, it appeared to him that he had misled his countrymen; and to correct the evil he had done, he saw no other course, but to attempt the cure by the means which had caused it. He therefore became the leader of the first and most powerful conspiracy, and was joined by the Bardi, Rossi, Frescobaldi, Scali Altoviti, Magalotti, Strozzi, and Mancini. Of the second, the principals were Manno and Corso Donati, and with them the Pazzi, Cavicciulli, Cerchi, and Albizzi. Of the third the first was Antonio Adimari, and with him the Medici, Bordini, Rucellai, and Aldobrandini. It was the intention of these last, to slay him in the house of the Albizzi, whither he was expected to go on St. John's day, to see the horses run, but he not having gone, their design did not succeed. They then resolved to attack him as he rode through the city; but they found this would be very difficult; for he was always accompanied with a considerable armed force, and never took the same road twice together, so that they had no certainty of where to find him. They had a design of slaying him in the council, although they knew that if he were dead, they would be at the mercy of his followers.

While these matters were being considered by the conspirators, Antonio Adimari, in expectation of getting assistance from them, disclosed the affair to some Siennese, his friends, naming certain of the conspirators, and assuring them that the whole city was ready to rise at once. One of them communicated the matter to Francesco Brunelleschi, not with a design to injure the plot, but in the hope that he would join them. Francesco, either from personal fear, or private hatred of some one, revealed the whole to the duke; whereupon, Pagolo del Mazecha and Simon da Monterappoli were taken, who acquainted him with the number and quality of the conspirators. This terrified him, and he was advised to request their presence rather than to take them prisoners, for if they fled, he might without disgrace, secure himself by banishment of the rest. He therefore sent for Antonio Adimari, who, confiding in his companions, appeared immediately, and was detained. Francesco Brunelleschi and Uguccione Buondelmonti advised the duke to take as many of the conspirators prisoners as he could, and put them to death; but he, thinking his strength unequal to his foes, did not adopt this course, but took another, which, had it succeeded, would have freed him from his enemies and increased his power. It was the custom of the duke to call the citizens together upon some occasions and advise with them. He therefore having first sent to collect forces from without, made a list of three hundred citizens, and gave it to his messengers, with orders to assemble them under the pretense of public business; and having drawn them together, it was his intention either to put them to death or imprison them.

The capture of Antonio Adimari and the sending for forces, which could not be kept secret, alarmed the citizens, and more particularly those who were in the plot, so that the boldest of them refused to attend, and as each had read the list, they sought each other, and resolved to rise at once and die like men, with arms in their hands, rather than be led like calves to the slaughter. In a very short time the chief conspirators became known to each other, and resolved that the next day, which was the 26th July, 1343, they would raise a disturbance in the Old Market place, then arm themselves and call the people to freedom.

The next morning being come, at nine o'clock, according to agreement, they took arms, and at the call of liberty assembled, each party in its own district, under the ensigns and with the arms of the people, which had been secretly provided by the conspirators. All the heads of families, as well of the nobility as of the people, met together, and swore to stand in each other's defense, and effect the death of the duke; except some of the Buondelmonti and of the Cavalcanti, with those four families of the people which had taken so conspicuous a part in making him sovereign, and the butchers, with others, the lowest of the plebeians, who met armed in the piazza in his favor.

The duke immediately fortified the place, and ordered those of his people who were lodged in different parts of the city to mount upon horseback and join those in the court; but, on their way thither, many were attacked and slain. However, about three hundred horse assembled, and the duke was in doubt whether he should come forth and meet the enemy, or defend himself within. On the other hand, the Medici, Cavicciulli, Rucellai, and other families who had been most injured by him, fearful that if he came forth, many of those who had taken arms against him would discover themselves his partisans, in order to deprive him of the occasion of attacking them and increasing the number of his friends, took the lead and assailed the palace. Upon this, those families of the people who had declared for the duke, seeing themselves boldly attacked, changed their minds, and all took part with the citizens, except Uguccione Buondelmonti, who retired into the palace, and Giannozzo Cavalcanti, who having withdrawn with some of his followers to the new market, mounted upon a bench, and begged that those who were going in arms to the piazza, would take the part of the duke. In order to terrify them, he exaggerated the number of his people and threatened all with death who should obstinately persevere in their undertaking against their sovereign. But not finding any one either to follow him, or to chastise his insolence, and seeing his labor fruitless, he withdrew to his own house.

In the meantime, the contest in the piazza between the people and the forces of the duke was very great; but although the place served them for defense, they were overcome, some yielding to the enemy, and others, quitting their horses, fled within the walls. While this was going on, Corso and Amerigo Donati, with a part of the people, broke open the stinche, or prisons; burnt the papers of the provost and of the public chamber; pillaged the houses of the rectors, and slew all who had held offices under the duke whom they could find. The duke, finding the piazza in possession of his enemies, the city opposed to him, and without any hope of assistance, endeavored by an act of clemency to recover the favor of the people. Having caused those whom he had made prisoners to be brought before him, with amiable and kindly expressions he set them at liberty, and made Antonio Adimari a knight, although quite against his will. He caused his own arms to be taken down, and those of the people to be replaced over the palace; but these things coming out of season, and forced by his necessities, did him little good. He remained, notwithstanding all he did, besieged in the palace, and saw that having aimed at too much he had lost all, and would most likely, after a few days, die either of hunger, or by the weapons of his enemies. The citizens assembled in the church of Santa Reparata, to form the new government, and appointed fourteen citizens, half from the nobility and half from the people, who, with the archbishop, were invested with full authority to remodel the state of Florence. They also elected six others to take upon them the duties of provost, till he who should be finally chosen took office, the duties of which were usually performed by a subject of some neighboring state.

Many had come to Florence in defense of the people; among whom were a party from Sienna, with six ambassadors, men of high consideration in their own country. These endeavored to bring the people and the duke to terms; but the former refused to listen to any whatever, unless Guglielmo da Scesi and his son, with Cerrettieri Bisdomini, were first given up to them. The duke would not consent to this; but being threatened by those who were shut up with him, he was forced to comply. The rage of men is certainly always found greater, and their revenge more furious upon the recovery of liberty, than when it has only been defended. Guglielmo and his son were placed among the thousands of their enemies, and the latter was not yet eighteen years old; neither his beauty, his innocence, nor his youth, could save him from the fury of the multitude; but both were instantly slain. Those who could not wound them while alive, wounded them after they were dead; and not satisfied with tearing them to pieces, they hewed their bodies with swords, tore them with their hands, and even with their teeth. And that every sense might be satiated with vengeance, having first heard their moans, seen their wounds, and touched their lacerated bodies, they wished even the stomach to be satisfied, that having glutted the external senses, the one within might also have its share. This rabid fury, however hurtful to the father and son, was favorable to Cerrettieri; for the multitude, wearied with their cruelty toward the former, quite forgot him, so that he, not being asked for, remained in the palace, and during night was conveyed safely away by his friends.

The rage of the multitude being appeased by their blood, an agreement was made that the duke and his people, with whatever belonged to him, should quit the city in safety; that he should renounce all claim, of whatever kind, upon Florence, and that upon his arrival in the Casentino he should ratify his renunciation. On the sixth of August he set out, accompanied by many citizens, and having arrived at the Casentino he ratified the agreement, although unwillingly, and would not have kept his word if Count Simon had not threatened to take him back to Florence. This duke, as his proceedings testified, was cruel and avaricious, difficult to speak with, and haughty in reply. He desired the service of men, not the cultivation of their better feelings, and strove rather to inspire them with fear than love. Nor was his person less despicable than his manners; he was short, his complexion was black, and he had a long, thin beard. He was thus in every respect contemptible; and at the end of ten months, his misconduct deprived him of the sovereignty which the evil counsel of others had given him.

Chapter IX: Many cities and territories, subject to the Florentines, rebel—Prudent conduct adopted upon this occasion—The city is divided into quarters—Disputes between the nobility and the people—The bishop endeavors to reconcile them, but does not succeed—The government reformed by the people—Riot of Andrea Strozzi—Serious disagreements between the nobility and the people—They come to arms, and the nobility are subdued—The plague in Florence of which Boccaccio speaks.

These events taking place in the city, induced all the dependencies of the Florentine state to throw off their yoke; so that Arezzo, Castiglione, Pistoia, Volterra, Colle, and San Gemigniano rebelled. Thus Florence found herself deprived of both her tyrant and her dominions at the same moment, and in recovering her liberty, taught her subjects how they might become free. The duke being expelled and the territories lost, the fourteen citizens and the bishop thought it would be better to act kindly toward their subjects in peace, than to make them enemies by war, and to show a desire that their subjects should be free as well as themselves. They therefore sent ambassadors to the people of Arezzo, to renounce all dominion over that city, and to enter into a treaty with them; to the end that as they could not retain them as subjects, they might make use of them as friends. They also, in the best manner they were able, agreed with the other places that they should retain their freedom, and that, being free, they might mutually assist each other in the preservation of their liberties. This prudent course was attended with a most favorable result; for Arezzo, not many years afterward, returned to the Florentine rule, and the other places, in the course of a few months, returned to their former obedience. Thus it frequently occurs that we sooner attain our ends by a seeming indifferent to them, than by more obstinate pursuit.

Having settled external affairs, they now turned to the consideration of those within the city; and after some altercation between the nobility and the people, it was arranged that the nobility should form one-third of the Signory and fill one-half of the other offices. The city was, as we have before shown, divided into sixths; and hence there would be six signors, one for each sixth, except when, from some more than ordinary cause, there had been twelve or thirteen created; but when this had occurred they were again soon reduced to six. It now seemed desirable to make an alteration in this respect, as well because the sixths were not properly divided, as that, wishing to give their proportion to the great, it became desirable to increase the number. They therefore divided the city into quarters, and for each created three signors. They abolished the office of Gonfalonier of Justice, and also the Gonfaloniers of the companies of the people; and instead of the twelve Buonuomini, or good men, created eight counsellors, four from each party. The government having been established in this manner, the city might have been in repose if the great had been content to live in that moderation which civil society requires. But they produced a contrary result, for those out of office would not conduct themselves as citizens, and those who were in government wished to be lords, so that every day furnished some new instance of their insolence and pride. These things were very grievous to the people, and they began to regret that for one tyrant put down, there had sprung up a thousand. The arrogance of one party and the anger of the other rose to such a degree, that the heads of the people complained to the bishop of the improper conduct of the nobility, and what unfit associates they had become for the people; and begged he would endeavor to induce them to be content with their share of administration in the other offices, and leave the magistracy of the Signory wholly to themselves.

The bishop was naturally a well-meaning man, but his want of firmness rendered him easily influenced. Hence, at the instance of his associates, he at first favored the duke of Athens, and afterward, by the advice of other citizens, conspired against him. At the reformation of the government, he had favored the nobility, and now he appeared to incline toward the people, moved by the reasons which they had advanced. Thinking to find in others the same instability of purpose, he endeavored to effect an amicable arrangement. With this design he called together the fourteen who were yet in office, and in the best terms he could imagine advised them to give up the Signory to the people, in order to secure the peace of the city; and assured them that if they refused, ruin would most probably be the result.

This discourse excited the anger of the nobility to the highest pitch, and Ridolfo de' Bardi reproved him in unmeasured terms as a man of little faith; reminding him of his friendship for the duke, to prove the duplicity of his present conduct, and saying, that in driving him away he had acted the part of a traitor. He concluded by telling him, that the honors they had acquired at their own peril, they would at their own peril defend. They then left the bishop, and in great wrath, informed their associates in the government, and all the families of the nobility, of what had been done. The people also expressed their thoughts to each other, and as the nobility made preparations for the defense of their signors, they determined not to wait till they had perfected their arrangements; and therefore, being armed, hastened to the palace, shouting, as they went along, that the nobility must give up their share in the government.

The uproar and excitement were astonishing. The Signors of the nobility found themselves abandoned; for their friends, seeing all the people in arms, did not dare to rise in their defense, but each kept within his own house.

The Signors of the people endeavored to abate the excitement of the multitude, by affirming their associates to be good and moderate men; but, not succeeding in their attempt, to avoid a greater evil, sent them home to their houses, whither they were with difficulty conducted. The nobility having left the palace, the office of the four councillors was taken from their party, and conferred upon twelve of the people. To the eight signors who remained, a Gonfalonier of Justice was added, and sixteen Gonfaloniers of the companies of the people; and the council was so reformed, that the government remained wholly in the hands of the popular party.

At the time these events took place there was a great scarcity in the city, and discontent prevailed both among the highest and the lowest classes; in the latter for want of food, and in the former from having lost their power in the state. This circumstance induced Andrea Strozzi to think of making himself sovereign of the city. Selling his corn at a lower price than others did, a great many people flocked to his house; emboldened by the sight of these, he one morning mounted his horse, and, followed by a considerable number, called the people to arms, and in a short time drew together about 4,000 men, with whom he proceeded to the Signory, and demanded that the gates of the palace should be opened. But the signors, by threats and the force which they retained in the palace, drove them from the court; and then by proclamation so terrified them, that they gradually dropped off and returned to their homes, and Andrea, finding himself alone, with some difficulty escaped falling into the hands of the magistrates.

This event, although an act of great temerity, and attended with the result that usually follows such attempts, raised a hope in the minds of the nobility of overcoming the people, seeing that the lowest of the plebeians were at enmity with them. And to profit by this circumstance, they resolved to arm themselves, and with justifiable force recover those rights of which they had been unjustly deprived. Their minds acquired such an assurance of success, that they openly provided themselves with arms, fortified their houses, and even sent to their friends in Lombardy for assistance. The people and the Signory made preparation for their defense, and requested aid from Perugia and Sienna, so that the city was filled with the armed followers of either party. The nobility on this side of the Arno divided themselves into three parts; the one occupied the houses of the Cavicciulli, near the church of St. John; another, the houses of the Pazzi and the Donati, near the great church of St. Peter; and the third those of the Cavalcanti in the New Market. Those beyond the river fortified the bridges and the streets in which their houses stood; the Nerli defended the bridge of the Carraja; the Frescobaldi and the Manelli, the church of the Holy Trinity; and the Rossi and the Bardi, the bridge of the Rubaconte and the Old Bridge. The people were drawn together under the Gonfalon of justice and the ensigns of the companies of the artisans.

Both sides being thus arranged in order of battle, the people thought it imprudent to defer the contest, and the attack was commenced by the Medici and the Rondinelli, who assailed the Cavicciulli, where the houses of the latter open upon the piazza of St. John. Here both parties contended with great obstinacy, and were mutually wounded, from the towers by stones and other missiles, and from below by arrows. They fought for three hours; but the forces of the people continuing to increase, and the Cavicciulli finding themselves overcome by numbers, and hopeless of other assistance, submitted themselves to the people, who saved their houses and property; and having disarmed them, ordered them to disperse among their relatives and friends, and remain unarmed. Being victorious in the first attack, they easily overpowered the Pazzi and the Donati, whose numbers were less than those they had subdued; so that there only remained on this side of the Arno, the Cavalcanti, who were strong both in respect of the post they had chosen and in their followers. Nevertheless, seeing all the Gonfalons against them, and that the others had been overcome by three Gonfalons alone, they yielded without offering much resistance. Three parts of the city were now in the hands of the people, and only one in possession of the nobility; but this was the strongest, as well on account of those who held it, as from its situation, being defended by the Arno; hence it was first necessary to force the bridges. The Old Bridge was first assailed and offered a brave resistance; for the towers were armed, the streets barricaded, and the barricades defended by the most resolute men; so that the people were repulsed with great loss. Finding their labor at this point fruitless, they endeavored to force the Rubaconte Bridge, but no better success resulting, they left four Gonfalons in charge of the two bridges, and with the others attacked the bridge of the Carraja. Here, although the Nerli defended themselves like brave men, they could not resist the fury of the people; for this bridge, having no towers, was weaker than the others, and was attacked by the Capponi, and many families of the people who lived in that vicinity. Being thus assailed on all sides, they abandoned the barricades and gave way to the people, who then overcame the Rossi and the Frescobaldi; for all those beyond the Arno took part with the conquerors.

There was now no resistance made except by the Bardi, who remained undaunted, notwithstanding the failure of their friends, the union of the people against them, and the little chance of success which they seemed to have. They resolved to die fighting, and rather see their houses burned and plundered, than submit to the power of their enemies. They defended themselves with such obstinacy, that many fruitless attempts were made to overcome them, both at the Old Bridge and the Rubaconte; but their foes were always repulsed with loss. There had in former times been a street which led between the houses of the Pitti, from the Roman road to the walls upon

Mount St. George. By this way the people sent six Gonfalons, with orders to assail their houses from behind. This attack overcame the resolution of the Bardi, and decided the day in favor of the people; for when those who defended the barricades in the street learned that their houses were being plundered, they left the principal fight and hastened to their defense. This caused the Old Bridge to be lost; the Bardi fled in all directions and were received into the houses of the Quaratesi, Panzanesi, and Mozzi. The people, especially the lower classes, greedy for spoil, sacked and destroyed their houses, and pulled down and burned their towers and palaces with such outrageous fury, that the most cruel enemy of the Florentine name would have been ashamed of taking part in such wanton destruction.

The nobility being thus overcome, the people reformed the government; and as they were of three kinds, the higher, the middle, and the lower class, it was ordered that the first should appoint two signors; the two latter three each, and that the Gonfalonier should be chosen alternately from either party. Besides this, all the regulations for the restraint of the nobility were renewed; and in order to weaken them still more, many were reduced to the grade of the people. The ruin of the nobility was so complete, and depressed them so much, that they never afterward ventured to take arms for the recovery of their power, but soon became humbled and abject in the extreme. And thus Florence lost the generosity of her character and her distinction in arms.

After these events the city remained in peace till the year 1353. In the course of this period occurred the memorable plague, described with so much eloquence by Giovanni Boccaccio, and by which Florence lost 96,000 souls. In 1348, began the first war with the Visconti, occasioned by the archbishop, then prince of Milan; and when this was concluded, dissensions again arose in the city; for although the nobility were destroyed, fortune did not fail to cause new divisions and new troubles.

Book III: Chapter I: Reflections upon the domestic discords of republics—A parallel between the discords of Rome and those of Florence—Enmities between the families of the Ricci and the Albizzi—Uguccione de' Ricci causes the laws against the Ghibellines to be renewed in order to injure the Albizzi—Piero degli Albizzi derives advantage from it—Origin of admonitions and the troubles which result from them—Uguccione de' Ricci moderates their injustice—Difficulties increase—A meeting of the citizens—They address the Signory—The Signory attempt to remedy the evils.

Those serious, though natural enmities, which occur between the popular classes and the nobility, arising from the desire of the latter to command, and the disinclination of the former to obey, are the causes of most of the troubles which take place in cities; and from this diversity of purpose, all the other evils which disturb republics derive their origin. This kept Rome disunited; and this, if it be allowable to compare small things with great, held Florence in disunion; although in each city it produced a different result; for animosities were only beginning with the people and nobility of Rome contended, while ours were brought to a conclusion by the contentions of our citizens. A new law settled the disputes of Rome; those of Florence were only terminated by the death and banishment of many of her best people. Those of Rome increased her military virtue, while that of Florence was quite extinguished by her divisions. The quarrels of Rome established different ranks of society, those of Florence abolished the distinctions which had previously existed. This diversity of effects must have been occasioned by the different purposes which the two people had in view. While the people of Rome endeavored to associate with the nobility in the supreme honors, those of Florence strove to exclude the nobility from all participation in them: as the desire of the Roman people was more reasonable, no particular offense was given to the nobility; they therefore consented to it without having recourse to arms; so that, after some disputes concerning particular points, both parties agreed to the enactment of a law which, while it satisfied the people, preserved the nobility in the enjoyment of their dignity.

On the other hand, the demands of the people of Florence being insolent and unjust, the nobility, became desperate, prepared for their defense with their utmost energy, and thus bloodshed and the exile of citizens followed. The laws which were afterward made, did not provide for the common good, but were framed wholly in favor of the conquerors. This too, must be observed, that from the acquisition of power, made by the people of Rome, their minds were very much improved; for all the offices of state being attainable as well by the people as the nobility, the peculiar excellencies of the latter exercised a most beneficial influence upon the former; and as the city increased in virtue she attained a more exalted greatness.

But in Florence, the people being conquerors, the nobility were deprived of all participation in the government; and in order to regain a portion of it, it became necessary for them not only to seem like the people, but to be like them in behavior, mind, and mode of living. Hence arose those changes in armorial bearings, and in the titles of families, which the nobility adopted, in order that they might seem to be of the people; military virtue and generosity of feeling became extinguished in them; the people not possessing these qualities, they could not appreciate them, and Florence became by degrees more and more depressed and humiliated. The virtue of the Roman nobility degenerating into pride, the citizens soon found that the business of the state could not be carried on without a prince. Florence had now come to such a point, that with a comprehensive mind at the head of affairs she would easily have been made to take any form that he might have been disposed to give her; as may be partly observed by a perusal of the preceding book.

Having given an account of the origin of Florence, the commencement of her liberty, with the causes of her divisions, and shown how the factions of the nobility and the people ceased with the tyranny of the duke of Athens, and the ruin of the former, we have now to speak of the animosities between the citizens and the plebeians and the various circumstances which they produced.

The nobility being overcome, and the war with the archbishop of Milan concluded, there did not appear any cause of dissension in Florence. But the evil fortune of the city, and the defective nature of her laws, gave rise to enmities between the family of the Albizzi and that of the Ricci, which divided her citizens as completely as those of the Buondelmonti and the Uberti, or the Donati and the Cerchi had formerly done. The pontiffs, who at this time resided in France, and the emperors, who abode in Germany, in order to maintain their influence in Italy, sent among us multitudes of soldiers of many countries, as English, Dutch, and Bretons. As these, upon the conclusion of a war, were thrown out of pay, though still in the country, they, under the standard of some soldier of fortune, plundered such people as were least prepared to defend themselves. In the year 1353 one of these companies came into Tuscany under the command of Monsignor Reale, of Provence, and his approach terrified all the cities of Italy. The Florentines not only provided themselves forces, but many citizens, among whom were the Albizzi and the Ricci, armed themselves in their own defense. These families were at the time full of hatred against each other, and each thought to obtain the sovereignty of the republic by overcoming his enemy. They had not yet proceeded to open violence, but only contended in the magistracies and councils. The city being all in arms, a quarrel arose in the Old Market place, and, as it frequently happens in similar cases, a great number of people were drawn together. The disturbance spreading, it was told the Ricci that the Albizzi had assailed their partisans, and to the Albizzi that the Ricci were in quest of them. Upon this the whole city arose, and it was all the magistrates could do to restrain these families, and prevent the actual occurrence of a disaster which, without being the fault of either of them, had been willfully though falsely reported as having already taken place. This apparently trifling circumstance served to inflame the minds of the parties, and make each the more resolved to increase the number of their followers. And as the citizens, since the ruin of the nobility, were on such an equality that the magistrates were more respected now than they had previously been, they designed to proceed toward the suppression of this disorder with civil authority alone.

We have before related, that after the victory of Charles I. the government was formed of the Guelphic party, and that it thus acquired great authority over the Ghibellines. But time, a variety of circumstances, and new divisions had so contributed to sink this party feeling into oblivion, that many of Ghibelline descent now filled the highest offices. Observing this, Uguccione, the head of the family of the Ricci, contrived that the law against the Ghibellines should be again brought into operation; many imagining the Albizzi to be of that faction, they having arisen in Arezzo, and come long ago to Florence. Uguccione by this means hoped to deprive the Albizzi of participation in the government, for all of Ghibelline blood who were found to hold offices, would be condemned in the penalties which this law provided. The design of Uguccione was discovered to Piero son of Filippo degli Albizzi, and he resolved to favor it: for he saw that to oppose it would at once declare him a Ghibelline; and thus the law which was renewed by the ambition of the Ricci for his destruction, instead of robbing Piero degli Albizzi of reputation, contributed to increase his influence, although it laid the foundation of many evils. Nor is it possible for a republic to enact a law more pernicious than one relating to matters which have long transpired. Piero having favored this law, which had been contrived by his enemies for his stumbling-block, it became the stepping-stone to his greatness; for, making himself the leader of this new order of things, his authority went on increasing, and he was in greater favor with the Guelphs than any other man.

As there could not be found a magistrate willing to search out who were Ghibellines, and as this renewed enactment against them was therefore of small value, it was provided that authority should be given to the Capitani to find out who were of this faction; and, having discovered, to signify and *admonish* them that they were not to take upon themselves any office of government; to which *admonitions*, if they were disobedient, they became condemned in the penalties. Hence, all those who in Florence are deprived of the power to hold offices are called *ammoniti*, or *admonished*.

The Capitani in time acquiring greater audacity, admonished not only those to whom the admonition was applicable, but any others at the suggestion of their own avarice or ambition; and from 1356, when this law was made, to 1366, there had been admonished above 200 citizens. The Captains of the Parts and the sect of the Guelphs were thus become powerful; for every one honored them for fear of being admonished; and most particularly the leaders, who were Piero degli Albizzi, Lapo da Castiglionchio, and Carlo Strozzi. This insolent mode of proceeding was offensive to many; but none felt so particularly injured with it as the Ricci; for they knew themselves to have occasioned it, they saw it involved the ruin of the republic, and their enemies, the Albizzi, contrary to their intention, became great in consequence.

On this account Uguccione de' Ricci, being one of the Signory, resolved to put an end to the evil which he and his friends had originated, and with a new law provided that to the six Captains of Parts an additional three should be appointed, of whom two should be chosen from the companies of minor artificers, and that before any party could be declared Ghibelline, the declaration of the Capitani must be confirmed by twenty-four Guelphic citizens, appointed for the purpose. This provision tempered for a time the power of the Capitani, so that the admonitions were greatly diminished, if not wholly laid aside. Still the parties of the Albizzi and the Ricci were continually on the alert to oppose each other's laws, deliberations, and enterprises, not from a conviction of their inexpediency, but from a hatred of their promoters.

In such distractions the time passed from 1366 to 1371, when the Guelphs again regained the ascendant. There was in the family of the Buondelmonti a gentleman named Benchi, who, as an acknowledgment of his merit in a war against the Pisans, though one of the nobility, had been admitted among the people, and thus became eligible to office among the Signory; but when about to take his seat with them, a law was made that no nobleman who had become of the popular class should be allowed to assume that office. This gave great offense to Benchi, who, in union with Piero degli Albizzi, determined to depress the less powerful of the popular party with *Admonitions*, and obtain the government for themselves. By the interest which Benchi possessed with the ancient nobility, and that of Piero with most of the influential citizens, the Guelphic party resumed their ascendancy, and by new reforms among the *Parts*, so remodeled the administration as to be able to dispose of the offices of the captains and the twenty-four citizens at pleasure. They then returned to the *Admonitions* with greater audacity than ever, and the house of the Albizzi became powerful as the head of this faction.

On the other hand, the Ricci made the most strenuous exertions against their designs; so that anxiety universally prevailed, and ruin was apprehended alike from both parties. In consequence of this a great number of citizens, out of love to their country, assembled in the church of St. Piero Scarraggio, and after a long consideration of the existing disorders, presented themselves before the Signors, whom one of the principal among them addressed in the following terms:—

"Many of us, magnificent Signors! were afraid of meeting even for consideration of public business, without being publicly called together, lest we should be noted as presumptuous or condemned as ambitious. But seeing that so many citizens daily assemble in the lodges and halls of the palace, not for any public utility, but only for the gratification of their own ambition, we have thought that as those who assemble for the ruin of the republic are fearless, so still less ought they to be apprehensive who meet together only for its advantage; nor ought we to be anxious respecting the opinion they may form of our assembling, since they are so utterly indifferent to the opinion of others. Our affection for our country, magnificent Signors! caused us to assemble first, and now brings us before you, to speak of grievances already great and daily increasing in our republic, and to offer our assistance for their removal: and we doubt not that, though a difficult undertaking, it will still be attended with success, if you will lay aside all private regards, and authoritatively use the public force.

"The common corruption of all the cities of Italy, magnificent Signors! has infested and still vitiates your own; for when this province had shaken off the imperial yoke, her cities not being subject to any powerful influence that might restrain them, administered affairs, not as free men do, but as a factious populace; and hence have arisen all the other evils and disorders that have appeared. In the first place, there cannot be found among the citizens either unity or friendship, except with those whose common guilt, either against their country or against private individuals, is a bond of union. And as the knowledge of religion and the fear of God seem to be alike extinct, oaths and promises have lost their validity, and are kept as long as it is found expedient; they are adopted only as a means of deception, and he is most applauded and respected whose cunning is most efficient and secure. On this account bad men are received with the approbation due to virtue, and good ones are regarded only in the light of fools.

"And certainly in the cities of Italy all that is corruptible and corrupting is assembled. The young are idle, the old lascivious, and each sex and every age abounds with debasing habits, which the good laws, by misapplication, have lost the power to correct. Hence arises the avarice so observable among the citizens, and that greediness, not for true glory, but for unworthy honors; from which follow hatred, animosities, quarrels, and factions; resulting in deaths, banishments, affliction to all good men, and the advancement of the most unprincipled; for the good, confiding in their innocence, seek neither safety nor advancement by illegal methods as the wicked do, and thus unhonored and undefended they sink into oblivion.

"From proceedings such as these, arise at once the attachment for and influence of parties; bad men follow them through ambition and avarice, and necessity compels the good to pursue the same course. And most lamentable is it to observe how the leaders and movers of parties sanctify their base designs with words that are all piety and virtue; they have the name of liberty constantly in their mouths, though their actions prove them her greatest enemies. The reward which they desire from victory is not the glory of having given liberty to the city, but the satisfaction of having vanquished others, and of making themselves rulers; and to attain their end, there is nothing too unjust, too cruel, too avaricious for them to attempt. Thus laws and ordinances, peace, wars, and treaties are adopted and pursued, not for the public good, not for the common glory of the state, but for the convenience or advantage of a few individuals.

"And if other cities abound in these disorders, ours is more than any infected with them; for her laws, statutes, and civil ordinances are not, nor have they ever been, established for the benefit of men in a state of freedom, but according to the wish of the faction that has been uppermost at the time. Hence it follows that, when one party is expelled, or faction extinguished, another immediately arises; for, in a city that is governed by parties rather than by laws, as soon as one becomes dominant and unopposed, it must of necessity soon divide against itself; for the private methods at first adapted for its defense will now no longer keep it united. The truth of this, both the ancient and modern dissensions of our city prove. Everyone thought that when the Ghibellines were destroyed, the Guelphs would long continue happy and honored; yet after a short time they divided into the Bianchi and Neri, the black faction and the white. When the Bianchi were overcome, the city was not long free from factions; for either, in favor of the emigrants, or on account of the animosity between the nobility and the people, we were still constantly at war. And as if resolved to give up to others, what in mutual harmony we either would not or were unable to retain, we confided the care of our precious liberty first to King Robert, then to his brother, next to his son, and at last to the duke of Athens. Still we have never in any condition found repose, but seem like men who can neither agree to live in freedom nor be content with slavery. Nor did we hesitate (so greatly does the nature of our ordinances dispose us to division), while yet under allegiance to the king, to substitute for his majesty, one of the vilest of men born at Agobbio.

"For the credit of the city, the name of the duke of Athens ought to be consigned to oblivion. His cruel and tyrannical disposition, however, might have taught us wisdom and instructed us how to live; but no sooner was he expelled than we handled our arms, and fought with more hatred, and greater fury than we had ever done on any former occasion; so that the ancient nobility were vanquished the city was left at the disposal of the people. It was generally supposed that no further occasion of quarrel or of party animosity could arise, since those whose pride and insupportable ambition had been regarded as the causes of them were depressed; however, experience proves how liable human judgment is to error, and what false impressions men imbibe, even in regard to the things that most intimately concern them; for we find the pride and ambition of the nobility are not extinct, but only transferred from them to the people who at this moment, according to the usual practice of ambitious men, are endeavoring to render themselves masters of the republic; and knowing they have no chance of success but what is offered by discord, they have again divided the city, and the names of Guelph and Ghibelline, which were beginning to be forgotten (and it would have been well if they had never been heard among us), are repeated anew in our ears.

"It seems almost necessarily ordained, in order that in human affairs there may be nothing either settled or permanent, that in all republics there are what may be called fatal families, born for the ruin of their country. Of this kind of pest our city has produced a more copious brood than any other; for not one but many have disturbed and harassed her: first the Buondelmonti and the Uberti; then the Donati and the Cerchi; and now, oh ridiculous! oh disgraceful thought! the Ricci and the Albizzi have caused a division of her citizens.

"We have not dwelt upon our corrupt habits or our old and continual dissensions to occasion you alarm, but to remind you of their causes; to show that as you doubtless are aware of them, we also keep them in view, and to remind you that their results ought not to make you diffident of your power to repress the disorders of the present time. The ancient families possessed so much influence, and were held in such high esteem, that civil force was insufficient to restrain them; but now, when the empire has lost its ascendancy, the pope is no longer formidable, and the whole of Italy is reduced to a state of the most complete equality, there can be no difficulty. Our republic might more especially than any other (although at first our former practices seem to present a reason to the contrary), not only keep itself united but be improved by good laws and civil regulations, if you, the Signory, would once resolve to undertake the matter; and to this we, induced by no other motive than the love of our country, would most strongly urge you. It is true the corruption of the country is great, and much discretion will be requisite to correct it; but do not impute the past disorders to the nature of the men, but to the times, which, being changed, give reasonable ground to hope that, with better government, our city will be attended with better fortune; for the malignity of the people will be overcome by restraining the ambition and annulling the ordinances of those who have encouraged faction, and adopting in their stead only such principles as are conformable to true civil liberty. And be assured, that these desirable ends will be more certainly attained by the benign influence of the laws, than by a delay which will compel the people to effect them by force and arms."

The Signory, induced by the necessity of the case, of which they were previously aware, and further encouraged by the advice of those who now addressed them, gave authority to fifty-six citizens to provide for the safety of the republic. It is usually found that most men are better adapted to pursue a good course already begun, than to discover one applicable to immediate circumstances. These citizens thought rather of extinguishing existing factions than of preventing the formation of new ones, and effected neither of these objects. The facilities for the establishment of new parties were not removed; and out of those which they guarded against, another more powerful arose, which brought the republic into still greater danger. They, however, deprived three of the family of the Albizzi, and three of that of the Ricci, of all the offices of government, except those of the Guelphic party, for three years; and among the deprived were Piero degli Albizzi and Uguccione de' Ricci. They forbade the citizens to assemble in the palace, except during the sittings of the Signory. They provided that if any one were beaten, or possession of his property detained from him, he might bring his case before the council and denounce the offender, even if he were one of the nobility; and that if it were proved, the accused should be subject to the usual penalties. This provision abated the boldness of the Ricci, and increased that of the Albizzi; since, although it applied equally to both, the Ricci suffered from it by far the most; for if Piero was excluded from the palace of the Signory, the chamber of the Guelphs, in which he possessed the greatest authority, remained open to him; and if he and his followers had previously been ready to *Admonish*, they became after this injury, doubly so. To this pre-disposition for evil, new excitements were added.

Chapter II: The war of the Florentines against the pope's legate, and the causes of it—League against the pope—The censures of the pope disregarded in Florence—The city is divided into two factions, the one the Capitani di Parte, the other of the eight commissioners of the war—Measures adopted by the Guelphic party against their adversaries—The Guelphs endeavor to prevent Salvestro de Medici from being chosen Gonfalonier—Salvestro de Medici Gonfalonier—His law against the nobility, and in favor of the Ammoniti—The *Collegi* disapprove of the law—Salvestro addresses the council in its favor—The law is passed—Disturbances in Florence.

The papal chair was occupied by Gregory XI. He, like his predecessors, residing at Avignon, governed Italy by legates, who, proud and avaricious, oppressed many of the cities. One of these legates, then at Bologna, taking advantage of a great scarcity of food at Florence, endeavored to render himself master of Tuscany, and not only withheld provisions from the Florentines, but in order to frustrate their hopes of the future harvest, upon the approach of spring, attacked them with a large army, trusting that being famished and unarmed, he should find them an easy conquest. He might perhaps have been successful, had not his forces been mercenary and faithless, and, therefore, induced to abandon the enterprise for the sum of 130,000 florins, which the Florentines paid them. People may go to war when they will, but cannot always withdraw when they like. This contest, commenced by the ambition of the legate, was sustained by the resentment of the Florentines, who, entering into a league with Bernabo of Milan, and with the cities hostile to the church, appointed eight citizens for the administration of it, giving them authority to act without appeal, and to expend whatever sums they might judge expedient, without rendering an account of the outlay.

This war against the pontiff, although Uguccione was now dead, reanimated those who had followed the party of the Ricci, who, in opposition to the Albizzi, had always favored Bernabo and opposed the church, and this, the rather, because the eight commissioners of war were all enemies of the Guelphs. This occasioned Piero degli Albizzi, Lapo da Castiglionchio, Carlo Strozzi, and others, to unite themselves more closely in opposition to their adversaries. The eight carried on the war, and the others admonished during three years, when the death of the pontiff put an end to the hostilities, which had been carried on which so much ability, and with such entire satisfaction to the people, that at the end of each year the eight were continued in office, and were called *Santi*, or holy, although they had set ecclesiastical censures at defiance, plundered the churches of their property, and compelled the priests to perform divine service. So much did citizens at that time prefer the good of their country to their ghostly consolations, and thus showed the church, that if as her friends they had defended, they could as enemies depress her; for the whole of Romagna, the Marches, and Perugia were excited to rebellion.

Yet while this war was carried on against the pope, they were unable to defend themselves against the captains of the parts and their faction; for the insolence of the Guelphs against the eight attained such a pitch, that they could not restrain themselves from abusive behavior, not merely against some of the most distinguished citizens, but even against the eight themselves; and the captains of the parts conducted themselves with such arrogance, that they were feared more than the Signory. Those who had business with them treated them with greater reverence, and their court was held in higher estimation: so that no ambassador came to Florence, without commission to the captains.

Pope Gregory being dead, and the city freed from external war; there still prevailed great confusion within; for the audacity of the Guelphs was insupportable, and as no available mode of subduing them presented itself, it was thought that recourse must be had to arms, to determine which party was the strongest. With the Guelphs were all the ancient nobility, and the greater part of the most popular leaders, of which number, as already remarked, were Lapo, Piero, and Carlo. On the other side, were all the lower orders, the leaders of whom were the eight commissioners of war, Giorgio Scali and Tommaso Strozzi, and with them the Ricci, Alberti, and Medici. The rest of the multitude, as most commonly happens, joined the discontented party.

It appeared to the heads of the Guelphic faction that their enemies would be greatly strengthened, and themselves in considerable danger in case a hostile Signory should resolve on their subjugation. Desirous, therefore, of being prepared against this calamity, the leaders of the party assembled to take into consideration the state of the city and that of their own friends in particular, and found the *ammoniti* so numerous and so great a difficulty, that the whole city was excited against them on this account. They could not devise any other remedy than, that as their enemies had deprived them of all the offices of honor, they should banish their opponents from the city, take possession of the palace of the Signory, and bring over the whole state to their own party; in imitation of the Guelphs of former times, who found no safety in the city, till they had driven all their adversaries out of it. They were unanimous upon the main point, but did not agree upon the time of carrying it into execution. It was in the month of April, in the year 1378, when Lapo, thinking delay inadvisable, expressed his opinion, that procrastination was in the highest degree perilous to themselves; as in the next Signory, Salvestro de' Medici would very probably be elected Gonfalonier, and they all knew he was opposed to their party. Piero degli Albizzi, on the other hand, thought it better to defer, since they would require forces, which could not be assembled without exciting observation, and if they were discovered, they would incur great risk. He thereupon judged it preferable to wait till the approaching feast of St. John on which, being the most solemn festival of the city, vast multitudes would be assembled, among whom they might conceal whatever numbers they pleased. To obviate their fears of Salvestro, he was to be ADMONISHED, and if this did not appear likely to be effectual, they would "ADMONISH" one of the Colleague of his quarter, and upon redrawing, as the ballot-boxes would be nearly empty, chance would very likely occasion that either he or some associate of his would be drawn, and he would thus be rendered incapable of sitting as Gonfalonier. They therefore came to the conclusion proposed by Piero, though Lapo consented reluctantly, considering the delay dangerous, and that, as no opportunity can be in all respects suitable, he who waits for the concurrence of every advantage, either never makes an attempt, or, if induced to do so, is most frequently foiled. They "admonished" the Colleague, but did not prevent the appointment of Salvestro, for the design was discovered by the Eight, who took care to render all attempts upon the drawing futile.

Salvestro Alammano de' Medici was therefore drawn Gonfalonier, and, being one of the noblest popular families, he could not endure that the people should be oppressed by a few powerful persons. Having resolved to put an end to their insolence, and perceiving the middle classes favorably disposed, and many of the highest of the people on his side, he communicated his design to Benedetto Alberti, Tommaso Strozzi, and Georgio Scali, who all promised their assistance. They, therefore, secretly draw up a law which had for its object to revive the restrictions upon the nobility, to retrench the authority of the Capitani di Parte, and recall the *ammoniti* to their dignity. In order to attempt and obtain their ends, at one and the same time, having to consult, first the Colleagues and then the Councils, Salvestro being Provost (which office for the time makes its possessor almost prince of the city), he called together the Colleagues and the Council on the same morning, and the Colleagues being apart, he proposed the law prepared by himself and his friends, which, being a novelty, encountered in their small number so much opposition, that he was unable to have it passed.

Salvestro, seeing his first attempt likely to fail, pretended to leave the room for a private reason, and, without being perceived, went immediately to the Council, and taking a lofty position from which he could be both seen and heard, said:—"That considering himself invested with the office of Gonfalonier, not so much to preside in private cases (for which proper judges were appointed, who have their regular sittings), as to guard the state, correct the insolence of the powerful, and ameliorate those laws by the influence of which the republic was being ruined, he had carefully attended to both these duties, and to his utmost ability provided for them, but found the perversity of some so much opposed to his just designs as to deprive him of all opportunity of doing good, and them not only of the means of assisting him with their counsel, but even hearing him. Therefore finding he no longer contributed either to the benefit of the republic or of the people generally, he could not perceive any reason for his longer holding the magistracy, of which he was either undeserving, or others thought him so, and would therefore retire to his house, that the people might appoint another in his stead, who would either have greater virtue or better fortune than himself." And having said this, he left the room as if to return home.

Those of the council who were in the secret, and others desirous of novelty, raised a tumult, at which the Signory and the Colleagues came together, and finding the Gonfalonier leaving them, entreatingly and authoritatively detained him, and obliged him to return to the council room, which was now full of confusion. Many of the noble citizens were threatened in opprobrious language; and an artificer seized Carlo Strozzi by the throat, and would undoubtedly have murdered him, but was with difficulty prevented by those around. He who made the greatest disturbance, and incited the city to violence, was Benedetto degli Alberti, who, from a window of the palace, loudly called the people to arms; and presently the courtyards were filled with armed men, and the Colleagues granted to threats, what they had refused to entreaty. The Capitani di Parte had at the same time drawn together a great number of citizens to their hall to consult upon the means of defending themselves against the orders of the Signors, but when they heard the tumult that was raised, and were informed of the course the Councils had adopted, each took refuge in his own house.

Let no one, when raising popular commotions, imagine he can afterward control them at his pleasure, or restrain them from proceeding to the commission of violence. Salvestro intended to enact his law, and compose the city; but it happened otherwise; for the feelings of all had become so excited, that they shut up the shops; the citizens fortified themselves in their houses; many conveyed their valuable property into the churches and monasteries, and everyone seemed to apprehend something terrible at hand. The companies of the Arts met, and each appointed an additional officer or Syndic; upon which the Priors summoned their Colleagues and these Syndics, and consulted a whole day how the city might be appeased with satisfaction to the different parties; but much difference of opinion prevailed, and no conclusion was come to. On the following day the Arts brought forth their banners, which the Signory understanding, and being apprehensive of evil, called the Council together to consider what course to adopt. But scarcely were they met, when the uproar recommenced, and soon the ensigns of the Arts, surrounded by vast numbers of armed men, occupied the courts. Upon this the Council, to give the Arts and the people hope of redress, and free themselves as much as possible from the charge of causing the mischief, gave a general power, which in Florence is called *Balia*, to the Signors, the Colleagues, the Eight, the Capitani di Parte, and to the Syndics of the Arts, to reform the government of the city, for the common benefit of all. While this was being arranged, a few of the ensigns of the Arts and some of the mob, desirous of avenging themselves for the recent injuries they had received from the Guelphs, separated themselves from the rest, and sacked and burnt the house of Lapo da Castiglionchio, who, when he learned the proceedings of the Signory against the Guelphs, and saw the people in arms, having no other resource but concealment or flight, first took refuge in Santa Croce, and afterward, being disguised as a monk, fled into the Casentino, where he was often heard to blame himself for having consented to wait till St. John's day, before they had made themselves sure of the government. Piero degli Albizzi and Carlo Strozzi hid themselves upon the first outbreak of the tumult, trusting that when it was over, by the interest of their numerous friends and relations, they might remain safely in Florence.

The house of Lapo being burnt, as mischief begins with difficulty but easily increases, many other houses, either through public hatred, or private malice, shared the same fate; and the rioters, that they might have companions more eager than themselves to assist them in their work of plunder, broke open the public prisons, and then sacked the monastery of the Agnoli and the convent of S. Spirito, whither many citizens had taken their most valuable goods for safety. Nor would the public chambers have escaped these destroyers' hands, except out of reverence for one of the Signors, who on horseback, and followed by many citizens in arms, opposed the rage of the mob.

Chapter III: Contrary measures adopted by the magistrates to effect a pacification—Luigi Guicciardini the Gonfalonier entreats the magistrates of the Arts to endeavor to pacify the people—Serious riot caused by the plebeians—The woolen Art—The plebeians assemble—The speech of a seditious plebeian—Their resolution thereupon—The Signory discover the designs of the plebeians—Measures adopted to counteract them.

This popular fury being abated by the authority of the Signors and the approach of night, on the following day, the Balia relieved the admonished, on condition that they should not for three years be capable of holding any magistracy. They annulled the laws made by the Guelphs to the prejudice of the citizens; declared Lapo da Castiglionchio and his companions, rebels, and with them many others, who were the objects of universal detestation. After these resolutions, the new Signory were drawn for, and Luigi Guicciardini appointed Gonfalonier, which gave hope that the tumults would soon be appeased; for everyone thought them to be peaceable men and lovers of order. Still the shops were not opened, nor did the citizens lay down their arms, but continued to patrol the city in great numbers; so that the Signory did not assume the magistracy with the usual pomp, but merely assembled within the palace, omitting all ceremony.

This Signory, considering nothing more advisable in the beginning of their magistracy than to restore peace, caused a relinquishment of arms; ordered the shops to be opened, and the strangers who had been called to their aid, to return to their homes. They appointed guards in many parts of the city, so that if the admonished would only have remained quiet, order would soon have been re-established. But they were not satisfied to wait three years for the recovery of their honours; so that to gratify them the Arts again met, and demanded of the Signory, that for the benefit and quiet of the city, they would ordain that no citizens should at any time, whether Signor, Colleague, Capitano di Parte, or Consul of any art whatever, be admonished as a Ghibelline; and further, that new ballots of the Guelphic party should be made, and the old ones burned. These demands were at once acceded to, not only by the Signors, but by all the Councils; and thus it was hoped the tumults newly excited would be settled.

But since men are not satisfied with recovering what is their own, but wish to possess the property of others and to revenge themselves, those who were in hopes of benefiting by these disorders persuaded the artificers that they would never be safe, if several of their enemies were not expelled from the city or destroyed. This terrible doctrine coming to the knowledge of the Signory, they caused the magistrates of the Arts and their Syndics to be brought before them, and Luigi Guicciardini, the Gonfalonier, addressed them in the following words: "If these Signors, and I with them, had not long been acquainted with the fate of this city, that as soon as external wars have ceased the internal commence, we should have been more surprised, and our displeasure would have been greater. But as evils to which we are accustomed are less annoying, we have endured past disturbances patiently, they having arisen for the most part without our fault; and we hoped that, like former troubles, they would soon have an end, after the many and great concessions we had made at your suggestion. But finding that you are yet unsettled, that you contemplate the commission of new crimes against your fellow-citizens, and are desirous of making new exiles, our displeasure increases in proportion to your misconduct. And certainly, could we have believed that during our magistracy the city was to be ruined, whether with or without your concurrence, we should certainly, either by flight or exile, have avoided these horrors. But trusting that we had to do with those who possessed some feelings of humanity and some love of their country, we willingly accepted the magistracy, thinking that by our gentleness we should overcome your ambition. But we perceive from experience that the more humble our behavior, the more concessions we make, the prouder you become, and the more exorbitant are your demands. And though we speak thus, it is not in order to offend, but to amend you. Let others tell you pleasing tales, our design is to communicate only what is for your good. Now we would ask you, and have you answer on your honor, What is there yet ungranted, that you can, with any appearance of propriety, require? You wished to have authority taken from the Capitani di Parte; and it is done. You wished that the ballotings should be burned, and a reformation of them take place; and we consent. You desired that the admonished should be restored to their honours; and it is permitted. At your entreaty we have pardoned those who have burned down houses and plundered churches; many honorable citizens have been exiled to please you; and at your suggestion new restraints have been laid upon the Great. When will there be an end of your demands? and how long will you continue to abuse our liberality? Do you not observe with how much more moderation we bear defeat than you your victory? To what end will your divisions bring our city? Have you forgotten that when disunited Castruccio, a low citizen of Lucca, subdued her? or that a duke of Athens, your hired captain did so too? But when the citizens were united in her defense, an archbishop of Milan and a pope were unable to subdue it, and, after many years of war, were compelled to retire with disgrace.

"Then why would you, by your discords, reduce to slavery in a time of peace, that city, which so many powerful enemies have left free, even in war? What can you expect from your disunion but subjugation? or from the property of which you already have plundered, or may yet plunder us, but poverty? for this property is the means by which we furnish occupation for the whole city, and if you take it from us, our means of finding that occupation is withdrawn. Besides, those who take it will have difficulty in preserving what is dishonestly acquired, and thus poverty and destitution are brought upon the city. Now, I, and these Signors command, and if it were consistent with propriety, we would entreat that you allow your minds to be calmed; be content, rest satisfied with the provisions that have been made for you; and if you should be found to need anything further, make your request with decency and order, and not with tumult; for when your demands are reasonable they will always be complied with, and you will not give occasion to evil designing men to ruin your country and cast the blame upon yourselves." These words conveying nothing but the truth, produced a suitable effect upon the minds of the citizens, who thanking the Gonfalonier for having acted toward them the part of a king Signor, and toward the city that of a good citizen, offered their obedience in whatever might be committed to them. And the Signors, to prove the sincerity of their intentions, appointed two citizens for each of the superior magistracies, who, with Syndics of the arts, were to consider what could be done to restore quite, and report their resolutions to the Signors.

While these things were in progress, a disturbance arose, much more injurious to the republic than anything that had hitherto occurred.

The greatest part of the fires and robberies which took place on the previous days were perpetrated by the very lowest of the people; and those who had been the most audacious, were afraid that when the greater differences were composed, they would be punished for the crimes they had committed; and that as usual, they would be abandoned by those who had instigated them to the commission of crime. To this may be added, the hatred of the lower orders toward the rich citizens and the principals of the arts, because they did not think themselves remunerated for their labor in a manner equal to their merits. For in the time of Charles I., when the city was divided into arts, a head or governor was appointed to each, and it was provided that the individuals of each art, should be judged in civil matters by their own superiors. These arts, as we have before observed, were at first twelve; in the course of time they were increased to twenty-one, and attained so much power, that in a few years they grasped the entire government of the city; and as some were in greater esteem than others, they were divided into *Major* and *Minor*; seven were called "major," and fourteen, the "minor arts." From this division, and from other causes which we have narrated above, arose the arrogance of the Capitani di Parte; for those citizens who had formerly been Guelphs, and had the constant disposal of that magistracy, favored the followers of the major and persecuted the minor arts and their patrons; and hence arose the many commotions already mentioned. When the companies of the arts were first organized, many of those trades, followed by the lowest of the people and the plebeians, were not incorporated, but were ranged under those arts most nearly allied to them; and, hence, when they were not properly remunerated for their labor, or their masters oppressed them, they had no one of whom to seek redress, except the magistrate of the art to which theirs was subject; and of him they did not think justice always attainable. Of the arts, that which had always had, and now has, the greatest number of these subordinates, is the woolen; which being both then, and still, the most powerful body, and first in authority, supports the greater part of the plebeians and lowest of the people.

The lower classes, then, the subordinates not only of the woolen, but also of the other arts, were discontented, from the causes just mentioned; and their apprehension of punishment for the burnings and robberies they had committed, did not tend to compose them. Meetings took place in different parts during the night, to talk over the past, and to communicate the danger in which they were, when one of the most daring and experienced, in order to animate the rest, spoke thus:

"If the question now were, whether we should take up arms, rob and burn the houses of the citizens, and plunder churches, I am one of those who would think it worthy of further consideration, and should, perhaps, prefer poverty and safety to the dangerous pursuit of an uncertain good. But as we have already armed, and many offenses have been committed, it appears to me that we have to consider how to lay them aside, and secure ourselves from the consequences of what is already done. I certainly think, that if nothing else could teach us, necessity might. You see the whole city full of complaint and indignation against us; the citizens are closely united, and the signors are constantly with the magistrates. You may be sure they are contriving something against us; they are arranging some new plan to subdue us. We ought therefore to keep two things in view, and have two points to consider; the one is, to escape with impunity for what has been done during the last few days, and the other, to live in greater comfort and security for the time to come. We must, therefore, I think, in order to be pardoned for our faults, commit new ones; redoubling the mischief, and multiplying fires and robberies; and in doing this, endeavor to have as many companions as we can; for when many are in fault, few are punished; small crimes are chastised, but great and serious ones rewarded. When many suffer, few seek vengeance; for general evils are endured more patiently than private ones. To increase the number of misdeeds will, therefore, make forgiveness more easily attainable, and will open the way to secure what we require for our own liberty. And it appears evident that the gain is certain; for our opponents are disunited and rich; their disunion will give us the victory, and their riches, when they have become ours, will support us. Be not deceived about that antiquity of blood by which they exalt themselves above us; for all men having had one common origin, are all equally ancient, and nature has made us all after one fashion. Strip us naked, and we shall all be found alike. Dress us in their clothing, and they in ours, we shall appear noble, they ignoble—for poverty and riches make all the difference. It grieves me much to think that some of you are sorry inwardly for what is done, and resolve to abstain from anything more of the kind. Certainly, if it be so, you are not the men I took you for; because neither shame nor conscience ought to have any influence with you. Conquerors, by what means soever, are never considered aught but glorious. We have no business to think about conscience; for when, like us, men have to fear hunger, and imprisonment, or death, the fear of hell neither can nor ought to have any influence upon them. If you only notice human proceedings, you may observe that all who attain great power and riches, make use of either force or fraud; and what they have acquired either by deceit or violence, in order to conceal the disgraceful methods of attainment, they endeavor to sanctify with the false title of honest gains. Those who either from imprudence or want of sagacity avoid doing so, are always overwhelmed with servitude and poverty; for faithful servants are always servants, and honest men are always poor; nor do any ever escape from servitude but the bold and faithless, or from poverty, but the rapacious and fraudulent. God and nature have thrown all human fortunes into the midst of mankind; and they are thus attainable rather by rapine than by industry, by wicked actions rather than by good. Hence it is that men feed upon each other, and those who cannot defend themselves must be worried. Therefore we must use force when the opportunity offers; and fortune cannot present us one more favorable than the present, when the citizens are still disunited, the Signory doubtful, and the magistrates terrified; for we may easily conquer them before they can come to any settled arrangement. By this means we shall either obtain the entire government of the city, or so large a share of it, as to be forgiven past errors, and have sufficient authority to threaten the city with a renewal of them at some future time. I confess this course is bold and dangerous, but when necessity presses, audacity becomes prudence, and in great affairs the brave never think of dangers. The enterprises that are begun with hazard always have a reward at last; and no one ever escaped from embarrassment without some peril. Besides, it is easy to see from all their preparations of prisons, racks, and instruments of death, that there is more danger in inaction than in endeavoring to secure ourselves; for in the first case the evils are certain, in the latter doubtful. How often have I heard you complain of the avarice of your superiors and the injustice of your magistrates. Now then is the time, not only to liberate yourself from them, but to become so much superior, that they will have more causes of grief and fear from you, than you from them. The opportunity presented by circumstances passes away, and when gone, it will be vain to think it can be recalled. You see the preparations of our enemies; let us anticipate them; and those who are first in arms will certainly be victors, to the ruin of their enemies and their own exaltation; and thus honors will accrue to many of us and security to all." These arguments greatly inflamed minds already disposed to mischief, so that they determined to take up arms as soon as they had acquired a sufficient number of associates, and bound themselves by oath to mutual defense, in case any of them were subdued by the civil power.

While they were arranging to take possession of the republic, their design became known to the Signory, who, having taken a man named Simone, learned from him the particulars of the conspiracy, and that the outbreak was to take place on the following day. Finding the danger so pressing, they called together the colleagues and those citizens who with the syndics of the arts were endeavoring to effect the union of the city. It was then evening, and they advised the signors to assemble the consuls of the trades, who proposed that whatever armed force was in Florence should be collected, and with the Gonfaloniers of the people and their companies, meet under arms in the piazza next morning. It happened that while Simone was being tortured, a man named Niccolo da San Friano was regulating the palace clock, and becoming acquainted with what was going on, returned home and spread the report of it in his neighborhood, so that presently the piazza of St. Spirito was occupied by above a thousand men. This soon became known to the other conspirators, and San Pietro Maggiore and St. Lorenzo, their places of assembly, were presently full of them, all under arms.

Chapter IV: Proceedings of the plebeians—The demand they make of the Signory—They insist that the Signory leave the palace—The Signory leave the palace—Michael di Lando Gonfalonier—Complaints and movements of the plebeians against Michael di Lando—Michael di Lando proceeds against the plebeians and reduces them to order—Character of Michael di Lando.

At daybreak on the 21st of July, there did not appear in the piazza above eighty men in arms friendly to the Signory, and not one of the Gonfaloniers; for knowing the whole city to be in a state of insurrection they were afraid to leave their homes. The first body of plebeians that made its appearance was that which had assembled at San Pietro Maggiore; but the armed force did not venture to attack them. Then came the other multitudes, and finding no opposition, they loudly demanded their prisoners from the Signory; and being resolved to have them by force if they were not yielded to their threats, they burned the house of Luigi Guicciardini; and the Signory, for fear of greater mischief, set them at liberty. With this addition to their strength they took the Gonfalon of Justice from the bearer, and under the shadow of authority which it gave them, burned the houses of many citizens, selecting those whose owners had publicly or privately excited their hatred. Many citizens, to avenge themselves for private injuries, conducted them to the houses of their enemies; for it was quite sufficient to insure its destruction, if a single voice from the mob called out, "To the house of such a one," or if he who bore the Gonfalon took the road toward it. All the documents belonging to the woolen trade were burned, and after the commission of much violence, by way of associating it with something laudable, Salvestro de Medici and sixty-three other citizens were made knights, among whom were Benedetto and Antonio degli Alberti, Tommaso Strozzi and others similarly their friends; though many received the honor against their wills. It was a remarkable peculiarity of the riots, that many who had their houses burned, were on the same day, and by the same party made knights; so close were the kindness and the injury together. This circumstance occurred to Luigi Guicciardini, Gonfalonier of Justice.

In this tremendous uproar, the Signory, finding themselves abandoned by their armed force, by the leaders of the arts, and by the Gonfaloniers, became dismayed; for none had come to their assistance in obedience to orders; and of the sixteen Gonfalons, the ensign of the Golden Lion and of the Vaio, under Giovenco della Stufa and Giovanni Cambi alone appeared; and these, not being joined by any other, soon withdrew. Of the citizens, on the other hand, some, seeing the fury of this unreasonable multitude and the palace abandoned, remained within doors; others followed the armed mob, in the hope that by being among them, they might more easily protect their own houses or those of their friends. The power of the plebeians was thus increased and that of the Signory weakened. The tumult continued all day, and at night the rioters halted near the palace of Stefano, behind the church of St. Barnabas. Their number exceeded six thousand, and before daybreak they obtained by threats the ensigns of the trades, with which and the Gonfalon of Justice, when morning came, they proceeded to the palace of the provost, who refusing to surrender it to them, they took possession of it by force.

The Signory, desirous of a compromise, since they could not restrain them by force, appointed four of the Colleagues to proceed to the palace of the provost, and endeavor to learn what was their intention. They found that the leaders of the plebeians, with the Syndics of the trades and some citizens, had resolved to signify their wishes to the Signory. They therefore returned with four deputies of the plebeians, who demanded that the woolen trade should not be allowed to have a foreign judge; that there should be formed three new companies of the arts; namely, one for the wool combers and dyers, one for the barbers, doublet-makers, tailors, and such like, and the third for the lowest class of people. They required that the three new arts should furnish two Signors; the fourteen minor arts, three; and that the Signory should provide a suitable place of assembly for them. They also made it a condition that no member of these companies should be expected during two years to pay any debt that amounted to less than fifty ducats; that the bank should take no interest on loans already contracted, and that only the principal sum should be demanded; that the condemned and the banished should be forgiven, and the admonished should be restored to participation in the honors of government. Besides these, many other articles were stipulated in favor of their friends, and a requisition made that many of their enemies should be exiled and admonished. These demands, though grievous and dishonorable to the republic, were for fear of further violence granted, by the joint deliberation of the Signors, Colleagues, and Council of the people. But in order to give it full effect, it was requisite that the Council of the Commune should also give its consent; and, as they could not assemble two councils during the same day it was necessary to defer it till the morrow. However the trades appeared content, the plebeians satisfied; and both promised, that these laws being confirmed, every disturbance should cease.

On the following morning, while the Council of the Commune were in consultation, the impatient and volatile multitude entered the piazza, under their respective ensigns, with loud and fearful shouts, which struck terror into all the Council and Signory; and Guerrente Marignolli, one of the latter, influenced more by fear than anything else, under pretense of guarding the lower doors, left the chamber and fled to his house. He was unable to conceal himself from the multitude, who, however, took no notice, except that, upon seeing him, they insisted that all the Signors should quit the palace, and declared that if they refused to comply, their houses should be burned and their families put to death.

The law had now been passed; the Signors were in their own apartments; the Council had descended from the chamber, and without leaving the palace, hopeless of saving the city, they remained in the lodges and courts below, overwhelmed with grief at seeing such depravity in the multitude, and such perversity or fear in those who might either have restrained or suppressed them. The Signory, too, were dismayed and fearful for the safety of their country, finding themselves abandoned by one of their associates, and without any aid or even advice; when, at this moment of uncertainty as to what was about to happen, or what would be best to be done, Tommaso Strozzi and Benedetto Alberti, either from motives of ambition (being desirous of remaining masters of the palace), or because they thought it the most advisable step, persuaded them to give way to the popular impulse, and withdraw privately to their homes. This advice, given by those who had been the leaders of the tumult, although the others yielded, filled Alamanno Acciajuoli and Niccolo del Bene, two of the Signors, with anger; and, reassuming a little vigor, they said, that if the others would withdraw they could not help it, but they would remain as long as they continued in office, if they did not in the meantime lose their lives. These dissensions redoubled the fears of the Signory and the rage of the people, so that the Gonfalonier, disposed rather to conclude his magistracy in dishonor than in danger, recommended himself to the care of Tommaso Strozzi, who withdrew him from the palace and conducted him to his house. The other Signors were, one after another, conveyed in the same manner, so that Alamanno and Niccolo, not to appear more valiant than wise, seeing themselves left alone, also retired, and the palace fell into the hands of the plebeians and the Eight Commissioners of War, who had not yet laid down their authority.

When the plebeians entered the palace, the standard of the Gonfalonier of Justice was in the hands of Michael di Lando, a wool comber. This man, barefoot, with scarcely anything upon him, and the rabble at his heels, ascended the staircase, and, having entered the audience chamber of the Signory, he stopped, and turning to the multitude said, "You see this palace is now yours, and the city is in your power; what do you think ought to be done?" To which they replied, they would have him for their Gonfalonier and lord; and that he should govern them and the city as he thought best. Michael accepted the command; and, as he was a cool and sagacious man, more favored by nature than by fortune, he resolved to compose the tumult, and restore peace to the city. To occupy the minds of the people, and give himself time to make some arrangement, he ordered that one Nuto, who had been appointed bargello, or sheriff, by Lapo da Castiglionchio, should be sought. The greater part of his followers went to execute this commission; and, to commence with justice the government he had acquired by favor, he commanded that no one should either burn or steal anything; while, to strike terror into all, he caused a gallows to be erected in the court of the palace. He began the reform of government by deposing the Syndics of the trades, and appointing new ones; he deprived the Signory and the Colleagues of their magistracy, and burned the balloting purses containing the names of those eligible to office under the former government.

In the meantime, Ser Nuto, being brought by the mob into the court, was suspended from the gallows by one foot; and those around having torn him to pieces, in little more than a moment nothing remained of him but the foot by which he had been tied.

The Eight Commissioners of War, on the other hand, thinking themselves, after the departure of the Signors, left sole masters of the city, had already formed a new Signory; but Michael, on hearing this, sent them an order to quit the palace immediately; for he wished to show that he could govern Florence without their assistance. He then assembled the Syndics of the trades, and created as a Signory, four from the lowest plebeians; two from the major, and two from the minor trades. Besides this, he made a new selection of names for the balloting purses, and divided the state into three parts; one composed of the new trades, another of the minor, and the third of the major trades. He gave to Salvestro de' Medici the revenue of the shops upon the Old Bridge; for himself he took the provostry of Empoli, and conferred benefits upon many other citizens, friends of the plebeians; not so much for the purpose of rewarding their labors, as that they might serve to screen him from envy.

It seemed to the plebeians that Michael, in his reformation of the state, had too much favored the higher ranks of the people, and that themselves had not a sufficient share in the government to enable them to preserve it; and hence, prompted by their usual audacity, they again took arms, and coming tumultuously into the court of the palace, each body under their particular ensigns, insisted that the Signory should immediately descend and consider new means for advancing their well-being and security. Michael, observing their arrogance, was unwilling to provoke them, but without further yielding to their request, blamed the manner in which it was made, advised them to lay down their arms, and promised that then would be conceded to them, what otherwise, for the dignity of the state, must of necessity be withheld. The multitude, enraged at this reply, withdrew to Santa Maria Novella, where they appointed eight leaders for their party, with officers, and other regulations to ensure influence and respect; so that the city possessed two governments, and was under the direction of two distinct powers. These new leaders determined that Eight, elected from their trades, should constantly reside in the palace with the Signory, and that whatever the Signory should determine must be confirmed by them before it became law. They took from Salvestro de' Medici and Michael di Lando the whole of what their former decrees had granted them, and distributed to many of their party offices and emoluments to enable them to support their dignity. These resolutions being passed, to render them valid they sent two of their body to the Signory, to insist on their being confirmed by the Council, with an intimation, that if not granted they would be vindicated by force. This deputation, with amazing audacity and surpassing presumption, explained their commission to the Signory, upbraided the Gonfalonier with the dignity they had conferred upon him, the honor they had done him, and with the ingratitude and want of respect he had shown toward them. Coming to threats toward the end of their discourse, Michael could not endure their arrogance, and sensible rather of the dignity of the office he held than of the meanness of his origin, determined by extraordinary means to punish such extraordinary insolence, and drawing the sword with which he was girt, seriously wounded, and cause them to be seized and imprisoned.

When the fact became known, the multitude were filled with rage, and thinking that by their arms they might ensure what without them they had failed to effect, they seized their weapons and with the utmost fury resolved to force the Signory to consent to their wishes. Michael, suspecting what would happen, determined to be prepared, for he knew his credit rather required him to be first to the attack than to wait the approach of the enemy, or, like his predecessors, dishonor both the palace and himself by flight. He therefore drew together a good number of citizens (for many began to see their error), mounted on horseback, and followed by crowds of armed men, proceeded to Santa Maria Novella, to encounter his adversaries. The plebeians, who as before observed were influenced by a similar desire, had set out about the same time as Michael, and it happened that as each took a different route, they did not meet in their way, and Michael, upon his return, found the piazza in their possession. The contest was now for the palace, and joining in the fight, he soon vanquished them, drove part of them out of the city, and compelled the rest to throw down their arms and escape or conceal themselves, as well as they could. Having thus gained the victory, the tumults were composed, solely by the talents of the Gonfalonier, who in courage, prudence, and generosity surpassed every other citizen of his time, and deserves to be enumerated among the glorious few who have greatly benefited their country; for had he possessed either malice or ambition, the republic would have been completely ruined, and the city must have fallen under greater tyranny than that of the duke of Athens. But his goodness never allowed a thought to enter his mind opposed to the universal welfare: his prudence enabled him to conduct affairs in such a manner, that a great majority of his own faction reposed the most entire confidence in him; and he kept the rest in awe by the influence of his authority. These qualities subdued the plebeians, and opened the eyes of the superior artificers, who considered how great must be the folly of those, who having overcome the pride of the nobility, could endure to submit to the nauseous rule of the rabble.

Chapter V: New regulations for the elections of the Signory—Confusion in the City—Piero degli Albizzi and other citizens condemned to death—The Florentines alarmed by the approach of Charles of Durazzo—The measures adopted in consequence thereof—Insolent Conduct of Giorgio Scali—Benedetto Alberti—Giorgio Scali beheaded.

By the time Michael di Lando had subdued the plebeians, the new Signory was drawn, and among those who composed it, were two persons of such base and mean condition, that the desire increased in the minds of the people to be freed from the ignominy into which they had fallen; and when, upon the first of September, the new Signory entered office and the retiring members were still in the palace, the piazza being full of armed men, a tumultuous cry arose from the midst of them, that none of the lowest of the people should hold office among the Signory. The obnoxious two were withdrawn accordingly. The name of one was Il Tira, of the other Baroccio, and in their stead were elected Giorgio Scali and Francesco di Michele. The company of the lowest trade was also dissolved, and its members deprived of office, except Michael di Lando, Lorenzo di Puccio and a few others of better quality. The honors of government were divided into two parts, one of which was assigned to the superior trades, the other to the inferior; except that the latter were to furnish five Signors, and the former only four. The Gonfalonier was to be chosen alternately from each.

The government thus composed, restored peace to the city for the time; but though the republic was rescued from the power of the lowest plebeians, the inferior trades were still more influential than the nobles of the people, who, however, were obliged to submit for the gratification of the trades, of whose favor they wished to deprive the plebeians. The new establishment was supported by all who wished the continued subjugation of those who, under the name of the Guelphic party, had practiced such excessive violence against the citizens. And as among others, thus disposed, were Giorgio Scali, Benedetto Alberti, Salvestro di Medici, and Tommaso Strozzi, these four almost became princes of the city. This state of the public mind strengthened the divisions already commenced between the nobles of the people, and the minor artificers, by the ambition of the Ricci and the Albizzi; from which, as at different times very serious effects arose, and as they will hereafter be frequently mentioned, we shall call the former the popular party, the latter the plebeian. This condition of things continued three years, during which many were exiled and put to death; for the government lived in constant apprehension, knowing that both within and without the city many were dissatisfied with them. Those within, either attempted or were suspected of attempting every day some new project against them; and those without, being under no restraint, were continually, by means of some prince or republic, spreading reports tending to increase the disaffection.

Gianozzo da Salerno was at this time in Bologna. He held a command under Charles of Durazzo, a descendant of the kings of Naples, who, designing to undertake the conquest of the dominions of Queen Giovanna, retained his captain in that city, with the concurrence of Pope Urban, who was at enmity with the queen. Many Florentine emigrants were also at Bologna, in close correspondence with him and Charles. This caused the rulers in Florence to live in continual alarm, and induced them to lend a willing ear to any calumnies against the suspected. While in this disturbed state of feeling, it was disclosed to the government that Gianozzo da Salerno was about to march to Florence with the emigrants, and that great numbers of those within were to rise in arms, and deliver the city to him. Upon this information many were accused, the principal of whom were Piero degli Albizzi and Carlo Strozzi: and after these Cipriano Mangione, Jacopo Sacchetti, Donato Barbadori, Filippo Strozzi, and Giovanni Anselmi, the whole of whom, except Carlo Strozzi who fled, were made prisoners; and the Signory, to prevent any one from taking arms in their favor, appointed Tommaso Strozzi and Benedetto Alberti with a strong armed force, to guard the city. The arrested citizens were examined, and although nothing was elicited against them sufficient to induce the Capitano to find them guilty, their enemies excited the minds of the populace to such a degree of outrageous and overwhelming fury against them, that they were condemned to death, as it were, by force. Nor was the greatness of his family, or his former reputation of any service to Piero degli Albizzi, who had once been, of all the citizens, the man most feared and honored. Some one, either as a friend to render him wise in his prosperity, or an enemy to threaten him with the fickleness of fortune, had upon the occasion of his making a feast for many citizens, sent him a silver bowl full of sweetmeats, among which a large nail was found, and being seen by many present, was taken for a hint to him to fix the wheel of fortune, which, having conveyed him to the top, must if the rotation continued, also bring him to the bottom. This interpretation was verified, first by his ruin, and afterward by his death.

After this execution the city was full of consternation, for both victors and vanquished were alike in fear; but the worst effects arose from the apprehensions of those possessing the management of affairs; for every accident, however trivial, caused them to commit fresh outrages, either by condemnations, admonitions, or banishment of citizens; to which must be added, as scarcely less pernicious, the frequent new laws and regulations which were made for defense of the government, all of which were put in execution to the injury of those opposed to their faction. They appointed forty-six persons, who, with the Signory, were to purge the republic of all suspected by the government. They admonished thirty-nine citizens, ennobled many of the people, and degraded many nobles to the popular rank. To strengthen themselves against external foes, they took into their pay John Hawkwood, an Englishman of great military reputation, who had long served the pope and others in Italy. Their fears from without were increased by a report that several bodies of men were being assembled by Charles of Durazzo for the conquest of Naples, and many Florentine emigrants were said to have joined him. Against these dangers, in addition to the forces which had been raised, large sums of money were provided; and Charles, having arrived at Arezzo, obtained from the Florentines 40,000 ducats, and promised he would not molest them. His enterprise was immediately prosecuted, and having occupied the kingdom of Naples, he sent Queen Giovanna a prisoner into Hungary. This victory renewed the fears of those who managed the affairs of Florence, for they could not persuade themselves that their money would have a greater influence on the king's mind than the friendship which his house had long retained for the Guelphs, whom they so grievously oppressed.

This suspicion increasing, multiplied oppressions; which again, instead of diminishing the suspicion, augmented it; so that most men lived in the utmost discontent. To this the insolence of Giorgio Scali and Tommaso Strozzi (who by their popular influence overawed the magistrates) also contributed, for the rulers were apprehensive that by the power these men possessed with the plebeians they could set them at defiance; and hence it is evident that not only to good men, but even to the seditious, this government appeared tyrannical and violent. To put a period to the outrageous conduct of Giorgio, it happened that a servant of his accused Giovanni di Cambio of practices against the state, but the Capitano declared him innocent. Upon this, the judge determined to punish the accuser with the same penalties that the accused would have incurred had he been guilty, but Giorgio Scali, unable to save him either by his authority or entreaties, obtained the assistance of Tommaso Strozzi, and with a multitude of armed men, set the informer at liberty and plundered the palace of the Capitano, who was obliged to save himself by flight. This act excited such great and universal animosity against him, that his enemies began to hope they would be able to effect his ruin, and also to rescue the city from the power of the plebeians, who for three years had held her under their arrogant control.

To the realization of this design the Capitano greatly contributed, for the tumult having subsided, he presented himself before the signors, and said "He had cheerfully undertaken the office to which they had appointed him, for he thought he should serve upright men who would take arms for the defense of justice, and not impede its progress. But now that he had seen and had experience of the proceedings of the city, and the manner in which affairs were conducted, that dignity which he had voluntarily assumed with the hope of acquiring honor and emolument, he now more willingly resigned, to escape from the losses and danger to which he found himself exposed." The complaint of the Capitano was heard with the utmost attention by the Signory, who promising to remunerate him for the injury he had suffered and provide for his future security, he was satisfied. Some of them then obtained an interview with certain citizens who were thought to be lovers of the common good, and least suspected by the state; and in conjunction with these, it was concluded that the present was a favorable opportunity for rescuing the city from Giorgio and the plebeians, the last outrage he had committed having completely alienated the great body of the people from him. They judged it best to profit by the occasion before the excitement had abated, for they knew that the favor of the mob is often gained or lost by the most trifling circumstance; and more certainly to insure success, they determined, if possible, to obtain the concurrence of Benedetto Alberti, for without it they considered their enterprise to be dangerous.

Benedetto was one of the richest citizens, a man of unassuming manners, an ardent lover of the liberties of his country, and one to whom tyrannical measures were in the highest degree offensive; so that he was easily induced to concur in their views and consent to Giorgio's ruin. His enmity against the nobles of the people and the Guelphs, and his friendship for the plebeians, were caused by the insolence and tyrannical proceedings of the former; but finding that the plebeians had soon become quite as insolent, he quickly separated himself from them; and the injuries committed by them against the citizens were done wholly without his consent. So that the same motives which made him join the plebeians induced him to leave them.

Having gained Benedetto and the leaders of the trades to their side, they provided themselves with arms and made Giorgio prisoner. Tommaso fled. The next day Giorgio was beheaded; which struck so great a terror into his party, that none ventured to express the slightest disapprobation, but each seemed anxious to be foremost in defense of the measure. On being led to execution, in the presence of that people who only a short time before had idolized him, Giorgio complained of his hard fortune, and the malignity of those citizens who, having done him an undeserved injury, had compelled him to honor and support a mob, possessing neither faith nor gratitude. Observing Benedetto Alberti among those who had armed themselves for the preservation of order, he said, "Do you, too, consent, Benedetto, that this injury shall be done to me? Were I in your place and you in mine, I would take care that no one should injure you. I tell you, however, this day is the end of my troubles and the beginning of yours." He then blamed himself for having confided too much in a people who may be excited and inflamed by every word, motion, and breath of suspicion. With these complaints he died in the midst of his armed enemies, delighted at his fall. Some of his most intimate associates were also put to death, and their bodies dragged about by the mob.

Chapter VI: Confusion and riots in the city—Reform of government in opposition to the plebeians—Injuries done to those who favored the plebeians—Michael di Lando banished—Benedetto Alberti hated by the Signory—Fears excited by the coming of Louis of Anjou—The Florentines purchase Arezzo—Benedetto Alberti becomes suspected and is banished—His discourse upon leaving the city—Other citizens banished and admonished—War with Giovanni Galeazzo, duke of Milan.

The death of Giorgio caused very great excitement; many took arms at the execution in favor of the Signory and the Capitano; and many others, either for ambition or as a means for their own safety, did the same. The city was full of conflicting parties, who each had a particular end in view, and wished to carry it into effect before they disarmed. The ancient nobility, called the *Great*, could not bear to be deprived of public honors; for the recovery of which they used their utmost exertions, and earnestly desired that authority might be restored to the Capitani di Parte. The nobles of the people and the major trades were discontented at the share the minor trades and lowest of the people possessed in the government; while the minor trades were desirous of increasing their influence, and the lowest people were apprehensive of losing the companies of their trades and the authority which these conferred.

Such opposing views occasioned Florence, during a year, to be disturbed by many riots. Sometimes the nobles of the people took arms; sometimes the major and sometimes the minor trades and the lowest of the people; and it often happened that, though in different parts, all were at once in insurrection. Hence many conflicts took place between the different parties or with the forces of the palace; for the Signory sometimes yielding, and at other times resisting, adopted such remedies as they could for these numerous evils. At length, after two assemblies of the people, and many Balias appointed for the reformation of the city; after much toil, labor, and imminent danger, a government was appointed, by which all who had been banished since Salvestro de' Medici was Gonfalonier were restored. They who had acquired distinctions or emoluments by the Balia of 1378 were deprived of them. The honors of government were restored to the Guelphic party; the two new Companies of the Trades were dissolved, and all who had been subject to them assigned to their former companies. The minor trades were not allowed to elect the Gonfalonier of Justice, their share of honors was reduced from a half to a third; and those of the highest rank were withdrawn from them altogether. Thus the nobles of the people and the Guelphs repossessed themselves of the government, which was lost by the plebeians after it had been in their possession from 1378 to 1381, when these changes took place.

The new establishment was not less injurious to the citizens, or less troublesome at its commencement than that of the plebeians had been; for many of the nobles of the people, who had distinguished themselves as defenders of the plebeians, were banished, with a great number of the leaders of the latter, among whom was Michael di Lando; nor could all the benefits conferred upon the city by his authority, when in danger from the lawless mob, save him from the rabid fury of the party that was now in power. His good offices evidently excited little gratitude in his countrymen. The neglect of their benefactors is an error into which princes and republics frequently fall; and hence mankind, alarmed by such examples, as soon as they begin to perceive the ingratitude of their rulers, set themselves against them.

As these banishments and executions had always been offensive to Benedetto Alberti, they continued to disgust him, and he censured them both publicly and privately. The leaders of the government began to fear him, for they considered him one of the most earnest friends of the plebeians, and thought he had not consented to the death of Giorgio Scali from disapprobation of his proceeding, but that he might be left himself without a rival in the government. His discourse and his conduct alike served to increase their suspicions, so that all the ruling party had their eyes upon him, and eagerly sought an opportunity of crushing him.

During this state of things, external affairs were not of serious importance, for some which ensued were productive of apprehension rather than of injury. At this time Louis of Anjou came into Italy, to recover the kingdom of Naples for Queen Giovanna, and drive out Charles of Durazzo. His coming terrified the Florentines; for Charles, according to the custom of old friends, demanded their assistance, and Louis, like those who seek new alliances, required their neutrality. The Florentines, that they might seem to comply with the request of Louis, and at the same time assist Charles, discharged from their service Sir John Hawkwood, and transferred him to that of Pope Urban, who was friendly to Charles; but this deceit was at once detected, and Louis considered himself greatly injured by the Florentines. While the war was carried on between Louis and Charles in Puglia, new forces were sent from France in aid of Louis, and on arriving in Tuscany, were by the emigrants of Arezzo conducted to that city, and took it from those who held possession for Charles. And when they were about to change the government of Florence, as they had already done that of Arezzo, Louis died, and the order of things in Puglia and in Tuscany was changed accordingly; for Charles secured the kingdom, which had been all but lost, and the Florentines, who were apprehensive for their own city, purchased Arezzo from those who held it for Louis.

Charles, having secured Puglia, went to take possession of Hungary, to which he was heir, leaving, with his wife, his children Ladislaus and Giovanna, who were yet infants. He took possession of Hungary, but was soon after slain there.

As great rejoicings were made in Florence on account of this acquisition as ever took place in any city for a real victory, which served to exhibit the public and private wealth of the people, many families endeavoring to vie with the state itself in displays of magnificence. The Alberti surpassed all others; the tournaments and exhibitions made by them were rather suitable for a sovereign prince than for any private individuals. These things increased the envy with which the family was regarded, and being joined with suspicions which the state entertained of Benedetto, were the causes of his ruin. The rulers could not endure him, for it appeared as if, at any moment, something might occur, which, with the favor of his friends, would enable him to recover his authority, and drive them out of the city. While in this state of suspicion and jealousy, it happened that while he was Gonfalonier of the Companies, his son-in-law, Filippo Magalotti, was drawn Gonfalonier of Justice; and this circumstance increased the fears of the government, for they thought it would strengthen Benedetto's influence, and place the state in the greater peril. Anxious to provide a remedy, without creating much disturbance, they induced Bese Magalotti, his relative and enemy, to signify to the Signory that Filippo, not having attained the age required for the exercise of that office, neither could nor ought to hold it.

The question was examined by the signors, and part of them out of hatred, others in order to avoid disunion among themselves, declared Filippo ineligible to the dignity, and in his stead was drawn Bardo Mancini, who was quite opposed to the plebeian interests, and an inveterate foe of Benedetto. This man, having entered upon the duties of his office, created a *Balia* for the reformation of the state, which banished Benedetto Alberti and admonished all the rest of his family except Antonio. Before his departure, Benedetto called them together, and observing their melancholy demeanor, said, "You see, my fathers, and you the elders of our house, how fortune has ruined me and threatened you. I am not surprised at this, neither ought you to be so, for it always happens thus to those who among a multitude of the wicked, wish to act rightly, and endeavor to sustain, what the many seek to destroy. The love of my country made me take part with Salvestro de Medici and afterward separated me from Giorgio Scali. The same cause compelled me to detest those who now govern, who having none to punish them, will allow no one to reprove their misdeeds. I am content that my banishment should deliver them from the fears they entertain, not of me only, but of all who they think perceives or is acquainted wit their tyrannical and wicked proceedings; and they have aimed their first blow at me, in order the more easily to oppress you. I do not grieve on my own account; for those honors which my country bestowed upon me while free, she cannot in her slavery take from me; and the recollection of my past life will always give me greater pleasure than the pain imparted by the sorrows of exile. I deeply regret that my country is left a prey to the greediness and pride of the few who keep her in subjection. I grieve for you; for I fear that the evils which this day cease to affect me, and commence with you, will pursue you with even greater malevolence than they have me. Comfort, then, each other; resolve to bear up against every misfortune, and conduct yourselves in such a manner, that when disasters befall you (and there will be many), every one may know they have come upon you undeservedly." Not to give a worse impression of his virtue abroad than he had done at home, he made a journey to the sepulcher of Christ, and while upon his return, died at Rhodes. His remains were brought to Florence, and interred with all possible honors, by those who had persecuted him, when alive, with every species of calumny and injustice.

The family of the Alberti was not the only injured party during these troubles of the city; for many others were banished and admonished. Of the former were Piero Benini, Matteo Alderotti, Giovanni and Francesco del Bene, Giovanni Benci, Andrea Adimari, and with them many members of the minor trades. Of the admonished were the Covini, Benini, Rinucci, Formiconi, Corbizzi, Manelli, and Alderotti. It was customary to create the Balia for a limited time; and when the citizens elected had effected the purpose of their appointment, they resigned the office from motives of good feeling and decency, although the time allowed might not have expired. In conformity with this laudable practice, the Balia of that period, supposing they had accomplished all that was expected of them, wished to retire; but when the multitude were acquainted with their intention, they ran armed to the palace, and insisted, that before resigning their power, many other persons should be banished and admonished. This greatly displeased the signors; but without disclosing the extent of their displeasure, they contrived to amuse the multitude with promises, till they had assembled a sufficient body of armed men, and then took such measures, that fear induced the people to lay aside the weapons which madness had led them to take up. Nevertheless, in some degree to gratify the fury of the mob, and to reduce the authority of the plebeian trades, it was provided, that as the latter had previously possessed a third of the honors, they should in future have only a fourth. That there might always be two of the signors particularly devoted to the government, they gave authority to the Gonfalonier of Justice, and four others, to form a ballot-purse of select citizens, from which, in every Signory, two should be drawn.

This government from its establishment in 1381, till the alterations now made, had continued six years; and the internal peace of the city remained undisturbed until 1393. During this time, Giovanni Galeazzo Visconti, usually called the Count of Virtu, imprisoned his uncle Bernabo, and thus became sovereign of the whole of Lombardy. As he had become duke of Milan by fraud, he designed to make himself king of Italy by force. In 1391 he commenced a spirited attack upon the Florentines; but such various changes occurred in the course of the war, that he was frequently in greater danger than the Florentines themselves, who, though they made a brave and admirable defense, for a republic, must have been ruined, if he had survived. As it was, the result was attended with infinitely less evil than their fears of so powerful an enemy had led them to apprehend; for the duke having taken Bologna, Pisa, Perugia, and Sienna, and prepared a diadem with which to be crowned king of Italy at Florence, died before he had tasted the fruit of his victories, or the Florentines began to feel the effect of their disasters.

Chapter VII: Maso degli Albizzi—His violence excites the anger of the people—They have recourse to Veri de' Medici—The modesty of Veri—He refuses to assume the dignity of prince, and appeases the people—Discourse of Veri to the Signory—The banished Florentines endeavor to return—They secretly enter the city and raise a tumult—Some of them slain, others taken to the church of St. Reparata—A conspiracy of exiles supported by the duke of Milan—The conspiracy discovered and the parties punished—Various enterprises of the Florentines—Taking of Pisa—War with the king of Naples—Acquisition of Cortona.

During the war with the duke of Milan the office of Gonfalonier of Justice fell to Maso degli Albizzi, who by the death of Piero in 1379, had become the inveterate enemy of the Alberti: and as party feeling is incapable either of repose or abatement, he determined, notwithstanding Benedetto had died in exile, that before the expiration of his magistracy, he would revenge himself on the remainder of that family. He seized the opportunity afforded by a person, who on being examined respecting correspondence maintained with the rebels, accused Andrea and Alberto degli Alberti of such practices. They were immediately arrested, which so greatly excited the people, that the Signory, having provided themselves with an armed force, called the citizens to a general assembly or parliament, and appointed a Balia, by whose authority many were banished, and a new ballot for the offices of government was made. Among the banished were nearly all the Alberti; many members of the trades were admonished, and some put to death. Stung by these numerous injuries, the trades and the lowest of the people rose in arms, considering themselves despoiled both of honor and life. One body of them assembled in the piazza; another ran to the house of Veri de' Medici, who, after the death of Salvestro, was head of the family. The Signory, in order to appease those who came to the piazza or court of the palace, gave them for leaders, with the ensigns of the Guelphs and of the people in their hands, Rinaldo Gianfigliazzi, and Donato Acciajuoli, both men of the popular class, and more attached to the interests of the plebeians than any other. Those who went to the house of Veri de' Medici, begged that he would be pleased to undertake the government, and free them from the tyranny of those citizens who were destroying the peace and safety of the commonwealth.

It is agreed by all who have written concerning the events of this period, that if Veri had had more ambition than integrity he might without any impediment have become prince of the city; for the unfeeling treatment which, whether right or wrong, had been inflicted upon the trades and their friends, had so excited the minds of men to vengeance, that all they required was some one to be their leader. Nor were there wanting those who could inform him of the state of public feeling; for Antonio de' Medici with whom he had for some time been upon terms of most intimate friendship, endeavored to persuade him to undertake the government of the republic. To this Veri replied: "Thy menaces when thou wert my enemy, never alarmed me; nor shall thy counsel, now when thou art my friend, do me any harm." Then, turning toward the multitude, he bade them be of good cheer; for he would be their defender, if they would allow themselves to be advised by him. He then went, accompanied by a great number of citizens, to the piazza, and proceeded directly to the audience chamber of the Signory, whom he addressed to this effect: That he could not regret having lived so as to gain the love of the Florentines; but he was sorry they had formed an opinion of him which his past life had not warranted; for never having done anything that could be construed as either factious or ambitious, he could not imagine how it had happened, that they should think him willing to stir up strife as a discontented person, or usurp the government of his country like an ambitious one. He therefore begged that the infatuation of the multitude might not injure him in their estimation; for, to the utmost of his power, their authority should be restored. He then recommended them to use good fortune with moderation; for it would be much better to enjoy an imperfect victory with safety to the city, than a complete one at her ruin. The Signory applauded Veri's conduct; begged he would endeavor to prevent recourse to arms, and promised that what he and the other citizens might deem most advisable should be done. Veri then returned to the piazza, where the people who had followed him were joined by those led by Donato and Rinaldo, and informed the united companies that he had found the Signory most kindly disposed toward them; that many things had been taken into consideration, which the shortness of time, and the absence of the magistrates, rendered incapable of being finished. He therefore begged they would lay down their arms and obey the Signory; assuring them that humility would prevail rather than pride, entreaties rather than threats; and if they would take his advice, their privileges and security would remain unimpaired. He thus induced them to return peaceably to their homes.

The disturbance having subsided, the Signory armed the piazza, enrolled 2,000 of the most trusty citizens, who were divided equally by Gonfalons, and ordered to be in readiness to give their assistance whenever required; and they forbade the use of arms to all who were not thus enrolled. Having adopted these precautionary measures, they banished and put to death many of those members of the trades who had shown the greatest audacity in the late riots; and to invest the office of Gonfalonier of Justice with more authoritative majesty, they ordered that no one should be eligible to it, under forty-five years of age. Many other provisions for the defense of the state were made, which appeared intolerable to those against whom they were directed, and were odious even to the friends of the Signory themselves, for they could not believe a government to be either good or secure, which needed so much violence for its defense, a violence excessively offensive, not only to those of the Alberti who remained in the city, and to the Medici, who felt themselves injured by these proceedings, but also to many others. The first who attempted resistance was Donato, the son of Jacopo Acciajuoli, who thought of great authority, and the superior rather than the equal of Maso degli Albizzi (who on account of the events which took place while he was Gonfalonier of Justice, was almost at the head of the republic), could not enjoy repose amid such general discontent, or, like many others, convert social evils to his own private advantage, and therefore resolved to attempt the restoration of the exiles to their country, or at least their offices to the admonished. He went from one to another, disseminating his views, showing that the people would not be satisfied, or the ferment of parties subside, without the changes he proposed; and declared that if he were in the Signory, he would soon carry them into effect. In human affairs, delay causes tedium, and haste danger. To avoid what was tedious, Donato Acciajuoli resolved to attempt what involved danger. Michele Acciajuoli his relative, and Niccolo Ricoveri his friend, were of the Signory. This seemed to Donato a conjuncture of circumstances too favorable to be lost, and he requested they would propose a law to the councils, which would include the restoration of the citizens. They, at his entreaty, spoke about the matter to their associates, who replied, that it was improper to attempt any innovation in which the advantage was doubtful and the danger certain. Upon this, Donato, having in vain tried all other means he could think of, excited with anger, gave them to understand that since they would not allow the city to be governed with peaceful measures, he would try what could be done with arms. These words gave so great offense, that being communicated to the heads of the government, Donato was summoned, and having appeared, the truth was proven by those to whom he had intrusted the message, and he was banished to Barletta. Alamanno and Antonio de' Medici were also banished, and all those of that family, who were descended from Alamanno, with many who, although of the inferior artificers, possessed influence with the plebeians. These events took place two years after the reform of government effected by Maso degli Albizzi.

At this time many discontented citizens were at home, and others banished in the adjoining states. Of the latter there lived at Bologna Picchio Cavicciulli, Tommaso de' Ricci, Antonio de' Medici, Benedetto degli Spini, Antonio Girolami, Cristofano di Carlone, and two others of the lowest order, all bold young men, and resolved upon returning to their country at any hazard. These were secretly told by Piggiello and Baroccio Cavicciulli, who, being admonished, lived in Florence, that if they came to the city they should be concealed in their house; from which they might afterward issue, slay Maso degli Albizzi, and call the people to arms, who, full of discontent, would willingly arise, particularly as they would be supported by the Ricci, Adimari, Medici, Manelli, and many other families. Excited with these hopes, on the fourth of August, 1397, they came to Florence, and having entered unobserved according to their arrangement, they sent one of their party to watch Maso, designing with his death to raise the people. Maso was observed to leave his house and proceed to that of an apothecary, near the church of San Pietro Maggiore, which he entered. The man who went to watch him ran to give information to the other conspirators, who took their arms and hastened to the house of the apothecary, but found that Maso had gone. However, undaunted with the failure of their first attempt, they proceeded to the Old Market, where they slew one of the adverse party, and with loud cries of "people, arms, liberty, and death to the tyrants," directed their course toward the New Market, and at the end of the Calimala slew another. Pursuing their course with the same cries, and finding no one join them in arms, they stopped at the Loggia Nighittosa, where, from an elevated situation, being surrounded with a great multitude, assembled to look on rather than assist them, they exhorted the men to take arms and deliver themselves from the slavery which weighed so heavily upon them; declaring that the complaints of the discontented in the city, rather than their own grievances, had induced them to attempt their deliverance. They had heard that many prayed to God for an opportunity of avenging themselves, and vowed they would use it whenever they found anyone to conduct them; but now, when the favorable circumstances occurred, and they found those who were ready to lead them, they stared at each other like men stupefied, and would wait till those who were endeavoring to recover for them their liberty were slain, and their own chains more strongly riveted upon them; they wondered that those who were wont to take arms upon slight occasions, remained unmoved under the pressure of so many and so great evils; and that they could willingly suffer such numbers of their fellow-citizens to be banished, so many admonished, when it was in their power to restore the banished to their country, and the admonished to the honors of the state. These words, although full of truth, produced no effect upon those to whom they were addressed; for they were either restrained by their fears, or, on account of the two murders which had been committed, disgusted with the parties. Thus the movers of the tumult, finding that neither words or deeds had force sufficient to stir anyone, saw, when too late, how dangerous a thing it is to attempt to set a people free who are resolved to be slaves; and, despairing of success, they withdrew to the temple of Santa Reparata, where, not to save their lives, but to defer the moment of their deaths, they shut themselves up. Upon the first rumor of the affair, the Signory being in fear, armed and secured the palace; but when the facts of the case were understood, the parties known, and whither they had betaken themselves, their fears subsided, and they sent the Capitano with a sufficient body of armed men to secure them. The gates of the temple were forced without much trouble; part of the conspirators were slain defending themselves; the remainder were made prisoners and examined, but none were found implicated in the affair except Baroccio and Piggiello Cavicciulli, who were put to death with them.

Shortly after this event, another occurred of greater importance. The Florentines were, as we have before remarked, at war with the duke of Milan, who, finding that with merely open force he could not overcome them, had recourse to secret practices, and with the assistance of the exiles of whom Lombardy was full, he formed a plot to which many in the city were accessory. It was resolved by the conspirators that most of the emigrants, capable of bearing arms, should set out from the places nearest Florence, enter the city by the river Arno, and with their friends hasten to the residences of the chiefs of the government; and having slain them, reform the republic according to their own will. Of the conspirators within the city, was one of the Ricci named Samminiato; and as it often happens in treacherous practices, few are insufficient to effect the purpose of the plot, and among many secrecy cannot be preserved, so while Samminiato was in quest of associates, he found an accuser. He confided the affair to Salvestro Cavicciulli, whose wrongs and those of his friends were thought sufficient to make him faithful; but he, more influenced by immediate fear than the hope of future vengeance, discovered the whole affair to the Signory, who, having caused Samminiato to be taken, compelled him to tell all the particulars of the matter. However, none of the conspirators were taken, except Tommaso Davizi, who, coming from Bologna, and unaware of what had occurred at Florence, was seized immediately upon his arrival. All the others had fled immediately upon the apprehension of Samminiato.

Samminiato and Tommaso having been punished according to their deserts, a Balia was formed of many citizens, which sought the delinquents, and took measures for the security of the state. They declared six of the family of the Ricci rebels; also, six of the Alberti; two of the Medici; three of the Scali; two of the Strozzi; Bindo Altoviti, Bernado Adimari, and many others of inferior quality. They admonished all the family of the Alberti, the Ricci, and the Medici for ten years, except a few individuals. Among the Alberti, not admonished, was Antonio, who was thought to be quiet and peaceable. It happened, however, before all suspicion of the conspiracy had ceased, a monk was taken who had been observed during its progress to pass frequently between Bologna and Florence. He confessed that he had often carried letters to Antonio, who was immediately seized, and, though he denied all knowledge of the matter from the first, the monk's accusation prevailed, and he was fined in a considerable sum of money, and banished a distance of three hundred miles from Florence. That the Alberti might not constantly place the city in jeopardy, every member of the family was banished whose age exceeded fifteen years.

These events took place in the year 1400, and two years afterward, died Giovanni Galeazzo, duke of Milan, whose death as we have said above, put an end to the war, which had then continued twelve years. At this time, the government having gained greater strength, and being without enemies external or internal, undertook the conquest of Pisa, and having gloriously completed it, the peace of the city remained undisturbed from 1400 to 1433, except that in 1412, the Alberti, having crossed the boundary they were forbidden to pass, a Balia was formed which with new provisions fortified the state and punished the offenders with heavy fines. During this period also, the Florentines made war with Ladislaus, king of Naples, who finding himself in great danger ceded to them the city of Cortona of which he was master; but soon afterward, recovering his power, he renewed the war, which became far more disastrous to the Florentines than before; and had it not, in 1414, been terminated by his death, as that of Lombardy had been by the death of the duke of Milan, he, like the duke, would have brought Florence into great danger of losing her liberty. Nor was the war with the king concluded with less good fortune than the former; for when he had taken Rome, Sienna, the whole of La Marca and Romagna, and had only Florence itself to vanquish, he died. Thus death has always been more favorable to the Florentines than any other friend, and more potent to save them than their own valor. From the time of the king's decease, peace was preserved both at home and abroad for eight years, at the end of which, with the wars of Filippo, duke of Milan, the spirit of faction again broke out, and was only appeased by the ruin of that government which continued from 1381 to 1434, had conducted with great glory so many enterprises; acquired Arezzo, Pisa, Cortona, Leghorn, and Monte Pulciano; and would have accomplished more if the citizens had lived in unity, and had not revived former factions; as in the following book will be particularly shown.

Book IV: Chapter I: License and Slavery peculiar defects in republican governments—Application of this reflection to the state of Florence—Giovanni di Bicci di' Medici re-establishes the authority of his family—Filippo Visconti, duke of Milan, endeavors to make amicable arrangements with the Florentines—Their jealousy of him—Precautionary measures against him—War declared—The Florentines are routed by the ducal forces.

Republican governments, more especially those imperfectly organized, frequently change their rulers and the form of their institutions; not by the influence of liberty or subjection, as many suppose, but by that of slavery and license; for with the nobility or the people, the ministers respectively of slavery or licentiousness, only the name of liberty is in any estimation, neither of them choosing to be subject either to magistrates or laws. When, however, a good, wise, and powerful citizen appears (which is but seldom), who establishes ordinances capable of appeasing or restraining these contending dispositions, so as to prevent them from doing mischief, then the government may be called free, and its institutions firm and secure; for having good laws for its basis, and good regulations for carrying them into effect, it needs not, like others, the virtue of one man for its maintenance. With such excellent laws and institutions, many of those ancient republics, which were of long duration, were endowed. But these advantages are, and always have been, denied to those which frequently change from tyranny to license, or the reverse; because, from the powerful enemies which each condition creates itself, they neither have, nor can possess any stability; for tyranny cannot please the good, and license is offensive to the wise: the former may easily be productive of mischief, while the latter can scarcely be beneficial; in the former, the insolent have too much authority, and in the latter, the foolish; so that each requires for their welfare the virtue and the good fortune of some individual who may be removed by death, or become unserviceable by misfortune.

Hence, it appears, that the government which commenced in Florence at the death of Giorgio Scali, in 1381, was first sustained by the talents of Maso degli Albizzi, and then by those of Niccolo da Uzzano. The city remained tranquil from 1414 to 1422; for King Ladislaus was dead, and Lombardy divided into several parts; so that there was nothing either internal or external to occasion uneasiness. Next to Niccolo da Uzzano in authority, were Bartolomeo Valori, Neroni di Nigi, Rinaldo degli Albizzi, Neri di Gino, and Lapo Niccolini. The factions that arose from the quarrels of the Albizzi and the Ricci, and which were afterward so unhappily revived by Salvestro de' Medici, were never extinguished; for though the party most favored by the rabble only continued three years, and in 1381 was put down, still, as it comprehended the greatest numerical proportion, it was never entirely extinct, though the frequent Balias and persecutions of its leaders from 1381 to 1400, reduced it almost to nothing. The first families that suffered in this way were the Alberti, the Ricci, and the Medici, which were frequently deprived both of men and money; and if any of them remained in the city, they were deprived of the honors of government. These oft-repeated acts of oppression humiliated the faction, and almost annihilated it. Still, many retained the remembrance of the injuries they had received, and a desire of vengeance remained pent in their bosoms, ungratified and unquenched. Those nobles of the people, or new nobility, who peaceably governed the city, committed two errors, which eventually caused the ruin of their party; the first was, that by long continuance in power they became insolent; the second, that the envy they entertained toward each other, and their uninterrupted possession of power, destroyed that vigilance over those who might injure them, which they ought to have exercised. Thus daily renewing the hatred of a mass of the people by their sinister proceedings, and either negligent of the threatened dangers, because rendered fearless by prosperity, or encouraging them through mutual envy, they gave an opportunity to the family of the Medici to recover their influence. The first to do so was Giovanni di Bicci de' Medici, who having become one of the richest men, and being of a humane and benevolent disposition, obtained the supreme magistracy by the consent of those in power. This circumstance gave so much gratification to the mass of the people (the multitude thinking they had now found a defender), that not without occasion the judicious of the party observed it with jealousy, for they perceived all the former feelings of the city revived. Niccolo da Uzzano did not fail to acquaint the other citizens with the matter, explaining to them how dangerous it was to aggrandize one who possessed so much influence; that it was easy to remedy an evil at its commencement, but exceedingly difficult after having allowed it to gather strength; and that Giovanni possessed several qualities far surpassing those of Salvestro. The associates of Niccolo were uninfluenced by his remarks; for they were jealous of his reputation, and desired to exalt some person, by means of whom he might be humbled.

This was the state of Florence, in which opposing feelings began to be observable, when Filippo Visconti, second son of Giovanni Galeazzo, having, by the death of his brother, become master of all Lombardy, and thinking he might undertake almost anything, greatly desired to recover Genoa, which enjoyed freedom under the Dogiate of Tommaso da Campo Fregoso. He did not think it advisable to attempt this, or any other enterprise, till he had renewed amicable relations with the Florentines, and made his good understanding with them known; but with the aid of their reputation he trusted he should attain his wishes. He therefore sent ambassadors to Florence to signify his desires. Many citizens were opposed to his design, but did not wish to interrupt the peace with Milan, which had now continued for many years. They were fully aware of the advantages he would derive from a war with Genoa, and the little use it would be to Florence. Many others were inclined to accede to it, but would set a limit to his proceedings, which, if he were to exceed, all would perceive his base design, and thus they might, when the treaty was broken, more justifiably make war against him. The question having been strongly debated, an amicable arrangement was at length effected, by which Filippo engaged not to interfere with anything on the Florentine side of the rivers Magra and Panaro.

Soon after the treaty was concluded, the duke took possession of Brescia, and shortly afterward of Genoa, contrary to the expectation of those who had advocated peace; for they thought Brescia would be defended by the Venetians, and Genoa would be able to defend herself. And as in the treaty which Filippo made with the Doge of Genoa, he had acquired Serezana and other places situated on this side the Magra, upon condition that, if he wished to alienate them, they should be given to the Genoese, it was quite palpable that he had broken the treaty; and he had, besides, entered into another treaty with the legate of Bologna, in opposition to his engagement respecting the Panaro. These things disturbed the minds of the citizens, and made them, apprehensive of new troubles, consider the means to be adopted for their defense.

The dissatisfaction of the Florentines coming to the knowledge of Filippo, he, either to justify himself, or to become acquainted with their prevailing feelings, or to lull them to repose, sent ambassadors to the city, to intimate that he was greatly surprised at the suspicions they entertained, and offered to revoke whatever he had done that could be thought a ground of jealousy. This embassy produced no other effect than that of dividing the citizens; one party, that in greatest reputation, judged it best to arm, and prepare to frustrate the enemy's designs; and if he were to remain quiet, it would not be necessary to go to war with him, but an endeavor might be made to preserve peace. Many others, whether envious of those in power, or fearing a rupture with the duke, considered it unadvisable so lightly to entertain suspicions of an ally, and thought his proceedings need not have excited so much distrust; that appointing the ten and hiring forces was in itself a manifest declaration of war, which, if undertaken against so great a prince, would bring certain ruin upon the city without the hope of any advantage; for possession could never be retained of the conquests that might be made, because Romagna lay between, and the vicinity of the church ought to prevent any attempt against Romagna itself. However the views of those who were in favor of war prevailed, the Council of Ten were appointed, forces were hired, and new taxes levied, which, as they were more burdensome upon the lower than the upper ranks, filled the city with complaints, and all condemned the ambition and avarice of the great, declaring that, to gratify themselves and oppress the people, they would go to war without any justifiable motive.

They had not yet come to an open rupture with the duke, but everything tended to excite suspicion; for Filippo had, at the request of the legate of Bologna (who was in fear of Antonio Bentivogli, an emigrant of Bologna at Castel Bolognese), sent forces to that city, which, being close upon the Florentine territory, filled the citizens with apprehension; but what gave every one greater alarm, and offered sufficient occasion for the declaration of war, was the expedition made by the duke against Furli. Giorgio Ordelaffi was lord of Furli, who dying, left Tibaldo, his son, under the guardianship of Filippo. The boy's mother, suspicious of his guardian, sent him to Lodovico Alidossi, her father, who was lord of Imola, but she was compelled by the people of Furli to obey the will of her deceased husband, to withdraw him from the natural guardian, and place him in the hands of the duke. Upon this Filippo, the better to conceal his purpose, caused the Marquis of Ferrara to send Guido Torello as his agent, with forces, to seize the government of Furli, and thus the territory fell into the duke's hands. When this was known at Florence, together with the arrival of forces at Bologna, the arguments in favor of war were greatly strengthened, but there were still many opposed to it, and among the rest Giovanni de' Medici, who publicly endeavored to show, that even if the ill designs of the duke were perfectly manifest, it would still be better to wait and let him commence the attack, than to assail him; for in the former case they would be justified in the view of the princes of Italy as well as in their own; but if they were to strike the first blow at the duke, public opinion would be as favorable to him as to themselves; and besides, they could not so confidently demand assistance as assailants, as they might do if assailed; and that men always defend themselves more vigorously when they attack others. The advocates of war considered it improper to await the enemy in their houses, and better to go and seek him; that fortune is always more favorable to assailants than to such as merely act on the defensive, and that it is less injurious, even when attended with greater immediate expense, to make war at another's door than at our own. These views prevailed, and it was resolved that the ten should provide all the means in their power for rescuing Furli from the hands of the duke.

Filippo, finding the Florentines resolved to occupy the places he had undertaken to defend, postponed all personal considerations, and sent Agnolo della Pergola with a strong force against Imola, that Ludovico, having to provide for the defense of his own possessions, might be unable to protect the interests of his grandson. Agnolo approached Imola while the forces of the Florentines were at Modigliana, and an intense frost having rendered the ditches of the city passable, he crossed them during the night, captured the place, and sent Lodovico a prisoner to Milan. The Florentines finding Imola in the hands of the enemy, and the war publicly known, sent their forces to Furli and besieged it on all sides. That the duke's people might not relieve it, they hired Count Alberigo, who from Zagonara, his own domain, overran the country daily, up to the gates of Imola. Agnolo della Pergola, finding the strong position which the Florentines had taken prevented him from relieving Furli, determined to attempt the capture of Zagonara, thinking they would not allow that place to be lost, and that in the endeavor to relieve it they would be compelled to give up their design against Furli, and come to an engagement under great disadvantage. Thus the duke's people compelled Alberigo to sue for terms, which he obtained on condition of giving up Zagonara, if the Florentines did not relieve him within fifteen days. This misfortune being known in the Florentine camp and in the city, and all being anxious that the enemy should not obtain the expected advantage, they enabled him to secure a greater; for having abandoned the siege of Furli to go to the relief of Zagonara, on encountering the enemy they were soon routed, not so much by the bravery of their adversaries as by the severity of the season; for, having marched many hours through deep mud and heavy rain, they found the enemy quite fresh, and were therefore easily vanquished. Nevertheless, in this great defeat, famous throughout all Italy, no death occurred except those of Lodovico degli Obizi and two of his people, who having fallen from their horses were drowned in the morass.

Chapter II: The Florentines murmur against those who had been advocates of the war—Rinaldo degli Albizzi encourages the citizens—Measures for the prosecution of the war—Attempt of the higher classes to deprive the plebeians of their share in the government—Rinaldo degli Albizzi addresses an assembly of citizens and advises the restoration of the *Grandi*—Niccolo da Uzzano wishes to have Giovanni de' Medici on their side—Giovanni disapproves of the advice of Rinaldo degli Albizzi.

The defeat at Zagonara spread consternation throughout Florence; but none felt it so severely as the nobility, who had been in favor of the war; for they perceived their enemies to be inspirited and themselves disarmed, without friends, and opposed by the people, who at the corners of streets insulted them with sarcastic expressions, complaining of the heavy taxes, and the unnecessary war, and saying, "Oh! they appointed the ten to frighten the enemy. Have they relieved Furli, and rescued her from the hands of the duke? No! but their designs have been discovered; and what had they in view? not the defense of liberty; for they do not love her; but to aggrandize their own power, which God has very justly abated. This is not the only enterprise by many a one with which they have oppressed the city; for the war against King Ladislaus was of a similar kind. To whom will they flee for assistance now? to Pope Martin, whom they ridiculed before the face of Braccio; or to Queen Giovanna, whom they abandoned, and compelled to throw herself under the protection of the king of Aragon?" To these reproaches was added all that might be expected from an enraged multitude.

Seeing the discontent so prevalent, the Signory resolved to assemble a few citizens, and with soft words endeavor to soothe the popular irritation. On this occasion, Rinaldo degli Albizzi, the eldest son of Maso, who, by his own talents and the respect he derived from the memory of his father, aspired to the first offices in the government, spoke at great length; showing that it is not right to judge of actions merely by their effects; for it often happens that what has been very maturely considered is attended with unfavorable results: that if we are to applaud evil counsels because they are sometimes followed by fortunate events, we should only encourage men in error which would bring great mischief upon the republic; because evil counsel is not always attended with happy consequences. In the same way, it would be wrong to blame a wise resolution, because if its being attended with an unfavorable issue; for by so doing, we should destroy the inclination of citizens to offer advice and speak the truth. He then showed the propriety of undertaking the war; and that if it had not been commenced by the Florentines in Romagna the duke would have assailed them in Tuscany. But since it had pleased God, that the Florentine people should be overcome, their loss would be still greater if they allowed themselves to be dejected; but if they set a bold front against adversity, and made good use of the means within their power, they would not be sensible of their loss or the duke of his victory. He assured them they ought not to be alarmed by impending expenses and consequent taxation; because the latter might be reduced, and the future expense would not be so great as the former had been; for less preparation is necessary for those engaged in self-defense than for those who design to attack others. He advised them to imitate the conduct of their forefathers, who, by courageous conduct in adverse circumstances, had defended themselves against all their enemies.

Thus encouraged, the citizens engaged Count Oddo the son of Braccio, and united with him, for directing the operations of the war, Niccolo Piccinino, a pupil of his father's, and one of the most celebrated of all who had served under him. To these they added other leaders, and remounted some of those who had lost their horses in the late defeat. They also appointed twenty citizens to levy new taxes, who finding the great quite subdued by the recent loss, took courage and drained them without mercy.

These burdens were very grievous to the nobility, who at first, in order to conciliate, did not complain of their own particular hardships, but censured the tax generally as unjust, and advised that something should be done in the way of relief; but their advice was rejected in the Councils. Therefore, to render the law as offensive as possible, and to make all sensible of its injustice, they contrived that the taxes should be levied with the utmost rigor, and made it lawful to kill any that might resist the officers employed to collect them. Hence followed many lamentable collisions, attended with the blood and death of citizens. It began to be the impression of all, that arms would be resorted to, and all prudent persons apprehended some approaching evil; for the higher ranks, accustomed to be treated with respect, could not endure to be used like dogs; and the rest were desirous that the taxation should be equalized. In consequence of this state of things, many of the first citizens met together, and it was resolved that it had become necessary for their safety, that some attempt should be made to recover the government; since their want of vigilance had encouraged men to censure public actions, and allowed those to interfere in affairs who had hitherto been merely the leaders of the rabble. Having repeatedly discussed the subject, they resolved to meet again at an appointed hour, when upwards of seventy citizens assembled in the church of St. Stephen, with the permission of Lorenzo Ridolfi and Francesco Gianfigliazzi, both members of the Signory. Giovanni de' Medici was not among them either because being under suspicion he was not invited or that entertaining different views he was unwilling to interfere.

Rinaldo degli Albizzi addressed the assembly, describing the condition of the city, and showing how by their own negligence it had again fallen under the power of the plebeians, from whom it had been wrested by their fathers in 1381. He reminded them of the iniquity of the government which was in power from 1378 to 1381, and that all who were then present had to lament, some a father, others a grandfather, put to death by its tyranny. He assured them they were now in the same danger, and that the city was sinking under the same disorders. The multitude had already imposed a tax of its own authority; and would soon, if not restrained by greater force or better regulations, appoint the magistrates, who, in this case, would occupy their places, and overturn the government which for forty-two years had ruled the city with so much glory; the citizens would then be subject to the will of the multitude, and live disorderly and dangerous, or be under the command of some individual who might make himself prince. For these reasons he was of opinion, that whoever loved his country and his honor must arouse himself, and call to mind the virtue of Bardo Mancini, who, by the ruin of the Alberti, rescued the city from the dangers then impending; and that the cause of the audacity now assumed by the multitude was the extensive Squittini or Pollings, which, by their negligence, were allowed to be made; for thus the palace had become filled with low men. He therefore concluded, that the only means of remedying the evil was to restore the government to the nobility, and diminish the authority of the minor trades by reducing the companies from fourteen to seven, which would give the plebeians less authority in the Councils, both by the reduction in their number and by increasing the authority of the great; who, on account of former enmities, would be disinclined to favor them. He added, that it is a good thing to know how to avail themselves of men according to the times; and that as their fathers had used the plebeians to reduce the influence of the great, that now, the great having been humbled, and the plebeians become insolent, it was well to restrain the insolence of the latter by the assistance of the former. To effect this they might proceed either openly or otherwise, for some of them belonging to the Council of Ten, forces might be led into the city without exciting observation.

Rinaldo was much applauded, and his advice was approved of by the whole assembly. Niccolo da Uzzano who, among others, replied to it, said, "All that Rinaldo had advanced was correct, and the remedies he proposed good and certain, if they could be adopted without an absolute division of the city; and this he had no doubt would be effected if they could induce Giovanni de' Medici to join them; for with him on their side, the multitude being deprived of their chief and stay, would be unable to oppose them; but that if he did not concur with them they could do nothing without arms, and that with them they would incur the risk of being vanquished, or of not being able to reap the fruit of victory." He then modestly reminded them of what he had said upon a former occasion, and of their reluctance to remedy the evil when it might easily have been done; that now the same remedy could not be attempted without incurring the danger of greater evils, and therefore there was nothing left for them to do but to gain him over to their side, if practicable. Rinaldo was then commissioned to wait upon Giovanni and try if he could induce him to join them.

He undertook this commission, and in the most prevailing words he could make use of endeavored to induce him to coincide with their views; and begged that he would not by favoring an audacious mob, enable them to complete the ruin both of the government and the city. To this Giovanni replied, that he considered it the duty of a good and wise citizen to avoid altering the institutions to which a city is accustomed; there being nothing so injurious to the people as such a change; for many are necessarily offended, and where there are several discontented, some unpropitious event may be constantly apprehended. He said it appeared to him that their resolution would have two exceedingly pernicious effects; the one conferring honors on those who, having never possessed them, esteemed them the less, and therefore had the less occasion to grieve for their absence; the other taking them from those who being accustomed to their possession would never be at rest till they were restored to them. It would thus be evident that the injury done to one party, was greater than the benefit they had conferred upon the other; so that whoever was the author of the proposition, he would gain few friends and make many enemies, and that the latter would be more resolutely bent on injuring him than the former would be zealous for his defense, for mankind are naturally more disposed to revenge than to gratitude, as if the latter could only be exercised with some inconvenience to themselves, while the former brings alike gratification and profit. Then, directing his discourse more particularly to Rinaldo, he said, "And you, if you could call to mind past events, and knew how craftily

affairs are conducted in this city, would not be so eager in this pursuit; for he who advises it, when by your aid he has wrested the power from the people, will, with the people's assistance, who will have become your enemies, deprive you of it. And it will happen to you as to Benedetto Alberti, who, at the persuasion of those who were not his friends, consented to the ruin of Giorgio Scali and Tommaso Strozzi, and shortly afterward was himself sent into exile by the very same men." He therefore advised Rinaldo to think more maturely of these things, and endeavor to imitate his father, who, to obtain the benevolence of all, reduced the price of salt, provided that whoever owed taxes under half a florin should be at liberty to pay them or not, as he thought proper, and that at the meeting of the Councils every one should be free from the importunities of his creditors. He concluded by saying, that as regarded himself, he was disposed to let the government of the city remain as it was.

Chapter III: Giovanni de' Medici acquires the favor of the people—Bravery of Biaggio del Melano—Baseness of Zanobi del Pino—The Florentines obtain the friendship of the lord of Faenza—League of the Florentines with the Venetians—Origin of the Catasto—The rich citizens discontented with it—Peace with the duke of Milan—New disturbances on account of the Catasto.

These events, and the circumstances attending them, becoming known to the people, contributed greatly to increase the reputation of Giovanni, and brought odium on those who had made the proposals; but he assumed an appearance of indifference, in order to give less encouragement to those who by his influence were desirous of change. In his discourse he intimated to every one that it is not desirable to promote factions, but rather to extinguish them; and that whatever might be expected of him, he only sought the union of the city. This, however, gave offense to many of his party; for they would have rather seen him exhibit greater activity. Among others so disposed, was Alamanno de' Medici, who being of a restless disposition, never ceased exciting him to persecute enemies and favor friends; condemning his coldness and slow method of proceeding, which he said was the cause of his enemies' practicing against him, and that these practices would one day effect the ruin of himself and his friends. He endeavored to excite Cosmo, his son, with similar discourses; but Giovanni, for all that was either disclosed or foretold him, remained unmoved, although parties were now declared, and the city in manifest disunion.

There were at the palace, in the service of the Signory, two chancellors, Ser Martino and Ser Pagolo. The latter favored the party of Niccolo da Uzzano, the former that of Giovanni; and Rinaldo, seeing Giovanni unwilling to join them, thought it would be advisable to deprive Ser Martino of his office, that he might have the palace more completely under his control. The design becoming known to his adversaries, Ser Martino was retained and Ser Pagolo discharged, to the great injury and displeasure of Rinaldo and his party. This circumstance would soon have produced most mischievous effects, but for the war with which the city was threatened, and the recent defeat suffered at Zagonara, which served to check the audacity of the people; for while these events were in progress at Florence, Agnolo della Pergola, with the forces of the duke, had taken all the towns and cities possessed by the Florentines in Romagna, except Castracaro and Modigliano; partly from the weakness of the places themselves, and partly by the misconduct of those who had the command of them. In the course of the campaign, two instances occurred which served to show how greatly courage is admired even in enemies, and how much cowardice and pusillanimity are despised.

Biaggio del Melano was castellan in the fortress of Monte Petroso. Being surrounded by enemies, and seeing no chance of saving the place, which was already in flames, he cast clothes and straw from a part which was not yet on fire, and upon these he threw his two little children, saying to the enemy, "Take to yourselves those goods which fortune has bestowed upon me, and of which you may deprive me; but those of the mind, in which my honor and glory consist, I will not give up, neither can you wrest them from me." The besiegers ran to save the children, and placed for their father ropes and ladders, by which to save himself, but he would not use them, and rather chose to die in the flames than owe his safety to the enemies of his country: an example worthy of that much lauded antiquity, which offers nothing to surpass it, and which we admire the more from the rarity of any similar occurrence. Whatever could be recovered from the ruins, was restored for the use of the children, and carefully conveyed to their friends; nor was the republic less grateful; for as long as they lived, they were supported at her charge.

An example of an opposite character occurred at Galeata, where Zanobi del Pino was governor; he, without offering the least resistance, gave up the fortress to the enemy; and besides this, advised Agnolo della Pergola to leave the Alps of Romagna, and come among the smaller hills of Tuscany, where he might carry on the war with less danger and greater advantage. Agnolo could not endure the mean and base spirit of this man, and delivered him to his own attendants, who, after many reproaches, gave him nothing to eat but paper painted with snakes, saying, that of a Guelph they would make him a Ghibelline; and thus fasting, he died in a few days.

At this time Count Oddo and Niccolo Piccinino entered the Val di Lamona, with the design of bringing the lord of Faenza over to the Florentines, or at least inducing him to restrain the incursions of Agnolo della Pergola into Romagna; but as this valley is naturally strong, and its inhabitants warlike, Count Oddo was slain there, and Niccolo Piccinino sent a prisoner to Faenza. Fortune, however, caused the Florentines to obtain by their loss, what, perhaps, they would have failed to acquire by victory; for Niccolo so prevailed with the lord of Faenza and his mother, that they became friends of the Florentines. By this treaty, Niccolo Piccinino was set at liberty, but did not take the advice he had given others; for while in treaty with the city, concerning the terms of his engagement, either the conditions proposed were insufficient, or he found better elsewhere; for quite suddenly he left Arezzo, where he had been staying, passed into Lombardy, and entered the service of the duke.

The Florentines, alarmed by this circumstance, and reduced to despondency by their frequent losses, thought themselves unable to sustain the war alone, and sent ambassadors to the Venetians, to beg they would lend their aid to oppose the greatness of one who, if allowed to aggrandize himself, would soon become as dangerous to them as to the Florentines themselves. The Venetians were advised to adopt the same course by Francesco Carmignuola, one of the most distinguished warriors of those times, who had been in the service of the duke, and had afterward quitted it; but they hesitated, not knowing how far to trust him; for they thought his enmity with the duke was only feigned. While in this suspense, it was found that the duke, by means of a servant of Carmignuola, had caused poison to be given him in his food, which, although it was not fatal, reduced him to extremity. The truth being discovered, the Venetians laid aside their suspicion; and as the Florentines still solicited their assistance, a treaty was formed between the two powers, by which they agreed to carry on the war at the common expense of both: the conquests in Lombardy to be assigned to the Venetians; those in Romagna and Tuscany to the Florentines; and Carmignuola was appointed Captain General of the League. By this treaty the war was commenced in Lombardy, where it was admirably conducted; for in a few months many places were taken from the duke, together with the city of Brescia, the capture of which was in those days considered a most brilliant exploit.

The war had continued from 1422 to 1427, and the citizens of Florence were so wearied of the taxes that had been imposed during that time, that it was resolved to revise them, preparatory to their amelioration. That they might be equalized according to the means of each citizen, it was proposed that whoever possessed property of the value of one hundred florins should pay half a florin of taxes. Individual contribution would thus be determined by an invariable rule, and not left to the discretion of parties; and as it was found that the new method would press heavily upon the powerful classes, they used their utmost endeavors to prevent it from becoming law. Giovanni de' Medici alone declared himself in favor of it, and by his means it was passed. In order to determine the amount each had to pay, it was necessary to consider his property in the aggregate, which the Florentines call *accatastare*, in which in this application of it would signify *to rate* or *value*, and hence this tax received the name of *catasto*. The new method of rating formed a powerful check to the tyranny of the great, who could no longer oppress the lower classes, or silence them with threats in the council as they had formerly done, and it therefore gave general satisfaction, though to the wealthy classes it was in the highest degree offensive. But as it is found men are never satisfied, but that the possession of one advantage only makes them desire more, the people, not content with the equality of taxation which the new law produced, demanded that the same rule should be applied to past years; that in investigation should be made to determine how much, according to the Catasto, the rich had paid less than their share, and that they should now pay up to an equality with those who, in order to meet the demand unjustly made, had been compelled to sell their possessions. This proposal alarmed the great more than the Catasto had done; and in self-defense they unceasingly decried it, declaring it in the highest degree unjust in being laid not only on immovable but movable property, which people possess to-day and lose to-morrow; that many persons have hidden wealth which the Catasto cannot reach; that those who leave their own affairs to manage those of the republic should be less burdened by her, it being enough for them to give their labour, and that it was unjust of the city to take both their property and their time, while of others she only took money. The advocates of the Catasto replied, that if movable property varies, the taxes would also vary, and frequently rating it would remedy the evil to which it was subject; that it was unnecessary to mention those who possessed hidden property; for it would be unreasonable to take taxes for that which produced no interest, and that if it paid anything, it could not fail to be discovered: that those who did not like to labor for the republic might cease to do so; for no doubt she would find plenty of loving citizens who would take pleasure in assisting her with both money and counsel: that the advantages and honors of a participation in the government are so great, that of themselves they are a sufficient remuneration to those who thus employ themselves, without wishing to be excused from paying their share of taxes. But, they added, the real grievance had not been mentioned: for those who were offended with the Catasto, regretted they could no longer involve the city in all the difficulties of war without injury to themselves, now that they had to contribute like the rest; and that if this law had then been in force they would not have gone to war with King Ladislaus, or the Duke Filippo, both which enterprises had been not through necessity, but to impoverish the citizens. The excitement was appeased by Giovanni de' Medici, who said, "It is not well to go into things so long past, unless to learn something for our present guidance; and if in former times the taxation has been unjust, we ought to be thankful, that we have now discovered a method of making it equitable, and hope that this will be the means of uniting the citizens, not of dividing them; which would certainly be the case were they to attempt the recovery of taxes for the past, and make them equal to the present; and that he who is content with a moderate victory is always most successful; for those who would more than conquer, commonly lose." With such words as these he calmed the disturbance, and this retrospective equalization was no longer contemplated.

The war with the duke still continued; but peace was at length restored by means of a legate of the pope. The duke, however, from the first disregarded the conditions, so that the league again took arms, and meeting the enemy's forces at Maclovio routed them. After this defeat the duke again made proposals for peace, to which the Florentines and Venetians both agreed; the former from jealousy of the Venetians, thinking they had spent quite enough money in the aggrandizement of others; the latter, because they found Carmignuola, after the defeat of the duke, proceed but coldly in their cause; so that they thought it no longer safe to trust him. A treaty was therefore concluded in 1428, by which the Florentines recovered the places they had lost in Romagna; and the Venetians kept Brescia, to which the duke added Bergamo and the country around it. In this war the Florentines expended three millions and a half of ducats, extended the territory and power of the Venetians, and brought poverty and disunion upon themselves.

Being at peace with their neighbors, domestic troubles recommenced. The great citizens could not endure the Catasto, and not knowing how to set it aside, they endeavored to raise up more numerous enemies to the measure, and thus provide themselves with allies to assist them in annulling it. They therefore instructed the officers appointed to levy the tax, that the law required them to extend the Catasto over the property of their nearest neighbors, to see if Florentine wealth was concealed among it. The dependent states were therefore ordered to present a schedule of their property against a certain time. This was extremely offensive to the people of Volterra, who sent to the Signory to complain of it; but the officers, in great wrath, committed eighteen of the complainants to prison. The Volterrani, however, out of regard for their fellow-countrymen who were arrested, did not proceed to any violence.

Chapter IV: Death of Giovanni de' Medici—His character—Insurrection of Volterra—Volterra returns to her allegiance—Niccolo Fortebraccio attacks the Lucchese—Diversity of opinion about the Lucchese war—War with Lucca—Astore Gianni and Rinaldo degli Albizzi appointed commissaries—Violence of Astorre Gianni.

About this time Giovanni de' Medici was taken ill, and finding his end approach, called his sons Cosmo and Lorenzo to him, to give them his last advice, and said, "I find I have nearly reached the term which God and nature appointed at my birth, and I die content, knowing that I leave you rich, healthy, and of such standing in society, that if you pursue the same course that I have, you will live respected in Florence, and in favor with everyone. Nothing cheers me so much at this moment, as the recollection that I have never willfully offended anyone; but have always used my utmost endeavors to confer benefits upon all. I would have you do so too. With regard to state affairs, if you would live in security, take just such a share as the laws and your countrymen think proper to bestow, thus you will escape both danger and envy; for it is not what is given to any individual, but what he has determined to possess, that occasions odium. You will thus have a larger share than those who endeavor to engross more than belongs to them; for they thus usually lose their own, and before they lose it, live in constant disquiet. By adopting this method, although among so many enemies, and surrounded by so many conflicting interests, I have not only maintained my reputation but increased my influence. If you pursue the same course, you will be attended by the same good fortune; if otherwise, you may be assured, your end will resemble that of those who in our own times have brought ruin both upon themselves and their families." Soon after this interview with his sons, Giovanni died, regretted by everyone, as his many excellencies deserved. He was compassionate; not only bestowing alms on those who asked them, but very frequently relieving the necessities of the poor, without having been solicited so to do. He loved all; praised the good, and pitied the infirmities of the wicked. He never sought the honors of government; yet enjoyed them all; and never went to the palace unless by request. He loved peace and shunned war; relieved mankind in adversity, and assisted them in prosperity; never applied the public money to his own uses, but contributed to the

public wealth. He was courteous in office; not a man of great eloquence, but possessed of extraordinary prudence. His demeanor expressed melancholy; but after a short time his conversation became pleasant and facetious. He died exceedingly rich in money, but still more in good fame and the best wishes of mankind; and the wealth and respect he left behind him were not only preserved but increased by his son Cosmo.

The Volterran ambassadors grew weary of lying in prison, and to obtain their liberty promised to comply with the commands of the Florentines. Being set free and returned to their city, the time arrived for the new Priors to enter upon office, and among those who were drawn, was one named Giusto, a plebeian, but possessing great influence with his class, and one of those who had been imprisoned at Florence. He, being inflamed with hatred against the Florentines on account of his public as well as personal injuries, was further stimulated by Giovanni di Contugi, a man of noble family, and his colleague in office, to induce the people, by the authority of the Priors and his own influence, to withdraw their country from the power of the Florentines, and make himself prince. Prompted by these motives, Giusto took arms, rode through the city, seized the Capitano, who resided in it, on behalf of the Florentines, and with the consent of the people, became lord of Volterra. This circumstance greatly displeased the Florentines; but having just made peace with the duke, and the treaty being yet uninfringed on either side, they bethought themselves in a condition to recover the place; and that the opportunity might not be lost, they immediately appointed Rinaldo degli Albizzi and Palla Strozzi commissaries, and sent them upon the expedition. In the meantime, Giusto, who expected the Florentines would attack him, requested assistance of Lucca and Sienna. The latter refused, alleging her alliance with Florence; and Pagolo Guinigi, to regain the favor of the Florentines, which he imagined he had lost in the war with the duke and by his friendship for Filippo, not only refused assistance to Giusto, but sent his messenger prisoner to Florence.

The commissaries, to come upon the Volterrani unawares, assembled their cavalry, and having raised a good body of infantry in the Val d'Arno Inferiore, and the country about Pisa, proceeded to Volterra. Although attacked by the Florentines and abandoned by his neighbors, Giusto did not yield to fear; but, trusting to the strength of the city and the ruggedness of the country around it, prepared for his defense.

There lived at Volterra one Arcolano, brother of that Giovanni Contugi who had persuaded Giusto to assume the command. He possessed influence among the nobility, and having assembled a few of his most confidential friends, he assured them that by this event, God had come to the relief of their necessities; for if they would only take arms, deprive Giusto of the Signory, and give up the city to the Florentines, they might be sure of obtaining the principal offices, and the place would retain all its ancient privileges. Having gained them over, they went to the palace in which Giusto resided; and while part of them remained below, Arcolano, with three others, proceeded to the chamber above, where finding him with some citizens, they drew him aside, as if desirous to communicate something of importance, and conversing on different subjects, let him to the lower apartment, and fell upon him with their swords. They, however, were not so quick as to prevent Giusto from making use of his own weapon; for with it he seriously wounded two of them; but being unable to resist so many, he was at last slain, and his body thrown into the street. Arcolano and his party gave up the city to the Florentine commissaries, who, being at hand with their forces, immediately took possession; but the condition of Volterra was worse than before; for among other things which operated to her disadvantage, most of the adjoining countryside was separated from her, and she was reduced to the rank of a vicariate.

Volterra having been lost and recovered almost at the same time, present circumstances afforded nothing of sufficient importance to occasion a new war, if ambition had not again provoked one. Niccolo Fortebraccio, the son of a sister of Braccio da Perugia, had been in the service of the Florentines during most of their wars with the duke. Upon the restoration of peace he was discharged; but when the affair of Volterra took place, being encamped with his people at Fucecchio, the commissaries availed themselves both of himself and his forces. Some thought that while Rinaldo conducted the expedition along with him, he persuaded him, under one pretext or another, to attack the Lucchese, assuring him, that if he did so, the Florentines would consent to undertake an expedition against them, and would appoint him to the command. When Volterra was recovered, and Niccolo returned to his quarters at Fucecchio, he, either at the persuasion of Rinaldo, or of his own accord, in November, 1429, took possession of Ruoti and Compito, castles belonging to the Lucchese, with three hundred cavalry and as many infantry, and then descending into the plain, plundered the inhabitants to a vast amount. The news of this incursion having reached Florence, persons of all classes were seen gathered in parties throughout the city discussing the matter, and nearly all were in favor of an expedition against Lucca. Of the Grandees thus disposed, were the Medici and their party, and with them also Rinaldo, either because he thought the enterprise beneficial to the republic, or induced by his own ambition and the expectation of being appointed to the command. Niccolo da Uzzano and his party were opposed to the war. It seems hardly credible that such contrary opinions should prevail, though at different times, in the same men and the same city, upon the subject of war; for the same citizens and people that, during the ten years of peace had incessantly blamed the war undertaken against Duke Filippo, in defense of liberty, now, after so much expense and trouble, with their utmost energy, insisted on hostilities against Lucca, which, if successful, would deprive that city of her liberty; while those who had been in favor of a war with the duke, were opposed to the present; so much more ready are the multitude to covet the possessions of others than to preserve their own, and so much more easily are they led by the hope of acquisition than by the fear of loss. The suggestions of the latter appear incredible till they are verified; and the pleasing anticipations of the former are cherished as facts, even while the advantages are very problematical, or at best, remote. The people of Florence were inspired with hope, by the acquisitions which Niccolo Fortebraccio had made, and by letters received from their rectors in the vicinity of Lucca; for their deputies at Vico and Pescia had written, that if permission were given to them to receive the castles that offered to surrender, the whole country of Lucca would very soon be obtained. It must, however, be added, that an ambassador was sent by the governor of Lucca to Florence, to complain of the attack made by Niccolo, and to entreat that the Signory would not make war against a neighbor, and a city that had always been friendly to them. The ambassador was Jacopo Viviani, who, a short time previously, had been imprisoned by Pagolo Guinigi, governor of Lucca, for having conspired against him. Although he had been found guilty, his life was spared, and as Pagolo thought the forgiveness mutual, he reposed confidence in him. Jacopo, more mindful of the danger he had incurred than of the lenity exercised toward him, on his arrival in Florence secretly instigated the citizens to hostilities; and these instigations, added to other hopes, induced the Signory to call the Council together, at which 498 citizens assembled, before whom the principal men of the city discussed the question.

Among the first who addressed the assembly in favor of the expedition, was Rinaldo. He pointed out the advantage that would accrue from the acquisition, and justified the enterprise from its being left open to them by the Venetians and the duke, and that as the pope was engaged in the affairs of Naples, he could not interfere. He then remarked upon the facility of the expedition, showing that Lucca, being now in bondage to one of her own citizens, had lost her natural vigor and former anxiety for the preservation of her liberty, and would either be surrendered to them by the people in order to expel the tyrant, or by the tyrant for fear of the people. He recalled the remembrance of the injuries done to the republic by the governor of Lucca; his malevolent disposition toward them; and their embarrassing situation with regard to him, if the pope or the duke were to make war upon them; and concluded that no enterprise was ever undertaken by the people of Florence with such perfect facility, more positive advantage, or greater justice in its favor.

In a reply to this, Niccolo da Uzzano stated that the city of Florence never entered on a more unjust or more dangerous project, or one more pregnant with evil, than this. In the first place they were going to attack a Guelphic city, that had always been friendly to the Florentine people, and had frequently, at great hazard, received the Guelphs into her bosom when they were expelled from their own country. That in the history of the past there was not an instance, while Lucca was free, of her having done an injury to the Florentines; and that if they had been injured by her enslavers, as formerly by Castruccio, and now by the present governor, the fault was not in the city, but in her tyrant. That if they could assail the latter without detriment to the people, he should have less scruple, but as this was impossible, he could not consent that a city which had been friendly to Florence should be plundered of her wealth. However, as it was usual at present to pay little or no regard either to equity or injustice, he would consider the matter solely with reference to the advantage of Florence. He thought that what could not easily be attended by pernicious consequences might be esteemed useful, but he could not imagine how an enterprise should be called advantageous in which the evils were certain and the utility doubtful. The certain evils were the expenses with which it would be attended; and these, he foresaw, would be sufficiently great to alarm even a people that had long been in repose, much more one wearied, as they were, by a tedious and expensive war. The advantage that might be gained was the acquisition of Lucca, which he acknowledged to be great; but the hazards were so enormous and immeasurable, as in his opinion to render the conquest quite impossible. He could not induce himself to believe that the Venetians, or Filippo, would willingly allow them to make the acquisition; for the former only consented in appearance, in order to avoid the semblance of ingratitude, having so lately, with Florentine money, acquired such an extent of dominion. That as regarded the duke, it would greatly gratify him to see them involved in new wars and expenses; for, being exhausted and defeated on all sides, he might again assail them; and that if, after having undertaken it, their enterprise against Lucca were to prove successful, and offer them the fullest hope of victory, the duke would not want an opportunity of frustrating their labors, either by assisting the Lucchese secretly with money, or by apparently disbanding his own troops, and then sending them, as if they were soldiers of fortune, to their relief. He therefore advised that they should give up the idea, and behave toward the tyrant in such a way as to create him as many enemies as possible; for there was no better method of reducing Lucca than to let them live under the tyrant, oppressed and exhausted by him; for, if prudently managed, that city would soon get into such a condition that he could not retain it, and being ignorant or unable to govern itself, it must of necessity fall into their power. But he saw that his discourse did not please them, and that his words were unheeded; he would, however, predict this to them, that they were about to commence a war in which they would expend vast sums, incur great domestic dangers, and instead of becoming masters of Lucca, they would deliver her from her tyrant, and of a friendly city, feeble and oppressed, they would make one free and hostile, and that in time she would become an obstacle to the greatness of their own republic.

The question having been debated on both sides, they proceeded to vote, as usual, and of the citizens present only ninety-eight were against the enterprise. Thus determined in favor of war, they appointed a Council of Ten for its management, and hired forces, both horse and foot. Astorre Gianni and Rinaldo degli Albizzi were appointed commissaries, and Niccolo Fortebraccio, on agreeing to give up to the Florentines the places he had taken, was engaged to conduct the enterprise as their captain. The commissaries having arrived with the army in the country of the Lucchese, divided their forces; one part of which, under Astorre, extended itself along the plain, toward Camaiore and Pietrasanta, while Rinaldo, with the other division, took the direction of the hills, presuming that when the citizens found themselves deprived of the surrounding country, they would easily submit. The proceedings of the commissaries were unfortunate, not that they failed to occupy many places, but from the complaints made against them of mismanaging the operations of the war; and Astorre Gianni had certainly given very sufficient cause for the charges against him.

There is a fertile and populous valley near Pietrasanta, called Seravezza, whose inhabitants, on learning the arrival of the commissary, presented themselves before him and begged he would receive them as faithful subjects of the Florentine republic. Astorre pretended to accept their proposal, but immediately ordered his forces to take possession of all the passes and strong positions of the valley, assembled the men in the principal church, took them all prisoners, and then caused his people to plunder and destroy the whole country, with the greatest avarice and cruelty, making no distinction in favor of consecrated places, and violating the women, both married and single. These things being known in Florence, displeased not only the magistracy, but the whole city.

Chapter V: The inhabitants of Seravezza appeal to the Signory—Complaints against Rinaldo degli Albizzi—The commissaries changed—Filippo Brunelleschi proposes to submerge the country about Lucca—Pagolo Guinigi asks assistance of the duke of Milan—The duke sends Francesco Sforza—Pagolo Guinigi expelled—The Florentines routed by the forces of the duke—The acquisitions of the Lucchese after the victory—Conclusion of the war.

A few of the inhabitants of the valley of Seravezza, having escaped the hands of the commissary, came to Florence and acquainted every one in the streets with their miserable situation; and by the advice of those who, either through indignation at his wickedness or from being of the opposite party, wished to punish the commissary, they went to the Council of Ten, and requested an audience. This being granted, one of them spoke to the following effect: "We feel assured, magnificent lords, that we shall find credit and compassion from the Signory, when you learn how your commissary has taken possession of our country, and in what manner he has treated us. Our valley, as the memorials of your ancient houses abundantly testify, was always Guelphic, and has often proved a secure retreat to your citizens when persecuted by the Ghibellines. Our forefathers, and ourselves too, have always revered the name of this noble republic as the leader and head of their party. While the Lucchese were Guelphs we willingly submitted to their government; but when enslaved by the tyrant, who forsook his old friends to join the Ghibelline faction, we have obeyed him more through force than good will. And God knows how often we have prayed, that we might have an opportunity of showing our attachment to our ancient party. But how blind are mankind in their wishes! That which we desired for our safety has proved our destruction. As soon as we learned that your ensigns were approaching, we hastened to meet your commissary, not as an enemy, but as the representative of our ancient lords; placed our valley, our persons, and our fortunes in his hands, and commended them to his good faith, believing him to possess the soul, if not of a Florentine, at least of a man. Your lordships will forgive us; for, unable to support his cruelties, we are compelled to speak. Your commissary has nothing of the man but the shape, nor of a Florentine but the name; a more deadly pest, a more savage beast, a more horrid monster never was imagined in the human mind; for, having assembled us in our church under pretense of wishing to speak with us, he made us prisoners. He then burned and destroyed the whole valley, carried off our property, ravaged every place, destroyed everything, violated the women, dishonored the virgins, and dragging them from the arms of their mothers, gave them up to the brutality of his soldiery. If by any injury to the Florentine people we merited such treatment, or if he had vanquished us armed in our defense, we should have less reason for complaint; we should have accused ourselves, and thought that either our mismanagement or our arrogance had deservedly brought the calamity upon us; but after having freely presented ourselves to him unarmed, to be robbed and plundered with such unfeeling barbarity, is more than we can bear. And though we might have filled Lombardy with complaints and charges against this city, and spread the story of our misfortunes over the whole of Italy, we did not wish to slander so just and pious a republic, with the baseness and perfidy of one wicked citizen, whose cruelty and avarice, had we known them before our ruin was complete, we should have endeavored to satiate (though indeed they are insatiable), and with one-half of our property have saved the rest. But the opportunity is past; we are compelled to have recourse to you, and beg that you will succor the distresses of your subjects, that others may not be deterred by our example from submitting themselves to your authority. And if our extreme distress cannot prevail with you to assist us, be induced, by your fear of the wrath of God, who has seen his temple plundered and burned, and his people betrayed in his bosom." Having said this they threw themselves on the ground, crying aloud, and praying that their property and their country might be restored to them; and that if the Signory could not give them back their honor, they would, at least, restore husbands to their wives, and children to their fathers. The atrocity of the affair having already been made known, and now by the living words of the sufferers presented before them, excited the compassion of the magistracy. They ordered the immediate return of Astorre, who being tried, was found guilty, and admonished. They sought the goods of the inhabitants of Seravezza; all that could be recovered was restored to them, and as time and circumstance gave opportunity, they were compensated for the rest.

Complaints were made against Rinaldo degli Albizzi, that he carried on the war, not for the advantage of the Florentine people, but his own private emolument; that as soon as he was appointed commissary, he lost all desire to take Lucca, for it was sufficient for him to plunder the country, fill his estates with cattle, and his house with booty; and, not content with what his own satellites took, he purchased that of the soldiery, so that instead of a commissary he became a merchant. These calumnies coming to his ears, disturbed the temper of this proud but upright man, more than quite became his dignity. He was so exasperated against the citizens and magistracy, that without waiting for or asking permission, he returned to Florence, and, presenting himself before the Council of Ten, he said that he well knew how difficult and dangerous a thing it was to serve an unruly people and a divided city, for the one listens to every report, the other pursues improper measures; they neglect to reward good conduct, and heap censure upon whatever appears doubtful; so that victory wins no applause, error is accused by all, and if vanquished, universal condemnation is incurred; from one's own party through envy, and from enemies through hatred, persecution results. He confessed that the baseness of the present calumnies had conquered his patience and changed the temper of his mind; but he would say, he had never, for fear of a false accusation, avoided doing what appeared to him beneficial to the city. However, he trusted the magistrates would in future be more ready to defend their fellow-citizens, so that the latter might continue anxious to effect the prosperity of their country; that as it was not customary at Florence to award triumphs for success, they ought at least to be protected from calumny; and that being citizens themselves, and at any moment liable to false accusations, they might easily conceive how painful it is to an upright mind to be oppressed with slander. The Ten endeavored, as well as circumstances would admit, to soothe the acerbity of his feelings, and confided the care of the expedition to Neri di Gino and Alamanno Salviati, who, instead of overrunning the country, advanced near to Lucca. As the weather had become extremely cold, the forces established themselves at Campannole, which seemed to the commissaries waste of time; and wishing to draw nearer the place, the soldiery refused to comply, although the Ten had insisted they should pitch their camp before the city, and would not hear of any excuse.

At that time there lived at Florence, a very distinguished architect, named Filippo di Ser Brunelleschi, of whose works our city is full, and whose merit was so extraordinary, that after his death his statue in marble was erected in the principal church, with an inscription underneath, which still bears testimony to those who read it, of his great talents. This man pointed out, that in consequence of the relative positions of the river Serchio and the city of Lucca, the wastes of the river might be made to inundate the surrounding country, and place the city in a kind of lake. His reasoning on this point appeared so clear, and the advantage to the besiegers so obvious and inevitable, that the Ten were induced to make the experiment. The result, however, was quite contrary to their expectation, and produced the utmost disorder in the Florentine camp; for the Lucchese raised high embankments in the direction of the ditch made by our people to conduct the waters of the Serchio, and one night cut through the embankment of the ditch itself, so that having first prevented the water from taking the course designed by the architect, they now caused it to overflow the plain, and compelled the Florentines, instead of approaching the city as they wished, to take a more remote position.

The design having failed, the Council of Ten, who had been re-elected, sent as commissary, Giovanni Guicciardini, who encamped before Lucca, with all possible expedition. Pagolo Guinigi finding himself thus closely pressed, by the advice of Antonio del Rosso, then representative of the Siennese at Lucca, sent Salvestro Trento and Leonardo Bonvisi to Milan, to request assistance from the duke; but finding him indisposed to comply, they secretly engaged, on the part of the people, to deliver their governor up to him and give him possession of the place; at the same time intimating, that if he did not immediately follow this advice, he would not long have the opportunity, since it was the intention of Pagolo to surrender the city to the Florentines, who were very anxious to obtain it. The duke was so much alarmed with this idea, that, setting aside all other considerations, he caused Count Francesco Sforza, who was engaged in his service, to make a public request for permission to go to Naples; and having obtained it, he proceeded with his forces directly to Lucca, though the Florentines, aware of the deception, and apprehensive of the consequences, had sent to the count, Boccacino Alamanni, his friend, to frustrate this arrangement. Upon the arrival of the count at Lucca, the Florentines removed their camp to Librafatta, and the count proceeded immediately to Pescia, where Pagolo Diacceto was lieutenant governor, who, promoted by fear rather than any better motive, fled to Pistoia, and if the place had not been defended by Giovanni Malavolti, to whom the command was intrusted, it would have been lost. The count failing in his attempt went to Borgo a Buggiano which he took, and burned the castle of Stigliano, in the same neighborhood.

The Florentines being informed of these disasters, found they must have recourse to those remedies which upon former occasions had often proved useful. Knowing that with mercenary soldiers, when force is insufficient, corruption commonly prevails, they offered the count a large sum of money on condition that he should quit the city, and give it up to them. The count finding that no more money was to be had from Lucca, resolved to take it of those who had it to dispense, and agreed with the Florentines, not to give them Lucca, which for decency he could not consent to, but to withdraw his troops, and abandon it, on condition of receiving fifty thousand ducats; and having made this agreement, to induce the Lucchese to excuse him to the duke, he consented that they should expel their tyrant.

Antonio del Rosso, as we remarked above, was Siennese ambassador at Lucca, and with the authority of the count he contrived the ruin of Pagolo Guinigi. The heads of the conspiracy were Pierro Cennami and Giovanni da Chivizzano. The count resided upon the Serchio, at a short distance from the city, and with him was Lanzilao, the son of Pagolo. The conspirators, about forty in number, went armed at night in search of Pagolo, who, on hearing the noise they made, came toward them quite astonished, and demanded the cause of their visit; to which Piero Cennami replied, that they had long been governed by him, and led about against the enemy, to die either by hunger or the sword, but were resolved to govern themselves for the future, and demanded the keys of the city and the treasure. Pagolo said the treasure was consumed, but the keys and himself were in their power; he only begged that as his command had begun and continued without bloodshed, it might conclude in the same manner. Count Francesco conducted Pagolo and his son to the duke, and they afterward died in prison.

The departure of the count having delivered Lucca from her tyrant, and the Florentines from their fear of his soldiery, the former prepared for her defense, and the latter resumed the siege. They appointed the count of Urbino to conduct their forces, and he pressed the Lucchese so closely, that they were again compelled to ask the assistance of the duke, who dispatched Niccolo Piccinino, under the same pretense as he previously sent Count Francesco. The Florentine forces met him on his approach to Lucca, and at the passage of the Serchio a battle ensued, in which they were routed, the commissary with a few of his men escaping to Pisa. This defeat filled the Florentines with dismay, and as the enterprise had been undertaken with the entire approbation of the great body of the people, they did not know whom to find fault with, and therefore railed against those who had been appointed to the management of the war, reviving the charges made against Rinaldo. They were, however, more severe against Giovanni Guicciardini than any other, declaring that if he had wished, he might have put a period to the war at the departure of Count Francesco, but that he had been bribed with money, for he had sent home a large sum, naming the party who had been intrusted to bring it, and the persons to whom it had been delivered. These complaints and accusations were carried to so great a length that the captain of the people, induced by the public voice, and pressed by the party opposed to the war, summoned him to trial. Giovanni appeared, though full of indignation. However his friends, from regard to their own character, adopted such a course with the Capitano as induced him to abandon the inquiry.

After this victory, the Lucchese not only recovered the places that had belonged to them, but occupied all the country of Pisa except Beintina, Calcinaja, Livorno, and Librafatta; and, had not a conspiracy been discovered that was formed in Pisa, they would have secured that city also. The Florentines again prepared for battle, and appointed Micheletto, a pupil of Sforza, to be their leader. The duke, on the other hand, followed up this victory, and that he might bring a greater power against the Florentines, induced the Genoese, the Siennese, and the governor of Piombino, to enter into a league for the defense of Lucca, and to engage Niccolo Piccinino to conduct their forces. Having by this step declared his design, the Venetians and the Florentines renewed their league, and the war was carried on openly in Tuscany and Lombardy, in each of which several battles were fought with variety of fortune. At length, both sides being wearied out, they came to terms for the cessation of hostilities, in May, 1433. By this arrangement the Florentines, Lucchese, and Siennese, who had each occupied many fortresses belonging to the others, gave them all up, and each party resumed its original possessions.

Chapter VI: Cosmo de' Medici, his character and mode of proceedings—The greatness of Cosmo excites the jealousy of the citizens—The opinion of Niccolo da Uzzano—Scandalous divisions of the Florentines—Death of Niccolo da Uzzano—Bernardo Guadagni, Gonfalonier, adopts measures against Cosmo—Cosmo arrested in the palace—He is apprehensive of attempts against his life.

During the war the malignant humors of the city were in constant activity. Cosmo de' Medici, after the death of Giovanni, engaged more earnestly in public affairs, and conducted himself with more zeal and boldness in regard to his friends than his father had done, so that those who rejoiced at Giovanni's death, finding what the son was likely to become, perceived they had no cause for exultation. Cosmo was one of the most prudent of men; of grave and courteous demeanor, extremely liberal and humane. He never attempted anything against parties, or against rulers, but was bountiful to all; and by the unwearied generosity of his disposition, made himself partisans of all ranks of the citizens. This mode of proceeding increased the difficulties of those who were in the government, and Cosmo himself hoped that by its pursuit he might be able to live in Florence as much respected and as secure as any other citizen; or if the ambition of his adversaries compelled him to adopt a different course, arms and the favor of his friends would enable him to become more so. Averardo de' Medici and Puccio Pucci were greatly instrumental in the establishment of his power; the former by his boldness, the latter by unusual prudence and sagacity, contributed to his aggrandizement. Indeed the advice of wisdom of Puccio were so highly esteemed, that Cosmo's party was rather distinguished by the name of Puccio than by his own.

By this divided city the enterprise against Lucca was undertaken; and the bitterness of party spirit, instead of being abated, increased. Although the friends of Cosmo had been in favor of it, many of the adverse faction were sent to assist in the management, as being men of greater influence in the state. Averardo de' Medici and the rest being unable to prevent this, endeavored with all their might to calumniate them; and when any unfavorable circumstance occurred (and there were many), fortune and the exertions of the enemy were never supposed to be the causes, but solely the want of capacity in the commissary. This disposition aggravated the offenses of Astorre Gianni; this excited the indignation of Rinaldo degli Albizzi, and made him resign his commission without leave; this, too, compelled the captain of the people to require the appearance of Giovanni Guicciardini, and from this arose all the other charges which were made against the magistrates and the commissaries. Real evils were magnified, unreal ones feigned, and the true and the false were equally believed by the people, who were almost universally their foes.

All these events and extraordinary modes of proceeding were perfectly known to Niccolo da Uzzano and the other leaders of the party; and they had often consulted together for the purpose of finding a remedy, but without effect; though they were aware of the danger of allowing them to increase, and the great difficulty that would attend any attempt to remove or abate them. Niccolo da Uzzano was the earliest to take offense; and while the war was proceeding without, and these troubles within, Niccolo Barbadoro desirous of inducing him to consent to the ruin of Cosmo, waited upon him at his house; and finding him alone in his study, and very pensive, endeavored, with the best reasons he could advance, to persuade him to agree with Rinaldo on Cosmo's expulsion. Niccolo da Uzzano replied as follows: "It would be better for thee and thy house, as well as for our republic, if thou and those who follow thee in this opinion had beards of silver instead of gold, as is said of thee; for advice proceeding from the hoary head of long experience would be wiser and of greater service to all. It appears to me, that those who talk of driving Cosmo out of Florence would do well to consider what is their strength, and what that of Cosmo. You have named one party, that of the nobility, the other that of the plebeians. If the fact corresponded with the name, the victory would still be most uncertain, and the example of the ancient nobility of this city, who were destroyed by the plebeians, ought rather to impress us with fear than with hope. We have, however, still further cause for apprehension from the division of our party, and the union of our adversaries. In the first place, Neri di Gino and Nerone di Nigi, two of our principal citizens, have never so fully declared their sentiments as to enable us to determine whether they are most our friends our those of our opponents. There are many families, even many houses, divided; many are opposed to us through envy of brothers or relatives. I will recall to your recollection two or three of the most important; you may think of the others at your leisure. Of the sons of Maso degli Albizzi, Luca, from envy of Rinaldo, has thrown himself into their hands. In the house of Guicciardini, of the sons of Luigi, Piero is the enemy of Giovanni and in favor of our adversaries. Tommaso and Niccolo Soderini openly oppose us on account of their hatred of their uncle Francesco. So that if we consider well what we are, and what our enemies, I cannot see why we should be called NOBLE any more than they. If it is because they are followed by the plebeians, we are in a worse condition on that account, and they in a better; for were it to come either to arms or to votes, we should not be able to resist them. True it is, we still preserve our dignity, our precedence, the priority of our position, but this arises from the former reputation of the government, which has now continued fifty years; and whenever we come to the proof, or they discover our weakness we shall lose it. If you were to say, the justice of our cause ought to augment our influence and diminish theirs I answer, that this justice requires to be perceived and believed by others as well as by ourselves, but this is not the case; for the justice of our cause is wholly founded upon our suspicion that Cosmo designs to make himself prince of the city. And although we entertain this suspicion and suppose it to be correct, others have it not; but what is worse, they charge us with the very design of which we accuse him. Those actions of Cosmo which lead us to suspect him are, that he lends money indiscriminately, and not to private persons only, but to the public; and not to Florentines only, but to the *condottieri*, the soldiers of fortune. Besides, he assists any citizen who requires magisterial aid; and, by the universal interest he possesses in the city, raises first one friend and then another to higher grades of honor. Therefore, to adduce our reasons for expelling him, would be to say that he is kind, generous, liberal, and beloved by all. Now tell me, what law is there which forbids, disapproves, or condemns men for being pious, liberal, and benevolent? And though they are all modes adopted by those who aim at sovereignty, they are not believed to be such, nor have we sufficient power to make them to be so esteemed; for our conduct has robbed us of confidence, and the city, naturally partial and (having always lived in faction) corrupt, cannot lend its attention to such charges. But even if we were successful in an attempt to expel him (which might easily happen under a favorable Signory), how could we (being surrounded by his innumerable friends, who would constantly reproach us, and ardently desire to see him again in the city) prevent his return? It would be impossible for they being so numerous, and having the good will of all upon their side, we should never be secure from them. And as many of his first discovered friends as you might expel, so many enemies would you make, so that in a short time he would return, and the result would be simply this, that we had driven him out a good man and he had returned to us a bad one; for his nature would be corrupted by those who recalled him, and he, being under obligation, could not oppose them. Or should you design to put him to death, you could not attain your purpose with the magistrates, for his wealth, and the corruption of your minds, will always save him. But let us suppose him put to death, or that being banished, he did not return, I cannot see how the condition of our republic would be ameliorated; for if we relieve her from Cosmo, we at once make her subject to Rinaldo, and it is my most earnest desire that no citizen may ever, in power and authority, surpass the rest. But if one of these must prevail, I know of no reason that should make me prefer Rinaldo to Cosmo. I shall only say, may God preserve the city from any of her citizens usurping the sovereignty, but if our sins have deserved this, in mercy save us from Rinaldo. I pray thee, therefore, do not advise the adoption of a course on every account pernicious, nor imagine that, in union with a few, you would be able to oppose the will of the many; for the citizens, some from ignorance and others from malice, are ready to sell the republic at any time, and fortune has so much favored them, that they have found a purchaser. Take my advice then; endeavor to live moderately; and with regard to liberty, you will find as much cause for suspicion in our party as in that of our adversaries. And when troubles arise, being of neither side, you will be agreeable to both, and you will thus provide for your own comfort and do no injury to any."

These words somewhat abated the eagerness of Barbadoro, so that tranquillity prevailed during the war with Lucca. But this being ended, and Niccolo da Uzzano dead, the city being at peace and under no restraint, unhealthy humors increased with fearful rapidity. Rinaldo, considering himself now the leader of the party, constantly entreated and urged every citizen whom he thought likely to be Gonfalonier, to take up arms and deliver the country from him who, from the malevolence of a few and the ignorance of the multitude, was inevitably reducing it to slavery. These practices of Rinaldo, and those of the contrary side, kept the city full of apprehension, so that whenever a magistracy was created, the numbers of each party composing it were made publicly known, and upon drawing for the Signory the whole city was aroused. Every case brought before the magistrates, however trivial, was made a subject of contention among them. Secrets were divulged, good and evil alike became objects of favor and opposition, the benevolent and the wicked were alike assailed, and no magistrate fulfilled the duties of his office with integrity.

In this state of confusion, Rinaldo, anxious to abate the power of Cosmo, and knowing that Bernardo Guadagni was likely to become Gonfalonier, paid his arrears of taxes, that he might not, by being indebted to the public, be incapacitated for holding the office. The drawing soon after took place, and fortune, opposed to our welfare, caused Bernardo to be appointed for the months of September and October. Rinaldo immediately waited upon him, and intimated how much the party of the nobility, and all who wished for repose, rejoiced to find he had attained that dignity; that it now rested with him to act in such a manner as to realize their pleasing expectations. He then enlarged upon the danger of disunion, and endeavored to show that there was no means of attaining the blessing of unity but by the destruction of Cosmo, for he alone, by the popularity acquired with his enormous wealth, kept them depressed; that he was already so powerful, that if not hindered, he would soon become prince, and that it was the part of a good citizen, in order to prevent such a calamity, to assemble the people in the piazza, and restore liberty to his country. Rinaldo then reminded the new Gonfalonier how Salvestro de' Medici was able, though unjustly, to restrain the power of the Guelphs, to whom, by the blood of their ancestors, shed in its cause, the government rightly belonged; and argued that what he was able unjustly to accomplish against so many, might surely be easily performed with justice in its favor against one! He encouraged him with the assurance that their friends would be ready in arms to support him; that he need not regard the plebeians, who adored Cosmo, since their assistance would be of no greater avail than Giorgio Scali had found it on a similar occasion; and that with regard to his wealth, no apprehension was necessary, for when he was under the power of the Signory, his riches would be so too. In conclusion, he averred that this course would unite and secure the republic, and crown the Gonfalonier with glory. Bernardo briefly replied, that he thought it necessary to act exactly as Rinaldo had advised, and that as the time was suitable for action, he should provide himself with forces, being assured from what Rinaldo had said, he would be supported by his colleagues.

Bernardo entered upon the duties of his office, prepared his followers, and having concerted with Rinaldo, summoned Cosmo, who, though many friends dissuaded him from it, obeyed the call, trusting more to his own innocence than to the mercy of the Signory. As soon as he had entered the palace he was arrested. Rinaldo, with a great number of armed men, and accompanied by nearly the whole of his party, proceeded to the piazza, when the Signory assembled the people, and created a Balia of two hundred persons for the reformation of the city. With the least possible delay they entered upon the consideration of reform, and of the life or death of Cosmo. Many wished him to be banished, others to be put to death, and several were silent, either from compassion toward him or for fear of the rest, so that these differences prevented them from coming to any conclusion.

There is an apartment in the tower of the palace which occupies the whole of one floor, and is called the Alberghettino, in which Cosmo was confined, under the charge of Federigo Malavolti. In this place, hearing the assembly of the Councils, the noise of arms which proceeded from the piazza, and the frequent ringing of the bell to assemble the Balia, he was greatly apprehensive for his safety, but still more less his private enemies should cause him to be put to death in some unusual manner. He scarcely took any food, so that in four days he ate only a small quantity of bread, Federigo, observing his anxiety, said to him, "Cosmo, you are afraid of being poisoned, and are evidently hastening your end with hunger. You wrong me if you think I would be a party to such an atrocious act. I do not imagine your life to be in much danger, since you have so many friends both within the palace and without; but if you should eventually lose it, be assured they will use some other medium than myself for that purpose, for I will never imbue my hands in the blood of any, still less in yours, who never injured me; therefore cheer up, take some food, and preserve your life for your friends and your country. And that you may do so with greater assurance, I will partake of your meals with you." These words were of great relief to Cosmo, who, with tears in his eyes, embraced and kissed Federigo, earnestly thanking him for so kind and affectionate conduct, and promising, if ever the opportunity were given him, he would not be ungrateful.

Chapter VII: Cosmo is banished to Padua—Rinaldo degli Albizzi attempts to restore the nobility—New disturbances occasioned by Rinaldo degli Albizzi—Rinaldo takes arms against the Signory—His designs are disconcerted—Pope Eugenius in Florence—He endeavors to reconcile the parties—Cosmo is recalled—Rinaldo and his party banished—Glorious return of Cosmo.

Cosmo in some degree recovered his spirits, and while the citizens were disputing about him, Federigo, by way of recreation, brought an acquaintance of the Gonfalonier to take supper with him, an amusing and facetious person, whose name was Il Farnagaccio. The repast being nearly over, Cosmo, who thought he might turn this visit to advantage, for he knew the man very intimately, gave a sign to Federigo to leave the apartment, and he, guessing the cause, under pretense of going for something that was wanted on the table, left them together. Cosmo, after a few friendly expressions addressed to Il Farnagaccio, gave him a small slip of paper, and desired him to go to the director of the hospital of Santa Maria Nuova, for one thousand one hundred ducats; he was to take the hundred for himself, and carry the thousand to the Gonfalonier, and beg that he would take some suitable occasion of coming to see him. Farnagaccio undertook the commission, the money was paid, Bernardo became more humane, and Cosmo was banished to Padua, contrary to the wish of Rinaldo, who earnestly desired his death. Averardo and many others of the house of Medici were also banished, and with them Puccio and Giovanni Pucci. To silence those who were dissatisfied with the banishment of Cosmo, they endowed with the power of a Balia, the Eight of War and the Capitano of the People. After his sentence, Cosmo on the third of October, 1433, came before the Signory, by whom the boundary to which he was restricted was specified; and they advised him to avoid passing it, unless he wished them to proceed with greater severity both against himself and his property. Cosmo received his sentence with a cheerful look, assuring the Signory that wherever they determined to send him, he would willingly remain. He earnestly begged, that as they had preserved his life they would protect it, for he knew there were many in the piazza who were desirous to take it; and assured them, that wherever he might be, himself and his means were entirely at the service of the city, the people, and the Signory. He was respectfully attended by the Gonfalonier, who retained him in the palace till night, then conducted him to his own house to supper, and caused him to be escorted by a strong armed force to his place of banishment. Wherever the cavalcade passed, Cosmo was honorably received, and was publicly visited by the Venetians, not as an exile, but with all the respect due to one in the highest station.

Florence, widowed of so great a citizen, one so generally beloved, seemed to be universally sunk in despondency; victors and the vanquished were alike in fear. Rinaldo, as if inspired with a presage of his future calamities, in order not to appear deficient to himself or his party, assembled many citizens, his friends, and informed them that he foresaw their approaching ruin for having allowed themselves to be overcome by the prayers, the tears, and the money of their enemies; and that they did not seem aware they would soon themselves have to entreat and weep, when their prayers would not be listened to, or their tears excite compassion; and that of the money received, they would have to restore the principal, and pay the interest in tortures, exile, and death; that it would have been much better for them to have done nothing than to have left Cosmo alive, and his friends in Florence; for great offenders ought either to remain untouched, or be destroyed; that there was now no remedy but to strengthen themselves in the city, so that upon the renewed attempts of their enemies, which would soon take place, they might drive them out with arms, since they had not sufficient civil authority to expel them. The remedy to be adopted, he said, was one that he had long before advocated, which was to regain the friendship of the grandees, restoring and conceding to them all the honors of the city, and thus make themselves strong with that party, since their adversaries had joined the plebeians. That by this means they would become the more powerful side, for they would possess greater energy, more comprehensive talent and an augmented share of influence; and that if this last and only remedy were not adopted, he knew not what other means could be made use of to preserve the government among so many enemies, or prevent their own ruin and that of the city.

Mariotto Baldovinetti, one of the assembly, was opposed to this plan, on account of the pride and insupportable nature of the nobility; and said, that it would be folly to place themselves again under such inevitable tyranny for the sake of avoiding imaginary dangers from the plebeians. Rinaldo, finding his advice unfavorably received, vexed at his own misfortune and that of his party, imputed the whole to heaven itself, which had resolved upon it, rather than to human ignorance and blunders. In this juncture of affairs, no remedial measure being attempted, a letter was found written by Agnolo Acciajuoli to Cosmo, acquainting him with the disposition of the city in his favor, and advising him, if possible, to excite a war, and gain the friendship of Neri di Gino; for he imagined the city to be in want of money, and as she would not find anyone to serve her, the remembrance of him would be revived in the minds of the citizens, and they would desire his return; and that if Neri were detached from Rinaldo, the party of the latter would be so weakened, as to be unable to defend themselves. This letter coming to the hands of the magistrates, Agnolo was taken, put to the torture, and sent into exile. This example, however, did not at all deter Cosmo's party.

It was now almost a year since Cosmo had been banished, and the end of August, 1434, being come, Niccolo di Cocco was drawn Gonfalonier for the two succeeding months, and with him eight signors, all partisans of Cosmo. This struck terror into Rinaldo and his party; and as it is usual for three days to elapse before the new Signory assume the magistracy and the old resign their authority, Rinaldo again called together the heads of his party. He endeavored to show them their certain and immediate danger, and that their only remedy was to take arms, and cause Donato Velluti, who was yet Gonfalonier, to assemble the people in the piazza and create a Balia. He would then deprive the new Signory of the magistracy, appoint another, burn the present balloting purses, and by means of a new Squittini, provide themselves with friends. Many thought this course safe and requisite; others, that it was too violent, and likely to be attended with great evil. Among those who disliked it was Palla Strozzi, a peaceable, gentle, and humane person, better adapted for literary pursuits than for restraining a party, or opposing civil strife. He said that bold and crafty resolutions seem promising at their commencement, but are afterward found difficult to execute, and generally pernicious at their conclusion; that he thought the fear of external wars (the duke's forces being upon the confines of Romagna), would occupy the minds of the Signory more than internal dissensions; but, still, if any attempt should be made, and it could not take place unnoticed, they would have sufficient time to take arms, and adopt whatever measures might be found necessary for the common good, which being done upon necessity, would occasion less excitement among the people and less danger to themselves. It was therefore concluded, that the new Signory should come in; that their proceedings should be watched, and if they were found attempting anything against the party, each should take arms, and meet in the piazza of San Pulinari, situated near the palace, and whence they might proceed wherever it was found necessary. Having come to this conclusion, Rinaldo's friends separated.

The new Signory entered upon their office, and the Gonfalonier, in order to acquire reputation, and deter those who might intend to oppose him, sent Donato Velluti, his predecessor, to prison, upon the charge of having applied the public money to his own use. He then endeavored to sound his colleagues with respect to Cosmo: seeing them desirous of his return, he communicated with the leaders of the Medici party, and, by their advice, summoned the hostile chiefs, Rinaldo degli Albizzi, Ridolfo Peruzzi, and Niccolo Barbadoro. After this citation, Rinaldo thought further delay would be dangerous: he therefore left his house with a great number of armed men, and was soon joined by Ridolfo Peruzzi and Niccolo Barbadoro. The force accompanying them was composed of several citizens and a great number of disbanded soldiers then in Florence: and all assembled according to appointment in the piazza of San Pulinari. Palla Strozzi and Giovanni Guicciardini, though each had assembled a large number of men, kept in their houses; and therefore Rinaldo sent a messenger to request their attendance and to reprove their delay. Giovanni replied, that he should lend sufficient aid against their enemies, if by remaining at home he could prevent his brother Piero from going to the defense of the palace. After many messages Palla came to San Pulinari on horseback, accompanied by two of his people on foot, and unarmed. Rinaldo, on meeting him, sharply reproved him for his negligence, declaring that his refusal to come with the others arose either from defect of principle or want of courage; both of which charges should be avoided by all who wished to preserve such a character as he had hitherto possessed; and that if he thought this abominable conduct to his party would induce their enemies when victorious to spare him from death or exile, he deceived himself; but for himself (Rinaldo) whatever might happen, he had the consolation of knowing, that previously to the crisis he had never neglected his duty in council, and that when it occurred he had used every possible exertion to repel it with arms; but that Palla and the others would experience aggravated remorse when they considered they had upon three occasions betrayed their country; first when they saved Cosmo; next when they disregarded his advice; and now the third time by not coming armed in her defense according to their engagement. To these reproaches Palla made no reply audible to those around, but, muttering something as he left them, returned to his house.

The Signory, knowing Rinaldo and his party had taken arms, finding themselves abandoned, caused the palace to be shut up, and having no one to consult they knew not what course to adopt. However, Rinaldo, by delaying his coming to the piazza, having waited in expectation of forces which did not join him, lost the opportunity of victory, gave them courage to provide for their defense, and allowed many others to join them, who advised that means should be used to induce their adversaries to lay down their arms. Thereupon, some of the least suspected, went on the part of the Signory to Rinaldo, and said, they did not know what occasion they had given his friends for thus assembling in arms; that they never had any intention of offending him, and if they had spoken of Cosmo, they had no design of recalling him; so if their fears were thus occasioned they might at once be dispelled, for that if they came to the palace they would be graciously received, and all their complaints attended to. These words produced no change in Rinaldo's purpose; he bade them provide for their safety by resigning their offices, and said that then the government of the city would be reorganized, for the mutual benefit of all.

It rarely happens, where authorities are equal and opinions contrary, that any good resolution is adopted. Ridolfo Peruzzi, moved by the discourse of the citizens, said, that all he desired was to prevent the return of Cosmo, and this being granted to them seemed a sufficient victory; nor would he, to obtain a greater, fill the city with blood; he would therefore obey the Signory; and accordingly went with his people to the palace, where he was received with a hearty welcome. Thus Rinaldo's delay at San Pulinari, Palla's want of courage, and Ridolfo's desertion, deprived their party of all chance of success; while the ardor of the citizens abated, and the pope's authority did not contribute to its revival.

Pope Eugenius was at this time at Florence, having been driven from Rome by the people. These disturbances coming to his knowledge, he thought it a duty suitable to his pastoral office to appease them, and sent the patriarch Giovanni Vitelleschi, Rinaldo's most intimate friend, to entreat the latter to come to an interview with him, as he trusted he had sufficient influence with the Signory to insure his safety and satisfaction, without injury or bloodshed to the citizens. By his friend's persuasion, Rinaldo proceeded with all his followers to Santa Maria Nuova, where the pope resided. Eugenius gave him to understand, that the Signory had empowered him to settle the differences between them, and that all would be arranged to his satisfaction, if he laid down his arms. Rinaldo, having witnessed Palla's want of zeal, and the fickleness of Ridolfo Peruzzi, and no better course being open to him, placed himself in the pope's hands, thinking that at all events the authority of his holiness would insure his safety. Eugenius then sent word to Niccolo Barbadoro, and the rest who remained without, that they were to lay down their arms, for Rinaldo was remaining with the pontiff, to arrange terms of agreement with the signors; upon which they immediately dispersed, and laid aside their weapons.

The Signory, seeing their adversaries disarmed, continued to negotiate an arrangement by means of the pope; but at the same time sent secretly to the mountains of Pistoia for infantry, which, with what other forces they could collect, were brought into Florence by night. Having taken possession of all the strong positions in the city, they assembled the people in the piazza and created a new balia, which, without delay, restored Cosmo and those who had been exiled with him to their country; and banished, of the opposite party, Rinaldo degli Albizzi, Ridolfo Peruzzi, Niccolo Barbadoro, and Palla Strozzi, with so many other citizens, that there were few places in Italy which did not contain some, and many others beyond her limits were full of them. By this and similar occurrences, Florence was deprived of men of worth, and of much wealth and industry.

The pope, seeing such misfortunes befall those who by his entreaties were induced to lay down their arms, was greatly dissatisfied, and condoled with Rinaldo on the injuries he had received through his confidence in him, but advised him to be patient, and hope for some favorable turn of fortune. Rinaldo replied, "The want of confidence in those who ought to have trusted me, and the great trust I have reposed in you, have ruined both me and my party. But I blame myself principally for having thought that you, who were expelled from your own country, could preserve me in mine. I have had sufficient experience of the freaks of fortune; and as I have never trusted greatly to prosperity, I shall suffer less inconvenience from adversity; and I know that when she pleases she can become more favorable. But if she should never change, I shall not be very desirous of living in a city in which individuals are more powerful than the laws; for that country alone is desirable in which property and friends may be safely enjoyed, not one where they may easily be taken from us, and where friends, from fear of losing their property, are compelled to abandon each other in their greatest need. Besides, it has always been less painful to good men to hear of the misfortunes of their country than to witness them; and an honorable exile is always held in greater esteem than slavery at home." He then left the pope, and, full of indignation, blaming himself, his own measures, and the coldness of his friends, went into exile.

Cosmo, on the other hand, being informed of his recall, returned to Florence; and it has seldom occurred that any citizen, coming home triumphant from victory, was received by so vast a concourse of people, or such unqualified demonstrations of regard as he was upon his return from banishment; for by universal consent he was hailed as the benefactor of the people, and the FATHER OF HIS COUNTRY.

Book V: Chapter I: The vicissitudes of empires—The state of Italy—The military factions of Sforza and Braccio—The Bracceschi and the Sforzeschi attack the pope, who is expelled by the Romans—War between the pope and the duke of Milan—The Florentines and the Venetians assist the pope—Peace between the pope and the duke of Milan—Tyranny practiced by the party favorable to the Medici.

It may be observed, that provinces amid the vicissitudes to which they are subject, pass from order into confusion, and afterward recur to a state of order again; for the nature of mundane affairs not allowing them to continue in an even course, when they have arrived at their greatest perfection, they soon begin to decline. In the same manner, having been reduced by disorder, and sunk to their utmost state of depression, unable to descend lower, they, of necessity, reascend; and thus from good they gradually decline to evil, and from evil again return to good. The reason is, that valor produces peace; peace, repose; repose, disorder; disorder, ruin; so from disorder order springs; from order virtue, and from this, glory and good fortune. Hence, wise men have observed, that the age of literary excellence is subsequent to that of distinction in arms; and that in cities and provinces, great warriors are produced before philosophers. Arms having secured victory, and victory peace, the buoyant vigor of the martial mind cannot be enfeebled by a more excusable indulgence than that of letters; nor can indolence, with any greater or more dangerous deceit, enter a well regulated community. Cato was aware of this when the philosophers, Diogenes and Carneades, were sent ambassadors to the senate by the Athenians; for perceiving with what earnest admiration the Roman youth began to follow them, and knowing the evils that might result to his country from this specious idleness, he enacted that no philosopher should be allowed to enter Rome. Provinces by this means sink to ruin, from which, men's sufferings having made them wiser, they again recur to order, if they be not overwhelmed by some extraordinary force. These causes made Italy, first under the ancient Tuscans, and afterward under the Romans, by turns happy and unhappy; and although nothing has subsequently arisen from the ruins of Rome at all corresponding to her ancient greatness (which under a well-organized monarchy might have been gloriously effected), still there was so much bravery and intelligence in some of the new cities and governments that afterward sprang up, that although none ever acquired dominion over the rest, they were, nevertheless, so balanced and regulated among themselves, as to enable them to live in freedom, and defend their country from the barbarians.

Among these governments, the Florentines, although they possessed a smaller extent of territory, were not inferior to any in power and authority; for being situated in the middle of Italy, wealthy, and prepared for action, they either defended themselves against such as thought proper to assail them, or decided victory in favor of those to whom they became allies. From the valor, therefore, of these new governments, if no seasons occurred of long-continued peace, neither were any exposed to the calamities of war; for that cannot be called peace in which states frequently assail each other with arms, nor can those be considered wars in which no men are slain, cities plundered, or sovereignties overthrown; for the practice of arms fell into such a state of decay, that wars were commenced without fear, continued without danger, and concluded without loss. Thus the military energy which is in other countries exhausted by a long peace, was wasted in Italy by the contemptible manner in which hostilities were carried on, as will be clearly seen in the events to be described from 1434 to 1494, from which it will appear how the barbarians were again admitted into Italy, and she again sunk under subjection to them. Although the transactions of our princes at home and abroad will not be viewed with admiration of their virtue and greatness like those of the ancients, perhaps they may on other accounts be regarded with no less interest, seeing what masses of high spirited people were kept in restraint by such weak and disorderly forces. And if, in detailing the events which took place in this wasted world, we shall not have to record the bravery of the soldier, the prudence of the general, or the patriotism of the citizen, it will be seen with what artifice, deceit, and cunning, princes, warriors, and leaders of republics conducted themselves, to support a reputation they never deserved. This, perhaps, will not be less useful than a knowledge of ancient history; for, if the latter excites the liberal mind to imitation, the former will show what ought to be avoided and decried.

Italy was reduced to such a condition by her rulers, that when, by consent of her princes, peace was restored, it was soon disturbed by those who retained their armies, so that glory was not gained by war nor repose by peace. Thus when the league and the duke of Milan agreed to lay aside their arms in 1433, the soldiers, resolved upon war, directed their efforts against the church. There were at this time two factions or armed parties in Italy, the Sforzesca and the Braccesca. The leader of the former was the Count Francesco, the son of Sforza, and of the latter, Niccolo Piccinino and Niccolo Fortebraccio. Under the banner of one or other of these parties almost all the forces of Italy were assembled. Of the two, the Sforzesca was in greatest repute, as well from the bravery of the count himself, as from the promise which the duke of Milan had made him of his natural daughter, Madonna Bianca, the prospect of which alliance greatly strengthened his influence. After the peace of Lombardy, these forces, from various causes attacked Pope Eugenius. Niccolo Fortebraccio was instigated by the ancient enmity which Braccio had always entertained against the church; the count was induced by ambition: so that Niccolo assailed Rome, and the count took possession of La Marca.

The Romans, in order to avoid the war, drove Pope Eugenius from their city: and he, having with difficulty escaped, came to Florence, where seeing the imminent danger of his situation, being abandoned by the princes (for they were unwilling again to take up arms in his cause, after having been so anxious to lay them aside), he came to terms with the count, and ceded to him the sovereignty of La Marca, although, to the injury of having occupied it, he had added insult; for in signing the place, from which he addressed letters to his agents, he said in Latin, according to the Latin custom, *Ex Girfalco nostro Firmiano, invito Petro et Paulo*. Neither was he satisfied with this concession, but insisted upon being appointed Gonfalonier of the church, which was also granted; so much more was Eugenius alarmed at the prospect of a dangerous war than of an ignominious peace. The count, having been thus been reconciled to the pontiff, attacked Niccolo Fortebraccio, and during many months various encounters took place between them, from all which greater injury resulted to the pope and his subjects, than to either of the belligerents. At length, by the intervention of the duke of Milan, an arrangement, by way of a truce, was made, by which both became princes in the territories of the church.

The war thus extinguished at Rome was rekindled in Romagna by Batista da Canneto, who at Bologna slew some of the family of the Grifoni, and expelled from the city the governor who resided there for the pope, along with others who were opposed to him. To enable himself to retain the government, he applied for assistance to Filippo; and the pope, to avenge himself for the injury, sought the aid of the Venetians and Florentines. Both parties obtained assistance, so that very soon two large armies were on foot in Romagna. Niccolo Piccinino commanded for the duke, Gattamelata and Niccolo da Tolentino for the Venetians and Florentines. They met near Imola, where a battle ensued, in which the Florentines and Venetians were routed, and Niccolo da Tolentino was sent prisoner to Milan where, either through grief for his loss or by some unfair means, he died in a few days.

The duke, on this victory, either being exhausted by the late wars, or thinking the League after their defeat would not be in haste to resume hostilities, did not pursue his good fortune, and thus gave the pope and his colleagues time to recover themselves. They therefore appointed the Count Francesco for their leader, and undertook to drive Niccolo Fortebraccio from the territories of the church, and thus terminate the war which had been commenced in favor of the pontiff. The Romans, finding the pope supported by so large an army, sought a reconciliation with him, and being successful, admitted his commissary into the city. Among the places possessed by Niccolo Fortebraccio, were Tivoli, Montefiascone, Citta di Castello, and Ascesi, to the last of which, not being able to keep the field, he fled, and the count besieged him there. Niccolo's brave defense making it probable that the war would be of considerable duration, the duke deemed to necessary to prevent the League from obtaining the victory, and said that if this were not effected he would very soon have to look at the defense of his own territories. Resolving to divert the count from the siege, he commanded Niccolo Piccinino to pass into Tuscany by way of Romagna; and the League, thinking it more important to defend Tuscany than to occupy Ascesi, ordered the count to prevent the passage of Niccolo, who was already, with his army, at Furli. The count accordingly moved with his forces, and came to Cesena, having left the war of La Marca and the care of his own territories to his brother Lione; and while Niccolo Piccinino was endeavoring to pass by, and the count to prevent him, Fortebraccio attacked Lione with great bravery, made him prisoner, routed his forces, and pursuing the advantage of his victory, at once possessed himself of many places in La Marca. This circumstance greatly perplexed the count, who thought he had lost all his territories; so, leaving part of his force to check Piccinino, with the remainder he pursued Fortebraccio, whom he attacked and conquered. Fortebraccio was taken prisoner in the battle, and soon after died of his wounds. This victory restored to the pontiff all the places that had been taken from him by Fortebraccio, and compelled the duke of Milan to sue for peace, which was concluded by the intercession of Niccolo da Esta, marquis of Ferrara; the duke restoring to the church the places he had taken from her, and his forces retiring into Lombardy. Batista da Canneto, as in the case with all who retain authority only by the consent and forces of another, when the duke's people had quitted Romagna, unable with his own power to keep possession of Bologna, fled, and Antonio Bentivogli, the head of the opposite party, returned to his country.

All this took place during the exile of Cosmo, after whose return, those who had restored him, and a great number of persons injured by the opposite party, resolved at all events to make themselves sure of the government; and the Signory for the months of November and December, not content with what their predecessors had done in favor of their party extended the term and changed the residences of several who were banished, and increased the number of exiles. In addition to these evils, it was observed that citizens were more annoyed on account of their wealth, their family connections or private animosities, than for the sake of the party to which they adhered, so that if these prescriptions had been accompanied with bloodshed, they would have resembled those of Octavius and Sylla, though in reality they were not without some stains; for Antonio di Bernardo Guadagni was beheaded, and four other citizens, among whom were Zanobi dei Belfratelli and Cosmo Barbadori, passing the confines to which they were limited, proceeded to Venice, where the Venetians, valuing the friendship of Cosmo de' Medici more than their own honor, sent them prisoners to him, and they were basely put to death. This circumstance greatly increased the influence of that party, and struck their enemies with terror, finding that such a powerful republic would so humble itself to the Florentines. This, however, was supposed to have been done, not so much out of kindness to Cosmo, as to excite dissensions in Florence, and by means of bloodshed make greater certainty of division among the citizens, for the Venetians knew there was no other obstacle to their ambition so great as the union of her people.

The city being cleared of the enemies, or suspected enemies of the state, those in possession of the government now began to strengthen their party by conferring benefits upon such as were in a condition to serve them, and the family of the Alberti, with all who had been banished by the former government, were recalled. All the nobility, with few exceptions, were reduced to the ranks of the people, and the possessions of the exiles were divided among themselves, upon each paying a small acknowledgment. They then fortified themselves with new laws and provisos, made new Squittini, withdrawing the names of their adversaries from the purses, and filling them with those of their friends. Taking advice from the ruin of their enemies, they considered that to allow the great offices to be filled by mere chance of drawing, did not afford the government sufficient security, they therefore resolved that the magistrates possessing the power of life and death should always be chosen from among the leaders of their own party, and therefore that the *Accoppiatori*, or persons selected for the imborsation of the new Squittini, with the Signory who had to retire from office, should make the new appointments. They gave to eight of the guard authority to proceed capitally, and provided that the exiles, when their term of banishment was complete, should not be allowed to return, unless from the Signory and Colleagues, which were thirty-seven in number, the consent of thirty-four was obtained. It was made unlawful to write to or to receive letters from them; every word, sign, or action that gave offense to the ruling party was punished with the utmost rigor; and if there was still in Florence any suspected person whom these regulations did not reach, he was oppressed with taxes imposed for the occasion. Thus in a short time, having expelled or impoverished the whole of the adverse party, they established themselves firmly in the government. Not to be destitute of external assistance, and to deprive others of it, who might use it against themselves, they entered into a league, offensive and defensive, with the pope, the Venetians, and the duke of Milan.

Chapter II: Death of Giovanni II.—Rene of Anjou and Alfonso of Aragon aspire to the kingdom—Alfonso is routed and taken by the Genoese—Alfonso being a prisoner of the duke of Milan, obtains his friendship—The Genoese disgusted with the duke of Milan—Divisions among the Genoese—The Genoese, by means of Francesco Spinola, expel the duke's governor—League against the duke of Milan—Rinaldo degli Albizzi advises the duke to make war against the Florentines—His discourse to the duke—The duke adopts measures injurious to the Florentines—Niccolo Piccinino appointed to command the duke's forces—Preparations of the Florentines—Piccinino routed before Barga.

The affairs of Florence being in this condition, Giovanna, queen of Naples, died, and by her will appointed Rene of Anjou to be her successor. Alfonso, king of Aragon, was at this time in Sicily, and having obtained the concurrence of many barons, prepared to take possession of the kingdom. The Neapolitans, with whom a greater number of barons were also associated, favored Rene. The pope was unwilling that either of them should obtain it; but desired the affairs of Naples to be administered by a governor of his own appointing.

In the meantime Alfonso entered the kingdom, and was received by the duke of Sessa; he brought with him some princes, whom he had engaged in his service, with the design (already possessing Capua, which the prince of Taranto held in his name) of subduing the Neapolitans, and sent his fleet to attack Gaeta, which had declared itself in their favor. They therefore demanded assistance of the duke of Milan, who persuaded the Genoese to undertake their defense; and they, to satisfy the duke their sovereign, and protect the merchandise they possessed, both at Naples and Gaeta, armed a powerful fleet. Alfonso hearing of this, augmented his own naval force, went in person to meet the Genoese, and coming up with them near the island of Ponzio, an engagement ensued, in which the Aragonese were defeated, and Alfonso, with many of the princes of his suite, made prisoners, and sent by the Genoese to the Filippo.

This victory terrified the princes of Italy, who, being jealous of the duke's power, thought it would give him a great opportunity of being sovereign of the whole country. But so contrary are the views of men, that he took a directly opposite course. Alfonso was a man of great sagacity, and as soon as an opportunity presented itself of communicating with Filippo, he proved to him how completely he contravened his own interests, by favoring Rene and opposing himself; for it would be the business of the former, on becoming king of Naples, to introduce the French into Milan; that in an emergency he might have assistance at hand, without the necessity of having to solicit a passage for his friends. But he could not possibly secure this advantage without effecting the ruin of the duke, and making his dominions a French province; and that the contrary of all this would result from himself becoming lord of Naples; for having only the French to fear, he would be compelled to love and caress, nay even to obey those who had it in their power to open a passage for his enemies. That thus the title of king of king of Naples would be with himself (Alfonso), but the power and authority with Filippo; so that it was much more the duke's business than his own to consider the danger of one course and the advantage of the other; unless he rather wished to gratify his private prejudices than to give security to his dominions. In the one case he would be a free prince, in the other, placed between two powerful sovereigns, he would either be robbed of his territories or live in constant fear, and have to obey them like a slave. These arguments so greatly influenced the duke, that, changing his design, he set Alfonso at liberty, sent him honorably to Genoa and then to Naples. From thence the king went to Gaeta, which as soon as his liberation had become known, was taken possession of by some nobles of his party.

The Genoese, seeing that the duke, without the least regard for them, had liberated the king, and gained credit to himself through the dangers and expense which they had incurred; that he enjoyed all the honor of the liberation, and they were themselves exposed to the odium of the capture, and the injuries consequent upon the king's defeat, were greatly exasperated. In the city of Genoa, while in the enjoyment of her liberty, a magistrate is created with the consent of the people, whom they call the Doge; not that he is absolutely a prince, or that he alone has the power of determining matters of government; but that, as the head of the state, he proposes those questions or subjects which have to be considered and determined by the magistrates and the councils. In that city are many noble families so powerful, that they are with great difficulty induced to submit to the authority of the law. Of these, the most powerful are the Fregosa and the Adorna, from whom arise the dissensions of the city, and the impotence of her civil regulations; for the possession of this high office being contested by means inadmissible in well-regulated communities, and most commonly with arms in their hands, it always occurs that one party is oppressed and the other triumphant; and sometimes those who fail in the pursuit have recourse to the arms of strangers, and the country they are not allowed to rule they subject to foreign authority. Hence it happens, that those who govern in Lombardy most commonly command in Genoa, as occurred at the time Alfonso of Aragon was made prisoner. Among the leading Genoese who had been instrumental in subjecting the republic to Filippo, was Francesco Spinola, who, soon after he had reduced his country to bondage, as always happens in such cases, became suspected by the duke. Indignant at this, he withdrew to a sort of voluntary exile at Gaeta, and being there when the naval expedition was in preparation, and having conducted himself with great bravery in the action, he thought he had again merited so much of the duke's confidence as would obtain for him permission to remain undisturbed at Genoa. But the duke still retained his suspicions; for he could not believe that a vacillating defender of his own country's liberty would be faithful to himself; and Francesco Spinola resolved again to try his fortune, and if possible restore freedom to his country, and honorable safety for himself; for he was there was no probability of regaining the forfeited affection of his fellow-citizens, but by resolving at his own peril to remedy the misfortunes which he had been so instrumental in producing. Finding the indignation against the duke universal, on account of the liberation of the king, he thought the moment propitious for the execution of his design. He communicated his ideas to some whom he knew to be similarly inclined, and his arguments ensured their co-operation.

The great festival of St. John the Baptist being come, when Arismeno, the new governor sent by the duke, was to enter Genoa, and he being already arrived, accompanied by Opicino, the former governor, and many Genoese citizens, Francesco Spinola thought further delay improper; and, issuing from his house with those acquainted with his design, all armed, they raised the cry of liberty. It was wonderful to see how eagerly the citizens and people assembled at the word; so that those who for any reason might be favorable to Filippo, not only had no time to arm, but scarcely to consider the means of escape. Arismeno, with some Genoese, fled to the fortress which was held for the duke, Opicino, thinking that if he could reach the palace, where two thousand men were in arms, and at his command, he might be able either to effect his own safety, or induce his friends to defend themselves, took that direction; but before he arrived at the piazza he was slain, his body divided into many pieces and scattered about the city. The Genoese having placed the government in the hands of free magistrates, in a few days recovered the castle, and the other strongholds possessed by the duke, and delivered themselves entirely from his yoke.

These transactions, though at first they had alarmed the princes of Italy with the apprehension that the duke would become too powerful, now gave them hope, seeing the turn they had taken, of being able to restrain him; and, notwithstanding the recent league, the Florentines and Venetians entered into alliance with the Genoese. Rinaldo degli Albizzi and the other leading Florentine exiles, observing the altered aspect of affairs, conceived hopes of being able to induce the duke to make war against Florence, and having arrived at Milan, Rinaldo addressed him in the following manner: "If we, who were once your enemies, come now confidently to supplicate your assistance to enable us to return to our country, neither you, nor anyone, who considers the course and vicissitudes of human affairs, can be at all surprised; for of our past conduct toward yourself and our present intentions toward our country, we can adduce palpable and abundant reasons. No good man will ever reproach another who endeavors to defend his country, whatever be his mode of doing so; neither have we had any design of injuring you, but only to preserve our country from detriment; and we appeal to yourself, whether, during the greatest victories of our league, when you were really desirous of peace, we were not even more anxious for it than yourself; so that we do not think we have done aught to make us despair altogether of favor from you. Nor can our country itself complain that we now exhort you to use those arms against her, from which we have so pertinaciously defended her; for that state alone merits the love of all her citizens, which cares with equal affection for all; not one that favors a few, and casts from her the great mass of her children. Nor are the arms that men use against their country to be universally condemned; for communities, although composed of many, resemble individual bodies; and as in these, many infirmities arise which cannot be cured without the application of fire or of steel, so in the former, there often occur such numerous and great evils, that a good and merciful citizen, when there is a necessity for the sword, would be much more to blame in leaving her uncured, than by using this remedy for her preservation. What greater disease can afflict a republic than slavery? and what remedy is more desirable for adoption than the one by which alone it can be effectually removed? No wars are just but those that are necessary; and force is merciful when it presents the only hope of relief. I know not what necessity can be greater than ours, or what compassion can exceed that which rescues our country from slavery. Our cause is therefore just, and our purpose merciful, as both yourself and we may be easily convinced. The amplest justice is on your side; for the Florentines have not hesitated, after a peace concluded with so much solemnity, to enter into league with those who have rebelled against you; so that if our cause is insufficient to excite you against them, let your own just indignation do so; and the more so, seeing the facility of the undertaking. You need be under no apprehension from the memory of the past, in which you may have observed the power of that people and their pertinency in self-defense; though these might reasonably excite fear, if they were still animated by the valor of former times. But now, all is entirely the reverse; for what power can be expected in a city that has recently expelled the greatest part of her wealth and industry? What indomitable resolution need be apprehended from the people whom so many and such recent enmities have disunited? The disunion which still prevails will prevent wealthy citizens advancing money as they used to do on former occasions; for though men willingly contribute according to their means, when they see their own credit, glory, and private advantage dependent upon it, or when there is a hope of regaining in peace what has been spent in war, but not when equally oppressed under all circumstances, when in war they suffer the injuries of the enemy, and in peace, the insolence of those who govern them. Besides this, the people feel more deeply the avarice of their rulers, than the rapacity of the enemy; for there is hope of being ultimately relieved from the latter evil, but none from the former. Thus, in the last war, you had to contend with the whole city; but now with only a small portion. You attempted to take the government from many good citizens; but now you oppose only a few bad ones. You then endeavored to deprive a city of her liberty, now you come to restore it. As it is unreasonable to suppose that under such disparity of circumstances, the result should be the same, you have now every reason to anticipate an easy victory; and how much it will strengthen your own government, you may easily judge; having Tuscany friendly, and bound by so powerful an obligation, in your enterprises, she will be even of more service to you than Milan. And, although, on former occasions, such an acquisition might be looked upon as ambitious and unwarrantable, it will now be considered merciful and just. Then do not let this opportunity escape, and be assured, that although your attempts against the city have been attended with difficulty, expense, and disgrace, this will with facility procure you incalculable advantage and an honorable renown."

Many words were not requisite to induce the duke to hostilities against the Florentines, for he was incited to it by hereditary hatred and blind ambition, and still more, by the fresh injuries which the league with the Genoese involved; yet his past expenses, the dangerous measures necessary, the remembrance of his recent losses, and the vain hopes of the exiles, alarmed him. As soon as he had learned the revolt of Genoa, he ordered Niccolo Piccinino to proceed thither with all his cavalry and whatever infantry he could raise, for the purpose of recovering her, before the citizens had time to become settled and establish a government; for he trusted greatly in the fortress within the city, which was held for him. And although Niccolo drove the Genoese from the mountains, took from them the valley of Pozeveri, where they had entrenched themselves, and obliged them to seek refuge within the walls of the city, he still found such an insurmountable obstacle in the resolute defense of the citizens, that he was compelled to withdraw. On this, at the suggestion of the Florentine exiles, he commanded Niccolo to attack them on the eastern side, upon the confines of Pisa in the Genoese territory, and to push the war with his utmost vigor, thinking this plan would manifest and develop the course best to be adopted. Niccolo therefore besieged and took Serezana, and having committed great ravages, by way of further alarming the Florentines he proceeded to Lucca, spreading a report that it was his intention to go to Naples to render assistance to the king of Aragon. Upon these new events Pope Eugenius left Florence and proceeded to Bologna, where he endeavored to effect an amicable arrangement between the league and the duke, intimating to the latter, that if he would not consent to some treaty, the pontiff must send Francesco Sforza to assist the league, for the latter was now his confederate, and served in his pay. Although the pope greatly exerted himself in this affair, his endeavors were unavailing; for the duke would not listen to any proposal that did not leave him the possession of Genoa, and the league had resolved that she should remain free; and, therefore, each party, having no other resource, prepared to continue the war.

In the meantime Niccolo Piccinino arrived at Lucca, and the Florentines, being doubtful what course to adopt, ordered Neri di Gino to lead their forces into the Pisan territory, induced the pontiff to allow Count Francesco to join him, and with their forces they halted at San Gonda. Piccinino then demanded admission into the kingdom of Naples, and this being refused, he threatened to force a passage. The armies were equal, both in regard of numbers and the capacity of their leaders, and unwilling to tempt fortune during the bad weather, it being the month of December, they remained several days without attacking each other. The first movement was made by Niccolo Piccinino, who being informed that if he attacked Vico Pisano by night, he could easily take possession of the place, made the attempt, and having failed, ravaged the surrounding country, and then burned and plundered the town of San Giovanni alla Vena. This enterprise, though of little consequence, excited him to make further attempts, the more so from being assured that the count and Neri were yet in their quarters, and he attacked Santa Maria in Castello and Filetto, both which places he took. Still the Florentine forces would not stir; not that the count entertained any fear, but because, out of regard to the pope, who still labored to effect an accommodation, the government of Florence had deferred giving their final consent to the war. This course, which the Florentines adopted from prudence, was considered by the enemy to be only the result of timidity, and with increased boldness they led their forces up to Barga, which they resolved to besiege. This new attack made the Florentines set aside all other considerations, and resolve not only to relieve Barga, but to invade the Lucchese territory. Accordingly the count proceeded in pursuit of Niccolo, and coming up with him before Barga, an engagement took place, in which Piccinino was overcome, and compelled to raise the siege.

The Venetians considering the duke to have broken the peace, send Giovan Francesco da Gonzaga, their captain, to Ghiaradadda, who, by severely wasting the duke's territories, induced him to recall Niccolo Piccinino from Tuscany. This circumstance, together with the victory obtained over Niccolo, emboldened the Florentines to attempt the recovery of Lucca, since the duke, whom alone they feared, was engaged with the Venetians, and the Lucchese having received the enemy into their city, and allowed him to attack them, would have no ground of complaint.

Chapter III: The Florentines go to war with Lucca—Discourse of a citizen of Lucca to animate the plebeians against the Florentines—The Lucchese resolve to defend themselves—They are assisted by the duke of Milan—Treaty between the Florentines and the Venetians—Francesco Sforza, captain of the league, refuses to cross the Po in the service of the Venetians and returns to Tuscany—The bad faith of the Venetians toward the Florentines—Cosmo de' Medici at Venice—Peace between the Florentines and the Lucchese—The Florentines effect a reconciliation between the pope and the Count di Poppi—The pope consecrates the church of Santa Reparata—Council of Florence.

The count commenced operations against Lucca in April, 1437, and the Florentines, desirous of recovering what they had themselves lost before they attacked others, retook Santa Maria in Castello, and all the places which Piccinino had occupied. Then, entering the Lucchese territory, they besieged Camaiore, the inhabitants of which, although faithful to their rulers, being influenced more by immediate danger than by attachment to their distant friends, surrendered. In the same manner, they obtained Massa and Serezana. Toward the end of May they proceeded in the direction of Lucca, burning the towns, destroying the growing crops, grain, trees, and vines, driving away the cattle, and leaving nothing undone to injure the enemy. The Lucchese, finding themselves abandoned by the duke, and hopeless of defending the open country, forsook it; entrenched and fortified the city, which they doubted not, being well garrisoned, they would be able to defend for a time, and that, in the interim, some event would occur for their relief, as had been the case during the former wars which the Florentines had carried on against them. Their only apprehension arose from the fickle minds of the plebeians, who, becoming weary of the siege, would have more consideration of their own danger than of other's liberty, and would thus compel them to submit to some disgraceful and ruinous capitulation. In order to animate them to defense, they were assembled in the public piazza, and some of the eldest and most esteemed of the citizens addressed them in the following terms: "You are doubtless aware that what is done from necessity involves neither censure nor applause; therefore, if you should accuse us of having caused the present war, by receiving the ducal forces into the city, and allowing them to commit hostilities against the Florentines, you are greatly mistaken. You are well acquainted with the ancient enmity of the Florentines against you, which is not occasioned by any injuries you have done them, or by fear on their part, but by our weakness and their own ambition; for the one gives them hope of being able to oppress us, and the other incites them to attempt it. It is then vain to imagine that any merit of yours can extinguish that desire in them, or that any offense you can commit, can provoke them to greater animosity. They endeavor to deprive you of your liberty; you must resolve to defend it; and whatever they may undertake against us for that purpose, although we may lament, we need not wonder. We may well grieve, therefore, that they attack us, take possession of our towns, burn our houses, and waste our country. But who is so simple as to be surprised at it? for were it in our power, we should do just the same to them, or even worse. They declare war against us now, they say, for having received Niccolo; but if we had not received him, they would have done the same and assigned some other ground for it; and if the evil had been delayed, it would most probably have been greater. Therefore, you must not imagine it to be occasioned by his arrival, but rather by your own ill fortune and their ambition; for we could not have refused admission to the duke's forces, and, being come, we could not prevent their aggressions. You know, that without the aid of some powerful ally we are incapable of self-defense, and that none can render us this service more powerfully or faithfully than the duke. He restored our liberty; it is reasonable to expect he will defend it. He has always been the greatest foe of our inveterate enemies; if, therefore, to avoid incensing the Florentines we had excited his anger, we should have lost our best friend, and rendered our enemy more powerful and more disposed to oppress us; so that it is far preferable to have this war upon our hands, and enjoy the favor of the duke, than to be in peace without it. Besides, we are justified in expecting that he will rescue us from the dangers into which we are brought on his account, if we only do not abandon our own cause. You all know how fiercely the Florentines have frequently assailed us, and with what glory we have maintained our defense. We have often been deprived of every hope, except in God and the casualties which time might produce, and both have proved our friends. And as they have delivered us formerly, why should they not continue to do so. Then we were forsaken by the whole of Italy; now we have the duke in our favor; besides we have a right to suppose that the Venetians will not hastily attack us; for they will not willingly see the power of Florence increased. On a former occasion the Florentines were more at liberty; they had greater hope of assistance, and were more powerful in themselves, while we were in every respect weaker; for then a tyrant governed us, now we defend ourselves; then the glory of our defense was another's, now it is our own; then they were in harmony, now they are disunited, all Italy being filled with their banished citizens. But were we without the hope which these favorable circumstances present, our extreme necessity should make us firmly resolved on our defense. It is reasonable to fear every enemy, for all seek their own glory and your ruin; above all others, you have to dread the Florentines, for they would not be satisfied by submission and tribute, or the dominion of our city, but they would possess our entire substance and persons, that they might satiate their cruelty with our blood, and their avarice with our property, so that all ranks ought to dread them. Therefore do not be troubled at seeing our crops destroyed, our towns burned, our fortresses occupied; for if we preserve the city, the rest will be saved as a matter of course; if we lose her, all else would be of no advantage to us; for while retaining our liberty, the enemy can hold them only with the greatest difficulty, while losing it they would be preserved in vain. Arm, therefore; and when in the fight, remember that the reward of victory will be safety, not only to your country, but to your homes, your wives, and your children." The speaker's last words were received with the utmost enthusiasm by the people, who promised one and all to die rather than abandon their cause, or submit to any terms that could violate their liberty. They then made arrangements for the defense of the city.

In the meantime, the Florentine forces were not idle; and after innumerable mischiefs done to the country took Monte Carlo by capitulation. They then besieged Uzzano, in order that the Lucchese, being pressed on all sides, might despair of assistance, and be compelled to submission by famine. The fortress was very strong, and defended by a numerous garrison, so that its capture would be by no means an easy undertaking. The Lucchese, as might be expected, seeing the imminent peril of their situation, had recourse to the duke, and employed prayers and remonstrances to induce him to render them aid. They enlarged upon their own merits and the offenses of the Florentines; and showed how greatly it would attach the duke's friends to him to find they were defended, and how much disaffection it would spread among them, if they were left to be overwhelmed by the enemy; that if they lost their liberties and their lives, he would lose his honor and his friends, and forfeit the confidence of all who from affection might be induced to incur dangers in his behalf; and added tears to entreaties, so that if he were unmoved by gratitude to them, he might be induced to their defense by motives of compassion. The duke, influenced by his inveterate hostility against the Florentines, his new obligation to the Lucchese, and, above all, by his desire to prevent so great an acquisition from falling into the hands of his ancient enemies, determined either to send a strong force into Tuscany, or vigorously to assail the Venetians, so as to compel the Florentines to give up their enterprise and go to their relief.

It was soon known in Florence that the duke was preparing to send forces into Tuscany. This made the Florentines apprehensive for the success of their enterprise; and in order to retain the duke in Lombardy, they requested the Venetians to press him with their utmost strength. But they also were alarmed, the marquis of Mantua having abandoned them and gone over to the duke; and thus, finding themselves almost defenseless, they replied, "that instead of increasing their responsibilities, they should be unable to perform their part in the war, unless the Count Francesco were sent to them to take the command of the army, and with the special understanding that he should engage to cross the Po in person. They declined to fulfil their former engagements unless he were bound to do so; for they could not carry on the war without a leader, or repose confidence in any except the count; and he himself would be useless to them, unless he came under an obligation to carry on the war whenever they might think needful." The Florentines thought the war ought to be pushed vigorously in Lombardy; but they saw that if they lost the count their enterprise against Lucca was ruined; and they knew well that the demand of the Venetians arose less from any need they had of the count, than from their desire to frustrate this expedition. The count, on the other hand, was ready to pass into Lombardy whenever the league might require him, but would not alter the tenor of his engagement; for he was unwilling to sacrifice the hope of the alliance promised to him by the duke.

The Florentines were thus embarrassed by two contrary impulses, the wish to possess Lucca, and the dread of a war with Milan. As commonly happens, fear was the most powerful, and they consented, after the capture of Uzzano, that the count should go into Lombardy. There still remained another difficulty, which, depending on circumstances beyond the reach of their influence, created more doubts and uneasiness than the former; the count would not consent to pass the Po, and the Venetians refused to accept him on any other condition. Seeing no other method of arrangement, than that each should make liberal concessions, the Florentines induced the count to cross the river by a letter addressed to the Signory of Florence, intimating that this private promise did not invalidate any public engagement, and that he might still refrain from crossing; hence it resulted that the Venetians, having commenced the war, would be compelled to proceed, and that the evil apprehended by the Florentines would be averted. To the Venetians, on the other hand, they averred that this private letter was sufficiently binding, and therefore they ought to be content; for if they could save the count from breaking with his father-in-law, it was well to do so, and that it could be of no advantage either to themselves or the Venetians to publish it without some manifest necessity. It was thus determined that the count should pass into Lombardy; and having taken Uzzano, and raised bastions about Lucca to restrain in her inhabitants, placed the management of the siege in the hands of the commissaries, crossed the Apennines, and proceeded to Reggio, when the Venetians, alarmed at his progress, and in order to discover his intentions, insisted upon his immediately crossing the Po, and joining the other forces. The count refused compliance, and many mutual recriminations took place between him and Andrea Mauroceno, their messenger on this occasion, each charging the other with arrogance and treachery: after many protestations, the one of being under no obligation to perform that service, and the other of not being bound to any payment, they parted, the count to return to Tuscany, the other to Venice.

The Florentines had sent the count to encamp in the Pisan territory, and were in hopes of inducing him to renew the war against the Lucchese, but found him indisposed to do so, for the duke, having been informed that out of regard to him he had refused to cross the Po, thought that by this means he might also save the Lucchese, and begged the count to endeavor to effect an accommodation between the Florentines and the Lucchese, including himself in it, if he were able, declaring, at the same time, the promised marriage should be solemnized whenever he thought proper. The prospect of this connection had great influence with the count, for, as the duke had no sons, it gave him hope of becoming sovereign of Milan. For this reason he gradually abated his exertions in the war, declared he would not proceed unless the Venetians fulfilled their engagement as to the payment, and also retained him in the command; that the discharge of the debt would not alone be sufficient, for desiring to live peaceably in his own dominions, he needed some alliance other than that of the Florentines, and that he must regard his own interests, shrewdly hinting that if abandoned by the Venetians, he would come to terms with the duke.

These indirect and crafty methods of procedure were highly offensive to the Florentines, for they found their expedition against Lucca frustrated, and trembled for the safety of their own territories if ever the count and the duke should enter into a mutual alliance. To induce the Venetians to retain the count in the command, Cosmo de' Medici went to Venice, hoping his influence would prevail with them, and discussed the subject at great length before the senate, pointing out the condition of the Italian states, the disposition of their armies, and the great preponderance possessed by the duke. He concluded by saying, that if the count and the duke were to unite their forces, they (the Venetians) might return to the sea, and the Florentines would have to fight for their liberty. To this the Venetians replied, that they were acquainted with their own strength and that of the Italians, and thought themselves able at all events to provide for their own defense; that it was not their custom to pay soldiers for serving others; that as the Florentines had used the count's services, they must pay him themselves; with respect to the security of their own states, it was rather desirable to check the count's pride than to pay him, for the ambition of men is boundless, and if he were now paid without serving, he would soon make some other demand, still more unreasonable and dangerous. It therefore seemed necessary to curb his insolence, and not allow it to increase till it became incorrigible; and that if the Florentines, from fear or any other motive, wished to preserve his friendship, they must pay him themselves. Cosmo returned without having effected any part of his object.

The Florentines used the weightiest arguments they could adopt to prevent the count from quitting the service of the League, a course he was himself reluctant to follow, but his desire to conclude the marriage so embarrassed him, that any trivial accident would have been sufficient to determine his course, as indeed shortly happened. The count had left his territories in La Marca to the care of Il Furlano, one of his principal condottieri, who was so far influenced by the duke as to take command under him, and quit the count's service. This circumstance caused the latter to lay aside every idea but that of his own safety, and to come to agreement with the duke; among the terms of which compact was one that he should not be expected to interfere in the affairs of Romagna and Tuscany. The count then urged the Florentines to come to terms with the Lucchese, and so convinced them of the necessity of this, that seeing no better course to adopt, they complied in April, 1438, by which treaty the Lucchese retained their liberty, and the Florentines Monte Carlo and a few other fortresses. After this, being full of exasperation, they despatched letters to every part of Italy, overcharged with complaints, affecting to show that since God and men were averse to the Lucchese coming under their dominion, they had made peace with them. And it seldom happens that any suffer so much for the loss of their own lawful property as they did because they could not obtain the possessions of others.

Though the Florentines had now so many affairs in hand, they did not allow the proceedings of their neighbors to pass unnoticed, or neglect the decoration of their city. As before observed, Niccolo Fortebraccio was dead. He had married a daughter of the Count di Poppi, who, at the decease of his son-in-law, held the Borgo San Sepolcro, and other fortresses of that district, and while Niccolo lived, governed them in his name. Claiming them as his daughter's portion, he refused to give them up to the pope, who demanded them as property held of the church, and who, upon his refusal, sent the patriarch with forces to take possession of them. The count, finding himself unable to sustain the attack, offered them to the Florentines, who declined them; but the pope having returned to Florence, they interceded with him in the count's behalf. Difficulties arising, the patriarch attacked the Casentino, took Prato Vecchio, and Romena, and offered them also to the Florentines, who refused them likewise, unless the pope would consent they should restore them to the count, to which, after much hesitation, he acceded, on condition that the Florentines should prevail with the Count di Poppi to restore the Borgo to him. The pope was thus satisfied, and the Florentines having so far completed the building of their cathedral church of Santa Reparata, which had been commenced long ago, as to enable them to perform divine service in it, requested his holiness to consecrate it. To this the pontiff willingly agreed, and the Florentines, to exhibit the wealth of the city and the splendor of the edifice, and do greater honor to the pope, erected a platform from Santa Maria Novella, where he resided, to the cathedral he was about to consecrate, six feet in height and twelve feet wide, covered with rich drapery, for the accommodation of the pontiff and his court, upon which they proceeded to the building, accompanied by those civic magistrates, and other officers who were appointed to take part in the procession. The usual ceremonies of consecration having been completed, the pope, to show his affection for the city, conferred the honor of knighthood upon Giuliano Davanzati, their Gonfalonier of Justice, and a citizen of the highest reputation; and the Signory, not to appear less gracious than the pope, granted to the new created knight the government of Pisa for one year.

There were at that time certain differences between the Roman and the Greek churches, which prevented perfect conformity in divine service; and at the last council of Bale, the prelates of the Western church having spoken at great length upon the subject, it was resolved that efforts should be made to bring the emperor and the Greek prelates to the council at Bale, to endeavor to reconcile the Greek church with the Roman. Though this resolution was derogatory to the majesty of the Greek empire, and offensive to its clergy, yet being then oppressed by the Turks, and fearing their inability for defense, in order to have a better ground for requesting assistance, they submitted; and therefore, the emperor, the patriarch, with other prelates and barons of Greece, to comply with the resolution of the council, assembled at Bale, came to Venice; but being terrified by the plague then prevailing, it was

resolved to terminate their differences at Florence. The Roman and Greek prelates having held a conference during several days, in which many long discussions took place, the Greeks yielded, and agreed to adopt the ritual of the church of Rome.

Chapter IV: New wars in Italy—Niccolo Piccinino, in concert with the duke of Milan, deceives the pope, and takes many places from the church—Niccolo attacks the Venetians—Fears and precautions of the Florentines—The Venetians request assistance of the Florentines and of Sforza—League against the duke of Milan—The Florentines resolve to send the count to assist the Venetians—Neri di Gino Capponi at Venice—His discourse to the senate—Extreme joy of the Venetians.

Peace being restored between the Lucchese and Florentines, and the duke and the count having become friends, hopes were entertained that the arms of Italy would be laid aside, although those in the kingdom of Naples, between Rene of Anjou and Alfonso of Aragon, could find repose only by the ruin of one party or the other. And though the pope was dissatisfied with the loss of so large a portion of his territories, and the ambition of the duke and the Venetians was obvious, still it was thought that the pontiff, from necessity, and the others from weariness, would be advocates of peace. However, a different state of feeling prevailed, for neither the duke nor the Venetians were satisfied with their condition; so that hostilities were resumed, and Lombardy and Tuscany were again harassed by the horrors of war. The proud mind of the duke could not endure that the Venetians should possess Bergamo and Brescia, and he was still further annoyed, by hearing, that they were constantly in arms, and in the daily practice of annoying some portion of his territories. He thought, however, that he should not only be able to restrain them, but to recover the places he had lost, if the pope, the Florentines, and the count could be induced to forego the Venetian alliance. He therefore resolved to take Romagna from the pontiff, imagining that his holiness could not injure him, and that the Florentines, finding the conflagration so near, either for their own sake would refrain from interference, or if they did not, could not conveniently attack him. The duke was also aware of the resentment of the Florentines against the Venetians, on account of the affair of Lucca, and he therefore judged they would be the less eager to take arms against him on their behalf. With regard to the Count Francesco, he trusted that their new friendship, and the hope of his alliance would keep him quiet. To give as little color as possible for complaint, and to lull suspicion, particularly, because in consequence of his treaty with the count, the latter could not attack Romagna, he ordered Niccolo Piccinino, as if instigated by his own ambition to do so.

When the agreement between the duke and the count was concluded, Niccolo was in Romagna, and in pursuance of his instructions from the duke, affected to be highly incensed, that a connection had been established between him and the count, his inveterate enemy. He therefore withdrew himself and his forces to Camurata, a place between Furli and Ravenna, which he fortified, as if designing to remain there some time, or till a new enterprise should present itself. The report of his resentment being diffused, Niccolo gave the pope to understand how much the duke was under obligation to him, and how ungrateful he proved; and he was persuaded that, possessing nearly all the arms of Italy, under the two principal generals, he could render himself sole ruler: but if his holiness pleased, of the two principal generals whom he fancied he possessed, one would become his enemy, and the other be rendered useless; for, if money were provided him, and he were kept in pay, he would attack the territories held of the church by the count, who being compelled to look to his own interests, could not subserve the ambition of Filippo. The pope giving entire credence to this representation, on account of its apparent reasonableness, sent Niccolo five thousand ducats and loaded him with promises of states for himself and his children. And though many informed him of the deception, he could not give credit to them, nor would he endure the conversation of any who seemed to doubt the integrity of Niccolo's professions. The city of Ravenna was held for the church by Ostasio da Polenta. Niccolo finding further delay would be detrimental, since his son Francesco had, to the pope's great dishonor, pillaged Spoleto, determined to attack Ravenna, either because he judged the enterprise easy, or because he had a secret understanding with Ostasio, for in a few days after the attack, the place capitulated. He then took Bologna, Imola, and Furli; and (what is worthy of remark) of twenty fortresses held in that country for the pope, not one escaped falling into his hands. Not satisfied with these injuries inflicted on the pontiff, he resolved to banter him by his words as well as ridicule him by his deeds, and wrote, that he had only done as his holiness deserved, for having unblushingly attempted to divide two such attached friends as the duke and himself, and for having dispersed over Italy letters intimating that he had quitted the duke to take part with the Venetians. Having taken possession of Romagna, Niccolo left it under the charge of his son, Francesco, and with the greater part of his troops, went into Lombardy, where joining the remainder of the duke's forces, he attacked the country about Brescia, and having soon completely conquered it, besieged the city itself.

The duke, who desired the Venetians to be left defenseless, excused himself to the pope, the Florentines, and the count, saying, that if the doings of Niccolo were contrary to the terms of the treaty, they were equally contrary to his wishes, and by secret messengers, assured them that when an occasion presented itself, he would give them a convincing proof that they had been performed in disobedience to his instructions. Neither the count nor the Florentines believed him, but thought, with reason, that these enterprises had been carried on to keep them at bay, till he had subdued the Venetians, who, being full of pride, and thinking themselves able alone to resist the duke, had not deigned to ask for any assistance, but carried on the war under their captain, Gattamelata.

Count Francesco would have wished, with the consent of the Florentines, to go to the assistance of king Rene, if the events of Romagna and Lombardy had not hindered him; and the Florentines would willingly have consented, from their ancient friendship to the French dynasty, but the duke was entirely in favor of Alfonso. Each being engaged in wars near home, refrained from distant undertakings. The Florentines, finding Romagna occupied with the duke's forces, and the Venetians defeated, as if foreseeing their own ruin in that of others, entreated the count to come to Tuscany, where they might consider what should be done to resist Filippo's power, which was now greater than it had ever before been; assuring him that if his insolence were not in some way curbed, all the powers of Italy would soon have to submit to him. The count felt the force of the fears entertained by the Florentines, but his desire to secure the duke's alliance kept him in suspense; and the duke, aware of this desire, gave him the greatest assurance that his hopes would be realized as shortly as possible, if he abstained from hostilities against him. As the lady was now of marriageable age, the duke had frequently made all suitable preparations for the celebration of the ceremony, but on one pretext or another they had always been wholly set aside. He now, to give the count greater confidence, added deeds to his words, and sent him thirty thousand florins, which, by the terms of the marriage contract, he had engaged to pay.

Still the war in Lombardy proceeded with greater vehemence than ever; the Venetians constantly suffered fresh losses of territory, and the fleets they equipped upon the rivers were taken by the duke's forces; the country around Verona and Brescia was entirely occupied, and the two cities themselves so pressed, that their speedy fall was generally anticipated. The marquis of Mantua, who for many years had led the forces of their republic, quite unexpectedly resigned his command, and went over to the duke's service. Thus the course which pride prevented them from adopting at the commencement of the war, fear compelled them to take during its progress; for knowing there was no help for them but in the friendship of the Florentines and the count, they began to make overtures to obtain it, though with shame and apprehension; for they were afraid of receiving a reply similar to that which they had given the Florentines, when the latter applied for assistance in the enterprise against Lucca and the count's affairs. However, they found the Florentines more easily induced to render aid than they expected, or their conduct deserved; so much more were the former swayed by hatred of their ancient enemy, than by resentment of the ingratitude of their old and habitual friends. Having foreseen the necessity into which the Venetians must come, they had informed the count that their ruin must involve his own; that he was deceived if he thought the duke, while fortune, would esteem him more than if he were in adversity; that the duke was induced to promise him his daughter by the fear he entertained of him; that what necessity occasions to be promised, it also causes to be performed; and it was therefore desirable to keep the duke in that necessity, which could be done without supporting the power of the Venetians. Therefore he might perceive, that if the Venetians were compelled to abandon their inland territories, he would not only lose the advantages derivable from them, but also those to be obtained from such as feared them; and that if he considered well the powers of Italy, he would see that some were poor, and others hostile; that the Florentines alone were not, as he had often said, sufficient for his support; so that on every account it was best to keep the Venetians powerful by land. These arguments, conjoined with the hatred which the count had conceived against Filippo, by supposing himself duped with regard to the promised alliance, induced him to consent to a new treaty; but still he would not consent to cross the Po. The agreement was concluded in February, 1438; the Venetians agreeing to pay two-thirds of the expense of the war, the Florentines one-third, and each engaging to defend the states which the count possessed in La Marca. Nor were these the only forces of the league, for the lord of Faenza, the sons of Pandolfo Malatesti da Rimino and Pietro Giampagolo Orsini also joined them. They endeavored, by very liberal offers, to gain over the marquis of Mantua, but could not prevail against the friendship and stipend of the duke; and the lord of Faenza, after having entered into compact with the league, being tempted by more advantageous terms, went over to him. This made them despair of being able to effect an early settlement of the troubles of Romagna.

The affairs of Lombardy were in this condition: Brescia was so closely besieged by the duke's forces, that constant apprehensions were entertained of her being compelled by famine to a surrender; while Verona was so pressed, that a similar fate was expected to await her, and if one of these cities were lost, all the other preparations for the war might be considered useless, and the expenses already incurred as completely wasted. For this there was no remedy, but to send the count into Lombardy; and to this measure three obstacles presented themselves. The first was, to induce him to cross the Po, and prosecute the war in whatever locality might be found most advisable; the second, that the count being at a distance, the Florentines would be left almost at the mercy of the duke, who, issuing from any of his fortresses, might with part of his troops keep the count at bay, and with the rest introduce into Tuscany the Florentine exiles, whom the existing government already dreaded; the third was, to determine what route the count should take to arrive safely in the Paduan territory, and join the Venetian forces. Of these three difficulties, the second, which particularly regarded the Florentines, was the most serious;

but, knowing the necessity of the case, and wearied out by the Venetians, who with unceasing importunity demanded the count, intimating that without him they should abandon all hope, they resolved to relieve their allies rather than listen to the suggestions of their own fears. There still remained the question about the route to be taken, for the safety of which they determined the Venetians should provide; and as they had sent Neri Capponi to treat with the count and induce him to cross the Po, they determined that the same person should also proceed to Venice, in order to make the benefit the more acceptable to the Signory, and see that all possible security were given to the passage of the forces.

Neri embarked at Cesena and went to Venice; nor was any prince ever received with so much honor as he was; for upon his arrival, and the matters which his intervention was to decide and determine, the safety of the republic seemed to depend. Being introduced to the senate, and in presence of the Doge, he said, "The Signory of Florence, most serene prince, has always perceived in the duke's greatness the source of ruin both to this republic and our own, and that the safety of both states depends upon their separate strength and mutual confidence. If such had been the opinion of this illustrious Signory, we should ourselves have been in better condition, and your republic would have been free from the dangers that now threaten it. But as at the proper crisis you withheld from us confidence and aid, we could not come to the relief of your distress, nor could you, being conscious of this, freely ask us; for neither in your prosperity nor adversity have you clearly perceived our motives. You have not observed, that those whose deeds have once incurred our hatred, can never become entitled to our regard; nor can those who have once merited our affection ever after absolutely cancel their claim. Our attachment to your most serene Signory is well known to you all, for you have often seen Lombardy filled with our forces and our money for your assistance. Our hereditary enmity to Filippo and his house is universally known, and it is impossible that love or hatred, strengthened by the growth of years, can be eradicated from our minds by any recent act either of kindness or neglect. We have always thought, and are still of the same opinion, that we might now remain neutral, greatly to the duke's satisfaction, and with little hazard to ourselves; for if by your ruin he were to become lord of Lombardy, we should still have sufficient influence in Italy in free us from any apprehension on our own account; for every increase of power and territory augments that animosity and envy, from which arise wars and the dismemberment of states. We are also aware what heavy expenses and imminent perils we should avoid, by declining to involve ourselves in these disputes; and how easily the field of battle may be transferred from Lombardy to Tuscany, by our interference in your behalf. Yet all these apprehensions are at once overborne by our ancient affection for the senate and people of Venice, and we have resolved to come to your relief with the same zeal with which we should have armed in our own defense, had we been attacked. Therefore, the senate of Florence, judging it primarily necessary to relieve Verona and Brescia, and thinking this impossible without the count, have sent me, in the first instance, to persuade him to pass into Lombardy, and carry on the war wherever it may be most needful; for you are aware he is under no obligation to cross the Po. To induce him to do so, I have advanced such arguments as are suggested by the circumstances themselves, and which would prevail with us. He, being invincible in arms, cannot be surpassed in courtesy, and the liberality he sees the Florentines exercise toward you, he has resolved to outdo; for he is well aware to what dangers Tuscany will be exposed after his departure, and since we have made your affairs our primary consideration, he has also resolved to make his own subservient to yours. I come, therefore, to tender his services, with seven thousand cavalry and two thousand infantry, ready at once to march against the enemy, wherever he may be. And I beg of you, so do my lords at Florence and the count, that as his forces exceed the number he has engaged to furnish you, out of your liberality, would remunerate him, that he may not repent of having come to your assistance, nor we, who have prevailed with him to do so." This discourse of Neri to the senate was listened to with that profound attention which an oracle might be imagined to command; and his audience were so moved by it, that they could not restrain themselves, till the prince had replied, as strict decorum on such occasions required, but rising from their seats, with uplifted hands, and most of them with tears in their eyes, they thanked the Florentines for their generous conduct, and the ambassador for his unusual dispatch; and promised that time should never cancel the remembrance of such goodness, either in their own hearts, or their children's; and that their country, thenceforth, should be common to the Florentines with themselves.

Chapter V: Francesco Sforza marches to assist the Venetians, and relieves Verona—He attempts to relieve Brescia but fails—The Venetians routed by Piccinino upon the Lake of Garda—Piccinino routed by Sforza; the method of his escape—Piccinino surprises Verona—Description of Verona—Recovered by Sforza—The duke of Milan makes war against the Florentines—Apprehensions of the Florentines—Cardinal Vitelleschi their enemy.

When their demonstrations of gratitude had subsided, the Venetian senate, by the aid of Neri di Gino, began to consider the route the count ought to take, and how to provide him with necessaries. There were four several roads; one by Ravenna, along the beach, which on account of its being in many places interrupted by the sea and by marshes, was not approved. The next was the most direct, but rendered inconvenient by a tower called the Uccellino, which being held for the duke, it would be necessary to capture; and to do this, would occupy more time than could be spared with safety to Verona and Brescia. The third was by the brink of the lake; but as the Po had overflowed its banks, to pass in this direction was impossible. The fourth was by the way of Bologna to Ponte Puledrano, Cento, and Pieve; then between the Bondeno and the Finale to Ferrara, and thence they might by land or water enter the Paduan territory, and join the Venetian forces. This route, though attended with many difficulties, and in some parts liable to be disputed by the enemy, was chosen as the least objectionable. The count having received his instructions, commenced his march, and by exerting the utmost celerity, reached the Paduan territory on the twentieth of June. The arrival of this distinguished commander in Lombardy filled Venice and all her dependencies with hope; for the Venetians, who only an instant before had been in fear for their very existence, began to contemplate new conquests.

The count, before he made any other attempt, hastened to the relief of Verona; and to counteract his design, Niccolo led his forces to Soave, a castle situated between the Vincentino and the Veronese, and entrenched himself by a ditch that extended from Soave to the marshes of the Adige. The count, finding his passage by the plain cut off, resolved to proceed by the mountains, and thus reach Verona, thinking Niccolo would imagine this way to be so rugged and elevated as to be impracticable, or if he thought otherwise, he would not be in time to prevent him; so, with provisions for eight days, he took the mountain path, and with his forces, arrived in the plain, below Soave. Niccolo had, even upon this route, erected some bastions for the purpose of preventing him, but they were insufficient for the purpose; and finding the enemy had, contrary to his expectations, effected a passage, to avoid a disadvantageous engagement he crossed to the opposite side of the Adige, and the count entered Verona without opposition.

Having happily succeeded in his first project, that of relieving Verona, the count now endeavored to render a similar service to Brescia. This city is situated so close to the Lake of Garda, that although besieged by land, provisions may always be sent into it by water. On this account the duke had assembled a large force in the immediate vicinity of the lake, and at the commencement of his victories occupied all the places which by its means might relieve Brescia. The Venetians also had galleys upon the lake, but they were unequal to a contest with those of the duke. The count therefore deemed it advisable to aid the Venetian fleet with his land forces, by which means he hoped to obtain without much difficulty those places which kept Brescia in blockade. He therefore encamped before Bardolino, a fortress situated upon the lake, trusting that after it was taken the others would surrender. But fortune opposed this design, for a great part of his troops fell sick; so, giving up the enterprise, he went to Zevio, a Veronese castle, in a healthy and plentiful situation. Niccolo, upon the count's retreat, not to let slip an opportunity of making himself master of the lake, left his camp at Vegasio, and with a body of picked men took the way thither, attacked the Venetian fleet with the utmost impetuosity, and took nearly the whole of it. By this victory almost all the fortresses upon the lake fell into his hands.

The Venetians, alarmed at this loss, and fearing that in consequence of it Brescia would surrender, solicited the count, by letters and messengers, to go to its relief; and he, perceiving that all hope of rendering assistance from the lake was cut off, and that to attempt an approach by land, on account of the ditches, bastions, and other defenses erected by Niccolo, was marching to certain destruction, determined that as the passage by the mountains had enabled him to relieve Verona, it should also contribute to the preservation of Brescia. Having taken this resolution, the count left Zevio, and by way of the Val d'Acri went to the Lake of St. Andrea, and thence to Torboli and Peneda, upon the Lake of Garda. He then proceeded to Tenna, and besieged the fortress, which it was necessary to occupy before he could reach Brescia.

Niccolo, on being acquainted with the count's design, led his army to Peschiera. He then, with the marquis of Mantua and a chosen body of men, went to meet him, and coming to an engagement, was routed, his people dispersed, and many of them taken, while others fled to the fleet, and some to the main body of his army. It was now nightfall, and Niccolo had escaped to Tenna, but he knew that if he were to remain there till morning, he must inevitably fall into the enemy's hands; therefore, to avoid a catastrophe which might be regarded as almost fatal, he resolved to make a dangerous experiment. Of all his attendants he had only with him a single servant, a Dutchman, of great personal strength, and who had always been devotedly attached to him. Niccolo induced this man to take him upon his shoulders in a sack, as if he had been carrying property of his master's, and to bear him to a place of security. The enemy's lines surrounded Tenna, but on account of the previous day's victory, all was in disorder, and no guard was kept, so that the Dutchman, disguised as a trooper, passed through them without any opposition, and brought his master in safety to his own troops.

Had this victory been as carefully improved as it was fortunately obtained, Brescia would have derived from it greater relief and the Venetians more permanent advantage; but they, having thoughtlessly let it slip, the rejoicings were soon over, and Brescia remained in her former difficulties. Niccolo, having returned to his forces, resolved by some extraordinary exertion to cancel the impression of his death, and deprive the Venetians of the change of relieving Brescia. He was acquainted with the topography of the citadel of Verona, and had learned from prisoners whom he had taken, that it was badly guarded, and might be very easily recovered. He perceived at once that fortune presented him with an opportunity of regaining the laurels he had lately lost, and of changing the joy of the enemy for their recent victory into sorrow for a succeeding disaster. The city of Verona is situated in Lombardy, at the foot of the mountains which divide Italy from Germany, so that it occupies part both of hill and plain. The river Adige rises in the valley of Trento, and entering Italy, does not immediately traverse the country, but winding to the left, along the base of the hills, enters Verona, and crosses the city, which it divides unequally, giving much the larger portion to the plain. On the mountain side of the river are two fortresses, formidable rather from their situation than from their actual strength, for being very elevated they command the whole place. One is called San Piero, the other San Felice. On the opposite side of the Adige, upon the plain, with their backs against the city walls, are two other fortresses, about a mile distant from each other, one called the Old the other the New Citadel, and a wall extends between them that may be compared to a bowstring, of which the city wall is the arc. The space comprehended within this segment is very populous, and is called the Borgo of St. Zeno. Niccolo Piccinino designed to capture these fortresses and the Borgo, and he hoped to succeed without much difficulty, as well on account of the ordinary negligence of the guard, which their recent successes would probably increase, as because in war no enterprise is more likely to be successful than one which by the enemy is deemed impossible. With a body of picked men, and accompanied by the marquis of Mantua, he proceeded by night to Verona, silently scaled the walls, and took the New Citadel: then entering the place with his troops, he forced the gate of S. Antonio, and introduced the whole of his cavalry. The Venetian garrison of the Old Citadel hearing an uproar, when the guards of the New were slaughtered, and again when the gate was forced, being now aware of the presence of enemies, raised an alarm, and called the people to arms. The citizens awaking in the utmost confusion, some of the boldest armed and hastened to the rector's piazza. In the meantime, Niccolo's forces had pillaged the Borgo of San Zeno; and proceeding onward were ascertained by the people to be the duke's forces, but being defenseless they advised the Venetian rectors to take refuge in the fortresses, and thus save themselves and the place; as it was more advisable to preserve their lives and so rich a city for better fortune, than by endeavoring to repel the present evil, encounter certain death, and incur universal pillage. Upon this the rectors and all the Venetian party, fled to the fortress of San Felice. Some of the first citizens, anxious to avoid being plundered by the troops, presented themselves before Niccolo and the marquis of Mantua, and begged they would rather take possession of a rich city, with honor to themselves, than of a poor one to their own disgrace; particularly as they had not induced either the favor of its former possessors, or the animosity of its present masters, by self-defense. The marquis and Niccolo encouraged them, and protected their property to the utmost of their power during such a state of military license. As they felt sure the count would endeavor to recover the city, they made every possible exertion to gain possession of the fortresses, and those they could not seize they cut off from the rest of the place by ditches and barricades, so that the enemy might be shut out.

The Count Francesco was with his army at Tenna; and when the report was first brought to him he refused to credit it; but being assured of the fact by parties whom it would have been ridiculous to doubt, he resolved, by the exertion of uncommon celerity, to repair the evil negligence had occasioned; and though all his officers advised the abandonment of Verona and Brescia, and a march to Vicenza, lest he might be besieged by the enemy in his present situation, he refused, but resolved to attempt the recovery of Verona. During the consultation, he turned to the Venetian commissaries and to Bernardo de' Medici, who was there as commissary for the Florentines, and promised them the recovery of the place if one of the fortresses should hold out. Having collected his forces, he proceeded with the utmost speed to Verona. Observing his approach, Niccolo thought he designed, according to the advice he had received, to go to Vicenza, but finding him continue to draw near, and taking the direction of San Felice, he prepared for its defense—though too late; for the barricades were not completed; his men were dispersed in quest of plunder, or extorting money from the inhabitants by way of ransom; and he could not collect them in time to prevent the count's troops from entering the fortress. They then descended into the city, which they happily recovered, to Niccolo's disgrace, and with the loss of great numbers of his men. He himself, with the marquis of Mantua, first took refuge in the citadel, and thence escaping into the country, fled to Mantua, where, having assembled the relics of their army, they hastened to join those who were at the siege of Brescia. Thus in four days Verona was lost and again recovered from the duke. The count, after this victory, it being now winter and the weather very severe, having first with considerable difficulty thrown provisions into Brescia, went into quarters at Verona, and ordered, that during the cold season, galleys should be provided at Torboli, that upon the return of spring, they might be in a condition to proceed vigorously to effect the permanent relief of Brescia.

The duke, finding the war suspended for a time, the hope he had entertained of occupying Brescia and Verona annihilated, and the money and counsels of the Florentines the cause of this, and seeing that neither the injuries they had received from the Venetians could alienate them, nor all the promises he had made attach them to himself, he determined, in order to make them feel more closely the effects of the course they had adopted, to attack Tuscany; to which he was strenuously advised by the Florentine exiles and Niccolo. The latter advocated this from his desire to recover the states of Braccio, and expel the count from La Marca; the former, from their wish to return home, and each by suitable arguments endeavored to induce the duke to follow the plan congenial to their own views. Niccolo argued that he might be sent into Tuscany, and continue the siege of Brescia; for he was master of the lake, the fortresses were well provided, and their officers were qualified to oppose the count should he undertake any fresh enterprise; which it was not likely he would do without first relieving Brescia, a thing impossible; and thus the duke might carry on the war in Tuscany, without giving up his attempts in Lombardy; intimating that the Florentines would be compelled, as soon as he entered Tuscany, to recall the count to avoid complete ruin; and whatever course they took, victory to the duke must be the result. The exiles affirmed, that if Niccolo with his army were to approach Florence, the people oppressed with taxes, and wearied out by the insolence of the great, would most assuredly not oppose him, and pointed out the facility of reaching Florence; for the way by the Casentino would be open to them, through the friendship of Rinaldo and the Count di Poppi; and thus the duke, who was previously inclined to the attempt, was induced by their joint persuasions to make it. The Venetians, on the other hand, though the winter was severe, incessantly urged the count to relieve Brescia with all his forces. The count questioned the possibility of so doing, and advised them to wait the return of spring, in the meantime strengthening their fleet as much as possible, and then assist it both by land and water. This rendered the Venetians dissatisfied; they were dilatory in furnishing provisions, and consequently many deserted from their army.

The Florentines, being informed of these transactions, became alarmed, perceiving the war threatening themselves, and the little progress made in Lombardy. Nor did the suspicion entertained by them of the troops of the church give them less uneasiness; not that the pope was their enemy, but because they saw those forces more under the sway of the patriarch, who was their greatest foe. Giovanni Vitelleschi of Corneto was at first apostolic notary, then bishop of Recanati, and afterward patriarch of Alexandria; but at last, becoming a cardinal, he was called Cardinal of Florence. He was bold and cunning; and, having obtained great influence, was appointed to command all the forces of the church, and conduct all the enterprises of the pontiff, whether in Tuscany, Romagna, the kingdom of Naples, or in Rome. Hence he acquired so much power over the pontiff, and the papal troops, that the former was afraid of commanding him, and the latter obeyed no one else. The cardinal's presence at Rome, when the report came of Niccolo's design to march into Tuscany, redoubled the fear of the Florentines; for, since Rinaldo was expelled, he had become an enemy of the republic, from finding that the arrangements made by his means were not only disregarded, but converted to Rinaldo's prejudice, and caused the laying down of arms, which had given his enemies an opportunity of banishing him. In consequence of this, the government thought it would be advisable to restore and indemnify Rinaldo, in case Niccolo came into Tuscany and were joined by him. Their apprehensions were increased by their being unable to account for Niccolo's departure from Lombardy, and his leaving one enterprise almost completed, to undertake another so entirely doubtful; which they could not reconcile with their ideas of consistency, except by supposing some new design had been adopted, or some hidden treachery intended. They communicated their fears to the pope, who was now sensible of his error in having endowed the cardinal with too much authority.

Chapter VI: The pope imprisons the cardinal and assists the Florentines—Difference of opinion between the count and the Venetians respecting the management of the war. The Florentines reconcile them—The count wishes to go into Tuscany to oppose Piccinino, but is prevented by the Venetians—Niccolo Piccinino in Tuscany—He takes Marradi, and plunders the neighborhood of Florence—Description of Marradi—Cowardice of Bartolomeo Orlandini—Brave resistance of Castel San Niccolo—San Niccolo surrenders—Piccinino attempts to take Cortona, but fails.

While the Florentines were thus anxious, fortune disclosed the means of securing themselves against the patriarch's malevolence. The republic everywhere exercised the very closest espionage over epistolary communication, in order to discover if any persons were plotting against the state. It happened that letters were intercepted at Monte Pulciano, which had been written by the patriarch to Niccolo without the pope's knowledge; and although they were written in an unusual character, and the sense so involved that no distinct idea could be extracted, the obscurity itself, and the whole aspect of the matter so alarmed the pontiff, that he resolved to seize the person of the cardinal, a duty he committed to Antonio Rido, of Padua, who had the command of the castle of St. Angelo, and who, after receiving his instructions, soon found an opportunity of carrying them into effect. The patriarch, having determined to go into Tuscany, prepared to leave Rome on the following day, and ordered the castellan to be upon the drawbridge of the fortress in the morning, for he wished to speak with him as he passed. Antonio perceived this to be the favorable moment, informed his people what they were to do, and awaited the arrival of the patriarch upon the bridge, which adjoined the building, and might for the purpose of security be raised or lowered as occasion required. The appointed time found him punctual; and Antonio, having drawn him, as if for the convenience of conversation, on to the bridge, gave a signal to his men, who immediately raised it, and in a moment the cardinal, from being a commander of armies, found himself a prisoner of the castellan. The patriarch's followers at first began to use threats, but being informed of the pope's directions they were appeased. The castellan comforting him with kind words, he replied, that "the great do not make each other prisoners to let them go again; and that those whom it is proper to take, it is not well to set free." He shortly afterward died in prison. The pope appointed Lodovico, patriarch of Aquileia, to command his troops; and, though previously unwilling to interfere in the wars of the league and the duke, he was now content to take part in them, and engaged to furnish four thousand horse and two thousand foot for the defense of Tuscany.

The Florentines, freed from this cause for anxiety, were still apprehensive of Niccolo, and feared confusion in the affairs of Lombardy, from the differences of opinion that existed between the count and the Venetians. In order the better to become acquainted with the intentions of the parties, they sent Neri di Gini Capponi and Giuliano Davanzati to Venice, with instructions to assist in the arrangement of the approaching campaign; and ordered that Neri, having discovered how the Venetians were disposed, should proceed to the count, learn his designs, and induce him to adopt the course that would be most advantageous to the League. The ambassadors had only reached Ferrara, when they were told that Niccolo Piccinino had crossed the Po with six thousand horse. This made them travel with increased speed; and, having arrived at Venice, they found the Signory fully resolved that Brescia should be relieved without waiting for the return of spring; for they said that "the city would be unable to hold out so long, the fleet could not be in readiness, and that seeing no more immediate relief, she would submit to the enemy; which would render the duke universally victorious, and cause them to lose the whole of their inland possessions." Neri then proceeded to Verona to ascertain the count's opinion, who argued, for many reasons, that to march to Brescia before the return of spring would be quite useless, or even worse; for the situation of Brescia, being considered in conjunction with the season, nothing could be expected to result but disorder and fruitless toil to the troops; so that, when the suitable period should arrive, he would be compelled to return to Verona with his army, to recover from the injuries sustained in the winter, and provide necessaries for the summer; and thus the time available for the war would be wasted in marching and countermarching. Orsatto Justiniani and Giovanni Pisani were deputed on the part of Venice to the count at Verona, having been sent to consider these affairs, and with them it was agreed that the Venetians should pay the count ninety thousand ducats for the coming year, and to each of the soldiers forty ducats; that he should set out immediately with the whole army and attack the duke, in order to compel him, for his own preservation, to recall Niccolo into Lombardy. After this agreement the ambassadors returned to Venice; and the Venetians, having so large an amount of money to raise, were very remiss with their commissariat.

In the meantime, Niccolo Piccinino pursued his route, and arrived in Romagna, where he prevailed upon the sons of Pandolfo Malatesti to desert the Venetians and enter the duke's service. This circumstance occasioned much uneasiness in Venice, and still more at Florence; for they thought that with the aid of the Malatesti they might resist Niccolo; but finding them gone over to the enemy, they were in fear lest their captain, Piero Giampagolo Orsini, who was in the territories of the Malatesti, should be disarmed and rendered powerless. The count also felt alarmed, for, through Niccolo's presence in Tuscany, he was afraid of losing La Marca; and, urged by a desire to look after his own affairs, he hastened to Venice, and being introduced to the Doge, informed him that the interests of the League required his presence in Tuscany; for the war ought to be carried on where the leader and forces of the enemy were, and not where his garrisons and towns were situated; for when the army is vanquished the war is finished; but to take towns and leave the armament entire, usually allowed the war to break out again with greater virulence; that Tuscany and La Marca would be lost if Niccolo were not vigorously resisted, and that, if lost, there would be no possibility of the preservation of Lombardy. But supposing the danger to Lombardy not so imminent, he did not intend to abandon his own subjects and friends, and that having come into Lombardy as a prince, he did not intend to return a mere condottiere. To this the Doge replied, it was quite manifest that, if he left Lombardy, or even recrossed the Po, all their inland territories would be lost; in that case they were unwilling to spend any more money in their defense. For it would be folly to attempt defending a place which must, after all, inevitably be lost; and that it is less disgraceful and less injurious to lose dominions only, then to lose both territory and money. That if the loss of their inland possessions should actually result, it would then be seen how highly important to the preservation of Romagna and Tuscany the reputation of the Venetians had been. On these accounts they were of quite a different opinion from the count; for they saw that whoever was victor in Lombardy would be so everywhere else, that conquest would be easily attainable now, when the territories of the duke were left almost defenseless by the departure of Niccolo, and that he would be ruined before he could order Niccolo's recall, or provide himself with any other remedy; that whoever attentively considered these things would see, that the duke had sent Niccolo into Tuscany for no other reason than to withdraw the count from his enterprise, and cause the war, which was now at his own door, to be removed to a greater distance. That if the count were to follow Niccolo, unless at the instigation of some very pressing necessity, he would find his plan successful, and rejoice in the adoption of it; but if he were to remain in Lombardy, and allow Tuscany to shift for herself, the duke would, when too late, see the imprudence of his conduct, and find that he had lost his territories in Lombardy and gained nothing in Tuscany. Each party having spoken, it was determined to wait a few days to see what would result from the agreement of the Malatesti with Niccolo; whether the Florentines could avail themselves of Piero Giampagolo, and whether the pope intended to join the League with all the earnestness he had promised. Not many days after these resolutions were adopted, it was ascertained that the Malatesti had made the agreement more from fear than any ill-will toward the League; that Piero Giampagolo had proceeded with his force toward Tuscany, and that the pope was more disposed than ever to assist them. This favorable intelligence dissipated the count's fears, and he consented to remain in Lombardy, and that Neri Capponi should return to Florence with a thousand of his own horse, and five hundred from the other parties. It was further agreed, that if the affairs of Tuscany should require the count's presence, Neri should write to him, and he would proceed thither to the exclusion of every other consideration. Neri arrived at Florence with his forces in April, and Giampagolo joined them the same day.

In the meantime, Niccolo Piccinino, the affairs of Romagna being settled, purposed making a descent into Tuscany, and designing to go by the mountain passes of San Benedetto and the valley of Montone, found them so well guarded by the contrivance of Niccolo da Pisa, that his utmost exertions would be useless in that direction. As the Florentines, upon this sudden attack, were unprovided with troops and officers, they had sent into the defiles of these hills many of their citizens, with infantry raised upon the emergency to guard them, among whom was Bartolomeo Orlandini, a cavaliere, to whom was intrusted the defense of the castle of Marradi and the adjacent passes. Niccolo Piccinino, finding the route by San Benedetto impracticable, on account of the bravery of its commander, thought the cowardice of the officer who defended that of Marradi would render the passage easy. Marradi is a castle situated at the foot of the mountains which separate Tuscany from Romagna; and, though destitute of walls, the river, the mountains, and the inhabitants, make it a place of great strength; for the peasantry are warlike and faithful, and the rapid current undermining the banks has left them of such tremendous height that it is impossible to approach it from the valley if a small bridge over the stream be defended; while on the mountain side the precipices are so steep and perpendicular as to render it almost impregnable. In spite of these advantages, the pusillanimity of Bartolomeo Orlandini rendered the men cowardly and the fortress untenable; for as soon as he heard of the enemy's approach he abandoned the place, fled with all his forces, and did not stop till he reached the town of San Lorenzo. Niccolo, entering the deserted fortress, wondered it had not been defended, and, rejoicing over his acquisition, descended into the valley of the Mugello, where he took some castles, and halted with his army at Pulicciano. Thence he overran the country as far as the mountains of Fiesole; and his audacity so increased that he crossed the Arno, plundering and destroying everything to within three miles of Florence.

The Florentines, however, were not dismayed. Their first concern was to give security to the government, for which they had no cause for apprehension, so universal was the good will of the people toward Cosmo; and besides this, they had restricted the principal offices to a few citizens of the highest class, who with their vigilance would have kept the populace in order, even if they had been discontented or desirous of change. They also knew by the compact made in Lombardy what forces Neri would bring with him, and expected the troops of the pope. These prospects sustained their courage till the arrival of Neri di Gino, who, on account of the disorders and fears of the city, determined to set out immediately and check Niccolo. With the cavalry he possessed, and a body of infantry raised entirely from the people, he recovered Remole from the hands of the enemy, where having encamped, he put a stop to all further depredations, and gave the inhabitants hopes of repelling the enemy from the neighborhood. Niccolo finding that, although the Florentines were without troops, no disturbance had arisen, and learning what entire composure prevailed in the city, thought he was wasting time, and resolved to undertake some other enterprise to induce them to send forces after him, and give him a chance of coming to an engagement, by means of which, if victorious, he trusted everything would succeed to his wishes.

Francesco, Count di Poppi, was in the army of Niccolo, having deserted the Florentines, with whom he was in league, when the enemy entered the Mugello; and though with the intention of securing him as soon as they had an idea of his design, they increased his appointments, and made him commissary over all the places in his vicinity; still, so powerful is the attachment to party, that no benefit or fear could eradicate the affection he bore toward Rinaldo and the late government; so that as soon as he knew Niccolo was at hand he joined him, and with the utmost solicitude entreated him to leave the city and pass into the Casentino, pointing out to him the strength of the country, and how easily he might thence harass his enemies. Niccolo followed his advice, and arriving in the Casentino, took Romena and Bibbiena, and then pitched his camp before Castel San Niccolo. This fortress is situated at the foot of the mountains which divide the Casentino from the Val d'Arno; and being in an elevated situation, and well garrisoned, it was difficult to take, though Niccolo, with catapults and other engines, assailed it without intermission. The siege had continued more than twenty days, during which the Florentines had collected all their forces, having assembled under several leaders, three thousand horse, at Fegghine, commanded by Piero Giampagolo Orsini, their captain, and Neri Capponi and Bernardo de' Medici, commissaries. Four messengers, from Castel San Niccolo, were sent to them to entreat succor. The commissaries having examined the site, found it could not be relieved, except from the Alpine regions, in the direction of the Val d'Arno, the summit of which was more easily attainable by the enemy than by themselves, on account of their greater proximity, and because the Florentines could not approach without observation; so that it would be making a desperate attempt, and might occasion the destruction of the forces. The commissaries, therefore, commended their fidelity, and ordered that when they could hold out no longer, they should surrender. Niccolo took the fortress after a siege of thirty-two days; and the loss of so much time, for the attainment of so small an advantage, was the principle cause of the failure of his expedition; for had he remained with his forces near Florence, he would have almost deprived the government of all power to compel the citizens to furnish money: nor would they so easily have assembled forces and taken other precautions, if the enemy had been close upon them, as they did while he was at a distance. Besides this, many would have been disposed to quiet their apprehensions of Niccolo, by concluding a peace; particularly, as the contest was likely to be of some duration. The desire of the Count di Poppi to avenge himself on the inhabitants of San Niccolo, long his enemies, occasioned his advice to Piccinino, who adopted it for the purpose of pleasing him; and this caused the ruin of both. It seldom happens, that the gratification of private feelings, fails to be injurious to the general convenience.

Niccolo, pursuing his good fortune, took Rassina and Chiusi. The Count di Poppi advised him to halt in these parts, arguing that he might divide his people between Chiusi, Caprese, and the Pieve, render himself master of this branch of the Apennines, and descend at pleasure into the Casentino, the Val d'Arno, the Val di Chiane, or the Val di Tavere, as well as be prepared for every movement of the enemy. But Niccolo, considering the sterility of these places, told him, "his horses could not eat stones," and went to the Borgo San Sepolcro, where he was amicably received, but found that the people of Citta di Castello, who were friendly to the Florentines, could not be induced to yield to his overtures. Wishing to have Perugia at his disposal, he proceeded thither with forty horse, and being one of her citizens, met with a kind reception. But in a few days he became suspected, and having attempted unsuccessfully to tamper with the legate and people of Perugia, he took eight thousand ducats from them, and returned to his army. He then set on foot secret measures, to seduce Cortona from the Florentines, but the affair being discovered, his attempts were fruitless. Among the principal citizens was Bartolomeo di Senso, who being appointed to the evening watch of one of the gates, a countryman, his friend, told him, that if he went he would be slain. Bartolomeo, requesting to know what was meant, he became acquainted with the whole affair, and revealed it to the governor of the place, who, having secured the leaders of the conspiracy, and doubled the guards at the gates, waited till the time appointed for the coming of Niccolo, who finding his purpose discovered, returned to his encampment.

Chapter VII: Brescia relieved by Sforza—His other victories—Piccinino is recalled into Lombardy—He endeavors to bring the Florentines to an engagement—He is routed before Anghiari—Serious disorders in the camp of the Florentines after the victory—Death of Rinaldo degli Albizzi—His character—Neri Capponi goes to recover the Casentino—The Count di Poppi surrenders—His discourse upon quitting his possessions.

While these events were taking place in Tuscany, so little to the advantage of the duke, his affairs in Lombardy were in a still worse condition. The Count Francesco, as soon as the season would permit, took the field with his army, and the Venetians having again covered the lake with their galleys, he determined first of all to drive the duke from the water; judging, that this once effected, his remaining task would be easy. He therefore, with the Venetian fleet, attacked that of the duke, and destroyed it. His land forces took the castles held for Filippo, and the ducal troops who were besieging Brescia, being informed of these transactions, withdrew; and thus, the city, after standing a three years' siege, was at length relieved. The count then went in quest of the enemy, whose forces were encamped before Soncino, a fortress situated upon the River Oglio; these he dislodged and compelled to retreat to Cremona, where the duke again collected his forces, and prepared for his defense. But the count constantly pressing him more closely, he became apprehensive of losing either the whole, or the greater part, of his territories; and perceiving the unfortunate step he had taken, in sending Niccolo into Tuscany, in order to correct his error, he wrote to acquaint him with what had transpired, desiring him, with all possible dispatch, to leave Tuscany and return to Lombardy.

In the meantime, the Florentines, under their commissaries, had drawn together their forces, and being joined by those of the pope, halted at Anghiari, a castle placed at the foot of the mountains that divide the Val di Tavere from the Val di Chiane, distant four miles from the Borgo San Sepolcro, on a level road, and in a country suitable for the evolutions of cavalry or a battlefield. As the Signory had heard of the count's victory and the recall of Niccolo, they imagined that without again drawing a sword or disturbing the dust under their horses' feet, the victory was their own, and the war at an end, they wrote to the commissaries, desiring them to avoid an engagement, as Niccolo could not remain much longer in Tuscany. These instructions coming to the knowledge of Piccinino, and perceiving the necessity of his speedy return, to leave nothing unattempted, he determined to engage the enemy, expecting to find them unprepared, and not disposed for battle. In this determination he was confirmed by Rinaldo, the Count di Poppi, and other Florentine exiles, who saw their inevitable ruin in the departure of Niccolo, and hoped, that if he engaged the enemy, they would either be victorious, or vanquished without dishonor. This resolution being adopted, Niccolo led his army, unperceived by the enemy, from Citta di Castello to the Borgo, where he enlisted two thousand men, who, trusting the general's talents and promises, followed him in hope of plunder. Niccolo then led his forces in battle array toward Anghiari, and had arrived within two miles of the place, when Micheletto Attendulo observed great clouds of dust, and conjecturing at once, that it must be occasioned by the enemy's approach, immediately called the troops to arms. Great confusion prevailed in the Florentine camp, for the ordinary negligence and want of discipline were now increased by their presuming the enemy to be at a distance, and they were more disposed to fight than to battle; so that everyone was unarmed, and some wandering from the camp, either led by their desire to avoid the excessive heat, or in pursuit of amusement. So great was the diligence of the commissaries and of the captain, that before the enemy's arrival, the men were mounted and prepared to resist their attack; and as Micheletto was the first to observe their approach, he was also first armed and ready to meet them, and with his troops hastened to the bridge which crosses the river at a short distance from Anghiari. Pietro Giampagolo having previous to the surprise, filled up the ditches on either side of the road, and leveled the ground between the bridge and Anghiari, and Micheletto having taken his position in front of the former, the legate and Simoncino, who led the troops of the church, took post on the right, and the commissaries of the Florentines, with Pietro Giampagolo, their captain, on the left; the infantry being drawn up along the banks of the river. Thus, the only course the enemy could take, was the direct one over the bridge; nor had the Florentines any other field for their exertions, excepting that their infantry were ordered, in case their cavalry were attacked in flank by the hostile infantry, to assail them with their cross bows, and prevent them from wounding the flanks of the horses crossing the bridge. Micheletto bravely withstood the enemy's charge upon the bridge; but Astorre and Francesco Piccinino coming up, with a picked body of men, attacked him so vigorously, that he was compelled to give way, and was pushed as far as the foot of the hill which rises toward the Borgo d'Anghiari; but they were in turn repulsed and driven over the bridge, by the troops that took them in flank. The battle continued two hours, during which each side had frequent possession of the bridge, and their attempts upon it were attended with equal success; but on both sides of the river, the disadvantage of Niccolo was manifest; for when his people crossed the bridge, they found the enemy unbroken, and the ground being leveled, they could manoeuvre without difficulty, and the weary be relieved by such as were fresh. But when the Florentines crossed, Niccolo could not relieve those that were harassed, on account of the hindrance interposed by the ditches and embankments on each side of the road; thus whenever his troops got possession of the bridge, they were soon repulsed by the fresh forces of the Florentines; but when the bridge was taken by the Florentines, and they passed over and proceeded upon the road, Niccolo having no opportunity to reinforce his troops, being prevented by the impetuosity of the enemy and the inconvenience of the ground, the rear guard became mingled with the van, and occasioned the utmost confusion and disorder; they were forced to flee, and hastened at full speed toward the Borgo. The Florentine troops fell upon the plunder, which was very valuable in horses, prisoners, and military stores, for not more than a thousand of the enemy's cavalry reached the town. The people of the Borgo, who had followed Niccolo in the hope of plunder, became booty themselves, all of them being taken, and obliged to pay a ransom. The colors and carriages were also captured. This victory was much more advantageous to the Florentines than injurious to the duke; for, had they been conquered, Tuscany would have been his own; but he, by his defeat, only lost the horses and accoutrements of his army, which could be replaced without any very serious expense. Nor was there ever an instance of wars being carried on in an enemy's country with less injury to the assailants than at this; for in so great a defeat, and in a battle which continued four hours, only one man died, and he, not from wounds inflicted by hostile weapons, or any honorable means, but, having fallen from his horse, was trampled to death. Combatants then engaged with little danger; being nearly all mounted, covered with armor, and preserved from death whenever they chose to surrender, there was no necessity for risking their lives; while fighting, their armor defended them, and when they could resist no longer, they yielded and were safe.

This battle, from the circumstances which attended and followed it, presents a striking example of the wretched state of military discipline in those times. The enemy's forces being defeated and driven into the Borgo, the commissaries desired to pursue them, in order to make the victory complete, but not a single condottiere or soldier would obey, alleging, as a sufficient reason for their refusal, that they must take care of the booty and attend to their wounded; and, what is still more surprising, the next day, without permission from the commissaries, or the least regard for their commanders, they went to Arezzo, and, having secured their plunder, returned to Anghiari; a thing so contrary to military order and all subordination, that the merest shadow of a regular army would easily and most justly have wrested from them the victory they had so undeservedly obtained. Added to this, the men-at-arms, or heavy-armed horse, who had been taken prisoners, whom the commissaries wished to be detained that they might not rejoin the enemy, were set at liberty, contrary to their orders. It is astonishing, that an army so constructed should have sufficient energy to obtain the victory, or that any should be found so imbecile as to allow such a disorderly rabble to vanquish them. The time occupied by the Florentine forces in going and returning from Arezzo, gave Niccolo opportunity of escaping from the Borgo, and proceeding toward Romagna. Along with him also fled the Florentine exiles, who, finding no hope of their return home, took up their abodes in various parts of Italy, each according to his own convenience. Rinaldo made choice of Ancona; and, to gain admission to the celestial country, having lost the terrestrial, he performed a pilgrimage to the holy sepulcher; whence having returned, he died suddenly while at table at the celebration of the marriage of one of his daughters; an instance of fortune's favor, in removing him from the troubles of this world upon the least sorrowful day of his exile. Rinaldo d'Albizzi appeared respectable under every change of condition; and would have been more so had he lived in a united city, for many qualities were injurious to him in a factious community, which in an harmonious one would have done him honor.

When the forces returned from Arezzo, Niccolo being then gone, the commissaries presented themselves at the Borgo, the people of which were willing to submit to the Florentines; but their offer was declined, and while negotiations were pending, the pope's legate imagined the commissaries designed to take it from the church. Hard words were exchanged and hostilities might have ensued between the Florentine and ecclesiastical forces, if the misunderstanding had continued much longer; but as it was brought to the conclusion desired by the legate, peace was restored.

While the affair of the Borgo San Sepolcro was in progress, Niccolo Piccinino was supposed to have marched toward Rome; other accounts said La Marca, and hence the legate and the count's forces moved toward Perugia to relieve La Marca or Rome, as the case might be, and Bernardo de Medici accompanied them. Neri led the Florentine forces to recover the Casentino, and pitched his camp before Rassina, which he took, together with Bibbiena, Prato Vecchio, and Romena. From thence he proceeded to Poppi and invested it on two sides with his forces, in one direction toward the plain of Certomondo, in the other upon the hill extending to Fronzole. The count finding himself abandoned to his fate, had shut himself up in Poppi, not with any hope of assistance, but with a view to make the best terms he could. Neri pressing him, he offered to capitulate, and obtained reasonable conditions, namely, security for himself and family, with leave to take whatever he could carry away, on condition of ceding his territories and government to the Florentines. When he perceived the full extent of his misfortune, standing upon the bridge which crosses the Arno, close to Poppi, he turned to Neri in great distress, and said, "Had I well considered my own position and the power of the Florentines, I should now have been a friend of the republic and congratulating you on your victory, not an enemy compelled to supplicate some alleviation of my woe.

The recent events which to you bring glory and joy, to me are full of wretchedness and sorrow. Once I possessed horses, arms, subjects, grandeur and wealth: can it be surprising that I part with them reluctantly? But as you possess both the power and the inclination to command the whole of Tuscany, we must of necessity obey you; and had I not committed this error, my misfortune would not have occurred, and your liberality could not have been exercised; so, that if you were to rescue me from entire ruin, you would give the world a lasting proof of your clemency. Therefore, let your pity pass by my fault, and allow me to retain this single house to leave to the descendants of those from whom your fathers have received innumerable benefits." To this Neri replied: "That his having expected great results from men who were capable of doing only very little, had led him to commit so great a fault against the republic of Florence; that, every circumstance considered, he must surrender all those places to the Florentines, as an enemy, which he was unwilling to hold as a friend: that he had set such an example, as it would be most highly impolitic to encourage; for, upon a change of fortune, it might injure the republic, and it was not himself they feared, but his power while lord of the Casentino. If, however, he could live as a prince in Germany, the citizens would be very much gratified; and out of love to those ancestors of whom he had spoken, they would be glad to assist him." To this, the count, in great anger, replied: "He wished the Florentines at a much greater distance." Attempting no longer to preserve the least urbanity of demeanor, he ceded the place and all its dependencies to the Florentines, and with his treasure, wife, and children, took his departure, mourning the loss of a territory which his forefathers had held during four hundred years. When all these victories were known at Florence, the government and people were transported with joy. Benedetto de' Medici, finding the report of Niccolo having proceeded either to Rome or to La Marca, incorrect, returned with his forces to Neri, and they proceeded together to Florence, where the highest honors were decreed to them which it was customary with the city to bestow upon her victorious citizens, and they were received by the Signory, the Capitani di Parte, and the whole city, in triumphal pomp.

Book VI: Chapter I: Reflections on the object of war and the use of victory—Niccolo reinforces his army—The duke of Milan endeavors to recover the services of Count Francesco Sforza—Suspicions of the Venetians—They acquire Ravenna—The Florentines purchase the Borgo San Sepolcro of the pope—Piccinino makes an excursion during the winter—The count besieged in his camp before Martinengo—The insolence of Niccolo Piccinino—The duke in revenge makes peace with the league—Sforza assisted by the Florentines.

Those who make war have always and very naturally designed to enrich themselves and impoverish the enemy; neither is victory sought or conquest desirable, except to strengthen themselves and weaken the enemy. Hence it follows, that those who are impoverished by victory or debilitated by conquest, must either have gone beyond, or fallen short of, the end for which wars are made. A republic or a prince is enriched by the victories he obtains, when the enemy is crushed and possession is retained of the plunder and ransom. Victory is injurious when the foe escapes, or when the soldiers appropriate the booty and ransom. In such a case, losses are unfortunate, and conquests still more so; for the vanquished suffers the injuries inflicted by the enemy, and the victor those occasioned by his friends, which being less justifiable, must cause the greater pain, particularly from a consideration of his being thus compelled to oppress his people by an increased burden of taxation. A ruler possessing any degree of humanity, cannot rejoice in a victory that afflicts his subjects. The victories of the ancient and well organized republics, enabled them to fill their treasuries with gold and silver won from their enemies, to distribute gratuities to the people, reduce taxation, and by games and solemn festivals, disseminate universal joy. But the victories obtained in the times of which we speak, first emptied the treasury, and then impoverished the people, without giving the victorious party security from the enemy. This arose entirely from the disorders inherent in their mode of warfare; for the vanquished soldiery, divesting themselves of their accoutrements, and being neither slain nor detained prisoners, only deferred a renewed attack on the conqueror, till their leader had furnished them with arms and horses. Besides this, both ransom and booty being appropriated by the troops, the victorious princes could not make use of them for raising fresh forces, but were compelled to draw the necessary means from their subjects' purses, and this was the only result of victory experienced by the people, except that it diminished the ruler's reluctance to such a course, and made him less particular about his mode of oppressing them. To such a state had the practice of war been brought by the sort of soldiery then on foot, that the victor and the vanquished, when desirous of their services, alike needed fresh supplies of money; for the one had to re-equip them, and the other to bribe them; the vanquished could not fight without being remounted, and the conquerors would not take the field without a new gratuity. Hence it followed, that the one derived little advantage from the victory, and the other was the less injured by defeat; for the routed party had to be re-equipped, and the victorious could not pursue his advantage.

From this disorderly and perverse method of procedure, it arose, that before Niccolo's defeat became known throughout Italy, he had again reorganized his forces, and harassed the enemy with greater vigor than before. Hence, also, it happened, that after his disaster at Tenna, he so soon occupied Verona: that being deprived of his army at Verona, he was shortly able to appear with a large force in Tuscany; that being completely defeated at Anghiari, before he reached Tuscany, he was more powerful in the field than ever. He was thus enabled to give the duke of Milan hopes of defending Lombardy, which by his absence appeared to be lost; for while Niccolo spread consternation throughout Tuscany, disasters in the former province so alarmed the duke, that he was afraid his utter ruin would ensue before Niccolo, whom he had recalled, could come to his relief, and check the impetuous progress of the count. Under these impressions, the duke, to insure by policy that success which he could not command by arms, had recourse to remedies, which on similar occasions had frequently served his turn. He sent Niccolo da Esti, prince of Ferrara, to the count who was then at Peschiera, to persuade him, "That this war was not to his advantage; for if the duke became so ruined as to be unable to maintain his position among the states of Italy, the count would be the first to suffer; for he would cease to be of importance either with the Venetians or the Florentines; and to prove the sincerity of his wish for peace, he offered to fulfill the engagement he had entered into with regard to his daughter, and send her to Ferrara; so that as soon as peace was established, the union might take place." The count replied, "That if the duke really wished for peace, he might easily be gratified, as the Florentines and the Venetians were equally anxious for it. True, it was, he could with difficulty credit him, knowing that he had never made peace but from necessity, and when this no longer pressed him, again desired war. Neither could he give credence to what he had said concerning the marriage, having been so repeatedly deceived; yet when peace was concluded, he would take the advice of his friends upon that subject."

The Venetians, who were sometimes needlessly jealous of their soldiery, became greatly alarmed at these proceedings; and not without reason. The count was aware of this, and wishing to remove their apprehensions, pursued the war with unusual vigor; but his mind had become so unsettled by ambition, and the Venetians' by jealousy, that little further progress was made during the remainder of the summer, and upon the return of

Niccolo into Lombardy, winter having already commenced, the armies withdrew into quarters, the count to Verona, the Florentine forces to Tuscany, the duke's to Cremona, and those of the pope to Romagna. The latter, after having been victorious at Anghiari, made an unsuccessful attack upon Furli and Bologna, with a view to wrest them from Niccolo Piccinino; but they were gallantly defended by his son Francesco. However, the arrival of the papal forces so alarmed the people of Ravenna with the fear of becoming subject to the church, that, by consent of Ostasio di Polenta their lord, they placed themselves under the power of the Venetians; who, in return for the territory, and that Ostasio might never retake by force what he had imprudently given them, sent him and his son to Candia, where they died. In the course of these affairs, the pope, notwithstanding the victory at Anghiari, became so in want of money, that he sold the fortress of Borgo San Sepolcro to the Florentines for 25,000 ducats.

Affairs being thus situated, each party supposed winter would protect them from the evils of war, and thought no more of peace. This was particularly the case with the duke, who, being rendered doubly secure by the season and by the presence of Niccolo, broke off all attempts to effect a reconciliation with the count, reorganized Niccolo's forces, and made every requisite preparation for the future struggle. The count being informed of this, went to Venice to consult with the senate on the course to be pursued during the next year. Niccolo, on the other hand, being quite prepared, and seeing the enemy unprovided, did not await the return of spring, but crossed the Adda during severe weather, occupied the whole Brescian territory, except Oddula and Acri, and made prisoners two thousand horse belonging to Francesco's forces, who had no apprehension of an attack. But the greatest source of anxiety to the count, and alarm to the Venetians, was the desertion of his service by Ciarpellone, one of his principal officers. Francesco, on learning these matters, immediately left Venice, and, arriving at Brescia, found that Niccolo, after doing all the mischief he could, had retired to his quarters; and therefore, finding the war concluded for the present was not disposed to rekindle it, but rather to use the opportunity afforded by the season and his enemies, of reorganizing his forces, so as to be able, when spring arrived, to avenge himself for his former injuries. To this end he induced the Venetians to recall the forces they had in Tuscany, in the Florentine service, and to order that to succeed Gattamelata, who was dead, Micheletto Attendulo should take the command.

On the approach of spring, Niccolo Piccinino was the first to take the field, and encamped before Cignano, a fortress twelve miles from Brescia; the count marched to its relief, and the war between them was conducted in the usual manner. The count, apprehensive for the city of Bergamo, besieged Martinengo, a castle so situated that the possession of it would enable him to relieve the former, which was closely pressed by Niccolo, who, having foreseen that the enemy could impede him only from the direction of Martinengo, had put the castle into a complete state of defense, so that the count was obliged to lend his whole force to the siege. Upon this, Niccolo placed his troops in a situation calculated to intercept the count's provisions, and fortified himself with trenches and bastions in such a manner that he could not be attacked without the most manifest hazard to his assailant. Hence the besiegers were more distressed than the people of Martinengo whom they besieged. The count could not hold his position for want of food, nor quit it without imminent danger; so that the duke's victory appeared certain, and defeat equally inevitable to the count and the Venetians.

But fortune, never destitute of means to assist her favorites, or to injure others, caused the hope of victory to operate so powerfully upon Niccolo Piccinino, and made him assume such a tone of unbounded insolence, that, losing all respect for himself and the duke, he sent him word that, having served under his ensign for so long, without obtaining sufficient land to serve him for a grave, he wished to know from himself what was to be the reward of his labors; for it was in his power to make him master of Lombardy, and place all his enemies in his power; and, as a certain victory ought to be attended by a sure remuneration, he desired the duke to concede to him the city of Piacenza, that when weary with his lengthened services he might at last betake himself to repose. Nor did he hesitate, in conclusion, to threaten, if his request were not granted, to abandon the enterprise. This injurious and most insolent mode of proceeding highly offended the duke, and, on further consideration, he determined rather to let the expedition altogether fail, than consent to his general's demand. Thus, what all the dangers he had incurred, and the threats of his enemies, could not draw from him, the insolent behavior of his friends made him willing to propose. He resolved to come to terms with the count, and sent Antonio Guido Buono, of Tortona, to offer his daughter and conditions of peace, which were accepted with great pleasure by the count, and also by the colleagues as far as themselves were concerned. The terms being secretly arranged, the duke sent to command Niccolo to make a truce with the count for one year; intimating, that being exhausted with the expense, he could not forego a certain peace for a doubtful victory. Niccolo was utterly astonished at this resolution, and could not imagine what had induced the duke to lose such a glorious opportunity; nor could he surmise that, to avoid rewarding his friends, he would save his enemies, and therefore to the utmost of his power he opposed this resolution; and the duke was obliged, in order to induce his compliance, to threaten that if he did not obey he would give him up to his soldiers and his enemies. Niccolo submitted, with the feelings of one compelled to leave country and friends, complaining of his hard fate, that fortune and the duke were robbing him of the victory over his enemies. The truce being arranged, the marriage of the duke's daughter, Bianca, to the count was solemnized, the duke giving Cremona for her portion. This being over, peace was concluded in November, 1441, at which Francesco Barbadico and Pagolo Trono were present for the Venetians, and for the Florentines Agnolo Acciajuoli. Peschiera, Asola, and Lonato, castles in the Mantuan territory, were assigned to the Venetians.

The war in Lombardy was concluded; but the dissensions in the kingdom of Naples continued, and the inability to compose them occasioned the resumption of those arms which had been so recently laid aside. Alfonso, of Aragon, had, during these wars, taken from Rene the whole kingdom except Naples; so that, thinking he had the victory in his power, he resolved during the siege of Naples to take Benevento, and his other possessions in that neighborhood, from the count; and thought he might easily accomplish this while the latter was engaged in the wars of Lombardy. Having heard of the conclusion of peace, Alfonso feared the count would not only come for the purpose of recovering his territories, but also to favor Rene; and Rene himself had hope of his assistance for the same reason. The latter, therefore, sent to the count, begging he would come to the relief of a friend, and avenge himself of an enemy. On the other hand, Alfonso entreated Filippo, for the sake of the friendship which subsisted between them, to find the count some other occupation, that, being engaged in greater affairs, he might not have an opportunity of interfering between them. Filippo complied with this request, without seeming to be aware that he violated the peace recently made, so greatly to his disadvantage. He therefore signified to pope Eugenius, that the present was a favorable opportunity for recovering the territories which the count had taken from the church; and, that he might be in a condition to use it, offered him the services of Niccolo Piccinino, and engaged to pay him during the war; who, since the peace of Lombardy, had remained with his forces in Romagna. Eugenius eagerly took the advice, induced by his hatred of the count, and his desire to recover his lost possessions; feeling assured that, although on a former occasion he had been duped by Niccolo, it would be improper, now that the duke interfered, to suspect any deceit; and, joining his forces to those of Niccolo, he assailed La Marca. The count, astonished at such an unexpected attack, assembled his troops, and went to meet the enemy. In the meantime, King Alfonso took possession of Naples, so that the whole kingdom, except Castelnuova, was in his power. Leaving a strong guard at Castelnuova Rene set out and came to Florence, where he was most honorably received; and having remained a few days, finding he could not continue the war, he withdrew to Marseilles.

In the meantime, Alfonso took Castelnuova, and the count found himself assailed in the Marca Inferiore, both by the pope and Niccolo. He applied to the Venetians and the Florentines for assistance, in men and money, assuring them that if they did not determine to restrain the pope and king, during his life, they would soon afterward find their very existence endangered, for both would join Filippo and divide Italy among them. The Florentines and Venetians hesitated for a time, both to consider the propriety of drawing upon themselves the enmity of the pope and the king, and because they were then engaged in the affairs of the Bolognese. Annibale Bentivoglio had driven Francesco Piccinino from Bologna, and for defense against the duke, who favored Francesco, he demanded and received assistance of the Venetians and Florentines; so that, being occupied with these matters they could not resolve to assist the count, but Annibale, having routed Francesco Piccinino, and those affairs seeming to be settled, they resolved to support him. Designing however to make sure of the duke, they offered to renew the league with him, to which he was not averse; for, although he consented that war should be made against the count, while King Rene was in arms, yet finding him now conquered, and deprived of the whole kingdom, he was not willing that the count should be despoiled of his territories; and therefore, not only consented that assistance should be given him, but wrote to Alfonso to be good enough to retire to his kingdom, and discontinue hostilities against the count; and although reluctantly, yet in acknowledgment of his obligations to the duke, Alfonso determined to satisfy him, and withdrew with his forces beyond the Tronto.

Chapter II: Discords of Florence—Jealousy excited against Neri di Gino Capponi—Baldaccio d'Anghiari murdered—Reform of government in favor of the Medici—Enterprises of Sforza and Piccinino—Death of Niccolo Piccinino—End of the war—Disturbances in Bologna—Annibale Bentivoglio slain by Battista Canneschi, and the latter by the people—Santi, supposed to be the son of Ercole Bentivoglio, is called to govern the city of Bologna—Discourse of Cosmo de' Medici to him—Perfidious designs of the duke of Milan against Sforza—General war in Italy—Losses of the duke of Milan—The duke has recourse to the count, who makes peace with him—Offers of the duke and the Venetians to the count—The Venetians furtively deprive the count of Cremona.

While the affairs of Romagna proceeded thus, the city of Florence was not tranquil. Among the citizens of highest reputation in the government, was Neri di Gino Capponi, of whose influence Cosmo de' Medici had more apprehension than any other; for to the great authority which he possessed in the city was added his influence with the soldiery. Having been often leader of the Florentine forces he had won their affection by his courage and talents; and the remembrance of his own and his father's victories (the latter having taken Pisa, and he himself having overcome Niccolo Piccinino at Anghiari) caused him to be beloved by many, and feared by those who were averse to having associates in the government. Among the leaders of the Florentine army was Baldaccio d'Anghiari, an excellent soldier, for in those times there was not one in Italy who surpassed him in vigor either of body or mind; and possessing so much influence with the infantry, whose leader he had always been, many thought they would follow him wherever he chose to lead them. Baldaccio was the intimate friend of Neri, who loved him for his talents, of which he had been a constant witness. This excited great suspicion in the other citizens, who, thinking it alike dangerous either to discharge or retain him in their service, determined to destroy him, and fortune seemed to favor their design. Bartolommeo Orlandini was Gonfalonier of Justice; the same person who was sent to the defense of Marradi, when Niccolo Piccinino came into Tuscany, as we have related above, and so basely abandoned the pass, which by its nature was almost impregnable. So flagrant an instance of cowardice was very offensive to Baldaccio, who, on many occasions, both by words and letters, had contributed to make the disgraceful fact known to all. The shame and vexation of Bartolommeo were extreme, so that of all things he wished to avenge himself, thinking, with the death of his accuser, to efface the stain upon his character.

This feeling of Bartolommeo Orlandini was known to other citizens, so that they easily persuaded him to put Baldaccio to death, and at one avenge himself, and deliver his country from a man whom they must either retain at great peril, or discharge to their greater confusion. Bartolommeo having therefore resolved to murder him, concealed in his own apartment at the palace several young men, all armed; and Baldaccio, entering the piazza, whither it was his daily custom to come, to confer with the magistrates concerning his command, the Gonfalonier sent for him, and he, without any suspicion, obeyed. Meeting him in the corridor, which leads to the chambers of the Signory, they took a few turns together discoursing of his office, when being close to the door of the apartments in which the assassins were concealed, Bartolommeo gave them the signal, upon which they rushed out, and finding Baldaccio alone and unarmed, they slew him, and threw the body out of the window which looks from the palace toward the dogano, or customhouse. It was thence carried into the piazza, where the head being severed, it remained the whole day exposed to the gaze of the people. Baldaccio was married, and had only one child, a boy, who survived him but a short time; and his wife, Annalena, thus deprived of both husband and offspring, rejected every proposal for a second union. She converted her house into a monastery, to which she withdrew, and, being joined by many noble ladies, lived in holy seclusion to the end of her days. The convent she founded, and which is named from her, preserves her story in perpetual remembrance.

This circumstance served to weaken Neri's power, and made him lose both influence and friends. Nor did this satisfy the citizens who held the reins of government; for it being ten years since their acquisition of power, and the authority of the Balia expired, many began to exhibit more boldness, both in words and deeds, than seemed consistent with their safety; and the leaders of the party judged, that if they wished to preserve their influence, some means must be adopted to increase it. To this end, in 1444 the councils created a new Balia, which reformed the government, gave authority to a limited number to create the Signory, re-established the Chancery of Reformations, depriving Filippo Peruzzi of his office of president in it, and appointing another wholly under their influence. They prolonged the term of exile to those who were banished; put Giovanni di Simone Vespucci in prison; deprived the Accoppiatori of their enemies of the honors of government, and with them the sons of Piero Baroncelli, the whole of the Seragli, Bartolommeo Fortini, Francesco Castellani, and many others. By these means they strengthened their authority and influence, and humbled their enemies, or those whom they suspected of being so.

Having thus recovered and confirmed their government, they then turned their attention to external affairs. As observed above, Niccolo Piccinino was abandoned by King Alfonso, and the count having been aggrandized by the assistance of the Florentines, attacked and routed him near Fermo, where, after losing nearly the whole of his troops, Niccolo fled to Montecchio, which he fortified in such a manner that in a short time he had again assembled so large an army as enabled him to make head against the count; particularly as the season was now come for them to withdraw into quarters. His principal endeavor during the winter was to collect troops, and in this he was assisted both by the pope and Alfonso; so that, upon the approach of spring, both leaders took the field, and Niccolo, being the strongest, reduced the count to extreme necessity, and would have conquered him if the duke had not contrived to frustrate his designs. Filippo sent to beg he would come to him with all speed, for he wished to have a personal interview, that he might communicate matters of the highest importance. Niccolo, anxious to hear them, abandoned a certain victory for a very doubtful advantage; and leaving his son Francesco to command the army, hastened to Milan. The count being informed of the circumstance, would not let slip the opportunity of fighting in the absence of Niccolo; and, coming to an engagement near the castle of Monte Loro, routed the father's forces and took the son prisoner. Niccolo having arrived at Milan saw that the duke had duped him, and learning the defeat of his army and the capture of his son, he died of grief in 1445, at the age of sixty-four, having been a brave rather than a fortunate leader. He left two sons, Francesco and Jacopo, who, possessing less talent than their father, were still more unfortunate; so that the arms of the family became almost annihilated, while those of Sforza, being favored by fortune, attained augmented glory. The pope, seeing Niccolo's army defeated and himself dead, having little hope of assistance from Aragon, sought peace with the count, and, by the intervention of the Florentines, succeeded. Of La Marca, the pope only retained Osimo, Fabriano, and Recanati; all the rest remained in the count's possession.

Peace being restored to La Marca, the whole of Italy would have obtained repose had it not been disturbed by the Bolognese. There were in Bologna two very powerful families, the Canneschi and the Bentivogli. Of the latter, Annibale was the head; of the former, Battista, who, as a means of confirming their mutual confidence, had contracted family alliances; but among men who have the same objects of ambition in view, it is easy to form connections, but difficult to establish friendship. The Bolognese were in a league with the Venetians and Florentines, which had been effected by the influence of Annibale, after they had driven out Francesco Piccinino; and Battista, knowing how earnestly the duke desired to have the city favorable to him, proposed to assassinate Annibale, and put Bologna into his power. This being agreed upon, on the twenty-fifth of June, 1445, he attacked Annibale with his men, and slew him: and then, with shouts of "the duke, the duke," rode through the city. The Venetian and Florentine commissaries were in Bologna at the time, and at first kept themselves within doors; but finding that the people, instead of favoring the murderers, assembled in the piazza, armed in great numbers, mourning the death of Annibale, they joined them; and, assembling what forces they could, attacked the Canneschi, soon overpowered them, slew part, and drove the remainder out of the city. Battista, unable to effect his escape, or his enemies his capture, took refuge in a vault of his house, used for storing grain. The friends of the Bentivogli, having sought him all day, and knowing he had not left the city, so terrified his servants, that one of them, a groom, disclosed the place of his concealment, and being drawn forth in complete armor he was slain, his body dragged about the streets, and afterward burned. Thus the duke's authority was sufficient to prompt the enterprise, but his force was not at hand to support it.

The tumults being settled by the death of Battista, and the flight of the Canneschi, Bologna still remained in the greatest confusion. There not being one of the house of Bentivogli of age to govern, Annibale having left but one son whose name was Giovanni, only six years old, it was apprehended that disunion would ensue among the Bentivogli, and cause the return of the Cannecshi, and the ruin both of their own country and party. While in this state of apprehension, Francesco, sometime Count di Poppi, being at Bologna, informed the rulers of the city, that if they wished to be governed by one of the blood of Annibale, he could tell them of one; and related that about twenty years ago, Ercole, cousin of Annibale, being at Poppi, became acquainted with a girl of the castle, of whom was born a son named Santi, whom Ercole, on many occasions acknowledged to be his own, nor could he deny it, for whoever knew him and saw the boy, could not fail to observe the strongest resemblance. The citizens gave credit to the tale, and immediately sent to Florence to see the young man, and procure of Cosmo and Neri permission to return with him to Bologna. The reputed father of Santi was dead, and he lived under the protection of his uncle, whose name was Antonio da Cascese. Antonio was rich, childless, and a friend of Neri, to whom the matter becoming known, he thought it ought neither to be despised nor too hastily accepted; and that it would be best for Santi and those who had been sent from Bologna, to confer in the presence of Cosmo. They were accordingly introduced, and Santi was not merely honored but adored by them, so greatly were they influenced by the spirit of party. However, nothing was done at the time, except that Cosmo, taking Santi apart, spoke to him thus: "No one can better advise you in this matter than yourself; for you have to take that course to which your own mind prompts you. If you be the son of Ercole Bentivoglio, you will naturally aspire to those pursuits which are proper to your family and worthy of your father; but if you be the son of Agnolo da Cascese, you will remain in Florence, and basely spend the remainder of your days in some branch of the woolen trade." These words greatly influenced the youth, who, though he had at first almost refused to adopt such a course, said, he would submit himself wholly to what Cosmo and Neri should determine. They, assenting to the request of the Bolognese, provided suitable apparel, horses, and servants; and in a few days he was escorted by a numerous cavalcade to Bologna, where the guardianship of Annibale's son and of the city were placed in his hands. He conducted himself so prudently, that although all his ancestors had been slain by their enemies, he lived in peace and died respected by everyone.

After the death of Niccolo Piccinino and the peace of La Marca, Filippo wishing to procure a leader of his forces, secretly negotiated with Ciarpellone, one of the principal captains of Count Francesco, and arrangements having been made, Ciarpellone asked permission to go to Milan to take possession of certain castles which had been given him by Filippo during the late wars. The count suspecting what was in progress, in order to prevent the duke from accommodating himself at his expense, caused Ciarpellone to be arrested, and soon afterward put to death; alleging that he had been detected plotting against him. Filippo was highly annoyed and indignant, which the Venetians and the Florentines were glad to observe, for their greatest fear was, that the duke and the count should become friends.

The duke's anger caused the renewal of war in La Marca. Gismondo Malatesti, lord of Rimino, being son-in-law of the count, expected to obtain Pesaro; but the count, having obtained possession, gave it to his brother, Alessandro. Gismondo, offended at this, was still further exasperated at finding that Federigo di Montefeltro, his enemy, by the count's assistance, gained possession of Urbino. He therefore joined the duke, and solicited the pope and the king to make war against the count, who, to give Gismondo a taste of the war he so much desired, resolved to take the initiative, and attacked him immediately. Thus Romagna and La Marca were again in complete confusion, for Filippo, the king, and the pope, sent powerful assistance to Gismondo, while the Florentines and Venetians supplied the count with money, though not with men. Nor was Filippo satisfied with the war in Romagna, but also desired to take Cremona and Pontremoli from the count; but Pontremoli was defended by the Florentines, and Cremona by the Venetians. Thus the war was renewed in Lombardy, and after several engagements in the Cremonese, Francesco Piccinino, the leader of the duke's forces, was routed at Casale, by Micheletto and the Venetian troops. This victory gave the Venetians hope of obtaining the duke's dominions. They sent a commissary to Cremona, attacked the Ghiaradadda, and took the whole of it, except Crema. Then crossing the Adda, they overran the country as far as Milan. Upon this the duke had recourse to Alfonso, and entreated his assistance, pointing out the danger his kingdom would incur if Lombardy were to fall into the hands of the Venetians. Alfonso promised to send him troops, but apprised him of the difficulties which would attend their passage, without the permission of the count.

Filippo, driven to extremity, then had recourse to Francesco, and begged he would not abandon his father-in-law, now that he had become old and blind. The count was offended with the duke for making war against him; but he was jealous of the increasing greatness of the Venetians, and he himself began to be in want of money, for the League supplied him sparingly. The Florentines, being no longer in fear of the duke, ceased to stand in need of the count, and the Venetians desired his ruin; for they thought Lombardy could not be taken from him except by this means; yet while Filippo sought to gain him over, and offered him the entire command of his forces, on condition that he should restore La Marca to the pope and quit the Venetian alliance, ambassadors were sent to him by that republic, promising him Milan, if they took it, and the perpetual command of their forces, if he would push the war in La Marca, and prevent Alfonso from sending troops into Lombardy. The offers of the Venetians were great, as also were their claims upon him, having begun the war in order to save him from losing Cremona; while the injuries received from the duke were fresh in his memory, and his promises had lost all influence, still the count hesitated; for on the one hand, were to be considered his obligations to the League, his pledged faith, their recent services, and his hopes of the future, all which had their influence on him; on the other, were the entreaties of his father-in-law, and above all, the bane which he feared would be concealed under the specious offers of the Venetians, for he doubted not, that both with regard to Milan and their other promises, if they were victorious, he would be at their mercy, to which no prudent men would ever submit if he could avoid it. These difficulties in the way of his forming a determination, were obviated by the ambition of the Venetians, who, seeing a chance of occupying Cremona, from secret intelligence with that city, under a different pretext, sent troops into its neighborhood; but the affair was discovered by those who commanded Cremona for the count, and measures were adopted which prevented its success. Thus without obtaining Cremona, they lost the count's friendship, who, now being free from all other considerations, joined the duke.

Chapter III: Death of Filippo Visconti, duke of Milan—The Milanese appoint Sforza their captain—Milan becomes a republic—The pope endeavors to restore peace to Italy—The Venetians oppose this design—Alfonso attacks the Florentines—The neighborhood of Piombino becomes the principal theater of war—Scarcity in the Florentine camp—Disorders occur in the Neapolitan and Florentine armies—Alfonso sues for peace and is compelled to retreat—Pavia surrenders to the count—Displeasure of the Milanese—The count besieges Caravaggio—The Venetians endeavor to relieve the place—They are routed by the count before Caravaggio.

Pope Eugenius being dead, was succeeded by Nicholas V. The count had his whole army at Cotignola, ready to pass into Lombardy, when intelligence was brought him of the death of Filippo, which happened on the last day of August, 1447. This event greatly afflicted him, for he doubted whether his troops were in readiness, on account of their arrears of pay; he feared the Venetians, who were his armed enemies, he having recently forsaken them and taken part with the duke; he was in apprehension from Alfonso, his inveterate foe; he had no hope from the pontiff or the Florentines; for the latter were allies of the Venetians, and he had seized the territories of the former. However, he resolved to face his fortune and be guided by circumstances; for it often happens, that when engaged in business valuable ideas are suggested, which in a state of inaction would never have occurred. He had great hopes, that if the Milanese were disposed to defend themselves against the ambition of the Venetians, they could make use of no other power but his. Therefore, he proceeded confidently into the Bolognese territory, thence to Modena and Reggio, halted with his forces upon the Lenza, and sent to offer his services at Milan. On the death of the duke, part of the Milanese were inclined to establish a republic; others wished to choose a prince, and of these, one part favored the count, and another Alfonso. However, the majority being in favor of freedom, they prevailed over the rest, and organized a republic, to which many cities of the Duchy refused obedience; for they, too, desired to live in the enjoyment of their liberty, and even those who did not embrace such views, refused to submit to the sovereignty of the Milanese. Lodi and Piacenza surrendered themselves to the Venetians; Pavia and Parma became free. This confused state of things being known to the count, he proceeded to Cremona, where his ambassadors and those of the Milanese arranged for him to command the forces of the new republic, with the same remuneration he had received from the duke at the time of his decease. To this they added the possession of Brescia, until Verona was recovered, when he should have that city and restore Brescia to the Milanese.

Before the duke's death, Pope Nicholas, after his assumption of the pontificate, sought to restore peace among the princes of Italy, and with this object endeavored, in conjunction with the ambassadors sent by the Florentines to congratulate him on his accession, to appoint a diet at Ferrara to attempt either the arrangement of a long truce, or the establishment of peace. A congress was accordingly held in that city, of the pope's legate and the Venetian, ducal, and Florentine representatives. King Alfonso had no envoy there. He was at Tivoli with a great body of horse and foot, and favorable to the duke; both having resolved, that having gained the count over to their side, they would openly attack the Florentines and Venetians, and till the arrival of the count in Lombardy, take part in the treaty for peace at Ferrara, at which, though the king did not appear, he engaged to concur in whatever course the duke should adopt. The conference lasted several days, and after many debates, resolved on either a truce for five years, or a permanent peace, whichsoever the duke should approve; and the ducal ambassadors, having returned to Milan to learn his decision, found him dead. Notwithstanding this, the Milanese were disposed to adopt the resolutions of the assembly, but the Venetians refused, indulging great hopes of becoming masters of Lombardy, particularly as Lodi and Piacenza, immediately after the duke's death, had submitted to them. They trusted that either by force or by treaty they could strip Milan of her power; and then so press her, as to compel her also to surrender before any assistance could arrive; and they were the more confident of this from seeing the Florentines involved in war with King Alfonso.

The king being at Tivoli, and designing to pursue his enterprise against Tuscany, as had been arranged between himself and Filippo, judging that the war now commenced in Lombardy would give him both time and opportunity, and wishing to have a footing in the Florentine state before he openly commenced hostilities, opened a secret understanding with the fortress of Cennina, in the Val d'Arno Superiore, and took possession of it. The Florentines, surprised with this unexpected event, perceiving the king already in action, and resolved to do them all the injury in his power, hired forces, created a council of ten for management of the war, and prepared for the conflict in their usual manner. The king was already in the Siennese, and used his utmost endeavors to reduce the city, but the inhabitants of Sienna were firm in their attachment to the Florentines, and refused to receive him within their walls or into any of their territories. They furnished him with provisions, alleging in excuse, the enemy's power and their inability to resist. The king, finding he could not enter by the Val d'Arno, as he had first intended, both because Cennina had been already retaken, and because the Florentines were now in some measure prepared for their defense, turned toward Volterra, and occupied many fortresses in that territory. Thence he proceeded toward Pisa, and with the assistance of Fazio and Arrigo de' Conti, of the Gherardesca, took some castles, and issuing from them, assailed Campiglia, but could not take it, the place being defended by the Florentines, and it being now in the depth of winter. Upon this the king, leaving garrisons in the places he had taken to harass the surrounding country, withdrew with the remainder of his army to quarters in the Siennese. The Florentines, aided by the season, used the most active exertions to provide themselves troops, whose captains were Federigo, lord of Urbino, and Gismondo Malatesti da Rimino, who, though mutual foes, were kept so united by the prudence of the commissaries, Neri di Gino and Bernardetto de' Medici, that they broke up their quarters while the weather was still very severe and recovered not only the places that had been taken in the territory of Pisa, but also the Pomerancie in the neighborhood of Volterra, and so checked the king's troops, which at first had overrun the Maremma, that they could scarcely retain the places they had been left to garrison.

Upon the return of the spring the commissaries halted with their whole force, consisting of five thousand horse and two thousand foot, at the Spedaletto. The king approached with his army, amounting to fifteen thousand men, within three miles of Campiglia, but when it was expected he would attack the place he fell upon Piombino, hoping, as it was insufficiently provided, to take it with very little trouble, and thus acquire a very important position, the loss of which would be severely felt by the Florentines; for from it he would be able to exhaust them with a long war, obtain his own provision by sea, and harass the whole territory of Pisa. They were greatly alarmed at this attack, and, considering that if they could remain with their army among the woods of Campiglia, the king would be compelled to retire either in defeat or disgrace. With this view they equipped four galleys at Livorno, and having succeeded in throwing three hundred infantry into Piombino, took up their own position at the Caldane, a place where it would be difficult to attack them; and they thought it would be dangerous to encamp among the thickets of the plain.

The Florentine army depended for provisions on the surrounding places, which, being poor and thinly inhabited, had difficulty in supplying them. Consequently the troops suffered, particularly from want of wine, for none being produced in that vicinity, and unable to procure it from more distant places, it was impossible to obtain a sufficient quantity. But the king, though closely pressed by the Florentines, was well provided except in forage, for he obtained everything else by sea. The Florentines, desirous to supply themselves in the same manner, loaded four vessels with provisions, but, upon their approach, they were attacked by seven of the king's galleys, which took two of them and put the rest to flight. This disaster made them despair of procuring provisions, so that two hundred men of a foraging party, principally for want of wine, deserted to the king, and the rest complained that they could not live without it, in a situation where the heat was so excessive and the water bad. The commissaries therefore determined to quit the place, and endeavor to recover those castles which still remained in the enemy's power; who, on his part, though not suffering from want of provisions, and greatly superior in numbers, found his enterprise a failure, from the ravages made in his army by those diseases which the hot season produces in marshy localities; and which prevailed to such an extent that many died daily, and nearly all were affected. These circumstances occasioned overtures of peace. The king demanded fifty thousand florins, and the possession of Piombino. When the terms were under consideration, many citizens, desirous of peace, would have accepted them, declaring there was no hope of bringing to a favorable conclusion a war which required so much money to carry it on. But Neri Capponi going to Florence, placed the matter in a more correct light, and it was then unanimously determined to reject the proposal, and take the lord of Piombino under their protection, with an alliance offensive and defensive, provided he did not abandon them, but assist in their defense as hitherto. The king being informed of this resolution, saw that, with his reduced army, he could not gain the place, and withdrew in the same condition as if completely routed, leaving behind him two thousand dead. With the remainder of his sick troops he retired to the Siennese territory, and thence to his kingdom, incensed against the Florentines, and threatening them with new wars upon the return of spring.

While these events were proceeding in Tuscany the Count Sforza, having become leader of the Milanese forces, strenuously endeavored to secure the friendship of Francesco Piccinino, who was also in their service, that he might support him in his enterprises, or be less disposed to do him injury. He then took the field with his army, upon which the people of Pavia, conscious of their inability to resist him, and unwilling to obey the Milanese, offered to submit themselves to his authority, on condition that he should not subject them to the power of Milan. The count desired the possession of Pavia, and considered the circumstance a happy omen, as it would enable him to give a color to his designs. He was not restrained from treachery either by fear or shame; for great men consider failure disgraceful,—a fraudulent success the contrary. But he was apprehensive that his possession of the city would excite the animosity of the Milanese, and perhaps induce them to throw themselves under the power of the Venetians. If he refused to accept the offer, he would have occasion to fear the duke of Savoy, to whom many citizens were inclined to submit themselves; and either alternative would deprive him of the sovereignty of Lombardy. Concluding there was less danger in taking possession of the city than in allowing another to have it, he determined to accept the proposal of the people of Pavia, trusting he would be able to satisfy the Milanese, to whom he pointed out the danger they must have incurred had he not complied with it; for her citizens would have surrendered themselves to the Venetians or to the duke of Savoy; so that in either case they would have been deprived of the government, and therefore they ought to be more willing to have himself as their neighbor and friend, than a hostile power such as either of the others, and their enemy. The Milanese were upon this occasion greatly perplexed, imagining they had discovered the count's ambition, and the end he had in view; but they thought it desirable to conceal their fears, for they did not know, if the count were to desert them, to whom they could have recourse except the Venetians, whose pride and tyranny they naturally dreaded. They therefore resolved not to break with the count, but by his assistance remedy the evils with which they were threatened, hoping that when freed from them they might rescue themselves from him also; for at that time they were assailed not only by the Venetians but by the Genoese and the duke of Savoy, in the name of Charles of Orleans, the son of a sister of Filippo, but whom the count easily vanquished. Thus their only remaining enemies were the Venetians, who, with a powerful army, determined to occupy their territories, and had already taken possession of Lodi and Piacenza, before which latter place the count encamped; and, after a long siege, took and pillaged the city. Winter being set in, he led his forces into quarters, and then withdrew to Cremona, where, during the cold season, he remained in repose with his wife.

In the spring, the Venetian and Milanese armies again took the field. It was the design of the Milanese, first to recover Lodi and then to come to terms with the Venetians; for the expenses of the war had become very great, and they were doubtful of their general's sincerity, so that they were anxious alike for the repose of peace, and for security against the count. They therefore resolved that the army should march to the siege of Carravaggio, hoping that Lodi would surrender, on that fortress being wrested from the enemy's hands. The count obeyed, though he would have preferred crossing the Adda and attacking the Brescian territory. Having encamped before Caravaggio, he so strongly entrenched himself, that if the enemy attempted to relieve the place, they would have to attack him at a great disadvantage. The Venetian army, led by Micheletto, approached within two bowshots of the enemy's camp, and many skirmishes ensued. The count continued to press the fortress, and reduced it to the very last extremity, which greatly distressed the Venetians, since they knew the loss of it would involve the total failure of their expedition. Very different views were entertained by their military officers respecting the best mode of relieving the place, but they saw no course open except to attack the enemy in his trenches, in spite of all obstacles. The castle was, however, considered of such paramount importance, that the Venetian senate, though naturally timid, and averse to all hazardous undertakings, chose rather to risk everything than allow it to fall into the hands of the enemy.

They therefore resolved to attack the count at all events, and early the next morning commenced their assault upon a point which was least defended. At the first charge, as commonly happens in a surprise, Francesco's whole army was thrown into dismay. Order, however, was soon so completely restored by the count, that the enemy, after various efforts to gain the outworks, were repulsed and put to flight; and so entirely routed, that of twelve thousand horse only one thousand escaped the hands of the Milanese, who took possession of all the carriages and military stores; nor had the Venetians ever before suffered such a thorough rout and overthrow. Among the plunder and prisoners, crouching down, as if to escape observation, was found a Venetian commissary, who, in the course of the war and before the fight, had spoken contemptuously of the count, calling him "bastard," and "base-born." Being made prisoner, he remembered his faults, and fearing punishment, being taken before the count, was agonized with terror; and, as is usual with mean minds (in prosperity insolent, in adversity abject and cringing), prostrated himself, weeping and begging pardon for the offenses he had committed. The count, taking him by the arm, raised him up, and encouraged him to hope for the best. He then said he wondered how a man so prudent and respectable as himself, could so far err as to speak disparagingly of those who did not merit it; and as regarded the insinuations which he had made against him, he really did not know how Sforza his father, and Madonna Lucia his mother, had proceeded together, not having been there, and having no opportunity of interfering in the matter, so that he was not liable either to blame or praise. However, he knew very well, that in regard to his own actions he had conducted himself so that no one could blame him; and in proof of this he would refer both the Venetian senate and himself to what had happened that day. He then advised him in future to be more respectful in speaking of others, and more cautious in regard to his own proceedings.

Chapter IV: The count's successes—The Venetians come to terms with him—Views of the Venetians—Indignation of the Milanese against the count—Their ambassador's address to him—The count's moderation and reply—The count and the Milanese prepare for war—Milanese ambassadors at Venice—League of the Venetians and Milanese—The count dupes the Venetians and Milanese—He applies for assistance to the Florentines—Diversity of opinions in Florence on the subject—Neri di Gino Capponi averse to assisting the count—Cosmo de' Medici disposed to do so—The Florentines sent ambassadors to the count.

After this victory, the count marched into the Brescian territory, occupied the whole country, and then pitched his camp within two miles of the city. The Venetians, having well-grounded fears that Brescia would be next attacked, provided the best defense in their power. They then collected the relics of their army, and, by virtue of the treaty, demanded assistance of the Florentines; who, being relieved from the war with Alfonso, sent them one thousand foot and two thousand horse, by whose aid the Venetians were in a condition to treat for peace. At one time it seemed the fate of their republic to lose by war and win by negotiation; for what was taken from them in battle was frequently restored twofold on the restoration of peace. They knew the Milanese were jealous of the count, and that he wished to be not their captain merely, but their sovereign; and as it was in their power to make peace with either of the two (the one desiring it from ambition, the other from fear), they determined to make choice of the count, and offer him assistance to effect his design; persuading themselves, that as the Milanese would perceive they had been duped by him, they would in revenge place themselves in the power of any one rather than in his; and that, becoming unable either to defend themselves or trust the count, they would be compelled, having no other resource, to fall into their hands. Having taken this resolution, they sounded the count, and found him quite disposed for peace, evidently desirous that the honor and advantage of the victory at Caravaggio should be his own, and not accrue to the Milanese. The parties therefore entered into an agreement, in which the Venetians undertook to pay the count thirteen thousand florins per month, till he should obtain Milan, and to furnish him, during the continuance of the war, four thousand horse and two thousand foot. The count engaged to restore to the Venetians the towns, prisoners, and whatever else had been taken by him during the late campaigns, and content himself with those territories which the duke possessed at the time of his death.

When this treaty became known at Milan, it grieved the citizens more than the victory at Caravaggio had exhilarated them. The rulers of the city mourned, the people complained, women and children wept, and all exclaimed against the count as false and perfidious. Although they could not hope that either prayers or promises would divert him from his ungrateful design, they sent ambassadors to see with what kind of color he would invest his unprincipled proceedings, and being admitted to his presence, one of them spoke to the following effect;—"It is customary with those who wish to obtain a favor, to make use either of prayers, presents, or threats, that pity, convenience, or fear, may induce a compliance with their requests. But as with cruel, avaricious, or, in their own conceit, powerful men, these arguments have no weight, it is vain to hope, either to soften them by prayers, win them by presents, or alarm them by menaces. We, therefore, being now, though late, aware of thy pride, cruelty, and ambition, come hither, not to ask aught, nor with the hope, even if we were so disposed, of obtaining it, but to remind thee of the benefits thou hast received from the people of Milan, and to prove with what heartless ingratitude thou hast repaid them, that at least, under the many evils oppressing us, we may derive some gratification from telling thee how and by whom they have been produced. Thou canst not have forgotten thy wretched condition at the death of the duke Filippo; the king and the pope were both thine enemies; thou hadst abandoned the Florentines and the Venetians, who, on account of their just indignation, and because they stood in no further need of thee, were almost become thy declared enemies. Thou wert exhausted by thy wars against the church; with few followers, no friends, or any money; hopeless of being able to preserve either thy territories or thy reputation. From these circumstances thy ruin must have ensued, but for our simplicity; we received thee to our home, actuated by reverence for the happy memory of our duke, with whom, being connected by marriage and renewed alliance, we believed thy affection would descend to those who had inherited his authority, and that, if to the benefits he had conferred on thee, our own were added, the friendship we sought to establish would not only be firm, but inseparable; with this impression, we added Verona or Brescia to thy previous appointments. What more could we either give or promise thee? What else couldst thou, not from us merely, but from any others, have either had or expected? Thou receivedst from us an unhoped-for benefit, and we, in return, an unmerited wrong. Neither hast thou deferred until now the manifestation of thy base designs; for no sooner wert thou appointed to command our armies, than, contrary to every dictate of propriety, thou didst accept Pavia, which plainly showed what was to be the result of thy friendship; but we bore with the injury, in hope that the greatness of the advantage would satisfy thy ambition. Alas! those who grasp at all cannot be satisfied with a part. Thou didst promise that we should possess the conquests which thou might afterward make; for thou wert well aware that what was given at many times might be withdrawn at once, as was the case after the victory at Caravaggio, purchased by our money and blood, and followed by our ruin. Oh! unhappy states, which have to guard against their oppressor; but much more wretched those who have to trust to mercenary and faithless arms like thine! May our example instruct posterity, since that of Thebes and Philip of Macedon, who, after victory over her enemies, from being her captain became her foe and her prince, could not avail us.

"The only fault of which we are conscious is our over-weening confidence in one whom we ought not to have trusted; for thy past life, thy restless mind, incapable of repose, ought to have put us on our guard; neither ought we to have confided in one who betrayed the lord of Lucca, set a fine upon the Florentines and the Venetians, defied the duke, despised the king, and besides all this, persecuted the church of God, and the Divinity himself with innumerable atrocities. We ought not to have fancied that so many potentates possessed less influence over the mind of Francesco Sforza, than the Milanese; or that he would preserve unblemished that faith towards us which he had on so many occasions broken with them. Still this want of caution in us does not excuse the perfidy in thee; nor can it obliterate the infamy with which our just complaints will blacken thy character throughout the world, or prevent the remorse of thy conscience, when our arms are used for our own destruction; for thou wilt see that the sufferings due to parricides are fully deserved by thee. And though ambition should blind thine eyes, the whole world, witness to thine iniquity, will compel thee to open them; God himself will unclose them, if perjuries, if violated faith, if treacheries displease him, and if, as ever, he is still the enemy of the wicked. Do not, therefore, promise thyself any certainty of victory; for the just wrath of the Almighty will weigh heavily upon thee; and we are resolved to lose our liberty only with our lives; but if we found we could not ultimately defend it, we would submit ourselves to anyone rather than to thee. And if our sins be so great that in spite of our utmost resolution, we should still fall into thy hands, be quite assured, that the sovereignty which is commenced in deceit and villainy, will terminate either in thyself or thy children with ignominy and blood."

The count, though not insensible to the just reproaches of the Milanese, did not exhibit either by words or gestures any unusual excitement, and replied, that "He willingly attributed to their angry feelings all the serious charges of their indiscreet harangue; and he would reply to them in detail, were he in the presence of anyone who could decide their differences; for it would be evident that he had not injured the Milanese, but only taken care that they should not injure him. They well knew how they had proceeded after the victory of Caravaggio; for, instead of rewarding him with either Verona or Brescia, they sought peace with the Venetians, that all the blame of the quarrel might rest on him, themselves obtaining the fruit of victory, the credit of peace, and all the advantages that could be derived from the war. It would thus be manifest they had no right to complain, when he had effected the arrangements which they first attempted to make; and that if he had deferred to do so a little longer, he would have had reason to accuse them of the ingratitude with which they were now charging him. Whether the charge were true or false, that God, whom they had invoked to avenge their injuries, would show at the conclusion of the war, and would demonstrate which was most his friend, and who had most justice on their side."

Upon the departure of the ambassadors, the count determined to attack the Milanese, who prepared for their defense, and appointed Francesco and Jacopo Piccinino (attached to their cause, on account of the ancient feud of the families of Braccio and Sforza) to conduct their forces in support of liberty; at least till they could deprive the count of the aid of the Venetians, who they did not think would long be either friendly or faithful to him. On the other hand, the count, perfectly aware of this, thought it not imprudent, supposing the obligation of the treaty insufficient, to bind them by the ties of interest; and, therefore, in assigning to each their portion of the enterprise, he consented that the Venetians should attack Crema, and himself, with the other forces, assail the remainder of the territory. The advantage of this arrangement kept the Venetians so long in alliance with the count, that he was enabled to conquer the whole of the Milanese territory, and to press the city so closely, that the inhabitants could not provide themselves with necessaries; despairing of success, they sent envoys to the Venetians to beg they would compassionate their distress, and, as ought to be the case between republics, assist them in defense of their liberty against a tyrant, whom, if once master of their city, they would be unable to restrain; neither did they think he would be content with the boundaries assigned him by the treaty, but would expect all the dependencies of Milan.

The Venetians had not yet taken Crema, and wishing before they changed sides, to effect this point, they *Publicly* answered the envoys, that their engagements with the count prevented them from defending the Milanese; but *Secretly*, gave them every assurance of their wish to do so.

The count had approached so near Milan with his forces, that he was disputing the suburbs with the inhabitants, when the Venetians having taken Crema, thought they need no longer hesitate to declare in favor of the Milanese, with whom they made peace and entered into alliance; among the terms of which was the defense of their liberty unimpaired. Having come to this agreement, they ordered their forces to withdraw from the count's camp and to return to the Venetian territory. They informed him of the peace made with the Milanese, and gave him twenty days to consider what course he would adopt. He was not surprised at the step taken by the Venetians, for he had long foreseen it, and expected its occurrence daily; but when it actually took place, he could not avoid feeling regret and displeasure similar to what the Milanese had experienced when he abandoned them. He took two days to consider the reply he would make to the ambassadors whom the Venetians had sent to inform him of the treaty, and during this time he determined to dupe the Venetians, and not abandon his enterprise; therefore, appearing openly to accept the proposal for peace, he sent his ambassadors to Venice with full credentials to effect the ratification, but gave them secret orders not to do so, and with pretexts or caviling to put it off. To give the Venetians greater assurance of his sincerity, he made a truce with the Milanese for a month, withdrew from Milan and divided his forces among the places he had taken. This course was the occasion of his victory and the ruin of the Milanese; for the Venetians, confident of peace, were slow in preparing for war, and the Milanese finding the truce concluded, the enemy withdrawn, and the Venetians their friends, felt assured that the count had determined to abandon his design. This idea injured them in two ways: one, by neglecting to provide for their defense; the next, that, being seed-time, they sowed a large quantity of grain in the country which the enemy had evacuated, and thus brought famine upon themselves. On the other hand, all that was injurious to his enemies favored the count, and the time gave him opportunity to take breath and provide himself with assistance.

The Florentines during the war of Lombardy had not declared in favor of either party, or assisted the count either in defense of the Milanese or since; for he never having been in need had not pressingly requested it; and they only sent assistance to the Venetians after the rout at Caravaggio, in pursuance of the treaty. Count Francesco, standing now alone, and not knowing to whom else he could apply, was compelled to request immediate aid of the Florentines, publicly from the state, and privately from friends, particularly from Cosmo de' Medici, with whom he had always maintained a steady friendship, and by whom he had constantly been faithfully advised and liberally supported. Nor did Cosmo abandon him in his extreme necessity, but supplied him generously from his own resources, and encouraged him to prosecute his design. He also wished the city publicly to assist him, but there were difficulties in the way. Neri di Gino Capponi, one of the most powerful citizens of Florence, thought it not to the advantage of the city, that the count should obtain Milan; and was of opinion that it would be more to the safety of Italy for him to ratify the peace than pursue the war. In the first place, he apprehended that the Milanese, through their anger against the count, would surrender themselves entirely to the Venetians, which would occasion the ruin of all. Supposing he should occupy Milan, it appeared to him that so great military superiority, combined with such an extent of territory, would be dangerous to themselves, and that if as count he was intolerable, he would become doubly so as duke. He therefore considered it better for the republic of Florence and for Italy, that the count should be content with his military reputation, and that Lombardy should be divided into two republics, which could never be united to injure others, and separately are unable to do so. To attain this he saw no better means than to refrain from aiding the count, and continuing in the former league with the Venetians. These reasonings were not satisfactory to Cosmo's friends, for they imagined that Neri had argued thus, not from a conviction of its advantage to the republic, but to prevent the count, as a friend of Cosmo, from becoming duke, apprehending that Cosmo would, in consequence of this, become too powerful.

Cosmo, in reply, pointed out, that to lend assistance to the count would be highly beneficial both to Italy and the republic; for it was unwise to imagine the Milanese could preserve their own liberty; for the nature of their community, their mode of life, and their hereditary feuds were opposed to every kind of civil government, so that it was necessary, either that the count should become duke of Milan, or the Venetians her lords. And surely under such circumstances, no one could doubt which would be most to their advantage, to have for their neighbor a powerful friend or a far more powerful foe. Neither need it be apprehended that the Milanese, while at war with the count, would submit to the Venetians; for the count had a stronger party in the city, and the Venetians had not, so that whenever they were unable to defend themselves as freemen, they would be more inclined to obey the count than the Venetians.

These diverse views kept the city long in suspense; but at length it was resolved to send ambassadors to the count to settle the terms of agreement, with instructions, that if they found him in such a condition as to give hopes of his ultimate success, they were to close with him, but, if otherwise, they were to draw out the time in diplomacy.

Chapter V: Prosecution of the war between the count and the Milanese—The Milanese reduced to extremity—The people rise against the magistrates—Milan surrenders to the count—League between the new duke of Milan and the Florentines, and between the king of Naples and the Venetians—Venetian and Neapolitan ambassadors at Florence—Answer of Cosmo de' Medici to the Venetian ambassador—Preparations of the Venetians and the king of Naples for the war—The Venetians excite disturbances in Bologna—Florence prepares for war—The emperor, Frederick III. at Florence—War in Lombardy between the duke of Milan and the Venetians—Ferrando, son of the king of Naples, marches into Tuscany against the Florentines.

The ambassadors were at Reggio when they heard that the count had become lord of Milan; for as soon as the truce had expired, he approached the city with his forces, hoping quickly to get possession of it in spite of the Venetians, who could bring no relief except from the side of the Adda, which route he could easily obstruct, and therefore had no apprehension (being then winter) of their arrival, and he trusted that, before the return of spring, he would be victorious, particularly, as by the death of Francesco Piccinino, there remained only Jacopo his brother, to command the Milanese. The Venetians had sent an ambassador to Milan to confirm the citizens in their resolution of defense, promising them powerful and immediate aid. During the winter a few slight skirmishes had taken place between the count and the Venetians; but on the approach of milder weather, the latter, under Pandolfo Malatesti, halted with their army upon the Adda, and considering whether, in order to succor the Milanese, they ought to risk a battle, Pardolfo, their general, aware of the count's abilities, and the courage of his army, said it would be unadvisable to do so, and that, under the circumstances, it was needless, for the count, being in great want of forage, could not keep the field, and must soon retire. He therefore advised them to remain encamped, to keep the Milanese in hope, and prevent them from surrendering. This advice was approved by the Venetians, both as being safe, and because, by keeping the Milanese in this necessity, they might be the sooner compelled to submit to their dominion; for they felt quite sure that the injuries they had received would always prevent their submission to the count.

In the meantime, the Milanese were reduced to the utmost misery; and as the city usually abounded with poor, many died of hunger in the streets; hence arose complaints and disturbances in several parts, which alarmed the magistrates, and compelled them to use their utmost exertions to prevent popular meetings. The multitude are always slow to resolve on commotion; but the resolution once formed, any trivial circumstance excites it to action. Two men in humble life, talking together near the Porta Nuova of the calamities of the city, their own misery, and the means that might be adopted for their relief, others beginning to congregate, there was soon collected a large crowd; in consequence of it a report was spread that the neighborhood of Porta Nuova had risen against the government. Upon this, all the lower orders, who only waited for an example, assembled in arms, and chose Gasparre da Vicomercato to be their leader. They then proceeded to the place where the magistrates were assembled, and attacked them so impetuously that all who did not escape by flight were slain: among the number, as being considered a principal cause of the famine, and gratified at their distress, fell Lionardo Veniero, the Venetian ambassador. Having thus almost become masters of the city, they considered what course was next to be adopted to escape from the horrors surrounding them, and to procure peace. A feeling universally prevailed, that as they could not preserve their own liberty, they ought to submit to a prince who could defend them. Some proposed King Alfonso, some the duke of Savoy, and others the king of France, but none mentioned the count, so great was the general indignation against him. However, disagreeing with the rest, Gasparre da Vicomercato proposed him, and explained in detail that if they desired relief from war, no other plan was open, since the people of Milan required a certain and immediate peace, and not a distant hope of succor. He apologized for the count's proceedings, accused the Venetians, and all the powers of Italy, of which some from ambition and others from avarice were averse to their possessing freedom. Having to dispose of their liberty, it would be preferable, he said, to obey one who knew and could defend them; so that, by their servitude they might obtain peace, and not bring upon themselves greater evils and more dangerous wars. He was listened to with the most profound attention; and, having concluded his harangue, it was unanimously resolved by the assembly, that the count should be called in, and Gasparre was appointed to wait upon him and signify their desire. By the people's command he conveyed the pleasing and happy intelligence to the count, who heard it with the utmost satisfaction, and entered Milan as prince on the twenty-sixth of February, 1450, where he was received with the greatest possible joy by those who, only a short time previously had heaped on him all the slanders that hatred could inspire.

The news of this event reaching Florence, orders were immediately sent to the envoys who were upon the way to Milan, that instead of treating for his alliance with the count, they should congratulate the duke upon his victory; they, arranging accordingly, had a most honorable reception, and were treated with all possible respect; for the duke well knew that in all Italy he could not find braver or more faithful friends, to defend him against the power of the Venetians, than the Florentines, who, being no longer in fear of the house of Visconti, found themselves opposed by the Aragonese and Venetians; for the Aragonese princes of Naples were jealous of the friendship which the Florentines had always evinced for the family of France; and the Venetians seeing the ancient enmity of the Florentines against the Visconti transferred to themselves, resolved to injure them as much as possible; for they knew how pertinaciously and invariably they had persecuted the Lombard princes. These considerations caused the new duke willingly to join the Florentines, and united the Venetians and King Alfonso against their common enemies; impelling them at the same time to hostilities, the king against the Florentines, and the Venetians against the duke, who, being fresh in the government, would, they imagined, be unable to resist them, even with all the aid he could obtain.

But as the league between the Florentines and the Venetians still continued, and as the king, after the war of Piombino, had made peace with the former, it seemed indecent to commence an open rupture until some plausible reason could be assigned in justification of offensive measures. On this account each sent ambassadors to Florence, who, on the part of their sovereigns, signified that the league formed between them was made not for injury to any, but solely for the mutual defense of their states. The Venetian ambassador then complained that the Florentines had allowed Alessandro, the duke's brother, to pass into Lombardy with his forces; and besides this, had assisted and advised in the treaty made between the duke and the marquis of Mantua, matters which he declared to be injurious to the Venetians, and inconsistent with the friendship hitherto subsisting between the two governments; amicably reminding them, that one who inflicts unmerited injury, gives others just ground of hostility, and that those who break a peace may expect war. The Signory appointed Cosmo de' Medici to reply to what had been said by the Venetian ambassador, and in a long and excellent speech he recounted the numerous advantages conferred by the city on the Venetian republic; showed what an extent of dominion they had acquired by the money, forces, and counsel of the Florentines, and reminded him that, although the friendship had originated with the Florentines, they had never given occasion of enmity; and as they desired peace, they greatly rejoiced when the treaty was made, if it had been entered into for the sake of peace, and not of war. True it was, he wondered much at the remarks which had been made, seeing that such light and trivial matters should give offense to so great a republic; but if they were worthy of notice he must have it universally understood, that the Florentines wished their country to be free and open to all; and that the duke's character was such, that if he desired the friendship of the marquis of Mantua, he had no need of anyone's favor or advice. He therefore feared that these cavils were produced by some latent motive, which it was not thought proper to disclose. Be this as it might, they would freely declare to all, that in the same proportion as the friendship of the Florentines was beneficial their enmity could be destructive.

The matter was hushed up; and the ambassadors, on their departure, appeared perfectly satisfied. But the league between the king and the Venetians made the Florentines and the duke rather apprehend war than hope for a long continuance of peace. They therefore entered into an alliance, and at the same time the enmity of the Venetians transpired by a treaty with the Siennese, and the expulsion of all Florentine subjects from their cities and territories. Shortly after this, Alfonso did the same, without any consideration of the peace made the year previous, and not having even the shadow of an excuse. The Venetians attempted to take Bologna, and having armed the emigrants, and united to them a considerable force, introduced them into the city by night through one of the common sewers. No sooner had they entered, than they raised a cry, by which Santi Bentivogli, being awakened, was told that the whole city was in possession of the rebels. But though many advised him to escape, saying that he could not save the city by his stay, he determined to confront the danger, and taking arms encouraged his followers, assembled a few friends, attacked and routed part of the rebels, slew many more, and drove the remainder out of the city. By this act of bravery all agreed he had fully proved himself a genuine scion of the house of the Bentivogli.

These events and demonstrations gave the Florentines an earnest of approaching war; they consequently followed their usual practice on similar occasions, and created the Council of Ten. They engaged new condottieri, sent ambassadors to Rome, Naples, Venice, Milan, and Sienna, to demand assistance from their friends, gain information about those they suspected, decide such as were wavering, and discover the designs of the foe. From the pope they obtained only general expressions of an amicable disposition and admonitions to peace; from the king, empty excuses for having expelled the Florentines, and offers of safe conduct for whoever should demand it; and although he endeavored, as much as possible, to conceal every indication of his hostile designs, the ambassadors felt convinced of his unfriendly disposition, and observed many preparations tending to the injury of the republic. The League with the duke was strengthened by mutual obligations, and through his means they became friends with the Genoese, the old differences with them respecting reprisals, and other small matters of dispute, being composed, although the Venetians used every possible means to prevent it, and entreated the emperor of Constantinople to expel all Florentines from his dominions; so fierce was the animosity with which they entered on this war, and so powerful their lust of dominion, that without the least hesitation they sought the destruction of those who had been the occasion of their own power. The emperor, however, refused to listen to them. The Venetian senate forbade the Florentine ambassadors to enter their territories, alleging, that being in league with the king, they could not entertain them without his concurrence. The Siennese received the ambassadors with fair words, fearing their own ruin before the League could assist them, and therefore endeavored to appease the powers whose attack they were unable to resist. The Venetians and the king (as was then conjectured) were disposed to send ambassadors to Florence to justify the war. But the Venetian envoy was not allowed to enter the Florentine dominions, and the king's ambassador, being unwilling to perform his office alone, the embassy was not completed; and thus the Venetians learned, that however little they might esteem the Florentines, the latter had still less respect for them.

In the midst of these fears, the emperor, Frederick III., came into Italy to be crowned. On the thirtieth of January, 1451, he entered Florence with fifteen hundred horse, and was most honorably received by the Signory. He remained in the city till the sixth of February, and then proceeded to Rome for his coronation, where, having been solemnly consecrated, and his marriage celebrated with the empress, who had come to Rome by sea, he returned to Germany, and again passed through Florence in May, with the same honors as upon his arrival. On his return, having derived some benefits from the marquis of Mantua, he conceded to him Modena and Reggio. In the meantime, the Florentines did not fail to prepare themselves for immediate war; and to augment their influence, and strike the enemy with terror, they, in conjunction with the duke, entered into alliance with the king of France for the mutual defense of their states. This treaty was published with great pomp throughout all Italy.

The month of May, 1452, having arrived, the Venetians thought it not desirable to defer any longer their attack upon the duke, and with sixteen thousand horse and six thousand foot assailed his territories in the direction of Lodi, while the marquis of Montferrat, instigated either by his own ambition or the entreaties of the Venetians, did the same on the side of Alexandria. The duke assembled a force of eighteen thousand cavalry and three thousand infantry, garrisoned Alexandria and Lodi, and all the other places where the enemy might annoy them. He then attacked the Brescian territory, and greatly harassed the Venetians; while both parties alike plundered the country and ravaged the smaller towns. Having defeated the marquis of Montferrat at Alexandria, the duke was able to unite his whole force against the Venetians and invade their territory.

While the war in Lombardy proceeded thus, giving rise to various trifling incidents unworthy of recital, King Alfonso and the Florentines carried on hostilities in Tuscany, but in a similarly inefficient manner, evincing no greater talent, and incurring no greater danger. Ferrando, the illegitimate son of Alfonso, entered the country with twelve thousand troops, under the command of Federigo, lord of Urbino. Their first attempt was to attack Fojano, in the Val di Chiane; for, having the Siennese in their favor, they entered the Florentine territory in that direction. The walls of the castle were weak, and it was small, and consequently poorly manned, but the garrison were, among the soldiers of that period, considered brave and faithful. Two hundred infantry were also sent by the Signory for its defense. Before this castle, thus provided, Ferrando sat down, and either from the valor of its defenders or his own deficiencies, thirty-six days elapsed before he took it. This interval enabled the city to make better provision for places of greater importance, to collect forces and conclude more effective arrangements than had hitherto been made. The enemy next proceeded into the district of Chiane, where they attacked two small towns, the property of private citizens, but could not capture them. They then encamped before the Castellina, a fortress upon the borders of the Chianti, within ten miles of Sienna, weak from its defective construction, and still more so by its situation; but, notwithstanding these defects, the assailants were compelled to retire in disgrace, after having lain before it forty-four days. So formidable were those armies, and so perilous those wars, that places now abandoned as untenable were then defended as impregnable.

While Ferrando was encamped in the Chianti he made many incursions, and took considerable booty from the Florentine territories, extending his depredations within six miles of the city, to the great alarm and injury of the people, who at this time, having sent their forces to the number of eight thousand soldiers under Astorre da Faenza and Gismondo Malatesti toward Castel di Colle, kept them at a distance from the enemy, lest they should be compelled to an engagement; for they considered that so long as they were not beaten in a pitched battle, they could not be vanquished in the war generally; for small castles, when lost, were recovered at the peace, and larger places were in no danger, because the enemy would not venture to attack them. The king had also a fleet of about twenty vessels, comprising galleys and smaller craft, which lay off Pisa, and during the siege of Castellina were moored near the Rocca di Vada, which, from the negligence of the governor, he took, and then harassed the surrounding country. However, this annoyance was easily removed by a few soldiers sent by the Florentines to Campiglia, and who confined the enemy to the coast.

Chapter VI: Conspiracy of Stefano Porcari against the papal government—The conspirators discovered and punished—The Florentines recover the places they had lost—Gherardo Gambacorti, lord of Val di Bagno, endeavors to transfer his territories to the king of Naples—Gallant conduct of Antonio Gualandi, who counteracts the design of Gambacorti—Rene of Anjou is called into Italy by the Florentines—Rene returns to France—The pope endeavors to restore peace—Peace proclaimed—Jacopo Piccinino attacks the Siennese.

The pontiff did not interfere in these affairs further than to endeavor to bring the parties to a mutual accommodation; but while he refrained from external wars he incurred the danger of more serious troubles at home. Stefano Porcari was a Roman citizen, equally distinguished for nobility of birth and extent of learning, but still more by the excellence of his character. Like all who are in pursuit of glory, he resolved either to perform or to attempt something worthy of memory, and thought he could not do better than deliver his country from the hands of the prelates, and restore the ancient form of government; hoping, in the event of success, to be considered a new founder or second father of the city. The dissolute manners of the priesthood, and the discontent of the Roman barons and people, encouraged him to look for a happy termination of his enterprise; but he derived his greatest confidence from those verses of Petrarch in the canzone which begins, "Spirto gentil che quelle membra reggi," where he says,—

"Sopra il Monte Tarpejo canzon vedra, Un cavalier, ch' Italia tutta onora, Pensoso piu d'altrui, che di se stesso."

Stefano, believing poets are sometimes endowed with a divine and prophetic spirit, thought the event must take place which Petrarch in this canzone seemed to foretell, and that he was destined to effect the glorious task; considering himself in learning, eloquence, friends, and influence, superior to any other citizen of Rome. Having taken these impressions, he had not sufficient prudence to avoid discovering his design by his discourse, demeanor, and mode of living; so that the pope becoming acquainted with it, in order to prevent the commission of some rash act, banished him to Bologna and charged the governor of the city to compel his appearance before him once every day. Stefano was not daunted by this first check, but with even greater earnestness prosecuted his undertaking, and, by such means as were available, more cautiously corresponded with his friends, and often went and returned from Rome with such celerity as to be in time to present himself before the governor within the limit allowed for his appearance. Having acquired a sufficient number of partisans, he determined to make the attempt without further delay, and arranged with his friends at Rome to provide an evening banquet, to which all the conspirators were invited, with orders that each should bring with him his most trust-worthy friends, and himself promised to be with him before the entertainment was served. Everything was done according to this orders, and Stefano Porcari arrived at the place appointed. Supper being brought in, he entered the apartment dressed in cloth of gold, with rich ornaments about his neck, to give him a dignified appearance and commanding aspect. Having embraced the company, he delivered a long oration to dispose their minds to the glorious undertaking. He then arranged the measures to be adopted, ordering that one part of them should, on the following morning, take possession of the pontiff's palace, and that the other should call the people of Rome to arms. The affair came to the knowledge of the pope the same night, some say by treachery among the conspirators, and others that he knew of Porcari's presence at Rome. Be this as it may, on the night of the supper Stefano, and the greater part of his associates, were arrested, and afterward expiated their crime by death. Thus ended his enterprise; and though some may applaud his intentions, he must stand charged with deficiency of understanding; for such undertakings, though possessing some slight appearance of glory, are almost always attended with ruin.

Gherardo Gambacorti was lord of Val di Bagno, and his ancestors as well as himself had always been in the pay or under the protection of the Florentines. Alfonso endeavored to induce him to exchange his territory for another in the kingdom of Naples. This became known to the Signory, who, in order to ascertain his designs, sent an ambassador to Gambacorti, to remind him of the obligations of his ancestors and himself to their republic, and induce him to continue faithful to them. Gherardo affected the greatest astonishment, assured the ambassador with solemn oaths that no such treacherous thought had ever entered his mind, and that he would gladly go to Florence and pledge himself for the truth of his assertions; but being unable, from indisposition, he would send his son as an hostage. These assurances, and the proposal with which they were accompanied, induced the Florentines to think Gherardo had been slandered, and that his accuser must be alike weak and treacherous. Gherardo, however, hastened his negotiation with redoubled zeal, and having arranged the terms, Alfonso sent Frate Puccio, a knight of Jerusalem, with a strong body of men to the Val di Bagno, to take possession of the fortresses and towns, the people of which, being attached to the Florentine republic, submitted unwillingly.

Frate Puccio had already taken possession of nearly the whole territory, except the fortress of Corzano. Gambacorti was accompanied, while transferring his dominions, by a young Pisan of great courage and address, named Antonio Gualandi, who, considering the whole affair, the strength of the place, the well known bravery of the garrison, their evident reluctance to give it up, and the baseness of Gambacorti, at once resolved to make an effort to prevent the fulfillment of his design; and Gherardo being at the entrance, for the purpose of introducing the Aragonese, he pushed him out with both his hands, and commanded the guards to shut the gate upon such a scoundrel, and hold the fortress for the Florentine republic. When this circumstance became known in Bagno and the neighboring places, the inhabitants took up arms against the king's forces, and, raising the Florentine standard, drove them out. The Florentines learning these events, imprisoned Gherardo's son, and sent troops to Bagno for the defense of the territory, which having hitherto been governed by its own prince, now became a vicariate. The traitor Gherardo escaped with difficulty, leaving his wife, family, and all his property, in the hands of those whom he had endeavored to betray. This affair was considered by the Florentines of great importance; for had the king succeeded in securing the territory, he might have overrun the Val di Tavere and the Casentino at his pleasure, and would have caused so much annoyance, that they could no longer have allowed their whole force to act against the army of the Aragonese at Sienna.

In addition to the preparations made by the Florentines in Italy to resist the hostile League, they sent as ambassador, Agnolo Acciajuoli, to request that the king of France would allow Rene of Anjou to enter Italy in favor of the duke and themselves, and also, that by his presence in the country, he might defend his friends and attempt the recovery of the kingdom of Naples; for which purpose they offered him assistance in men and money. While the war was proceeding in Lombardy and Tuscany, the ambassador effected an arrangement with King Rene, who promised to come into Italy during the month of June, the League engaging to pay him thirty thousand florins upon his arrival at Alexandria, and ten thousand per month during the continuance of the war. In pursuance of this treaty, King Rene commenced his march into Italy, but was stopped by the duke of Savoy and the marquis of Montferrat, who, being in alliance with the Venetians, would not allow him to pass. The Florentine ambassador advised, that in order to uphold the influence of his friends, he should return to Provence, and conduct part of his forces into Italy by sea, and, in the meantime, endeavor, by the authority of the king of France, to obtain a passage for the remainder through the territories of the duke. This plan was completely successful; for Rene came into Italy by sea, and his forces, by the mediation of the king of France, were allowed a passage through Savoy. King Rene was most honorably received by Duke Francesco, and joining his French with the Italian forces, they attacked the Venetians with so much impetuosity, that they shortly recovered all the places which had been taken in the Cremonese. Not content with this, they occupied nearly the whole Brescian territory; so that the Venetians, unable to keep the field, withdrew close to the walls of Brescia.

Winter coming on, the duke deemed it advisable to retire into quarters, and appointed Piacenza for the forces of Rene, where, having passed the whole of the cold season of 1453, without attempting anything, the duke thought of taking the field, on the approach of spring, and stripping the Venetians of the remainder of their possessions by land, but was informed by the king that he was obliged of necessity to return to France. This determination was quite new and unexpected to the duke, and caused him the utmost concern; but though he immediately went to dissuade Rene from carrying it into effect, he was unable either by promises or entreaties to divert him from his purpose. He engaged, however, to leave part of his forces, and send his son for the service of the League. The Florentines were not displeased at this; for having recovered their territories and castles, they were no longer in fear of Alfonso, and on the other hand, they did not wish the duke to obtain any part of Lombardy but what belonged to him. Rene took his departure, and send his son John into Italy, according to his promise, who did not remain in Lombardy, but came direct to Florence, where he was received with the highest respect.

The king's departure made the duke desirous of peace. The Venetians, Alfonso, and the Florentines, being all weary of the war, were similarly disposed; and the pope continued to wish it as much as ever; for during this year the Turkish emperor, Mohammed, had taken Constantinople and subdued the whole of Greece. This conquest alarmed the Christians, more especially the Venetians and the pope, who already began to fancy the Mohammedans at their doors. The pope therefore begged the Italian potentates to send ambassadors to himself, with authority to negotiate a general peace, with which all complied; but when the particular circumstances of each case came to be considered, many difficulties were found in the war of effecting it. King Alfonso required the Florentines to reimburse the expenses he had incurred in the war, and the Florentines demanded some compensation from him. The Venetians thought themselves entitled to Cremona from the duke; while he insisted upon the restoration of Bergamo, Brescia, and Crema; so that it seemed impossible to reconcile such conflicting claims. But what could not be effected by a number at Rome was easily managed at Milan and Venice by two; for while the matter was under discussion at Rome, the duke and the Venetians came to an arrangement on the ninth of April, 1454, by virtue of which, each party resumed what they possessed before the war, the duke being allowed to recover from the princes of Montferrat and Savoy the places they had taken. To the other Italian powers a month was allowed to ratify the treaty. The pope and the Florentines, and with them the Siennese and other minor powers, acceded to it within the time. Besides this, the Florentines, the Venetians, and the duke concluded a treaty of peace for twenty-five years. King Alfonso alone exhibited dissatisfaction at what had taken place, thinking he had not been sufficiently considered, that he stood, not on the footing of a principal, but only ranked as an auxiliary, and therefore kept aloof, and would not disclose his intentions. However, after receiving a legate from the pope, and many solemn embassies from other powers, he allowed himself to be persuaded, principally by means of the pontiff, and with his son joined the League for thirty years. The duke and the king also contracted a twofold relationship and double marriage, each giving a daughter to a son of the other. Notwithstanding this, that Italy might still retain the seeds of war, Alfonso would not consent to the peace, unless the League would allow him, without injury to themselves, to make war upon the Genoese, Gismondo Malatesti, and Astorre, prince of Faenza. This being conceded, his son Ferrando, who was at Sienna, returned to the kingdom, having by his coming into Tuscany acquired no dominion and lost a great number of his men.

Upon the establishment of a general peace, the only apprehension entertained was, that it would be disturbed by the animosity of Alfonso against the Genoese; yet it happened otherwise. The king, indeed, did not openly infringe the peace, but it was frequently broken by the ambition of the mercenary troops. The Venetians, as usual on the conclusion of a war, had discharged Jacopo Piccinino, who with some other unemployed condottieri, marched into Romagna, thence into the Siennese, and halting in the country, took possession of many places. At the commencement of these disturbances, and the beginning of the year 1455, Pope Nicholas died, and was succeeded by Calixtus III., who, to put a stop to the war newly broken out so near home, immediately sent Giovanni Ventimiglia, his general, with what forces he could furnish. These being joined by the troops of the Florentines and the duke of Milan, both of whom furnished assistance, attacked Jacopo, near Bolsena, and though Ventimiglia was taken prisoner, yet Jacopo was worsted, and retreated in disorder to Castiglione della Pescaia, where, had he not been assisted by Alfonso, his force would have been completely annihilated. This made it evident that Jacopo's movement had been made by order of Alfonso, and the latter, as if palpably detected, to conciliate his allies, after having almost alienated them with this unimportant war, ordered Jacopo to restore to the Siennese the places he had taken, and they gave him twenty thousand florins by way of ransom, after which he and his forces were received into the kingdom of Naples.

Chapter VII: Christendom alarmed by the progress of the Turks—The Turks routed before Belgrade—Description of a remarkable hurricane—War against the Genoese and Gismondo Malatesti—Genoa submits to the king of France—Death of Alfonso king of Naples—Succeeded by his son Ferrando—The pope designs to give the kingdom of Naples to his nephew Piero Lodovico Borgia—Eulogy of Pius II.—Disturbances in Genoa between John of Anjou and the Fregosi—The Fregosi subdued—John attacks the kingdom of Naples—Ferrando king of Naples routed—Ferrando reinstated—The Genoese cast off the French yoke—John of Anjou routed in the kingdom of Naples.

The pope, though anxious to restrain Jacopo Piccinino, did not neglect to make provision for the defense of Christendom, which seemed in danger from the Turks. He sent ambassadors and preachers into every Christian country, to exhort princes and people to arm in defense of their religion, and with their persons and property to contribute to the enterprise against the common enemy. In Florence, large sums were raised, and many citizens bore the mark of a red cross upon their dress to intimate their readiness to become soldiers of the faith. Solemn processions were made, and nothing was neglected either in public or private, to show their willingness to be among the most forward to assist the enterprise with money, counsel, or men. But the eagerness for this crusade was somewhat abated, by learning that the Turkish army, being at the siege of Belgrade, a strong city and fortress in Hungary, upon the banks of the Danube, had been routed and the emperor wounded; so that the alarm felt by the pope and all Christendom, on the loss of Constantinople, having ceased to operate, they proceeded with deliberately with their preparations for war; and in Hungary their zeal was cooled through the death of Giovanni Corvini the Waiwode, who commanded the Hungarian forces on that memorable occasion, and fell in the battle.

To return to the affairs of Italy. In the year 1456, the disturbances occasioned by Jacopo Piccinino having subsided, and human weapons laid aside, the heavens seemed to make war against the earth; dreadful tempestuous winds then occurring, which produced effects unprecedented in Tuscany, and which to posterity will appear marvelous and unaccountable. On the twenty-fourth of August, about an hour before daybreak, there arose from the Adriatic near Ancona, a whirlwind, which crossing from east to west, again reached the sea near Pisa, accompanied by thick clouds, and the most intense and impenetrable darkness, covering a breadth of about two miles in the direction of its course. Under some natural or supernatural influence, this vast and overcharged volume of condensed vapor burst; its fragments contended with indescribable fury, and huge bodies sometimes ascending toward heaven, and sometimes precipitated upon the earth, struggled, as it were, in mutual conflict, whirling in circles with intense velocity, and accompanied by winds, impetuous beyond all conception; while flashes of awful brilliancy, and murky, lurid flames incessantly broke forth. From these confused clouds, furious winds, and momentary fires, sounds issued, of which no earthquake or thunder ever heard could afford the least idea; striking such awe into all, that it was thought the end of the world had arrived, that the earth, waters, heavens, and entire universe, mingling together, were being resolved into their ancient chaos. Wherever this awful tempest passed, it produced unprecedented and marvelous effects; but these were more especially experienced near the castle of St. Casciano, about eight miles from Florence, upon the hill which separates the valleys of Pisa and Grieve. Between this castle and the Borgo St. Andrea, upon the same hill, the tempest passed without touching the latter, and in the former, only threw down some of the battlements and the chimneys of a few houses; but in the space between them, it leveled many buildings quite to the ground. The roofs of the churches of St. Martin, at Bagnolo, and Santa Maria della Pace, were carried more than a mile, unbroken as when upon their respective edifices. A muleteer and his beasts were driven from the road into the adjoining valley, and found dead. All the large oaks and lofty trees which could not bend beneath its influence, were not only stripped of their branches but borne to a great distance from the places where they grew, and when the tempest had passed over and daylight made the desolation visible, the inhabitants were transfixed with dismay. The country had lost all its habitable character; churches and dwellings were laid in heaps; nothing was heard but the lamentations of those whose possessions had perished, or whose cattle or friends were buried beneath the ruins; and all who witnessed the scene were filled with anguish or compassion. It was doubtless the design of the Omnipotent, rather to threaten Tuscany than to chastise her; for had the hurricane been directed over the city, filled with houses and inhabitants, instead of proceeding among oaks and elms, or small and thinly scattered dwellings, it would have been such a scourge as the mind, with all its ideas of horror, could not have conceived. But the Almighty desired that this slight example should suffice to recall the minds of men to a knowledge of himself and of his power.

To return to our history. King Alfonso was dissatisfied with the peace, and as the war which he had unnecessarily caused Jacopo Piccinino to make against the Siennese, had produced no important result, he resolved to try what could be done against those whom the conditions of the League permitted him to attack. He therefore, in the year 1456, assailed the Genoese, both by sea and by land, designing to deprive the Fregosi of the government and restore the Adorni. At the same time, he ordered Jacopo Piccinino to cross the Tronto, and attack

Gismondo Malatesti, who, having fortified his territories, did not concern himself, and this part of the king's enterprise produced no effect; but his proceedings against Genoa occasioned more wars against himself and his kingdom than he could have wished. Piero Fregoso was then doge of Genoa, and doubting his ability to sustain the attack of the king, he determined to give what he could not hold, to some one who might defend it against his enemies, in hope, that at a future period, he should obtain a return for the benefit conferred. He therefore sent ambassadors to Charles VII. of France, and offered him the government of Genoa. Charles accepted the offer, and sent John of Anjou, the son of King Rene, who had a short time previously left Florence and returned to France, to take possession with the idea, that he, having learned the manners and customs of Italy, would be able to govern the city; and also that this might give him an opportunity of undertaking the conquest of Naples, of which Rene, John's father, had been deprived by Alfonso. John, therefore, proceeded to Genoa, where he was received as prince, and the fortresses, both of the city and the government, given up to him. This annoyed Alfonso, with the fear that he had brought upon himself too powerful an enemy. He was not, however, dismayed; but pursued his enterprise vigorously, and had led his fleet to Porto, below Villamarina, when he died after a sudden illness, and thus John and the Genoese were relieved from the war. Ferrando, who succeeded to the kingdom of his father Alfonso, became alarmed at having so powerful an enemy in Italy, and was doubtful of the disposition of many of his barons, who being desirous of change, he feared would take part with the French. He was also apprehensive of the pope, whose ambition he well knew, and who seeing him new in the government, might design to take it from him. He had no hope except from the duke of Milan, who entertained no less anxiety concerning the affairs of the kingdom than Ferrando; for he feared that if the French were to obtain it, they would endeavor to annex his own dominions; which he knew they considered to be rightfully their own. He, therefore, soon after the death of Alfonso, sent letters and forces to Ferrando; the latter to give him aid and influence, the former to encourage him with an intimation that he would not, under any circumstances, forsake him. The pontiff intended, after the death of Alfonso, to give the kingdom of Naples to his nephew Piero Lodovico Borgia, and, to furnish a decent pretext for his design and obtain the concurrence of the powers of Italy in its favor he signified a wish to restore that realm to the dominion of the church of Rome; and therefore persuaded the duke not to assist Ferrando. But in the midst of these views and opening enterprises, Calixtus died, and Pius II. of Siennese origin, of the family of the Piccolomini, and by name AEneas, succeeded to the pontificate. This pontiff, free from the ties of private interest, having no object but to benefit Christendom and honor the church, at the duke's entreaty crowned Ferrando king of Naples; judging it easier to establish peace if the kingdom remained in the hands which at present held it, than if he were to favor the views of the French, or, as Calixtus purposed, take it for himself. Ferrando, in acknowledgment of the benefit, created Antonio, one of the pope's nephews, prince of Malfi, gave him an illegitimate daughter of his own in marriage, and restored Benevento and Terracina to the church.

It thus appeared that the internal dissensions of Italy might be quelled, and the pontiff prepared to induce the powers of Christendom to unite in an enterprise against the Turks (as Calixtus had previously designed) when differences arose between the Fregosi and John of Anjou, the lord of Genoa, which occasioned greater and more important wars than those recently concluded. Pietrino Fregoso was at his castle of Riviera, and thought he had not been rewarded by John in proportion to his family's merits; for it was by their means the latter had become prince of the city. This impression drove the parties into open enmity; a circumstance gratifying to Ferrando, who saw in it relief from his troubles, and the sole means of procuring his safety: he therefore assisted Pietrino with money and men, trusting to drive John out of the Genoese territory. The latter being aware of his design, sent for aid to France; and, on obtaining it, attacked Pietrino, who, through his numerous friends, entertained the strongest assurance of success; so that John was compelled to keep within the city, into which Pietrino having entered by night, took possession of some parts of it; but upon the return of day, his people were all either slain or made prisoners by John's troops, and he himself was found among the dead.

This victory gave John hopes of recovering the kingdom; and in October, 1459, he sailed thither from Genoa, with a powerful fleet, and landed at Baia; whence he proceeded to Sessa, by the duke of which place he was favorably received. The prince of Taranto, the Aquilani, with several cities and other princes, also joined him; so that a great part of the kingdom fell into his hands. On this Ferrando applied for assistance to the pope and the duke of Milan; and, to diminish the number of his enemies, made peace with Gismondo Malatesti, which gave so much offense to Jacopo Piccinino, the hereditary enemy of Gismondo, that he resigned his command under Ferrando, and joined his rival. Ferrando also sent money to Federigo, lord of Urbino, and collected with all possible speed what was in those times considered a tolerable army; which, meeting the enemy upon the river Sarni, an engagement ensued in which Ferrando was routed, and many of his principal officers taken. After this defeat, the city of Naples alone, with a few smaller places and princes of inferior note, adhered to Ferrando, the greater part having submitted to John. Jacopo Piccinino, after the victory, advised an immediate march upon Naples; but John declined this, saying, he would first reduce the remainder of the kingdom, and then attack the seat of government.

This resolution occasioned the failure of his enterprise; for he did not consider how much more easily the members follow the head than the head the members.

After his defeat, Ferrando took refuge in Naples, whither the scattered remnants of his people followed him; and by soliciting his friends, he obtained money and a small force. He sent again for assistance to the pope and the duke, by both of whom he was supplied more liberally and speedily than before; for they began to entertain most serious apprehensions of his losing the kingdom. His hopes were thus revived; and, marching from Naples, he regained his reputation in his dominions, and soon obtained the places of which he had been deprived. While the war was proceeding in the kingdom, a circumstance occurred by which John of Anjou lost his influence, and all chance of success in the enterprise. The Genoese had become so weary of the haughty and avaricious dominion of the French, that they took arms against the viceroy, and compelled him to seek refuge in the castelletto; the Fregosi and the Adorni united in the enterprise against him, and were assisted with money and troops by the duke of Milan, both for the recovery and preservation of the government. At the same time, King Rene coming with a fleet to the assistance of his son, and hoping to recover Genoa by means of the castelletto, upon landing his forces was so completely routed, that he was compelled to return in disgrace to Provence. When the news of his father's defeat reached Naples, John was greatly alarmed, but continued the war for a time by the assistance of those barons who, being rebels, knew they would obtain no terms from Ferrando. At length, after various trifling occurrences, the two royal armies came to an engagement, in which John was routed near Troia, in the year 1463. He was, however, less injured by his defeat than by the desertion of Jacopo Piccinino, who joined Ferrando; and, being abandoned by his troops, he was compelled to take refuge in Istria, and thence withdrew to France. This war continued four years. John's failure was attributable to negligence; for victory was often within his grasp, but he did not take proper means to secure it. The Florentines took no decisive part in this war. John, king of Aragon, who succeeded upon the death of Alfonso, sent ambassadors to request their assistance for his nephew Ferrando, in compliance with the terms of the treaty recently made with his father Alfonso. The Florentines replied, that they were under no obligation; that they did not think proper to assist the son in a war commenced by the father with his own forces; and that as it was begun without either their counsel or knowledge, it must be continued and concluded without their help. The ambassadors affirmed the engagement to be binding on the Florentines, and themselves to be answerable for the event of the war; and then in great anger left the city.

Thus with regard to external affairs, the Florentines continued tranquil during this war; but the case was otherwise with their domestic concerns, as will be particularly shown in the following book.

Book VII: Chapter I: Connection of the other Italian governments with the history of Florence—Republics always disunited—Some differences are injurious; others not so—The kind of dissensions prevailing at Florence—Cosmo de' Medici and Neri Capponi become powerful by dissimilar means—Reform in the election of magistrates favorable to Cosmo—Complaints of the principal citizens against the reform in elections—Luca Pitti, Gonfalonier of Justice, restrains the imborsations by force—Tyranny and pride of Luca Pitti and his party—Palace of the Pitti—Death of Cosmo de' Medici—His liberality and magnificence—His modesty—His prudence—Sayings of Cosmo.

It will perhaps appear to the readers of the preceding book that, professing only to write of the affairs of Florence, I have dilated too much in speaking of those which occurred in Lombardy and Naples. But as I have not already avoided, so it is not my intention in future to forbear, similar digressions. For although we have not engaged to give an account of the affairs of Italy, still it would be improper to neglect noticing the most remarkable of them. If they were wholly omitted, our history would not be so well understood, neither would it be so instructive or agreeable; since from the proceedings of the other princes and states of Italy, have most commonly arisen those wars in which the Florentines were compelled to take part. Thus, from the war between John of Anjou and King Ferrando, originated those serious enmities and hatreds which ensued between Ferrando and the Florentines, particularly the house of Medici. The king complained of a want of assistance during the war, and of the aid afforded to his enemy; and from his anger originated the greatest evils, as will be hereafter seen. Having, in speaking of external affairs, come down to the year 1463, it will be necessary in order to make our narrative of the contemporaneous domestic transactions clearly understood, to revert to a period several years back. But first, according to custom, I would offer a few remarks referring to the events about to be narrated, and observe, that those who think a republic may be kept in perfect unity of purpose are greatly deceived. True it is, that some divisions injure republics, while others are beneficial to them. When accompanied by factions and parties they are injurious; but when maintained without them they contribute to their prosperity. The legislator of a republic, since it is impossible to prevent the existence of dissensions, must at least take care to prevent the growth of faction. It may therefore be observed, that citizens acquire reputation and power in two ways; the one public, the other private. Influence is acquired publicly by winning a battle, taking possession of a territory, fulfilling the duties of an embassy with care and prudence, or by giving wise counsel attended by a happy result. Private methods are conferring benefits upon individuals, defending them against the magistrates, supporting them with money, and raising them to undeserved honors; or with public games and entertainments gaining the affection of the populace. This mode of procedure produces parties and cliques; and in proportion as influence thus acquired is injurious, so is the former beneficial, if quite free from party spirit; because it is founded upon the public good, and not upon private advantage. And though it is impossible to prevent the existence of inveterate feuds, still if they be without partisans to support them for their own individual benefit, they do not injure a republic, but contribute to its welfare; since none can attain distinction, but as he contributes to her good, and each party prevents the other from infringing her liberties. The dissensions of Florence were always accompanied by factions, and were therefore always pernicious; and the dominant party only remained united so long as its enemies held it in check. As soon as the strength of the opposition was annihilated, the government, deprived of the restraining influence of its adversaries, and being subject to no law, fell to pieces. The party of Cosmo de' Medici gained the ascendant in 1434; but the depressed party being very numerous, and composed of several very influential persons, fear kept the former united, and restrained their proceedings within the bounds of moderation, so that no violence was committed by them, nor anything done calculated to excite popular dislike. Consequently, whenever this government required the citizens' aid to recover or strengthen its influence, the latter were always willing to gratify its wishes; so that from 1434 to 1455, during a period of twenty-one years, the authority of a balia was granted to it six times.

There were in Florence, as we have frequently observed, two principally powerful citizens, Cosmo de' Medici and Neri Capponi. Neri acquired his influence by public services; so that he had many friends but few partisans. Cosmo, being able to avail himself both of public and private means, had many partisans as well as friends. While both lived, having always been united, they obtained from the people whatever they required; for in them popularity and power were united. But in the year 1455, Neri being dead, and the opposition party extinct, the government found a difficulty in resuming its authority; and this was occasioned, remarkably enough, by Cosmo's private friends, and the most influential men in the state; for, not fearing the opposite party, they became anxious to abate his power. This inconsistency was the beginning of the evils which took place in 1456; so that those in power were openly advised in the deliberative councils not to renew the power of the balia, but to close the balloting purses, and appoint the magistrates by drawing from the pollings or squittini previously made. To restrain this disposition, Cosmo had the choice of two alternatives, either forcibly to assume the government, with the partisans he possessed, and drive out the others, or to allow the matter to take its course, and let his friends see they were not depriving him of power, but rather themselves. He chose the latter; for he well knew that at all events the purses being filled with the names of his own friends, he incurred no risk, and could take the government into his own hands whenever he found occasion. The chief offices of state being again filled by lot, the mass of the people began to think they had recovered their liberty, and that the decisions of the magistrates were according to their own judgments, unbiased by the influence of the Great. At the same time, the friends of different grandees were humbled; and many who had commonly seen their houses filled with suitors and presents, found themselves destitute of both. Those who had previously been very powerful were reduced to an equality with men whom they had been accustomed to consider inferior; and those formerly far beneath them were now become their equals. No respect or deference was paid to them; they were often ridiculed and derided, and frequently heard themselves and the republic mentioned in the open streets without the least deference; thus they found it was not Cosmo but themselves that had lost the government. Cosmo appeared not to notice these matters; and whenever any subject was proposed in favor of the people he was the first to support it. But the greatest cause of alarm to the higher classes, and his most favorable opportunity of retaliation, was the revival of the catasto, or property-tax of 1427, so that individual contributions were determined by statute, and not by a set of persons appointed for its regulation.

This law being re-established, and a magistracy created to carry it into effect, the nobility assembled, and went to Cosmo to beg he would rescue them and himself from the power of the plebeians, and restore to the government the reputation which had made himself powerful and them respected. He replied, he was willing to comply with their request, but wished the law to be obtained in the regular manner, by consent of the people, and not by force, of which he would not hear on any account. They then endeavored in the councils to establish a new balia, but did not succeed. On this the grandees again came to Cosmo, and most humbly begged he would assemble the people in a general council or parliament, but this he refused, for he wished to make them sensible of their great mistake; and when Donato Cocchi, being Gonfalonier of Justice, proposed to assemble them without his consent, the Signors who were of Cosmo's party ridiculed the idea so unmercifully, that the man's mind actually became deranged, and he had to retire from office in consequence. However, since it is undesirable to allow matters to proceed beyond recovery, the Gonfalon of Justice being in the hands of Luca Pitti, a bold-spirited man, Cosmo determined to let him adopt what course he thought proper, that if any trouble should arise it might be imputed to Luca and not to himself. Luca, therefore, in the beginning of his magistracy, several times proposed to the people the appointment of a new balia; and, not succeeding, he threatened the members of the councils with injurious and arrogant expressions, which were shortly followed by corresponding conduct; for in the month of August, 1458, on the eve of Saint Lorenzo, having filled the piazza, and compelled them to assent to a measure to which he knew them to be averse. Having recovered power, created a new balia, and filled the principal offices according to the pleasure of a few individuals, in order to commence that government with terror which they had obtained by force, they banished Girolamo Machiavelli, with some others, and deprived many of the honors of government. Girolamo, having transgressed the confines to which he was limited, was declared a rebel. Traveling about Italy, with the design of exciting the princes against his country, he was betrayed while at Lunigiana, and, being brought to Florence, was put to death in prison.

This government, during the eight years it continued, was violent and insupportable; for Cosmo, being now old, and through ill health unable to attend to public affairs as formerly, Florence became a prey to a small number of her own citizens. Luca Pitti, in return for the services he had performed for the republic, as made a knight, and to be no less grateful than those who had conferred the dignity upon him, he ordered that the priors, who had hitherto been called priors of the trades, should also have a name to which they had no kind of claim, and therefore called them priors of liberty. He also ordered, that as it had been customary for the gonfalonier to sit upon the right hand of the rectors, he should in future take his seat in the midst of them. And that the Deity might appear to participate in what had been done, public processions were made and solemn services performed, to thank him for the recovery of the government. The Signory and Cosmo made Luca Pitti rich presents, and all the citizens were emulous in imitation of them; so that the money given amounted to no less a sum than twenty thousand ducats. He thus attained such influence, that not Cosmo but himself now governed the city; and his pride so increased, that he commenced two superb buildings, one in Florence, the other at Ruciano, about a mile distant, both in a style of royal magnificence; that in the city, being larger than any hitherto built by a private person. To complete them, he had recourse to the most extraordinary means; for not only citizens and private individuals made him presents and supplied materials, but the mass of people, of every grade, also contributed. Besides this, any exiles who had committed murders, thefts, or other crimes which made them amenable to the laws, found a safe refuge within their walls, if they were able to contribute toward their decoration or completion. The other citizens, though they did not build like him, were no less violent or rapacious, so that if Florence were not harassed by external wars, she was ruined by the wickedness of her own children. During this period the wars of Naples took place. The pope also commenced hostilities in Romagna against the Malatesti, from whom he wished to take Rimino and Cesena, held by them. In these designs, and his intentions of a crusade against the Turks, was passed the pontificate of Pius II.

Florence continued in disunion and disturbance. The dissensions continued among the party of Cosmo, in 1455, from the causes already related, which by his prudence, as we have also before remarked, he was enabled to tranquilize; but in the year 1464, his illness increased, and he died. Friends and enemies alike grieved for his loss; for his political opponents, perceiving the rapacity of the citizens, even during the life of him who alone restrained them and made their tyranny supportable, were afraid, lest after his decease, nothing but ruin would ensue. Nor had they much hope of his son Piero, who though a very good man, was of infirm health, and new in the government, and they thought he would be compelled to give way; so that, being unrestrained, their rapacity would pass all bounds. On these accounts, the regret was universal. Of all who have left memorials behind them, and who were not of the military profession, Cosmo was the most illustrious and the most renowned. He not only surpassed all his contemporaries in wealth and authority, but also in generosity and prudence; and among the qualities which contributed to make him prince in his own country, was his surpassing all others in magnificence and generosity. His liberality became more obvious after his death, when Piero, his son, wishing to know what he possessed, it appeared there was no citizen of any consequence to whom Cosmo had not lent a large sum of money; and often, when informed of some nobleman being in distress, he relieved him unasked. His magnificence is evident from the number of public edifices he erected; for in Florence are the convents and churches of St. Marco and St. Lorenzo, and the monastery of Santa Verdiana; in the mountains of Fiesole, the church and abbey of St. Girolamo; and in the Mugello, he not only restored, but rebuilt from its foundation, a monastery of the Frati Minori, or Minims. Besides these, in the church of Santa Croce, the Servi, the Agnoli, and in San Miniato, he erected splendid chapels and altars; and besides building the churches and chapels we have mentioned, he provided them with all the ornaments, furniture, and utensils suitable for the performance of divine service. To these sacred edifices are to be added his private dwellings, one in Florence, of extent and elegance adapted to so great a citizen, and four others, situated at Careggi, Fiesole, Craggiulo, and Trebbio, each, for size and grandeur, equal to royal palaces. And, as if it were not sufficient to be distinguished for magnificence of buildings in Italy alone, he erected an hospital at Jerusalem, for the reception of poor and infirm pilgrims. Although his habitations, like all his other works and actions, were quite of a regal character, and he alone was prince in Florence, still everything was so tempered with his prudence, that he never transgressed the decent moderation of civil life; in his conversation, his servants, his traveling, his mode of living, and the relationships he formed, the modest demeanor of the citizen was always evident; for he was aware that a constant exhibition of pomp brings more envy upon its possessor than greater realities borne without ostentation. Thus in selecting consorts for his sons, he did not seek the alliance of princes, but for Giovanni chose Corneglia degli Allesandri, and for Piero, Lucrezia de' Tornabuoni. He gave his granddaughters, the children of Piero, Bianca to Guglielmo de' Pazzi, and Nannina to Bernardo Ruccellai. No one of his time possessed such an intimate knowledge of government and state affairs as himself; and hence amid such a variety of fortune, in a city so given to change, and among a people of such extreme inconstancy, he retained possession of the government thirty-one years; for being endowed with the utmost prudence, he foresaw evils at a distance, and therefore had an opportunity either of averting them, or preventing their injurious results. He thus not only vanquished domestic and civil ambition, but humbled the pride of many princes with so much fidelity and address, that whatever powers were in league with himself and his country, either overcame their adversaries, or remained uninjured by his alliance; and whoever were opposed to him, lost either their time, money, or territory. Of this the Venetians afford a sufficient proof, who, while in league with him against Duke Filippo were always victorious, but apart from him were always conquered; first by Filippo and then by Francesco. When they joined Alfonso against the Florentine republic, Cosmo, by his commercial credit, so drained Naples and Venice of money, that they were glad to obtain peace upon any terms it was thought proper to grant. Whatever difficulties he had to contend with, whether within the city or without, he brought to a happy issue, at once glorious to himself and destructive to his enemies; so that civil discord strengthened his government in Florence, and war increased his power and reputation abroad. He added to the Florentine dominions, the Borgo of St. Sepolcro, Montedoglio, the Casentino and Val di Bagno. His virtue and good fortune overcame all his enemies and exalted his friends. He was born in the year 1389, on the day of the saints Cosmo and Damiano. His earlier years were full of trouble, as his exile, captivity, and personal danger fully testify; and having gone to the council of Constance, with Pope John, in order to save his life, after the ruin of the latter, he was obliged to escape in disguise. But after the age of forty, he enjoyed the greatest felicity; and not only those who assisted him in public business, but his agents who conducted his commercial speculations throughout Europe, participated in his prosperity. Hence many enormous fortunes took their origin in different families of Florence, as in that of the Tornabuoni, the Benci, the Portinari, and the Sassetti. Besides these, all who depended upon his advice and patronage became rich; and, though he was constantly expending money in building churches, and in charitable purposes, he sometimes complained to his friends that he had never been able to lay out so much in the service of God as to find the balance in his own favor, intimating that all he had done or could do, was still unequal to what the Almighty had done for him. He was of middle stature, olive complexion, and venerable aspect; not learned but exceedingly eloquent, endowed with great natural capacity, generous to his friends, kind to the poor, comprehensive in discourse, cautious in advising, and in his speeches and replies, grave and witty. When Rinaldo degli Albizzi, at the beginning of his exile, sent to him to say, "the hen had laid," he replied, "she did ill to lay so far from the nest." Some other of the rebels gave him to understand they were "not dreaming." He said, "he believed it, for he had robbed them of their sleep." When Pope Pius was endeavoring to induce the different governments to join in an expedition against the Turks, he said, "he was an old man, and had undertaken the enterprise of a young one." To the Venetians ambassadors, who came to Florence with those of King Alfonso to complain of the republic, he uncovered his head, and asked them what color it was; they said, "white;" he replied, "it is so; and it will not be long before your senators have heads as white as mine." A few hours before his death, his wife asked him why he kept his eyes shut, and he said, "to get them in the way of it." Some citizens saying to him, after his return from exile, that he injured the city, and that it was offensive to God to drive so many religious persons out of it; he replied that, "it was better to injure the city, than to ruin it; that two yards of rose-colored cloth would make a gentleman, and that it required something more to direct a government than to play with a string of beads." These words gave occasion to his enemies to slander him, as a man who loved himself more than his country, and was more attached to this world than to the next. Many others of his sayings might be adduced, but we shall omit them as unnecessary. Cosmo was a friend and patron of learned men. He brought Argiripolo, a Greek by birth, and one of the most erudite of his time, to Florence, to instruct the youth in Hellenic literature. He entertained Marsilio Ficino, the reviver of the Platonic philosophy, in his own house; and being much attached to him, have him a residence near his palace at Careggi, that he might pursue the study of letters with greater convenience, and himself have an opportunity of enjoying his company. His prudence, his great wealth, the uses to which he applied it, and his splendid style of living, caused him to be beloved and respected in Florence, and obtained for him the highest consideration, not only among the princes and governments of Italy, but throughout all Europe. He thus laid a foundation for his descendants, which enabled them to equal him in virtue, and greatly surpass him in fortune; while the authority they possessed in Florence and throughout Christendom was not obtained without being merited. Toward the close of his life he suffered great affliction; for, of his two sons, Piero and Giovanni, the latter, of whom he entertained the greatest hopes, died; and the former was so sickly as to be unable to attend either to public or private business. On being carried from one apartment to another, after Giovanni's death, he remarked to his attendants, with a sigh, "This is too large a house for so small a family." His great mind also felt distressed at the idea that he had not extended the Florentine dominions by any valuable acquisition; and he regretted it the more, from imagining he had been deceived by Francesco Sforza, who, while count, had promised, that if he became lord of Milan, he would undertake the conquest of Lucca for the Florentines, a design, however, that was never realized; for the count's ideas changed upon his becoming duke; he resolved to enjoy in peace, the power he had acquired by war, and would not again encounter its fatigues and dangers, unless the welfare of his own dominions required it. This was a source of much annoyance to Cosmo, who felt he had incurred great expense and trouble for an ungrateful and perfidious friend. His bodily infirmities prevented him from attending either to public or private affairs, as he had been accustomed, and he consequently witnessed both going to decay; for Florence was ruined by her own citizens, and his fortune by his agents and children. He died, however, at the zenith of his glory and in the enjoyment of the highest renown. The city, and all the Christian princes, condoled with his son Piero for his loss. His funeral was conducted with the utmost pomp and solemnity, the whole city following his corpse to the tomb in the church of St. Lorenzo, on which, by public decree, he was inscribed, "*Father of His Country*." If, in speaking of Cosmo's actions, I have rather imitated the biographies of princes than general history, it need not occasion wonder; for of so extraordinary an individual I was compelled to speak with unusual praise.

Chapter II: The duke of Milan becomes lord of Genoa—The king of Naples and the duke of Milan endeavor to secure their dominions to their heirs—Jacopo Piccinino honorably received at Milan, and shortly afterward murdered at Naples—Fruitless endeavors of Pius II. to excite Christendom against the Turks—Death of Francesco Sforza, duke of Milan—Perfidious counsel given to Piero de' Medici by Diotisalvi Neroni—Conspiracy of Diotisalvi and others against Piero—Futile attempts to appease the disorders—Public spectacles—Projects of the conspirators against Piero de' Medici—Niccolo Fedini discloses to Piero the plots of his enemies.

While Florence and Italy were in this condition, Louis XI. of France was involved in very serious troubles with his barons, who, with the assistance of Francis, duke of Brittany, and Charles, duke of Burgundy, were in arms against him. This attack was so serious, that he was unable to render further assistance to John of Anjou in his enterprise against Genoa and Naples; and, standing in need of all the forces he could raise, he gave over Savona (which still remained in the power of the French) to the duke of Milan, and also intimated, that if he wished, he had his permission to undertake the conquest of Genoa. Francesco accepted the proposal, and with the influence afforded by the king's friendship, and the assistance of the Adorni, he became lord of Genoa. In acknowledgment of this benefit, he sent fifteen hundred horse into France for the king's service, under the command of Galeazzo, his eldest son. Thus Ferrando of Aragon and Francesco Sforza became, the latter, duke of Lombardy and prince of Genoa, and the former, sovereign of the whole kingdom of Naples. Their families being allied by marriage, they thought they might so confirm their power as to secure to themselves its enjoyment during life, and at their deaths, its unencumbered reversion to their heirs. To attain this end, they considered it necessary that the king should remove all ground of apprehension from those barons who had offended him in the war of John of Anjou, and that the duke should extirpate the adherents of the Bracceschi, the natural enemies of his family, who, under Jacopo Piccinino, had attained the highest reputation. The latter was now the first general in Italy, and possessing no territory, he naturally excited the apprehension of all who had dominions, and especially of the duke, who, conscious of what he had himself done, thought he could neither enjoy his own estate in safety, nor leave them with any degree of security to his son during Jacopo's lifetime. The king, therefore, strenuously endeavored to come to terms with his barons, and using his utmost ingenuity to secure them, succeeded in his object; for they perceived their ruin to be inevitable if they continued in war with their sovereign, though from submission and confidence in him, they would still have reason for apprehension. Mankind are always most eager to avoid a certain evil; and hence inferior powers are easily deceived by princes. The barons, conscious of the danger of continuing the war, trusted the king's promises, and having placed themselves in his hands, they were soon after destroyed in various ways, and under a variety of pretexts. This alarmed Jacopo Piccinino, who was with his forces at Sulmona; and to deprive the king of the opportunity of treating him similarly, he endeavored, by the mediation of his friends, to be reconciled with the duke, who, by the most liberal offers, induced Jacopo to visit him at Milan, accompanied by only a hundred horse.

Jacopo had served many years with his father and brother, first under Duke Filippo, and afterward under the Milanese republic, so that by frequent intercourse with the citizens he had acquired many friends and universal popularity, which present circumstances tended to increase; for the prosperity and newly acquired power of the Sforzeschi had occasioned envy, while Jacopo's misfortunes and long absence had given rise to compassion and a great desire to see him. These various feelings were displayed upon his arrival; for nearly all the nobility went to meet him; the streets through which he passed were filled with citizens, anxious to catch a glimpse of him, while shouts of "The Bracceschi! the Bracceschi!" resounded on all sides. These honors accelerated his ruin; for the duke's apprehensions increased his desire of destroying him; and to effect this with the least possible suspicion, Jacopo's marriage with Drusiana, the duke's natural daughter, was now celebrated. The duke then arranged with Ferrando to take him into pay, with the title of captain of his forces, and give him 100,000 florins for his maintenance. After this agreement, Jacopo, accompanied by a ducal ambassador and his wife Drusiana, proceeded to Naples, where he was honorably and joyfully received, and for many days entertained with every kind of festivity; but having asked permission to go to Sulmona, where his forces were, the king invited him to a banquet in the castle, at the conclusion of which he and his son Francesco were imprisoned, and shortly afterward put to death. It was thus our Italian princes, fearing those virtues in others which they themselves did not possess, extirpated them; and hence the country became a prey to the efforts of those by whom it was not long afterward oppressed and ruined.

At this time, Pope Pius II. having settled the affairs of Romagna, and witnessing a universal peace, thought it a suitable opportunity to lead the Christians against the Turks, and adopted measures similar to those which his predecessors had used. All the princes promised assistance either in men or money; while Matthias, king of Hungary, and Charles, duke of Burgundy, intimated their intention of joining the enterprise in person, and were by the pope appointed leaders of the expedition. The pontiff was so full of expectation, that he left Rome and proceeded to Ancona, where it had been arranged that the whole army should be assembled, and the Venetians engaged to send ships thither to convey the forces to Sclavonia. Upon the arrival of the pope in that city, there was soon such a concourse of people, that in a few days all the provisions it contained, or that could be procured from the neighborhood, were consumed, and famine began to impend. Besides this, there was no money to provide those who were in want of it, nor arms to furnish such as were without them. Neither Matthias nor Charles made their appearance. The Venetians sent a captain with some galleys, but rather for ostentation and the sake of keeping their word, than for the purpose of conveying troops. During this position of affairs, the pope, being old and infirm, died, and the assembled troops returned to their homes. The death of the pontiff occurred in 1465, and Paul II. of Venetian origin, was chosen to succeed him; and that nearly all the principalities of Italy might change their rulers about the same period, in the following year Francesco Sforza, duke of Milan, also died, having occupied the dukedom sixteen years, and Galleazzo, his son, succeeded him.

The death of this prince infused redoubled energy into the Florentine dissensions, and caused them to produce more prompt effects than they would otherwise have done. Upon the demise of Cosmo, his son Piero, being heir to the wealth and government of his father, called to his assistance Diotisalvi Neroni, a man of great influence and the highest reputation, in whom Cosmo reposed so much confidence that just before his death he recommended Piero to be wholly guided by him, both with regard to the government of the city and the management of his fortune. Piero acquired Diotisalvi with the opinion Cosmo entertained of him, and said that as he wished to obey his father, though now no more, as he always had while alive, he should consult him concerning both his patrimony and the city. Beginning with his private affairs, he caused an account of all his property, liabilities, and assets, to be placed in Diotisalvi's hands, that, with an entire acquaintance with the state of his affairs, he might be able to afford suitable advice, and the latter promised to use the utmost care. Upon examination of these accounts the affairs were found to be in great disorder, and Diotisalvi, instigated rather by his own ambition than by attachment to Piero or gratitude to Cosmo, thought he might without difficulty deprive him of both the reputation and the splendor which his father had left him as his inheritance. In order to realize his views, he waited upon Piero, and advised him to adopt a measure which, while it appeared quite correct in itself, and suitable to existing circumstances, involved a consequence destructive to his authority. He explained the disorder of his affairs, and the large amount of money it would be necessary to provide, if he wished to preserve his influence in the state and his reputation of wealth; and said there was no other means of remedying these disorders so just and available as to call in the sums which his father had lent to an infinite number of persons, both foreigners and citizens; for Cosmo, to acquire partisans in Florence and friends abroad, was extremely liberal of his money, and the amount of loans due to him was enormous. Piero thought the advice good, because he was only desirous to repossess his own property to meet the demands to which he was liable; but as soon as he had ordered those amounts to be recalled, the citizens, as if he had asked for something to which he had no kind of claim, took great offense, loaded him with opprobrious expressions, and accused him of being avaricious and ungrateful.

Diotisalvi, noticing the popular excitement against Piero, occasioned by his own advice, obtained an interview with Luca Pitti, Agnolo Acciajuoli, and Niccolo Soderini, and they resolved to unite their efforts to deprive him both of the government and his influence. Each was actuated by a different motive; Luca Pitti wished to take the position Cosmo had occupied, for he was now become so great, that he disdained to submit to Piero; Diotisalvi Neroni, who knew Luca unfit to be at the head of a government, thought that of necessity on Piero's removal, the whole authority of the state would devolve upon himself; Niccolo Soderini desired the city to enjoy greater liberty, and for the laws to be equally binding upon all. Agnolo Acciajuoli was greatly incensed against the Medici, for the following reasons: his son, Raffaello, had some time before married Alessandra de' Bardi, and received with her a large dowry. She, either by her own fault or the misconduct of others, suffered much ill-treatment both from her father-in-law and her husband, and in consequence Lorenzo d' Ilarione, her kinsman, out of pity for the girl, being accompanied by several armed men, took her away from Agnolo's house. The Acciajuoli complained of the injury done them by the Bardi, and the matter was referred to Cosmo, who decided that the Acciajuoli should restore to Alessandra her fortune, and then leave it to her choice either to return to her husband or not. Agnolo thought Cosmo had not, in this instance, treated him as a friend; and having been unable to avenge himself on the father, he now resolved to do his utmost to ruin the son. These conspirators, though each was influenced by a different motive from the rest, affected to have only one object in view, which was that the city should be governed by the magistrates, and not be subjected to the counsels of a few individuals. The odium against Piero, and opportunities of injuring him, were increased by the number of merchants who failed about this time; for it was reported that he, in having, quite unexpectedly to all, resolved to call in his debts, had, to the disgrace and ruin of the city, caused them to become insolvent. To this was added his endeavor to obtain Clarice degli Orsini as wife of Lorenzo, his eldest son; and hence his enemies took occasion to say, it was quite clear, that as he despised a Florentine alliance, he no longer considered himself one of the people, and was preparing to make himself prince; for he who refuses his fellow-citizens as relatives, desires to make them slaves, and therefore cannot expect to have them as friends. The leaders of the sedition thought they had the victory in their power; for the greater part of the citizens followed them, deceived by the name of liberty which they, to give their purpose a graceful covering, adopted upon their ensigns.

In this agitated state of the city, some, to whom civil discord was extremely offensive, thought it would be well to endeavor to engage men's minds with some new occupation, because when unemployed they are commonly led by whoever chooses to excite them. To divert their attention from matters of government, it being now a year since the death of Cosmo, it was resolved to celebrate two festivals, similar to the most solemn observed in the city. At one of them was represented the arrival of the three kings from the east, led by the star which announced the nativity of Christ; which was conducted with such pomp and magnificence, that the preparations for it kept the whole city occupied many months. The other was a tournament (for so they call the exhibition of equestrian combats), in which the sons of the first families in the city took part with the most celebrated cavaliers of Italy. Among the most distinguished of the Florentine youth was Lorenzo, eldest son of Piero, who, not by favor, but by his own personal valor, obtained the principal prize. When these festivals were over, the citizens reverted to the same thoughts which had previously occupied them, and each pursued his ideas with more earnestness than ever. Serious differences and troubles were the result; and these were greatly increased by two circumstances: one of which was, that the authority of the balia had expired; the other, that upon the death of Duke Francesco, Galeazzo the new duke sent ambassadors to Florence, to renew the engagements of his father with the city, which, among other things, provided that every year a certain sum of money should be paid to the duke. The principal opponents of the Medici took occasion, from this demand, to make public resistance in the councils, on pretense that the alliance was made with Francesco and not Galeazzo; so that Francesco being dead, the obligation had ceased; nor was there any necessity to revive it, because Galeazzo did not possess his father's talents, and consequently they neither could nor ought to expect the same benefits from him; that if they had derived little advantage from Francesco, they would obtain still less from Galeazzo; and that if any citizen wished to hire him for his own purposes, it was contrary to civil rule, and inconsistent with the public liberty. Piero, on the contrary, argued that it would be very impolitic to lose such an alliance from mere avarice, and that there was nothing so important to the republic, and to the whole of Italy, as their alliance with the duke; that the Venetians, while they were united, could not hope either by feigned friendship or open war to injure the duchy; but as soon as they perceived the Florentines alienated from him they would prepare for hostilities, and, finding him young, new in the government, and without friends, they would, either by force or fraud, compel him to join them; in which case ruin of the republic would be inevitable.

The arguments of Piero were without effect, and the animosity of the parties began to be openly manifested in their nocturnal assemblies; the friends of the Medici meeting in the Crocetta, and their adversaries in the Pieta. The latter being anxious for Piero's ruin, had induced many citizens to subscribe their names as favorable to the undertaking. Upon one occasion, particularly when considering the course to be adopted, although all agreed that the power of the Medici ought to be reduced, different opinions were given concerning the means by which it should be effected; one party, the most temperate and reasonable, held that as the authority of the balia had ceased, they must take care to prevent its renewal; it would then be found to be the universal wish that the magistrates and councils should govern the city, and in a short time Piero's power would be visibly diminished, and, as a consequence of his loss of influence in the government, his commercial credit would also fail; for his affairs were in such a state, that if they could prevent him from using the public money his ruin must ensue. They would thus be in no further danger from him, and would succeed in the recovery of their liberty, without the death or exile of any individual; but if they attempted violence they would incur great dangers; for mankind are willing to allow one who falls of himself to meet his fate, but if pushed down they would hasten to his relief; so that if they adopted no extraordinary measures against him, he will have no reason for defense or aid; and if he were to seek them it would be greatly to his own injury, by creating such a general suspicion as would accelerate his ruin, and justify whatever course they might think proper to adopt. Many of the assembly were dissatisfied with this tardy method of proceeding; they thought delay would be favorable to him and injurious to themselves; for if they allowed matters to take their ordinary course, Piero would be in no danger whatever, while they themselves would incur many; for the magistrates who were opposed to him would allow him to rule the city, and his friends would make him a prince, and their own ruin would be inevitable, as happened in 1458; and though the advice they had just heard might be most consistent with good feeling, the present would be found to be the safest. That it would therefore be best, while the minds of men were yet excited against him, to effect his destruction. It must be their plan to arm themselves, and engage the assistance of the marquis of Ferrara, that they might not be destitute of troops; and if a favorable Signory were drawn, they would be in condition to make use of them. They therefore determined to wait the formation of the new Signory, and be governed by circumstances.

Among the conspirators was Niccolo Fedini, who had acted as president of their assemblies. He, being induced by most certain hopes, disclosed the whole affair to Piero, and gave him a list of those who had subscribed their names, and also of the conspirators. Piero was alarmed on discovering the number and quality of those who were opposed to him; and by the advice of his friends he resolved to take the signatures of those who were inclined to favor him. Having employed one of his most trusty confidants to carry his design into effect, he found so great a disposition to change and instability, that many who had previously set down their names among the number of his enemies, now subscribed them in his favor.

Chapter III: Niccolo Soderini drawn Gonfalonier of Justice—Great hopes excited in consequence—The two parties take arms—The fears of the Signory—Their conduct with regard to Piero—Piero's reply to the Signory—Reform of government in favor of Piero de' Medici—Dispersion of his enemies—Fall of Lucca Pitti—Letter of Agnolo Acciajuoli to Piero de' Medici—Piero's answer—Designs of the Florentine exiles—They induce the Venetians to make war on Florence.

In the midst of these events, the time arrived for the renewal of the supreme magistracy; and Niccolo Soderini was drawn Gonfalonier of Justice. It was surprising to see by what a concourse, not only of distinguished citizens, but also of the populace, he was accompanied to the palace; and while on the way thither an olive wreath was placed upon his head, to signify that upon him depended the safety and liberty of the city. This, among many similar instances, serves to prove how undesirable it is to enter upon office or power exciting inordinate expectations; for, being unable to fulfil them (many looking for more than it is possible to perform), shame and disappointment are the ordinary results. Tommaso and Niccolo Soderini were brothers. Niccolo was the more ardent and spirited, Tommaso the wiser man; who, being very much the friend of Piero, and knowing that his brother desired nothing but the liberty of the city, and the stability of the republic, without injury to any, advised him to make new Squittini, by which means the election purses might be filled with the names of those favorable to his design. Niccolo took his brother's advice, and thus wasted the period of his magistracy in vain hopes, which his friends, the leading conspirators, allowed him to do from motives of envy; for they were unwilling that the government should be reformed by the authority of Niccolo, and thought they would be in time enough to effect their purpose under another gonfalonier. Thus the magistracy of Niccolo expired; and having commenced many things without completing aught, he retired from office with much less credit than when he had entered upon it.

This circumstance caused the aggrandizement of Piero's party, whose friends entertained stronger hopes, while those who had been neutral or wavering became his adherents; so that both sides being balanced, many months elapsed without any open demonstration of their particular designs. Piero's party continuing to gather strength, his enemies' indignation increased in proportion; and they now determined to effect by force what they either could not accomplish, or were unwilling to attempt by the medium of the magistrates, which was assassination of Piero, who lay sick at Careggi, and to this end order the marquis of Ferrara nearer to the city with his forces, that after Piero's death he might lead them into the piazza, and thus compel the Signory to form a government according to their own wishes; for though all might not be friendly, they trusted they would be able to induce those to submit by fear who might be opposed to them from principle.

Diotisalvi, the better to conceal his design, frequently visited Piero, conversed with him respecting the union of the city, and advised him to effect it. The conspirators' designs had already been fully disclosed to Piero; besides this, Domenico Martelli had informed him, that Francesco Neroni, the brother of Diotisalvi, had endeavored to induce him to join them, assuring him the victory was certain, and their object all but attained. Upon this, Piero resolved to take advantage of his enemies' tampering with the marquis of Ferrara, and be first in arms. He therefore intimated that he had received a letter from Giovanni Bentivogli, prince of Bologna, which informed him that the marquis of Ferrara was upon the river Albo, at the head of a considerable force, with the avowed intention of leading it to Florence; that upon this advice he had taken up arms; after which, in the midst of a strong force, he came to the city, when all who were disposed to support him, armed themselves also. The adverse party did the same, but not in such good order, being unprepared. The residence of Diotisalvi being near that of Piero, he did not think himself safe in it, but first went to the palace and begged the Signory would endeavor to induce Piero to lay down his arms, and thence to Luca Pitti, to keep him faithful in their cause. Niccolo Soderini displayed the most activity; for taking arms, and being followed by nearly all the plebeians in his vicinity, he proceeded to the house of Luca, and begged that he would mount his horse, and come to the piazza in support of the Signory, who were, he said, favorable, and that the victory would, undoubtedly, be on their side; that he should not stay in the house to be basely slain by their armed enemies, or ignominiously deceived by those who were unarmed; for, in that case, he would soon repent of having neglected an opportunity irrecoverably lost; that if he desired the forcible ruin of Piero, he might easily effect it; and that if he were anxious for peace, it would be far better to be in a condition to propose terms than to be compelled to accept any that might be offered. These words produced no effect upon Luca, whose mind was now quite made up; he had been induced to desert his party by new conditions and promises of alliance from Piero; for one of his nieces had been married to Giovanni Tornabuoni. He, therefore, advised Niccolo to dismiss his followers and return home, telling him he ought to be satisfied, if the city were governed by the magistrates, which would certainly be the case, and that all ought to lay aside their weapons; for the Signory, most of whom were friendly, would decide their differences. Niccolo, finding him impracticable, returned home; but before he left, he said, "I can do the city no good alone, but I can easily foresee the evils that will befall her. This resolution of yours will rob our country of her liberty; you will lose the government, I shall lose my property, and the rest will be exiled."

During this disturbance the Signory closed the palace and kept their magistrates about them, without showing favor to either party. The citizens, especially those who had followed Luca Pitti, finding Piero fully prepared and his adversaries unarmed, began to consider, not how they might injure him, but how, with least observation, glide into the ranks of his friends. The principal citizens, the leaders of both factions, assembled in the palace in the presence of the Signory, and spoke respecting the state of the city and the reconciliation of parties; and as the infirmities of Piero prevented him from being present, they, with one exception, unanimously determined to wait upon him at his house. Niccolo Soderini having first placed his children and his effects under the care of his brother Tommaso, withdrew to his villa, there to await the event, but apprehended misfortune to himself and ruin to his country. The other citizens coming into Piero's presence, one of them who had been appointed spokesman, complained of the disturbances that had arisen in the city, and endeavored to show, that those must be most to blame who had been first to take up arms; and not knowing what Piero (who was evidently the first to do so) intended, they had come in order to be informed of his design, and if it had in view the welfare of the city, they were desirous of supporting it. Piero replied, that not those who first take arms are the most to blame, but those who give the first occasion for it, and if they would reflect a little on their mode of proceeding toward himself, they would cease to wonder at what he had done; for they could not fail to perceive, that nocturnal assemblies, the enrollment of partisans, and attempts to deprive him both of his authority and his life, had caused him to take arms; and they might further observe, that as his forces had not quitted his own house, his design was evidently only to defend himself and not to injure others. He neither sought nor desired anything but safety and repose; neither had his conduct ever manifested a desire for ought else; for when the authority of the Balia expired, he never made any attempt to renew it, and was very glad the magistrates had governed the city and had been content. They might also remember that Cosmo and his sons could live respected in Florence, either with the Balia or without it, and that in 1458, it was not his family, but themselves, who had renewed it. That if they did not wish for it at present, neither did he; but this did not satisfy them; for he perceived that they thought it impossible to remain in Florence while he was there. It was entirely beyond all his anticipations that his own or his father's friends should think themselves unsafe with him in Florence, having always shown himself quiet and peaceable. He then addressed himself to Diotisalvi and his brothers, who were present, reminding them with grave indignation, of the benefits they had received from Cosmo, the confidence he had reposed in them and their subsequent ingratitude; and his words so strongly excited some present, that had he not interfered, they would certainly have torn the Neroni to pieces on the spot. He concluded by saying, that he should approve of any determination of themselves and the Signory; and that for his own part, he only desired peace and safety. After this, many things were discussed, but nothing determined, excepting generally, that it was necessary to reform the administration of the city and government.

The Gonfalon of Justice was then in the hands of Bernardo Lotti, a man not in the confidence of Piero, who was therefore disinclined to attempt aught while he was in office; but no inconvenience would result from the delay, as his magistracy was on the point of expiring. Upon the election of Signors for the months of September and October, 1466, Roberto Lioni was appointed to the supreme magistracy, and as soon as he assumed its duties, every requisite arrangement having been previously made, the people were called to the piazza, and a new Balia created, wholly in favor of Piero, who soon afterward filled all the offices of government according to his own pleasure. These transactions alarmed the leaders of the opposite faction, and Agnolo Acciajuoli fled to Naples, Diotisalvi Neroni and Niccolo Soderini to Venice. Luca Pitti remained in Florence, trusting to his new relationship and the promises of Piero. The refugees were declared rebels, and all the family of the Neroni were dispersed. Giovanni di Neroni, then archbishop of Florence, to avoid a greater evil, became a voluntary exile at Rome, and to many other citizens who fled, various places of banishment were appointed. Nor was this considered sufficient; for it was ordered that the citizens should go in solemn procession to thank God for the preservation of the government and the reunion of the city, during the performance of which, some were taken and tortured, and part of them afterward put to death and exiled. In this great vicissitude of affairs, there was not a more remarkable instance of the uncertainty of fortune than Luca Pitti, who soon found the difference between victory and defeat, honor and disgrace. His house now presented only a vast solitude, where previously crowds of citizens had assembled. In the streets, his friends and relatives, instead of accompanying, were afraid even to salute him. Some of them were deprived of the honors of government, others of their property, and all alike threatened. The superb edifices he had commenced were abandoned by the builders; the benefits that had been conferred upon him, where now exchanged for injuries, the honors for disgrace. Hence many of those who had presented him with articles of value now demanded them back again, as being only lent; and those who had been in the habit of extolling him as a man of surpassing excellence, now termed him violent and ungrateful. So that, when too late, he regretted not having taken the advice of Niccolo Soderini, and preferred an honorable death in battle, than to a life of ignominy among his victorious enemies.

The exiles now began to consider various means of recovering that citizenship which they had not been able to preserve. However, Agnolo Acciajuoli being at Naples, before he attempted anything else, resolved to sound Piero, and try if he could effect a reconciliation. For this purpose, he wrote to him in the following terms: "I cannot help laughing at the freaks of fortune, perceiving how, at her pleasure, she converts friends into enemies, and enemies into friends. You may remember that during your father's exile, regarding more the injury done to him than my own misfortunes, I was banished, and in danger of death, and never during Cosmo's life failed to honor and support your family; neither have I since his death ever entertained a wish to injure you. True, it is, that your own sickness, and the tender years of your sons, so alarmed me, that I judged it desirable to give such a form to the government, that after your death our country might not be ruined; and hence, the proceedings, which not against you, but for the safety of the state, have been adopted, which, if mistaken, will surely obtain forgiveness, both for the good design in view, and on account of my former services. Neither can I apprehend, that your house, having found me so long faithful, should now prove unmerciful, or that you could cancel the impression of so much merit for so small a fault." Piero replied: "Your laughing in your present abode is the cause why I do not weep, for were you to laugh in Florence, I should have to weep at Naples. I confess you were well disposed toward my father, and you ought to confess you were well paid for it; and the obligation is so much the greater on your part than on ours, as deeds are of greater value than words. Having been recompensed for your good wishes, it ought not to surprise you that you now receive the due reward of your bad ones. Neither will a pretense of your patriotism excuse you, for none will think the city less beloved or benefited by the Medici, than by the Acciajuoli. It, therefore, seems but just, that you should remain in dishonor at Naples, since you knew not how to live with honor at home."

Agnolo, hopeless of obtaining pardon, went to Rome, where, joining the archbishop and other refugees, they used every available means to injure the commercial credit of the Medici in that city. Their attempts greatly annoyed Piero; but by his friends' assistance, he was enabled to render them abortive. Diotisalvi Neroni and Niccolo Soderini strenuously urged the Venetian senate to make war upon their country, calculating, that in case of an attack, the government being new and unpopular, would be unable to resist. At this time there resided at Ferrara, Giovanni Francesco, son of Palla Strozzi, who, with his father, was banished from Florence in the changes of 1434. He possessed great influence, and was considered one of the richest merchants. The newly banished pointed out to Giovanni Francesco how easily they might return to their country, if the Venetians were to undertake the enterprise, and that it was most probable they would do so, if they had pecuniary assistance, but that otherwise it would be doubtful. Giovanni Francesco, wishing to avenge his own injuries, at once fell in with their ideas, and promised to contribute to the success of the attempt all the means in his power. On this they went to the Doge, and complained of the exile they were compelled to endure, for no other reason, they said, than for having wished their country should be subject to equal laws, and that the magistrates should govern, not a few private individuals; that Piero de' Medici, with his adherents, who were accustomed to act tyrannically, had secretly taken up arms, deceitfully induced them to lay their own aside, and thus, by fraud, expelled them from their country; that, not content with this, they made the Almighty himself a means of oppression to several, who, trusting to their promises, had remained in the city and were there betrayed; for, during public worship and solemn supplications, that the Deity might seem to participate in their treachery, many citizens had been seized, imprisoned, tortured, and put to death; thus affording to the world a horrible and impious precedent. To avenge themselves for these injuries, they knew not where to turn with so much hope of success as to the senate, which, having always enjoyed their liberty, ought to compassionate those who had lost it. They therefore called upon them as free men to assist them against tyrants; as pious, against the wicked; and would remind the Venetians, that it was the family of the Medici who had robbed them of their dominions in Lombardy, contrary to the wish of the other citizens, and who, in opposition to the interests of the senate, had favored and supported Francesco, so, that if the exiles' distresses could not induce them to undertake the war, the just indignation of the people of Venice, and their desire of vengeance ought to prevail.

Chapter IV: War between the Venetians and the Florentines—Peace re-established—Death of Niccolo Soderini—His character—Excesses in Florence—Various external events from 1468 to 1471—Accession of Sixtus IV.—His character—Grief of Piero de' Medici for the violence committed in Florence—His speech to the principal citizens—Plans of Piero de' Medici for the restoration of order—His death and character—Tommaso Soderini, a citizen of great reputation, declares himself in favor of the Medici—Disturbances at Prato occasioned by Bernardo Nardi.

The concluding words of the Florentine exiles produced the utmost excitement among the Venetian senators, and they resolved to send Bernardo Coglione, their general, to attack the Florentine territory. The troops were assembled, and joined by Ercole da Esti, who had been sent by Borgo, marquis of Ferrara. At the commencement of hostilities, the Florentines not being prepared, their enemies burned the Borgo of Dovadola, and plundered the surrounding country. But having expelled the enemies of Piero, renewed their league with Galeazzo, duke of Milan, and Ferrando, king of Naples, they appointed to the command of their forces Federigo, count of Urbino; and being thus on good terms with their friends, their enemies occasioned them less anxiety. Ferrando sent Alfonso, his eldest son, to their aid, and Galeazzo came in person, each at the head of a suitable force, and all assembled at Castrocaro, a fortress belonging to the Florentines, and situated among the roots of the Appennines which descend from Tuscany to Romagna. In the meantime, the enemy withdrew toward Imola. A few slight skirmishes took place between the armies; yet, in accordance with the custom of the times, neither of them acted on the offensive, besieged any town, or gave the other an opportunity of coming to a general engagement; but each kept within their tents, and conducted themselves with most remarkable cowardice. This occasioned general dissatisfaction among the Florentines; for they found themselves involved in an expensive war, from which no advantage could be derived. The magistrates complained of these spiritless proceedings to those who had been appointed commissaries to the expedition; but they replied, that the entire evil was chargeable upon the Duke Galeazzo, who possessing great authority and little experience, was unable to suggest useful measures, and unwilling to take the advice of those who were more capable; and therefore any demonstration of courage or energy would be impracticable so long as he remained with the army. Hereupon the Florentines intimated to the duke, that his presence with the force was in many ways advantageous and beneficial, and of itself sufficient to alarm the enemy; but they considered his own safety and that of his dominions, much more important than their own immediate convenience; because so long as the former were safe, the Florentines had nothing to fear, and all would go well; but if his dominions were to suffer, they might then apprehend all kinds of misfortune. They assured him they did not think it prudent for him to be absent so long from Milan, having recently succeeded to the government, and being surrounded by many powerful enemies and suspected neighbors; while any who were desirous of plotting against him, had an opportunity of doing so with impunity. They would, therefore, advise him to return to his territories, leaving part of his troops with them for the use of the expedition. This advice pleased Galeazzo, who, in consequence, immediately withdrew to Milan. The Florentine generals being now left without any hindrance, to show that the cause assigned for their inaction was the true one, pressed the enemy more closely, so that they came to a regular engagement, which continued half a day, without either party yielding. Some horses were wounded and prisoners taken, but no death occurred. Winter having arrived, and with it the usual time for armies to retire into quarters, Bartolommeo Coglione withdrew to Ravenna, the Florentine forces into Tuscany, and those of the king and duke, each to the territories of their sovereign. As this attempt had not occasioned any tumult in Florence, contrary to the rebels' expectation, and the troops they had hired were in want of pay, terms of peace were proposed, and easily arranged. The revolted Florentines, thus deprived of hope, dispersed themselves in various places. Diotisalvi Neroni withdrew to Ferrara, where he was received and entertained by the Marquis Borso. Niccolo Soderini went to Ravenna, where, upon a small pension allowed by the Venetians, he grew old and died. He was considered a just and brave man, but over-cautious and slow to determine, a circumstance which occasioned him, when Gonfalonier of Justice, to lose the opportunity of victory which he would have gladly recovered when too late.

Upon the restoration of peace, those who remained victorious in Florence, as if unable to convince themselves they had conquered, unless they oppressed not merely their enemies, but all whom they suspected, prevailed upon Bardo Altoviti, then Gonfalonier of Justice, to deprive many of the honors of government, and to banish several more. They exercised their power so inconsiderately, and conducted themselves in such an arbitrary manner, that it seemed as if fortune and the Almighty had given the city up to them for a prey. Piero knew little of these things, and was unable to remedy even the little he knew, on account of his infirmities; his body being so contracted that he could use no faculty but that of speech. All he could do was to admonish the leading men, and beg they would conduct themselves with greater moderation, and not by their violence effect their country's ruin. In order to divert the city, he resolved to celebrate the marriage of his son Lorenzo with Clarice degli Orsini with great splendor; and it was accordingly solemnized with all the display suitable to the exalted rank of the parties. Feasts, dancing, and antique representations occupied many days; at the conclusion of which, to exhibit the grandeur of the house of Medici and of the government, two military spectacles were presented, one performed by men on horseback, who went through the evolutions of a field engagement, and the other representing the storming of a town; everything being conducted with admirable order and the greatest imaginable brilliancy.

During these transactions in Florence, the rest of Italy, though at peace, was filled with apprehension of the power of the Turks, who continued to attack the Christians, and had taken Negropont, to the great disgrace and injury of the Christian name. About this time died Borso, marquis of Ferrara, who was succeeded by his brother Ercole. Gismondo da Rimini, the inveterate enemy of the church also expired, and his natural brother Roberto, who was afterward one of the best generals of Italy, succeeded him. Pope Paul died, and was succeeded by Sixtus IV. previously called Francesco da Savona, a man of the very lowest origin, who by his talents had become general of the order of St. Francis, and afterward cardinal. He was the first who began to show how far a pope might go, and how much that which was previously regarded as sinful lost its iniquity when committed by a pontiff. Among others of his family were Piero and Girolamo, who, according to universal belief, were his sons, though he designated them by terms reflecting less scandal on his character. Piero being a priest, was advanced to the dignity of a cardinal, with the title of St. Sixtus. To Girolamo he gave the city of Furli, taken from Antonio Ordelaffi, whose ancestors had held that territory for many generations. This ambitious method of procedure made him more regarded by the princes of Italy, and all sought to obtain his friendship. The duke of Milan gave his natural daughter Caterina to Girolamo, with the city of Imola, which he had taken from Taddeo degli Alidossi, as her portion. New matrimonial alliances were formed between the duke and king Ferrando; Elisabetta, daughter of Alfonso, the king's eldest son, being united to Giovan Galeazzo, the eldest son of the duke.

Italy being at peace, the principal employment of her princes was to watch each other, and strengthen their own influence by new alliances, leagues, or friendships. But in the midst of this repose, Florence endured great oppression from her principal citizens, and the infirmities of Piero incapacitated him from restraining their ambition. However, to relieve his conscience, and, if possible, to make them ashamed of their conduct, he sent for them to his house, and addressed them in the following words: "I never thought a time would come when the behavior of my friends would compel me to esteem and desire the society of my enemies, and wish that I had been defeated rather than victorious; for I believed myself to be associated with those who would set some bounds to their avarice, and who, after having avenged themselves on their enemies, and lived in their country with security and honor, would be satisfied. But now I find myself greatly deceived, unacquainted with the ambition of mankind, and least of all with yours; for, not satisfied with being masters of so great a city, and possessing among yourselves those honors, dignities, and emoluments which used to be divided among many citizens; not contented with having shared among a few the property of your enemies, or with being able to oppress all others with public burdens, while you yourselves are exempt from them, and enjoy all the public offices of profit you must still further load everyone with ill usage. You plunder your neighbors of their wealth; you sell justice; you evade the law; you oppress the timid and exalt the insolent. Nor is there, throughout all Italy, so many and such shocking examples of violence and avarice as in this city. Has our country fostered us only to be her destroyer? Have we been victorious only to effect her ruin? Has she honored us that we may overwhelm her with disgrace? Now, by that faith which is binding upon all good men, I promise you, that if you still conduct yourselves so as to make me regret my victory, I will adopt such measures as shall cause you bitterly to repent of having misused it." The reply of the citizens accorded with the time and circumstances, but they did not forego their evil practices; so that, in consequence, Piero sent for Agnolo Acciajuoli to come secretly to Cafaggiolo, and discussed with him at great length the condition of the city; and doubtless, had he not been prevented by death, he would have called home the exiles as a check upon the rapine of the opposite party. But these honorable designs were frustrated; for, sinking under bodily infirmities and mental anguish, he expired in the fifty-third year of his age. His goodness and virtue were not duly appreciated by his country, principally from his having, until almost the close of his life, been associated with Cosmo, and the few years he survived being spent in civil discord and constant debility. Piero was buried in the church of St. Lorenzo, near his father, and his obsequies were performed with all the pomp and solemnity due to his exalted station. He left two sons, Lorenzo and Guiliano, whose extreme youth excited alarm in the minds of thinking men, though each gave hopes of future usefulness to the republic.

Among the principal citizens in the government of Florence, and very superior to the rest, was Tommaso Soderini, whose prudence and authority were well known not only at home, but throughout Italy. After Piero's death, the whole city looked up to him; many citizens waited upon him at his own house, as the head of the government, and several princes addressed him by letter; but he, impartially estimating his own fortune and that of the house of Medici, made no reply to the princes' communications, and told the citizens, it was not his house, but that of the Medici they ought to visit. To demonstrate by his actions the sincerity and integrity of his advice he assembled all the heads of noble families in the convent of St. Antonio, whither he also brought Lorenzo and

Guiliano de' Medici, and in a long and serious speech upon the state of the city, the condition of Italy, and the views of her princes, he assured them, that if they wished to live in peace and unity in Florence, free both from internal dissensions and foreign wars, it would be necessary to respect the sons of Piero and support the reputation of their house; for men never regret their continuance in a course sanctioned by custom while new methods are soon adopted and as speedily set aside; and it has always been found easier to maintain a power which by its continuance has outlived envy, than to raise a new one, which innumerable unforeseen causes may overthrow. When Tommaso had concluded, Lorenzo spoke, and, though young, with such modesty and discretion that all present felt a presentiment of his becoming what he afterward proved to be; and before the citizens departed they swore to regard the youths as their sons, and the brothers promised to look upon them as their parents. After this, Lorenzo and Guiliano were honored as princes, and resolved to be guided by the advice of Tommaso Soderini.

While profound tranquillity prevailed both at home and abroad, no wars disturbing the general repose, there arose an unexpected disturbance, which came like a presage of future evils. Among the ruined families of the party of Luca Pitti, was that of the Nardi; for Salvestro and his brothers, the heads of the house, were banished and afterward declared rebels for having taken part in the war under Bartolommeo Coglione. Bernardo, the brother of Salvestro, was young, prompt, and bold, and on account of his poverty being unable to alleviate the sorrows of exile, while the peace extinguished all hopes of his return to the city, he determined to attempt some means of rekindling the war; for a trifling commencement often produces great results, and men more readily prosecute what is already begun than originate new enterprises. Bernardo had many acquaintances at Prato, and still more in the district of Pistoia, particularly among the Palandra, a family which, though rustic, was very numerous, and, like the rest of the Pistolesi, brought up to slaughter and war. These he knew to be discontented, on account of the Florentine magistrates having endeavored, perhaps too severely, to check their partiality for inveterate feuds and consequence bloodshed. He was also aware that the people of Prato considered themselves injured by the pride and avarice of their governors, and that some were ill disposed toward Florence; therefore all things considered, he hoped to be able to kindle a fire in Tuscany (should Prato rebel) which would be fostered by so many, that those who might wish to extinguish it would fail in the attempt. He communicated his ideas to Diotisalvi Neroni, and asked him, in case they should succeed in taking possession of Prato, what assistance might be expected from the princes of Italy, by his means? Diotisalvi considered the enterprise as imminently dangerous, and almost impracticable; but since it presented a fresh chance of attaining his object, at the risk of others, he advised him to proceed, and promised certain assistance from Bologna and Ferrara, if he could retain Prato not less than fifteen days. Bernardo, whom this promise inspired with a lively hope of success, proceeded secretly to Prato, and communicated with those most disposed to favor him, among whom were the Palandra; and having arranged the time and plan, informed Diotisalvi of what had been done.

Chapter V: Bernardo takes possession of Prato, but is not assisted by the inhabitants—He is taken, and the tumult appeased—Corruption of Florence—The duke of Milan in Florence—The church of Santo Spirito destroyed by fire—The rebellion of Volterra, and the cause of it—Volterra reduced to obedience by force, in accordance with the advice of Lorenzo de' Medici—Volterra pillaged.

Cesare Petrucci held the office of Provost of Prato for the Florentine people, at this period. It is customary with governors of towns, similarly situated, to keep the keys of the gates near their persons; and whenever, in peaceful times, they are required by any of the inhabitants, for entrance or exit, they are usually allowed to be taken. Bernardo was aware of this custom, and about daybreak, presented himself at the gate which looks toward Pistoia, accompanied by the Palandra and about one hundred persons, all armed. Their confederates within the town also armed themselves, and one of them asked the governor for the keys, alleging, as a pretext, that some one from the country wished to enter. The governor not entertaining the slightest suspicion, sent a servant with them. When at a convenient distance, they were taken by the conspirators, who, opening the gates, introduced Bernardo and his followers. They divided themselves into two parties, one of which, led by Salvestro, an inhabitant of Prato, took possession of the citadel; the other following Bernardo, seized the palace, and placed Cesare with all his family in the custody of some of their number. They then raised the cry of liberty, and proceeded through the town. It was now day, and many of the inhabitants hearing the disturbance, ran to the piazza where, learning that the fortress and the palace were taken and the governor with all his people made prisoners, they were utterly astonished, and could not imagine how it had occurred. The eight citizens, possessing the supreme authority, assembled in their palace to consider what was best to be done. In the meantime, Bernardo and his followers, on going round the town, found no encouragement, and being told that the Eight had assembled, went and declared the nature of their enterprise, which he said was to deliver the country from slavery, reminding them how glorious it would be for those who took arms to effect such an honorable object, for they would thus obtain permanent repose and everlasting fame. He called to recollection their ancient liberty and present condition, and assured them of certain assistance, if they would only, for a few days, aid in resisting the forces the Florentines might send against them. He said he had friends in Florence who would join them as soon as they found the inhabitants resolved to support him. His speech did not produce the desired effect upon the Eight, who replied that they knew not whether Florence was free or enslaved, for that was a matter which they were not called upon to decide; but this they knew very well, that for their own part, they desired no other liberty than to obey the magistrates who governed Florence, from whom they had never received any injury sufficient to make them desire a change. They therefore advised him to set the governor at liberty, clear the place of his people, and, as quickly as possible, withdraw from the danger he had so rashly incurred. Bernardo was not daunted by these words, but determined to try whether fear could influence the people of Prato, since entreaties produced so little effect. In order to terrify them, he determined to put Cesare to death, and having brought him out of prison, ordered him to be hanged at the windows of the palace. He was already led to the spot with a halter around his neck, when seeing Bernardo giving directions to hasten his end, he turned to him, and said: "Bernardo, you put me to death, thinking that the people of Prato will follow you; but the direct contrary will result; for the respect they have for the rectors which the Florentine people send here is so great, that as soon as they witness the injury inflicted upon me, they will conceive such a disgust against you as will inevitably effect your ruin. Therefore, it is not by my death, but by the preservation of my life, that you can attain the object you have in view; for if I deliver your commands, they will be much more readily obeyed, and following your directions, we shall soon attain the completion of your design." Bernardo, whose mind was not fertile in expedients, thought the advice good, and commanded Cesare, on being conducted to a veranda which looked upon the piazza, to order the people of Prato to obey him, and having done which, Cesare was led back to prison.

The weakness of the conspirators was obvious; and many Florentines residing in the town, assembled together, among whom, Giorgio Ginori, a knight of Rhodes, took arms first against them, and attacked Bernardo, who traversed the piazza, alternately entreating and threatening those who refused to obey him, and being surrounded by Giorgio's followers, he was wounded and made prisoner. This being done, it was easy to set the governor at liberty and subdue the rest, who being few, and divided into several parties, were nearly all either secured or slain. An exaggerated report of these transactions reached Florence, it being told there that Prato was taken, the governor and his friends put to death, and the place filled with the enemy; and that Pistoia was also in arms, and most of the citizens in the conspiracy. In consequence of this alarming account, the palace as quickly filled with citizens, who consulted with the Signory what course ought to be adopted. At this time, Roberto da San Severino, one of the most distinguished generals of this period, was at Florence, and it was therefore determined to send him, with what forces could be collected, to Prato, with orders that he should approach the place, particularly observe what was going on, and provide such remedies as the necessity of the case and his own prudence should suggest. Roberto had scarcely passed the fortress of Campi, when he was met by a messenger from the governor, who informed him that Bernardo was taken, his followers either dispersed or slain, and everything restored to order. He consequently returned to Florence, whither Bernardo was shortly after conveyed, and when questioned by the magistracy concerning the real motives of such a weak conspiracy, he said, he had undertaken it, because, having resolved to die in Florence rather than live in exile, he wished his death to be accompanied by some memorable action.

This disturbance having been raised and quelled almost at the same time, the citizens returned to their accustomed mode of life, hoping to enjoy, without anxiety, the state they had now established and confirmed. Hence arose many of those evils which usually result from peace; for the youth having become more dissolute than before, more extravagant in dress, feasting, and other licentiousness, and being without employment, wasted their time and means on gaming and women; their principal study being how to appear splendid in apparel, and attain a crafty shrewdness in discourse; he who could make the most poignant remark being considered the wisest, and being most respected. These manners derived additional encouragement from the followers of the duke of Milan, who, with his duchess and the whole ducal court, as it was said, to fulfill a vow, came to Florence, where he was received with all the pomp and respect due to so great a prince, and one so intimately connected with the Florentine people. Upon this occasion the city witnessed an unprecedented exhibition; for, during Lent, when the church commands us to abstain from animal food, the Milanese, without respect for either God or his church, ate of it daily. Many spectacles were exhibited in honor of the duke, and among others, in the temple of Santo Spirito, was represented the descent of the Holy Ghost among the apostles; and in consequence of the numerous fires used upon the occasion, some of the woodwork became ignited, and the church was completely destroyed by the flames. Many thought that the Almighty being offended at our misconduct, took this method of signifying his displeasure. If, therefore, the duke found the city full of courtly delicacies, and customs unsuitable to well-regulated conduct, he left it in a much worse state. Hence the good citizens thought it necessary to restrain these improprieties, and made a law to put a stop to extravagance in dress, feasts, and funerals.

In the midst of this universal peace, a new and unexpected disturbance arose in Tuscany. Certain citizens of Volterra had discovered an alum-mine in their district, and being aware of the profit derivable from it, in order to obtain the means of working and securing it, they applied to some Florentines, and allowed them to share in the profits. This, as is frequently the case with new undertakings, at first excited little attention from the people of Volterra; but in time, finding the profits derived from it had become considerable, they fruitlessly endeavored to effect what at first might have been easily accomplished. They began by agitating the question in their councils, declaring it grossly improper that a source of wealth discovered in the public lands should be converted to the emolument of private individuals. They next sent advocates to Florence, and the question was referred to the consideration of certain citizens, who, either through being bribed by the party in possession, or from a sincere conviction, declared the aim of the people of Volterra to be unjust in desiring to deprive their citizens of the fruit of their labor; and decided that the alum-pit was the rightful property of those who had hitherto wrought it; but, at the same time, recommended them to pay an annual sum by way of acknowledgment to the city. This answer instead of abating, served only to increase the animosities and tumult in Volterra, and absorbed entire attention both in the councils and throughout the city; the people demanding the restitution of what they considered their due, and the proprietors insisting upon their right to retain what they had originally acquired, and what had been subsequently been confirmed to them by the decision of the Florentines. In the midst of these disturbances, a respectable citizen, named Il Pecorino, was killed, together with several others, who had embraced the same side, whose houses were also plundered and burned; and the fury of the mob rose to such a height, that they were with difficulty restrained from putting the Florentine rectors to death.

After the first outrage, the Volterrani immediately determined to send ambassadors to Florence, who intimated, that if the Signory would allow them their ancient privileges, the city would remain subject to them as formerly. Many and various were the opinions concerning the reply to be made. Tommaso Soderini advised that they should accept the submission of the people of Volterra, upon any conditions with which they were disposed to make it; for he considered it unreasonable and unwise to kindle a flame so near home that it might burn their own dwelling; he suspected the pope's ambition, and was apprehensive of the power of the king; nor could he confide in the friendship either of the duke or the Venetians, having no assurance of the sincerity of the latter, or the valor of the former. He concluded by quoting that trite proverb, "Meglio un magro accordo che una grassa vittoria."[*] On the other hand, Lorenzo de' Medici, thinking this an opportunity for exhibiting his prudence and wisdom, and being strenuously supported by those who envied the influence of Tommaso Soderini, resolved to march against them, and punish the arrogance of the people of Volterra with arms; declaring that if they were not made a striking example, others would, without the least fear or respect, upon every slight occasion, adopt a similar course. The enterprise being resolved on, the Volterrani were told that they could not demand the observance of conditions which they themselves had broken, and therefore must either submit to the direction of the Signory or expect war. With this answer they returned to their city, and prepared for its defense; fortifying the place, and sending to all the princes of Italy to request assistance, none of whom listened to them, except the Siennese and the lord of Piombino, who gave them some hope of aid. The Florentines on the other hand, thinking success dependent principally upon celerity, assembled ten thousand foot and two thousand horse, who, under the command of Federigo, lord of Urbino, marched into the country of Volterra and quickly took entire possession of it. They then encamped before the city, which, being in a lofty situation, and precipitous on all sides, could only be approached by a narrow pass near the church of St. Alessandro. The Volterrani had engaged for their defense about one thousand mercenaries, who, perceiving the great superiority of the Florentines, found the place untenable, and were tardy in their defensive operations, but indefatigable in the constant injuries they committed upon the people of the place. Thus these poor citizens were harassed by the enemy without, and by their own soldiery within; so, despairing of their safety, they began to think of a capitulation; and, being unable to obtain better terms, submitted to the discretion of the Florentine commissaries, who ordered the gates to be opened, and introduced the greater part of their forces. They then proceeded to the palace, and commanded the priors to retire to their homes; and, on the way thither, one of them was in derision stripped by the soldiers. From this beginning (so much more easily are men predisposed to evil than to good) originated the pillage and destruction of the city; which for a whole day suffered the greatest horrors, neither women nor sacred places being spared; and the soldiery, those engaged for its defense as well as its assailants, plundered all that came within their reach. The news of this victory was received with great joy at Florence, and as the expedition had been undertaken wholly by the advice of Lorenzo, he acquired great reputation. Upon which one of the intimate friends of Tommaso Soderini, reminding him of the advice he had given, asked him what he thought of the taking of Volterra; to which he replied, "To me the place seems rather lost than won; for had it been received on equitable terms, advantage and security would have been the result; but having to retain it by force it will in critical junctures, occasion weakness and anxiety, and in times of peace, injury and expense."

[*] A lean peace is better than a fat victory.

Chapter VI: Origin of the animosity between Sixtus IV. and Lorenzo de' Medici—Carlo di Braccio da Perugia attacks the Siennese—Carlo retires by desire of the Florentines—Conspiracy against Galeazzo, duke of Milan—His vices—He is slain by the conspirators—Their deaths.

The pope, anxious to retain the territories of the church in obedience, had caused Spoleto to be sacked for having, through internal factions, fallen into rebellion. Citta di Castello being in the same state of contumacy, he besieged that place; and Niccolo Vitelli its prince, being on intimate terms with Lorenzo de' Medici, obtained assistance from him, which, though inadequate, was quite enough to originate that enmity between Sixtus IV. and the Medici afterward productive of such unhappy results. Nor would this have been so long in development had not the death of Frate Piero, cardinal of St. Sixtus, taken place; who, after having traveled over Italy and visited Venice and Milan (under the pretense of doing honor to the marriage of Ercole, marquis of Ferrara), went about sounding the minds of the princes, to learn how they were disposed toward the Florentines. But upon his return he died, not without suspicion of having been poisoned by the Venetians, who found they would have reason to fear Sixtus if he were allowed to avail himself of the talents and exertions of Frate Piero. Although of very low extraction, and meanly brought up within the walls of a convent, he had no sooner attained the distinction of the scarlet hat, than he exhibited such inordinate pride and ambition, that the pontificate seemed too little for him, and he gave a feast in Rome which would have seemed extraordinary even for a king, the expense exceeding twenty thousand florins. Deprived of this minister, the designs of Sixtus proceeded with less promptitude. The Florentines, the duke, and the Venetians having renewed their league, and allowed the pope and the king to join them if they thought proper, the two latter also entered into a league, reserving an opening for the others if they were desirous to become parties to it. Italy was thus divided in two factions; for circumstances daily arose which occasioned ill feeling between the two leagues; as occurred with respect to the island of Cyprus, to which Ferrando laid claim, and the Venetians occupied. Thus the pope and the king became more closely united. Federigo, prince of Urbino, was at this time one of the first generals of Italy; and had long served the Florentines. In order, if possible, to deprive the hostile league of their captain, the pope advised, and the king requested him to pay a visit to them. To the surprise and displeasure of the Florentines, Federigo complied; for they thought the same fate awaited him as had befallen Niccolo Piccinino. However, the result was quite different; for he returned from Naples and Rome greatly honored, and with the appointment of general to their forces. They also endeavored to gain over to their interest the lords of Romagna and the Siennese, that they might more easily injure the Florentines, who, becoming aware of these things, used their utmost endeavors to defend themselves against the ambition of their enemies; and having lost Federigo d'Urbino, they engaged Roberto da Rimino in his place, renewed the league with the Perugini and formed one with the prince of Faenza. The pope and the king assigned, as the reasons of their animosity against the Florentines, that they wished to withdraw them from the Venetian alliance, and associate them with their own league; for the pope did not think the church could maintain her reputation, nor the Count Girolamo retain the states of Romagna, while the Florentines and the Venetians remained united. The Florentines conjectured their design was to set them at enmity with the Venetians, not so much for the sake of gaining their friendship as to be able the more easily to injure them. Two years passed away in these jealousies and discontents before any disturbance broke out; but the first which occurred, and that but trivial, took place in Tuscany.

Braccio of Perugia, whom we have frequently mentioned as one of the most distinguished warriors of Italy, left two sons, Oddo and Carlo; the latter was of tender years; the former, as above related, was slain by the people of Val di Lamona; but Carlo, when he came to mature age, was by the Venetians, out of respect for the memory of his father, and the hopes they entertained from himself, received among the condottieri of their republic. The term of his engagement having expired, he did not design to renew it immediately, but resolved to try if, by his own influence and his father's reputation, he could recover possession of Perugia. To this the Venetians willingly consented, for they usually extended their dominion by any changes that occurred in the neighboring states. Carlo consequently came into Tuscany, but found more difficulties in his attempt upon Perugia than he had anticipated, on account of its being allied with the Florentines; and desirous of doing something worthy of memory, he made war upon the Siennese, alleging them to be indebted to him for services performed by his father in the affairs of that republic, and attacked them with such impetuosity as to threaten the total overthrow of their dominion. The Siennese, ever ready to suspect the Florentines, persuaded themselves that this outrage had been committed with their cognizance, and made heavy complaints to the pope and the king against them. They also sent ambassadors to Florence to complain of the injuries they had suffered, and adroitly intimated, that if Carlo had not been secretly supported he could not have made war upon them with such perfect security. The Florentines denied all participation in the proceedings of Carlo, expressed their most earnest wish to do everything in their power to put a stop to them, and allowed the ambassadors to use whatever terms they pleased in the name of the Signory, to command him to desist. Carlo complained that the Florentines, by their unwillingness to support him, had deprived themselves of a most valuable acquisition and him of great glory; for he could have insured them the possession of the whole territory in a short time, from the want of courage in the people and the ineffectual provision they had made for their defense. He then withdrew to his engagement under the Venetians; but the Siennese, although delivered from such imminent peril by the Florentines, were still very indignant against them; considering themselves under no obligation to those who had delivered them from an evil to which they had first exposed them.

While the transactions between the king and the pope were in progress, and those in Tuscany in the manner we have related, an event of greater importance occurred in Lombardy. Cola Montano, a learned and ambitious man, taught the Latin language to the youth of the principal families in Milan. Either out of hatred to the character and manners of the duke, or from some other cause, he constantly deprecated the condition of those who live under a bad prince; calling those glorious and happy who had the good fortune to be born and live in a republic. He endeavored to show that the most celebrated men had been produced in republics, and not reared under princes; that the former cherish virtue, while the latter destroy it; the one deriving advantage from virtuous men, while the latter naturally fear them. The youths with whom he was most intimate were Giovanni Andrea Lampognano, Carlo Visconti, and Girolamo Ogliato. He frequently discussed with them the faults of their prince, and the wretched condition of those who were subject to him; and by constantly inculcating his principles, acquired such an ascendancy over their minds as to induce them to bind themselves by oath to effect the duke's destruction, as soon as they became old enough to attempt it. Their minds being fully occupied with this design, which grew with their years, the duke's conduct and their own private injuries served to hasten its execution. Galeazzo was licentious and cruel, of both which vices he had given such repeated proofs, that he became odious to all. Not content with corrupting the wives of the nobility, he also took pleasure in making it notorious; nor was he satisfied with murdering individuals unless he effected their deaths by some unusual cruelty. He was suspected of having destroyed his own mother; for, not considering himself prince while she was present, he conducted himself in such a manner as induced her to withdraw from his court, and, travelling toward Cremona, which she obtained as part of her marriage portion, she was seized with a sudden illness, and died upon the road; which made many think her son had caused her death. The duke had dishonored both Carlo and Girolamo in respect to their wives or other female relatives, and had refused to concede to Giovanandrea possession of the monastery of Miramondo, of which he had obtained a grant from the pope for a near relative. These private injuries increased the young men's desire for vengeance, and the deliverance of their country from so many evils; trusting that whenever they should succeed in destroying the duke, many of the nobility and all the people would rise in their defense. Being resolved upon their undertaking, they were often together, which, on account of their long intimacy, did not excite any suspicion. They frequently discussed the subject; and in order to familiarize their minds with the deed itself, they practiced striking each other in the breast and in the side with the sheathed daggers intended to be used for the purpose. On considering the most suitable time and place, the castle seemed insecure; during the chase, uncertain and dangerous; while going about the city for his own amusement, difficult if not impracticable; and, at a banquet, of doubtful result. They, therefore, determined to kill him upon the occasion of some procession or public festivity when there would be no doubt of his presence, and where they might, under various pretexts, assemble their friends. It was also resolved that if one of their number were prevented from attending, on any account whatever, the rest should put him to death in the midst of their armed enemies.

It was now the close of the year 1476, near Christmas, and as it was customary for the duke to go upon St. Stephen's day, in great solemnity, to the church of that martyr, they considered this the most suitable opportunity for the execution of their design. Upon the morning of that day they ordered some of their most trusty friends and servants to arm, telling them they wished to go to the assistance of Giovanandrea, who, contrary to the wish of some of his neighbors, intended to turn a watercourse into his estate; but that before they went they wished to take leave of the prince. They also assembled, under various pretenses, other friends and relatives, trusting that when the deed was accomplished, everyone would join them in the completion of their enterprise. It was their intention, after the duke's death, to collect their followers together and proceed to those parts of the city where they imagined the plebeians would be most disposed to take arms against the duchess and the principal ministers of state, and they thought the people, on account of the famine which then prevailed, would easily be induced to follow them; for it was their design to give up the houses of Cecco Simonetta, Giovanni Botti, and Francesco Lucani, all leading men in the government, to be plundered, and by this means gain over the populace and restore liberty to the community. With these ideas, and with minds resolved upon their execution, Giovanandrea, together with the rest, were early at the church, and heard mass together; after which, Giovanandrea, turning to a statue of St. Ambrose, said, "O patron of our city! thou knowest our intention, and the end we would attain, by so many dangers; favor our enterprise, and prove, by protecting the oppressed, that tyranny is offensive to thee." To the duke, on the other hand, when intending to go to the church, many omens occurred of his approaching death; for in the morning, having put on a cuirass, as was his frequent custom, he immediately took it off again, either because it inconvenienced him, or that he did not like its appearance. He then wished to hear mass in the castle, and found that the priest who officiated in the chapel had gone to St. Stephen's, and had taken with him the sacred utensils. On this he desired the service to be performed by the bishop of Como, who acquainted him with preventing circumstances. Thus, almost compelled, he determined to go to the church; but before his departure, caused his sons, Giovan Galeazzo and Ermes, to be brought to him, whom he embraced and kissed several times, seeming reluctant to part with them. He then left the castle, and, with the ambassadors of Ferrara and Mantua on either hand, proceeded to St. Stephen's. The conspirators, to avoid exciting suspicion, and to escape the cold, which was very severe, had withdrawn to an apartment of the archpriest, who was a friend of theirs, but hearing the duke's approach, they came into the church, Giovanandrea and Girolamo placing themselves upon the right hand of the entrance, and Carlo on the left. Those who led the procession had already entered, and were followed by the duke, surrounded by such a multitude as is usual on similar occasions. The first attack was made by Lampognano and Girolamo, who, pretending to clear the way for the prince, came close to him, and grasping their daggers, which, being short and sharp, were concealed in the sleeves of their vests, struck at him. Lampognano gave him two wounds, one in the belly, the other in the throat. Girolamo struck him in the throat and breast. Carlo Visconti, being nearer the door, and the duke having passed, could not wound him in front: but with two strokes, transpierced his shoulder and spine. These six wounds were inflicted so instantaneously, that the duke had fallen before anyone was aware of what had happened, and he expired, having only once ejaculated the name of the Virgin, as if imploring her assistance. A great tumult immediately ensued, several swords were drawn, and as often happens in sudden emergencies, some fled from the church, and others ran toward the scene of tumult, both without any definite motive or knowledge of what had occurred. Those, however, who were nearest the duke and had seen him slain, recognizing the murderers, pursued them. Giovanandrea, endeavoring to make his way out of the church, proceeded among the women, who being numerous, and according to their custom, seated upon the ground, was prevented in his progress by their apparel, and being overtaken, he was killed by a Moor, one of the duke's footmen. Carlo was slain by those immediately around him. Girolamo Olgiato passed through the crowd, and got out of the church; but seeing his companions dead, and not knowing where else to go, he proceeded home, where his father and brothers refused to receive him; his mother only, having compassion on her son recommended him to a priest, an old friend of the family, who, disguising him in his own apparel, led him to his house. Here he remained two days, not without hope that some disturbance might arise in Milan which would contribute to his safety. This not occurring, and apprehensive that his hiding place would be discovered, he endeavored to escape in disguise, but being observed, he was given over to justice, and disclosed all the particulars of the conspiracy. Girolamo was twenty-three years of age, and exhibited no less composure at his death than resolution in his previous conduct, for being stripped of his apparel, and in the hands of the executioner, who stood by with the sword unsheathed, ready to deprive him of life, he repeated the following words, in the Latin tongue, in which he was well versed: "Mors acerba, fama perpetua, stabit vetus memoria facti."

The enterprise of these unfortunate young men was conducted with secrecy and executed with resolution; and they failed for want of the support of those whom they expected would rise in their defense. Let princes therefore learn to live, so as to render themselves beloved and respected by their subjects, that none may have hope of safety after having destroyed them; and let others see how vain is the expectation which induces them to trust so much to the multitude, as to believe, that even when discontented, they will either embrace or ward off their dangers. This event spread consternation all over Italy; but those which shortly afterward occurred in Florence caused much more alarm, and terminated a peace of twelve years' continuance, as will be shown in the following book; which, having commenced with blood and horror, will have a melancholy and tearful conclusion.

Book VIII: Chapter I: State of the family of the Medici at Florence—Enmity of Sixtus IV. toward Florence—Differences between the family of the Pazzi and that of the Medici—Beginning of the conspiracy of the Pazzi—Arrangements to effect the design of the conspiracy—Giovanni Batista da Montesecco is sent to Florence—The pope joins the conspiracy—The king of Naples becomes a party to it—Names of the conspirators—The conspirators make many ineffectual attempts to kill Lorenzo and Giuliano de' Medici—The final arrangement—Order of the conspiracy.

This book, commencing between two conspiracies, the one at Milan already narrated, the other yet to be recorded, it would seem appropriate, and in accordance with our usual custom, were we to treat of the nature and importance of these terrible demonstrations. This we should willingly do had we not discussed the matter elsewhere, or could it be comprised in few words. But requiring much consideration, and being already noticed in another place, it will be omitted, and we shall proceed with our narrative. The government of the Medici having subdued all its avowed enemies in order to obtain for that family undivided authority, and distinguish them from other citizens in their relation to the rest, found it necessary to subdue those who secretly plotted against them. While Medici contended with other families, their equals in authority and reputation, those who envied their power were able to oppose them openly without danger of being suppressed at the first demonstration of hostility; for the magistrates being free, neither party had occasion to fear, till one or other of them was overcome. But after the victory of 1466, the government became so entirely centred in the Medici, and they acquired so much authority, that discontented spirits were obliged either to suffer in silence, or, if desirous to destroy them, to attempt it in secrecy, and by clandestine means; which plots rarely succeed and most commonly involve the ruin of those concerned in them, while they frequently contribute to the aggrandizement of those against whom they are directed. Thus the prince of a city attacked by a conspiracy, if not slain like the duke of Milan (which seldom happens), almost always attains to a greater degree of power, and very often has his good disposition perverted to evil. The proceedings of his enemies give him cause for fear; fear suggests the necessity of providing for his own safety, which involves the injury of others; and hence arise animosities, and not unfrequently his ruin. Thus these conspiracies quickly occasion the destruction of their contrivers, and, in time, inevitably injure their primary object.

Italy, as we have seen above, was divided into two factions; the pope and the king on one side; on the other, the Venetians, the duke, and the Florentines. Although the flames of war had not yet broken out, every day gave rise to some new occasion for rekindling them; and the pope, in particular, in all his plans endeavored to annoy the Florentine government. Thus Filippo de' Medici, archbishop of Pisa, being dead, Francesco Salviati, a declared enemy of the Medici, was appointed his successor, contrary to the wish of the Signory of Florence, who being unwilling to give him possession, there arose between them and the pope many fresh grounds of offense, before the matter was settled. Besides this, he conferred, at Rome, many favors upon the family of the Pazzi, and opposed that of the Medici, whenever an opportunity offered. The Pazzi were at this time, both on account of nobility of birth and their great wealth, the most brilliant in France. The head of this family was Jacopo, whom the people, on account of his distinguished pre-eminence, had made a knight. He had no children, except one natural daughter, but many nephews, sons of his brothers Piero and Antonio, the first of whom were Guglielmo, Francesco, Rinato, Giovanni, and then, Andrea, Niccolo, and Galeotto. Cosmo de' Medici, noticing the riches and rank of this family, had given his granddaughter, Bianca, to Guglielmo, hoping by this marriage to unite the houses, and obviate those enmities and dissensions so frequently occasioned by jealousy. However (so uncertain and fallacious are our expectations), very different feelings were thus originated; for Lorenzo's advisers pointed out to him how dangerous it was, and how injurious to his authority, to unite in the same individuals so much wealth and power. In consequence, neither Jacopo nor his nephews obtained those degrees of honor, which in the opinion of other citizens were their due. This gave rise to anger in the Pazzi, and fear on the part of the Medici; as the former of these increased, so did the latter; and upon all occasions, when the Pazzi came in competition with other citizens, their claims to distinction, however strong, were set aside by the magistracy. Francesco de' Pazzi, being at Rome, the Council of Eight, upon some trivial occasion, compelled him to return, without treating him with the respect usually observed toward great citizens, so that the Pazzi everywhere bitterly complained of the ill usage they experienced, and thus excited suspicion in others, and brought down greater evils upon themselves. Giovanni de' Pazzi had married the daughter of Giovanni Buonromei, a very wealthy man, whose riches on his decease, without other children, came to his daughter. His nephew, Carlo, however, took possession of part, and the question being litigated, a law was passed, by virtue of which the wife of Giovanni de' Pazzi was robbed of her inheritance, and it was given to Carlo. In this piece of injustice the Pazzi at once recognized the influence of the Medici. Giuliano de' Medici often complained to his brother Lorenzo of the affair, saying he was afraid that by grasping at too much they would lose all.

Lorenzo, flushed with youth and power, would assume the direction of everything, and resolved that all transactions should bear an impress of his influence. The Pazzi, with their nobility and wealth unable to endure so many affronts, began to devise some means of vengeance. The first who spoke of any attempt against the Medici, was Francesco, who, being more sensitive and resolute than the others, determined either to obtain what was withheld from him, or lose what he still possessed. As the government of Florence gave him great offense, he resided almost constantly at Rome, where, like other Florentine merchants, he conducted extensive commercial operations; and being a most intimate friend of Count Girolamo, they frequently complained to each other of the conduct of the Medici. After a while they began to think that for the count to retain his estates, or the Pazzi their rights in the city, it would be necessary to change the government of Florence; and this they considered could not be done without the death of Giuliano and Lorenzo. They imagined the pope and the king would be easily induced to consent, because each could be convinced of the facility of the enterprise. Having acquired these ideas, they communicated them to Francesco Salviati, archbishop of Pisa, who, being ambitious and recently offended by the Medici, willingly adopted their views. Considering their next step, they resolved, in order to facilitate the design, to obtain the consent of Jacopo de' Pazzi, without whose concurrence they feared it would be impracticable. With this view, it was resolved that Francesco de' Pazzi should go to Florence, while the archbishop and the count were to remain at Rome, to be ready to communicate with the pope when a suitable opportunity occurred. Francesco found Jacopo de' Pazzi more cautious and difficult to persuade than he could have wished, and on imparting this to his friends at Rome, it was thought he desired the sanction of some greater authority to induce him to adopt their views. Upon this, the archbishop and the count communicated the whole affair to Giovanni Batista da Montesecco, a leader of the papal forces, possessing military reputation, and under obligations to the pope and the count. To him the affair seemed difficult and dangerous, while the archbishop endeavored to obviate his objections by showing how much assistance the pope and the king would lend to the enterprise; the hatred of the Florentines toward the Medici, the numerous friends the Salviati and the Pazzi would bring with them, the readiness with which the young men might be slain, on account of their going about the city unaccompanied and without suspicion, and the facility with which the government might then be changed. These things Giovanni Batista did not in reality believe, for he had heard from many Florentines quite contrary statements.

While occupied with these deliberations, Carlo, lord of Faenza, was taken ill, and tears were entertained for his life. This circumstance seemed to the archbishop and the count to offer an opportunity for sending Giovanni Batista to Florence, and thence to Romagna, under pretence of recovering certain territories belonging to the latter, of which the lord of Faenza had taken possession. The count therefore commissioned Giovanni Batista to have an interview with Lorenzo de' Medici, and on his part request his advice how to proceed with respect to the affair of Romagna; that he should then see Francesco de' Pazzi, and in conjunction with him endeavor to induce his uncle Jacopo to adopt their ideas. To render the pope's authority available in their behalf, Giovanni Batista was ordered, before his departure, to communicate with the pontiff, who offered every means at his disposal in favor of their enterprise. Giovanni Batista, having arrived at Florence, obtained an interview with Lorenzo, by whom he was most graciously received; and with regard to the advice he was commissioned to ask, obtained a wise and friendly answer; so that he was astonished at finding him quite a different character from what he had been represented, and considered him to possess great sagacity, an affectionate heart, and most amicably disposed toward the count. He found Francesco de' Pazzi had gone to Lucca, and spoke to Jacopo, who was at first quite opposed to their design, but before they parted the pope's authority seemed to have influenced him; for he told Giovanni Batista, that he might go to Romagna, and that before his return Francesco would be with him, and they would then consult more particularly upon the subject. Giovanni Batista proceeded to Romagna, and soon returned to Florence. After a pretended consultation with Lorenzo, upon the count's affairs, he obtained an interview with Francesco and Jacopo de' Pazzi, when the latter gave his consent to their enterprise. They then discussed the means of carrying it into effect. Jacopo de' Pazzi was of opinion that it could not be effected while both the brothers remained at Florence; and therefore it would be better to wait till Lorenzo went to Rome, whither it was reported he had an intention of going; for then their object would be more easily attained. Francesco de' Pazzi had no objection to Lorenzo being at Rome, but if he were to forego the journey, he thought that both the brothers might be slain, either at a marriage, or at a play, or in a church. With regard to foreign assistance, he supposed the pope might assemble forces for the conquest of the fortress of Montone, being justified in taking it from Count Carlo, who had caused the tumults already spoken of in Sienna and Perugia.

Still no definite arrangement was made; but it was resolved that Giovanni Batista and Francesco de' Pazzi should go to Rome and settle everything with the pontiff. The matter was again debated at Rome; and at length it was concluded that besides an expedition against Montone, Giovan Francesco da Tolentino, a leader of the papal troops, should go into Romagna, and Lorenzo da Castello to the Val di Tavere; that each, with the forces of the country, should hold himself in readiness to perform the commands of the archbishop de' Salviati and Francesco de Pazzi, both of whom were to come to Florence, and provide for the execution of their design, with the assistance of Giovanni Batista da Montesecco. King Ferrando promised, by his ambassador, to contribute all in his power to the success of their undertaking. Francesco de' Pazzi and the archbishop having arrived at Florence, prevailed upon Jacopo di Poggio, a well educated youth, but ambitious and very desirous of change, to join them, and two others, each of the name of Jacopo Salviati, one a brother, the other a kinsman, of the archbishop. They also gained over Bernardo Bandini and Napoleone Franzeni, two bold young men, under great obligations to the family of the Pazzi. Besides those already mentioned, they were joined by Antonio da Volterra and a priest named Stefano, who taught Latin to the daughter of Jacopo de' Pazzi. Rinato de' Pazzi, a grave and prudent man, being quite aware of the evils resulting from such undertakings, refused all participation in the conspiracy; he held it in abhorrence, and as much as possible, without betraying his kinsmen, endeavored to counteract it.

The pope had sent Raffaello di Riario, a nephew of Count Girolamo, to the college of Pisa, to study canon law, and while there, had advanced him to the dignity of a cardinal. The conspirators determined to bring this cardinal to Florence, as they would thus be better able to conceal their design, since any persons requisite to be introduced into the city might easily be made to appear as a part of his retinue, and his arrival might facilitate the completion of their enterprise. The cardinal came, and was received by Jacopo de' Pazzi at his villa of Montughi, near Florence. By his means it was also intended to bring together Giuliano and Lorenzo, and whenever this happened, to put them both to death. They therefore invited them to meet the cardinal at their villa of Fiesole; but Giuliano, either intentionally or through some preventing cause, did not attend; and this design having failed, they thought that if asked to an entertainment at Florence, both brothers would certainly be present. With this intention they appointed Sunday, the twenty-sixth of April, 1478, to give a great feast; and, resolving to assassinate them at table, the conspirators met on the Saturday evening to arrange all proceedings for the following day. In the morning it was intimated to Francesco that Giuliano would be absent; on which the conspirators again assembled and finding they could no longer defer the execution of their design, since it would be impossible among so many to preserve secrecy, they determined to complete it in the cathedral church of Santa Reparata, where the cardinal attending, the two brothers would be present as usual. They wished Giovanni Batista da Montesecco to undertake the murder of Lorenzo, while that of Giuliano was assigned to Francesco de' Pazzi and Bernardo Bandini. Giovanni Batista refused, either because his familiarity with Lorenzo had created feelings in his favor, or from some other reason, saying he should not have resolution sufficient to commit such a deed in a church, and thus add sacrilege to treachery. This caused the failure of their undertaking; for time pressing, they were compelled to substitute Antonio da Volterra and Stefano, the priest, two men, who, from nature and habit, were the most unsuitable of any; for if firmness and resolution joined with experience in bloodshed be necessary upon any occasion, it is on such as these; and it often happens that those who are expert in arms, and have faced death in all forms on the field of battle, still fail in an affair like this. Having now decided upon the time, they resolved that the signal for the attack should be the moment when the priest who celebrated high mass should partake of the sacrament, and that, in the meantime, the Archbishop de' Salviati, with his followers, and Jacopo di Poggio, should take possession of the palace, in order that the Signory, after the young men's death, should voluntarily, or by force, contribute to their assistance.

Chapter II: Giuliano de' Medici slain—Lorenzo escapes—The archbishop Salviati endeavors to seize the palace of the Signory—He is taken and hanged—The enterprise of the conspirators entirely fails—Manifestations of the Florentines in favor of Lorenzo de' Medici—The conspirators punished—The funeral of Giuliano—The pope and the king of Naples make war upon the Florentines—Florence excommunicated—Speech of Lorenzo de' Medici to the citizens of Florence.

The conspirators proceeded to Santa Reparata, where the cardinal and Lorenzo had already arrived. The church was crowded, and divine service commenced before Giuliano's arrival. Francesco de' Pazzi and Bernardo Bandini, who were appointed to be his murderers, went to his house, and finding him, they, by earnest entreaties, prevailed upon him to accompany them. It is surprising that such intense hatred, and designs so full of horror as those of Francesco and Bernardo, could be so perfectly concealed; for while conducting him to the church, and after they had reached it, they amused him with jests and playful discourse. Nor did Francesco forget, under pretense of endearment, to press him in his arms, so as to ascertain whether under his apparel he wore a cuirass or other means of defense. Giuliano and Lorenzo were both aware of the animosity of the Pazzi, and their desire to deprive them of the government; but they felt assured that any design would be attempted openly, and in conjunction with the civil authority. Thus being free from apprehension for their personal safety both affected to be on friendly terms with them. The murderers being ready, each in his appointed station, which they could retain without suspicion, on account of the vast numbers assembled in the church, the preconcerted moment arrived, and Bernardo Bandini, with a short dagger provided for the purpose, struck Giuliano in the breast, who, after a few steps, fell to the earth. Francesco de' Pazzi threw himself upon the body and covered him with wounds; while, as if blinded by rage, he inflicted a deep incision upon his own leg. Antonio and Stefano, the priest, attacked Lorenzo, and after dealing many blows, effected only a slight incision in the throat; for either their want of resolution, the activity of Lorenzo, who, finding himself attacked, used his arms in his own defense, or the assistance of those by whom he was surrounded, rendered all attempts futile. They fled and concealed themselves, but being subsequently discovered, were put to death in the most ignominious manner, and their bodies dragged about the city. Lorenzo, with the friends he had about him, took refuge in the sacristy of the church. Bernardo Bandini, after Giuliano's death, also slew Francesco Nori, a most intimate friend of the Medici, either from some previous hatred or for having endeavored to render assistance to Giuliano; and not content with these murders, he ran in pursuit of Lorenzo, intending, by his own promptitude, to make up for the weakness and inefficiency of the others; but finding he had taken refuge in the vestry, he was prevented.

In the midst of these violent and fearful deeds, during which the uproar was so terrible, that it seemed almost sufficient to bring the church down upon its inmates, the cardinal Riario remained close to the altar, where he was with difficulty kept in safety by the priests, until the Signory, upon the abatement of the disturbance, could conduct him to their palace, where he remained in the utmost terror till he was set at liberty.

There were at this time in Florence some people of Perugia, whom party feuds had compelled to leave their homes; and the Pazzi, by promising to restore them to their country, obtained their assistance. The Archbishop de' Salviati, going to seize the palace, together with Jacopo di Poggio, and the Salviati, his friends, took these Perugini with him. Having arrived, he left part of his people below, with orders that when they heard a noise they should make themselves masters of the entrance, while himself, with the greater part of the Perugini, proceeded above, and finding the Signory at dinner (for it was now late), was admitted after a short delay, by Cesare Petrucci, the Gonfalonier of Justice. He entered with only a few of his followers, the greater part of them being shut up in the cancelleria into which they had gone, whose doors were so contrived, that upon closing they could not be opened from either side, without the key. The archbishop being with the gonfalonier, under pretense of having something to communicate on the part of the pope, addressed him in such an incoherent and hesitating manner, that the gonfalonier at once suspected him, and rushing out of the chamber to call assistance, found Jacopo di Poggio, whom he seized by the hair of the head, and gave into the custody of his attendants. The Signory hearing the tumult, snatched such arms as they could at the moment obtain, and all who had gone up with the archbishop, part of them being shut up, and part overcome with terror, were immediately slain or thrown alive out of the windows of the palace, at which the archbishop, the two Jacopi Salviati, and Jacopodi Poggio were hanged. Those whom the archbishop left below, having mastered the guard and taken possession of the entrance occupied all the lower floors, so that the citizens, who in the uproar, hastened to the palace, were unable to give either advice or assistance to the Signory.

Francesco de' Pazzi and Bernardo Bandini, perceiving Lorenzo's escape, and the principal agent in the enterprise seriously wounded, became immediately conscious of the imminent peril of their position. Bernardo, using the same energy in his own behalf that had served him against the Medici, finding all lost, saved himself by flight. Francesco, wounded as he was, got to his house, and endeavored to get on horseback, for it had been arranged they should ride through the city and call the people to arms and liberty; but he found himself unable, from the nature of his wound, and, throwing himself naked upon his bed, begged Jacopo de' Pazzi to perform the part for which he was himself incapacitated. Jacopo, though old and unaccustomed to such business, by way of making a last effort, mounted his horse, and, with about a hundred armed followers, collected without previous preparation, hastened to the piazza of the palace, and endeavored to assemble adherents by cries of "people," and "liberty;" but the former, having been rendered deaf by the fortune and liberty of the Medici, the latter was unknown in Florence, and he found no followers. The signors, who held the upper part of the palace, saluted him with stones and threats. Jacopo, while hesitating, was met by Giovanni Seristori, his brother-in-law, who upbraided him with the troubles he had occasioned, and then advised him to go home, for the people and liberty were as dear to other citizens as to himself. Thus deprived of every hope, Lorenzo being alive, Francesco seriously wounded, and none disposed to follow him, not knowing what to do, he resolved, if possible, to escape by flight; and, accompanied by those whom he had led into the piazza, left Florence with the intention of going into Romagna.

In the meantime the whole city was roused to arms, and Lorenzo de' Medici, accompanied by a numerous escort, returned to his house. The palace was recovered from its assailants, all of whom were either slain or made prisoners. The name of the Medici echoed everywhere, and portions of dead bodies were seen borne on spears and scattered through the streets; while everyone was transported with rage against the Pazzi, and pursued them with relentless cruelty. The people took possession of their houses, and Francesco, naked as they found him, was led to the palace, and hanged beside the archbishop and the rest. He could not be induced, by any injurious words or deeds, to utter a syllable, but regarding those around with a steady look, he silently sighed. Guglielmo de' Pazzi, brother-in-law to Lorenzo, fled to the latter's house, and by his innocence and the intercession of his wife, Bianca, he escaped death. There was not a citizen of any rank whatever who did not, upon this occasion, wait upon Lorenzo with an offer of his services; so great were the popularity and good fortune which this family had acquired by their liberality and prudence. Rinato de' Pazzi was at his villa when the event took place, and on being informed of it, he endeavored to escape in disguise, but was arrested upon the road and brought to Florence. Jacopo de' Pazzi was taken while crossing the mountains of Romagna, for the inhabitants of these parts having heard what had occurred, and seeing him in flight, attacked and brought him back to the city; nor could he, though he frequently endeavored, prevail with them to put him to death upon the road. Jacopo and Rinato were condemned within four days after the murder of Giuliano. And though so many deaths had been inflicted that the roads were covered with fragments of human bodies, not one excited a feeling of regret, except that of Rinato; for he was considered a wise and good man, and possessed none of the pride for which the rest of his family were notorious. As if to mark the event by some extraordinary circumstance, Jacopo de' Pazzi, after having been buried in the tomb of his ancestors, was disinterred like an excommunicated person, and thrown into a hole at the outside of the city walls; from this grave he was taken, and with the halter in which he had been hanged, his body was dragged naked through the city, and, as if unfit for sepulture on earth, thrown by the populace into the Arno, whose waters were then very high. It was an awful instance of the instability of fortune, to see so wealthy a man, possessing the utmost earthly felicity, brought down to such a depth of misery, such utter ruin and extreme degradation. It is said he had vices, among which were gaming and profane swearing, to which he was very much addicted; but these seem more than balanced by his numerous charities, for he relieved many in distress, and bestowed much money for pious uses. It may also be recorded in his favor, that upon the Saturday preceding the death of Giuliano, in order that none might suffer from his misfortunes, he discharged all his debts; and whatever property he possessed belonging to others, either in his own house or his place of business, he was particularly careful to return to its owners. Giovanni Batista da Montesecco, after a long examination, was beheaded; Napoleone Franzesi escaped punishment by flight; Giulielmo de' Pazzi was banished, and such of his cousins as remained alive were imprisoned in the fortress of Volterra. The disturbances being over, and the conspirators punished, the funeral obsequies of Giuliano were performed amid universal lamentation; for he possessed all the liberality and humanity that could be wished for in one of his high station. He left a natural son, born some months after his death, named Giulio, who was endowed with that virtue and felicity with which the whole world is now acquainted; and of which we shall speak at length when we come to our own times, if God spare us. The people who had assembled in favor of the Pazzi under Lorenzo da Castello in the Val di Tavere, and under Giovan Francesco da Tolentino in Romagna, approached Florence, but having heard of the failure of the conspiracy, they returned home.

The changes desired by the pope and the king in the government of Florence, not having taken place, they determined to effect by war what they had failed to accomplish by treachery; and both assembled forces with all speed to attack the Florentine states; publicly declaring that they only wished the citizens to remove Lorenzo de' Medici, who alone of all the Florentines was their enemy. The king's forces had already passed the Tronto, and the pope's were in Perugia; and that the citizens might feel the effect of spiritual as well as temporal weapons, the pontiff excommunicated and anathematized them. Finding themselves attacked by so many armies, the Florentines prepared for their defense with the utmost care. Lorenzo de' Medici, as the enemy's operations were said to be directed against himself alone, resolved first of all to assemble the Signory, and the most influential citizens, in the palace, to whom, being above three hundred in number, he spoke as follows:—"Most excellent signors, and you, magnificent citizens, I know not whether I have more occasion to weep with you for the events which have recently occurred, or to rejoice in the circumstances with which they have been attended. Certainly, when I think with what virulence of united deceit and hatred I have been attacked, and my brother murdered, I cannot but mourn and grieve from my heart, from my very soul. Yet when I consider with what promptitude, anxiety, love, and unanimity of the whole city my brother has been avenged and myself defended, I am not only compelled to rejoice, but feel myself honored and exalted; for if experience has shown me that I had more enemies than I apprehended, it has also proved that I possess more warm and resolute friends than I could ever have hoped for. I must therefore grieve with you for the injuries others have suffered, and rejoice in the attachment you have exhibited toward myself; but I feel more aggrieved by the injuries committed, since they are so unusual, so unexampled, and (as I trust you believe) so undeserved on our part. Think, magnificent citizens, to what a dreadful point ill fortune has reduced our family, when among friends, amidst our own relatives, nay, in God's holy temple, we have found our greatest foes. Those who are in danger turn to their friends for assistance; they call upon their relatives for aid; but we found ours armed, and resolved on our destruction. Those who are persecuted, either from public or private motives, flee for refuge to the altars; but where others are safe, we are assassinated; where parricides and assassins are secure, the Medici find their murderers. But God, who has not hitherto abandoned our house, again saved us, and has undertaken the defense of our just cause. What injury have we done to justify so intense desire of our destruction? Certainly those who have shown themselves so much our enemies, never received any private wrong from us; for, had we wished to injure them, they would not have had an opportunity of injuring us. If they attribute public grievances to ourselves (supposing any had been done to them), they do the greater injustices to you, to this palace, to the majesty of this government, by assuming that on our account you would act unfairly to any of your citizens; and such a supposition, as we all know, is contradicted by every view of the circumstances; for we, had we been able, and you, had we wished it, would never have contributed to so abominable a design. Whoever inquires into the truth of these matters, will find that our family has always been exalted by you, and from this sole cause, that we have endeavored by kindness, liberality, and beneficence, to do good to all; and if we have honored strangers, when did we ever injure our relatives? If our enemies' conduct has been adopted, to gratify their desire for power (as would seem to be the case from their having taken possession of the palace and brought an armed force into the piazza), the infamous, ambitious, and detestable motive is at once disclosed. If they were actuated by envy and hatred of our authority, they offend you rather than us; for from you we have derived all the influence we possess. Certainly usurped power deserves to be detested; but not distinctions conceded for acts of kindness, generosity, and magnificence. And you all know that our family never attained any rank to which this palace and your united consent did not raise it. Cosmo, my grandfather, did not return from exile with arms and violence, but by your unanimous desire and approbation. It was not my father, old and inform, who defended the government against so many enemies, but yourselves by your authority and benevolence defended him; neither could I, after his death, being then a boy, have maintained the position of my house except by your favor and advice. Nor should we ever be able to conduct the affairs of this republic, if you did not contribute to our support. Therefore, I know not the reason of their hatred toward us, or what just cause they have of envy. Let them direct their enmity against their own ancestors, who, by their pride and avarice, lost the reputation which ours, by very opposite conduct, were enabled to acquire. But let it be granted we have greatly injured them, and that they are justified in seeking our ruin; why do they come and take possession of the palace? Why enter into league with the pope and the king, against the liberties of this republic? Why break the long-continued peace of Italy? They have no excuse for this; they ought to confine their vengeance to those who do them wrong, and not confound private animosities with public grievances. Hence it is that since their defeat our misfortune is the greater; for on their account the pope and the king make war upon us, and this war, they say, is directed against my family and myself. And would to God that this were true; then the remedy would be sure and unfailing, for I would not be so base a citizen as to prefer my own safety to yours; I would at once resolve to ensure your security, even though my own destruction were the immediate and inevitable consequence. But as the wrongs committed by princes are usually concealed under some less offensive covering, they have adopted this plea to hide their more abominable purpose. If, however, you think otherwise, I am in your hands; it is with you to do with me what you please. You are my fathers, my protectors, and whatever you command me to do I will perform most willingly; nor will I ever refuse, when you find occasion to require it, to close the war with my own blood which was commenced with that of my brother." While Lorenzo spoke, the citizens were unable to refrain from tears, and the sympathy with which he had been heard was extended to their reply, delivered by one of them in the name of the rest, who said that the city acknowledged many advantages

derived from the good qualities of himself and his family; and encouraged them to hope that with as much promptitude as they had used in his defense, and in avenging his brother's death, they would secure to him his influence in the government, which he should never lose while they retained possession of the country. And that their deeds might correspond with their words, they immediately appointed a number of armed men, as a guard for the security of his person against domestic enemies.

Chapter III: The Florentines prepare for war against the pope—They appeal to a future council—Papal and Neapolitan movements against the Florentines—The Venetians refuse to assist the Florentines—Disturbances in Milan—Genoa revolts from the duke—Futile endeavors to effect peace with the pope—The Florentines repulse their enemies from the territory of Pisa—They attack the papal states—The papal forces routed upon the borders of the Lake of Perugia.

The Florentines now prepared for war, by raising money and collecting as large a force as possible. Being in league with the duke of Milan and the Venetians, they applied to both for assistance. As the pope had proved himself a wolf rather than a shepherd, to avoid being devoured under false accusations, they justified their cause with all available arguments, and filled Italy with accounts of the treachery practiced against their government, exposing the impiety and injustice of the pontiff, and assured the world that the pontificate which he had wickedly attained, he would as impiously fill; for he had sent those whom he had advanced to the highest order of prelacy, in the company of traitors and parricides, to commit the most horrid treachery in the church in the midst of divine service and during the celebration of the holy sacrament, and that then, having failed to murder the citizens, change the government, and plunder the city, according to his intention, he had suspended the performance of all religious offices, and injuriously menaced and injured the republic with pontifical maledictions. But if God was just, and violence was offensive to him, he would be displeased with that of his viceregent, and allow his injured people who were not admitted to communion with the latter, to offer up their prayers to himself. The Florentines, therefore, instead of receiving or obeying the interdict, compelled the priests to perform divine service, assembled a council in Florence of all the Tuscan prelates under their jurisdiction, and appealed against the injuries suffered from the pontiff to a future general council.

The pope did not neglect to assign reasons in his own justification, and maintained it was the duty of a pontiff to suppress tyranny, depress the wicked, and exalt the good; and that this ought to be done by every available means; but that secular princes had no right to detain cardinals, hang bishops, murder, mangle, and drag about the bodies of priests, destroying without distinction the innocent with the guilty.

Notwithstanding these complaints and accusations, the Florentines restored to the pope the cardinal whom they had detained, in return for which he immediately assailed them with his own forces and those of the king. The two armies, under the command of Alfonso, eldest son of Ferrando, and duke of Calabria, who had as his general, Federigo, count of Urbino, entered the Chianti, by permission of the Siennese, who sided with the enemy, occupied Radda with many other fortresses, and having plundered the country, besieged the Castellina. The Florentines were greatly alarmed at these attacks, being almost destitute of forces, and finding their friends slow to assist; for though the duke sent them aid, the Venetians denied all obligation to support the Florentines in their private quarrels, since the animosities of individuals were not to be defended at the public expense. The Florentines, in order to induce the Venetians to take a more correct view of the case, sent Tommaso Soderini as their ambassador to the senate, and, in the meantime, engaged forces, and appointed Ercole, marquis of Ferrara, to the command of their army. While these preparations were being made, the Castellina was so hard pressed by the enemy, that the inhabitants, despairing of relief, surrendered, after having sustained a siege of forty-two days. The enemy then directed their course toward Arezzo, and encamped before San Savino. The Florentine army being now in order, went to meet them, and having approached within three miles, caused such annoyance, that Federigo d'Urbino demanded a truce for a few days, which was granted, but proved so disadvantageous to the Florentines, that those who had made the request were astonished at having obtained it; for, had it been refused, they would have been compelled to retire in disgrace. Having gained these few days to recruit themselves, as soon as they were expired, they took the castle in the presence of their enemies. Winter being now come, the forces of the pope and king retired for convenient quarters to the Siennese territory. The Florentines also withdrew to a more commodious situation, and the marquis of Ferrara, having done little for himself and less for others, returned to his own territories.

At this time, Genoa withdrew from the dominion of Milan, under the following circumstances. Galeazzo, at his death, left a son, Giovan Galeazzo, who being too young to undertake the government, dissensions arose between Sforza, Lodovico, Ottaviano, and Ascanio, his uncles, and the lady Bona, his mother, each of whom desired the guardianship of the young duke. By the advice and mediation of Tommaso Soderini, who was then Florentine ambassador at the court of Milan, and of Cecco Simonetta, who had been secretary to Galeazzo, the lady Bona prevailed. The uncles fled, Ottaviano was drowned in crossing the Adda; the rest were banished to various places, together with Roberto da San Severino, who in these disputes had deserted the duchess and joined the uncles of the duke. The troubles in Tuscany, which immediately followed, gave these princes hope that the new state of things would present opportunities for their advantage; they therefore quitted the places to which their exile limited them, and each endeavored to return home. King Ferrando, finding the Florentines had obtained assistance from none but the Milanese, took occasion to give the duchess so much occupation in her own government, as to render her unable to contribute to their assistance. By means of Prospero Adorno, the Signor Roberto, and the rebellious uncles of the duke, he caused Genoa to throw off the Milanese yoke. The Castelletto was the only place left; confiding in which, the duchess sent a strong force to recover the city, but it was routed by the enemy; and perceiving the danger which might arise to her son and herself if the war were continued, Tuscany being in confusion, and the Florentines, in whom alone she had hope, themselves in trouble, she determined, as she could not retain Genoa in subjection, to secure it as an ally; and agreed with Battistino Fregoso, the enemy of Prospero Adorno, to give him the Castelletto, and make him prince of Genoa, on condition that he should expel Prospero, and do nothing in favor of her son's uncles. Upon this agreement, Battistino, by the assistance of the Castelletto and of his friends, became lord of Genoa; and according to the custom of the city, took the title of Doge. The Sforzeschi and the Signor Roberto, being thus expelled by the Genoese, came with their forces into Lunigiana, and the pope and the king, perceiving the troubles of Lombardy to be composed, took occasion with them to annoy Tuscany in the Pisan territory, that the Florentines might be weakened by dividing their forces. At the close of winter they ordered Roberto da San Severino to leave Lunigiana and march thither, which he did, and with great tumult plundered many fortresses, and overran the country around Pisa.

At this time, ambassadors came to Florence from the emperor, the king of France, and the king of Hungary, who were sent by their princes to the pontiff. They solicited the Florentines also to send ambassadors to the pope, and promised to use their utmost exertion to obtain for them an advantageous peace. The Florentines did not refuse to make trial, both for the sake of publicly justifying their proceedings, and because they were really desirous of peace. Accordingly, the ambassadors were sent, but returned without coming to any conclusion of their differences. The Florentines, to avail themselves of the influence of the king of France, since they were attacked by one part of the Italians and abandoned by the other, sent to him as their ambassador, Donato Acciajuoli, a distinguished Latin and Greek scholar, whose ancestors had always ranked high in the city, but while on his journey he died at Milan. To relieve his surviving family and pay a deserved tribute to his memory, he was honorably buried at the public expense, provision was made for his sons, and suitable marriage portions given to his daughters, and Guid' Antonio Vespucci, a man well acquainted with pontifical and imperial affairs, was sent as ambassador to the king in his stead.

The attack of Signor Roberto upon the Pisan territory, being unexpected, greatly perplexed the Florentines; for having to resist the foe in the direction of Sienna, they knew not how to provide for the places about Pisa. To keep the Lucchese faithful, and prevent them from furnishing the enemy either with money or provisions, they sent as ambassador Piero di Gino Capponi, who was received with so much jealousy, on account of the hatred which that city always cherishes against the Florentines from former injuries and constant fear, that he was on many occasions in danger of being put to death by the mob; and thus his mission gave fresh cause of animosity rather than of union. The Florentines recalled the marquis of Ferrara, and engaged the marquis of Mantua; they also as earnestly requested the Venetians to send them Count Carlo, son of Braccio, and Deifobo, son of Count Jacopo, and after many delays, they complied; for having made a truce with the Turks, they had no excuse to justify a refusal, and could not break through the obligation of the League without the utmost disgrace. The counts, Carlo and Deifobo, came with a good force, and being joined by all that could be spared from the army, which, under the marquis of Ferrara, held in check the duke of Calabria, proceeded toward Pisa, to meet Signor Roberto, who was with his troops near the river Serchio, and who, though he had expressed his intention of awaiting their arrival, withdrew to the camp at Lunigiana, which he had quitted upon coming into the Pisan territory, while Count Carlo recovered all the places that had been taken by the enemy in that district.

The Florentines, being thus relieved from the attack in the direction of Pisa, assembled the whole force between Colle and Santo Geminiano. But the army, on the arrival of Count Carlo, being composed of Sforzeschi and Bracceschi, their hereditary feuds soon broke forth, and it was thought that if they remained long in company, they would turn their arms against each other. It was therefore determined, as the smaller evil, to divide them; to send one party, under Count Carlo, into the district of Perugia, and establish the other at Poggibonzi, where they formed a strong encampment in order to prevent the enemy from penetrating the Florentine territory. By this they also hoped to compel the enemy to divide their forces; for Count Carlo was understood to have many partisans in Perugia, and it was therefore expected, either that he would occupy the place, or that the pope would be compelled to send a large body of men for its defense. To reduce the pontiff to greater necessity, they ordered Niccolo Vitelli, who had been expelled from Citta di Castello, where his enemy Lorenzo Vitelli commanded, to lead a force against that place, with the view of driving out his adversary and withdrawing it from obedience to the pope. At the beginning of the campaign, fortune seemed to favor the Florentines; for Count Carlo made rapid advances in the Perugino, and Niccolo Vitelli, though unable to enter Castello, was superior in the field, and plundered the surrounding country without opposition. The forces also, at Poggibonzi, constantly overran the country up to the walls of Sienna. These hopes, however, were not realized; for in the first place, Count Carlo died, while in the fullest tide of success; though the consequences of this would have been less detrimental to the Florentines, had not the victory to which it gave occasion, been nullified by the misconduct of others. The death of the count being known, the forces of the church, which had already assembled in Perugia, conceived hopes of overcoming the Florentines, and encamped upon the lake, within three miles of the enemy. On the other side, Jacopo Guicciardini, commissary to the army, by the advice of Roberto da Rimino, who, after the death of Count Carlo, was the principal commander, knowing the ground of their sanguine expectations, determined to meet them, and coming to an engagement near the lake, upon the site of the memorable rout of the Romans, by Hannibal, the Carthaginian general, the papal forces were vanquished. The news of the victory, which did great honor to the commanders, diffused universal joy at Florence, and would have ensured a favorable termination of the campaign, had not the disorders which arose in the army at Poggibonzi thrown all into confusion; for the advantage obtained by the valor of the one, was more than counterbalanced by the disgraceful proceedings of the other. Having made considerable booty in the Siennese territory, quarrels arose about the division of it between the marquis of Mantua and the marquis of Ferrara, who, coming to arms, assailed each other with the utmost fury; and the Florentines seeing they could no longer avail themselves of the services of both, allowed the marquis of Ferrara and his men to return home.

Chapter IV: The duke of Calabria routs the Florentine army at Poggibonzi—Dismay in Florence on account of the defeat—Progress of the duke of Calabria—The Florentines wish for peace—Lorenzo de' Medici determines to go to Naples to treat with the king—Lodovico Sforza, surnamed the Moor, and his brothers, recalled to Milan—Changes in the government of that city in consequence—The Genoese take Serezana—Lorenzo de' Medici arrives at Naples—Peace concluded with the king—The pope and the Venetians consent to the peace—The Florentines in fear of the duke of Calabria—Enterprises of the Turks—They take Otranto—The Florentines reconciled with the pope—Their ambassadors at the papal court—The pope's reply to the ambassadors—The king of Naples restores to the Florentines all the fortresses he had taken.

The army being thus reduced, without a leader, and disorder prevailing in every department, the duke of Calabria, who was with his forces near Sienna, resolved to attack them immediately. The Florentines, finding the enemy at hand, were seized with a sudden panic; neither their arms, nor their numbers, in which they were superior to their adversaries, nor their position, which was one of great strength, could give them confidence; but observing the dust occasioned by the enemy's approach, without waiting for a sight of them, they fled in all directions, leaving their ammunition, carriages, and artillery to be taken by the foe. Such cowardice and disorder prevailed in the armies of those times, that the turning of a horse's head or tail was sufficient to decide the fate of an expedition. This defeat loaded the king's troops with booty, and filled the Florentines with dismay; for the city, besides the war, was afflicted with pestilence, which prevailed so extensively, that all who possessed villas fled to them to escape death. This occasioned the defeat to be attended with greater horror; for those citizens whose possessions lay in the Val di Pesa and the Val d'Elsa, having retired to them, hastened to Florence with all speed as soon as they heard of the disaster, taking with them not only their children and their property, but even their laborers; so that it seemed as if the enemy were expected every moment in the city. Those who were appointed to the management of the war, perceiving the universal consternation, commanded the victorious forces in the Perugino to give up their enterprise in that direction, and march to oppose the enemy in the Val d'Elsa, who, after their victory, plundered the country without opposition; and although the Florentine army had so closely pressed the city of Perugia that it was expected to fall into their hands every instant, the people preferred defending their own possessions to endeavoring to seize those of others. The troops, thus withdrawn from the pursuit of their good fortune, were marched to San Casciano, a castle within eight miles of Florence; the leaders thinking they could take up no other position till the relics of the routed army were assembled. On the other hand, the enemy being under no further restraint at Perugia, and emboldened by the departure of the Florentines, plundered to a large amount in the districts of Arezzo and Cortona; while those who under Alfonso, duke of Calabria, had been victorious near Poggibonzi, took the town itself; sacked Vico and Certaldo, and after these conquests and pillagings encamped before the fortress of Colle, which was considered very strong; and as the garrison was brave and faithful to the Florentines, it was hoped they would hold the enemy at bay till the republic was able to collect its forces. The Florentines being at Santo Casciano, and the enemy continuing to use their utmost exertions against Colle, they determined to draw nearer, that the inhabitants might be more resolute in their defense, and the enemy assail them less boldly. With this design they removed their camp from Santo Casciano to Santo Geminiano, about five miles from Colle, and with light cavalry and other suitable forces were able every day to annoy the duke's camp. All this, however, was insufficient to relieve the people of Colle; for, having consumed their provisions, they were compelled to surrender on the thirteenth of November, to the great grief of the Florentines, and joy of the enemy, more especially of the Siennese, who, besides their habitual hatred of the Florentines, had a particular animosity against the people of Colle.

It was now the depth of winter, and the weather so unsuitable for war, that the pope and the king, either designing to hold out a hope of peace, or more quietly to enjoy the fruit of their victories, proposed a truce for three months to the Florentines, and allowed them ten days to consider the reply. The offer was eagerly accepted; but as wounds are well known to be more painful after the blood cools than when they were first received, this brief repose awakened the Florentines to a consciousness of the miseries they had endured; and the citizens openly laid the blame upon each other, pointing out the errors committed in the management of the war, the expenses uselessly incurred, and the taxes unjustly imposed. These matters were boldly discussed, not only in private circles, but in the public councils; and one individual even ventured to turn to Lorenzo de' Medici, and say, "The city is exhausted, and can endure no more war; it is therefore necessary to think of peace." Lorenzo was himself aware of the necessity, and assembled the friends in whose wisdom and fidelity he had the greatest confidence, when it was at once concluded, that as the Venetians were lukewarm and unfaithful, and the duke in the power of his guardians, and involved in domestic difficulties, it would be desirable by some new alliance to give a better turn to their affairs. They were in doubt whether to apply to the king or to the pope; but having examined the question in all sides, they preferred the friendship of the king as more suitable and secure; for the short reigns of the pontiffs, the changes ensuing upon each succession, the disregard shown by their church toward temporal princes, and the still greater want of respect for them exhibited in her determinations, render it impossible for a secular prince to trust a pontiff, or safely to share his fortune; for an adherent of the pope will have a companion in victory, but in defeat must stand alone, while the pontiff is sustained by his spiritual power and influence. Having therefore decided that the king's friendship would be of the greatest utility to them, they thought it would be most easily and certainly obtained by Lorenzo's presence; for in proportion to the confidence they evinced toward him, the greater they imagined would be the probability of removing his impressions of past enmities. Lorenzo having resolved to go to Naples, recommended the city and government to the care of Tommaso Soderini, who was at that time Gonfalonier of Justice. He left Florence at the beginning of December, and having arrived at Pisa, wrote to the government to acquaint them with the cause of his departure. The Signory, to do him honor, and enable him the more effectually to treat with the king, appointed him ambassador from the Florentine people, and endowed him with full authority to make such arrangements as he thought most useful for the republic.

At this time Roberto da San Severino, with Lodovico and Ascanio (Sforza their elder brother being dead) again attacked Milan, in order to recover the government. Having taken Tortona, and the city and the whole state being in arms, the duchess Bona was advised to restore the Sforzeschi, and to put a stop to civil contentions by admitting them to the government. The person who gave this advice was Antonio Tassino, of Ferrara, a man of low origin, who, coming to Milan, fell into the hands of the duke Galeazzo, and was given by him to his duchess for her valet. He, either from his personal attractions, or some secret influence, after the duke's death attained such influence over the duchess, that he governed the state almost at his will. This greatly displeased the minister Cecco, whom prudence and long experience had rendered invaluable; and who, to the utmost of his power, endeavored to diminish the authority of Tassino with the duchess and other members of the government. The latter, aware of this, to avenge himself for the injury, and secure defenders against Cecco, advised the duchess to recall the Sforzeschi, which she did, without communicating her design to the minister, who, when it was done, said to her, "You have taken a step which will deprive me of my life, and you of the government." This shortly afterward took place; for Cecco was put to death by Lodovico, and Tassino, being expelled from the dukedom, the duchess was so enraged that she left Milan, and gave up the care of her son to Lodovico, who, becoming sole governor of the dukedom, caused, as will be hereafter seen, the ruin of Italy.

Lorenzo de' Medici had set out for Naples, and the truce between the parties was in force, when, quite unexpectedly, Lodovico Fregoso, being in correspondence with some persons of Serezana, entered the place by stealth, took possession of it with an armed force, and imprisoned the Florentine governor. This greatly offended the Signory, for they thought the whole had been concerted with the connivance of King Ferrando. They complained to the duke of Calabria, who was with the army at Sienna, of a breach of the truce; and he endeavored to prove, by letters and embassies, that it had occurred without either his own or his father's knowledge. The Florentines, however, found themselves in a very awkward predicament, being destitute of money, the head of the republic in the power of the king, themselves engaged in a long-standing war with the latter and the pope, in a new one with the Genoese, and entirely without friends; for they had no confidence in the Venetians, and on account of its changeable and unsettled state they were rather apprehensive of Milan. They had thus only one hope, and that depended upon Lorenzo's success with the king.

Lorenzo arrived at Naples by sea, and was most honorably received, not only by Ferrando, but by the whole city, his coming having excited the greatest expectation; for it being generally understood that the war was undertaken for the sole purpose of effecting his destruction, the power of his enemies invested his name with additional lustre. Being admitted to the king's presence, he spoke with so much propriety upon the affairs of Italy, the disposition of her princes and people, his hopes from peace, his fears of the results of war, that Ferrando was more astonished at the greatness of his mind, the promptitude of his genius, his gravity and wisdom, than he had previously been at his power. He consequently treated him with redoubled honor, and began to feel compelled rather to part with him as a friend, than detain him as an enemy. However, under various pretexts he kept Lorenzo from December till March, not only to gain the most perfect knowledge of his own views, but of those of his city; for he was not without enemies, who would have wished the king to detain and treat him in the same manner as Jacopo Piccinino; and, with the ostensible view of sympathizing for him, pointed out all that would, or rather that they wished should, result from such a course; at the same time opposing in the council every proposition at all likely to favor him. By such means as these the opinion gained ground, that if he were detained at Naples much longer, the government of Florence would be changed. This caused the king to postpone their separation more than he would have otherwise done, to see if any disturbance were likely to arise. But finding everything go quietly on, Ferrando allowed him to depart on the sixth of March, 1479, having, with every kind of attention and token of regard, endeavored to gain his affection, and formed with him a perpetual alliance for their mutual defense. Lorenzo returned to Florence, and upon presenting himself before the citizens, the impressions he had created in the popular mind surrounded him with a halo of majesty brighter than before. He was received with all the joy merited by his extraordinary qualities and recent services, in having exposed his own life to the most imminent peril, in order to restore peace to his country. Two days after his return, the treaty between the republic of Florence and the king, by which each party bound itself to defend the other's territories, was published. The places taken from the Florentines during the war were to be taken up at the discretion of the king; the Pazzi confined in the tower of Volterra were to be set at liberty, and a certain sum of money, for a limited period, was to be paid to the duke of Calabria.

As soon as this peace was publicly known, the pope and the Venetians were transported with rage; the pope thought himself neglected by the king; the Venetians entertained similar ideas with regard to the Florentines, and complained that, having been companions in the war, they were not allowed to participate in the peace. Reports of this description being spread abroad, and received with entire credence at Florence, caused a general fear that the peace thus made would give rise to greater wars; and therefore the leading members of the government determined to confine the consideration of the most important affairs to a smaller number, and formed a council of seventy citizens, in whom the principal authority was invested. This new regulation calmed the minds of those desirous of change, by convincing them of the futility of their efforts. To establish their authority, they in the first place ratified the treaty of peace with the king, and sent as ambassadors to the pope Antonio Ridolfi and Piero Nasi. But, notwithstanding the peace, Alfonso, duke of Calabria, still remained at Sienna with his forces, pretending to be detained by discords among the citizens, which, he said, had risen so high, that while he resided outside the city they had compelled him to enter and assume the office of arbitrator between them. He took occasion to draw large sums of money from the wealthiest citizens by way of fines, imprisoned many, banished others, and put some to death; he thus became suspected, not only by the Siennese but by the Florentines, of a design to usurp the sovereignty of Sienna; nor was any remedy then available, for the republic had formed a new alliance with the king, and were at enmity with the pope and the Venetians. This suspicion was entertained not only by the great body of the Florentine people, who were subtle interpreters of appearances, but by the principal members of the government; and it was agreed, on all hands, that the city never was in so much danger of losing her liberty. But God, who in similar extremities has always been her preserver, caused an unhoped-for event to take place, which gave the pope, the king, and the Venetians other matters to think of than those in Tuscany.

The Turkish emperor, Mahomet II. had gone with a large army to the siege of Rhodes, and continued it for several months; but though his forces were numerous, and his courage indomitable, he found them more than equalled by those of the besieged, who resisted his attack with such obstinate valor, that he was at last compelled to retire in disgrace. Having left Rhodes, part of his army, under the Pasha Achmet, approached Velona, and, either from observing the facility of the enterprise, or in obedience to his sovereign's commands, coasting along the Italian shores, he suddenly landed four thousand soldiers, and attacked the city of Otranto, which he easily took, plundered, and put all the inhabitants to the sword. He then fortified the city and port, and having assembled a large body of cavalry, pillaged the surrounding country. The king, learning this, and aware of the redoubtable character of his assailant, immediately sent messengers to all the surrounding powers, to request assistance against the common enemy, and ordered the immediate return of the duke of Calabria with the forces at Sienna.

This attack, however it might annoy the duke and the rest of Italy, occasioned the utmost joy at Florence and Sienna; the latter thinking it had recovered its liberty, and the former that she had escaped a storm which threatened her with destruction. These impressions, which were not unknown to the duke, increased the regret he felt at his departure from Sienna; and he accused fortune of having, by an unexpected and unaccountable accident, deprived him of the sovereignty of Tuscany. The same circumstance changed the disposition of the pope; for although he had previously refused to receive any ambassador from Florence, he was now so mollified as to be anxious to listen to any overtures of peace; and it was intimated to the Florentines, that if they would condescend to ask the pope's pardon, they would be sure of obtaining it. Thinking it advisable to seize the opportunity, they sent twelve ambassadors to the pontiff, who, on their arrival, detained them under different pretexts before he would admit them to an audience. However, terms were at length settled, and what should be contributed by each in peace or war. The messengers were then admitted to the feet of the pontiff, who, with the utmost pomp, received them in the midst of his cardinals. They apologized for past occurrences; first showing they had been compelled by necessity, then blaming the malignity of others, or the rage of the populace, and their just indignation, and enlarging on the unfortunate condition of those who are compelled either to fight or die; saying, that since every extremity is endured in order to avoid death, they had suffered war, interdicts, and other inconveniences, brought upon them by recent events, that their republic might escape slavery, which is the death of free cities. However, if in their necessities they had committed any offense, they were desirous to make atonement, and trusted in his clemency, who, after the example of the blessed Redeemer, would receive them into his compassionate arms.

The pope's reply was indignant and haughty. After reiterating all the offenses against the church during the late transactions, he said that, to comply with the precepts of God, he would grant the pardon they asked, but would have them understand, that it was their duty to obey; and that upon the next instance of their disobedience, they would inevitably forfeit, and that most deservedly, the liberty which they had just been upon the point of losing; for those merit freedom who exercise themselves in good works and avoid evil; that liberty, improperly used, injures itself and others; that to think little of God, and less of his church, is not the part of a free man, but a fool, and one disposed to evil rather than good, and to effect whose correction is the duty not only of princes but of every Christian; so that in respect of the recent events, they had only themselves to blame, who, by their evil deeds, had given rise to the war, and inflamed it by still worse actions, it having been terminated by the kindness of others rather than by any merit of their own. The formula of agreement and benediction was then read; and, in addition to what had already been considered and agreed upon between the parties, the pope said, that if the Florentines wished to enjoy the fruit of his forgiveness, they must maintain fifteen galleys, armed, and equipped, at their own expense, as long as the Turks should make war upon the kingdom of Naples. The ambassadors complained much of this burden in addition to the arrangement already made, but were unable to obtain any alleviation. However, after their return to Florence, the Signory sent, as ambassador to the pope, Guidantonio Vespucci, who had recently returned from France, and who by his prudence brought everything to an amicable conclusion, obtained many favors from the pontiff, which were considered as presages of a closer reconciliation.

Having settled their affairs with the pope, Sienna being free, themselves released from the fear of the king, by the departure of the duke of Calabria from Tuscany, and the war with the Turks still continuing, the Florentines pressed the king to restore their fortresses, which the duke of Calabria, upon quitting the country, had left in the hands of the Siennese. Ferrando, apprehensive that if he refused, they would withdraw from the alliance with him, and by new wars with the Siennese deprive him of the assistance he hoped to obtain from the pope and other Italian powers, consented that they should be given up, and by new favors endeavored to attach the Florentines to his interests. It is thus evident, that force and necessity, not deeds and obligations, induce princes to keep faith.

The castles being restored, and this new alliance established, Lorenzo de' Medici recovered the reputation which first the war and then the peace, when the king's designs were doubtful, had deprived him of; for at this period there was no lack of those who openly slandered him with having sold his country to save himself, and said, that in war they had lost their territories, and in peace their liberty. But the fortresses being recovered, an honorable treaty ratified with the king, and the city restored to her former influence, the spirit of public discourse entirely changed in Florence, a place greatly addicted to gossip, and in which actions are judged by the success attending them, rather than by the intelligence employed in their direction; therefore, the citizens praised Lorenzo extravagantly, declaring that by his prudence he had recovered in peace, what unfavorable circumstances had taken from them in war, and that by his discretion and judgment he had done more than the enemy with all the force of their arms.

Chapter V: New occasions of war in Italy—Differences between the marquis of Ferrara, and the Venetians—The king of Naples and the Florentines attack the papal states—The pope's defensive arrangements—The Neapolitan army routed by the papal forces—Progress of the Venetians against the marquis of Ferrara—The pope makes peace, and enters into a league against the Venetians—Operations of the League against the Venetians—The Venetians routed at Bondeno—Their losses—Disunion among the League—Lodovico Sforza makes peace with the Venetians—Ratified by the other parties.

The invasion of the Turks had deferred the war which was about to break forth from the anger of the pope and the Venetians at the peace between the Florentines and the king. But as the beginning of that invasion was unexpected and beneficial, its conclusion was equally unlooked for and injurious; for Mahomet dying suddenly, dissensions arose among his sons, and the forces which were in Puglia being abandoned by their commander, surrendered Otranto to the king. The fears which restrained the pope and the Venetians being thus removed, everyone became apprehensive of new troubles. On the one hand, was the league of the pope and the Venetians, and with them the Genoese, Siennese, and other minor powers; on the other, the Florentines, the king, and the duke, with whom were the Bolognese and many princes. The Venetians wished to become lords of Ferrara, and thought they were justified by circumstances in making the attempt, and hoping for a favorable result. Their differences arose thus: the marquis of Ferrara affirmed he was under no obligation to take salt from the Venetians, or to admit their governor; the terms of convention between them declaring, that after seventy years, the city was to be free from both impositions. The Venetians replied, that so long as he held the Polesine, he was bound to receive their salt and their governor. The marquis refusing his consent, the Venetians considered themselves justified in taking arms, and that the present moment offered a suitable opportunity; for the pope was indignant against the Florentines and the king; and to attach the pope still further, the Count Girolamo, who was then at Venice, was received with all possible respect; first admitted to the privileges of a citizen, and then raised to the rank of a senator, the highest distinctions the Venetian senate can confer. To prepare for the war, they levied new taxes, and appointed to the command of the forces, Roberto da San Severino, who being offended with Lodovico, governor of Milan, fled to Tortona, whence, after occasioning some disturbances, he went to Genoa, and while there, was sent for by the Venetians, and placed at the head of their troops.

These circumstances becoming known to the opposite league, induced it also to provide for war. The duke of Milan appointed as his general, Federigo d'Urbino; the Florentines engaged Costanzo, lord of Pesaro; and to sound the disposition of the pope, and know whether the Venetians made war against Ferrara with his consent or not, King Ferrando sent Alfonso, duke of Calabria, with his army across the Tronto, and asked the pontiff's permission to pass into Lombardy to assist the marquis, which was refused in the most peremptory manner. The Florentines and the king, no longer doubtful about the pope's intentions, determined to harass him, and thus either compel him to take part with them, or throw such obstacles in his way, as would prevent him from helping the Venetians, who had already taken the field, attacked the marquis, overran his territory, and encamped before Figaruolo, a fortress of the greatest importance. In pursuance of the design of the Florentines and the king, the duke of Calabria, by the assistance of the Colonna family (the Orsini had joined the pope), plundered the country about Rome and committed great devastation; while the Florentines, with Niccolo Vitelli, besieged and took Citta di Castello, expelling Lorenzo Vitelli, who held it for the pope, and placing Niccolo in it as prince.

The pope now found himself in very great straits; for the city of Rome was disturbed by factions and the country covered with enemies. But acting with courage and resolution, he appointed Roberto da Rimino to take the command of his forces; and having sent for him to Rome, where his troops were assembled, told him how great would be the honor, if he could deliver the church from the king's forces, and the troubles in which it was involved; how greatly indebted, not only himself, but all his successors would be, and, that not mankind merely, but God himself would be under obligations to him. The magnificent Roberto, having considered the forces and preparations already made, advised the pope to raise as numerous a body of infantry as possible, which was done without delay. The duke of Calabria was at hand, and constantly harassed the country up to the very gates of Rome, which so roused the indignation of the citizens, that many offered their assistance to Roberto, and all were thankfully received. The duke, hearing of these preparations, withdrew a short distance from the city, that in the belief of finding him gone, the magnificent Roberto would not pursue him, and also in expectation of his brother Federigo, whom their father had sent to him with additional forces. But Roberto, finding himself nearly equal to the duke in cavalry, and superior in infantry, marched boldly out of Rome and took a position within two miles of the enemy. The duke, seeing his adversaries close upon him, found he must either fight or disgracefully retire. To avoid a retreat unbecoming a king's son, he resolved to face the enemy; and a battle ensued which continued from morning till midday. In this engagement, greater valor was exhibited on both sides than had been shown in any other during the last fifty years, upward of a thousand dead being left upon the field. The troops of the church were at length victorious, for her numerous infantry so annoyed the ducal cavalry, that they were compelled to retreat, and Alfonso himself would have fallen into the hands of the enemy, had he not been rescued by a body of Turks, who remained at Otranto, and were at that time in his service. The lord of Rimino, after this victory, returned triumphantly to Rome, but did not long enjoy the fruit of his valor; for having, during the heat of the engagement, taken a copious draught of water, he was seized with a flux, of which he very shortly afterward died. The pope caused his funeral to be conducted with great pomp, and in a few days, sent the Count Girolamo toward Citta di Castello to restore it to Lorenzo, and also endeavor to gain Rimino, which being by Roberto's death left to the care of his widow and a son who was quite a boy, his holiness thought might be easily won; and this certainly would have been the case, if the lady had not been defended by the Florentines, who opposed him so effectually, as to prevent his success against both Castello and Rimino.

While these things were in progress at Rome and in Romagna, the Venetians took possession of Figaruolo and crossed the Po with their forces. The camp of the duke of Milan and the marquis was in disorder; for the count of Urbino having fallen ill, was carried to Bologna for his recovery, but died. Thus the marquis's affairs were unfortunately situated, while those of the Venetians gave them increasing hopes of occupying Ferrara. The Florentines and the king of Naples used their utmost endeavors to gain the pope to their views; and not having succeeded by force, they threatened him with the council, which had already been summoned by the emperor to assemble at Basle; and by means of the imperial ambassadors, and the co-operation of the leading cardinals, who were desirous of peace, the pope was compelled to turn his attention toward effecting the pacification of Italy. With this view, at the instigation of his fears, and with the conviction that the aggrandizement of the Venetians would be the ruin of the church and of Italy, he endeavored to make peace with the League, and sent his nuncios to Naples, where a treaty was concluded for five years, between the pope, the king, the duke of Milan, and the Florentines, with an opening for the Venetians to join them if they thought proper. When this was accomplished, the pope intimated to the Venetians, that they must desist from war against Ferrara. They refused to comply, and made preparations to prosecute their design with greater vigor than they had hitherto done; and having routed the forces of the duke and the marquis at Argenta, they approached Ferrara so closely as to pitch their tents in the marquis's park.

The League found they must no longer delay rendering him efficient assistance, and ordered the duke of Calabria to march to Ferrara with his forces and those of the pope, the Florentine troops also moving in the same direction. In order to direct the operations of the war with greater efficiency, the League assembled a diet at Cremona, which was attended by the pope's legate, the Count Girolamo, the duke of Calabria, the Signor Lodovico Sforza, and Lorenzo de' Medici, with many other Italian princes; and when the measures to be adopted were fully discussed, having decided that the best way of relieving Ferrara would be to effect a division of the enemy's forces, the League desired Lodovico to attack the Venetians on the side of Milan, but this he declined, for fear of bringing a war upon the duke's territories, which it would be difficult to quell. It was therefore resolved to proceed with the united forces of the League to Ferrara, and having assembled four thousand cavalry and eight thousand infantry, they went in pursuit of the Venetians, whose force amounted to two thousand two hundred men at arms, and six thousand foot. They first attacked the Venetian flotilla, then lying upon the river Po, which they routed with the loss of above two hundred vessels, and took prisoner Antonio Justiniano, the purveyor of the fleet. The Venetians, finding all Italy united against them, endeavored to support their reputation by engaging in their service the duke of Lorraine, who joined them with two hundred men at arms: and having suffered so great a destruction of their fleet, they sent him, with part of their army, to keep their enemies at bay, and Roberto da San Severino to cross the Adda with the remainder, and proceed to Milan, where they were to raise the cry of "The duke and the Lady Bona," his mother; hoping by this means to give a new aspect to affairs there, believing that Lodovico and his government were generally unpopular. This attack at first created great consternation, and roused the citizens in arms; but eventually produced consequences unfavorable to the designs of the Venetians; for Lodovico was now desirous to undertake what he had refused to do at the entreaty of his allies. Leaving the marquis of Ferrara to the defense of his own territories, he, with four thousand horse and two thousand foot, and joined by the duke of Calabria with twelve thousand horse and five thousand foot, entered the territory of Bergamo, then Brescia, next that of Verona, and, in defiance of the Venetians, plundered the whole country; for it was with the greatest difficulty that Roberto and his forces could save the cities themselves. In the meantime, the marquis of Ferrara had recovered a great part of his territories; for the duke of Lorraine, by whom he was attacked, having only at his command two thousand horse and one thousand foot, could not withstand him. Hence, during the whole of 1483, the affairs of the League were prosperous.

The winter having passed quietly over, the armies again took the field. To produce the greater impression upon the enemy, the League united their whole force, and would easily have deprived the Venetians of all they possessed in Lombardy, if the war had been conducted in the same manner as during the preceding year; for by the departure of the duke of Lorraine, whose term of service had expired, they were reduced to six thousand horse and five thousand foot, while the allies had thirteen thousand horse and five thousand foot at their disposal. But, as is often the case where several of equal authority are joined in command, their want of unity decided the victory to their enemies. Federigo, marquis of Mantua, whose influence kept the duke of Calabria and Lodovico Sforza within bounds, being dead, differences arose between them which soon became jealousies. Giovan Galeazzo, duke of Milan, was now of an age to take the government on himself, and had married the daughter of the duke of Calabria, who wished his son-in-law to exercise the government and not Lodovico; the latter, being aware of the duke's design, studied to prevent him from effecting it. The position of Lodovico being known to the Venetians, they thought they could make it available for their own interests; and hoped, as they had often before done, to recover in peace all they had lost by war; and having secretly entered into treaty with Lodovico, the terms were concluded in August, 1484. When this became known to the rest of the allies, they were greatly dissatisfied, principally because they found that the places won from the Venetians were to be restored; that they were allowed to keep Rovigo and the Polesine, which they had taken from the marquis of Ferrara, and besides this retain all the pre-eminence and authority over Ferrara itself which they had formerly possessed. Thus it was evident to everyone, they had been engaged in a war which had cost vast sums of money, during the progress of which they had acquired honor, and which was concluded with disgrace; for the places wrested from the enemy were restored without themselves recovering those they had lost. They were, however, compelled to ratify the treaty, on account of the unsatisfactory state of their finances, and because the faults and ambition of others had rendered them unwilling to put their fortunes to further proof.

Chapter VI: Affairs of the pope—He is reconciled to Niccolo Vitelli—Discords between the Colonnesi and the Orsini—Various events—The war of Serezana—Genoa occupied by her archbishop—Death of Sixtus IV.—Innocent VIII. elected—Agostino Fregoso gives Serezana to the bank of St. Giorgio—Account of the bank of St. Giorgio—War with the Genoese for Serezana—Stratagem of the Florentines to attack Pietra Santa—Difficulties and final surrender of Pietra Santa—The Lucchese lay claim to Pietra Santa—The city of L'Aquila revolts against the king of Naples—War between him and the pope—The Florentines take the king's party—Peace between the pope and the king.

During these events in Lombardy, the pope sent Lorenzo to invest Citta di Castello, for the purpose of expelling Niccolo Vitelli, the place having been abandoned to him by the League, for the purpose of inducing the pontiff to join them. During the siege, Niccolo's troops were led out against the papal forces and routed them. Upon this the pope recalled the Count Girolamo from Lombardy with orders first to recruit his army at Rome, and then proceed against Citta di Castello. But thinking afterward, that it would be better to obtain Niccolo Vitello as his friend than to renew hostilities with him, an arrangement was entered into by which the latter retained Citta di Castello, and the pope pacified Lorenzo as well as he could. He was induced to both these measures rather by his apprehension of fresh troubles than by his love of peace, for he perceived dissensions arising between the Colonessi and the Orsini.

In the war between the king of Naples and the pope, the former had taken the district of Tagliacozzo from the Orsini, and given it to the Colonnesi, who had espoused his cause. Upon the establishment of peace, the Orsini demanded its restoration by virtue of the treaty. The pope had frequently intimated to the Colonnesi that it ought to be restored; but they, instead of complying with the entreaties of the Orsini, or being influenced by the pope's threats, renewed hostilities against the former. Upon this the pontiff, unable to endure their insolence, united his own forces with those of the Orsini, plundered the houses they possessed in Rome, slew or made prisoners all who defended them, and seized most of their fortresses. So that when these troubles were composed, it was rather by the complete subjugation of one party than from any desire for peace in the other.

Nor were the affairs of Genoa or of Tuscany in repose, for the Florentines kept the Count Antonio da Marciano on the borders of Serezana; and while the war continued in Lombardy, annoyed the people of Serezana by inroads and light skirmishes. Battistino Fregoso, doge of Genoa, trusting to Pagolo Fregoso, the archbishop, was taken prisoner, with his wife and children, by the latter, who assumed the sovereignty of the city. The Venetian fleet had attacked the kingdom of Naples, taken Gallipoli, and harassed the neighboring places. But upon the peace of Lombardy, all tumults were hushed except those of Tuscany and Rome; for the pope died in five days after its declaration, either in the natural course of things, or because his grief for peace, to which he was always opposed, occasioned his end.

Upon the decease of the pontiff, Rome was immediately in arms. The Count Girolamo withdrew his forces into the castle; and the Orsini feared the Colonnesi would avenge the injuries they had recently sustained. The Colonnesi demanded the restitution of their houses and castles, so that in a few days robberies, fires, and murders prevailed in several parts of the city. The cardinals entreated the count to give the castle into the hands of the college, withdraw his troops, and deliver Rome from the fear of his forces, and he, by way of ingratiating himself with the future pontiff obeyed, and retired to Imola. The cardinals, being thus divested of their fears, and the barons hopeless of assistance in their quarrels, proceeded to create a new pontiff, and after some discussion, Giovanni Batista Cibo, a Genoese, cardinal of Malfetta, was elected, and took the name of Innocent VIII. By the mildness of his disposition (for he was peaceable and humane) he caused a cessation of hostilities, and for the present restored peace to Rome.

The Florentines, after the pacification of Lombardy, could not remain quiet; for it appeared disgraceful that a private gentleman should deprive them of the fortress of Serezana; and as it was allowed by the conditions of peace, not only to demand lost places, but to make war upon any who should impede their restoration, they immediately provided men and money to undertake its recovery. Upon this, Agostino Fregoso, who had seized Serezana, being unable to defend it, gave the fortress to the Bank of St. Giorgio. As we shall have frequent occasion to speak of St. Giorgio and the Genoese, it will not be improper, since Genoa is one of the principal cities of Italy, to give some account of the regulations and usages prevailing there. When the Genoese had made peace with the Venetians, after the great war, many years ago, the republic, being unable to satisfy the claims of those who had advanced large sums of money for its use, conceded to them the revenue of the Dogano or customhouse, so that each creditor should participate in the receipts in proportion to his claim, until the whole amount should be liquidated, and as a suitable place for their assembling, the palace over the Dogano was assigned for their use. These creditors established a form of government among themselves, appointing a council of one hundred persons for the direction of their affairs, and a committee of eight, who, as the executive body, should carry into effect the determinations of the council. Their credits were divided into shares, called *Luoghi*, and they took the title of the Bank, or Company of St. Giorgio. Having thus arranged their government, the city fell into fresh difficulties, and applied to San Giorgio for assistance, which, being wealthy and well managed, was able to afford the required aid. On the other hand, as the city had at first conceded the customs, she next began to assign towns, castles, or territories, as security for moneys received; and this practice has proceeded to such a length, from the necessities of the state, and the accommodation by the San Giorgio, that the latter now has under its administration most of the towns and cities in the Genoese dominion. These the Bank governs and protects, and every year sends its deputies, appointed by vote, without any interference on the part of the republic. Hence the affections of the citizens are transferred from the government to the San Giorgio, on account of the tyranny of the former, and the excellent regulations adopted by the latter. Hence also originate the frequent changes of the republic, which is sometimes under a citizen, and at other times governed by a stranger; for the magistracy, and not the San Giorgio, changes the government. So when the Fregosi and the Adorni were in opposition, as the government of the republic was the prize for which they strove, the greater part of the citizens withdrew and left it to the victor. The only interference of the Bank of St. Giorgio is when one party has obtained a superiority over the other, to bind the victor to the observance of its laws, which up to this time have not been changed; for as it possesses arms, money, and influence, they could not be altered without incurring the imminent risk of a dangerous rebellion. This establishment presents an instance of what in all the republics, either described or imagined by philosophers, has never been thought of; exhibiting within the same community, and among the same citizens, liberty and tyranny, integrity and corruption, justice and injustice; for this establishment preserves in the city many ancient and venerable customs; and should it happen (as in time it easily may) that the San Giorgio should have possession of the whole city, the republic will become more distinguished than that of Venice.

Agostino Fregoso conceded Serezana to the San Giorgio, which readily accepted it, undertook its defense, put a fleet to sea, and sent forces to Pietra Santa to prevent all attempts of the Florentines, whose camp was in the immediate vicinity. The Florentines found it would be essentially necessary to gain possession of Pietra Santa, for without it the acquisition of Serezana lost much of its value, being situated between the latter place and Pisa; but they could not, consistently with the treaty, besiege it, unless the people of Pietra Santa, or its garrison, were to impede their acquisition of Serezana. To induce the enemy to do this, the Florentines sent from Pisa to the camp a quantity of provisions and military stores, accompanied by a very weak escort; that the people of Pietra Santa might have little cause for fear, and by the richness of the booty be tempted to the attack. The plan succeeded according to their expectation; for the inhabitants of Pietra Santa, attracted by the rich prize took possession of it.

This gave legitimate occasion to the Florentines to undertake operations against them; so leaving Serezana they encamped before Pietra Santa, which was very populous, and made a gallant defense. The Florentines planted their artillery in the plain, and formed a rampart upon the hill, that they might also attack the place on that side. Jacopo Guicciardini was commissary of the army; and while the siege of Pietra Santa was going on, the Genoese took and burned the fortress of Vada, and, landing their forces, plundered the surrounding country. Biongianni Gianfigliazzi was sent against them, with a body of horse and foot, and checked their audacity, so that they pursued their depredations less boldly. The fleet continuing its efforts went to Livorno, and by pontoons and other means approached the new tower, playing their artillery upon it for several days, but being unable to make any impression they withdrew.

In the meantime the Florentines proceeded slowly against Pietra Santa, and the enemy taking courage attacked and took their works upon the hill. This was effected with so much glory, and struck such a panic into the Florentines, that they were almost ready to raise the siege, and actually retreated a distance of four miles; for their generals thought that they would retire to winter quarters, it being now October, and make no further attempt till the return of spring.

When the discomfiture was known at Florence, the government was filled with indignation; and, to impart fresh vigor to the enterprise, and restore the reputation of their forces, they immediately appointed Antonio Pucci and Bernardo del Neri commissaries, who, with vast sums of money, proceeded to the army, and intimated the heavy displeasure of the Signory, and of the whole city, if they did not return to the walls; and what a disgrace, if so large an army and so many generals, having only a small garrison to contend with, could not conquer so poor and weak a place. They explained the immediate and future advantages that would result from the acquisition, and spoke so forcibly upon the subject, that all became anxious to renew the attack. They resolved, in the first place, to recover the rampart upon the hill; and here it was evident how greatly humanity, affability, and condescension influence the minds of soldiers; for Antonio Pucci, by encouraging one and promising another, shaking hands with this man and embracing that, induced them to proceed to the charge with such impetuosity, that they gained possession of the rampart in an instant. However, the victory was not unattended by misfortune, for Count Antonio da Marciano was killed by a cannon shot. This success filled the townspeople with so much terror, that they began to make proposals for capitulation; and to invest the surrender with imposing solemnity, Lorenzo de' Medici came to the camp, when, after a few days, the fortress was given up. It being now winter, the leaders of the expedition thought it unadvisable to make any further effort until the return of spring, more particularly because the autumnal air had been so unhealthy that numbers were affected by it. Antonio Pucci and Biongianni Gianfigliazzi were taken ill and died, to the great regret of all, so greatly had Antonio's conduct at Pietra Santa endeared him to the army.

Upon the taking of Pietra Santa, the Lucchese sent ambassadors to Florence, to demand its surrender to their republic, on account of its having previously belonged to them, and because, as they alleged, it was in the conditions that places taken by either party were to be restored to their original possessors. The Florentines did not deny the articles, but replied that they did not know whether, by the treaty between themselves and the Genoese, which was then under discussion, it would have to be given up or not, and therefore could not reply to that point at present; but in case of its restitution, it would first be necessary for the Lucchese to reimburse them for the expenses they had incurred and the injury they had suffered, in the death of so many citizens; and that when this was satisfactorily arranged, they might entertain hopes of obtaining the place.

The whole winter was consumed in negotiations between the Florentines and Genoese, which, by the pope's intervention, were carried on at Rome; but not being concluded upon the return of spring, the Florentines would have attacked Serezana had they not been prevented by the illness of Lorenzo de' Medici, and the war between the pope and King Ferrando; for Lorenzo was afflicted not only by the gout, which seemed hereditary in his family, but also by violent pains in the stomach, and was compelled to go the baths for relief.

The more important reason was furnished by the war, of which this was the origin. The city of L'Aquila, though subject to the kingdom of Naples, was in a manner free; and the Count di Montorio possessed great influence over it. The duke of Calabria was upon the banks of the Tronto with his men-at-arms, under pretense of appeasing some disturbances among the peasantry; but really with a design of reducing L'Aquila entirely under the king's authority, and sent for the Count di Montorio, as if to consult him upon the business he pretended then to have in hand. The count obeyed without the least suspicion, and on his arrival was made prisoner by the duke and sent to Naples. When this circumstance became known at L'Aquila, the anger of the inhabitants arose to the highest pitch; taking arms they killed Antonio Cencinello, commissary for the king, and with him some inhabitants known partisans of his majesty. The L'Aquilani, in order to have a defender in their rebellion, raised the banner of the church, and sent envoys to the pope, to submit their city and themselves to him, beseeching that he would defend them as his own subjects against the tyranny of the king. The pontiff gladly undertook their defense, for he had both public and private reasons for hating that monarch; and Signor Roberto of San Severino, an enemy of the duke of Milan, being disengaged, was appointed to take the command of his forces, and sent for with all speed to Rome. He entreated the friends and relatives of the Count di Montorio to withdraw their allegiance from the king, and induced the princes of Altimura, Salerno, and Bisignano to take arms against him. The king, finding himself so suddenly involved in war, had recourse to the Florentines and the duke of Milan for assistance. The Florentines hesitated with regard to their own conduct, for they felt all the inconvenience of neglecting their own affairs to attend to those of others, and hostilities against the church seemed likely to involve much risk. However, being under the obligation of a League, they preferred their honor to convenience or security, engaged the Orsini, and sent all their own forces under the Count di Pitigliano toward Rome, to the assistance of the king. The latter divided his forces into two parts; one, under the duke of Calabria, he sent toward Rome, which, being joined by the Florentines, opposed the army of the church; with the other, under his own command, he attacked the barons, and the war was prosecuted with various success on both sides. At length, the king, being universally victorious, peace was concluded by the intervention of the ambassadors of the king of Spain, in August, 1486, to which the pope consented; for having found fortune opposed to him he was not disposed to tempt it further. In this treaty all the powers of Italy were united, except the Genoese, who were omitted as rebels against the republic of Milan, and unjust occupiers of territories belonging to the Florentines. Upon the peace being ratified, Roberto da San Severino, having been during the war a treacherous ally of the church, and by no means formidable to her enemies, left Rome; being followed by the forces of the duke and the Florentines, after passing Cesena, found them near him, and urging his flight reached Ravenna with less than a hundred horse. Of his forces, part were received into the duke's service, and part were plundered by the peasantry. The king, being reconciled with his barons, put to death Jacopo Coppola and Antonello d'Aversa and their sons, for having, during the war, betrayed his secrets to the pope.

Chapter VII: The pope becomes attached to the Florentines—The Genoese seize Serezanello—They are routed by the Florentines—Serezana surrenders—Genoa submits to the duke of Milan—War between the Venetians and the Dutch—Osimo revolts from the church—Count Girolamo Riario, lord of Furli, slain by a conspiracy—Galeotto, lord of Faenza, is murdered by the treachery of his wife—The government of the city offered to the Florentines—Disturbances in Sienna—Death of Lorenzo de' Medici—His eulogy—Establishment of his family—Estates bought by Lorenzo—His anxiety for the defense of Florence—His taste for arts and literature—The university of Pisa—The estimation of Lorenzo by other princes.

The pope having observed in the course of the war, how promptly and earnestly the Florentines adhered to their alliances, although he had previously been opposed to them from his attachment to the Genoese, and the assistance they had rendered to the king, now evinced a more amicable disposition, and received their ambassadors with greater favor than previously. Lorenzo de' Medici, being made acquainted with this change of feeling, encouraged it with the utmost solicitude; for he thought it would be of great advantage, if to the friendship of the king he could add that of the pontiff. The pope had a son named Francesco, upon whom designing to bestow states and attach friends who might be useful to him after his own death, saw no safer connection in Italy than Lorenzo's, and therefore induced the latter to give him one of his daughters in marriage. Having formed this alliance, the pope desired the Genoese to concede Serezana to the Florentines, insisting that they had no right to detain what Agostino had sold, nor was Agostino justified in making over to the Bank of San Giorgio what was not his own. However, his holiness did not succeed with them; for the Genoese, during these transactions at Rome, armed several vessels, and, unknown to the Florentines, landed three thousand foot, attacked Serezanello, situated above Serezana, plundered and burnt the town near it, and then, directing their artillery against the fortress, fired upon it with their utmost energy. This assault was new and unexpected by the Florentines, who immediately assembled their forces under Virginio Orsino, at Pisa, and complained to the pope, that while he was endeavoring to establish peace, the Genoese had renewed their attack upon them. They then sent Piero Corsini to Lucca, that by his presence he might keep the city faithful; and Pagolantonio Soderini to Venice, to learn how that republic was disposed. They demanded assistance of the king and of Signor Lodovico, but obtained it from neither; for the king expressed apprehensions of the Turkish fleet, and Lodovico made excuses, but sent no aid. Thus the Florentines in their own wars are almost always obliged to stand alone, and find no friends to assist them with the same readiness they practice toward others. Nor did they, on this desertion of their allies (it being nothing new to them) give way to despondency; for having assembled a large army under Jacopo Guicciardini and Pietro Vettori, they sent it against the enemy, who had encamped upon the river Magra, at the same time pressing Serezanello with mines and every species of attack. The commissaries being resolved to relieve the place, an engagement ensued, when the Genoese were routed, and Lodovico dal Fiesco, with several other principal men, made prisoners. The Serezanesi were not so depressed at their defeat as to be willing to surrender, but obstinately prepared for their defense, while the Florentine commissaries proceeded with their operations, and instances of valor occurred on both sides. The siege being protracted by a variety of fortune, Lorenzo de' Medici resolved to go to the camp, and on his arrival the troops acquired fresh courage, while that of the enemy seemed to fail; for perceiving the obstinacy of the Florentines' attack, and the delay of the Genoese in coming to their relief, they surrendered to Lorenzo, without asking conditions, and none were treated with severity except two or three who were leaders of the rebellion. During the siege, Lodovico had sent troops to Pontremoli, as if with an intention of assisting the Florentines; but having secret correspondence in Genoa, a party was raised there, who, by the aid of these forces, gave the city to the duke of Milan.

At this time the Dutch made war upon the Venetians, and Boccolino of Osimo, in the Marca, caused that place to revolt from the pope, and assumed the sovereignty. After a variety of fortune, he was induced to restore the city to the pontiff and come to Florence, where, under the protection of Lorenzo de' Medici, by whose advice he had been prevailed upon to submit, he lived long and respected. He afterward went to Milan, but did not experience such generous treatment; for Lodovico caused him to be put to death. The Venetians were routed by the Dutch, near the city of Trento, and Roberto da S. Severino, their captain, was slain. After this defeat, the Venetians, with their usual good fortune, made peace with the Dutch, not as vanquished, but as conquerors, so honorable were the terms they obtained.

About this time, there arose serious troubles in Romagna. Francesco d'Orso, of Furli, was a man of great authority in that city, and became suspected by the count Girolamo, who often threatened him. He consequently, living under great apprehensions, was advised by his friends to provide for his own safety, by the immediate adoption of such a course as would relieve him from all further fear of the count. Having considered the matter and resolved to attempt it, they fixed upon the market day, at Furli, as most suitable for their purpose; for many of their friends being sure to come from the country, they might make use of their services without having to bring them expressly for the occasion. It was the month of May, when most Italians take supper by daylight. The conspirators thought the most convenient hour would be after the count had finished his repast; for his household being then at their meal, he would remain in the chamber almost alone. Having fixed upon the hour, Francesco went to the count's residence, left his companions in the hall, proceeded to his apartment, and desired an attendant to say he wished for an interview. He was admitted, and after a few words of pretended communication, slew him, and calling to his associates, killed the attendant. The governor of the place coming by accident to speak with the count, and entering the apartment with a few of his people, was also slain. After this slaughter, and in the midst of a great tumult, the count's body was thrown from the window, and with the cry of "church and liberty," they roused the people (who hated the avarice and cruelty of the count) to arms, and having plundered his house, made the Countess Caterina and her children prisoners. The fortress alone had to be taken to bring the enterprise to a successful issue; but the Castellan would not consent to its surrender. They begged the countess would desire him to comply with their wish, which she promised to do, if they would allow her to go into the fortress, leaving her children as security for the performance of her promise. The conspirators trusted her, and permitted her to enter; but as soon as she was within, she threatened them with death and every kind of torture in revenge for the murder of her husband; and upon their menacing her with the death of her children, she said she had the means of getting more. Finding they were not supported by the pope, and that Lodovico Sforza, uncle to the countess, had sent forces to her assistance, the conspirators became terrified, and taking with them whatever property they could carry off, they fled to Citta di Castello. The countess recovered the state, and avenged the death of her husband with the utmost cruelty. The Florentines hearing of the count's death, took occasion to recover the fortress of Piancaldoli, of which he had formerly deprived them, and, on sending some forces, captured it; but Cecco, the famous engineer, lost his life during the siege.

To this disturbance in Romagna, another in that province, no less important, has to be added. Galeotto, lord of Faenza, had married the daughter of Giovanni Bentivogli, prince of Bologna. She, either through jealousy or ill treatment by her husband, or from the depravity of her own nature, hated him to such a degree, that she determined to deprive him of his possessions and his life; and pretending sickness, she took to her bed, where, having induced Galeotto to visit her, he was slain by assassins, whom she had concealed for that purpose in the apartment. She had acquainted her father with her design, and he hoped, on his son-in-law's death, to become lord of Faenza. A great tumult arose as soon as the murder was known, the widow, with an infant son, fled into the fortress, the people took up arms, Giovanni Bentivogli, with a condottiere of the duke of Milan, named Bergamino, engaged for the occasion, entered Faenza with a considerable force, and Antonio Boscoli, the Florentine commissary, was also there. These leaders being together, and discoursing of the government of the place, the men of Val di Lamona, who had risen unanimously upon learning what had occurred, attacked Giovanni and Bergamino, the latter of whom they slew, made the former prisoner, and raising the cry of "Astorre and the Florentines," offered the city to the commissary. These events being known at Florence, gave general offense; however, they set Giovanni and his daughter at liberty, and by the universal desire of the people, took the city and Astorre under their protection. Besides these, after the principal differences of the greater powers were composed, during several years tumults prevailed in Romagna, the Marca, and Sienna, which, as they are unimportant, it will be needless to recount. When the duke of Calabria, after the war of 1478, had left the country, the distractions of Sienna became more frequent, and after many changes, in which, first the plebeians, and then the nobility, were victorious, the latter and length maintained the superiority, and among them Pandolfo and Jacopo Petrucci obtained the greatest influence, so that the former being distinguished for prudence and the latter for resolution, they became almost princes in the city.

The Florentines after the war of Serezana, lived in great prosperity until 1492, when Lorenzo de' Medici died; for he having put a stop to the internal wars of Italy, and by his wisdom and authority established peace, turned his thoughts to the advancement of his own and the city's interests, and married Piero, his eldest son, to Alfonsina, daughter of the Cavaliere Orsino. He caused Giovanni, his second son, to be raised to the dignity of cardinal. This was the more remarkable from its being unprecedented; for he was only fourteen years of age when admitted to the college; and became the medium by which his family attained to the highest earthly glory. He was unable to make any particular provision for Guiliano, his third son, on account of his tender years, and the shortness of his own life. Of his daughters, one married Jacopo Salviati; another, Francesco Cibo; the third, Piero Ridolfi; and the fourth, whom, in order to keep his house united, he had married to Giovanni de' Medici, died. In his commercial affairs he was very unfortunate, from the improper conduct of his agents, who in all their proceedings assumed the deportment of princes rather than of private persons; so that in many places, much of his property was wasted, and he had to be relieved by his country with large sums of money. To avoid similar inconvenience, he withdrew from mercantile pursuits, and invested his property in land and houses, as being less liable to vicissitude. In the districts of Prato, Pisa, and the Val di Pesa, he purchased extensively, and erected buildings, which for magnificence and utility, were quite of regal character. He next undertook the improvement of the city, and as many parts were unoccupied by buildings, he caused new streets to be erected in them, of great beauty, and thus enlarged the accommodation of the inhabitants. To enjoy his power in security and repose, and conquer or resist his enemies at a distance, in the direction of Bologna he fortified the castle of Firenzuola, situated in the midst of the Appennines; toward Sienna he commenced the restoration and fortification of the Poggio Imperiale; and he shut out the enemy in the direction of Genoa, by the acquisition of Pietra Santa and Serezana. For the greater safety of the city, he kept in pay the Baglioni, at Perugia, and the Vitelli, at Citta di Castello, and held the government of Faenza wholly in his own power; all which greatly contributed to the repose and prosperity of Florence. In peaceful times, he frequently entertained the people with feasts, and exhibitions of various events and triumphs of antiquity; his object being to keep the city abundantly supplied, the people united, and the nobility honored. He was a great admirer of excellence in the arts, and a patron of literary men, of which Agnolo da Montepulciano, Cristofero Landini, and Demetrius Chalcondylas, a Greek, may afford sufficient proofs. On this account, Count Giovanni della Mirandola, a man of almost supernatural genius, after visiting every court of Europe, induced by the munificence of Lorenzo, established his abode at Florence. He took great delight in architecture, music, and poetry, many of his comments and poetical compositions still remaining. To facilitate the study of literature to the youth of Florence, he opened a university at Pisa, which was conducted by the most distinguished men in Italy. For Mariano da Chinazano, a friar of the order of St. Augustine, and an excellent preacher, he built a monastery in the neighborhood of Florence. He enjoyed much favor both from fortune and from the Almighty; all his enterprises were brought to a prosperous termination, while his enemies were unfortunate; for, besides the conspiracy of the Pazzi, an attempt was made to murder him in the Carmine, by Batista Frescobaldi, and a similar one by Baldinetto da Pistoja, at his villa; but these persons, with their confederates, came to the end their crimes deserved. His skill, prudence, and fortune, were acknowledged with admiration, not only by the princes of Italy, but by those of distant countries; for Matthias, king of Hungary, gave him many proofs of his regard; the sultan sent ambassadors to him with valuable presents, and the Turkish emperor placed in his hands Bernardo Bandini, the murderer of his brother. These circumstances raised his fame throughout Italy, and his reputation for prudence constantly increased; for in council he was eloquent and acute, wise in determination, and prompt and resolute in execution. Nor can vices be alleged against him to sully so many virtues; though he was fond of women, pleased with the company of facetious and satirical men, and amused with the games of the nursery, more than seemed consistent with so great a character; for he was frequently seen playing with his children, and partaking of their infantine sports; so that whoever considers this gravity and cheerfulness, will find united in him dispositions which seem almost incompatible with each other. In his later years, he was greatly afflicted; besides the gout, he was troubled with excruciating pains in the stomach, of which he died in April, 1492, in the forty-fourth year of his age; nor was there ever in Florence, or even in Italy, one so celebrated for wisdom, or for whose loss such universal regret was felt. As from his death the greatest devastation would shortly ensue, the heavens gave many evident tokens of its approach; among other signs, the highest pinnacle of the church of Santa Reparata was struck with lightning, and great part of it thrown down, to the terror and amazement of everyone. The citizens and all the princes of Italy mourned for him, and sent their ambassadors to Florence, to condole with the city on the occasion; and the justness of their grief was shortly after apparent; for being deprived of his counsel, his survivors were unable either to satisfy or restrain the ambition of Lodovico Sforza, tutor to the duke of Milan; and hence, soon after the death of Lorenzo, those evil plants began to germinate, which in a little time ruined Italy, and continue to keep her in desolation.

www.ingramcontent.com/pod-product-compliance
Lightning Source LLC
LaVergne TN
LVHW031149200826
846147LV00012B/86
9798880922871